ENERGY LAW AND POLICY

Third Edition

■ ■ ■

Lincoln L. Davies
Dean and Frank R. Strong Chair in Law
The Ohio State University Moritz College of Law

Alexandra B. Klass
Distinguished McKnight University Professor
University of Minnesota Law School

Hari M. Osofsky
Dean and Myra and James Bradwell Professor of Law
Northwestern University Pritzker School of Law

Joseph P. Tomain
Dean Emeritus and Professor of Law
University of Cincinnati College of Law

Elizabeth J. Wilson
Professor and Director of the Arthur L. Irving
Institute for Energy and Society
Dartmouth College

AMERICAN CASEBOOK SERIES®

WEST
ACADEMIC
PUBLISHING

American Casebook Series is a trademark registered in the U.S. Patent and Trademark Office.

© 2015, 2018 LEG, Inc. d/b/a West Academic
© 2022 LEG, Inc. d/b/a West Academic
      444 Cedar Street, Suite 700
      St. Paul, MN 55101
      1-877-888-1330

West, West Academic Publishing, and West Academic are trademarks of West Publishing Corporation, used under license.

Printed in the United States of America

ISBN: 978-1-64708-430-1

PREFACE

Energy is one of the foremost issues of our time. The energy sector is immense—touching every part of the economy and every one of our lives. At the same time, the energy policy conversation is changing. Climate change, energy security, and environmental responsibility mean that the energy law of the future must address the ecological consequences of unconstrained fossil fuel consumption. However, much of the public dialogue about these important transitions is highly politicized and fails to situate individual issues within the energy system as a whole. In *Energy Law and Policy*, we break away from the traditional approach of looking at energy resources one at a time and instead try to provide that more holistic view of energy in society and law. The design of our book seeks to account for the complex, interrelated energy systems that buttress society, while addressing the grand energy challenges humanity faces today.

The book is organized into three parts that introduce students to the fundamental aspects of the energy sector, energy law, and the most pressing energy topics of the 21st century. Part I presents an overview of energy resources and markets. It identifies the book's primary themes: (1) the relationship between regulation, markets, and technological innovation; (2) the federalism issues that arise from the interaction of key regulatory actors; and (3) the transition to cleaner energy and increasing efforts to ensure energy burdens and benefits are distributed more equitably throughout our society. This Part also introduces the major sources of energy and the evolving law governing their extraction. In Part II, we discuss energy in terms of the electricity and transportation sectors that rely upon these energy resources. The U.S. energy profile can be roughly divided into oil for transportation and electricity for cooling, lighting, and other uses. This Part introduces traditional regulation in both of these sectors, and the ways in which law and policy for transportation and electricity are now in transition. Part III turns to the pressing energy challenges of the day. It presents case studies on grid modernization and cybersecurity; new and expanding energy extraction technologies such as deepwater oil and gas extraction, offshore wind development, and hydraulic fracturing; transportation electrification and carbon capture and storage (CCS); and the role of nuclear power in a clean energy future. *Energy Law and Policy* thus seeks to provide a solid understanding of the current energy regulatory regime, while also equipping students to anticipate future challenges and opportunities.

The book contains cases, sample statutes and regulations, and pertinent excerpts from energy law and policy experts. These policy-oriented, often empirical materials offer the necessary building blocks for a public law course, particularly one that covers a rapidly transitioning field. The book aims to introduce energy law and policy to students who seek to practice in the field and to those simply interested in gaining a better understanding this fascinating, critical area of law. The book describes the key jurisdictional actors that play differing roles in energy controversies and provides students with an understanding of the multi-jurisdictional approach to energy regulation pervasive in the United States. Throughout, the book highlights the debate over whether and how society can transition to a clean energy future. Trillions of dollars of sunk costs, and current institutions bound by the multitude of laws that favor and support the dominant energy model, challenge efforts to create a significant clean energy transition. Our book seeks to orient students with the existing modes of energy regulation, while also equipping them to address the challenges that will be faced by the energy lawyer of the future. We think it is critical for the next generation of energy lawyers to understand the energy system holistically and to think creatively about our options in this time of transition.

We want to thank The Ohio State University, University of Minnesota, Dartmouth College, and University of Cincinnati for providing us with generous research and financial support. Brandon Crawford (Minnesota Law '22); Ellie Burnett, Shynelle Kissi, Paul Stammen, Allison Thurwanger (Ohio State '23); Hillary Davis (Dartmouth '23); and Elias Nielsen provided excellent research support. Finally, we are forever grateful to our families for their unfailing support and patience.

As you use this book, please send us comments and suggestions so that we can incorporate them into future editions.

LLD
ABK
HMO
JPT
EJW

August 2021

COPYRIGHT ACKNOWLEDGMENTS

SUMMARY OF CONTENTS

———————

TABLE OF CONTENTS

PART II. MAJOR ENERGY SYSTEMS: ELECTRICITY AND TRANSPORTATION

TABLE OF CASES

The principal cases are in bold type.

ENERGY LAW AND POLICY

Third Edition

INTRODUCTION

■ ■ ■

Energy law undergirds modern society and every aspect of how the energy system works, as well as its efforts to adapt to the rapidly changing technologies, environmental demands, and risks. Transforming how we create and use energy throughout society requires fundamental changes in policies, regulations, and institutions, with energy law playing a central role. Responding to global cyber-attacks means coordinating energy law and security across end use devices and globally networked infrastructures. Ensuring that people have enough heat, food and clean water after storms, heat waves, fires or ice vortexes requires redesigning how energy law works to allow our energy system to become resilient and reliable in a rapidly changing world.

Energy law must evolve quickly to meet these new challenges. In California and the West, a new climate normal is emerging and droughts, fires, and heat waves are putting people's lives at risk. These changes are producing major shifts in the electric grid, requiring it to operate very differently from how it was originally designed. Reducing GHG emissions through the large-scale deployment of renewable energy resources and low-carbon distributed energy resources like rooftop solar PV also requires changes in our policies and regulations. Allowing demand management to play a role in energy markets and grid operations means energy law shifts are fundamentally altering the relationships between customers and utilities. Cyberattacks on critical infrastructure, like the May 2021 Colonial Pipeline cyber-ransomware attack can paralyze critical energy infrastructure and underlie the legal responsibilities for ensuring the system is safe. Energy law and policy is at the center of this transformation, as we explore in this book.

Modern energy law, as a legal discipline, began during turbulent times in domestic and international oil and gas markets in the 1970s. International oil markets had been experiencing dramatic changes during the preceding decades as the oil rich Middle Eastern countries increased the royalties demanded from foreign oil companies; took ownership interests in those same companies; and, ultimately, created competing state-run oil producing and exporting firms of their own. These countries contained most of the world's oil reserves and, consequently, became not only major competitors to United States oil companies, but also oligopolists who could, and did, exercise market power to our detriment. DANIEL YERGIN, THE PRIZE: THE EPIC QUEST FOR OIL, MONEY AND POWER (1992). However, it was the Arab Oil Embargo in October 1973 that roiled world

1

markets and destabilized the domestic economy of the United States. It also gave birth to the field of energy law.

Even prior to the Arab Embargo, there was trouble on the oil horizon. In the mid-1950s, the U.S. domestic oil supply was insufficient to provide all of our oil needs and we began importing foreign oil. The Arabian Peninsula had long been known for its substantial oil resources. Importing relatively inexpensive foreign oil, however, threatened domestic oil producers. In a protective measure, President Eisenhower, by executive proclamation, inaugurated the Mandatory Oil Import Quota Program (MOIP) arguing that cheap oil threatened national security because of the growing dependence on foreign oil and threatened an economic decline in the petroleum sector of the domestic economy.[1] The MOIP had two immediate effects. First, the quantity of imports was limited and, therefore, oil prices rose. Second, several oil producing nations formed the Organization of Petroleum Exporting Countries (OPEC) in response to the import limitations.[2]

Our need for foreign oil only increased when, in 1970, domestic oil production peaked, which helped set the stage for the Oil Embargo. Quite simply, in retaliation for the United States' decision to supply the Israeli military during the 1973 Arab-Israeli War, or the Yom Kippur War, the Arab members of OPEC, together with Egypt, Syria and Tunisia, imposed an embargo on oil being shipped to the United States. *See, e.g.,* U.S. Department of State, Office of the Historian, *Milestones: 1969–1976: Oil Embargo, 1973–1974.* The United States economy was already strained as a result of Vietnam War expenditures. However, that strain was exacerbated when the price of world oil quadrupled from $10 per barrel to $40 per barrel. The direct consequence of the price spike was that the United States experienced double-digit inflation and other economic dislocations.

In response to the Arab Oil Embargo, President Nixon launched Project Independence, which, as its name implies, was intended to reduce our reliance on imported oil. Every president since then has echoed the need for energy independence. No president, however, has achieved that goal. Still, oil independence, especially from Middle East oil, has been and remains a central goal of our domestic energy policy.

---

[1]   *See* Charles J. Ciccheti & William J. Gillen, *The Mandatory Oil Import Quota Program: A Consideration of Economic Efficiency and Equity*, 13 NAT. RES. J. 399 (1973).

[2]   The original five countries that created OPEC in 1960 were: Iran, Iraq, Kuwait, Saudi Arabia and Venezuela. Those countries were later joined by: Qatar (1961), Indonesia (1962), Libya (1962), the United Arab Emirates (1967), Algeria (1969), Nigeria (1971), Ecuador (1973), Gabon (1975) and Angola (2007). Gabon terminated its membership in 1995. Indonesia suspended its membership effective January 2009. OPEC estimates that it controls approximately 80% of the world's oil reserves. *OPEC Share of World Crude Oil Reserves* 2018, Organization of the Petroleum Exporting Countries (2019).

In addition to articulating an energy policy of independence, President Nixon also tried to stabilize the whole economy through a series of wage and price controls that were also imposed on the oil industry. Wage and price controls are very difficult to implement and sustain. They tend to have a limited effect before exceptions are granted and the price control edifice crumbles, as did President Nixon's.

Once wage and price controls were eliminated, the United States' difficulties with its energy markets remained. We continued to increase imports of foreign oil. Our natural gas markets had been regulated in a way that caused natural gas shortages. Additionally, the costs of constructing nuclear power plants greatly exceeded estimates, sometimes by multiples of five or more. Given these pressures on traditional energy markets, alternatives were sought. Legislation during the Nixon and Ford administrations was aimed at encouraging the use of coal rather than oil to produce electricity, and to promote conservation on a limited basis. It was President Jimmy Carter, though, who aggressively pursued energy legislation in an attempt to remove economic impediments in the energy sector and to coordinate policy across energy industries and markets.

President Carter's National Energy Act of 1978 and his Energy Security Act of 1980 were major legislative initiatives. Each of those acts consisted of multiple pieces of legislation addressing oil, natural gas, electricity, conservation, and renewable resources, as well as energy taxes. It was that legislation, more than any other single event, that helped crystallize a corpus of law and regulations that effectively created the discipline of energy law as we know it today.

Predecessors

Energy law, as a legal discipline, has its predecessors. The most direct source of energy law is public utilities regulation. Public utilities texts and casebooks have been around for over a century.[3] At the end of the 19th century, gas and electricity companies began as small, local businesses that, due to technological limitations, served relatively small geographical areas. These businesses were local, competitive, and were unregulated. With technological improvements, those companies grew to serve more customers and, to achieve economies of scale, consolidated.

That consolidation revealed two things. First, these local, growing utilities could exercise market power over their customers. Second, the firms that were already in the gas or electricity business would exercise market power to set barriers to competition. Nevertheless, the threat of new entrants continued, and incumbent firms sought to prevent competition with the help of government. In 1898, for example, Samuel

---

[3] *See, e.g.,* JOSEPH ASBURY JOYCE, A TREATISE ON FRANCHISES: ESPECIALLY THOSE OF PUBLIC SERVICE CORPORATIONS (1909); OSCAR L. POND, A TREATISE ON THE LAW OF PUBLIC UTILITIES OPERATING IN CITIES AND TOWNS (1913).

Insull, the president of Chicago's Commonwealth Edison Company, proposed a grand bargain where the local electricity company would receive an exclusive service territory (a monopoly) "coupled with the conditions of public control, requiring all charges for services fixed by public bodies to be based on cost plus a reasonable profit."[4] Through this arrangement, which was often referred to as a "regulatory compact," a privately owned energy firm would be given an exclusive monopoly service territory in exchange for the government's authority to set rates at just and reasonable levels. Thus began the government regulation of energy utilities that continues today.

Traditional energy policy is heavily based on fossil fuels, especially oil, natural gas, and coal. Indeed, all energy resources are natural resources that must be extracted, processed, and transformed to create usable energy. Consequently, another source for contemporary energy law is the oil and gas law of producing states.[5] While oil and gas law is often taught independently of energy law, the connection between the two is direct and important and we will introduce you to the fundamentals of that subject.

The third source of energy law is natural resources law. Like oil and gas, energy resources such as coal, water, and uranium must be extracted from public and private lands. Courses on natural resources law typically examine these resources among others.[6] Also, like oil and gas law, natural resources law is an independent field of study. Yet, it has a direct connection with energy law and policy. Thus, today's energy law has its antecedents in oil and gas, public utilities, and natural resources laws.

The Dominant Model of U.S. Energy Policy

Conventional wisdom is that the United States has no cohesive or comprehensive national energy policy. To some extent, the conventional wisdom is correct. Even though the president is required to submit a National Energy Plan biannually to Congress, that plan lacks the force of law. Instead, existing energy policy is derived from the many statutes, regulations, and cases that affect the energy sector. However, as we review the history of energy legislation and other legal activities, a more or less cohesive energy policy does emerge. This book, then, moves beyond first generation casebook approaches by providing a holistic look at U.S. energy law and policy and by examining its future direction.

Part of that holistic examination involves describing past and current shifts in energy law and recognizing the dominant model that underlies

---

[4]   Insull quoted in GE Digital Energy & The Analysis Group, *Results-Based Regulation: A Modern Approach to Modernize the Grid* 7 (2013), http://www.gedigitalenergy.com/regulation/.

[5]   *See, e.g.*, OWEN L. ANDERSON ET AL., HEMINGWAY OIL AND GAS LAW AND TAXATION (4th ed. 2004).

[6]   *See, e.g.*, CHRISTINE A. KLEIN ET AL., NATURAL RESOURCES LAW: A PLACE-BASED BOOK OF PROBLEMS AND CASES (4th ed. 2018).

current changes. During the last quarter of the 19th century, modern energy industries and markets began to take shape. In that period, the country experienced two notable transitions. First, there was a transition in energy resources. The movement from wood to coal ended and the movement from coal to oil, electricity, and natural gas began. The second transition was a shift from local and state to regional and national energy markets. The transition in energy resources and the transition in markets mirrored each other. As an energy industry, such as electricity or oil, moved from local to interstate commerce, so did regulation move from local and state to federal regulators. Additionally, the traditional model of energy policy began to reveal identifiable characteristics.

A first characteristic of this model—and one that has shaped energy law and the way that it has been traditionally taught—is that government regulates energy sources independently of each other. As a matter of policy, the country's preference of regulating energy resources independently is consistent with a preference for private markets and private investment. If resources are treated separately, the idea goes, competition will be encouraged. Separate legal treatment allows resources to compete with each other, thus increasing energy production, increasing the number of energy producers, and, in turn, reducing prices. The policy preference in energy law, in short, mirrors the nation's general preference for competition and markets. Nevertheless, if energy markets did not behave competitively—or if there was a supervening public policy, such as war mobilization—then government regulators could intervene. They could do so by attempting to stimulate energy markets, or by seeking to create incentives for the further development of energy resources and their expansion. In short, national energy policy has always been a matter of the relationship between privately owned energy firms and government regulation. Thus, a core tension involves whether, and if so how, to regulate energy firms and markets.

The emphasis on private ownership is important. The post-World War II United States has operated on the presumption that democratic capitalism is the preferred form of social ordering. The United States also recognizes that energy is a basic input to the economy and that energy production and distribution should be made as available as possible. Instead of coordinating several energy resources and markets, a core belief is that government will allow energy resources and markets to develop independently of each other but not necessarily independent of the helping hand of government. Energy policy often is industrial policy, and in this context, fossil fuels have been the big winners. During both World Wars government activity promoted the use of oil, coal, and natural gas. Although careful to ensure no particular firm or industry exercised market power, government has promoted these fuels throughout their fuel cycles from extraction through transportation, production, and consumption.

In the early decades of the 20th century, energy markets were structured by: (1) seemingly inexhaustible supplies of oil, natural gas, and coal; (2) a shift from local to regional and interstate resource production and distribution; (3) continuous growth in energy markets and the continued realization of economies of scale; (4) increasing industry concentration and large-scale production; and (5) transportation bottlenecks in each industry. Government regulation of energy sought to capitalize on resource abundance; promote economic growth; check industry concentration and the exercise of market power; and address the monopoly problems caused by transportation bottlenecks.

Government regulation, however, neither coordinated energy production nor addressed energy markets comprehensively. Instead, energy policy was driven by one overarching goal: keep energy as available, affordable, and reliable as possible because energy was a primary input into the economy and largely responsible for the economic growth that the United States enjoyed throughout the 20th century.

Indeed, the political economy of energy in the United States is based upon the symbiotic relationship between government and industry. Both government and industry recognize energy is indispensable to economic health and have developed policies to further that goal. By treating energy industries roughly independently of each other, some competition is fostered without energy industries necessarily taking market share from each other, thus allowing several energy industries to flourish.

Today, oil and electricity divide the energy pie into two roughly equal shares. These energy resources are currently complementary to each other, but things are changing rapidly. Oil has dominated the transportation sector and generates little electricity. Electricity has been used for heating, cooling, lighting, and end use devices like computers and has historically played a minor role in the transportation sector. The rise of electric vehicles (EVs) is beginning to change this.

Finally, because the federal government owns one-third of the lands on the continental United States and controls offshore resources, it is a part of the public policy of the United States to encourage the development of those lands for energy production. Government support of energy is perhaps most noticeable in times of economic disequilibrium. The government response to the Arab Oil Embargo, the protection of shipping lanes in the Mideast, and the general sensitivity of our foreign policy to the geopolitics of oil all speak to the government's efforts to keep oil supplies available.

We can summarize the dominant model of national energy policy by delineating its primary goals:

(1) maintain abundant supplies of energy resources;

(2) monitor prices for reasonableness;

(3) limit the market power of large-scale, concentrated firms, especially firms in the transportation segment;

(4) promote multiple, but limited, energy producers;

(5) support conventional fuels of oil, natural gas, coal, and nuclear power;

(6) encourage some development of alternative energy resources;

(7) avoid a heavy hand of coordinated and comprehensive energy policy; and

(8) allow energy decision-making and policymaking to occur within an active federal-state regulatory system.

In short, government has supported the dominant model of fossil-fuel energy production and distribution for decades. It has done so based upon a fundamental assumption that there is a direct and positive correlation between the level of energy production and consumption and the country's economic health. Further, the United States continues to believe that economies of scale in energy production can still be realized. Simply, our policy is that the more natural resources that are extracted and processed, the more energy will be produced and consumed, which will result in either stable or relatively low prices to consumers and, more importantly, strong economic growth.

As a consequence of a belief in the above principles, domestic energy policy has strongly favored large-scale, high-technology, capital-intensive, integrated, and centralized production of energy from fossil fuels.[7] This type of energy firm has been favored over alternatives, such as small-scale or decentralized power producers such as wind or solar.

But times are changing as energy policymakers begin to shift their beliefs that traditional energy industries are sufficient for the future, resulting in a large-scale transition of the energy system. Policymakers are promoting renewable energy resources, distributed energy resources, energy efficiency, and demand management through mandates, tax incentives, and other forms of support. Nevertheless, our continued reliance on fossil fuels remains strong. Indeed, in the wake of heightened use of technologies like hydraulic fracturing, domestic production of oil and natural gas is higher than ever before.

Energy and the Environment

It should occur to the reader that little has been said about environmental law and policy. Under the dominant model, energy law and environmental law operate under separate statutes implemented by

---

[7] *See* AMORY LOVINS, SOFT ENERGY PATHS: TOWARD A DURABLE PEACE 1–31 (1977).

different government agencies. However, there are two notable anomalies with the disconnection between energy law and environmental law.

The first anomaly is that energy resources follow a natural, physical fuel cycle. Natural resources are extracted, processed into usable energy, consumed, and then waste products must be disposed of. At every point along the fuel cycle, there are environmental consequences. The second anomaly is the fact that environmental law, notably the National Environmental Policy Act of 1970 and several associated environmental laws, preceded the development of modern energy law that occurred in the late 1970s. It would seem, then, that energy law and environmental law should be coordinated with each other.

The most significant change in energy policy from the first two editions of this casebook to the third edition deals with the issue of the integration of energy and environmental law. During the Obama administration, several efforts were undertaken to merge these two disciplines. In December 2015, under the auspices of the UN Framework Convention on Climate Change, 195 nations, including the United States, signed the Paris Agreement, which aims to reduce global greenhouse gas emissions through increasingly ambitious national commitments. Also during the Obama administration, U.S. Department of Energy Research and Development funds were shifted to clean energy technologies, and the U.S. Environmental Protection Agency issued a Clean Power Plan that directed states to reduce carbon emissions from the electricity sector. Each of these efforts can be seen as an attempt to coordinate energy and environmental policies.

After the 2016 election, however, the Trump administration moved to reverse each of these efforts. President Trump withdrew the United States from the Paris Agreement, repealed the Clean Power Plan, and attempted to defund clean energy research and development, among other efforts to return to a traditional fossil fuel policy.

In 2021, the Biden administration provided another reversal as it rejoined the Paris Agreement and made addressing climate change and transforming the energy sector a central focus. His "Plan for Climate Change and Environmental Justice" set a target of 100% carbon-free electricity generation by 2035, with a goal of net-zero emissions by 2050. Multiple executive orders and additional plans focused on promoting clean energy technologies, EVs, and limiting fossil fuel leases on federal lands, highlight this dramatic shift in direction.

There are at least three significant lessons to take from these shifts from one administration to another. First, energy markets are deeply intertwined with government regulations, which can be revised even when political consensus is insufficient to allow for statutory change. Second, while the prior administration preferred a return to a traditional fuel energy policy, the Biden administration has made clean energy development and decarbonization a centerpiece of its domestic and foreign policy. And third, even though the federal government has not taken a leadership role in climate change until recently, multiple local, state, and private sector initiatives are underway to reduce pollution, promote clean energy, and consider energy and environmental laws and policies together.

The Practice of Energy Law and Policy

This book provides an introduction to energy law and policy for those intending to go into the field, as well as for others who are simply interested in this increasingly important area of law. Lawyers and other professionals, including those with advanced degrees in economics, public policy, engineering, or other sciences, practice in the continually changing and expanding field of energy law and policy.

Regarding law practice, energy law attorneys in private practice and in-house counsel at energy firms represent companies in the oil, gas, coal, nuclear, electricity, hydropower, and other renewable energy industries. These attorneys assist with project development, due diligence, project financing, mergers and acquisitions, power marketing, energy regulation before FERC and state public utility commissions, antitrust, transmission planning and development, lobbying at the state and federal levels, facility licensing and permitting, real estate transactions, regulatory compliance, pipeline regulation, and fuel supply and transportation agreements, among many other practice areas.

Energy lawyers also work for government, representing federal agencies such as FERC in various permitting and licensing proceedings, for national laboratories, and at state agencies, including state public utility commissions and state energy offices. Like their counterparts in private practice, their work involves a full range of licensing, permitting, ratemaking, litigation, and regulatory proceedings.

Finally, energy lawyers are active in a range of energy and environmental nongovernmental organizations as well as trade associations. Sometimes these organizational actors attempt to reduce the environmental externalities of energy development, promote alternative energy, and represent consumer and producer interests in electric and natural gas utility ratemaking proceedings in state public utility commissions across the country. At other times, organizational actors attempt to further the specific interests of their members' interests and promote wind, solar, natural gas, coal, and the like. Thus, energy lawyers advise a wide range of clients on a broad variety of substantive issues in energy and related fields. To meet these different substantive needs in energy law, the field of energy lawyers is complemented by transactional lawyers, regulatory attorneys, real estate lawyers, litigators, tax lawyers, and public finance lawyers, just to name a few.

Given the range of legal and policy issues that confront energy lawyers, students should be aware that a regulatory lawyer's skill set differs, at least in part, from both litigation lawyers and transactional lawyers. The stock in trade for a litigator often is advocacy. Courtroom lawyers zealously defend their clients within the bounds of the law. Transactional lawyers rely less on advocacy skills than they do on negotiation skills. The ability to "get to yes" or to walk away from the negotiation table when a client's needs will not be satisfied are essential skills for the transactional lawyer. Regulatory lawyers, on the other hand, must develop a set of political and policy skills. The political skills consist of the ability to understand various political positions, build a consensus when possible, and compromise when necessary. The policy skills for the regulatory lawyer may not require the lawyer to engage in complex econometric analyses. However, the regulatory lawyer must be familiar with the empirical bases for the regulatory positions or proposals she or he is advancing. Also, the regulatory lawyer who only acts as a zealous advocate will likely be at a disadvantage. Instead, the regulatory lawyer often must learn to balance the private interests of the clients with the public interest of the policies that they favor—and to cast the client's objectives in terms of those public interests. These distinctions blur at times, of course, as many litigators use political and negotiations skills to get to a settlement, and transactional lawyers often negotiate with potential litigation in mind.

There are many longstanding bar associations at the state and federal levels that provide excellent resources for lawyers and other professionals practicing energy law. For instance, the American Bar Association's Section of Environment, Energy, and Resources (SEER) is a premier forum for lawyers working in a broad range of areas related to energy and the environment. SEER represents more than 10,000 members and offers conferences, networking opportunities, and publications to inform members of developing trends, current court decisions, legislative initiatives, and statutes in the area. Active SEER committees focusing on energy and resources include Energy and Environmental Markets and Finance; Energy and Natural Resources Litigation; Energy and Natural Resources Market Regulation; Energy Infrastructure and Siting; Nuclear Law; Oil and Gas; Petroleum Marketing; Renewable, Alternative, and Distributed Energy Resources; Electricity; and Gas. The ABA also has a Section of Public Utilities, Communications, and Transportation Law. This Section includes committees on electricity, gas, maritime, nuclear energy, oil pipelines, renewable energy, water, and antitrust. Likewise, the Energy Bar Association in Washington, D.C. is an international, nonprofit association of attorneys, non-attorney professionals, and students active in all areas of energy law, which include antitrust, international energy transactions, legislation and regulatory reform, electric utility regulation, alternative dispute resolution, finance and transactions, and environment and public lands. It has over 2400 members, six regional chapters and an increasing number of members across the United States and Canada. Finally, virtually every state bar association has a section devoted to environmental and energy issues, public utilities regulation, and the like.

On the policy side, public policy professionals work on government relations, project and policy creation and evaluation, and management throughout the energy industry. In private firms, many practitioners begin in government relations but also work across different analytic and evaluative functions. In government, public policy professionals work at federal, state, and local levels in the executive, legislative, and judicial branches on energy and natural resource-focused topics. Some work in Congress or at the state-level as legislative aides or on staff committees focused on energy resources or electricity. Others work at state agencies or commissions researching energy-related issues, developing and evaluating energy policies, and implementing energy-related programs. Many also work in energy lobbying groups like the Edison Electric Institute, the American Petroleum Institute, the American Public Power Association, the Solar Energy Industries Association, or the American Natural Gas Alliance. Much like their lawyer counterparts, public policy professionals also focus on energy work at non-profit organizations at the federal, regional, state, and local levels. Policy practitioners can participate in professional organizations like the National Association of Regulatory Utility Commissioners (NARUC) or the National Association of State Energy Officials (NASEO), which organize trainings and policy development.

Lessons

A course on energy law, like courses in environmental law, securities regulation, or labor law, among others, differ from first-year law courses in one significant way. First-year courses in torts, contracts, and property, as the key examples, are foundational private law courses that introduce you to the common law method of case analysis. The other upper-level courses just mentioned are distinguishable as heavily regulatory and statute-based public law courses. Both sets of courses are necessary to understand and practice law.

Still, for some students, a course on energy law may, to some extent, look esoteric and narrow. After all, most students do not come to law school with the desire to practice energy law. Indeed, when the authors were in law school, very few schools had regular courses in the subject taught by full-time faculty. Recognizing that a mix of students will take this course— both those set on practicing in the field and those with an interest in the issues it raises—we have written this book to give students a foundation in energy law and policy and to convey lessons with salience beyond this course. Many of the key points in this book are transferable to other areas of practice, particularly practices in public or regulatory law. In Chapter 1, we describe those lessons in more detail. Here, though, by way of preview, we hope to orient you to the themes and lessons that should have value beyond the study of energy law and policy.

In this book, in addition to case extracts, we present you with a wide range of materials. Where appropriate, we provide you with examples of statutes and regulations. Often, in addition, you will be reading excerpts from government reports, white papers, and other professional studies. These policy-oriented, and often empirical, materials constitute the necessary building blocks of a public law course, particularly one that is experiencing significant evolution.

Globally, annual energy investments are valued at approximately $1.9 trillion, INT'L ENERGY AGENCY, WORLD ENERGY INVESTMENTS 2021 (2021). Domestically, the energy sector is estimated to be 6.2% of the country's GDP or valued at $1.3 trillion. UNIV. OF MICHIGAN CENTER FOR SUSTAINABLE SYSTEMS, U.S. ENERGY SYSTEM FACTSHEET (Sept. 2020). The energy sector is also complex, touching every part of the economy and every one of our lives. Throughout the book we will introduce you to what may sometimes appear to be a bewildering array of public and private actors participating in a wide variety of disciplines and activities. Nonetheless, a lawyer's ability to understand and address complex multi-dimensional problems is a necessary practical skill. It is abundantly present in energy law.

We hope to break down that complexity into understandable as well as digestible portions. As complex as the energy sector is, it can be understood by recognizing that the physical resources used to produce and consume energy are ordered by specific energy markets together with specific energy regulations. Thus, appreciating the physical, market, and regulatory dimensions of the energy sector will give you a solid grounding for the materials that follow.

We will explain in more detail the relationship between government and markets. The United States today prefers markets as a tool for the production and distribution of goods and services. Markets, however, are not always competitive nor do they always produce the goods and services necessary for a healthy political economy or a healthy environment. We explain how markets fail and how government can respond—and has responded—to those failures. We examine the energy regulatory tools used to correct market defects, manage market externalities, and to achieve other ends that markets neglect. This understanding of the relationship between government and markets is one that pervades the practice of public law as well as the development of public policy more generally.

The complexity of the energy system, the magnitude of a century of financial investment, and the regulatory structures created and designed to support the production, distribution, consumption, and disposal of energy resources have generated rules and regulations at every level of government. Local land use law, state statutory and common law, regional and interstate agreements, and federal legislation and regulation all touch the energy sector. Unlike a contract dispute that may be restricted to two private parties, disputes about energy regularly involve multiple actors, the public and private sectors, and several jurisdictions. Thus, another lesson of this casebook is that energy problems cannot be solved without an appreciation for the several jurisdictional actors that play differing roles in energy controversies. Throughout this book, we explore the various federalism conflicts between state and federal actors, which are often the dominant conflicts of energy law and policy.

The array of federal and state legislation affecting energy is vast. It also seems to be the case that federal energy policy has been stuck in its traditional mode as described above for over a century. The challenges posed by climate change for future energy policy remain largely unaddressed by Congress. The Biden administration is undertaking measures to promote a clean energy economy, but the pace of the energy transition is likely to be constrained by existing statutes and regulations. A gridlocked legislative branch, and political and legal challenges to its approach slow energy system change further. Moreover, states and localities are deeply divided in their support of an energy transition; Eastern and Western coastal states—with their greater immediate risks from climate change and generally lower investments in the fossil fuel industry—are leading the way.

This disconnection between governmental entities at multiple levels of government creates what may be the most important challenge facing the development of our future energy policy: the need for coordinated energy and environmental leadership. Incumbent energy industries that have operated under a federal framework and often resist new energy policies and new entrants and thus exacerbates federalism conflicts.

Finally, the book discusses the promises and the challenges of moving towards a clean energy future. Even assuming that there is a policy consensus in favor of clean energy, the challenge of how to address evolving energy legal systems remains. Some levels of government are institutionalizing clean energy policy in law, and those changes bring conflict, debate, and opportunity for further policy innovation. Nevertheless, current institutions, trillions of dollars of sunk costs, and the existence of a multitude of laws that favor and support the dominant model, slow energy law transition. The road to the energy future will be bumpy, unpredictable, and uneven. The challenge for every energy lawyer of the future, then, is not only how to manage these various problems and conflicts but to equip herself with the skills to help shape and implement policies supporting a new energy regime.

We hope that you enjoy this course on energy law and policy. You are certainly taking it at an exciting moment for the field. We also encourage you to embrace the complexity and think creatively; you represent the future of energy law.

PART I

THEMES, ENERGY SOURCES, AND EXTRACTION OF NATURAL RESOURCES

■ ■ ■

Energy begins in the physical world. Energy, therefore, is subject to physical laws. We can start with Einstein's famous equation, $E = MC^2$ (Energy = Mass × Speed of Light × Speed of Light). The significant relationship for us, though, is the relationship between matter and energy that physicists began exploring long before Einstein's revolutionary contributions. For our purposes, "matter" is constituted by natural resources such as coal, oil, uranium, natural gas, wind, and sunlight. Each of those resources is comprised of *potential* energy. Energy, in turn, is simply defined as the ability to do work. To release the potential energy and turn it into *kinetic* energy or *work* energy, those resources must be processed.

This need to process potential energy into kinetic energy—plus two long-standing principles of physics—are at the core of the challenges facing energy law and the energy system.

The First Law of Thermodynamics—Conservation of Mass—holds that energy changes form but does not dissipate. Problems arise with the Second Law of Thermodynamics—Entropy. The law of entropy holds that over time, potential energy decreases and is released as heat. Thus, even though all the potential energy in a natural resource is conserved, when natural resources are processed from potential to kinetic energy, some of their potential energy is lost. Simple examples of the Second Law are that ice warms as it melts and that hot pans cool down into the air around them.

The significance of these two laws for our study, however, can be characterized as "energy efficiency." Imagine, for example, that a ton of coal has 100 units of potential energy. To generate the kinetic energy of coal in the form of electricity, the coal must be burned to create heat, which boils water to create steam, which turns turbines to generate and then distribute usable electricity. At every stage of that process, units of energy are lost. The result is that we will capture about 30 units of coal's 100 potential units of energy after this process has run its course. The other 70 units will

15

be dissipated as waste heat, some of which may be recovered by still other processes.

The material form of the natural resources that we use to produce energy also has significant implications for our study of energy law and policy. Consider coal and uranium. Both are examples of solid matter. Then consider oil, natural gas, and water, each of which is an example of a fugacious or a migrating resource. Finally, consider wind and sunlight. These are common resources incapable of being captured. The legal regimes for each of these natural resources are different. Coal and uranium, for example, are located in a specific space and can be mined and relatively easily stored. Oil and natural gas, to the contrary, migrate easily and are not site-specific, although both can be relatively easily stored. Again, by contrast, wind and sunlight can neither be specifically located nor easily stored.

As you begin your study of energy law and policy in this Part, it is useful to keep in mind that the different physical characteristics of the natural resources used to produce energy impact the way we regulate them. However, every part of energy law grapples in some way with the same problem: the dissipation of energy as it is processed from one form to another.

Part I focuses on the legal implications of the energy system and the primary sources that it uses. Chapter 1 begins with an overview of the integrated physical, market, and regulatory aspects of the energy system, and introduces core themes of the book. Chapter 2 furthers that discussion by introducing you to some of the basic metrics used by energy industries and their regulators, and by providing an overview of the primary sources of energy. Chapter 3 focuses on energy extraction and the various ways in which natural resources are obtained to produce useable energy.

CHAPTER 1

THE COMPLEX ENERGY SYSTEM: PHYSICAL, MARKET, AND REGULATORY ELEMENTS

■ ■ ■

A. OVERVIEW

In February 2021, Arctic winds broke free of the polar vortex that swirls around the North Pole and blew south, bringing a winter snow and ice storm and freezing temperatures to the southern United States. The frigid weather resulted in catastrophic failures of energy and water infrastructure not weatherized for cold weather for days or weeks in multiple states. In particular, Texas suffered a massive electric grid failure that resulted in over 150 deaths; millions of people left without light, clean water, or heat; and billions of dollars in damages to homes, businesses, and infrastructure. *See, e.g.*, Rob Hotakainen, *Feb. Winter Storms Most Expensive on Record—NOAA*, E&E NEWS (Apr. 8, 2021); Brian K. Sullivan, *Texas Deep Freeze Could Cost $90 Billion in Losses, Modeler Says*, BLOOMBERG LAW (Feb. 24, 2021). Texas's grid failed primarily because Texas power plant operators were not legally required to insulate their facilities for sustained cold temperatures and did not invest to do so. In other parts of the country, by contrast, states require such insulation or energy markets create financial incentives to prompt such investments. Because of the lack of weatherization of energy infrastructure in Texas, pipes and equipment needed to run the state's natural gas wells, distribution system, gas plants, nuclear plants, and wind turbines froze, taking nearly half the state's electric generation capacity (over 52,000 MW) offline at precisely the moment that energy demand statewide skyrocketed as residents attempted to heat homes and businesses. *See* Matt Largey, *Texas' Power Grid Was 4 Minutes And 37 Seconds Away from Collapsing. Here's How It Happened*, HOUSTON PUB. MEDIA (Feb. 24, 2021); Alexandra B. Klass, *Lessons from the Texas Grid Disaster: Planning and Investing for a Different Future*, LAWFARE (Feb. 22, 2021).

Less than three months after freezing temperatures disrupted the Texas grid and surrounding states, extended high temperatures placed renewed strain on the region's electricity supply, resulting in significant power plant outages, and prompting grid operators to call for residents and businesses to drastically reduce electricity consumption to avoid widespread blackouts and brownouts. *See* Eric Levenson, *Electric Grid Operator Asks Texans to Stop Blasting AC as Unplanned Outages and Heat Collide*, CNN NEWS (June 15, 2021); Brad Plumer et al., *Climate Change Batters the West Before Summer Even Begins*, N.Y. TIMES (June 17, 2021) (discussing strain on electric grids and water supplies).

Notably, California experienced a similar problem in the summer of 2020, when soaring temperatures spurred an overwhelming surge in electricity use that drained power reserves and necessitated cutting off power to millions of people to avoid further damaging the state's infrastructure. *See* Peter Behr, *"Everything Went Wrong." Experts Revisit Calif. Blackouts*, E&E NEWS (Dec. 3, 2020). High temperatures likewise caused power to be shut off in particularly dry locations to prevent power lines from sparking wildfires. *See* Zeeshan Aleem, *California's Heat Wave Caused Rolling Blackouts for Millions*, VOX (Aug. 15, 2020); Dale Kasler, *PG&E Lowers Numbers in Preparation for Largest California Wildfire Blackout of 2020*, SACRAMENTO BEE (Oct. 23, 2020). The relationship between transmission lines and wildfires is not new to Californians. In 2018, a broken power line sparked one of the deadliest wildfires in the state's history. The Camp Fire spread throughout the northern part of the state taking lives and destroying lands, businesses, and houses. Pacific Gas & Electric, which owned the transmission lines that caused the fire, pled guilty in 2020 to 84 counts of involuntary manslaughter and one felony count of unlawfully causing a fire. *See* Phil Helsel, *PG&E Pleads Guilty to 84 Counts of Manslaughter in Devastating Camp Fire*, NBC NEWS (Jun. 17, 2020); *see also* Katie Worth & Karen Pinchin, *After Deadly Fire, Regulators and Consumers Question PG&E Blackouts,* FRONTLINE (Nov. 15, 2019) (discussing PG&E's role in the Camp Fire and its failure to take adequate preventative measures).

The electric grid failures in Texas and elsewhere go beyond the physical aspects of repairing downed power lines and making sure wind and water have not rendered buildings' electrical and mechanical systems unsafe. Electricity infrastructure can be especially vulnerable because a patchwork of applicable laws makes it hard to obtain needed upgrades and complicates collaboration among key public and private entities. For example, Texas operates its own single state power grid, the Electric Reliability Council of Texas (ERCOT), while the rest of the continental United States is comprised of two, major multi-state power grids, the Eastern and Western Interconnections. By establishing its own self-contained electric grid many decades ago, Texas avoided transmitting electricity in interstate commerce, thus exempting itself from federal regulatory oversight under the Federal Power Act (discussed later in this chapter) and granting it more authority than most states to chart its own course in developing energy markets and regulations. But ERCOT's isolation was a liability, not an asset, in the cold weather of February 2021.

Texas could not call on energy resources from other parts of the nation, as is done elsewhere in the country, because of its physical and regulatory barriers. Likewise, ERCOT's lack of a "capacity market," which pays generators in advance to have reserve power available in times of high demand, meant that when ERCOT's energy demand forecasts proved too low, there was no extra power available as backup. The impact of extreme weather events on the nation's energy infrastructure is no surprise; the number of outages caused by severe weather is expected to rise as a changing climate increases the frequency and intensity of such events. *See* JUDSON BRUZGUL & NEIL WEISENFELD, ICF INT'L, RESILIENT POWER: HOW UTILITIES CAN IDENTIFY AND PREPARE FOR INCREASING CLIMATE RISKS (2021) (highlighting utilities' vulnerabilities to climate stressors and the need to improve infrastructure resilience); *see also* NAT'L ACAD. OF SCI., ENG'G, & MED., ENHANCING THE RESILIENCE OF THE NATION'S ELECTRICITY SYSTEM 50–68 (2017) (discussing the causes of grid failure and how climate change may increase the frequency and severity of floods, wildfires, and regional weather impacts).

Just as the grid failure in Texas was not limited to the physical aspects of the problem, neither was it limited to the electricity sector. The difficulties after the Texas freeze highlight the physical ways in which electricity and transportation—the two major components of our energy system—are linked despite often separate laws and agencies governing them. For instance, the weaknesses in the electric grid in Texas did not simply limit the flow of electricity crucial to repairs. It also constrained transportation well beyond the immediate shutdown of planes, trains, and roads from the storm. Gas stations, pipelines, and terminals that supply them need electricity to function. The cold crippled some of Texas's—and the continent's—largest oil refineries and caused fuel deliveries to be delayed or halted, resulting in 15% of Texas gas stations to be without fuel a week after freezing temperatures arrived. *See* Jeffrey Blair, *Gasoline Crisis Paralyzes One of Every Seven Texas Stations*, BLOOMBERG NEWS (Feb. 24, 2021). The gasoline shortage triggered food supply chain disruptions across the state; many stores implemented purchase limits on groceries as suppliers struggled to deliver products. Restaurants and stores were forced to throw out spoiled food and Texas residents lined up for hours in the hope of finding food. *See* Leslie Patton, *Texas is Facing a Food Supply Nightmare in Wake of Blackouts*, BLOOMBERG NEWS (Feb. 19, 2021).

The energy fallout from severe weather events often has unequal impacts, as reflected in the crisis in Texas. There are no express standards for equity or public safety when implementing rolling blackouts in Texas. Rather, when the storm struck in February 2021, the blackout allocation was based on critical infrastructure and engineering considerations alone. Arianna Skibell, *Texas Grid Crisis Exposes Environmental Justice Rifts*, ENERGYWIRE (Feb. 23, 2021). This resulted in predominantly white areas having an 11% chance of experiencing an outage while predominantly non-white areas had a 47% chance. Mary Dettloff, *Frozen Out: Minorities Suffered Four Times More Power Outages in Texas Blackouts*, UMASS.EDU (April 14, 2021).

Before the storms hit Texas and the blackouts began, legislators and public utility commissioners knew of natural gas shortages and the potential impacts of the cold. *See* Edward Klump et al., *Documents Reveal Natural Gas Chaos in Texas Blackouts*, ENERGYWIRE (May 20, 2021). Despite facing similar weather-induced power outages in 2011, the state's energy generation infrastructure was not sufficiently weatherized to survive the storm unscathed. In the months after Texas's energy crisis, state lawmakers grappled with identifying the root cause of the grid failure and how to address future challenges. State-level disagreements represent a microcosm of national interests and concerns over the role of fossil fuels and renewable energy sources and of free markets and regulation in the future of the nation's energy production. Some political figures blamed renewable energy for the grid's failure and proposed imposing costs on renewable facilities to ensure grid reliability; others stood steadfastly in support of renewables and highlighted how natural gas shortages contributed to the blackouts. *See* Herman K. Trabish, *'A Terrible Idea': Texas Legislators Fight Over Renewables' Role in Power Crisis, Aiming to Avert a Repeat*, UTIL. DIVE (May 17, 2021). As lawmakers continue to debate the role of renewable energy, weatherization, and the role of energy markets, one thing is certain: changes to the energy system will be needed to adapt to our changing climate and prevent the recurrence of such disasters.

This small sampling of the issues arising from increasingly severe weather events illustrates the complexity of energy law and its many components. U.S. energy law, the primary subject of this book, frames and is framed by the physical characteristics of our energy sources and system, by the markets that value and distribute them, and by the policies that shape them. "Energy law" is made up of different statutes and regulations created at multiple levels of government. A myriad of individuals, corporations, government agencies, and nongovernmental organizations have an interest in how individual energy issues are resolved.

While energy law interacts extensively with environmental law, the two areas have different goals, statutory regimes, and key regulatory agencies. Energy law's primary focus is on providing reliable, affordable energy. It covers extraction and transportation of energy resources, electricity production and transmission, and transportation of goods and people. Energy law has an additional focus on regulating markets, in part due to the major industries it covers, but also because perceived market failures have led to government price-setting. Environmental law, by contrast, focuses on addressing pollution and on conserving and protecting key natural resources. For a more in-depth discussion of these issues, see Lincoln L. Davies, *Alternative Energy and the Energy-Environment Disconnect*, 46 IDAHO L. REV. 473 (2010); Alexandra B. Klass, *Climate Change and the Convergence of Environmental and Energy Law*, 24 FORDHAM ENV'T L. REV. 180 (2013); Jody Freeman, *The Uncomfortable Convergence of Energy and Environmental Law*, 41 HARV. ENV'T L. REV. 339 (2017).

In the past, the primary direct interface between energy and environmental law has occurred when energy projects have environmental implications. Today, however, we face a new set of challenges—including concerns about climate change and the need for new approaches to economic growth and energy justice—that take place against the backdrop of longstanding commitments like those to energy security. This has brought the fields of energy law and environmental law closer together while creating new challenges for both fields. For instance, as discussed later in this chapter and in Chapter 6, the Obama administration's regulation of motor vehicle greenhouse gas (GHG) emissions combined regulation of fuel economy, an "energy" issue, and tailpipe emissions, an "environmental" issue, for the first time. The interface of energy and environmental law also arises in the electricity regulation context. The largely federal-state approach to environmental law does not always mesh neatly with regional energy markets. *See* Hannah J. Wiseman & Hari M. Osofsky, *Regional Energy Governance and U.S. Carbon Emissions*, 43 ECOLOGY L.Q. 143 (2016).

The introductory examples of the Texas and California power outages illustrate the complexity of the energy system and how seldom people "look behind the plug." Most people think little about where their energy comes from until a crisis occurs, whether a serious one—like persistent blackouts after increasingly frequent hurricanes and winter storms or oil spilling into the Gulf of Mexico—or a relatively minor one like the power outage during the 2013 Super Bowl or a passing thunderstorm. At those moments, consumers simply want the lights back on and would prefer not to grapple with the complicated reasons that the power loss occurred.

At its core, this book is about understanding what happens behind the plug from a physical, market, and regulatory perspective. The book grapples with the complexity of energy law's interaction with the energy system and environmental law. It discusses the laws applicable to sources of energy and to the two main components of the energy system—electricity and transportation. Throughout its exploration of that complexity, the book focuses both on how the system has historically evolved and how it is currently transitioning.

In considering these transitions, the book focuses on three major themes. First, it considers the way in which assumptions about energy markets drive regulatory strategies around ensuring fair pricing and spurring innovation. In other words, should energy production, distribution, and consumption be handled by the market, by government regulation, or by some combination of the two? Second, it highlights the ways in which the fragmentation of crucial legal authority across key actors at different levels of government creates difficult federalism questions. Energy is subject to regulation by local and state governments, by regional authorities on occasion, and by the federal government, thus raising thorny federalism concerns. Third, it analyzes how the public pressure for cleaner energy, especially in the context of climate change, has begun to change regulatory approaches to electricity and transportation. In short, the country and the world are experiencing a significant energy transition from a traditional fossil fuel energy economy to one in which non-fossil fuels, renewable resources, and energy efficiency are playing increasingly important roles. Across the three themes, this book explores problems of inequality in access to energy resources, and in the pollution created by them, and considers possibilities for enhanced energy justice.

This introductory chapter begins the book's discussion of contemporary energy law and policy by (1) introducing the energy system; (2) highlighting the key government and private actors in the energy system; (3) providing a basic introduction to administrative law—the framework within which most energy system rules are made and many energy system disputes are resolved; and (4) providing an exposition of the three themes of energy law described in the previous paragraph.

B. INTRODUCTION TO THE ENERGY SYSTEM

Energy is the lifeblood of the global and U.S. economies and our societies. It fuels our transportation system, lights and heats our homes, and allows businesses to produce goods and services for the global economy. The energy system consists of both primary sources—coal, natural gas, oil, nuclear, renewables—and the secondary systems that use them—electricity and transportation. This book will focus on both aspects of the energy system.

Moments of crisis like the frigid cold in Texas or the blistering heat in California highlight how dependent we are on readily available primary energy sources and on our secondary electricity and transportation systems for our daily lives. As the graph below illustrates, our energy consumption has increased over the past decades, with minor dips during recessionary periods. Throughout 2020, COVID-19 and its related economic impacts resulted in a significant decrease in energy production and consumption.

U.S. Primary Energy Overview, 1949–2020

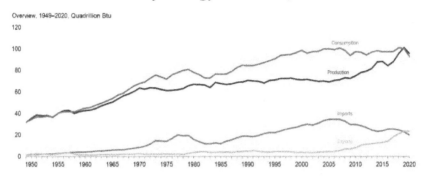

Source: U.S. Energy. Info. Admin.

Although our demand for energy continues to grow, starting in about 2008, U.S. energy prices for gasoline, heating oil, and natural gas began to decline. Likewise, electricity prices had been declining for decades and began to level off. *See* U.S. ENERGY INFO. ADMIN., MONTHLY ENERGY REVIEW 17 (Aug. 2021) (Table 1.6 showing "Cost of Fuel to End Users in Real (1982–1984) Dollars"). There are two significant reasons for this phenomenon. First, the 2008 economic recession reduced the spending power of most Americans. Second, as energy consumers, we continue to realize energy efficiencies, thus reducing overall costs even while our population increases spur increasing energy demand.

As illustrated in the diagram below, fossil fuel sources continue to dominate the U.S. energy system, despite the recent growth in renewable energy resources. In 2020, 79% of the primary energy consumed in the United States came from oil, natural gas, and coal. Nuclear power, another large-scale energy source, contributed 9% to our energy profile, leaving an array of renewable energy resources to round out the profile. Among renewable sources, wind and solar now make up over one-third of renewable energy production—a greater amount than hydropower—a big increase over just a few years ago. Biofuels and wood also comprise a significant portion of renewable sources; although their benefits and limitations are debated, they are considered renewable because they can be regrown if sustainably harvested.

U.S. primary energy consumption by energy source, 2020

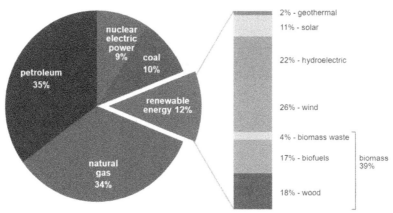

total = 92.94 quadrillion
British thermal units (Btu)

total = 11.59 quadrillion Btu

nuclear electric power 9%
coal 10%
petroleum 35%
renewable energy 12%
natural gas 34%

2% - geothermal
11% - solar
22% - hydroelectric
26% - wind
4% - biomass waste
17% - biofuels
18% - wood

biomass 39%

Note: Sum of components may not equal 100% because of independent rounding.
Source: U.S. Energy Information Administration, *Monthly Energy Review*, Table 1.3 and 10.1,
April 2021, preliminary data

eia

Source: U.S. Energy Info. Admin.

However, simply knowing these percentages only scratches the surface of the energy system's complexity. What makes energy law so complex from a physical perspective are variations in primary energy sources, their locations around the planet and within the United States, and the different ways in which they are transported, transformed, and used. These issues are discussed in Chapter 2.

The fossil and non-fossil fuel sources we rely on are used primarily for electricity and transportation. Different fuels dominate the transportation and electricity systems with oil providing nearly all transportation-related energy and natural gas, coal, nuclear energy, and renewables all powering the electricity sector. The electricity system also is subdivided into three customer classes: residential, commercial, and industrial users, with different patterns of energy use in each. The residential and commercial sectors of the economy generally consume energy for heating, cooling, and lighting purposes and powering end use devices. The industrial sector also consumes energy for these purposes, as well as for manufacturing. Energy is consumed in the transportation sector by cars, trucks, buses, and other motor vehicles, as well as by planes, trains, and ships. *See, e.g., U.S. Energy Facts, Explained*, U.S. Energy Info. Admin. (last updated May 14, 2021) (showing 2020 energy flow diagrams, including energy use by sector).

The ever-increasing energy use in both the electricity and transportation systems—dominated by fossil fuel sources—provides three primary challenges for energy law that help to drive some of the transitions discussed in the next section. First, fossil fuel sources of energy comprise the lion's share of U.S. and global GHG emissions. To the extent that regulators want to mitigate these emissions as part of a climate change strategy, they must grapple with how we use these sources of energy.

The following chart illustrates the fundamental interconnection between energy consumption and the emission of carbon dioxide (CO_2), one of the key GHGs. Note that coal and oil provide a higher percentage of carbon dioxide emissions than their percentage consumed as compared to natural gas because they emit more CO_2 when consumed. This is part of why natural gas was initially heralded by many as a "bridge fuel" to a lower carbon energy footprint. Because horizontal drilling paired with hydraulic fracturing gives access to large reserves of natural gas and drives down its price, it will likely continue to be a key energy source over the century despite the efforts by many groups, and now the Biden administration, to phase out fossil fuels—including natural gas—entirely.

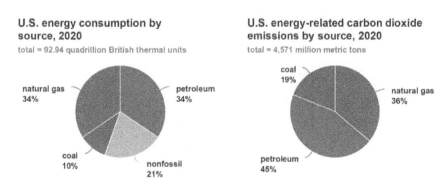

U.S. energy consumption by source, 2020
total = 92.94 quadrillion British thermal units

natural gas 34%
petroleum 34%
coal 10%
nonfossil 21%

U.S. energy-related carbon dioxide emissions by source, 2020
total = 4,571 million metric tons

coal 19%
natural gas 36%
petroleum 45%

Source: U.S. Energy Information Administration, *Monthly Energy Review*, Tables 1.3 and 11.1, April 2021, preliminary data
Note: nonfossil is nuclear and renewable energy.

Source: U.S. Energy Info. Admin.

When discussing U.S. contributions to climate change, a focus on domestic resource uses only provides a partial picture. Oil, natural gas, and coal are globally traded commodities and increasing demand for energy in other regions of the world is driving energy markets. If we use less coal domestically but still produce the same amount of coal and export more, that coal results in the same quantity of GHG emissions globally. Not counting these exports in our total contribution to climate change misses some of the ongoing ways that U.S. coal production affects global GHG emissions. For instance, the states of Wyoming and Montana have actively worked with coal companies to build export terminals on the U.S. West Coast to export U.S. coal to Asia. *See* Alexandra B. Klass & Shantal Pai, *The Law of Energy Exports*, 103 CALIF. L. REV. 733 (2021).

Second, even if nonconventional fuel extraction methods like deepwater drilling and hydraulic fracturing paired with horizontal drilling allow us to increase our domestic production of fossil fuels to meet our energy needs for longer than we originally thought, important questions remain surrounding the public health and climate consequences of continuing to use them. Thus, even though domestic oil production has increased significantly, and oil imports are declining, as illustrated by the following figure, imports remain substantial. *See Oil Imports and Exports*, U.S. Energy Info. Admin. (last updated Apr. 13, 2021) (explaining that the United States became a net petroleum exporter in 2020 for the first time since 1949, while still importing some crude oil for domestic use and for export).

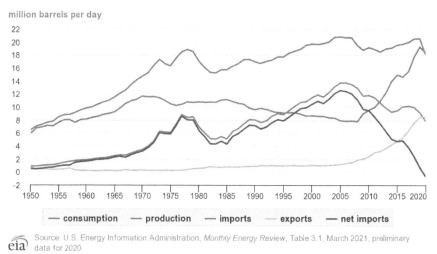

U.S. petroleum consumption, production, imports, exports, and net imports, 1950-2020

Source: U.S. Energy Information Administration, *Monthly Energy Review*, Table 3.1, March 2021, preliminary data for 2020

Source: U.S. Energy Info. Admin.

Moreover, many of the oil supplies outside of the United States are in Middle Eastern countries with which we have complex relationships or that remain geopolitically challenging. Likewise, cyberattacks on energy facilities in the United States, such as the one involving the Colonial Pipeline on the East Coast in May 2021, are a growing threat. Thus, while the advent of hydraulic fracturing paired with horizontal drilling in the United States has significantly reduced longstanding concerns surrounding supply-related risks to U.S. "energy independence," increasing concerns over cyberattacks as well as the disruptive impacts of climate change on energy facilities means that a truly "resilient" U.S. energy system remains elusive. *See, e.g.*, Clifford Krauss, *Hackers and Climate Change Threaten Energy Independence*, N.Y. TIMES (May 18, 2021).

Finally, the electricity and transportation systems have physical characteristics that pose difficult market regulatory questions. A key issue in both systems is the optimal level of centralization versus decentralization. In the context of electricity, this issue arises due to fundamental infrastructure questions. As explored in depth in Chapters 4 and 5, providing electricity was long believed to be a natural monopoly, an industry in which competition in a particular physical area was impractical due to the high costs of generation plants, transmission lines, and distribution networks. For natural monopolies, governments tend to engage in price-setting regulation because there is inadequate competition to let the market set a fair, low price for consumers. Over time, regulators have increasingly treated electricity generation and, to some extent, certain aspects of electricity transmission and distribution, as capable of supporting competitive markets. In addition, efforts have been made to shift away from relying exclusively on big power plants that transport electricity over long distances to incorporating a distributed generation model where localized energy sources (renewable and non-renewable) power more local sections of the distribution network. The questions of when markets are capable of setting prices and the appropriate role of government in supporting a transition to a more decentralized grid pose complex dilemmas that will be explored throughout the electricity chapters of the book.

In the context of transportation, as explored in Chapter 6, there have been complex dynamics around centralization and decentralization as well, driven by patterns of urbanization, the national highway program, and the power of the automobile industry. Many metropolitan areas initially expanded in ways that aligned with their physical topography and placement of trolley lines. With the advent of the automobile era, many streetcar lines were ripped from the streets. Automobiles made massive suburban and exurban expansion possible, leading to wide-ranging metropolitan areas where some of the larger suburbs became developed job centers. However, pressures around cleaner energy and environmental justice have led some cities to invest in a rebuilding of light rail systems, and movements to locate work, school, and play closer to where people live. The COVID-19 crisis that began in 2020 has created new opportunities for remote work which, in turn, has shifted electricity and transportation energy use. There have also been growing efforts to recognize and address the continuing adverse effects of decades of highway expansion that destroyed and fundamentally altered low-income and minority urban neighborhoods. These challenges interact with other social, market, and legal concerns to create major transitions for the energy system.

NOTES AND QUESTIONS

1.   How should law deal with the varying characteristics of physical energy sources? Right now, different legal regimes address almost every source. If you want to decrease this fragmentation, how should a more holistic approach to energy law incorporate these differences?

2.   To what extent has the shift from coal to natural gas helped the United States transition to cleaner energy? On the one hand, natural gas emits fewer GHG emissions and other air pollutants than coal when burned in power plants. On the other hand, low prices for natural gas may make it harder for even "cleaner" renewable energy sources like solar and wind to enter the market more fully now and in the future. What role might energy storage play in this dynamic moving forward?

3.   Another crucial physical challenge to modernizing the grid, as discussed in later chapters, is that it can be extremely difficult to obtain regulatory approval to build interstate, long-distance electric transmission lines due to a lack of federal authority and sometimes conflicting regional, state, and local authority. These "siting" issues also serve as a barrier to bringing new renewable energy generators on-line, as wind and solar are often located far from existing transmission lines. For a discussion of these issues, see Alexandra B. Klass & Elizabeth J. Wilson, *Interstate Transmission Challenges for Renewable Energy: A Federalism Mismatch*, 65 VAND. L. REV. 1801 (2012).

C. KEY GOVERNMENTAL AND NONGOVERNMENTAL ACTORS IN THE ENERGY SYSTEM

This chapter thus far has focused on the energy system's complicated physical dimensions that help to frame legal approaches to energy law. This section introduces an additional complexity—the myriad of governmental, nongovernmental, and hybrid participants in the energy system. It begins by discussing the many different types of governmental regulators, and then turns to the nongovernmental and hybrid entities that play a critical role in how energy law operates.

Several federal agencies play an important regulatory role and in some energy sectors, the primary role. The most important of those agencies are the Department of Energy (DOE), Federal Energy Regulatory Commission (FERC), Nuclear Regulatory Commission (NRC), Department of the Interior (DOI), and Environmental Protection Agency (EPA). However, many other agencies are also relevant. For example, as discussed more in Chapter 6, the Department of Transportation (DOT) plays a significant role in highway planning and funding, setting federal vehicle fuel economy standards, and funding and facilitating the transition to electric vehicles.

The cabinet-level DOE was established in 1977 by the Department of Energy Organization Act of 1977, 42 U.S.C. §§ 7101, *et seq.* Prior to its creation, energy was regulated by several agencies and departments. Indeed, agencies such as the Department of the Interior, the Department of Agriculture, and the Department of Defense continue to have energy regulatory responsibilities.

The DOE came out of two notable traditions. First, DOE regulates defense related energy projects and laboratories stemming from the creation of the atomic bomb through the Manhattan Project. Second, in response to the Arab Oil Embargo in 1973, the DOE was created to satisfy a desire for a more coordinated and centralized energy regulator. Throughout this book, we will provide citations to a wide array of statutes that address traditional regulation of the coal, oil, and natural gas industries. Further, an additional set of statutes addresses alternative and renewable resources as well as energy efficiency. The DOE has significant responsibility in both arenas. *See generally* Sharon B. Jacobs, *The Statutory Separation of Powers*, 129 YALE L.J. 378 (2019) (discussing history of DOE and its relationship with other federal agencies).

In addition to its regulatory authority, the DOE is responsible for conducting planning, research, and development. Section 801 of the Department of Energy Organization Act, for example, requires the President to submit to Congress a biannual national energy plan in consultation with regional, state, and local agencies as well as the private sector. Energy research and development (R&D) is wide-ranging and includes funding for projects ranging from clean coal to green hydrogen and from advanced battery systems to hydrogen fuel cells. These several R&D initiatives as well as the scope of DOE activities can be seen on its website, http://energy.gov/. The U.S. DOE's National Laboratories are also active in energy research. The historic nuclear weapons labs—Los Alamos, Livermore, Sandia, and the Pacific Northwest National Lab (PNNL)—all have strong energy research portfolios focusing on technology and materials development as well as energy modeling and cybersecurity. Additionally, other national labs also specialize in energy research. The National Renewable Energy Laboratory (NREL) performs world-class research on renewable technologies like wind, biomass, geothermal, and solar; Lawrence Berkeley National Laboratory has leading groups focused on energy storage, energy efficiency, and transportation; the National Energy Technology Laboratory (NETL) works on carbon capture and storage as well as advanced coal technologies; and Oak Ridge and Argonne have become leaders in energy and transportation.

FERC—previously the Federal Power Commission—is another important federal energy regulatory agency and plays a prominent role throughout this book. Congress established FERC to oversee the country's interstate transmission and the pricing of a variety of energy resources, including electricity, natural gas, and oil. FERC is responsible for assisting consumers in obtaining reliable, efficient, and sustainable energy services at a reasonable cost through appropriate regulatory and market means by (1) ensuring that rates, terms, and conditions are just, reasonable and not unduly discriminatory or preferential; and (2) promoting the development of safe, reliable, and efficient energy infrastructure that serves the public interest. More specifically, FERC's responsibilities include:

- Regulating the interstate transmission of natural gas, oil, and electricity;

- Regulating the wholesale sale of electricity (individual states regulate retail sales);

- Licensing and inspecting hydropower projects;

- Approving the construction of interstate natural gas pipelines, storage facilities, and Liquefied Natural Gas (LNG) terminals;

- Monitoring and investigating energy markets; and

- Maintaining the reliability of the electric grid.

The President appoints FERC's five commissioners for 5-year terms with the advice and consent of the Senate. One member of the Commission is designated by the President to serve as chair and FERC's administrative head; all commissioners have an equal vote on regulatory matters. To avoid undue political influence or pressure, no more than three commissioners may belong to the same political party. The Commission is funded through costs recovered by the fees and annual charges from the industries it regulates. To maintain FERC's independence as a regulatory agency capable of providing fair and unbiased decisions, neither the President nor Congress reviews FERC decisions in advance of issuance.

FERC and the other federal agencies listed above have designated roles in regulating the energy system that at times overlap not only with other federal agencies, but also with state governments. The chapters that follow will explore the enabling authority Congress has granted to each federal agency and how that authority has changed over time because of new legislation, judicial decisions, and changing Presidential administrations that have altered agency priorities.

Despite the prominence of federal agencies in regulating energy law, much of the lawmaking critical to energy takes place at the state and local levels. The nuanced differences among each state's legal system generally and approach to energy law in particular can make a unified understanding of energy law difficult. In the context of electricity, the state public utility commissions described in the notes and questions below play a crucial role in regulating the utilities that provide power in that state, which often includes setting prices. For both electricity and transportation, state and local land use planning and environmental regulation determine where the crucial infrastructure can be placed. Moreover, state-based legislation and administrative regulation interact with that state's common law. For instance, as discussed in depth in Chapters 3 and 9 in the context of oil and gas production, the rule of capture articulated in *Pierson v. Post*, 3 Cai. R. 175, 2 Am. Dec. 264 (N.Y. 1805), continues to play an important role.

Energy regulation is not created by governmental entities alone. Corporations, utilities, banks, nongovernmental organizations, and individuals also play crucial roles in the development of formal energy law and the informal norms that influence behavior. Some of the most important entities in the energy regulation process are not clearly definable as either governmental or nongovernmental. Rather, they are hybrid public-private entities that are governmentally constituted but have private members that play a decision-making role. Later chapters explore many variations on such entities, which are often regional or national in scope. For example, in the electricity context, Regional Transmission Organizations (RTOs) and Independent System Operators (ISOs) help manage the grid and are key players in addressing renewable energy integration, and the North American Electric Reliability Corporation (NERC) sets standards to maintain grid reliability, including promulgating new cybersecurity standards.

NOTES AND QUESTIONS

1.   Jonas Monast and Sarah Adair describe the different types of state agencies involved with energy regulation:

> States wield the primary authority to regulate electric utilities and play a critical role in implementing and enforcing both state and federal environmental law. While states seek to provide citizens with affordable electricity, reliable electricity, and a healthy environment, they commonly delegate portions of these interrelated goals to multiple state agencies with very different mandates. For instance, state public utility commissions (PUCs) or public service commissions (PSCs) primarily serve to protect consumers, balancing consumers' interest in affordable rates against the utility's financial health, which is necessary to attract capital and provide reliable service. State environmental agencies protect the public health and the environment by developing and enforcing standards that may require utilities to install costly pollution controls, retire plants, and raise rates. A third type of agency, the state energy office, influences the affordability, reliability, and environmental impact of electricity production within the state by developing and implementing

additional state energy goals, such [as] encouraging investment in energy efficiency and renewable energy.

Jonas J. Monast & Sarah K. Adair, *A Triple Bottom Line for Electric Utility Regulation: Aligning State-Level Energy, Environmental, and Consumer Protection Goals*, 38 COLUM. J. ENV'T L. 1, 3–4 (2013).

2. Energy companies vary greatly in their responses to environmental initiatives such as GHG emissions regulations. Several energy companies, like Shell Oil, were among the coalition of business leaders urging President Trump to remain in the Paris Agreement. Ben Popken, *Big Business Urges Trump to Stick with Paris Climate Accord*, NBC NEWS (May 31, 2017). At the same time, numerous U.S. states, cities, and private parties have sued fossil fuel companies in recent years seeking damages and restitution for harms associated with climate change in their jurisdictions caused by the defendants' emission of GHGs as well as for alleged false statements made by these companies over decades regarding the relationship between the use of their products and climate change. Similar lawsuits have also been filed in other countries seeking injunctive relief and damages. *See, e.g.*, Maxine Joselow, *Big Tobacco Had to Pay $206B. Is Big Oil Next?*, CLIMATEWIRE (Mar. 10, 2021); Sam Meredith, *Big Oil's Increasing Number of Climate Lawsuits Draws Parallels to Big Tobacco*, CNBC (June 25, 2021); Jacqueline Peel & Hari M. Osofsky, *Climate Change Litigation*, 16 ANN. REV. OF L. & SOC. SCI. 21 (2020); Rupert F. Stuart-Smith, *Filling the Evidentiary Gap in Climate Litigation*, NATURE CLIMATE CHANGE (June 28, 2021). What role should lawsuits like these play in the energy transition? Does this litigation support or work at cross purposes with clean energy legislation and regulation?

Moreover, individual energy companies may have a complex relationship to energy transition. For example, although Shell Oil was one of the companies supporting the Paris Agreement, it also has been the subject of lawsuits and protests. One of the most significant critiques was of its operations in Nigeria, particularly in the aftermath of that government's execution of Ken Saro-Wiwa—a poet, lawyer, and activist protesting Shell's activities—on trumped up charges. Shell faced lawsuits in Nigeria, the Netherlands, and the United States over its operations there. For a discussion of these lawsuits, see Hari M. Osofsky, *Climate Change and Environmental Justice: Reflections on Litigation over Oil Extraction and Rights Violations in Nigeria*, 1 J. HUM. RTS & ENV'T 189 (2010). For a broader discussion of Shell's operations in Nigeria, see IKE OKONTA & ORONTO DOUGLAS, WHERE VULTURES FEAST: SHELL, HUMAN RIGHTS, AND OIL (2003); OGONI'S AGONIES: KEN SARO-WIWA AND THE CRISIS IN NIGERIA (Abdul-Rasheed Na'Allah ed., 1998).

D. ADMINISTRATIVE LAW BASICS

As noted in the previous section, many departments, bureaus, and agencies of the federal government are directly involved in establishing rules and regulations for the energy industry. Understanding how the law interacts with these agencies requires a basic understanding of administrative law. While administrative law is not the only type of law relevant to energy law—common law property cases help to frame the law of oil and natural gas extraction—it plays an important role in energy law and is often not taught in the first year of law school. This section provides a basic introduction to administrative law, explaining when it is relevant to energy law and some core tenets of how it works.

When agencies make rules pursuant to energy law statutes, administrative law becomes relevant. For example, to name a few examples of federal agency regulation of the production, distribution and consumption of energy, the DOE sets standards for energy efficiency, conducts energy R&D, and oversees energy defense activities. The Interior Department makes decisions regarding leasing of federal onshore and offshore lands for oil, natural gas, and coal extraction as well as for solar and wind projects. The Department of Transportation issues rules concerning the safety of pipelines, oil tankers, and the like as well as vehicle fuel economy standards. The Internal Revenue Service implements a range of taxes on energy industry actors. The Department of Justice and the Federal Trade Commission monitor monopoly activities in energy industries.

Additionally, the EPA issues rules and regulations concerning clean air and clean water, thus affecting power plants and their emissions. The Occupational Safety and Health Administration oversees workplace safety throughout the energy sector, though miners are protected by the Department of Labor's Mine Safety and Health Administration. Finally, FERC oversees the interstate regulation of electricity and natural gas markets. More importantly, as you will read throughout this book, many energy decisions are made by state administrative agencies such as public utility commissions and public service commissions. While states have their own administrative procedures as well, we focus in this section on the general principles of federal administrative procedure.

Notably, administrative law is distinguishable from first-year law school common law courses such as torts, property, and contracts. The common law, also known as judge-made law, as the name implies, is forged in courts on a case-by-case basis. Regulatory lawmaking occurs in administrative agencies that have been directed by Congress to address issues set forth in statutes. Further, most often, judicial review will be available to oversee agency behavior. Many, if not most, energy issues will begin with a rule or decision made by an administrative agency. Consequently, energy lawyers must understand and be familiar with administrative law in order to practice effectively.[1]

---

[1]   A useful general text is WILLIAM F. FOX, UNDERSTANDING ADMINISTRATIVE LAW (6th ed. 2012).

In addition to the fact that courts develop common law and agencies develop administrative law, there are at least three other important distinguishing factors between the common law and regulatory law. First, common law decisions are made after a conflict between identifiable parties has occurred and after a court analyzes and decides how to retrospectively resolve that conflict. Regulatory decisions may be adjudicative in the same way. However, most regulatory decisions do not resolve retrospective disputes. Instead, regulatory decisions are forward-looking in that they are intended to apply not only to litigants in a controversy, but also prospectively to a general class of regulated parties. Thus, regulatory actions resemble legislative activity more than the resolution of past disputes.

Second, most common law controversies involve private parties trying to resolve disputes between them. Regulatory law controversies, however, will most often involve several private parties and a government actor or agency. A private party may seek individual redress against a government rule or decision. However, it is more often the case that private litigants are challenging the future application of a government rule or regulation that will have implications beyond their own individual interests.

Third, Congress authorizes administrative agencies through broad— but not unbridled—delegations of authority to perform certain actions.[2] The agency, then, has the obligation of implementing as well as executing the tasks assigned to it by the legislative branch. In this way, administrative agencies serve a judicial function by resolving individual disputes, a legislative function by promulgating forward-looking rules and regulations, and an executive function by implementing and enforcing directives from Congress.

Administrative agencies are sometimes referred to as the "fourth branch of government." With very rare exceptions, however, this is a misnomer. Administrative agencies are virtually all under the control of the executive branch. A handful of "independent regulatory agencies," such as FERC, are independent of the executive branch to the extent that the president lacks the power to remove officers. Nevertheless, all regulatory agencies are governed by three important legal principles. First, all agency action must pass constitutional muster. Second, all agency action must be consistent with the enabling statute that created the agency and with subsequent legislation that delegates responsibilities to it. And third, all

---

[2] In the beginning of the New Deal, the Supreme Court twice invalidated congressional delegations of authority to administrative agencies. See *Panama Refining Co. v. Ryan*, 293 U.S. 388 (1935); *A.L.A. Schechter Poultry Corp. v. United States*, 295 U.S. 495 (1935) (both cases invalidated portions of the National Industrial Recovery Act). Since those decisions, however, the Court has given Congress broad authority to delegate. *See, e.g., FPC v. Hope Natural Gas Co.*, 320 U.S. 591 (1944); *Gundy v. United States*, 139 S. Ct. 2116 (2019).

agencies must satisfy the minimum procedural requirements of the Administrative Procedure Act (APA), 5 U.S.C. §§ 551, *et seq.*

Regulatory lawyers must be familiar with the statutory requirements of the agencies with whom they work and with statutory administrative procedures. Additionally, to the extent that a controversy continues beyond the administrative process, the regulatory lawyer must also understand the extent and availability of judicial review. While a full course on administrative law is advisable for the regulatory lawyer, here we highlight the requirements of the APA and the basic principles of judicial review.

1. THE ADMINISTRATIVE PROCEDURE ACT

The APA sets out the general procedural framework and the minimum procedural requirements for administrative agencies. The APA also establishes rules for the judicial review of their actions. The APA, however, is not always controlling because an agency's organic statute, such as the Department of Energy Organization Act, 42 U.S.C. §§ 7101, *et seq.*, also contains procedural provisions that take precedence over the APA. Nevertheless, under the APA, agencies basically engage in two functions— adjudication and rulemaking. The APA sets out requirements for both formal and informal adjudication and formal and informal rulemaking. Still, agencies have any number of procedures available, and in this short space we highlight only the general principles of these basic procedures.

a. Adjudication

Formal adjudication is a non-jury trial-type hearing, also known as an "on-the-record-hearing," conducted by an administrative law judge (ALJ). Adjudication is available when a statute requires a decision "to be determined on the record after opportunity for an agency hearing" with exceptions set out in the statute. 5 U.S.C. § 554(a). Persons who have a right to an agency hearing are also entitled to notice of the time, place, and nature of the hearing; the legal authority and jurisdiction under which the hearing is to be held; and the matters of fact and law to be addressed. 5 U.S.C. § 554(b). Parties to such a hearing shall be given the opportunity to submit facts and arguments and make settlement offers. 5 U.S.C. § 554(c). Similar to a trial, the ALJ receives evidence under oath pursuant to APA § 556 and makes a decision pursuant to § 557. Further, parties to an adjudication can cross-examine witnesses. The rules of evidence apply, but are more liberally construed than in court proceedings. Hearsay evidence, for example, otherwise inadmissible in court, is generally admissible in administrative proceedings. Thus, in every case of formal adjudication required by statute to be determined on the record after an opportunity for hearing, the procedures in § 554 must be followed.

While discovery is generally available to parties in judicial proceedings, the APA has no provision for discovery in agency actions. Instead, most formal agency adjudications are preceded by staff investigations that do uncover a wide range of evidence. A formal hearing is concluded with the issuance of a written decision and the APA has detailed requirements governing its contents. The statute requires that the parties receive an opportunity to provide proposed findings and conclusions as well as exceptions to the proposed decision before the agency announces a recommended, initial, or final decision. 5 U.S.C. § 557(c). The APA then provides that decisions must include "findings and conclusions and the reasons or basis therefore, on all material issues of fact, law, or discretion presented on the record." *Id.* These requirements gain importance because they elaborate an agency's reasoning for its decision for a reviewing court, and thus make agency administrators publicly accountable for their decisions.

At the conclusion of the hearing, the ALJ makes an initial decision or recommends one. If the ALJ makes an initial decision, that decision becomes the agency's decision unless it is timely appealed. When the ALJ recommends a decision, the final decision is rendered by the commissioners or by the members of an agency's governing body. The agency is not required to accept the determination of the ALJ on either matters of fact or law. However, if the agency rejects the initial determination by the ALJ, it must provide persuasive reasons for doing so. While the APA sets out general requirements for adjudicatory procedures and subsequent appeals, other enabling legislation can set out its own procedural requirements. The Federal Power Act, for example, establishes specific procedures for rate hearings. *See, e.g.*, 16 U.S.C. § 824d(e).

Agencies also use informal adjudication when neither a formal adjudication nor a rulemaking is required. Because these actions are informal, generalization is difficult. These agency actions range from an individual face-to-face meeting involving an applicant for Social Security benefits to the Department of Veterans Affairs Board deciding thousands of disability cases each year where formal adjudication is not required by statute.[3]

b. Rulemaking

Rulemaking is the procedure used most extensively by administrative agencies. More particularly, informal or "notice and comment" rulemaking is a procedure by which agencies conduct their business. Rulemaking is how an agency exercises its legislative function. Importantly, a rule is defined as "the whole or a part of an agency statement of general or

---

[3] *See* WILLIAM F. FOX, UNDERSTANDING ADMINISTRATIVE LAW ch. 9 (6th ed. 2012).

particular applicability and future effect designed to implement, interpret, or prescribe law or policy . . ." 5 U.S.C. § 551(4).

At the most basic level, pursuant to § 553(b), an agency must issue a "notice of proposed rulemaking" (NOPR) in the Federal Register. As examples, the EPA can issue a NOPR for clean air regulations or the DOE can issue a NOPR for efficiency standards. The notice must contain certain information such as the time, place, and nature of the rule making proceeding and the legal authority for it. After the notice is given, interested parties can review the proposed rule and submit their comments and arguments either in favor of or in opposition to the proposal. Once the comments are received, an agency publishes the final rule which must be consistent with its statutory and policy goals and must include a concise general statement of its basis and purpose. § 553(c).

If a statute requires that a rule be made on the record after opportunity for a hearing, then §§ 556 and 557 apply, a formal rulemaking occurs, and a hearing is conducted. The difficulty for an agency or regulated party lies in determining whether a particular statute requires a formal trial-type proceeding or will allow informal notice and comment rulemaking. There is a general preference for informal rulemaking; nevertheless, statutes may require more procedural protections and an agency is free to engage in "hybrid rulemaking" that utilizes procedures other than the APA minima. *See, e.g., Vermont Yankee Nuclear Power Corp. v. NRDC*, 435 U.S. 519 (1978).

For the last 30 years or so, the use of informal notice and comment rulemaking has grown substantially. Rulemaking processes can be more efficient than case-by-case adjudication simply because the rulemaking can resolve many issues in a single proceeding. At the same time, rulemaking elicits participation by interested parties and is often more transparent than adjudicatory processes. Generally, courts have been liberal in permitting agencies to use notice and comment rulemaking. More specifically, the APA does not contain any requirement that an announcement of an agency's new policy must be done by adjudication or rulemaking. Courts, in turn, have not made it mandatory for agencies to use one or the other procedure in setting policy. Rather, courts have largely left the determination of policymaking procedure to the agency's discretion.

In recent years, notice and comment rulemaking has come under criticism. A rule can languish either in an agency or in an oversight bureau, such as the Office of Information and Regulatory Affairs (OIRA) within the White House.[4] Since President Reagan, the White House, by Executive Order, has exercised substantial authority over proposed rules, discussed in more detail in later chapters. Specifically, "major rules," defined as rules

---

[4] *See, e.g.,* Michael L. Livermore & Richard L. Revesz, *Regulatory Review, Capture and Agency Inaction,* 101 GEO. L.J. 1338 (2013).

that can have an annual effect on the economy of $100 million or more, must be reviewed by the White House to assess the costs and benefits of those rules to reduce costly regulatory burdens on the economy. More recently, this process has been criticized for slowing down the rulemaking process and advantaging industry interests over public interests.[5] That criticism has met with responses that OIRA functions well to gather data for more informed and more coordinated and efficient decisions.[6] More recently, in 2021, President Biden issued a Presidential Memorandum calling for the modernization of regulatory review processes, including "ways that OIRA can play a more proactive role in partnering with agencies to explore, promote, and undertake regulatory initiatives that are likely to yield significant benefits." *Presidential Memorandum—Modernizing Regulatory Review* (Jan. 20, 2021).

During the Trump administration, federal agencies faced additional restraints. To manage the costs that private parties had to spend to comply with federal regulations, the administration imposed a requirement that for each new regulation issued, agencies had to identify at least two prior regulations for elimination. *See* Executive Order 13771, 82 Fed. Reg. 9339 (2017). President Biden subsequently revoked this requirement. *See* Executive Order 13992, 86 Fed. Reg. 7049 (2021).

2. JUDICIAL REVIEW

"A person suffering legal wrong because of agency action, or adversely affected or aggrieved by agency action within the meaning of a relevant statute, is entitled to judicial review thereof." 5 U.S.C. § 702. This grant of authority from the APA seems quite broad; however, it is subject to important limitations. Congress, by statute, can preclude judicial review or require a party to take additional actions prior to judicial review. The Natural Gas Act, for example, requires that persons aggrieved by a FERC order must first seek agency appeal before seeking judicial review: "No objection to the order of the Commission shall be considered by the court unless such objection shall have been urged before the Commission in the application for rehearing unless there is reasonable ground for failure so to do." 15 U.S.C. § 717r(b). In general, an appeal of a FERC order can be filed in either the U.S. Court of Appeals for the District of Columbia Circuit or in the U.S. Court of Appeals for the circuit in which the regulated entity is located or has its principal place of business. *See* 15 U.S.C. § 717r(b) (Natural Gas Act); 16 U.S.C. § 825*l*(b) (Federal Power Act). Further, before judicial review is available, an agency action must be final as defined by

---

[5] *See, e.g., Eyes on OIRA*, CENTER FOR PROGRESSIVE REFORM, http://www.progressivereform. org/EyeonOIRA.cfm. *But see* Gabriel Scheffler, *Failure to Capture: Why Business Does Not Control the Rulemaking Process*, 79 MD. L. REV. 700 (2020).

[6] *See, e.g.*, Cass Sunstein, *The Office of Information and Regulatory Affairs: Myths and Realities*, 126 HARV. L. REV. 1838 (2013) (note that Professor Sunstein served as head of OIRA under President Obama from September 2009 to August 2012).

statute. 5 U.S.C. § 704. Also, the decision must involve a matter that has not been committed to agency discretion by law. 5 U.S.C. § 701(a)(2).

The discretion requirement is tricky. Administrative decisions generally involve discretion and are ordinarily reviewable. However, if an action has been "committed to agency discretion," judicial review is unavailable. Determining the dividing line between abuse of discretion and discretion that is committed to an agency is difficult. In attempting to identify that dividing line, courts will look to whether "meaningful standards" for review are available. In the absence of any meaningful standard, review will be denied. Compare *Citizens to Preserve Overton Park v. Volpe*, 401 U.S. 402, 410 (1971) (finding discretion exception to judicial review did not apply because federal statute at issue conditioned Secretary of Transportation's approval of funds for highways through parks on there being no "feasible and prudent" alternative to the selected route) with *Heckler v. Cheney*, 470 U.S. 821 (1985) (refusal of Food and Drug Administration to determine whether injection of inmates sentenced to death with legal drugs alleged to be in noncompliance with agency's regulation was subject to prosecutorial discretion and thus not susceptible to meaningful judicial review). *See* ALFRED C. AMAN, JR. & WILLIAM T. MAYTON, ADMINISTRATIVE LAW (3d ed. 2014).

Under the APA, the scope of judicial review is substantial: "the reviewing court shall decide all relevant questions of law, interpret constitutional and statutory provisions, and determine the meaning or applicability of the terms of an agency action." 5 U.S.C. § 706. Further, the reviewing court can "compel agency action unlawfully withheld or unreasonably delayed." 5 U.S.C. § 706(1). Additionally, the reviewing court can:

hold unlawful and set aside agency action, findings, and conclusions found to be—

(A) arbitrary, capricious, an abuse of discretion, or otherwise not in accordance with law;

(B) contrary to constitutional right, power, privilege, or immunity;

(C) in excess of statutory jurisdiction, authority, or limitations, or short of statutory right;

(D) without observance of procedure required by law;

(E) unsupported by substantial evidence in a case subject to sections 556 and 557 of this title or otherwise reviewed on the record of an agency hearing provided by statute; or

(F) unwarranted by the facts to the extent that the facts are subject to trial de novo by the reviewing court.

5 U.S.C. § 706(2).

As specific as the statutory guidance may appear, the regulatory lawyer understands that keen attention must be paid to standing and to the standards of review used by courts in assessing agency action. Standing is a requirement imposed on courts by Article III of the Constitution, which provides that courts can only hear "cases or controversies." Over the years, that requirement has been repeatedly litigated and refined.

In the 1970s, the Supreme Court established a requirement that someone seeking judicial review of an agency action must allege individualized injury. *Sierra Club v. Morton*, 405 U.S. 727 (1972). The Supreme Court has established strict standards for proving an "injury-in-fact" that would meet standing requirements to challenge agency action. For example, in 1978, the Supreme Court allowed an environmental group to challenge the constitutionality of the Price-Anderson Act that set a $600 million limit on damages from a single nuclear power plant accident. *See Duke Power Co. v. Carolina Environmental Study Group*, 438 U.S. 59 (1978). In later cases, the Court tightened the standing requirement and held that plaintiffs who challenge agency action as general taxpayers or as citizens will generally not be given standing. Instead, they must allege injury that is personal, and more than the type of injury suffered by any other citizen of the country. *See, e.g., Valley Forge Christian College v. Americans United for Separation of Church and State*, 454 U.S. 464 (1982). *See also Lujan v. National Wildlife Federation*, 497 U.S. 871 (1990) (allegations of injury associated with reclassifying federal lands for commercial development insufficient where plaintiffs alleged they had visited those lands and agency action had damaged their enjoyment of those lands); *Summers v. Earth Island Institute*, 555 U.S. 488 (2009) (standing denied for failure to allege sufficient injuries in fact). Nevertheless, environmental lawsuits do not always lose in the Court. Indeed, in *Massachusetts v. EPA*, 549 U.S. 497 (2007), the Court granted standing to the state of Massachusetts when it sought to have the EPA address GHG emissions from automobiles pursuant to the Clean Air Act.

Once standing has been granted, litigants who challenge federal agency action must then satisfy the requirements of § 706 as set out above, which empower a court to set aside agency action for legal or factual reasons. As a matter of law, an agency action may be set aside if it is arbitrary, capricious, or an abuse of discretion; contrary to constitutional law; or, in excess of an agency's statutory jurisdiction. § 706(2)(A)–(C). Under the doctrine of separation of powers, courts purport to be the ultimate authority to decide cases because of their judicial independence. Nevertheless, courts must be careful to observe and uphold the congressional delegation of power to an agency. Further, courts are well aware of agencies' technical expertise and, therefore, will grant agencies a significant degree of deference on that basis. *See, e.g., Industrial Union Department, AFL-CIO v. American Petroleum Institute*, 448 U.S. 607 (1980); *Baltimore Gas & Elec. Co. v. NRDC*, 462 U.S. 87 (1983).

Another essentially legal issue involves an agency's interpretation of a statute, a context in which courts exercise a good deal of deference. The Supreme Court has established a policy for reviewing an agency's construction of a statute. The reviewing court must first determine whether "Congress has directly addressed the precise question at issue." If so, then the reviewing court should "give effect to the unambiguously expressed intent of Congress." If the statute, however, is "silent or ambiguous with respect to the specific issue," the issue becomes whether the agency's interpretation is either "permissible" or a "reasonable interpretation." If the statute remains ambiguous after this analysis, then it must be presumed that Congress delegated to the agency the task of filling statutory gaps in some reasonable way. *Chevron U.S.A., Inc. v. NRDC*, 467 U.S. 837 (1984). The literature on the *Chevron* decision is vast, and courts continue to take seriously their judicial independence in the reviewing process. It is often the case, for example, that determining ambiguity presents ambiguities of its own, and courts are not reluctant to make their own interpretations rather than simply rely on an agency's construction. *See, e.g., MCI Telecommunications Corp. v. AT & T*, 512 U.S. 218 (1994); *United States v. Mead*, 533 U.S. 218 (2001).

Courts likewise defer to agency interpretations of their own ambiguous regulations through what is commonly termed *Auer* deference. For this form of deference to apply, the regulations must be genuinely ambiguous and there must be a presumption that Congress intended to defer to the agency. Further, the agency's regulatory interpretation must implicate the agency's substantive expertise, reflect "fair and considered judgment," and must not be an *ad hoc* rationalization. *See Kisor v. Wilkie*, 139 S. Ct. 2400 (2019) (citing *Auer v. Robbins*, 519 U.S. 452 (1997)). Even if agency interpretations are not afforded *Chevron* or *Auer* deference, courts will defer to agency readings to the extent that they have the power to persuade. *See id.* at 2414; *Skidmore v. Swift & Co.*, 323 U.S. 134, 140 (1944).

As to matters of fact, the reviewing court will only overturn an agency action that is "unsupported by substantial evidence." § 706(2)(E). Substantial evidence has been defined as "such relevant evidence as a reasonable mind might accept as adequate to support a conclusion." *Consolidated Edison Co. v. NLRB*, 305 U.S. 197 (1938). The reviewing court is engaged in an inquiry to make sure that the agency has carefully reviewed the evidence. Sometimes a court will take a "hard look"[7] at the agency's factual review and at other times a court will give that review a "soft glance."[8] In either case, the court is required to examine the whole record when looking at an agency's evidentiary analysis.

Agencies are required to explain their findings and the reasons for their decisions so that the reviewing court can examine the decision fully based on the "whole record." *See* § 706. If an agency, for example, issues an order not based on substantial evidence, does not consider alternatives that are contained in the record, or does not explain why it ignored those evidentiary alternatives, then its decision can be overturned. To substantiate its decision, the agency must discuss the available evidence and provide "a rational connection between the facts found and the choice made." *Motor Vehicle Mfrs. Ass'n v. State Farm Mut. Auto Ins.,* 463 U.S. 29 (1983). In other words, the reviewing court is not to look only for evidence that supports an agency's decision, but also must consider all the relevant evidence both for and against an agency's finding to determine whether the finding and decision are within a zone of reasonableness. *See* Sidney A. Shapiro & Richard W. Murphy, *Arbitrariness Review Made Reasonable: Structural And Conceptual Reform of the "Hard Look,"* 92 NOTRE DAME L. REV. 331 (2016); Richard W. Murphy, *Un Foxing Judicial Review of Agency Policy Reversals or "We Were Told to Like the New Policy Better" is Not a Good Reason to Change,* 54 U. RICH. L. REV. 1045 (2020).

Administrative law, then, is at the heart of energy law and policymaking. Many of the cases that follow were generated by agency decisions which were subject to the rules, principles, and procedures of administrative law. Additionally, many of the policy extracts that follow also have been part of the administrative lawmaking process. Students of regulatory law, then, should have some sense of rulemaking and adjudication as well as the circumstances under which judicial review of agency action is available.

E. THREE THEMES OF *ENERGY LAW AND POLICY*

An important part of what makes energy law so complicated is that the physical energy system is in transition. Our reliance on different energy sources has shifted over time through a combination of emerging technologies, market forces, policies, and regulations. As discussed in later chapters, a major market shift has taken place from coal to natural gas in the United States. This shift was complemented by the Obama administration's GHG regulations in the energy sector—which the Trump administration substantially reversed but the Biden administration is

---

[7] Citizens to Preserve Overton Park, Inc. v. Volpe, 401 U.S. 410 (1971); Harold Leventhal, *Environmental Decision Making and the Role of the Courts,* 122 U. PA. L. REV. 509, 525 (1974).

[8] William H. Rodgers Jr., *Benefits, Costs and Risks: Oversight of Health and Environmental Decisionmaking,* 4 HARV. ENV'T L. REV. 191, 210–14 (1980).

restoring and supplementing—and lawsuits against the coal industry. *See Climate Deregulation Tracker*, Sabin Center for Climate Change Law; *Climate Reregulation Tracker*, Sabin Center for Climate Change Law.

Additionally, technological developments over the last two decades have revived domestic fossil fuel production and at the same time bolstered renewable energy development. Today, ultra-deepwater drilling is possible in oceans and more widespread shale extraction methods have increased the domestic supplies of oil and natural gas and increased recoverable fossil fuel supplies globally. Technological developments and favorable tax treatment have also allowed wind and solar energy to increasingly undercut the costs of fossil fuels in the electric sector, making these renewable energy resources more competitive in many energy markets. *See, e.g.*, Benjamin Storrow, *Building Wind, Solar Can be Cheaper Than Existing Gas*, CLIMATEWIRE (Oct. 21, 2020). Even as these developments transform the energy system, further technological and policy challenges remain. For example, although there is general agreement that we need to expand and modernize our electricity system, grid improvements face technological as well as regulatory and social barriers, including concerns about siting, privacy, and cybersecurity.

In considering these transitions, as noted above, three main themes emerge: (1) the appropriate relationship between regulation, markets, and technological innovation; (2) the federalism issues that arise from the interaction of key regulatory actors; and (3) the transition to cleaner energy. Each of these themes will be explored in more detail through the remainder of this book.

1. WHAT ROLE SHOULD REGULATION PLAY IN ENERGY MARKETS?

The United States, like any country, must decide how to treat a critical societal input, such as energy. Often the basic choice has been framed as a choice between so-called "free markets" or government regulation. In fact, that choice is hardly simple. First, markets require government rules to operate fairly and effectively. Without contract, property, or tort rules, for example, no modern market can function because no contract could be enforced, no injury could be compensated, and no property could be protected. In short, the oft-stated choice between markets or government is a false choice. Markets are tools for organizing society and need rules— *i.e.*, government regulations—to operate.

Second, competitive markets are very difficult to create and sustain. For example, a market imperfection, such as pollution, will cause inefficiencies that can be remedied only by some sort of outside intervention, often by the government. Thus, the question of how to address energy issues is always a question about what the proper mix between government intervention and competition ought to be.

One other point needs to be stressed. In the United States, competitive markets are viewed as important tools to support wealth creation, efficient resource distribution, and the encouragement of innovation. Still, given market imperfections and negative externalities (and other public policies that we discuss throughout the book) the United States is a mixed economy: it relies on the combination of markets enabled by government rules to promote the common good. Consequently, "how free" a market should be, and how much the law should tip its weight to favor one energy outcome or another, repeatedly emerges as a fundamental inquiry in energy law. Should coal plant emissions be more closely regulated? Should Congress encourage nuclear power because it is a relatively "clean" energy source with virtually no GHG emission from the plants used to produce power? Should Congress provide significant tax subsidies for wind and solar energy to make them more competitive with fossil fuels? Should federal and state governments create tax credits or mandates for electric vehicles? Or should the market decide? Debates about the extent, as well as the nature, of government regulation permeate our energy economy.

Thus, as discussed in more depth in Chapter 2, energy law must make choices about when and how to intervene in energy markets. Specifically, the law's regulation of markets aims to address four primary economic problems: (1) a firm's market power, or influence over a market; (2) physical and economic waste; (3) negative externalities, largely environmental and social harm; and (4) free-riding, where some market participants aim to make money based on someone else's monetary and time investments.

Efforts to address these problems through law take multiple forms with respect to energy sources and the two main secondary systems of electricity and transportation. Much of energy regulation ends up influencing prices charged and options available. Some of that influence is direct. Laws explicitly authorize price setting or production incentives in some markets. In other cases, the law does not explicitly address markets, but ends up affecting them significantly, for instance by leaving crude oil pricing primarily to competitive forces or by taxing gasoline sales at the pump.

One of the most fundamental areas in which law interacts with markets is electric utility regulation—the body of law governing our providers of electricity. Even in a country committed to private capital markets, we find the government exercising the extraordinary power to set the prices of a private firm's product. For even though the bulk of electric utilities that serve retail customers are called "public utilities," they are, for the most part, privately owned. Federal and state government regulators have the constitutional and statutory authority to set the prices of those private utilities' products, and have traditionally exercised it, because those utilities had monopoly power and might not set prices fairly. In particular, utilities were viewed as "natural monopolies," which are monopolies arising in situations where infrastructure costs are sufficiently high that it only makes sense for one firm to participate in a market.

Traditional electric utility regulation focused on "vertically integrated" utilities that controlled electric generation, transmission, and distribution for a region. It treated those vertically integrated utilities as natural monopolies in all phases of electricity production. However, as electricity markets in some states have been restructured, many states allow for varying levels of competition in electricity generation, transportation, and distribution. Competition has also been encouraged at a federal level with interstate sales. This growth in competitive markets has taken place in some of these sectors more than others. For example, electric distribution largely retains natural monopoly characteristics, but as distributed generation and microgrids expand, opportunities for competition arise.

As electric generation becomes more competitive but transmission—and distribution for the most part—continue to be natural monopolies, an additional dilemma arises—generators need access to transmission lines to sell electricity. The following case excerpt, which involves a challenge to FERC's requirements on transmission access, provides an overview of this growth in competitive markets as well as an introduction to some of the key players in this market transition.

In particular, the case focuses on a dilemma resulting from the "unbundling"—separating out—the cost of generation of electricity at power plants from the cost of transmitting it from those power plants to distribution centers and end users. Traditionally, states "bundled" generation, transmission, and distribution, so customers received one bill for all these services. "Unbundling" these functions allows a state to support more competition in its energy markets if it chooses to do so.

The case also addresses the extent to which utilities transmitting energy should be forced to carry electricity generated by their competitors. Should the answer to that question depend upon whether the utility transmitting electricity has "unbundled" its services? As you read it, focus on what you believe to be the appropriate role of government in shaping markets and how the different levels of government are interacting with each other and the utilities.

NEW YORK V. FERC
535 U.S. 1 (2002)

JUSTICE STEVENS delivered the opinion of the Court.

These cases raise two important questions concerning the jurisdiction of the Federal Energy Regulatory Commission (FERC or Commission) over the transmission of electricity. First, if a public utility "unbundles"—i.e., separates—the cost of transmission from the cost of electrical energy when billing its retail customers, may FERC require the utility to transmit competitors' electricity over its lines on the same terms that the utility applies to its own energy transmissions? Second, must FERC impose that requirement on utilities that continue to offer only "bundled" retail sales?

In Order No. 888, issued in 1996 with the stated purpose of "Promoting Wholesale Competition Through Open Access Non-Discriminatory Transmission Services by Public Utilities," FERC answered yes to the first question and no to the second. It based its answers on provisions of the Federal Power Act (FPA), as added by § 213, and as amended, 16 U.S.C. § 824 *et seq.*, enacted in 1935. Whether or not the 1935 Congress foresaw the dramatic changes in the power industry that have occurred in recent decades, we are persuaded, as was the Court of Appeals, that FERC properly construed its statutory authority.

In 1935, when the FPA became law, most electricity was sold by vertically integrated utilities that had constructed their own power plants, transmission lines, and local delivery systems. Although there were some interconnections among utilities, most operated as separate, local monopolies subject to state or local regulation. Their sales were "bundled," meaning that consumers paid a single charge that included both the cost of the electric energy and the cost of its delivery. Competition among utilities was not prevalent.

Prior to 1935, the States possessed broad authority to regulate public utilities, but this power was limited by our cases holding that the negative impact of the Commerce Clause prohibits state regulation that directly burdens interstate commerce. When confronted with an attempt by Rhode Island to regulate the rates charged by a Rhode Island plant selling electricity to a Massachusetts company, which resold the electricity to the city of Attleboro, Massachusetts, we invalidated the regulation because it imposed a "direct burden upon interstate commerce." *Public Util. Comm'n of R.I. v. Attleboro Steam & Elec. Co.*, 273 U.S. 83, 89 (1927). Creating what has become known as the "Attleboro gap," we held that this interstate transaction was not subject to regulation by either Rhode Island or Massachusetts, but only "by the exercise of the power vested in Congress." *Id.* at 90.

When it enacted the FPA in 1935, . . . Congress authorized federal regulation of electricity in areas beyond the reach of state power, such as the gap identified in *Attleboro*, but it also extended federal coverage to some areas that previously had been state regulated. . . . The FPA charged the Federal Power Commission (FPC), the predecessor of FERC, "to provide effective federal regulation of the expanding business of transmitting and selling electric power in interstate commerce." . . . Specifically, in § 201(b) of the FPA, Congress recognized the FPC's jurisdiction as including "the transmission of electric energy in interstate commerce" and "the sale of electric energy at wholesale in interstate commerce." . . . Furthermore, § 205 of the FPA prohibited, among other things, unreasonable rates and undue discrimination "with respect to any transmission or sale subject to the jurisdiction of the Commission," . . . and § 206 gave the FPC the power to correct such unlawful practices. . . .

Since 1935, and especially beginning in the 1970's and 1980's, the number of electricity suppliers has increased dramatically. Technological advances have made it possible to generate electricity efficiently in different ways and in smaller plants. In addition, unlike the local power networks of the past, electricity is now delivered over three major networks, or "grids," in the continental United States. Two of these grids— the "Eastern Interconnect" and the "Western Interconnect"—are connected to each other. It is only in Hawaii and Alaska and on the "Texas Interconnect"—which covers most of that State—that electricity is distributed entirely within a single State. In the rest of the country, any electricity that enters the grid immediately becomes a part of a vast pool of energy that is constantly moving in interstate commerce. As a result, it is now possible for power companies to transmit electric energy over long distances at a low cost. As FERC has explained, "the nature and magnitude of coordination transactions" have enabled utilities to operate more efficiently by transferring substantial amounts of electricity not only from plant to plant in one area, but also from region to region, as market conditions fluctuate. . . .

As amici explain in less technical terms, "[e]nergy flowing onto a power network or grid energizes the entire grid, and consumers then draw undifferentiated energy from that grid." . . . As a result, explain amici, any activity on the interstate grid affects the rest of the grid. Amici dispute the States' contentions that electricity functions "the way water flows through a pipe or blood cells flow through a vein" and "can be controlled, directed and traced" as these substances can be, calling such metaphors "inaccurate and highly misleading." . . .

Despite these advances in technology that have increased the number of electricity providers and have made it possible for a "customer in Vermont [to] purchase electricity from an environmentally friendly power producer in California or a cogeneration facility in Oklahoma," . . . public utilities retain ownership of the transmission lines that must be used by their competitors to deliver electric energy to wholesale and retail customers. The utilities' control of transmission facilities gives them the power either to refuse to deliver energy produced by competitors or to deliver competitors' power on terms and conditions less favorable than those they apply to their own transmissions. . . .

Congress has addressed these evolving conditions in the electricity market on two primary occasions since 1935. First, Congress enacted the Public Utility Regulatory Policies Act of 1978 (PURPA) . . . to promote the development of new generating facilities and to conserve the use of fossil fuels. Because the traditional utilities controlled the transmission lines and were reluctant to purchase power from "nontraditional facilities," PURPA directed FERC to promulgate rules requiring utilities to purchase electricity from "qualifying cogeneration and small power production facilities." . . .

Over a decade later, Congress enacted the Energy Policy Act of 1992 (EPAct), 106 Stat. 2776. This law authorized FERC to order individual utilities to provide transmission services to unaffiliated wholesale generators (i.e., to "wheel" power) on a case-by-case basis. . . . Exercising its authority under the EPAct, FERC ordered a utility to "wheel" power for a complaining wholesale competitor 12 times, in 12 separate proceedings. . . . FERC soon concluded, however, that these individual proceedings were too costly and time consuming to provide an adequate remedy for undue discrimination throughout the market.

Thus, in 1995, FERC initiated the rulemaking proceeding that led to the adoption of the order presently under review. FERC proposed a rule that would "require that public utilities owning and/or controlling facilities used for the transmission of electric energy in interstate commerce have on file tariffs providing for nondiscriminatory open-access transmission services." Notice of Proposed Rulemaking, 60 Fed. Reg. 17662 (hereinafter NPRM). The stated purpose of the proposed rule was "to encourage lower electricity rates by structuring an orderly transition to competitive bulk power markets." The NPRM stated:

> The key to competitive bulk power markets is opening up transmission services. Transmission is the vital link between sellers and buyers. To achieve the benefits of robust, competitive bulk power markets, all wholesale buyers and sellers must have equal access to the transmission grid. Otherwise, efficient trades cannot take place and ratepayers will bear unnecessary costs. Thus, market power through control of transmission is the single greatest impediment to competition. Unquestionably, this market power is still being used today, or can be used, discriminatorily to block competition. . . .

Rather than grounding its legal authority in Congress' more recent electricity legislation, FERC cited §§ 205–206 of the 1935 FPA—the provisions concerning FERC's power to remedy unduly discriminatory practices—as providing the authority for its rulemaking. . . .

In 1996, after receiving comments on the NPRM, FERC issued Order No. 888. It found that electric utilities were discriminating in the "bulk power markets," in violation of § 205 of the FPA, by providing either inferior access to their transmission networks or no access at all to third-party wholesalers of power. . . . Invoking its authority under § 206, it prescribed a remedy containing three parts that are presently relevant.

First, FERC ordered "functional unbundling" of wholesale generation and transmission services. FERC defined "functional unbundling" as requiring each utility to state separate rates for its wholesale generation, transmission, and ancillary services, and to take transmission of its own wholesale sales and purchases under a single general tariff applicable equally to itself and to others.

Second, FERC imposed a similar open access requirement on unbundled retail transmissions in interstate commerce. Although the NPRM had not envisioned applying the open access requirements to retail transmissions, but rather "would have limited eligibility to wholesale transmission customers," FERC ultimately concluded that it was "irrelevant to the Commission's jurisdiction whether the customer receiving the unbundled transmission service in interstate commerce is a wholesale or retail customer." . . . Thus, "if a public utility voluntarily offers unbundled retail access," or if a State requires unbundled retail access, "the affected retail customer must obtain its unbundled transmission service under a non-discriminatory transmission tariff on file with the Commission." . . .

Third, FERC rejected a proposal that the open access requirement should apply to "the transmission component of bundled retail sales." . . . Although FERC noted that "the unbundling of retail transmission and generation . . . would be helpful in achieving comparability," it concluded that such unbundling was not "necessary" and would raise "difficult jurisdictional issues" that could be "more appropriately considered" in other proceedings. . . .

In 1997, in response to numerous petitions for rehearing and clarification, FERC issued Order No. 888–A. . . . With respect to various challenges to its jurisdiction, FERC acknowledged that it did not have the "authority to order, sua sponte, open-access transmission services by public utilities," but explained that § 206 of the FPA explicitly required it to remedy the undue discrimination that it had found. . . . FERC also rejected the argument that its failure to assert jurisdiction over bundled retail transmissions was inconsistent with its assertion of jurisdiction over unbundled retail transmissions. FERC repeated its explanation that it did not believe that regulation of bundled retail transmissions (i.e., the "functional unbundling" of retail transmissions) "was necessary," and again stated that such unbundling would raise serious jurisdictional questions. . . . FERC did not, however, state that it had no power to regulate the transmission component of bundled retail sales. . . . Rather, FERC reiterated that States have jurisdiction over the retail sale of power, and stated that, as a result, "[o]ur assertion of jurisdiction . . . arises only if the [unbundled] retail transmission in interstate commerce by a public utility occurs voluntarily or as a result of a state retail program." . . .

The first question is whether FERC exceeded its jurisdiction by including unbundled retail transmissions within the scope of its open access requirements in Order No. 888. New York argues that FERC overstepped in this regard, and that such transmissions—because they are part of retail transactions—are properly the subject of state regulation. New York insists that the jurisdictional line between the States and FERC falls between the wholesale and retail markets.

As the Court of Appeals explained, however, the landscape of the electric industry has changed since the enactment of the FPA, when the electricity universe was "neatly divided into spheres of retail versus wholesale sales." . . . As the Court of Appeals also explained, the plain language of the FPA readily supports FERC's claim of jurisdiction. Section 201(b) of the FPA states that FERC's jurisdiction includes "the transmission of electric energy in interstate commerce" and "the sale of electric energy at wholesale in interstate commerce.". . . The unbundled retail transmissions targeted by FERC are indeed transmissions of "electric energy in interstate commerce," because of the nature of the national grid. There is no language in the statute limiting FERC's transmission jurisdiction to the wholesale market, although the statute does limit FERC's sale jurisdiction to that at wholesale. . . .

Th[e] statutory text . . . unambiguously authorizes FERC to assert jurisdiction over two separate activities—transmitting and selling. It is true that FERC's jurisdiction over the sale of power has been specifically confined to the wholesale market. However, FERC's jurisdiction over electricity transmissions contains no such limitation. Because the FPA authorizes FERC's jurisdiction over interstate transmissions, without regard to whether the transmissions are sold to a reseller or directly to a consumer, FERC's exercise of this power is valid. . . .

Order No. 888 does not even arguably affect the States' jurisdiction over three of these subjects: generation facilities, transmissions in intrastate commerce, or transmissions consumed by the transmitter. Order No. 888 does discuss local distribution facilities, and New York argues that, as a result, FERC has improperly invaded the States' authority "over facilities used in local distribution." . . . However, FERC has not attempted to control local distribution facilities through Order No. 888. To the contrary, FERC has made clear that it does not have jurisdiction over such facilities, and has merely set forth a seven-factor test for identifying these facilities, without purporting to regulate them. . . .

Our evaluation of the extensive legislative history reviewed in New York's brief is affected by the importance of the changes in the electricity industry that have occurred since the FPA was enacted in 1935. No party to these cases has presented evidence that Congress foresaw the industry's transition from one of local, self-sufficient monopolies to one of nationwide competition and electricity transmission. Nor is there evidence that the 1935 Congress foresaw the possibility of unbundling electricity transmissions from sales. More importantly, there is no evidence that if Congress had foreseen the developments to which FERC has responded, Congress would have objected to FERC's interpretation of the FPA. Whatever persuasive effect legislative history may have in other contexts, here it is not particularly helpful because of the interim developments in the electric industry. Thus, we are left with the statutory text as the clearest guidance. That text unquestionably supports FERC's jurisdiction to order unbundling of wholesale transactions (which none of the parties before us questions), as well as to regulate the unbundled transmissions of electricity retailers. . . .

Accordingly, the judgment of the Court of Appeals is affirmed.

It is so ordered.

Law interacts with markets beyond price setting and access to markets. Indeed, law can promote and advance technological innovation. Technological innovation can certainly come from two people fooling around with electronics in their garage. Such innovation can also come from large-scale government research and development projects like the Manhattan Project, which ultimately yielded commercial nuclear power, or the Apollo Project, which yielded any number of innovations. In addition, innovation can emerge through public-private collaborations, as was the case with the development of SO_2 scrubbers for coal-fired power plants. Energy innovation is discussed more fully in Chapter 11.

Thus, the question of whether to "leave it to the market" or to engage government involvement is not an either-or question. It is one of degree— how much government involvement do we want or need, and how much should society rely solely on markets, which inevitably have their own logics and flaws? Government regulation, for example, can create incentives for new technologies related to energy production from fossil fuels and renewable sources. The following excerpt involves a controversy around the appropriateness of government mandates requiring companies to achieve a minimum level of energy efficiency for appliances like refrigerators, heating systems, and air conditioners and the metrics regulators use to set those mandates.

ZERO ZONE, INC. V. U.S. DEP'T OF ENERGY
832 F.3d 654 (7th Cir. 2016)

The United States Department of Energy (DOE) published [a final rule to improve] the energy efficiency of commercial refrigeration equipment (CRE). . . . 79 Fed. Reg. 17,726 (Mar. 28, 2014) (the "New Standards Rule"). . . .

Petitioners Zero Zone, Inc. (Zero Zone), a small business specializing in CRE, and Air-Conditioning, Heating and Refrigeration Institute (AHRI), a trade association of CRE manufacturers, petitioned for review . . . .

The Energy Policy and Conservation Act (EPCA), Pub. L. No. 94–163, §§ 321–339, 89 Stat. 871, 917–32 (1975) (codified as amended at 42 U.S.C. §§ 6201–6422) was enacted in part to improve the energy efficiency of specific types of equipment and appliances. Congress enacted the EPCA in the wake of the 1973–1974 embargo of petroleum exports to the United States by the Organization of Arab Petroleum Exporting Countries. S. Rep. No. 94–26, at 26 (1975). It viewed the embargo as presenting a need for "legislation which would facilitate the reduction of the nation's petroleum consumption through energy conservation." *Id.* at 27; *see also* H.R. Rep. No. 94–340, at 1 (1975) ("This legislation is directed to the attainment of the collective goals of increasing domestic supply, *conserving and managing energy demand*, and establishing standby programs for minimizing this nation's vulnerability to major interruptions in the supply of petroleum imports." (emphasis added)).

As originally enacted, the EPCA authorized the Federal Energy Administration (FEA)—the predecessor to DOE—to implement voluntary "energy efficiency improvement target[s]" that would encourage manufacturers to decrease the energy consumption of their equipment. However, Congress determined shortly thereafter that, "[u]nder the target approach, there would be little incentive by a manufacturer to exceed a target, and to do so might place a given manufacturer at a competitive disadvantage." H.R. Rep. No. 95–496, at 45 (1977). It therefore amended the EPCA to impose *mandatory* energy conservation standards. National Energy Conservation Policy Act, Pub. L. No. 95–619, § 422, 92 Stat. 3206, 3259 (1978). As amended, the EPCA directs DOE to review these standards and implement new ones when appropriate. 42 U.S.C. §§ 6313(c), 6316(e), 6295(m).

When establishing new energy conservation standards, DOE must follow certain statutory requirements. First, standards may not "increase[ ] the maximum allowable energy use" of any individual unit. *Id.* § 6295(*o*)(1). Second, standards must be "designed to achieve the maximum improvement in energy efficiency" and be "technologically feasible and economically justified." *Id.* § 6295(*o*)(2)(A). . . .

Congress amended the EPCA in 2005, and in doing so added CRE to the industrial equipment category. Energy Policy Act of 2005, Pub. L. No. 109–58, § 136, 119 Stat. 594, 638–39 (codified at 42 U.S.C. § 6313(c)(2)–(3)) (EPACT). The EPACT prescribed standards for six different classes of CRE. § 136, 119 Stat. at 639. It also required DOE to set standards for additional classes of CRE that were not yet covered by the EPCA. *Id.*

Accordingly, DOE published a final rule on January 9, 2009, that prescribed energy conservation standards for thirty-eight additional equipment classes. These classes were defined by a combination of the equipment's geometry (vertical, semivertical, or horizontal), door type (solid, transparent, or open), condensing-unit configuration (self-contained or remote-condensing), and operating temperature (medium, low, or ice-cream). . . .

The New Standards Rule establishes energy conservation standards for forty-nine classes of CRE. Just as in DOE's earlier 2009 Final Rule, the classes were defined by a combination of the equipment's geometry, door type, condensing-unit configuration, and operating temperature. For each class, the maximum daily energy consumption is determined by a function of either the unit's refrigerated volume (V) or the unit's total display area (TDA). For eight equipment classes, DOE made no changes from the 2009 Final Rule. For the remaining forty-one equipment classes, DOE set forth a higher standard that it determined was both technologically feasible and economically justified. DOE estimated that the revised standards were likely to result in a savings of 2.89 quadrillion British thermal units of energy in 2014—an "annualized energy savings equivalent to 0.5 percent of total U.S. commercial primary energy consumption in 2014." . . .

The resulting energy conservation standards do not compel manufacturers to use any particular components to achieve improved efficiency. Instead, as DOE explained, "should manufacturers value some features over others, they are free to use different design paths in order to attain the performance levels required." . . .

. . . DOE concluded in the Final Rule, published on March 28, 2014, that the new standards would result in lower energy use and thus produce a net benefit to consumers between $4.93 and $11.74 billion. In addition, DOE noted the monetary benefits of the reductions in greenhouse gas emissions. DOE then determined that the development of new CRE would cost manufacturers between $93.9 and $165 million. DOE concluded that the benefits outweighed the costs and that the standards therefore would be economically justified. . . .

In our review, "[w]e give great deference to an agency's predictive judgments about areas that are within the agency's field of discretion and expertise." . . . However, we also note that the Supreme Court "has stressed the importance of not simply rubber-stamping agency factfinding." *Dickinson v. Zurko*, 527 U.S. 150, 162 (1999). . . .

The EPCA requires that efficiency standards be "economically justified." 42 U.S.C. § 6295(o)(2)(A). In addressing this statutory mandate, DOE established five different "trial standard levels," and determined which "level" would be economically and technologically feasible. . . . DOE concluded that [the third-highest] level of standards would produce a net benefit to consumers between $4.93 and $11.74 billion and reduce greenhouse gas emissions. Conversely, the new standards would cost manufacturers between $93.9 and $165 million. DOE determined therefore that the standards were justified. The petitioners fault DOE's economic analysis in several ways. We now address each of those arguments.

The petitioners first contend that DOE acted arbitrarily and capriciously when it assumed that the new standards would not result in significant changes in purchasing behavior. DOE essentially treated CRE as "price inelastic," meaning that an increase in the price of CRE would not impact the amount of CRE purchased. The petitioners object to that assumption, noting that consumers could refurbish used equipment or switch to cheaper, less-efficient models of CRE.

Our review of the record convinces us that DOE's consideration of this issue was certainly more balanced and careful than the petitioners suggest. DOE explained in the New Standards Rule that it "did not have enough information on CRE customer behavior to explicitly model" the effects of the new standards on demand, and therefore it had to make a prediction about the market for CRE. In its technical support document, DOE reasoned:

> In general, when the data are available[,] DOE incorporates a purchase price elasticity into the shipments model. This allows for the possibility that total shipments will fall under a standard, due to a rise in the first cost of the equipment. For commercial refrigeration equipment, DOE did not have access to any data that would allow the estimation of purchase price elasticities. Therefore the total shipments in the standards case scenarios are the same as the total shipments in the base case scenario. As most users of this equipment are subject to health codes and other regulations, it is not very likely that a business owner would forego the purchase of needed equipment even under a price increase. Price sensitivity is more likely to occur in the form of increased equipment lifetimes. However, equipment lifetimes for food sales and service are driven primarily by the remodeling

cycle, and so are unlikely to be affected on the average by a standard.

DOE's analysis hardly is arbitrary and capricious. A business must store food at a proper temperature in order to comply with health code regulations. Consequently, in DOE's view, restaurants and other businesses will purchase CRE regardless of its price. A refrigerator cannot easily be substituted. DOE reasonably concluded that CRE is a "necessity" for restaurants and other businesses, which makes demand relatively inelastic. That conclusion is worthy of our deference. . . .

DOE considered the environmental benefits of the amended standards when determining whether the New Standards Rule was "economically justified." In particular, DOE employed "an estimate of the monetized damages associated with an incremental increase in carbon emissions in a given year," known as the Social Cost of Carbon (SCC). The petitioners contend that the EPCA does not allow DOE to consider environmental factors and that DOE abused its discretion when it considered them. In the alternative, the petitioners contend that DOE's analysis of the SCC was itself arbitrary and capricious.

We turn first to DOE's statutory authority under the EPCA. An agency decision is arbitrary and capricious when the agency "has relied on factors which Congress had not intended it to consider." *Nat'l Ass'n of Home Builders*, 551 U.S. at 658 (internal quotation marks omitted). Here, however, the EPCA specifically *requires* DOE to consider "the need for national energy . . . conservation." 42 U.S.C. § 6295(o)(2)(B)(i)(VI). In the New Standards Rule, DOE explained that the "Need of the Nation to Conserve Energy" includes the "potential environmental benefits" which would result. To determine whether an energy conservation measure is appropriate under a cost-benefit analysis, the expected reduction in environmental costs needs to be taken into account. We have no doubt that Congress intended that DOE have the authority under the EPCA to consider the reduction in SCC.

Alternatively, [petitioners] contend that DOE's calculation of SCC was irredeemably flawed. They submit that DOE failed to address three concerns about these calculations raised by the Chamber of Commerce in a letter during the notice and comment period. That letter complained that: (1) who exactly worked on the SCC analysis had not been made public; (2) the inputs to the models were not peer reviewed; and (3) the "damages functions," or variables based on problems like sea level rise, were determined in an arbitrary manner. DOE responded to the letter in general, noting that it "acknowledge[d] the limitations in the SCC estimates." DOE then referenced letters from multiple parties that supported the SCC values, a 2010 interagency group report on the discount rates used, and the OMB's Final Information Quality Bulletin for Peer

Review. Although DOE did not respond to the specific points laid out in the Chamber of Commerce letter, it did respond to the Chamber of Commerce's general concerns and made clear that, despite those concerns, the calculation of SCC could be used. . . . DOE's determination of SCC was neither arbitrary nor capricious.

The petitioners raise a series of objections to DOE's general approach to weighing the costs and benefits of its new standards. . . .

The petitioners first contend that DOE arbitrarily considered indirect *benefits* like carbon reduction over hundreds of years but ignored indirect *costs* like the long-term effects on displaced workers. DOE fully responded to that objection in the New Standards Rule . . .

[Petitioners] next contend that DOE arbitrarily considered the *global* benefits to the environment but only considered the *national* costs. They emphasize that the EPCA only concerns "national energy and water conservation." 42 U.S.C. § 6295(*o*)(2)(B)(i)(VI). In the New Standards Rule, DOE did not let this submission go unanswered. It explained that climate change "involves a global externality," meaning that carbon released in the United States affects the climate of the entire world. According to DOE, national energy conservation has global effects, and, therefore, those global effects are an appropriate consideration when looking at a national policy. Further, [petitioners] point to no global costs that should have been considered alongside these benefits. Therefore, DOE acted reasonably when it compared global benefits to national costs. . . .

NOTES AND QUESTIONS

1.   Order No. 888 relies on jurisdictional powers granted to FERC by the Federal Power Act—a statute, as the courts note, that has been around since 1935. Given that statute's age, and the massive changes that have occurred in the electricity industry since its passage, do you agree with FERC's decision to use that statute, which clearly anticipated a traditional, cost-based regulation model, to push electricity into new competitive frontiers? Should FERC instead have sought a more specific authorization from Congress to reform the industry in the way it did? For instance, does Congress' grant of authority to FERC to order power wheeling on a case-by-case basis cut against the Commission's claim of general Federal Power Act jurisdiction to reform the entire wholesale market? Or does the adaptability of the Federal Power Act's core provisions to modern times merely speak to the statute's durability (and Congress' intention that the statute's regulatory regime be flexible)?

2.   On its face, FERC's reliance on examining market structure and market power seems to make eminent sense. However, how much confidence should the public have in FERC's ability to adequately assess market structure? Does

the criticism that bureaucrats are poor at policing utilities in the cost-of-service ratemaking context equally apply to a market-based ratemaking regime?

3.   The *Zero Zone* case provides an example of Congress directing a federal agency—DOE—to set energy conservation standards for appliances to conserve energy. What aspects of the market for commercial and residential appliances might cause Congress to intervene through legislation like EPCA rather than letting market competition drive efficiency standards? If consumers will save money in the long run by using more energy efficiency appliances, why are labels about energy costs not enough to lead to more energy efficient appliances without the need for regulations?

4.   One of the primary points of contention in *Zero Zone* was whether DOE was justified in using a social cost of carbon (SCC) in determining whether the standards it set for commercial refrigeration equipment were "economically justified" under EPCA. As discussed in more detail in Chapter 6, In 2010, a federal interagency working group was tasked with establishing SCC values to estimate the climate benefits of federal agency rulemakings. The SCC is an estimate of the economic damages associated with a small increase in CO_2 emissions, generally one metric ton, in a given year. The SCC dollar figure represents the benefit of a CO_2 reduction or the value of damages avoided for reducing emissions. Between 2010 and 2016, a variety of federal agencies, including DOE, used in SCC in numerous rulemaking proceedings with the SCC set at approximately $51 per ton. *See* U.S. EPA, EPA FACT SHEET, THE SOCIAL COST OF CARBON (Dec. 2016). In 2017, the Trump administration reduced the SCC to $1 per ton by excluding all climate damages outside the continental United States. In 2021, President Biden directed federal agencies to reinstate use of the SCC in rulemaking proceedings at an interim value of $51 per ton and to conduct further study. For more information on the SCC, see VALUING CLIMATE DAMAGES: UPDATING ESTIMATION OF THE SOCIAL COST OF CARBON (The Nat'l Academies Press 2017); Jean Chemnick, *Cost of Carbon Pollution Pegged at $51 Per Ton*, SCI. AM. (Mar. 1, 2021) (discussing Biden administration actions). What provisions in EPCA allow consideration of a SCC in determining whether an appliance efficiency standard is "economically justified"?

5.   What would you be willing to do to reduce the amount of energy that you personally consume? What actions could you take that would have the greatest impact on energy demand?

2.   FEDERALISM

Energy law and policymaking consistently struggle with the question of who regulates what at which levels of government. The first case in the previous section introduces these issues in addition to highlighting evolving views of electricity markets. The battles over the appropriateness of FERC forcing open access to electricity transmission were not simply about the relationship between government and markets. In addition, the opinion explored debates over whether FERC was inappropriately stepping into state territory.

Disputes over federal versus state regulation have been a core concern of federalism since the founding of this country. Many disagreements over energy resources, electricity, and transportation include heated arguments over when federal versus state governments can and should exercise jurisdiction.

The following case, brought before the Federal Power Commission transitioned into FERC, illustrates another type of traditional federalism dispute that often arises in energy law. Here, the issue focuses on the limits of state authority rather than on the limits of federal authority. The court must determine whether a state-based utility has enough connection to interstate commerce to make federal regulation appropriate. As you read it, consider whether you think the majority opinion or the dissent more accurately captures the federalism issues.

FEDERAL POWER COMMISSION V. FLORIDA POWER & LIGHT CO.
404 U.S. 453 (1972)

MR. JUSTICE WHITE delivered the opinion of the Court.

We are asked to determine whether the Federal Power Commission [FPC] exceeded its statutory authorization when it asserted jurisdiction over the Florida Power & Light Co. Section 201(b) of the Federal Power Act . . . grants the Federal Power Commission jurisdiction over "the transmission of electric energy in interstate commerce and . . . the sale of electric energy at wholesale in interstate commerce, but . . . not (over) any other sale of electric energy. . . ." Section 201(c) defines energy transmitted in interstate commerce as energy "transmitted from a State and consumed at any point outside thereof." In *Connecticut Light & Power Co. v. FPC*, 324 U.S. 515 (1945), we noted that by this definition the initial jurisdictional determination "was to follow the flow of electric energy, an engineering and scientific, rather than a legalistic or governmental, test."

In the case now before us the FPC hearing examiner and the Commission itself, utilizing two scientific tests, determined that the Florida Power & Light Co. (FP & L) generates energy that is transmitted in interstate commerce. They therefore held the company subject to the Commission's jurisdiction. Respondent FP & L argues that an alternative model better represents the flow of its electricity; by use of this model it purports to demonstrate that its power has not flowed in interstate commerce. The Court of Appeals for the Fifth Circuit rejected the FPC's tests as "not sufficient to prove the actual transmission of energy interstate." It [also] did not approve FP & L's test . . ., but because the FPC must shoulder the burden of proof, its finding of jurisdiction was set aside.

We granted certiorari to determine if either of the FPC's tests provides an acceptable basis at law and a sufficient basis in fact for the establishment of jurisdiction.

I

FP & L is Florida's largest electric utility. At the time relevant to this litigation it served nearly one million customers, ranked ninth nationally among electric companies in revenues, 14th in investment in gross utility electric plant, and 16th in kilowatt-hour sales. Despite this significant size, the peninsular nature of Florida, the concentration of the company's sales in the southern part of the State, and the recurrent threat of hurricanes which might sever power lines combine to make the operations of the company unusually insular and independent of the operations of like companies in other States. All of FP & L's equipment, including transmission lines, is confined to Florida and none of its lines directly connect with those of out-of-state companies.

FP & L does, however, indirectly connect with out-of-state companies. As a member of the Florida Pool, it is interconnected with the Florida Power Corp. (Corp), the Tampa Electric Co., the Orlando Utilities Commission, and the City of Jacksonville. These interconnected utilities and authorities coordinate their activities and exchange power as circumstances require. In 1964 FP & L transferred over 107 million kwh to Corp and received over 61 million kWh from Corp. If power from FP & L flows in interstate commerce it is because Corp interconnects just short of Florida's northern border with Georgia Power Co. and regularly exchanges power with it. Georgia's lines transmit the power out of or into Florida. There are numerous instances in which transfers between Georgia and Corp are recorded as coinciding with transfers between Corp and FP & L.

The Georgia-Corp interconnection serves another function. Corp, FP & L, and the other Florida Pool participants are members of the Interconnected Systems Group (ISG), a national interlocking of utilities that automatically provides power in case of emergencies. In time of emergency this power also would flow through Corp's links with Georgia. To date FP & L has had no occasion to call for ISG power. But when a midwestern utility sustained a 580-megawatt generating loss, a regularly scheduled 8-megawatt FP & L contribution to the Florida Pool coincided with an 8-megawatt contribution from the pool to the ISG system.

These relationships establish the focal issue in this case. The FPC may exercise jurisdiction only if there is substantial evidentiary support for the Commission's conclusion that FP & L power has reached Georgia via Corp or that Georgia's power has reached FP & L because of exchanges with Corp. What happens when FP & L gives power to Corp and Corp gives power to Georgia (or vice versa)? Is FP & L power commingled with Corp's own supply, and thus passed on with that supply, as the Commission contends? Or is it diverted to handle Corp's independent power needs, displacing a like amount of Corp power that is then passed on, as respondent argues? Or, as the Commission also contends, do changes in FP & L's load or generation, or that of others in the interconnected system, stimulate a reaction up and down the line by a signal or a chain reaction that is, in essence, electricity moving in interstate commerce? Upon answer to these questions, jurisdiction rides.

If FP & L were directly involved in power exchanges with Georgia, there would be no serious question about the resolution of this case. Section 201 of the Federal Power Act owes its origin to the determination of this Court that a direct transfer of power from a utility in Rhode Island to a utility in Massachusetts is in interstate commerce. *See Public Utilities Comm'n v. Attleboro Steam & Electric Co.*, 273 U.S. 83 (1927). "Part II (of the Act) is a direct result of Attleboro." There can be no doubt that § 201 achieves its end and fills the "Attleboro gap" by giving the FPC jurisdiction over direct exchanges.

Nor would there be any difficulty in resolving this case if the company or companies that stood between FP & L and the out-of-state power companies could be shown to be sometimes no more than a funnel. In *Jersey Central Power & Light Co. v. FPC*, 319 U.S. 61 (1943), the first of the major FPC jurisdictional cases to be considered by this Court, Jersey Central supplied power to the Public Service Electric & Gas Co. (also a New Jersey company), which in turn had exchange arrangements with Staten Island Edison Corp. (a New York company). The transfer from PSE & G to Staten Island was effected through a "bus"—a transmission line of three conductors into which a number of subsidiary lines connect. The FPC showed through extensive sampling of the logs of the relevant companies, that on at least a dozen occasions when Staten Island drew power from the bus only Jersey Central was supplying the bus. Thus, the intermediate presence of PSE & G was shown to be, in some circumstances, a null factor, and it was established that Jersey Central energy was moving in interstate commerce.

In the litigation before us the record does not disclose situations in which Corp operated as a null or insufficient factor. Thus, the FPC has not in this litigation demonstrated with the clarity and certainty obtaining in the *Jersey Central* case that the energy flows that are a prerequisite to jurisdiction occurred. . . .

II

The Federal Power Commission followed alternate routes to its conclusion that FP & L energy moved in interstate commerce. The first course, based on what the Commission called the electromagnetic unity of response of interconnected electrical systems, is best represented in the words of the hearing examiner:

> (N)one of the connected electric systems including that of Florida, Corp, and Georgia has any control over the actual transfers of power at each point of interconnection because of the free flow characteristics of electric networks. . . .

> An electric utility system such as Florida (Power & Light) is essentially an electro-mechanical system to which all operating generators on the interconnected network are interlocked electromagnetically. This means that electric generators, under ordinary operating conditions run either at exactly the same speed or at speeds which will result in a frequency of 60 cycles. No operating generator can change its speed by itself as long as it operates connected to the network.

> . . .

> The cause and effect relationship in electric energy occurring throughout every generator and point on the Georgia, Corp and Florida systems constitutes interstate transmission of electric energy by, to, and from Florida. It is the electromagnetic unity of response of Florida, Corp, Georgia and other interconnecting systems that constitutes the interstate transmission of electric energy by Florida.

By this analysis a change in FP & L's load or generating pattern depletes or adds to the force available in out-of-state lines; therefore FP & L is transmitting energy in interstate commerce.

The alternative analysis by the Commission and its staff experts concentrates on power flow within the "Turner bus"—the point of connection between Corp's and FP & L's systems. Power supplied to the bus from a variety of sources is said to merge at a point and to be commingled just as molecules of water from different sources (rains, streams, etc.) would be commingled in a reservoir. On this basis the FPC need only show (1) FP & L power entering the bus and (2) power leaving the bus for out-of-state destinations at the same moment, in order to establish the fact that some FP & L power goes out of state. The FPC purported to make this demonstration by a series of tracing studies.

III

We do not find it necessary to approve or disapprove the Federal Power Commission's analysis based on unity of electromagnetic response. Its alternative assertion that energy commingles in a bus is, in our opinion, sufficient to sustain jurisdiction.

In evaluating this second approach, the courts are called upon to do no more than assess the Commission's judgment of technical facts. If the Commission's conclusion of commingling is not overturned, then the legal consequences are clear.

The conclusion of the FPC that FP & L energy commingled with that of Corp and was transmitted in commerce rested on the testimony of expert witnesses. The major points expounded by these witnesses were probed, and in our opinion not undercut, by the hearing examiner's questions, FP & L's cross-examination, and rebuttal testimony of FP & L witnesses. The hearing examiner found the testimony persuasive and held that his conclusions could be independently reached upon it. A majority of the Commission, reasoning similarly, endorsed these conclusions. . . .

The decision of the Court of Appeals is reversed and the case is remanded for reinstatement of the order of the Federal Power Commission. . . .

MR. JUSTICE DOUGLAS, with whom THE CHIEF JUSTICE concurs, dissenting.

There can be no doubt that Congress has constitutional power to regulate under the Commerce Clause the interstate "commingling" of electric power involved in the instant case. The question is whether it has done so. . . .

Evidently undesirous of explicitly overruling the proposition that "(m)ere connection determines nothing," *Jersey Central Power & Light Co. v. FPC*, 319 U.S. 61, 72 (1943), the Court avoids validating the FPC's electromagnetic unity theory as the jurisdictional hold over the respondent. Instead, relying on the Commission's expertise, the Court purports to hold a narrower ground that actual flows of FP & L's electricity were in fact measured passing out of Florida through the employment of the Commission's "commingled" tracing method. . . .

The Commission's abandonment of the conventional test in favor of the commingled method will now mean that every privately owned interconnected facility in the United States (except for those isolated in Texas) is within the FPC's jurisdiction. Both tracing methods assume that a momentary increase in FP & L's generation over its local needs will be passed on to the interconnecting Florida Power Corp. (Corp) system located between FP & L and the state line. The conventional system assumes that such excesses will be absorbed by the first few loads reached in the Corp system and therefore will never cross the state line. On the other hand, the commingled approach assumes that the first load which the FP & L excess reaches will continue to rely upon other utilities' power to a large extent and therefore will absorb only a part of the FP & L excess. The leftover FP & L excess will then travel to the next load, but again, will only supply part of those consumers' needs, with the remainder passing on to the next load,

and so on, until some fractional part of the original FP & L excess crosses the state line. Extending the assumption's application, it is clear that any momentary increase in output by any generator located at any point in the ISG grid will send a surge of power throughout the entire network. If this assumption is approved, then it is difficult to perceive what remains of the *Jersey Central* proposition that "(m)ere connection determines nothing."
. . .

While federal regulation was to be pervasive, once fastened onto a company, Congress expressed an unambiguous policy to preserve and to rely upon effective and adequate state regulation:

> The revised bill would impose Federal regulation only over those matters which cannot effectively be controlled by the States. The limitation on the Federal Power Commission's jurisdiction in this regard has been inserted in each section in an effort to prevent the expansion of Federal authority over State matters.

And this objective is presented in the statute's language:

> It is hereby declared . . . that Federal regulation . . . is necessary in the public interest, such Federal regulation, however, to extend only to those matters which are not subject to regulation by the States. Public Utility Holding Company Act of 1935, § 201(a), 49 Stat. 847.

The Commission does not assert that Florida's regulation of FP & L is inadequate. Each year the Florida Public Service Commission conducts field audits of electric utilities to ensure compliance with its accounting practices and depreciation rates. Other than enhancing the slogan of "federal leadership" the Commission cites no function which it might better fulfill than the state regime. . . .

In light of these congressional purposes I would not superimpose federal regulation on top of state regulation in case of de minimis transmissions not made by prearrangement or in case of wholesale transactions. . . .

In the instant case apart from the infinitesimal and sporadic exchanges the Commission only found that "FPL (respondent) contributed 8 mw to ISG to assist a midwestern utility which had sustained a 580-mw generator loss." And that single episode could be measured in terms of seconds only. Such fleeting episodes are not in my view sufficient to displace a state regime with the federal one, since the Congress promised that as much as possible be left to the States. I would not make that a hollow promise.

If we allow federal pre-emption in this case, then we have come full cycle, leaving local authorities control of electric energy only insofar as municipal plants are concerned. The federal camel has a tendency to occupy permanently any state tent.

That may be a wise course; but if so, Congress should make the decision.

NOTES AND QUESTIONS

1.   Do you agree with the majority or the dissent in the *Florida Power & Light Co.* case? Do you think federal authority is appropriate in this context? Since that decision, the Supreme Court has made clear that all transmissions of electricity, no matter how de minimis, are subject to FERC jurisdiction. This means that FERC has jurisdiction over all "transmission" of electricity (although not necessarily all "sales" of electricity) in the United States other than in Texas, Alaska, and Hawaii, which each have their own grid and do not, for the most part, transmit electricity to or from other states. *See, e.g., New York v. FERC*, 535 U.S. 1, 7 (1992) ("It is only in Hawaii and Alaska and on the "Texas Interconnect"—which covers most of that State—that electricity is distributed entirely within a single State. In the rest of the country, any electricity that enters the grid immediately becomes a part of a vast pool of energy that is constantly moving in interstate commerce."). Based on the discussion earlier in this chapter regarding the Texas electric grid disaster in 2021, should Texas rethink its physical and regulatory isolation from the rest of the United States when it comes to electricity transmission? If it refuses, in order to remain free from FERC regulation under the Federal Power Act, should Congress step in? Why or why not? For a discussion of this issue, see Catherine Morehouse, *Congress, Texas Should "Rethink" ERCOT's "Go It Alone" Approach: FERC Chair Glick*, UTIL. DIVE (Feb. 19, 2021).

2.   Are there some portions of the energy system that seem particularly appropriate for federal regulation? For state or local regulation? Which ones require multi-level strategies? For a detailed discussion of these issues, see Hari M. Osofsky & Hannah J. Wiseman, *Dynamic Energy Federalism*, 72 MD. L. REV. 773 (2013).

3.   A TRANSITION TO CLEAN ENERGY

Energy use always involves tradeoffs. How do we balance the environmental demands of our energy use against our ever-growing thirst for more power? By flipping a light switch, starting our cars, or turning up (or down) our thermostats, we make individual choices that in the aggregate impact consumption significantly. However, these behavioral choices only represent part of the picture. When we look behind the plug, it becomes clear that complex choices around sources of energy and their infrastructure have important environmental and social impacts. Questions about the appropriate role of law in influencing these consumption choices arise again and again in energy law. Answering them is made harder by the deep fragmentation of energy law and regulation, as well as the traditional separation between energy law and environmental law.

Moreover, U.S. energy choices interact with those made around the world because of the global aspects of many energy sources, technologies, and products. Many multinational companies with a home base in the United States are involved in the extraction of fossil fuels or choose to do their manufacturing in other places, and many energy resources are fungible, globally traded commodities. Our transition to "cleaner" energy is thus intertwined with choices made by a wide range of individuals and entities here, as well as in China, the Middle East, Nigeria, and India, just to name a few key places.

Thus, almost every aspect of energy law involves choices that impact environmental protection. As highlighted in more depth in Chapters 2 and 3, each source of energy raises different environmental concerns, from localized pollution, land use conflicts, threats to endangered species, and environmental justice impacts, to more national and global impacts such as interstate air and water pollution and climate change. Moreover, technological decisions made around each source and conversion of energy can alter those environmental considerations because different technologies using the same resources involve different risks. However, for the most part, these issues cannot be resolved under a single legal regime. Often a variety of energy and environmental laws apply to a project. These laws, moreover, often have diverse aims that do not easily align and often conflict with one another.

Throughout this book, you will see reference in the case excerpts and other materials to many of the landmark environmental laws that apply in various ways to energy projects. For instance, the National Environmental Policy Act of 1969, 42 U.S.C. §§ 4321, *et seq.* (NEPA) requires federal administrative agencies to evaluate the potential for significant environmental effects of "federal actions," which include not only federally funded projects but any private projects that require a federal approval such as a wetland permit, federal oil or gas lease, water discharge permit, air permit, or certificate of public convenience and necessity for a natural gas pipeline. Likewise, many energy projects may impact federally protected endangered or threatened plant or animal species, triggering provisions of the Endangered Species Act, 16 U.S.C. §§ 1531, *et seq.* In many cases, these federal requirements provide the most effective way for opponents of energy projects to challenge the project in court, thus delaying or canceling the project. Thus, these federal statutes, particularly NEPA, loom large in the chapters that follow, in addition to federal energy-specific statutes and applicable state and local laws.

One of the most hotly contested areas in which energy and environmental law questions come together involves the regulation of climate change. The two major energy systems—electricity and transportation—both rely heavily on fossil fuels that create significant GHG emissions. Moreover, as the Texas grid disaster and recent wildfire and hurricane examples illustrate, our energy systems need to be made more resilient to adapt to the impacts of climate change like sea level rise, coastal erosion, droughts, increased fires and flooding, and less predictability of storms and weather patterns. Numerous government and academic reports describe the many ways in which the energy sector is currently vulnerable to climate change and extreme weather. *See, e.g.,* ENHANCING THE RESILIENCE OF THE NATION'S ELECTRICITY SYSTEM, *supra* at 58–66; U.S. DEPARTMENT OF ENERGY, U.S. ENERGY SECTOR VULNERABILITIES TO CLIMATE CHANGE AND EXTREME WEATHER (July 2013).

Existing energy and environmental laws both have provisions that apply to climate change mitigation and adaptation. But they are deeply fragmented and often initially conceptualized to address other types of emissions, such as those that create smog. Political contestation in Congress has prevented comprehensive climate change legislation from passing, which has made lawsuits under a variety of types of environmental statutes an important mechanism through which people are trying to force limits on GHG emissions arising from electricity and transportation. For a summary of the huge number of cases over climate change, see *Climate Change Litigation Database*, Sabin Center for Climate Change Law, http://climatecasechart.com/.

The most significant of these cases is the 2007 U.S. Supreme Court opinion in *Massachusetts v. EPA*, 549 U.S. 497 (2007), which involved whether the EPA had the authority to regulate motor vehicle GHG emissions under the Clean Air Act. As discussed in Chapter 6, this opinion became the basis for the Obama administration's regulation of GHG emissions in both the transportation and electricity sectors, some of which the Trump administration later moved to eliminate. The following case from the U.S. Court of Appeals for the D.C. Circuit discusses *Massachusetts v. EPA* in the context of evaluating actions taken by the Trump administration EPA to repeal the Obama administration's signature regulatory effort to reduce GHG emissions from existing power plants— known as the Clean Power Plan—and replace it with a more modest regulation. As you read the excerpt of the opinion below, consider the many complicated issues that this case raises. How should courts deal with complex science and emerging technologies? How should agencies and courts apply older, broad statutes in new contexts? How much discretion should the EPA have in its regulatory approach to a politically contested issue?

AM. LUNG ASS'N V. EPA

985 F.3d 914 (D.C. Cir. 2021)

Opinion for the Court filed PER CURIAM.

As the Supreme Court recognized nearly fourteen years ago, climate change has been called "the most pressing environmental challenge of our time." *Massachusetts v. EPA*, 549 U.S. 497, 505 (2007). Soon thereafter, the United States government determined that greenhouse gas emissions are polluting our atmosphere and causing significant and harmful effects on the human environment. And both Republican and Democratic administrations have agreed: Power plants burning fossil fuels like coal "are far and away" the largest stationary source of greenhouse gases and, indeed, their role in greenhouse gas emissions "dwarf[s] other categories[.]".

The question in this case is whether the Environmental Protection Agency (EPA) acted lawfully in adopting the 2019 Affordable Clean Energy Rule (ACE Rule), 84 Fed. Reg. 32,520 (July 8, 2019), as a means of regulating power plants' emissions of greenhouse gases. It did not. Although the EPA has the legal authority to adopt rules regulating those emissions, the central operative terms of the ACE Rule and the repeal of its predecessor rule, the Clean Power Plan, 80 Fed. Reg. 64,662 (Oct. 23, 2015), hinged on a fundamental misconstruction of . . . the Clean Air Act. . . .

In 1963, Congress passed the Clean Air Act, 42 U.S.C. § 7401 *et seq.*, "to protect and enhance the quality of the Nation's air resources so as to promote the public health and welfare and the productive capacity of its population[,]" *id.* § 7401(b)(1). Animating the Act was Congress' finding that "growth in the amount and complexity of air pollution brought about by urbanization, industrial development, and the increasing use of motor vehicles[ ] has resulted in mounting dangers to the public health and welfare[.]" *Id.* § 7401(a)(2).

Section 111 of the Clean Air Act, which was added in 1970 and codified at 42 U.S.C. § 7411, directs the EPA to regulate any new and existing stationary sources of air pollutants that "cause[ ], or contribute[ ] significantly to, air pollution" and that "may reasonably be anticipated to endanger public health or welfare." 42 U.S.C. § 7411(b)(1)(A); *see id.* § 7411(d), (f) (providing that the EPA Administrator "shall" regulate existing and new sources of air pollution). A "stationary source" is a source of air pollution that cannot move, such as a power plant. *See id.* § 7411(a)(3) (defining "stationary source" as "any building, structure, facility, or installation which emits or may emit any air pollutant[ ]"). An example of a common non-stationary source of air pollution is a gas-powered motor vehicle. *See Utility Air Regulatory Group v. EPA (UARG)*, 573 U.S. 302, 308 (2014).

Within 90 days of the enactment of Section 7411, the EPA Administrator was to promulgate a list of stationary source categories that "cause[ ], or contribute[ ] significantly to, air pollution[.]" 42 U.S.C. § 7411(b)(1)(A). In 1971, the Administrator included fossil-fuel-fired steam-generating power plants on that list. Today's power plants fall in that same category.

Once a stationary source category is listed, the Administrator must promulgate federal "standards of performance" for all newly constructed sources in the category. 42 U.S.C. § 7411(b)(1)(B). The Act defines a "standard of performance" as

> a standard for emissions of air pollutants which reflects the degree of emission limitation achievable through the application of the best system of emission reduction which (taking into account the cost of achieving such reduction and any nonair quality health and environmental impact and energy requirements) the Administrator determines has been adequately demonstrated.

Id. § 7411(a)(1). . . .

While the new source standards are promulgated and enforced entirely by the EPA, the Clean Air Act prescribes a process of cooperative federalism for the regulation of existing sources. Under that structure, the statute delineates three distinct regulatory steps involving three sets of actors—the EPA, the States, and regulated industry—each of which has a flexible role in choosing how to comply. *See* 42 U.S.C. § 7411(a)(1), (d). . . .

Electricity powers the world. Chances are that you are reading this opinion on a device that consumes electricity. Yet two distinct characteristics of electricity make its production and delivery in the massive quantities demanded by consumers an exceptionally complex process. First, unlike most products, electricity is a perfectly fungible commodity. A watt of electricity is a watt of electricity, no matter who makes it, how they make it, or where it is purchased. Second, at least as of now, this highly demanded product cannot be effectively stored at scale after it is created. Paul L. Joskow, *Creating a Smarter U.S. Electricity Grid*, 26 J. Econ. Persp. 29, 31–33 (2012). Instead, electricity must constantly be produced, and is almost instantaneously consumed.

Those unique attributes led to the creation of the American electrical grid. The grid has been called the "supreme engineering achievement of the 20th century," MIT, The Future of the Electric Grid 1 (2011), and it is an exceptionally complex, interconnected system. "[A]ny electricity that enters the grid immediately becomes a part of a vast pool of energy that is constantly moving[.]" *New York v. FERC*, 535 U.S. 1, 7 (2002). That means that units of electricity as delivered to the user are identical, no matter their source. On the grid, there is no coal-generated electricity or renewable-generated electricity; there is just electricity. . . .

Most generators of electricity on the American grid create power by burning fossil fuels like coal, oil, and natural gas. *See* United States Energy Information Administration (EIA), *Frequently Asked Questions: What Is U.S. Electricity Generation by Energy Source?* (Nov. 2, 2020) (fossil fuels represented 62.6 percent of electricity generation in 2019). Some of those power plants take a fossil fuel (usually coal) and burn it in a water boiler to make steam. Other power plants take a different fossil fuel (usually natural gas), mix it with highly compressed air, and ignite it to release a combination of super-hot gases. Either way, that steam or superheated mixture is piped into giant turbines that catch the gases and rotate at extreme speeds. Those turbines turn generators, which spin magnets within wire coils to produce electricity. EIA, *Electricity Explained* (Nov. 9, 2020).

Electrical power has become virtually as indispensable to modern life as air itself. But electricity generation has come into conflict with air quality in ways that threaten human health and well-being when power generated by burning fossil fuels emits carbon dioxide and other polluting greenhouse gases into the air.

Since the late 1970s, the federal government has focused "serious attention" on the effects of carbon dioxide pollution on the climate. *Massachusetts v. EPA*, 549 U.S. at 507. In 1978, Congress adopted the National Climate Program Act, Pub. L. No. 95–367, 92 Stat. 601, which directed the President to study and devise an appropriate response to "man-induced climate processes and their implications[,]" *id.* § 3; *see Massachusetts v. EPA*, 549 U.S. at 507–508. In response, the National Academy of Sciences' National Research Council reported "no reason to doubt that climate changes will result" if "carbon dioxide continues to increase," and "[a] wait-and-see policy may mean waiting until it is too late." *Massachusetts v. EPA*, 549 U.S. at 508. . . .

It was not until the Supreme Court's 2007 decision in *Massachusetts v. EPA*, however, that the Court confirmed that carbon dioxide and other greenhouse gas emissions constituted "air pollutant[s]" covered by the Clean Air Act. *See* 549 U.S. at 528. . . .

Given that statutory command, the Supreme Court ruled that the EPA "can avoid taking further action" to regulate such pollution "only if it determines that greenhouse gases do not contribute to climate change" or offers some reasonable explanation for not resolving that question. *Massachusetts v. EPA*, 549 U.S. at 533.

Taking up the mantle, the EPA in 2009 found "compelling[ ]" evidence that emissions of greenhouse gases are polluting the atmosphere and are endangering human health and welfare by causing significant damage to

the environment. 2009 Endangerment Finding, 74 Fed. Reg. at 66,497 . . .
The EPA concluded that " 'compelling' evidence supported the 'attribution
of observed climate change to anthropogenic' [that is, human-influenced]
emissions of greenhouse gases[.]" *AEP*, 564 U.S. at 417 (quoting 74 Fed.
Reg. at 66,518). The "[c]onsequent dangers of greenhouse gas emissions,"
the EPA determined, include

> increases in heat-related deaths; coastal inundation and erosion
> caused by melting icecaps and rising sea levels; more frequent and
> intense hurricanes, floods, and other "extreme weather events"
> that cause death and destroy infrastructure; drought due to
> reductions in mountain snowpack and shifting precipitation
> patterns; destruction of ecosystems supporting animals and
> plants; and potentially "significant disruptions" of food
> production.

Id. (quoting 74 Fed. Reg. at 66,524–66,535). . . .

In 2015, with the 2009 carbon dioxide endangerment finding
continuing in effect, the EPA reaffirmed that greenhouse gases "endanger
public health, now and in the future." New Source Rule, 80 Fed. Reg. at
64,518. The EPA explained that, "[b]y raising average temperatures,
climate change increases the likelihood of heat waves, which are associated
with increased deaths and illnesses[,]" particularly among "[c]hildren, the
elderly, and the poor[.]" *Id.* at 64,517. In addition, the EPA found that
"[c]limate change impacts touch nearly every aspect of public welfare." *Id.*
Among the "multiple threats caused by human emissions of [greenhouse
gases]," the EPA pointed to climate changes that "are expected to place
large areas of the country at serious risk of reduced water supplies,
increased water pollution, and increased occurrence of extreme events such
as floods and droughts." *Id.* The EPA "emphasize[d] the urgency of
reducing [greenhouse gas] emissions due to * * * projections that show
[greenhouse gas] concentrations climbing to ever-increasing levels in the
absence of mitigation[,]" citing independent assessments finding that,
"without a reduction in emissions, CO_2 concentrations by the end of the
century would increase to levels that the Earth has not experienced for
more than 30 million years." *Id.* at 64,518. . . .

That endangerment finding provided the essential factual
foundation—and triggered a statutory mandate—for the EPA to regulate
greenhouse gas emissions from both new and existing power plants. . . .

In the Clean Power Plan, the EPA determined that a combination of
three existing methods of emission reduction—which the Plan referred to
as building blocks, 80 Fed. Reg. at 64,667—formed the "best system of
emission reduction," 42 U.S.C. § 7411(a)(1).

First, the system incorporated heat-rate improvements—that is,
technological measures that improve efficiency at coal-fired steam power

plants and, in that way, reduce the amount of coal that must be burned to produce each watt of electricity to the grid.

Second, the system added the "substitut[ion of] increased generation from lower-emitting existing natural gas combined cycle units for generation from higher-emitting affected steam generating" power plants, which are mostly coal-fired.

Third, the system prioritized the use of electricity generated from zero-emitting renewable-energy sources over electricity from the heavily greenhouse-gas-polluting fossil-fuel-fired power plants.

Those second and third methods of emission control are often referred to as "generation shifting" because the reductions occur when the source of power generation shifts from higher-emission power plants to less-polluting sources of energy. As the EPA observed, such shifts in generation already occur all the time as a matter of grid mechanics. That is, within the grid's "Constrained Least-Cost Dispatch" system, production from "generators with the lowest variable costs" will be dispatched "first, as system operational limits allow, until all demand is satisfied." "[R]enewable energy generators typically receive dispatch priority because they have lower variable costs than fossil-fuel-fired generators, which must purchase fuel." The EPA found that most electricity is generated by diversified utilities that could achieve most or all of the shift to lower- or no-emission generation by reassessing the dispatch priority of their own assets. . . .

The Clean Power Plan was challenged in this court. After we heard argument *en banc*, but before we issued a decision, that litigation was held in abeyance and ultimately dismissed as the EPA reassessed its position.

In 2019, the EPA issued a new rule that repealed and replaced the Clean Power Plan: The Affordable Clean Energy (ACE) Rule. *See* Repeal of the Clean Power Plan; Emission Guidelines for Greenhouse Gas Emissions from Existing Electric Utility Generating Units; Revisions to Emission Guidelines Implementing Regulations, 84 Fed. Reg. 32,520 (July 8, 2019). That Rule is the subject of this litigation.

At the outset, the ACE Rule repealed the Clean Power Plan. The EPA explained that it felt itself statutorily compelled to do so because, in its view, "the plain meaning" of Section 7411(d) "unambiguously" limits the best system of emission reduction to only those measures "that can be put into operation *at* a building, structure, facility, or installation." Because the Clean Power Plan's best system was determined by using some emission control measures that the EPA characterized as physically operating off the site of coal-fired power plants—such as some forms of generation shifting and emissions trading—the EPA concluded that it had no choice but to repeal the Plan. . . .

Considering its authority under Section 7411 to be confined to physical changes to the power plants themselves, the EPA's ACE Rule determined a new best system of emission reduction for coal-fired power plants only. The EPA left unaddressed in this rulemaking (or elsewhere) greenhouse gas emissions from other types of fossil-fuel-fired power plants, such as those fired by natural gas or oil.

The EPA's proposed system relied solely on heat-rate improvement technologies and practices that could be applied at and to existing coal-fired power plants. . . . The EPA limited itself to techniques that could be "applied broadly" to the Nation's coal-fired plants, which primarily amounted to upgrades to existing equipment. . . .

The EPA predicted that its ACE Rule would reduce carbon dioxide emissions by less than 1% from baseline emission projections by 2035. . .

Twelve petitions for review of the ACE Rule were timely filed in this court and consolidated in this case [by a coalition of states and municipal governments, power utilities, trade associations from the renewable energy industry, and public health and advocacy groups]. . . .

We may set aside the ACE Rule if it is "arbitrary, capricious, an abuse of discretion, or otherwise not in accordance with law." 42 U.S.C. § 7607(d)(1)(C), (d)(9)(A); *see also Maryland v. EPA*, 958 F.3d 1185, 1196 (D.C. Cir. 2020) ("[W]e apply the same standard of review under the Clean Air Act as we do under the Administrative Procedure Act.") (quoting *Allied Local & Reg'l Mfrs. Caucus v. EPA*, 215 F.3d 61, 68 (D.C. Cir. 2000)). . . .

The issue before us arises at . . . the EPA's determination of the best system of emission reduction. In the Clean Power Plan, the Agency determined that the best system was one that both improved the heat rate at power plants and prioritized generation from lower-emitting plants ahead of high-emitting plants. The EPA then calculated specific emission reductions achievable through application of that best system that it published as emission guidelines for States. . . .

In the Agency's current view, the only pollution-control methods the Administrator can consider in selecting the "best system of emission reduction" within the meaning of Section 7411(a) are add-ons or retrofits confined to the level of the individual fossil-fuel-fired power plant. That is so even though the record before the EPA shows that generation shifting to prioritize use of the cleanest sources of power is one of the most cost-effective means of reducing emissions that plants have already adopted and that have been demonstrated to work, and that generation shifting is capable of achieving far more emission reduction than controls physically confined to the source. In other words, the EPA reads the statute to require the Agency to turn its back on major elements of the systems that the power sector is actually and successfully using to efficiently and cost-effectively achieve the greatest emission reductions. . . .

All of that is wrong, the EPA has since decided. . . . The EPA insists that its current reading is mandated by the statutory text.

It is the EPA's current position that is wrong. Nothing in Section 7411(a)(1) itself dictates the "at and to the source" constraint on permissible ingredients of a "best system" that the Agency now endorses. . . .

Because promulgation of the ACE Rule and its embedded repeal of the Clean Power Plan rested critically on a mistaken reading of the Clean Air Act, we vacate the ACE Rule and remand to the Agency. . .

NOTES AND QUESTIONS

1.   In *Massachusetts v. EPA*, the Supreme Court held for the first time that GHG emissions were an "air pollutant" subject to regulation under the Clean Air Act. During the Bush II administration, the EPA took the position that GHGs were not the types of "pollutants" Congress envisioned when it enacted the relevant amendments to the Clean Air Act in the 1970s. Should that matter? Once the Court charged EPA with addressing GHG emissions, how far should that power extend in terms of the ability to create a framework to guide reduction of GHG emissions in the electric power sector?

2.   According to the D.C. Circuit in the *American Lung Association* case, what, precisely, did the Trump administration EPA do wrong in limiting its authority under the Clean Air Act regarding the "best system of emission reduction"? What should the Biden administration do as a legal matter in response to this decision? As a political matter? As it turns out, the Supreme Court will weigh in on these questions. As this book went to print in late 2021, the Court had granted certiorari in this case to review multiple questions regarding the scope of EPA's authority to address GHG emissions under Section 7411 of the Clean Air Act.

3.   Unlike some more localized environmental impacts, climate change is global in its scope. In 2021, the International Energy Agency issued its first comprehensive analysis of the policies required to decarbonize the global economy, and why nations must put those policies in place prior to 2030 to significantly reduce the use of fossil fuels in all sectors of the economy and reach "net-zero" carbon emission by 2050. *See* INT'L ENERGY AGENCY, NET-ZERO BY 2050: A ROADMAP FOR THE GLOBAL ENERGY SECTOR (May 2021).

PRACTICE PROBLEM

In the aftermath of the cold-weather power outages in 2021, the Texas legislature held hearings to discuss the contributing factors and response to the blackouts. ERCOT's CEO, Bill Magness, stated that nearly half of the state's power supply went down at one point due to the snowstorm and cold. He also shared that Texas's power grid was four minutes and thirty-seven seconds away from "catastrophe": degradation of electric grid infrastructure to a point where the damage would have resulted in long-term outages for millions of residents lasting weeks or possibly months. Governor Abbott of Texas is shaken by this harrowing testimony and has become skeptical of Texas's go-it-alone approach to its power grid. He reaches out to you for advice. He would like your opinion on the following questions:

1.   Which levels of government are relevant to the response to an extreme weather disaster like the recent Texas blackouts and why?

2.   Which aspects of preparing the energy system for and responding to extreme weather might each of these levels of government handle best? What type of multi-level structure would you recommend establishing to ensure coordination of key actors and expeditious resolution of conflicts? Are there certain aspects, such as weatherization requirements for natural gas plants, wind turbines, and related energy infrastructure, that should be subject to regulation rather than left solely to markets?

3.   What is the appropriate role of government in paying for the costs of the disaster and what aspects of the response should be left "to the market" and private insurance? When, if at all, should government step in and help defray those costs? If government should have a role, which level of government should defray which costs?

4.   How should the government balance the need to restore energy as quickly as possible with the need for environmental protection? Should the government relax environmental regulations to get the system online faster? How should the government address and prevent inequalities in how impacts are distributed?

5.   Governor Abbott appeared on national television and asserted that Texas's renewable sources of energy (wind and solar) were largely to blame for the grid disaster. He claimed that fossil fuels are necessary to ensure the reliability and resiliency of the electric grid. To what extent does Texas's experience illustrate the wider issues of fuel diversity and grid security? Does grid reliability require the continued use of fossil fuels? Or is reliability a function of transmission and distribution? For an in-depth report on grid reliability, see U.S. DEP'T OF ENERGY, STAFF REPORT TO THE SECRETARY ON ELECTRICITY MARKETS AND RELIABILITY (Aug. 2017).

6.   The Texas grid disaster had far-reaching effects beyond the state. Frozen natural gas wellheads and the shutdown of processing plants in Texas decreased natural gas production and processing. Market prices around the country rose significantly, and many utilities were forced to purchase natural gas at inflated prices. Some of these utilities attempted to pass through those costs to consumers through rate increases. Other utilities with excess natural gas reserves were able to sell in wholesale markets and profit off the market volatility. Still others, such as Brazos Electric Cooperative, declared

bankruptcy rather than pass on exorbitant costs to its member co-ops. Because ERCOT is an isolated grid, utilities in other states that would otherwise have been able to help with the Texas disaster were unable to because of the absence of transmission lines into the state. Taking these various factors into account, what potential regulatory changes could be proposed to ensure future extreme weather events have less drastic effects on utilities and consumers?

CHAPTER 2

ENERGY RESOURCES, METRICS, AND LEGAL TOOLS

■ ■ ■

A. OVERVIEW

Understanding energy law requires a grasp of the physical and economic systems that energy law governs. This is true whether you represent a company in the energy industry, are a government regulator, work in energy policy, advocate for a non-governmental organization, or interact with energy law in some other way. You cannot effectively participate in the energy law and policy conversation unless you also understand the energy industry both in the United States and internationally. In energy, the physical, industrial, legal, social, political, and technological systems are deeply intertwined.

This chapter introduces three aspects of energy to help you develop the basic vocabulary to understand energy systems.

First, the chapter introduces key energy metrics such as megawatts (MW), megawatt-hours (MWh), barrels of oil, million cubic feet of natural gas, and other units. Although some law students—and law professors—may cringe at the idea of grappling with anything that resembles mathematics, we are convinced that a basic grasp of energy metrics is essential to being conversant in energy law. You do not have to be an engineer or an economist to be a good energy lawyer, but you must be able to understand these concepts to address your clients' problems effectively. From Washington, D.C. to Sacramento, from New York City to Houston, from Qatar to The Hague, the world's best energy lawyers are fluent in the language of energy.

Second, the chapter surveys the energy resources on which society relies. It provides an overview of their physical characteristics, availability, uses, and environmental profiles. These resources fall into two primary categories: (1) nonrenewables such as coal, oil, natural gas, and uranium and (2) renewables such as wind, solar, geothermal, biomass, hydropower, and energy efficiency.

Third, the chapter highlights four recurring economic issues in energy law. At its core, energy law, like most government regulation, seeks to address failures in the market system. There are four recurring failures:

(1) the ability of firms to exercise market power; (2) waste, both physical and economic; (3) externalities, also known as environmental and social costs; and (4) free-riding problems, which, among other dilemmas, can lead to underinvestment in energy innovation. While not all these problems occur in every part of energy law, they do appear again and again. The last part of the chapter thus seeks to introduce you to the legal tools used to address these common economic problems faced by the energy sector, so you can recognize what types of issues energy law confronts across different contexts and throughout the book.

B. MEASURING ENERGY

Just as energy lawyers must understand the physical and market characteristics of energy resources, it is also important to understand how energy is measured. Different energy units are used in different contexts. There are three types of measurements to keep in mind. First, some units describe *the quantity* of energy produced or used, such as "calories," "BTUs," or "quads." Second, there are resource-specific metrics, such as "barrels" for oil, "mcf" (thousand cubic feet) for natural gas, or "kilowatt-hours" for electricity. Third, there are prefixes used to describe larger amounts of the same metric, such as "watt," "kilowatt," "megawatt," "gigawatt," and "terawatt." Fourth, there are units which describe the *rate* of energy being used, such as "watts" or "million barrels per day." This section aims to build your energy vocabulary by introducing you to these different energy units.

1. ENERGY AND POWER UNITS

There are two common systems for measuring and calculating energy production and consumption: English units (used in the United States and also referred to as the "Imperial System" or the "U.S. Customary System") and International Standard units (abbreviated as SI, from the French and used everywhere else). The English system typically uses British Thermal Units (BTUs) to describe energy. The SI system uses joules. Other energy measurements include therms, watts, and calories. Thus, familiarity with energy conversion is helpful for energy law- and policy-makers.

An important distinction is the difference between energy and power. Energy comes in many forms, but there are two basic types: (1) stored, or "potential," energy, and (2) working, or "kinetic," energy. By contrast, power is energy per unit of time. So there is a big difference between BTUs and BTUs per hour or megawatts (MW) and megawatt-hours (MWh). And a big difference between joules and watts (one watt is one joule per second). The first is a unit of energy; the second is a unit of power.

BTUs and joules measure energy. A BTU is the energy required to raise a pound of water by one degree Fahrenheit. By the same token, a calorie is the energy needed to raise 1 gram of water by 1 degree Celsius. A calorie is about four times the size of a joule. So what is a joule?

A joule is the equivalent of the force of one Newton for the distance of a meter. Let's unravel that. In science, force is equal to mass times acceleration ($F = M \times A$). The force of 1 Newton on a scale on the Earth's surface is 0.2448 pounds, or about the weight of a small apple. The force of one Newton causes a mass of 1 kilogram to accelerate at the rate of 1 meter per second squared. A joule, then, is simply the energy needed to do this over the distance of a meter, essentially the energy needed to raise a small apple one meter. A BTU is equivalent to just over 1,000 Joules. The table below provides a sheet to help convert energy units between the English and SI systems.

Basic Energy and Power Conversions

1 BTU	= 1055 joules
	= 252 calories
	= 0.2930 watt-hours
1 joule	= 0.000948 BTU
	= 0.239 calories
	= 1 Newton-meter
1 kilocalorie	= 1000 calories
	= 4.187 kilojoules
	= 3.968 BTU
1 Quad	= 10^{15} BTU
	= 1.055^{18} joules
	= 1.055 Exajoule

Source: MIT Energy Club, Units and Conversions Fact Sheet.

Another common energy unit used at the society- or economy-wide level is the "quad." A quad is shorthand for a quadrillion BTU, or 10^{15} BTU. A quad is *a lot* of energy. To give you a sense of what a quad is, the United States uses roughly 100 quads of energy per year. Countries that use the SI system describe gross energy consumption in exajoules (EJ) instead of quads. An EJ is equal to 10^{18} joules, or 0.95 quads. You will also sometimes see large-scale energy use expressed in terawatt-years. A terawatt-year (TWyr) is equal to 31.54 EJ, 29.89 quads, or 8.76×10^{12} kilowatt-hours.

2.   RESOURCE-SPECIFIC ENERGY UNITS

Energy resources have their own energy units. You have probably heard of most of these units before, but it may not have been clear exactly what they mean or how to convert from one to another. The table below presents a short list of the basic units for each type of resource.

Resource-Specific Energy Units

Energy Type	Unit(s)
Coal	Short ton (2,000 pounds)
	Metric ton (2,200 pounds, 1,000 kilograms)
Electricity	Kilowatt-hours
	Megawatt-hours
	Gigawatt-hours
	Terawatt-hours
Oil	Barrels
	Tons of oil (metric tons of oil equivalent, "toe")
Natural Gas	Cubic feet, usually thousand cubic feet (mcf)
	Cubic meters (m^3) at standard temperature and pressure (STP)

Source: MIT Energy Club, Units and Conversions Fact Sheet.

Some of these units developed for historical reasons. For instance, when oil was first extracted from the Pennsylvania oil fields by Edwin Drake, the most convenient container available was whiskey barrels, so that's what he used. The measurement stuck, and we still use it today. Crude oil is measured in barrels, or 42 gallons (159 liters). Oil production is measured in barrels/day and annual oil consumption in millions of barrels/day (MMB/D).

Resource-Specific Energy and Power Values

Energy Type (Lower heating value)	BTU Value
1 short ton of coal	19–28,000 000 BTU
1 barrel of oil	5,800,000 BTU
1 gallon of diesel fuel or heating oil	128,000 BTU
1 gallon of gasoline	115,000 BTU
1 gallon of ethanol	76,000 BTU
1 kilowatt hour of electricity	3,412 BTU
1 cubic foot of natural gas	1,027 BTU
1 billion metric tons of oil equivalent	3.97×10^{16} BTU
1 quad	1×10^{15} BTU

Source: MIT Energy Club, Units and Conversions Fact Sheet.

A good way to understand how much energy is in each of these units is to convert them to the same unit of measurement. Let's use BTUs. The table above presents the energy potential of different resources in BTUs.

As energy resources are chemically different, burning them releases different levels of carbon dioxide and other pollutants. We can compare CO_2 emissions per unit of energy of different fossil fuel resources. The table below summarizes these comparisons.

Resource-Specific Carbon Dioxide Emissions

Energy Type	CO_2 Emissions (lbs/ million BTU)	CO_2 Emissions kg/GJ	Other Units
Lignite coal	215	93	2791 lb/short ton
Sub-bituminous coal	212	92	3716 lb/short ton
Bituminous coal	205	88.3	4931 lb/short ton
Diesel fuel	161	69.4	22.38 lb/gallon
Gasoline	156	67.2	19.56 lb/gallon
Natural gas	117	50.3	121 lb/mcf

Source: MIT Energy Club, Units and Conversions Fact Sheet.

When discussing electricity, there is another important distinction to keep in mind. One can talk about power plants in two ways.

First, you might refer to the size of the plant, which determines how much electricity it can produce—its "capacity" or "installed capacity." This sometimes is referred to as the facility's "nameplate capacity." For instance, a coal-fired power plant might be said to have an "installed capacity" of 600 megawatts (MW)—that is, the plant has the capability of producing 600 MW of energy. However, just because that is the plant's rated capacity does not mean it will actually produce energy to its full capacity potential. Rather, the amount of energy it produces will be measured in kilowatt hours (kWh) or megawatt hours (MWh). You probably already have a good idea of what a kWh is. A kilowatt is 1,000 Watts. So if you run one hundred 10-watt LED bulbs in your house for one hour, you have consumed a kWh. Part of your home electricity bill is probably expressed in cents per kWh. Thus, to figure out how much you have to pay for energy from electricity each month, you multiply that rate by the kilowatt-hours you consumed (¢/kWh x kWh = $ owed).

Second, the relationship between how much energy the power plant can theoretically produce compared to what it actually produces is called the plant's "capacity factor." The capacity factor measures the percent of time (hours) a power plant operates during a specific time period (usually a year). It compares how much electricity a generator actually produces with the maximum it could produce at continuous full power operation during the same period. If a one-megawatt (MW) plant generated 7,000 megawatt-hours (MWh) in a year (8,760 hours), the capacity factor would be .80 or 80% (to calculate divide 7000 MWh by 8,760 MWh (the MWh if the plant ran 100% of the time in a year)). Generators with capacity factors of 70% or higher run close to year-round and are known as "baseload" generation. Generators that run sporadically to meet the highest demand periods (sometimes only a few hours a year) are called "peaking" generation. They must be able to ramp up quickly to satisfy increases in consumption. Intermediate generation is known as "shoulder" or "load following." These facilities run for longer periods than peakers but less than baseload generation. They get their name from tracking the amount of electricity demand above what is satisfied by baseload (and until peaking power is needed). This traditional stack order of plants is changing across many systems as large-scale deployment of variable renewable resources and the dropping price of natural gas shifts the order in which plants are dispatched. The table below shows average capacity factors of different kinds of U.S. power plants in 2011 and 2020, which have changed slightly due to relative changes in fuel cost and technological changes.

Average U.S. Electricity Generation Capacity Factors 2011 and 2020

Generation Type	2011 Capacity Factor (%)	2020 Capacity Factor (%)
Nuclear	89.1	92.5
Coal	62.8	40.2
Natural Gas—Combined Cycle	44.3	56.6
Hydroelectric	45.8	41.5
Geothermal	71.5	74.3
Wind	32.1	35.4
Solar PV	19	24.9
Petroleum—Steam Turbine	12.6	13.4

Source: U.S. Energy Info. Admin.

3. SIZE AND QUANTITY UNITS

A third set of energy metrics describe the size or quantity of a given item. These are not difficult to learn. They are basically shorthand for multiplication in math. However, they are important to understand as you learn about the energy system.

Common prefixes in energy include "kilo" for thousand, "mega" for million, "giga" for billion, "tera" for trillion, and "peta" or "quad" for quadrillion. Thus, a "kilowatt" is a thousand watts, a "megawatt" is a million watts, a "gigawatt" is a billion watts, and so on. The table below summarizes common energy unit prefixes, their symbols, descriptions, and mathematical representations.

Energy Measurement Prefixes

Prefix	Symbol	Meaning	Mathematical Representation
kilo	k	Thousand	10^3
mega	M	Million	10^6
giga	G	Billion	10^9
tera	T	Trillion	10^{12}
peta / quad	P / Q	Quadrillion	10^{15}
exa	E	Quintillion	10^{18}

For a more comprehensive series of conversion factors and energy metrics that you may find useful, see MIT, Units & Conversions Fact Sheet and American Physical Society, Energy Units.

C. ENERGY CONSUMPTION AND RESOURCES

People use energy to power human activities. From heating our homes, producing, transporting, storing, and cooking our food, running our schools, hospitals, industries and businesses, energy flows through human activities. For the most part, people do not *want* energy, they want the services that energy provides. They want warm showers and cold beer, not fossil fuels or electric currents. How we use energy has varied over time and across locations. It is driven by local weather and climate conditions, and local practices and norms of energy use. It is shaped by the size (and insulation!) in our homes, the types of industry, and also by available resources and technologies, environmental and energy laws and policies, and geopolitical opportunities and constraints. *See, e.g.*, Hannah Ritchie, *Energy Production and Consumption*, OUR WORLD IN DATA.

Global energy use has increased over fourfold since 1960, while the global population has only increased by 2.6 percent. We fly, ship, and drive enormous quantities of goods and people all over the world. This increase in global energy use depends on diverse energy resources.

Energy resources—the raw materials society uses to create energy— can be divided into two categories: renewable and nonrenewable. Nonrenewable resources include coal, oil, natural gas, and uranium (nuclear power). Renewables include solar, wind, hydropower, biomass, geothermal, and energy efficiency. There are many other ways to classify energy resources, but because a resource's renewability speaks to lower greenhouse gas intensity (except for uranium used for nuclear), the renewable versus nonrenewable dichotomy has particular resonance and can address which energy technologies can reduce greenhouse gas emissions and address climate change.

Nonrenewable fossil fuel energy resources—coal, oil, and natural gas—have dominated global and U.S. energy use for over a century. On a global scale, oil, coal, and natural gas accounted for the majority (83%) of global energy use in 2020. Nuclear (4.3%), hydropower (6.8%) and other renewables (5.7%) made up a much smaller share. *See* BP STATISTICAL REVIEW OF WORLD ENERGY 11 (July 2021). As for the United States, in 2020, fossil fuels made up nearly 80% of primary energy use, with nuclear accounting for 9% and renewables up to 12%. *See U.S. Energy Facts Explained*, U.S. Energy Info. Admin. (last updated May 14, 2021).

Fossil fuels have been used by humans for millennia. Archeologists believe that coal was mined 6,000 years ago in ancient China, and the Persians used oil-soaked arrows when laying siege to Athens. Ming Dynasty texts in China report a flammable gas extracted from the earth with long bamboo tubes, stored in pig bladders, and then lit to provide light. *See* BARBARA FREESE, COAL: A HUMAN HISTORY (2003). In ancient Greece, a temple was built on Mount Parnassus over an ignited natural gas leak that a sheepherder found around 1000 B.C.E. *History*, NATURALGAS.ORG. The temple housed a priestess known as the Oracle of Delphi who would give out prophecies "inspired" by this "eternal flame." *Id.* In North America, Native Americans used asphaltum[1] from oil seeps to caulk canoes, hold together weapons, create watertight baskets, and to make walnut-shell dice used in games. U.S. Geological Survey, *Native American Uses of Asphaltum*.

Fossil fuels' dominance in the global energy economy is a relatively recent development. It is only in the last 150 years that fossil fuel use grew exponentially, outpacing reliance on resources like wind, water, and wood as the Industrial Revolution ushered in modern society. The advent of both electricity and the gasoline-powered automobile cemented fossil fuels' lock on the world's energy profile.

Today, fossil fuels are used in every sector of the economy. Products made from petroleum are wide-ranging and include beauty products, paint, perfume, contact lenses, carpet, plastic bottles, glue, and toothpaste. Coal is used in the production of steel, cement, chemicals, pharmaceuticals, and other everyday products like kitchen knives, mountain bikes, and billiard

---

[1]   Ashpaltum is a tar-like substance created when oil seeps to the surface and the lighter components evaporate out.

balls. Natural gas and other fossil fuels are used to make agricultural fertilizers, plastics, preservatives, raincoats, and bug nets.

Different fossil fuels have different end uses in the energy system and economy that vary regionally. Thus, understanding the variety of ways fossil fuels are used across the economy is an important piece to understanding the complexities of energy law and policy. Coal is currently used almost exclusively for electricity generation, with a small portion used directly in industry in the United States. Most oil, by contrast, is used for transportation. Natural gas is used across sectors: one-third goes directly to industry; a smaller fraction is used for commercial and residential heating and almost 40% is used for electricity generation. Other regions of the world use fossil fuels in different proportions.

Nuclear and most renewables have their own stories and geographies. Today they are used almost exclusively for electricity generation, although some sources, like biomass, solar and geothermal energy, are used for heating, cooling, and electricity production, especially when consumed directly by end users. The standout exception among renewables is biomass. Very little of the biomass consumed in the United States is used for electricity generation, though some is used for home heating. The bulk of commercial biomass is used in the transportation sector to produce ethanol and biodiesel. The figures below depict the overall use of energy resources by source and sector in the United States in 2020 and over time. Notably, total U.S. energy consumption in 2020 declined from 2019 levels (100.2 quads v. 92.9 quads) due to the COVID-19 pandemic and is expected to rebound in 2021. For an interactive diagram showing changing energy use and consumption over the decades, see *U.S. Energy History Visualization*, https://us-sankey.rcc.uchicago.edu/.

U.S. Energy Consumption by Sector (2020)

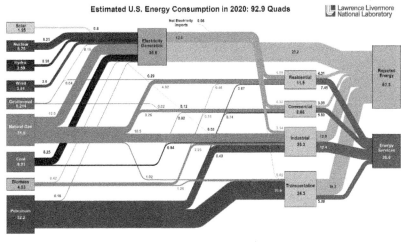

Energy consumption in the United States (1776–2019)
quadrillion British thermal units

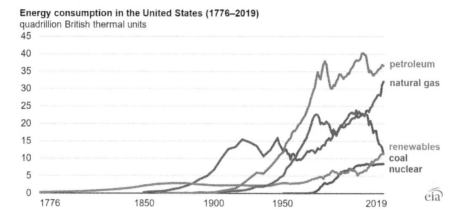

Source: U.S. Energy Info. Admin.

As the figures above show, renewable resources today play a much smaller role in energy production than nonrenewables. This is largely due to path dependency and the historical development and investment in nonrenewable resources, technologies, and infrastructure. Adding more renewables requires fundamental system changes and evolution of technologies, policies, and laws. First, these resources, while universally more abundant than fossil fuels, tend to pack less energy punch. That is, their energy is less concentrated as compared to fossil fuels. A gallon of gasoline refined from crude oil, for instance, contains 116,090 BTUs of energy, whereas the amount of electricity produced in an hour from a single solar panel is only 1/50 (or less) of that amount. When combined with the fact that fossil fuels are relatively easy to transport—coal moves by train or barge, oil and natural gas by tanker and pipeline—nonrenewable resources maintain some advantages over renewables.

Second, until recently, renewables cost more than many fossil fuel resources. While many observers rightly note that some of the cost differential between renewables and nonrenewables must be attributed to subsidies for conventional fuels and the failure of political systems to force these technologies to internalize all the costs they impose on society, the fact remains that historically renewables have cost more, though this has changed dramatically in recent years. Economists and social scientists often speak of "path dependency" or "technological lock-in," where the decisions made today are shaped by those of the past. Technology lock-in is especially prevalent in large socio-technical systems like the energy system, with long technology lifetimes (decades); high capital costs of change (trillions of dollars); and a complex set of institutions, laws, and policies that favor the status quo and incumbents.

Third, when it comes to electricity generation, the variable nature of wind and solar resources requires new grid management systems and operating practices to seamlessly integrate them into the system. It is a common adage in the electricity industry that "electricity cannot be stored." A more accurate phrasing might be "electricity cannot be cheaply stored at large scale." But the point remains. When it comes to renewables, solar panels produce electricity when the sun is shining, and wind turbines spin when the wind is blowing. A combined cycle natural gas plant, on the other hand, can be fired up when electricity is needed and run to meet demand, assuming there is gas to power it. Thus, while the sun delivers more than 10,000 times the energy we use each day on Earth, nonrenewables continue to dominate global energy production and consumption.

Levelized Cost of Energy

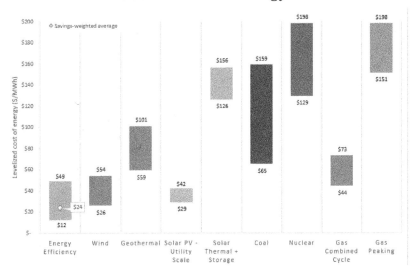

Source: CHARLOTTE COHN, AM. COUNCIL FOR AN ENERGY-EFFICIENT ECON. (ACEEE), THE COST OF SAVING ELECTRICITY FOR THE LARGEST U.S. UTILITIES: RATEPAYER-FUNDED EFFICIENCY PROGRAMS IN 2018, at 9 (June 2021).

Despite these continuing barriers to greater use of renewable energy, the long-term prospects for energy transition are promising from a cost perspective. Renewable energy technologies, particularly wind and solar, have seen dramatic cost reductions in recent years due to supply and demand-side innovation and policy. As shown in the chart above, utility-scale solar and wind are now cost competitive with all other forms of new electricity generation on an unsubsidized, levelized cost basis. *See also* LAZARD, LEVELIZED COST OF ENERGY AND LEVELIZED COST OF STORAGE—2020. If renewable resources are cost competitive or cheaper to build than new nonrenewables, why does the assertion that renewables are "more expensive" than conventional energy sources persist? At least part of the answer lies in the fact that energy infrastructure is long-lived. Thus, many existing generation facilities have a cost advantage over renewables because their capital costs have been amortized over decades and were paid off long ago. However, as renewable energy costs continue to decline, electric utilities are increasingly closing existing coal plants before the end of their expected lives because replacing them with lower cost renewable energy plants, coupled with investments in energy efficiency, will save customers money in both the short and long term. These issues are discussed in more detail in Chapters 4 and 5.

***

NOTES AND QUESTIONS

1.   The focus of this book is on energy consumption and production. However, many of the resources discussed here are used for other, non-energy purposes. Petroleum is used to make many products such as plastics. Biomass like corn can be used as food for livestock and people. Nuclear materials can be used for electricity production, the medical field, and in military weapons. The tradeoffs among the potential uses of these resources underscore the complexity and inter-linkages between our energy system and the rest of society and, consequently, the difficulty of good energy governance.

2.   Look again at the figure above entitled "U.S. Energy Consumption by Sector (2020)." Note the light gray lines labeled "Rejected Energy." What do these lines represent? How do they compare to the energy our society actually consumes? The fact that so much energy is lost can be attributed in part to the Second Law of Thermodynamics, also referred to as "entropy," which broadly states that disorder in the universe only increases. In energy terms, this means that as energy shifts from one form to another, some energy is lost and energy available for use decreases. Thus, these conversion losses mean that there is less energy available in the form of electricity created from combusted coal than there was stored in the coal before it was burned. More efficient technologies can reduce this loss. Most energy losses are due to inefficiencies in our energy systems. Energy is lost through inefficient combustion technologies, transporting electricity from distant power plants to the cities where it is used, and through inefficient end uses. If more efficient turbines were used or the plants generated electricity closer to the users, less energy would be lost. Better insulation in buildings coupled with more efficient appliances and end use technologies can also save energy at extremely low cost, as shown in the chart above. For example, an LED light uses roughly one-tenth of the energy as an incandescent bulb for the same light emitted. What does the vast amount of energy lost in the U.S. energy infrastructure say about energy efficiency as an energy resource itself? Energy efficiency as a resource is discussed in more detail later in this chapter.

3.   As we transition to more renewable energy, it is important that we do so in a way that does not exacerbate energy inequality. For an analysis of these concerns, including the fact and women and people of color are underrepresented in clean energy jobs, see Sanya Carley & David M. Konisky, *The Justice and Equity Implications of the Clean Energy Transition*, 5 NATURE ENERGY 569 (2020).

1. NONRENEWABLE RESOURCES

Nonrenewable energy resources—primarily fossil fuels plus nuclear power—share some common features. They occur naturally in the earth's surface. Fossil fuels are geologically compressed plant and animal matter from millions of years ago, while uranium is a naturally occurring element that is mined and processed to produce nuclear fuel. And, except for uranium, when they are burned, they release carbon dioxide and other pollutants into the atmosphere. In this way, even fossil fuels are a form of solar energy: sunlight captured millions or billions of years ago and stored in living creatures that died and became part of the earth.

Modern civilization is built on the back of two billion years of energy reserves. David R. Hodas, *Ecosystem Subsidies of Fossil Fuels*, 22 J. LAND USE & ENV'T L. 599 (2007). While the absolute amount of these reserves *is* limited, fossil fuel availability depends on the interplay between their discovery, technology, and economics. For example, extraction of oil resources like oil or tar sands is only economical if oil prices are over $50/barrel. Likewise, improved technologies like directional drilling and hydraulic fracturing make production of previously unavailable natural gas and oil resources viable economic commodities. The same is true with deep offshore oil and gas reserves. As neither markets nor technological innovation can be predicted, nonrenewable energy resources raise questions that strike at the heart of the dilemmas energy law and policy address. What are the environmental and climatic risks of burning cheap fossil fuels before looking for energy alternatives? What tools can law use to encourage development of different and cleaner energy sources? What role should markets or new tax policies play?

Nonrenewable energy resources are so-called because they are finite and cannot be regenerated in the scale of human time. Nonrenewables also share a common legacy of imposing significant environmental impacts. Nuclear energy has extensive environmental consequences both at the front and back ends of its fuel cycle—from the toxic uranium tailings piles that dot the western United States to the tens of thousands of tons of highly radioactive waste stockpiled at nuclear generation stations. Fossil fuels also impose extensive ecological and human health costs. From runoff caused by mountaintop coal removal to water contamination from oil and gas operations to toxic air pollutants and smog-forming emissions, it is fair to say that many of the nation's environmental laws were a direct response to society's dependence on nonrenewable fuels.

Pollution from energy plants, industrial facilities, and roadways has been found to disproportionately fall on poor communities and communities of color. Roadway noise and pollution coupled with industrial smoke and emissions from power plants affect the air, water, and land in many communities. In turn, this leads to adverse health impacts, lower property values, urban heat islands, and shapes community morbidities and mortality. Preferential lending, redlining, and targeting communities of color for the siting of industrial facilities contributed to these inequities. As a result, pollution associated with these environmental externalities systematically and disproportionately affects people of color in the United States. *See, e.g.,* Hiroko Tabuchi & Nadja Popovich, *People of Color Breathe More Hazardous Air. The Sources Are Everywhere,* N.Y. TIMES (Apr. 28, 2021); Christopher W. Tessum et al., *PM$_{2.5}$ Polluters Disproportionately and Systemically Affect People of Color in the United States,* 7 SCI. ADVANCES (Apr. 28, 2021).

At the same time, as the nation undergoes a clean energy transition, there is concern that many low-income, rural communities that are dependent on fossil fuel extraction and production for jobs and related economic support will be left behind. Thus, legislators, policy experts, and advocates have focused on the need for a "just transition" for communities that receive current economic benefits from fossil fuel resources as well as those communities that may bear new burdens associated with replacement energy production facilities. *See, e.g.,* Ann Eisenberg, *Just Transitions,* 92 S. CAL. L. REV. 273 (2019); DANIEL RAIMI, RES. FOR THE FUTURE, MAPPING THE US ENERGY ECONOMY TO INFORM TRANSITION PLANNING (May 2021); Devarshee Saha & Jillian Neuberger, *Steps to Aid US Fossil Fuel Workers in the Clean Energy Transition,* WORLD RES. INST. (Jan. 25, 2021); *Who Pays to Make Big Tech Green?,* BLOOMBERG BUSINESSWEEK (Mar. 2, 2021) (discussing impacts to tax revenues of small towns when coal plants close); Carley & Konisky, *supra.*

a. Coal

Coal consists of ancient plant and animal matter decomposed and compressed over millions of years deep in geological formations. Today, coal is found in seams within sedimentary rock and is extracted from underground and surface mines around the world.

Humans have used coal for thousands of years, with the earliest mining possibly occurring in modern-day China in 1000 B.C.E. In the United States, coal has been used since colonial times. Prior to 1950, Americans used coal for electricity generation, fuel for rail and water transport, and commercial and residential heating. Today, however, it is used predominantly in the electricity sector. *See Coal,* Encyclopedia Britannica; *U.S. Coal Flow, 2020,* U.S. ENERGY INFO. ADMIN.

Not all coal is created equally; there are four ranks of coal: anthracite, bituminous, sub-bituminous, and lignite. These classifications differ based on age, heating value, and carbon content of the coal. Anthracite coal, or metallurgic coal, is the oldest and hardest coal and has the highest heat content, while lignite is at the other end of the age and heat spectrum. Anthracite coal is mainly used by the metals industry in the United States;

the other three classes are used for combustion. Coal composition and quality varies; it is a mixture of complex organic molecules and trace contaminants, and quality is determined by energy content or heating values (BTU/lb or MJ/kg), sulfur content, and ash content, all of which affect combustion and requisite environmental controls.

Coal is available and widely used throughout the world. Coal production increased 65% from 2000 until 2014 and declined slightly until 2016. Since 2016, global coal production has increased, totaling 8.7 billion short tons (7.9 billion metric tons) in 2019. A few countries dominate coal production. While the United States had been called the "Saudi Arabia of coal," China is now its largest producer, mining 4 billion short tons (3.7 billion metric tons) in 2019 (almost 47% of global production). While U.S. mining decreased from 1.1 billion tons in 2011 to 705 million short tons in 2019, it was still the third largest producer globally, and has the largest reserves in the world. Other countries with large coal production include India, Indonesia, Australia, and Russia. *See Coal Information Overview*, Int'l Energy Agency (last updated July 2020); BP STATISTICAL REVIEW OF WORLD ENERGY 44 (June 2020).

Coal Rank Characteristics

Coal Rank	Heat Value	Carbon Content (%C)	Global Locations	U.S. Locations (percent of U.S. production)
Anthracite	Not used for combustion	87+	U.S., China, Russia	Pennsylvania (0.4% of U.S. production)
Bituminous	25–28 mmBtu/ton	45–86	U.S., China, India, Russia	Appalachia and the Midwest (48%)
Sub-Bituminous	19–24 mmBtu/ton	35–45	U.S., China, Russia, Ukraine	Wyoming, Colorado, New Mexico, Montana, Alaska (44%)
Lignite	9–18 mmBtu/ton	25–35	Germany, Australia, U.S., China	Texas, North Dakota, Louisiana, Mississippi, Montana (7.5%)

Sources: *Coal Data*, U.S. Dep't of Interior, Bureau of Land Mgmt.; *Annual Coal Report*, U.S. ENERGY INFO. ADMIN. (Oct. 5, 2020).

In the past, most coal was consumed domestically, but international trade in coal has expanded over the last decades. In 2019, Indonesia exported 455 million metric tons (31.7% of world coal export) and Australia 393 million tons (27.4% of world coal export). Russia, the United States, South Africa, and Colombia also serve as major exporters, but both the United States and Colombia reduced their exports in 2019 by 21 and 12 million tons, respectively. The largest importing countries are China, India, and Japan (together over half, or 51.3% of global coal imports), and South Korea (9%). Remaining coal reserves are large, with an estimated 1.07 trillion recoverable tons remaining (or over 130 years at current usage rates). *See* INT'L ENERGY AGENCY, COAL INFORMATION OVERVIEW (2020); BP STATISTICAL REVIEW OF WORLD ENERGY, *supra*, at 44. As the United States has reduced its domestic consumption of coal to generate electricity, coal companies have increasingly looked to increase exports to overseas markets and construct new coal export terminals in states like Washington, which have often opposed granting required permits. *See* Alexandra B. Klass & Shantal Pai, *The Law of Energy Exports*, 109 CALIF. L. REV. 733 (2021) (discussing litigation over coal export terminals).

In the United States, roughly half of the produced coal is mined underground (bituminous coal), mostly in the East, and the other half in surface mines with large coal seams (subbituminous coal) in the West. Over 71% of U.S. coal production comes from just five states—Wyoming, West Virginia, Pennsylvania, Illinois, and Kentucky. MELISSA N. DIAZ, CONG. RESEARCH SERV., U.S. ENERGY IN THE 21ST CENTURY: A PRIMER 16 (Mar. 16, 2021). The figure below shows coal resources in the United States.

Coal Resources in the United States

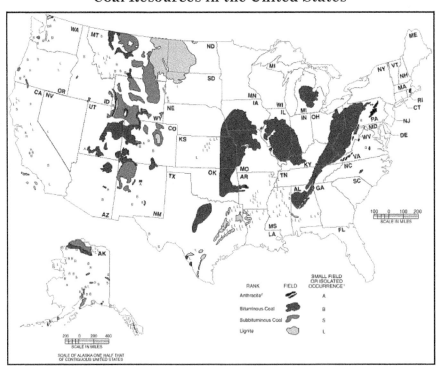

Source: U.S. Dep't of Energy.

Underground mining digs deep into the subsurface to extract the coal seam through three different approaches: (1) conventional techniques, or "room and pillar" mining, where large pillars of coal support the weight of the remaining rock; (2) continuous mining, where a mobile machine with spinning teeth gouges the coal from the rock face and the coal is continuously transported to the surface; and (3) longwall mining, where a 1000-foot face of the coal seam is continuously sheared and conveyed to the surface, and the roof is supported in the working area but allowed to collapse behind the working zone. (Video showing longwall mining: http://www.youtube.com/watch?v=bXORrVmxwbM.)

Surface mining includes three key types: (1) contour mining along sloping terrain; (2) area mining, where a large "box" of overburden is removed to extract the coal, and the overburden is then placed in the previous "box" to remediate the area; and (3) mountaintop mining, where the overburden is removed from the mountaintop (often taking off 200–600 feet of Appalachian mountains and ridges) and the coal seams are mined.

Coal-fired power accounted for roughly 19% of electricity production in the United States in 2020, down from over 50% in 2004. *What is U.S. Electricity Generation by Energy Source?*, U.S. Energy Info. Admin. (last updated Mar. 6, 2021). This decrease is driven by electric utilities closing older coal plants and switching to relatively cheaper natural gas and renewable energy technologies, as well as stricter environmental regulations on coal-fired power plants. *See* Michael R. Drysdale, *Farewell to Coal?*, 62 ROCKY MT. MIN. L. INST. 17–1 (2016). Nevertheless, coal still plays a major role in the electricity sector in the United States and worldwide, although within the United States that role differs significantly from state to state. Some states, like California, generate no electricity in-state from coal but still import it from the regional electric grid while others, like Kentucky, Wyoming, and West Virginia—all of which have economies tied to coal extraction—continue to generate significant amounts of electricity from coal-fired power. While these states are slowly transitioning to add additional renewable energy resources to their electricity mix, state legislatures often enact policies to slow or halt that process to protect coal interests. *See, e.g.*, Emma Penrod, *Wyoming Bill to Slow Coal Plant Closures Sent to Governor as 4 Other States Pursue Similar Steps*, UTIL. DIVE (Apr. 7, 2021); Dionne Searcey, *Wyoming Coal Country Pivots, Reluctantly, to Wind Farms*, N.Y. TIMES (Mar. 5, 2021).

To produce electricity, coal is washed to remove impurities (either at the mine or on-site), pulverized, and then fed by conveyer belt into large boilers where it is burned. This combustion process heats water to power a steam turbine that drives a generator and produces electricity. Coal-fired power plants in the United States are typically 35–40% efficient, meaning that 60–65% of the initial energy in the coal is lost to heat. Both the extraction and consumption of coal have significant environmental impacts. The environmental impacts of underground mining include subsidence, where the collapse of the underground mine causes the overburden to shift, creating sinkholes or troughs in the surface. This can lead to surface property damage. Acid mine drainage—which also results from hard rock mining—occurs when a mine is abandoned and pumping to remove water ceases. The mine subsequently floods and the exposed mine rock (often containing sulfides) reacts with the water, creating sulfuric acid and lowering the water pH. This acidic water can contaminate groundwater, streams, and drinking water.

Burning coal also creates air pollution. Fine particulates (PM), sulfur dioxide (SO_2), mercury, and oxides of nitrogen (NO_x) from coal fired power plants can affect air quality locally or travel hundreds of miles, depending on the pollutant and atmospheric conditions. PM, especially ultra-fine particulates, affects human respiratory function. NO_x, created during combustion, can react with other atmospheric compounds and form tropospheric ozone (O_3), which causes respiratory problems in humans and damage to agricultural crops. SO_2 reacts with water in the atmosphere and falls back to earth as acid rain, where it pollutes lakes and harms forests. Coal combustion is also an important source of GHGs; while coal produced only 24% of U.S. electricity in 2019, it accounted for 61% of the CO_2 emissions from the electric sector. *Sources of Greenhouse Gas Emissions, Electricity Sector Emissions*, U.S. Env't Prot. Agency.

Pollution from coal is not new. Infamous cases of deaths caused by coal-induced air pollution and coal extraction underscore the importance of controlling these emissions and enhancing mine safety. In 1930, in the Meuse Valley, Belgium, for instance, a coal-based smog killed 60 people. In 1948, in Donora, Pennsylvania, half of the town of 14,000 became ill and 20 people perished from coal pollution. And in December 1952, pollution levels in London elevated so high for five days that visibility reduced to one foot and 12,000 people died. *See* William H. Helfand et al., *Donora, Pennsylvania: An Environmental Disaster of the 20th Century*, 91 AM. J. PUB. HEALTH 553 (2001); Michelle L. Bell et al., Commentary, *A Retrospective Assessment of Mortality from the London Smog Episode of 1952: The Role of Influenza and Pollution*, 112 ENV'T HEALTH PERSP. 6 (2004); John Nielson, *The Killer Fog of '52: Thousands Died as Poisonous Air Smothered London*, NPR (Dec. 11, 2002). More recently, in April 2010, 29 mineworkers were killed in the West Virginia Upper Big Branch mining disaster as a direct result of the mine owners' failure to implement safety standards. *See Upper Big Branch Mine-South, Performance Coal Company, Massey Energy* Company, Mine Safety & Health Admin., U.S. Dep't of Labor (Apr. 5, 2012).

The first U.S. cities to adopt smoke control ordinances were Chicago and Cincinnati in 1881. By 1950, 80 municipalities and two counties had adopted policies to control smoke pollution, but air pollution management remained largely a local issue. Ultimately, Congress enacted the Clean Air Act of 1970 (amending an earlier Clean Air Act of 1963), with subsequent amendments in 1977 and 1990. The Clean Air Act and its amendments now form the backbone of U.S. air pollution control efforts, with a significant emphasis on regulating emissions from coal-fired power plants.

One 2011 study placed the cost that coal imposes on U.S. society at a third to over one-half a trillion dollars per year. Paul R. Epstein et al., *Full Cost Accounting for the Life Cycle of Coal*, 1219 ANN. N.Y. ACAD. SCI. 73 (2011); *see also* Nicholas Muller, Robert Mendelsohn & William Nordhaus, *Environmental Accounting for Pollution in the United States Economy*, 101 AM. ECON. REV. 1649 (2011); Matthew J. Kotchen, *The Producer Benefits of Implicit Fossil Fuel Subsidies in the United States*, 118 PROC. OF THE NAT'L ACAD. OF SCI. (Apr. 2021). To help address this problem, in 1990, Congress enacted Title IV of the Clean Air Act and created a tradable emissions approach to air emissions from power plants, which included a nationwide cap on SO_2 emissions.

Beyond SO_2 and NO_x, another pollutant of concern associated with coal-fired power plants is mercury. Mercury is a persistent, bio-accumulative neurotoxin that can cause adverse health effects such as delayed development, low IQ, and neurological defects in children at very low concentrations. Mercury emitted from power plants and other sources enters water bodies and is consumed by fish, which are then consumed by humans. Millions of acres of lakes, millions of river miles, and coastal waters of many states are subject to fish consumption advisories due to mercury pollution.

EPA enacted a series of regulations to control mercury emissions from power plants throughout the 2000s. Most recently, in 2012, EPA promulgated what is known as the "utility MACT" or the Mercury Air Toxics Standards (MATS). The MATS required coal-fired power plants to achieve a 91% reduction of uncontrolled emissions of mercury, nine other toxic metals, and three acid gases, all of which Congress listed as hazardous air pollutants in the Clean Air Act Amendments of 1990. The costs of the rule were estimated at $9.6 billion annually and the benefits, in the form of avoidance of premature deaths and reduction of non-fatal heart attacks, asthma attacks, and developmental effects on children, were estimated at $37 billion to $90 billion annually. *See, e.g.,* JAMES E. MCCARTHY, CONG. RESEARCH SERV., CLEAN AIR ACT ISSUES IN THE 113TH CONGRESS: AN OVERVIEW (Nov. 4, 2013). Although the U.S. Supreme Court ultimately remanded the MATS to EPA for further analysis of its costs and benefits in *Michigan v. EPA*, 576 U.S. 743 (2015), by that time most electric utilities had already complied with the rule.

Finally, 80% of all energy used in the United States comes from fossil fuels, which account for 75% of total GHG emissions and 93% of CO_2

emissions. While coal was only 11% of total energy used in the United States in 2019, coal-fired power plants produced 21% of all CO_2. The Obama administration worked to limit these GHG emissions through regulations imposed on the electric power sector under the Clean Air Act. The *American Lung Association v. EPA* case excerpt in Chapter 1 discusses the Obama administration's Clean Power Plan and the Trump administration's Affordable Clean Energy Rule governing existing power plants. The Obama administration EPA also enacted an earlier rule, in 2013, imposing the first regulations to limit CO_2 emissions from new power plants.

Certain states have also attempted to limit the use of coal-fired power through a variety of means. These include (1) state renewable portfolio standards, discussed in detail in Chapter 5, which require a certain percentage of electricity in the state be generated from renewable energy sources and (2) laws limiting CO_2 emissions from power generated or used in the state, which effectively limits the use of coal-fired power in the state. States that have placed direct limits on CO_2 emissions from electricity used or generated in the state include New York, California, Washington, Oregon, and Minnesota. *See* Alexandra B. Klass & Elizabeth Henley, *Energy Policy, Extraterritoriality, and the Dormant Commerce Clause*, 5 SAN. DIEGO J. OF CLIMATE & ENERGY L. 127, 156–67 (2013–14). The coal industry and electric power providers have challenged some of these provisions on dormant Commerce Clause grounds, with mixed success, as discussed in detail in Chapter 4. *Compare North Dakota v. Heydinger*, 825 F.3d 912 (8th Cir. 2016) (striking down portion of Minnesota law that banned imports of new coal-fired power) *with Energy and Environment Legal Institute v. Epel*, 793 F.3d 1169, 1174 (10th Cir. 2015) (upholding Colorado renewable portfolio standard, which requires a certain percentage of electricity be generated from renewable resources, thus disfavoring the use of coal-fired power).

Carbon capture and storage (CCS) is a set of technologies which could allow the continued combustion of fossil fuels, separating out the carbon dioxide and injecting it deep into the subsurface. This technology could be used to avoid carbon dioxide emissions from coal plants, cement factories, or upstream oil and gas operations. While research into CCS is over two decades old with demonstration projects around the world, costs remain high and, at least in the United States, renewable energy, battery storage, and energy efficiency provide lower cost means of reducing GHG emissions in the electric power sector. However, support for the technology continues both in the United States and abroad.

For instance, fossil fuel extraction states, like North Dakota and Wyoming, along with the fossil fuel industry itself, are wary of a clean energy transition that does not involve continued economic returns from their fossil fuel resources and thus seek ways to continue to use coal and other fossil fuels without the associated GHG emissions. Others continue to support developing CCS technologies for use in carbon-emitting industries outside the electric power sector, like cement making, that do not have readily available clean energy substitutes, and for exporting the technology abroad to developing nations that remain reliant on new fossil fuel plants. CCS is also referred to as CCUS or "carbon capture utilization, and storage," to encompass technologies that would not only capture and store CO_2 but also use them in products such as food, fuel, cement, or fertilizers. For more information on CCS and CCUS, see Chapter 11 and *Carbon Capture Utilization and Storage*, Int'l Energy Agency; PETER FOLGER, CONG. RSCH. SERV., CARBON CAPTURE AND SEQUESTRATION IN THE UNITED STATES (Aug. 9, 2018); *Coal-Fired Plant Carbon Capture Projects Face Headwinds*, S&P GLOBAL MARKET INTELLIGENCE (June 25, 2021); ALEX BRECKEL, ET AL., BUILDING TO NET-ZERO: A U.S. POLICY BLUEPRINT FOR GIGATON-SCALE CO_2 TRANSPORT AND STORAGE INFRASTRUCTURE (June 30, 2021); COUNCIL ON ENV'T QUALITY REPORT TO CONGRESS ON CARBON CAPTURE, UTILIZATION, AND SEQUESTRATION (June 2021).

b.   Oil

Crude oil is composed of complex hydrocarbons, and, like coal, it is created through the decomposition and transformation of ancient organic material. Millions of years ago, sand and silt deposits covered dead organic material at the bottom of watery ecosystems. Over time, these layers were exposed to intense geologic heat and pressure that converted the organic layer into what we know today as crude oil. Humans have been using oil for thousands of years, with the first evidence of use dating back to the time of the ancient Sumerians, Assyrians, and Babylonians and the surface seeps on the banks of the Euphrates River. "[I]t is impossible to date the earliest instance of human familiarity with crude oil because in some locales the fuel was known for millennia. . . . In ancient Mesopotamia asphalts and bitumens were used in floor and wall mosaics and as protective coatings and lighter oils were burned in fire pans for illumination. . . ." VACLAV SMIL, ENERGY TRANSITIONS: HISTORY, REQUIREMENTS, PROSPECTS 33 (2010). Before the late 1800s, oil often was not used for energy purposes. "Oil from natural seeps in western Pennsylvania was collected . . . and bottled to be sold as a medicinal 'Seneca oil, . . .'" *Id.* Indeed, even in its early days as an energy source, oil was not used to fuel transportation but rather to replace diminishing supplies of whale oil as a lighting source. DANIEL YERGIN, THE PRIZE: THE EPIC QUEST FOR OIL, MONEY & POWER (3d ed. 2008).

Oil is often described in one of two ways: conventional or unconventional. Conventional oil is found in structural geologic traps, confined by tight formations in layers of sedimentary rock, while unconventional oil—shale oil and oil (or tar) sands—is located within the rock matrix or as heavy bitumen. Despite the commonly used terms like "reservoir" or "pool," conventional oil does not exist underground in vast subsurface lakes but instead looks like many other rock formations. *See* U.S. DEPT. OF ENERGY, FOSSIL ENERGY STUDY GUIDE: OIL 1 (2013). "Oil exists in this underground formation as tiny droplets trapped inside the open spaces, called 'pores,' inside rocks. The 'pores' and the oil droplets can be seen only through a microscope. The droplets cling to the rock, like drops of water cling to a window pane." *Id.*

Oil is recovered through onshore and offshore oil wells using primary, secondary (water flooding), and tertiary (enhanced oil recovery using CO_2 floods to swell and produce more oil) recovery methods, which produce oil, associated natural gas, and accompanying saline waters (roughly 3–10 barrels for every barrel of oil produced). Crude oil is a black to yellow liquid with a strong smell. To convert crude oil into usable fuels, it is refined in a three-step process of separation, conversion, and treatment. Separation involves piping the crude oil through hot furnaces to vaporize it so that it is separated into different fuel streams. These streams are then "fractioned" in a distillation tower according to weight and boiling point. Next, the conversion process transforms the fractions into streams that will become finished products. Conversion can be done by "cracking" heavy compounds in a bullet-shaped reactor to make lighter and more valued compounds, or by using heat and pressure to arrange the molecules to add value. Finally, at the treatment stage, the refinery combines a variety of streams to create a finished product such as propane, gasoline, or jet fuel. The different products created are then pumped into storage tanks near the refinery to await shipment to other storage tanks across the country and world. Commonly used products produced from crude oil include gasoline and liquid petroleum gas, which are the lightest fractions; kerosene, and diesel, which are middle weight; and heavy gas oil and residuum, which are the heaviest crude oil byproducts.

Oil is a fungible, globally traded commodity and a cornerstone of world energy and economic markets. But oil prices can also be volatile and subject to economic fluctuations, with prices over \$100/barrel in the summer of 2014 to below \$20/barrel in April 2020 during the COVID-19 pandemic. Global prices at a range of \$40 to \$57 per barrel in 2019–20 stalled many oil extraction projects around the world because those prices cannot support profits when balanced against the costs of extraction and development.

While oil is found throughout the world, approximately half of the global oil supplies are located in the Middle East. Central and South America have 19% of global reserves, while the United States, Canada, the former Soviet Union, and Africa have less than 10% of global conventional reserves each. *See* BP STATISTICAL REVIEW OF WORLD ENERGY, *supra*, at 14. However, new, non-conventional oil resources like oil shale and oil sands, as well as deep offshore oil fields, are changing the distribution and politics of global oil supply.

Oil is transported by pipeline and rail and shipped throughout the world. Globally, oil supplies over 33% of total energy used, over 98 million barrels per day. Oil trade is dominated by large national oil companies, which control the majority of reserves (up to 90%) and production (55%). These include Saudi Aramco, National Iranian Oil Company, Kuwait Petroleum Corporation, Iraq National Oil Company, and PEMEX (Mexico), among others. By contrast, international oil companies like Exxon Mobil, BP, Shell, ConocoPhillips, Chevron, and ENI produce roughly 26% of crude oil. *See* BP STATISTICAL REVIEW OF WORLD ENERGY, *supra* at 9, 31 (data on global energy consumption and map depicting major trade movements of oil for 2019); *The National Oil Company Database*, NAT. RES. GOVERNANCE INST. (Apr. 2019); *Oil,* Int'l Energy Agency. Oil drives the transportation sector, but petrochemical products are also important feedstocks for industry. The largest consumers of oil are the United States, the European Union, and China. *See* BP STATISTICAL REVIEW OF WORLD ENERGY, *supra* (data from 2019).

In the United States, oil supplies approximately 35% of total U.S. energy needs, which includes supplying 90% of the transportation sector's energy needs and about 33% of industrial sector needs in 2020. *See U.S. Energy Facts Explained*, U.S. Energy Info. Admin. (last updated May 14, 2021). The United States produced a record 17 million barrels per day of oil in 2019, with the majority of oil produced onshore in Texas, North Dakota, New Mexico, Oklahoma, and Colorado. Offshore oil production in the Gulf of Mexico was also significant, accounting for approximately 15% of all oil production. *See U.S. Petroleum Flow, 2019*, U.S. ENERGY INFO. ADMIN. (July 20, 2020); *Where Our Oil Comes From*, U.S. Energy Info. Admin. (last updated Apr. 8, 2021).

Like other fossil fuels, oil has many environmental effects, chief among them being the air pollutants and GHG emissions that result from the combustion of crude oil. The extraction of oil causes both air and water pollution. "Among the toxic chemicals that can be released during oil and gas operations are benzene, toluene, ethylbenzene, and xylene (known as the "BTEX" chemicals); radioactive materials; hydrogen sulfide; arsenic; and mercury. . . . According to the State of Colorado, oil and gas production facilities can release more than 50 toxic air pollutants from a variety of sources. . . ." AMY MALL ET AL., NATURAL RESOURCES DEFENSE COUNCIL, DRILLING DOWN: PROTECTING WESTERN COMMUNITIES FROM THE HEALTH AND ENVIRONMENTAL EFFECTS OF OIL AND GAS PRODUCTION (Oct. 2007). The production and transport of crude oil and its refined products can lead to oil spills both large and small, such as the crash of the *Exxon Valdez* tanker in Alaska in 1989 and the blowout of the *Deepwater Horizon* oil rig off the Gulf Coast in 2010 (discussed in Chapter 9). And the refining and combustion of oil products in cars, trucks, ships, and planes also creates air and water pollution, even as environmental regulations in the United States have substantially improved these emissions over the last decades.

Despite new techniques like hydraulic fracturing and deepwater drilling, U.S. oil production has historically fallen short of domestic demand for oil, though that has shifted recently. U.S. oil consumption began to outstrip domestic production in the 1950s, and by 2005, over 60% of oil consumed in the United States was imported from overseas, highlighting geopolitical and security vulnerabilities. But due to increased production, by 2020, the United States became a net petroleum exporter for the first time since 1949, while still importing some crude oil both for domestic supply and for international export. *See Oil Imports and Exports*, U.S. Energy Info. Admin. (last updated Apr. 13, 2021).

c. Natural Gas

Natural gas consists primarily of methane, or CH_4. It is less complex than other fossil fuels—lighter than air, highly flammable, odorless in its pure state, and burns almost completely, producing relatively little air pollution and no ash waste, though it does produce carbon dioxide. Thus, for years, many viewed natural gas as "a relatively benign fossil fuel for the environment." U.S. ENERGY INFO. ADMIN. & U.S. DEP'T OF ENERGY, DOE/EIA-0560(98), NATURAL GAS 1998: ISSUES AND TRENDS (1999). You probably know natural gas well. For many Americans, it heats our homes, fuels our fireplaces, runs our water heaters, and cooks our food in ovens and on ranges. And what about that rotten egg smell that comes with natural gas? That's not the natural state of natural gas at all; it's an odorant that utilities add to the fuel for safety.

Natural gas is an ancient energy source that has only become widely useful in modern times. "The ancient 'eternal fires' in [the Middle East] . . . reported in Plutarch's writings around 100 to 125 A.D. probably were from natural gas escaping from cracks in the ground and ignited by lightning." *Natural Gas: Fueling the Blue Flame—The History of Natural Gas*, U.S. Dep't of Energy. The Chinese, around 500 B.C.E., also used bamboo as "pipes" to capture gas seeping to the surface to boil ocean water to make it drinkable. French explorers discovered natural gas in and around Lake Erie in the early 1600s. In 1821, William Hart "dug the first successful natural gas well in the U.S. in Fredonia, New York." *A Brief History of Natural Gas,* Am. Public Gas Ass'n. Fifteen years after that, in 1836, Philadelphia formed the first municipally owned natural gas distribution company. Yet for most of the nineteenth century—and well into the twentieth—discovered natural gas was allowed to simply escape into the atmosphere or was burned ("flared") when found with oil or coal.

The first commercial natural gas pipeline in the United States was not built until 1891, a 120-mile segment from Indiana to Chicago. The natural gas was used to supplement the town gas supplies. Still, until metal, welding, and pipe making technologies improved, very few natural gas pipelines were built pre-World War II, often rendering natural gas stranded and unusable. Following the war, the country constructed thousands of miles of pipeline, so that today, "the U.S. pipeline network, laid end-to-end, would stretch to the moon and back twice." Natural gas largely replaced coal and town gas as a home heating and cooking fuel, resulting in major improvements in urban air quality. *Natural Gas: Fueling the Blue Flame—The History of Natural Gas*, U.S. Dep't of Energy.

Natural gas can be produced in three primary ways: (1) from wells devoted to natural gas extraction, (2) co-produced with oil, or (3) from coal beds as coal bed methane. Like oil, natural gas is typically classified as "conventional" or "unconventional." Conventional gas is found in geological basins, generally referred to as "plays," or reservoirs made of porous and permeable rocks, which hold significant natural gas in the spaces within the rock. Technological advancements in directional drilling coupled with hydraulic fracturing (also referred to as "hydro-fracking," "fraccing," or "fracking") have opened up new natural gas resources that were previously inaccessible.

These "unconventional" reserves now supply more than half of U.S. natural gas needs and consist of tight sands gas, coalbed methane (CBM) gas, and shale gas. Tight sands gas is natural gas contained in sandstone, siltstone, and carbonate reservoirs of low permeability, meaning gas will not flow naturally when a well is drilled. To extract tight sands gas, the rock is fractured to stimulate production. Coal bed methane (CBM) gas is natural gas trapped in coal seams held in place by water. The gas is extracted by drilling wells into the coal seams and removing the groundwater, which reduces the pressure in the coal seam and allows the CBM to flow to the surface through the well. Most CBM production is in Wyoming and other Rocky Mountain states.

Shale gas is found in fine-grained sedimentary rock with low permeability and porosity, known as shale. Extracting the gas from the tight pore spaces requires technologies associated with hydraulic fracturing. The procedure uses horizontal directional drilling to precisely drill a well into a shale formation, and then hydro-fracture the well by injecting a high-pressure mix of water, "proppants" (such as sand or ceramic beads), and various chemicals, which are pumped into the well at high pressure. The pressure fractures the rock, creating small cracks which radiate outward from the well bore and, held open by the proppants, allows the oil or natural gas to flow to the production well. This process has allowed what were once considered unproductive shale formations to become major supplies of oil and gas for the United States and the world.

As a result of abundant shale gas production, the United States became the world's largest natural gas producer in 2009 (surpassing Russia) and became a net exporter of natural gas in 2018, a dramatic shift from the mid-2000s. As of 2021, the top five gas producing states were Texas, Pennsylvania, Louisiana, Oklahoma, and Ohio. *See Where Our Natural Gas Comes From*, U.S. Energy Info. Admin. (last updated Mar. 11, 2021).

Natural gas is difficult to transport. Thus, unless linked by a pipeline or close to a liquefied natural gas (LNG) terminal, natural gas in remote fields is often "stranded": unable to be sold or traded. Because of these transport challenges, international trade in natural gas is smaller than for oil, but it is increasing with international investments in LNG infrastructure. Natural gas becomes LNG by cooling it to −260°F at normal pressure. This is done by removing water, mercury, and CO_2, and then compressing and cooling the gas with propane refrigerant. The resulting LNG takes up to 600 times less space than conventional natural gas— roughly equivalent to reducing a beach ball to the size of a ping- pong ball. Once in liquid form, LNG can be used either as a fuel in vehicles or shipped for subsequent use. Following shipping, LNG can be reheated to a gaseous state and transported via established transportation methods, such as pipelines, to end users. With the advent of hydraulic fracturing, FERC has approved several applications for new LNG export terminals and has many more under review. *See LNG*, Fed. Energy Reg. Comm'n. For a diagram of global natural gas trades by pipeline and LNG shipments between regions, see BP STATISTICAL REVIEW OF WORLD ENERGY, *supra* at 43. These LNG terminals, like natural gas pipelines and other fossil fuel transport infrastructure, have become subject to a growing number of legal challenges as concerns of over climate change and the environmental justice impacts of energy infrastructure have grown, as discussed in more detail in Chapter 7.

Natural gas is used widely in the industrial sector, for electricity production, and for residential and commercial heating. Because natural gas is used for space heating in buildings, its consumption follows a seasonal trend, with gas stored in the summer and fall in underground storage sites and used in the winter for space heating. Within the industrial sector, natural gas is used for process heat, to fire boilers, for combined heat and power, and as an industrial feedstock. *See U.S. Natural Gas Flow, 2020*, U.S. Energy Info. Admin. (flow chart).

Natural gas comes with both environmental benefits and costs. Positively, electricity produced using natural gas has fewer ecological impacts than electricity from other fossil fuels, particularly coal and oil. As compared to a coal plant, a natural gas plant produces fewer criteria air pollutants (no particulate matter, one third as much NO_x and 1% of the sulfur) and half of the CO_2. This has led some to call natural gas the "bridge fuel" to the future—from our carbon-intensive energy systems dominated by oil and coal toward a more sustainable energy world. *See, e.g.,* Richard J. Pierce, Jr., *Natural Gas: A Long Bridge to a Promising Destination,* 32 UTAH ENV'T L. REV. 245 (2012); JOHN D. PODESTA & TIMOTHY WIRTH, CTR. FOR AM. PROGRESS, NATURAL GAS: A BRIDGE FUEL FOR THE 21ST CENTURY 3 (Aug. 10, 2009); Joel Kirkland, *Natural Gas Could Serve as "Bridge Fuel" to a Low-Carbon Future,* SCI. AM. (June 25, 2010). Over one-third of natural gas is used in the electricity sector, and this share has been growing. In the past, higher natural gas prices meant that electric utilities dispatched natural gas plants primarily as load following or "peaker" plants in times of high electricity demand. However, increased North American supply due to shale gas extraction and corresponding consistently lower prices prompted many electric utilities to replace their coal-fired units with natural gas combined cycle plants. As a result, many gas-fired plants now run around the clock as "baseload" generation.

On the negative side, while natural gas produces fewer air emissions than oil or coal, it is not pollution-free and has a range of adverse impacts on air, water, and land. These impacts include: (1) air pollution emissions from drilling equipment, escaped methane and hydrocarbons, natural gas flaring, and emissions from support vehicles or leaks from pipelines; (2) water pollution from wastewater produced during the drilling process, improper disposal of wastes to surface and groundwater, and spills and leaks from pipelines, storage tanks, and transport trucks; and (3) interference with plants and animals by habitat destruction and disturbance as well as the air pollution and water pollution just described. *See* Margriat F. Carswell, *Balancing Energy and the Environment, in* THE ENVIRONMENT OF OIL 179, 182–85 (Richard J. Gilbert, ed. 1993). Moreover, as discussed in Chapters 3 and 9, because natural gas consists primarily of methane—a potent GHG—the release of methane into the atmosphere during the extraction, transportation, and use phases can have significant climate-related impacts.

These environmental impacts are often exacerbated when natural gas is extracted using hydraulic fracturing technologies, which can result not only in the pollution described above but also earthquakes ("induced seismicity") associated with underground injection of wastewater, enhanced truck traffic, and land use disruption. *See, e.g.,* David B. Spence, *Federalism, Regulatory Lags, and the Political Economy of Energy Production,* 161 U. PA. L. REV. 431, 507 (2013). This is a topic that Chapter 9 explores in depth. There remains considerable debate regarding the benefits natural gas-fired power provides over coal-fired power when it comes to life cycle GHG emissions, considering the significant methane emissions associated with the extraction, transport, and use of natural gas domestically and worldwide. *See, e.g.,* ENVIRONMENTAL DEFENSE FUND, METHANE RESEARCH: THE 16 STUDIES (2017) (summarizing series of collaborative studies with academic institutions and industry to determine the extent of methane loss during natural gas production, distribution, and transport); U.S. DEP'T OF ENERGY, LIFE CYCLE GREENHOUSE GAS PERSPECTIVE ON EXPORTING LIQUEFIED NATURAL GAS FROM THE UNITED STATES (May 29, 2014); JAMES LITTLEFIELD ET AL., NAT'L ENERGY TECH. LAB., LIFE CYCLE ANALYSIS OF NATURAL GAS EXTRACTION AND POWER GENERATION (Apr. 19, 2019).

d. Nuclear Power

Nuclear reactors use uranium to produce electricity. As further detailed in Chapter 10, nuclear reactors create electricity by boiling water to produce steam and turn a turbine. The reactor produces heat from the fission (splitting) of atoms within the reactor core. While there long has been hope for nuclear fusion energy—where atoms are joined, as stars like the sun do to produce energy—this technology remains in the research phase. However, new developments in China, the United Kingdom, and the United States are creating hope that the long sought-after technology could become commercialized sooner rather than later. *See, e.g.,* Caroline Delbert, *China's Artificial Sun Just Smashed a Fusion World Record,* POPULAR MECHANICS (Jun. 7, 2021); Caroline Delbert, *This Reactor May Have Finally Solved Nuclear Fusion's Biggest Problem,* POPULAR MECHANICS (May 28, 2021); David Nield, *MIT Physicists Just Majorly Advanced the Quest Towards Actual Fusion Power,* SCIENCE ALERT (Sept. 10, 2021).

Unlike fossil fuels, which have been used for centuries, nuclear energy has a short history. It started during World War II with the Manhattan Project in Los Alamos, New Mexico led by General Leslie Groves and Dr. J. Robert Oppenheimer. After the war, the U.S. Government enacted the Atomic Energy Act of 1946, which, among other things, established the Atomic Energy Commission (the predecessor to today's Nuclear Regulatory Commission). At that point, to address the public concerns regarding nuclear power as well as industry's desire to commercialize nuclear energy, Congress enacted the Atomic Energy Act of 1954, which moved nuclear power from the military realm to the private sector to take advantage of what was thought to be power "too cheap to meter." With the enactment of the Price Anderson Act in 1957, which significantly limited liability for nuclear accidents, U.S. utilities invested heavily in constructing nuclear power plants. This building boom in the 1960s, which included plant sizes ranging from 800 to 1100 MW, resulted in nuclear power becoming 20% of U.S. electricity production. *See* Joseph P. Tomain, *Nuclear Futures,* 15 DUKE ENV'T L. & POL'Y F. 221 (2005).

The nuclear fuel cycle can be divided into three stages: front-end, use or operation, and back-end. In the "front-end" part of the cycle, uranium is mined, milled, enriched, and then turned into usable nuclear fuel (fuel "fabrication"). Nuclear reactors use this fuel to create the chain reactions that heat the water that turns their turbines. On the "back-end," spent nuclear fuel must either be reprocessed for reuse, as is common in France, or stored for "disposal," which is what the United States does.

"Uranium is a slightly radioactive metal that occurs throughout the Earth's crust. It is about 500 times more abundant than gold and about as common as tin. It is present in most rocks and soils as well as in many rivers and in sea water. It is, for example, found in concentrations of about four parts per million (ppm) in granite, which makes up 60% of the Earth's crust." *Nuclear Fuel Cycle Overview*, World Nuclear Ass'n (updated Apr. 2021). Uranium ore is mined in either underground or open pit mines (55%) or, increasingly, through *in situ* leach mining (45%). In 2019, global uranium ore production was 54,752 metric tons (64,566 short tons of U_3O_8), with Kazakhstan (42%), Canada (13%), Australia (12%), Namibia (10%), and Uzbekistan (6%) counting themselves as the highest producing countries. The United States produced only 67 metric tons, down from 1919 metric tons in 2014, with most domestic uranium mining occurring in the western part of the nation. *See* WORLD NUCLEAR ASS'N, URANIUM PRODUCTION FIGURES 2010–2019 (2020).

Once mined, uranium ore is milled, chemically processed to leach the uranium from the ore, and then dried and filtered to create yellowcake. "Milling, which is generally carried out close to a uranium mine, extracts the uranium from the ore. Most mining facilities include a mill, although where mines are close together, one mill may process the ore from several mines." *Nuclear Fuel Cycle Overview, supra*. The mills work by crushing the ore to a fine slurry. This slurry is then leached using sulfuric acid or a strong alkaline solution to separate the uranium from waste rock. Following the leaching process, it is precipitated as uranium oxide (U_3O_8), which is then dried and heated. Uranium oxide is the product sold in the market. Roughly 2000 tons of U_3O_8 is needed to keep "a large (1000 MWe) nuclear power reactor generating electricity for one year." *Id.*

The uranium oxide yielded from the milling and leaching process is called yellowcake. Yellowcake typically contains 70–90% U_3O_8, but it usually is not yellow—it is khaki or brown. The leftovers from the milling process—unused ore "and nearly all the rock material"—are what are referred to as uranium tailings. *Id.* They contain radioactive materials, requiring treatment and separation from the environment.

Most nuclear reactors require "fissile," or fissionable uranium: U_{235}. However, most naturally occurring uranium is not U_{235}; about 99.3% is U_{238}. Thus, the yellowcake produced from the milling and leaching process must undergo further refining, or "enrichment," to be useable in light water reactors. Enrichment increases the U_{235} content to 3.5 to 5% (by contrast, weapons-grade uranium is enriched to 90-plus percent). Enrichment is a complicated process that uses chemicals, centrifuges, and lasers to gasify the uranium into uranium hexafluoride and eventually produce enriched uranium oxide. A good explanation of uranium enrichment is available at http://www.youtube.com/watch?v=69UpMhUnEeY. "A small number of reactors, notably the Canadian and Indian heavy water type, do not require uranium to be enriched." *Id.*

Before use, the last stage of the front-end uranium cycle is fabrication. Here, the enriched uranium is made into ceramic pellets and stacked into nuclear fuel rods. These rods are bundled, and the rod assemblies are used in the reactors, lasting about 6 years. After the fuel rod is used, the U_{235} levels decrease to 1%, and the hot rods are moved to storage in spent fuel pools to allow them to further cool. In theory, the cooler rods are supposed to be moved to long-term disposal sites, but in practice, most remain in spent fuel pools or are moved to dry cask storage. Only France reprocesses the fuel and vitrifies the waste. The challenges raised by long-term nuclear fuel storage are addressed further in Chapter 10.

Nuclear energy has many benefits; it provided nearly 20% of U.S. electricity production and over 50% of the nation's carbon-free electricity in 2020. The plants produce no traditional air emissions, such as SO_x, NO_x, or toxic emissions, and generally affects water systems at the site of electricity production only through thermal waste. Because it produces 90% of its potential output, nuclear boasts the highest capacity factor of any kind of electricity generation fleet in the country. Thus, nuclear epitomizes "baseload" generation. While the United States holds only a fraction of the world's uranium reserves, it leads the world in nuclear energy production. Nevertheless, significant cost overruns in the construction of planned nuclear plants, overestimations of how much energy the nation would use, increasing regulation of atomic energy production, and the 1979 incident at the Three Mile Island facility in Pennsylvania brought construction of new nuclear power facilities in the United States "to a screeching halt." Dan C. Perry, *Uranium Law and Leasing*, 55 RMMLF-INST 27–1 (2009).

There had been four AP1000 nuclear power plants under construction at Vogtle (Georgia Power) and Summer (licensed for South Carolina Electric & Gas Company) in the United States in recent years. But high costs for advanced nuclear ($5,880/kW), cost overruns at the facilities, low natural gas prices, liberalized electricity markets, and subsidies and rapid penetration of renewable power all undermined the business case for new nuclear plants, leading to the cancellation of the two South Carolina reactors in 2017 and the bankruptcy of Westinghouse Corporation. *See, e.g.,* Tom Hals & Emily Flitter, *How Two Cutting Edge U.S. Nuclear Projects Bankrupted Westinghouse*, REUTERS (May 2, 2017); Brad Plumer, *U.S. Nuclear Comeback Stalls as Two Reactors are Abandoned*, N.Y. TIMES (July 31, 2017). The Vogtle project continues, but with significant delays and cost overruns. *See* Matt Kemper, *Georgia Power Discloses More Vogtle Nuclear Delays, Big Extra Costs*, ATLANTA J.-CONST. (July 29, 2021).

Today, public opposition to nuclear persists in the United States. For many, a culture of fear surrounds nuclear, and for others, the technology's historical ties to military weapons and testing makes the energy source too much to stomach. Indeed, in the 1970s and 1980s, many states enacted moratoria prohibiting the construction of new nuclear facilities in those states. Moreover, the potential risk of nuclear accidents at these facilities—as evidenced by the 1979 incident at Three Mile Island in Pennsylvania, the 1986 disaster at Chernobyl in the U.S.S.R., and the 2011 triple meltdown at the Fukushima Daiichi plant in Japan—demands extensive regulation of the industry to ensure safe operation. But perhaps most damning for the industry, finding solutions to store spent nuclear fuel has proven extraordinarily difficult.

There is good reason why the nuclear waste dilemma is so intractable. Spent nuclear fuel is highly radioactive and fatal to humans for hundreds of thousands of years. In the face of this, it is not just the United States that has had trouble finding a solution for nuclear waste. All countries that house nuclear facilities struggle with the safe disposal of spent nuclear fuel. Today, the United States lacks a permanent storage facility, and the fight over the location that had been chosen—Yucca Mountain, Nevada—is an ongoing, some might say "never ending," saga. *See* Chapter 10. Nevertheless, in recent years environmental groups, states, and others have also expressed concern that inexpensive natural gas and the rising costs of nuclear may threaten a major source of existing carbon-free electricity in the United States. *See, e.g.,* Brad Plumer, *How Retiring Nuclear Power Plants May Undercut U.S. Climate Goals*, N.Y. TIMES (June 13, 2017).

Globally, nuclear is a growing technology. As of 2021 there was over 396 GW of nuclear power generated by around 440 reactors located in 31 countries, with the United States, France, China, Russia, and South Korea having the largest installed nuclear fleets. Nuclear power plants produce 10% of global electricity. *See Nuclear Power in the World Today*, Int'l Atomic Energy Agency (last updated Mar. 2021).

The figure below shows the global energy production from nuclear energy. Although the United States is the largest producer of electricity from nuclear energy, with 94 nuclear reactors as of 2020, the percentage contribution of nuclear energy to each country's electricity mix tells a different story. In France, nuclear produces 71% of the country's electricity; in the Ukraine, Hungary, Belgium, and Slovakia, around 50%.

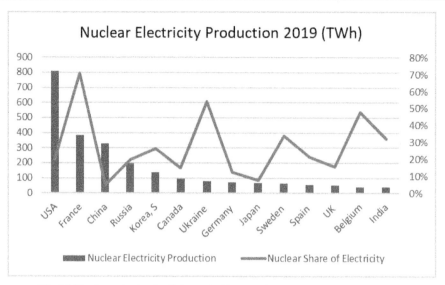

Sources: World Nuclear Ass'n; Int'l Atomic Energy Agency.

2. RENEWABLE RESOURCES

Renewable energy resources have many advantages but also present novel challenges. Their operating costs tend to be very low—in many cases, effectively zero other than maintenance because renewable "fuels" like wind, sun, and water are free. Renewables, as their name implies, also are effectively unlimited in supply. Because they regenerate continuously, or can be regenerated, renewables offer the promise of energy security that nonrenewables cannot. (Note: this is not strictly true for high-temperature geothermal energy, which "mines" the heat of the subsurface.) And renewables can provide extensive environmental benefits, including lower air emissions than fossil fuels, lower or zero carbon emissions, and, in many cases, significantly reduced environmental impacts at the point of extraction. There are, of course, environmental costs involved in extracting the materials needed to construct renewable energy technologies, such as critical minerals for wind turbines and solar panels, but the life-cycle impacts can be much lower than those that accompany many "traditional" energy sources. Growth in renewable energy in the United States and worldwide over the past two decades has far exceeded expectations and is on track to continue as prices for wind and solar decrease and electric utilities across the country gain more experience integrating utility-scale renewable projects into their operations.

Although the beneficial qualities of renewable energy make them a crucial part of a sustainable energy solution, there are many barriers that limit their ability to serve as a "one-size fits all" answer to a new energy transition. Unlike fossil fuels, which can be fairly easily stored and transported, electricity produced by variable renewable technologies cannot, at least without greater integration of commercial-scale energy storage or more sophisticated demand management technologies. Chapter 11 discusses innovative efforts to develop storage technologies in more depth, but until such technologies are widely deployed, electricity produced from renewables needs to be used as it is produced. In addition, the places with the greatest renewable resources are often located far from major population centers; this creates the need for additional investment in high voltage transmission lines to transport utility-scale renewable electricity to distant load centers. Chapter 7 discusses the complexities of siting and paying for these needed transmission lines. Finally, although renewable energy has made significant inroads in the electricity sector, the transportation sector is in transition and still dominated by oil. The potential for electrifying the transportation sector is discussed in Chapter 11.

Because of the potential benefits of renewable energy as well as the recognition that the renewable energy industry has not received the decades of financial and other support historically provided to fossil fuel industries, federal and state governments have created various financial incentives and tax credits to promote renewable energy development. A good summary of tax incentive programs for both fossil fuels and renewable energy is contained in MOLLY F. SHERLOCK, CONG. RSCH. SERV., THE VALUE OF ENERGY TAX INCENTIVES FOR DIFFERENT TYPES OF ENERGY RESOURCES (Mar. 19, 2019). Many of the incentives for renewable energy are focused on supporting wind and solar energy resources for electricity, but some also support small hydropower projects and other types of low or zero-carbon energy as well as CCS projects.

A partial list of these programs is presented below, with some of them discussed in more detail in later chapters. It is important to note, however, that these more recent and time-limited tax incentives to support renewable energy must be evaluated against the backdrop of many decades of permanent federal tax subsidies for fossil fuel extraction activities such as the expensing of intangible drilling costs and the percentage depletion allowance. *See* SHERLOCK, *supra*, at 9–12; Carlos Anchondo & Lesley Clark, *Key to the Shale Boom? 3 Federal Subsidies*, ENERGYWIRE (July 23, 2021) (discussing tax subsidies for fossil fuels); Scott Waldman, *Biden Wants to End Oil Subsidies. First He Has To Find Them*, ENERGYWIRE (Mar. 9, 2021).

Plug-In Electric Vehicle Tax Credit: Established as part of the Energy Improvement and Extension Act of 2008, this credit allows taxpayers to claim a tax credit for qualified purchases of electric vehicles. Depending on the type of vehicle and its battery capacity, credits range from $2,500 to $7,500 and begin to phase out once manufacturers have sold 200,000 qualifying vehicles. *See* MOLLY F. SHERLOCK, CONG. RSCH. SERV., THE PLUG-IN ELECTRIC VEHICLE TAX CREDIT (May 14, 2019).

Section 45Q Tax Credit for Carbon Oxide Sequestration: Since 2008, the Section 45Q tax credit has incentivized CCS by providing credits per metric ton of qualified carbon oxides captured and disposed of. The tax credit applies to industrial sources employing carbon capture equipment to prevent the release of carbon dioxide and carbon oxide that would otherwise be emitted into the atmosphere. Originally, the tax credit was set to expire once 75 million metric tons of CO_2 had been captured and the credit claimed. The Bipartisan Budget Act of 2018 modified the sequestration credit by eliminating the 75 million metric ton cap in favor of a construction deadline for qualifying equipment and a 12-year claim period extending from the date of construction. Although the construction deadline was initially set at the end of 2023, Congress extended 45Q to apply to projects beginning construction before 2026 as part of the Taxpayer Certainty and Disaster Relief Act of 2020. *See* ANGELA C. JONES & MOLLY F. SHERLOCK, CONG. RSCH. SERV., THE TAX CREDIT FOR CARBON SEQUESTRATION (SECTION 45Q) (Mar. 12, 2020).

Production Tax Credit (PTC): Since 1992, the federal government has granted a PTC (currently 1.3 to 2.5 cents per kWh) first for wind, closed-loop biomass, and poultry waste energy resources and later expanded to include several other renewable energy sources. The PTC is for the first 10 years of operation and is a major driver for wind energy development, allowing wind to be more cost-competitive with fossil-fuel electricity resources. The PTC has sunset (and almost sunset) numerous times, but Congress has often renewed it at the last hour. Legislation in 2015 extended it further until 2020, with gradual reductions leading up to that date: wind facilities which started construction in 2017 had the PTC reduced by 20%; 2018 by 40%; and 2019 by 60%. Congress subsequently extended PTCs for all technologies in 2020 through the end of the year and retroactively extended PTCs for non-wind resources that expired in 2017. The tax credit was renewed by a stimulus bill in 2020 and extended through the end of 2021 at a reduced rate of 60% of the total credit. *See, e.g., Renewable Energy Production Tax Credit (PTC)*, DSIRE; MOLLY SHERLOCK, CONG. RESEARCH SERV., THE RENEWABLE ELECTRICITY PRODUCTION TAX CREDIT: IN BRIEF (Apr. 29, 2020).

Section 48 Investment Tax Credit (ITC): First created as part of the American Recovery and Reinvestment Act (ARRA) in 2009, the ITC allows qualified renewable energy sources to take the PTC as a 30% investment tax credit for the year the facility is placed in service, which helps offshore wind projects, certain solar projects, and other projects where developers lack a history of operations, thus requiring them to take a significant discount when monetizing the PTC. Originally set to continue until 2022, the ITC was extended by a stimulus package for different periods of time depending on the type of resource project. The amount of the tax credit is reduced over time, with qualifying solar projects beginning construction before 2023 receiving a 26% credit; 2024 a 22% credit; and 10% for all projects commenced thereafter. For tax credits of more than 10%, solar facilities must be placed in service prior to 2026. For qualifying wind projects, ITCs can be claimed in lieu of the PTC if construction begins prior to 2022 and are based on the initial construction year (2017, 24%; 2018, 18%; 2019, 12%; 2020–21, 18%). Offshore wind projects were included in the stimulus bill for the first time and qualify for the full 30% tax credit so long as construction begins prior to 2026. *See* Michael Rodgers & Brandon Dubov, *Stimulus Bill Brings Welcomed Changes to the Renewable Energy Industry*, WHITE & CASE, LLP (Jan. 6, 2021); *Business Energy Investment Tax Credit (ITC)*, DSIRE.

Renewable Portfolio Standards (RPSs) and Clean Energy Standards (CESs): More than half the states and the District of Columbia have RPSs, which require utilities and other electricity providers to generate a certain percentage of electricity sales each year by a set date, often 15% to 20%, by 2020 or 2030, measured in MWs, from renewable energy sources. There is significant variation among the states over which electricity providers must comply with the RPS and which renewable resources count toward meeting the RPS. Several additional states now also have CESs, which mandate that up to 100% of electricity sales come from carbon-free energy resources (generally renewable energy plus nuclear power and/or fossil fuel plants equipped with CCS) by dates ranging from 2030 to 2050. RPSs and CESs are discussed in detail in Chapter 5.

Feed-in Tariffs (FiTs): FiTs provide a secure contract for renewable power at a set price that provides a rate of return to investors and developers. FiTs are used widely in Europe in the form of a mandate to purchase renewable power at a set rate. Some municipalities, such as Gainesville, Florida, have employed FiTs. California, Vermont, New York, Washington, Hawaii, and Indiana have also begun to implement them.

U.S. Department of Energy Loan Guarantees: The U.S. Department of Energy has a loan guarantee program, expanded through ARRA, for projects that employ new renewable energy technologies that reduce or sequester GHGs.

Clean Renewable Energy Bonds (CREBs): CREBs were created as part of the Energy Policy Act of 2005 to finance public sector renewable energy projects. ARRA provided for $1.6 billion in new CREBs to finance wind, biomass, hydropower, landfill gas, and other renewable energy projects.

State, Local Government, and Utility Subsidies and Incentives: Many states, local governments, and utilities provide a wide variety of tax incentives and other financial benefits for renewable energy projects. For more information, see *Financial Incentives for Renewable Energy*, DSIRE.

As introduced in Chapter 1, every energy choice has tradeoffs, including renewables sources. Beyond the storage and transmission issues described above, renewable energy sources also come with their own environmental and social costs. The remainder of this section introduces various renewable energy resources, including their comparative advantages and disadvantages.

a. Hydropower

Hydropower is perhaps the oldest and, historically, one of the simplest renewable technologies. Hydropower has been used since Mesopotamia for irrigation, to mill grain, and to power lumber and textile mills. Since the first commercial hydroelectric power plant was built on the Fox River in Appleton, Wisconsin in 1882, hydropower has also been used to produce electricity.

Traditionally, hydroelectric facilities were located on rivers, but many facilities built in the 1900s include dams on lakes—or dams that effectively created lakes, such as Lake Powell at the Glen Canyon Dam or Lake Mead near Las Vegas from the Hoover Dam. Hydropower plants produce electricity, and also provide regulation and black start services to support grid resilience.

Today, in addition to re-powering existing facilities, new forms of hydropower from ocean sources (tidal, current, and thermal) are under development, as are low-head, run-of-the-river, and other micro-hydro projects. *See* CONG. RSCH. SERV., SMALL HYDRO AND LOW-HEAD HYDROPOWER TECHNOLOGIES AND PROSPECTS (Mar. 1, 2010). Other forms of hydropower include pumped storage and conduit hydropower. Pumped storage operates by moving water between two reservoirs at different elevations. At times of low electricity demand, this technology uses cheap electricity to pump the water up to a reservoir. Then, in times of high demand, the water is released to flow through turbines and create higher cost electricity. Pumped storage has an installed capacity of 23 GW in the United States and is in use in every region of the country. Conduit hydropower utilizes existing waterways such as canals, tunnels, aqueducts, and pipelines. Electricity generating equipment is installed into the structure without the use of a large dam or reservoir. This technology is utilized throughout the country, including by the San Diego County Water Authority at the Ranchos Penasquitos Pressure Control Hydroelectric Facility. This facility has a 4.5 MW production capacity. *Conduit Hydropower,* Nat'l Hydropower Ass'n, Hydro.org.

Hydroelectricity Worldwide

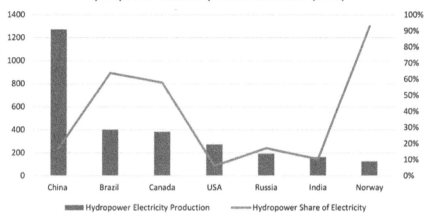

Hydropower Electricity Production 2019 (TWh)

Source: BP Global Energy.

While hydropower is used in over 150 countries, just seven countries—China, Brazil, the United States, Canada, India, Japan, and Russia—accounted for approximately 61% of global hydropower capacity in 2019. At home in the United States, 103 GW of capacity (hydropower with 80 GW and pumped hydro with 23 GW) produced 6.6% of electricity in 2019, with Washington, Oregon, California, and New York producing the most electricity from hydropower. U.S. ENERGY INFO. ADMIN., ELEC. POWER ANNUAL 2019 tbls. 3.14, 3.16 (Oct. 21, 2020); INT'L HYDROPOWER ASS'N, 2020 HYDROPOWER STATUS REPORT (2020). Moreover, while over half of the world's installed hydropower capacity is in these countries, some smaller countries are almost wholly dependent on hydropower for electricity. For example, Albania, Bhutan, Lesotho, Paraguay, and another eight countries generate over 90% of their electricity using hydropower. *See Share of Electricity Production from Hydropower, 2020*, OUR WORLD IN DATA (2021).

Hydroelectric power plants generate electricity when water runs through a turbine, causing it to spin and produce electricity. The amount of electricity produced from a hydropower project depends on the hydraulic head (the mass of the water) and rate of the fluid flow (how much water is flowing). Hydroelectric power plants vary greatly in size. The largest four hydro plants in the world are over 13 GW each: Three Gorges (22 GW), Baihetan (to be 16 GW when fully completed in 2022) and Xiluodu (13.8 GW), all in China and Itaipu (14 GW) in Brazil and Paraguay. At the other end of the scale, micro-hydro (less than 100 kW) and run-of-the river projects are also gaining popularity, although they still comprise a small share of total hydropower capacity. In addition, hydropower can be adversely affected by rainfall, meaning that drought years can reduce power production.

Hydropower capacity is particularly sensitive to the effects of climate change and shifts in rainfall patterns and drought. Over the last 50 years, average global temperatures have increased by 1.8°F, and this warming trend is expected to continue. U.S. GLOBAL CHANGE RSCH. PROGRAM, IMPACTS, RISKS, AND ADAPTATION IN THE UNITED STATES: FOURTH NATIONAL CLIMATE ASSESSMENT, VOLUME II (2018). While overall precipitation across the United States has increased, regional and seasonal variation and extensive droughts in southern and western states have also been observed. *Id. See also* Henry Fountain, *Against Expectations, Southwestern Summers Are Getting Even Drier*, N.Y. TIMES (June 22, 2021). Because electricity production depends on the mass and flow rate of water, climate change poses a looming threat to the future of hydropower as a viable source of electricity, particularly in the western states that are home to the nation's largest hydropower facilities. *See, e.g.*, Alexandra Meeks, *A California Reservoir is Expected to Fall So Low That a Hydropower Plant is Expected to Shut Down for the First Time*, CNN (June 18, 2021) (reporting on drought-related threats to large hydropower facilities and, thus, electricity supply, throughout the western United States in 2021); Scott Van Voorhis, *Historic Drought Slashes Hydropower Generation in California, Other Western States*, UTIL. DIVE (Aug. 24, 2021).

Nevertheless, hydropower has much untapped promise. Today, hydropower produces roughly 16% of global electricity, the largest share of any non-fossil renewables: an installed capacity of over 1,300 GW. *See* BP STATISTICAL REVIEW OF WORLD ENERGY, *supra*, at 61; 2020 HYDROPOWER STATUS REPORT, *supra*. Moreover, global hydropower capacity is increasing at roughly 3% per year. The International Energy Agency estimates that capacity could double to 2,000 GW by 2050, with much untapped hydro potential in Africa, Latin America, and Asia. In China, massive projects are coming online in 2021 to 2022. *See China Starts Baihetan Hydro Project, Biggest Since Three Gorges*, REUTERS (June 28, 2021). In the United States, 2,400 conventional hydropower facilities provide nearly 80 GW of installed capacity (6.7% of total capacity) and produce 38% of renewable electricity. Repowering old facilities and adding electricity generation to existing non-powered dams are both ways to increase U.S. hydropower capacity without building more dams. *See* U.S. DEP'T OF ENERGY, U.S. HYDROPOWER MARKET REPORT (Jan. 2021). The figure below shows existing hydroelectric power plants in the United States as of 2015.

U.S. Hydroelectric Capacity (79.6 GW) (2015)

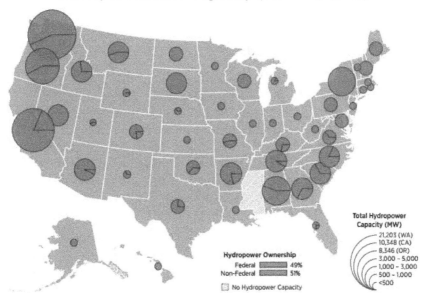

Source: U.S. DEPT. OF ENERGY, HYDROPOWER VISION: A NEW CHAPTER FOR AMERICA'S FIRST RENEWABLE ENERGY SOURCE ES-1 (July 2016).

Like other renewables, hydroelectricity has many environmental and climate benefits. After construction hydropower plants are usually inexpensive to operate and can operate indefinitely. This carbon free electricity generation is important, but so is the ability of hydropower plants to provide other electricity services including load following, peaking power, regulation, and black start services. Additionally, hydropower dams are often linked to other societal uses including flood control, agricultural irrigation, and public water supplies.

Like all energy technologies, hydropower has costs. Most prominent is the adverse impact of hydropower on fish species that rely on impacted waterways. Specifically, dams fragment river ecosystems and affect the connectivity of species' migration and spawning habitats. *See* Valeria Barbarossa et al., *Impacts of Current and Large Dams on the Geographic Range Connectivity of Freshwater Fish Worldwide*, PROCEEDINGS OF THE NAT'L ACADEMY OF SCIENCES (Feb. 2020). This, in turn, can result in significant harm to local communities, particularly native tribes, that have historically relied on the impacted fish and free flowing rivers for their food supply, culture, and religious practices. *See, e.g.*, Sarah Krakoff, *Not Yet America's Best Idea: Law, Inequality, and Grand Canyon National Park*, 91 U. COLO. L. REV. 559 (2020) (discussing impact of western dam building on native tribes); Liam Patton, Note, *The Little Colorado River Project: Is New Hydropower Development the Key to a Renewable Energy Future, Or*

the Vestige of a Failed Past, 32 COLO. NAT. RES. ENERGY & ENV'T L. REV.
41 (2021) (same).

On a global scale, the "social groups bearing the social and
environmental costs and risks of large dams, especially the poor,
vulnerable, and future generations, are often not the same groups that
receive the water and electricity services, nor the social and economic
benefits from these." *The Report of the World Commission on Dams*, 16 AM.
U. INT'L L. REV. 1435, 1442 (2001). For example, China's Three Gorges Dam
displaced 1.35 million people and Chinese officials anticipated relocation
up to 4 million more over the subsequent 10 to 15 years to protect the
ecology of the reservoir area. Brooke Wilmsen et al., *Development for
Whom? Rural to Urban Resettlement at Three Gorges Dam, China*, 35
ASIAN STUDIES REV. 21, 22 (2011). Scholars worry that those displaced
because of development projects such as Three Gorges will face heightened
threats of increased poverty, landlessness, unemployment, food insecurity,
and social marginalization. Peter H. Gleick, *Water Brief 3: Three Gorges
Dam Project, Yangtze River, China*, WORLDWATER.ORG (2009).

As a result of these adverse environmental, community, and cultural
impacts, debates over large-scale dams incite sharp political battles. In the
United States, Congress has delegated the licensing and relicensing of
most non-federal hydropower facilities to FERC under Part I of the Federal
Power Act, as discussed in more detail in Chapter 3. These licensing and
relicensing proceedings at FERC are often fraught with controversy.
However, in recent years, former adversaries have taken steps toward
finding common ground. In 2020, the hydroelectric industry and
environmental groups reached agreement on establishing a set of policy
measures to increase the production of electricity from existing dams,
retrofit many dams to reduce their environmental externalities, and
accelerate removal of older, underutilized dams to restore local ecological
conditions. *See* Brad Plumer, *Environmentalists and Dam Operators, At
War for Years, Start Making Peace*, N.Y. TIMES (Oct. 13, 2020). Moreover,
there is growing support for smaller, run of the river, hydropower projects
that can help increase the generation of carbon-free electricity in the
United States without the environmental costs of larger dam projects.

Notably, in 2021, FERC agreed to allow a large electric utility in the
Pacific Northwest, PacifiCorp, to transfer its license for four, large
hydroelectric dams on the Klamath River to the Klamath River Renewal
Corporation and the states of Oregon and California, paving the way for
the ultimate decommissioning and removal of the dams. This would help
restore the river ecosystem and improve salmon runs the Yurok, Karuk,
Hoopa and Klamath Tribes depend upon as cultural resources. *See* Alex
Schwartz, *FERC Decision Pushes Klamath Dam Removal Forward*,
HERALD & NEWS (June 17, 2021). For more on the potential benefits and
challenges associated with decommissioning and removing dams, see, e.g.,

Margaret A. Walls & Vincent Gonzales, *Dismantling Dams Can Help Address US Infrastructure Problems*, RESOURCES (Oct. 22, 2020); Dan Tarlock, *The Legal-Political Barriers to Ramping Up Hydro*, 86 CHI.-KENT L. REV. 259 (2011); Michael C. Blumm & Andrew B. Erickson, *Dam Removal in the Pacific Northwest: Lessons for the Nation*, 42 ENV'T L. 1043 (2012). For a detailed discussion of U.S. hydropower resources, opportunities, and challenges, see U.S. DEP'T OF ENERGY, U.S. HYDROPOWER LICENSING REPORT (Jan. 2021); KELSI BRACMORT ET AL., CONG. RSCH. SERV., HYDROPOWER: FEDERAL AND NONFEDERAL INVESTMENT (July 7, 2015); U.S. DEP'T OF ENERGY, HYDROPOWER VISION: A NEW CHAPTER FOR AMERICA'S FIRST RENEWABLE ENERGY SOURCE (July 2016). Hydropower licensing under the Federal Power Act is discussed in Chapter 3.

b. Wind

Wind rivals hydropower as the earth's oldest renewable energy technology. Wind has been powering human civilizations for millennia. Early windmills pumped water and milled grain in Persia and China as early as 200 B.C.E. By the eleventh century, wind power had spread to Europe and was used to pump water, grind grain, and help the Dutch drain Rhine Valley marshes and build the Netherlands. In North America, Midwest farmers used wind power to pump water in the 1800s. Wind was first used to create electricity in Scotland, the United States and Denmark in the late 1880s, but the technology languished until the oil crisis and high energy prices of the 1970s spurred U.S. and global development of modern turbines. However, low energy prices in the 1980s and 1990s shifted political priorities; funds for U.S. wind research decreased significantly. *History of U.S. Wind Energy*, U.S. Dep't of Energy; *Mr. Brush's Wind Dynamo*, SCI. AM. 383 (Dec. 20, 1890).

Blowing wind creates electricity by rotating the blades of a turbine, which in turn spins a shaft connected to a generator. The wind harnessed to make power from a turbine is formed by a combination of factors, including the uneven heating of the earth's atmosphere, the shape of the earth's surface, and the earth's rotation, which combine to form varying wind patterns across the planet. For a nice view of real-time wind patterns, see http://hint.fm/wind/. Modern wind facilities use the same concept as ancient windmills, but the technologies have evolved significantly, with wind turbines today over 50 times more powerful than only a few decades ago. Wind turbines have improved due to developments in mechanical and aeronautical engineering and use sophisticated control systems. Turbines better use available wind by controlling blade pitch (the angle of the blades into or out of the wind) and yaw (the rotation of the entire wind turbine in the horizontal axis) and are integrated with real time energy markets. Indeed, the blades of today's turbines look much like angled wings, as opposed to the sail-like panels of yesteryear. Today's wind turbines also dwarf those of the past and have been increasing in size, capturing more wind energy and requiring less overall space, because fewer turbines are needed to generate the same amount of energy. *See, e.g.*, Mike Hughlett, *Next Generation Wind Turbines in Minnesota Could Be 60 Stories High*, STAR TRIB. (Aug. 28, 2021); RYAN WISER ET AL., U.S. DEP'T OF ENERGY, LAND-BASED WIND MARKET REPORT: 2021 EDITION (Aug. 2021) (reporting on improved wind plant performance due to larger turbines mounted on taller towers as well as greater capacity factors). The figure below shows wind resources in the United States, as reflected by annual average wind speeds at 100 meters. As the figure shows, the strongest U.S. wind resources are in the Midwest, Plains states, Texas, and offshore.

Wind Resources in the United States

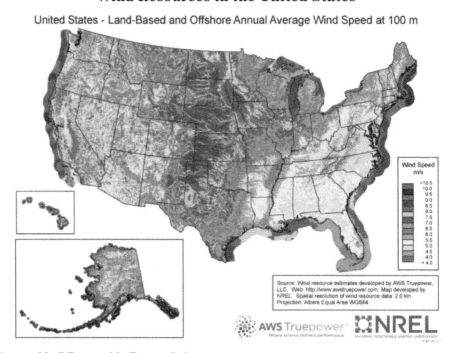

United States - Land-Based and Offshore Annual Average Wind Speed at 100 m

Source: Nat'l Renewable Energy Lab.

While wind turbines can be used on a small scale to power individual homes, farms, or businesses, most of the installed capacity is from utility-scale wind farms. In 2020 wind produced about 8.5% of U.S. electricity, up from 4% in 2013 and is expected to produce 10% by 2021. *See The United States Installed More Wind Turbine Capacity in 2020 Than in Any Other Year*, ENERGY INFO. ADMIN. (Mar. 3, 2021). It is common to install groups of turbines together to create a utility-scale "wind plant." Computerized controls—control systems—provide information on plant operations to owners and grid operators and help the turbine adjust to changing weather and market conditions. Modern turbines also automatically curtail operations in dangerously high winds. They do this by turning their blades into the wind, allowing the air to pass, and with mechanical brakes akin to those used in cars.

743 GW of wind power had been installed worldwide as of 2020, with 288 GW in China, 122 GW in the United States, 62 GW in Germany, 38 GW in India, 27 GW in Spain, and 24 GW in the United Kingdom. *See* GLOBAL WIND ENERGY COUNCIL, GLOBAL WIND REPORT 2021 (Mar. 2021). A 2010 study by DOE's National Renewable Energy Laboratory (NREL) found that overland wind energy resources in the contiguous 48 states could generate 37 billion MW-hours of electrical power per year, equal to roughly 10 times the current electrical power usage in the continental United States. As of August 2021, the total capacity of onshore wind energy in the United States was approximately 122 GW. The top five states for installed wind power capacity were Texas (nearly 33 GW), Iowa (11 GW), Oklahoma (9 GW), Kansas (7 GW), and Illinois (6 GW). *See* WISER ET AL., *supra*.

As of 2020, U.S. offshore wind capacity was only 42 MW, with many projects planned. The Biden administration has set a goal of developing 30 GW of offshore wind over the next decade. *See* WALTER MUSIAL ET AL., U.S. DEP'T OF ENERGY, OFFSHORE WIND MARKET REPORT: 2021 EDITION (Aug. 2021); *Q4 Installed Wind Power Capacity*, Am. Clean Power Ass'n; *Installed Wind Capacity*, WINDExchange, U.S. Dept. of Energy; Erin Baker & Matthew Lackner, *The US Just Set Ambitious Offshore Wind Power Targets—What Will It Take To Meet Them?*, THE CONVERSATION (March 31, 2021). Although U.S. offshore wind development is far behind that of Europe (with 25 GW of offshore wind installed as of 2020 and a plan for 60 GW by 2030 and 300 GW by 2050), the industry appears to be nearing a breakthrough. In 2021, the U.S. Department of the Interior granted approval for the construction of the 800 MW Vineyard Wind project off the coast of Massachusetts, and more projects are in the pipeline. *See, e.g.*, MUSIAL ET AL., *supra*, at ix (map of offshore wind projects in permitting process); Anmar Frangoul, *"A Huge Moment": U.S. Gives Go-Ahead For its First Major Offshore Wind Farm*, CNBC NEWS: SUSTAINABLE FUTURE (May 12, 2021). Offshore wind is discussed in more detail in Chapter 9.

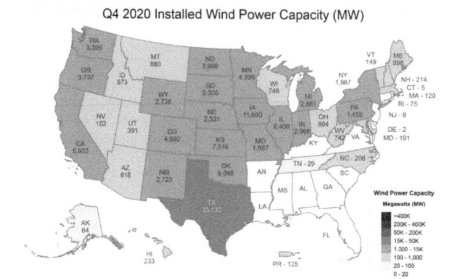

Q4 2020 Installed Wind Power Capacity (MW)

Total Installed Wind Capacity: 122,465 MW

Source: American Clean Power Association (https://cleanpower.org/)

Source: WINDExchange, U.S. Dep't of Energy.

From an environmental perspective, wind energy provides a clean, domestic source of electricity. It reduces GHGs and eliminates other environmental emissions associated with fossil fuel combustion. Among renewables, wind is the cheapest energy source for electricity production. While wind, solar, and geothermal all use free "fuel," the electricity produced from a wind facility today costs between 3 and 8¢/kWh and operational costs have decreased over time, though these costs vary regionally. *See* WISER, ET AL., WIND ENERGY TECHNOLOGY DATA UPDATE: 2020 EDITION (Aug. 2020).

There are, however, some drawbacks to wind power. Wind is a variable resource; it does not produce electricity around the clock. Thus, capacity factors for wind farms average 36%, with a good capacity factor for a newer wind farm above 40%, meaning that the turbines produce electricity an average of 36% of the time, with newer and better facilities producing much more. Instead, wind turbines only produce electricity when the wind blows which varies with the site, time of day, season, and year. To address this limitation, many new wind projects are being sited in conjunction with energy storage technologies. Wind power sites also tend to be in rural areas, which can provide economic benefits in the form of jobs and income for communities and landowners. However, as discussed in Chapters 5 and 7, the remote location of many wind farms means that new transmission lines are often needed to move the electricity to the grid.

Moreover, while wind tends to have much less extensive environmental impacts than fossil fuel resources, there are still impacts.

Perhaps most prominently, wind turbines, like other modern structures such as skyscrapers, cars, and oil and gas containment ponds, present a danger to wildlife, specifically birds and bats. It is estimated that each year vehicles kill approximately 214 million birds, building collisions kill 599 million birds, and collisions with electric transmission lines kill 25 million birds. *See Threats to Birds,* U.S. Fish & Wildlife Service (last updated Sept. 14, 2018). In comparison, some studies estimate that U.S. wind farms kill roughly 234,000 birds each year, although these risks are being reduced through proper siting, technological developments, and trends towards bigger turbines which are taller and rotate more slowly to reduce bird deaths. *Id.* The impacts can also differ by bird species. *See* Jay E. Diffendorfer et al., *Demographic and Potential Biological Removal Models Identify Raptor Species Sensitive to Current and Future Wind Energy,* 12 ECOSPHERE (June 2021). Of course, all these man-made threats to birds pale in comparison to the threats posed by outdoor and stray cats, which kill an estimated 2.4 billion birds each year. *See id.*

c. Solar

Solar energy produces electricity primarily using two technologies: photovoltaics and concentrating solar power. Photovoltaics (PV) are the most common way of creating electricity from the sun. They generally consist of ground- or roof-mounted panels that contain several individual solar cells or a single thin layer of semiconductors. Most PV cells today are made from one of two substances—crystalline silicon (95% of installed PV) or "thin film" semiconductors (3–5% of the global market). Today, silicon is more efficient but also more expensive; thin film is less efficient but cheaper to manufacture. Thin film cells are traditionally made of cadmium telluride (CdTe), copper indium gallium selenide (CIGS), or amorphous silicon (a-Si). Other innovations in PV design aimed at improving performance and boosting efficiencies include bifacial panels, multijunction units, and using alternative materials known as perovskites, which may become more efficient and easier to use than today's silicon. *See* U.S. DEP'T OF ENERGY, SOLAR TECHNOLOGIES OFFICE, PV CELLS 101, PART 2: SOLAR PHOTOVOLTAIC CELL RESEARCH DIRECTIONS (Dec. 3, 2019). All these substances work because they are "semiconductors." That is, when sunlight hits them, electrons are freed. The freed electrons then travel through an electrical circuit, producing electricity.

Photovoltaics are a much older technology than most people think. Alexandre Edmund Becquerel first observed the PV effect of semiconductors in 1839, which opened the door for further scientific study for decades to come. In 1954, Bell Labs created the first solar PV device capable of producing useable electricity. "[B]y 1958, solar cells were being used in a variety of small-scale scientific and commercial applications." *History of Photovoltaic Technology,* Solar Energy Indus. Ass'n. In more recent times, the price of PV technology has dropped dramatically spurring rapid growth worldwide, with over 125 GW of additional capacity installed in 2020. As a result, PV is increasingly cost-competitive. With over 707 GW of PV installed globally in 2020 (up from 291 GW in 2016), China leads the world in PV installations (254 GW), followed by the United States (74 GW), Japan (67 GW), Germany (54 GW), and India (39 GW). *See* INT'L RENEWABLE ENERGY AGENCY, RENEWABLE CAPACITY STATISTICS 2021 (Mar. 2021).

In contrast to PV, concentrating solar power (CSP) technologies, or solar thermal power, harness the sun's energy to heat liquid, create steam, and turn a turbine. CSP generation systems function in essentially the same manner as fossil fuel systems, but they utilize a much cleaner input fuel: sunlight. Today's CSP systems utilize one of three technologies: (1) parabolic troughs; (2) solar dishes; or (3) solar towers. Parabolic troughs are much what they sound like: a collection of parabolic-shaped reflectors that concentrate solar rays on a pipe that carries heat transfer fluid. This fluid is transported to a heat exchanger, where heat from the fluid is used to generate superheated steam that is, in turn, fed into a conventional turbine to produce electricity. The largest solar power facility in the world, located in California's Mojave Desert, utilizes this technology. Solar dishes track the sun throughout the day and concentrate solar rays on the focal point of the dish, where power-generating equipment is located. This equipment converts heat and mechanical energy into electricity through a system of transfer fluid. Finally, solar tower installations use hundreds to thousands of ground mirrors, or heliostats, to concentrate solar rays onto a tower-mounted heat exchanger. The exchanger then creates steam, which in turn is used to produce electricity.

As with other energy sources, different CSP technologies provide different advantages. In power tower systems utilizing molten salt, the liquid retains its heat and can be used immediately or stored for later use. This storage capability allows these CSP facilities to function during peak electricity demand periods or at night, and alleviates some concerns that CSP, like wind, can function only as an intermittent generation resource. Implementation of concentrating solar power is increasing worldwide. At the end of 2016 there was almost 6.5 GW of CSP worldwide, with 1.7 GW in the United States and 2.3 GW in Spain. Recently, CSP growth has been most prominent in China, Morocco, and South Africa; each of these countries installed between 300 and 500 GW of CSP since 2016. *See* RENEWABLE CAPACITY STATISTICS 2021, *supra.*

Because the most cost-efficient CSP plants are often large, they are typically associated with companies that supply energy to utilities or with the utilities themselves. In contrast, PV systems are both "distributed" (if they are located on residential and commercial rooftops) and "utility-scale" if they are larger and more centralized. Many utilities have built large PV-based solar farms, both to comply with state renewable portfolio standards and because the declining costs of solar make them a cost competitive investment. Distributed solar systems located at residential sites added 3.2 GW_{dc} in 2020 and non-residential PV another 2.1 GW_{dc}; utility PV added 14 GW_{dc}. *See* SOLAR ENERGY INDUS. ASS'N, SOLAR MARKET INSIGHT REPORT: 2020 YEAR IN REVIEW (2021). (Note: PV systems create DC power. To convert from GW_{dc} to GW_{ac} (or the power which would be available to the grid), 100 GW_{dc} is roughly equivalent to 85 GW_{ac}, so multiply the GW_{dc} number by .85 to get GW_{ac}.).

As of the end of 2020, the United States had installed a total of 76 GW of solar capacity—46 GW of utility-scale PV, 28 GW of distributed PV, and 2 GW of CSP—constituting 3% of total U.S. electricity generation that year. *See* U.S. DEP'T OF ENERGY, SOLAR FUTURES STUDY 22 (Sept. 2021). The location of solar projects depends on solar resources, policy incentives, and local siting rules, just like other energy technologies. In the United States solar potential is much higher in the sunnier regions, such as in the West and in Hawaii, with the Southwest having the highest potential of any region. California has 17 GW_{dc}, followed by North Carolina with 3 GW_{dc}, Arizona at 2.7 GW_{dc}, and Nevada with 2 GW_{dc}. The state-level policies in New Jersey, North Carolina, and New York have pushed these jurisdictions into the top 10 states for installed solar PV. While not as popular in the United States, solar energy can also be used for direct thermal heating, with 479 $GW_{thermal}$ installed worldwide, though this is much more common in other parts of the world, like China, Germany, Turkey, and Israel. *See* WERNER WEISS & MONIKA SPÖRK-DÜR, SOLAR HEAT WORLDWIDE (2020); INT'L ENERGY AGENCY, RENEWABLES 2020 (Nov. 2020); REN21, RENEWABLES 2020: GLOBAL STATUS REPORT (2020).

U.S. Installed and Projected Solar Capacity by State: 2020

Q4 2020 (MW) (top states)

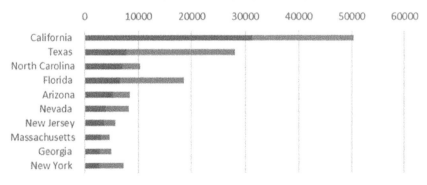

■ Installed Solar Capacity, Q4 2020 (MW)   ■ Growth Projection for Next 5 Years (MW)

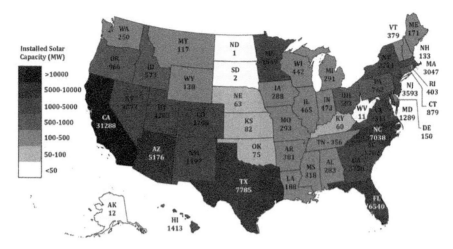

Source: Data used to create these figures were sourced from SOLAR ENERGY INDUSTRIES ASS'N & WOOD MACKENZIE, POWER & RENEWABLES U.S. SOLAR MARKET INSIGHT 2020 YEAR IN REVIEW (2021).

Solar energy offers many benefits. First, electricity production from solar power generates few traditional air pollutants and GHGs compared to fossil-powered generation facilities (although the environmental impacts of PV manufacturing remain). Second, solar can reduce the use of fossil fuels, which helps to decarbonize the U.S. energy supply. Additionally, solar can provide economic benefits such as employment during the construction and operation of the facility.

Like wind, the sun is a variable resource. PV systems only produce electricity when the sun shines. Low solar capacity factors of 20–30% for PV, and just over 40% for CSP (as compared to 90% or higher for nuclear plants) are one of the reasons why some new solar projects are being co-located with energy storage technologies. *See Utility-Scale Energy Technology Capacity Factors*, Nat'l Renewable Energy Lab. In California, high penetrations of solar PV have led to grid integration challenges. When smoke from western wildfires in 2020 blocked the sun, California electricity production from solar PV dipped by 30%. *See* Peter Behr, *Solar Power Plunges as Smoke Shrouds Calif.,* ENERGYWIRE (Sept. 11, 2020). Also, some of the materials used to produce PV cells are critical minerals, which can present geopolitical risks and affect the price of new solar. *See Energy Basics*, U.S. Dep't of Energy.

As environmentally friendly as solar can be, it also has environmental costs. For instance, ground-mounted utility-scale solar facilities require large areas of land, meaning facilities can disrupt other land uses such as agriculture, grazing, or wildlife use. When sensitive, threatened, or endangered species live in the area, siting is problematic and solar plant construction can lead to habitat degradation and loss when land is cleared and graded, due in part to soil compaction, erosion, and alteration of drainage channels. Uma Outka, *The Renewable Energy Footprint*, 30 STAN. ENV'T L.J. 241 (2011). And, like all energy generation technologies, solar requires connections to the electric transmission grid, which in remote locations can present a major hurdle to the successful integration of solar into the grid.

Solar installed on residential and commercial rooftops can pose new challenges for low-voltage distribution network management. Distribution networks were originally built to handle flows of power from large central power generating stations to end consumers, not to manage two-way flows of power from those consumers. Thus, if not properly designed and managed, fluctuations in electricity production from rooftop PV solar could adversely affect the distribution network. These challenges can include voltage stability, frequency stability, and power quality. *See* K.N. Nwaigwe et al., *An Overview of Solar Power (PV systems) Integration into Electricity Grids*, 2 MATERIALS SCIENCE FOR ENERGY TECHNOLOGIES 629 (2019). However, development of new inverter designs and additional utility experience with managing PV solar has reduced these issues. The improved integration of solar energy into the electric grid is discussed in more detail in Chapter 8.

d. Geothermal

Low-temperature geothermal resources are widely used for district and building heating and cooling (about 30 $GW_{thermal}$ globally). High-temperature conventional geothermal mines energy from hot spots in the Earth's crust. It does this by producing hot water or steam (~150C) from an underground well (usually within a depth of 3km from the surface). This steam is used to drive a turbine and produce electricity; spent, warm water is reinjected back into the subsurface. The United States is the leading producer of geothermal energy—35 GW in 2019—although this constituted only 0.4% of total U.S. electricity that year. *See* REN21, RENEWABLES 2020: GLOBAL STATUS REPORT 92–97 (2020) (0.7 GW of geothermal added globally in 2019); *How Geothermal Energy Works*, UNION OF CONCERNED SCIENTISTS (Dec. 22, 2014); CENTER FOR SUSTAINABLE SYSTEMS, UNIV. OF MICHIGAN, GEOTHERMAL ENERGY FACT SHEET (Sept. 2020).

Geothermal energy has been used by humans around the globe since prehistory; warm thermal pools and vents used for cooking or space heating are documented throughout ancient civilizations. Geothermal heat use in modern buildings uses a heat exchanger to preheat or precool air and depends on stable underground temperatures. As energy to heat and cool buildings currently represents 12% of U.S. GHG emissions, geothermal technologies could allow for reductions in natural gas, oil, and propane for home heating and electricity for home cooling. This technology, using low temperature geothermal heat pumps, has been used since the 1940s.

Though the drilling of shallow geothermal wells has historically made this technology costly to install, it is inexpensive to operate. As it pre-heats or pre-cools air coming into the home, it can substantially reduce the use of fossil fuels to heat and cool (electricity) buildings. See a video of how the process works here: https://www.energy.gov/energysaver/heat-and-cool/heat-pump-systems/geothermal-heat-pumps.

Low temperature geothermal systems can also be linked to district heating systems. Cities like Boise, Idaho have been using geothermal energy since the 1890s, tapping into a 177°F subterranean river to heat homes, businesses, swimming pools, and the Idaho state capitol and to keep sidewalks ice-free. The technology is also most famously used in Reykjavík, Iceland, where over 99% of the heat for the 1930s district energy system comes from geothermal energy. Paris also partially uses geothermal energy for its district heating system.

High temperature geothermal has been used since the 1960s to drive turbines and directly produce electricity. Globally, 13.9 GW of geothermal electric capacity has been installed to date. The United States has the largest share, at 3.7 GW (2.5 GW$_{net}$), mostly in California and Nevada. However, some countries, like Iceland, El Salvador, and the Philippines, generate over 20% of their electricity from geothermal resources.

Geothermal power plants mine subsurface heat and have high capacity factors, operating 90–98% of the time. Geothermal electricity plants operate using one of two technologies—binary or steam. Most plants are binary plants which route hot water through a heat exchanger, reinjecting the "spent" water back into the subsurface. Steam plants can use the steam to drive a turbine or use a "flash plant" to depressurize the hot water and produce steam to drive a turbine. *See* NAT'L ACADEMY OF SCIENCES, ELECTRICITY FROM RENEWABLE RESOURCES: STATUS, PROSPECTS, AND IMPEDIMENTS (2010).

New technologies could expand opportunities for geothermal energy in the United States and globally. For example, enhanced geothermal reservoirs can be engineered to extract geothermal energy from low-permeability and low-porosity sites. This technology would drill deeper into the Earth's surface (from 3 to 10 km) to access heat resources. *Id.* An MIT study on geothermal energy estimated that the U.S. geothermal resource is over 13 million EJ (3.6 trillion GWh), or over 100,000 times greater than current U.S. energy use, and the extractable enhanced geothermal resource is estimated at 2,000 times greater than current U.S. energy use. *See* MIT, THE FUTURE OF GEOTHERMAL ENERGY: IMPACT OF ENHANCED GEOTHERMAL SYSTEMS (EGS) ON THE UNITED STATES IN THE 21ST CENTURY (2006). Concerns with enhanced geothermal development (EGS) include induced seismicity (human-made earthquakes), land subsidence, and water requirements. NAT'L ACADEMY OF SCIENCES, *supra.* The figure below shows the distribution of high temperature geothermal resources across the country.

Source: Nat'l Renewable Energy Lab.

As geothermal energy has historically been more costly than other alternatives, its growth is expected to be modest in the absence of new policies and incentives. The best high temperature geothermal resources occur primarily in the Western United States, but lower temperature geothermal energy for heating and cooling buildings can be used almost anywhere. The cost effectiveness is also determined by the relative cost of other energy technologies.

Geothermal is even more environmentally benign than other renewables. Most geothermal power plants release less than 1% of the carbon monoxide of a fossil fuel plant, and roughly 3% of a fossil plant's sulfur emissions. Likewise, geothermal heat pumps that use a closed-loop system for residential heating are the most energy efficient and cost effective method of heating a home. *Geothermal Basics*, U.S. Dep't of Energy.

However, there are some drawbacks to geothermal energy. Viable high temperature geothermal sites often are limited to areas with geothermal hotspots, such as tectonic and volcanic regions. Geothermal power stations also require significant upfront investments and can be expensive to build and maintain in remote locations. Furthermore, once a geothermal power station is built, there is some risk that the water it uses to generate steam can chill the rocks buried beneath the ground, rendering the site ineffectual for future energy production. Additionally, recent concerns about induced seismicity, e.g., geothermal projects causing small earthquakes, have been raised, with documented events in and around the Geysers project in California. *See* NAT'L RESEARCH COUNCIL, INDUCED SEISMICITY POTENTIAL IN ENERGY TECHNOLOGIES (2013); ERNIE MAIER ET AL., U.S. DEP'T OF ENERGY, PROTOCOL FOR ADDRESSING INDUCED SEISMICITY ASSOCIATED WITH ENHANCED GEOTHERMAL SYSTEMS (Jan. 2012).

e. Biomass, Biofuels, and Waste-to-Energy

Biomass was the most prominent form of energy used by humans from pre-history to the industrial revolution when fossil fuels became dominant. Biomass contributes 13–14% of primary global energy use—fourth after oil, coal, and natural gas. Most global direct biomass use is for cooking or heating in developing countries, and a sizeable proportion is used for industrial process heat in the forestry and paper industries. While 2.3 billion people worldwide depend on biomass for cooking, over 1 billion people living in Sub-Saharan Africa (83%) depend on biomass as a cooking fuel. *See* WORLD BIOENERGY ASS'N, GLOBAL BIOENERGY STATISTICS 2020 (2020); *Access to Clean Cooking*, SDG7, INT'L ENERGY AGENCY (2021)

"Biomass" is an exceptionally broad term. It refers to a vast array of non-fossil biological materials, ranging from firewood to charcoal to crop residue and from dung to liquid fuels like ethanol produced from sugarcane, corn, or cellulosic material. Other kinds of biomass include biodiesel from algae or palm oil and methane captured from municipal landfills. The figure below shows biomass resources in the continental United States.

While most biomass use comes from solid biomass, about 5% of biomass used comes from industrial and municipal solid waste which is burned or gasified to produce electricity and/or heat in Waste-to Energy plants. Most of these plants (over 500) are located in the EU, where they are an important part of waste management and future renewables policies. Asia also has many plants burning industrial and municipal waste. The Waste-to-Energy plants can be configured to produce electricity only, or electricity and heat, or heat only. *See* Nicolae Scarlat et al., *Status and Opportunities for Energy Recovery from Municipal Solid Waste in Europe*, 10 WASTE & BIOMASS VALORIZATION 2425 (2019).

Biomass is touted as one of the largest potential renewable energy resources, and many studies suggest that more efficient methods of biomass production and consumption could increase future use by two- to tenfold. *See* GLOBAL BIOENERGY STATISTICS, *supra*. Because biomass absorbs CO_2 when it grows and then releases it when it is burned, an ideal biomass system might be considered "carbon neutral." However, the biomass lifecycle often produces GHG emissions, in part from fossil fuel consumption and fertilizers used to grow, harvest, and transport these fuels. Moreover, wood pellet processing facilities, which can emit harmful air pollutants, are often located in environmental justice communities in the rural, southeastern United States with high percentages of low-income and minority residents. Additionally, incomplete combustion of biomass can create indoor and outdoor air pollution. *See, e.g.,* Gabriel Popkin, *There's A Booming Business in America's Forests. Some Aren't Happy About It,* N.Y. TIMES (Apr. 19, 2021).

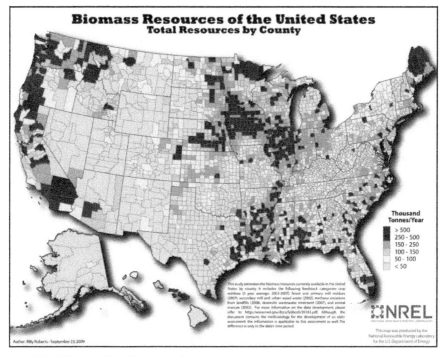

Source: Nat'l Renewable Energy Lab.

Biomass use presents logistical and technical challenges too. It is costly to transport bulky, dense, low-energy cellulosic materials and converting biomass into solid, gas, or liquid fuels remains difficult. However, while much attention in the United States has been focused on creating liquid fuels from biomass, it also can be combusted to produce electricity—either through direct burning or by pelletizing it to make it more transportable and then combusted. Traditional burning of biomass is relatively inefficient, but modern combustion, gasification, and fermentation processes can more efficiently capture the energy in biomass to create heat, electricity, or liquid fuels. As of 2019, there was around 139 GW of bio-power capacity, generating an estimated 591 TWh. *See* REN21, RENEWABLES 2020: GLOBAL STATUS REPORT (2020).

The most prominent use of biomass in the United States is as liquid biofuels. There is a good chance the car you drive today uses some biofuels, probably ethanol. Other popular biofuels include biodiesel, methanol, and dimethyl ether (DME). The idea is that liquid biofuels can replace oil in the transportation sector. Globally, over 80% of world ethanol production is from the United States and Brazil, driven by subsides and policies promoting production. Although ethanol production hit an all-time high in 2019, equivalent to 1,143 thousand barrels equivalent per day, it decreased almost 15% in 2020 due to demand reductions from COVID-19. The primary crops used to make ethanol are corn (U.S.) and sugarcane (Brazil). Biodiesel and HVO (hydrogenated vegetable oils) saw similar demand declines in 2020, after a record production of 699 thousand barrels equivalent per day in 2019, with production dominated by Indonesia, the United States, Brazil and Germany.

Crops used to make biodiesel include canola, soy, palm or other vegetable oils, and animal oils. Two key factors affect the utility of biofuels: (1) the land they require and (2) their overall energy balance, or the amount of energy actually captured in the fuel compared to the energy inputs needed to grow, harvest, and manufacture the fuel. Different biofuels fare better than others under these metrics.

Biofuel sources—and the challenges they raise—differ across the globe. In the United States, the most popular biofuel is ethanol made from corn. Ethanol production currently consumes roughly 40% of the U.S. corn crop. In Brazil, most of the ethanol is made from sugarcane, and in Germany rapeseed often is used to produce biodiesel. Oil palm production on peat lands to create biodiesel for domestic use and export in Indonesia has become very controversial for environmentalists, as the high GHG emissions from land conversion could offset any savings from biofuel use for many decades. *See* Jonathan Foley, *It's Time to Rethink America's Corn System*, SCI. AM. (Mar. 5, 2013).

Proponents of biomass and biofuels long have argued for them based on their environmental benefits. Biofuels such as biodiesel burn cleaner in engines by reducing particulate matter, sulfates, hydrocarbons, and carcinogens. For gasoline, adding ethanol can decrease carbon monoxide emissions, though it results in higher emissions of acetaldehyde. Indeed, many biofuels have both environmental advantages and costs. Thus, from a climate perspective, biofuels are less attractive than other renewable resources that virtually eliminate these emissions. Overall, however, recent analyses suggest that widespread ethanol use *has* decreased the lifecycle carbon intensity of fuels. Yet, challenges of increasing corn-based biomass use for ethanol production include competing land and water uses, including effects on biodiversity, soil erosion, and conflicts with local and global food needs. *See, e.g.,* Elisabeth Rosenthal, *As Biofuel Demand Grows, So Do Guatemala's Hunger Pangs*, N.Y. TIMES (Jan. 5, 2013); Uisung Lee et al., *Retrospective Analysis of the U.S. Corn Ethanol Industry for 2005–2019: Implications for Greenhouse Gas Emission Reductions,* BIOFUELS, BIOPRODUCTS AND BIOREFINING (May 4, 2021). Biofuels used in the transportation sector are discussed in more detail in Chapter 6.

f.   End Use Energy: Efficiency, Demand Response, and Conservation

Americans use a lot of energy. And, because of our current electric grid mix, this energy usage emits 6.5 billion metric tons of CO_2 equivalent GHGs (roughly 15% of global emissions, though the U.S. has only 4.3% of the global population). In 2019 a person in the United States used an average of 287 GJ of energy per capita. By contrast, a citizen of Denmark used about 120 GJ, the UK 116 GJ, China 99 GJ, and Sri Lanka 17 GJ. In some countries, energy use is decreasing, like in Denmark where the per capita rate fell 2.2% per year between 2008 and 2018 or is flat, like in the United States, where the rate fell 0.6% during the same time period. In other countries, energy use is increasing, with Chinese growth up 3.3% per year during the same decade. How energy is used depends on many things like weather and climate, natural resources, legacy infrastructure and industries, population changes and settlement patterns, economic development, and social norms. *See BP Statistical Review of Energy: Consumption Per Capita*, BP (2020). New energy-intensive industries like Bitcoin and legalized marijuana highlight the need for increased energy efficiency across the economy and across the globe. *See, e.g.*, Jon Huang et al., *Bitcoin Uses More Electricity Than Many Countries. How Is That Possible?*, N.Y. TIMES (Sept. 3, 2021) (maps and graphs showing growth in Bitcoin's electricity use over time and how to address the associated energy use and climate impacts); Natalie Fertig & Gavin Bade, *An Inconvenient Truth (About Weed)*, POLITICO (Aug. 10, 2021).

As mentioned previously, we produce energy to help people do things. People don't want energy *per se*, they want energy services like cold milk and warm homes. Using energy more efficiently means that less energy is needed to do the same things. Any end use energy savings are amplified through the energy system—making appliances, buildings, industry, and transportation more efficient benefits the whole energy system. A refrigerator using 50% less electricity reduces consumer costs by saving energy. Increasing efficiency lowers the amount of energy lost through electricity generation (30–50%) and across the distribution and transmission networks (5–10%). It also avoids the environmental impacts of extracting and combusting the fuel that would otherwise be used to generate the electricity. These cumulative system-wide energy savings reduce emissions, peak demand, and the cost of building more infrastructure like new power plants. Thus, while we often measure the value of energy efficiency (EE) on kWh saved for the consumer, the entire system benefits can be far more important.

EE is a tool which encompasses all sectors of the economy and stretches from product design and system planning to product use and final disposal. The promise of EE is huge: the International Energy Agency estimates that large-scale adoption of EE measures could cut the growth of global energy demand in half by 2050. This would reduce or slow global GHG emissions and save money needed for energy infrastructure. Indeed, experts around the world focus on energy efficiency as one of the most important means of reducing global GHG emissions. *See* INT'L ENERGY AGENCY, ENERGY EFFICIENCY 2020, at 10 (2021) ("energy efficiency delivers more than 40% of the reduction in energy-related greenhouse gas emissions over the next 20 years in the IEA's Sustainable Development Scenario"). Moreover, as shown earlier in this chapter, energy efficiency is the least-cost energy resource on a levelized basis.

In practice, implementing EE is tricky and involves high transaction costs and a multitude of decision makers with different and often conflicting interests. For example, in a rented apartment, the landlord buying the appliances will not be paying the energy costs of inefficient appliance choices, the renter will. Retrofitting a home or business to make it more efficient takes time and money that could be spent elsewhere. Overcoming these split incentives and competing priorities often makes implementing EE tricky. The utility business model has historically been based on selling energy, not saving it; changing incentives are necessary to change behavior. EE programs also raise important equity considerations, and analyses of who uses and benefits from EE incentives highlight challenges in ensuring distributional equity. *See* Tony Reames, *Targeting Energy Justice: Exploring Spatial, Racial/Ethnic and Socioeconomic Disparities in Urban Residential Heating Energy Efficiency,* 97 ENERGY POL'Y 549 (2016).

From a pragmatic perspective, programs promoting EE cut across the energy system—from appliance standards and building codes to fuel economy standards and technology performance rates. EE is usually divided into three categories: (1) buildings (electric use plus space conditioning); (2) transportation (discussed in Chapter 6); and (3) industrial energy use. Promoting EE in the absence of a carbon pricing mechanism requires both targeting by sector (building, industrial, transportation), *and* focusing on end use technologies like appliances and electronics. In the United States, transportation and appliance efficiency standards are set at the federal level but the bulk of EE policies are regulated under state and local laws and vary significantly across the country.

Buildings use an estimated 40% of U.S. energy and 76% of produced electricity. As buildings last for decades, technologies to retrofit existing buildings and reduce their energy consumption are as important as making new buildings as efficient as possible. Within buildings, air conditioning, heating, and ventilation use 37% of energy; major appliances 18%; lighting 11%; and other uses, including electronics, 36%. The Department of Energy estimates that adopting the best available technologies for energy efficiency could reduce residential energy consumption by 50% and commercial consumption by 46%. *See* U.S. DEP'T OF ENERGY, QUADRENNIAL TECHNOLOGY REVIEW (QTR), ch. 5 (Sept. 2015).

After the first appliance standards were adopted in California in the 1970s, Congress followed suit. In 1974, it enacted the Energy Policy and Conservation Act (EPCA) (discussed in the *Zero Zone* case in Chapter 1). EPCA and later amendments created the national framework for setting minimum appliance efficiency standards. The resulting appliance standards have saved American consumers on average about $500 per year, resulting in an estimated cumulative savings of $2 trillion by 2030, and avoiding an estimated 8 billion metric tons of CO_2 emissions. Clothes washers purchased today use 70% less energy than those made in 1990 and refrigerators and air conditioners use 50% less energy to provide the same energy services. The potential for further energy savings is well documented; updating standards for appliances like water heaters, fans, and dryers enables additional savings for consumers and substantial emissions reductions. The law requires DOE to review and update the standards every six years but politics can often interfere. For example, the DOE under the Trump administration missed 28 appliance standard review deadlines, prompting numerous lawsuits and creating a backlog for the Biden administration. *See, e.g.*, Robert Walton, *DOE Begins "Repairing Damage" Done by Trump to Energy Efficiency Program, Say Advocates*, UTIL. DIVE (Apr. 5, 2021); Lesley Clark, *DOE Releases Rule to Overturn Trump Efficiency Plan*, ENERGYWIRE (July 1, 2021).

For products not covered by DOE established federal standards, states can choose to create their own, with many choosing to do so. *See, e.g., States*, Appliance Standards Awareness Project; *Appliance Standards Summary*, Am. Council for an Energy-Efficient Economy (last updated June 2019). But where a federal standard exists, states are preempted (i.e., prohibited) under EPCA from setting standards that are stricter than the federal standards. Federal courts have differed in their analyses regarding the scope of preemption of state and local building code standards under EPCA. *Compare Air Conditioning, Heating & Refrigeration Institute v. City of Albuquerque*, 2008 WL 5586316 (D.N.M., Oct. 3, 2008) (enjoining city's energy conservation standards for new and remodeled buildings because it found the only feasible compliance pathway was through installing HVAC and water heater equipment that were more energy efficient than required by EPCA standards) *with Building Industry Ass'n v. Wash. State Building Code Council*, 683 F.3d 1144, 1151–52 (9th Cir. 2012) (upholding state building code on grounds that regulated parties could meet energy savings requirements through multiple means and the code did not "create any penalty or legal compulsion to use higher efficiency products."). For a discussion of the preemption provisions of EPCA, see Alexandra B. Klass, *State Standards for Nationwide Products Revisited: Federalism, Green Building Codes, and Appliance Efficiency Standards*, 34 HARV. ENV'T L. REV. 335 (2010). For a detailed discussion of how the DOE rulemaking process works, see Kit Kennedy, *Chapter 9: Lighting Appliances and Other Equipment, in* LEGAL PATHWAYS TO DEEP DECARBONIZATION 217 (Gerrard and Dernbach, eds. 2019).

In addition to the mandatory appliance standards which set an efficiency floor and ceiling, EPA introduced ENERGY STAR in 1992 as a voluntary labeling program to identify and promote the most energy efficient products. EPA has since partnered with DOE to certify and label many different products as energy efficient, including computers, major appliances, office equipment, and lighting, as well as new homes and commercial buildings and industrial plants. Many states and municipalities have enacted ordinances encouraging or requiring that appliances in new construction or new buildings also be certified as ENERGY STAR compliant. Likewise, at least forty states have enacted building energy codes requiring both new construction and existing buildings undergoing major renovations to meet minimum energy efficiency requirements. EPA estimated that ENERGY STAR and similar state and federal programs resulted in $450 billion in cost savings to consumers since the program began and $39 billion in 2019 alone.

Local, state, and federal policies have also attempted to overcome barriers to EE. Policy tools at the state and local levels include: (1) personal and corporate tax incentives and state sales tax exemptions; (2) property tax incentives; (3) rebates to encourage purchasing more energy efficient appliances or products; (4) policies promoting energy audits provided by utilities; (5) efforts to help utilities recover costs of EE programs and lost revenue from decreased electricity demand; (6) standards requiring utilities to provide a certain percentage of electricity demand through EE; and (7) more stringent building codes. These efforts can include programs through electric and natural gas utilities, with over $8.4 billion spent by utilities for energy efficiency in 2019. *See generally* Alexandra B. Klass & John K. Harting, *State and Municipal Energy Efficiency Laws, in* THE LAW OF CLEAN ENERGY: EFFICIENCY AND RENEWABLES 57 (Michael B. Gerrard ed. 2011); Kennedy, *supra*. For summaries of these policies and regulations, see *Rules, Regulations & Policies for Energy Efficiency*, DSIRE. *See also* AM. COUNCIL FOR AN ENERGY EFFICIENT ECON., POLICY

BRIEF: THE COST OF SAVING ELECTRICITY FOR THE LARGEST U.S. UTILITIES: RATEPAYER-FUNDED EFFICIENCY PROGRAMS IN 2018 (June 2021).

Changes in the building envelope and operations standards can reduce energy use for building space conditioning (heating, cooling, and ventilation) and lighting. Improving the building envelope can include better insulation in walls, roofs, windows, and doors to manage conduction and solar gain. Improving building operations and maintenance can ensure better thermal comfort and air quality while helping building systems operate as efficiently as possible (for example, no windows open for cooling when the heat is on!). In addition to the ENERGY STAR building program mentioned above, the U.S. Green Building Council has developed standards for Leadership in Energy and Environmental Design (LEED), which aim to use less energy (and reduce other environmental impacts) in the construction and operation of buildings. *See What is LEED?*, U.S. Green Building Council. Although LEED is administered by a nongovernmental entity, it has become increasingly popular in recent years with over 100,000 projects completed worldwide.

New efforts to certify buildings which use no or very little energy are also underway. Zero energy buildings, or Net-Zero energy buildings, often use passive design, work to limit thermal conductivity, and use natural elements to reduce or eliminate the need for heating, ventilation, and cooling systems. Technologies like better metering and control systems and the addition of geothermal heat pumps, or PV on rooftops or nearby, can help to further decrease a building's energy load. LEED, ENERGY STAR, and PassiveHaus standards, among others, are helping to ensure the next generation of buildings use as little energy as possible. *See* Lee Paddock & Caitlin McCoy, *New Buildings, in* LEGAL PATHWAYS TO DEEP DECARBONIZATION 256 (Gerrard and Dernbach, eds. 2019). Efforts to pass national legislation to establish building energy efficiency and performance standards have repeatedly stumbled, often with strong opposition from builders who do not welcome government standards despite the benefits they could bring to consumers, the environment, and the economy. *See NAHB Opposes Portman-Shaheen Energy Bill*, NAT'L ASS'N OF HOMEBUILDERS (July 17, 2019).

Reducing industrial energy use (36% of 2020 U.S. energy use) also offers important opportunities for EE. The most energy intensive sectors are bulk chemicals, petroleum refining, and forest products, which together use almost 20% of U.S. energy. Unlike EE in the residential and commercial sectors, industrial sector EE is well aligned with business objectives: save energy to make money. Indeed, the energy intensity of U.S. industry has decreased 26% between 1998 and 2018, while gross manufacturing output increased by 12%. *See Energy Use in Industry*, U.S. Energy Info. Admin. (last updated May 5, 2021); *Manufacturing Energy and Carbon Footprints (2018 MECS)*, U.S. Dep't of Energy (providing data on energy use and carbon emissions in various manufacturing sectors).

As discussed in Chapters 4 and 8, demand response is another valuable energy management tool which helps the grid operate more flexibly. In addition to reducing energy use through EE programs, shifting *when* and *where* energy is used is also an extremely valuable resource. As electricity is still expensive to store, changing the shape of the demand curve by shifting or reducing energy demand peaks can provide important benefits for system operators and planners. This allows for a more efficient use of resources and enables better integration of renewables and distributed generation. This last point is particularly important in the context of grid decarbonization and adapting to a changing climate.

Many utilities and system operators run "demand response" programs, enabling customers to contribute to energy load reduction during times of peak demand in exchange for financial incentives and shift that load to times when electricity resources are more available and therefore cheaper. Peak electricity production is usually the most expensive and utilities have long worked to develop programs to help customers cut demand during peak times. While these programs are not new (rural electric co-operatives in Minnesota have been cycling customers' water heaters to reduce peak demand since the 1990s), advances in control systems, industrial energy use management, and "smart" home systems and appliances now allow a much greater degree of responsiveness and reliability. Integration with demand response and electricity markets can allow customers to bid demand into markets and be compensated for the load reduction. Together with these efforts, grid integrated buildings and communities present the next frontier in managing energy use, incorporating variable renewable resources, and managing carbon. *See* Chapter 8.

For large industrial customers that pay for energy used as well as a peak demand charge, implementing demand management programs and shifting energy use for process heat or other areas of production can reduce energy costs significantly. These programs can also provide important societal benefits, as flexible industrial facility energy use can accommodate more variable energy resources and help to ensure greater grid reliability. *See* Raphael Heffron et al., *Industrial Demand-side Flexibility: A Key Element of a Just Energy Transition and Industrial Development*, 269 APPLIED ENERGY 115026 (2020).

Emergency demand management programs have long played a critical role in ensuring system reliability. These systems have been called upon more frequently in recent years as the climate changes and extreme weather patterns showcase how our energy infrastructure no longer meets operational demands. In the event of a crisis on the grid, emergency load shedding is critical to keep the system operating at a base level and avoid system blackouts. There are many incentive-based programs that compensate customers for participating in emergency direct load control programs or interruptible/curtailable load management. *See* Mohamed El-Shimy, *The Art of Load Shedding and Online Applications in a Power System Under an Emergency State*, ELEC. ENG'G PORTAL (Feb. 24, 2021).

D. ENERGY MARKET FAILURES AND ENERGY LEGAL TOOLS

Just as the related field of environmental law seeks to regulate interconnected problems occurring in ecosystems, energy law also tries to address economic failures in energy markets. This is one key dividing line between environmental law and energy law. The former roots itself in biophysical systems, risk assessment, and science. Energy law focuses on market systems, competition and innovation, and economics.

There are four primary economic problems that energy law seeks to address. *First*, energy law often attempts to mitigate or limit firms' **market power**—a company's ability to exclude competitors from a market or to charge too high ("supracompetitive") prices. *Second*, energy law often seeks to limit **waste**, both physical and economic, that can occur in energy production and consumption. *Third*, energy law sometimes aims to prevent **negative externalities** or "spillover effects" created from energy use, such as pollution from coal mining or uranium production or tailpipe emissions from cars. These externalities typically appear when the entity consuming or producing energy foists the costs of that activity onto the rest of society rather than itself. *Fourth*, energy law often attempts to correct **free-riding** or **public good** problems, which can result in underinvestment in energy innovation. As developers and adapters of new technologies cannot fully capture all the social benefits that their innovations create—society inevitably absorbs some of those benefits—there is a risk that energy system evolution is too slow and is suboptimal.

Each of these market failures reoccur throughout energy law. However, while more than one problem can arise in a single context, it is rare that all four do. Rather, different segments of the energy industry tend to face certain types of economic problems. The utility industries, for instance, both electric and natural gas, raise market power questions. As these firms were long viewed as natural monopolies, they often had the ability to exercise market power by excluding other firms from competition or raising prices above otherwise competitive levels. By contrast, a common problem in oil and gas production is the risk of waste. If an oil or gas field is developed too quickly, not all the resource can be extracted. Overproduction also causes economic waste because the market becomes flooded with too much supply. Over the years, energy law has sought to correct these market flaws.

The legal tools used in energy regulation respond to these energy market failures. The following cases introduce each of these economic problems and some of the legal tools used to address them.

1. MARKET POWER

Economists define market power as "the power to raise prices above competitive levels without losing so many sales that the price increase is unprofitable." HERBERT HOVENKAMP, FEDERAL ANTITRUST POLICY: THE LAW OF COMPETITION AND ITS PRACTICE § 3.1, at 79 (1994). "Market power generally is defined as the power of a firm to restrict output and thereby increase the selling price of its goods in the market." *Ryko Mfg. Co. v. Eden Servs.*, 823 F.2d 1215, 1232 (8th Cir. 1987). Market power problems are pervasive throughout different segments of the energy industry, so this is a core dilemma that energy law confronts at multiple levels.

One historical market power problem in energy arose at the end of the nineteenth century. Led by John D. Rockefeller, Standard Oil Company, came to dominate oil production in the United States. Standard Oil grew its share of domestic refining capacity from 10% at its founding in 1870 to 90% by 1879. "What Rockefeller aspired to was nothing less than world conquest. . . ." CARL SOLBERG, OIL POWER 42 (1976). "General Motors, IBM, and the rest of the hundred supercorporations that dominate modern life are but later likenesses of Standard Oil. . . . Tiger, octopus, anaconda— these were the images of Rockefeller's monster that . . . filled the public eye." *Id.* at 48. *See also* DANIEL YERGIN, THE PRIZE: THE EPIC QUEST FOR OIL, MONEY & POWER (3d ed. 2008). Eventually, the Supreme Court broke up Standard Oil in an antitrust suit, but the kind of virtual monopoly that Standard Oil erected is only one example of how energy firms can exercise market power.

Creating a monopoly—that is, commanding so much of the market that your firm can control prices by withholding supply—is the classic way to exercise market power. It is often called "horizontal" market power because it involves controlling prices across a market. Another way to exercise market power is to erect barriers to entry, or to control critical industrial inputs. For example, patents are government-granted mini-monopolies that create barriers to using certain products. Law school and the bar exam are barriers to entry to the practice of law. In energy, the license required to operate a nuclear power plant is a kind of government-regulated barrier to entry. Similarly, an electric company that owns substantial natural gas reserves might be able to unfairly influence prices because that fuel is an important input to electricity generation. This ability to exclude or unfairly disadvantage competitors from entering a downstream market by blocking them upstream is sometimes referred to as "vertical" market power.

Other kinds of market power include leverage, reciprocal dealing, and discrimination. "Leverage is loosely defined here as a supplier's power to induce his customer for one product to buy a second product from him that would not otherwise be purchased solely on the merit of that second product." 5 AREEDA & TURNER, ANTITRUST LAW ¶ 1134a, at 202 (1980). Reciprocal dealing involves "sweetheart deals" or inappropriate information sharing among related companies. For example, if one part of a corporate family is regulated and another branch is not, a regulated electric utility might be tempted to give confidential information about generation dispatch to its affiliated (but unregulated) power marketing system company. Discrimination includes blocking out, or giving worse terms, to possible competitors or certain classes of competitors. Electricity transmission and natural gas pipeline owners long have been accused of discrimination—entering into favorable deals with incumbent companies but offering unpalatable terms to new entrants or competitors that want to encroach on their territory.

Finally, another kind of market power problem that has arisen in the energy context is market manipulation. Enron may be the most infamous example of this. In 2001, the company engaged in a series of practices to make it look like California was experiencing extreme electricity shortages, when in fact it was not. By structuring trades and transactions the right way, Enron was able to drive up energy costs and profit substantially in the aftermath—until it got caught. Enron's manipulation of energy markets in California is discussed in Chapters 4 and 5.

As you read the following case, consider what kind of market power the statutory provision at issue sought to address. Ask whether the provision was successful in addressing the market power problem, or if there are signs that some form of market power persisted, nevertheless.

OTTER TAIL POWER CO. V. UNITED STATES
410 U.S. 366 (1973)

MR. JUSTICE DOUGLAS delivered the opinion of the Court.

Otter Tail sells electric power at retail in 465 towns in Minnesota, North Dakota, and South Dakota. . . . In towns where Otter Tail distributes at retail, it operates under municipally granted franchises which are limited from 10 to 20 years. Each town in Otter Tail's service area generally can accommodate only one distribution system, making each town a natural monopoly market for the distribution and sale of electric power at retail. The aggregate of towns in Otter Tail's service area is the geographic market in which Otter Tail competes for the right to serve the towns at retail. That competition is generally for the right to serve the entire retail market within the composite limits of a town, and that competition is generally between Otter Tail and a prospective or existing municipal system. These towns number 510 and of those Otter Tail serves 91%, or 465.

Otter Tail's policy is to acquire, when it can, existing municipal systems within its service areas. It has acquired six since 1947. Between 1945 and 1970, there were contests in 12 towns served by Otter Tail over proposals to replace it with municipal systems. In only three ... were municipal systems actually established. Proposed municipal systems have great obstacles; they must purchase the electric power at wholesale. To do so they must have access to existing transmission lines. The only ones available belong to Otter Tail. . . .

The antitrust charge against Otter Tail does not involve the lawfulness of its retail outlets, but only its methods of preventing the towns it served from establishing their own municipal systems when Otter Tail's franchises expired. The critical events centered largely in four towns— Elbow Lake, Minnesota, Hankinson, North Dakota, Colman, South Dakota, and Aurora, South Dakota. When Otter Tail's franchise in each of these towns terminated, the citizens voted to establish a municipal distribution system. Otter Tail refused to sell the new systems energy at wholesale and refused to agree to wheel power from other suppliers of wholesale energy.

Colman and Aurora had access to other transmission. Against them, Otter Tail used the weapon of litigation.

As respects Elbow Lake and Hankinson, Otter Tail simply refused to deal, although according to the findings it had the ability to do so. Elbow Lake, cut off from all sources of wholesale power, constructed its own generating plant. Both Elbow Lake and Hankinson requested the Bureau of Reclamation and various cooperatives to furnish them with wholesale power; they were willing to supply it if Otter Tail would wheel it. But Otter Tail refused, relying on provisions in its contracts which barred the use of its lines for wheeling power to towns which it had served at retail. Elbow Lake after completing its plant asked the Federal Power Commission, under § 202(b) of the Federal Power Act to require Otter Tail to interconnect with the town and sell it power at wholesale. The Federal Power Commission ordered first a temporary and then a permanent connection. Hankinson tried unsuccessfully to get relief from the North Dakota Commission and then filed a complaint with the federal commission seeking an order to compel Otter Tail to wheel. While the application was pending, the town council voted to withdraw it and subsequently renewed Otter Tail's franchise. . . .

The decree of the District Court enjoins Otter Tail from "(r)efusing to sell electric power at wholesale to existing or proposed municipal electric power systems in cities and towns located in (its service area)" and from refusing to wheel electric power over its transmission lines from other electric power lines to such cities and towns. But the decree goes on to provide:

> "The defendant shall not be compelled by the Judgment in this case to furnish wholesale electric service or wheeling service to a municipality except at rates which are compensatory and under terms and conditions which are filed with and subject to approval by the Federal Power Commission."

So far as wheeling is concerned, there is no authority granted the Commission under Part II of the Federal Power Act to order it, for the bills originally introduced contained common carrier provisions which were deleted. The Act as passed contained only the interconnection provision set forth in § 202(b).[7] The common carrier provision in the original bill and the power to direct wheeling were left to the "voluntary coordination of electric facilities." Insofar as the District Court ordered wheeling to correct anticompetitive and monopolistic practices of Otter Tail, there is no conflict with the authority of the Federal Power Commission.

As respects the ordering of interconnections, there is no conflict on the present record. Elbow Lake applied to the Federal Power Commission for an interconnection with Otter Tail and, as we have said, obtained it. Hankinson renewed Otter Tail's franchise. So the decree of the District Court, as far as the present record is concerned, presents no actual conflict between the federal judicial decree and an order of the Federal Power Commission. . . .

Otter Tail argues that, without the weapons which it used, more and more municipalities will turn to public power and Otter Tail will go downhill. The argument is a familiar one. . . .

[But t]he fact that three municipalities which Otter Tail opposed finally got their municipal systems does not excuse Otter Tail's conduct. That fact does not condone the antitrust tactics which Otter Tail sought to impose. . . . The proclivity for predatory practices has always been a consideration for the District Court in fashioning its antitrust decree.

We do not suggest, however, that the District Court, concluding that Otter Tail violated the antitrust laws, should be impervious to Otter Tail's assertion that compulsory interconnection or wheeling will erode its integrated system and threaten its capacity to serve adequately the public.

---

[7]   Section 202(b) provides: "Whenever the Commission, upon application of any State commission or of any person engaged in the transmission or sale of electric energy . . . finds such action necessary or appropriate in the public interest it may by order direct a public utility (if the Commission finds that no undue burden will be placed upon such public utility thereby) to establish physical connection of its transmission facilities with the facilities of one or more other persons engaged in the transmission or sale of electric energy, to sell energy to or exchange energy with such persons: Provided, That the Commission shall have no authority to compel the enlargement of generating facilities for such purposes, nor to compel such public utility to sell or exchange energy when to do so would impair its ability to render adequate service to its customers. . . ."

As the dissent properly notes, the Commission may not order interconnection if to do so "would impair (the utility's) ability to render adequate service to its customers." 16 U.S.C. § 824a(b). Since[, however,] the District Court has made future connections subject to Commission approval and in any event has retained jurisdiction to enable the parties to apply for "necessary or appropriate" relief and presumably will give effect to the policies embodied in the Federal Power Act, we cannot say under these circumstances that it has abused its discretion.

Except for the provision of the order discussed in part IV of this opinion, the judgment is affirmed.

MR. JUSTICE STEWART, with whom THE CHIEF JUSTICE and MR. JUSTICE REHNQUIST join, concurring in part and dissenting in part.

The Court in this case has followed the District Court into a misapplication of the Sherman Act to a highly regulated, natural-monopoly industry wholly different from those that have given rise to ordinary antitrust principles. In my view, Otter Tail's refusal to wholesale power through interconnection or to perform wheeling services was conduct entailing no antitrust violation.

It is undisputed that Otter Tail refused either to wheel power or to sell it at wholesale to the towns of Elbow Lake, Minnesota, and Hankinson, North Dakota ... The District Court concluded that Otter Tail had substantial monopoly power at retail and "strategic dominance" in the subtransmission of power in most of its market area. The District Court then mechanically applied the familiar Sherman Act formula: since Otter Tail possessed monopoly power and had acted to preserve that power, it was guilty of an antitrust violation. Nowhere did the District Court come to grips with the significance of the Federal Power Act, either in terms of the specific regulatory apparatus it established or the policy considerations that moved the Congress to enact it. Yet it seems to me that these concerns are central to the disposition of this case.

... The problem that Congress addressed in fashioning a regulatory system reflected a purpose to prevent unnecessary financial concentration while recognizing the "natural monopoly" aspects, and concomitant efficiencies, of power generation and transmission. The report stated that

"(w)hile the distribution of gas or electricity in any given community is tolerated as a "natural monopoly" to avoid local duplication of plants, there is no justification for an extension of that idea of local monopoly to embrace the common control, by a few powerful interests, of utility plants scattered over many States and totally unconnected in operation."

The resulting statutory system left room for the development of economies of large scale, single company operations. One of the stated mandates to the Federal Power Commission was for it to assure "an abundant supply of electric energy throughout the United States with the greatest possible economy and with regard to the proper utilization and conservation of natural resources," 16 U.S.C. § 824a. In the face of natural monopolies at retail and similar economies of scale in the subtransmission of power, Congress was forced to address the very problem raised by this case—use of the lines of one company by another. One obvious solution would have been to impose the obligations of a common carrier upon power companies owning lines capable of the wholesale transmission of electricity. Such a provision was originally included in the bill. . . .

Had these provisions been enacted, the Commission would clearly have had the power to order interconnections and wheeling for the purpose of making available to local power companies wholesale power obtained from or through companies with subtransmission systems. The latter companies would equally clearly have had an obligation to provide such services upon request. Yet, after substantial debate, the Congress declined to follow this path. . . .

This legislative history, especially when viewed in the light of repeated subsequent congressional refusals to impose common carrier obligations in this area, indicates a clear congressional purpose to allow electric utilities to decide for themselves whether to wheel or sell at wholesale as they see fit. This freedom is qualified by a grant of authority to the Commission to order interconnection (but not wheeling) in certain circumstances. But the exercise of even that power is limited by a consideration of the ability of the regulated utility to function. The Commission may not order interconnection where this would entail an "undue burden" on the regulated utility. In addition, the Commission has "no authority to compel the enlargement of generating facilities for such purposes, nor to compel such public utility to sell or exchange energy when to do so would impair its ability to render adequate service to its customers." 16 U.S.C. § 824a(b).

As the District Court found, Otter Tail is a vertically integrated power company. But the bulk of its business—some 90% of its income—derives from sales of power at retail. Left to its own judgment in dealing with its customers, it seems entirely predictable that Otter Tail would decline wholesale dealing with towns in which it had previously done business at retail. If the purpose of the congressional scheme is to leave such decisions to the power companies in the absence of a contrary requirement imposed by the Commission, it would appear that Otter Tail's course [here] was foreseeably within the zone of freedom specifically created by the statutory scheme. As a retailer of power, Otter Tail asserted a legitimate business interest in keeping its lines free for its own power sales and in refusing to lend a hand in its own demise. . . .

Both because I believe Otter Tail's refusal to wheel or wholesale power was conduct exempt from the antitrust laws and because I believe the District Court's decree improperly pre-empted the jurisdiction of the Federal Power Commission, I would reverse the judgment before us.

NOTES AND QUESTIONS

1. In antitrust circles, *Otter Tail* is best known for helping define the limits of a federal preemption defense to antitrust claims. From an energy perspective, the case squarely presents the question of market power and one of the core statutes Congress has adopted to regulate it, the Federal Power Act. As we will see in Chapter 4, the Federal Power Act, and its twin statute, the Natural Gas Act, seek to prevent utility companies from frustrating competition (and from charging higher-than-reasonable prices). The statutes do this by regulating prices of energy sales and by granting the Commission regulatory authority to review sales of jurisdictional energy facilities and mergers of energy firms. The power in question here falls into the latter category—the authority of the Federal Power Commission to order a regulated utility to let competitors connect to and use its transmission lines. As the case makes plain, Congress engaged in some debate about how extensive this power should be. When we revisit electricity in Chapters 4 and 5, and the transportation of energy in Chapter 7, you will see that regulatory authority to order the use of energy transportation—or what are sometimes called "bottleneck"—facilities, remains a key issue.

2. All three of the major historical players in the electricity industry are present in the *Otter Tail* decision. Otter Tail itself is an investor-owned utility (IOU). IOUs dominate electricity service nationwide. The four cities that wanted to connect to Otter Tail's system are examples of municipal utilities or "munis", some of which supply their own power like Elbow Lake did, and some of which buy power from others and are in the business of delivering electricity to residents. The decision also mentions rural electric cooperatives, which are member owned and were instrumental in electrifying rural communities. *See* Alexandra B. Klass & Gabriel Chan, *Cooperative Clean Energy*, 100 N.C. L. REV. 1 (2021) (discussing the history of rural electric cooperatives). Which of these types of entities provides power to your home? In the modern electricity industry, other kinds of companies, such as merchant power producers, ISO/RTOs, and merchant transmission companies, are also part of the mix. Some regions also have power aggregators, like the Utah Associated Municipal Power System, a political subdivision of the State of Utah that buys, develops, and acquires electric power supplies for its municipal utility and electric cooperative members in Arizona, California, Idaho, Nevada, New Mexico, and Utah. Chapters 4 and 5 provide more detail on the evolution of the electricity sector and electricity regulation.

3.   Otter Tail, incorporated in 1907, is still an operating electric utility today. It has almost 760 employees, owns roughly 800 MW of generation, 5,800 miles of transmission line, and serves approximately 132,000 customers across 70,000 square miles in 422 communities in Minnesota, North Dakota, and South Dakota. *See* https://www.otpco.com/about-us/.

4.   What reasons might Otter Tail have had for denying the different cities' requests for interconnection? Are those reasons well founded, or are they simply an indication of exercising market power? In either case, was Otter Tail's taking that position economically rational? Why or why not? Couldn't Otter Tail have made money by charging the cities for the electricity-related services they desired?

5.   As noted in *Otter Tail*, the Federal Power Act as originally passed gave FERC the authority to order interconnections between electric utilities so long as the utility being forced to interconnect is adequately compensated. 16 U.S.C. § 824a(b). FERC also has the power to order interconnections in emergencies, war, or crises. *Id.* § 824a(c). Although these powers have been reaffirmed by the courts, FERC has not wielded them often, and there are few examples in the case law where FERC has ordered interconnections between utilities. *See, e.g., New England Power Co. v. FPC*, 349 F.2d 258 (1st Cir. 1965); *Am. Paper Inst., Inc. v. Am. Elec. Power Serv. Corp.*, 461 U.S. 402 (1983). What reasons might FERC have for using this power sparingly when regulating electric utilities? For a discussion of how FERC regulates electricity, natural gas, and oil markets, see ENERGY PRIMER: A HANDBOOK FOR ENERGY MARKET BASICS, FED. ENERGY REG. COMM'N (Apr. 2020).

6.   In 1978, Congress gave FERC further interconnection authority. The Public Utility Regulatory Policies Act of 1978 (PURPA) added Sections 210, 211, and 212 to the Federal Power Act. *See* 16 U.S.C. §§ 824i, 824j, 824k. Under Section 210, FERC could now order the interconnection of many non-utilities, such as renewables facilities, cogenerators, and independent power producers, to utilities. Section 211 gave FERC the authority to order the "wheeling," or shipment, of electricity across utilities' transmission lines in limited circumstances. And Section 212 governed the rates, terms, and conditions for FERC's orders under Sections 210 and 211. In the Energy Policy Act of 1992, Congress expanded FERC's wheeling authority under Section 211. "This law authorized FERC to order individual utilities to provide transmission services to unaffiliated wholesale generators (*i.e.*, to 'wheel' power) on a case-by-case basis. Exercising its authority under the EPAct, FERC ordered a utility to 'wheel' power for a complaining wholesale competitor 12 times, in 12 separate proceedings." *New York v. FERC*, 535 U.S. 1, 9 (2002); *see also* Suedeen G. Kelly, *Electricity*, *in* JAMES E. HICKEY, JR. ET AL., ENERGY LAW AND POLICY FOR THE 21ST CENTURY 12–1, 12–24 to –25 (Rocky Mtn. Min. L. Found. 2000).

2. WASTE

Waste can be defined many ways. The most conventional definition is that of physical waste, or when a resource is used to produce less than it possibly can. This might occur for many reasons. An activity might ruin a resource. The resource might be consumed in a way that uses part of it but renders the rest unusable. It might be underused. Or it might be used in a way that does not create the most useful social output. You are likely familiar with waste in your life. A half-eaten ice cream cone dropped on the floor is an example of waste (unless the five-second rule applies). A doctor capable of brain surgery but forced to work in a job as a janitor is an example of an underemployed resource, or waste. Some economists suggest that much of marketing and advertising is waste, because the resources employed by one company to get you to buy their product only cancel out their competitors' efforts in the same vein.

In economic terms, waste occurs when a market produces an inefficient outcome. By "efficient," economists typically mean Pareto-efficient. Pareto efficiency, or "Pareto optimality," occurs when "resources cannot be reallocated so as to make one person better off without making someone else worse off." NICHOLAS MERCURO & STEVEN G. MEDEMA, ECONOMICS AND THE LAW: FROM POSNER TO POST-MODERNISM AND BEYOND 21 (2d ed. 2006). Thus, waste occurs in economic terms when the absence of a resource "would not reduce the output of society, or if their reallocation would increase the output of society." Ken McCormick, *Towards a Definition of Waste in Economics: A Neoinstitutionalist Approach*, 44 REV. SOC. ECON. 80, 83 (1986). So, "resources that are unemployed, working at cross purposes, or involved in the process of planned obsolescence would not be missed if they were suddenly removed. Hence, they are currently being wasted. Likewise, a reduction in inefficiency would increase output, so the existence of inefficiency implies the existence of waste." *Id.* "If a society can be better off without an increase in resources, it must not be using its resources to their full potential." *Id.* at 81; *see also* Phillip W. Lear, *Utah Oil and Gas Conservation Law and Practice*, 1998 UTAH L. REV. 89 (summarizing one statutory definition of waste as "the inefficient dissipation of reservoir energy, inefficient transportation or storing of oil and gas, the drilling of unnecessary wells, and production of oil and gas in excess of transportation and storing capacity").

These kinds of physical waste occur in many energy contexts. Advocates of an advanced grid argue that energy can be used more efficiently if demand can be shifted to use energy at different times of the day. Proponents of distributed generation similarly contend that energy consumption will be more efficient if we locate electricity production closer to where it is consumed, consequently reducing loss through transport. Perhaps most famously, the oil and gas industry is notorious for waste. Especially early in the industry's history, waste was profligate. One prominent example is the story of Spindletop in Texas:

> In the first week of January, 1901, the largest gusher the world had ever seen spewed 800,000 barrels of oil across the coastal

plain just southeast of Houston. Oil in unimaginable torrents flowed from this well. Thousands of people traveled to the see this sensation, many pressing close enough to feel the black mist on their faces.

Within five years of its discovery, the Spindletop field had gone from boom to bust. Drillers swarmed into the Beaumont area, leased every acre, including pig sties, drilled as many wells as they could squeeze on to each lease, and then produced oil at full flow in order to out-drain the rival operator next door. Under the Rule of Capture, the race is to the quickest. Five percent of the oil underlying the field was produced using the natural pressure in the field but 95% of the oil remained locked in the pore spaces of the underground reservoir. This pattern repeated itself in newly discovered oil fields in West Texas. During the first two decades of the 20th century, millions of barrels of oil ran down creeks and streams or were put in earthen storage subject to fire, evaporation and floods. Gas, then an unwanted byproduct of the production of oil, was flared or vented by the billions and even trillions of cubic feet.

Jacqueline Lang Weaver, *The Federal Government as a Useful Enemy: Perspectives on the Bush Energy/Environmental Agenda From the Texas Oilfields*, 19 PACE ENV'T L. REV. 1 (2001).

A second kind of waste is "economic waste" which can be defined as overproduction of a resource so that the resource is priced too low. That is, economic waste occurs when a slower (or longer-term) production of a good would result in a larger maximization of profits, or when there is an unnecessary overinvestment in a resource. Lear, *supra* ("Economic waste is recognized in some states, and might include expending financial resources in excess of the usual, ordinary, and necessary sums for such projects.").

Again, the oil and gas industry has a history of economic waste. A contemporary account from the early 1930s surveyed some of the economic waste problems the industry faced early on:

The heroics of Governor Murray in calling out the troops to close the oil wells of Oklahoma until such time as purchasers would pay one dollar a barrel has dramatized the acute problem of low prices and overproduction which has haunted the petroleum industry in the past few years. The competitive exploitation of oil lands has resulted not only in dissipating huge quantities of both oil and gas through the wasteful rush to market but also in diminishing profits through the production of oil and gas in excess of current demands. . . .

The physical losses of oil and gas and the waste of gas energy have been accompanied by huge economic costs. The intense duplication of wells has saddled the industry with a great overhead of fixed charges. While lifting and storage costs may be delayed—if the oil can be kept in the ground until a market is found—drilling costs are already incurred and add to the total costs of production even though production is restricted. . . . These economic wastes have made the industry grimly aware of the need for "conservation."

J. Howard Marshall & Norman L. Meyers, *Legal Planning of Petroleum Production*, 41 YALE L. J. 33 (1931). In 2020, during the COVID-19 pandemic, the sudden halt to travel worldwide sent oil prices plummeting to record low levels, prompting Texas regulators to consider for the first time in decades imposing limits on production in order to reduce supply and increase prices. The regulators ultimately declined to impose such limits. *See* Sergio Chapa, *Texas Railroad Commission Rejects Statewide Oil Production Cuts*, HOUSTON CHRON. (May 6, 2020). Can you think of reasons why they might have declined to act? Should they have?

The following case involves an Indiana statute that sought to prevent waste of natural gas. The statute provided: "[I]t shall be unlawful for any person, firm or corporation having possession or control of any natural gas or oil well . . . to allow or permit the flow of gas or oil from any such well to escape into the open air without being confined within wells or proper pipes, or other safe receptacle for a longer period than two (2) days next after gas or oil shall have been struck in such well. . . ." As you read the case, consider if there are any parallels between statutes, such as Indiana's at the end of the nineteenth century, and the practices of hydraulic fracturing for oil and gas extraction today.

STATE V. OHIO OIL CO.

49 N.E. 809 (Ind. 1898)

MCCABE, J.

The state of Indiana . . . brought suit against the . . . Ohio Oil Company, seeking to enjoin it from wasting natural gas. . . . The substance of the complaint is that: For many years . . . there has been underlying Madison, Grant, Howard, Delaware, Blackford, Tipton, Hamilton, Wells, and other counties in Indiana a large deposit of natural gas utilized for fuel and light by the people of those counties, and of many other counties and cities in Indiana, including Indianapolis, Ft. Wayne, Richmond, Logansport, Lafayette, and others of the most populous cities of the state, to which cities the gas is conducted, after being brought through wells to the surface of the ground, by pipes and conduits, by means of which many hundreds of thousands of the people of Indiana are supplied with gas for light and fuel.

The natural gas ... is contained in and percolates freely through a stratum of rock known as "Trenton Rock," comprising a vast reservoir, in which the gas is confined under great pressure, and from which it escapes, when permitted to do so, with great force. The fuel supplied by the natural gas thus obtained is the cheapest and best known to civilization, and the value of the natural gas deposit to the state and its citizens is many millions of dollars. Since the discovery of the gas deposit in 1886, vast sums of money have come into the state, and have been invested in building up large manufacturing interests, and vast sums of money belonging to the people of Indiana have been invested in similar enterprises, causing a great increase of population, principally in the territory underlying which gas is found.

Many cities in and adjacent to the gas territory, including those named, are almost wholly dependent for fuel supply upon natural gas, and for that reason the people of Indiana have become and are greatly interested in the protection and continued preservation of the gas supply.

Many millions of dollars invested in manufacturing and other properties in and near the gas territory are wholly dependent for their continued operation, and for the permanent value of their property, upon the gas supply. Their location and establishment in the gas territory was due to the presence of natural gas underlying it, without which such enterprises could not be operated at a profit; and, in the event that the supply of gas is exhausted in the territory, many of such manufacturing enterprises, in which thousands of citizens of Indiana find employment at remunerative wages, will be compelled to suspend operations. Their employés will be thrown out of employment, and many of them, being wholly dependent upon their labor for support, may and will become charges upon the state and its municipal subdivisions. The property of the manufacturing enterprises, and the vast investments depending on them and related to them, will become worthless, and the owners will be driven to remove to other parts of the country, taking away from Indiana great wealth now invested in these enterprises.

In the cities named, and in all the territory known as the "Gas Belt," the inhabitants have for years used practically no other fuel than natural gas. Their houses, in many instances, are constructed with a view to the use of natural gas, and will have to be differently equipped before other kinds of fuel can be used. The cost of natural gas as fuel to the people in the gas belt, who number several hundreds of thousands, is very much less than that of any other fuel that has ever been or can be procured by them, and to the other inhabitants of the state using natural gas it has become and is a source of great convenience, comfort, and increased happiness, because of its cheapness, convenience, and cleanliness as fuel. Many small villages in and near the gas territory have within a few years became flourishing and opulent cities.

The state's wealth, and its revenues derived from taxation on account of such increased population and the various interests that have been fostered and supported by natural gas, have been greatly increased, and will, in the event gas is exhausted, be correspondingly curtailed. The state of Indiana, relying upon the permanent supply of gas, has, at great expense, equipped many of its public institutions, including the State House, the Central and other hospitals for the insane, the asylums for the blind and deaf and dumb, the institutions for the care of the orphans of American soldiers and sailors, and other public institutions . . ., together with the court houses in many counties and a vast number of public schools, for the use of natural gas as fuel, by which the cost of maintaining the public buildings and institutions named has been materially lessened, and the comfort and happiness of their inmates and occupants immensely increased.

Natural gas exists in large reservoirs, or a series of reservoirs connected with each other, underlying the gas territory, and the diminution or consumption of natural gas taken from any part of them affects or reduces correspondingly the common supply. If the gas supply is accordingly husbanded and protected, it will last for many years, and continue to supply the various interests named with abundant fuel, and the population, wealth, and other material interests of the state will continue to be benefited and enhanced, and the comfort, enjoyment, and happiness of the people of the state greatly increased.

It is charged that about May 25, 1897, the Ohio Oil Company . . . caused a well to be drilled near Alexandria, Madison county, which produces natural gas and petroleum in large quantities. The location of this well is described, as well as that of five other wells, drilled at about the same time as the one first named, all of which produce both natural gas and petroleum, and have done so ever since their completion. It is charged that, instead of securely anchoring the wells as drilled, so as to confine the gas produced by them, within two days next after their completion, the defendant . . . has "unlawfully permitted the gas produced therein to flow and escape into the open air, whereby many millions of cubic feet of natural gas have been wasted and lost, and whereby the state's supply of natural gas has been greatly diminished. . . ." It is also charged that the defendant avows its purpose to permit the gas to escape continuously and indefinitely hereafter from said wells, and refuses to make any effort to confine it, and declares its purpose to drill other wells in the gas territory, and permit the gas therefrom to flow and escape into the open air, and that, if the gas continues to flow from the wells, the supply of natural gas upon which the citizens of the state depend will be greatly diminished; that the pressure of gas, as found in said Trenton rock, will be greatly diminished, and that by the diminution of such pressure, water will accumulate in the rock stratum, and ultimately and entirely displace and overcome the gas supply; that because of the wrongful acts of the defendant above described, heretofore committed and now continuing, its property and that of its citizens has been and will continue to be essentially interfered with, and the comfortable enjoyment of the lives of its citizens greatly interrupted. . . .

[Defendant contends] that there is no authority or right of action in the state at common law, and especially that the state cannot maintain a suit in equity. . . . The reason assigned in argument why the state cannot maintain the action for an injunction is that the statute provides a different remedy, namely, the recovery of a penalty of $200 for each violation of the act, and a further penalty of $200 for each 10 days during which such violation shall continue, to be recovered in a civil action in the name of the state, for the use of the county in which such well is located, with attorney's fees and costs of suit. And another remedy, provided in another section of the act, is that certain persons in the vicinity are authorized to go upon the land where any well is situate from which gas or oil is allowed to escape in violation of the act, and shut up the same, and pack and tube said well, so as to prevent the escape of gas or oil, and maintain a civil suit against the owner for the costs of such closing of said well, with attorney's fees and costs of suit. But this court has gone much further than to hold that the fact that the civil remedy given to recover penalties and the other remedies for violations of the act does not bar the right to an injunction. In the case of *Gas Co. v. Tyner*, it was said: "No authority has been cited, and we know of none, supporting the position of the appellants that the appellee is not entitled to an injunction because the accumulation of nitroglycerin within the corporate limits of a town or city. . . ." . . .

The supreme court of Kansas, in *State v. Crawford*, said: "Every place where a public statute is openly, publicly, repeatedly, continuously, persistently, and intentionally violated is a public nuisance." . . . The complaint shows that by the repeated and continuing acts of defendant this public property right is being and will continue to be greatly interfered with and impaired; and that such acts constitute a nuisance, both under our statute and at common law, is not open to serious question. . . .

It is true that, as a result of the principles announced in the previous part of this opinion, natural gas, when reduced to actual possession by the land owner, when drawn into his well, pipes, tanks, or other receptacles, thereby becomes his personal property, subject to his dominion. But, as said by this court in *Gas Co. v. Tyner*: "The rule that the owner has the right to do as he pleases with or upon his own property is subject to many limitations and restrictions, one of which is that he must have due regard for the rights of others." Appellee's counsel have conceded that the pressure in gas wells since the discovery of gas in this state has fallen from 350 pounds to 150 pounds. This very strongly indicates the possibility, if not the probability, of exhaustion. In the light of these facts, one who recklessly, defiantly, persistently, and continuously wastes natural gas, and boldly declares his purpose to continue to do so, as the complaint charges appellee with doing, all of which it admits to be true by its demurrer, ought not to complain of being branded as the enemy of mankind. . . . It is not the use of unlimited quantities of gas that is prohibited, but it is the waste of it that is forbidden. The object and policy of that inhibition is to prevent, if possible, the exhaustion of the store house of nature, wherein is deposited an element that ministers more to the comfort, happiness, and wellbeing of society than any other of the bounties of the earth. . . . The continued waste and exhaustion of the natural gas of Indiana through appellee's wells would not only deny to the inhabitants the many valuable uses of the gas, but the state, whose many quasi public corporations have many millions of dollars invested in supplying gas to the state and its inhabitants, will suffer the destruction of such corporations, the loss of such investments and a source of large revenues. To use appellee's wells as they have been doing, they injure thousands, and perhaps millions, of the people of Indiana, and the injury—the exhaustion of natural gas—is not only an irreparable one, but it will be a great public calamity. . . .

We had petroleum oil for more than a third of a century before its discovery in this state, imported from other states, and we could continue to do so if the production of oil should cease in this state. But we cannot have the blessings of natural gas unless the measures for the preservation thereof in this state are enforced against the lawless. . . .

NOTES AND QUESTIONS

1.   Indiana's complaint in *Ohio Oil* includes lengthy descriptions of the value of natural gas to the state. If natural gas was so valuable to Indianans, why didn't Ohio Oil capture the gas and sell it?

2.   By the same token, if Ohio Oil believed that the way it was extracting oil in Indiana was necessary, why didn't it appeal to the Indiana legislature for an exemption from the statute in question? What do you think Ohio Oil's chances of success would have been at the Indiana state house?

3.   Ohio Oil challenged the Indiana Supreme Court's rulings in the U.S. Supreme Court. Ruling that the Indiana law addressed "the preservation and protection of rights of an essentially local character," a subject that was

"especially . . . within [the state's] lawful authority," the Court upheld the statute against Ohio Oil's constitutional takings challenge:

> [T]he legislative power . . . can be manifested for the purpose of protecting all the collective owners, by securing a just distribution . . . and . . . by preventing waste. . . . Viewed, then, as a statute to protect or to prevent the waste of the common property of the surface owners, the law of the state of Indiana which is here attacked because it is asserted that it devested private property without due compensation, in substance, is a statute protecting private property and preventing it from being taken by one of the common owners without regard to the enjoyment of the others.

Ohio Oil Co. v. State of Indiana, 177 U.S. 190, 210 (1900).

4.   Many states responded to the waste caused by the rule of capture by creating well-spacing requirements, conservation measures, and mandatory unitization or "forced pooling" laws in the 1920s, which created procedures for merging multiple landowners' oil and gas interests into a single unit, setting rules for extraction, and allocating costs and revenues. For more detail on these procedures, see Chapter 3.

5.   The issue of waste in the oil industry has become prominent again since the advent of hydraulic fracturing for oil and natural gas in 2007. In Texas, New Mexico, and North Dakota, for example, significantly increased oil production and the lack of adequate state regulations requiring operators to capture associated gas has led to an increase in intentional flaring and unintentional venting of methane during natural gas production. These developments are discussed in detail in Chapter 9. Why might producers burn off such a large amount of a valuable energy resource rather than capturing it and selling it? Why have the states allowed it? How might state courts, regulators, or mineral owners respond?

3. NEGATIVE EXTERNALITIES

The concept of externalities, or "spillover effects," is a common one. For economists, externalities can be both positive and negative. An externality occurs when an individual (or a firm) acts or without bearing the full benefits or costs of that action. A positive externality is when the individual does not capture all the benefits of her decision. A negative externality takes place when the individual does not bear all the costs.

Examples of positive externalities are all around us. Immunizations create positive externalities as they not only protect the person receiving the vaccination but also decrease the risk that others will be infected. If you keep your yard and house well maintained, your neighbors receive a positive externality through higher property values. Likewise, my uncle's neighbors benefit from the bees he keeps, because in addition to making honey for him, they pollinate the neighbors' flowers—a positive externality.

Negative externalities are also common. If you sit on the end of an empty row at a movie theater, forcing others to climb over you, that is a type of negative externality. The thirteen-year-old who refuses to shower or wear deodorant imposes negative externalities on the people around him or her. The classic example of a negative externality is pollution. When a firm manufactures a good but sends pollution into the air or water as part of the process, that pollution is a negative externality. The firm profits from its production, but it does not bear the full cost of the emitted pollution.

Pollution is pervasive in the energy sector. Whether it is water pollution from an abandoned coal mine, air pollution a gas well, or uranium tailings or toxic emissions from a coal plant, much energy use leads to pollution. Likewise, energy extraction, production, and consumption inflict other kinds of environmental effects that can be considered negative externalities. Moreover, as discussed above and throughout this book, these negative pollution impacts are distributed unequally.

A primary objective of environmental law is to control negative externalities, often in energy. Environmental law does this both by trying to limit pollution and to clean up after it has occurred. To the extent environmental law touches on energy, it is an important field to understand for the energy lawyer. One might think of environmental law as an external break on energy processes, restricting to some degree how energy can be made and used. That said, energy law itself addresses negative externalities in certain instances. Sometimes this occurs when environmental and energy objectives overlap; efficiency measures are a good example. They both maximize energy use and reduce pollution. Sometimes energy law also includes limiting negative externalities as an objective, or as one objective among others.

The following case addresses negative externalities in the context of hydroelectricity production. As you read the court's decision, consider how the law in question seeks to grapple with negative externalities, and if that is the law's primary goal.

SHAFER & FREEMAN LAKES ENV'T CONSERV. CORP. V. FERC

992 F.3d 1071 (D.C. Cir. 2021)

MILLETT, CIRCUIT JUDGE:

. . . The Federal Power Act gives the Federal Energy Regulatory Commission (Commission) responsibility for licensing the construction, maintenance, and operation of hydroelectric projects, including dams, on waters subject to federal jurisdiction. *See* 16 U.S.C. § 797(e).[2] When

---

[2] Congress's jurisdiction over certain waters derives from its authority to regulate interstate and foreign commerce under the Constitution. *See* U.S. CONST. Art. I, § 8, cl. 3; *Federal Power Comm'n v. Oregon*, 349 U.S. 435, 442 (1955). In particular, the Federal Power Act requires the

deciding whether to issue a license to a hydropower project, the Commission not only must consider "the power and development purposes for which licenses are issued," but also must "give equal consideration to the purposes of energy conservation, the protection, mitigation of damage to, and enhancement of, fish and wildlife (including related spawning grounds and habitat), the protection of recreational opportunities, and the preservation of other aspects of environmental quality." 16 U.S.C. § 797(e) . . .

Like all federal agency actions, Commission licensing decisions must comply with the Endangered Species Act's requirement to avoid jeopardy to listed species. To that end, the Commission consults with that Act's statutorily designated wildlife agencies when deciding whether to issue or amend licenses for hydroelectric facilities.

Two dams sit on the Tippecanoe River in northern Indiana. These dams use the flow of the river to generate electricity, and they also typically provide enough water to sustain two large reservoirs. The Norway Dam, built in 1923, creates a ten-mile-long reservoir called Lake Shafer. Further downstream, the Oakdale Dam, built in 1925, creates a reservoir of similar length called Lake Freeman. The dams are owned and operated by a privately owned utility company, the Northern Indiana Public Service Company LLC (NIPSCO).

The lakes are centers of economic and recreational activity for the region. More than four thousand private lakefront properties surround the reservoirs, and the lakes support substantial boating, fishing, tourism, and related activities.

For almost eighty years, the Commission took the position that the portion of the Tippecanoe River near the dams was not a navigable water for purposes of federal jurisdiction, and so the dams did not require a license from the Commission. But in 2000, the agency changed course and determined that the Norway Dam and Oakdale Dam portions of the Tippecanoe River constitute a navigable waterway within the federal government's jurisdiction. In 2007, the Commission issued a 30-year license to NIPSCO to operate the two dams.

As relevant here, that license required that NIPSCO operate the dams "in an instantaneous run-of-river mode." In this mode, NIPSCO must ensure that "the outflow from the Norway Dam approximates the sum of inflows to Lake Shafer and the outflow from the Oakdale Dam approximates the sum of inflows to Lake Freeman." More specifically, the license required NIPSCO to prevent the water level of the lakes from fluctuating more than three inches above or below a target elevation. For

Commission to regulate dams on "navigable waters," which means waters "used or suitable for use" for transporting people or property in interstate or foreign commerce. *See* 16 U.S.C. §§ 796(8), 817(1); *Turlock Irrigation Dist. v. FERC*, 786 F.3d 18, 26 (D.C. Cir. 2015).

Lake Freeman, that elevation is roughly 610 feet above sea level (technically, 612.45 feet NGVD). The license allowed deviation from this rule only during periods of "abnormal river conditions[,]" meaning abnormally high flows, not abnormally low flows.

In the summer of 2012, Indiana experienced an extreme drought, and water levels on the Tippecanoe River reached historic lows. Residents living along the stretch of the Tippecanoe downstream of the dams alerted the Indiana Department of Natural Resources that the river was drying up and large numbers of mussels were dying. That July, biologists from Indiana and the U.S. Fish and Wildlife Service surveyed the river over several days, and found "substantial numbers of fresh dead mussels [and] stranded live mussels[.]" Among the dead were numerous mussels listed as endangered or threatened under the Endangered Species Act, including fanshell, clubshell, sheepnose, and rabbitsfoot mussels. *See* 16 U.S.C. § 1533.

The Service determined that low water flow out of the dams was contributing to the mussel deaths. In the Service's view, the way in which the dams were being operated caused less water to reach the lower Tippecanoe River than would reach it in the absence of the dams, and so the dams partially caused the mussel deaths in the dried-out river. The Service then wrote a letter to NIPSCO informing the company that it must increase water flow out of the Oakdale Dam or risk potential liability under the Endangered Species Act for "take" of listed mussels. Alternatively, the Service said, NIPSCO could try to avoid liability by demonstrating that the dams were "maintaining the 'run of the river' rate of discharge"—in other words, demonstrate that the dams had no effect on the flow of the river or the mussel deaths caused by insufficient water.

NIPSCO opted to increase the water flow out of the Oakdale Dam. Over the subsequent years, NIPSCO continued to work with the Service to ensure that enough water was released from the dams to avoid killing mussels. This cooperation required NIPSCO to perform a regulatory balancing act: The increased releases that the Fish and Wildlife Service requested to protect the mussels forced the company to violate the Commission's license requirement that the company maintain relatively stable lake elevations. To remedy the situation, NIPSCO sought and received variances from the Commission allowing temporary violations of the license's water-level terms.

In 2014, the Service devised a plan for protecting the Tippecanoe River mussels. As described in a "Technical Assistance Letter" sent to NIPSCO, the Service suggested that NIPSCO could avoid liability under the Endangered Species Act by releasing enough water to mimic the natural run-of-river flow that would occur if the dams were not there. While recognizing that NIPSCO's license from the Commission already required the company to operate the dams in what the Commission called "instantaneous run-of-river mode," the Service defined "run-of-river" operations differently in its new plan. Rather than focusing on keeping the lake levels steady, as the Commission had required, the Service advised NIPSCO to calculate the amount of water needed to approximate the natural flow of water out of the Oakdale Dam during low-flow conditions.

The Service then calculated that, in the absence of the dams, more water would flow into the river downstream than entered it upstream because of the large watershed surrounding the downstream portions of the river. More specifically, the water flow directly beneath the Oakdale Dam under natural conditions would be 1.9 times the flow measured upstream of the dams (as measured at the Winamac gauge on the River). To that end, the Service advised NIPSCO to release enough water during low-flow events so that the flow directly below the Oakdale Dam was 1.9 times the 24-hour daily average flow at the Winamac gauge. In addition, the Service instructed NIPSCO to cease electricity generation during low-flow events, because the Service concluded that engaging the dam's turbines caused large fluctuations in water flow that harmed mussels.

Two months later, NIPSCO sought permission from the Commission to implement the Service's plan. Technically, this request came in the form of an application to amend the definition of "abnormal river conditions" in NIPSCO's license. The proposed amendment removed the lower limit on the elevation of Lake Freeman during low-flow events, allowing the lake level to fall more than three inches below the target elevation.

After the Commission opened the proceedings, a group of local entities (the "Coalition") intervened to oppose the proposed amendment to NIPSCO's license. The Coalition included the Shafer & Freeman Lakes Environmental Conservation Corporation, a local non-profit that owns much of the land beneath the lakes. It also included Carroll and White Counties and the City of Monticello, each of which encompasses or borders part of Lake Freeman. The Coalition argued that the dams do not alter the natural run of the Tippecanoe River, and that the Service's formula for calculating river flow was " 'junk' science[.]" In the Coalition's view, the amendment would provide an "unnatural" benefit to the mussels by releasing more water from Lake Freeman than the Tippecanoe River would provide in its natural state. In support, the Coalition submitted two reports from professors with expertise in hydrology.

In practical terms, the Coalition was concerned that Lake Freeman could be drawn down "in excess of 12 feet," preventing almost all recreational use of the lake, with concomitant effects on homeowners, local businesses, and tourism. The Coalition also voiced concern that a large drawdown could cause significant environmental and aesthetic harm to the lakes and lakeshore. For those reasons, the Coalition asked the

Commission to deny the amendment application and to require NIPSCO to operate the dams as it previously had.

As required by the National Environmental Policy Act (NEPA), 42 U.S.C. § 4332, the Commission conducted an environmental assessment analyzing the consequences of the proposed amendment. The Commission's draft environmental assessment was released for public comment. The assessment evaluated three alternative courses of action: (1) a "no-action" alternative, in which the Oakdale Dam would continue operating without change under its current license; (2) NIPSCO's "proposed alternative" to operate in accordance with the Fish and Wildlife Service's guidance in the Technical Assistance Letter; and (3) the Commission's "staff alternative," which reflected a potential compromise position. Under the staff alternative, during periods of low flow, NIPSCO would cease diverting water for the generation of electricity, but would still be obligated to prevent Lake Freeman's elevation from falling more than three inches below its target elevation.

Citing its obligation under the Federal Power Act to balance wildlife conservation with other interests, the Commission proposed its "staff alternative" as the best option, reasoning that it would "avoid adverse effects from project operations on endangered mussels, while protecting the numerous resources of Lake Freeman that depend on stable lake levels." The Commission also agreed with the Coalition's experts that "[t]here are legitimate concerns" with the Service's approach to calculating water flow.

The Fish and Wildlife Service submitted comments on the draft that strongly opposed adoption of the Commission staff alternative, and defended the proposed NIPSCO amendment that incorporated the Service's recommendation. The Service explained that the Commission staff alternative was "essentially the same" as the no-action status quo because the staff alternative maintained the status quo limits on lake level fluctuations, and so would continue to result in inadequate water flow for mussels.

The Commission's final environmental assessment adhered to its original conclusion, rejecting the NIPSCO amendment and concluding that the Commission staff alternative best balanced the interests of mussels with those interests that depend on stable lake levels. . . . At the same time, the Commission acknowledged that, under the consultation provisions of the Endangered Species Act, 16 U.S.C. § 1536, it needed to obtain the Fish and Wildlife Service's agreement that its staff alternative would not adversely affect endangered mussels.

Because the Service decidedly did not agree with the Commission's conclusion, the two agencies entered into "formal consultation," and the Service prepared a Biological Opinion. See 16 U.S.C. § 1536(a)(2), (b); 50 C.F.R. § 402.14. The Biological Opinion laid out the Service's scientific evaluation of the competing options and critiqued the reasoning underlying the staff alternative. . . . Nonetheless, the Service concluded that, under the governing Endangered Species Act standard, the staff alternative "is not likely to jeopardize the continued existence of the clubshell, fanshell, sheepnose, or rabbitsfoot mussels and is not likely to destroy or adversely modify designated critical habitat." That "no jeopardy" finding cleared the way for the Commission to proceed with the staff alternative.

The Service then . . . concluded that the staff alternative would result in some incidental take of mussels. *See* 16 U.S.C. § 1536(b)(4). While this level of incidental take would not result in jeopardy to the species, the Service proposed a "reasonable and prudent measure" to "minimize impacts of incidental take[.]" Specifically, the Service advised that NIPSCO should "restor[e] a more natural flow regime downstream of Oakdale Dam during low-flow periods" by "[a]dopt[ing] the alternative proposed by NIPSCO in its request for a license amendment and implement[ing] the Service [Technical Assistance Letter] of 2014[.]"

In other words, the "reasonable and prudent measure" to minimize incidental take from the staff alternative was to proceed with the approach to water-flow management originally recommended by the Service . . . underscoring that the reasonable and prudent measure and associated terms and conditions were "non-discretionary, and must be undertaken by the [Commission] so that they become binding conditions of any grant or permit issued to NIPSCO, as appropriate, for the exemption" from civil and criminal liability under the Endangered Species Act to apply. . . .

In June 2018, almost a year after receiving the Biological Opinion, the Commission issued its ruling. The Commission acknowledged that there was "a difference in opinion [between the two agencies] regarding how best to approximate run-of-river operations at the Oakdale development." The Commission reiterated its view that its own method was best, and described the Service's approach as containing "inaccuracies" that would "provide greater flows than would otherwise occur naturally."

But the Commission concluded that the Endangered Species Act "constrains [the Commission's] discretion to implement staff's recommended alternative." The Commission explained that, while it is required to balance a range of interests under the Federal Power Act, its obligations under the Endangered Species Act are "more narrowly focused on protecting threatened and endangered species." So while the Commission "might ordinarily prefer staff's alternative to balance non-developmental and developmental uses under [the Federal Power Act], in this case the [Endangered Species Act] compels a different result." The Commission added that the risk of "civil and criminal penalties, including imprisonment" for actions not in compliance with an Incidental Take Statement weighed against the staff alternative. . . .

Under 16 U.S.C. § 825*l*(b), this court has jurisdiction to review not only the Commission's order amending NIPSCO's license, but also the Service's Biological Opinion that was prepared in the course of the Commission licensing proceeding. . . .

We must uphold the Biological Opinion, as well as the Commission's licensing decision based on it, unless either decision was "arbitrary and capricious" or unsupported by substantial evidence. 5 U.S.C. § 706(2); *see City of Tacoma*, 460 F.3d at 75–76. . . .

Under the Endangered Species Act, both the Fish and Wildlife Service and the Commission are required to "use the best scientific and commercial data available" when making their respective decisions. 16 U.S.C. § 1536(a)(2); 50 C.F.R. § 402.14(g)(8). This means that the agency "may not base its [decisions] on speculation or surmise or disregard superior data[.]" *Building Indus. Ass'n of Superior Cal. v. Norton*, 247 F.3d 1241, 1246–1247 (D.C. Cir. 2001). But when the science is uncertain, courts must "proceed with particular caution, avoiding all temptation to direct the agency in a choice between rational alternatives." *American Wildlands v. Kempthorne*, 530 F.3d 991, 1000–1001 (D.C. Cir. 2008) (internal quotation omitted). . . .

The Coalition's central scientific complaint is that, in its view, the Service wrongly relied on a method of river-flow calculation called "linear scaling." The theory of linear scaling holds that, in a comparatively homogeneous landscape, a river's flow at a given point is correlated linearly to the size of the river's watershed at that point. In other words, if a river downstream at point B has a total watershed three times the size of the watershed upstream at point A, then the river's flow rate at point B will be three times the flow rate at point A. . . .

In [the Coalition's] view, the better method for ensuring "natural" flow rates on the Tippecanoe River is not linear scaling, but instead keeping lake levels relatively constant. If the lakes are not gaining any elevation, the argument goes, then water is leaving the lakes at more or less the same rate as it is entering them—that is, the "natural" run-of-river flow. . . .

The record is replete with briefs, letters, scientific reports, and agency and expert opinions elaborating and debating the merits of the Service's linear scaling methodology. But the only question before us is whether the Fish and Wildlife Service acted reasonably in its analysis and used the "best scientific and commercial data available," *see* 16 U.S.C. § 1536(a)(2). The Service's analysis passes muster.

First, the agency offered a thorough and reasoned explanation of its scientific decision-making. The Service's methodology is based on a "fundamental characteristic of watersheds"—namely, that a river's flow "increases from the headwaters to the mouth of the river." To use the Service's example: "At its source downstream of Lake Itasca in Minnesota, the Mississippi River is 18 feet wide and can be waded—[whereas] about

1,300 miles downstream, south of Cairo, Illinois, the Mississippi is more than 3,500 feet wide." . . .

The Service emphasized that a key benefit of its linear-scaling approach was to mimic not just the *quantity* of water being released from the Oakdale Dam but also the *timing* of those releases. . . . The Service explained that mussels can be adversely affected by "even relatively brief episodes of inadequate flow downstream." And according to the Service, low-flow data between 2012 and 2014 shows that, prior to the issuance of the Service's Technical Assistance Letter, NIPSCO routinely permitted "dramatic" and "highly unnatural" fluctuations in flow out of the dam. The Service's recommendation aimed to avoid inadequate water flows by ensuring a particular amount of outflow during low-flow periods. . . .

The Coalition also presses a legal objection to the Biological Opinion and the Commission's reliance on it. By regulation, the Fish and Wildlife Service requires that the "reasonable and prudent measures" it proposes to reduce incidental take cannot work more than a "minor change" in the proposed agency action. 50 C.F.R. § 402.14(i)(2). The Coalition contends that, by requiring water flow measures that accord with its linear scaling model and that can materially reduce the level of Lake Freeman during low-flow events, the Service's reasonable and prudent measure is a major change, in violation of that regulation. Because neither the Service nor the Commission adequately explained why the Service's reasonable and prudent measure qualified as a minor change, we conclude that the agencies acted in an arbitrary manner, and we remand this issue for consideration by the agencies in the first instance. . . .

NIPSCO argues that the appropriate remedy for any agency error in this case is to remand without vacating either the Incidental Take Statement or the Commission's orders. NIPSCO explains that if the Incidental Take Statement were vacated, NIPSCO would lose the legal protection from Endangered Species Act liability that its compliance with that Statement currently provides. And if the Commission's orders are vacated, NIPSCO will be required to revert to maintaining Lake Freeman at a stable elevation, trapping it once again between the Scylla and Charybdis of violating its Commission license or violating the Endangered Species Act.

We agree with NIPSCO that remand without vacatur is warranted. . . . It is possible that the Commission and the Service "can redress [their] failure of explanation on remand while reaching the same result." *Black Oak Energy, LLC v. FERC*, 725 F.3d 230, 244 (D.C. Cir. 2013). And the conflicting regulatory obligations that vacatur would leave NIPSCO betwixt and between also favor remand without vacatur. *Cf. Oglala Sioux Tribe v. United States Nuclear Regulatory Comm'n*, 896 F.3d 520, 538 (D.C. Cir. 2018) (declining to vacate operating license when licensee had reasonably relied on agency ruling and faced grave economic harm if license were vacated).

NOTES AND QUESTIONS

1.   How should FERC evaluate the impact of dams on environmental interests? Does it make sense to engage in a cost-benefit analysis? For instance, should FERC weigh the benefits of hydroelectricity against harm to endangered mussels? How should it weigh impacts on mussels against the economic benefits associated with tourism and recreation? Or is some other approach better?

2.   Consider the conflict that arose between the two federal agencies in this case. Can you articulate each of their positions? How did FERC's ultimate decision resolve the conflict? How did the court evaluate the mandate of each agency's governing statute in its review of the FERC order amending NIPSCO's license? Did the court reach the right decision? Why or why not?

3.   In the face of a changing climate, drought is becoming more widespread, creating new uncertainties regarding the role of hydropower as a long-term, reliable source of renewable electricity in the United States and worldwide. What changes in management and approach may be necessary to continue to use the nation's hydropower resources? Do the current federal laws governing hydropower supply the tools needed to address these challenges?

4.   FREE-RIDING

Free-riding is the mirror image of the negative externality problem. It is created by positive externalities. Specifically, when an actor cannot capture all of the benefits that are generated from something it does, there is a risk that the activity will be underprovided in society. This is referred to as a "free-riding" problem because everyone else in society is able to take advantage of the action without paying for it—*i.e.*, for free—or without paying their fair share for the benefit they receive. For instance, a teenager who jumps the gate and takes the New York subway without paying is a "free rider."

The problem is also referred to as a "public good" problem in certain contexts, as the benefits created by the positive externality are public in nature. They are what economists call "non-excludable" because the actor providing them cannot stop others from consuming them, and they are "non-rivalrous," meaning that when one person benefits from the good, that consumption does not reduce the amount of the good available to others. Common examples of public goods include street lighting, national defense, government R&D, and beautiful gardens.

Free-riding problems abound in energy. You may be familiar with the "I drink your milkshake" scene from the movie *There Will Be Blood,* loosely based upon Upton Sinclair's 1927 novel *Oil!.* The issue presented is a free-rider problem known as "The Tragedy of the Commons," or the overconsumption of a common pool resource. One oil developer can reduce the total amount of oil available to all by drilling and overproducing on the land before others can do the same.

Free riding problems are contentious in the context of decisions regarding how electric utilities within a multi-state region should share the costs of new, long-distance electric transmission lines that benefit all utility customers as precise cost allocation is difficult to quantify. In attempting to address these concerns, FERC issued an important order, Order 1000 (discussed in Chapter 5), that defines free-riders as "entities who are being subsidized by those who pay the costs of the benefits that free riders receive for nothing. . . ." Order No. 1000–A ¶ 578, 77 Fed. Reg. at 32,274. According to FERC, in the electric transmission line development context, free riders "do not bear cost responsibility for benefits that they receive in their use of the transmission grid. . . ." *Id.* at ¶ 576, 77 Fed. Reg. at 32,273; *see also El Paso Elec. Co. v. FERC*, 832 F.3d 495, 499 (5th Cir. 2016).

Similarly, transmission and distribution operators in Europe and the United States have complained that customers with rooftop solar PV are free-riding because they underpay for the use of electric transmission and distribution lines and related grid infrastructure needed to ensure reliable power when the sun is not shining. A common dispute in utility rate design is "cross-subsidization"—arguments by one class of customers that they are paying more than their fair share of the system costs, and thus, cross-subsidizing another class of customers. In that context, "cross-subsidization" is simply another name for "free-riding."

The case excerpt below explores the "cross-subsidization" aspects of free-riding in the context of rooftop PV supported by a "net metering" policy. As explained in more detail in later chapters, "net metering" takes account of the flow of electricity both to and from a customer's site when the customer's solar panels are generating electricity and credits the customer's account. When a customer's generation exceeds its use, the excess electricity from the customer site flows back to the electric grid, offsetting the customer's electricity consumption at a later time (for instance, when the sun is not shining and the solar panels are not generating electricity). Thus, net metering policies credit such customers for the excess electricity they produce, up to the total amount they consume from the system in a given time period.

Many states require utilities to offer net metering, but policies differ on how many customers can participate, how large the rooftop solar system can be, and what price the utility will credit to the customer for electricity produced. Altogether, as of 2021, 39 states had net metering policies in place for some utilities, six states offered some kind of distributed generation compensation other than net metering, and two were in transition to some other kind of distributed generation compensation. Only three states had no net metering or distributed generation rules in place. *See Status of Net Metering Reforms*, DSIRE INSIGHT (May 25, 2021).

As U.S. adoption of rooftop solar has increased rapidly, concerns about free-riding and cross-subsidization have grown. Disputes over whether— and if so, in what form—to continue net metering policies abound. *See, e.g.,* Edward Klump & Jeffrey Tomich, *4 Solar Fights Critical for 100% Clean Electricity*, ENERGYWIRE (Dec. 1, 2021). Typically, utilities and consumer groups argue that solar customers are not paying their "fair share" of the fixed costs of the electric grid because of their significantly reduced electric bills, and that these benefits mainly go to wealthier customers who can afford the upfront costs to install rooftop solar. By contrast, solar users, the solar industry, and many environmental groups counter that rooftop solar is a grid asset because it provides carbon-free energy, reduces "peak load" during the summer, and consequently reduces costs for all the utility's customers.

MATTER OF WESTAR ENERGY, INC.
460 P.3d 821 (Kan. 2020)

The opinion of the court was delivered by STEGALL, J.:

In 2018, claiming declining sales and rising costs, Westar Energy, Inc. and Kansas Gas and Electric Company (Utilities) applied to the Kansas Corporation Commission (Commission) for a rate increase. The application included a proposed net rate increase of $52.6 million a year, as well as changes in the residential rate design. . . .

[T]he Utilities have traditionally "recovered the costs of providing electricity through a two-part rate involving a flat service charge and a variable energy charge based on the number of kilowatt hours (kWh) used in a monthly billing period." The Utilities, however, don't recover all their fixed costs through the flat service charge and have opted instead to fold some of those fixed costs into the variable energy charge. "A utility company could apportion its fixed costs among its customers at a flat rate and limit the variable rate to the recovery of actual generation costs, but utilities have traditionally sought to recover fixed costs through the variable rate as an incentive for customers to exercise prudent energy consumption."

This same interplay between designing a sound economic model of electricity generation and delivery, on the one hand, and promoting a policy of responsible energy production and use, on the other, is at the heart of today's dispute. This is because some of the Utilities' customers are less dependent than others on the primarily fossil-fueled electricity sold by the Utilities. These customers are known as "partial requirements customers" or "residential distributed generation customers" (DG customers) because they generate their own electricity from a renewable source such as wind or the sun.

Still connected to the utility grid, so-called DG customers have always paid the flat service charge, just like everyone else. But as a class, they use less utility generated electricity and thus the variable energy portion of their utility bills is lower. In fact, in some cases, if the DG customer is generating more electricity than they use and selling the excess back to the grid, the variable energy portion of the bill may amount to a net-zero.

According to the Utilities, this has created what is sometimes referred to in economic parlance as a "free rider" problem. Malm, *An Actions-Based Estimate of the Free Rider Fraction in Electric Utility DSM Programs*, 17 The Energy Journal No. 3, 41 (1996) (defining free riders as individuals who impose costs on the system without providing benefits such as payment). As one study, procured by the Utilities and made part of the record before the Commission, put it:

> When a customer conserves energy, the utility produces less energy, and thus incurs less energy production cost (e.g. fuel or purchased power). This should amount to a dollar-for-dollar savings for both the customer and the utility. However, when a customer conserves energy, the utility does not incur lower fixed costs, like capital investments in power plants (production demand), or substations and poles (distribution demand), or meters, billing, or customer service representatives (customer). When some customers are able to reduce their energy consumption by installing DG they avoid paying fixed costs that the utility continues to incur to provide the customer with needed services. Ultimately, those costs will be shifted to customers that do not have DG, resulting in a hidden subsidy from non-DG to DG customers.

To remedy this alleged economic imbalance, the Utilities sought and obtained approval of a new rate structure applicable only to DG customers—the residential distributed generation (RS-DG) rate design. . . . Two of the objecting intervenors—the Sierra Club and Vote Solar (Renewable Energy Advocates)—appealed the Commission's action to the Court of Appeals.

All along, the Utilities' arguments have been driven by their view that the ongoing viability of their economic model depends on fixing the inequities created by DG customers not paying their "fair share." Of course, the overall rate structure chosen by the Utilities—which puts a portion of fixed costs into the variable energy charge—is itself designed to incentivize reduced energy consumption. As such, one would be justified in wondering whether the free rider problem identified by the Utilities is a feature of the system rather than a bug (because lower energy users will necessarily pay a smaller per-unit share of the fixed costs).

In any event, though we are not insensible to the economic arguments, we find that in this particular case we can move past them with relative ease. This is because the policy favoring customers who generate a portion of their own energy from renewable sources was chosen by the policy makers in our Legislature and is cemented in Kansas law. And interpreting and enforcing statutes as they are written is the job of this court, not deciding whether those statutes effect good or bad policy.

Distributed generation systems are not new. On the heels of several energy and oil shortages in the 1970s, President Jimmy Carter and his administration confronted America's crisis relationship with fossil fuels. President Carter addressed the nation several times reiterating the need for "strict conservation" and the use of "permanent renewable energy sources like solar power" to protect the environment, achieve economic growth, and gain independence as a country. Carter, *The Energy Problem*, Address to the Nation (April 18, 1977), *in* 1 Public Papers of the Presidents of the United States: Jimmy Carter 656, 657 (1977); *see also* Tomain, *The Dominant Model of United States Energy Policy*, 61 U. Colo. L. Rev. 355, 369–72 (1990) (highlighting President Carter's energy addresses and legislative developments). President Carter described these efforts as the " 'moral equivalent of war.' " Carter, at 656. To show dedication to the cause, he even installed solar panels on the White House. *See* Outka, *Environmental Law and Fossil Fuels: Barriers to Renewable Energy*, 65 Vand. L. Rev. 1679, 1691 (2012).

At the same time, growing concerns that fossil fuels were contributing to global climate change also began to drive efforts to incentivize conservation and alternative-source energy generation. "In general, the process of balancing energy and environmental objectives has been a common theme underlying many of the major actions of Congress, the courts, the executive branch, and the independent agencies during the past year." *Report of Committee on the Environment*, 1 Energy L.J. 119 (1980). . . .

This history is significant not because it is (or is not) dispositive of the underlying claims about fossil fuels and their relative benefit or harm to society, but because it describes the political, economic, and cultural context within which Kansas law developed. States such as Kansas responded in this historical moment by developing their own conservation programs. . . . Thus, in 1980, the Kansas Legislature enacted K.S.A. 66–117d, L. 1980, ch. 201, § 1:

"No electric or gas utility providing electrical or gas service in this state shall consider the use of any renewable energy source other than nuclear by a customer as a basis for establishing higher rates or charges for any service or commodity sold to such customer nor shall any such utility subject any customer utilizing any renewable energy source other than nuclear to any other prejudice or disadvantage on account of the use of any such renewable energy source."

Contrary to the Utilities' current economic arguments, at least at the time K.S.A. 66–117d was enacted, there was a widely held belief that incentivizing consumer generation of electricity was economically beneficial to the entire electric generation system. The basic idea was that "[p]roperly designed and integrated solar devices" would "reduce consumers' need for electricity during peak demand periods" which would in turn allow "utilities to achieve load management control." Lawrence & Minan, *Financing Solar Energy Development Through Public Utilities*, 50 Geo. Wash. L. Rev. 371, 378 (1982). . . .

The Utilities in this case appear to have given up on the economic promise once attached to the private generation of electricity from renewable resources. Indeed, the Utilities admitted at oral argument that under their proposed RS-DG rate design, DG customers will pay more for their electricity than other customers and that, considered in isolation, this violates K.S.A. 66–117d. But the Utilities argue K.S.A. 66–117d is invalid and cannot be applied to the RS-DG rate design because it conflicts with a more recent statute—K.S.A. 66–1265(e). And, being the more recent statute, the Utilities argue that K.S.A. 66–1265(e) preempts K.S.A. 66–117d and allows the Utilities to charge more to DG customers than they do to non-DG customers—all for providing the same services and selling the same energy.

Under K.S.A. 66–1265(e):

"Each utility shall: . . .

> "(e) for any customer-generator which began operating its renewable energy resource under an interconnect agreement with the utility on or after July 1, 2014, have the option to propose, within an appropriate rate proceeding, the application of time-of-use rates, minimum bills or other rate structures that would apply to all such customer-generators prospectively."

We must now determine whether the RS-DG rate design violates Kansas law. . . . Our review of the Commission's actions requires us to interpret both K.S.A. 66–117d and K.S.A. 66–1265(e). Interpretation of a statute is a question of law over which we exercise plenary review. *Midwest*

Crane & Rigging, LLC v. Kansas Corporation Comm'n, 397 P.3d 1205 (Kan. 2017).

. . . When interpreting and comparing K.S.A. 66–117d and K.S.A. 66–1265(e), we abide by the most fundamental rule of statutory interpretation—that the intent of the Legislature governs if that intent can be ascertained. *Harsay v. University of Kansas*, 430 P.3d 30 (Kan. 2018). In ascertaining this intent, we begin with the plain language of the statute, giving common words their ordinary meaning. *Nauheim v. City of Topeka*, 432 P.3d 647 (Kan. 2019). We will only review legislative history or use canons of construction if the statute's language or text is unclear or ambiguous. 432 P.3d 647.

Under this plain language analysis, we can discern no conflict between the statutes. On the one hand, K.S.A. 66–117d is an antidiscrimination provision that prohibits utilities from charging DG customers a higher price than non-DG customers for the same service. K.S.A. 66–117d focuses on the price of the goods and services sold by the Utilities. On the other hand, K.S.A. 66–1265(e) addresses rate structure rather than price. K.S.A. 66–1265(e) allows utilities to propose separate rate structures that would apply to all DG customers that began generating their own electricity after 2014. The Utilities argue that K.S.A. 66–1265(e)'s language permits utilities to charge DG customers a higher price than they charge to non-DG customers, reasoning that a change in rate structure necessarily impacts price. And this means the two statutes conflict, evincing a legislative desire to repeal K.S.A. 66–117d.

But while it is clearly true that a change in rate structure could impact the ultimate price charged by Utilities for providing their goods and services, we can imagine a rate structure change that would not result in price discrimination against DG customers. The two statutes can coexist. . . .

By glossing over this price versus structure distinction, both the Utilities and the Court of Appeals effectively write K.S.A. 66–117d out of the books. This runs contrary to a bedrock principle of statutory interpretation that " '[r]epeal by implication is not favored.' " *In re City of Wichita*, 59 P.3d 336 (Kan. 2002) . . . .

By its plain text, K.S.A. 66–117d clearly prohibits the Utilities from price discrimination against DG customers, something the Utilities admit they are trying to do. By its plain text, K.S.A. 66–1265(e) authorizes the Utilities to apply alternative rate structures to DG customers. Examples of such rate structures given in the statute are "time-of-use rates" or "minimum bills." But there is nothing in K.S.A. 66–1265(e) suggesting that such a rate structure does not also have to comply with the price nondiscrimination provisions of K.S.A. 66–117d. In other words, while utilities may try to alter the rate structure applicable to DG customers, they must do so within the larger context of a nondiscriminatory price regime. . . .

Here, the proposed rate does not reflect an added service justifying a higher cost. The Utilities want to impose a mandatory three-part rate design for DG customers as opposed to the two-part rate design applied to non-DG customers. Both rate designs include a basic service fee and a kilowatt hour energy charge. The three-part rate design, however, adds an additional "demand charge" for DG customers. This demand charge includes a flat fee of $3 in the winter and $9 in the summer. There is no question that the RS-DG rate at issue here is not built on a time-of-use rate or a minimum bill. It is simply price discrimination. And this price discrimination undermines the policy preferences of our Legislature—as expressed in K.S.A. 66–117d—which has codified the goal of incentivizing renewable energy production by private parties as we have already described.

We can think of several ways the Utilities could attempt to reduce or eliminate their economic "free rider" problem without creating a regime of price discrimination. For example, the Utilities could simply restructure their rates so that their fixed costs are fully recovered by the flat fee charged to each customer hooked to the grid. Alternatively, the Utilities could impose a nondiscriminatory time-of-use rate, or a sliding scale rate that decreased the per-unit price as the customer purchased a higher volume of energy—thus rewarding high volume purchasers. Of course it is beyond the scope of this opinion to predict whether these alternative price schemes would clear either the political or legal hurdles they might face. These examples simply illustrate that price discrimination is not the only way to achieve an equitable market for the sale of electricity within statutory parameters. Our decision today does not impose any restrictions on the Utilities' and Commission's economic judgments concerning how best to structure the generation and sale of electricity other than the restriction imposed by the Kansas Legislature in K.S.A. 66–117d. . . .

NOTES AND QUESTIONS

1.   Who are the free riders in *Matter of Westar Energy*? Are you sure? For an in-depth discussion of free riding arguments in state policies relating to distributed solar, energy efficiency, and EV charging infrastructure see Alexandra B. Klass, *Regulating the Energy "Free Riders,"* 100 B.U. L. REV. 581 (2020).

2.   Is it fair to compensate rooftop solar owners at the full retail rate that residential customers pay the utility for electricity? Would your answer be the same if you knew that the utility could purchase "utility-scale" solar energy on the wholesale market at a fraction of the cost? *See, e.g.,* ENERGY INFO. ADMIN.,

ALTERNATIVE POLICIES—UTILITY RATE STRUCTURE (Mar. 2020); Dan Gearino, *Solar Industry Wins Big in Kentucky Ruling*, INSIDE CLIMATE NEWS (May 20, 2021). The question of how to appropriately compensate rooftop solar owners for the electricity they generate and send back to the grid is discussed in more detail in Chapters 4 and 8.

3. Another common free-riding problem is energy technology innovation. Because innovators and early adopters of clean energy technology cannot capture all the benefits of creating and using these technologies, both their development and their deployment are suboptimal in society. An example of this is vehicle fuel efficiency—one car company invests time and money to improve the fuel economy of its vehicles and then other car companies can adopt that technology without the same level of expenditures. This free-riding problem is the target of the federally mandated Corporate Average Fuel Economy (CAFE) standards, discussed in detail in Chapter 6.

CHAPTER 3

EXTRACTION OF NATURAL RESOURCES FOR ENERGY

■ ■ ■

A. OVERVIEW

This chapter focuses on the legal issues surrounding how we obtain the sources of energy introduced in Chapter 2. As described there, each source has physical characteristics that affect how it is extracted and the environmental and social impacts of that extraction. Moreover, as technology evolves, we can extract previously inaccessible energy resources, but also face new risks that accompany this resource production.

The chapter reviews issues regarding the extraction of both fossil fuel and renewable energy sources. Specifically, it examines coal, oil, natural gas, hydropower, wind, and solar resources. It does not cover nuclear energy, which is covered in depth in Chapter 10. Similarly, more recent extraction techniques such as hydraulic fracturing, offshore oil and gas drilling, and offshore wind development are addressed in Chapter 9. Finally, biofuels are covered in Chapter 6 with vehicle transportation.

Across these different energy resources, with their specific legal regimes, issues of markets, federalism, and the energy-environment interface arise. For example, changing prices, extraction technology, physical location of resources, and regulatory restrictions affect which resources are taken out of the ground, as well as how and where they are extracted. Complex federalism regimes create conflicts between states and the federal government about which one is the decisionmaker, and similar conflicts arise between state and local governments. Conflicts also arise between public and private parties. For all these resources, their extraction creates local externalities, which raise concerns for those living nearby. The chapter highlights these issues as it considers how a mix of statutory and common law at different levels of government regulates the extraction of these resources.

B. FOSSIL FUEL SOURCES

As described in depth in Chapter 2, coal, oil, and natural gas continue to provide the vast majority of energy in the United States and around the world. However, they are obtained through different methods governed by different legal regimes. This section first describes the law pertinent to coal extraction and then turns to oil and natural gas.

1. COAL

Coal has long been a core source of energy in the United States, although its use has decreased substantially in recent years, declining over 60% since 2008. By 2020, coal contributed less than 20% of total U.S. electricity generation and only 10% of total U.S. energy consumption. *See, e.g., Less Electricity Was Generated by Coal Than Nuclear in the United States in 2020*, ENERGY INFO. ADMIN. (Mar. 18, 2021); *What is U.S. Electricity Generation by Energy Source?,* Energy Info. Admin. (last updated Mar. 5, 2021). Regulating coal extraction is complicated by (1) difficult questions over ownership rights on private land, (2) significant extraction taking place on public land, and (3) conflicts under the existing federal regime over whether federal or state governments should have control over extraction.

In all three of these areas, concerns over the serious environmental and health impacts of coal mining and its waste products arise. As discussed in Chapter 2, coal extraction, especially surface mining, has environmental costs through landscape disruption and tailings. Over time, these costs can grow, as tailings enter the water system and old mines produce acid drainage, damaging streams, rivers, and lakes. Throughout this discussion, the section considers how these concerns interact with extraction disputes.

Coal mining also interacts with labor concerns, as coal miners often have faced treacherous conditions that produced deadly accidents and long-term health consequences. The chapter does not address these labor issues in depth, but more information on the evolution of the laws governing worker health and safety is available in *Legislative History of U.S. Mine Safety and Health*, U.S. Dep't of Labor.

As discussed in Chapter 2, the United States has the largest coal reserves and resources in the world, with five states—Wyoming, West Virginia, Pennsylvania, Illinois, and Kentucky—constituting over 71% of U.S. coal production. MELISSA N. DIAZ, CONG. RSCH. SERV., U.S. ENERGY IN THE 21ST CENTURY: A PRIMER 16 (Mar. 16, 2021). Approximately 41% of total domestic coal production came from federal lands in 2019, primarily in the western United States, with the remainder from nonfederal lands. *See, e.g.,* CONG., RSCH. SERV., FEDERAL LANDS AND RELATED RESOURCES: OVERVIEW AND SELECTED ISSUES FOR THE 117TH CONGRESS 15 (Feb. 16, 2021). This section explores common ownership disputes over coal extraction on private lands, followed by a discussion of the laws governing the leasing of coal on federal lands.

a. Ownership Disputes on Private Lands

The property rights surrounding coal extraction have been contentious because those rights frequently are divided among different people on any given tract of land. For example, in Pennsylvania, where the following case is based, as well as in virtually all states with significant oil, gas, or coal resources, different people or companies may own the rights to the coal, the surface land, and support for the surface land. These "split estate" property questions are further complicated as extraction methods vary in the externalities that they create. Shaft mining, which takes place underground, causes fewer impacts on the surface land than surface mining (also known as "strip mining"), where surface layers are removed as part of the mining process. The following case explores the confluence of a dispute over divided property rights, based on the desire to strip mine.

STEWART V. CHERNICKY
266 A.2d 259 (Pa. 1970)

Before Bell, C.J., and Jones, Cohen, Eagen, O'Brien, Roberts, and Pomeroy, JJ.

EAGEN, JUSTICE.

This action results from an alleged unauthorized strip mining of a portion of a tract of land by Peter Chernicky and E. G. Kriebel, Trading as C & K Coal Company (C & K Company), a partnership.

The tract consists of 21 1/4 acres located in Perry Township, Clarion County. By deed dated December 8, 1902, the then owner, D. W. Bartow, granted and conveyed to Horace A. Noble et al., all the coal in and under the tract with the right to remove the same without liability for injury to the surface. Bartow retained ownership of the surface. On the dates here involved, the Thomas M. Stewart Estate, as Bartow's successor in title, was the owner of the surface. Vincent C. Conner and Lois Conner, as successors in title to Noble et al., were the owners of the coal. C & K Company was the lessee of the coal rights vested in the Conners.

The tract was remote, uncultivated woodland, not easily accessible, and its boundaries were not clearly distinguishable from those of the surrounding lands. It was but one of 33 separate properties which the Conners had leased to the C & K Company in a single document dated March 8, 1962. The Conners owned both the surface and the coal rights in a portion of these, while in others they owned only the coal. In the lease this particular tract (the Stewart Tract) had been designated the "V. C. Conner Tract (Coal)," leading some to believe the Conners owned both the surface and the coal. C & K Company never had it or the land adjacent to it surveyed, whereby the divided ownership might have been realized. As a result of these circumstances, six or seven acres of it were stripped in

1963 without the consent of the Stewart Estate, causing extensive damage to the surface. The Stewart Estate instituted this action seeking damages from C & K Company and the Conners. At trial, the jury returned a verdict in favor of the plaintiff and against all defendants in the amount of $10,200. Motions for judgment notwithstanding the verdict or a new trial were filed by all defendants. The court below granted the motions for judgment n.o.v. The Stewart Estate appealed.

The central issue is: Did the C & K Company have the right to remove the coal under the land involved by the strip mining method without liability for injury to or destruction of the surface, regardless who owned that surface, or was such removal to be limited to shaft or deep mining? In the latter situation, the C & K Company would be liable for what occurred.

A party engaged in strip mining must either own (or lease from one who owns) both the estate of coal and the surface estate Or own (or lease from one who owns) a coal estate which includes the right to employ the strip mining method, for such a process entails the actual stripping away of the outer covering of the terrain.

Any interest and rights that the C & K Company has in the tract of land in issue derives from the lease it obtained from the Conners on March 8, 1962. Such lease contains the following pertinent provisions:

> Nothing herein or hereinafter contained shall be construed as warranting the said leased premises or the quantity or quality of the coal that may be found in the thirty-three tracts listed under Exhibit "A" herein.

> Subject to the exceptions, reservations, covenants and conditions referred to in the preceding paragraph hereof, lessors do hereby grant and let unto lessees, All mining rights which Lessors now have in and upon the real estate described in Exhibit "A" hereto annexed.

> It is expressly understood and agreed between the parties hereto, that as to those parcels or tracts of land set forth in Exhibit "A" in which lessors do not own surface that lessors intend to grant hereby Only such mining rights in such lands as lessors may actually have or own therein. (Emphasis added.)

The land in issue is admittedly one of the thirty-three tracts listed in Exhibit "A" of the above lease. This lease, in effect if not in form, is a quitclaim deed of all the mining rights of which the lessors were seized in the above tract. The interest and rights of the C & K Company in the specific tract in issue are thus co-extensive with those previously possessed by its lessors, the Conners.

The Conners clearly owned only the coal under the tract. Therefore, any right which the C & K Company might have had to strip mine this property must derive from the coal estate alone. To determine the nature and extent of this estate, which had been carved from the fee, reference must be made to the deed of severance wherein the separation in ownership occurred. This was the deed of December 8, 1902, *supra*.

This deed, after granting and conveying title to the coal in and under the tract to the Conners' predecessors in title, stated in pertinent part:

> Together with the right of ingress, egress and regress over and through said lands for the purpose of Mining, storing, manufacturing and removing said coal and such other coal as may be now owned or hereafter acquired by the said second parties, their heirs or assigns; Also the right to drain and Ventilate said mines by shafts or otherwise and to deposit the waste from said mines, and to build roads and structures with the necessary curtilege (sic) for said purposes; With a full release of and without liability for damages for injury to the surface, waters or otherwise arising From any of said Operations.
>
> Together with all and singular the said property, rights, privileges, hereditaments, and appurtenances whatsoever thereunto belonging or in anywise appertaining, and the reversion and the remainders thereof, and all the estate, right, title, interest, property, claim and demand whatsoever of the said party of the first part, in law, equity or otherwise howsoever of, in and to the said coal, coal space, mining rights, and Release of damages. (Emphasis added.)

In construing this deed, it is the intention of the parties at the time of the transaction that governs, and such intention is to be gathered from a reading of the entire deed. If the deed is ambiguous, then all of the attending circumstances existing at the time of the execution of the instrument should be considered to aid in determining the apparent object of the parties.

There is no express intent of the parties in this deed concerning the means by which the coal granted was to be mined, neither strip mining nor deep mining being specifically mentioned. The deed merely refers to "mining" in general. The intent of the parties must therefore be implied. . . .

In this regard, this Court recognizes that "strip mining is an accepted Manner or Method of coal mining, which, with the use of modern huge and efficient machinery, has become progressively more in vogue." *Mt. Carmel Railroad Co. v. M. A. Hanna Co.*, 371 Pa. at 240, 89 A.2d at 512, *supra*. And this Court does not wish to interfere with its use or hinder its economic viability. Yet we cannot help but realize that "in view of the surface violence, destruction and disfiguration which inevitably attend strip or open mining, * * * no land owner would lightly or casually grant strip mining rights, nor would any purchaser of land treat lightly any reservation of mining rights which would permit the grantor or his assignee to come upon his land and turn it into a battleground with strip mining". *Rechez Bros., Inc. v. Duricka*, 374 Pa. at 265, 97 A.2d at 826, *supra*. Therefore, "the burden rests upon him who seeks to assert the right to destroy or injure the surface" (*Merrill v. Manufacturers Light and Heat Co.*, 409 Pa. at 73, 185 A.2d at 576, *supra*) to show some positive indication that the parties to the deed agreed to authorize practices which may result in these consequences. Particularly is this so where such operations were not common at the time the deed was executed.

The most critical clause in the above deed relevant to the method of mining authorized is: "also the right to drain and ventilate said mines by shafts or otherwise * * *." Ventilating is a feature only of shaft or deep mining. Yet this particular clause begins with "also," which could imply that to ventilate was an additional right to those already previously granted rather than a word of limitation. Such an interpretation, however, fails to take into account that "ventilate" refers to "said mines." This seems to connote that the mines for which provisions were made in prior clauses were expected to require ventilation, leading to the conclusion that the parties contemplated shaft mining.

Under this interpretation, the clause in the deed of severance granting a "full release of and without liability for injury to the surface, waters, or otherwise" would not relieve the C & K Company of liability. It is a limited release from liability, because it is only applicable if the injury arises "from any of the said operations." If there is only the right to shaft or deep mine, the reference to "said operations" limits the release to damages caused by such shaft or deep mining. It would not be applicable to damage caused by the use of strip mining processes.

Yet, it is argued, this deed was a Grant of certain mineral rights rather than a reservation of such rights. "If a person grants a portion of his property to another and the grant is susceptible of more than one interpretation, the words of the grant are to be construed most strongly against the grantor and more favorably to the grantee * * * unless, of course, the grantee drafted the grant and was therefore responsible for the ambiguity." *New Charter Coal Co. v. McKee*, 411 Pa. at 312, 191 A.2d at 833, *supra*; accord, *Merrill v. Manufacturers Light and Heat Co.*, *supra*. Therefore, it is urged that doubts should be resolved so as to enlarge the rights of the grantee, which in this case means resolving ambiguities in favor of permitting strip mining.

This factor does distinguish this case from *Rochez Bros., Inc. v. Duricka*, *supra*, since the language there construed by the Court was contained in a Reservation rather than a grant. Yet, although these rules of construction are valuable aids of interpretation, they ought not to be so liberally applied as to make a contract for the parties that they did not intend to make between themselves.

The right to mine and remove coal by deeds conveying land in language peculiarly applicable to underground mining does not include the right to remove such coal by strip mining methods. *Rochez Bros., Inc. v. Duricka, supra.* Nor will a mere authorization to "mine," without more, encompass the right to strip mine, for the reasons expressed before. The jury apparently concluded that the C & K Company had not met its burden of establishing a right to strip mine, either by the plain meaning of the words of the deed or by the interpretation of those words in the light of the surrounding circumstances at the time of the execution of the deed. This conclusion of the jury was a permissible one in the circumstances, and we find it was error to have set aside that verdict by the granting of a judgment non obstante veredicto. . . .

NOTES AND QUESTIONS

1.   Do you agree with the court's distinction between authorizing shaft and surface mining? Should the extent to which extraction methods create surface damage matter in construing property rights grants in contracts? In what situations, if any, might it be appropriate to construe a broader authorization?

2.   Courts have varied from state to state and over time regarding whether they construe a deed to the underlying mineral estate as allowing surface mining as well. Compare the outcome in this case, for example, with that in *Martin v. Kentucky Oak Mining Company*, 429 S.W.2d 395 (Ky. 1968), in which the court reached the opposite result and construed the deed more broadly. The evolution of Kentucky case law in the decades since that opinion shows a notable shift in views toward surface mining. Almost twenty years later, the Kentucky Supreme Court upheld the decision's broad construction of the deeds to include surface mining, but overruled the earlier opinion's approach to damages, allowing damages for the harms from surface mining. *See Akers v. Baldwin*, 736 S.W.2d 294 (Ky. 1987). A few years later, the Kentucky courts fully overruled *Martin*, and ceased interpreting broad form deeds to permit surface mining. *See Ward v. Harding*, 860 S.W.2d 280 (Ky. 1993).

3.   These questions about how to construe property rights in relation to surface mining represent only one area in which property disputes have occurred concerning coal extraction. For example, there have been disputes over how to handle subsidence—when mining coal causes the land above the coal mine to collapse. Initially, the U.S. Supreme Court was skeptical about whether states could pass laws limiting mining that risked subsidence without providing compensation. In *Pennsylvania Coal Co. v. Mahon*, 260 U.S. 393 (1922), the Supreme Court ruled that such a law—the Kohler Act—constituted an unconstitutional taking of private property, explaining: "The general rule at least is that while property may be regulated to a certain extent, if

regulation goes too far it will be recognized as a taking." *Id.* at 415. Over time, the Supreme Court became more accepting of this type of regulation. Years later, in *Keystone Bituminous Coal Assoc. v. DeBenedictis*, 480 U.S. 470 (1987), for example, the Supreme Court upheld the Pennsylvania Subsidence Act's requirement that half of the coal beneath particular structures be left in the ground to provide surface support after coal companies challenged the law as an unconstitutional taking. *See id.*

b. Coal Leasing on Federal Land

Coal mining on federal public land, primarily in the western United States, also raises complex legal questions. Unlike coal mining operations in the eastern United States, which historically used a combination of underground and surface mining practices, coal mining in the western United States is dominated by surface mining. There are several different types of surface mining where coal is removed from surface outcrops or where the overburden (over-lying rock) is removed to extract the coal including: (1) contour mining, which is surface mining along sloping terrain and (2) area mining where a large "box" of overburden is removed to extract the coal and the overburden is then placed in the previous "box" to remediate the area.

Approximately half of U.S. coal comes from surface mines, and much of that underlies federal public lands in the West. For a video of the largest coal mine, Black Thunder Mine in Wyoming, see, http://www.youtube.com/watch?v=2LQwxTm94Ps. Until the early 1900s, federal land and mineral policy was to dispose of lands in the public domain by selling them outright in fee simple. However, several statutes enacted in the homesteading era of the early 1900s required the United States to retain coal and other mineral resources, conveying only the surface estate to private parties. In 1920, Congress enacted the Mineral Leasing Act, 30 U.S.C. §§ 181, *et seq.* to govern the private exploration, development, and removal of coal and other fuel minerals. The Mineral Leasing Act authorizes the Secretary of the Interior, through the Bureau of Land Management (BLM), to lease coal and other subsurface mineral rights for development. Congress has amended the Mineral Leasing Act through the Federal Coal Leasing Act Amendments Act of 1976 to address, among other things, competitive leasing, diligent development, and BLM's receipt of fair market value of use of public resources. Federal regulations governing coal leasing are at 43 C.F.R. 3000 and 3400. Today, all federal coal is issued through competitive leasing, except for preference right lease applications submitted prior to the Federal Coal Leasing Amendments Act of 1976 or modifications to existing leases. For additional detail on the laws and regulations governing federal coal leasing, see Michael R. Drysdale, *Farewell to Coal?*, 62 ROCKY MT. MIN. L. INST. 17–1 (2016).

The Mineral Leasing Act and the Mineral Leasing Act for Acquired Lands of 1947, 30 U.S.C. §§ 351, *et seq.*, give the BLM responsibility over approximately 570 million acres of the 700 million acres of mineral estate owned by the federal government where coal development is allowed. In some cases, the federal government owns the coal estate while states or private parties own the surface estate. For coal leases issued through the competitive leasing process, the federal government receives a statutory royalty rate of 12.5% for coal extracted using surface mining methods, and 8% for coal extracted using underground mining methods. *See generally* BRANDON S. TRACY, CONG. RSCH. SERV., POLICY TOPICS AND BACKGROUND RELATED TO MINING ON FEDERAL LANDS 8–9 (Mar. 19, 2020); *Coal Data*, BLM.

The federal government's practice of issuing leases to private companies to extract coal on federal public lands has led to disputes over how the BLM should conduct the leasing process, the factors that it should evaluate in issuing leases, and how economic and environmental impacts should be balanced. The next case—and the notes following it—explore some of these issues in the context of leases in the Powder River Basin in Wyoming and Montana, which today provides nearly half of the coal used to produce electricity in the United States. As is true of several of the cases excerpted in this chapter, the plaintiffs' primary legal claim is under the National Environmental Policy Act of 1969, 42 U.S.C. §§ 4321, *et seq.* (NEPA). As discussed in Chapter 1, NEPA requires federal agencies to evaluate the potential for significant environmental effects associated with "federal actions," which include federal funding, federal permits, federal leases, or other federal approvals of private projects. In recent years, opponents of federal approvals for a variety of fossil fuel projects—coal, oil, and gas leases; natural gas pipeline certificates; wetland permits; and the like—have used NEPA to require federal agencies to provide more detailed analyses of project impacts on future GHG emissions, other air pollution emissions, and land and water impacts prior to issuing project permits, leases, or other approvals. When successful, such claims can serve to delay projects, increase their costs, and in some cases, lead to their ultimate demise.

WILDEARTH GUARDIANS V. BLM
870 F.3d 1222 (10th Cir. 2017)

BRISCOE, CIRCUIT JUDGE.

Appellants WildEarth Guardians and Sierra Club (Plaintiffs) challenge the Bureau of Land Management's (BLM) decision to approve four coal leases in Wyoming's Powder River Basin. Plaintiffs brought an Administrative Procedure Act (APA) claim arguing that the BLM failed to comply with the National Environmental Policy Act (NEPA) when it concluded that issuing the leases would not result in higher national carbon dioxide emissions than would declining to issue them. The district court upheld the leases. We reverse and remand with instructions to the BLM to revise its Environmental Impact Statements (EISs) and Records of Decision (RODs). . . .

The Powder River Basin (PRB) region is the largest single contributor to United States' domestic coal production. In 2008, PRB coal represented 55.5% of the United States's surface-mined coal, and 38.5% of the country's total coal production. The BLM controls much of the region and is often in the business of approving mining infrastructure and issuing mining leases under the Federal Land Policy and Management Act (FLPMA), 43 U.S.C. §§ 1701–1787, the Mineral Leasing Act, 30 U.S.C. §§ 181–287, and BLM's own regulations and plans. See 43 C.F.R. §§ 1601.0–1610.8, 43 C.F.R. §§ 3400.0–3–3487.1.

At issue in this case are four coal tracts that extend the life of two existing surface mines near Wright, Wyoming: the Black Thunder mine and the North Antelope Rochelle mine. The four "Wright Area Leases" at issue here are North Hilight, South Hilight, North Porcupine, and South Porcupine. The tracts are also near, and partially within, the Thunder Basin National Grassland, a national forest.

Alone, the two existing mines account for approximately 19.7% of the United States's annual domestic coal production. The North and South Hilight leases will extend the life of the Black Thunder mine by approximately four years; the North and South Porcupine leases will extend the life of the North Antelope Rochelle mine by approximately nine years. Without these leases, the existing mines would cease operations after the currently leased reserves are depleted. . . . In total, the tracts at issue contain approximately two billion tons of recoverable coal.

Pursuant to NEPA, BLM prepared a Draft Environmental Impact Statement (DEIS) for the leases. In the DEIS, BLM compared its preferred action (denominated Alternative 2 in the DEIS) to a no action alternative in which none of the coal leases would be issued, as it was required to do under [Council on Environmental Quality] CEQ regulations. 40 C.F.R. § 1502.14. Regarding carbon dioxide emissions and impacts on climate change, BLM concluded that there was no appreciable difference between the United States's total carbon dioxide emissions under its preferred alternative and the no action alternative. BLM concluded that, even if it did not approve the proposed leases, the same amount of coal would be sourced from elsewhere, and thus there was no difference between the proposed action and the no action alternative in this respect.

BLM then received comments on the DEIS, including from Plaintiffs. WildEarth Guardians commented that BLM's conclusion on carbon dioxide emissions under the no action alternative was "at best a gross oversimplification, and at worst entirely impossible." They argued that if the tracts were not leased, "it will be very difficult for domestic coal mines," or international coal mines, to replace that quantity of coal at the same price, making "other sources of electricity," with lower carbon dioxide emissions rates, "more competitive with coal." WildEarth Guardians concluded that the authorization of the leases would have a significant effect on national carbon dioxide emissions as compared to the no action alternative, and that BLM therefore failed to adequately compare the alternatives. . . .

The BLM published its Final Environmental Impact Statement (FEIS) for the Wright Area Leases in July, 2010. The FEIS acknowledges some basic presumptions that no one in this litigation contests: the quantity of coal proposed in these leases would result in approximately 382 million tons of annual carbon dioxide emissions from electricity generation, which is the equivalent of roughly 6% of the United States's total emissions in 2008, anthropogenic carbon dioxide emissions contribute to climate change, climate change presents a litany of environmental harms disbursed throughout the globe, and if the nation's energy mix shifts towards non-coal energy sources, less carbon dioxide would be emitted.

However, the BLM's contested conclusion regarding comparative carbon dioxide emissions from the no action alternative remained in the FEIS:

> It is not likely that selection of the No Action alternative[ ] would result in a decrease of U.S. CO_2 emissions attributable to coal mining and coal-burning power plants in the longer term, because there are multiple other sources of coal that, while not having the cost, environmental, or safety advantages, could supply the demand for coal beyond the time that the Black Thunder . . . and North Antelope Rochelle mines complete recovery of the coal in their existing leases.

For purposes of this conclusion, the BLM "assum[ed] that all forms of electric generation would grow at a proportional rate to meet forecast electric demand" in 2010, 2015, and 2020. The FEIS relies on various governmental reports, including the EIA's Annual Energy Outlook reports from 2008, 2009, and 2010. Under these projections, coal's share of the energy mix continues to represent the largest portion of the United States's energy mix. The BLM predicted that overall demand for coal in the United States was predicted to grow during the life of the Wright Area Leases.

The BLM then concluded that, because overall demand for coal was predicted to increase, the effect on the supply of coal of the no action alternative would have no consequential impact on that demand. This long logical leap presumes that either the reduced supply will have no impact on price, or that any increase in price will not make other forms of energy more attractive and decrease coal's share of the energy mix, even slightly. . . .

Following the FEIS, BLM issued a ROD for each of the four tracts, deciding to offer them for lease. . . .

The Plaintiffs argue the BLM's substitution assumption rendered its comparison of the preferred alternative (issuing the leases) and the no action alternative arbitrary and capricious . . . because it lacks support in the administrative record and ignores basic supply and demand principles . . . . Plaintiffs argue that the FEIS and RODs therefore do not comply with NEPA and CEQ regulations and should be vacated. . . .

The Plaintiffs' . . . argument is persuasive. . . . The BLM did not point to any information (other than its own unsupported statements) indicating that the national coal deficit of 230 million tons per year incurred under the no action alternative could be easily filled from elsewhere, or at a comparable price. It did not refer to the nation's stores of coal or the rates at which those stores may be extracted. Nor did the BLM analyze the specific difference in price between PRB coal and other sources; such a price difference would [a]ffect substitutability. . . .

That this perfect substitution assumption lacks support in the record is enough for us to conclude that the analysis which rests on this assumption is arbitrary and capricious. True, "the mere presence of contradictory evidence does not invalidate the Agencies' actions or decisions." *Wyo. Farm Bureau Fed'n v. Babbitt*, 199 F.3d 1224, 1241 (10th Cir. 2000). If the agency is faced with conflicting evidence or interpretations, "[w]e cannot displace the agencies' choice between two conflicting views, even if we would have made a different choice had the matter been before us de novo." [citations omitted].

But this assumption nevertheless falls below the required level of data necessary to reasonably bolster the Bureau's choice of alternatives. A number of our cases discuss the quality of evidentiary support sufficient to avoid our concluding that a challenged NEPA analysis is arbitrary and capricious. The evidence must be sufficient in volume and quality to "sharply defin[e] the issues and provid[e] a clear basis for choice among options." *Citizens' Comm. to Save Our Canyons v. Krueger*, 513 F.3d 1169, 1179 (10th Cir. 2008) (quoting 40 C.F.R. § 1502.14); . . . Here, the blanket assertion that coal would be substituted from other sources, unsupported by hard data, does not provide "information sufficient to permit a reasoned choice" between the preferred alternative and no action alternative. It provided no information.

Even if we could conclude that the agency had enough data before it to choose between the preferred and no action alternatives, we would still conclude this perfect substitution assumption arbitrary and capricious because the assumption itself is irrational (i.e., contrary to basic supply and demand principles). . . .

In *Baltimore Gas & Electric Co. v. NRDC*, 462 U.S. 87 (1983), the Supreme Court upheld the Nuclear Regulatory Commission's conclusion that permanent nuclear waste storage would not have a significant environmental impact, which was based on the Commission's assumption that the waste repositories would perform perfectly. The Court upheld the agency's decision based on the zero release assumption after considering three factors: (1) it had a limited purpose in the overall environmental analysis, i.e., it was not the key to deciding between two alternatives; (2) overall, the agency's estimation of the environmental effects was overstated, so this single assumption did not determine the overall direction the NEPA analysis took; and (3) courts are most deferential to agency decisions based not just on "simple findings of fact," but in the agency's "special expertise, at the frontiers of science." *Id.* at 102–04.

Here, the BLM's substitution assumption appears to be quite different from the Commission's zero release assumption under the three factor analysis in *Baltimore Gas*. First, the BLM's perfect substitution assumption was key to the ultimate decision to open bidding on the leases. In each of the four RODs, the "Reasons for Decision" section first discusses the leases' effect on coal combustion in the nation overall, then lists the other facts that influenced its decision in bullet points. In each ROD, the discussion opens with the assertion that: "Denying this proposed coal leasing is not likely to affect current or future domestic coal consumption used for electric generation." Prioritizing the carbon emissions and global warming analysis in the RODs suggests that this question was critical to the decision to open the leases for bidding. . . .

Second, the BLM's carbon emissions analysis seems to be liberal (i.e., underestimates the effect on climate change). The RODs assume that coal will continue to be a much used source of fuel for electricity and that coal use will increase with population size. We do not owe the BLM any greater deference on the question at issue here because it does not involve "the frontiers of science." The BLM acknowledged that climate change is a scientifically verified reality. Climate science may be better in 2017 than in 2010 when the FEIS became available, but it is not a scientific frontier as defined by the Supreme Court in *Baltimore Gas*, i.e., as barely emergent knowledge and technology. *Balt. Gas*, 462 U.S. at 92. . . .

BALDOCK, J., concurring.

. . . Because the question before us is an economic one, and because in resolving that question we dispose of this appeal, I see no need to comment on matters of climate science, as the Court does when it attempts to distinguish this appeal from *Baltimore Gas & Elec. Co. v. Nat. Res. Def. Council, Inc.*, 462 U.S. 87 (1983). . . .

The assertion that climate science is settled science is, in my view, both unnecessary to this appeal and questionable as a factual matter. Such an assertion is not necessary to this appeal because there is no disputed issue of climate science before us and thus no question of climate science we must decide whether to defer to the BLM on. . . .

. . . Accordingly, I concur with the Court's analysis of the BLM's economic assumption and disposition of this appeal on that basis, without joining its conclusion about climate science.

NOTES AND QUESTIONS

1.   Did the court in *WildEarth Guardians* apply an appropriate level of deference under the APA regarding the BLM's "perfect substitution" argument? How should the courts review agency decisions made under a set of assumptions that may no longer be valid? Did you agree with the concurring judge that the majority's discussion of climate change was unnecessary?

2.   One of the plaintiffs' main arguments in the case was that it was arbitrary and capricious for the BLM to fail to compare the GHG emissions associated with the coal leases in question with the GHG emissions that would result from denying the leases and obtaining the equivalent amount of energy from other sources. The extent to which regulators must compare the potential GHG emissions that may flow from energy-related project permitting has been subject to significant litigation and scholarly commentary in recent years. For competing analyses of whether regulators should evaluate the "upstream" and "downstream" GHG emissions associated with coal leasing, oil and gas pipelines, and other energy projects, see Michael Burger & Jessica Wentz, *Upstream and Downstream Greenhouse Gas Emissions: The Proper Scope of NEPA Review*, 41 HARV. ENV'T L. REV. 109 (2017); James W. Coleman, *Beyond the Pipeline Wars: Reforming Environmental Assessment of Energy Transport Infrastructure*, 2018 UTAH L. REV. 119 (2018). *See also Vecinos para el Bienstar de la Commundad Costera v. FERC*, 6 F.4th 1321 (D.C. Cir. 2021) (finding FERC approvals for LNG terminals and associated interstate natural gas pipelines in Texas were arbitrary and capricious for failure to adequately evaluate the projects' impacts on GHG emissions and nearby environmental justice communities).

3.   During the Obama administration, the BLM became subject to growing criticism that the federal government was not receiving fair market value for Powder River Basin coal leases, in large part because of a lack of competition in the industry. In 2014, the U.S. District Court for the Southern District of New York summarized the situation as follows, based heavily on a 2013 U.S. Government Accountability Office report:

> . . . Coal production from federal leases averages about 450 million
> tons per year and produces about $1 billion in annual revenue. Of

that revenue, some two-thirds come from royalties for the sale of coal; one-third comes from payments for leases. Four lessee companies [Alpha Natural Resources, Arch Coal, Cloud Peak Energy, and Peabody Energy] account for more than 90 percent of federal coal sales. . . .

Under the Mineral Leasing Act, BLM cannot accept less than "fair market value" (or "FMV") for the award, known as a sale, of a coal lease. Accordingly, before every lease sale, BLM must make an assessment of the fair market value of the lease tract's coal. Fair market value is defined under federal regulations as the cash value at which a knowledgeable owner would sell or lease the land to a knowledgeable purchaser. The estimate of fair market value, generally expressed in cents per ton of recoverable coal, is kept confidential.

BLM then publicly announces the sale and solicits sealed bids. At the close of the sale period, BLM awards the lease to the company submitting the highest bid, as long as the company is qualified to hold the lease and the bid meets or exceeds BLM's confidential estimate of fair market value.

In 23 of the 28 Powder River Basin coal lease sales conducted during the past 20 years, BLM has received only one bid; in the remaining five cases, BLM received two bids. In lease sales where there is only one bid, BLM's confidential estimate of fair market value, therefore, effectively supplies the sole price competition for the applicant. There is a similar lack of competition in other states where BLM leases coal tracts. . . .

Nat. Res. Defense Council v. U.S. Dept. of Interior, 36 F. Supp. 3d 384, 390–93 (S.D.N.Y. 2014). *See also* U.S. GOV'T ACCOUNTABILITY OFFICE, OIL, GAS, AND COAL ROYALTIES: RAISING FEDERAL RATES COULD DECREASE PRODUCTION ON FEDERAL LANDS BUT INCREASE FEDERAL REVENUE (June 2017).

4.   In 2016, President Obama issued a controversial Executive Order placing a moratorium on all new coal leasing on federal lands. The stated purpose of the moratorium was to review the leasing program's impacts on public health and the environment, to address concerns that the government was not receiving fair market value for coal leases, and to evaluate whether to increase the statutory royalty rates for federal coal extraction. In 2017, President Trump reversed the moratorium and re-opened federal lands for coal leasing. In 2021, President Biden stopped short of reinstating the Obama-era moratorium but pledged to conduct a comprehensive review of the program. *See* James Marshall, *Biden Admin to Review Federal Coal Leasing Program*, GREENWIRE (Aug. 17, 2021). Should the federal government revisit the royalty rates in place for federal coal? On what grounds might those rates be increased? Should Congress or BLM address the lack of competition for federal coal leases? If so, how should it do so?

c. Federalism and the Surface Mining Control and Reclamation Act of 1977 (SMCRA)

As described in Chapter 2, the practice of coal mining varies across the United States. The prior sections have highlighted some of the ways in which these different contexts—such as underground versus surface mining and private property rights versus federal public land leasing—create specific legal disputes. This section builds on that discussion to consider the bigger picture question of federal versus state roles in regulating coal extraction. The variation in coal mining techniques among states with very different geographies and physical conditions has led at times to difficult federalism questions about which level of government should regulate. As Steven and Michael Braverman explain:

> Coal is actively mined in twenty-four states. There are five principal coal basins: Appalachia (Northern, Central, and Southern), the Illinois (Interior) Basin, Gulf Lignite (Texas and Louisiana), Western Bituminous (Colorado and Utah), the Powder River Basin (Wyoming and Montana), and numerous minor and sub-basins within these principal basins. The principal methods of mining—underground and surface—have very different environmental and safety challenges. The diversity of conditions and mining methods in the various regions would suggest that local or state-level regulation of mining would be the best approach; experience has proven otherwise. Historically, mining states have been reluctant to enact and enforce stringent regulation, the effect of which would be to increase production costs and thereby put the particular state at a competitive disadvantage in relation to other states or regions. . . .

Steven C. Braverman & Michael R. Braverman, *Regulation of Surface Coal Mining: The End of a Thirty-Year Balancing Act?*, 27 NAT. RESOURCES & ENV'T 28 (2012).

Many of these federalism issues arise under one of the most important federal statutes on coal mining, the Surface Mining Control and Reclamation Act of 1977, 30 U.S.C. §§ 1201, *et seq.* (SMCRA, often referred to colloquially as "Smack-ra"). The law resulted from the federal government's decision in the late 1970s to address some of the environmental and social concerns surrounding the extraction of coal. From the start, the statute faced many challenges from the coal industry, including to its constitutionality. In *Hodel v. Virginia Surface Mining and Reclamation Ass'n*, 452 U.S. 264 (1981), the U.S. Supreme Court held that Congress had authority under the Commerce Clause of the U.S. Constitution to enact SMCRA, which was intended to "establish a nationwide program to protect society and the environment from the adverse effects of surface coal mining operations." *Hodel*, 452 U.S. at 268 (citing 30 U.S.C. § 1202(a)). The following case discusses SMCRA in more detail as well as the relationship between the federal government and the states in implementing the law.

BRAGG V. W. VA. COAL ASS'N

248 F.3d 275 (4th Cir. 2001), *cert. denied*, 534 U.S. 1113 (2002)

NIEMEYER, CIRCUIT JUDGE.

This case, which is of great importance to the citizens of West Virginia, was commenced by some of its citizens and an environmental group against the Director of the West Virginia Division of Environmental Protection to challenge his issuance of permits for mountaintop-removal coal mining in the State. The complaint alleged that the Director "has routinely approved surface coal mining permits which decapitate the State's mountains and dump the resulting waste in nearby valleys, burying hundreds of miles of headwaters of West Virginia's streams," and it requested an injunction prohibiting the further issuance of such permits.

The public concern over this issue is demonstrated by the remarkably broad spectrum of interests represented in these proceedings, as well as by their unusual alliances, in both the political and legal arenas. On one side of the dispute are plaintiffs, consisting of a group of private citizens and environmental groups who oppose West Virginia's current permitting practices, and they enjoy the support of the U.S. Environmental Protection Agency. On the other side are the coal mining companies, who are allied with the United Mine Workers of America and the West Virginia State political establishment, all of whom favor current mining practices. . . .

Following extensive and careful consideration of motions for summary judgment on the substantive issues presented and cross-motions to dismiss, the district court denied the motions to dismiss, found that West Virginia's approval of mountaintop mining practices violated both federal and State law, and enjoined the State from issuing further permits that authorize dumping of mountain rock within 100 feet of intermittent and perennial streams.

Because we conclude that the doctrine of sovereign immunity bars the citizens from bringing their claims against an official of West Virginia in federal court, we vacate the district court's injunction and remand with instructions to dismiss the citizens' complaint without prejudice so that they may present their claims in the proper forum. . . .

Mountaintop-removal coal mining, while not new, only became widespread in West Virginia in the 1990s. Under this method, to reach horizontal seams of coal layered in mountains, the mountaintop rock above the seam is removed and placed in adjacent valleys; the coal is extracted; and the removed rock is then replaced in an effort to achieve the original contour of the mountain. But because rock taken from its natural state and broken up naturally "swells," perhaps by as much as 15 to 25%, the excess rock not returned to the mountain—the "overburden"—remains in the valleys, creating "valley fills." Many valley fills bury intermittent and perennial streams and drainage areas that are near the mountaintop. Over the years, the West Virginia Director of Environmental Protection (the "Director" or "State Director"), as well as the U.S. Army Corps of Engineers, has approved this method of coal mining in West Virginia.

The disruption to the immediate environment created by mountaintop mining is considerable and has provoked sharp differences of opinion between environmentalists and industry players. *See, e.g.,* Penny Loeb, *Shear Madness,* U.S. NEWS & WORLD REPT., Aug. 11, 1997. As Loeb reported these differences of opinion, environmentalists decry the "startling" change in the topography, which leaves the land more subject to floods, results in the pollution of streams and rivers, and has an "incalculable" impact on wildlife. The environmentalists also criticize the mining process itself, which cracks foundations of nearby houses, causes fires, creates dust and noise, and disrupts private wells. The coal companies concede that the process changes the landscape, but note on the positive side that land is reclaimed, that grass, small shrubs, and trees are planted, and that waterfowl ponds are added. Moreover, the companies observe that mining is critical to the West Virginia economy and creates high-paying jobs in the State.

In July 1998, Patricia Bragg, along with eight other West Virginia citizens and the West Virginia Highlands Conservancy (collectively "Bragg"), commenced this action against officials of the U.S. Army Corps of Engineers and the State Director [under the citizen suit provisions of the Surface Mining Control and Reclamation Act of 1977 (SMCRA)]. Bragg alleged that the State Director, in granting surface coal mining permits, . . . consistently issued permits to mining operations, without making requisite findings, that (1) authorized valley fills, (2) failed to assure the restoration of original mountain contours, and (3) violated other environmental protection laws. . . .

[SMCRA] was enacted to strike a balance between the nation's interests in protecting the environment from the adverse effects of surface coal mining and in assuring the coal supply essential to the nation's energy requirements. The Act accomplishes these purposes through a "cooperative federalism," in which responsibility for the regulation of surface coal mining in the United States is shared between the U.S. Secretary of the Interior and State regulatory authorities. Under this scheme, Congress established in SMCRA "minimum national standards" for regulating surface coal mining and encouraged the States, through an offer of exclusive regulatory jurisdiction, to enact their own laws incorporating these minimum standards, as well as any more stringent, but not inconsistent, standards that they might choose. . . .

Thus, SMCRA provides for *either* State regulation of surface coal mining within its borders *or* federal regulation, but not both. The Act expressly provides that one or the other is exclusive, *see* 30 U.S.C. §§ 1253(a), 1254(a), with the exception that an approved State program is always subject to revocation when a State fails to enforce it, *see id.* §§ 1253(a); 1271(b). Federal oversight of an approved State program is provided by the Secretary's obligation to inspect and monitor the operations of State programs. *See id.* §§ 1267, 1271. Only if an approved State program is revoked, as provided in § 1271, however, does the *federal* program become the operative regulation for surface coal mining in any State that has previously had its program approved. *See id.* §§ 1254(a), 1271.

In the case before us, West Virginia submitted a program to the Secretary in 1980 for approval, and the Secretary approved the program in 1981, thus granting West Virginia "primacy" status—a status under which its law exclusively regulates coal mining in the State. As part of this program, the West Virginia legislature enacted its own statute entitled the "Surface Coal Mining and Reclamation Act" (the "West Virginia Coal Mining Act"). As amended, the West Virginia Coal Mining Act vests the Director of the State Division of Environmental Protection with the authority to administer the Act and otherwise to provide for the regulation of surface coal mining within the State. The West Virginia Act sets out minimum performance standards that mirror those found in SMCRA, and the State Director has exercised his statutorily granted power to promulgate State regulations that parallel those issued by the Secretary of the Interior pursuant to the federal Act. Thus, since the Secretary's approval of the West Virginia program in 1981, the Director has served as the exclusive permitting authority in the State, and West Virginia has maintained "exclusive jurisdiction," with certain exceptions inherent in the federal oversight provisions, over surface mining regulation within its borders.

The State Director asserted below and now contends that, as an official of West Virginia who has been sued in his official capacity, he is immune from suit in federal court under the doctrine of sovereign immunity guaranteed by the Eleventh Amendment. In response to the district court's reliance on *Ex parte Young*, 209 U.S. 123 (1908), to overcome the Eleventh Amendment bar, the Director argues that the *Ex parte Young* exception does not apply because the issues in this case involve enforcement of West Virginia law, not federal law. Acknowledging that Bragg nominally asserts violations of both federal and State law, the Director argues that Bragg actually seeks to compel the Director "to comply with the approved West Virginia surface mining program" because once a State program is approved by the Secretary of the Interior, it is State law, not federal law, that governs. Thus, the Director concludes that the *Ex parte Young* exception for ongoing *federal* violations does not apply; rather, *Pennhurst State School & Hospital v. Halderman*, 465 U.S. 89 (1984), controls. In *Pennhurst,* the Supreme Court held the *Ex parte Young* doctrine inapplicable to a suit brought against a State official to compel his compliance with State law. *See* 465 U.S. at 106.

Although the *Ex parte Young* exception to the Eleventh Amendment is well established, its precise contours are not. . . .

The respective federal and State interests revealed in this case make the analysis complex because SMCRA was expressly designed to hand over to the States the task of enforcing minimum national standards for surface coal mining, providing only limited federal mechanisms to oversee State enforcement. Thus, because the federal enactment, in furtherance of its design to advance State interests, creates the potential for exclusive State regulatory authority, the federal interest would seem to be better served by encouraging private citizens to enforce their claims relating to the State enforcement efforts in State, rather than federal, court. A more precise evaluation of this interest, however, as it might affect application of *Ex parte Young,* requires us to return to the statutory structure of SMCRA and the methods by which it employs a cooperative federalism.

As we have noted, under SMCRA Congress intended to divide responsibility for the regulation of surface coal mining between the federal government and the States. But characterizing the regulatory structure of SMCRA as "cooperative" federalism is not entirely accurate, as the statute does not provide for *shared* regulation of coal mining. Rather, the Act provides for enforcement of either a federal program or a State program, but not both. Thus, in contrast to other "cooperative federalism" statutes, SMCRA exhibits extraordinary deference to the States. The statutory federalism of SMCRA is quite unlike the cooperative regime under the Clean Water Act, 33 U.S.C. § 1251 *et seq.*, which was construed in *Arkansas v. Oklahoma*, 503 U.S. 91 (1992). As the Supreme Court noted there, one of the Clean Water Act's regulations "effectively *incorporate[d]* "State law into the unitary federal enforcement scheme, making State law, in certain circumstances, federal law. *Id.* at 110 (emphasis added). Under SMCRA, in contrast, Congress designed a scheme of mutually exclusive regulation by either the U.S. Secretary of the Interior or the State regulatory authority, depending on whether the State elects to regulate itself or to submit to federal regulation. Because West Virginia is a primacy state, its regulation of surface coal mining on nonfederal lands within its borders is "exclusive." *See* 30 U.S.C. § 1253(a); 30 C.F.R. § 948.10. This federal policy of encouraging "exclusive" State regulation was careful and deliberate. The Act's preliminary findings explain that "because of the diversity in terrain, climate, biologic, chemical, and other physical conditions in areas subject to mining operations, the primary governmental responsibility for developing, authorizing, issuing, and enforcing regulations for surface mining and reclamation operations subject to this chapter should rest with the States." 30 U.S.C. § 1201(f). . . . To make this point absolutely clear, SMCRA provides explicitly that when States regulate, they do so exclusively, *see id.* § 1253(a), and when the Secretary regulates, he does so exclusively, *see id.* § 1254(a).

Even so, SMCRA does manifest an ongoing federal interest in assuring that minimum national standards for surface coal mining are enforced. But when a State fails to enforce these minimum national standards, it does not automatically forfeit the right of exclusive regulation. SMCRA vindicates its national-standards policy through a limited and ordered federal oversight, grounded in a process that can lead ultimately to the withdrawal of the State's exclusive control. Until that withdrawal occurs, because an approved State program must include "a *State law* which provides for the regulation of surface coal mining and reclamation operations in accordance with the requirements of this chapter," 30 U.S.C. § 1253(a)(1) (emphasis added), the minimum national standards are attained by State enforcement of its own law. . . .

In sum, even though the States ultimately remain subject to SMCRA, the Act grants "exclusive jurisdiction" to a primacy State (one with an approved program), thereby conditionally divesting the federal government of *direct* regulatory authority. Therefore, when a State's program has been approved by the Secretary of the Interior, we can look only to State law on matters involving the enforcement of the minimum national standards; whereas, on matters relating to the good standing of a State program, SMCRA remains directly applicable. . . .

Accordingly, we conclude that Bragg's claims filed against the State Director in federal court are not authorized by the *Ex parte Young* exception to the Eleventh Amendment. . . .

NOTES AND QUESTIONS

1.   As is evident from the *Bragg* case excerpt, mountaintop removal mining has been controversial from its inception. Concerns over its environmental effects on waterways and landscapes have led to stricter regulation of the practice since the late 2000s. Three different federal agencies regulate mountaintop mining—the U.S. Army Corps of Engineers and the EPA under the Clean Water Act—and the Department of Interior's Office of Surface Management, Reclamation, and Enforcement (OSMRE) under SMCRA. SMCRA states that mining companies should not cause "material damage to the environment to the extent that it is technologically and economically feasible." Based on this language, OSMRE first enacted the "stream buffer

zone rule" in 1979 and revised it in 1983. As mining practices changed over subsequent decades, environmental and community groups in the Appalachian region urged the agency to tighten the regulations to prevent environmental harm. In 2008, the Bush administration amended and updated the stream buffer zone rule but it was immediately subject to legal challenge that continued during the Obama administration. Ultimately, the U.S. District Court for the District of Columbia invalidated the new rule for failure to comply with the Endangered Species Act consultation requirements. *Nat'l Parks Conserv. Ass'n v. Jewell*, 62 F. Supp. 3d 7 (D.D.C. 2014).

A few years later, OSMRE issued a new rule, called the "Stream Protection Rule," which went into effect in the final days of the Obama administration, in January 2017. The new rule required coal operators to avoid causing damage to the hydrologic balance of waterways outside the permit area and required them to conduct a baseline assessment of nearby ecosystems, monitor affected streams during mining operations, and develop a plan for restoring waterway after mining is complete. Industry and coal mining states strongly opposed the rule from the outset and Congress invalidated it in February 2017 under the Congressional Review Act (CRA). The CRA, which was enacted in 1996, allows the House and Senate to nullify any "recently finalized" regulation by a simple majority vote in both houses of Congress so long as the President approves it. The CRA generally applies to any regulation finalized after June of a Presidential election year. *See, e.g.,* RICHARD S. BETH, CONG. RSCH. SERV., DISAPPROVAL OF REGULATIONS BY CONGRESS: PROCEDURE UNDER THE CONGRESSIONAL REVIEW ACT (Oct. 10, 2001).

2.   A separate provision of SMCRA requires coal companies to obtain bonds to help ensure money is available for reclaiming (i.e., restoring) the mine site after coal extraction is complete in the event the mine operator goes bankrupt or otherwise has insufficient funds for reclamation. As domestic demand for coal continues to decline, and the number of coal companies going bankrupt has increased significantly, regulators, local communities, and advocates have expressed concern over significant shortfalls in reclamation funds. *See, e.g.,* Stephen Lee, *Modern Coal Mines' Cleanup Has Big Unbudgeted Costs, Group Says*, BLOOMBERG LAW (July 8, 2021); Taylor Mayhall, *Reclaiming Reclamation: Rule Changes Proposed To Ensure Coal Companies Fund Mandatory Clean-Ups*, 102 MINN. L. REV. 1451 (2018). Do you think that current legal approaches to regulating coal mining set the right balance between the federal and state governments and between allowing mining while limiting environmental and social costs? Why or why not? How might you change the regime?

2. OIL AND GAS

Unlike coal, where domestic production from federal lands dominates, oil and gas production from federal lands is more modest, but still significant. In 2019, oil production from federal lands constituted 9% of total domestic production, as compared to 76% from nonfederal lands and the remainder from offshore federal lands. As for natural gas, in 2019, production from federal lands constituted 9% of total domestic production as compared to 88% from nonfederal lands and the remainder from offshore federal lands. *See* CONG. RSCH. SERV., REVENUES AND DISBURSEMENTS FROM OIL AND NATURAL GAS PRODUCTION ON FEDERAL LANDS 1–5 (Sept. 2, 2020). *See also* DIAZ, *supra* at 5–12 (discussing recent trends in oil and natural gas production, consumption, and exports).

Unlike with coal, where the federal government has engaged in extensive regulation of the extraction process on both public and private lands through SMCRA, state law has historically dominated the extraction of oil and natural gas on nonfederal lands. As a result, when the BLM under the Obama administration enacted rules governing venting and flaring of natural gas from oil wells on federal lands, there was strong opposition from the industry as well as from oil and gas producing states, leading to litigation discussed in Chapter 9.

This section first discusses ownership issues and state laws governing onshore oil and gas development on private lands, followed by an exploration of the laws governing onshore oil and gas development on federal lands. As noted earlier, laws governing offshore oil and gas extraction, as well as state and federal laws specifically governing hydraulic fracturing, are addressed in detail in Chapter 9.

a.   Oil and Gas Development on Private Lands

Onshore oil and gas extraction on private lands is primarily regulated through state common law and statutes, complemented by federal environmental statutes and limited direct federal oil and gas law. Two basic ideas compete. First, property law aims to maximize productive use of the land. In the case of oil and gas, this traditionally has meant that the law encourages people to invest in extracting it as quickly as possible. Second, as people rush to extract oil and gas resources, the law seeks to prevent what Garrett Hardin termed *the tragedy of the commons*. That is, the law aims to constrain wasteful behavior that can result in the competitive push to extract the common pool resources of oil and gas.

These two competing goals illustrate the dilemmas around energy markets and environmental externalities described in Chapter 1. Law shapes markets by distributing property rights in a manner that encourages rapid development. But those market choices then lead to externalities, which the law aims to constrain without unduly limiting markets.

Regarding common law, many of you have previously encountered the case *Pierson v. Post*, 3 Cai. R. 175, 2 Am. Dec. 264 (N.Y. 1805) in property law. In that case, the court had to decide who owned a fox that one person had chased but another person had killed. This dispute over a fox established "the rule of capture," which became a dominant rule in oil and gas extraction. As early as 1889, the Pennsylvania Supreme Court declared:

> Water and oil, and still more strongly gas, may be classed by themselves, if the analogy be not too fanciful, as minerals *feroe naturoe*. In common with animals, and unlike other minerals, they have the power and the tendency to escape without the volition of the owner. Their "fugitive and wandering existence within the limits of a particular tract was uncertain," as said by Chief Justice AGNEW in *Brown v. Vandegrift*, 80 Pa. St. 147, 148. They belong to the owner of the land, and are part of it, so long as they are on or in it, and are subject to his control; but when they escape, and go into other land, or come under another's control, the title of the former owner is gone. Possession of the land, therefore, is not necessarily possession of the gas. If an adjoining, or even a distant, owner, drills his own land, and taps your gas, so that it comes into his well and under his control, it is no longer yours, but his. And equally so as between lessor and lessee in the present case, the one who controls the gas—has it in his grasp, so to speak—is the one who has possession in the legal as well as in the ordinary sense of the word.

Westmoreland & Cambria Nat. Gas Co. v. De Witt, 18 A. 724 (Pa. 1889).

In its purest form, the rule of capture allows landowners to extract as much as possible from their wells even if they end up taking oil and gas from under someone else's land due to the shared nature of the reservoir. However, from the start, states have limited the rule of capture in several ways. As Professors Bruce M. Kramer and Owen L. Anderson explain:

> The rule of capture has been an integral part of oil and gas law since the completion of the first commercial oil well in Pennsylvania in the 1840s. The early development of the rule was subsumed within the larger question of whether oil and gas was a possessory or non-possessory interest or whether it was real property or personal property. Many early cases relied on the *ferae naturae* or percolating waters analogy as they developed the rule of capture, which recognizes ownership of oil and gas in the party that brings it to the surface regardless of where the oil and gas lay in its natural state.

> As the rule of capture moved on to more complex issues, other than pure ownership, it was modified in a number of significant ways. A series of Indiana and Kentucky cases limited the rule by recognizing the correlative rights of others to capture oil or gas from the common source of supply. Thus, owners who employed artificial methods to produce the hydrocarbons, owners who

negligently drilled into the common source of supply, and owners who wasted the hydrocarbons were not insulated from liability by the rule of capture.

Modern oil and gas cases typically involve more complex issues than ownership of oil and gas. Thus, where an oil and gas operator directionally drills a well that is bottomed on the land of another, he may not assert a rule of capture defense to limit liability to the amount of oil and gas originally located under the neighbor's land. Oil and gas conservation statutes have had the greatest impact on the rule of capture by limiting the ability of oil and gas owners to drill wells. Where an oil and gas operator violates conservation regulations by appropriating more oil and gas than was authorized by the state regulations, the operator may not plead the rule of capture to defend his actions. Nevertheless, the rule of capture continues to apply to the extent conservation law or orders do not preempt it. Indeed, continued recognition of the rule, together with recognition of correlative rights, is essential to the efficient administration of conservation laws.

Bruce M. Kramer & Owen L. Anderson, *The Rule of Capture—An Oil and Gas Perspective*, 35 ENV'T L. 899, 899 (2005).

In addition to these constraints described by Professors Kramer and Anderson, states have used the property law doctrine of waste in both statutes and case law to limit the rule of capture. This doctrine applies because the incentives created by the rule of capture can often create wasteful behavior. Chapter 2 detailed the physical waste that occurred in the Spindletop field in Texas in 1901 as producers rushed to drill as many wells as possible, leading to pressure depletion in the field, massive wasting of oil during the production process, and flaring of large quantities of natural gas. Chapter 2 also highlighted the economic waste that occurred in the oil and gas fields of Oklahoma in the 1930s as overproduction led to plummeting prices; the Oklahoma governor responded by calling out the troops to close the oil wells until such time as purchasers would pay one dollar a barrel.

The case excerpts that follow explore in more detail the application of the rule of capture and related property doctrines to oil and gas resources. This includes issues surrounding the rights of multiple parties regarding both surface and mineral interests of the same parcel of property. One common situation is that one party owns the surface rights while another party owns the subsurface mineral rights, creating what is known as a "split estate" (first introduced in the materials before the *Stewart* case in the prior section), which can lead to conflicts between the owner of the mineral estate (which, by law, is the "dominant" estate) and the owner of the surface estate (which, by law, is the "servient estate"). Another common situation is where the owner of the mineral estate (who may or may not also be the owner of the surface estate) leases the rights to develop the subsurface oil and gas resources to a third-party developer. In this situation, it is standard for the oil and gas developer to pay the lessor a "royalty," which is typically 1/8 (or 12%) of the value of oil or gas the developer produces from the property. As you read the case excerpts below, consider the financial interests and legal rights of the parties to the disputes and how they drive the parties' positions in the lawsuits.

ELLIFF V. TEXON DRILLING CO.
210 S.W.2d 558 (Tex. 1948)

FOLLEY, JUSTICE.

This is a suit by the petitioners, Mrs. Mabel Elliff, Frank Elliff, and Charles C. Elliff, against the respondents, Texon Drilling Company, a Texas corporation, Texon Royalty Company, a Texas corporation, Texon Royalty Company, a Delaware corporation, and John L. Sullivan, for damages resulting from a "blowout" gas well drilled by respondents in the Agua Dulce Field in Nueces County.

The petitioners owned the surface and certain royalty interests in 3054.9 acres of land in Nueces County, upon which there was a producing well known as Elliff No. 1. They owned all the mineral estate underlying the west 1500 acres of the tract, and an undivided one-half interest in the mineral estate underlying the east 1554.9 acres. Both tracts were subject to oil and gas leases, and therefore their royalty interest in the west 1500 acres was one-eighth of the oil or gas, and in the east 1554.9 acres was one-sixteenth of the oil and gas.

It was alleged that these lands overlaid approximately fifty per cent of a huge reservoir of gas and distillate and that the remainder of the reservoir was under the lands owned by Mrs. Clara Driscoll, adjoining the lands of petitioners on the east. Prior to November 1936, respondents were engaged in the drilling of Driscoll-Sevier No. 2 as an offset well at a location 466 feet east of petitioners' east line. On the date stated, when respondents had reached a depth of approximately 6838 feet, the well blew out, caught fire and cratered. Attempts to control it were unsuccessful, and huge quantities of gas, distillate and some oil were blown into the air, dissipating large quantities from the reservoir into which the offset well was drilled. When the Driscoll-Sevier No. 2 well blew out, the fissure or opening in the ground around the well gradually increased until it enveloped and destroyed Elliff No. 1. The latter well also blew out, cratered, caught fire and burned for several years. Two water wells on petitioners' land became involved in the cratering and each of them blew out. Certain damages also resulted to the surface of petitioners' lands and to their cattle thereon. The cratering process and the eruption continued until large quantities of gas and distillate were drained from under petitioners' land and escaped into the air, all of which was alleged to be the direct and proximate result of the negligence of respondents in permitting their well to blow out. The extent of the emissions from the Driscoll-Sevier No. 2 and Elliff No. 1, and the two water wells on petitioners' lands, was shown at various times during the several years between the blowout in November 1936, and the time of the trial in June 1946. There was also expert testimony from petroleum engineers showing the extent of the losses from the underground reservoir, which computations extended from the date of the blowout only up to June 1938. It was indicated that it was not feasible to calculate the losses subsequent thereto, although lesser emissions of gas continued even up to the time of the trial. All the evidence with reference to the damages included all losses from the reservoir beneath petitioners' land without regard to whether they were wasted and dissipated from above the Driscoll land or from petitioners' land.

The jury found that respondents were negligent in failing to use drilling mud of sufficient weight in drilling their well, and that such negligence was the proximate cause of the well blowing out. It also found that petitioners had suffered $4620 damage to sixty acres of the surface, and $1350 for the loss of 27 head of cattle. The damages for the gas and distillate wasted "from and under" the lands of petitioners, due to respondents' negligence, was fixed by the jury at $78,580.46 for the gas, and $69,967.73 for the distillate. These figures were based upon the respective fractional royalty interests of petitioners in the whole amount wasted under their two tracts of land, and at a value, fixed by the court without objection by the parties, of two cents per 1000 cubic feet for the gas and $1.25 per barrel for the distillate. . . .

On the findings of the jury the trial court rendered judgment for petitioners for $154,518.19, which included $148,548.19 for the gas and distillate, and $5970 for damages to the land and cattle. The Court of Civil Appeals reversed the judgment and remanded the cause. 210 S.W.2d 553. . . .

[O]ur attention will be confined to the sole question as to whether the law of capture absolves respondents of any liability for the negligent waste or destruction of petitioners' gas and distillate, though substantially all of such waste or destruction occurred after the minerals had been drained from beneath petitioners' lands. . . .

. . . In our state the landowner is regarded as having absolute title in severalty to the oil and gas in place beneath his land. The only qualification of that rule of ownership is that it must be considered in connection with the law of capture and is subject to police regulations. The oil and gas beneath the soil are considered a part of the realty. Each owner of land owns separately, distinctly and exclusively all the oil and gas under his land and is accorded the usual remedies against trespassers who appropriate the minerals or destroy their market value.

. . . In the absence of common law precedent, and owing to the lack of scientific information as to the movement of these minerals, some of the courts have sought by analogy to compare oil and gas to other types of property such as wild animals, birds, subterranean waters and other migratory things, with reference to which the common law had established rules denying any character of ownership prior to capture. However, as was said by Professor A. W. Walker, Jr., of the School of Law of the University of Texas: "There is no oil or gas producing state today which follows the wild-animal analogy to its logical conclusion that the landowner has no property interest in the oil and gas in place." 16 T.L.R. 370, 371. In the light of modern scientific knowledge these early analogies have been disproven, and courts generally have come to recognize that oil and gas, as commonly found in underground reservoirs, are securely entrapped in a static condition in the original pool, and, ordinarily, so remain until disturbed by penetrations from the surface. It is further established, nevertheless, that these minerals will migrate across property lines towards any low pressure area created by production from the common pool. This migratory character of oil and gas has given rise to the so-called rule or law of capture. That rule simply is that the owner of a tract of land acquires title to the oil or gas which he produces from wells on his land, though part of the oil or gas may have migrated from adjoining lands. He may thus appropriate the oil and gas that have flowed from adjacent lands without the consent of the owner of those lands, and without incurring liability to him for drainage. The non-liability is based upon the theory that after the drainage the title or property interest of the former owner is gone. This rule, at first blush, would seem to conflict with the view of absolute ownership of the minerals in place, but it was otherwise decided in the early case of *Stephens County v. Mid-Kansas Oil & Gas Co.*, 1923, 254 S.W. 290. Mr. Justice Greenwood there stated, 254 S.W. 292:

> The objection lacks substantial foundation that gas or oil in a certain tract of land cannot be owned in place, because subject to appropriation, without the consent of the owner of the tract, through drainage from wells on adjacent lands. If the owners of adjacent lands have the right to appropriate, without liability, the gas and oil underlying their neighbor's land, then their neighbor has the correlative right to appropriate, through like methods of drainage, the gas and oil underlying the tracts adjacent to his own.

Thus it is seen that, notwithstanding the fact that oil and gas beneath the surface are subject both to capture and administrative regulation, the fundamental rule of absolute ownership of the minerals in place is not affected in our state. In recognition of such ownership, our courts, in decisions involving well-spacing regulations of our Railroad Commission, have frequently announced the sound view that each landowner should be afforded the opportunity to produce his fair share of the recoverable oil and gas beneath his land, which is but another way of recognizing the existence of correlative rights between the various landowners over a common reservoir of oil or gas.

It must be conceded that under the law of capture there is no liability for reasonable and legitimate drainage from the common pool. The landowner is privileged to sink as many wells as he desires upon his tract of land and extract therefrom and appropriate all the oil and gas that he may produce, so long as he operates within the spirit and purpose of conservation statutes and orders of the Railroad Commission. These laws and regulations are designed to afford each owner a reasonable opportunity to produce his proportionate part of the oil and gas from the entire pool and to prevent operating practices injurious to the common reservoir. In this manner, if all operators exercise the same degree of skill and diligence, each owner will recover in most instances his fair share of the oil and gas. This reasonable opportunity to produce his fair share of the oil and gas is the landowner's common law right under our theory of absolute ownership of the minerals in place. But from the very nature of this theory the right of each land holder is qualified, and is limited to legitimate operations. Each owner whose land overlies the basin has a like interest, and each must of necessity exercise his right with some regard to the rights of others. No owner should be permitted to carry on his operations in reckless or lawless irresponsibility, but must submit to such limitations as are necessary to enable each to get his own. *Hague v. Wheeler*, 27 A. 714.

While we are cognizant of the fact that there is a certain amount of reasonable and necessary waste incident to the production of oil and gas to which the non-liability rule must also apply, we do not think this immunity should be extended so as to include the negligent waste or destruction of the oil and gas.

In 1 SUMMERS, OIL AND GAS, PERM. ED., s 63 correlative rights of owners of land in a common source of supply of oil and gas are discussed and described in the following language:

> These existing property relations, called the correlative rights of the owners of land in the common source of supply, were not created by the statute, but held to exist because of the peculiar physical facts of oil and gas. The term "correlative rights" is merely a convenient method of indicating that each owner of land in a common source of supply of oil and gas has legal privileges as against other owners of land therein to take oil or gas therefrom by lawful operations conducted on his own land; that each such owner has duties to the other owners not to exercise his privileges

of taking so as to injure the common source of supply; and that each such owner has rights that other owners not exercise their privileges of taking so as to injure the common source of supply.

In 85 A.L.R. 1156, in discussing the case of *Hague v. Wheeler, supra,* the annotator states:

> * * * The fact that the owner of the land has a right to take and to use gas and oil, even to the diminution or exhaustion of the supply under his neighbor's land, does not give him the right to waste the gas. His property in the gas underlying his land consists of the right to appropriate the same, and permitting the gas to escape into the air is not an appropriation thereof in the proper sense of the term.

In like manner, the negligent waste and destruction of petitioners' gas and distillate was neither a legitimate drainage of the minerals from beneath their lands nor a lawful or reasonable appropriation of them. Consequently, the petitioners did not lose their right, title and interest in them under the law of capture. At the time of their removal they belonged to petitioners, and their wrongful dissipation deprived these owners of the right and opportunity to produce them. That right is forever lost, the same cannot be restored, and petitioners are without an adequate legal remedy unless we allow a recovery under the same common law which governs other actions for damages and under which the property rights in oil and gas are vested. This remedy should not be denied.

In common with others who are familiar with the nature of oil and gas and the risks involved in their production, the respondents had knowledge that a failure to use due care in drilling their well might result in a blowout with the consequent waste and dissipation of the oil, gas and distillate from the common reservoir. In the conduct of one's business or in the use and exploitation of one's property, the law imposes upon all persons the duty to exercise ordinary care to avoid injury or damage to the property of others. Thus under the common law, and independent of the conservation statutes, the respondents were legally bound to use due care to avoid the negligent waste or destruction of the minerals imbedded in petitioners' oil and gas-bearing strata. This common-law duty the respondents failed to discharge. For that omission they should be required to respond in such damages as will reasonably compensate the injured parties for the loss sustained as the proximate result of the negligent conduct. The fact that the major portion of the gas and distillate escaped from the well on respondents' premises is immaterial. Irrespective of the opening from which the minerals escaped, they belonged to the petitioners and the loss was the same. They would not have been dissipated at any opening except for the wrongful conduct of the respondents. Being responsible for the loss they are in no position to deny liability because the gas and distillate did not escape through the surface of petitioners' lands.

We are therefore of the opinion the Court of Civil Appeals erred in holding that under the law of capture the petitioners cannot recover for the damages resulting from the wrongful drainage of the gas and distillate from beneath their lands. . . .

VIRTEX OPERATING CO. v. BAUERLE

No. 04–16–00549–CV, 2017 WL 5162546 (Tex. Ct. App., Nov. 8, 2017)

Opinion by: MARIALYN BARNARD, JUSTICE.

This appeal arises from a dispute between the Bauerles and VirTex concerning the installation of overhead power lines across the Bauerles' ranch property—known as the Todos Santos Ranch—in Dilley, Texas. The Todos Santos Ranch comprises approximately 8,500 acres in Frio and Zavala Counties. It is undisputed that the Bauerles own the surface estate of the 8,500-acre tract as well as a 2% royalty interest in the property. The Bauerles primarily use the ranch property to run a commercial hunting business and a cattle operation. The ranch is equipped with a hunting lodge, cookhouse, three bunkhouses, and a man-made lake. The Bauerles lease the ranch and its facilities to hunters on a yearly basis, and under these leases, hunters have the opportunity to hunt deer, turkey, and quail. In addition to the hunting leases, the Bauerles also maintain cattle on the ranch; however, the main source of income for the ranch stems from the hunting leases.

Under the hunting leases, hunters use helicopters several times throughout the year on the ranch for a number of game operations, including brush and predator control, game surveys, and deer captures. Of these operations, deer captures are arguably the most important. In an effort to manage the number of Whitetail deer on the ranch, hunters use helicopters to locate and capture deer quickly. Once pilots locate a deer, they are able to push the deer into an open area, where the deer can be captured with a net gun. The operation requires pilots to fly alongside the deer—approximately 4 to 5 feet above ground—weaving in and out of brush, while at the same time, dodging trees and other obstacles. The process has been described as one of "the most extreme [forms of] flying that you can possibly do." According to several hunters, this method of deer capture is less stressful for the deer and more cost efficient for hunters. Additionally, this method has, to date, eliminated injuries to the deer. Ultimately, the captured deer are relocated to a fenced enclosure for breeding or to another nearby ranch in the event the Bauerles' ranch has a surplus of deer. . . .

As indicated above, it is undisputed the Bauerles own the entire surface estate and a 2% royalty interest in the ranch property. ExxonMobil owns the full mineral fee estate underlying the property and executed an oil and gas lease—known as the Mars Mclean Lease—to VirTex. The Mars Mclean Lease covers approximately 3,000 acres of the Bauerles' ranch. Although there was no oil and gas activity on the property when the Bauerles first acquired the property, a VirTex landman informed Mr. Bauerle that VirTex was interested in drilling a well to determine whether there was oil and gas on the property. Because the well was productive, VirTex drilled several more wells, paying monthly royalties to the Bauerles. By the fall of 2008, the Bauerles had entered into a surface use agreement with VirTex, allowing VirTex to install tank batteries. Currently, VirTex operates nine wells on approximately 2,000 acres of the leased acreage.

Each of the existing wells on the property is equipped with a pumpjack, which extracts crude oil from the ground so that the oil can be refined and placed on the market. VirTex currently operates each of the pump jacks with four portable diesel generators that it rents. According to VirTex, the generators were intended to be a temporary means of generating power to the pump jacks until the installation of permanent overhead power lines. In 2012, VirTex approached the Bauerles and asked them to sign an easement for the installation of power lines. Currently, the property has a single power line that runs alongside a black paved road to the hunting lodge and other facilities on the ranch. VirTex's proposed power line configuration consists of a box with overhead power lines running to the individual wells; overall, the design would create a perimeter the Bauerles describe as a spiderweb. It is undisputed VirTex would pay for the costs of the proposed power lines.

Due to a concern that the overhead power lines would interfere with the helicopter operations, the Bauerles refused to sign the easement. The Bauerles also asked VirTex to halt any construction plans concerning the installation of the overhead power lines. VirTex agreed. The Bauerles then filed a declaratory judgment action, requesting the trial court to render judgment declaring that VirTex's installation of the proposed overhead power lines would substantially impair their preexisting use of the "lateral surface and super-adjacent airspace" of the property, which included use of the helicopters for game operations. . . . In response, VirTex counterclaimed, asserting the Bauerles were unreasonably interfering with its right to extract the minerals by prohibiting the installation of the overhead power lines. According to VirTex, the installation of the overhead power lines is a reasonable and customary practice operators use to generate power to wells, and there is no other industry accepted method available.

The parties proceeded to trial, and the jury returned a verdict in favor of the Bauerles . . . .

"Texas law has always recognized that a landowner may sever the mineral and surface estates and convey them separately." *Coyote Lake Ranch, LLC v. City of Lubbock*, 498 S.W.3d 53, 60 (Tex. 2016). The severed mineral estate is known as the dominant estate because it receives the benefit of an implied right to use as much of the surface estate as reasonably necessary to produce and remove minerals; however this right must be exercised with "due regard" for the rights of the surface estate owner. *Id.* (citing *Getty Oil Co. v. Jones*, 470 S.W.2d 618, 621 (Tex. 1971)); *Merriman v. XTO Energy, Inc.*, 407 S.W.3d 244, 249–50 (Tex. 2013) (stating dominant mineral estate owner has not only right to go onto surface to extract minerals, but also all incidental rights reasonably necessary for extraction). This concept of "due regard" is known as the accommodation doctrine and is aimed at balancing the rights of the surface owner and the mineral owner with regard to the use of the surface while at the same time recognizing the dominant nature of the mineral estate. *Coyote Lake Ranch*, 498 S.W.3d at 62–63; *Tex. Genco, LP v. Valence Operating Co.*, 187 S.W.3d [at] 121 (Tex. App.-Waco 2006, pet. denied).

Under the accommodation doctrine, "if the mineral owner or lessee has only one method for developing and producing the minerals, [then] that method may be used regardless of whether it precludes or substantially impairs the surface estate owner's existing use of the surface." *Merriman*, 407 S.W.3d at 248–49. On the other hand, "if the mineral owner has reasonable alternative uses of the surface, one of which permits the surface estate owner to continue to use the surface in the manner intended . . . and one of which would preclude that use by the surface owner, [then] the mineral owner *must* use the alternative that allows continued use of the surface by the surface owner." *Id.* . . .

Based on [Texas case law] the Bauerles had the burden of producing evidence conclusively establishing that VirTex's installation of overhead power lines would completely preclude or substantially impair their existing use of the surface, and there were no reasonable alternative methods available to them by which their existing use of the surface could be continued. *See Coyote Lake Ranch*, 498 S.W.3d at 62; *Merriman*, 407 S.W.3d at 249. Only after the Bauerles established these two elements were they required to further prove there were alternative reasonable, customary, and industry-accepted methods available to VirTex which would allow VirTex to recover the minerals and them to continue their existing use. *See Coyote Lake Ranch*, 498 S.W.3d at 62; *Merriman*, 407 S.W.3d at 249. . . .

VirTex argues that although the evidence shows the overhead power lines would admittedly make the Bauerles' use of helicopters more difficult and dangerous, the evidence did not establish the power lines would make helicopter use impossible. In support of this contention, VirTex points to the testimony by the Bauerles' helicopter witness, Freddie Graf, who conducts much of the ranch work on the property with a helicopter. Graf testified it would be possible—albiet, more dangerous—to fly a helicopter within the proposed grid. VirTex also points to testimony from its witness, Ben Ellis, who testified the proposed power lines did not substantially impair the Bauerles' use of the surface because many of the power lines would be in wooded areas, which are areas where deer capture and predator control do not occur.

The Bauerles, however, argue the evidence . . . establishes that a large part of the ranch work requires the use of helicopters on the property, and the use of helicopters would become extremely dangerous once the overhead power lines were installed. The Bauerles point to Graf's testimony, as well as testimony from Will Nichols, who also leases use of the ranch and flies helicopters on the ranch. Both Graf and Nichols testified the proposed power lines would make the area extremely difficult to fly and drastically hinder their ability to conduct game operations.

. . . Nichols, as well as Graf, testified the Bauerles' property currently had one power line across the property, and the installation of the proposed grid would make flying "so extremely dangerous" that neither of them would want to perform game operations on the property. . . . Viewing this evidence in the light most favorable to the verdict, as well as considering and weighing all the evidence, we conclude such evidence is legally and factually sufficient to establish that VirTex's installation of the power lines would substantially impair the existing use of helicopters over the lateral surface and super-adjacent airspace of the property. . . .

VirTex next contends the Bauerles failed to establish that no reasonable alternative methods existed by which they could continue leasing property to hunters interested in using helicopters. In support of its position, VirTex argues the evidence shows hunters could continue using helicopters for game operations in the 5,500 acres of unleased property and could use four-wheelers to capture and transport deer in the leased acreage with the proposed power lines. . . .

Here, the jury heard testimony from hunters, who testified the use of helicopters for game operations made the Bauerles' large property possible to manage in an efficient manner. When given the option of using four-wheelers, Graf and Nichols testified the amount of terrain they had to cover with a four-wheeler was too large. Furthermore, with regard to the idea of keeping helicopter operations restricted to the other parts of the ranch, Graf and Nichols testified that due to the unpredictable nature of deer, there was no guarantee helicopters could successfully capture deer without flying into VirTex's leased area. Both Graf and Nichols further testified they would not lease the property from the Bauerles unless they had the option to use helicopters. . . .

We disagree with VirTex that the Bauerles failed to meet their burden of proof with respect to the second element of the accommodation doctrine. . . .

Having held the Bauerles produced sufficient evidence establishing the first and second prongs of the accommodation doctrine, we now turn to whether the Bauerles proved an alternative reasonable, customary, and industry-accepted method was available to VirTex. *See Coyote Lake Ranch*, 498 S.W.3d at 62; *Merriman*, 407 S.W.3d at 249. . . . According to VirTex, the proposed alternative suggested by the Bauerles to power the pump jacks with natural gas failed to include the ancillary costs of "sweetening" the gas—a process that was necessary because the acid in natural gas could destroy the generators for each pump jack. Moreover, according to VirTex, the Bauerles' expert, Mike Kramer, presumed VirTex could obtain an easement over neighboring property for a natural gas line and access to an amine plant. VirTex further points out Kramer calculated the cost increase of using natural gas as to only the nine existing wells on the property as opposed to the forty-five proposed wells VirTex planned to drill. . . .

With regard to sufficiency of the evidence, the record reflects the Bauerles produced evidence that other reasonable, customary, and industry-accepted methods existed by which VirTex could power the wells. The Bauerles produced evidence that the wells could be powered by natural gas, a method VirTex had used in the other operations across South Texas. . . . Specifically, the jury heard testimony from Kramer, who opined that although the cheapest option for powering the pump jacks would be with overhead power lines, powering the wells by natural gas was the next best alternative at $200–$300 more per month per well. Kramer also opined this method was industry-accepted, explaining he had worked on past operations in which the pump jacks were powered by natural gas. . . .

After viewing this evidence in the light most favorable to the verdict and crediting favorable evidence and disregarding contrary evidence, we conclude the evidence is legally sufficient to support the jury's finding that reasonable and industry-accepted alternatives existed by which VirTex could power the pump jacks. . . . Accordingly, we hold the evidence was legally and factually sufficient to support the jury's finding with respect to the third element of the accommodation doctrine. . . .

State legislatures have enacted many statutes that shape oil and gas extraction. For example, although the *VirTex* case illustrates the application of the accommodation doctrine as a matter of common law in Texas, other oil and gas states, including Colorado and Wyoming, have enacted statutes codifying the doctrine in order to encourage the use of private surface use agreements to avoid disputes between mineral owners and surface owners. *See, e.g.*, Wyo. Split Estate Act, WYO. STAT. ANN.

§§ 30–5–401, *et seq.* (codifying accommodation doctrine and setting forth requirements for mineral estate owner with regard to notice, sharing of work plans, and documentation of efforts to reach agreement on surface access); Colorado Oil and Gas Conservation Act, COLO. REV. STAT. §§ 34–60–101, *et seq.* (similar requirements). *See also EME Wyoming v. BRW East*, 486 P.3d 980 (Wyo. 2021) (describing Wyoming Split Estate Act as codifying oil and gas operators' access to surface lands and placing additional conditions on access); Joseph C. Pierzchala, *Surface Use Law: Colorado, New Mexico, Wyoming*, OIL & GAS AGREEMENTS: SURFACE USE IN THE 21ST CENTURY 2D-1 (Rocky Mt. Min. L. Fdn. 2017).

To avoid concerns associated with physical and economic waste under the rule of capture, many states set statutory and regulatory requirements for oil and gas operations to promote more efficient and productive oil and gas extraction. *See* Northcutt Ely, *The Conservation of Oil*, 51 HARV. L. REV. 1209 (1932); Northcutt Ely & John C. Jacobs, *Unit Operations of Oil and Gas Fields*, 57 YALE L.J. 1207 (1948). *See also* David B. Spence, *Federalism, Regulatory Lags, and the Political Economy of Energy Production*, 161 U. PA. L. REV. 431, 447–48 (2013) (discussing how the rule of capture led to waste in the oil fields in the late 19th and early 20th centuries, resulting in states enacting "conservation statutes" designed to organize production, promote efficiency, and set standards for well construction).

Each state takes a somewhat different statutory approach. Many states responded to the poor use of energy resources by creating well spacing requirements, conservation measures, and mandatory unitization or "forced pooling" laws, beginning in the 1920s. These laws created procedures allowing for the merger of multiple landowners' oil and gas interests into a single unit, imposed rules and standards for extraction, and established requirements for sharing costs and revenues. In a number of these states, once a certain percentage of landowners over a common field agree to unitization, any remaining landowners are bound by the agreement, thus overriding their individual property rights in the oil and gas resources underlying their land. According to a study in 2011, 38 states had some form of compulsory unitization or forced pooling laws governing the extraction of oil and gas resources. *See* Maria Baca, *State Laws Can Compel Landowners to Accept Gas and Oil Drilling*, PROPUBLICA (May 19, 2011); Sharon O. Flanery & Ryan J. Morgan, *Overview of Pooling and Unitization Affecting Appalachian Shale Development*, 32 ENERGY & MIN. L. INST. 13 (2011) (describing development and provisions of state well spacing laws and pooling and unitization laws).

The following Texas statutory provisions define some of these key measures and the role of its commission in implementing them. As you read them, consider how waste is defined and what measures are being used to prevent it.

TEXAS NATURAL RESOURCES CODE

Title 3. Oil and Gas

Subtitle B. Conservation and Regulation of Oil and Gas

Chapter 85. Conservation of Oil and Gas

A. General Provisions

Sec. 85.001. DEFINITIONS. (a) In this chapter:

(1) "Commission" means the Railroad Commission of Texas.

(2) "Pool," "common pool," "field," or "common source of supply" means a common reservoir.

(3) "Pool" means an underground reservoir containing a connected accumulation of crude petroleum oil, or natural gas, or both. . . .

Subchapter C. Provisions Generally Applicable to the Conservation of Oil and Gas

Sec. 85.041. ACTS PROHIBITED IN VIOLATION OF LAWS, RULES, AND ORDERS. (a) The purchase, acquisition, or sale, or the transporting, refining, processing, or handling in any other way, of oil or gas, produced in whole or in part in violation of any oil or gas conservation statute of this state or of any rule or order of the commission under such a statute, is prohibited.

(b) The purchase, acquisition, or sale, or the transporting, refining, processing, or handling in any other way, of any product of oil or gas which is derived in whole or in part from oil or gas or any product of either, which was in whole or part produced, purchased, acquired, sold, transported, refined, processed, or handled in any other way, in violation of any oil or gas conservation statute of this state, or of any rule or order of the commission under such a statute, is prohibited.

Sec. 85.042. RULES AND ORDERS. (a) The commission may promulgate and enforce rules and orders necessary to carry into effect the provisions of Section 85.041 of this code and to prevent that section's violation.

(b) When necessary, the commission shall make and enforce rules either general in their nature or applicable to particular fields for the prevention of actual waste of oil or operations in the field dangerous to life or property.

Sec. 85.043. APPLICATION OF CERTAIN RULES AND ORDERS. If the commission requires a showing that refined products were manufactured from oil legally produced, the requirement shall be of uniform application throughout the state; provided that, if the rule or order is promulgated for the purpose of controlling a condition in any local area or preventing a violation in any local area, then on the complaint of a person that the same or similar conditions exist in some other local area and the promulgation and enforcement of the rule could be beneficially applied to that additional area, the commission may determine whether or not those conditions do exist, and if it is shown that they do, the rule or order may be enlarged to include the additional area. . . .

Sec. 85.045. WASTE ILLEGAL AND PROHIBITED. The production, storage, or transportation of oil or gas in a manner, in an amount, or under conditions that constitute waste is unlawful and is prohibited.

Sec. 85.046. WASTE. (a) The term "waste," among other things, specifically includes:

(1) operation of any oil well or wells with an inefficient gas-oil ratio and the commission may determine and prescribe by order the permitted gas-oil ratio for the operation of oil wells;

(2) drowning with water a stratum or part of a stratum that is capable of producing oil or gas or both in paying quantities;

(3) underground waste or loss, however caused and whether or not the cause of the underground waste or loss is defined in this section;

(4) permitting any natural gas well to burn wastefully;

(5) creation of unnecessary fire hazards;

(6) physical waste or loss incident to or resulting from drilling, equipping, locating, spacing, or operating a well or wells in a manner that reduces or tends to reduce the total ultimate recovery of oil or gas from any pool;

(7) waste or loss incident to or resulting from the unnecessary, inefficient, excessive, or improper use of the reservoir energy, including the gas energy or water drive, in any well or pool; however, it is not the intent of this section or the provisions of this chapter that were formerly a part of Chapter 26, Acts of the 42nd Legislature, 1st Called Session, 1931, as amended, to require repressuring of an oil pool or to require that the separately owned properties in any pool be unitized under one management, control, or ownership;

(8) surface waste or surface loss, including the temporary or permanent storage of oil or the placing of any product of oil in open pits or earthen storage, and other forms of surface waste or surface loss including unnecessary or excessive surface losses, or destruction without beneficial use, either of oil or gas;

(9) escape of gas into the open air in excess of the amount necessary in the efficient drilling or operation of the well from a well producing both oil and gas;

(10) production of oil in excess of transportation or market facilities or reasonable market demand, and the commission may determine when excess production exists or is imminent and ascertain the reasonable market demand; and

(11) surface or subsurface waste of hydrocarbons, including the physical or economic waste or loss of hydrocarbons in the creation, operation, maintenance, or abandonment of an underground hydrocarbon storage facility.

(b) Notwithstanding the provisions contained in this section or elsewhere in this code or in other statutes or laws, the commission may permit production by commingling oil or gas or oil and gas from multiple stratigraphic or lenticular accumulations of oil or gas or oil and gas where the commission, after notice and opportunity for hearing, has found that producing oil or gas or oil and gas in a commingled state will prevent waste, promote conservation, or protect correlative rights.

(c) The commission, after notice and opportunity for hearing, may permit surface commingling of production of oil or gas or oil and gas from two or more tracts of land producing from the same reservoir or from one or more tracts of land producing from different reservoirs if the commission finds that the commingling will prevent waste, promote conservation, or protect correlative rights. The commission may permit the commingling regardless of whether the tracts or commission-designated reservoirs have the same working or royalty interest ownership. The amount of production attributable to each tract or commission-designated reservoir shall be determined in a manner consistent with this title. The commission has broad discretion in administering this subsection and shall adopt and enforce rules or orders as necessary to administer this subsection.

Sec. 85.047. EXCLUSION FROM DEFINITION OF WASTE. The use of gas produced from an oil well within the permitted gas-oil ratio for manufacture of natural gasoline shall not be included in the definition of waste.

Sec. 85.048. AUTHORITY TO LIMIT PRODUCTION. (a) Under the provisions of Subsection (10), Section 85.046 of this code, the commission shall not restrict the production of oil from any new field brought into production by exploration until the total production from that field is 10,000 barrels of oil a day in the aggregate.

(b) The commission's authority to restrict production from a new field under other provisions of Section 85.046 of this code is not limited by this section. . . .

Sec. 85.053. DISTRIBUTION, PRORATION, AND APPORTIONMENT OF ALLOWABLE PRODUCTION. (a) If a rule or order of the commission limits or fixes in a pool or portion of a pool the production of oil, or the production of gas from wells producing gas only, the commission, on written complaint by an affected party or on its own initiative and after notice and an opportunity for a hearing, shall distribute, prorate, or otherwise apportion or allocate the allowable production among the various producers on a reasonable basis if the commission finds that action to be necessary to:

(1) prevent waste; or

(2) adjust the correlative rights and opportunities of each owner of oil or gas in a common reservoir to produce and use or sell the oil or gas as permitted in this chapter.

(b) When, as provided in Subsection (b) of Section 85.046 or Subsection (b) of Section 86.012 of this code, as amended, the commission has permitted production by commingling oil or gas or oil and gas from multiple stratigraphic or lenticular accumulations of oil or gas or oil and gas, the commission may distribute, prorate, apportion, or allocate the production of such commingled separate multiple stratigraphic or lenticular accumulations of oil or gas or oil and gas as if they were a single pool; provided, however, that:

(i) such commingling shall not cause the allocation of allowable production from a well producing from any separate accumulation or accumulations to be less than that which would result from the commission applying the provisions of Section 86.095 of this code to such accumulation or accumulations; and

(ii) the allocation of the allowable for such commingled production shall be based on not less than two factors which the Railroad Commission shall take into account as directed by Section 86.089 of this code.

Sec. 85.054. ALLOWABLE PRODUCTION OF OIL. (a) To prevent unreasonable discrimination in favor of one pool as against another, and on written complaint and proof of such discrimination or if the commission on its own initiative finds such an action to be necessary, the commission may allocate or apportion the allowable production of oil on a fair and reasonable basis among the various pools in the state.

(b) In allocating or ascertaining the reasonable market demand for the entire state, the reasonable market demand of one pool shall not be discriminated against in favor of another pool.

(c) The commission may determine the reasonable market demand of the respective pool as the basis for determining the allotments to be assigned to the respective pool so that discrimination may be prevented.

Sec. 85.055. ALLOWABLE PRODUCTION OF GAS. (a) If, on written complaint by an affected party or on its own initiative and after notice and an opportunity for a hearing, the commission finds that full production from wells producing gas only from a common source of supply of gas in this state is in excess of the reasonable market demand, the commission shall inquire into the production and reasonable market demand for the gas and shall determine the allowable production from the common source of supply.

(b) The allowable production from a prorated common source of supply is that portion of the reasonable market demand that can be produced without waste.

(c) The commission shall allocate, distribute, or apportion the allowable production from the prorated common source of supply among the various producers on a reasonable basis and shall limit the production of each producer to the amount allocated or apportioned to the producer.

(d) When, as provided in Subsection (b) of Section 85.046 or Subsection (b) of Section 86.012 of this code, as amended, the commission has permitted production by commingling oil or gas or oil and gas from multiple stratigraphic or lenticular accumulations of oil or gas or oil and gas, the commission may allocate, distribute, or apportion the production of such commingled separate multiple stratigraphic or lenticular accumulations of oil or gas or oil and gas as if they were a single common source of supply; provided, however, that:

(i) such commingling shall not cause the allocation of allowable production from a well producing from any separate accumulation or accumulations to be less than that which would result from the commission applying the provisions of Section 86.095 of this code to such accumulation or accumulations; and

(ii) the allocation of the allowable for such commingled production shall be based on not less than two factors which the Railroad Commission shall take into account as directed by Section 86.089 of this code.

Sec. 85.056. PUBLIC INTEREST. In the administration of the provisions of this chapter that were formerly a part of Chapter 2, Acts of the 42nd Legislature, 4th Called Session, 1932, as amended, the commission shall take into consideration and protect the rights and interests of the purchasing and consuming public in oil and all its products, such as gasoline and lubricating oil. . . .

NOTES AND QUESTIONS

1. How does the court in *Elliff* balance encouraging extraction through the rule of capture and limiting it through the doctrine of waste? Do you think it strikes the balance correctly? As the court details the approaches of different states, which one seems the most appropriate?

2.   How does the Texas statute strike this balance? Do you agree with its approach? What are the benefits and limitations of having commissioners determine pooling, proration, apportionment, and production limits to constrain waste? At the start of the COVID-19 pandemic in the spring of 2020, oil prices plummeted as the United States and other nations imposed lockdowns, and travel by car, bus, and plane ground to a halt. When oil prices ventured into negative territory as a result, there were numerous calls for the Texas Railroad Commission to use its authority under the statute to impose limits on oil production to boost prices. After extended hearings on the topic, the Commission declined to do so, choosing to let markets address the crisis rather than regulation. Should the commission have stepped in to reduce the economic waste associated with oversupply? For a discussion of the arguments at the Commission, see Mitchell Ferman, *Texas Agency Won't Cut Production Despite Cratering Prices*, TEXAS TRIB. (May 5, 2020); Sergio Chapa, *Texas Railroad Commission Rejects Statewide Oil Production Cuts*, HOUSTON CHRON. (May 6, 2020).

3.   Consider the waste provisions of the Texas statute contained in Sections 85.045–.047. Which subsections of the statute deal directly with the waste issue in the *Ohio Oil* case excerpted in Chapter 2? Does the statute address this issue in the same way as the court did using the common law nuisance doctrine in *Ohio Oil*? In light of concerns associated with increased flaring of natural gas from oil wells since the advent of hydraulic fracturing, along with other environmental impacts of oil and gas production, both Colorado and New Mexico have enacted stricter regulations on the practice. *See, e.g.*, Sam Brasch, *Colorado Has a New Set of Oil and Gas Rules with a Focus on Regulating the Industry*, CPR NEWS (Nov. 23, 2020) (discussing new state legislation and implementing rules); Susan Montoya Bryan, *New Mexico Proposes More Rules to Curb Oil and Gas Emissions*, AP (May 6, 2021). These regulations, along with federal regulations governing flaring and venting of natural gas from oil and gas wells on federal lands, are discussed in more detail in Chapter 9.

4.   As you might imagine, most disputes over the accommodation doctrine discussed in the *VirTex* case do not involve conflicts between oil and gas extraction and the use of helicopters for deer capture, but instead involve conflicts between oil and gas extraction and surface uses such as ranching, farming, or residential activities. However, in recent years, other conflicts have arisen, such as one in Texas involving the use of the surface estate for solar energy. *See Lyle v. Midway Solar LLC*, 618 S.W.3d 857 (Tex. Ct. App. 2020) (finding accommodation doctrine applied to dispute between large scale solar operation and subsurface mineral owner but that subsurface mineral owner could not enjoin solar operation prior to attempting to develop those minerals and showing that the solar plant interfered with the ability to drill for oil and gas). For more on the accommodation doctrine, see *EQT Prod. Co. v. Crowder*, 828 S.E.2d 800 (W. Va. 2019) (mineral owner does not have right to use surface lands to benefit mining or drilling on other property); Brandy R. Manning & Daniel B. Mathis, *The Accommodation Doctrine in Texas (and Elsewhere)*, ABA ENV'T & ENERGY LITIG. (Mar. 11, 2014); Meredith Wegener, *Balancing Rights*

in a New Energy Era: Will the Mineral Estate's Dominance Continue?, 57 HOUS. L. REV. 1037 (2020).

5.   Should the rule of capture apply in the context of hydraulic fracturing of oil and gas, where the oil or gas cannot be produced or flow freely without horizontal drilling, fracturing the rocks, and injecting sand and chemicals to hold open the pores in the rock to allow the gas to flow? In a controversial decision discussed in depth in Chapter 9, the Texas Supreme Court in 2008 held that the rule of capture did apply to hydraulic fracturing activities that resulted in natural gas being drained from a neighbor's property. The court thus dismissed the neighbor's trespass action even though the jury had found that the hydraulic fracturing actions had constituted a trespass. The court held that the rule of capture applied in part because the landowner could drill a well of his own to offset drainage from the property, the landowner could seek forced pooling if an offer to pool was rejected, and the rule of capture was well established in Texas and the court did not wish to alter it. *See Coastal Oil & Gas Corp. v. Garza Energy Trust*, 268 S.W.3d 1 (Tex. 2008). *See also Briggs v. Southwestern Energy Prod. Co.*, 224 A.3d 334 (Pa. 2020) (reaching a similar conclusion). What public policy goals are promoted by applying the rule of capture in these situations? By allowing the trespass action to prevail?

6.   As you might imagine, there is a wealth of common law doctrine and state regulation that governs oil and gas ownership, leasing, and conservation. For a summary of these regulations and doctrines, see generally ALEXANDRA B. KLASS & HANNAH J. WISEMAN, ENERGY LAW: CONCEPTS AND INSIGHTS ch. 2 (2d ed. 2020).

b. Oil and Gas Development on Federal Lands

The Mineral Leasing Act of 1920 is the primary law granting authority to the U.S. Department of Interior, through BLM, to lease federal oil and natural gas resources. As discussed in the earlier section on coal leasing, the federal government retained title to the bulk of subsurface mineral resources in the western United States even while it conveyed the surface lands to private parties under the various homesteading acts. Congress amended the Mineral Leasing Act in 1987 with the enactment of the Federal Onshore Oil and Gas Leasing Reform Act (FOOGLRA or "Reform Act"), 30 U.S.C. §§ 188, 195, 226. FOOGLRA revised the federal leasing system to ensure all leases are awarded through a competitive bidding process and to ensure protection of surface resources potentially impacted by oil and gas production. The bulk of oil and gas extraction on federal lands occurs on lands managed by BLM (within the Department of Interior) or the U.S. Forest Service (within the Department of Agriculture). Under FOOGLRA, BLM manages the mineral leasing process with regard to oil and gas resources on all federal lands, but with respect to leasing on federal forest lands, the Forest Service retains authority to determine whether oil and gas leasing is compatible with surface use and protection of those lands. The following case explores the application of these laws.

CITIZENS FOR A HEALTHY COMMUNITY V. BLM

377 F. Supp. 3d 1223 (D. Colo. 2019)

BABCOCK, DISTRICT JUDGE.

This matter is before me on Plaintiffs' Amended Complaint for Declaratory and Injunctive Relief and Petition for Review of Agency Action. Plaintiffs seek judicial review of: (1) Defendant Bureau of Land Management's (BLM) approval of a master development plan; (2) Defendant United States Forest Service's (USFS) approval of certain natural gas wells, well pads, and related infrastructure; and (3) both Defendants' approval of related applications for permits to drill. . . .

Through the Mineral Leasing Act, 30 U.S.C. §§ 181–287, the Federal Land Policy and Management Act, 43 U.S.C. §§ 1701–1787, and related regulations, BLM has authority to lease public lands with oil and gas reserves to private industry for development. *W. Energy All. v. Zinke*, 877 F.3d 1157, 1161 (10th Cir. 2017). Lands contained in national forests have additional oversight from the Secretary of Agriculture. 30 U.S.C. § 226(h).

In enacting the Federal Land Policy and Management Act, Congress aimed to empower the Secretary of the Interior to manage the United States' public lands. 43 U.S.C. § 1701. The Secretary, through BLM, "shall manage the public lands under principles of multiple use and sustained yield." 43 U.S.C. § 1732(a). "Multiple use" means "a combination of balanced and diverse resource uses that takes into account the long-term needs of future generations for renewable and nonrenewable resources, including, but not limited to, recreation, range, timber, minerals, watershed, wildlife and fish, and natural scenic, scientific and historical values. . . ."43 U.S.C. § 1702(c). Congress entrusts BLM with the "orderly and efficient exploration, development and production of oil and gas." 43 C.F.R. § 3160.0–4; 43 U.S.C. § 1732(b). This is done by using a "three-phase decision-making process." *W. Energy All. v. Zinke*, 877 F.3d at 1161 (quoting *Pennaco Energy, Inc. v. U.S. Dep't of Interior*, 377 F.3d 1147, 1151 (10th Cir. 2004)).

In the first phase, BLM creates a resource management plan (RMP), which is "designed to guide and control future management actions and the development of subsequent, more detailed and limited scope plans for resources and uses." 43 C.F.R. § 1601.0–2. Part of an RMP indicates the lands open or closed to the development of oil and gas, and subsequent development must abide by the terms of the RMP. *W. Energy All.*, 877 F.3d at 1161–62. The approval of an RMP "is considered a major Federal action significantly affecting the quality of the human environment" and thus requires an [Environmental Impact Statement] EIS [under the National Environmental Policy Act]. 43 C.F.R. § 1601.0–6.

In the second phase, through state offices, BLM identifies parcels that it will offer for lease, responds to potential protests of the suggested parcels, and conducts "a competitive lease sale auction." *W. Energy All.*, 877 F.3d at 1162 (citing 43 C.F.R. Subpart 3120). During the identification of parcels available for leasing, a 2010 Department of Interior policy mandates additional review, including: (1) an interdisciplinary team reviewing the parcels proposed for leasing and conducting site visits; (2) identifying issues BLM must consider; and (3) obliging BLM to consult other stakeholders "such as federal agencies, and State, tribal, and local governments." *Id.*

In the final phase, after the sale of a lease, BLM "decides whether specific development projects will be permitted on the leased land." *Id.*; see 43 C.F.R. § 3162.3–1; 30 U.S.C. § 226. BLM must approve applications for permits to drill after parcels of land are leased. 30 U.S.C. § 226(g). . .

The Bull Mountain Unit (the "Unit") is located in the Colorado River basin, approximately 30 miles northeast of the town of Paonia and is bisected by State Highway 133. The Unit consists of: 440 acres of federal surface lands underlain by a mineral estate administered by BLM; 12,900 acres of split-estate lands consisting of private surface and BLM-administered minerals; and 6,330 acres of fee land consisting of private surface and private minerals regulated by the Colorado Oil and Gas Conservation Commission.

In 2008 and 2009, BLM sought input for a master development plan (MDP) concerning 2,300 acres of land owned by Intervenor-Defendants within the Unit. An MDP typically provides infrastructural information regarding a planned cluster of wells and associated facilities adjacent to an oil and gas unit or field. BLM completed a preliminary [Environmental Assessment] EA [under the National Environmental Policy Act], but then elected to complete an EIS regarding the Unit's MDP. In January 2015, BLM published a draft EIS with an opportunity for public comment. In July 2016, BLM published a final EIS.

In the final EIS, BLM considered four alternatives: alternative A was a no-action alternative and alternatives B, C, and D contained a development of 146 new gas wells and four new water disposal wells. Alternatives B, C, and D contained 36, 35, and 33 new well pads, respectively. BLM selected alternative D as its preferred alternative. It assumed the life of the project would be at least 50 years. In October 2017, BLM approved the MDP in a Record of Decision. This Record of Decision additionally approved an application for permit to drill (APD) by Intervenor-Defendants. BLM notes that since the commencement of this suit, it has approved: (1) three other APDs in the same well pad location as the original APD; (2) two lateral extensions for an existing well bore on a different well pad; and (3) two APDs on well pads located on private surface lands.

The 25-well Project addressed six APDs—three from Intervenor-Defendants and three from another company. The 25-well Project is situated between Paonia and Carbondale. It involves the construction of 25 natural gas wells on four new well pads and one existing well pad and the approval of 19 additional APDs. One proposed well pad occurs on split estate lands with federal minerals underneath private surface land. Three other well pads are located on federally managed lands. The fifth well pad is located on private surface lands over private mineral estate, but is planned to bore horizontally into adjacent federal mineral estate. . . .

Plaintiffs are non-profit organizations who focus on environmental issues. . . . Plaintiffs challenge the NEPA review process performed by Defendants regarding the Unit's MPD and the 25-well Project, alleging generally that Defendants "failed to consider a reasonable range of alternatives" and "failed to take a hard look at the direct, indirect, and cumulative impacts to people and the environment." . . .

In an EIS or EA, federal agencies must consider the direct, indirect, and cumulative predicted impacts of a proposed action. . . . "The significance of an impact is determined by the action's context and its intensity." . . . "Applicable regulations require agencies to consider ten factors when assessing intensity, including the proposed action's effects on public health, the unique characteristics of the geographic area, the uncertainty of potential effects, and the degree of controversy surrounding the effects on the human environment." *Id.* (citing 40 C.F.R. § 1508.27(b)).

Plaintiffs contend that Defendants failed in their analysis of: (1) the foreseeable indirect impacts of oil and gas; (2) the cumulative impacts of GHG pollution and climate change; and (3) the magnitude and severity of GHG emissions from the Unit's EIS and the 25-well Project's EA. . . .

Plaintiffs argue that in the EIS and EA, Defendants provided no analysis of the indirect impacts of oil and gas production, specifically the emissions resulting from the eventual combustion of those fuels. Defendants respond that they have "repeatedly explained that available scientific models could not perform such precise calculations." Defendants continue that "it is unknown which specific uses will be made of those minerals, where those uses will occur, what type and amount of GHG emissions will result from those uses, and what incremental effects those emissions may have on climate change." Intervenor-Defendants add that it would be inappropriate and irrelevant for Defendants to analyze downstream combustion at this time because: (1) the Unit's MDP is an umbrella analysis "meant to facilitate separate actions that will actually authorize resource extraction. . ."; (2) BLM's rejection of the MDP would not invalidate Intervenor-Defendants' existent leases; and (3) if BLM denied the 25-well Project, "federal minerals would be drained through oil and gas development on private mineral estate adjacent to the 25-Well Project. . . ."

"Indirect impacts are defined as being caused by the action and are later in time or farther removed in distance but still reasonably foreseeable." *Utahns for Better Transp.* [*v. U.S. Dep't of Transp.*], 305 F.3d [1152, 1177 (10th Cir. 2002)] (citing 40 C.F.R. § 1508.8(b)). An effect is considered reasonably foreseeable if it is "sufficiently likely to occur that a person of ordinary prudence would take it into account in reaching a decision." *Colo. Env't Coal. v. Salazar*, 875 F.Supp.2d 1233, 1251 (D. Colo. 2012) (citing cases).

Courts with persuasive authority have found that combustion emissions are an indirect effect of an agency's decision to extract those natural resources. *See San Juan Citizens All. v. U.S. Bureau of Land Mgmt.*, 326 F. Supp. 3d 1227, 1242–43 (D.N.M. 2018) (collecting cases) (*San Juan*). I found similarly in *Wilderness Workshop v. United States Bureau of Land Management*, when I held that "BLM acted in an arbitrary and capricious manner and violated NEPA by not taking a hard look at the indirect effects resulting from the combustion of oil and gas in the planning area under the RMP." 342 F. Supp. 3d 1145, 1156 (D. Colo. 2018). . . .

. . . . Further, Defendants relied upon Intervenor-Defendants' production estimations when conducting its economic analysis. . . . *see also Michael Burger & Jessica Wentz, Downstream and Upstream Greenhouse Gas Emissions: The Proper Scope of NEPA Review*, 41 Harv. Env't L. Rev. 109, 183 (2017) (listing a variety of available of tools that can be used to estimate the indirect greenhouse gas emissions from fossil fuel production).

Simply put, an agency cannot rely on production estimates while simultaneously claiming it would be too speculative to rely upon the predicted emissions from those same production estimates. *Wilderness Workshop* [*v. BLM*], 342 F. Supp. 3d [1145, 1155–56 (D. Colo. 2018)] (quoting *High Country Conservation Advocates v. United States Forest Service*, 52 F. Supp. 3d 1174, 1196 (D. Colo. 2014)). . . .

As such, Defendants acted in an arbitrary and capricious manner and violated NEPA by not taking a hard look at the foreseeable indirect effects resulting from the combustion of oil and gas in the EIS and EA. Defendants must quantify and reanalyze the foreseeable indirect effects the emissions.

[The court proceeded to find that the defendants sufficiently analyzed the cumulative climate change impacts as well as the economic and socio-economic impacts of the GHG emissions associated with the projects. It also found that the defendants appropriately analyzed the water quantity and wildlife impacts associated with the projects but did not adequately analyze the cumulative impacts on wildlife associated with the projects.— Eds.]

NOTES AND QUESTIONS

1.   Can you list some of the additional regulatory hurdles associated with developing oil and gas resources on public lands as compared to private lands based on the *Citizens for a Healthy Community* excerpt? Are such additional hurdles justified? Regarding GHG emissions, how might BLM and the USFS comply with the court's order? What information will the agencies be required to compile? How difficult will that be?

2.   The *Citizens for a Healthy Community* excerpt illustrates that split estate lands exist not only between two private parties, but also between private parties and the federal government. What additional challenges exist for split estate lands when one of the parties is the federal government?

3.   As discussed in the Practice Problem at the end of this chapter, soon after President Biden took office in 2021, he issued an executive order that directed the Secretary of Interior to "pause" new oil and natural gas leases on public lands to allow completion of a comprehensive review of federal oil and gas permitting and leasing practices in light of the Secretary's "broad stewardship responsibilities over the public lands," including potential climate and other impacts. Is such a "pause" consistent with the Secretary's multiple use mandate under the Federal Land Policy and Management Act or its obligations to lease lands for oil and gas development under the Mineral Leasing Act? Why or why not? For a discussion of this issue, see *Louisiana v. Biden*, 2021 WL 2446010 (W.D. La., June 15, 2021) (granting preliminary injunction against leasing pause); Heather Richards, *Interior Announces First Oil Drilling Sales of the Biden Era*, ENERGYWIRE (Aug. 25, 2021) (reporting on Interior Department announcement of first lease sales to comply with court order while appealing same).

C. RENEWABLE ENERGY SOURCES

As Chapter 2 explores in depth, renewable energy sources constitute a rapidly increasing share of the fuels used for electricity and transportation. The law sometimes supports that transition, such as through state clean energy standards (discussed in Chapter 5) and financial incentives, and at times does not. For example, the royalty program that helps to foster offshore oil and gas drilling, described in Chapter 9, provides financial incentives for fossil fuel expansion and the federal Production Tax Credit provides financial incentives for wind power and other renewables.

Given renewables' importance in addressing climate change, their rapid worldwide growth, and the goals of those who advocate for a transition to a cleaner energy economy, it is crucial to consider the laws governing extraction of renewable energy. In general, renewable sources have fewer externalities associated with extraction than fossil fuels, particularly with respect to pollution of land and water, but they still raise concerns addressed by the law. These externalities interact with federalism questions as some of them, like risks to endangered species, implicate federal environmental laws, while others arise in the context of state and local land use planning.

In addition, the physical characteristics of renewable energy sources create issues for regulating their extraction. Namely, unlike coal, oil, and gas, most renewable energy sources—except for biofuels—produce their energy at the time of extraction. While storage technologies are improving and becoming more cost competitive, this physical reality means that renewables need to be close to where they are being used and connected to a low voltage distribution network or have access to a high-voltage transmission grid. They also need to be integrated into electricity system operations and linked to electricity markets. Chapters 4 and 5 on the electricity system, Chapter 7 on energy transportation, and Chapter 8 on grid modernization address some of these difficult grid integration issues.

This section first addresses hydropower and then discusses wind and solar energy. We treat hydropower separately because it has a distinct and long-standing federal regime regulating it, in addition to the state and local issues that it raises. Its extraction is also arguably the most controversial, with fights over the benefits and harms of dams taking place throughout the 20th century and into the present.

1. HYDROPOWER ENERGY

Hydropower extraction through dams has long been a source of non-fossil fuel energy in the United States. Many large dam projects were built with federal involvement. In addition to serving as major new sources of electricity, these projects played a crucial role in helping provide employment in the first half of the 20th century, including in the New Deal period. Today, the federal government owns and operates approximate one-half of U.S. hydroelectric generating capacity, primarily through the U.S. Army Corps of Engineers and U.S. Bureau of Reclamation. These large hydropower facilities are located primarily in the western United States. Federal Power Marketing Administrations (PMAs) within the U.S. Department of Energy sell federal hydropower resources to utilities and other power distributors. *See* KELSI BRACMORT ET AL., CONG. RSCH. SERV., HYDROPOWER: FEDERAL AND NONFEDERAL INVESTMENT (July 2015). The remainder of U.S. hydropower is owned and operated by local governments and private utilities. This "non-federal hydropower" is subject to FERC jurisdiction and must meet FERC licensing requirements. Although both federal hydropower and non-federal hydropower have provided accessible and inexpensive electricity to large portions of the United States, the construction—and presence—of dams became a controversial topic over time, with many environmental interests calling for dam decommissioning in various parts of the country, as discussed in Chapter 2.

The following excerpt by Professor Gina Warren describes the evolution of FERC regulation of non-federal hydropower as the industry expanded in the early 20th century.

GINA S. WARREN, HYDROPOWER: IT'S A SMALL WORLD AFTER ALL

91 Neb. L. Rev. 925, 933–38 (2013)

The Federal Water Power Act of 1920 (enacted in 1920, amended in 1935 and 1986, and renamed the Federal Power Act) (FPA) was the first national policy for the regulation of hydropower development. The purpose of the FPA was to set forth a comprehensive plan for development of the Nation's water resources that were within the jurisdiction of the federal government. This comprehensive plan would replace "the piecemeal, restrictive, negative approach of the River and Harbor Acts and other federal laws previously enacted." It created a new commission—the Federal Power Commission, now known as the Federal Energy Regulatory Commission (FERC)—with the exclusive regulatory and licensing authority over hydropower facilities. Under the FPA, licenses are required for all new and already-built hydroelectric facilities located within the Act's jurisdiction. The Act's jurisdiction includes all navigable waters or waters that affect interstate commerce, dams or reservoirs that occupy federal land, or dams that utilize surplus water or water power from a government dam. When enacted, the FPA was thought to be a detailed and comprehensive plan, which left "no room or need for conflicting state controls." Provisions of the Clean Water Act . . . somewhat altered this view. Nevertheless, the Commission remains the preeminent regulatory body, deciding whether development should occur and if so, by whom and how.

The Act authorizes the Commission to grant a fifty-year license to a hydropower operator as long as the project is: (1) in the public interest and (2) "best adapted to a comprehensive plan for improving or developing a waterway." . . . [T]he FPA was later amended [in 1986] to require the Commission to "give equal consideration to the purposes of energy conservation, the protection, mitigation of damage to, and enhancement of, fish and wildlife (including related spawning grounds and habitat), the protection of recreational opportunities, and the preservation of other aspects of environmental quality." In short, the Commission must now weigh the need for hydropower energy development within a national waterway against (1) the availability of alternative sources of power; (2) other potential uses of the river, including recreational uses; and (3) the protection of the environment, fish, and wildlife. Unfortunately, the statute provides the Commission little guidance—and allows for significant leeway—in balancing these values. . . .

While the Commission had exclusive authority to license and regulate private and municipal hydropower facilities, federally-owned hydropower facilities could be constructed and operated outside the FPA. In the mid-twentieth century, the U.S. Army Corps of Engineers (Corps) and the U.S. Bureau of Reclamation worked together to build the largest dams in the United States. In fact, "85 were built between 1902 and 1930, and 203 were built between 1930 and 1970," including the well-known Hoover Dam. Construction of the Hoover Dam (originally known as the Colorado River's Boulder Dam) began in 1931 with the first electric generation from the facility occurring in 1936. Construction on the dam continued until 1961. As completed, Hoover Dam is 726.4 feet high and 1,244 feet long, containing a total of 7.65 million cubic yards of concrete. According to the Bureau of Reclamation, Hoover Dam generates an average of four billion kilowatt-hour (kWh) of electricity annually, making it one of the largest electric power generating facilities in the world. It remains the "highest and third largest concrete dam in the United States." . . .

. . . [W]hen hydropower first came to prominence in the United States, there was little concern, or at least little understanding, about what the dams and reservoirs could do to the surrounding ecosystem. However, "[a]s scientists began to study ecosystems and the life cycles of various water dependent species, they came to realize the decline of certain fish and animal species could be traced to the dams, which can destroy entire river habitats." Many environmentalists had a growing concern that FERC was too autonomous, with too much authority, and failed to take into account the environmental concerns when issuing licenses or relicenses. In an effort to give environmental issues more importance in the FERC review process, Congress enacted the Electric Consumers Protection Act of 1986 [ECPA], which amended the Federal Power Act. . . . "[T]he Act added environmental protection provisions that require FERC [in FPA §§ 4(e) and 10(a)] to "give equal consideration" to energy development and the protection of and conservation of our natural resources, including fish, wildlife and the environment. To facilitate the balancing of these interests, FERC is required [under FPA § 10(j)] to consult with state and federal environmental agencies prior to issuing licenses. These state and federal resource agencies evaluate the project and place conditions and recommendations on the proposed license for the "protection, mitigation, and enhancement" of the environment, fish, and wildlife. FERC must then accept the conditions and recommendations as part of the license or provide a written explanation as to why the recommendations or conditions are "inconsistent with the purposes and requirements of applicable law." Whether this added provision has made any difference—other than to increase administrative costs—is unclear. As one commentator notes, "both the FERC and the courts have interpreted the language as merely procedural, rejecting the notion that environmental concerns be accorded any particular weight." . . .

As the above excerpt makes clear, licensing of hydropower projects is a core area of regulation. Theoretically, FERC jurisdiction over initial licensing and relicensing can be a complicated question, but in practice, FERC has jurisdiction over virtually all non-federal hydroelectricity facilities in the United States. Charles R. Sensiba, *Hydropower, in* THE LAW OF CLEAN ENERGY: EFFICIENCY AND RENEWABLES (Michael B. Gerrard, ed. 2011); BRACMORT ET AL., *supra*.

Under Part I of the FPA, FERC's licensing of hydroelectric facilities takes place under a four-stage lifecycle. First, under § 4(f) of the FPA, 16 U.S.C. § 797(f), FERC issues "preliminary permits." These permits do not actually allow the construction or operation of a hydroelectricity facility, but rather, give license applicants a chance to collect data, prepare maps, and make other plans necessary for their license application. Second, under § 4(e), FERC issues licenses for the actual construction and operation of hydroelectric facilities. These licenses can be issued for fifty years. Third, upon the expiration of the original license, FERC can relicense a facility for thirty to fifty years under FPA § 15, 16 U.S.C. § 808. Finally, FERC may decommission facilities or accept the surrender of licenses pursuant to FPA § 6, *Id.* § 799. A license might be surrendered for various reasons, including escalating construction costs, technical infeasibility of a planned dam, or a project that has become uneconomic because of new environmental or other conditions in the relicensing process. FERC provides extensive guidance on hydroelectric licensing in its handbook, which covers how to apply the traditional, integrated, and alternative licensing processes; exemptions from licensing; and competing applications. *See* FED. ENERGY REGULATORY COMM'N, HANDBOOK FOR HYDROELECTRIC PROJECT LICENSING AND 5 MW EXEMPTIONS FROM LICENSING (Apr. 2004). *See also* FED. ENERGY REGULATORY COMM'N, HYDROPOWER LICENSING—GET INVOLVED: A GUIDE FOR THE PUBLIC (2020); FED. ENERGY REGULATORY COMM'N, HYDROPOWER PRIMER: A HANDBOOK OF HYDROPOWER BASICS (Feb. 2017).

Courts give FERC a wide berth in determining its licensing procedures. As the Ninth Circuit has put it, the FPA "establishes an elaborate regulatory regime which charges [FERC] with the responsibility to balance the interests of hydropower licenses and other participants in the licensing process." *Am. Rivers v. FERC*, 201 F.3d 1186, 1201 (9th Cir. 1999). As a consequence, Congress "left the complex policy decision about how far FERC should extend its regulatory tentacles up to FERC itself." *Bear Lake Watch, Inc. v. FERC*, 324 F.3d 1071, 1074 (9th Cir. 2003). Nevertheless, the FPA does put some limits on FERC's discretion. For instance, FERC must adhere to the § 7 and § 106 consultation requirements of, respectively, the Endangered Species Act and the National Historic Preservation Act; conduct consistency reviews under the Coastal Zone Management Act; and ensure that licenses satisfy the § 401 water quality certification requirements of the Clean Water Act, as discussed below.

Today, most of FERC's work is at the relicensing stage with regard to large hydropower facilities, coupled with an increased focus on licensing new small and medium size hydropower projects. *See* U.S. DEP'T OF ENERGY, U.S. HYDROPOWER MARKET REPORT 49 (Jan. 2021) (showing size of projects receiving new licenses). Environmentalists often raise concerns during the licensing and relicensing process about the ways in which hydroelectric dams change river landscapes and water flows, and adversely impact fish and other river-based species.

When reading the case below, consider how the opinion treats environmental concerns and the role that deference to agency decision-making plays in the resolution of this dispute. Also pay attention to the court's description of the nuts and bolts of the FERC licensing process itself.

U.S. DEP'T OF INTERIOR V. FERC

952 F.2d 538 (D.C. Cir. 1992)

HARRY T. EDWARDS, CIRCUIT JUDGE:

This case presents another skirmish in the continuing battle between utilities and municipalities seeking to produce electricity and agencies and individuals seeking to protect the environment. Here, the Federal Energy Regulatory Commission (FERC or Commission) licensed sixteen projects in the Upper Ohio River Basin over objections from the United States Department of Interior (Interior) and several state agencies and interest groups. In the case at hand, the petitioners now claim that FERC (i) granted the disputed licenses without sufficient data to assess the environmental impacts of the projects, and (ii) gave insufficient weight to environmental concerns raised by the projects. . . .

Beginning in 1979, Allegheny Electric Cooperative and others filed applications to operate hydroelectric power projects at 19 existing dams in the Upper Ohio River Basin. A total of 25 applications were filed, five of which were mutually exclusive. In early 1987, FERC determined that, because the projects presented a danger of reducing the rivers' water quality, the National Environmental Policy Act, 42 U.S.C. § 4332(2)(C) (1988), required the preparation of an Environmental Impact Statement (EIS).

In May 1988, FERC staff published a draft EIS. The Commission solicited comments from interested parties, including the petitioners in this case, and FERC staff held a public meeting in Pittsburgh, Pennsylvania. The petitioners submitted written comments which focused on three concerns: the effect of the projects on dissolved oxygen (DO) levels in the river, the level of fish mortality resulting from entrainment (passage of fish through turbines), and the disruption of public sport fishing. The dissolved oxygen level of water determines the capacity of the river to support marine life and absorb waste. The dams in the Ohio River Basin increase the DO level by aerating water as it passes over the dam. Hydropower projects tend to reduce aeration because water passes over turbines instead of falling freely over the crest of the dam. Fish mortality from entrainment obviously lowers fish populations, but also tends disproportionately to affect desirable sport fish species which live near dams. Sport fishing is an important recreational use of the existing properties, and could be disrupted by project development.

On September 29, 1988, FERC issued its final EIS (FEIS). The FEIS analyzed the proposed projects from a number of different perspectives, including power generation, impact on water quality and fishery resources, effects on recreational facilities, and socioeconomic conditions. In responding to the concerns expressed by Interior and the state environmental agencies, the FEIS offered five alternatives ranging from denial of all license applications to granting each license as proposed. . . .

In deciding which projects to license, FERC opted for a moderately protective construction scheme. In addition to the option of denying all license applications, the FEIS had analyzed four alternatives wherein differing numbers of the projects would be built or operated at different power levels. The Commission opted to license 16 of the proposed 19 sites, concluding that the alternative selected, "[i]n addition to protecting water quality, . . . would protect target resources by avoiding the significant adverse impacts to wetlands, fisheries, and recreation that would occur if the proposed projects at [the three unlicensed sites] were built." "The FEIS considered the adverse impacts of these [unlicensed] projects to be unavoidable, because no adequate site-specific mitigative measures were found to currently exist." Balancing the power benefits against potential environmental harms, the Commission concluded that the alternative best advanced competing goals.

The Commission addressed the DO level concern by adopting a 6.5 mg/l minimum for all projects where current levels met or exceeded that mark. The FEIS had considered four options for different DO standards: no conditions, conditioning operation on 5.0 mg/l DO, conditioning operation on 6.5 mg/l DO, and conditioning operation on maintenance of pre-project DO levels. The Commission rejected a 5.0 mg/l DO standard, the current standard set by the three bordering states, as too low to ensure continued fish development. A study by the United States Environmental Protection Agency had established 6.5 mg/l as the level necessary to maintain unimpeded fish development. . . .

. . . The Commission estimated that the 6.5 mg/l standard would cause "an annual fuel displacement loss of 246,000 barrels of oil" and would

> result in a loss of approximately $11 million in annual revenues for local governments when compared to [the least restrictive alternative]. However, on balance, we do not believe that these lost displacement benefits and lost local government revenues outweigh the potential adverse impacts to the resurgent fishery resources in the basin that could occur if the proposed projects were allowed to reduce DO levels below 6.5 mg/L.

48 F.E.R.C. at 62,364.

FERC also took several other steps to protect water quality. First, the Commission included license conditions "requiring the licensees with projects located at the 11 dams that are moderate to good aerators to cease generation or take other appropriate steps, should DO levels at their projects fall below 6.5 mg/L even with the required spill flows." Second, the Commission retained authority to modify the other five projects to improve water quality if necessary. Third, FERC required all licensees to join a water quality management group (WQMG), which included members of the federal and state agencies, and "to submit for Commission approval any recommendations for modifications in the spill flows or other conditions at the project" coming from the WQMG. Fourth, the Commission included in each license a reservation of authority, enabling it on its own motion or the motion of the federal and state agencies to "order reasonable modifications in project structures or operations to conserve or develop fish and wildlife resources." Finally, although rejecting the state agencies' requests to require DO to remain at pre-project levels, the Commission acknowledged that the states were empowered by section 401(a)(1) of the Clean Water Act to impose the more stringent requirement if they so desired.

As to fish entrainment, the FEIS evaluated data from several other projects, including two on the Ohio River. The Commission concluded that minimal mortality would occur to fish eggs and larvae entrained. . . .

. . . While acknowledging that "existing studies have not provided definitive answers to questions regarding the magnitude of entrainment" that would occur on the proposed projects, the Commission concluded that, "on the basis of the existing credible scientific evidence and . . . their best professional judgment," juvenile and adult mortality would be between zero and 10 percent of fish entrained. In balancing, the Commission assumed the worst case, 10 percent mortality rate, and concluded that licensing the 16 projects was in the public interest, even at that mortality level.

Despite its conclusion that the projects should be constructed even at the 10 percent mortality rate, the Commission imposed other conditions to reduce the number of fish killed, including:

> (1) monitoring of actual entrainment once project operations have begun; (2) compensation to the state resource agency for project-related losses unless and until site-specific mitigation is installed; (3) a basin-wide cooperative effort to develop prototype facilities for fish protection and guidance (bioengineering test facility); and (4) reevaluation of mitigation options, based on the results of such testing.

Id. at 62,377. . . .

Finally, to protect sport fishing opportunities in the tailwaters below dams, FERC required project licensees to provide access to powerhouse tailwaters, consistent with safety requirements, wherever physically possible. Licensees were charged with acquiring additional land where necessary to guarantee public access. Where on-site access was physically obstructed, FERC required licensees to provide off-site recreational facilities. . . .

Our review of the Commission's decision is deferential. In a licensing decision such as this, where few explicit statutory provisions govern, our role is narrowly circumscribed. . . .

Under the FPA, FERC may license hydroelectric projects on federal lands and on waterways that are subject to congressional regulation under the Commerce Clause. 16 U.S.C. § 797(e) (1988). Under sections 4(e) and 10(a) of the FPA, 16 U.S.C. §§ 797(e), 803(a), as amended by the Electric Consumers Protection Act (ECPA), Pub. L. No. 99–495, 100 Stat. 1243 (1986), FERC must consider environmental issues when deciding whether to issue hydropower licenses.

> In deciding whether to issue any license under [the FPA] for any project, the Commission, in addition to the power and development purposes for which licenses are issued, shall give equal consideration to the purposes of energy conservation, the protection, mitigation of damage to, and enhancement of, fish and wildlife (including related spawning grounds and habitat), the protection of recreational opportunities, and the preservation of other aspects of environmental quality.

16 U.S.C. § 797(e) (1988).

> All licenses issued under this subchapter shall be on the following conditions: That the project adopted . . . will be best adapted to a comprehensive plan . . . for the adequate protection, mitigation,

and enhancement of fish and wildlife (including related spawning grounds and habitat). . . .

16 U.S.C. § 803(a) (1988).

Additionally, under section 10(j) of the FPA, 16 U.S.C. § 803(j), FERC must impose conditions on licenses "based on recommendations received pursuant to the Fish and Wildlife Coordination Act (16 U.S.C. § 661 *et seq.*) from the National Marine Fisheries Service, the United States Fish and Wildlife Service, and State fish and wildlife agencies." § 803(j)(1). FERC retains ultimate authority, however, to decide whether any recommended conditions are "inconsistent with the purposes of" the FPA or other laws. § 803(j)(2). When it acts contrary to a recommendation received from a wildlife agency, FERC must make an appropriate finding on the record to justify its decision. *Id.* . . .

The agencies . . . contend, first, that FERC violated the statute and its own regulations in refusing to conduct studies that the agencies thought vital to the section 10(j) recommendation process, and, second, that the FERC licensing decisions here violate the mandate of sections 4(e) and 10(a) that environmental concerns be given "equal consideration." The agencies' first objection may be disposed of easily. Nothing in the statute requires *FERC* to conduct the studies that the fish and wildlife agencies deem necessary to the section 10(j) process. Section 10(j)(1) requires the Commission to consider recommendations "received pursuant to the Fish and Wildlife Coordination Act (16 U.S.C. § 661, *et seq*)." 16 U.S.C. § 803(j)(1). Under the Coordination Act, agency recommendations are made "based on surveys and investigations *conducted by* the United States Fish and Wildlife Service and such state agenc[ies]." 16 U.S.C. § 662(b) (1988) (emphasis added). . . .

We also reject the agencies' contentions founded on sections 4(e) and 10(a). The statutory "equal consideration" requirement does not change the standard of review that we, as an appeals court, apply. The ECPA amendments to the FPA, which added the "equal consideration" language to section 4(e) and created the section 10(j) process, were aimed primarily at increasing FERC's sensitivity to environmental concerns. *See* H.R. REP. No. 507, 99th Cong., 2d Sess. 21–22 (1986) ("It is intended that the Commission give significant attention to, and demonstrate a high level of concern for all environmental aspects of hydropower development. . . ."); H.R. CONF. REP. No. 934, 99th Cong., 2d Sess. 21 (1986) ("The amendments expressly identify fish and wildlife protection, mitigation, and enhancement, recreational opportunities, and energy conservation as nondevelopmental values that must be adequately considered by FERC when it decides whether and under what condition to issue a hydroelectric license for a project.").

Furthermore, the ECPA amendments do not give environmental factors preemptive force. First, FERC still is charged with determining the "public interest," *i.e.*, balancing power and non-power values. Even where the fish and wildlife agencies make formal section 10(j) recommendations, those agencies have no veto power. *See National Wildlife Fed'n v. FERC,* 912 F.2d 1471, 1480 (D.C. Cir. 1990) ("While the Commission must address each recommendation, the discretion ultimately vests in the Commission as to how to incorporate each recommendation. If we read the statute any other way, the Commission would be held hostage to every agency recommendation, and the Commission's role of reconciling all competing interests would be compromised.").

Second, the Conference Report makes clear that the substantial evidence review of section 825*l* is not abrogated simply because FERC decides an "environmental" fact instead of a power fact.

> To address concerns that the input from [the fish and wildlife] agencies could be ignored, watered down, or undervalued, the Commission may only reject, in part or whole, a recommendation of any of these agencies concerning any specific project after attempting to resolve the difference with the agencies and after publishing a finding (and reasons therefor) that such recommendation is inconsistent with the purposes and requirements of the Federal Power Act and that the conditions selected by FERC meet the statutory standard in section 10(j)(1). Such findings would be subject to judicial challenge with the standard for review being the statutory language *and the arbitrary and capricious standard.*

H.R. CONF. REP. No. 934, at 23 (emphasis added) . . . .

For us, then, the question is whether FERC's licensing decision here is supported by substantial evidence and is not arbitrary and capricious. We think the decision easily passes muster. FERC staff recognized the dissolved oxygen concern early, addressing it in the draft and final environmental impact statements. The Commission recognized that existing studies were inconclusive, but reasonably concluded that the 1986 EPA report established a DO standard that would protect fishery resources. The EPA report constitutes substantial evidence in support of FERC's action, especially since there is no weighty evidence to refute it with respect to the critical points here in issue. . . .

FERC staff also confronted the fish entrainment issue early and consistently. The FEIS examined several studies and concluded that mortality would not exceed 10 percent and that, even at that worst-case level, the projects licensed were in the public interest. The 10 percent figure was based on substantial evidence: FERC pointed to studies conducted at several sites and noted that higher mortality levels in some experiments were not controlling because the turbines to be used in the licensed projects were substantially different. . . .

Petitioners nonetheless contend that because FERC recognized that the data it had gathered were inconclusive, the Commission violated its duty under *Confederated Tribes and Bands of the Yakima Indian Nation v. FERC*, 746 F.2d 466 (9th Cir. 1984) (*Yakima*), *cert. denied*, 471 U.S. 1116 (1985), fully to consider environmental issues before licensing. In *Yakima*, FERC issued a hydropower license without studying the impact on anadromous fish resources. Instead, FERC conditioned the license on results to be reached in other proceedings already underway in which fishery issues in the project area would be studied. The Ninth Circuit reversed, holding that "FERC must consider fishery issues *before*, not after, issuance of a license. . . . [T]he statute requires that public interest concerns be evaluated as a *condition* to licensing." *Id.* at 471. . . .

On the record before us, we hold that FERC's disposition of this case presents no infirmity warranting reversal or reconsideration. Furthermore, contrary to petitioners' assertions, we do not read *Yakima* to require FERC to have perfect information before it takes any action. Indeed, such a requirement would be contrary to the statutory standard that requires us to affirm any FERC factual finding supported by substantial evidence. 16 U.S.C. § 825*l*(b). More practically, a perfect information standard would hamstring the agency. Virtually every decision must be made under some uncertainty; the question is whether the Commission's response, *given uncertainty*, is supported by substantial evidence and not arbitrary and capricious. . . .

Most importantly, FERC liberally used license conditions to protect against unknown risks. Despite a finding on minimum flows necessary to maintain DO levels at the eleven dams rated fair-to-good aerators, FERC not only conditioned the licenses on flow maintenance but also conditioned them on maintaining the 6.5 mg/l level—thereby eliminating any uncertainty due to the flow prediction model. The Commission also required licensees to participate in study projects designed to discover better approaches to maintaining DO levels and reducing fish mortality from entrainment. FERC additionally required that licensees build their projects to accommodate the future addition of fish protective devices, such as screens over intake pipes, should the bioengineering test facility find them to be beneficial. Finally, FERC included a general reservation of authority permitting it to impose "reasonable modifications . . . to conserve and develop fish and wildlife resources." 48 F.E.R.C. at 62,367.

These conditions and the "reopener" clause are not merely references to otherwise restrictive modification procedures. *See, e.g.,* FPA § 6, 16 U.S.C. § 799 (1988). When conditions are inserted into the license by FERC, they become integral, substantive parts of the license. As contemplated by the plain language of the license clause, any party, including petitioners here, may petition FERC to enforce the license conditions or exercise its retained authority under the reopener clause. The Commission's action, or lack thereof, would then be subject to judicial review. . . .

NOTES AND QUESTIONS

1.   How does the administrative law context influence the way in which this case is resolved? Do you think the required deference to agency decision-making is positive or problematic? How does it influence the balancing of environmental and development concerns? How does this case compare to the *Shafer & Freeman Lakes Environmental and Conservation Corporation* case that you read in Chapter 2 involving the intersection of the Federal Power Act and the Endangered Species Act?

2.   Other federal statutes also have relevance for hydroelectric permitting and licensing. The Clean Water Act, for example, provides an overall scheme for protecting water quality that includes state-implemented regulations and responsibility. Section 401 of the Clean Water Act in particular often applies to the federal licensing process, as explained by the Supreme Court in *PUD No. 1 of Jefferson County v. Washington Dept. of Ecology*, 511 U.S. 700 (1994):

> [Section 401 of the Clean Water Act] requires States to provide a water quality certification before a federal license or permit can be issued for activities that may result in any discharge into intrastate navigable waters. Specifically, § 401 requires an applicant for a federal license or permit to conduct any activity "which may result in any discharge into the navigable waters" to obtain from the State a certification "that any such discharge will comply with the applicable provisions of sections [1311, 1312, 1313, 1316, and 1317 of this title]." 33 U.S.C. § 1341(a). Section 401(d) further provides that "[a]ny certification . . . shall set forth any effluent limitations and other limitations, and monitoring requirements necessary to assure that any applicant . . . will comply with any applicable effluent limitations and other limitations, under section [1311 or 1312 of this title] . . . and with any other appropriate requirement of State law set forth in such certification." 33 U.S.C. § 1341(d). The limitations included in the certification become a condition on any federal license.

Id. at 707–08.

In that case, which involved a city and local utility district wanting to build a hydroelectric project on Washington State's Dosewallips River, the Supreme Court addressed whether the state environmental agency could impose project conditions under § 401 of the Clean Water Act that required the applicant to maintain minimum stream flows to protect salmon and steelhead runs. *Id.* at 703, 710. The Court held that "the State may include minimum stream flow requirements in a certification issued pursuant to § 401 of the Clean Water Act insofar as necessary to enforce a designated use contained in a state water quality standard." *Id.* at 723. In recent years, there has been significant litigation, as well as EPA rulemaking, regarding the Clean Water Act one-year time limit on state water quality certifications for federally approved projects. *See Hoopa Valley Tribe v. FERC*, 913 F.3d 1099 (D.C. Cir. 2019) (placing limits on one-year statutory time period for state to grant or deny § 401 Clean Water Act certification by holding that state could not use a process of requiring a licensee to withdraw and resubmit its application to extend the review period); *North Carolina v. FERC*, 3 F.4th 655 (4th Cir. 2021) (distinguishing the "egregious set of facts" in *Hoopa Valley Tribe* and holding that North Carolina did not waive its § 401 Clean Water Act certification rights by requiring applicant to withdraw and resubmit its application to include updated environmental information related to the project, and finding FERC decision to the contrary was arbitrary and capricious). Litigation over state Clean Water Act certification for a range of energy projects, including natural gas pipelines and liquefied natural gas (LNG) import and export terminals, is discussed in Chapter 7.

3.   There is a wealth of fascinating material on the role of hydropower in the modern world. For a discussion of dam disputes, old and new, and the role of hydroelectricity, see ROBERT W. ADLER, RESTORING COLORADO RIVER ECOSYSTEMS: A TROUBLED SENSE OF IMMENSITY (2007); KARL BOYD BROOKS, PUBLIC POWER, PRIVATE DAMS: THE HELLS CANYON HIGH DAM CONTROVERSY (2009); DANIEL MCCOOL, RIVER REPUBLIC: THE FALL AND RISE OF AMERICA'S RIVERS (2012); PATRICK MCCULLY, SILENCED RIVERS: THE ECOLOGY AND POLITICS OF LARGE DAMS (2001); JACQUES LESLIE, DEEP WATER: THE EPIC STRUGGLE OVER DAMS, DISPLACED PEOPLE, AND THE ENVIRONMENT (2006); JOHN MCPHEE, ENCOUNTERS WITH THE ARCHDRUID (1980); ZYGMUND J.B. PLATER, THE SNAIL DARTER AND THE DAM (2013); JAMES LAWRENCE POWELL, DEAD POOL: LAKE POWELL, GLOBAL WARMING, AND THE FUTURE OF WATER IN THE WEST (2008); MARC REISNER, CADILLAC DESERT (1986); ROBERT W. RIGHTER, THE BATTLE OVER HETCH HETCHY: AMERICA'S MOST CONTROVERSIAL DAM AND THE BIRTH OF MODERN ENVIRONMENTALISM (2006); RICHARD WHITE, THE ORGANIC MACHINE: THE REMAKING OF THE COLUMBIA RIVER (1996).

4.   Unlike renewable wind and solar resources, which are expanding rapidly in the United States, U.S. hydropower generation has grown more slowly in recent years, mostly through "capacity increases at existing facilities, new hydropower in conduits and canals, and by powering non-powered dams (NPDs)." U.S. HYDROPOWER MARKET REPORT, *supra* at iv. Another major part of FERC's work has been the approval of pumped storage projects, a topic discussed in Chapter 2. Moreover, both the U.S. Department of Energy and the National Hydropower Association have touted the potential expansion of hydropower to meet the nation's decarbonization and renewable energy goals. *See, e.g.,* NAT'L HYDROPOWER ASS'N AND CHELEN CTY. PUB. UTIL. DIST., REINVIGORATING HYDROPOWER (Apr. 2019); U.S. DEP'T OF ENERGY, HYDROPOWER VISION: A NEW CHAPTER FOR AMERICA'S 1ST RENEWABLE

ELECTRICITY SOURCE (July 2016). To speed the licensing process, Congress enacted the American Water Infrastructure Act of 2018, which, among other things, directed FERC to introduce an expedited licensing process for new licenses at existing NPDs and for closed-loop pumped storage projects, creating a timeline of two years from application to final decision. *See* Fed. Energy Reg. Comm'n, Final Rule, Hydroelectric Licensing Regulations Under America's Water Infrastructure Act of 2018, 84 Fed. Reg. 17,064 (Apr. 24, 2019). What are the benefits and drawbacks of such an expedited process?

5.   While the era of building new, large-scale hydropower projects in the United States may be over, states and electric utilities near the Canadian border have increased efforts to import large amounts of Canadian hydropower from expanding facilities in Manitoba and Quebec to meet corporate and state clean energy goals and mandates. For instance, in 2019, Minnesota Power, an investor-owned utility in northern Minnesota, completed a new 500 kV electric transmission line, called the Great Northern Transmission Line, to import hydropower energy from Manitoba Hydro. *See Great Northern Transmission Line*, Minnesota Power. In Massachusetts, the state enacted legislation to allow it to solicit bids for large-scale renewable energy procurement to meet its state renewable energy mandates. After accepting bids from Hydro-Québec, the state has attempted to develop a new transmission line to transport the contracted energy to the state's electric grid. Unfortunately for Massachusetts, unlike Minnesota, it does not share a border with Canada, and opponents in New Hampshire defeated the proposed Northern Pass transmission line after years in the permitting process. Iulia Gheorgiu, *New Hampshire Supreme Court Strikes Down Appeal for Northern Pass Transmission Permit*, UTIL. DIVE (July 22, 2019); James W. Coleman & Alexandra B. Klass, *Energy and Eminent Domain*, 104 MINN. L. REV. 659 (2019) (discussing Northern Pass project). As of 2021, Massachusetts was working with Avangrid (the U.S. subholding company of the Spanish energy company Iberdrola) to build the Clean Energy Connect transmission line through Maine to facilitate the hydropower imports. *See New England Clean Energy Connect*, Iberdrola. What are the economic and environmental benefits and drawbacks of importing large amounts of hydropower across the U.S.-Canadian border? *See, e.g.*, Nia Williams & Allison Lampert, *Canada Plans Hydropower Push As Biden Looks to Clean Up U.S. Grid*, REUTERS (Feb, 9, 2021); Tara Lohan, *Promise or Peril? Importing Hydropower to Fuel the Clean Energy Transition*, ECOWATCH (Oct. 21, 2020).

6.   The Supreme Court has become involved in many disputes involving hydropower, beyond the ones already noted above. For examples of a few of the Supreme Court cases involving hydropower, see *California v. FERC*, 495 U.S. 490 (1990) (considering whether the Federal Power Act preempted California's requirements for minimum stream flow); *Chemehuevi Tribe of Indians v. Federal Power Commission*, 420 U.S. 395 (1975) (involving whether the Federal Power Commission had authority to license thermal-electric power plants that would require large amounts of river water); *Udall v. Federal Power Commission*, 387 U.S. 428 (1967) (focusing on the question of whether Federal Water Power Act § 7(b) requires a showing that licensing of a private,

state, or municipal agency serves as a satisfactory alternative to federal development); *First Iowa Hydro-Elec. Co-op. v. Federal Power Commission*, 328 U.S. 152 (1946) (addressing state versus federal roles in hydroelectric licensing, and finding federal authority in the context of the case).

7.   Both President Reagan in the 1980s and President Trump in the 2010s called for selling off federal hydropower facilities to the private sector. *See* Kirk Johnson, *Down the Mighty Columbia River, Where a Power Struggle Looms*, N.Y. TIMES (July 28, 2017); Jeremy P. Jacobs, *Anatomy of a "Bloodbath,"* GREENWIRE (Sept. 16, 2019) (discussing various proposals to restructure or sell hydropower and transmission line assets of Bonneville Power Administration and history of same). With the federal government currently owning and operating about half the hydropower resources in the United States, what impacts would that have on hydropower users such as the agricultural sector and local communities near these facilities? On endangered species and other river-dependent animals and plants?

2. SOLAR AND WIND ENERGY

Like oil and natural gas and unlike hydropower, solar and wind energy tend to be regulated largely at state and local levels. Moreover, states vary in the extent to which they regulate these resources and whether state agencies or local governments have permitting authority. This lack of extensive federal regulation and variability of resource location has created a piecemeal approach across the United States and makes many renewable energy projects particularly vulnerable to local opposition. For instance, in 2009, Professors Ashira Ostrow and Patricia Salkin described the patchwork of regulation that exists for renewable energy facility siting, with some states like Iowa, Texas Idaho, Utah, and Illinois leaving wind farm approval solely to local governments and other states, like New Hampshire and Connecticut, granting authority to a state siting agency when the facility exceeds a certain size. *See* Patricia E. Salkin & Ashira Pelman Ostrow, *Cooperative Federalism and Wind: A New Framework for Achieving Sustainability*, 37 HOFSTRA L. REV. 1049, 1065–67 (2009). More recently, Uma Outka has explored the continuing variability among the states regarding permitting authority for renewable energy projects, which results in "barriers and delays for new projects." Uma Outka, *Renewable Energy Siting for the Critical Decade*, 69 U. KAN. L. REV. 857 (2021). *See also* Hannah J. Wiseman, *Taxing Local Energy Externalities*, 96 NOTRE DAME L. REV. 563, 591–92 (2020) (discussing differences between states to the extent they allow local governments to completely ban renewable energy projects within their jurisdictions or limit local authority to facilities below a certain size).

In states where local governments have strong siting authority, some localities may constrain wind or solar energy development even if broader state policy is supportive of renewable energy development. The following cases illustrate this dilemma.

ECOGEN, LLC v. TOWN OF ITALY

438 F. Supp. 2d 149 (W.D.N.Y. 2006)

LARIMER, DISTRICT JUDGE.

The development of wind power projects, which convert wind energy into electricity, seems to be on the upswing in this country, but that growth has not been universally welcomed. As in *Don Quixote*, where one person sees a windmill, another sees a "monstrous giant" looming over the countryside. This case involves one such proposed project that has met with local opposition.

Plaintiff, Ecogen, LLC (Ecogen), commenced this action under 42 U.S.C. § 1983,[1] seeking relief from a moratorium (the Moratorium) enacted by the Town of Italy (N.Y.) Town Board (the Board), which, for the duration of the moratorium prohibits the "construction or erection of wind turbine towers, relay stations and/or other support facilities in the Town of Italy." Ecogen has moved for an order preliminarily enjoining defendants from enforcing or continuing the Moratorium insofar as it relates to the construction and operation of an electrical substation within the Town of Italy. Defendants, who include the Town of Italy (the Town or Italy), the Town supervisor, and the Board, have moved to dismiss the complaint . . .

Ecogen is an independent power producer engaged in the development of wind-energy projects (sometimes referred to as "wind farms") in New York State. Wind farms produce electrical energy through the use of wind turbines, which are windmill-like structures that use a wind-driven rotor mounted on a tower to create electricity through the use of a generator. According to plaintiff, only certain types of areas are suitable for the construction of wind farms. In particular, wind farms should ideally be located in areas with strong winds and nearby electrical transmission lines.

In 2001, Ecogen identified certain ridge tops in the contiguous Towns of Prattsburgh and Italy as viable spots for wind energy projects (the Prattsburgh Project and the Italy Project). Ecogen determined that it would be feasible to build about 30 wind turbines in Prattsburgh, and another 23 in Italy. None have been built to date. . . .

In anticipation of the Prattsburgh and Italy Projects, Ecogen has acquired property rights and easements to an assemblage of properties in both towns. The Town of Prattsburgh has allegedly welcomed the

---

[1] [42 U.S.C. § 1983 creates a right of civil action under federal law against state and local governments for violations of federal constitutional and statutory rights, including, as in this case, for violations of due process of law under the Fourteenth Amendment.—Eds.]

Prattsburgh Project, and Ecogen has been proceeding with that project, but it cannot be completed until the substation is built.

The Town of Italy Board was apparently less receptive to the project for that town, however. On June 8, 2004, the Board passed a "local law Establishing a Moratorium on Construction or Erection of Wind Turbine Towers, Relay Stations and/or other support facilities in the Town of Italy." Dkt. #11 Ex. D. The stated purpose of the Moratorium is to prohibit the construction of such structures "for a reasonable time pending the completion of a plan for control of construction of such structures in the Town of Italy as part of the adoption of comprehensive zoning regulations. . . ." *Id.* § 3(A). The Board also stated that it took this action "to protect the value, use and enjoyment of property in the Town" by its citizens. *Id.* § 3(B). Specifically, the Board stated that "a principal concern is the scenic and aesthetic attributes of the Town of Italy as they relate to the use of land in the Town for residential, recreational and tourism purposes," and that "the installation of wind turbine facilities in the Town of Italy may have an adverse affect [sic] upon the scenic and aesthetic attributes of the Town of Italy and a correspondingly detrimental influence upon residential and recreational uses as well as real estate values in the Town of Italy, unless properly controlled through zoning regulations." *Id.* § 3(C).

To fulfill these stated objectives, the Board decreed that "[f]or a period of six (6) months from and after the effective date of this Local Law, no construction or erection of wind turbine towers, relay stations and/or support facilities shall be permitted within the geographical limits of the Town of Italy," nor could any permits for such facilities be filed during that period. *Id.* § 4. The Moratorium became effective upon its filing with the New York Secretary of State on June 15, 2004. *Id.* at 1.

The Moratorium also contains a provision, entitled "Alleviation of Extraordinary Hardship," which provides that the Board "may authorize exceptions to the moratorium imposed by this Law when it finds, based upon evidence presented to it, that deferral of action on an application for facility construction, or the deferral of approval of the application for the duration of the moratorium would impose an extraordinary hardship on a landowner or applicant." *Id.* § 5(A). . . .

As stated, the original duration of the Moratorium was six months. However, the Board has renewed the Moratorium several times since its original passage. It most recently did so on March 29, 2006, and the Moratorium, which has now been in effect for about two years, is currently scheduled to expire-if it is not again renewed-in October 2006.

Because of the Moratorium, then, Ecogen has been unable to erect any wind turbines or related facilities within the Town of Italy, including the substation. Ecogen claims that this is holding up not only the Italy Project but also the Prattsburgh Project, which requires completion of the substation. Ecogen also contends that it has been unable to take certain procedural steps that are necessary to both projects (such as the completion of environmental impact studies), and that it is in jeopardy of losing certain tax credits, which are contingent upon the Prattsburgh Project's completion by December 31, 2007. . . .

Ecogen commenced this action on March 29, 2006. . . .

Plaintiff alleges that insofar as the Moratorium relates to the proposed substation, defendants' actions in passing and renewing the Moratorium have denied plaintiff the use of property without due process of law, in violation of the Fourteenth Amendment [to the U.S. Constitution]. Defendants respond that the Moratorium is a valid exercise of the Town's police and zoning powers.

In the context of land use regulation, the constitutional guarantee of substantive due process protects a person with an interest in property from arbitrary or irrational governmental action depriving the person of that interest. In order to prevail on its substantive due process claim, Ecogen must establish that the Moratorium, at least insofar as it prohibits Ecogen's construction of a substation, bears no rational relationship to any legitimate governmental purpose. . . .

Applying these standards to the case at bar, I find that plaintiff has not stated a valid claim that the Moratorium is invalid on its face. Whatever its shortcomings, I am not able to say that it is so arbitrary or irrational as to violate plaintiff's substantive due process rights.

First, I note that, at least for purposes of the pending motions, plaintiff does not appear to dispute that in general the Town has an interest in preserving its aesthetic character. Plaintiff contends, though, that the modest substation presents no aesthetic concerns.

The question, then, is whether the Moratorium's prohibition of the construction of "wind turbine towers, relay stations and/or other support facilities" is rationally related to that interest. Again, I am unable to say that it is not. Assuming that the Town has a legitimate concern in restricting the construction of wind towers, the Moratorium is not completely irrational. If the aim is to prevent wind towers from being built in Italy, certainly it makes some sense to prohibit the construction of wind tower support facilities, such as substations, as well.

Plaintiff's contention that the substation itself would have no adverse aesthetic impact, and that it makes no sense to single out substations related to wind power projects, therefore miss the mark. Prohibiting the construction of wind power substations is not an end in itself, but a means to an end: prohibiting (for the duration of the Moratorium, a matter which is further discussed below) the construction of wind farms in Italy.

It may be that defendants' means of attaining that end are not the most efficacious, wisest or fairest possible, but that is not the standard by which they are to be judged by this Court, especially at this stage of the litigation. . . .

Mindful of the competing interests of the Town in preserving the status quo pending completion of a comprehensive zoning plan, and of Ecogen in obtaining a prompt decision on its proposal to build a substation in Italy to service its project in Prattsburgh, I deny plaintiff's motion for a preliminary injunction at this time, but with the added provision that defendants must either: (1) enact a comprehensive zoning plan within ninety days of the date of issuance of this Decision and Order; or (2) render a decision on plaintiff's application for a hardship exception within ninety days of its filing. If defendants fail to do either of these things, plaintiff may again seek injunctive relief in this Court.

BOARD OF CTY. COMM'RS V. PERENNIAL SOLAR
212 A.3d 868 (Md. Ct. App. 2019)

BOOTH, J.

> "Here comes the sun, and I say, It's all right."
>
> — The Beatles, "Here Comes the Sun"

This case involves the intersection of the State's efforts to promote solar electric generation as part of its renewable energy policies, and local governments' interest in ensuring compliance with local planning and zoning prerogatives. In this matter, we are asked to determine whether state law preempts local zoning authority with respect to solar energy generating systems that require a Certificate of Public Convenience and Necessity (CPCN) issued by the Maryland Public Service Commission [(PSC)].

This case began with an application by Perennial Solar, LLC (Perennial) to the Washington County Board of Zoning Appeals (Board) for a special exception and variance to construct a Solar Energy Generating System (SEGS) adjacent to the rural village of Cearfoss in Washington County, Maryland. After the Board granted the variance and special exception, a group of aggrieved landowners sought judicial review of the Board's decision in the Circuit Court for Washington County. The Board of County Commissioners of Washington County, Maryland (Washington County or the County) intervened in the case. . . .

Perennial's contention is that the PSC's regulatory authority established by the Public Utilities Article over the siting and construction of SEGS preempts local zoning approval by implication. Perennial argues that the General Assembly has given the PSC broad authority to take final action to determine the siting of SEGS which require a certificate of public convenience and necessity, and that the comprehensive nature of the statute indicates the Legislature's intent to occupy the entire field. . . .

This Court has frequently explained that Maryland state law may preempt local law in one of three ways: (1) preemption by conflict; (2) express preemption; or (3) implied preemption. *Altadis U.S.A., Inc. v. Prince George's Cty.*, 65 A.3d 118 (Md. 2013); *Talbot Cty. v. Skipper*, 620 A.2d 880 (Md. 1993); *Allied Vending, Inc. v. City of Bowie*, 631 A.2d 77 (Md. 1993). . . .

Perennial argues that the local zoning ordinances are preempted by implication. State law can preempt local ordinances by implication when "the ordinance deals with an area in which the General Assembly has acted with such force that an intent to occupy the entire field must be implied." *Howard Cty.* [*v. Potomac Elec. Power Co.*, 573 A.2d 821 (1990)].

There is no particular formula for determining whether the General Assembly intended to preempt an entire area. *Howard Cty.*, 573 A.2d 821. Nevertheless, we have stated repeatedly that "[t]he primary indicia of legislative purpose to preempt an entire field of law is the comprehensiveness with which the General Assembly has legislated in the field." *Id.* . . .

In addition to reviewing the comprehensiveness of the legislation that is the subject of the preemption analysis, in *Allied Vending*, we summarized the secondary factors in which the Court has previously considered in determining whether a local law is preempted by implication:

> 1) whether local laws existed prior to the enactment of state laws governing the same subject matter, 2) whether the state laws provide for pervasive administrative regulation, 3) whether the local ordinance regulates an area in which some local control has traditionally been allowed, 4) whether the state law expressly provides concurrent legislative authority to local jurisdictions or requires compliance with local ordinances, 5) whether a state agency responsible for administering and enforcing the state law has recognized local authority to act in the field, 6) whether the particular aspect of the field sought to be regulated by local government has been addressed by state legislation, and 7) whether a two-tiered regulatory process existing if local laws were not preempted would engender chaos and confusion.

Allied Vending, 631 A.2d 77 (internal citations omitted).

With the principles of implied preemption in mind, we turn to the language of the Public Utilities Article [(PU)] and consider the duties and authority delegated to the PSC by the General Assembly in the area of solar energy generating station approvals.

In response to the growing concern over climate change, the Maryland General Assembly enacted legislation intended to reduce Maryland greenhouse gas emissions. The legislation included a specific intent to move the Maryland energy market away from historical reliance on fossil fuels and enacted a Renewable Energy Portfolio Standard (RPS). *See* Maryland Code, Environment Article (EN) § 2–1201, *et seq.*; PU § 7–701.

. . . As part of its enactment, the General Assembly specifically determined that: "the benefits of electricity from renewable energy resources, including long term decreased emissions, a healthier environment, increased energy security, and decreased reliance on and vulnerability from imported energy sources, accrue to the public at large;" and that the State needed to "develop a minimum level of these resources in the electricity supply portfolio of the State." PU § 7–702(b). The RPS includes specific targets for the share of electricity coming from solar electric generation. PU § 7–703.

In 2009, the Maryland General Assembly enacted the Greenhouse Gas Emissions Reduction Act of 2009 (GRRA), a law that requires the State to reduce greenhouse gas emissions from a 2006 baseline by 25% by 2020 and by 40% by 2030. During the 2019 legislative session, the General Assembly adopted the Clean Energy Jobs Act, which increases the State's RPS target to 50% by 2030. The Clean Energy Jobs Act also includes a significant increase in electricity sales derived from solar energy from 1.9% to 5.5% in 2019, and to 14.5% in 2028. . . .

The General Assembly has delegated to the PSC the authority to "implement a renewable energy portfolio standard" that applies to retail electricity sales in the State by electricity suppliers consistent with the specific timetable established by the statute. PU § 7–703(a). . . .

Consistent with the PSC's duties to ensure compliance with the RPS, including the specific targets for the share of electricity coming from solar electric generation, the General Assembly has also delegated to the PSC the exclusive authority to approve generating stations in Maryland. Unless exempt by the statute, a generating station cannot be constructed unless the PSC issues a CPCN, which is only issued after a detailed application and approval process. PU § 7–207.

The PSC's review process of a generating station is extensive. Upon receipt of an application, the PSC provides notice of the application to: (i) the Maryland Department of Planning; (ii) the governing body, and if applicable, the executive of each county or municipal corporation in which a portion of the generating station is proposed to be constructed; (iii) the governing body of any county or municipal corporation within one-mile of the proposed location of the generating station; (iv) each member of the General Assembly representing any part of the county in which any portion of the generating station is proposed to be constructed; (v) each member of the General Assembly representing any portion of each county within one-mile of the proposed location of the generating station; and (vi) all other interested persons. PU § 7–207(c)(1). A copy of the application is also provided to each appropriate State unit and unit of local government for review, evaluation, and comment regarding the significance of the proposal to the State, area wide, and local plans or programs (see PU § 7–207(c)(2)), and to each member of the General Assembly who is provided with the statutory notice pursuant to PU § 7–207(c)(1). Id. . . .

Under the express language of the PU, the PSC is the final approving authority for the siting and construction of generating stations, which require a CPCN, after giving "due consideration" to the following statutory factors [that include "the recommendation of the governing body of each county or municipal corporation in which any portion of the construction of the generating station . . . is proposed to be located."]. PU § 7–207.

Not surprisingly, as the State's energy market moves toward renewable energy sources, such as solar energy, land use conflicts often arise, particularly in rural areas where land historically zoned for agricultural use is proposed as a site for large scale solar projects. With the proliferation of solar facilities, counties such as Washington, Kent and Queen Anne's Counties (collectively, "the Counties") have adopted specific solar regulations as part of their planning and zoning authority.

The Counties argue that PU § 7–207 does not preempt their right to regulate SEGS through their planning and zoning authority conferred by the Express Powers Act, Maryland Code, Local Government Article (LG) § 10–324(b)(1), in which the General Assembly has determined that it is a state policy that "the orderly development and use of land and structures requires comprehensive regulation through the implementation of planning and zoning controls." The General Assembly has expressly delegated planning and zoning authority to local government. LG § 110–324(b)(2); Maryland Code, Land Use Article (LU) § 4–101(a)(2). . . .

The pertinent provision of the County's Zoning Ordinance is Section 4.26, added by amendment in 2011, which permits SEGS as a land use by special exception in certain zoning districts in the County.

Section 4.26 of the Zoning Ordinance also provides specific design standards for SEGS, including minimum lot size, buffer yards, controlled access, electrical wire placement, diffused lighting and glare, appearance, color and finish, signage, noise, electromagnetic interference, code compliance, and the establishment of a reclamation or decommissioning plan. The design standards also expressly require that the SEGS comply with PSC regulations. Zoning Ordinance, Section 4.26(A)(13). The standards also require that an applicant obtain PSC approval for a CPCN-exempt SEGS prior to construction and the issuance of a county building permit. Id., Section 4.26(A)(14).

... SEGS are permitted in the Agricultural (Rural) Zoning District by special exception. Under Article 28A of the Zoning Ordinance, a "special exception" is defined as "[a] grant of a specific use that would not be appropriate generally or without restriction; and shall be based upon a finding that the use conforms to the plan and is compatible with the existing neighborhood." . . .

Perennial's application involved not only a special exception but also a request for a variance from the strict application of the Zoning Ordinance to enable Perennial to construct its solar arrays over the internal property lines. We have held that "[a] variance refers to administrative relief which may be granted from the strict application of a particular development limitation in the zoning ordinance (i.e., setback, area and height limitations, etc.)." *Mayor & Council of Rockville v. Rylyns Enters., Inc.*, 814 A.2d 469 (Md. 2002) . . . .

Comparing the comprehensive provisions of PU § 7–207 against the applicable provisions of the Zoning Ordinance, both the statute enacted by the General Assembly and the local ordinance adopted by the County attempt to regulate the siting and location of SEGS. Under the statute, the PSC is given the final authority to approve the location of SEGS, while under the Zoning Ordinance, the Board has the final authority to approve site-specific special exceptions and variances for the construction of SEGS. Clearly, only one of these bodies can have the final say on the matter.

Applying the principles of implied preemption to PU § 7–207, it is clear that the General Assembly intended to vest final authority with the PSC for the siting and location of generating stations requiring a CPCN. The statute manifests the general legislative purpose to create an all-compassing statutory scheme of solar energy regulation. . . .

The statute grants the PSC broad authority to determine whether and where SEGS may be constructed. In making such a determination, the PSC undertakes a multi-faceted review, which includes input from other state agencies, as well as from local government. In addition to considering the recommendations of other state agencies, the PSC is also required to consider the stability and reliability of the system; economics; esthetics; historic sites; aviation safety; air quality and water pollution; and the availability of means of the required timely disposal of wastes produced by any generating station. PU § 7–207(e)(2). Ultimately, the final decision regarding whether to approve a generating station lies exclusively with the PSC.

The General Assembly's intent to preempt local government's zoning approval authority over generating stations is clear from the plain text of the statute, which specifically defines the role of local government, as well as planning and zoning considerations, in the PSC review and approval process. Contrary to Washington County's "all or nothing" approach to preemption, the General Assembly has carved out a key role for local government in the PSC's review and approval process.

For example, as part of the CPCN application process, the PSC holds public hearings within each local jurisdiction where the construction is proposed, with the governing body of the local jurisdiction invited to jointly preside over and participate in those hearings. PU § 7–207(d). Local land use interests are also designated by statute as a factor requiring "due consideration" by the PSC in evaluating and approving generating stations. This includes the "*recommendation* of the governing body of each county or municipal corporation in which any portion of the construction of the generating station . . . is proposed to be located," PU § 7–207(e)(1), as well as several other factors typically considered in local land use decisions, including esthetics, historic sites, pollution, and waste disposal. PU § 7–207(e)(2) (emphasis added). . . .

While our review of the comprehensive nature of PU § 7–207 leads us to our conclusion that the General Assembly has acted with such a force in this field that local zoning authority over generating systems is impliedly preempted, our conclusion is further bolstered by our consideration of the secondary factors that we summarized in *Allied Vending*, 631 A.2d 77.

First, as stated above, "state law . . . provide[s] for pervasive administrative regulation." *Id.* PU § 7–207 addresses all regulatory matters associated with the approval and operation of generating stations, including siting and locational approvals.

Second, the statute does not "expressly provide concurrent legislative authority to the local jurisdiction or require compliance with local planning and zoning ordinances." *Allied Vending*, 631 A.2d 77. To the contrary, the statute expressly identifies the local governing body's role as a participant in a public hearing process, with the ability to make a "recommendation," which the PSC is required to give "due consideration" before taking "final action". *See* PU § 7–207(a) and (b). . . .

Third, "the particular aspect of the field sought to be regulated by the local government"—comprehensive planning and local zoning regulations—"ha[s] been addressed by the state legislation." *Allied Vending*, 631 A.2d 77. The statute gives the PSC the final approval authority over the siting and location of generating stations—the same authority sought to be exercised by the local government as part of its special exception and variance process. The statute also specifically addresses the role of the comprehensive plan and local zoning regulations in the PSC approval process, which is that they must be given "due consideration" by the PSC. The statute, however, does not mandate or otherwise require that the local zoning authority approve a generating station prior to PSC approval.

Finally, a two-tiered regulatory process as proposed by the County "would engender chaos and confusion" if local zoning authority was not preempted. Under the Zoning Ordinance, the Board's process for approving a variance and special exception for Perennial's SEGS is a process for approving the *siting and location* of a SEGS on a particular property. The Board is required to consider and apply the comprehensive plan and the zoning ordinance when considering the application. That process requires a public hearing and a final decision by the Board, which is appealable to the circuit court.

By comparison, the PSC approval process also involves a determination of whether to approve a SEGS at a particular location. Thus, a two-tiered process could create confusion, particularly if the Board does not grant the special exception or variance, or establishes conditions for the use that are inconsistent with the PSC's ultimate approval. Such an interpretation is consistent with the plain language of the statute, which vests in the PSC the authority to take "final action" after giving due consideration to the local comprehensive plan and zoning regulations. . . .

———————

As discussed in Chapter 2, renewable energy projects, while generally less risky to human health and ecosystems than many fossil fuel projects, can still produce significant externalities. For instance, they can pose threats to bats and birds, and many projects take up large amounts of land and use scarce resources such as water. Likewise, when the entire life cycle of renewable technologies is accounted for, additional externalities arise related to the extraction of critical minerals used in wind turbines, electric vehicles, solar panels, and batteries. While the energy sources these technologies utilize may be renewable, the minerals they require are not. As clean energy deployment increases, the global demand for minerals such as copper, nickel, cobalt, zinc, and aluminum is projected to as much as quadruple by 2040. *See* INT'L ENERGY AGENCY, THE ROLE OF CRITICAL MINERALS IN CLEAN ENERGY TRANSITIONS (May 2021).

In addition, these projects can raise cultural and tribal concerns. The following case addresses such claims in the context of solar energy development on federal public lands, with a focus on the procedural issue of whether the federal government adequately consulted with the concerned tribe prior to authorizing the project.

QUECHAN TRIBE OF FORT YUMA INDIAN RESERVATION V. U.S. DEPT. OF INTERIOR

755 F. Supp. 2d 1104 (S.D. Cal. 2010)

LARRY ALAN BURNS, DISTRICT JUDGE.

On October 29, 2010, Plaintiff (the "Tribe") filed its complaint, alleging Defendants' decision to approve a solar energy project violated various provisions of federal law. On November 12, the Tribe filed a motion for preliminary injunction, asking the Court to issue an order to preserve the status quo by enjoining proceeding with the project, pending the outcome of this litigation. . . .

The Quechan Tribe is a federally-recognized Indian tribe whose reservation is located mostly in Imperial County, California and partly in Arizona. A large solar energy project is planned on 6500 acres of federally-owned land known as the California Desert Conservation Area (CDCA). The Department of the Interior, as directed by Congress, developed a binding management plan for this area.

The project is being managed by a company called Tessera Solar, LLC. Tessera plans to install about 30,000 individual "suncatcher" solar collectors, expected to generate 709 megawatts when completed. The suncatchers will be about 40 feet high and 38 feet wide, and attached to pedestals about 18 feet high. Support buildings, roads, a pipeline, and a power line to support and service the network of collectors are also planned. Most of the project will be built on public lands. Tessera submitted an application to the state of California to develop the Imperial Valley Solar project. The project is planned in phases. . . .

The area where the project would be located has a history of extensive use by Native American groups. The parties agree 459 cultural resources have been identified within the project area. These include over 300 locations of prehistoric use or settlement, and ancient trails that traverse the site. The tribes in this area cremated their dead and buried the remains, so the area also appears to contain archaeological sites and human remains. The draft environmental impact statement (EIS) prepared by the BLM indicated the project "may wholly or partially destroy all archaeological sites on the surface of the project area."

The Tribe believes the project would destroy hundreds of their ancient cultural sites including burial sites, religious sites, ancient trails, and probably buried artifacts. . . . The Tribe maintains Defendants were required to comply with the National Environmental Policy Act (NEPA), the National Historical Preservation Act (NHPA), and the Federal Land Policy and Management Act of 1976 (FLPMA) by making certain analyses and taking certain factors into account deciding to go ahead with the project. The Tribe now seeks judicial intervention under the Administrative Procedures Act (APA). . . .

The parties agree that, under NHPA Section 106 (16 U.S.C. § 470f) and its implementing regulations, the Bureau of Land Management (BLM) is required to consult with certain parties before spending money on or approving any federally-assisted undertaking such as the project at issue here, and that the Tribe is one of those parties. The Tribe maintains BLM didn't adequately or meaningfully consult with them, but instead approved the project before completing the required consultation. According to the Tribe, BLM simply didn't consider what the tribe had to say before approving the project.

The Court finds this to be the strongest basis for issuance of injunctive relief and therefore focuses on it.

The NHPA's purpose is to preserve historic resources, and early consultation with tribes is encouraged "to ensure that all types of historic properties and all public interests in such properties are given due consideration. . . ." *Te-Moak Tribe v. U.S. Dep't of Interior*, 608 F.3d 593, 609 (9th Cir. 2010) (quoting 16 U.S.C. § 470a(d)(1)(A)). . . .

The Section 106 process is described in 36 C.F.R. §§ 800.2–800.6. After preliminary identification of the project and consulting parties, Section 106 requires identifying historic properties within a project's affected area, evaluating the project's potential effects on those properties, and resolving any adverse effects. The Tribe insists this consultation must be completed at least for Phase 1 of the project, before construction begins.

Throughout this process, the regulations require the agency to consult extensively with Indian tribes that fall within the definition of "consulting party," including here the Quechan Tribe. Section 800.4 alone requires at least seven issues about which the Tribe, as a consulting party, is entitled to be consulted before the project was approved. . . .

Furthermore, under § 800.2, consulting parties that are Indian tribes are entitled to *special consideration* in the course of an agency's fulfillment of its consultation obligations. . . .

Preliminarily, several points bear noting. First, the sheer volume of documents is not meaningful. The number of letters, reports, meetings, etc. and the size of the various documents doesn't in itself show the NHPA-required consultation occurred.

Second, the BLM's communications are replete with recitals of law (including Section 106), professions of good intent, and solicitations to consult with the Tribe. But mere *pro forma* recitals do not, by themselves, show BLM actually complied with the law. As discussed below, documentation that might support a finding that true government-to-government consultation occurred is painfully thin.

At oral argument, the Tribe described the meetings as cursory information sessions and the reports and other communications as inadequate. Its briefing also argues that Defendants have confused "contact" with required "consultation." . . .

Although BLM invited the Tribe to attend public informational meetings about the project, the invitations do not appear to meet the requirements set forth in 36 C.F.R. § 800.2(c)(2)(ii). . . .

The documentary evidence also confirms the Tribe's contention that the number of identified sites continued to fluctuate. And Defendants have admitted the evaluation of sites eligible for inclusion in the National Register hasn't *yet* been completed.

BLM's invitation to "consult," then, amounted to little more than a general request for the Tribe to gather its own information about all sites within the area and disclose it at public meetings. Because of the lack of information, it was impossible for the Tribe to have been consulted meaningful as required in applicable regulations. The documentary evidence also discloses almost no "government-to-government" consultation. . . .

Defendants have emphasized the size, complexity, and expense of this project, as well as the time limits, and the facts are sympathetic. . . .

That said, government agencies are not free to glide over requirements imposed by Congressionally-approved statutes and duly adopted regulations. The required consultation must at least meet the standards set forth in 36 C.F.R. § 800.2(c)(2)(ii), and should begin early. The Tribe was entitled to be provided with adequate information and time, consistent with its status as a government that is entitled to be consulted. The Tribe's consulting rights should have been respected. It is clear that did not happen here.

The Court therefore determines the Tribe is likely to prevail at least on its claim that it was not adequately consulted as required under NHPA before the project was approved. Because the project was approved "without observance of procedure required by law," the Tribe is entitled to have the BLM's actions set aside under 5 U.S.C. § 706(2)(D).

The evidence shows, and the parties do not dispute, that the planned project is extensive. The size and number of suncatchers, not to mention roads, buildings, and other supporting infrastructure, ensures this will be a massive project. The undisputed evidence also shows the 459 historic properties extend from one end of the area to the other, so some type of impact on the properties is likely. In fact, phase 1 of the plan acknowledges that one such property *will* be adversely impacted; because of the property's size, power lines cannot span it, and one power pole must be installed on the property.

The Court therefore holds the FLPMA claim at least raises "serious questions" for purposes of injunctive relief. . . .

Having determined that the Tribe is likely to succeed on the merits, at least as to its claim that required NHPA consulting must be completed before phase 1 of the project begins, the Court turns to the remaining factors [for injunctive relief].

To obtain preliminary injunctive relief, the Tribe must show it is likely to suffer irreparable harm in the absence of preliminary relief. *Winter* [*v. Nat. Res. Def. Council*, 555 U.S. 7, 20 (2008)]. . . . This is the easiest and most straightforward part of the inquiry, because the Court finds it is very likely the Tribe will suffer irreparable harm.

The parties agree there are hundreds of known historical sites on the land, and the Tribe attaches cultural and religious significance to many if not most of these. Hundreds of these sites have been identified as prehistoric, and many contain human remains. Damage to or destruction of any of them would constitute irreparable harm in some degree. Second, if the tribe hasn't been adequately consulted and the project goes ahead anyway, this legally-protected procedural interest would effectively be lost.

The briefing didn't focus extensively on the risk of specific damage, but the massive size of the project and the large number of historic properties and incomplete state of the evaluation virtually ensures some loss or damage. . . .

The Court therefore finds this key requirement is easily met, and turns to the remaining two *Winter* factors.

To obtain injunctive relief under *Winter*, the Tribe must establish the balance of equities tips in its favor. 555 U.S. at 20. *Winter* also refers to this as the "balance of hardships" inquiry.

Here, Defendants held most of the power—including the power to control the timing of the project and the review process. . . .

The Ninth Circuit has emphasized that consultation with tribes must begin early, and that if consultation begins after other parties may have invested a great deal of time and money, the other parties may become entrenched and inflexible, and the government agency may be inclined to tolerate degradation it would otherwise have insisted be avoided. *Te-Moak Tribe*, 608 F.3d at 609. This appears to be happening here. While the Court is sympathetic to the problems Defendants face, the fact that they are now pressed for time and somewhat desperate after having invested a great deal of effort and money is a problem of their own making and does not weigh in their favor.

It bears considering, too, that two of the Defendants are Secretary of the Interior Salazar and BLM, who represent part of the United States government, and that Congress and the Department of the Interior created the requirements that Defendants are finding so onerous. Congress and, to a lesser extent, the Department of the Interior could have made these consulting requirements less stringent, but they didn't. Congress could also have exempted renewable energy projects such as this from the Section 106 review process, but didn't. . . .

The Court is mindful that Defendants face hardships as well. For example, Imperial Valley Solar has already spent millions of dollars preparing this project, and faces difficulties obtaining investment and financing if the project is held up. Even so, the Court finds the balance of equities tips heavily in the Tribe's favor.

The final step in the *Winter* analysis requires the Court to consider whether a preliminary injunction is in the public interest. Obviously there are many competing interests here. The interests the Tribe urges the Court to consider involve historic and cultural preservation, in this case of hundreds of prehistoric sites and other sites whose significance has yet to be completely evaluated. The Tribe itself is a sovereign, and both it and its members have an interest in protecting their cultural patrimony. The culture and history of the Tribe and its members are also part of the culture and history of the United States more generally.

The value of a renewal energy project of this magnitude to the public is also great. It provides the public with a significant amount of power while reducing pollution and dependence on fossil fuels. As Defendants point out, it is a goal of the federal government and the state of California to promote the development of such projects. . . .

That being said, the Court looks to the statutes enacted by Congress rather than to its own analysis of desirable priorities in the first instance. Here, in enacting NHPA Congress has adjudged the preservation of historic properties and the rights of Indian tribes to consultation to be in the public interest. Congress could have, but didn't, include exemptions for renewable energy projects such as this one. . . . But because Congress didn't do that, and instead made the determination that preservation of historical properties takes priority here, the Court must adopt the same view.

NOTES AND QUESTIONS

1.   How does the balance of authority between state and local governments regarding renewable energy development on private lands differ between the *Ecogen* case and the *Perennial Solar* case? Which state has set the balance in a way you find preferable? Should there be a different balance of authority when it comes to wind energy projects as compared to solar energy projects?

For a discussion of the variation among states in the extent to which they grant local governments siting authority in the context of wind, see ENV'T L. INST., STATE ENABLING LEGISLATION FOR COMMERCIAL-SCALE WIND POWER SITING AND THE LOCAL GOVERNMENT ROLE (2011). The Environmental Law Institute has also prepared a resource for local government officials on wind energy siting. ENV'T L. INST., SITING WIND ENERGY FACILITIES—WHAT DO LOCAL OFFICIALS NEED TO KNOW? (2013).

2.   Litigation over the Ecogen wind project in New York dragged on for years. The town of Prattsburgh, which originally did not oppose the project, changed its position when a new town board was elected and enacted its own moratorium on wind development in the town in 2009. Ecogen sued, a state court invalidated the moratorium in 2013, and a state appellate court affirmed that decision. *See* John Christenson, *Wind Farm Prevails in Prattsburgh*, THE CHRONICLE EXPRESS (Feb. 6, 2014). In other parts of the United States, wind and solar development remain controversial in local communities even as it continues to receive strong support from electric utilities and states. *See, e.g.,* KATE MARSH ET AL., COLUMBIA LAW SCHOOL, OPPOSITION TO RENEWABLE ENERGY FACILITIES IN THE UNITED STATES, SABIN CENTER FOR CLIMATE CHANGE LAW (Feb. 2021) (detailing state and local laws prohibiting and regulating renewable energy development and discussing contested projects in each state); Veronica Penny, *Where Wind and Solar Power Need to Grow for America to Meet It's Energy Needs*, N.Y. TIMES (May 28, 2021) (showing areas of United States with good wind and solar potential and discussing barriers to building same).

3.   In 2020, New York enacted the Accelerated Renewable Energy Growth and Community Benefit Act. Among other provisions, the state law constrains the role of local governments in the siting of "major" renewable energy facilities by creating a state override provision for local laws that are "unreasonably burdensome" considering the state's renewable energy and zero emission targets and other environmental benefits of such renewable energy facilities. The law also places new, strict time limits on the approval process. The Act established a new Office of Renewable Energy Siting (ORES) within the NY Department of State to streamline the siting process for major renewable energy projects. The ORES promulgated final regulations implementing the law in March 2021. *See Regulations*, N.Y. Office of Renewable Energy Siting, https://ores.ny.gov/regulations; Outka, *supra* (discussing New York statute); Michael B. Gerrard & Edward McTiernan, *New York's New Statute on Siting Renewable Energy Facilities*, N.Y. L.J. (May 14, 2020). Would application of the new law in New York result in a different outcome in *Ecogen*? What would be the benefits and drawbacks of that result?

4.   Tessera Solar ultimately decided to sell the project at issue in the *Quechan Tribe of Fort Yuma Indian Reservation* case to another company, which chose to deploy PV rather than SunCatcher technology. The decision to sell the project was due in large part to the company's struggles to finance the project, and the lawsuit may have played a role in that choice. *See* Jason Deign, *What Happened to Tessera Solar's Projects?*, REUTERS EVENTS (Mar. 4, 2011). How

should courts balance the need for procedural protections with the need for efficiency in regulatory approvals? Did the court strike the right balance in the case?

5.   One of the most widely publicized controversies over wind siting took place in the context of the Cape Wind project, an offshore wind project near affluent areas of Cape Cod in Massachusetts. Many residents opposed the project, including members of the Kennedy family. The project went through extensive regulatory processes at both the state and federal levels. For a description of that process, see *Cape Wind*, Bureau of Ocean Energy Mgmt. Ultimately, the owners abandoned the project at the end of 2017. *See* Joe Ryan & Brian Eckhouse, *What Was Once Hailed as First U.S. Offshore Wind Farm is No More*, BLOOMBERG (Dec. 4, 2017). Nevertheless, other U.S. offshore wind projects have learned from the Cape Wind saga and are beginning to come online. Deepwater Wind (now owned by the Danish wind company Ørsted) built the nation's first offshore wind farm off the coast of Block Island, Rhode Island that began operation at the end of 2016 and has other U.S. projects underway. *See Our Offshore Wind Projects in the U.S.*, ØRSTED, https://us. orsted.com/wind-projects. Another company, Vineyard Wind (proposed by Avangrid and Copenhagen Infrastructure Partners), received approval in 2021 for the construction and operation of the nation's largest offshore wind project 15 miles off the coast of Massachusetts. *See Vineyard Wind*, Bureau of Ocean Energy Mgmt, https://www.boem.gov/vineyard-wind. Offshore wind is discussed in detail in Chapter 9.

6.   Even after a renewable energy project is approved and built, it still may be at risk from neighbors. If a nearby property owner blocks the sun or wind, the installation may produce significantly less energy. Some states have created statutory protections to prevent this from occurring. *See, e.g.,* Troy A. Rule, *Shadow on the Cathedral: Solar Access Laws in a Different Light*, 2010 U. ILL. L. REV. 851 (2010) (describing the enactment of state solar access laws first between 1978 and 1981 as a result of the oil embargos of the 1970s, and 30 years later, in the late 2000s, during another spike in energy prices). New Mexico is one of a few states that has enacted a solar rights statute that uses a first-in-time "prior appropriation" approach to protect investments in "solar collector devices" from structures or buildings that might later block the device's access to solar resources. *See* New Mexico Solar Rights Act, N.M. STAT. ANN. §§ 47–3–1, *et seq.* The New Mexico law also creates a process for recording the solar right as part of the property title, making it transferable to subsequent owners upon sale of the property. *See id.* Other states, like Massachusetts and Iowa, grant authority to local governments to enact permitting processes and zoning ordinances to protect solar access within their jurisdictions. Alison Holm, *Solar Rights: Issues and Policy Options*, NAT'L RENEWABLE ENERGY LAB. (June 6, 2017) (discussing laws in California, New Mexico, Iowa, and Massachusetts).

7.   At the local level, the City of Chicago has enacted streamlined permitting and zoning processes for rooftop solar PV systems to facilitate quicker and easier local approval of solar projects. *See* CITY OF CHICAGO SOLAR ZONING

POLICY (Nov. 2015). Also in the Midwest, Indiana University and a group of energy nonprofits created a Model Solar Ordinance for Indiana local governments. *See* INDIANA UNIVERSITY AND GREAT PLAINS INST., MODEL SOLAR ORDINANCE FOR INDIANA LOCAL GOVERNMENTS (last updated Dec. 2020). Likewise, the Michigan Office of Climate and Energy within the state's Department of Environment, Great Lakes, and Energy has created a "Zoning for Renewable Energy Database" tracking local government permitting, zoning, and other rules for clean energy projects. *Zoning for Renewable Energy Database*, Michigan.gov. Considering all the potential approaches, what do you think is the optimal approach for solar development on private lands—uniform statewide regulation, local regulation, or model regulation that creates uniformity within a state while leaving the implementation to local governments? For a discussion of state laws governing solar rights, see Holm, *supra*.

8.   Many types of laws can apply to renewable energy projects beyond those discussed in this Section. For example, as wind turbines have grown taller, making elevators necessary, it was important to create a uniform standard for them to address the wide variation in state laws. Brad Kelechava, *Wind Turbine Tower Elevators*, AM. NAT'L STANDARDS INST. (Nov. 30, 2016).

PRACTICE PROBLEM

On January 27, 2021, President Biden issued an executive order (EO) entitled "Executive Order on Tackling the Climate Crisis at Home and Abroad." Some of the key provisions of the EO are as follows:

Sec. 201. Policy. Even as our Nation emerges from profound public health and economic crises borne of a pandemic, we face a climate crisis that threatens our people and communities, public health and economy, and, starkly, our ability to live on planet Earth. Despite the peril that is already evident, there is promise in the solutions—opportunities to create well-paying union jobs to build a modern and sustainable infrastructure, deliver an equitable, clean energy future, and put the United States on a path to achieve net-zero emissions, economy-wide, by no later than 2050. . . .

Sec. 207. Renewable Energy on Public Lands and in Offshore Waters. The Secretary of the Interior shall review siting and permitting processes on public lands and in offshore waters to identify to the Task Force steps that can be taken, consistent with applicable law, to increase renewable energy production on those lands and in those waters, with the goal of doubling offshore wind by 2030 while ensuring robust protection for our lands, waters, and biodiversity and creating good jobs. . . . The Secretary of the Interior shall engage with Tribal authorities regarding the development and management of renewable and conventional energy resources on Tribal lands.

Sec. 208. Oil and Natural Gas Development on Public Lands and in Offshore Waters. To the extent consistent with applicable law, the Secretary of the Interior shall pause new oil and natural gas leases on public lands or in offshore waters pending completion of a comprehensive review and reconsideration of Federal oil and gas permitting and leasing practices in light of the Secretary of the Interior's broad stewardship responsibilities over the public lands and in offshore waters, including potential climate and other impacts associated with oil and gas activities on public lands or in offshore waters. . . . In conducting this analysis, and to the extent consistent with applicable law, the Secretary of the Interior shall consider whether to adjust royalties associated with coal, oil, and gas resources extracted from public lands and offshore waters, or take other appropriate action, to account for corresponding climate costs.

Sec. 209. Fossil Fuel Subsidies. The heads of agencies shall identify for the Director of the Office of Management and Budget and the National Climate Advisor any fossil fuel subsidies provided by their respective agencies, and then take steps to ensure that, to the extent consistent with applicable law, Federal funding is not directly subsidizing fossil fuels. The Director of the Office of Management and Budget shall seek, in coordination with the heads of agencies and the National Climate Advisor, to eliminate fossil fuel subsidies from the budget request for Fiscal Year 2022 and thereafter. . . .

Sec. 218. Interagency Working Group on Coal and Power Plant Communities and Economic Revitalization. There is hereby established an Interagency Working Group on Coal and Power Plant Communities and Economic Revitalization (Interagency Working Group). The National Climate Advisor and the Assistant to the President for Economic Policy shall serve as Co-Chairs of the Interagency Working Group. . . .

(b) Mission and Work.

(i) The Interagency Working Group shall coordinate the identification and delivery of Federal resources to revitalize the economies of coal, oil and gas, and power plant communities; develop strategies to implement the policy set forth in section 217 of this order and for economic and social recovery; assess opportunities to ensure benefits and protections for coal and power plant workers; and submit reports to the National Climate Advisor and the Assistant to the President for Economic Policy on a regular basis on the progress of the revitalization effort. . . .

Sec. 219. Policy. To secure an equitable economic future, the United States must ensure that environmental and economic justice are key considerations in how we govern. That means investing and building a clean energy economy that creates well-paying union jobs, turning disadvantaged communities—historically marginalized and overburdened—into healthy, thriving communities, and undertaking robust actions to mitigate climate change while preparing for the impacts of climate change across rural, urban, and Tribal areas. Agencies shall make achieving environmental justice part of their missions by developing programs, policies, and activities to address the disproportionately high and adverse human health, environmental, climate-related and other cumulative impacts on disadvantaged communities, as well as the accompanying economic challenges of such impacts. . . .

Based on President Biden's EO, consider the following scenarios:

1.   You are counsel to the American Petroleum Institute, the trade organization that represents the interests of the U.S. oil and natural gas industry. What concerns you the most about this EO? What legal challenges might you bring to limit implementation of its provisions? Are there any policy statements in the EO that you and your members can support? What changes would you like to see from Congress to combat any objectionable provisions of the EO?

2.   You are counsel to the American Clean Power Association, the national trade association representing large-scale wind energy and other renewable power interests. What policies set forth in the EO help your members and why?

3.   You are counsel to Climate Justice Alliance, a network of urban and rural frontline communities focused on "the social, racial, economic and environmental justice issues of climate change." Your members are "locally, tribally, and regionally-based racial and economic justice organizations of Indigenous Peoples, Black, Latinx, Asian Pacific Islander, and poor white communities who share legacies of racial and economic oppression and social justice organizing." *See About*, Climate Justice Alliance, https://climatejustice alliance.org/about/. What statements in the EO are you most excited about and why? Is there anything in the EO that causes you concern?

PART II

MAJOR ENERGY SYSTEMS: ELECTRICITY AND TRANSPORTATION

■ ■ ■

This book began with an overview of the energy system as a whole and its primary and secondary components. Once the sources of energy discussed in Part I are extracted from the primary system, they are then used in secondary systems that provide their energy to consumers. The core secondary systems that this book focuses on are electricity and transportation. Part II introduces these two systems, considers how they and the law that regulates them have evolved over time, and explores the major transitions that they face.

As you will see, the law largely treats these two secondary energy systems separately. Moreover, as a physical matter, electricity and transportation rely upon different energy sources for the most part. For example, oil is the predominant fuel in the transportation sector and less than 1% of our oil consumption is currently dedicated to electricity production. Similarly, coal, natural gas, uranium, water, sunlight, and wind, among other resources, are all used to generate electricity with less than 1% of that electricity used in the transportation sector today.

Chapters 4 and 5 describe the electricity system. Chapter 4 explains traditional utility regulation including how it evolved and what it entails. Many of the fundamentals of the energy system have remained constant for over 100 years. It is often said at energy conferences, for example, that if Alexander Graham Bell were to return to contemporary America he would not understand or recognize today's telephony. Thomas Alva Edison, on the contrary, would easily understand the generation and distribution of electricity because today's electricity industry is only at a larger scale than the first power station that Edison built. However, regulatory models have been shifting and both the federal and state governments are experimenting with new incentives, approaches to price setting, and better coordination of grid management. Chapter 5 discusses the changes and challenges that the electricity industry has confronted over the last few decades as parts of the industry have undergone significant restructuring.

Part II then examines the transportation sector. It divides transportation into road and non-road-focused regulation and considers both "traditional" and transitional approaches and issues in each area.

Chapter 6 considers three dimensions of road transportation: (1) infrastructure, (2) vehicles, and (3) fuels. For each of these dimensions, we discuss both the traditional system and transitional issues. Chapter 7, on non-road transportation, examines the laws and regulations affecting railways, pipelines, and electric transmission lines.

CHAPTER 4

TRADITIONAL ELECTRICITY REGULATION

■ ■ ■

A. OVERVIEW

Electricity is the first of the two major systems covered in this book. Unlike the sources we cover in Part I of the book—coal, oil, natural gas, nuclear, and renewables—electricity is not a natural resource. Electricity is produced from other primary energy resources, which is why we refer to it as a "secondary" system—the transformation of primary energy sources through combustion or other means generates electricity.

Electricity has four important physical characteristics that interact with the law regulating it. First, as discussed in Chapter 1 in the context of the fallout from devastating weather events such as the Texas grid disaster in 2021 and the recent California wildfires, we depend on electricity being continuously available. Indeed, we tend to take electricity for granted; any breakdown in that service, through brownouts, blackouts, or downed power lines, is seen as an inconvenience at best and civic crisis at worst. Second, electricity has not been easily—or at least cheaply—stored, as we know from having to recharge our cell phones, iPads, and the like. Third, electricity is completely fungible. There is no difference in the quality of the electricity generated by one resource or another despite the significant differences in the environmental externalities of different energy resources. Finally, because electrons operate literally near the speed of light, we cannot identify the source or physical path of the electricity that we consume. Even though we pay our electric bills to the local utility, it is not likely that we are only consuming the electricity generated by the local utility.

From the title of this chapter, *Traditional Electricity Regulation*, we are signaling the fact that this is an industry undergoing transition. As we describe here, over a century of electricity regulation was based upon certain assumptions about the industry. These assumptions, however, are starting to erode. Historically, the country successfully developed a national infrastructure based on large central power stations. That model of electricity production served as the foundation for the regulations used to govern it and has largely persisted for over a century. As we explore in Chapter 5, however, the industry and its regulations are changing significantly.

This chapter describes the development of electricity regulation through roughly the end of the 20th century. We first present an overview of the industry before discussing electricity regulation in more detail. Understanding this traditional regulation of the electricity sector is important both because it forms the backdrop for new and emerging forms of law, and because traditional electricity regulation still largely predominates in many areas of the country and in the electricity industry.

1.   RESOURCE OVERVIEW

As is also true for transportation, fossil fuels continue to dominate the electricity sector. Of the nearly 100 quads of energy consumed in the United States, nearly 80% comes from fossil fuels. Oil accounts for 94% of the energy consumed in the transportation sector, while roughly 60% of electricity production comes from coal and natural gas. Nuclear power and renewable energy each comprise 20% of the electricity produced. *See What Is U.S. Electricity Generation by Energy Source?*, U.S. Energy Info. Admin. (May 5, 2021).

Critically, the electricity and transportation sectors and the resources used to fuel them have been for the most part mutually exclusive. Even though oil can be used to generate electricity, today this resource makes up only about 1% of electricity production. Similarly, electricity itself provides only about 1% of U.S. transportation resources. If the country is going to transition to a full-blown clean energy economy, however, then that division must be breached. We will explore that development in later chapters, particularly with respect to the adoption of electric vehicles and the push to electrify building-related energy use.

What is noticeable about the electricity system is that a significant amount of electricity is lost from generation to consumption. Consider that when 40 quads of energy are used to generate electricity, following the Second Law of Thermodynamics, conversion losses amount to over 25 quads. In other words, as resources are burned to generate electricity and as that electricity is transported and distributed to end users, over 60% of the potential energy is lost.

The figures below depict the major resources used to generate electricity. The first figure shows the resources relied upon for the last 75 years, while the second is a snapshot of current generation.

Major Sources of Electricity
1950–2020

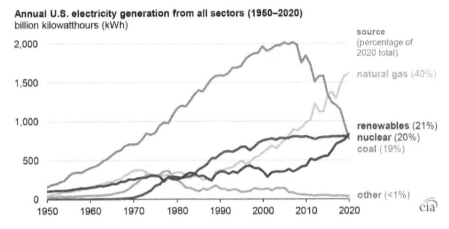

Source: U.S. Energy Info. Admin.

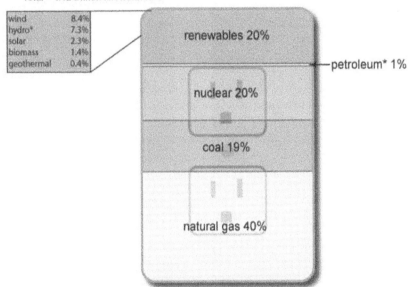

Source: U.S. Energy Info. Admin.

Until recently, the profile of the natural resources used to produce electricity was quite stable. For instance, for the last 50 years, hydroelectricity has generally maintained its contribution of between 6% and 8% of electricity production. Similarly, no new nuclear power plants have come online for over 30 years although two, Vogtle 3 and 4, are preparing to go online in Georgia. As depicted in the first figure above, starting in 2005, this profile began to change, particularly with respect to the mix of fossil fuels that we use to produce electricity. For graphs showing the changing electricity mix by state between 2001 and 2019, see Nadja Popovich & Brad Plumer, *How Does Your State Make Electricity?*, N.Y. TIMES (Oct. 28, 2020).

These changes have been particularly important because low natural gas prices and declining prices for solar and wind power have contributed to the reduction of coal-generated electricity and the retirement of coal plants. In fact, solar and wind power projects are coming online at a greater pace than either new coal or new nuclear power plants. Wind and solar power are already cost-competitive with coal and gas in most of the country. *See* LAZARD, LAZARD'S LEVELIZED COST OF ENERGY ANALYSIS VERSION 14.0 (Oct. 2020).

Not only is the mix of sources we use for electricity evolving, but how we use electricity is also changing. First, projections indicate a continuing, but slow, rise in overall demand for energy, including electricity. Simultaneously, however, rising demand for electricity may be offset by lower per capita expenditures on energy. In other words, while overall demand is increasing, consumers, as individuals, are spending less on energy than they have for decades. There are at least three causes for this shift. First, the Great Recession that began in 2007 reduced the spending power of most Americans. Second, as a society, we have shifted from a manufacturing economy to a services and information economy, which is less energy intensive. Third, as consumers, we are using energy more efficiently in our cars, appliances and devices, and buildings. A few open questions that we will address later in the book include the role of EVs and the impact of the clean energy transition on the electricity sector as a whole.

2. INDUSTRY OVERVIEW

In this section, we discuss the historic background and the basic design of the electricity industry. The industry is comprised primarily of privately owned utilities but also includes non-profit and government-owned utilities. We also describe the basic operations of a power plant. To achieve greater efficiencies and economies of scale, private utilities are connected to an expansive electric grid. We close the section with a brief discussion about how to measure electricity for the purposes of making comparisons among different plants and different consumer classes.

a. History

Historically, the development and expansion of the electric industry occurred rapidly. On September 4, 1882, Thomas Edison flipped a switch at his Pearl Street station in lower Manhattan and lit 400 incandescent light bulbs. At the time, Edison relied on direct electric current that generated heat, limiting electricity's ability to travel long distances. Edison's company initially served 85 local customers. George Westinghouse, one of Edison's rivals, correctly believed that alternating current was a preferred method for transporting electricity because it did not generate as much heat and, therefore, could travel longer distances. Westinghouse took his idea to Niagara Falls and, working with former Edison employee Nikola Tesla, harnessed waterpower to generate electricity to serve the city of Buffalo nearly 30 miles away.

Edison expanded his enterprise to capture economies of scale and scope by building generators, conductors, fixtures, light bulbs, and other ancillary products that we continue to use today. Indeed, Edison's business continues as General Electric, one of the world's largest public companies, with annual revenues of over $115 billion.

Edison's secretary, Samuel Insull, helped proliferate the use of electricity across the United States. Insull took the knowledge and expertise that he developed working with Edison to Chicago, where he created Commonwealth Edison. Insull also brought an innovation to the electric industry—a new corporate form, the electric holding company. Insull's financial manipulation of his holding company, however, would have two consequences. First, it led to his decline and ultimate demise. He was pursued by prosecutors for stock fraud and fled to Europe. Eventually, Insull was extradited to the United States and was tried but not convicted. He ultimately died penniless. *See, e.g.*, Richard D. Cudahy & William D. Henderson, *From Insull to Enron: Corporate (Re) Regulation After the Rise and Fall of Two Energy Icons*, 26 ENERGY L.J. 35 (2005). Second, partially in response to Insull's tactics, Congress passed important New Deal legislation, the Public Utility Holding Company Act of 1935 (PUHCA) (P.L. 74–333), to rein in corporate abuse in the electric industry. The statute played a heavy role in electricity regulation in the United States for most of the 20th century until recently, when federal oversight of utility holding companies was seen as too restrictive and led to the repeal of PUHCA by the Energy Policy Act of 2005 (Pub. L. 109–58). Nevertheless, extensive federal financial oversight of the electricity sector continues via other means by the Federal Energy Regulatory Commission, the Federal Trade Commission, the Securities and Exchange Commission, and the Department of Justice. *See* ADAM VANN, CONG. RSCH. SERV., THE REPEAL OF THE PUBLIC UTILITY HOLDING COMPANY ACT OF 1935 (PUHCA) AND ITS IMPACT ON THE ELECTRIC AND GAS UTILITIES (Nov. 20, 2006).

Despite the ignominious way his life ended, Insull's legacy continues to this day in two important ways. First, his company, Commonwealth Edison, serves nearly 3.8 million customers in Illinois and is a subsidiary of Chicago-based Exelon Corporation, one of the nation's largest electric utilities. Second, the legal model that Insull helped create and proliferate— the so-called "grand bargain" or "regulatory compact," by which utilities receive a monopoly service territory but become subject to government price controls—became the key cornerstone of traditional electricity regulation and continues to play a core role in the nation's legal treatment of the industry today.

b. Electric Utilities

The electricity industry, with revenues over $400 billion, is comprised of both public and private firms. There are roughly 168 privately owned electric utilities, which are referred to in the industry as investor-owned utilities (IOUs). The law calls IOUs "public utilities," even though they are privately owned because they have a legal obligation to serve the public. IOUs serve approximately 72% of the electricity customers in the United States. Other players serve the remainder, including municipally or state-owned generators ("munis" and public power producers), rural electric cooperatives (co-ops), private non-utility entities, and large federal power marketing administrations, such as the Tennessee Valley Authority (TVA) and the Bonneville Power Administration (BPA). The United States also imports energy from Canada and Mexico. *See Industry Data*, Edison Elec. Inst.

The Vertically Integrated Utility

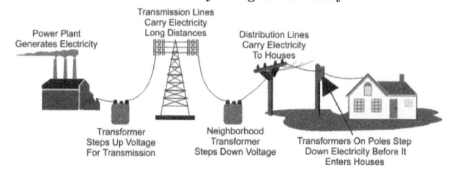

Source: U.S. Energy Info. Admin. (as adapted from the National Energy Education Development Project).

Traditionally, IOUs were structured as vertically integrated firms, meaning that the utility owned and operated all the functions necessary to generate electricity, transport it, and deliver it to end-users. The figure above depicts the operations of an IOU. These operations are generally discussed in terms of three stages: *generation* at the power plant; high voltage *transmission*, including "stepping up" and "stepping down" the voltage of electricity; and *distribution* of the stepped down lower voltage electricity to the consumer.

In addition to the traditional entities that generate electricity, over the last three decades the electricity market has seen an expansion in independent power producers (IPPs), which are sometimes referred to as non-utility generators. Below, we will discuss how and why IPPs came into existence. Simply, an IPP only produces power and then sells it to a larger entity for transmission and distribution.

The electric industry serves three major classes of customers: residential, commercial, and industrial. The residential class is by far the largest numerically, comprising over 87% of customers served, while at the other end of the spectrum, industry constitutes roughly .5% of customers served. Nevertheless, each class consumes relatively comparable amounts of electricity.

c. What Is a Utility?

Above, we described a "utility" (or an IOU) as a large company that generates, distributes, and transmits electricity to its ultimate consumers. IOUs are granted a monopoly in a defined service territory in exchange for the government's right to set its prices or rates. This means that the utility has the exclusive right (and obligation) to serve every customer within its service territory. As noted, this industry-government arrangement is often referred to as the "regulatory compact," explored below.

In recent years, the traditional role and scope of the public utility has come under scrutiny. More specifically, the question arises whether certain companies that provide energy services (including electricity) to consumers should be regulated as utilities. This concern arises with various forms of distributed generation, which basically means electricity generated on-site or near an end-user from a producer other than a traditional large-scale utility. Think, for example, of installing a wind turbine on your farm or solar panels on your roof. These are known as distributed generation, distributed energy resources (DERs), or "behind-the-meter" installations. The rise of distributed generation has created conflicts between local utilities and entities that generate their own power.

Take, for instance, rooftop solar installations. Instead of installing your own solar panels, imagine you hire a company such as Sunrun to install a system on your home. Should Sunrun, or similar companies, be treated as public utilities? Historically, solar power generated barely a sliver of the nation's electricity, but as PV prices plummet, that is rapidly changing, especially in some areas. Consequently, traditional utilities are concerned that distributed technologies such as rooftop solar PV, energy efficiency, energy storage, lower demand, and other less expensive resources can become "game changers" that will dramatically affect traditionally structured electric utilities by reducing their sales. *See, e.g.,* PETER KIND, DISRUPTIVE CHALLENGES: FINANCIAL IMPLICATIONS AND

STRATEGIC RESPONSES TO A CHANGING RETAIL ELECTRIC BUSINESS (Edison Elec. Inst., Jan. 2013).

Indeed, traditional utilities are sensitive to emerging technologies and are challenging companies such as Sunrun by arguing that they are utilities and should be regulated as such. The issue is significant because if the company that finances and installs rooftop solar panels is deemed to be selling electricity within the local utility's protected service territory, then that company may be in violation of the traditional public utility's protected franchise. In other words, if the rooftop solar company is determined to be a public utility, it may face the choice of either being put out of business in that service territory or being regulated as though it is a utility and bearing the associated costs.

The issue of whether a rooftop solar company should be considered a utility is presented in our next case from the Iowa Supreme Court. As you read the excerpt, consider the implications for emerging behind-the-meter technologies. As defined in the Iowa Revised Code § 476.1(3)(a), a "public utility" includes "a person, partnership, business association, or corporation ... owning or operating any facilities for ... furnishing ... electricity to the public for compensation." In the proceedings below, the Iowa Utilities Board (IUB)—the state's public utility commission—ruled that Eagle Point, a third-party solar provider, was acting as a "public utility," and thus could not sell electricity in the local utility's service territory. Eagle Point appealed to the state district court, which reversed the IUB. The case was then appealed to the Iowa Supreme Court, which, among other things, faced the question of whether Eagle Point was a public utility.

SZ ENTERPRISES, LLC D/B/A EAGLE POINT SOLAR V. IOWA UTILITIES BOARD

850 N.W.2d 441 (Iowa 2014)

APPEL, JUSTICE.

Eagle Point is in the business of providing design, installation, maintenance, monitoring, operational, and financing assistance services in connection with photovoltaic solar electric (PV) generation systems. The city of Dubuque desires to develop renewable energy for the use of the city.

Eagle Point proposed to enter into a business relationship known as a third-party power purchase agreement (PPA) with the city that would provide the city with renewable energy. Under the PPA, Eagle Point would own, install, operate, and maintain an on-site PV generation system at a city-owned building to supply a portion of the building's electric needs. The city would purchase the full electric output of Eagle Point's solar power generation facility on a per kWh basis, which escalated at a rate of three percent annually. The payments by the city would not only provide consideration for the electricity provided by the project, but would also finance the cost of acquiring the generation system, monetize offsetting renewable energy incentives related to the system, and cover Eagle Point's costs of operating and maintaining the system. Eagle Point would also own any renewable energy credits associated with the generation system but would credit to the city one third of any revenues received from the sale of those credits. At the conclusion of the agreement, Eagle Point would transfer all ownership rights of the PV generation system to the city.

The PV generation system constructed by Eagle Point would be on the customer side of the electric meter provided by the city's electric utility, Interstate Power. This means that electricity generated by the system would not pass through Interstate Power's electric meter. Due to size limitations, Eagle Point's PV generation system would not be able to generate enough electricity to power the entire building. The city would remain connected to the electric grid and continue to purchase electric power from Interstate Power to meet its remaining needs at the premises. . . .

We now consider whether the IUB applied the correct legal standard when it determined that Eagle Point's proposed third-party PPA with the city would bring it within the term public utility under Iowa Code section 476.1. . . .

In [*Iowa State Commerce Commission v. Northern Natural Gas, Co.,* 161 N.W.2d 111 (Iowa 1968)] we emphasized that "to the public" meant [sufficient sales to the public] to "clothe the operation with a public interest." In order to determine whether the sales were clothed with the public interest, we utilized the eight-factor . . . test [from *Natural Gas Service Co. v. Serv-Yu Cooperative, Inc.,* 219 P.2d 324 (Ariz. 1950)][1]. . . .

A review of the IUB decision in this case reveals that the IUB did not undertake the analysis required by *Northern Natural Gas I* and the *Serv-Yu* factors, but instead sought to apply a different bright-line test, namely, a test that whenever an entity sold electricity on a per kWh basis, it would be, as a matter of law, a public utility.

We decline to introduce such an innovation into our established law. The very purpose of *Northern Natural Gas I* was to escape a rigid test that required a finding that an entity was involved in providing a commodity in a fashion that gave rise to a duty to serve all members of the public. Having

---

[1]   [The eight factors set out in the *Serv-Yu* case, not all of which are discussed in this case excerpt are: (1) what the corporation actually does; (2) a dedication to public use; (3) articles of incorporation, authorization, and purposes; (4) dealing with the service of a commodity in which the public has been generally held to have an interest; (5) monopolizing or intending to monopolize the territory with a public service commodity; (6) acceptance of substantially all requests for service; (7) service under contracts and reserving the right to discriminate is not always controlling; (8) actual or potential competition with other corporations whose business is clothed with public interest. *See Serv-Yu,* 290 P.2d at 325–26.—Eds.]

abandoned the rigid test influenced by the common law, we do not think the proper approach is to substitute another equally rigid test at the other end of the spectrum. Indeed, under the IUB approach, a behind-the-meter solar generating project built by an engineering class at Iowa State University that furnished electricity on a per kWh basis to a nearby farm would be considered a public utility subject to a wide gamut of regulatory requirements. Even if the students obtained a waiver of the territorial exclusivity of the local electric utility, students would be required to stay after class to handle the paperwork associated with filing tariffs with the IUB.

We reject the approach of the IUB in this case. Instead . . . we conclude that the proper test is to examine the facts of a particular transaction on a case-by-case basis to determine whether the transaction cries out for public regulation. We believe the *Serv-Yu* factors provide a reasoned approach when considering the question of whether the activity involved is sufficiently clothed with the public interest to justify regulation. . . .

Before examining the *Serv-Yu* factors individually, we note generally two different types of considerations which could give rise to a public interest in the transaction. On the one hand, there could be a public interest in regulating the transaction between the developer-owner in a third-party PPA and the consumer. This type of public interest usually arises because the provider of the public utility, due to the nature of the service and the barriers to entry, is often in a vastly superior bargaining position compared to the consumer. On the other hand, because the commodities involved may be essential to commerce or everyday life, the continued provision of the service on a reliable basis may trigger a public interest.

We now move to consideration of the *Serv-Yu* factors. The first factor requires a pragmatic assessment of what is actually happening in the transaction. The transaction may be characterized as a sale of electricity or a method of financing a solar rooftop operation. Neither characterization is inaccurate. But most importantly, we have little doubt that the transaction is an arms-length transaction between a willing buyer and a willing seller. There is no reason to suspect any unusual potential for abuse. From a consumer protection standpoint, there is no reason to impose regulation on this type of individualized and negotiated transaction.

We also note that the IUB would not seek to regulate behind-the-meter solar installations that are owned by the host or which operate pursuant to a standard lease. If this is true, the actual issue here is not the supplying of electricity through behind-the-meter solar facilities, but the method of financing. Yet, financing of renewable energy methods is not something that public utilities are required to do. As pointed out by the Consumer Advocate in this case, if providing financing for renewable energy is not required of public utilities, the converse should also be true, namely, that providing financing for solar activities should not draw an entity into the fly trap of public regulation.

With respect to the second *Serv-Yu* factor, we agree with the district court that it cannot be said that the solar panels on the city's rooftop are dedicated to public use. The installation is no more dedicated to public use than the thermal windows or extra layers of insulation in the building itself. The behind-the-meter solar generating facility represents a private transaction between Eagle Point and the city.

On the fourth *Serv-Yu* factor, it seems clear that the provisions of on-site solar energy are not an indispensable service that ordinarily cries out for public regulation. All of Eagle Point's customers remain connected to the public grid, so if for some reason the solar system fails, no one goes without electric service. Although some may wish it so, behind-the-meter solar equipment is not an essential commodity required by all members of the public. It is, instead, an option for those who seek to lessen their utility bills or who desire to promote "green" energy. . . .

The fifth *Serv-Yu* factor relating to monopoly clearly cuts against a finding that Eagle Point is a public utility. There is simply nothing in the record to suggest that Eagle Point is a six hundred pound economic gorilla that has cornered defenseless city leaders in Dubuque. Indeed, the nature of the third-party PPA suggests the opposite, as the city has entered into what amounts to be a low risk transaction—it owes nothing unless the contraption on its rooftop actually produces valuable electricity.

The sixth and seventh *Serv-Yu* factors relate to the ability to accept all requests for service and, conversely, the ability to discriminate among members of the public. These twin factors cut in favor of finding that Eagle Point is not a public utility. Eagle Point is not producing a fungible commodity that everyone needs. It is not producing a substance like water that everyone old or young will drink, or natural gas necessary to run the farms throughout the county. More specifically, Eagle Point is not providing electricity to a grid that all may plug into to power their devices and associated "aps," or, more prosaically, their ovens, refrigerators, and lights.

Instead, Eagle Point is providing a customized service to individual customers. Whether Eagle Point can even provide the service will depend on a number of factors, including the size and structure of the rooftop, the presence of shade or obstructions, and the electrical use profile of the potential customer. Further, if Eagle Point decides not to engage in a transaction with a customer, the customer is not left high and dry, but may seek another vendor while continuing to be served by a regulated electric utility. These are not characteristics ordinarily associated with activity "clothed with a public interest."

The eighth *Serv-Yu* factor is perhaps the most interesting. Under the eighth factor, the actual or potential competition with other corporations whose business is clothed with the public interest is considered. Here, the IUB strenuously argues that allowing third-party PPAs will have decidedly negative impacts on regulated electric utilities charged with providing reliable electricity at a fair price to the public. . . . The fighting issue in this case is whether factor eight in the *Serv-Yu* litany trumps the preceding factors and requires that Eagle Point be treated as a public utility providing services to the public.

The position of the IUB has considerable appeal. Certainly, the case can be made that if Eagle Point is allowed to "cream skim" the most profitable customers, there may be impacts on the regulated utility. If the third-party-PPA movement gets legs in Iowa, it is conceivable that demand for electricity from traditional utilities will be materially impacted in the long run. There is nothing in the record of this administrative proceeding, however, to gauge the likelihood or degree of material impact, and there was no suggestion that the integrity of the grid or economic health of regulated providers has been adversely affected in states such as California, Nevada, Arizona, and Colorado, where third-party PPAs are not considered public utilities for purposes of regulation.

There are also mitigating factors. As pointed out by Eagle Point, it does not seek to replace the traditional electric supplier but only to reduce demand. Although an Eagle Point sale brochure promoting its services is in the record, there is nothing to suggest that its services will be attractive to, or even practical to, many customers of the traditional electric supplier. Further, the parties to third-party PPAs have the ability to convert their business arrangements into conventional leases which are outside the scope of regulation. Indeed, in this case, Eagle Point and the city have done just that to avoid unnecessary legal entanglements.

In addition to mitigating factors, there are also countervailing positive impacts. Behind-the-meter solar facilities tend to generate electricity during peak hours when the grid is under the greatest pressure. Further, Iowa Code section 476.8 requires regulated electric utilities to provide reasonably adequate service, and such service must "include[ ] programs for customers to encourage the use of energy efficiency and renewable energy sources." Thus, third-party PPAs like the one proposed by Eagle Point actually further one of the goals of regulated electric companies, namely, the use of energy efficient and renewable energy sources.

In the end, whether an activity is sufficient to draw an entity within the scope of utilities regulation is a matter of assessing the strength of the *Serv-Yu* factors on a case-by-case basis. The weighing of *Serv-Yu* factors is not a mathematical exercise but instead poses a question of practical judgment. In our view, in this case, the balance of factors point away from a finding that the third-party PPA for a behind-the-meter solar generation facility is sufficiently "clothed with the public interest" to trigger regulation. . . .

NOTES AND QUESTIONS

1.   The local utility, Interstate Power & Light (IPL), is concerned about losing electricity sales in its service territory. Consequently, it argues that Eagle Point is a competing public utility. What economic arguments does Eagle Point make to counter that claim? Do you find them credible?

2.   IPL also argues that Eagle Point is a competitor in its territory and, therefore, should be regulated like a utility. Eagle Point, however, counters by saying that it cannot provide all the electricity needed in the area and, therefore, cannot be deemed a competitor. Do you agree? Isn't Eagle Point directly competing for electricity sales with IPL, in IPL's service territory? More to the point, should regulators restrict competition in regulated areas? Even if Eagle Point cannot provide all the City's needs, it is taking sales away from IPL. And what might be the impacts, if any, on IPL or its remaining customers of allowing Eagle Point to provide power to the City?

3.   Many states are beginning to determine whether and how third-party vendors like Eagle Point should be able provide solar power to customers without running afoul of state laws providing exclusive service territories. In 2018, the North Carolina Supreme Court reached the opposite conclusion of the Iowa Supreme Court in *SZ Enterprises*, and held that a third party provider of solar power to a church was operating as a public utility in violation of Duke Energy's service agreement. *State ex rel. Utils. Comm'n v. N.C. Waste Awareness & Reduction Network*, 805 S.E.2d 712 (N.C. Ct. App. 2017), *aff'd*, 812 S.E.2d 804 (N.C. 2018) (mem. op.). What might explain the differing results? For a map showing which states do and do not allow third-party vendors as of 2019, see *3rd Party Solar PV Power Purchase Agreement (PPA)*, Database of State Incentives for Renewable Energy (DSIRE) (Aug. 2021) (map showing at least 29 states that allow such agreements).

4.   Traditional IOUs across the country have expressed increased concern about rooftop solar power because it can reduce sales. As discussed in Chapter 2 in connection with the *Matter of Westar Energy* case, to the extent that a homeowner relies on rooftop solar or other distributed energy resources, they are not buying electricity from their local utility. Moreover, as of 2021, 45 states and the District of Columbia have a "net metering" requirement or another type of distributed generation compensation rule. Utilities in an additional two states offer net metering despite no state requirements. *See Status of Net Metering Reforms*, DSIRE INSIGHT (May 25, 2021) (summary map). In its simplest form, net metering means that to the extent an individual homeowner generates more electricity than needed, the consumer is allowed to sell that electricity back to the utility and the utility gives the customer-

producer a credit on their electricity bill, often at the full retail electricity rate. Notably, in almost all cases, regulated utilities can obtain "utility-scale" solar energy at a significantly lower wholesale cost than the full retail rate (which includes a portion of the transmission and distribution costs of that energy) under net metering rules.

The issue that regulators must address, then, is how to set rates for customers that generate their own electricity and, therefore, may not be paying their full share of a utility's fixed costs. These net metering "battles" have been very contentious, with commissions and courts in some states accepting utilities' requests to reduce net metering incentives and impose new charges on rooftop solar users, while others, like the Kansas Supreme Court in *Matter of Westar Energy*, have rejected them. *See, e.g.*, Edward Klump & Jeffrey Tomich, *4 Solar Fights Critical for 100% Clean Electricity*, ENERGYWIRE (Dec. 1, 2020) (discussing regulatory debates and litigation in several states); Alexandra B. Klass, *Regulating the Energy "Free Riders,"* 100 B.U. L. REV. 581 (2020) (same); Emma Penrod, *South Carolina to Implement Net Metering Settlement with Time of Use Pricing*, UTIL. DIVE (May 21, 2021); Dan Gearino, *Solar Industry Wins Big in Kentucky Ruling*, INSIDE CLIMATE NEWS (May 20, 2021) (discussing Kentucky commission decision rejecting proposal from IOU to significantly reduce the price per kilowatt-hour the utility must pay rooftop solar generators on grounds that the utility was "undercounting the financial benefits of rooftop solar for the grid."); *Status of Net Metering Reforms, supra.* The question of how to value the grid-scale benefits of rooftop solar and appropriately compensate residential solar generators is also discussed in Chapter 8.

PRACTICE PROBLEM

Like Iowa and many other states, Minnesota does not have legislation expressly allowing for third-party solar power purchase agreements (PPAs) like the one at issue in the *Eagle Point Solar* case. *See 3rd Party Solar PV Power Purchase Agreement, supra* (map showing states that allow such agreements). At the same time, residential solar installations in Minnesota have become very popular, and there are numerous grants available for new solar projects. As a result of the growth of solar generation in the state, assume the Minnesota legislature is considering expressly authorizing third-party solar PPAs and a legislative committee is holding a hearing on the subject. Based on MINN. STAT. §§ 216B.37–.40 and 216B.02 (available on the Internet) and the materials in this chapter, consider the following questions:

1. Does the Iowa Supreme Court decision support an argument that third-party solar PPAs are legal in Minnesota? If you think that the decision does not support such an argument, what options might you propose for amending the Minnesota law? If you represent solar providers, what arguments might you make in favor of expanding the solar power market? What regulations might you suggest?

2.   If you represent electric utilities in the state, what arguments might you make to caution the Minnesota legislature against allowing third-party solar PPAs? What problems have states that have allowed such arrangements faced?

3.   If you represent environmental groups in the state, how might you suggest the legislature draft the law? How might your approach differ from that of the solar providers?

d.   Utility Plants

We have noted three important characteristics about electricity. First, we expect our electricity to be continuously available. Second, we are largely indifferent about where it comes from because, as a product, electricity is fungible. Third, electricity cannot yet be easily or inexpensively stored. These three simple facts reveal a significant complication about the electricity industry—there must always be a constant balance between the supply of and demand for electricity.

Utilities use a variety of resources to generate electricity, in part because they want to be flexible enough to use different fuels depending upon cost and plant operating characteristics. Further, demand varies at different times of the day, during different seasons of the year, and among different classes of customers. Also, to make sure that there is a reliable supply of electricity, utilities will acquire resources to ensure that they have a "reserve margin." For example, assume a utility serves 1 million customers with a peak summer load of 1,000 MW; it is then required to have 1,150 MW of capacity to ensure an adequate reserve margin.

Traditionally, there were three basic types of power plants, each with different comparative advantages as to cost, operation, and maintenance demands.

First, what have historically been called *"base load plants"*—almost always nuclear or coal plants—are expensive to build but have low fuel costs and cannot be ramped up or down rapidly. Therefore, they are most efficient when run as constantly as possible at full capacity. They are called "base load" because they tend to operate at relatively constant levels throughout the year. Today, however, cheap natural gas prices mean that combined-cycle natural gas plants are cheaper to construct and operate than either coal or nuclear power plants and thus have significantly expanded their footprint in the generation mix. This has resulted in coal and nuclear plants experiencing declining revenues and declining market share. Consequently, the term "base load" is being reevaluated given the increased complexity and diversity in the electricity market. *See, e.g.*, JUDY W. CHANG ET AL., ADVANCING PAST "BASELOAD" TO A FLEXIBLE GRID: HOW GRID PLANNERS AND POWER MARKETERS ARE BETTER DEFINING SYSTEM NEEDS TO ACHIEVE A COST-EFFECTIVE AND RELIABLE SUPPLY MIX (June 26, 2017).

Second, *intermediate load, shoulder load,* or *load-following* plants were often older coal plants or simple cycle natural gas, which were more expensive to operate than base load plants and were brought into service depending upon demand. Some older gas combustion plants and hydropower plants also served this purpose.

Third, at times of highest demand, such as on the hottest days of the year or at the busiest hour of the day, *peaking plants* are pulled into service to place electricity onto the grid. Prior to 2007, peaking plants were often simple cycle natural gas plants. Although such plants were not particularly expensive to construct, they were costlier to operate than coal or nuclear plants because natural gas costs were volatile and often high. Today, however, with continued low natural gas prices resulting from hydraulic fracturing technologies (discussed in Chapters 2, 3, and 9), natural gas plants more commonly serve as a "base load" or "shoulder load" resource.

All these factors mean that our electric system of multiple providers with differently configured generators and with varying inputs and varying demands must be continuously balanced. It might seem that keeping the system in balance would be a relatively straightforward proposition that can be addressed using computer systems and control technologies. That is partially correct. However, all balancing of generation, transmission, and distribution must take place on a real-time basis. This coordination takes place on the electric grid.

e.   **The Grid**

It may be a bit surprising that the United States does not operate a single transmission grid. Instead, the continental United States utilizes three regionally based grids, which operate largely independently (asynchronously) of each other. As shown on the map below, the Eastern Interconnection covers east of the Rocky Mountains while the Western Interconnection serves the western United States from the Rocky Mountains to the Pacific coast. The Texas or "ERCOT" Interconnection serves the bulk of Texas with small portions of the state connected to the Eastern and Western Interconnections. Within each grid, power generators are synchronously connected over high-voltage transmission networks and system-wide coordination takes place. Each interconnection is large and complex enough to need several balancing authorities, also known as dispatchers. Because these three grids are not synchronized with each other, power does not flow freely among them. The following map depicts the three current interconnections.

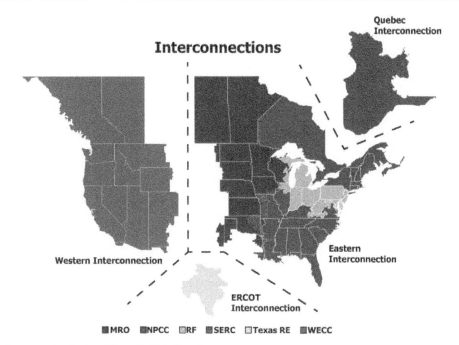

Source: North Am. Elec. Reliability Corp.

Perhaps more notably, the current grid has been resistant to change even though it needs significant improvements, upgrades, and modernization. *See, e.g., Reimagining and Rebuilding America's Energy Grid,* U.S. Dep't of Energy (June 10, 2021). In Chapters 5 and 8, we explore in depth efforts to improve grid coordination as well as the transition to a modern, "smart grid." For a detailed description of the current grid and trends for the future, see NAT'L ACADS. OF SCIENCES, ENG'G, AND MED., ENHANCING THE RESILIENCE OF THE NATION'S ELECTRICITY SYSTEM, CH. 2: TODAY'S GRID AND THE EVOLVING SYSTEM OF THE FUTURE (2017); NAT'L ACADS. OF SCIENCES, ENG'G, AND MED., THE FUTURE OF ELECTRIC POWER IN THE UNITED STATES (2021).

f. Measuring Electricity

Electricity is measured by how much we consume over time. We start with the concept of wattage. Because a watt is such a small amount of power, we generally measure electricity by 1,000-watt units known as the kilowatt-hour (kWh). We are all familiar with a 50- or 100-watt incandescent light bulb (or an 8- or 18-watt LED). For further context, the average U.S. household consumed 875 kWh per month in 2019, though this varies by location, from a low of 525 kWh per month in Hawaii to a high of 1230 kWh per month in Louisiana. *See How Much Electricity Does an American Home Use?,* U.S. Energy Info. Admin. (last updated Oct. 9, 2021).

The kW and kWh measurements are useful in several ways, and it is important to understand the difference between the two. First, we can measure electricity consumption by time period, such as hourly, daily, or monthly. Look at your electricity bill. You will see that you are billed on a kWh basis. Next, we can also measure the size and cost of a power plant. We typically measure power plants by their "nameplate capacity," which is the output of a power plant as usually stated by the manufacturer in megawatts (MW). A MW is 1000 kilowatts. Because plants do not always operate at full capacity, a more accurate measurement would be a plant's output, or net capacity factor. Nevertheless, nameplate capacity provides a useful basis for comparison. An average coal plant, for example, is between 500–600 MW. Nuclear power plants typically run in the 1,000 MW range. An individual wind turbine is 2–5 MW onshore and up to 13 MW offshore. While wind and solar plants are generally much smaller, utility-scale projects increasingly are being planned and developed. For a plain language explanation of the difference between "energy" measured in kWh and "power" measured in kW or MW, see *kW and kWh Explained*, BizEE Energy Lens.

Finally, the cost of electricity depends upon where customers live and on the utility serving those customers. Each utility, as noted, has a different resource mix. Low-cost hydropower will lower a consumer's electric bill, while higher cost power raises it. By way of example, one estimate places the cost of electricity production from *existing* (as opposed to new) electric generating plants at $37/MWh for "fossil steam" facilities such as coal, $24/MWh for nuclear, and $11/MWh for hydroelectricity. U.S. ENERGY INFO. ADMIN., ELECTRIC POWER ANNUAL tbl. 8.4 (Oct. 21, 2020) (2019 data). Electricity costs also vary according to the state or region, including transmission constraints that may limit a utility's ability to enter into contracts with neighboring providers. Therefore, a customer's electricity bill will vary according to: (1) region; (2) legacy resource mix used to generate the electricity; (3) a utility's customer costs and charges; and (4) the amount of electricity a customer uses. The U.S. Energy Information Administration reports, for example, that the average retail price of electricity in the residential sector can range from ¢30.32/kWh in Hawaii (which relies heavily on imported oil to generate electricity) to ¢10.00/kWh in Idaho and ¢9.74/kWh in Washington (both of which have access to inexpensive hydropower resources). U.S. ENERGY INFO. ADMIN., ELECTRIC POWER MONTHLY tbl. 5.6.B (Feb. 19, 2021); *Electricity Explained: Factors Affecting Electricity Prices*, U.S. Energy Info. Admin. (last updated Apr. 12, 2021).

In addressing electricity costs, it is also important to keep in mind that technology evolves over time. Thus, in contrast to the price of different *existing* generation types noted above, the EIA projects that the per-megawatt hour cost of building and operating *new* electric power plants is rather different in part due to finance costs: combined cycle natural gas ($37/MWh); advanced nuclear ($63/MWh); onshore wind ($37/MWh); solar standalone ($33/MWh); and hydropower ($55/MWh). *See* U.S. ENERGY INFO. ADMIN., LEVELIZED COSTS OF NEW GENERATION RESOURCES IN THE *ANNUAL ENERGY OUTLOOK 2021* tbl. 1b (Feb. 2021). Note, however, that such estimates do not include broader costs imposed by electricity consumption, including transmission costs (which can vary widely depending on where the plant is constructed) or the externalities, e.g., the health-related or other social costs associated with traditional air pollutants and GHG emissions (high for some energy resources, lower for others). Tax incentives and other subsidies and policies used to promote specific energy sources are also significant.

NOTES AND QUESTIONS

1.   Energy in general and electricity in particular is a critical input to any modern economy. Indeed, we generally assume that, to a certain point, there is a significant correlation between energy consumption and economic growth. Yet there are reasons to question the correlation for highly developed countries, such as the United States, that both use more energy per capita than other nations with equally high qualities of life and that emit high amounts of pollution that can have a negative impact on the economy. Moreover, deep energy inequality exists. Of the world's 7.9 billion people, approximately 800 million have no electricity at all, and many more have only intermittent access, thus raising significant issues of energy and economic justice. *See Access to Electricity, in* SDG7: DATA AND PROJECTIONS, INT'L ENERGY AGENCY (Oct. 2020).

2.   While electricity access is a key issue in many developing economies, countries that do have widespread electricity access still worry about reliability. Indeed, many utilities will attest that their number one objective is to always "keep the lights on." As described earlier in this book, however, natural disasters such as the 2021 Texas winter storm, western wildfires, and coastal hurricanes can interrupt the electricity supply for hours, days, or weeks, with particularly dire consequences for low-income communities and communities of color. Yet natural disasters are not the only causes of electricity service disruption. Poor regulatory designs can also lead to them. In the summer of 2000, for instance, California experienced a series of rolling brownouts precisely because its newly adopted set of rate regulations for electricity were susceptible to market manipulation and thus resulted in electricity shortages. *See, e.g.,* Sidney A. Shapiro & Joseph P. Tomain, *Rethinking Reform of Electricity Markets*, 40 WAKE FOREST L. REV. 497 497 (2005); Joseph P. Tomain, *The Past and Future of Electricity Regulation*, 32 ENV'T L. 435 (2002). The electricity market manipulation occurred at the direction of companies such as Enron, and ultimately led to electricity market regulatory reforms, as discussed in Chapter 5. *See* Jacqueline Lang Weaver,

Can Energy Markets Be Trusted? The Effect of the Rise and Fall of Enron on Energy Markets, 4 HOUSTON BUS. & TAX L.J. 1 (2004); NANCY B. RAPOPORT ET AL., ENRON AND OTHER CORPORATE FIASCOS: THE CORPORATE SCANDAL READER (2d ed. 2008).

3.   Above, we described ways to measure and compare the cost of electricity. What cost issues arise regarding electricity production as jurisdictions consider moving from fossil fuel economies to clean energy economies? More particularly, what are the consequences of substituting solar or wind power for coal to generate electricity? What other system changes are required?

4.   We described how traditional IOUs were vertically integrated. What are the advantages and disadvantages of vertical integration? How would you imagine that a utility that owned generation, transmission, and distribution facilities would behave towards its customers? How would it behave towards its competitors? The answers to these questions bear a direct connection to the justifications for government intervention into the electricity industry, to which we now turn.

B. REGULATORY OVERVIEW

In Chapter 5, we will discuss various industry restructuring efforts over the last four decades. Here, though, we concentrate on the traditionally structured utility and its regulation. Despite challenges and changes over the years, in many respects, the industry retains its fundamental purpose—to sell low-cost and reliable electricity. In this chapter and the next, one issue we address is how the fundamental purpose of the electricity industry has begun to change, and how utilities, under pressure from the public, new technologies, and new regulatory requirements, must now sell clean energy. In turn, utilities are reconsidering their traditional business models and changing the way they do business. These changes can be facilitated through smart regulation.

This section presents a brief history of electricity regulation. Roughly, from the industry's beginning until 1907 when Wisconsin and New York began electricity utility regulation, the industry was unregulated. The industry was local and competitive largely because transmission was limited. It was the switch from direct to alternating current (DC to AC) that allowed electricity to travel safely over longer distances. This technological advantage enabled electricity to be sold first between cities, then across state lines, and later, regionally. In economic terms, the industry enjoyed significant economies of scale, and the industry quickly went from a competitive one to a regulated one. Initially, regulation intervened at the municipal and state levels. However, as private utilities continued to realize economies of scale, interstate electricity sales increased dramatically. Along with this increase came industry concentration, and with that, various corporate abuses that led to state regulation and, eventually, federal attention.

The electric industry has been robust for most of its life, and it continued to realize economies of scale through most of the 20th century. In the early decades, federal regulation was relatively light, and state regulators were able to impose rates that both rewarded producers and were not burdensome to consumers. As interstate electricity transmission grew, as the size of electric utilities increased, and as industry concentration also increased, federal regulation likewise expanded. For the most part, though, state and federal regulation was non-controversial.

In the mid-1960s, however, the electric industry went through significant changes that necessitated closer regulatory scrutiny. Traditionally regulated public utilities appeared to reach a technological plateau, after which consumer prices began to rise. Until that time, prices to consumers stayed either flat or, in some instances, declined because economies of scale were still being realized. Yet once those economies of scale had run their course, consumers began to experience rising prices and, sometimes, rate shock, partially due to the significant investments (and cost overruns) in nuclear power.

Over the course of the last forty years, federal and state regulators have been attempting to address the changing landscape in the electric industry and consumer behavior, although in fits and starts.

For retail electric sales, regulators have been applying basically the same rate formula that they have always used. This formula balances the profit interest of producers against the consumer interest of having relatively cheap, reliable, and abundant electricity. Additionally, the intent of utility regulators to provide affordable, reliable, and accessible electricity became the bedrock principle of our national energy policy. As a matter of U.S. energy policy, cheap, reliable energy is seen as a key input to economic growth. As a matter of economics, many believe that the utility industry was successful *through* government regulation. Indeed, the public-private partnership enabled the creation of a national electricity infrastructure and made electricity widely available and relatively inexpensive, supporting strong economic growth over most of the last century.

C. REGULATING ELECTRIC UTILITIES

The basic tool used to regulate the electricity industry is price setting. In a country that prides itself on free market capitalism, the idea that government can intervene and set the prices of a privately owned corporation seems out of place. Nevertheless, price setting has deep and historic roots in electricity and natural gas utility regulation in the United States. More importantly, government price setting can be justified by an economic argument. All markets do not function competitively. Indeed, there are situations, referred to as market failures or market imperfections, in which a specific market does not operate efficiently. Those market failures, then, as discussed at length in the last portion of Chapter 2, become justifications for government intervention.

1. NATURAL MONOPOLY

The electricity industry is a classic example of a network industry. The natural gas, water, telephone, railroad, and internet industries share similar characteristics. Refer back to the figure above entitled *The Vertically Integrated Utility.* At the generation end, there is one electric power provider. At the other end, there are tens or hundreds of thousands or millions of customers. Producers and customers are linked together through transmission and distribution lines just as social networks are connected through the internet. In short, the transmission and distribution lines constitute a bottleneck in the entire delivery system for electricity. Customers of a vertically integrated utility are at the mercy of the producer's pricing. Consequently, if left unregulated, a vertically integrated utility that owns generation, transmission, and distribution can exercise monopoly power.

A monopolist operates under a different set of incentives than a firm in a competitive marketplace. Those incentives are depicted in the figure below entitled *Monopoly Power.*

Monopoly Power

If you have not taken a basic course in economics, this graph may appear a little busy. However, it demonstrates the consequences of monopoly power. The reduction of goods produced (moving from *Point C* to *Point B*), has four consequences. First, it shows that a monopolist can *reduce output* (moving from Q_c to Q_m) and second, *increase prices* (P_c to P_m)

at the same time. *Point C* represents the equilibrium point for a competitive market; this is the point where price equals marginal cost—the cost of a producer making the next unit of the good. Third, the consequence of the exercise of monopoly power is higher than competitive prices for consumers but also less consumer choice, which economists see as a loss to society and have termed "deadweight loss," or "social welfare loss" shown in the shaded section between points D, C and B. Fourth, also as a direct result of the move from *C* to *B*, there is a *transfer of consumer surplus* or *monopoly profits* from consumers to the monopolist, as indicated by the darker shaded portion of the graph.

In short, a monopolist can set prices above competitive levels and, simultaneously, reduce output to maximize its profit while lowering social welfare and consumer surplus. Our vertically integrated utility described above is a monopolist.

In the utility business, however, the argument is made that utilities are "natural monopolies," which can be economically useful if properly regulated. Judge Richard Posner has aptly described the situation of a natural monopoly in the telecommunications business, a description that also applies to the electric industry.

> The cost of the cable grid appears to be the biggest cost of a cable television system and to be largely invariant to the number of subscribers the system has. We said earlier that once the grid is in place—once every major street has a cable running above or below it that can be hooked up to the individual residences along the street—the cost of adding another subscriber probably is small. If so, the average cost of cable television would be minimized by having a single company in any given geographical area; for if there is more than one company and therefore more than one grid, the cost of each grid will be spread over a smaller number of subscribers, and the average cost per subscriber, and hence price, will be higher.

> If the foregoing accurately describes conditions in Indianapolis— again a question on which the record of the preliminary injunction proceeding is sketchy at best—it describes what economists call a "natural monopoly," wherein the benefits, and indeed the very possibility, of competition are limited. You can start with a competitive free-for-all—different cable television systems frantically building out their grids and signing up subscribers in an effort to bring down their average costs faster than their rivals—but eventually there will be only a single company, because until a company serves the whole market it will have an incentive to keep expanding in order to lower its average costs. In the interim there may be wasteful duplication of facilities. This

duplication may lead not only to higher prices to cable television subscribers, at least in the short run, but also to higher costs to other users of the public ways, who must compete with the cable television companies for access to them. An alternative procedure is to pick the most efficient competitor at the outset, give him a monopoly, and extract from him in exchange a commitment to provide reasonable service at reasonable rates.

Omega Satellite Products Co. v. City of Indianapolis, 694 F.2d 119 (7th Cir. 1982).

There are two basic electricity markets—wholesale and retail. A utility's generation plants are usually very large-scale operations. For the utility to achieve economies of scale, generation assets produce electricity which is dispatched through the high-voltage transmission grid. Those lines may travel in interstate commerce. The wholesale market is the first sale of electricity to the grid, to other utilities, to power marketers, or to local distribution companies for resale to end-users or other power providers. *See, e.g.,* FED. ENERGY REGULATORY COMM'N, ENERGY PRIMER: A HANDBOOK OF ENERGY MARKET BASICS (Apr. 2020). The high-voltage transmission lines also deliver electricity to local utilities, which in turn "step-down" the voltage to lower voltage distribution networks to resell it to local consumers. This resale for consumption constitutes the retail market.

Generally, the Federal Energy Regulatory Commission (FERC) regulates interstate wholesale electricity sales, while state public utility commissions or public service commissions (PUCs or PSCs) regulate the retail market. At the retail level, IOUs are regulated monopolies. Further, the transportation segments of the electricity and natural gas industries (the wires and the pipelines) are natural monopolies in the same way as the telecommunications cable grid discussed above. *See, e.g.,* Joseph P. Tomain, *The Persistence of Natural Monopoly,* 16 NAT. RES. & ENV'T 242 (Spring 2002). Once an electric utility installs transmission or distribution lines or a natural gas company lays a pipeline, then there is no good economic reason to add additional competing transmission lines or pipelines. So, utilities can act as monopolists because they do not operate in competitive environments.

How can the exercise of a utility's monopoly power be avoided? Refer back to the figure depicting monopoly power. The simple answer is that prices need to be moved from *Point B,* the monopoly price, to *Point C,* the competitive price. But how does that move occur? Can government set prices in private markets? We explore that question next.

2. PRICE SETTING

Price setting occurs in contexts where there are market flaws. Because of the way in which precedent operates in a common law system, cases about price setting in other contexts have ended up shaping price setting in electricity. In the following case, the question before the Court was whether to uphold a statute enacted by the Illinois legislature to set the prices charged by grain elevators, or whether such action violated the U.S. Constitution. As you read the excerpt, consider the conditions under which the Court says that government can set prices. Do you agree? What conditions would you require?

MUNN V. ILLINOIS
94 U.S. 113 (1876)

MR. CHIEF JUSTICE WAITE delivered the opinion of the Court.

Every statute is presumed to be constitutional. The courts ought not to declare one to be unconstitutional unless it is clearly so. If there is doubt, the expressed will of the legislature should be sustained. . . .

When one becomes a member of society, he necessarily parts with some rights or privileges which, as an individual not affected by his relations to others, he might retain. "A body politic," as aptly defined in the preamble of the Constitution of Massachusetts, "is a social compact by which the whole people covenants with each citizen, and each citizen with the whole people, that all shall be governed by certain laws for the common good". . . .

Under these [police] powers, the government regulates the conduct of its citizens one towards another, and the manner in which each shall use his own property, when such regulation becomes necessary for the public good. In their exercise, it has been customary in England from time immemorial, and in this country from its first colonization, to regulate ferries, common carriers, hackmen, bakers, millers, wharfingers, innkeepers, & c., and, in so doing, to fix a maximum of charge to be made for services rendered, accommodations furnished, and articles sold. To this day, statutes are to be found in many of the States upon some or all these subjects; and we think it has never yet been successfully contended that such legislation came within any of the constitutional prohibitions against interference with private property. . . .

From this it is apparent that, down to the time of the adoption of the Fourteenth Amendment, it was not supposed that statutes regulating the use, or even the price of the use, of private property necessarily deprived an owner of his property without due process of law. Under some circumstances they may, but not under all. The amendment does not change the law in this particular; it simply prevents the States from doing that which will operate as such a deprivation.

This brings us to inquire as to the principles upon which this power of regulation rests, in order that we may determine what is within and what without its operative effect. Looking, then, to the common law, from whence came the right which the Constitution protects, we find that, when private property is "affected with a public interest, it ceases to be *juris privati* only." This was said by Lord Chief Justice Hale more than two hundred years ago, in his treatise *De Portibus Maris,* and has been accepted without objection as an essential element in the law of property ever since. Property does become clothed with a public interest when used in a manner to make it of public consequence and affect the community at large. When, therefore, one devotes his property to a use in which the public has an interest, he, in effect, grants to the public an interest in that use, and must submit to be controlled by the public for the common good, to the extent of the interest he has thus created. He may withdraw his grant by discontinuing the use, but, so long as he maintains the use, he must submit to the control. . . .

It remains only to ascertain whether the warehouses of these plaintiffs in error, and the business which is carried on there, come within the operation of this principle.

For this purpose, we accept as true the statements of fact contained in the elaborate brief of one of the counsel of the plaintiffs in error. From these it appears that "the great producing region of the West and Northwest sends its grain by water and rail to Chicago, where the greater part of it is shipped by vessel for transportation to the seaboard by the Great Lakes, and some of it is forwarded by railway to the Eastern ports. . . . Vessels, to some extent, are loaded in the Chicago harbor, and sailed through the St. Lawrence directly to Europe. . . . The quantity [of grain] received in Chicago has made it the greatest grain market in the world. This business has created a demand for means by which the immense quantity of grain can be handled or stored, and these have been found in grain warehouses, which are commonly called elevators, because the grain is elevated from the boat or car, by machinery operated by steam, into the bins prepared for its reception, and elevated from the bins, by a like process, into the vessel or car which is to carry it on. . . . In this way, the largest traffic between the citizens of the country north and west of Chicago and the citizens of the country lying on the Atlantic coast north of Washington is in grain which passes through the elevators of Chicago. In this way, the trade in grain is carried on by the inhabitants of seven or eight of the great States of the West with four or five of the States lying on the seashore, and forms the largest part of interstate commerce in these States. The grain warehouses or elevators in Chicago are immense structures, holding from 300,000 to 1,000,000 bushels at one time, according to size. They are divided into bins of large capacity and great strength. . . . They are located with the river harbor on one side and the railway tracks on the other, and the grain is run through them from car to vessel, or boat to car, as may be demanded in the course of business. It has been found impossible to preserve each owner's grain separate, and this has given rise to a system of inspection and grading by which the grain of different owners is mixed, and receipts issued for the number of bushels which are negotiable, and redeemable in like kind, upon demand. This mode of conducting the business was inaugurated more than twenty years ago, and has grown to immense proportions. The railways have found it impracticable to own such elevators, and public policy forbids the transaction of such business by the carrier; the ownership has, therefore, been by private individuals, who have embarked their capital and devoted their industry to such business as a private pursuit."

In this connection, it must also be borne in mind that, although in 1874 there were in Chicago fourteen warehouses adapted to this particular business, and owned by about thirty persons, nine business firms controlled them, and that the prices charged and received for storage were such "as have been from year to year agreed upon and established by the different elevators or warehouses in the city of Chicago, and which rates have been annually published in one or more newspapers printed in said city, in the month of January in each year, as the established rates for the year then next ensuing such publication." Thus, it is apparent that all the elevating facilities through which these vast productions "of seven or eight great States of the West" must pass on the way "to four or five of the States on the seashore" may be a "virtual" monopoly.

Under such circumstances, it is difficult to see why, if the common carrier, or the miller, or the ferryman, or the innkeeper, or the wharfinger, or the baker, or the cartman, or the hackney-coachman, pursues a public employment and exercises "a sort of public office," these plaintiffs in error do not. They stand, to use again the language of their counsel, in the very "gateway of commerce," and take toll from all who pass. Their business most certainly "tends to a common charge, and is become a thing of public interest and use." Every bushel of grain for its passage "pays a toll, which is a common charge," and, therefore, according to Lord Hale, every such warehouseman "ought to be under public regulation, *viz.,* that he . . . take but reasonable toll." Certainly, if any business can be clothed "with a public interest, and cease to be *juris privati* only," this has been. It may not be made so by the operation of the Constitution of Illinois or this statute, but it is by the facts. . . .

The Court's opinion is notable for several reasons. First, it signifies the importance of a social compact among the citizens of the nation, including their businesses, and their government. We will see, shortly, that this idea of a social compact between utilities and government is alive and well. Second, the Court noted that some businesses are affected with a "public interest." And third, the Court noted the monopoly practices of the grain elevators, which the Illinois law at issue sought to address by setting maximum prices for grain storage. In short, we learned that government has intervened in private markets throughout our nation's history, and that it was a practice we inherited from England. We also learned that government intervention can be justified (1) if the business is in the "public interest" and (2) in the face of a market failure such as the exercise of monopoly power.

Almost sixty years after *Munn*, the Court recognized an even broader scope of power for legislatures to intervene in markets. In *Nebbia v. New York*, 291 U.S. 502 (1934), the Court addressed New York's setting of minimum and maximum milk prices and—importantly—lifted the "public interest" requirement it had imposed in *Munn*. Noting that "[l]egislation concerning sales of goods, and incidentally affecting prices, has repeatedly been held valid," the Court found no constitutional problem with New York's action:

> So far as the requirement of due process is concerned, and in the absence of other constitutional restriction, a state is free to adopt whatever economic policy may reasonably be deemed to promote public welfare, and to enforce that policy by legislation adapted to its purpose. The courts are without authority either to declare such policy, or, when it is declared by the legislature, to override it. If the laws passed are seen to have a reasonable relation to a proper legislative purpose, and are neither arbitrary nor discriminatory, the requirements of due process are satisfied, and judicial determination to that effect renders a court *functus officio*.

291 U.S. at 537. Which version of limits on economic regulation—*Munn*'s or *Nebbia*'s—do you prefer? Why? For a more in-depth discussion of *Nebbia* and its broader implications, see, e.g., BARRY CUSHMAN, RETHINKING THE NEW DEAL COURT: THE STRUCTURE OF A CONSTITUTIONAL REVOLUTION 134–215 (1998).

3. REGULATORY COMPACT

At this point, we have learned that it is constitutional for government to set prices in industries affected with the public interest and in which there is a demonstrated market imperfection. We have also learned that electric utilities have natural monopoly characteristics that constitute a market imperfection and, therefore, price regulation of them can be justified. Economically, the justification is that government wishes to capture scale economies and to avoid waste. Politically, or from a policy viewpoint, regulation is justified because electricity, as well as other energy products, are affected with the public interest—as noted earlier, energy is a primary input to any economy. However, even though price setting has constitutional imprimatur, the Fifth Amendment prohibits government from taking private property without just compensation. The issue then becomes: can price setting be so onerous as to constitute an unconstitutional taking? To avoid an unconstitutional taking, private utilities and their local, state, or federal regulators enter into what is often called the "regulatory compact." We must emphasize that the so-called "compact" is not a legally enforceable contract as much as it sets reciprocal duties and obligations among government, the utility, and its customers. *See* Ari Peskoe, *Utility Regulation Should Not Be Characterized as a "Regulatory Compact,"* HARV. ENV'T POL'Y INITIATIVE (2016).

Judge Kenneth Starr has offered a textbook description of that relationship:

> The utility business represents a compact of sorts; a monopoly on service in a particular geographical area (coupled with state-conferred rights of eminent domain or condemnation) is granted to the utility in exchange for a regime of intensive regulation, including price regulation, quite alien to the free market. . . . Each party to the compact gets something in the bargain. As a general rule, utility investors are provided a level of stability in earnings and value less likely to be attained in the unregulated or moderately regulated sector; in turn, ratepayers are afforded universal, non-discriminatory service and protection from monopolistic profits through political control over an economic enterprise. Whether this regime is wise or not is, needless to say, not before us.

Jersey Central Power & Light Company v. FERC, 810 F.2d 1168, 1189 (D.C. Cir. 1987) (Starr, J., concurring).

As Judge Starr points out, the relationship between government and the utility is such that in exchange for allowing government to set its prices and require it to provide utility services, the utility obtains an exclusive sales territory and economic stability. In short, the way that government responds to the threat of natural monopoly power is to establish a governmentally protected monopoly. This may seem counterintuitive. However, price and profit controls are now in the hands of government regulators to avoid the losses caused by the exercise of monopoly power.

Another way of viewing this relationship is that a balance must be found so neither consumers nor producers are unfairly burdened. From the utility's perspective, prices must be set in a way that it will earn a reasonable rate of return on its invested capital and will not be driven out of business. From the consumer's perspective, utility prices must not be higher than would be set in a competitive market.

At the heart of the government-utility relationship is the idea that utility prices will not be confiscatory relative to producers or to consumers.

The question thus becomes, how do prices get set and on what basis? For the most part, regulators have chosen cost-based ratemaking as the method for setting utility prices. We address that topic in the next section.

NOTES AND QUESTIONS

1.   One might argue that in a pure free market economy, the role of government should be quite limited. For instance, the role of government could be restricted to enforcing the common law rules of property, torts, and contracts. Sometimes referred to as the "common law baseline," the rules of property, torts, and contracts operate to establish the working rules of markets. Property, as you are aware, defines the legal relationships among claimants over different types of possessory interests. Contract rules provide for the exchange of property. And tort rules protect property (as well as persons) from injury or damage. Do you read the *Munn* excerpt above as limiting government to the enforcement of common-law rules, or as opening the door for government intervention beyond those rules? Either way, how far may government go in intervening in private markets? How far should it go?

2.   *Munn* and *Nebbia* establish the constitutionality of government price setting. In this regard, regulators will pay attention to the interest of consumers as well as the interests of utilities. Are there other public interest arguments that you can make for regulating utilities (for instance, environmental protection)? Even more broadly, should regulators consider economic factors, such as a transition to a clean energy economy or encouraging technological innovation? If environmental or clean energy issues are legitimate regulatory objectives, then what regulatory approaches should be considered to achieve those goals?

3.   For one take on what it means for utilities to serve the public interest in the modern economy, including in the face of climate change, see William Boyd, *Public Utility and the Low-Carbon Future*, 61 UCLA L. REV. 1614 (2014).

D. RATEMAKING

In industries where the government sets prices, the regulator must have a reasonable process for doing so. The term "ratemaking" is a government price setting mechanism for utility industries such as electricity, gas, water, and telephone. By statute, electricity rates are set mostly in adjudicatory hearings. In other words, the utility will propose rates for different customer classes. Administrative hearing officers will conduct a proceeding that will review and examine the utility's supporting information for those proposed rates. The hearing officers will take evidence and hear arguments from customer intervenors and other interested parties such as environmental interest groups and competitor utilities. In some instances, state agencies have been created, such as the

Ohio Office of Consumers' Counsel, to represent customers, particularly small customers, in rate hearings. In the following section we describe the elements of a rate case and the general ratemaking process.

1. OVERVIEW OF THE RATEMAKING PROCESS

Electric utilities are regulated in many ways, including finances and accounting, plant and transmission line siting, state and federal environmental regulation, local land use laws, safety regulation, and the like. Nevertheless, the core of electric utility regulation is ratemaking. Ratemaking takes place at federal and state levels. Basically, federal regulation addresses the interstate sales of "wholesale" power and electricity transmission in interstate commerce, while state regulation involves setting rates that are paid directly by a utility's "retail" customers.

Rate regulation balances the utility's interests against its customers' interests. Another way of characterizing these two groups is to equate the utility's interest with that of its shareholders and the customers' interests with those of utility ratepayers.

Because regulators set prices to try to correct a market failure, the main objective is to establish prices to replicate what a competitive marketplace would produce. Such governmentally established rates aim to "mimic the market." Of course, this is all by way of analogy. There are, in fact, no comparable markets for electricity prices, because electric utilities have their own industrial structure and retain natural monopoly characteristics. Nevertheless, rates are intended to approach competitive prices.

Ratemaking has both political and economic dimensions. Ratemaking is political because it occurs through a political process that determines the rate that is set and the product that is regulated. Ratemaking is economic because it attempts to set prices at efficient, *i.e.*, competitive, not monopolistic, levels. Consequently, both political and economic considerations justify the ends ratemaking seeks to achieve.

Traditionally, ratemaking has been said to serve five functions:

(1) capital attraction;

(2) reasonably priced energy;

(3) efficiency;

(4) demand control or consumer rationing; and

(5) income transfer.

See, e.g., JAMES C. BONBRIGHT ET AL., PRINCIPLES OF PUBLIC UTILITY RATES ch. 4 (2d ed. 1988); CHARLES F. PHILLIPS, JR., THE REGULATION OF PUBLIC UTILITIES ch. 5 (1988).

It should be apparent that these goals do not necessarily converge with one another. Setting reasonably priced energy, for example, may be inconsistent with demand control or income transfers. Imagine that electricity costs ¢6/kWh for coal-fired power. A PUC may determine that it is in the public interest to improve air quality and reduce carbon emissions, such that the service area should instead receive electricity from a nuclear plant, which is more expensive than ¢6/kWh. Although coal-fired electricity may be "reasonably priced," the PUC is reducing the demand for coal-fired electricity and increasing consumption of nuclear power.

Indeed, it is the responsibility of many state PUCs to oversee both the *cost* of electricity resources and the *type* of resources in which utilities invest. Regulators use different methods to determine the mix of an electric utility's generation fleet. As we will discuss in Chapter 5, in much of the country, price dominates, as policymakers and regulators have chosen to use wholesale power markets to determine a mix of electricity producers. However, many jurisdictions use other tools that seek to broaden relevant considerations beyond economics alone. Nearly two-thirds of the states, for instance, now use renewable portfolio standards (RPSs) or clean energy standards (CESs), also discussed in Chapter 5, that require a percentage of electricity to come from renewable or zero-carbon energy sources.

Another tool, employed since at least the late 1970s, is integrated resource planning. Many jurisdictions require some or all electricity providers to regularly prepare and submit an Integrated Resource Plan (IRP) to the PUC for review and approval. An IRP is the electricity provider's plan "for meeting forecasted annual peak and energy demand, plus some established reserve margin, through a combination of supply-side and demand-side resources over a specified future period." RACHEL WILSON & BRUCE BIEWALD, REG. ASSISTANCE PROJECT, BEST PRACTICES IN ELECTRIC UTILITY INTEGRATED RESOURCE PLANNING 4 (June 2013). In many states, the specified review period is 10–20 years, and the IRP must be updated every 2–5 years. For example, the 2020 IRP for Dominion Energy, a Virginia utility, outlined its plan to satisfy the state's net-zero energy goals by 2035. *See* 2020 DOMINION ENERGY, INTEGRATED RESOURCE PLAN (May 1, 2020). In 2020 Duke Energy opened an online portal for stakeholder engagement in developing its IRP for North and South Carolina. *See IRP Reference Information Portal,* Duke Energy, https://www.duke-energy.com/our-company/about-us/irp-carolinas. *See also* DUKE ENERGY CAROLINAS INTEGRATED RESOURCE PLAN: 2020 MODIFIED (filed Aug. 27, 2021).

The IRP process can raise contentious questions about utility investments: Should it invest more heavily in renewable energy resources like wind and solar? Should it retire aging coal plants? For instance, in 2021, in response to stakeholder criticism, Xcel Energy revised its proposed IRP for its upper Midwest operations to eliminate a proposed 800 MW combined-cycle natural gas plant in favor of significantly increasing renewable energy investments and extending the life of one of its nuclear plants to replace the energy from coal plants it was retiring early. *See, e.g.,* XCEL ENERGY, UPPER MIDWEST INTEGRATED RESOURCE PLAN 2020–2034 REPLY COMMENTS (June 25, 2021); Mike Hughlett, *Xcel Drops Plan for Big New Gas Power Plant in Becker*, STAR TRIB. (June 25, 2021). Likewise, Duke Energy was forced to revise its IRP filed in South Carolina after state regulators rejected its first filing. *See* Scott Van Voorhis, *Duke Explores Shutting Coal-Fired Plants by 2030 in South Carolina Plans*, UTIL. DIVE (Sept. 1, 2021) (reporting on Duke Energy's revised IRP intended to address regulators' questions regarding the utility's estimates of the capacity of solar power to meet its customers' energy needs and directing the utility to choose a single "preferred" alternative among the planning scenarios presented in the IRP). IRP requirements vary widely by state. For a detailed analysis of IRPs and state laws governing them, see WILSON & BIEWALD, *supra;* REGULATORY ASSISTANCE PROJECT, ELECTRICITY REGULATION IN THE U.S.: A GUIDE 106–09 (2d ed. 2016). The Xcel Energy and Duke IRPs are also discussed in Chapter 11.

The following sections explore these complexities of ratemaking through a more in-depth description of its five core functions listed above.

a. Capital Attraction

Even though utilities are heavily regulated, IOUs are privately owned. For a private business to function effectively, it must either borrow money or find investors. Whether the private firm takes on debt or issues equity, both forms of corporate finance can be called capital attraction. As a matter of constitutional law, government is prohibited from taking property without just compensation. In the case of a privately owned utility, a PUC cannot set prices so low as to effectively take a utility's property or capital. Instead, government-set rates must ensure a fair return on a utility's investments; otherwise, the firm would not be able to borrow or attract investors. PUCs, then, must balance the competing demands of a private firm's desire for profit and the ratepayers' interest in not being gouged. In short, rates must be not too low (non-confiscatory, so they are "just") and not too high (non-gouging, so they are "reasonable").

Below, we examine in detail what a utility does with the rates it collects. In brief, the utility will use collected revenues to cover its operating costs and its capital investments. Collected rates must allow the utility to invest capital for growth. Until the 1970s, utility investments were considered relatively safe with little financial risk. Utilities were not risky investments as the country's demand for electricity continued to grow steadily, utilities continued to serve that demand, and they were assured a reasonable return on their investments by government regulators.

Following the heyday of utility growth, however, the utility business became riskier for several reasons: nuclear power proved to be extraordinarily expensive; the cost of electricity produced by traditionally structured utilities increased; and utilities had overbuilt generation, in part because consumer demand for power flattened. Simultaneously, the electricity market began to open to new entrants, i.e., non-traditional power producers. Overall, the electric industry began to experience competition and with that competition, PUC ratemaking hearings became more contentious as consumers demanded less costly electricity while traditional utilities attempted to protect their service territories from new entrants.

b.　Reasonably Priced Energy

We have long attempted to keep the price of energy low as a matter of national energy policy. Compare, for example, the cost of a gallon of gasoline in the United States to that in Europe, where it is generally twice as expensive. Similarly, electricity in the United States is relatively cheap. Indeed, for most of the 20th century, electricity prices declined or stayed flat.

The idea behind cheap energy is economic growth. Yet, fossil fuel electricity emits GHGs and creates air pollution, and cleaner resources historically were more expensive. The trade-offs between cheap energy and a clean environment with more expensive electricity presented a challenge for PUC commissioners as clean energy agendas were often inconsistent with the goal of inexpensive electricity. However, that has changed significantly in recent years, as illustrated earlier in this chapter. Further, statutes charge PUC commissioners with keeping prices reasonable, making them take a hard look at utility requests for rate increases.

Similarly, consumer pressure to keep prices low plays a role in PUC hearings. Even if we assume that regulators favor keeping local utilities in business, they are also wary of raising rates on consumers. As we enter an era of energy transition, this tension faced by regulators is heightened and exacerbated by the rising income inequality in the United States.

c.　Efficiency

Rates should be set at the efficient price, which is deemed to be the price that a product would reach in a hypothetical competitive market. Determining the efficient price of electricity is no easy matter. As noted above, there are no comparable industries to the electric industry. Nevertheless, rates can be set so that the return to a utility's investors is like the risk that investors would undertake in other markets. In that way we can say that the rate is an efficient one. In short, the rate will be one that keeps the utility competitive compared with other firms with similar financial risks, thus approximating economic efficiency. Still, finding that approximation is not easy. Indeed, regulators will never price electricity exactly right. At any given point in time, electricity prices are almost certain to be either too high or too low. Utilities and consumers both argue their cases in rate hearings, with countervailing points and evidence.

d. Demand Control or Consumer Rationing

As a matter of basic economics, the lower the price of an item, the more of that product people will buy. Consequently, a firm, or its regulator, can either encourage or discourage consumption depending on the price it sets. For electricity ratemaking, controlling consumption—also known as demand control or consumer rationing—can be accomplished primarily through what is known as "rate design."

When the electricity industry was expanding and was realizing economies of scale, electricity rates either declined or stayed flat as noted above. In this scenario, rates could be designed to encourage consumption—and encourage industry expansion—by a method known as the "declining block" rate structure, with the utility offering lower prices per kWh as consumption increases. For instance, assume that a large house consumes 2,000 kWh per month. A utility can charge ¢8/kWh for the first 600 kWh consumed; ¢7/kWh for the next 600 kWh; followed by ¢6/kWh; and, finally, ¢4/kWh for all of the electricity consumed. Because price declines as more electricity is purchased, this rate design encourages consumption.

With this rate design, utilities sell as much as they can, and they will recover their fixed cost in the first block of early purchases. Consumers are satisfied because supplies are plentiful, and rates are relatively low. A declining block rate structure encourages more consumption (and subsequently more pollution).

Over time, use of the declining block rate came under criticism for at least three reasons. First, this rate structure does not work well in a non-expanding economy. Second, many suggested that declining block rates encourage waste or lead to inequities, because such structures offer lower prices to entities that buy more power. Third, as declining block rates favor those who use more energy, they charge small users, often poorer customers, more per kWh. Thus, a different method, the "inverted block rate" was proposed to encourage conservation. This rate structure acts to ensure that the more electricity that is consumed, the higher the cost consumers will pay. Regulators can use inverted block rates in many circumstances, including to encourage conservation or to discourage consumption at peak times.

e. Income Transfer

At its most general level, ratemaking distributes money from consumers to utility investors. So, ratemaking is a form of price control and a form of profit control. Ratemaking is also social policy; it can be used to redistribute income among classes of customers. Utilities generally serve three customer classes—residential, industrial, and commercial. Those groups can be further subdivided, for example, into low-income customers, renters and homeowners, or among large and small firms. Each of these categories has different costs associated with it. A large industrial plant consumes large amounts of electricity but does not require costly distribution lines nor extensive customer service. Individual residential consumers, by way of contrast, consume quite a bit less electricity but require a distribution line into each home and incur relatively higher service and customer costs.

Regulators, if they choose, can allocate costs differently among different consumer classes. A PUC can lower the cost of electricity to residential consumers by slightly raising the price of electricity to larger consumers and subsidizing costs to residential classes. In the past, PUCs have adopted "lifeline rates," which subsidize utility service to poor or elderly consumers. An emerging issue involving wealth transfer in electricity rate design is what portion of system costs rooftop solar users should pay. Many utilities have argued that rooftop PV customers are not paying their fair share of system costs. If accurate, solutions to this include charging solar customers a specific fee or moving more of the price of electricity into fixed fees for all customers, rather than having utilities recover the costs of running the grid through volumetric charges based on how much power consumers use. It should be no surprise that these changes are precisely what many utilities have proposed.

———————

As we experience an energy transition and changes in the electricity industry, ratemaking can be used to accomplish goals other than the traditional five objectives listed above. Below is a list of policy objectives adopted by the Ohio legislature in 2012.

OHIO REVISED CODE § 4928.02: STATE POLICY

It is the policy of this state to do the following throughout this state:

(A) Ensure the availability to consumers of adequate, reliable, safe, efficient, nondiscriminatory, and reasonably priced retail electric service;

(B) Ensure the availability of unbundled[2] and comparable retail electric service that provides consumers with the supplier, price, terms, conditions, and quality options they elect to meet their respective needs;

(C) Ensure diversity of electricity supplies and suppliers, by giving consumers effective choices over the selection of those supplies and suppliers and by encouraging the development of distributed and small generation facilities;

(D) Encourage innovation and market access for cost-effective supply- and demand-side retail electric service including, but not limited to, demand-side management, time-differentiated pricing, waste energy recovery systems, smart grid programs, and implementation of advanced metering infrastructure;

(E) Encourage cost-effective and efficient access to information regarding the operation of the transmission and distribution systems of electric utilities in order to promote both effective customer choice of retail electric service and the development of performance standards and targets for service quality for all consumers, including annual achievement reports written in plain language;

(F) Ensure that an electric utility's transmission and distribution systems are available to a customer-generator or owner of distributed generation, so that the customer-generator or owner can market and deliver the electricity it produces;

(G) Recognize the continuing emergence of competitive electricity markets through the development and implementation of flexible regulatory treatment;

(H) Ensure effective competition in the provision of retail electric service by avoiding anticompetitive subsidies flowing from a noncompetitive retail electric service to a competitive retail electric service or to a product or service other than retail electric service, and vice versa, including by prohibiting the recovery of any generation-related costs through distribution or transmission rates;

(I) Ensure retail electric service consumers protection against unreasonable sales practices, market deficiencies, and market power;

(J) Provide coherent, transparent means of giving appropriate incentives to technologies that can adapt successfully to potential environmental mandates;

(K) Encourage implementation of distributed generation across customer classes through regular review and updating of

---

[2] "Unbundling" means that an integrated utility must either divest its generation or transmission activities or treat them as separate corporate entities.

administrative rules governing critical issues such as, but not limited to, interconnection standards, standby charges, and net metering;

(L) Protect at-risk populations, including, but not limited to, when considering the implementation of any new advanced energy or renewable energy resource;

(M) Encourage the education of small business owners in this state regarding the use of, and encourage the use of, energy efficiency programs and alternative energy resources in their businesses;

(N) Facilitate the state's effectiveness in the global economy.

In carrying out this policy, the commission shall consider rules as they apply to the costs of electric distribution infrastructure, including, but not limited to, line extensions, for the purpose of development in this state.

NOTES AND QUESTIONS

1. What types of innovative energy technologies might be supported by the Ohio policy?

2. Can clean energy proponents use this statute to promote those industries? Can the statute be used to support energy efficiency? How? What will be the cost consequences of adding new technologies or diversifying the resource mix to serve Ohio consumers?

3. Above we listed and discussed five common ratemaking principles. As the clean energy transition accelerates, new ratemaking principles are developing. By way of example, the California PUC lists 10 principles for residential electricity ratemaking: (1) provide low income and medical baseline customers with enough access to ensure basic needs (such as health and comfort) are met at an affordable cost; (2) be based on marginal cost; (3) be based on cost-causation principles; (4) encourage conservation and energy efficiency; (5) encourage reduction of peak demand; (6) be stable and understandable and provide customer choice; (7) generally avoid cross-subsidies; (8) be explicit and transparent; (9) encourage economically efficient decision-making; and (10) emphasize customer education and outreach. CAL. PUB. UTIL. COMM'N, ENERGY DIVISION STAFF PROPOSAL, TRANSPORTATION ELECTRIFICATION FRAMEWORK 99 (Feb. 3, 2020).

4. Several states, including New York, Illinois, and Ohio have adopted or proposed legislation designed to support nuclear power plants using zero emission credits (ZECs). As discussed in more detail in Chapter, 5, under such programs, qualifying nuclear utilities are awarded a certain number of ZECs that are priced by the PUC. Electric utilities are required to purchase these credits to provide financial support for the state's nuclear plants to reduce carbon emissions and promote reliability. In effect, then, the ZECs provide a

subsidy to nuclear power plants. Do the ZEC programs satisfy the goals of ratemaking?

2.　RATEMAKING FORMULA

The traditional rate formula is known as cost-of-service ratemaking. It is akin to a cost-plus contract, in which the contractor is fully reimbursed for all expenses and is also contractually entitled to receive a percentage profit often based on the amount of capital investment it makes. Thus, as the name implies, cost-of-service ratemaking presumes that a utility is entitled to earn revenue by recouping its expenses and by earning a return on its investments. For the utility to maintain its service territory, expand its business, repay its loans, and provide a return to its investors, it must earn revenue. Although a utility is not "guaranteed" a profit under cost-of-service ratemaking, it will be profitable if its business decisions are reasonable.

Cost-of-service regulation determines a utility's revenue through a simple rate formula:

$$R = O + (V - D)r$$

These variables are defined as:

R　　The utility's total revenue requirement. This is the total amount of money that the utility is allowed to earn in the regulated portions of its business.

O　　The utility's operating expenses.

V　　The total value of a utility's tangible and intangible property.

D　　The utility's accrued depreciation. The calculation of (V-D) equals the value of the utility's property minus depreciation; this constitutes the utility's *rate base*, or its capital investments.

r　　The rate of return that a utility is allowed to earn on its capital investment, *i.e.*, its rate base.

a.　Operating Expenses

A utility's operating expenses are comprised of such things as fuel, wages and salaries, materials and supplies, payments to vendors, depreciation and taxes, and the like. These expenses must be recouped if the utility is to stay in business. Operating costs are often the largest component of the revenue requirement, and they are the easiest to determine. If the expenses were prudently incurred, they will be reimbursed dollar for dollar under the rate formula. Occasionally, however, operating expenses are questioned. Should, for example, a regulated utility be extensively involved in making charitable contributions or engaged in extensive advertising? From the ratepayer's standpoint, such expenses may seem unnecessary. From a utility's standpoint, though, charitable contributions in a utility's local service area may very well be considered a good business practice, just as advertising can encourage customer loyalty. But if charitable contributions are used to influence policy, they can be illegal. *See* Matt Kasper, *FirstEnergy Scandal is Latest Example of Utility Corruption, Deceit,* ENERGY & POL'Y INST. (July 23, 2020).

Regulators generally make two determinations with respect to operating expenses. First, should a particular item be treated as an expense? Second, what is the value of that item? The second determination is relatively easy because it is broadly left to the management of the utility, under the idea that these are business decisions that generally should not be second-guessed by a regulator or court. That is, regulators presume good faith: unless there is an abuse of managerial discretion, these expenses will be returned to the utility.

b. Rate Base

Determining the rate base is more difficult and more controversial than evaluating operating expenses. Notice that in the cost-of-service formula, the rate base represents the total value of a utility's property (including investments), with accumulated depreciation deducted. Depreciation is determined by assessing the value of a particular piece of property, such as a building or a generation facility, and calculating its useful life. Each year, then, an amount will be deducted from the value of the company's assets. Note that the utility recovers this annual amount of depreciation as an operating expense.

The important part of determining the rate base is assessing the value of a utility's capital investment. Valuation methods will vary, and courts have adopted different approaches over the years. Consider the example of building a new nuclear power plant. How should we calculate the investment in that plant? If we were going to value a commercial or residential building, the valuation would be relatively easy because comparable sales provide good data. There are no markets, however, for new nuclear power plants (or at least international markets are too divergent to make extrapolations), and thus, comparable sales data is unavailable.

The nuclear plant may be valued based on its original cost of construction. Or it might be valued based on its reproduction cost. Or, we might simply look at a company's books and calculate the cost of borrowed money. Things get more complicated still when we recognize that building a nuclear power plant will take a decade or more, and that during that period, monies will be borrowed and spent. How should such investments be treated for ratemaking purposes while the plant is being constructed but has not yet gone into operation? If we further consider that over time inflation is not static, then assessing the full value of a multi-year investment like a nuclear power plant becomes even more difficult. Not surprisingly, utilities will argue for higher valuations rather than lower ones; customers vice-versa; and regulators face the difficult task of arriving at a reasonable valuation.

c.   Rate of Return

A fair rate of return must be accorded to the utility and its investors. Indeed, it is the rate of return that attracts capital. Utilities make two basic types of investment: debt (bonds) and equity (preferred and common stock). The return to each class, based on risk, will differ. In 2019, for example, the average return on *equity* was about 9.5%. While that figure may appear high during a period of slow economic growth, it reflects the return in equity markets and is, in fact, down over the last two decades from a high of nearly 13%. *See* EDISON ELEC. INST., 2019 FINANCIAL REVIEW: ANNUAL REPORT OF THE U.S. INVESTOR-OWNED ELECTRIC UTILITY INDUSTRY (2019).

The rate of return, then, reflects the interest on debt and a return to shareholders for the capital that they have invested. Thus, the final variable (r) represents a weighted average of the different types of investments made by the utility, calculated to attract investors. In short, the rate of return must reflect risk to investors and, therefore, is most often higher than inflation. *See* LEONARD S. HYMAN ET AL., AMERICA'S ELECTRIC UTILITIES: PAST, PRESENT AND FUTURE 255–56 (8th ed. 2005).

Greater returns can also be used as an incentive to reward utilities for desirable behavior. Utilities that operate with greater efficiency by lowering costs may be awarded a slightly higher rate of return, to encourage continued efficiency measures. Naturally, the higher return cannot be confiscatory towards consumers, even as it is used as an incentive to utilities. And lesser returns will be imposed on a utility for mismanagement. *See In re Citizens Utilities Co.,* 769 A.2d 19 (Vt. 2000).

There is no precise economic or financial calculation to determine the appropriate rate. Instead, experts testify at rate hearings and regulators must choose a rate that is within a "zone of reasonableness."

NOTES AND QUESTIONS

1.   The history of ratemaking reveals that different authorities have been responsible for setting utility prices over time. Initially, in cases like *Munn*, legislatures set rates. Later, courts took on the responsibility for rate setting, by paying particular attention to the valuation of companies' property. In the early case of *Smyth v. Ames*, 169 U.S. 466 (1898), the Court explained:

> The basis of all calculations as to the reasonableness of rates to be charged by a corporation maintaining a highway under legislative

sanction must be the fair value of the property being used by it for the convenience of the public, and in order to ascertain that value, the original cost of construction, the amount expended in permanent improvements, the amount and market value of its bonds and stock, the present as compared with the original cost of construction, the probable earning capacity of the property under particular rates prescribed by statute, and the sum required to meet operating expenses, are all matters for consideration, and are to be given such weight as may be just and right in each case. What the company is entitled to ask is a fair return upon the value of that which it employs for the public convenience, and on the other hand, what the public is entitled to demand is that no more be exacted from it for the use of a public highway than the services rendered by it are reasonably worth.

2.   Justice Brandeis was a critic of the *Smyth* decision because he found some elements of its formula contradictory and others circular. He thus suggested reformulating the calculation in a concurring opinion in *Southwestern Bell Tel. Co. v. Missouri Pub. Serv. Comm'n*, 262 U.S. 276, 290–91, 306–07 (1923):

> The so-called rule of *Smyth v. Ames* is, in my opinion, legally and economically unsound. The thing devoted by the investor to the public use is not specific property, tangible and intangible, but capital embarked in the enterprise. Upon the capital so invested the federal Constitution guarantees to the utility the opportunity to earn a fair return. Thus, it sets the limit to the power of the state to regulate rates. The Constitution does not guarantee to the utility the opportunity to earn a return on the value of all items of property used by the utility, or of any of them. The several items of property constituting the utility, taken singly, and freed from the public use, may conceivably have an aggregate value greater than if the items are used in combination. The owner is at liberty, in the absence of controlling statutory provision, to withdraw his property from the public service, and, if he does so, may obtain for it exchange value. But, so long as the specific items of property are employed by the utility, their exchange value is not of legal significance.

> The investor agrees, by embarking capital in a utility, that its charges to the public shall be reasonable. His company is the substitute for the state in the performance of the public service, thus becoming a public servant. The compensation which the Constitution guarantees an opportunity to earn is the reasonable cost of conducting the business. Cost includes, not only operating expenses, but also capital charges. Capital charges cover the allowance, by way of interest, for the use of the capital, whatever the nature of the security issued therefor, the allowance for risk incurred, and enough more to attract capital. The reasonable rate to be prescribed by a Commission may allow an efficiently managed utility much more. But a rate is constitutionally compensatory if it allows to the utility the opportunity to earn the cost of the service as thus defined. . . .

The adoption of the amount prudently invested as the rate base and the amount of the capital charge as the measure of the rate of return would give definiteness to these two factors involved in rate controversies which are now shifting and treacherous, and which render the proceedings peculiarly burdensome and largely futile. Such measures offer a basis for decision which is certain and stable. The rate base would be ascertained as a fact, not determined as matter of opinion. It would not fluctuate with the market price of labor, or materials, or money. It would not change with hard times or shifting populations. It would not be distorted by the fickle and varying judgments of appraisers, commissions, or courts. It would, when once made in respect to any utility, be fixed for all time, subject only to increases to represent additions to plant, after allowance for the depreciation included in the annual operating charges. The wild uncertainties of the present method of fixing the rate base under the so-called rule of *Smyth v. Ames* would be avoided, and likewise the fluctuations which introduce into the enterprise unnecessary elements of speculation, create useless expense, and impose upon the public a heavy, unnecessary burden.

3.   The Brandeis formula, although an improvement on *Smyth*, did not remove the courts from making valuation determinations. That move came later, in *FPC v. Hope Natural Gas*, discussed below. We will soon see, however, that courts could not remove themselves completely from ratemaking review. More particularly, at the end of the 20th century, as PUCs had to grapple with setting rates during the period of significant investment in nuclear power plants that never came online, rate base determinations became complex, controversial, and, ultimately, subject to judicial intervention.

E. A BASIC RATE CASE

Electricity rates are most often set in adversarial rate hearings at both the federal and state levels. While this dual jurisdiction can present its own set of difficulties, both state and federal regulators tend to broadly employ the same fundamental principles of ratemaking. Here, we examine the federal statutory requirements for setting electricity rates as the basic model.

1. RATE HEARINGS

Sections 205 and 206 of Part II of the Federal Power Act (16 U.S.C. §§ 824d and 824e), enacted in 1935, set out the basic requirements for all rates:[3] they must be just and reasonable and cannot be discriminatory or preferential. Further, the rate setting process requires that once a rate has

---

[3] For a useful FERC presentation of its jurisdiction and § 205 and § 206 ratemaking, see LAWRENCE R. GREENFIELD, AN OVERVIEW OF THE FEDERAL ENERGY REGULATORY COMMISSION AND THE FEDERAL REGULATION OF PUBLIC UTILITIES IN THE UNITED STATES (2010).

been filed, it must stay in effect unless there is a notice and a new FERC hearing.

FEDERAL POWER ACT § 205
16 U.S.C. § 824d

(a) Just and reasonable rates

All rates and charges made, demanded, or received by any public utility for or in connection with the transmission or sale of electric energy subject to the jurisdiction of the Commission, and all rules and regulations affecting or pertaining to such rates or charges shall be just and reasonable, and any such rate or charge that is not just and reasonable is hereby declared to be unlawful.

(b) Preference or advantage unlawful

No public utility shall, with respect to any transmission or sale subject to the jurisdiction of the Commission,

(1) make or grant any undue preference or advantage to any person or subject any person to any undue prejudice or disadvantage, or

(2) maintain any unreasonable difference in rates, charges, service, facilities, or in any other respect, either as between localities or as between classes of service.

(c) Schedules

Under such rules and regulations as the Commission may prescribe, every public utility shall file with the Commission, within such time and in such form as the Commission may designate, and shall keep open in convenient form and place for public inspection schedules showing all rates and charges for any transmission or sale subject to the jurisdiction of the Commission, and the classifications, practices, and regulations affecting such rates and charges, together with all contracts which in any manner affect or relate to such rates, charges, classifications, and services.

(d) Notice required for rate changes

Unless the Commission otherwise orders, no change shall be made by any public utility in any such rate, charge, classification, or service, or in any rule, regulation, or contract relating thereto, except after sixty days' notice to the Commission and to the public. Such notice shall be given by filing with the Commission and keeping open for public inspection new schedules stating plainly the change or changes to be made in the schedule or schedules then in force and the time when the change or changes will go into effect. The Commission, for good cause shown, may allow changes to take effect without requiring the sixty days' notice herein provided for by an order specifying the changes so to be made and the time when they shall take effect and the manner in which they shall be filed and published.

Once a utility files a rate with FERC under § 205, FERC can take one of four actions: (1) accept the rate, (2) reject the rate, (3) accept the rate conditionally and set it for a trial-like hearing, or (4) do nothing, in which case the rate takes automatic effect under the statute.

FPA § 205 thus establishes the "key pattern" for FERC regulation. *See* JAMES H. MCGREW, FERC: FEDERAL ENERGY REGULATORY COMMISSION 21 (2d ed. 2009). As noted in the statute, FERC will only approve a rate that is just, reasonable, and nondiscriminatory. In this way, the government avoids a challenge from either the utility for taking its property (*i.e.,* its invested capital) or from ratepayers for extracting excessive rates. Once filed, FERC's approved rate becomes the "legal rate" or "filed rate"—that is, the only rate that can be legally charged and collected. Even a court cannot set a different rate from the filed rate, including if the court believes it has found a "more reasonable one." *Montana-Dakota Utils. Co. v. Northwestern Pub. Serv. Co.*, 341 U.S. 246, 252 (1950). This idea is known as the "filed rate doctrine" and will be discussed in greater depth below.

Although the filed rate doctrine forecloses the collection of any rate other than the one approved by FERC, this does not mean that the rate becomes frozen in perpetuity. In fact, the FPA specifically includes a provision for changing filed rates. Under that provision, § 206, either FERC itself or parties can seek the modification of any rate that can be shown to be unjust, unreasonable, or unduly discriminatory.

FEDERAL POWER ACT § 206
16 U.S.C. § 824e

(a) Unjust or preferential rates, etc.; statement of reasons for changes; hearing; specification of issues

Whenever the Commission, after a hearing held upon its own motion or upon complaint, shall find that any rate, charge, or classification, demanded, observed, charged, or collected by any public utility for any transmission or sale subject to the jurisdiction of the Commission, or that any rule, regulation, practice, or contract affecting such rate, charge, or classification is unjust, unreasonable, unduly discriminatory or preferential, the Commission shall determine the just and reasonable rate, charge, classification, rule, regulation, practice, or contract to be thereafter observed and in force, and shall fix the same by order. Any complaint or motion of the Commission to initiate a proceeding under this section shall state the change or changes to be made in the rate, charge, classification, rule, regulation, practice, or contract then in force, and the reasons for any proposed change or changes therein. If, after review of any motion or complaint and answer, the Commission shall decide to hold a hearing, it shall fix by order the time and place of such hearing and shall specify the issues to be adjudicated.

(b) Refund effective date; preferential proceedings; statement of reasons for delay; burden of proof; scope of refund order; refund orders in cases of dilatory behavior; interest

Whenever the Commission institutes a proceeding under this section, the Commission shall establish a refund effective date. In the case of a proceeding instituted on complaint, the refund effective date shall not be earlier than the date of the filing of such complaint nor later than 5 months after the filing of such complaint. In the case of a proceeding instituted by the Commission on its own motion, the refund effective date shall not be earlier than the date of the publication by the Commission of notice of its intention to initiate such proceeding nor later than 5 months after the publication date.

Thus, § 206 authorizes FERC to change rates after a hearing that is held by its own motion or by complaint from a third party if those rates that are already on file are found to be unjust or unreasonable. In such a case, FERC will set a just and reasonable rate to be prospectively applied. MCGREW, *supra* at 22; *see also City of Girard v. FERC*, 790 F.2d 919 (D.C. Cir. 1986). Additionally, FERC has the statutory authority to authorize refunds for limited periods of time.

2. COMMISSION DISCRETION TO SET RATES

When the government intervened in private markets to set rates, it first did so through legislative action as in the case of *Munn v. Illinois, supra*. Then, as in the cases of *Smyth v. Ames* and *Southwestern Bell, supra*, courts also became involved with reviewing and then actually setting rates. Given the complexity of ratemaking, administrative agencies soon were given this task, thus raising the issue of whether agencies or courts should be the ultimate arbiters of utility rates. The next landmark case lays out the principles that led the Supreme Court to hold that the federal commission should be granted a large degree of discretion in rate setting. In *FPC v. Hope Natural Gas*, the Supreme Court took the judiciary out of the valuation business by establishing what is known as the "end result" test. *Hope* thus began an era of deference to public utility commissions. Although *Hope* is a natural gas case, it has been repeatedly applied to both electricity and natural gas ratemaking.

Hope also provides an excellent example of a basic rate case. The Hope Natural Gas Company sold gas in interstate commerce and therefore fell under the jurisdiction of what was then the Federal Power Commission (FPC) and is now FERC. Customers complained that rates were excessive, and the FPC conducted a hearing to determine the reasonableness of the rates. The FPC ordered a reduction in future rates and established a new, "just and reasonable" rate. The utility then went to court, arguing that the FPC rate was confiscatory.

FEDERAL POWER COMMISSION V. HOPE NATURAL GAS CO.
320 U.S. 591 (1944)

MR. JUSTICE DOUGLAS delivered the opinion of the Court.

The Commission established an interstate rate base of $33,712,526 which, it found, represented the "actual legitimate cost" of the company's interstate property less depletion and depreciation and plus unoperated acreage, working capital and future net capital additions. The Commission, beginning with book cost, made certain adjustments not necessary to relate here, and found the "actual legitimate cost" of the plant in interstate service to be $51,957,416, as of December 31, 1940. It deducted accrued depletion and depreciation, which it found to be $22,328,016 on an "economic service life" basis. And it added $1,392,021 for future net capital additions, $566,105 for useful unoperated acreage, and $2,125,000 for working capital. It used 1940 as a test year to estimate future revenues and expenses. It allowed over $16,000,000 as annual operating expenses— about $1,300,000 for taxes, $1,460,000 for depletion and depreciation, $600,000 for exploration and development costs, $8,500,000 for gas purchased. The Commission allowed a net increase of $421,160 over 1940 operating expenses, which amount was to take care of future increase in wages, in West Virginia property taxes, and in exploration and development costs. The total amount of deductions allowed from interstate revenues was $13,495,584.

Hope introduced evidence from which it estimated reproduction cost of the property at $97,000,000. It also presented a so-called trended "original cost" estimate which exceeded $105,000,000. The latter was designed to indicate what the original cost of the property would have been if 1938 material and labor prices had prevailed throughout the whole period of the piecemeal construction of the company's property since 1898. Hope estimated by the "percent condition" method accrued depreciation at about 35% of reproduction cost new. On that basis, Hope contended for a rate base of $66,000,000. The Commission refused to place any reliance on reproduction cost new, saying that it was "not predicated upon facts," and was "too conjectural and illusory to be given any weight in these proceedings." It likewise refused to give any "probative value" to trended "original cost," since it was "not founded in fact," but was "basically erroneous" and produced "irrational results." In determining the amount of accrued depletion and depreciation, the Commission ... based its computation on "actual legitimate cost." It found that Hope, during the years when its business was not under regulation, did not observe "sound depreciation and depletion practices," but "actually accumulated an excessive reserve" of about $46,000,000. One member of the Commission thought that the entire amount of the reserve should be deducted from "actual legitimate cost" in determining the rate base. The majority of the Commission concluded, however, that where, as here, a business is brought under regulation for the first time, and where incorrect depreciation and depletion practices have prevailed, the deduction of the reserve requirement (actual existing depreciation and depletion), rather than the excessive reserve, should be made so as to lay "a sound basis for future regulation and control of rates." As we have pointed out, it determined accrued depletion and depreciation to be $22,328,016; and it allowed approximately $1,460,000 as the annual operating expense for depletion and depreciation.

Hope's estimate of original cost was about $69,735,000— approximately $17,000,000 more than the amount found by the Commission. The item of $17,000,000 was made up largely of expenditures which, prior to December 31, 1938, were charged to operating expenses. Chief among those expenditures was some $12,600,000 expended in well drilling prior to 1923. Most of that sum was expended by Hope for labor, use of drilling rigs, hauling, and similar costs of well drilling. Prior to 1923, Hope followed the general practice of the natural gas industry and charged the cost of drilling wells to operating expenses. Hope continued that practice until the Public Service Commission of West Virginia, in 1923, required it to capitalize such expenditures, as does the Commission under its present Uniform System of Accounts. The Commission refused to add such items to the rate base, stating that "No greater injustice to consumers could be done than to allow items as operating expenses and at a later date include them in the rate base, thereby placing multiple charges upon the consumers."

For the same reason, the Commission excluded from the rate base about $1,600,000 of expenditures on properties which Hope acquired from other utilities, the latter having charged those payments to operating expenses. The Commission disallowed certain other overhead items amounting to over $3,000,000 which also had been previously charged to operating expenses. And it refused to add some $632,000 as interest during construction, since no interest was in fact paid.

Hope contended that it should be allowed a return of not less than 8%. The Commission found that an 8% return would be unreasonable, but that 6 1/2% was a fair rate of return. That rate of return, applied to the rate base of $33,712,526, would produce $2,191,314 annually, as compared with the present income of not less than $5,801,171.

The Circuit Court of Appeals set aside the order of the Commission for the following reasons. (1) It held that the rate base should reflect the "present fair value" of the property, that the Commission, in determining the "value," should have considered reproduction cost and trended original cost, and that "actual legitimate cost" (prudent investment) was not the proper measure of "fair value" where price levels had changed since the investment. (2) It concluded that the well drilling costs and overhead items in the amount of some $17,000,000 should have been included in the rate base. (3) It held that accrued depletion and depreciation and the annual allowance for that expense should be computed on the basis of "present fair value" of the property, not on the basis of "actual legitimate cost." . . .

Congress has provided in § 4(a) of the Natural Gas Act that all natural gas rates subject to the jurisdiction of the Commission "shall be just and reasonable, and any such rate or charge that is not just and reasonable is hereby declared to be unlawful." Section 5(a) gives the Commission the power, after hearing, to determine the "just and reasonable rate" to be thereafter observed and to fix the rate by order. Section 5(a) also empowers the Commission to order a "decrease where existing rates are unjust . . . unlawful, or are not the lowest reasonable rates." And Congress has provided in § 19(b) that, on review of these rate orders, the "finding of the Commission as to the facts, if supported by substantial evidence, shall be conclusive. Congress, however, has provided no formula by which the "just and reasonable" rate is to be determined. It has not filled in the details of the general prescription of § 4(a) and § 5(a). It has not expressed in a specific rule the fixed principle of "just and reasonable."

When we sustained the constitutionality of the Natural Gas Act in the *Natural Gas Pipeline Co.* case, we stated that the "authority of Congress to regulate the prices of commodities in interstate commerce is at least as great under the Fifth Amendment as is that of the states under the Fourteenth to regulate the prices of commodities in intrastate commerce." Ratemaking is indeed but one species of price-fixing. The fixing of prices, like other applications of the police power, may reduce the value of the property which is being regulated. But the fact that the value is reduced does not mean that the regulation is invalid. It does, however, indicate that "fair value" is the end product of the process of ratemaking, not the starting point, as the Circuit Court of Appeals held. The heart of the matter is that rates cannot be made to depend upon "fair value" when the value of the going enterprise depends on earnings under whatever rates may be anticipated.

We held in *Federal Power Commission v. Natural Gas Pipeline Co.* that the Commission was not bound to the use of any single formula or combination of formulae in determining rates. Its ratemaking function, moreover, involves the making of "pragmatic adjustments." And when the Commission's order is challenged in the courts, the question is whether that order, "viewed in its entirety," meets the requirements of the Act. Under the statutory standard of "just and reasonable," it is the result reached, not the method employed, which is controlling. It is not theory, but the impact of the rate order, which counts. If the total effect of the rate order cannot be said to be unjust and unreasonable, judicial inquiry under the Act is at an end. The fact that the method employed to reach that result may contain infirmities is not then important. Moreover, the Commission's order does not become suspect by reason of the fact that it is challenged. It is the product of expert judgment which carries a presumption of validity. And he who would upset the rate order under the Act carries the heavy burden of making a convincing showing that it is invalid because it is unjust and unreasonable in its consequences.

The ratemaking process under the Act, *i.e.,* the fixing of "just and reasonable" rates, involves a balancing of the investor and the consumer interests. Thus, we stated in the *Natural Gas Pipeline Co.* case that "regulation does not insure that the business shall produce net revenues." But, such considerations aside, the investor interest has a legitimate concern with the financial integrity of the company whose rates are being regulated. From the investor or company point of view, it is important that there be enough revenue not only for operating expenses, but also for the capital costs of the business. These include service on the debt and dividends on the stock. By that standard, the return to the equity owner should be commensurate with returns on investments in other enterprises having corresponding risks. That return, moreover, should be sufficient to assure confidence in the financial integrity of the enterprise, so as to maintain its credit and to attract capital. The conditions under which more or less might be allowed are not important here. Nor is it important to this case to determine the various permissible ways in which any rate base on which the return is computed might be arrived at. For we are of the view that the end result in this case cannot be condemned under the Act as unjust and unreasonable from the investor or company viewpoint.

We have already noted that Hope is a wholly owned subsidiary of the Standard Oil Co. (N.J.). It has no securities outstanding except stock. All of that stock has been owned by Standard since 1908. The par amount presently outstanding is approximately $28,000,000, as compared with the rate base of $33,712,526 established by the Commission. Of the total outstanding stock, $11,000,000 was issued in stock dividends. The balance, or about $17,000,000, was issued for cash or other assets. During the four decades of its operations, Hope has paid over $97,000,000 in cash dividends. It had, moreover, accumulated by 1940 an earned surplus of about $8,000,000. It had thus earned the total investment in the company nearly seven times. Down to 1940, it earned over 20% per year on the average annual amount of its capital stock issued for cash or other assets. On an average invested capital of some $23,000,000, Hope's average earnings have been about 12% a year. And, during this period, it had accumulated in addition reserves for depletion and depreciation of about $46,000,000. Furthermore, during 1939, 1940, and 1941, Hope paid dividends of 10% on its stock. And in the year 1942, during about half of which the lower rates were in effect, it paid dividends of 7 1/2%. From 1939–1942, its earned surplus increased from $5,250,000 to about $13,700,000, *i.e.,* to almost half the par value of its outstanding stock.

As we have noted, the Commission fixed a rate of return which permits Hope to earn $2,191,314 annually. In determining that amount, it stressed the importance of maintaining the financial integrity of the company. It considered the financial history of Hope and a vast array of data bearing on the natural gas industry, related businesses, and general economic conditions. It noted that the yields on better issues of bonds of natural gas companies sold in the last few years were "close to 3 percent." It stated that the company was a "seasoned enterprise whose risks have been minimized" by adequate provisions for depletion and depreciation (past and present) with "concurrent high profits," by "protected established markets, through affiliated distribution companies, in populous and industrialized areas," and by a supply of gas locally to meet all requirements, "except on certain peak days in the winter, which it is feasible to supplement in the future with gas from other sources." The Commission concluded, "The company's efficient management, established markets, financial record, affiliations, and its prospective business place it in a strong position to attract capital upon favorable terms when it is required."

In view of these various considerations, we cannot say that an annual return of $2,191,314 is not "just and reasonable" within the meaning of the Act. Rates which enable the company to operate successfully, to maintain its financial integrity, to attract capital, and to compensate its investors for the risks assumed certainly cannot be condemned as invalid, even though they might produce only a meager return on the so-called "fair value" rate base. In that connection, it will be recalled that Hope contended for a rate base of $66,000,000 computed on reproduction cost new. The Commission points out that, if that rate base were accepted, Hope's average rate of return for the four-year period from 1937–1940 would amount to 3.27%. During that period, Hope earned an annual average return of about 9% on the average investment. It asked for no rate increases. Its properties were well maintained and operated. As the Commission says, such a modest rate of 3.27% suggests an "inflation of the base on which the rate has been computed." The incongruity between the actual operations and the return computed on the basis of reproduction cost suggests that the Commission was wholly justified in rejecting the latter as the measure of the rate base. . . .

It is suggested that the Commission has failed to perform its duty under the Act in that it has not allowed a return for gas production that will be enough to induce private enterprise to perform completely and efficiently its functions for the public. The Commission, however, was not oblivious of those matters. It considered them. It allowed, for example, delay rentals and exploration and development costs in operating expenses. No serious attempt has been made here to show that they are inadequate. We certainly cannot say that they are, unless we are to substitute our opinions for the expert judgment of the administrators to whom Congress entrusted the decision. Moreover, if, in light of experience, they turn out to be inadequate for development of new sources of supply, the doors of the Commission are open for increased allowances. This is not an order for all time. The Act contains machinery for obtaining rate adjustments.

NOTES AND QUESTIONS

1.   As noted above, Section 4 of the Natural Gas Act of 1938, 15 U.S.C. § 717d, and Section 205 of the Federal Power Act, 16 U.S.C. § 824e(a), both require that rates be "just and reasonable" and not "grant any undue preference or advantage" or reflect "any unreasonable difference" in prices. These requirements seek to conform to constitutional principles, so that rates are not confiscatory and so that similarly situated classes of customers are treated similarly. As an example of an unjust or unreasonable rate, when President Trump's Energy Secretary, Rick Perry, proposed a rule for FERC to enact subsidizing coal and nuclear plants, FERC rejected the proposed rule because, in its opinion, the plan was inconsistent with FERC's duty under the Federal Power Act to set rates that are just, reasonable, and non-discriminatory. *See* Brad Plumer, *Rick Perry's Plan to Rescue Struggling Coal and Nuclear Plants Is Rejected*, N.Y. TIMES (Jan. 8, 2018); Order Terminating Rulemaking Proceeding, Initiating New Proceeding, and Establishing Additional Procedures, 162 FERC ¶ 61,012, 61,036 (2018); *see also* 16 U.S.C. § 824e(a); Sharon B. Jacobs, *The Statutory Separation of Powers*, 192 YALE L.J. 378, 415–19 (2019) (discussing FERC rejection of proposed rule).

2.   Apply the basic cost-of-service rate formula to the facts in *Hope Natural Gas*. How did the FPC determine the rate base? What rate of return did the FPC use? What rate base and rate of return did the company want? The FPC disallowed a $17 million item. Why? How did the Court respond to the constitutional argument lodged by the company?

3.   Utility rates—also sometimes referred to as tariffs—are complicated. This is truer than ever today. First, regulated utilities operate under a series of federal and state regulations that require compliance and careful attention to how the costs of those regulations are treated in ratemaking. For example, a requirement that a utility undertake a study to integrate wind power into its operations can be recovered as a legitimate expense. Second, calculating the revenue requirement can become complicated. As noted, operating expenses are relatively easy to calculate, but deciding which items to expense and

applying the proper rate of return on each investment is not straightforward. Thus, different PUCs have used multiple approaches over the years. Third, a single tariff must incorporate different classes of customers, different types of service, and different charges for each. For example, the tariffs for the Ohio Power Company issued on September 27, 2021 are over 200 pages. *See* Ohio Pub. Utils. Comm'n, Tariffs: Utility and Telecom, Ohio Power Company, PUCO No. 20 (last modified Oct. 1, 2021).

Rates must be fair for each class of customers—residential, commercial, and industrial. Each class, in turn, has different needs and is charged accordingly. Rates should also be fair among customer classes. In the attempt to even out charges to each class of customers, a utility bill typically consists of three components—a demand charge, an energy charge, and a service charge. The demand charge represents the utility's fixed costs of electric capacity required to meet peak electric loads. The energy charge represents the amount of electricity consumed by each user. And the service charge represents certain fixed costs to provide electricity service to each consumer, including metering, billing, and maintenance.

Below, as an example, we have excerpted some of the monthly electric rates charged to various customer classes in Minnesota by Northern States Power Co., the Xcel Energy utility operating in that state. *See* Northern States Power Co., Minnesota Electric Rate Book—MPUC No. 2 (Nov. 2020). Even this simple example of a tariff should give you an idea of how complex ratemaking can be.

Monthly Customer Service Charges (2020)	
CUSTOMER CLASSIFICATION	**RATE**
Residential	
Overhead line	$ 8.00
Overhead line—electric heating	$ 10.00
Underground line	$ 10.00
Underground line—electric heating	$ 12.00
Commercial and Industrial	
General	$ 25.64
General Time-of-Day	$ 29.64
Peak-Controlled	$ 55.00
Peak-Controlled Time-of-Day	$ 55.00

Energy (Per kWh) and Demand (Per kW) Rates	
CUSTOMER CLASSIFICATION	RATE
Residential	
Energy: Summer (June–September)	10.301¢
Energy: Winter (Other months)	8.803¢
Energy: Winter-electric heating	5.988¢
Residential Time-of-Day	
Energy: On-Peak Summer	20.497¢
Energy: On-Peak Winter (standard)	16.508¢
Energy: On-Peak Winter (electric heating)	9.284¢
Energy: Off-Peak Summer	4.170¢
Energy: Off-Peak Winter	4.170¢
General	
Energy	3.407¢
Demand: Summer	$14.79
Demand: Winter	$10.49
General Time-of-Day	
Energy: On-Peak	4.855¢
Energy: Off-Peak	2.341¢
Demand: Summer	$14.79
Demand: Winter	$10.49

Note that Northern States Power assesses a separate monthly demand charge, measured per kW, only on commercial and industrial customers. This is for the fixed costs of the electric capacity required to meet the peak electric loads on its system and applies to the highest 15-minute kW demand during the billing period. *See Understanding Your Bill— Minnesota*, Xcel Energy. Why do you think this charge applies to commercial and industrial customers but not residential ratepayers? Residential customers pay for the fixed costs in their "bundled" energy charge. You can also see that the demand charges are roughly the same for each class.

Note also that customers who elect time-of-day service and have a special meter installed receive a significantly lower rate, measured in cents per kWh, during off-peak hours when overall electricity demand is less, and thus cheaper to generate. For residential customers, off-peak hours are 9 pm to 9 am Monday through Friday and all weekends and holidays. What effect should this have on electricity use? It aims to incentivize those customers to shift electricity use to those times of day. By contrast, all customer classes in this example pay higher seasonal rates during the summer months when air conditioning use is at its peak.

Finally, as discussed earlier in this chapter and in Chapter 2, as more customers install rooftop solar, their need to purchase electricity from the utility declines. Yet they still may need the utility to provide power when the sun is not shining. One problem arising under net metering regulation (which gives such customers a credit on their bill for any energy they send back to the grid) is that as these customers' bills are reduced, other customers will have to make up for a utility's fixed costs. One way to avoid what some suggest is an unfair "cross-subsidization" of rooftop solar users by non-rooftop solar users is to impose an additional demand charge on solar rooftop customers, as is being done in some states.

3. FILED RATE DOCTRINE

Once a rate is filed, it has the force and effect of law. Consumers, utilities, regulators, and, indeed, even competitors, have a right to rely on that rate. The filed rate doctrine began with railroad rates set under the jurisdiction of the Interstate Commerce Commission (ICC), in many ways the predecessor to many modern agencies, including FERC. The doctrine also applies to natural gas rates, telecommunications rates, insurance rates, and the like. The significance of the filed rate doctrine is that the legally established rates are on public notice. As simple as this concept appears, complications can arise, such as those noted by Scott Hempling:

(1) Courts must respect rates authorized by commissions.

(2) State commissions must respect rates authorized by federal commissions.

(3) Commissions must respect the rates that they set.

(4) Courts cannot award antitrust damages to customers of utilities with filed rates.

(5) The doctrine also applies to market-based (utility-set) rates.

(6) The doctrine also applies to non-rate terms and conditions.

(7) Fraud and misrepresentation do not block the filed rate defense.

See SCOTT HEMPLING, REGULATING PUBLIC UTILITY PERFORMANCE: THE LAW OF MARKET STRUCTURE, PRICING, AND JURISDICTION (2013). *See also* Joshua C. Macey, *Zombie Energy Laws*, 73 VAND. L. REV. 1077, 1102–05, 1117–21 (2020) (discussing the history and application of the filed rate doctrine).

The next case should give you a basic understanding of the filed rate doctrine. At issue was a controversy between the city of Girard, Kansas and Kansas Gas and Electric (KG & E). While the specific facts of the case are particular to this dispute, the general pattern is not, as disagreements between utilities over long-term contracts—and whether the terms of such agreements can be modified—tend to be common in the electricity industry. The filed rate doctrine, as you will see, has much to say on that question.

CITY OF GIRARD V. FERC
790 F.2d 919 (D.C. Cir. 1986)

McGOWEN, J.

Petitioner Girard, Kansas, is a municipality that purchases wholesale power from intervenor Kansas Gas and Electric (KG & E). Girard maintains its own power generation facilities but purchases its excess requirements from KG & E. Girard then resells some or all of its power to retail customers. In this case, Girard challenges an order of the Federal Energy Regulatory Commission (Commission or FERC) refusing to grant retroactive effect to a KG & E rate filing. Based on the filed rate doctrine, we reject Girard's claim of entitlement to a retroactive effective date. . . .

II. THE GIRARD DISPUTE

As with all customers, Girard's rates are determined by a tariff on file with the Commission. The particular filing applicable to Girard is entitled "Schedule 147." . . . Schedule 147 was filed with the Commission on March 24, 1981. It detailed the terms under which KG & E would sell power to Girard, and had a term of five years. Under Schedule A of Schedule 147, the precise amount of prearranged, or "firm," power supplied each year by KG & E to Girard was to be expressed in yearly letters of intent signed by each of the parties. These letters of intent obligated KG & E to sell, and Girard to buy, an agreed-upon amount of power during the term of the letter. On September 24, 1981, Girard and KG & E executed a letter of intent specifying the quantity to be purchased by Girard over a fourteen-month period beginning July 1, 1981. On September 20, 1982, the parties executed a new letter of intent covering the period from August 1, 1982, to July 31, 1983.

Sometime prior to July 31, 1983, Girard's power generation facilities failed. Since Girard was incapable of generating any power on its own, it became fully dependent on purchases from KG & E. The City requested that KG & E charge Girard under a lower rate schedule, reflecting Girard's new status as a full-requirements customer. KG & E did have a tariff on file with the Commission (Schedule PWM-883) setting the rate it charged certain full-requirements municipal customers. Prior to this dispute, however, it was KG & E's policy to file PWM-883 as the rate schedule applicable to a particular full-requirements customer only if that customer executed a full-requirements contract with the utility. Since Girard and KG & E were still in the process of negotiating such a contract, the utility did not immediately accede to Girard's request. After July 31, 1983, the parties' contract, as memorialized by the second letter of intent, had expired. KG & E continued to charge Girard under Schedule 147, the partial-requirements tariff, while the parties attempted to negotiate a new contract.

On December 5, 1983, after four months of unsuccessful negotiations, KG & E filed a new, full-requirements rate schedule applicable to Girard. Girard intervened, challenging the new rate on the merits, as well as KG & E's proposed effective date of January 31, 1984. Girard argued that it was entitled to purchase power under the lower, full-requirements schedule as of August 1, 1983, when its contract expired and it was a "de facto" full-requirements user. On February 3, 1984, the Commission rejected Girard's claims and implemented the new full-requirements rate as of January 31, 1984, subject to some limitations not relevant here. . . .

III. THE FILED RATE DOCTRINE

The filed rate doctrine "forbids a regulated entity to charge rates for its service other than those properly filed with the appropriate federal regulatory authority." *Arkansas Louisiana Gas Co. v. Hall*, 453 U.S. 571, 577 (1981); *see Montana-Dakota Utils. Co. v. Northwestern Pub. Serv. Co.*, 341 U.S. 246 (1950). The purpose of the filed rate doctrine is to assure effective Commission oversight of the rates at which power is sold. "The considerations underlying the [filed rate] doctrine . . . are preservation of the agency's primary jurisdiction over reasonableness of rates and the need to insure that regulated companies charge only those rates of which the agency has been made cognizant." *City of Cleveland v. FPC*, 525 F.2d 845, 854 (D.C. Cir. 1976).

In both its Initial Decision and Rehearing, the Commission relied on the filed rate doctrine to reject Girard's claim that it was entitled unilaterally to choose the applicable rate schedule.

Girard argues that the filed rate doctrine does not apply to this case. At the time the last letter of intent expired, KG & E had two types of tariffs on file with the Commission: partial-requirements rates and full-requirements rates. Since the Commission had already determined the lawfulness of the full-requirements rate as applied to other municipalities, Girard argues that it does no damage to the filed rate doctrine to allow it to choose between rates already on file. Girard contends that it did not request a rate that the Commission had not approved; rather, it merely sought application of a rate that the Commission had already accepted.

Girard finds support for its position in *New England Power Co. v. FPC*, 349 F.2d 258 (1st Cir. 1965). In that case, the court affirmed an order of the Federal Power Commission (the predecessor to FERC) that required a utility to accede to a city's request to receive power directly from the utility, rather than through an intermediary. Girard argues that if the Commission has the power to order a substitute interconnection, it must have the lesser power to order application of a more appropriate rate.

Girard's argument misses the mark, however. The City is claiming it is entitled to choose its own rate. Assuming for the sake of argument that *New England Power* is at all relevant, it stands only for the proposition that the Commission itself has power to order an interconnection. *Id.* at 263; *see* 16 U.S.C. § 824a(b) (1982) (Commission may order interconnection when necessary or appropriate). It does not state that a customer is necessarily entitled to the interconnections it desires.

Moreover, Girard's characterization of the filed rate doctrine misconstrues the thrust of the prohibition contained in that rule. Girard argues that "[t]he Commission's regulatory convenience is not disrupted by simply allowing a customer to move from one established wholesale class to another." The City also asserts that its demand that the full-requirements rate be applied "did not call for subversion of an approved rate." The City's position, however, would undermine the very heart of the filed rate doctrine. If wholesale customers could choose for themselves which rate they desired, the Commission would soon effectively lose its power to review rates. Indeed, the Commission could no longer assure that "regulated companies charge only those rates of which the agency has been made cognizant," *City of Cleveland*, 525 F.2d at 854, if customers could choose among rates willy-nilly. While Girard seeks application of a rate that by its terms seems appropriate to its situation, Girard is simply not empowered to make that decision. The Commission's jurisdiction over rates encompasses review of each rate charged to each customer. When a utility changes service to any customer, it must file a new tariff with the Commission. 16 U.S.C. § 824d(d) (1982). Only the Commission may determine the lawfulness of the new rate.

Girard also argues that the filed rate doctrine is inapplicable because no rate was on file as of August 1, 1983. Schedule A of Schedule 147 requires the parties' firm-power contract to be evidenced by annual letters of intent. Girard argues that since the filed rate itself requires a letter of intent, and none was in effect on August 1, there was no filed rate in effect.

We find this an unacceptably strained reading of Schedule A. Schedule A applies only to firm power: "electrical capacity and accompanying energy held in readiness and made available by one party (Seller) for the other party (Buyer) on a prearranged basis." Schedule 147 has two more schedules, applicable to emergency and supplemental service, that do not require annual letters of intent in order to govern relations between the parties. At oral argument, Girard conceded that as of August 1, 1983, KG & E was under no obligation to deliver any power to Girard at all, since the contract had expired. If so, then the parties certainly were not operating under Schedule A, which governs prearranged firm power sales. This does not mean that the rest of Schedule 147 was inapplicable. Girard's contention, that Schedule A's admonition that contracts be in writing overrides the five-year term embodied in the filing itself, presents a case of the tail wagging the dog. The terms of the filing bound both KG & E and Girard until the Commission approved changes. Any other conclusion would undermine the filed rate doctrine.

We therefore reject the petitioner's challenge to the Commission's application of the filed rate doctrine. The City was not *entitled* to choose the applicable rate *unilaterally.* . . .

NOTES AND QUESTIONS

1.   Which item in Scott Hempling's list of filed rate doctrine issues is at issue in the *City of Girard* case? Note that the court deferred to FERC's judgment rather than making its own independent interpretation of the just and reasonable rate. If, however, a court believes that the filed rate is unjust or unreasonable, the court will remand to FERC for its review and reexamination of the rate.

2.   FERC must also honor its own rates and cannot revise a filed rate through a rulemaking proceeding. *See Maislin Industries, U.S., Inc. v. Primary Steel, Inc.*, 497 U.S. 116 (1990). Nor, with limited exceptions, can FERC set new rates retroactively. "The rule against retroactive ratemaking"—the close corollary to the filed rate doctrine—"prohibits a commission from prescribing rates to recoup the utility's past losses for transactions that have already taken place." *Qwest Corp. v. Koppendrayer*, 436 F.3d 859, 863 (8th Cir. 2006); *Associated Gas Distribs. v. FERC*, 893 F.2d 349 (D.C. Cir. 1989). For a list of exceptions to retroactive ratemaking, such as to correct a commission mistake or to honor a court's remand of a rate that the court found unjust or unreasonable, see Hempling, *supra*, at ch. 10.

3.   Courts have observed that the filed rate doctrine and the rule against retroactive ratemaking have two core purposes. First, by giving parties notice of what rates they can expect to be charged, these doctrines help order markets. Second, by limiting utilities to rates approved by a regulator, they prevent companies from exercising market power and entering into sweetheart deals or excluding competitors. The doctrines thus "serv[e] the dual purposes of 'ensur[ing] rate predictability' for purchasers of regulated electricity and promoting equity among customers by 'preventing discriminatory pricing.'" *NSTAR Electric & Gas Corp. v. FERC*, 481 F.3d 794, 800 (D.C. Cir. 2007).

4.   As noted above, neither fraud nor misrepresentation claims invalidate a filed rate. In the case of *Medco Energi US, L.L.C. v. Sea Robin Pipeline, L.L.C.*, 729 F.3d 394 (5th Cir. 2013), for example, Medco Energi US, a natural gas producer, brought a state law claim against Sea Robin Pipeline Company, a natural gas transporter. Medco argued that Sea Robin materially misrepresented how long it would take to complete repairs to its gas pipeline that had been damaged by a hurricane. However, Sea Robin's filed rate—a tariff that contained non-price terms—included a liability disclaimer. The court ruled that this portion of the tariff was controlling, even in the face of a

misrepresentation claim. *Medco Energi*, 729 F.3d at 398. Does this seem like the right result? Why or why not? For an argument regarding why the courts should abolish the filed rate doctrine because it has outlived its purpose, see Macey, *Zombie Energy Laws*, *supra*, at 1102–05, 1117–21.

4. THE *MOBILE-SIERRA* DOCTRINE

The core idea behind the filed rate doctrine is that the rate on file is the legal rate, and thus, the only one that can be charged to customers by a utility. Utilities and their customers, however, can have another relationship. Particularly in the market for wholesale power, they may enter into a bilateral contract under certain terms and conditions for a set period of time. That contract governs the relationship between the utility and its customers, and because it too is filed with FERC, it cannot be abrogated by either side simply by filing a new or different rate with FERC. "The contract between the parties governs the legality of the filing. Rate filings consistent with contractual obligations are valid; rate filings inconsistent with contractual obligations are invalid." *Richmond Power & Light Co. v. FPC*, 481 F.2d 490, 493 (D.C. Cir. 1973).

Nonetheless, parties sometimes seek to unilaterally change contracts that they believe have become unfair. One court has described how this problem arises this way:

> [I]f a power company makes a contract that turns out to be disadvantageous to it but does no harm to the broader public, a regulatory commission has no business bailing the company out. It's a big boy; it took a risk; the risk materialized; but the adverse consequences are contained, they do not ramify, so there is no occasion for regulatory intervention.

MISO Transmission Owners v. FERC, 819 F.3d 329, 335 (7th Cir. 2016). Whether such an unhappy company can get out of a contract is governed by a now longstanding rule in utility regulation. That rule is known as the *Mobile-Sierra* doctrine.

It should come as no surprise that legal rules, even those that appear simple on their face, have complications. The *Mobile-Sierra* doctrine took its name from a pair of United States Supreme Court opinions decided in 1956: *United Gas Pipe Line Co. v. Mobile Gas Service Corp.*, 350 U.S. 332 (1956) and *FPC v. Sierra Pacific Power Co.*, 350 U.S. 348 (1956).

Mobile and *Sierra* shared a similar problem. In *Mobile*, United Gas entered into a contract to supply natural gas to Mobile. Similarly, in *Sierra*, Pacific Gas & Electric entered into a contract to supply Sierra with electricity at a set amount. In both cases, the suppliers filed their contracts with the Federal Power Commission, FERC's predecessor, and the FPC approved those contract rates. Later, both suppliers sought to raise prices above the contract rate by instituting rate proceedings at the FPC. Despite the language of FPA § 206—which allows parties to challenge a filed rate as unlawful if it is unjust, unreasonable, or unduly discriminatory—the Supreme Court rejected the suppliers' attempt to unilaterally raise the price of their sales. In so ruling, the Court held that once the FPC approved the contract rates, the suppliers could not unilaterally change them. The Court reasoned that the statute did not grant suppliers the right to abrogate contracts by simply filing a new rate schedule with the Commission.

Mobile-Sierra remains important law today. The Court has upheld the prohibition against deviating from the filed tariff even when a supplier and purchaser entered into a contract for a *lower* rate. The Court reasoned that the nondiscrimination provision of the statute prevented even that form of renegotiation. *See Maislin Industries, U.S., Inc., v. Primary Steel, Inc.,* 497 U.S. 116 (1990).

Nevertheless, economic conditions can be such that a utility feels compelled to file a new rate even when it has an outstanding contract on file with FERC. The issue then becomes whether the utility can file a unilateral rate increase or decrease that is not authorized in the filed contract. Courts have entertained such arguments, but they have repeatedly cautioned that the standard for granting such requests is a very high one.

POTOMAC ELEC. POWER CO. V. FERC

210 F.3d 403 (D.C. Cir 2000)

ROGERS, CIRCUIT JUDGE.

Potomac Electric Power Company (PEPCO) petitions for review of two orders of the Federal Energy Regulatory Commission (FERC) denying its request under § 206 of the Federal Power Act (FPA) for unilateral modification of the rates prescribed by a long-term, fixed rate, power transmission service agreement between PEPCO and the Allegheny Power System (APS). Because FERC did not abuse its discretion in applying the stringent *Mobile-Sierra* public interest standard, and because a mere rate disparity or a benefit to the purchasing utility or its customers from a rate modification does not suffice, without more, to satisfy that standard, we conclude that FERC's decision to dismiss the complaint was a reasonable exercise of its authority. Accordingly, we deny the petition.

In 1987, PEPCO entered into an 18.5 year power supply agreement with the Ohio Edison System, which was comprised of Ohio Edison Company and Pennsylvania Power Company. In order to effect delivery of the power to PEPCO's service area, PEPCO and the Ohio Edison System each entered into a transmission service agreement with the APS, an integrated electric utility system directly connected to both PEPCO and the Ohio Edison System. Under the three agreements, PEPCO would purchase contract entitlements to a share of the Ohio Edison System's installed generating capacity and associated energy, APS would purchase from the Ohio Edison System the power intended for PEPCO, and APS would, in turn, resell the power purchased from the Ohio Edison System to PEPCO. The dispute in the instant case involves the agreement between PEPCO and APS.

PEPCO's agreement with APS provided in relevant part that the base rate for the APS transmission service would commence at $1.70 per kW-month, increase to $2.255 per kW-month in 1994, and increase again to $2.815 per kW-month in 1999. In addition, the agreement required PEPCO to pay an "adder" of $1.00 per megawatt-hour for each megawatt-hour of energy that APS delivered. Furthermore, the agreement was a "fixed rate" contract, meaning that the parties agreed not to unilaterally request a rate change from the Commission, as provided in section 9.3 of the agreement, which stated:

> It is the intention of the parties that the rates and terms of service specified herein shall remain in effect for the entire term set forth in this Article, and shall not be subject to change pursuant to the Federal Power Act absent mutual agreement of the parties or as provided in section 3.4.

Section 3.4, in turn, provided for renegotiation "[i]n the event that reasonably unforeseeable circumstances beyond the control of any party to this Agreement result in a gross inequity to any party" and outlined a procedure for dispute resolution in case parties fail to reach a new agreement.

APS submitted the three agreements for FERC approval in March 1987. In its review of the filing, FERC noted that PEPCO represented that "the rate levels are completely justified on the basis of cost factors." Also as recounted by FERC at the time, PEPCO maintained that "once rates are determined to be cost-justified, the noncost factors such as the potential savings to PEPCO are superfluous, and the filing cannot be deemed deficient even if the noncost support were deemed insufficient." FERC also noted that "[n]o party to [the] proceeding has alleged that the rates under the three proposed agreements are unjust and unreasonable," and that "[o]ur review indicates that the rates to PEPCO will not generate excessive revenues and should be accepted for filing without suspension." FERC accepted the three contracts for filing to become effective June 1, 1987.

In 1996, FERC issued the first in a series of orders known collectively as "Order No. 888" to address problems associated with electric transmission monopolies in the bulk power markets. The Order required all public utilities that own, operate, or control interstate transmission facilities to file an open access nondiscriminatory transmission tariff. In its open access transmission tariff (OATT) proceeding pursuant to Order No.

888, APS agreed to charge a rate of $1.49 per kW-month for its transmission service, a rate substantially less than the rate PEPCO was obligated to pay under its 1987 agreement with APS.

Thereafter, PEPCO filed a complaint against APS, requesting that FERC summarily order APS to reduce the rate for transmission services under the 1987 agreement to the same level as APS's rate for comparable service under its OATT. The Federal Power Act provides that electricity rates may be modified in one of two ways: under § 205, the seller may attempt to prompt rate changes by filing a new rate schedule, which will be reviewed by FERC to determine whether the proposed rates are just and reasonable and under § 206, FERC may reform the rates "upon its own motion or upon complaint" if it determines the rates have become "unjust, unreasonable, unduly discriminatory or preferential." PEPCO's request for a rate decrease, claiming that APS's rate was "excessive and unreasonable," asked FERC to exercise its authority under § 206 to modify existing contracts and reduce the contractual transmission rate to the OATT rate. . . .

FERC dismissed PEPCO's complaint. Emphasizing that it "does not take contract modification lightly," FERC reasoned that the mere fact that PEPCO was subject to higher rates under its agreement with APS than it would be under APS's OATT was insufficient reason for abrogating an agreement that PEPCO had fully supported at the time of filing and FERC had approved as just and reasonable. FERC also rejected PEPCO's request that it act *sua sponte* to reduce the rates for the benefit of PEPCO's ratepayers, reasoning that it would be inappropriate to convert PEPCO's unilateral request for reformation into a FERC-initiated contract modification where the parties' agreement contained a *Mobile-Sierra* provision, and where PEPCO had failed to satisfy the public interest standard. . . .

The court will uphold FERC's orders unless they are "arbitrary, capricious, an abuse of discretion, or otherwise not in accordance with law." Likewise, the court will uphold FERC's factual findings as long as they are supported by substantial evidence. We hold that FERC's decision to dismiss the complaint was not an unreasonable exercise of its authority.

PEPCO concedes, implicitly in its briefs and explicitly at oral argument, that the public interest standard set out in *Mobile* and *Sierra*, and not the just and reasonable standard, controls PEPCO's § 206 request. The court has observed that the *Mobile-Sierra* public interest standard is much more restrictive than the FPA's "just and reasonable" standard, even characterizing the burden under the public interest standard as "practically insurmountable," [*Papago Tribal Util. Auth. v. FERC*, 729 F.2d 950 (D.C. Cir. 1983)] and "almost insurmountable." PEPCO challenges such a restrictive characterization of the standard, and contends that

FERC was bound by its own precedent to adopt an approach "less restrictive" than the *Papago* court's phrase "practically insurmountable" suggests.

For this proposition, PEPCO relies on *Northeast Utilities Service Company*, 66 F.E.R.C. ¶ 61,332 (1994), *aff'd* 55 F.3d 686 (1st Cir. 1995). In *Northeast Utilities*, FERC, reviewing a rate agreement in connection with a utility merger, modified a fixed-rate contract "under the public interest standard required by the *Mobile-Sierra* doctrine." In modifying the contract, FERC rejected the proposition that the *Mobile-Sierra* doctrine requires a generally applicable standard that is so stringent as to be "practically insurmountable." FERC explained:

> [I]f the Commission is to comply with both the *Mobile-Sierra* imperative to respect contractual arrangements, on the one hand, and our statutory mandate to protect the public interest and ensure that rates are just and reasonable and not unduly discriminatory or preferential, on the other, the "public interest" standard of review under the *Mobile-Sierra* doctrine cannot be "practically insurmountable" in all cases.

In other words, FERC took the position that the court's characterization of the standard in *Papago* did not "preclude[ ] the Commission from concluding in other circumstances that the interests of third parties sufficiently outweigh the contracting parties' interests in contract stability to justify the Commission's ordering contract modifications." FERC distinguished *Papago* on the basis that "*Papago* expressly addressed rate changes, not the scope of the Commission's authority upon its initial review of a newly-filed contract," and declared that in situations where it is reviewing a fixed-rate agreement "for the first time, without having had any previous opportunity to determine whether its terms are lawful," a more relaxed public interest standard is warranted. The First Circuit affirmed.

FERC, in two subsequent cases that PEPCO also relies on, reaffirmed its position in *Northeast Utilities* . . . .

Thus, as PEPCO contends, FERC has at times expressed an intent to apply a standard that is more flexible than the "practically insurmountable" standard that *Papago* described. However, unlike the circumstances in which FERC has stated it would apply a more flexible standard, PEPCO's § 206 request does not involve "the Commission proceed[ing] *sua sponte* or at the request of non-parties to change rates . . . in order to protect non-parties to a contract." PEPCO is not itself a non-party. Nor did it offer any evidence (beyond speculation) that the only potential nonparties here, its ratepayers, were adversely affected by the existing rates; it did not, for example, even attempt to show how much if any of the rate disparity was passed on to PEPCO ratepayers rather than borne by the utility itself. Nor does PEPCO's request involve a "newly-filed or previously unreviewed agreement." FERC was clear in *Northeast Utilities* that it was "not being asked to allow a party a unilateral rate change from a fixed-rate contract whose terms [it] previously accepted," and that it was instead "reviewing the . . . [c]ontract for the first time, without having had any previous opportunity to determine whether its terms are lawful." As FERC explained, applying the "practically insurmountable" standard in first review cases would mean that "[its] ability to protect the public interest would be negligible and public regulation would consist of little more than rubber-stamping private contracts." By contrast, FERC had approved PEPCO's 1987 agreement with APS long before it was presented in 1998 with a complaint by one party to the agreement seeking a unilateral rate change. The concerns that FERC raised in *Northeast Utilities* with regard to applying the "practically insurmountable" public interest standard when reviewing a contract for the first time thus do not apply here.

The question remains whether FERC abused its discretion in concluding that PEPCO failed to meet its burden under the *Mobile-Sierra* public interest standard. PEPCO contends that FERC, in its public interest analysis, failed to consider the excessive burden on PEPCO's ratepayers and the discriminatory impact of the disparity between the transmission rates set by the 1987 agreement and APS's OATT transmission rate. The problem with PEPCO's position is that, other than pointing out that the contract rate is twice APS's OATT rate, it has presented no evidence regarding how the contract rates are unduly discriminatory or excessively burdensome on PEPCO ratepayers. The court has repeatedly emphasized the importance of contractual stability in a number of cases involving the *Mobile-Sierra* doctrine. Furthermore, the court has consistently stated that rate disparity attributable to the operation of the *Mobile-Sierra* doctrine is not on that basis alone unduly discriminatory. In addition, FERC precedent makes clear that the fact that a contract has become uneconomic to one of the parties does not necessarily render the contract contrary to the public interest. Considering such precedent in favor of protecting contractual stability, PEPCO's failure to provide any evidence of undue discrimination or excessive burden, other than the disparity in rates and a bald claim that PEPCO ratepayers would derive benefit from a rate modification, renders its request wholly inadequate. Therefore, FERC's summary dismissal of PEPCO's public interest argument was within its authority.

Ultimately, PEPCO's case suffers from a failure of proof. PEPCO's counsel explained at oral argument that PEPCO did not seek a hearing before FERC on its § 206 complaint because PEPCO considered its allegations regarding the impact of the 1987 agreement on its ratepayers to be unrebutted. The court strains, in light of precedent, to imagine how

PEPCO could conclude that it did not have a burden to offer evidence on this and other relevant factual issues, such as whether and the extent to which the agreement rates adversely impact PEPCO's ratepayers and whether APS had market power at the time the 1987 agreements were signed. PEPCO's position would undoubtedly have been strengthened had there been evidence in the record to support the assertions in its briefs regarding the asserted impact on ratepayers and APS's market power, although we express no opinion on the outcome under those circumstances.

In sum, given the practically insurmountable standard that it faced, PEPCO was obligated to do more than point to the disparity between the agreement rates and the rates it would pay under the APS open access tariff. FERC reasonably concluded that PEPCO failed to demonstrate that the APS rates in the 1987 agreement are contrary to the public interest. While FERC retains the statutory authority and duty to correct or prevent an electric rate schedule that " 'might impair the financial ability of the public utility to continue its service, cast upon other consumers an excessive burden, or be unduly discriminatory,' " it acted within its discretion to conclude from the face of the complaint that the rates in the previously approved agreement that PEPCO fully supported and claimed was justified were not contrary to the public interest. Accordingly, we deny the petition.

NOTES AND QUESTIONS

1.   In *Potomac Electric*, PEPCO, as a consumer of electricity from APS, sought to have transmission rates reduced for its own electric customers. In deciding the case, the court balanced contract stability with the public interest in just and reasonable rates. In your opinion, did the courts strike the correct balance? If not, how should it have ruled, and what impact would that have for future cases?

2.   As the electricity industry moves toward competition-based regulation, detailed in Chapter 5, the question of when the *Mobile-Sierra* doctrine applies takes on increasing importance. The Supreme Court, in *Morgan Stanley Capital Group v. Public Util. Dist. No. 1 of Snohomish Cty.*, 554 U.S. 527 (2008), addressed that issue for market-based electricity sales. *Morgan Stanley* involved market-based contracts executed during the time Enron was manipulating the California electricity market. In the 1990s, California engaged in a rate design that was intended to usher in competition but that was significantly flawed in its structure. As a result, in 2000–2001, electricity rates hit unprecedented highs due to manipulation by parties like Enron. Utilities and other electricity purchasers attempted to stabilize their budgets by entering into long-term contracts with electricity suppliers. Once it was learned, however, that market manipulation was the basis of higher electricity prices, purchasers (primarily western utilities that purchased power under

long-term contracts during that period) challenged contract rates as unjust and unreasonable at FERC. FERC applied the *Mobile-Sierra* doctrine and found that the contracts did not "seriously harm the public interest," and thus, should be upheld.

On review of the Ninth Circuit decision vacating the FERC order, the Supreme Court clarified that FERC retains the right to review market-based contract rates if they violate the public interest, or if a claim is lodged that the rate of return is unfair. The Court also noted that contracting parties can agree to suspend the *Mobile-Sierra* doctrine, that is, they can allow unilateral modification of their contracts via § 206 FERC rate filings. However, the Court rejected the rule the Ninth Circuit had applied to the contracts at issue in the case, which required FERC to ask whether a contract was formed in an environment of market "dysfunction" in applying the doctrine. The Court found that rule unsupported by its precedent and inconsistent with the important role of contracts in the FPA's statutory scheme. Nevertheless, the Court affirmed the Ninth Circuit's decision to remand the contracts to FERC for further evaluation on the ground that the purchasing utilities were entitled to attempt to establish a causal connection between the sellers' unlawful market activities and the contract rate. The Court emphasized: "[T]he mere fact of a party's engaging in unlawful activity in the spot market does not deprive its forward contracts of the benefit of the *Mobile-Sierra* presumption. . . . Where, however, causality has been established, the *Mobile-Sierra* presumption should not apply." *Id.* at 554.

3.   Because *Morgan Stanley* involved challenges brought by parties to the contract, an open question after that case was whether non-contract parties can challenge rates as unjust and unreasonable. The Court then decided that issue in *NRG Power Marketing, LLC v. Maine Public Util. Comm'n*, 558 U.S. 165 (2010). *NRG* involved a settlement agreement among numerous parties in the New England market. The key parties to the settlement agreement were a group of generators who entered into a contract with the New England Independent System Operator (NE-ISO). As explained in more detail in Chapter 5, the ISO operates the transmission portion of the electricity system in the New England states as well as the formal wholesale power markets in that region. FERC approved the settlement agreement, but that agreement was challenged by entities that objected to the settlement—and, therefore, were not parties to the contract. The Court confirmed that nonparties have the right to challenge a contract as contrary to the public interest, as required by the *Mobile-Sierra* doctrine—and that the same standard applies to challenges by contract parties and non-parties alike. In so holding, the Court reversed the D.C. Circuit, which had held that the more rigorous *Mobile-Sierra* presumption (as opposed to the FPA's traditional unjust and unreasonable standard) did not apply when non-parties challenged a market-based contract. The Supreme Court, relying on *Morgan Stanley*, clarified that the public interest standard defines "what it means for a rate to satisfy the just-and-reasonable standard in the contract context." 558 U.S. at 174. "[I]f FERC itself must presume just and reasonable a contract rate resulting from fair, arms-length negotiations,"

the Court reasoned, "how can it be maintained that noncontracting parties nevertheless may escape that presumption?" *Id.*

4. *Mobile-Sierra*, however, does not always apply. Following FERC's adoption of Order 1000 (described in more detail in Chapter 5), for instance, incumbent utilities argued in court that the *Mobile-Sierra* doctrine prevented FERC-ordered changes to transmission tariffs. Order 1000 sought to enhance regional coordination, planning, and competition in markets for electric transmission line project developments. One controversial provision of Order 1000 was the removal of federal "rights of first refusal" that existed in many FERC-approved transmission tariffs. These provisions gave incumbent utilities the right "to have a first crack at constructing an electricity transmission project—that is, having the opportunity to build it without having to face competition from other firms that might also like to build it." *MISO Transmission Owners v. FERC*, 819 F.3d 329 (7th Cir. 2016). In Order 1000, FERC required removal of these provisions from federal transmission tariffs, to encourage non-incumbent transmission providers to propose transmission infrastructure projects, and thus, increase competition and presumably reduce the costs of such projects. On review, the D.C. Circuit rejected the challenging utilities' *Mobile-Sierra* arguments, holding that *Mobile-Sierra* does not apply to "anti-competitive measures that were not arrived at through arms-length bargaining." *Oklahoma Gas & Elec. Co. v. FERC*, 827 F.3d 75, 79 (D.C. Cir. 2016). In a later case, the court went even further, holding that even if *Mobile-Sierra* applied, FERC provided adequate justification for Order 1000's command to remove the right of first refusal provisions, as the agency had determined that such provisions "significantly harm the public interest," thus overcoming the *Mobile-Sierra* presumption in favor of stability. *See Emera Maine v. FERC*, 854 F.3d 662 (D.C. Cir. 2017).

F. ELECTRICITY FEDERALISM

Traditionally, electricity regulation has been an area where federal agencies and state governments had Congressionally defined boundaries. However, those boundaries have not always been as clear cut as either the states or the federal government would like. This jurisdictional divide can be seen in ratemaking. As noted above, both federal and state agencies regulate electricity prices. FERC sets rates for interstate wholesale electricity sales and electricity transmission, and state PUCs have jurisdiction over electricity retail rates and distribution charges. Unsurprisingly, in such a bifurcated regulatory setting, conflicts between federal and state regulators can and do arise. This section addresses such conflicts.

1. ESTABLISHING ELECTRICITY FEDERALISM: THE *ATTLEBORO* GAP

Before FERC, there was the FPC. And before the FPC—and even for a time after it—state PUCs regulated the burgeoning electric utility industry without federal involvement. *See, e.g.*, Sharon B. Jacobs, *Agency Genesis and the Energy Transition*, 121 COLUM. L. REV. 835 (2021) (discussing the creation and work of state PUCs). Inevitably, the industry started crossing state lines, with utilities trading power with each other, and some even forming "power pools" where they voluntarily coordinated their systems' operations.

With jurisdiction fractured among different states, conflicts were bound to arise, and they did. The case excerpt below was the first such conflict to take the national stage, exposing the problems that occur when competing authorities claimed jurisdiction.

PUBLIC UTILITIES COMMISSION OF RHODE ISLAND V. ATTLEBORO STEAM & ELECTRIC CO.
273 U.S. 83 (1927)

MR. JUSTICE SANFORD delivered the opinion of the Court.

This case involves the constitutional validity of an order of the Public Utilities Commission of Rhode Island putting into effect a schedule of prices applying to the sale of electric current in interstate commerce.

The Narragansett Electric Lighting Company is a Rhode Island corporation engaged in manufacturing electric current at its generating plant in the city of Providence and selling such current generally for light, heat and power. The Attleboro Steam & Electric Company is a Massachusetts corporation engaged in supplying electric current for public and private use in the city of Attleboro and its vicinity in that state.

In 1917 these companies entered into a contract by which the Narragansett Company agreed to sell, and the Attleboro Company to buy, for a period of twenty years, all the electricity required by the Attleboro Company for its own use and for sale in the city of Attleboro and the adjacent territory, at a specified basic rate; the current to be delivered by the Narragansett Company at the state line between Rhode Island and Massachusetts and carried over connecting transmission lines to the station of the Attleboro Company in Massachusetts, where it was to be metered. The Narragansett Company filed with the Public Utilities Commission of Rhode Island a schedule setting out the rate and general terms of the contract and was authorized by the Commission to grant the Attleboro Company the special rate therein shown; and the two companies then entered upon the performance of the contract. Current was thereafter supplied in accordance with its terms; and the generating plant of the Attleboro Company was dismantled.

In 1924 the Narragansett Company—having previously made an unsuccessful attempt to obtain an increase of the special rate to the Attleboro Company—filed with the Rhode Island Commission a new schedule, purporting to cancel the original schedule and establish an increased rate for electric current supplied, in specified minimum quantities, to electric lighting companies for their own use or sale to their customers and delivered either in Rhode Island or at the state line.

The Attleboro Company was in fact the only customer of the Narragansett Company to which this new schedule would apply.

The Commission thereupon instituted an investigation as to the contract rate and the proposed rate. After a hearing at which both companies were represented, the Commission found that, owing principally to the increased cost of generating electricity, the Narragansett Company in rendering service to the Attleboro Company was suffering an operating loss, without any return on the investment devoted to such service, while the rates to its other customers yielded a fair return; that the contract rate was unreasonable and a continuance of service to the Attleboro Company under it would be detrimental to the general public welfare and prevent the Narragansett Company from performing its full duty to its other customers; and that the proposed rate was reasonable and would yield a fair return, and no more, for the service to the Attleboro Company. And the Commission thereupon made an order putting into effect the rate contained in the new schedule.

From this order the Attleboro Company prosecuted an appeal to the Supreme Court of Rhode Island which ... held ... that the order of the Commission imposed a direct burden on interstate commerce and was invalid because of conflict with the commerce clause of the Constitution.

It is conceded, rightly, that the sale of electric current by the Narragansett Company to the Attleboro Company is a transaction in interstate commerce, notwithstanding the fact that the current is delivered at the state line. The transmission of electric current from one state to another, like that of gas, is interstate commerce and its essential character is not affected by a passing of custody and title at the state boundary not arresting the continuous transmission to the intended destination.

The petitioners contend, however, that the Rhode Island Commission cannot effectively exercise its power to regulate the rates for electricity furnished by the Narragansett Company to local consumers, without also regulating the rates for the other service which it furnishes; that if the Narragansett Company continues to furnish electricity to the Atteboro Company at a loss this will tend to increase the burden on the local consumers and impair the ability of the Narragansett Company to give them good service at reasonable prices; and that, therefore, the order of the Commission prescribing a reasonable rate for the interstate service to the Attleboro Company should be sustained as being essentially a local regulation, necessary to the protection of matters of local interest, and affecting interstate commerce only indirectly and incidentally. In support of this contention they rely chiefly upon *Pennsylvania Gas Co. v. Pub. Serv. Com.*, 252 U.S. 23 (1920); and the controlling question presented is whether the present case comes within the rule of the *Pennsylvania Gas Co.* case or that of the [*Missouri v.*] *Kansas Gas Co.*[, 265 U.S. 298 (1924)] case upon which the Attleboro Company relies.

In the *Pennsylvania Gas Co.* case, the company transmitted natural gas by a main pipe line from the source of supply in Pennsylvania to a point of distribution in a city in New York, which it there subdivided and sold at retail to local consumers supplied from the main by pipes laid through the streets of the city. In holding that the New York Public Service Commission might regulate the rate charged to these consumers, the court said that while a state may not 'directly' regulate or burden interstate commerce, it may in some instances, until the subject matter is regulated by Congress, pass laws 'indirectly' affecting such commerce, when needed to protect or regulate matters of local interest; that the thing which the New York Commission had undertaken to regulate, while part of an interstate transmission, was 'local in its nature,' pertaining to the furnishing of gas to local consumers, and the service rendered to them was 'essentially local,' being similar to that of a local plant furnishing gas to consumers in a city; and that such 'local service' was not of the character which required general and uniform regulation of rates by congressional action, even if the local rates might 'affect' the interstate business of the company.

In the *Kansas Gas Co.* case the company, whose business was principally interstate, transported natural gas by continuous pipe lines from wells in Oklahoma and Kansas into Missouri, and there sold and delivered it to distributing companies, which then sold and delivered it to local consumers. In holding that the rate which the company charged for the gas sold to the distributing companies—those at which these companies sold to the local consumers not being involved—was not subject to regulation by the Public Utilities Commission of Missouri, the court said that, while in the absence of congressional action a state may generally enact laws of internal police, although they have an indirect effect upon interstate commerce, 'the commerce clause of the Constitution, of its own force, restrains the states from imposing direct burdens upon interstate commerce,' and a state enactment imposing such a 'direct burden' must fall, being a direct restraint of that which in the absence of federal regulation should be free; that the sale and delivery to the distributing companies was 'an inseparable part of a transaction in interstate commerce—not local but essentially national in character—and enforcement of a selling price in such a transaction places a direct burden upon such commerce inconsistent with that freedom of interstate trade which it was the purpose of the commerce clause to secure and preserve;' that in the *Pennsylvania Gas Co.* case the decision rested on the ground that the service to the consumers for which the regulated charge was made, was 'essentially local,' and the things done were after the business in its essentially national aspect had come to an end . . .; but that in the sale of gas in wholesale quantities, not to consumers, but to distributing companies for resale to consumers, where the transportation, sale and delivery constitutes an unbroken chain, fundamentally interstate from beginning to end, 'the paramount interest is not local but national, admitting of and requiring uniformity of regulation,' which, 'even though it be the uniformity of governmental nonaction, may be highly necessary to preserve equality of opportunity and treatment among the various communities and states concerned.'

It is clear that the present case is controlled by the *Kansas Gas Co.* case. The order of the Rhode Island Commission is not, as in the *Pennsylvania Gas Co.* case, a regulation of the rates charged to local consumers, having merely an incidental effect upon interstate commerce, but is a regulation of the rates charged by the Narragansett Company for the interstate service to the Attleboro Company, which places a direct burden upon interstate commerce. Being the imposition of a direct burden upon interstate commerce, from which the state is restrained by the force of the commerce clause, it must necessarily fall, regardless of its purpose. It is immaterial that the Narragansett Company is a Rhode Island corporation subject to regulation by the Commission in its local business, or that Rhode Island is the state from which the electric current is transmitted in interstate commerce, and not that in which it is received, as in the *Kansas Gas Co.* case. The forwarding state obviously has no more authority than the receiving state to place a direct burden upon interstate commerce. Nor is it material that the general business of the Narragansett Company appears to be chiefly local, while in the *Kansas Gas Co.* case the company was principally engaged in interstate business. The test of the validity of a state regulation is not the character of the general business of the company, but whether the particular business which is regulated is essentially local or national in character. . . . Furthermore, if Rhode Island could place a direct burden upon the interstate business of the Narragansett Company because this would result in indirect benefit to the customers of the Narragansett Company in Rhode Island, Massachusetts could, by parity of reasoning, reduce the rates on such interstate business in order to benefit the customers of the Attleboro Company in that state, who would have, in the aggregate, an interest in the interstate rate correlative to that of the customers of the Narragansett Company in Rhode Island. Plainly, however, the paramount interest in the interstate business carried on between the two companies is not local to either state, but is essentially national in character. The rate is therefore not subject to regulation by either of the two states in the guise of protection to their respective local interests; but, if such regulation is required it can only be attained by the exercise of the power vested in Congress.

The decree is accordingly affirmed.

MR. JUSTICE BRANDEIS (dissenting).

The business of the Narragansett Company is an intrastate one. The only electricity sold for use without the state is that agreed to be delivered to the Attleboro Company. That company takes less than 3 per cent. of the electricity produced and manufactured by the Narragansett, which has over 70,000 customers in Rhode Island. The problem is essentially local in character. The Commission found as a fact that continuance of the service to the Attleboro Company at the existing rate would prevent the Narragansett from performing its full duty towards its other customers and would be detrimental to the general public welfare. It issued the order specifically to prevent unjust discrimination and to prevent unjust increase in the price to other customers. The Narragansett, a public service corporation of Rhode Island, is subject to regulation by that state. The order complained of is clearly valid as an exercise of the police power, unless it violates the commerce clause.

The power of the state to regulate the selling price of electricity produced and distributed by it within the state and to prevent discrimination is not affected by the fact that the supply is furnished under a long term contract. If the commission lacks the power exercised, it is solely because the electricity is delivered for use in another state. That fact makes the transaction interstate commerce, and Congress has power to legislate on the subject. It has not done so, nor has it legislated on any allied subject, so there can be no contention that it has occupied the field. . . . The burden resulting from the order here in question resembles more nearly that increase in the cost of an article produced and to be delivered which arises by reason of higher taxes laid upon plant, operations or profits; or which arises by reason of expenditures required under police regulations. It is like the regulation sustained in *Pennsylvania Gas Co. v. Public Service Commission* where an order of the New York Public Service Commission fixed the rates at which gas piped from without the state and delivered directly to the consumers might be sold. . . .

In my opinion the judgment below should be reversed.

NOTES AND QUESTIONS

1. Notice the last line in Justice Sanford's majority opinion: "The rate is therefore not subject to regulation by either of the two states in the guise of protection to their respective local interests; but, if such regulation is required it can only be attained by the exercise of the power vested in Congress." Indeed, it was the failure of Congress to foresee the possibility that a state rate may affect interstate commerce that gave rise to the Court creating the "*Attleboro*

gap." Eight years later, in 1935, Congress closed this gap when it enacted Part II of the FPA. In § 201 of the FPA, Congress declared that "the business of transmitting and selling electric energy for ultimate distribution to the public is affected with a public interest," and thus, that federal regulation would govern, with limited exceptions, "the transmission of electric energy in interstate commerce and the sale of such energy at wholesale in interstate commerce. . . ." FPA §§ 201(a) and (b). Thus, as discussed in the *New York v. FERC* case excerpted in Chapter 1, FERC regulates the interstate transmission of electricity as well as the wholesale sale of electricity (*i.e.*, a sale for re-sale) in interstate commerce in all states with the exceptions of Hawaii, Alaska, and Texas. This leaves intrastate retail sales of electricity and intrastate transmission of electricity to state regulation.

2.   Justice Brandeis argued in his dissent that the effect of the Rhode Island Supreme Court's holding threatened the economic security of the Narragansett Company. He further argued that the Rhode Island PUC had an obligation to protect the economic integrity of the utility. With which opinion do you agree? Was the majority right to declare that the Rhode Island PUC did not have authority to set the rates of electricity sold in Massachusetts? Or do you side with Justice Brandeis that the PUC had an obligation to protect the utility and the consumers of a Rhode Island public utility? Why? For a critique of the *Attleboro* Court's dormant Commerce Clause analysis, see *Ark. Elec. Co-op. Corp. v. Ark. Pub. Serv. Comm'n*, 461 U.S. 375, 389–94 (1983) (referring to the dormant Commerce Clause analysis in *Attleboro* as "mechanical" and "anachronistic" and rejecting it in favor of a "less formalistic" approach developed in more recent cases).

3.   For more on the rise of utility regulation in the early stages of the electric industry, see, e.g., THOMAS HUGHES, NETWORKS OF POWER: ELECTRIFICATION IN WESTERN SOCIETY (1983); JOHN NEUFELD, SELLING POWER: ECONOMICS, POLICY, AND ELECTRIC UTILITIES BEFORE 1940 (2016); *see also* William Hausman & John Neufeld, *The Market for Capital and the Origins of State Regulation of Electric Utilities in the United States*, 62 J. ECON. HIST. 1050 (2002); Christopher Knittel, *The Adoption of State Electricity Regulation: The Role of Interest Groups*, 54 J. INDUS. ECON. 201–222 (2006); Thomas Lyon & Nathan Wilson, *Capture or Contract? The Early Years of Electric Utility Regulation*, 42 J. REG. ECON. 225 (2012); Jacobs, *Agency Genesis and the Energy Transition*, *supra*; Boyd, *Public Utility and the Low Carbon Future*, *supra*.

2. CONTEMPORARY FEDERALISM ISSUES

Congress's adoption of Part II of the Federal Power Act had significant implications for electricity federalism. Not only did it close the *Attleboro* gap, creating federal jurisdiction over wholesale and interstate transmission rates, it meant that states could not disturb that authority. Because the Supremacy Clause of the U.S. Constitution gives primacy to federal law over state law, the FPC's—and now FERC's—decisions on wholesale and transmission rates preempt what states may have to say on those topics. For instance, if FERC approves a $50/MWh power sale between Detroit Edison and Commonwealth Edison in Chicago, neither the Michigan Public Service Commission nor the Illinois Commerce Commission can unravel FERC's approval. Either state commission might, perhaps, foreclose the utility from recovering a reasonable rate of return on its retail rates, deeming it an imprudent decision, but those state agencies lack the power to modify the actual federally set rate, or the utilities' obligation to buy and sell the power.

Even though federal law constitutionally preempts (i.e., overrides) conflicting state power, states often attempt to find ways to circumvent federally made decisions they do not like. In those circumstances, the Supreme Court has held that rates filed with FERC cannot be reexamined by a state PUC. Otherwise, if a state PUC seeks to protect its citizen-consumers by lowering federal rates, those unrecovered rates are "trapped" and imposed on shareholders in violation of the Supremacy Clause. *See Entergy La., Inc. v. Louisiana Pub. Serv. Comm'n*, 539 U.S. 39 (2003). Thus, FERC's acceptance of a rate preempts state regulators from second-guessing FERC's approval of the rate.

As noted, prior to the FPA, states could regulate intrastate and retail electricity sales but could not regulate interstate sales. The FPA then granted interstate sales jurisdiction to the federal government. Historically, jurisdiction was said to follow this "bright line." States would regulate retail electricity sales, and the Federal Power Commission would regulate wholesale interstate sales.

Today's evolving electricity industry challenges that bright line of regulation. Indeed, the Supreme Court recently addressed another *Attleboro*-like jurisdictional gap in the case below involving "demand response." Demand response is an energy management strategy where a utility or third party reduces customers' energy use when prices are high and then pays customers for not using the saved electricity. For example, on the hottest day of the year electricity demand is at its highest as people turn on their air conditioners and the cost of producing (and purchasing) peak power increases for the utility. The cost of peak power can be reduced through demand response, for example, by having customers turn off (or cycle off) their air conditioners. Reduce demand and electricity prices will decline accordingly. Demand response programs target all customer classes, from industrial consumers shifting large electric loads, to residential load shifting through automatic cycling of air conditioners, water heaters, thermostats, or other appliances.

FERC initiated a demand response program in 2008 by adopting Order 719, 125 FERC ¶ 61,071, following Congressional encouragement in the Energy Policy Act of 2005. In 2011, FERC supplemented Order 719 with

Order 745, 134 FERC ¶ 61,187 (2011). Basically, Order 745 required regional transmission organizations (described in more detail in Chapter 5) to compensate demand response bids into wholesale markets at market rates. In other words, a demand response bid under this Order is a promise to not consume electricity. In the words of the Supreme Court, "demand response providers . . . receive as much for conserving electricity as generators do for producing it." Order 745, like Order 719, allowed states to opt out of the program.

The D.C. Circuit invalidated Order 745, *see Electric Power Supply Ass'n v. FERC*, 753 F.3d 216 (D.C. Cir. 2014), and the case went to the Supreme Court, which reversed the D.C. Circuit in the opinion below. The federal demand response program at issue in the case presented an *Attleboro*-like gap problem. While Order 745 expressly addressed demand response bids in wholesale interstate markets, the program would invariably affect retail prices. The Supreme Court, then, was faced with two questions. First, did the FPA allow FERC to regulate demand response in wholesale markets even though retail prices were affected, or was demand response solely the province of state regulators? And second, should a demand response bid receive the same payment as a bid to consume electricity?

FERC v. ELEC. POWER SUPPLY ASS'N
577 U.S. 260 (2016)

JUSTICE KAGAN delivered the opinion of the Court.

The FPA delegates responsibility to FERC to regulate the interstate wholesale market for electricity—both wholesale rates and the panoply of rules and practices affecting them. . . . [T]he Act establishes a scheme for federal regulation of "the sale of electric energy at wholesale in interstate commerce." 16 U.S.C. § 824(b)(1). Under the statute, "[a]ll rates and charges made, demanded, or received by any public utility for or in connection with" interstate wholesale sales "shall be just and reasonable"; so too shall "all rules and regulations affecting or pertaining to such rates or charges." § 824d(a). And if FERC sees a violation of that standard, it must take remedial action. More specifically, whenever the Commission "shall find that any rate [or] charge"—or "any rule, regulation, practice, or contract affecting such rate [or] charge"—is "unjust [or] unreasonable," then the Commission "shall determine the just and reasonable rate, charge[,] rule, regulation, practice or contract" and impose "the same by order." § 824e(a). That means FERC has the authority—and, indeed, the duty—to ensure that rules or practices "affecting" wholesale rates are just and reasonable.

Taken for all it is worth, that statutory grant could extend FERC's power to some surprising places. For that reason, an earlier D.C. Circuit decision [*California Indep. Sys. Operator Corp. v. FERC*, 372 F.3d 395, 403 (D.C. Cir. 2004)] adopted, and we now approve, a common-sense construction of the FPA's language, limiting FERC's "affecting" jurisdiction to rules or practices that "*directly* affect the [wholesale] rate." . . .

[T]he rules [in FERC Order 745] governing wholesale demand response programs meet that standard with room to spare. In general, wholesale market operators employ demand response bids in competitive auctions that balance wholesale supply and demand and thereby set wholesale prices. The operators accept such bids if and only if they bring down the wholesale rate by displacing higher-priced generation. And when that occurs (most often in peak periods), the easing of pressure on the grid, and the avoidance of service problems, further contributes to lower charges. Wholesale demand response, in short, is all about reducing wholesale rates; so too, then, the rules and practices that determine how those programs operate.

And that is particularly true of the formula that operators use to compensate demand response providers. As in other areas of life, greater pay leads to greater participation. If rewarded at [the locational marginal price (LMP)], rather than at some lesser amount, more demand response providers will enter more bids capable of displacing generation, thus necessarily lowering wholesale electricity prices. Further, the Commission found, heightened demand response participation will put "downward pressure" on generators' own bids, encouraging power plants to offer their product at reduced prices lest they come away empty-handed from the bidding process. That, too, ratchets down the rates wholesale purchasers pay. Compensation for demand response thus directly affects wholesale prices. Indeed, it is hard to think of a practice that does so more.

The above conclusion does not end our inquiry into the Commission's statutory authority; to uphold the Rule, we also must determine that it does not regulate *retail* electricity sales. That is because, as earlier described, § 824(b) "limit[s] FERC's sale jurisdiction to that at wholesale," reserving regulatory authority over retail sales (as well as intrastate wholesale sales) to the States. . . .

Yet a FERC regulation does not run afoul of § 824(b)'s proscription just because it affects—even substantially—the quantity or terms of retail sales. It is a fact of economic life that the wholesale and retail markets in electricity, as in every other known product, are not hermetically sealed from each other. To the contrary, transactions that occur on the wholesale market have natural consequences at the retail level. And so too, of necessity, will FERC's regulation of those wholesale matters. . . . When FERC sets a wholesale rate, when it changes wholesale market rules, when it allocates electricity as between wholesale purchasers—in short, when it takes virtually any action respecting wholesale transactions—it has some effect, in either the short or the long term, on retail rates. That is of no legal consequence. *See, e.g., Mississippi Power & Light Co.* v. *Mississippi ex rel. Moore*, 487 U.S. 354, 365, 370–373 (1988) (holding that an order regulating wholesale purchases fell within FERC's jurisdiction, and preempted contrary state action, even though it clearly affected retail prices); *Nantahala Power & Light Co.* v. *Thornburg*, 476 U.S. 953, 959–961, 970 (1986) (same). When FERC regulates what takes place on the wholesale market, as part of carrying out its charge to improve how that market runs, then no matter the effect on retail rates, § 824(b) imposes no bar.

And in setting rules for demand response, that is all FERC has done. [FERC Order 745] addresses—and addresses only—transactions occurring on the wholesale market. Recall once again how demand response works.... *Wholesale* market operators administer the entire program, receiving every demand response bid made. Those operators accept such a bid at the mandated price when (and only when) the bid provides value to the *wholesale* market by balancing supply and demand more "cost effective[ly]"—*i.e.*, at a lower cost to *wholesale* purchasers—than a bid to generate power. The compensation paid for a successful bid (LMP) is whatever the operator's auction has determined is the marginal price of *wholesale* electricity at a particular location and time. And those footing the bill are the same *wholesale* purchasers that have benefited from the lower *wholesale* price demand response participation has produced. In sum, whatever the effects at the retail level, every aspect of the regulatory plan happens exclusively on the wholesale market and governs exclusively that market's rules.

What is more, the Commission's justifications for regulating demand response are all about, and only about, improving the wholesale market. ...

EPSA's primary argument that FERC has usurped state power (echoed in the dissent) maintains that the Rule "effectively," even though not "nominal[ly]," regulates retail prices. The argument begins on universally accepted ground: Under § 824(b), only the States, not FERC, can set retail rates. But as EPSA concedes, that tenet alone cannot make its case, because FERC's Rule does not set actual rates: States continue to make or approve all retail rates, and in doing so may insulate them from price fluctuations in the wholesale market. Still, EPSA contends, rudimentary economic analysis shows that the Rule does the "functional equivalen[t]" of setting—more particularly, of raising—retail rates. That is because the opportunity to make demand response bids in the wholesale market changes consumers' calculations. In deciding whether to buy electricity at retail, economically-minded consumers now consider *both* the cost of making such a purchase *and* the cost of forgoing a possible demand response payment. ...

[T]he impetus [for federal demand response] came from wholesale market operators. In designing their newly organized markets, those operators recognized almost at once that demand response would lower wholesale electricity prices and improve the grid's reliability. So they quickly sought, and obtained, FERC's approval to institute such programs. Demand response, then, emerged not as a Commission power grab, but instead as a market-generated innovation for more optimally balancing wholesale electricity supply and demand.

And when, years later (after Congress, too, endorsed the practice), FERC began to play a more proactive role, it did so for the identical reason: to enhance the wholesale, not retail, electricity market. Like the market operators, FERC saw that sky-high demand in peak periods threatened network breakdowns, compelled purchases from inefficient generators, and consequently drove up wholesale prices. Addressing those problems—which demand response does—falls within the sweet spot of FERC's statutory charge. So FERC took action promoting the practice. . . .

[T]he finishing blow to both of EPSA's arguments comes from FERC's notable solicitude toward the States. As explained earlier, the Rule allows any State regulator to prohibit its consumers from making demand response bids in the wholesale market. . . . Although claiming the ability to negate such state decisions, the Commission chose not to do so in recognition of the linkage between wholesale and retail markets and the States' role in overseeing retail sales. . . . Wholesale demand response as implemented in the Rule is a program of cooperative federalism, in which the States retain the last word. That feature of the Rule removes any conceivable doubt as to its compliance with § 824(b)'s allocation of federal and state authority.

One last point, about how EPSA's position would subvert the FPA.

EPSA's jurisdictional claim, as may be clear by now, stretches very far. Its point is not that this single Rule, relating to compensation levels, exceeds FERC's power. Instead, EPSA's arguments—that rewarding energy conservation raises effective retail rates and that "luring" consumers onto wholesale markets aims to disrupt state policies—suggest that the entire practice of wholesale demand response falls outside what FERC can regulate. EPSA proudly embraces that point: FERC, it declares, "has no business regulating 'demand response' at all." Under EPSA's theory, FERC's earlier Order No. 719, although never challenged, would also be ultra vires because it requires operators to open their markets to demand response bids. And more: FERC could not even approve an operator's voluntary plan to administer a demand response program. That too would improperly allow a retail customer to participate in a wholesale market.

Yet state commissions could not regulate demand response bids either. EPSA essentially concedes this point. And so it must. The FPA "leaves no room either for direct state regulation of the prices of interstate wholesales" or for regulation that "would indirectly achieve the same result." A State could not oversee offers, made in a wholesale market operator's auction, that help to set wholesale prices. Any effort of that kind would be preempted.

And all of that creates a problem. If neither FERC nor the States can regulate wholesale demand response, then by definition no one can. But under the Act, no electricity transaction can proceed unless it is regulable by someone. As earlier described, Congress passed the FPA precisely to eliminate vacuums of authority over the electricity markets. The Act makes federal and state powers "complementary" and "comprehensive," so that "there [will] be no 'gaps' for private interests to subvert the public welfare." Or said otherwise, the statute prevents the creation of any regulatory "no man's land." Some entity must have jurisdiction to regulate each and every practice that takes place in the electricity markets, demand response no less than any other. . . .

NOTES AND QUESTIONS

1.   In a portion of the opinion not included in the above excerpt, the Court rejected EPSA's challenge that FERC's rule in Order 745 compensating demand response bidders at the same rate as purchasing bidders resulted in a "double payment" to demand response bidders because they received both the FERC-regulated payment for demand response services and, simultaneously, did not have to pay for electricity. Are you persuaded by EPSA's double payment argument? Consider the situation of the air traveler who takes a payment rather than getting on a specific flight. That traveler may choose not to fly or may choose another flight. Does the air traveler who takes a payment receive a "double payment?"

2.   In addition to demand response, can you think of other energy initiatives that could run into similar jurisdictional problems?

3.   Why did FERC allow states to "opt out" or ban electricity users and third-party aggregators of demand response resources from participating in wholesale electricity markets in Orders 719 and 745? Doesn't that undermine the core purpose of the Order?

4.   FERC has continued to enact rules to create greater opportunities for emerging electricity resources to access wholesale electricity markets. For instance, after the Supreme Court upheld Order 745, FERC enacted Order 841, governing participation of energy storage resources in wholesale markets and Order 2222, governing market participation of distributed energy resources (DERs) such as rooftop solar, electric vehicles, and behind-the-meter storage

batteries. In a 2020 decision, the D.C. Circuit rejected a challenge to Order 841 even though, unlike Order 745, it did not contain an "opt-out" provision that allowed states to block energy storage resources within their jurisdiction from participating in wholesale markets. Is such a decision consistent with *FERC v. EPSA*? Why or why not? *See Nat'l Ass'n Reg. Util. Comm'rs v. FERC*, 964 F.3d 1177, 1189–90 (D.C. Cir. 2020) (upholding Order 841); Joshua C. Macey & Matthew R. Christiansen, *Long Live the Federal Power Act's Bright Line*, 134 HARV. L. REV. 1360 (2021). *See also* FED. ENERGY REG. COMM'N, FACT SHEET, FERC ORDER NO. 2222: A NEW DAY FOR DISTRIBUTED ENERGY RESOURCES (Sept. 17, 2020). Could FERC revise Order 745 to remove the opt-out for states?

3. DORMANT COMMERCE CLAUSE

Because the electric grid (except for Texas, Alaska, Hawaii, and Puerto Rico) operates in interstate commerce, federalism problems can arise because both federal and state regulators may be operating in the same sphere. Federalism issues in electricity also arise, however, because state regulation of electricity in one state will affect market participants in neighboring states. For this issue, the question becomes: at what point does one state's actions "affecting" other states rise to the level of an impermissible "burden" on interstate commerce in violation of the dormant Commerce Clause? Recall that in *Attleboro*, the reason the Supreme Court held that the Rhode Island PUC could not set a rate on interstate electricity sales was because doing so would impermissibly burden interstate commerce. That holding was premised on the Court's interpretation of U.S. Const. Art. 1, § 8, cl. 3, which provides that Congress shall have exclusive power "[t]o regulate Commerce with foreign Nations, and among the several States, and with the Indian Tribes." Although this provision sets forth Congress's affirmative power to regulate interstate commerce, the Supreme Court long has held that there is a "dormant" or "negative" aspect of the Commerce Clause which prevents state action that discriminates against or "unduly burdens" interstate commerce.

Since the Supreme Court's decision in *Attleboro* in 1927, the Court has created a more complex framework for evaluating claims that a state law violates the dormant Commerce Clause. In general, a state law violates the dormant Commerce Clause if it (1) discriminates against interstate commerce on its face, in its purpose, or in its effect, making the law subject to "strict scrutiny" or (2) does not discriminate against interstate commerce but imposes burdens on interstate commerce that are "clearly excessive" in relation to the law's local benefits, subjecting the law to a more favorable balancing test under *Pike v. Bruce Church, Inc.*, 397 U.S. 137, 142 (1970). Beyond these two options, as explained in the case excerpt below, many courts also consider as part of the dormant Commerce Clause analysis whether a state law is "extraterritorial" in its impact, meaning that it is attempting to control conduct beyond its borders. Thus, under the "extraterritoriality principle," a court may hold a state law invalid, even if it does not discriminate against interstate commerce, if it has the "practical effect" of regulating commerce outside the state's borders or controls the conduct of those engaged in commerce occurring wholly outside the state.

With these constitutional principles in mind, consider state energy policies. Some states are more aggressive than others in supporting a clean energy transition, including efforts to reduce GHG emissions, increase electricity from renewable energy, promoting energy efficiency, or other goals. To promote such goals, states often invoke, directly or indirectly, their power to regulate the in-state activities of utilities, including their retail sales. Further, with the rise of regional grids and electricity markets (described earlier in this chapter and in more detail in Chapter 5), utilities and other electricity market actors are participating in interstate energy markets that can be affected by state policies. The tricky question that arises—in many forms—is whether a state policy that favors a local utility or generator or disadvantages a utility or generator outside of its borders, can pass constitutional muster under the dormant Commerce Clause.

In the next case, the U.S. Court of Appeals for the Eighth Circuit was asked to review provisions of Minnesota's Next Generation Energy Act, Minn. Stat. § 216H.03, subd. 3. The relevant provisions of the statute provide that "no person shall . . . import or commit to import from outside the state power from a new large energy facility that would contribute to statewide power production carbon dioxide emissions; or enter into a new long-term power purchase agreement that would increase statewide power sector carbon dioxide emissions." In short, the Minnesota statute is largely an anti-coal measure. The state of North Dakota, three non-profit multi-state electric cooperatives, North Dakota lignite coal interests, and others sued the Minnesota Public Utilities Commission claiming a dormant Commerce Clause violation. The following decision resulted.

STATE OF NORTH DAKOTA V. HEYDINGER
825 F.3d 912 (8th Cir. 2016)

LOKEN, CIRCUIT JUDGE.

Technology has substantially changed the electric power industry since 1935, reducing the cost of generating and transmitting electricity and enabling new entrants to challenge the generating monopolies of traditional utilities. To encourage "robust competition in the wholesale electricity market," FERC encouraged utilities participating in regional transmission grids to create independent system operators (ISOs) and regional transmission organizations (RTOs), entities that "would assume operational control—but not ownership—of the transmission facilities owned by its member utilities [and] then provide open access to the regional transmission system to all electricity generators at rates established in a single . . . tariff that applies to all eligible users." Today, these regional organizations control most of the nation's transmission grid. *FERC v. Elec. Power Supply Ass'n*, 136 S. Ct. 760, 768 (2016).

Basin, Minnkota, and MRES, [the three multi-state electric cooperative plaintiffs in this case] are members of the Midcontinent Independent Transmission System Operator (MISO), an ISO established in 1998 and approved by FERC as the first RTO in 2001. MISO controls over 49,000 miles of transmission lines, a grid that spans fifteen States, including Minnesota, and parts of Canada. Its thirty transmission-owning members include investor-owned utilities, public power utilities, independent power producers, and rural electric cooperatives. In Minnesota, most retail distribution utilities, now referred to as load-serving entities or "LSEs," are either members of MISO or non-members who participate in its energy markets.

FERC requires that an approved RTO such as MISO has operational authority for all transmission facilities under its control, be the only provider of transmission services over those facilities, and have sole authority to approve or deny all requests for transmission service. . . . The Supreme Court recently explained how an RTO such as MISO efficiently allocates the supply and demand for electric power:

> [RTOs] obtain (1) orders from LSEs indicating how much electricity they need at various times and (2) bids from generators specifying how much electricity they can produce at those times and how much they will charge for it. [RTOs] accept the generators' bids in order of cost (least expensive first) until they satisfy the LSEs' total demand. The price of the last unit of electricity purchased is then paid to every supplier whose bid was accepted, regardless of its actual offer; and the total cost is split among the LSEs in proportion to how much energy they have ordered.

Elec. Power Supply, 136 S. Ct. at 768. MISO generators commit their electricity to be sold to the MISO market; LSE buyers take electricity out of the market without regard to its generation source. MISO—not individual generators—controls which generation facilities operate at any given time. Though utilities still enter into bilateral purchase agreements as a way to meet their reserve capacity requirements, "any electricity that enters the grid immediately becomes a part of a vast pool of energy that is constantly moving in interstate commerce."

The Minnesota statute at issue is part of the Next Generation Energy Act (NGEA), a statute [enacted in 2007] intended to reduce "statewide power sector carbon dioxide emissions" by prohibiting utilities from meeting Minnesota demand with electricity generated by a "new large energy facility" in a transaction that will contribute to or increase "statewide power sector carbon dioxide emissions." The statute regulates "the total annual emissions of carbon dioxide from the generation of electricity within the state and all emissions of carbon dioxide from the generation of electricity imported from outside of the state and consumed in Minnesota."

[Plaintiffs submitted evidence showing the harmful effects of the statute on their businesses, such as prohibiting them from dispatching coal-fired power that was generated outside of the state of Minnesota to the regional MISO grid.—Eds.]

The Commerce Clause grants to Congress the power to "regulate Commerce . . . among the several States." Although the Clause does not expressly limit the States' ability to regulate commerce, the Supreme Court has interpreted it as including a " 'dormant' limitation on the authority of the States to enact legislation affecting interstate commerce." A state statute that discriminates against interstate commerce in favor of in-state commerce is usually a per se violation of this constitutional limitation. Likewise, a statute that has the practical effect of exerting extraterritorial control over "commerce that takes place wholly outside of the State's borders" is likely to be invalid per se. Beyond those limitations, a statute will run afoul of the Commerce Clause as construed in *Pike v. Bruce Church, Inc.*, 397 U.S. 137 (1970), if it imposes an undue burden on interstate commerce that outweighs its local benefits.

The Supreme Court has applied the extraterritoriality doctrine in relatively few cases. The "critical inquiry is whether the practical effect of the regulation is to control conduct beyond the boundaries of the State." A state statute has undue extraterritorial reach and "is per se invalid" when it "requires people or businesses to conduct their out-of-state commerce in a certain way." The State argues the district court erred in ruling that "§ 216H.03, subd. 3(2)–(3), violates the extraterritoriality doctrine and is per se invalid." . . .

The State and its supporting amici argue that only price-control and price-affirmation laws can violate the extraterritoriality doctrine, an argument that would seemingly insulate all environmental prohibitions from this Commerce Clause scrutiny. This categorical approach to the Commerce Clause would be contrary to well-established Supreme Court jurisprudence. . . .

The district court correctly noted the Supreme Court has never so limited the doctrine, and indeed has applied it more broadly. . . . We have twice applied the doctrine outside the price-control context. Our sister circuits have considered whether a variety of non-price laws were unconstitutionally extraterritorial. . . .

A panel of the Tenth Circuit recently took a somewhat contrary position in *Energy & Environment Legal Institute v. Epel*, 793 F.3d 1169 (10th Cir.), *cert. denied*, 136 S. Ct. 595 (2015). At issue was the validity of a Colorado statute requiring "electricity generators to ensure that 20% of the electricity they sell to Colorado consumers comes from renewable sources." In upholding the law, the court ruled that "non-price standards for products sold in-state" may be amenable to Commerce Clause scrutiny under the *Pike* balancing test, or "for traces of discrimination" in favor of in-state commerce, but they do not warrant "near automatic condemnation" under the extraterritoriality doctrine. *Whether* a state statute with extraterritorial effect should be deemed "per se invalid," or should be analyzed under the *Pike* balancing test, is a difficult issue we have not previously addressed. In this case the State has not argued that the district court erred in applying the per se standard, as opposed to the *Pike* balancing test. . . .

The State primarily argues that the prohibitions in § 216H.03, subd. 3(2) and (3), do not apply to the "MISO short-term energy markets" and therefore do not violate the extraterritoriality doctrine. The State contends that the statute regulates only "contracts or other commitments to import electricity in the future" and the "persons who contract with a generating facility to import electricity into Minnesota for use by Minnesota customers." By contrast, the MISO markets are for *short-term* energy and thus do not implicate the NGEA prohibition on *long-term* power purchase agreements. Thus, the statute as the State would have us read it leaves non-Minnesota entities free to transact business with other non-Minnesota entities.

The district court concluded that this contention is contrary to the plain language of the statute. Subdivision 2 of § 216H.03 expressly defines "statewide power sector carbon dioxide emissions" as including emissions from the generation of electricity that is "imported from outside the state and consumed in Minnesota." Clause (2) of subdivision 3 provides that "no person" shall "import or commit to import" power from a large new energy facility located "outside the state," a command plainly encompassing both present and future transactions. Clause (3) prohibits entering into a new long-term power purchase agreement "that would increase emissions" from an out-of-state generating facility, whether presently existing or not. These broad prohibitions plainly encompass non-Minnesota entities and transactions. The presumption against extraterritoriality does not apply when the statute's text is clear. . . .

Not only do the challenged prohibitions apply to non-Minnesota utilities, they regulate activity and transactions taking place *wholly outside* of Minnesota. In the regional MISO transmission grid, a person who "imports" electricity does not know the origin of the electrons it receives, whether or not the transaction is pursuant to a long-term purchase agreement with an out-of-state generator. As a State expert described the energy market, the "contract path" between the importer and generator "represents a flow of dollars, not a flow of electrons." In the MISO grid, electrons flow freely without regard to state borders, entirely under MISO's control. Thus, when a non-Minnesota generating utility injects electricity into the MISO grid to meet its commitments to *non*-Minnesota customers, it cannot ensure that those electrons will not flow into and be consumed in Minnesota. Likewise, non-Minnesota utilities that enter into power purchase agreements to serve *non*-Minnesota members cannot guarantee that the electricity eventually bid into the MISO markets pursuant to those agreements will not be imported into and consumed in Minnesota. As [the Minnesota Department of Commerce] MDOC observed in the Dairyland [Power Cooperative] proceeding, "it is impossible to determine that no electrons from a generation unit reach a particular end-use customer, unless the generation resource and end-use customer are completely disconnected from each other physically." Thus, generators such as [plaintiffs] Basin, Minnkota, and MRES cannot prevent energy they place in the MISO grid to serve *non*-Minnesota customers from being imported into Minnesota, and a Minnesota LSE cannot do business with those out-of-state generators without "importing" electrons from their coal-fired facilities.

Like persons who post information on an out-of-state internet website, out-of-state utilities entering into purchases and sales of electricity in the MISO transmission grid "cannot prevent [electricity users in Minnesota] from accessing the [electrons]." And the statute provides that all MISO participants must comply with the challenged prohibitions any time they enter into a transaction or agreement that may "import" electricity into Minnesota. To avoid this direct impact on activities and transactions that are otherwise entirely out-of-state commerce, integrated regional utilities like Basin must either unplug from MISO or seek regulatory approval from MDOC and [the Minnesota Public Utilities Commission] MPUC. "Forcing a merchant to seek regulatory approval in one State before undertaking a transaction in another directly regulates interstate commerce." For this reason, the district court correctly concluded that the challenged prohibitions have "the practical effect of controlling conduct beyond the boundaries of" Minnesota.

The State argues that "§ 216H.03 merely regulates in an area of traditional state authority." Without question, Minnesota and other States have long regulated the siting, construction, and operation of electric generating facilities located within their borders. Minnesota "retains broad regulatory authority to protect the health and safety of its citizens and the integrity of its natural resources." Consistent with that authority, plaintiffs did not challenge, and the district court did not enjoin, enforcement of § 216H.03, subd. 3(1), which prohibits constructing within Minnesota a new large energy facility that would contribute to statewide carbon dioxide emissions.

But unlike Clause (1), Clauses (2) and (3) of § 216H.03, subd. 3, seek to reduce emissions that occur outside Minnesota by prohibiting transactions that originate outside Minnesota. And their practical effect is to control activities taking place *wholly* outside Minnesota. In determining whether a law has extraterritorial reach, the Supreme Court has instructed us to consider "how the challenged statute may interact with the legitimate regulatory regimes of other States." Other States in the MISO region have not adopted Minnesota's policy of increasing the cost of electricity by restricting use of the currently most cost-efficient sources of generating capacity. Yet the challenged statute will impose that policy on neighboring States by preventing MISO members from adding capacity from prohibited sources anywhere in the grid, absent Minnesota regulatory approval or the dismantling of the federally encouraged and approved MISO transmission system. This Minnesota may not do without the approval of Congress.

NOTES AND QUESTIONS

1.   Judge Loken found the law invalid on dormant Commerce Clause grounds. By contrast, in a separate opinion not excerpted above, Judge Murphy disagreed with Judge Loken's decision that the law had an unlawful extraterritorial effect on interstate commerce but concurred in the result because she found the Minnesota law was preempted under the Federal Power Act. According to Judge Murphy, the law purported to regulate wholesale electricity sales and transmission of electricity in interstate commerce, which is subject to exclusive FERC jurisdiction. The third judge on the panel, Judge Colloton, did not address the dormant Commerce Clause question but agreed with Judge Murphy that the state statute was preempted by the Federal Power Act. He also held that the statute was preempted by the Clean Air Act. Considering the various opinions in the case, how broadly (or narrowly) should its precedential effect be construed?

2.   Consider further the Minnesota law at issue in *Heydinger*, enacted in 2007. It prohibits (1) the construction of "new" (*i.e.*, after the statute was enacted) large energy facilities in the state that would contribute to statewide power sector carbon dioxide emissions, (2) the "import" of power from a large new energy facility located "outside the state," and (3) entering into a new long-term power purchase agreement "that would increase statewide power sector carbon dioxide emissions." What types of energy facilities is the state attempting to target? Why not simply limit utilities from building those facilities within the state (which the court said would not implicate the Constitution)? How has the U.S. energy landscape changed regarding carbon dioxide emissions from electric generating facilities since 2007, and what are the reasons for those changes? For a more detailed discussion of the Minnesota statute and the subsequent lawsuit (although published prior to the Eighth

Circuit's opinion), see Alexandra B. Klass & Elizabeth Henley, *Energy Policy, Extraterritoriality, and the Dormant Commerce Clause*, 5 SAN DIEGO J. OF CLIMATE & ENERGY LAW 127 (2013–14). If a state wanted to draft a statute that would achieve the same goals as Minnesota's without running afoul of the dormant Commerce Clause, what would it look like?

3.   In *Heydinger*, Judge Loken cites to *Energy and Environment Legal Institute v. Epel*, 793 F.3d 1169, 1174 (10th Cir. 2015) (*EELI*), written by then-Judge (now Justice) Gorsuch, before he joined the Supreme Court. Judge Loken accurately notes that Justice Gorsuch was skeptical about using the extraterritoriality doctrine to strike down a Colorado law that required electric utilities to obtain 20% of the electricity they sell from renewable energy sources. Such "renewable portfolio standards" or "RPSs" are discussed in more detail in Chapter 5. Justice Gorsuch wrote in *EELI*:

> Can Colorado's renewable energy mandate survive an encounter with the most dormant doctrine in dormant commerce clause jurisprudence? . . . It may be that Colorado's scheme will require Coloradans to pay more for electricity, but that's a cost they are apparently happy to bear for the ballot initiative proposing the renewable energy mandate passed with overwhelming support. So what does this policy choice by Coloradans affecting Colorado energy consumption preferences and Colorado consumer prices have to do with the United States Constitution and its provisions regarding interstate commerce? [EELI] points out that Colorado consumers receive their electricity from an interconnected grid serving eleven states and portions of Canada and Mexico. Because electricity can go anywhere on the grid and come from anywhere on the grid, and because Colorado is a net importer of electricity, Colorado's renewable energy mandate effectively means some out-of-state coal producers, like an EELI member, will lose business with out-of-state utilities who feed their power onto the grid. And this harm to out-of-state coal producers, EELI says, amounts to a violation of one of the three branches of dormant commerce clause jurisprudence.

In rejecting this argument, Justice Gorsuch explained:

> How can we have the sort of steadfast conviction . . . that interstate commerce will be harmed when, if anything, Colorado's mandate seems most obviously calculated to raise price for *in-state* consumers? EELI offers no story suggesting how Colorado's mandate disproportionately harms out-of-state businesses. To be sure, fossil fuel producers like EELI's member[s] will be hurt. But as far as we know, all fossil fuel producers in the area served by the grid will be hurt equally and all renewable energy producers in the area will be helped equally. . . . And it's far from clear how the mandate might hurt out-of-state consumers either. The mandate does have the effect of increasing demand for electricity generated using renewable sources and (under the law of demand) you might expect that to lead

to higher prices for electricity of that sort for everyone in the market (here, presumably, everyone connected to the grid). But the mandate also reduces demand for and might be expected to reduce the price everyone in the market has to pay for electricity generated using fossil fuels. So the net price impact on out-of-state consumers is far from obviously negative and, for all we know, may tip in favor of those willing to shift usage toward fossil fuel generated electricity.

Id. at 1174. Which court's—the Eight Circuit's or the Tenth Circuit's—dormant Commerce Clause analysis do you find most convincing?

4.   It is not surprising that coal interests in North Dakota and the state itself challenged the Minnesota law in *Heydinger*. One of North Dakota's major industries is lignite coal extraction, and for decades, electric utilities and cooperatives serving both North Dakota and Minnesota have built and operated coal-fired power plants near the Minnesota-North Dakota border. Thus, the provisions of Minnesota's Next Generation Energy Act purporting to limit the ability of coal-fired power plants in North Dakota to send energy to Minnesota was perceived as a significant threat to this entrenched industry.

5.   Dormant Commerce Clause challenges to state energy laws have a rich and long history, with regulated parties and states themselves attempting to invalidate state laws that allegedly protect in-state industries or otherwise treat in-state and out-of-state actors or activities differently in circumstances where Congress has not yet spoken on the issue. *See, e.g., Wyoming v. Oklahoma*, 502 U.S. 437 (1992) (invalidating Oklahoma statute that required in-state utilities to burn a minimum percentage of in-state coal in their coal-fired power plants on grounds it discriminated against out-of-state coal interests without a legitimate reason unrelated to economic protectionism); *Rocky Mountain Farmers Union v. Corey*, 913 F.3d 940 (9th Cir. 2019) (upholding California statute that assigned a higher "carbon intensity" value to ethanol produced in the Midwest under the state's Low Carbon Fuel Standard on grounds that distinction was grounded in environmental protection rather than economic protection and also did not regulate extraterritorially) (discussed in Chapter 6); *LSP Transmission Holdings, LLC v. Sieben*, 954 F.3d 1018 (8th Cir. 2020), *cert. denied*, 141 S. Ct. 1510 (2021) (upholding Minnesota statute that granted in-state utilities the "right of first refusal" to build transmission lines in their service territories) (discussed in Chapter 5). *See also* Niina H. Farrah, *Supreme Court Rejects Coal Export Appeal*, ENERGYWIRE (June 29, 2021) (reporting on U.S. Supreme Court decision to reject an original jurisdiction lawsuit by Montana and Wyoming against Washington alleging the latter state's denial of permits for a proposed coal export terminal violated the dormant Commerce Clause and blocked coal industry access to Asian markets). How much leeway should states have in setting state energy policy in a way that impacts other states? Is federal policy necessary to address this issue (like the enactment of the Federal Power Act after the Court's decision in *Attleboro*), or should the courts give states more room to innovate? For a discussion of these issues, see Alexandra B. Klass & Jim Rossi, *Reconstituting the Federalism Battle in Energy Transportation*, 41

HARV. ENV'T L. REV. 423 (2017); Alexandra B. Klass & Shantal Pai, *The Law of Energy Exports*, 103 CALIF. L. REV. 733 (2021).

G. CONTEMPORARY RATEMAKING ISSUES

1. COST-OF-SERVICE RATEMAKING

Traditionally, utility rates were set using a cost-of-service ratemaking methodology. As noted above, cost-of-service rates essentially repaid utilities dollar-for-dollar for their expenses and allowed them to earn a reasonable rate of return on their invested capital. Toward the end of the 20th century, however, generation from traditional IOUs became more expensive, and cheaper electricity was available from nonutility producers. Here, we discuss problems with cost-of-service ratemaking and alternatives to it.

One reason electricity costs rose was due to nuclear power plants. Utilities constructing nuclear units ran into many problems, including cost overruns, plant cancellations, and the conversion of nuclear facilities to coal plants. The issue for regulators then became: What should be done with these expensive investments that will not receive a return on investment, often referred to as "stranded costs"? Should they be included in the rate base and paid for by ratepayers? Or should they be denied rate base treatment, in which case the costs would be absorbed by the shareholders? Today, the stranded cost problem arises with early retirement of coal plants due to competition from low-cost natural gas and renewable energy, coupled with flat electricity demand and stronger environmental regulations. *See, e.g.*, U.S. DEP'T OF ENERGY, STAFF REPORT TO THE SECRETARY ON ELECTRICITY MARKETS AND RELIABILITY 13–14 (Aug. 2017).

As noted, federal regulation of the natural gas and electricity industries began in earnest in the mid-1930s. From then until the mid-1960s, especially after World War II, the electricity industry enjoyed significant expansion. Several federal policy initiatives facilitated the American Dream of individual homeownership, including the G.I. Bill that sent veterans to college, the Federal Highway Act of 1957 that made travel easier, and large-scale home developers that made the suburbs possible. Electricity was needed to serve those residential developments and the commercial facilities and industries driving post-war economic growth.

During the post-war period from 1945 to 1965, the electric industry's growth was steady and predictable. Electricity production and sales expanded, with prices stable and often decreasing. After 1965, production costs increased, as did rates. The traditional rate formula fit well with an expanding industry, as it provided a return on investment on the utility's capital investment.

The consequence of the traditional rate formula is that utilities had an incentive to continue to invest in capital expansion. The larger the rate base, the larger the capital investment, and the greater the return to shareholders.

Growth, however, cannot continue indefinitely. Once this infrastructure was constructed and as post-war economic growth slowed, electric utilities could not continue to expand at the same breakneck pace. In fact, utilities eventually overbuilt their generation, and PUCs had to address the issue of overinvestment.

To make matters worse, the nuclear industry experienced significant turbulence. Utilities ordered nuclear units under the belief that nuclear-powered electricity would be inexpensive for generations. However, they underestimated construction costs, and so experienced significant cost overruns. This was the beginning of utilities' decisions to cancel nuclear plants: an attempt to staunch escalating costs. The industry took another blow with the accident at Three Mile Island in 1979, which effectively stopped nuclear construction for over 40 years. *See* JOSEPH P. TOMAIN, NUCLEAR POWER TRANSFORMATION (1987).

The regulatory problem thus became clear. The traditional rate formula encouraged utilities to construct more plants—even if they were not necessary. When this occurred, who should pay for what were clearly "mistake[s] in retrospect"? Richard J. Pierce, *The Regulatory Treatment of Mistakes in Retrospect: Canceled Plants and Excess Capacity*, 122 U. PENN. L. REV. 497, 498 (1984). Should ratepayers absorb these costly mistakes when they are receiving no electricity? Or should shareholders pay, even if utilities made the mistakes in good faith as business decisions that appeared prudent at the time?

PUCs invoked two core principles to solve this problem. The first was the "used and useful" test. Under this approach, ratepayers are only responsible for the costs that result in electricity generated for their use. Thus, if a plant is built but never brought online, ratepayers will not be charged for that investment. The second was the "prudent investment" test. Under this approach, if the investment was considered prudently made, those investments can be placed into the rate base and charged to consumers.

Both principles can appear harsh; each shifts the full cost to either ratepayers or shareholders. Regulators were aware of this either-or dichotomy and attempted to fashion a better balance. Both the "used and useful" and "prudency" tests reached the courts as shown in the excerpts below.

DUQUESNE LIGHT CO. V. BARASCH
488 U.S. 299 (1989)

CHIEF JUSTICE REHNQUIST delivered the opinion of the Court.

Pennsylvania law required that rates for electricity be fixed without consideration of a utility's expenditures for electrical generating facilities which were planned but never built, even though the expenditures were prudent and reasonable when made. The Supreme Court of Pennsylvania held that such a law did not take the utilities' property in violation of the Fifth Amendment to the United States Constitution. We agree with that conclusion, and hold that a state scheme of utility regulation does not "take" property simply because it disallows recovery of capital investments that are not "used and useful in service to the public."

In response to predictions of increased demand for electricity, Duquesne Light Company (Duquesne) and Pennsylvania Power Company (Penn Power) joined a venture in 1967 to build more generating capacity. The project, known as the Central Area Power Coordination Group (CAPCO), involved three other electric utilities and had as its objective the construction of seven large nuclear generating units. In 1980, the participants canceled plans for construction of four of the plants. Intervening events, including the Arab oil embargo and the accident at Three Mile Island, had radically changed the outlook both for growth in the demand for electricity and for nuclear energy as a desirable way of meeting that demand. At the time of the cancellation, Duquesne's share of the preliminary construction costs associated with the four halted plants was $34,697,389. Penn Power had invested $9,569,665. . . .

In 1982, Duquesne again came before the PUC to obtain a rate increase. Again, it sought to amortize its expenditures on the canceled plants over 10 years. In January, 1988, the PUC issued a final order which granted Duquesne the authority to increase its revenues $106.8 million to a total yearly revenue in excess of $800 million. The rate increase included $3.6 million in revenue representing the first payment of the 10-year amortization of Duquesne's $36 million loss in the CAPCO plants.

The Pennsylvania Office of the Consumer Advocate (Consumer Advocate) moved the PUC for reconsideration in light of a state law enacted about a month before the close of the 1982 Duquesne rate proceeding. The Act . . . amended the Pennsylvania Utility Code by limiting "the consideration of certain costs in the rate base." It provided that "the cost of construction or expansion of a facility undertaken by a public utility producing . . . electricity shall not be made a part of the rate base nor otherwise included in the rates charged by the electric utility until such time as the facility is used and useful in service to the public." . . .

The [Pennsylvania Supreme Court] held that the controlling language of the Act prohibited recovery of the costs in question either by inclusion in the rate base or by amortization. The court rejected appellants' constitutional challenge to the statute thus interpreted, observing that "[t]he 'just compensation' safeguarded to a utility by the fourteenth amendment of the federal constitution is a reasonable return on the fair value of its property at the time it is being used for public service." Since the instant CAPCO investment was not serving the public and did not constitute an operating expense, no constitutional rights to recovery attached to it. The court remanded to the PUC for further proceedings to correct its rate order, giving effect to the exclusion required by Act 335. Duquesne and Penn Power appealed to this Court, arguing that the effect of Act 335 excluding their prudently incurred costs from the rate violated the Takings Clause of the Fifth Amendment, applicable to the States under the Fourteenth Amendment. . . .

Forty-five years ago in the landmark case of *FPC v. Hope Natural Gas Co.,* this Court abandoned the rule of *Smyth v. Ames,* and held that the "fair value" rule is not the only constitutionally acceptable method of fixing utility rates. In *Hope,* we ruled that historical cost was a valid basis on which to calculate utility compensation. We also acknowledged in that case that all of the subsidiary aspects of valuation for ratemaking purposes could not properly be characterized as having a constitutional dimension, despite the fact that they might affect property rights to some degree. Today we reaffirm these teachings of *Hope Natural Gas*: "[I]t is not theory, but the impact, of the rate order which counts. If the total effect of the rate order cannot be said to be unreasonable, judicial inquiry . . . is at an end. The fact that the method employed to reach that result may contain infirmities is not then important." This language, of course, does not dispense with all of the constitutional difficulties when a utility raises a claim that the rate which it is permitted to charge is so low as to be confiscatory: whether a particular rate is "unjust" or "unreasonable" will depend to some extent on what is a fair rate of return, given the risks under a particular rate setting system, and on the amount of capital upon which the investors are entitled to earn that return. . . .

Pennsylvania determines rates under a slightly modified form of the historical cost/prudent investment system. Neither Duquesne nor Penn Power alleges that the total effect of the rate order arrived at within this system is unjust or unreasonable. In fact, the overall effect is well within the bounds of *Hope,* even with total exclusion of the CAPCO costs. Duquesne was authorized to earn a 16.14% return on common equity and an 11.64% overall return on a rate base of nearly $1.8 billion. Its $35 million investment in the canceled plants comprises roughly 1.9% of its total base. The denial of plant amortization will reduce its annual allowance by .4%. Similarly, Penn Power was allowed a charge of 15.72%

return on common equity and a 12.02% overall return. Its investment in the CAPCO plants comprises only 2.4% of its $401.8 million rate base. The denial of amortized recovery of its $9.6 million investment in CAPCO will reduce its annual revenue allowance by only 0.5%.

Given these numbers, it appears that the PUC would have acted within the constitutional range of reasonableness if it had allowed amortization of the CAPCO costs but set a lower rate of return on equity, with the result that Duquesne and Penn Power received the same revenue they will under the instant orders on remand. The overall impact of the rate orders, then, is not constitutionally objectionable. No argument has been made that these slightly reduced rates jeopardize the financial integrity of the companies, either by leaving them insufficient operating capital or by impeding their ability to raise future capital. Nor has it been demonstrated that these rates are inadequate to compensate current equity holders for the risk associated with their investments under a modified prudent investment scheme. . . .

Finally we address the suggestion of the Pennsylvania Electric Association as *amicus* that the prudent investment rule should be adopted as the constitutional standard. We think that the adoption of any such rule would signal a retreat from 45 years of decisional law in this area which would be as unwarranted as it would be unsettling. . . .

The adoption of a single theory of valuation as a constitutional requirement would be inconsistent with the view of the Constitution this Court has taken since *Hope Natural Gas*. As demonstrated in *Wisconsin v. FPC*, [373 U.S. 294 (1963)], circumstances may favor the use of one ratemaking procedure over another. The designation of a single theory of ratemaking as a constitutional requirement would unnecessarily foreclose alternatives which could benefit both consumers and investors. The Constitution within broad limits leaves the States free to decide what rate setting methodology best meets their needs in balancing the interests of the utility and the public.

Unlike the "used and useful" question, the prudency issue did not make its way to the Supreme Court. It was, however, the subject of three lengthy decisions by the U.S. Court of Appeals for the D.C. Circuit, culminating in the following decision, *Jersey Central Power & Light v. FERC (Jersey Central III)*.

JERSEY CENTRAL POWER & LIGHT CO.
v. FERC (*JERSEY CENTRAL III*)

810 F.2d 1168 (D.C. Cir 1987)

BORK, CIRCUIT JUDGE.

At issue is the utility's proposed treatment of the $397 million investment lost when it suspended construction of its nuclear generating station at Forked River, New Jersey. The Forked River project was initiated about a decade and a half ago, when federal and state agencies were encouraging utilities to commit substantial amounts of capital to nuclear generating plants that required lead times of eight to twelve years. The consensus prediction was of substantial and steady increases in the demand for electricity and substantial and continued increases in the price of oil due to the operation of an international oil cartel. . . .

The forecasts of both demand and supply proved wrong. Due to conservation, demand did not rise nearly as much as expected, and, with the collapse of the international cartel, the oil market has experienced a world-wide glut and a dramatic decline in prices. Furthermore, the protracted litigation and political controversy which attended the construction of nuclear power projects resulted in extensive delays and dramatic increases in their ultimate cost. Thus, many investments which were prudent, indeed considered essential, when made, have now by necessity been cancelled. Forked River was one, and in 1980 Jersey Central abandoned it . . . .

Jersey Central sought to recover the cost of the Forked River investment by amortizing the $397 million over a fifteen-year period, a proposal to which the Commission agreed. Jersey Central also requested, however, that the unamortized portions be included in the rate base, with a rate of return sufficient to cover the carrying charges on the debt and the preferred stock portions of that unamortized investment.

The Commission responded by issuing an order summarily excluding the unamortized portion of the investment from the rate base. No discussion or analysis accompanied this portion of the order. The Commission simply noted that "consistent with Commission precedent . . . unamortized investment in cancelled plants must be excluded from rate base." . . .

[Before us, t]he parties offer radically differing views of the Commission's obligations under *Hope Natural Gas.* . . . [A]t oral argument before the court *en banc*, counsel [for the Commission] advanced the novel proposition that the "end result" test [of *Hope*] empowers a court to set aside a rate order on the utility's petition only if the order would put the utility into bankruptcy.

Hope Natural Gas reaffirmed a doctrinal shift . . . away from the more exacting and detailed standard of judicial review exemplified by *Smyth v. Ames*, 169 U.S. 466 (1898). Under *Smyth v. Ames*, courts had meticulously scrutinized rate orders to ensure that investors received the "fair value" of the property dedicated to public use. The "fair value" standard required courts to estimate the current market value of the property, and rates that provided anything less were deemed confiscatory. . . . The Supreme Court cases of the 1940's eliminated the requirement that the market value of the property be recovered, and regulated industries now collect rates calculated to generate a reasonable return on the original cost of the investment. The companies are still generally permitted to include in the rate base only property considered used and useful, but with the demise of "fair value," "used and useful" ceased to have any constitutional significance, and the Commission has at times departed from this standard. It is now simply one of several permissible tools of ratemaking, one that need not be, and is not, employed in every instance. . . .

The *Hope* Court made clear that when a rate was claimed to be beyond "just and reasonable" boundaries, the focus of analysis was to be the end result of that order:

> [I]t is the result reached not the method employed which is controlling. . . . It is not theory but the impact of the rate order which counts. If the total effect of the rate order cannot be said to be unjust and unreasonable, judicial inquiry under the Act is at an end. . . . And he who would upset the rate order under the Act carries the heavy burden of making a convincing showing that it is invalid because it is unjust and unreasonable in its consequences. . . .

The Supreme Court has repeatedly reaffirmed the "end result" standard of *Hope Natural Gas*[, including in *Permian Basin Area Rate Cases*, 390 U.S. 747 (1968)]. . . .

The teaching of these cases is straightforward. In reviewing a rate order courts must determine whether or not the end result of that order constitutes a reasonable balancing, based on factual findings, of the investor interest in maintaining financial integrity and access to capital markets and the consumer interest in being charged non-exploitative rates. Moreover, an order cannot be justified simply by a showing that each of the choices underlying it was reasonable; those choices must still add up to a reasonable result. . . .

The allegations made by Jersey Central and the testimony it offered track the standards of *Hope* and *Permian Basin* exactly. . . . *Permian Basin* reaffirmed that the reviewing court "must determine" whether the Commission's rate order may reasonably be expected to "maintain financial integrity" and "attract necessary capital." Jersey Central alleged that it had paid no dividends on its common stock for four years and faced a further prolonged inability to pay such dividends. . . . [that] "[a]dequate and prompt relief is necessary in order to maintain the past high quality of service"; and that the rate increase requested was "the minimum necessary to restore the financial integrity of the Company." . . .

Inexplicably, the Commission ruled that Jersey Central's showing did not require a hearing because there were "no testimony or exhibits which would support a higher return." That ruling is flatly at odds with *Hope* and *Permian Basin.* . . .

The Commission maintains that because excluding the unamortized portion of a cancelled plant investment from the rate base had previously been upheld as permissible, any rate order that rests on such a decision is unimpeachable. The fact that a particular ratemaking standard is generally permissible does not per se legitimate the end result of the rate orders it produces. . . .

In addition to prohibiting rates so low as to be confiscatory, the holding of *Hope Natural Gas* makes clear that exploitative rates are illegal as well. If the inclusion of property not currently used and useful in the rate base automatically constituted exploitation of consumers, as one of the amici maintains, then the Commission would be justified in excluding such property summarily even in cases where the utility pleads acute financial distress. A regulated utility has no constitutional right to a profit, and a company that is unable to survive without charging exploitative rates has no entitlement to such rates. *Market Street Ry. v. Railroad Comm'n of Cal.*, 324 U.S. 548 (1945). . . .

The central point, however, is this: it is impossible for us to say at this juncture whether including the unamortized portion of Forked River in the rate base would exploit consumers in this case, or whether its exclusion, on the facts of this case, constitutes confiscation, for no findings of fact have been made concerning the consequences of the rate order. Nor, for the same reason, can we make a judgment about the higher rate of return the utility sought as an alternative to inclusion in the rate base of its unamortized investment. Jersey Central has presented allegations which, if true, suggest that the rate order almost certainly does not meet the requirements of *Hope Natural Gas*, for the company has been shut off from long-term capital, is wholly dependent for short-term capital on a revolving credit arrangement that can be cancelled at any time, and has been unable to pay dividends for four years. The necessary findings are simply not there for us to review. The case should therefore be remanded to the Commission for a hearing at which the Commission can determine whether the rate order it issued constituted a reasonable balancing of the interests the Supreme Court has designated as relevant to the setting of a just and reasonable rate.

STARR, CIRCUIT JUDGE, concurring.

The Commission's stated justification for summarily dismissing these allegations was the weight of its prior "used and useful" precedent. But as the court's opinion shows, that body of precedent did not constitute as ironclad a rule as the Commission would have us believe.

Indeed, the Commission as a matter of policy has departed over the years from the strictures of the "used and useful" rule. This is illustrated by its treatment of "construction work in progress" (CWIP), part of which, the Commission recently determined, can be included in a utility's rate base. In that proceeding, the Commission recognized that its own practice admits of "widely recognized exceptions and departures" from the "used and useful" rule, "particularly when there are countervailing public interest considerations." In that setting, financial difficulties in the electric utility industry played a significant role in the Commission's decision to bend the rule.

This policy of flexibility, it seems to me, reflects the practical reality of the electric utility industry, namely that investments in plant and equipment are enormously costly. Rigid adherence to "used and useful" doctrines would doubtless imperil the viability of some utilities; thus, while not articulating its results in *Hope* or "takings" terms, the Commission—whether as a matter of policy or perceived constitutional obligation—has in the past taken these realities into account and provided relief for utilities in various forms. . . .

Requiring an investment to be prudent when made is one safeguard imposed by regulatory authorities upon the regulated business for benefit of ratepayers. As I see it, the "used and useful" rule is but another such safeguard.

For me, the prudent investment rule is, taken alone, too weighted for constitutional analysis in favor of the utility. It lacks balance. But so too, the "used and useful" rule, taken alone, is skewed heavily in favor of ratepayers. It also lacks balance. In the modern setting, neither regime, mechanically applied with full rigor, will likely achieve justice among the competing interests of investor and ratepayers so as to avoid confiscation of the utility's property or a taking of the property of ratepayers through unjustifiably exorbitant rates. Each approach, however, provides important insights about the ultimate object of the regulatory process, which is to achieve a just result in rate regulation. And that is the mission commanded by the Fifth Amendment.

Thus it is that a taking occurs not when an investment is made (even one under legal obligation), but when the balance between investor and ratepayer interests—the very function of utility regulation—is struck unjustly. Although the agency has broad latitude in striking the balance, the Constitution nonetheless requires that the end result reflect a reasonable balancing of the interests of investors and ratepayers. As we have seen, both investors and ratepayers were the intended beneficiaries of the Forked River investment; both should presumptively have to share in the loss. Filling in the gaps, the making of the specific judgments that constitutes the difficult part of this enterprise, belongs in the first instance to the politically accountable branches, specifically to the experts in the agency, not to generalist judges.

MIKVA, CIRCUIT JUDGE, with whom CHIEF JUDGE WALD, and CIRCUIT JUDGES SPOTTSWOOD W. ROBINSON, III and HARRY T. EDWARDS join, dissenting.

The real mischief of today's decision lies not in the majority's belief that the utility has raised an issue of fact necessitating a hearing, but in its determination that Jersey Central has actually made out a case of constitutional confiscation. The majority believes that Jersey Central can meet this burden. We simply cannot swallow the majority's assertion that "it is probable that the facts alleged [by Jersey Central], if true, would establish an invasion of the company's rights." In our view, it is beyond cavil that Jersey Central has not presented allegations which, if true, would establish that the Commission's orders result in unjust and unreasonable rates. . . .

Permian Basin teaches that if the Commission reasonably balances consumer and investor interests, then the resulting rate is not confiscatory. The separate opinion ably translates this into a working definition of a confiscatory rate: it exists when "an unreasonable balance has been struck in the regulation process so as unreasonably to favor ratepayer interests at the substantial expense of investor interests." . . .

The *Hope* Court did not define "unjust or unreasonable"; nor did it articulate when a rate would be confiscatory. It certainly did not hold that the end result could be condemned if the investor criteria defined in the case were not fulfilled. Indeed, it expressly noted that its holding made no suggestion that more or less might not be allowed.

This understanding of *Hope* is the only way to reconcile the Court's recitation of investor interests with its avowal that "regulation does not insure that the business shall produce net revenues." Investor interests are only one factor in the assessment of constitutionally reasonable, therefore non-confiscatory, rates. In any instance, the rate must also "provide appropriate protection to the relevant public interests, both existing and foreseeable." A just and reasonable rate which results from balancing these conflicting interests might not provide "enough revenue not only for operating expenses but also for the capital costs of the business ... includ[ing] service on the debt and dividends on the stock." The Court made this abundantly clear in *Market Street*. The Commission rate order in *Market Street* was claimed to be confiscatory. Like *Jersey Central*, the complaining company asserted that *Hope* "entitled [it] to a return 'sufficient to assure confidence in the financial integrity of the enterprise, so as to maintain its credit and to attract capital' and to " 'enable the company to operate successfully, to maintain its financial integrity, to attract capital, and to compensate its investors for the risks assumed.' " The Court dismissed the argument out of hand. In approving a rate that concededly consigned the company to operating at a loss, the Court made clear that a just and reasonable rate might not satisfy the investor "considerations" expounded in *Hope*.

Application of this principle is readily apparent in the Commission's current treatment of electric utility plants, investments prudent when made but sometimes frustrated in fruition. If the investment is successful, the customer benefits from controlled rates for the service provided. But the ratepayer also shares the costs if the investment fails; he must pay for the expenditure made on an unproductive facility from which he obtains no service. From the investor's viewpoint, price regulation cabins both his upside and downside risk. He cannot collect the windfall benefits if the project is a boon; he does not bear all costs if the project is a bust. Electric utility stockholders do not lose equity in the non-serviceable facility, as they might in the marketplace. They simply do not procure a return on the investment.

The majority quibbles with this risk allocation; it would prefer a world in which the investor is guaranteed a return on his investment, if prudent when made. Its resultant holding today is directly at odds with fundamental principles laid out in *Hope* and its progeny. Adherence to the majority's insistence on the inclusion of prudent investments in the rate base would virtually insulate investors in public utilities from the risks involved in free market business. This would drastically diminish protection of the public interest by thrusting the entire risk of a failed investment onto the ratepayers. *Jersey Central* and the majority would convert utility stockholders from risk-takers into annuity holders. Neither *Hope* nor the Fifth Amendment takings clause sanctions such radical results.

NOTES AND QUESTIONS

1. The *Duquesne Light* and *Jersey Central III* cases are noteworthy for several reasons, but a headline is their reaffirmation of the Supreme Court's decision in *Hope Natural Gas*, discussed earlier in this chapter. Note, however, that both cases treat *Hope Natural Gas* slightly differently. Do you think that treatment is in tension, or are they both in line with *Hope Natural Gas*? Why?

2. Another interesting feature of *Duquesne Light* is the role of the Pennsylvania Consumer Advocate. The Consumer Advocate is a statutorily

created state office charged with representing consumers in PUC proceedings. Other states also have established such agencies. The idea is that PUCs historically may have been more receptive to utilities' interests than to consumer concerns, especially small consumers. Agencies such as the Consumer Advocate thus seek to give voice to the interests of ratepayers. How effective do you think this model is? Can you imagine a better approach?

3.   The issue of rate recovery for canceled nuclear power plants is not simply a historical anomaly. In 2017, SCANA Corporation, a South Carolina investor-owned utility, and Santee Cooper, a South Carolina state-owned utility, canceled the construction of two nuclear power plants due to massive cost overruns that also led to the bankruptcy of Westinghouse Corporation. Soon after, SCANA proposed to the South Carolina Public Service Commission that it recover $4.9 billion from customers over a 60-year period. SCANA argued that, by law, it was entitled to recover its prudent investments. Amid a flurry of lawsuits brought by ratepayers and investors, Santee's customers sued the utility and received a $520 million settlement for the overcharge. *See* Avery G. Wilks & Andrew Brown, *Judge Approves Santee Cooper Ratepayer Settlement Over Failed VC Summer Nuclear Plant*, THE POST AND COURIER (Nov. 20, 2020); Avery G. Wilks & Andrew Brown, *3 Years Later: How the Fallout from SC's $9 Billion Nuclear Fiasco Continues*, THE POST AND COURIER (Jul. 31, 2020). These events also led to criminal charges for fraud against former SCANA and Westinghouse executives. *See, e.g.,* Lydia Beyoud, *Ex-Westinghouse Exec Charged with Fraud Over Nixed Nuclear Plant*, BLOOMBERG LAW (Aug. 19, 2021).

4.   The early retirement of coal plants also has been the focus of policy debates over stranded costs this century. Because coal-fired power plants are now generally more expensive than natural gas and renewable energy facilities, utilities are retiring coal plants years earlier than originally planned. For example, in 2018, Wisconsin's largest utility, We Energies, shut down its 1.2 GW coal-fired Pleasant Prairie plant years before the remaining balance on the plant would be repaid. One estimate showed that the recovery of stranded costs would cost ratepayers about $1 billion over 20 years. Jeffrey Tomich, *"Stranded Costs" Mount as Coal Vanishes from the Grid*, ENERGYWIRE (May 29, 2019). Consumers, with the support of the Citizens Utility Board of Wisconsin (CUB), a utility watchdog, argued against the recovery. The parties reached a settlement in which the company was allowed to continue earning a return on about $151 million of its investment (as compared to the utility's requested amount of $646 million of capital plus $220 million in profits). Chris Hubbuch, *PSC Approves Refinancing of Shuttered Coal Plant but Warns Strategy Not "A Template,"* WIS. STATE J. (Nov. 1, 2019); *see also* RON LEHR & MIKE O'BOYLE, DEPRECIATION AND EARLY PLANT RETIREMENT (Dec. 2018). How should regulators balance the interests of electric customers and utilities when presented with these challenges? When a facility like Pleasant Prairie was built, few would have predicted that coal would diminish in the electricity landscape so quickly. Should this matter? How should the costs of the clean energy transition be partitioned across parties? *See, e.g.,* Emma Penrod, *Push*

*for Green Energy Could Strand More than $68B in Coal and Gas Assets, S&P
Says*, UTIL. DIVE (Aug. 9, 2021).

5.   More recently, studies have shown that coal plant retirements coupled
with investments in renewable energy, natural gas, energy efficiency, and
demand management can benefit both customers and investors, resulting in
billions of dollars of savings. For instance, in 2021, Consumers Energy in
Michigan sought approval from the state commission to retire several coal-
fired power plants up to fifteen years sooner than scheduled. The utility
planned to replace the plants' output with the purchase of existing natural gas
plants and investments in renewable energy, energy efficiency, and demand
management, with an estimated savings to electricity customers of $650
million through 2040. Jeffrey Tomich, *Mich. Utility to Quit Coal by 2025, Buy
Natural Gas Plants*, ENERGYWIRE (June 24, 2025); *see* PAUL BODNAR ET AL.,
HOW TO RETIRE EARLY: MAKING ACCELERATED COAL PHASEOUT FEASIBLE AND
JUST 14 (2020). Does that change your answers to the questions posed above?
Why or why not? Even if electric customers, utilities, and their investors are
not financially impacted by coal plant closures, are there other stakeholders
who might be?

6.   Both the majority and the dissent in *Jersey Central III* discuss *Market
Street Ry. v. Railroad Comm'n of Cal.*, 324 U.S. 548 (1945). In that case,
regulators reduced streetcar passenger fares from $0.07 to $0.06, with the
intent that a rate reduction would stimulate passenger traffic. The streetcar
company complained that the rate was unconstitutionally confiscatory. The
Supreme Court, however, characterized the situation as reviewing an "ailing
unit of a generally sick industry." The Court referenced *Hope Natural Gas* and
emphasized that, while a regulated business is allowed to earn a return, there
is no guarantee that it makes a profit: "The due process clause has been applied
to prevent governmental destruction of existing economic values. It has not
and cannot be applied to ensure values or to restore values that have been lost
by the operation of economic forces." In short, the Court recognized that while
the property owner has an interest in continuing its business, government
cannot guarantee its profitability; some industries will decline, and some
businesses will fail. If the rate reflects a fair return on the capital investment,
it is constitutional. How might you apply this analysis to uncompetitive coal
plants in the present day?

7.   In his *Jersey Central III* concurrence, Judge Starr noted that the used and
useful test can have harsh consequences for utilities. In particular, the need
for long-term investments means that utilities will tie up tens or even
hundreds of millions of dollars during construction. How should such
construction investments be treated? Judge Starr noted one approach used by
regulators, including FERC, called "construction work in progress" (CWIP).
Under CWIP, a regulator will judge the prudence of the investment and allow
some of that investment to be placed into the rate base. The idea is to afford
shareholders a return on investment during construction. The second approach
is known as an "allowance for funds used during construction" (AFUDC). The
argument against CWIP is that ratepayers pay for an investment but

meanwhile do not receive electricity in return. AFUDC operates differently. Instead of including investment in the rate base during construction, AFUDC calculates the financing costs incurred during the construction process and adds it to the cost of the total investment. Once the project is completed, the costs are amortized over the life of the investment as depreciation.

8.   On remand from the D.C. Circuit, FERC reaffirmed its prior decision not to allow Jersey Central to include in its rate base the unamortized wholesale portion of its $397 million investment in the Forked River plant, based in part on the fact that only a small fraction of Jersey Central's income was subject to FERC (as opposed to state) jurisdiction. The Administrative Law Judge found that the New Jersey state commission had "exclusive jurisdiction over operations that generated 98.5% of JCPL's revenues, so it should be obvious that that agency's actions and policies had a far greater effect on JCPL's financial condition than did those of this Commission." This, the ALJ said, "demonstrates the impropriety of automatically attributing JCPL's difficulties to this Commission's rate order alone." It also found that "the revenues available to JCPL after summary disposition were only 4.2% lower than JCPL's originally proposed revenues and, because of JCPL's voluntary settlement reductions, higher than its potential recovery if it were now to prevail on the summary disposition issue in this proceeding." *Jersey Central Power & Light Co.*, 49 FERC ¶ 63,004 (1989). Are you convinced? If taken to its logical end, what is its impact on how and when utilities can raise *Hope Natural Gas* claims in FERC proceedings? FERC summarily affirmed this decision. *See Jersey Central Power & Light Co.*, 49 FERC ¶ 61,338 (1989).

2. ALTERNATIVES TO COST-OF-SERVICE RATEMAKING

As detailed above, after utilities moved out of an expansion mode, PUCs began looking for alternatives to cost-of-service ratemaking, in part to encourage conservation. The current energy transition is causing PUCs to rethink their electricity systems and their regulations, including ratemaking. Two initiatives stand out. First, PUCs are establishing new ratemaking principles in addition to the five discussed: capital attraction, reasonable rates, efficiency, demand control, and income transfer. Second, PUCs are investigating new rate designs.

a. New Ratemaking Principles

In 2014, New Hampshire, like other states, began examining its electricity distribution system. N.H. OFFICE OF ENERGY AND PLANNING, 10-YEAR STATE ENERGY STRATEGY (Sept. 2014). The following year, the legislature ordered the New Hampshire PUC to investigate grid modernization. The PUC, in turn, published guidance in 2020 detailing its plans for the future of the state's electricity system. The excerpt below discusses the investigation and the rate design recommendations.

ELECTRIC DISTRIBUTION UTILITIES: GUIDANCE
ON UTILITY DISTRIBUTION SYSTEM PLANNING AND
ORDER REQUIRING CONTINUED INVESTIGATION

IR 15–296, Order No. 26,358, 2020 WL 3077501 (N.H.P.U.C., May 22, 2020)

I. NEED FOR REFORM AND PATH FORWARD

New England's energy landscape has changed dramatically in recent years. Restructured electricity markets have led to a regional generation profile that has lowered the cost of energy supply and reduced carbon emissions. While the region has seen energy costs and emissions decline, costs and rates associated with the transmission and distribution systems have continued to rise. That increase in rates is the result of a combination of limited sales growth, declining system productivity, and a century-old regulatory structure that encourages investment in capital assets and focuses on commodity sales rather than rewarding efficiency and performance.

At the same time, rapid technological advances are creating opportunities to enhance grid reliability and resilience, capture efficiencies, and improve customer services. The growth of distributed energy resources, including energy efficiency, demand response, distributed generation, electric vehicles, and energy storage, is changing how customers expect to interact with their utility. Advanced technologies have the potential to save customers money, reduce emissions, and enable flexible energy services.

In light of those trends, it is incumbent on the Commission to re-align the utility planning and investment process, as well as compensation methods, to ensure that customers of regulated utilities continue to receive safe, adequate, and reliable service at just and reasonable rates. . . .

[Staff Recommended Rate Principles]

Staff embraced the rate design principles set forth in the Working Group Report, which suggested rates should: (1) provide fair compensation to utilities and consumers; (2) provide appropriate and efficient price signals; (3) incentivize customers to use electricity wisely and to invest in cost-effective DERs; (4) maximize consumer choice and control and protect vulnerable customers; and (5) reflect cost causation principles. . . .

[The Commission then adopted the following principles.]

Rate Design Principles. In our Order on Scope and Process, we required that any rate design recommendations of the grid modernization working group must be consistent with the principles of rate design that this Commission has historically supported, including efficiency, equity, simplicity, continuity, and revenue sufficiency. We adopt the Working Group recommendations cited in the Staff Report as consistent with the Commission's approach to rate design.

Customer Charges. We find that customer charges should only be used to recover customer-related costs as identified in a cost of service study. Such costs include the cost of the ratepayer-funded investments required to serve the customer, which in the Commission's experience for residential customers are typically identified as the service drop, the portion of the meter directly related to billing for usage, and the costs of billing and collection.

Peak-Coincident Demand Charges. We find that if demand charges are meant to inform recovery of distribution system costs for commercial and industrial customers, they should be coincident with the distribution system peak. Such an approach should only be implemented if peak coincident demand charge can be cost-effectively incorporated into company metering and billing systems.

Investment-Specific Rate Designs. [Some parties] supported the consensus on rate design issues in the Staff Memorandum with the caveat that, in order to maximize ratepayer benefits and stimulate private investment in DERs, certain investments must be paired with new rates that are a departure from current rate designs. We agree that certain investments may need to be paired with new rate designs in order to maximize customer benefits. For example, customer benefits associated with advanced metering functionality would likely only be maximized if rate designs meant to encourage reductions in demand coincident with system peak are adopted. We find that such pairings are more properly evaluated based on a full review of the facts and circumstances surrounding a specific investment or group of investments when proposed.

Cost-Allocation and Marginal Benefit. The [Office of Consumer Advocate] suggested that, in cases where the incremental benefits accrue disproportionately to a given class of customers, the Commission could direct a utility to allocate and recover the costs of such investments based on an apportionment of marginal benefits justifying the individual investment, rather than the embedded and marginal costs of the overall system. While consistent with the rate design principles of cost causation and equity, this would be a major deviation from the Commission's currently accepted practices of cost allocation and rate design. . . .

NOTES AND QUESTIONS

1.   How would the above rate principles apply to proposals for: (1) net metering; (2) utility pilot projects for EV charging; (3) investing in utility-scale solar or wind farms; (4) energy subsidies for low-income consumers; or (5) clean electricity? How different would use of these principles be from a more traditional approach?

2.   Another approach to rate setting is to offer customers a menu of choices. For example, a utility may offer the traditional option: a base rate, a demand charge to cover fixed costs, and an energy charge for electricity consumed. Or a utility may offer something different, for instance: a flat rate per month, without breaking down the charges; an upcharge if the customer wants 100% renewable power; a simple rate per kWh; or special charges for installing DERs or EV charging capabilities. If you were the consumer, which rate would you prefer? Why?

3.   Many of the new rates have the potential to raise customer costs. Marginal cost pricing, for example, will likely raise rates—at least some of the time— because if the rate is based on the next unit produced rather than historic costs, higher cost electricity will be charged to customers. The idea is that all rates rise in the short term, but in the long-term, energy efficiency and reduced demand will lower a customer's overall bill.

4.   Another issue to consider is known as the "rebound effect." To the extent that electricity rates fall, usage should increase. With an increase of usage, rates may also rise. This is particularly true as we try to electrify everything as part of the clean energy transition. *See* SAUL GRIFFITH, SAM CALISCH & LAURA FRASER, REWIRING AMERICA: A HANDBOOK FOR WINNING THE CLIMATE FIGHT (2020). Similarly, if the price of oil and natural gas declines and marginal pricing governs rates, consumption will rise. What do these economic laws tell us about how rates should be designed?

5.   Another approach to new rate designs is called "value stack pricing," which is an itemization of the different components of electricity service: (1) the value of energy consumed; (2) the capacity value of the system; (3) environmental values based on a clean energy standard; and (4) a "demand reduction value" based largely on the utility's marginal cost of service. The intent is to provide a more precise value of DERs while attempting to meet the need for predictable prices. *New Rate Revamp for Distributed Energy Resources (DERs)*, ENERGYWATCH (Mar. 13, 2017). The New York PSC adopted value stack pricing and discontinued its net metering regulations to promote DERs. *In the Matter of the Value of Distributed Energy Resources*, 2020 WL 4059532 (N.Y.P.S.C., July 16, 2020); *see also* N.Y. PUB. SERV. COMM'N, STAFF WHITEPAPER ON RATE DESIGN FOR MASS MARKET NET METERING SUCCESSOR TARIFF, Case No. 15–E–0751, Matter No. 17–01277 (Dec. 2019).

6.   Additionally, new rate designs should pay attention to (1) equitable cost allocation between shareholders and ratepayers; (2) compensation to customers for benefits they may provide, such as storage and balancing; (3) charging customers for the use of the grid; and (4) sending accurate price signals to end users for efficient use of electricity. Coley Girouard, *Rate Design for a DER Future: Designing Rates to Better Integrate and Value Distributed Energy Resources*, UTIL. DIVE (Feb. 12, 2018).

b. New Rate Designs

Rate principles are only guides for PUCs. The agencies must operationalize the principles through particular cases. The excerpt below from the Pennsylvania Public Utilities Commission overviews many of the benefits and drawbacks of alternatives to cost-of service ratemaking. The Commission issued the policy statement against the background of a state statute enacted in 2008—Act 129—that requires Pennsylvania's electric utilities "to develop energy efficiency and conservation (EE&C) plans and adopt other methods of reducing the amount of electricity consumed by customers." *See Energy Efficiency & Conservation*, Pa. Pub. Util. Comm'n. As you read the excerpt, consider the parties' positions—and what they may gain or lose by a departure from cost-of-service rates.

FIXED UTILITY DISTRIBUTION RATES POLICY STATEMENT
Docket No. M–2015–2518883, 2018 WL 2717449 (Pa. P.U.C., May 3, 2018)

BY THE COMMISSION:

On March 3, 2016, the Pennsylvania Public Utility Commission (Commission) held an *en banc* hearing to seek information from interested stakeholders on the efficacy and appropriateness of alternatives to traditional ratemaking principles for public utilities. Invited parties, including researchers, energy companies and consumer advocates testified before the Commission, giving views on whether alternative rate methodologies can encourage energy utilities to better implement energy efficiency and conservation (EE&C) programs, are just and reasonable and in the public interest, and are cost-effective. . . .

A. ALTERNATIVE RATE METHODOLOGIES

1. Revenue Decoupling

Decoupling mechanisms introduce a process of recovering authorized revenues between base rate cases and explicitly breaking the link between revenues and sales. Decoupling makes a utility theoretically indifferent to energy efficiency and conservation by removing the throughput incentive. Decoupling involves two separate steps. First, there is a ratemaking proceeding for determining the amount of revenues the utility is authorized to collect. Second, there is a decoupling mechanism to set an appropriate rate to ensure collection of the authorized revenue. There are three ways in which allowed revenues can be determined:

- Revenue Cap Decoupling: With revenue cap decoupling, the authorized revenues are typically set in a base rate case and then held constant until the next base rate case.

- Inflation and Productivity Decoupling: With inflation and productivity decoupling, the authorized revenues are adjusted between base rate cases, based on assumed known changes in inflation and company productivity. Inflation is often based on recognized government published indexes, such as the consumer price index.

- Revenue Per Customer (RPC) Decoupling: With RPC decoupling, the average revenue per customer for each volumetric rate is computed at the end of the base rate case. In subsequent periods between base rate cases, authorized revenues are derived by multiplying the actual number of customers served by the RPC value. The underlying premise for RPC decoupling is that, between rate cases, a utility's underlying cost structure is driven primarily by changes in the number of customers served. The utility is likely to require smaller rate increases in base rate cases because RPC increases occur more frequently, base rate case increases may be simpler to implement, and through the interim recalibration of revenues on a monthly basis through RPC increases, the risk of revenue recovery related to changes in weather between rate cases can be reduced or eliminated. . . .

Several utilities and stakeholders that filed comments support revenue decoupling in one form or another, while most consumer advocates do not. [PECO Energy Company (PECO)] states that its preferred approach is the revenue per customer decoupling model for all but very large customers and certain street lighting customers. PECO states that this model would mitigate revenue losses from energy efficiency and DERs but notes that it could exacerbate intra-class cost shifting, particularly in the residential class due to distributed energy resources. To address this intra-class cost shifting PECO states that it would move its fixed charge to be fully cost based and establish a separate rate class for net metered residential customers. [PPL Electric Utilities Corp. (PPL)] states that in conjunction with a multi-year rate plan, its preferred method is full revenue decoupling as it is the most appropriate method to encourage DERs and EE&C measures. PPL asserts that under its method, it will have assurance that its capital investments will be recovered, while providing a limit on revenues, will reduce rate case frequency and reduce regulation related costs and maintains incentives for EE&C measures and DERs. . . .

The other commenters that support revenue decoupling are [Natural Resources Defense Council (NRDC)], [Advanced Energy Economy (AEE)], [Keystone Energy Efficiency Alliance (KEEA)] and [American Council for an Energy-Efficient Economy (ACEEE)]. NRDC states that the Commission should clearly state a willingness to implement decoupling in connection with Act 129 lost revenues through a deferral mechanism, with recovery to be made in a subsequent base rate proceeding. . . . NRDC also states that the process should include a thorough review of potential rate and bill impacts and consider impacts on a wide variety of households, including low-usage customers, low-income customers, renters and customers with inelastic usage due to health needs. AEE states that revenue decoupling is an important way to remove financial disincentives by removing the threat of lowered revenue. . . .

Several commenters, however, do not support revenue decoupling. [Office of Consumer Advocate (OCA)] states that low to moderate income households that are unable to participate in energy efficiency programs for various reasons would bear the brunt of the increases caused by revenue decoupling. . . .

In addition to OCA, the [large industrial customers (Industrials)] assert that revenue decoupling cannot be implemented for several reasons. Industrials assert that decoupling is illegal under the current statutory framework, it constitutes single-issue ratemaking, prevents the Commission from ensuring that rates are just and reasonable, . . .

We agree that revenue decoupling may result in just and reasonable rates for fixed utilities in certain forms and in certain circumstances, so long as the revenue decoupling plan includes appropriate consumer safeguards. Among the consumer protections that could be considered are (1) a revenue adjustment cap (to limit the consumer's rate adjustment exposure) and (2) a reduced return on equity (to reflect possible reduced business risk for the utility). We recognize that revenue decoupling . . . removes the throughput incentive in such a way that may promote adoption of cost-effective efficiency and conservation measures.

At the same time, we note that revenue decoupling may not be appropriate, may not result in just and reasonable rates, or may not be authorized by the Public Utility Code for certain fixed utilities in certain circumstances. We recognize that if done inappropriately, revenue decoupling may adversely impact customers who, due to personal circumstances, are unable to take advantage of efficiency or conservation measures to reduce their consumption. . . .

3. Straight Fixed/Variable (SFV) Pricing

As a matter of rate design theory, SFV is based on the fact that most, if not all, of the utility's distribution system costs may be fixed in the short run and therefore customers should pay for those costs through fixed charges on their bills that reflect the amount of fixed costs of the distribution system for each customer class. The main advantage of utilizing SFV pricing is the revenue certainty for the utility. The utility is assured recovery of its allowed revenues through higher fixed charges and lower volume-based charges. Customers will have lower variations in their monthly electric bill because more charges are fixed, and bills will vary less due to variations in usage.

While SFV has the effect of decoupling the utility's earnings from consumption, it also has the effect of decoupling the customer's usage from the bill as to the fixed costs of the utility's distribution system. SFV may diminish the value of customer usage reduction methods, such as energy efficiency and distributed generation, as some of the charges are fixed. High fixed charges may also challenge low-income customers. . . .

[Duquesne Light Company (Duquense)] states that while it supports continuing use of cost trackers as well as the distribution system improvement charge (DSIC) and is considering new methodologies, including select performance incentives, revenue normalization adjustment clauses and formulaic approaches, in the interim, it supports a move toward more SFV pricing. . . .

OCA asserts that SFV with high fixed charges often involves an expanded definition of fixed costs to the point where it severs the relationship between usage and the embedded costs of the utility system, becomes contrary to effective EE&C efforts and is contrary to prior Commission decisions. . . . AEE states that they are particularly concerned about the risk of decoupling bills from consumption as a disincentive to efficient use of electricity. ACEEE asserts that SFV is not cost based and sends very poor price signals to customers to conserve electricity that would drive higher utility costs due to increased infrastructure investments to meet the higher demand.

The Commission recognizes that SFV will reduce the price signals to customers in regard to the actual consumption of supply, particularly in those situations where a utility's fixed costs make up a significant portion of a customer's entire bill. Alternatively, in situations where the fixed costs comprise a relatively small part of a customer's total bill, SFV will have little impact on a customer's incentive to employ efficiency measures and more appropriately aligns the utility's costs with the long-term causes of those costs. However, to the extent that fixed costs are used to amplify the price signals for consumption of supply, this is, in economic terms, an artificially high price signal because the costs of the distribution system, in the short run, are fixed and do not vary by day or by month. . . .

Furthermore, we agree with the parties that note that SFV provides utilities with greater revenue stability and reduces the disincentives for utilities to promote efficiency and conservation measures. Regarding impacts on high usage customers and low-income customers, the Commission again recognizes that in certain circumstances, these customers may be negatively impacted, but also recognize that these impacts may vary by utility and may be appropriately mitigated by other programs, such as the Low-Income Usage Reduction Program (LIURP), the Low-Income Heating Assistance Program (LIHEAP) and utility consumer assistance programs (CAPs). . . .

7.   DSM Performance Incentive Mechanism

As part of the *en banc* hearing, several witnesses and commentators suggested that in order to remove barriers for utilities to promote EE&C programs, both revenue decoupling and performance incentive mechanisms should be implemented together. . . .

FirstEnergy states that establishing true performance incentive mechanisms for exceeding goals would better align the Commission's public policy goals relative to EE&C performance with an EDC's operating performance, as well as the utility's revenue. FirstEnergy advocates for a shared savings approach to incentivize utilities to exceed their statutorily-mandated EE&C reduction goals. . . .

NRDC asserts that a well-designed PIM would not only provide more incentive for EDCs to spend up to their Act 129 budgets and achieve more cost-effective energy savings; it would also provide additional efficiency measures and other assistance to low-income consumers, alleviating the significant energy burdens that they face. AEE supports implementing broad PIMs that tie designated financial rewards and penalties to specific performance metrics. AEE states that PIMs shift the focus of the utility from static cost minimization to enhancement of value as utilities are incented to improve performance. . . .

As stated previously, we are not adopting, nor precluding, any particular rate methodology or performance incentive in this proceeding. Under the proposed policy statement, any utility proposing a rate plan that includes performance incentives will need to demonstrate, in addition to the Commission's authority to approve it, that the proposed rate plan including performance incentives does not discourage efficiency measures, appropriately aligns costs in accordance with cost causation principles, and does not inappropriately impact low-income customers or appropriately mitigates such impacts, among other things. . . .

[The commission then set forth its policy statement, which included a list of factors to guide future utility proposals reflective of the discussion in the excerpt above.—Eds.]

NOTES AND QUESTIONS

1.   Evaluate the various parties that favored and disfavored decoupling above. Did any positions surprise you? Why? For further discussion of various rate designs, see JOSEPH P. TOMAIN, CLEAN POWER POLITICS: THE DEMOCRATIZATION OF ENERGY 167–72 (2017); JANINE MIGDEN-OSTRANDER & RICH SEDANO, REGULATORY ASSISTANCE PROJECT, DECOUPLING DESIGN: CUSTOMIZING REVENUE REGULATION TO YOUR STATE'S PRIORITIES (Nov. 2016).

2.   A key focus of the excerpt is the potential adverse effects on low-income utility customers. What overarching principles of utility rate design require this emphasis? Notably, during the COVID-19 pandemic, state commissions around the country enacted emergency orders and reviewed existing policies to address the "energy burden" on residential utility customers—the percentage of monthly income spent on home energy costs. Studies show there are significant racial disparities in energy burdens. For instance, Black and Latinx households face, respectively, a 64 percent and a 24 percent higher energy burden than white households. Moreover, during the summer of 2020, "20% of African-American households and nearly 33% of Hispanic households reported that they could not afford their energy bills, compared to 12% of White respondents." COLLETTE BRASHEARS ET AL., INITIATIVE FOR ENERGY JUSTICE, UTILITY SHUT-OFFS AND THE COVID-19 PANDEMIC 2 (Dec. 2020).

3.   In recent years, communities of color and their advocates have urged state commissions, utilities, and policymakers to incorporate principles of "energy justice" into their actions. Energy justice expresses the idea that "all individuals should have access to energy that is affordable, safe, sustainable and able to sustain a decent lifestyle, as well as the opportunity to participate in and lead energy decision-making processes with the authority to make change." Sanya Carley & David M. Konisky, *The Justice and Equity Implications of the Clean Energy Transition*, 5 NATURE ENERGY 569, 570 (Aug. 2020). Without a focus on these principles, Professor Shalanda Baker has argued that even well-meaning utility programs designed to support a clean energy transition may still leave people of color without a voice in energy choices that impact their communities. *See* SHALANDA BAKER, REVOLUTIONARY POWER (2021); Shalanda Baker, *Anti-Resilience: A Roadmap for Transformational Justice Within the Energy System*, 54 HARV. CIVIL RIGHTS-CIVIL LIBERTIES L. REV. 1, 29 (2019). What provisions of the *Fixed Utility Distribution Rates Policy Statement* can be used to address both energy burden disparities and the ideal of energy justice in future ratemaking proceedings?

4.   The Pennsylvania Commission discusses the benefits and drawbacks of using "performance incentive mechanisms" to compensate utilities as an alternative to cost-of-service ratemaking. In 2017, a major utility in the Netherlands, Eneco, started moving from selling energy as a commodity to energy as a "service." The latter includes a range of features, such as EV charging units, solar panel repair services, smart meters, and battery storage services. *See* Stanley Reed, *Dutch Utility Bets Its Future on an Unusual Strategy: Selling Less Power*, N.Y. TIMES (Aug. 18, 2017). Based on your reading, what are the tradeoffs of this approach?

5.   Another alternative the Pennsylvania Commission discusses is Straight Fixed/Variable (SFV) Pricing, where all the utility's costs claimed to be "fixed"—like distribution costs and some transmission costs—are recovered from customers as a fixed monthly charge, rather than including some of those costs on a per kWh basis as has traditionally been the case. What existing problems with utility compensation does SFV pricing address? What new problems might it create? What types of customers would be benefitted or

harmed by its use? For additional information on SFV pricing, see JIM LAZAR, REG. ASSISTANCE PROJECT, THE SPECTER OF STRAIGHT FIXED/VARIABLE RATE DESIGNS AND THE EXERCISE OF MONOPOLY POWER (Aug. 31, 2015).

6.   Decoupling differs from cost-of-service ratemaking in that it seeks to divorce revenues from the amount of electricity sold. Instead, revenues hinge on the number of customers. The regulator must choose between allowing the recovery of revenue per customer or setting a net revenue requirement and apportioning it among all customers. Under a revenue per customer approach, the utility loses income if it loses customers. A net revenue design, however, will raise rates for remaining customers as others depart the system. How does the Pennsylvania PUC address these concerns?

CHAPTER 5

ELECTRICITY REGULATION
IN TRANSITION

■ ■ ■

A. OVERVIEW

As the century turned, electricity regulation in the United States also began to change. The change was long in coming. In retrospect, it really began to unfold in the 1970s, but its full effects were not obvious until the 1990s. In the history books, 1996—when FERC issued its landmark Order No. 888[1]—may go down as the red-letter year electricity regulation began to shift to something different and new.

Several factors caused this regulatory transition, as Chapter 4 noted. First, many industries in the United States were being swept up in a wave of deregulation and market restructuring; the pivot in electricity regulation was part of this broader societal shift. Second, new competitors were entering the electricity sector, primarily in generation, which opened up power markets. Third, rate increases caused by the growing use of nuclear generation put pressure on politicians to consider electricity competition. Fourth, the rising tide of environmental regulation that emerged at the end of the 1960s and early 1970s impacted the industry—and changed how the public saw it. While providing an abundant, cheap power supply arguably was and remains the primary expectation of electric utilities, the nation's burgeoning environmental consciousness prompted growing demand for clean energy. Finally, legislative and technological innovations played a heavy role in the evolution of electricity regulation.

One of the key policy innovations that drove this change was the Public Utility Regulatory Policies Act of 1978 (PURPA), 16 U.S.C. §§ 2601 *et seq.* Passed in the wake of the oil crises of the 1970s, PURPA had many aims, but two key objectives were promoting renewable energy and fostering competition. Thus, PURPA instituted what some modern commentators have acknowledged as the predecessor to today's "feed-in tariffs." It

---

[1] Of course, the immediate precursor to Order No. 888 was the Energy Policy Act of 1992, which augmented FERC's authority to compel electricity "wheeling" over utilities' transmission systems. *See* Energy Policy Act of 1992, Pub. L. 102–486, §§ 721–722, 106 Stat. 2915, 2915–19 (1992) (codified as amended at 16 U.S.C. § 824j); *see also, e.g.,* Joseph T. Kelliher, Comment, *Pushing the Envelope: Development of Federal Electric Transmission Access Policy,* 42 AM. U. L. REV. 543 (1993); Joseph T. Kelliher & Maria Farinella, *The Changing Landscape of Federal Energy Law,* 61 ADMIN. L. REV. 611 (2009).

imposed an obligation on incumbent, vertically integrated utilities to buy power from small and renewable energy competitors. Moreover, the utilities had to buy this power at premium prices. In PURPA-speak, these competitors were called "qualifying facilities"—"QFs" for short—and the premium prices utilities paid were "avoided cost rates," or the price the utility would have had to pay to build or acquire the energy on its own.

PURPA had two immediate effects, and at least one long-term one. Right away, PURPA encouraged more renewable and cogeneration facilities to produce power, and consequently, it challenged incumbent utilities' dominance in electricity generation. This latter effect—and utilities' disdain for it—cannot be overstated. PURPA effectively sought to force utilities to support the very companies that wanted to compete with them. Moreover, the small cracks in utilities' virtual monopoly control over electricity production eventually became larger fissures. As more generators took advantage of PURPA's incentives, it became apparent that other kinds of companies could provide electricity at lower prices. Indeed, as the 1990s beckoned, many companies—some utilities but some non-utilities—started building natural gas units that were cleaner, more efficient, and more modular than the large-scale generation of the past. *See* Chapter 2. This effect became even stronger when, in the Energy Policy Act of 1992, Congress created a new type of company, exempt wholesale generators, or "EWGs," that were not subject to Public Utility Holding Company Act (PUHCA) regulation. The effect was to allow a flood of generators into the market that did not need to meet PUHCA's technology and ownership restrictions. *See, e.g.*, Jeffrey D. Watkiss & Douglas W. Smith, *The Energy Policy Act of 1992—A Watershed for Competition in the Wholesale Power Market*, 10 YALE J. ON REG. 447 (1993).

Thus, with all these factors in play, many state and federal regulators took notice and began rethinking how they approached electricity regulation.

Another important innovation for electricity was the deregulatory experience occurring more broadly in society, such as in telecommunications and aviation, and including other energy fields. As detailed in Chapter 7, restructuring in the natural gas sector, in particular, gave regulators a template they could follow for the electricity sector. In natural gas, it became clear that certain parts of the industrial cycle were more competitive than others. Natural gas production, for instance, was quite competitive, because many firms could find natural gas deposits, drill, and sell their product on the market. Shipping the natural gas, however, was not economically competitive, because the pipelines needed to send gas long distances were natural monopolies with high capital costs. Thus, wellhead gas prices were deregulated, and FERC imposed on pipeline owners an "open access" mandate to allow all gas producers to ship their fuel on a first-come, first-served basis. This fostered competition by allowing firms to compete on price for the resource itself, without the constraint of getting their product to market. Pipeline owners thus effectively became common carriers.

Electricity parallels natural gas in many ways. Like natural gas providers, electric utilities long had been vertically integrated—producing the power, sending it long distances from their generators to their customers or "load" centers, and then distributing it to those customers. Also like natural gas, PURPA and the increasing use of combined cycle units made it clear that not all parts of the electricity industry needed to be insulated from competition. On the contrary, while the transmission and distribution of electricity were arguably natural monopolies forming inherent "bottlenecks" in the system, many kinds of companies could generate electricity using a variety of resources. Thus, FERC borrowed from its natural gas restructuring playbook. It started allowing electricity producers to sell power at market rates they negotiated rather than at cost-of-service rates that FERC set. And in its landmark ruling that forever shifted how the electricity sector functions—so-called Order No. 888[2]—the Commission compelled utilities to open up their transmission lines to all comers on a first-come, first-served, nondiscriminatory basis, after meeting their native load obligations. Thus, just as in the natural gas sector, FERC began promoting electricity competition among generators by trying to ensure that competitive generation could get to market through open access electron "pipelines"—the nation's transmission grids.

Meanwhile, states also got in on the action. A number of state legislatures and PUCs ordered incumbent utilities to divest their generation assets, blowing open the initial cracks in utility dominance that PURPA had formed into vast chasms of competition. *See, e.g.*, Susan Kelly & Elise Caplan, *Time for A Day 1.5 Market: A Proposal to Reform RTO-Run Centralized Wholesale Electricity Markets*, 29 ENERGY L.J. 491, 492 (2008). Roughly fifteen to twenty jurisdictions, including the District of Columbia, required their utilities to divest their generation assets and implemented retail electricity competition of one form or another. However, as detailed later in this chapter, the rush to adopt these laws quickly stalled out after the California energy crisis of 2000 and Enron's manipulation of electricity markets in the West. Moreover, powerful IOUs in southern states opposed restructuring, with the result that states in that region, along with others in the Midwest and intermountain west, remained traditionally regulated. *See, e.g.*, Conor Harrison & Shelley Welton, *The States That Opted Out: Power, Politics, and Exceptionalism in the Quest for Electricity Deregulation in the United States South*, 79 ENERGY RES. & SOC. SCI. 102147 (2020). Today, many states that had previously adopted retail competition laws are continuing with this

---

[2]   It is not coincidental that the address of FERC's headquarters in Washington, D.C. is 888 First Street N.E.

experiment, and their success is mixed. Texas stands out as the state where retail competition has perhaps been most influential.

Finally, growing attention to climate change unquestionably altered how regulators saw electricity. While various proposals for climate regulation were introduced (but failed to pass) in Congress, states stepped into the breach and started forging solutions on their own. Because of the industry's heavy reliance on fossil fuels, many of these solutions focused on electricity. *See, e.g.*, David E. Adelman & Kirsten H. Engel, *Reorienting State Climate Change Policies to Induce Technological Change*, 50 ARIZ. L. REV. 835, 862–63 (2008).

As the century turned, then, regulation of the electricity sector was in full transition. This transition consisted of three key pivots:

1. *Competition.* Perhaps most significantly, and certainly most pervasively, the electricity industry became a more competitive one, at least at the wholesale level. Regulation reflected—and encouraged—this shift. Thus, the prevalence of market-based rather than cost-based ratemaking abounded. Transmission lines became treated as a kind of hybrid public-private resource that had to be shared among the industry. And many consumers gained the power to choose where their electricity comes from.

2. *Coordination.* The electricity sector became more coordinated in many ways. Like the shift to competition, this also was a slowly unfolding process. From electricity's early days, bordering utilities long had coordinated with each other. Eventually, groups of neighboring utilities, especially in geographically smaller states, formed "power pools," or "tight power pools," that operated in sync with each other. These pools gave utilities a way to reduce operating costs by leveraging low-cost baseload units regardless of ownership, allowing them to defer running higher-cost peaking units except in very high demand periods. The shift at the end of the century, then, was as much a regulatory change as a physical one. FERC encouraged power pools to cede operation of their transmission systems to an independent party—known as "independent system operators" (ISOs) or "regional transmission organizations" (RTOs)—who would also run power markets in the region.[3] This facilitated both competition and coordination. In addition, FERC sought and obtained limited transmission siting authority in the Energy

---

[3] In the run-up to its ill-fated Order No. 2000, FERC tried to force utilities to join RTOs, but this move stalled under vehement political resistance from utilities in the Southeast and West. *See, e.g.*, John S. Moot, *Economic Theories of Regulation and Electricity Restructuring*, 25 ENERGY L.J. 273 (2004). Nevertheless, many RTOs have continued to expand their footprints.

Policy Act of 2005, and the same statute mandated formation of an Electric Reliability Organization (ERO) that would ensure utilities plan and run their systems reliably. Finally, FERC's Order No. 1000, issued in 2011 and upheld by the D.C. Circuit in 2014, sought to spur greater transmission planning and coordination among utilities. In short, in many ways, electricity regulation at the beginning of the 21st century sought to encourage utilities to work together.

3. *Clean energy.* Many regulatory innovations sought to imbue energy regulation with more environmental goals. At a high level, this might be seen as part of an increasing convergence of energy law and environmental law—fields that historically have been divorced from each other.[4] More specifically, the electricity sector saw the rapid emergence of laws like state renewable portfolio standards (RPSs) and their successors, clean energy standards (CESs), that, in the absence of federal action on climate change, mandated greater use of renewable resources in electricity production; innovations in ratemaking aimed at encouraging efficiency; provisions giving preferred transmission access for clean fuels; and a host of other measures encouraging electricity to become "greener."

This chapter picks up where Chapter 4 left off. Building on the base of historical electricity regulation, we focus here on how that regulation is changing. We do so in three sections, each of which pulls on different strands of the competition-coordination-clean energy transition. The first addresses rate regulation; the second, transmission regulation; and the third, transitions in electricity supply and the emerging shift toward renewable energy, which implicates federalism.

B. ELECTRICITY RATEMAKING IN TRANSITION

The changes over the last decades in how electricity rates are regulated can be divided into two broad categories. First, ratemaking changes occurred at the wholesale level, regulated by FERC. Second, there was a less dramatic shift in the regulation of electricity in a number of states. We address each of these two areas in this section. In addition, there have been other ratemaking innovations over time, particularly rate *design*

---

[4] *See* Todd S. Aagaard, *Energy-Environment Policy Alignments*, 90 WASH. L. REV. 1517 (2015); Lincoln L. Davies, *Alternative Energy and the Energy-Environment Disconnect*, 46 IDAHO L. REV. 473 (2010); Jody Freeman, *The Uncomfortable Convergence of Energy and Environmental Law*, 41 HARV. ENV'T L. REV. 339 (2017); Alexandra B. Klass, *Climate Change and the Convergence of Environmental and Energy Law*, 24 FORDHAM ENV'T L. REV. 180 (2013); Amy J. Wildermuth, *The Next Step: The Integration of Energy Law and Environmental Law*, 31 UTAH ENV'T L. REV. 369 (2011).

changes such as rate decoupling and declining block rates, which were highlighted briefly in Chapter 4.

1. WHOLESALE COMPETITION: MARKET-BASED RATES

The idea behind market-based rates is simple. Its implementation is much more difficult. The theory is this: Using actual competition should be more effective and efficient than expert regulators trying to approximate the outcome of a competitive, well-functioning market.

Cost-of-service rates try to *replicate* the outcome a competitive market would produce, by examining utilities' costs, whether those costs were prudently accrued, how they benefit customers, and then allowing the company to earn a "reasonable" return on its investment. As Chapter 4 details, that "reasonable" return should be neither too high nor too low—it should not gouge customers, but it should allow the company to attract capital and provide reliable service. The company's return on investment, in short, should be comparable to what a company operating in a fully competitive market might make.

There are several problems inherent in this cost-of-service approach. It relies on regulators to understand what the utility is doing and then accurately approximate the outcome of a competitive market that does not exist. This means that there are administrative costs both for the government and for utilities. Cost-of-service ratemaking is a time-intensive process. In fact, many rate cases can take years, and the ensuing litigation can easily last a decade. *See, e.g., Pub. Serv. Co. of New Mexico v. FERC*, 832 F.2d 1201 (10th Cir. 1987).[5] There is also the likelihood that government bureaucrats will not accurately replicate the price a competitive market would have set. This may be because of simple error, or because government employees by definition cannot have the intimate knowledge of an industry that firms themselves do, or because firms do not always have an incentive to give regulators complete information. Moreover, the very notion of cost-of-service ratemaking contemplates that utilities will recover all of their prudently incurred costs, plus a reasonable return. Thus, even if regulators can accurately determine what a reasonable, competitive return should be, the system includes a built-in bias allowing for the recovery of high-cost generation—something a truly competitive market seeks to drive out.

This chink in the cost-of-service system bears out in multiple ways for electricity. Regulators face political pressure to keep electricity prices down, and utilities have a natural incentive to maximize their profits. This creates a tension that makes cost-of-service ratemaking inherently messy.

---

[5] Underscoring the point, former FERC Commissioner Charles Stalon reportedly once told a member of his staff, "FERC doesn't set rates. It sets refunds."

It is also a reason why, some observe, utilities overbuilt generation in the latter half of the 20th century. *See, e.g.,* Joseph P. Tomain, *networkindustries.gov.reg,* 48 U. KAN. L. REV. 829, 846 (2000); Susan D. Fendell, *Public Ownership of Public Utilities: Have Stockholders Outlived Their Useful Economic Lives?,* 43 OHIO ST. L.J. 821, 828 (1982). Not only did utilities misestimate that electricity demand would continue to grow as rapidly as it had in the past, cost-of-service ratemaking encouraged them to keep building at a quick pace because the rate of return is calculated based on their aggregate amount of investment.

Market-based ratemaking seeks to avoid these problems. It suggests that rather than replicating the price a competitive market would establish, the *market itself* should *set* the price. To do this, a number of conditions have to be met. Everyone knows that the theoretical, perfectly competitive market used in economics textbooks does not exist; all markets have some imperfections. But a market used to set electricity prices must be sufficiently, or "functionally," competitive such that the public can have confidence that market-based rates do not result in a worse—and, hopefully, afford a better—outcome than cost-of-service rates. *See, e.g.,* G. William Stafford, *Electric Wholesale Power Sales at Market-Based Rates,* 12 ENERGY L.J. 291, 291 (1991). The idea has merit in part because many new competitors in electricity generation lack native load "rate bases" that can cover their risks, so the market should send a strong signal to them whether to even take the chance of building a power plant.

Regulation of market-based rates thus focuses not on the costs that a firm has actually incurred, but rather, on the firm's share of ownership in the market. If the market works properly, the price it sets should be an efficient one. Markets function when they have enough competitors, if there are not barriers to entry, and if no party can exercise market power (*i.e.,* set and sustain prices above competitive levels). When these conditions exist, the market price should be more efficient than one set using administratively established cost-of-service rates.

Today, at the wholesale level, FERC's market-based rate rules seek to do just this. FERC's rules aim to ensure that only parties which lack market power can charge market-based rates. Before allowing those parties to use market-based pricing, FERC analyzes how much of the market the party controls, to make sure there is enough competition. Contracts entered into at market-based prices also must be between non-affiliated entities, *i.e.,* arms-length transactions that are not "sweetheart deals." And the very purpose of Order No. 888 was to open up one area where utilities long held market power—transmission—so that the competitive playing field would be level.

As market-based rates became more prevalent, however, a few other issues emerged. One was whether FERC's reliance on market-based rates satisfied the "just and reasonable" and "filed rate" mandates of the Federal Power Act. Another was how FERC would design and apply its market-based rate test to ensure that market-based rates are fair. A third was what to do when parties manipulated market prices, despite regulators' best efforts to keep market-based prices fair. The remainder of this section addresses these issues.

a.   Challenges to Competitively Set Electricity Rates

Resistance to change in electricity ratemaking came from many angles. FERC built its model of competition on the backbone of Order No. 888. That rule was challenged on the ground that FERC exceeded its statutory authority by forcing utilities to share their transmission lines. The D.C. Circuit and then the U.S. Supreme Court rejected this challenge, culminating in the *New York v. FERC* decision excerpted in Chapter 1.

But opponents did not stop there. They also argued that using market-based rates to set electricity prices violated the Federal Power Act's mandate that all rates be filed, because the rate could not be known until parties agreed on it. Further, they asserted that market-based rates were an abdication of FERC's duty to ensure the justness and reasonableness of prices, because under a market-based rate regime FERC does not examine every contract for electricity sales—*ex ante* or individually.

These arguments were not just theory. They often arose from market failures with real monetary impacts. Nonetheless, the courts repeatedly have rejected these claims. As you read the following case, consider a fundamental question at the core of the cost-of-service versus market-based rate debate: What is more likely to guarantee fair power prices— neutral regulators doing their best, or a self-interested market that neutral regulators attempt to closely monitor?

PUBLIC CITIZEN V. FERC

7 F.4th 1177 (D.C. Cir. 2021)

MILLETT, CIRCUIT JUDGE.

This case is about the price of wholesale electricity—electricity sold from, for example, a power plant to a consumer-serving utility company. More precisely, this case concerns sales of capacity, which is typically a commitment by a power plant to provide electricity to a utility in the future. In April 2015, an auction for electrical capacity in Illinois produced a striking result. Capacity in neighboring regions (from Louisiana up to Minnesota) uniformly sold for less than $3.50 per megawatt-day. But in a region covering much of Illinois, the auction resulted in capacity prices of $150 per megawatt-day—more than 40 times the price in those neighboring regions and a nearly ninefold increase from the prior year's price of $16.75. . . .

I

A

Since the end of the last century, electricity production has been increasingly characterized by competitive markets. In light of that trend, Congress added a new provision to the Federal Power Act in 2005, which is referred to as Section 222. Entitled "Prohibition of energy market manipulation[,]" Section 222 makes it unlawful for any entity "to use or employ, in connection with the purchase or sale of electric energy or the purchase or sale of transmission services subject to the jurisdiction of the Commission, any manipulative or deceptive device or contrivance" in contravention of Commission rules. Section 222, though, does not "create a private right of action." Instead, enforcement of the prohibition on manipulation is assigned exclusively to the Commission. Nonetheless, private persons may bring allegations of market manipulation to the attention of the Commission by filing a complaint under Section 306 . . . .

Implementing the 2005 Act, the Commission has defined market manipulation more precisely, modeling it on the Securities Exchange Act's anti-manipulation provisions. In that way, the prohibition "is not intended to regulate negligent practices or corporate mismanagement, but rather to deter or punish fraud in wholesale energy markets." The Commission's regulations make it unlawful, in connection with the purchase or sale of electricity or transmission services, to (1) "use or employ any device, scheme, or artifice to defraud," (2) "make any untrue statement of a material fact or * * * omit to state a material fact necessary in order to make the statements made, in the light of the circumstances under which they were made, not misleading," or (3) "engage in any act, practice, or course of business that operates or would operate as a fraud or deceit." . . .

B

Before the advent of competitive electricity markets, a utility would commonly comply with the Federal Power Act by determining the dollar prices it wanted to charge for units of electricity, and then filing a schedule of those rates—known as a "tariff"—with the Commission. *See Morgan Stanley Cap. Group Inc. v. Public Util. Dist. No. 1 of Snohomish County*, 554 U.S. 527, 531 (2008). Those rates generally reflected the utility's costs plus a reasonable rate of return.

Since 1988, however, the Commission has permitted wholesale electricity sellers, such as utilities that own power plants, to file "market-based" tariffs instead. Market-based tariffs do not list any actual prices for electricity, but instead "simply state that the seller will enter into freely negotiated contracts with purchasers."

This court has held that the Commission's market-based approach is consistent with the Federal Power Act's requirement of "just and reasonable" rates, reasoning that, in a "competitive market, where neither buyer nor seller has significant market power, it is rational to assume that the terms of their voluntary exchange are reasonable, and specifically to infer that price is close to marginal cost, such that the seller makes only a normal return on its investment." *Tejas Power Corp. v. FERC*, 908 F.2d 998, 1004 (D.C. Cir. 1990).

Even though market-based tariffs do not identify a specific price for electricity, the Commission is still statutorily bound to ensure that the resulting rates are just and reasonable. To do that, the Commission requires assurance for any market-based tariff that the seller cannot exercise anticompetitive market power. *See Blumenthal v. FERC*, 552 F.3d 875, 882 (D.C. Cir. 2009). More specifically, the Commission has laid out three mandatory conditions that must exist for a market-based tariff to be approved.

First, the seller of electricity must demonstrate to the Commission's satisfaction that it and its affiliates either lack, or have adequately mitigated, any horizontal or vertical market power, and the seller cannot erect any barriers to entry against potential competitors.

Second, some sellers participate in organized regional markets for electrical power operated by Regional Transmission Organizations. Sellers in those markets "must also abide by additional rules" contained in the tariffs filed by the Regional Transmission Organizations. Those rules are "designed to help ensure that market power cannot be exercised in those organized markets and include additional protections," such as mitigation measures, when "appropriate to ensure that prices in those markets are just and reasonable."

Third, the Commission must continually perform "ongoing oversight of market-based rate authorizations and market conditions[.]" This oversight includes reviewing periodic reports that sellers and Regional Transmission Organizations are required to file, detailing their activities. The Commission also requires the Regional Transmission Organizations to submit data about their markets on an ongoing basis, which helps the Commission "detect anti-competitive or manipulative behavior, or ineffective market rules, thereby helping to ensure just and reasonable rates." . . .

D

Midcontinent Independent System Operator (MISO) is a Transmission Organization that, among its other responsibilities, conducts annual capacity auctions in portions of fifteen states in the Midwest and South.

For purposes of the auctions, MISO's operational area is divided into nine separate regional "zones." For each zone, MISO determines how much capacity will be required. It also determines a "local clearing requirement," which is "the minimum amount of procured capacity that must be physically located within the Zone (rather than imported [from another Zone or region])" to meet anticipated need.

In the auction, electricity generators offer to sell set amounts of capacity at specific prices. MISO accepts offers, beginning with the lowest, until the zone's capacity requirements are met. The price of the last increment of capacity needed to meet the zone's capacity requirements is the "auction clearing price" for that zone, and all the capacity for that zone is then purchased at that price.

In addition to those basic rules, MISO applies specific rules intended to mitigate the risk that, if the marketplace is insufficiently competitive, a seller might exercise market power, resulting in an unjust and unreasonable rate. In the auction for the 2015–2016 planning year—the year at issue in this case—several such rules were in effect.

First, offers to sell capacity could not exceed the "cost of new entry" in a particular zone—that is, the estimated cost of building a new power plant to provide capacity in that zone.

Second, to prevent generators from selling capacity at prices substantially higher than the amount they would receive from exporting their capacity to another market, MISO calculated an "initial reference level" that was "based on the estimated opportunity cost" of selling capacity in MISO rather than exporting it to a neighboring region. Specifically, MISO set the initial reference level by estimating how much generators could earn by exporting capacity to PJM Interconnection, a Transmission Organization region that covers portions of thirteen states in the Midwest and Mid-Atlantic, rather than selling it to MISO. Simplifying somewhat, if an offer exceeded the sum of (i) the initial reference level and (ii) ten percent of the cost of new entry—a sum known as the "conduct threshold"— the offer was automatically lowered to the initial reference level.

E

This case involves a seemingly anomalous result in the 2015 Auction for MISO's Zone 4—a zone that covers a large portion of Illinois. For that auction, MISO had calculated the cost of new entry for Zone 4 at $247.40 per megawatt (MW)day, and the initial reference level (again, based on the estimated opportunity cost of not selling energy to PJM) at $155.79 per MW-day. Based on these figures, the operating rule to ensure fair prices in the auction was that any offer over $180.53 per MW-day ($155.79 plus ten percent of $247.40) would be automatically reduced to $155.79.

The Auction took place in April 2015, and when the dust settled, the auction clearing price in most of the zones was quite uniform. Zones 1, 2, 3, 5, 6, and 7 all cleared at $3.48 per MW-day. Similarly, Zones 8 and 9 cleared at $3.29 per MW-day. But in Zone 4, the auction clearing price was far higher—$150 per MW-day. That was not only more than 40 times the price set in the other zones, but it was also out of keeping with historical rates in Zone 4. For example, in MISO's immediately preceding 2014–2015 auction, the price in Zone 4 (along with five other zones) was $16.75 per MW-day. Similarly, in MISO's capacity auction for the 2013–2014 planning year, the clearing price for Zone 4 (and for the entire region) was $1.05 per MW-day.

The month after the 2015 Auction, four complaints were filed with the Commission challenging the exceptionally high Zone 4 auction results. . . .

Public Citizen, the State of Illinois, and Southwestern Electric Cooperative alleged that the 2015 Auction had resulted in electricity rates for Zone 4 that were unjust and unreasonable in violation of Section 206 of the Federal Power Act. The State of Illinois explained that the $150 per MW-day capacity price would result in an additional $102.1 million in total capacity charges in the coming year, and that the average residential customer in Zone 4 would pay an additional $131 that year.

Those complainants pointed the finger at Dynegy, a power company in Illinois that, in 2013, had purchased four additional power plants in Zone 4. The State of Illinois alleged that Dynegy had become a "pivotal supplier" for Zone 4, meaning that Zone 4 could not meet its local clearing requirement without purchasing Dynegy's capacity. As a result, as the auction rules were designed, Dynegy could offer—and would receive—any price it wanted in the auction, so long as that price was beneath the conduct threshold set by the auction rules. In other words, Dynegy could exercise market power and garner an unreasonably high price for its electricity because the demand for capacity could not be met without it. [Public Citizen also alleged that Dynegy engaged in] "illegal market manipulation of the auction through withholding" competitive offers . . . .

II

A

Public Citizen's first contention is that Section 205 of the Federal Power Act requires the Commission to give its affirmative approval to each individual market-based price resulting from an auction for electricity or electrical capacity before that price can go into effect. That is incorrect.

Market-based rate regulation is based on the premise that, "[i]n a competitive market, where neither buyer nor seller has significant market power, * * * the terms of their voluntary exchange are reasonable, and * * * [the] price" they negotiate will be "close to marginal cost, such that the seller makes only a normal return on its investment." On that understanding, we have held that the Commission can rationally allow markets to set "just and reasonable" prices as long as the Commission takes the necessary steps to ensure that market participants cannot wield anticompetitive market power.

The Commission has developed a two-part supervisory process for ensuring that market rates are just and reasonable, and we have held that this process satisfies the Commission's statutory obligations .... First, before approving the use of a market-based tariff, the Commission must make a finding that the seller lacks or has adequately mitigated market power. Second, the Commission must conduct "continuing oversight" of the market by reviewing the mandatory transaction reports filed with it to make sure [they corroborate the market's "continued competitiveness."]

This second step is just as critical as the first. The Commission must review auction results—including prices—as part of its obligation to conduct "active ongoing review" of markets and market participants. But in conducting that active monitoring, the Commission examines auction prices not to determine whether the prices themselves are intrinsically just and reasonable, but instead "to ensure that the reported transactions are consistent with the data expected of a competitive, unmanipulated market." So while prices provide important and relevant evidence of the market's functioning, prices are not themselves the object of the Commission's inquiry.

This reasonable regulatory regime gives no quarter to Public Citizen's demand that the Commission must examine and approve every individual price resulting from every single auction to reconfirm that the price is "just and reasonable" in its own right. The whole premise of the Commission's market-based system is that a properly competitive market will necessarily produce just and reasonable prices. The Commission satisfies its statutory obligations under Section 205 by giving sellers *ex ante* approval for market-based pricing so long as (1) sellers participating in regional markets obey the rules designed to ensure fair and competitive markets, and (2) the Commission's continuing and vigilant monitoring of transaction reports verify that the markets work properly when the rubber meets the road. Public Citizen's desire to pile on another layer of agency review ignores longstanding precedent upholding this regulatory scheme.

Public Citizen insists that the statute's multiple references to "rates and charges" indicates that sellers must seek Commission approval of all auction prices. But what those references to rates and charges require is that they be just and reasonable. Nothing in the statute dictates the precise methodology the Commission must use to ensure the justness and reasonableness of rates, whether through individualized review or through reviewing and monitoring the process by which rates are computed.

Public Citizen points us to *Farmers Union Central Exchange v. FERC*, 734 F.2d 1486 (D.C. Cir. 1984), but that case is of no help to its argument. The Commission's protections of *ex ante* review, approval of the market design, and active post-approval monitoring do not involve "largely undocumented reliance on market forces as the principal means of rate regulation," which was the problem in *Farmers*. . . .

B

Public Citizen next challenges the Commission's conclusory statement that Dynegy did not engage in market manipulation, which the Commission made in explaining its wholly discretionary decision to close its investigation into Dynegy. Because that brief statement was made for the sole purpose of explaining the Commission's decision not to pursue an enforcement action, we have no power to review it.

It has long been settled that "an agency's decision not to prosecute or enforce, whether through civil or criminal process, is a decision generally committed to an agency's absolute discretion." In deciding whether to bring an enforcement action, an agency must not only determine whether a violation of the law occurred, but also whether "agency resources are best spent on this violation or another, whether the agency is likely to succeed if it acts, whether the particular enforcement action requested best fits the agency's overall policies, and, indeed, whether the agency has enough resources to undertake the action at all."

In this case, the Commission conducted a lengthy investigation into whether the 2015 Auction's localized rate spike was the product of market manipulation. The Commission's investigation spanned more than three years, produced 500,000 pages of documents, and involved seventeen days of testimony from eleven witnesses. After that, the Commission concluded that "the conduct investigated did not violate the Commission's regulations regarding market manipulation[,]" and for that reason, "no further action [was] appropriate to address the allegations of market manipulation raised in the complaints."

That type of Commission decision not to pursue further investigation or enforcement "is a paradigmatic instance of an agency exercising its presumptively nonreviewable enforcement discretion." *Baltimore Gas & Elec. Co. v. FERC*, 252 F.3d 456, 460 (D.C. Cir. 2001). That the Commission offered a brief and non-substantive passing word of explanation—whether on the question of liability or resource limitations—by itself does not open the door to judicial review of the non-enforcement decision.

In short, under the Federal Power Act, we cannot review either the Commission's discretionary decision to close its Section 222 investigation into Dynegy, or the fleeting explanation the Commission gave for its action.

C

[The court went on to grant Public Citizen's petition in part because FERC's reasoning was arbitrary and capricious. Specifically, FERC had ordered prospective tariff changes but did not reconcile why those changes were not needed in the 2015 auction as well. Further, FERC failed to address the argument that Dynegy's alleged market manipulation caused the 2015 auction rates to be unjust and unreasonable. Accordingly, remand to FERC was necessary.—Eds.]

NOTES AND QUESTIONS

1.   *Public Citizen* is another entry in what is now a long line of cases rejecting challenges to FERC's use of market-based rates to set electricity prices. In perhaps the most notable prior decision, *California ex rel. Lockyer v. FERC*, 383 F.3d 1006 (9th Cir. 2004), the Ninth Circuit rejected arguments that, because the price for each transaction itself is not submitted to FERC before it is charged, the filed rate doctrine forecloses use of market-based rates. Instead, the court said, having a tariff on file that allows the entity to charge market-based rates is sufficient. Do you agree with this reasoning, and that of the D.C. Circuit in *Public Citizen*? Or do you think the challengers had the better logic? Which approach do you think better protects consumers?

2.   *Lockyer*, like *Public Citizen*, was decided in the wake of alleged market manipulation. In *Lockyer*, that manipulation was quite real. The events that gave rise to the case stemmed from what widely became known as the California—or western—energy crisis. Driven heavily by market manipulation, prices in California skyrocketed. Electricity delivery was curtailed. Rolling brownouts and blackouts were common. *See, e.g.*, CONG. BUDGET OFFICE, CAUSES AND LESSONS OF THE CALIFORNIA ELECTRICITY CRISIS (2001); Paul L. Joskow, *California's Electricity Crisis*, 17 OXFORD REV. ECON. POL'Y 365 (2001).

How did market players manipulate prices in California? In part, traders took advantage of what they viewed as loopholes in FERC's market rules. In turn, they sought to drive up prices to artificial highs and reap massive profits. Enron had several names for the deceptive trades it used to manipulate the market, including "Death Star," "Get Shorty," "Ricochet," and "Fat Boy." The specific mechanics of each of these strategies varied, but the basic premise was to make the market look more constrained than it actually was—to create a false perception that there were energy shortages when there actually were not. Enron then capitalized on this perception by selling power into the market at artificially elevated prices. One Enron worker described the strategy this way: "What we did was overbook the transmission line we had the rights on and said to California utilities, 'if you want to use the line pay us.' By the time they agreed to meet our price, rolling black outs had already hit California and the price of electricity went through the roof." ENRON: THE SMARTEST GUYS IN THE ROOM (Magnolia Pictures 2005).

Much of this activity occurred in 2000 and 2001. In California, this manipulation tripled the cost of electricity between May 2000 and June 2001. In 1999, the total cost of electricity in California was $7.4 billion and rose to

$27.1 billion in 2000 and then $26 billion in 2001. In the end, these practices cost California consumers tens of billions of dollars. *See, e.g.*, Office of the Attorney General of California, *The California Energy Crisis 2000–2001: Update on Post-Crisis Developments, Briefing for the Little Hoover Commission* (Sept. 26, 2011); Richard A. Oppel Jr. & Jeff Gerth, *Enron Forced Up California Prices, Documents Show*, N.Y. TIMES (May 2, 2002).

When FERC discovered Enron's misdoings, it aggressively pursued the company. However, because market-based rate tariffs at the time typically lacked specific language about market manipulation, FERC found itself conscribed to using the rather blunt instruments of FPA §§ 205 and 206 as remedies. As a result, Congress and FERC made changes. As noted in *Public Citizen*, the FPA now forecloses such manipulation. FERC too now requires all firms selling at market-based rates to include in their tariffs specific prohibitions against market manipulation, including bans on: (1) "us[ing] or employ[ing] any device, scheme, or artifice to defraud," (2) "mak[ing] any untrue statement of a material fact or . . . omit[ting] to state a material fact necessary in order to make the statements made, in the light of the circumstances under which they were made, not misleading," and (3) "engag[ing] in any act, practice, or course of business that operates or would operate as a fraud or deceit upon any entity." 18 C.F.R. § 1c.2 (2021). The Energy Policy Act of 2005 also granted FERC authority to assess penalties of up to $1 million per day for each violation of the FPA. *See* 16 U.S.C. § 825o–1.

3.   Risk of market manipulation is not just a relic of the past or specific to California or the *Public Citizen* case. The issue persists. Questions of possible market manipulation arose in Texas, for instance, in the summer of 2021, when multiple thermal generators (coal, natural gas, and nuclear) went offline for "forced" (*i.e.*, non-planned) outages. As happened with Enron in California, the possibility exists in the Texas market that parties could fake an outage to make prices spike, and then reap a windfall through futures contracts or selling power at the inflated price. The idea is so basic that one University of Houston professor said, "We teach this in school." Edward Klump & Mike Lee, *"Outrageous." Texas Grid Scare Reignites Blackout Concerns*, ENERGYWIRE (June 15, 2021). *See also* Scott Disavino & Stephanie Kelly, *Texas Power Consumers to Pay the Price of Winter Storm*, REUTERS (Feb. 18, 2021) ("[T]here is enormous opportunity for market manipulation" in Texas."). And, because ERCOT is not subject to federal jurisdiction, FERC's anti-market-manipulation rules do not apply.

4.   Beyond the bar on market manipulation FERC required parties to add to their market-based rate tariffs, the Commission has also used "independent market monitors" to ensure market competition. As the name implies, these entities—which are often economics firms—are charged with watching for malfeasance or irregular behavior in electricity markets. If they spot problems, they can seek to have them addressed, including through filings with FERC—though some RTOs have pressed to limit such authority. *See PJM Interconnection, LLC*, 167 FERC ¶ 61,084 (2019).

5.   FERC's filing system for market-based sales is quite similar to what it uses for some kinds of transmission service under Order No. 888. There, utilities file a (largely generic, FERC-specified) tariff for transmission service. This is called the utility's OATT, or "Open Access Transmission Tariff." All transmission sales are made under the OATT, but many of the sales are never actually filed with FERC. Instead, transmission customers use the utility's OASIS, or "Open Access Same-time Information System," to make transmission reservations and purchases. OASIS is an internet-based computer interface, through which customers can see what transmission capacity is available. Only long-term transmission contracts (one year or longer) get filed with FERC; short-term contracts simply get made over OASIS and are provided pursuant to general agreements the customers enter into with the transmission provider. *See S. Montana Elec. Generation & Transmission Coop., Inc. Nw. Corp.*, 133 FERC ¶ 61,163 (Nov. 18, 2010). The difference between the OATT-OASIS regime and the one for market-based rates is that the OATT specifies the price of transmission in advance, after FERC approves it using cost-of-service ratemaking. The price of market-based rate contracts, by contrast, cannot be known in advance and are only reported to FERC after they are consummated. To see a sample OASIS, go to http:// www.oasis.oati.com/ipco/.

b.   Wholesale Market-Based Rate Authority

To police electricity rates charged at market prices, FERC had to devise a method to determine that the market which sets the price is competitive. For this, FERC turned to antitrust theory. In addition to approving electricity rates, FERC long has had the authority to monitor certain acquisitions of electricity facilities. *See* 16 U.S.C. § 824b. FERC also uses this power to exercise authority over proposed mergers of public utilities. *See* 18 C.F.R. §§ 33.1 *et seq.* (2021). Typically, those mergers are subject to further scrutiny by state PUCs and by either the U.S. Department of Justice (DOJ) or the Federal Trade Commission (FTC). DOJ and the FTC use joint "merger guidelines" to evaluate proposed corporate combinations, to make sure that the newly merged entity cannot unfairly raise market prices by exercising market power in a way the previously separate entities could not. U.S. DEP'T OF JUSTICE & FEDERAL TRADE COMMISSION, HORIZONTAL MERGER GUIDELINES (Aug. 19, 2010). To do so, the merger guidelines set forth various tests for assessing the "concentration" of the market. That is, they utilize economic measures of whether any one competitor has "too much" of a market share, such that it might be able to unduly impact prices. One of these tests is referred to as the HHI, or "Herfindahl-Hirschman Index."

FERC's own merger rules draw heavily on the DOJ/FTC merger guidelines, and FERC's market-based rate tests in turn borrow generously from the theory and tests the Commission's merger rules set forth. *See* 18 C.F.R. §§ 33.3, 33.4 (2021). That is, FERC's market-based rate test seeks to determine whether a party asking for permission to sell electricity at negotiated rates can unduly influence the price of electricity in the market.

As Chapter 4 explained, a utility has an incentive to manipulate prices if it can "withhold" supply from the market, thus increasing the price for everyone while also increasing its own profits. However, if other competitors have excess supply available, they can use that supply to compete against the firm that is withholding electricity. For example, if Utility A withheld power to raise prices, Utility B could offer to sell its supply into the market at a lower price, negating Utility A's ability to artificially raise prices, *i.e.,* to exercise "market power." In other words, a company lacks market power when other firms can out-compete it. Thus, the core of the market-based rate test is determining how much supply a utility has available that it theoretically could use to affect market prices.

FERC's market-based rate test first evolved organically through case-by-case decisions (*i.e.,* agency adjudications). Over time, this test underwent three major changes: first, in 2001, when FERC switched from its so-called "hub and spoke" analysis to a "supply margin assessment"; second, in 2004, when FERC replaced the "supply margin assessment" with two "indicative screens" for measuring market power, namely, the so-called "pivotal supplier" test and the "market share analysis"; and third, in 2007, when FERC codified its market-based rate tests in Order No. 697.

While FERC's market-based rate analysis has evolved over time, its overriding feature has remained constant: It seeks to determine whether a firm has market power. If the firm has market power, it may not charge market-based rates. If it does not have market power, it can exercise market-based rate authority. As the U.S. Supreme Court has noted, "FERC will grant approval of a market-based tariff only if a utility demonstrates that it lacks or has adequately mitigated market power, lacks the capacity to erect other barriers to entry, and has avoided giving preferences to its affiliates." *Morgan Stanley Capital Grp. Inc. v. Pub. Util. Dist. No. 1 of Snohomish Cnty., Wash.,* 554 U.S. 527, 537 (2008).

The FERC market-based rate analysis tests for three primary kinds of possible market power:

- Horizontal Market Power—This tends to be the primary focus of the analysis. Here, FERC questions how much direct control over market prices a firm might have by, for example, withholding electricity from the market. This is where FERC utilizes the market share analysis and the pivotal supplier test. That is, this part of the test assesses a firm's market power across the relevant product market—wholesale electricity generation. It is called "horizontal" for this reason.

- Vertical Market Power—This tends to be much less central to FERC's assessment. Here, FERC questions how much indirect control a firm might exercise over market prices—that is, whether firms can use their market power in upstream markets (*e.g.*, gas pipelines) to constrain competition in downstream markets (*e.g.*, electric sales). For instance, a utility might own natural gas or coal resources, thereby forcing wholesale electricity prices to rise by limiting others' access to these resources or charging discriminatory prices for them. Likewise, a firm might discriminate over access to its transmission lines (and thus, prevent access to the wholesale electricity market). Because this part of FERC's market-based rate test examines one type of market (*e.g.*, electricity transmission) "stacked" in the production chain on top of another (*i.e.*, electricity generation), it is referred to as assessing "vertical" market power.

- Affiliate Abuse/Preference—As competition became a bigger part of the electricity industry, many traditional utilities created or spun off marketing entities that broker electricity. If a utility that owns transmission or generation can sell power to one of its own corporate affiliates, there is a risk that "sweetheart deals" will result. That is, FERC worries that companies in the same corporate family—a regulated utility and an unregulated power marketer—will go into cahoots and use rates charged by the regulated utility to subsidize the profits of the unregulated trading company. FERC's market-based rate test thus compels parties engaging in market-based sales to institute rules that keep corporate affiliates separate and forecloses[6] market-based electricity sales between them. *See* 18 C.F.R. § 35.39 (2021).

Today, FERC conducts its market-based rate assessment under Order No. 697. Under this analysis, FERC generally assumes that the second and third types of market power—vertical market power and affiliate preferences—are solved by its regulations. Thus, market-based rate applicants have to supply information about vertical market power (such as ownership of natural gas resources), but FERC treats their compliance with Order No. 888 and its affiliate abuse rules as effectively resolving the vertical market power and affiliate abuse issues. This is why the focus in market-based rate cases is on horizontal market power—that is, how much generation the applicant controls.

---

[6] This is true unless there is a showing that the prices reflect market prices. *See, e.g., So. Cal. Edison Co. on behalf of Mountainview Power Co., L.L.C.,*106 FERC ¶ 61,183 (2004); *Boston Edison Co. re: Edgar Elec. Energy Co.,* 55 FERC ¶ 61,382 (1991).

FERC's analysis of horizontal market power can be summarized around the two tests Order No. 697 mandates, the "market share" and "pivotal supplier" tests:

> Sellers must pass both the "market share" and "pivotal supplier" screens. The market share screen compares the seller's total generating capacity to its average load in each of the four seasons (net of NERC[7] operating reserves, native load obligations, and long-term firm sales commitments). Sellers whose market shares are less than 20 percent pass the screen. The pivotal supplier screen compares a seller's uncommitted capacity at the time of its annual peak to average load during the month when the peak occurs. Sellers pass the screen if their uncommitted capacity is less than the total capacity available in the market on the peak day.
>
> Franchised utility sellers (and their affiliates) that are not part of an RTO typically fail one or both screens (usually the market share screen) in their home markets. Franchised utility sellers that are part of an RTO with day-ahead and realtime energy markets normally pass the screen because the market analyzed usually covers the entire RTO region, not just the utility's home control area (which FERC now refers to as the metered "balancing authority area"). Exceptions may arise in RTOs with well-defined submarkets created by persistent transmission constraints (Southwestern Connecticut in the New England Independent System Operator RTO is an example). . . .
>
> Sellers who fail the screens can submit a more robust, price sensitive, delivered price test analysis, which is the same analysis that FERC uses to screen merger applicants for market power concerns. . . . Several sellers that have failed the competitive screens have passed the delivered price test analysis.

Winston & Strawn LLP, *FERC Codifies Rules for Market-Based Power Sales* (June 21, 2007).

The cases that follow highlight FERC's application of its market-based rate test. As you read the materials, consider how well FERC's policy polices whether electricity rates are fair.

---

[7] [NERC, the North American Electric Reliability Corporation, is a not-for-profit entity composed of utility and other members. It long has served as an umbrella organization providing standards to help maintain electricity reliability in the United States. Following passage of the Energy Policy Act of 2005, FERC designated NERC the Electric Reliability Organization (ERO) charged with ensuring grid reliability and security, under FERC's oversight, pursuant to that Act. NERC is discussed in more detail later in this chapter.—Eds.]

ZEPHYR WIND, LLC
141 FERC ¶ 61,113 (2012)

Before Commissioners: Jon Wellinghoff, Chairman; Philip D. Moeller, John R. Norris, Cheryl A. LaFleur, and Tony T. Clark.

In this order, the Commission grants Zephyr Wind, LLC (Zephyr Wind) authority to make wholesale sales of electric energy, capacity, and ancillary services at market-based rates, effective September 25, 2012, as requested. We grant Zephyr Wind waiver of the obligation to file an Open Access Transmission Tariff (OATT), to establish and maintain an Open Access Same-Time Information System (OASIS), and other waivers commonly granted to market-based rate sellers. . . .

Zephyr Wind states that it is a Delaware limited liability company engaged in the business of constructing a wind-powered electric facility (Facility) in Nobles County, Minnesota, and selling electric products exclusively at wholesale from the Facility. Zephyr Wind explains that the Facility is currently under construction and will have a capacity of approximately 30.75 megawatts (MW). Zephyr Wind states that it expects to begin selling test power from the Facility on or about September 25 . . . and to commence commercial operations on or about October 31, 2012.

Zephyr Wind explains that the Facility is located in the Central region within the MISO market and that the Facility will consist of 15 wind turbines, each of 2.05 MW capacity, and will include associated interconnection facilities necessary to interconnect the Facility to the MISO grid. Specifically, the Facility will include an approximately 5-mile 34.5 kV generation tie line used to interconnect the Facility to the Nobles County Substation on Northern States Power Company's (Northern States) transmission system. Zephyr Wind states that, under three 20-year power purchase agreements, Northern States is entitled to all of the Facility's output and that, other than the Facility, Zephyr Wind does not own any other generation or transmission assets. . . .

A. Market-Based Rate Authorization

The Commission allows power sales at market-based rates if the seller and its affiliates do not have, or have adequately mitigated, horizontal and vertical market power.

1. Horizontal Market Power

The Commission has adopted two indicative screens for assessing horizontal market power: the pivotal supplier screen and the wholesale market share screen. The Commission has stated that passage of both screens establishes a rebuttable presumption that the applicant does not possess horizontal market power, while failure of either screen creates a rebuttable presumption that the applicant has horizontal market power.

Zephyr Wind represents that it will own and/or control approximately 30.75 MW of generation capacity in the MISO market and that it and its affiliates do not own or control any generation in the first-tier markets. Zephyr Wind adds that the entire capacity is committed to a non-affiliated third party under long-term sales agreements and that it and its affiliates do not control uncommitted generation through power purchase agreements.

Zephyr Wind represents that it relies on Tuscola Bay Wind, LLC's (Tuscola Bay) recently accepted market power analysis to demonstrate that Zephyr Wind passes both the pivotal supplier and the wholesale market share screens for the MISO market. In addition, we note that Zephyr Wind's capacity in the MISO market is fully committed. Accordingly, we find that Zephyr Wind's submittal satisfies the Commission's requirements for market-based rate authority regarding horizontal market power.

2. Vertical Market Power

In cases where a public utility, or any of its affiliates, owns, operates, or controls transmission facilities, the Commission requires that there be a Commission-approved OATT on file or that the seller has received waiver of the OATT requirement . . . .

Zephyr Wind seeks waiver of the requirements to file an OATT and establish and maintain an OASIS with respect to its generator interconnection line. In support of its request for waiver, Zephyr Wind states that the generator interconnection line is limited and discrete, and will be used solely by Zephyr Wind to interconnect the Facility to the transmission system. . . .

Based on the statements in Zephyr Wind's application, we find that its transmission facilities qualify as limited and discrete. Accordingly, we will grant Zephyr Wind waiver of the requirements of Order Nos. 888 and 890 and section 35.28 of the Commission's regulations to have an OATT on file. However, if Zephyr Wind receives a request for transmission service, it must file with the Commission a *pro forma* OATT within 60 days of the date of the request. . . .

AEP POWER MARKETING, INC.

124 FERC ¶ 61,274 (2008)

Before Commissioners: Joseph T. Kelliher, Chairman; Suedeen G. Kelly, Marc Spitzer, Philip D. Moeller, and Jon Wellinghoff.

In this order, the Commission accepts the updated market power analysis filed by AEP Power Marketing, Inc. (AEP Power), AEP Service Corporation (AEP Service), AEP Energy Partners, Inc. (AEP Energy), CSW Energy Services, Inc. (CSW Energy), and Central and South West Services, Inc. (CSW Services) (collectively, Applicants). As discussed below, the

Commission concludes that Applicants satisfy the Commission's standards for market-based rate authority. . . .

Applicants state that they and several affiliates known as the AEP East Companies own transmission and generation facilities in the PJM Interconnection, L.L.C. (PJM). . . . According to Applicants' filing, they own or control approximately 28,439 megawatts (MW) in and around PJM, and provide retail electric service in seven states. Applicants also operate to serve wholesale load within PJM. They have submitted a market power analysis for the PJM market. . . .

B. Market-Based Rate Authorization

The Commission allows power sales at market-based rates if the seller and its affiliates do not have, or have adequately mitigated, horizontal and vertical market power. . . .

C. Horizontal Market Power

The Commission adopted two indicative screens for assessing horizontal market power, the pivotal supplier screen and the wholesale market share screen.

Applicants have prepared the pivotal supplier and wholesale market share screens for the PJM market consistent with the requirements of Order No. 697.

We address below concerns raised by protesters regarding the relevant geographic market, Applicants' use of historical data, and whether the Commission should require Applicants to submit a delivered price test (DPT).

1. Relevant Geographic Market

a. Protests and Answers

The Ohio Commission argues that the relevant market is not the entirety of the PJM footprint, but rather is a subset of the generation in that footprint. . . . The Ohio Commission alleges that transmission constraints in PJM limit the amount of AEP generation that can serve load in eastern PJM, and further claims that "not all of the uncommitted capacity behind the principal constraints in PJM . . . was deliverable or available to serve load that AEP could serve. . . ."

Applicants state that the Ohio Commission does not provide evidence that there are persistent transmission constraints that limit imports into the AEP East area. Applicants conversely state that the PJM Market Monitoring Unit's 2007 State of the Market Report shows that the AEP East area is predominately export, not import, limited, and that the data does not in any way suggest that deliveries into the AEP East area are restricted by transmission limitations within PJM. . . .

b. Commission Determination

We find Applicant's use of the PJM footprint as the relevant geographic market to be appropriate. In Order No. 697, the Commission stated that it would continue the practice of using the seller's balancing authority area or RTO/ISO region as the default relevant geographic market. Although the Commission also stated that it would consider submarkets as the relevant geographic market in certain instances, we do not find it appropriate to do so here. As stated in Order No. 697, where the Commission has made a specific finding that there is a submarket within an RTO/ISO, that submarket will be considered as the default relevant geographic market. Here, no such finding has been made. And although the Commission stated in Order No. 697 that it would allow sellers and intervenors to present evidence on a case-by-case basis to show that some other geographic market should be considered as the relevant market in a particular case, we are not persuaded that some other relevant market should be considered here.

The Commission has stated that "[a]ny proposal to use an alternative geographic market (i.e., a market other than the default geographic market) must include a demonstration regarding whether there are frequently binding transmission constraints during historical seasonal peaks examined in the screens and at other competitively significant times that prevent competing supply from reaching customers within the proposed alternative geographic market." The requirement to address transmission constraints was found to be a "necessary condition" for those advocating adoption of an alternative geographic market. The Ohio Commission has not made a showing that binding transmission constraints exist that would support a finding of a separate geographic market for the AEP East area. Any binding transmission constraints in PJM are west to east, rather than east to west. . . .

2. Historical Data

a. Protests and Answers

The West Virginia and Ohio Industrial Customers object to Applicants' use of 2005/2006 data, as required by Order No. 697 and Order No. 697–A. They argue that the December 2005–December 2006 study period data provided by Applicants in compliance with Order No. 697 does not provide an accurate picture of the current and near-future regulatory environment and generation peak load requirements for Applicants' utilities in Ohio. They contend that the conditions in this historical period have no necessary relationship to current or future conditions. . . . They submit that the load the Ohio Power and Columbus Southern was serving during the December 2005–December 2006 study period may become "uncommitted" as a result of the procurement processes required by Ohio law[, that] the corresponding amount of Applicants' generation may also become "uncommitted," [and that in light of] . . . Applicants' failure to [model] this imminent ... change ..., the Commission should reject Applicants' filing. . . .

b.   Commission Determination

With respect to Applicants' use of 2005/2006 data, we note that in Order Nos. 697 and 697–A, the Commission considered the use of historical data. . . . The Commission stated:

> First, as we explained in the Final Rule, historical data are more objective, readily available, and less subject to manipulation by applicants than future projections. If the Commission were to allow applicants to submit studies based on their future projections or that reflect "imminent changes," then sellers would be able to selectively "cherry pick" those changes that benefited the seller in obtaining market-based rate authorization while ignoring other equally likely future changes that would undermine the seller's chances for obtaining such authorization. Second, this approach benefits customers, state commissions and other affected intervenors because it requires the use of a consistent methodology that can be replicated by intervenors, rather than allowing sellers to submit customized market power studies that, due to myriad selective adjustments, are difficult to analyze and can hide the presence of market power. . . .

Additionally, the Commission went on to state that accounting for "imminent changes" would be excessively burdensome because a review of all expiring contracts and all contracts being negotiated in the relevant market and the seller's first-tier markets might be necessary. Also, a long-term contract may be expiring in a year, but until it expires, it often can be renewed. However, we recognize that the Commission, in Order No. 697–A, stated that it would review, on a case-by-case basis, evidence presented by sellers and intervenors that seek to demonstrate that certain changes in the market have taken place and should be recognized in the analysis. The Commission stated that it will address countervailing factors that affect whether the seller will have the ability to exercise market power. We emphasize that the Commission stated that the evidence presented must be clear and compelling. However, in this proceeding, since the protestors argue of changes that "may" happen, we do not find it appropriate to reconsider the use of the 2005/2006 study period. Rather, if such changes do happen, Applicants would be obligated to inform the Commission of any change in status from the circumstances on which the Commission relied in granting them market-based rate authority in accordance with 18 C.F.R. § 35.42 (2008). In light of this, and based on . . . Order No. 697–A, we find that the use of historical data is more appropriate than relying on possible future changes. . . .

D. Vertical Market Power

In cases where a public utility, or any of its affiliates, owns, operates, or controls transmission facilities, the Commission requires that there be a Commission-approved Open Access Transmission Tariff (OATT) on file before granting a seller market-based rate authorization.

The Commission also considers a seller's ability to erect other barriers to entry as part of the vertical market power analysis. The Commission requires a seller to provide a description of its ownership or control of, or affiliation with an entity that owns or controls, intrastate natural gas transportation, storage or distribution facilities; sites for generation capacity development; and sources of coal supplies and equipment for the transportation of coal supplies, such as barges and rail cars (collectively, inputs to electric power production). The Commission also requires sellers to make an affirmative statement that they have not erected barriers to entry into the relevant market and will not erect barriers to entry into the relevant market.

Applicants state that all AEP East Companies' transmission facilities in PJM have been turned over to the operational control of PJM, which has an OATT on file with the Commission.

Further, Applicants state that they do not own or control, and are not affiliated with any entity that owns or controls, any intrastate natural gas transportation, storage, or distribution facilities. Applicants further state that they presently own or have options on six sites for development of generation capacity and explain that in PJM they own coal reserves in the Appalachian Basin, which are used mainly to fuel Applicants' generation stations. Lastly, Applicants state that they own and control lignite mines and reserves in Louisiana and Texas, and have lease agreements on a fleet of coal rail cars for private use.

The Commission adopted a rebuttable presumption that the ownership or control of, or affiliation with any entity that owns or controls, inputs to electric power production does not allow a seller to raise entry barriers but will allow intervenors to demonstrate otherwise.

Applicants affirmatively state that neither they nor their affiliates have erected barriers to entry into the relevant market and that they will not erect barriers into the relevant market.

Based on Applicants' representations we find that Applicants satisfy the Commission's requirements for market-based rates regarding vertical market power. . . .

NOTES AND QUESTIONS

1.   FERC makes quick work of approving Zephyr Wind's market-based rate application. Conversely, justifying its approval of AEP's application takes more explanation and time. Why? How much generation does each applicant own? How much does it matter that some of the AEP affiliates are traditional (*i.e.,* incumbent) utilities as opposed to Zephyr Wind, which is a small, new entrant into the market?

2.   The back story to the *Zephyr Wind* case highlights both the overlapping nature of state and federal electricity jurisdiction as well as the evolving shape of the electricity market. The project arose out of a 2003 Minnesota PUC order approving the development of four high-voltage transmission lines in southwestern Minnesota by Xcel Energy. In granting Xcel approval to build these lines, the PUC imposed conditions on the project—including that Xcel purchase up to 60 MW of wind energy from small, locally owned facilities. Originally, Community Wind South (CWS) sought and obtained approval from the PUC to build the wind project to fulfill the 2003 order's mandate. Subsequently, however, a multinational company headquartered in Germany purchased the vast majority of CWS, and that change in ownership went unreported to the Minnesota PUC. When the PUC later found out about this ownership shift (through a compliance filing by Xcel), it chose not to reopen its prior approval of the project. Zephyr did, however, disclose its multinational ownership in its FERC application for market-based rate authority. What issues does this fact pattern raise about the nature of electricity? Why do you think the Minnesota PUC wanted the wind projects to be community-based? Do you think it should matter whether electricity is produced by a local, regional, national, or international firm? Why or why not? Why do you think the Minnesota PUC effectively looked the other way when it found out the project's ownership had changed?

3.   As competition in electricity has grown, the shape of the market also has evolved. A large number of energy marketers that own no physical energy assets now participate in these markets. These firms often function much like stock traders on Wall Street and, in fact, many of them are staffed by former stockbrokers. It is also very easy for them to obtain market-based rate authority, precisely because they own no physical generation or transmission assets, and thus, it is very difficult for them to fail the Order No. 697 tests. For one example of such an entity that easily obtained market-based rate authority, see *Google Energy LLC*, 130 FERC ¶ 61,107 (2010).

4.   FERC approved AEP's market-based rate application despite various protests. In part, FERC pointed to the protestors' failure to supply hard data contradicting AEP's claims of an absence of market power or proving the market conditions the protestors said existed. If the protestors were so concerned with AEP's ability to influence market price, why didn't they submit the data FERC said was needed?

5.   Companies selling at market-based rates must conduct analyses for two different kinds of markets: a product market and a geographic market.

Understanding the difference is simple. The product market is merely the product sold. So, if you run Coca-Cola or Pepsi, your product market might be defined as soft drinks or beverages. If you are a cable television company, or a satellite TV company like DIRECTV or Dish Network, your product market is defined as bundles of television programming—or what the industry refers to as multichannel video programming distribution (MVPD).

Many product markets in the United States are national in nature. You can buy a Coke, Pepsi, or MVPD services anywhere in the country. Electricity, however, is not distributed this way. Thus, because the transmission system is limited and power can only flow from certain parts of the country to others, geographic markets are important in assessing market power in electricity: Unless it wants to pay exorbitant transmission charges, Exelon cannot wheel electricity from its Zion nuclear power station in Illinois to customers of Florida Power & Light in Miami.

For market-based rates, the product market is relatively straightforward. The product is wholesale electricity, which can also include energy capacity (the ability to generate electricity) and ancillary services (such as spinning and non-spinning reserves—generation products used to help maintain system stability).[8] By contrast, the geographic market is simply where the product of wholesale electricity will be sold. FERC defines geographic markets based on what it calls the "balancing area." In RTOs, the balancing area tends to be large—the entire RTO. For companies not in RTOs, however, the balancing area tends to be smaller—typically the historical footprint of each incumbent utility's franchised service area. This is why incumbent utilities that are not part of RTOs tend to fail the horizontal market power screens in their home franchise area. They built up a lot of generation there over time to serve their customers. Is it fair that FERC effectively forces these parties out of charging market-based rates in these areas? Many incumbent utilities would very much like to sell power at market-based rates in their home areas. Why do you think that is?

6.   Geographic markets were part of the fight in the *AEP* decision. AEP asserted that the entire RTO was the geographic market. Intervenors, on the other hand, wanted FERC to find two geographic markets: PJM West and PJM East. FERC declined. What would have been the effect had FERC agreed with the intervenors? Why did the intervenors argue for these smaller markets? Note also that FERC effectively said that in some circumstances there are two different markets in PJM. Why did that not apply to AEP?

7.   To satisfy the market share analysis and the pivotal supplier test, firms often hire economists to conduct these assessments. This is, in part, because an outside economist adds some measure of impartiality to their applications and, in part, because the analyses require sifting through large amounts of data—something energy economists are adept at. Hiring these economists, however, can be rather expensive, especially if they also have to conduct a

---

[8]   Some observers would note that determining which ancillary service products matter, and in which time periods, complicates the FERC market-based rate analysis.

delivered price test (*i.e.*, when the applicant fails one of the first two presumptive screens). Does this explain why Zephyr Wind relied on another party's analysis rather than submitting its own?

8.   Order No. 697's market share analysis and pivotal supplier test might sound complicated, but their objective is quite simple: Assess whether the applicant has "too much" generation it owns or controls compared to other players in the market.

The "market share" analysis looks at what percentage of generation in the market the applicant owns or controls. If the firm has 20% or more of the generation, it fails the test. If it has less than 20%, it passes. Passing the test creates a rebuttable presumption that the firm does not have market power, thus placing the burden on any challengers to show that market power exists.

That is straightforward enough. It is a bit more complicated how FERC calculates the percentage. First, the percentage is not calculated once in each market but four times: once for each season (winter, spring, summer, fall). Second, there are additions and subtractions that must be made to the utility's generation share before the percentage is calculated. You start with what the firm owns, based on its generation capacity. Then you add other long-term firm energy purchases and power the company makes or imports. Then you subtract generation that the company will not have available to compete in the market. This includes long-term firm energy sales, planned outages of its generation facilities, and, importantly, the company's average peak native load in the season. The company also gets to subtract its "balancing authority area reserve requirement," which is the excess generation capacity it must have available for reliability purposes. Native load is deducted for the same reason: It is treated as not "available" to compete in the market because the utility needs generation to serve those franchised customers. Once this calculation is completed for the applicant company, the same calculation is performed for all other companies in the geographic market (*i.e.*, the balancing area). The remaining amount of the applicant's generation is then compared against all the other companies' remaining generation to see if the applicant exceeds the 20% threshold.

Assume, for instance, a company has 19,500 MW of installed capacity, plus 500 MW of long-term firm purchases. It also sells off 1,000 MW of energy on a long-term firm basis, has planned maintenance outages worth 4,000 MW for the winter season, has a peak native load of 11,500 MW in that season and a balancing authority area reserve requirement of 1,500 MW. Then its total seasonal uncommitted capacity is 2,000 MW:

Installed Capacity	19,500
Long-Term Firm Purchases	500
Imported Power	0
Long-Term Firm Sales	−1,000
Seasonal Average Planned Outages	−4,000
Average Peak Native Load	−11,500
Balancing Authority Area Reserve Requirement	−1,500
Seller's Uncommitted Capacity	**2,000**

If all the other companies in the balancing area have a cumulative uncommitted capacity of 10,200 during this season, the applicant would pass the screen because it would have a 16.39% share of the available generation (2,000 divided by 12,200). The applicant could, however, still fail the screen in other seasons. If, for instance, the applicant had 4,680 MW of uncommitted capacity in the spring and the rest of the balancing area had 10,300, its share would be 31.24% (4,680 MW divided by 14,980)—too high to pass FERC's market share analysis. Market-based rate applicants must pass the market share analysis for all four seasons of the year, not just one. Further, they have to do so for the relevant geographic markets, which can change depending on how transmission constraints limit power movements.

The "pivotal supplier" analysis is based on a mathematical inequality rather than a percentage. If the seller's uncommitted capacity is less than all of the market's net uncommitted supply (including the applicant's own supply), then it passes the pivotal supplier test. If the applicant's uncommitted supply is greater than the cumulative net uncommitted supply for the market, then it fails the test. The idea here is straightforward: If other companies have enough generation to displace everything the applicant might be able to withhold from the market, FERC assumes that the applicant cannot artificially raise prices.

Again, adjustments are made to the companies' supply to determine what they have available to compete. As in the market share analysis, you start by adding installed capacity plus long-term firm purchases and power imports. You then deduct long-term firm sales, balancing area authority reserves, and native load. One difference, however, is that rather than using the seasonal average peak load, here the average of the daily peak loads for the month with the highest load for the year is used. For most of North America, this will usually be July or August, when everyone runs their air conditioners to keep cool. Also, planned generator outages are not counted in the pivotal supplier analysis because it is a yearly calculation rather than a seasonal one.

For instance, use again the hypothetical utility above. It has 19,5000 MW of installed capacity, 500 MW of long-term firm purchases, 1,000 MW of long-term firm sales, and a balancing area authority reserve requirement of 2,160. If its needle peak for the year is 16,500 MW, then its net uncommitted capacity is 340:

Installed Capacity	19,500
Long-Term Firm Purchases	500
Imported Power[9]	0
Long-Term Firm Sales	−1,000
Average Daily Peak Native Load in Peak Month	−16,500
Balancing Authority Area Reserve Requirement	−2,160
Seller's Uncommitted Capacity	**340**

That number (340) then gets compared against the market's net cumulative uncommitted supply. That figure is calculated by determining the uncommitted capacity for all the suppliers in the area, including the applicant, less the difference between the market's annual peak load (the so-called "needle peak," or the day on which the most power is consumed in the market) and the average daily peak native load in the month in which the needle peak occurs. So, if the market has a net uncommitted supply of 8,340 MW, the applicant passes the pivotal supplier test because 340 < 8,340. The applicant company would need another 8,000-plus MW of generation capacity to fail. Why might this utility so easily pass the pivotal supplier test but fail the market share analysis?

Do you see why companies hire economists to help with these analyses? Not only here but in many other contexts as well, this is a key skill that modern energy lawyers need to cultivate: being able to work with—and understand, test, and explain—smart economists.

9.   As the *AEP* case notes, if a firm fails FERC's initial market-power screens, a rebuttable presumption is created that the firm has market power. It can rebut this presumption by providing a more sophisticated economic analysis, called the "delivered price test." If the firm still fails that test, it typically will be denied market-based rate authority. The firm then has two options. It can propose some form of market power "mitigation" that it wants FERC to accept, or it can utilize the Commission's "default" mitigation. The default measures, perhaps not surprisingly, rely on cost-of-service ratemaking principles to set the price the seller can charge: "Default mitigation consists of three distinct products: (1) Sales of power of one week or less priced at the Seller's incremental cost plus a 10% adder; (2) Sales of power of more than one week but less than one year priced at no higher than a cost-based ceiling reflecting the costs of the unit(s) expected to provide the service; and (3) New contracts filed for review under [FPA] section 205 . . . for sales of power for one year or more priced at a rate not to exceed embedded cost of service." 18 C.F.R. § 35.38(b) (2021). While FERC regulations recognize all three of these categories of default pricing, generally when companies fail the market-power tests, they file cost-of-service rates that allow them to recover up to (i) the

---

[9]   A big challenge here is determining how much imported power is "in" the market. To assess this, FERC has to determine both (i) how much transmission import capacity is available, and (ii) how much available capacity exists in outside markets that can exert competitive pressure inside the market. FERC has complex rules in place for calculating this number, and determining it often is the most difficult and contentious part of the market share calculation, both in electricity mergers and market rate cases.

capacity costs of the units likely to provide service plus (ii) 110% of their incremental costs.

10. Note that the focus of FERC's market-based rate test is whether *a given company* should be able to exercise market power. FERC does not, *ex ante*, look at the *complete market structure* in determining whether market-based rates are appropriate. Is this effective? If so, then how could companies like Enron manipulate the electricity market in California? Effectively, FERC does examine complete market structure *ex post*, when it appears there is a problem, by applying its market manipulation prohibition. Is that effective? Or is it too late? Or too reactionary?

11. The rules FERC applies to companies selling at market-based rates that have traditionally regulated affiliates are called its "Code of Conduct" or "Affiliate Restrictions." These rules restrict the business relationship between utilities with captive customers and their marketing affiliates. FERC does not allow electricity sales between these corporate siblings unless the Commission first gives authorization. The Code of Conduct also limits the sharing of information between affiliates, unless that information is simultaneously shared with the public, and it restricts how affiliates can share employees and non-power goods or services. *See* 18 C.F.R. § 35.39 (2021).

12. FERC continues to tweak implementation of its market-based rate approvals. Recent clarifications FERC has made include: not needing to show passage of the market screens if the entity's generation is fully committed; inclusion of long-term firm power purchases in the entity's controlled generation; exclusion of behind-the-meter generation; changing how energy-constrained generators, such as solar, report capacity; and no reporting of quarterly land acquisitions that may be used for generation. *Refinements to Policies and Procedures for Market-Based Rates for Wholesale Sales of Electric Energy, Capacity and Ancillary Services by Public Utilities*, Order No. 816, 153 FERC ¶ 61,065 (2015), *order on reh'g and clarification*, Order No. 816–A, 155 FERC ¶ 61,188 (2016).

2. RETAIL COMPETITION: RESTRUCTURING AND THE STRUGGLE TO CONSUMER CHOICE

With the wholesale market in full-scale transition to competition, the next logical step was to make retail electricity markets competitive as well. At the end of the 20th century, this was indeed what many states did. These jurisdictions passed electricity restructuring laws that, to varying degrees, tried to pivot regulation to competition in the retail market. Many of these laws went so far as to force incumbent utilities to sell off their generation assets.

The rationales for retail competition were plain. Foremost was the suggestion that shifting to retail competition could push prices down. By giving incumbent utilities pressure from competitors, the theory went, the price of electricity would decrease. An additional rationale was that competition could spur product diversification so that consumers who wanted, for instance, more reliable power or cleaner generation could buy it. One group in favor of retail competition put it this way:

> *Different people value things differently!* That simple statement provides one reason that market transactions are an efficient mechanism for the allocation of resources. . . . Some people want the electric commodity delivered at the lowest possible cost, while others place a premium on the reliability of service, the quality of power, or the lowest emissions. Others want a blend of these factors. . . . Each value-based preference imposes costs on other people if it is forced on other people. . . .
>
> Consumer choice mitigates some problems of central decision making by offering a diverse set of options that meet people's diverse preferences. Rather than a one-size-fits-all approach or a government-mandated outcome, a competitive market is comprised of companies that offer a range of products and services. . . . There are still compromises to be made with respect to the regulated or monopoly components of the system; however, the less we mandate, the lower the shared costs.

DISTRIBUTED ENERGY FINANCIAL GROUP LLC, ABACCUS: AN ASSESSMENT OF RESTRUCTURED ELECTRICITY MARKETS 3–4 (2011).

Like the move to wholesale competition, however, switching to a retail electricity market was not short on complicated policy design and regulatory questions. Suedeen Kelly, a former law professor and subsequently a Commissioner at FERC, identified at least seven challenges in transitioning to a retail electricity market:

(1) *Stranded cost recovery*, or deciding whether and how to allow incumbent utilities to be paid for costs they incurred when regulated;

(2) *Incumbent utilities' market power*, or ensuring that incumbent utilities will not have an unfair advantage in the new market because of their ownership of distribution lines or large amounts of existing customers;

(3) *Non-market cost measures*, or regulators' efforts to ensure price decreases and lower rates despite moving generally to competition;

(4) *Regulating externalities*, which often was tackled along with restructuring, so that these laws tend to move both to competition and include surcharges to "fund programs variously designed to promote electricity efficiency, demand side management programs . . ., environmental improvement, universal electricity service, low income

assistance, and utility employee health, retirement and retraining programs";

(5) *Public, municipal, or cooperatively owned utilities*, or whether to compel these types of electric providers to participate in the retail market or to continue to allow them to sell on a cost-of-service rate basis;

(6) *Competition in ancillary services*, or whether the retail market extends only to energy or also to retail ancillary services such as billing, collections, metering, and meter reading; and

(7) *Consumer protection*, or the degree to which PSCs or incumbent utilities are allowed to educate customers about the switch to retail competition.

Suedeen G. Kelly, *Electricity, in* JAMES E. HICKEY, JR. ET AL., ENERGY LAW AND POLICY FOR THE 21ST CENTURY 12–1, 12–32 to –37 (Rocky Mtn. Min. L. Found. 2000).

It should thus be clear that switching to retail competition was no easy feat. Still, there were two common features that tended to be included in state restructuring legislation. First, because incumbent utilities could otherwise exercise vertical market power, they were required to offer open-access distribution service. Second, because states were concerned that competition might not come to fruition as fully or quickly as they hoped, legislation tended to require incumbent utilities to serve as "default" electricity providers—that is, "providers of last resort" or "POLRs." This requirement, too, generated several thorny policy design questions. For instance, what should the price of POLR service be? "If regulated POLR service is to be a proxy for efficient price signals, POLR rates must closely approximate a competitive price, which is based on supply and demand at any given time. If the POLR service price does not closely match the competitive price, it is likely to distort consumption and investment decisions." THE ELECTRIC ENERGY MARKET COMPETITION TASK FORCE, REPORT TO CONGRESS ON COMPETITION IN WHOLESALE AND RETAIL MARKETS FOR ELECTRICITY 7 (2007). Likewise, when should POLR rates change and how long should POLR service be available? "If POLR prices remain fixed while prices for fuel and wholesale power are rising, customers may experience rate shock when the transition period ends. . . ." *Id.* at 7–8.

Overall, between sixteen and twenty states, plus the District of Columbia, moved to retail competition, depending on how retail competition is defined. Broad-scale, nationwide retail competition, however, has failed to flourish, at least according to some:

Retail competition was expected to result in lower retail prices, innovative services and pricing options. It also was expected to shift the risks of assuring adequate new generation construction from ratepayers to competitive market providers. . . . In most profiled states, retail competition has not developed as expected for all customer classes. Few residential customers have switched to alternative providers. (Exceptions include Massachusetts, New York, and Texas.) In most of the profiled states, few residential customers have a wide variety of alternative suppliers and pricing options. Commercial and industrial (C & I) customers have more choices and options, but in several states large industrial customers have become increasingly dissatisfied with retail market prices. To the extent that multiple suppliers serve retail customers, prices have not decreased as expected, and the range of new options and services is often limited.

Id. at 6–7.

According to other reports, however, retail competition is working quite well in many of the states that adopted it. The Distributed Energy Financial Group has come up with a metric—coined "ABACCUS"—for rating retail electricity competition. The group releases summaries of North American retail competition. In their most recent report, they found:

One third of the states and provinces in North America have taken some steps to allow the direct sale of electric power to retail energy consumers by non-utilities. . . .

Eighteen jurisdictions in North America give non-utilities direct retail access to residential electricity consumers. Eligibility extends to at least 39.2 million residential accounts. Of these, 17.1 million (44%) received generation service (power only) or comprehensive electric service from a competitive retail energy provider or REP by the end of 2014. . . . In seven states, net switching declined in 2014. That is, in these states, more customers returned to default service than moved from default service to competitive service during the year. . . .

Nineteen jurisdictions in North America allow direct retail access to significant numbers of commercial and industrial customers. . . . These businesses acquire electricity just as they contract for other goods and services, reflecting their risk tolerance and taking into account many other issues . . . . [They] are sophisticated and . . . fully able to manage and sign a contract that best suits their operations.

Texas is the competitive residential electricity market leader for the eighth consecutive year. . . . The primary reason for Texas' success has been its market structure and especially the treatment of default service. . . . Texas is the only jurisdiction in North America that has carried through with its planned default service phase out. After the regulated "price to beat" was offered through the incumbent provider . . . from 2002 through 2006 in Texas, it was retired. Customers who had not selected an alternative provider remained with their current [provider]. Price regulation was removed and customers were advised to shop if they were not satisfied with the price or type of service.

DISTRIBUTED ENERGY FINANCIAL GROUP LLC, 2015 ABACCUS: AN ASSESSMENT OF RESTRUCTURED ELECTRICITY MARKETS 1, 5, 21 (Jul. 2015).

The ABACCUS scorecard also lists the percentage of retail customers that have switched suppliers—"the percent of residential customer accounts that have moved or migrated from the incumbent provider or moved off the default service product." *Id.* at 19. The report notes that only nine jurisdictions in North America have seen a switching rate of 20% or higher in the residential sector. For the United States, these residential switching rates, as of 2014, were as follows for eligible customers (they are different if all residential customers in the states are considered):

Jurisdiction	Residential Switching	Jurisdiction	Residential Switching
Texas	100.0%	Maryland	23.9%
Illinois	60.6%	New York	22.8%
Ohio	53.7%	Maine	22.4%
Connecticut	34.7%	Massachusetts	17.8%
Pennsylvania	36.0%	New Jersey	13.7%
District of Columbia	14.1%		

NOTES AND QUESTIONS

1. It is typical in states where retail restructuring is employed for the incumbent utilities to be designated as providers of last resort, or POLRs. The idea is that POLRs act as a safety net; customers must obtain service from somewhere, and what if a new competitor fails? How the POLR question is addressed appears to be one issue that plays heavily into how effective retail competition regimes are.

2. This raises an additional, important point: In retail competition efforts, legislatures, utility commissions, and courts are faced with intricate regulatory questions. Inevitably, this leads to additional regulations—for instance, the level of POLR rates, how to certify new competitors, whether to regulate them

at all, how to design the retail market, etc. Wholesale markets also include massive amounts of regulation, from FERC's market share and pivotal supplier screens to its Code of Conduct and anti-manipulation rules. If one of the aims of moving to competition is reducing regulatory costs, does the prevalence of regulations adopted to ensure that electricity markets properly function dilute that argument?

3.　Different states have used different models for retail competition. As noted above, Texas has been the most successful in having customers switch from incumbent providers. One court summarized Texas's statute:

> In 1999, the Texas Legislature . . . created a statutory scheme whereby the regulated utility industry would be separated or "unbundled" into three distinct entities: (1) power generation companies; (2) retail electric providers (REPs); and (3) transmission and distribution utilities. Once the statute goes into effect, electric providers formerly affiliated with regulated utilities will be required to provide electricity to residential and small commercial customers at a rate of six percent less than the rate in effect on January 1, 1999, adjusted to reflect the fuel factor as determined by the Commission. This price is referred to as the "price-to-beat." In enacting the price-to-beat statute, the Legislature intended for new REPs not affiliated with the regulated utility industry to enter the market and compete for customers with affiliated REPs, those that were formerly part of the bundled utility companies.

Reliant Energy, Inc. v. Public Utility Commission of Texas, 62 S.W.3d 833 (Tex. Ct. App. 2001). In other words, the Texas model put in place a discounted cost-of-service rate that must be provided, until the POLR lost 40% of its customers. Then, that discounted "price-to-beat" no longer applied. Why might the legislature require a discounted rate as the initial benchmark? And why might this model be more effective than others at getting customers to switch? For an assessment of Texas' transition to retail competition, see Phillip G. Oldham & Joseph P. Younger, *Lighting the Lone Star: The Texas Experience with a Competitive Electricity Market*, 40 WAKE FOREST L. REV. 709, 722 (2005).

4.　Residential retail competition, as noted, has not been as pervasive or as successful as many hoped. The Enron scandal and the California energy crisis immediately stunted the spread of retail restructuring laws. Virtually no state since has adopted such a law, and many that were considering proposals scrapped their plans. "Texas was the only state to proceed with its retail market in 2002—no other state has bothered to introduce retail competition or restructure its electricity market over the past decade, and few are contemplating to do so." *U.S. Retail Competition Is Alive, and Seemingly Managing Well*, 26 ELECTRICITY J. 2, 5 (Mar. 2013).

5.　In 2021, Tesla announced it would seek to become a retail electricity provider in Texas. One unique aspect of Tesla's proposal is that the company owns solar power and storage capacity, so it will not act as a middleman as many retail providers do. Would buying power from Tesla be attractive to you as a consumer? If you have access to retail electricity choice, what makes one provider more attractive than another?

6. Despite Texas often being held out as the model example of retail competition, brandishing that title does not come without downsides. At least one of those drawbacks was on full display during Winter Storm Uri in 2021, when Texas and neighboring states suffered what came to be known as the Big Freeze. The polar vortex and accompanying storm caused temperatures in the state to plummet. That, in turn, drove up electricity demand, as many Texans heat their homes using electricity. At the same time, supply shrunk, because many natural gas-fired facilities were not properly winterized—and others could not get fuel when natural gas wells, pipelines, and other infrastructure froze.

The result? Disaster. ERCOT was forced to employ rotating outages, water treatment plants failed, and over 700 people died. Worst hit were low-income communities of color—communities who had already been disproportionately impacted by the COVID-19 pandemic.

Not far from the center of this fray was a familiar figure: retail electricity competition. While many Texans were protected by fixed-price rates they had chosen in the retail market, others had selected variable rates that were tied to wholesale electricity prices which, in "normal" times, are lower than retail prices. Those wholesale costs exploded. "February's 'Big Freeze' winter storm exposed Texas energy market failures, racking up an unimaginable $52.6 billion in incremental electric system costs despite leaving residents short 1.6 million megawatt-hours of electricity—a deficit 1,000 times worse than California's August 2020 outages." Dan Esposito & Eric Gimon, *The Texas Big Freeze: How Much Were Markets to Blame for Widespread Outages*, UTIL. DIVE (June 3, 2021). This put some customers in the position where they might have to pay electricity bills "in excess of $5,000 or even $10,000." Edward Klump et al., *"Heads Will Roll": Grid Crisis Sparks Political Firestorm*, ENERGYWIRE (Feb. 22, 2021).

One company that garnered particular attention was Griddy. Oft likened to Costco, Uber, and Southwest Airlines, Griddy entered the Texas retail market in 2017. It sought to compete by offering customers up to 30% savings on their electricity bills, by tying its prices directly to wholesale market costs. Following the Big Freeze, Griddy—along with at least two other large Texas electricity suppliers—went bankrupt. As part of that bankruptcy plan, the state Attorney General secured releases of $29.1 million for roughly 24,000 of Griddy's 29,000 former customers. Edward Klump & Niina H. Farah, *Top Electricity Official Resigns After Blackout Crisis*, ENERGYWIRE (Mar. 17, 2021).

7. What do you think of retail competition? Would you want to promote it if you were a commissioner on your state's PSC? A report prepared for the Electric Markets Research Foundation highlights several effects retail competition has had:

- In U.S. jurisdictions with retail choice, roughly half of commercial and industrial load has switched to competitive suppliers, while under a tenth of residential load has done so. Because the gross benefits of switching suppliers are roughly proportional to a customer's size, larger customers are better able to overcome the transaction costs of switching than are smaller customers.

- Retail choice promotes renewable resources. To the extent that this raises the market penetration of intermittent resources such as wind and solar, it may raise resource adequacy issues because of the non-dispatchability of such resources.

- Retail choice has a mixed record in promoting demand response.

- Retail choice has not generally promoted smart metering.

- Retail choice states, from the beginning of retail choice up to the present, have had retail prices persistently higher than those in other states . . . . The overall trend has been toward a lower price gap . . . .

- The numerous statistical studies of the relationship of electricity prices to restructuring have reached contradictory conclusions about the price impacts of retail choice.

- Retail choice exacerbates the resource adequacy problem by materially adding to the financial uncertainties faced by investors in generating resources . . . .

- Under retail choice, retail suppliers incur marketing costs that must be recovered from customers.

- Some retail energy suppliers cherry pick customers. Some of the most attractive customers, namely industrial and large commercial customers, take advantage of lower prices in either the retail choice market or the regulated market, which may result in other customers bearing disproportionate shares of utilities' generation costs.

- There does not seem to be a clear relationship between retail choice and customer satisfaction. Results for U.S. residential customers are mixed. The EU experience suggests that retail choice, when well implemented, improves customer satisfaction.

- Retail choice decisions require business savvy that many consumers lack. Less educated or low-income consumers are more likely than other consumers to make poor retail supplier choices.

MATHEW J. MOREY ET AL., RETAIL CHOICE IN ELECTRICITY: WHAT HAVE WE LEARNED IN 20 YEARS? v–vii (2016); *see also* ADAM SWADLEY & MINE YÜCEL,

FEDERAL RESERVE BANK OF DALLAS, DID RESIDENTIAL ELECTRICITY RATES
FALL AFTER RETAIL COMPETITION? A DYNAMIC PANEL ANALYSIS (2011).

C. ELECTRICITY TRANSMISSION IN TRANSITION

While FERC's efforts to promote competition in electricity markets
have had profound effects on the industry, particularly from a ratemaking
and generation perspective, movement on the transmission side of the
ledger has been slower. In one important way, however, that was not true.
Early on, FERC recognized that it would need to change transmission
policy to promote wholesale competition, and thus was born Order No. 888.
After Order No. 888, FERC pushed hard for regional transmission
organizations (RTOs), which it believed would help coordinate markets and
open up the transmission system even more. Yet in other ways, particularly
with respect to rates and siting, transmission regulation at the beginning
of the 21st century looks very much like it did throughout the 20th. Several
overtures, including legislative ones, have sought to facilitate more top-
down transmission planning—most recently via FERC's own Order No.
1000—but states remain the center of authority for how transmission lines
are built and sited. This has obvious, and important, implications for the
country's ability to pivot to a new kind of energy economy.

This section of the chapter addresses both these issues: transmission
coordination through groups such as RTOs and transmission planning.

1. TRANSMISSION COORDINATION: RTOs AND ISOs

Modern groups that coordinate transmission systems—regional
transmission organizations (RTOs) and independent system operators
(ISOs)—go hand-in-hand with the shift to wholesale competition in
electricity. This is because one of the key goals of an RTO is to make
markets function more effectively. The theory is that they should do this in
at least two ways: (1) by having a neutral, non-self-interested organization
run the transmission system (and thus remove the risk of discriminatory
transmission access) and (2) by coordinating the market's operation so
there is a transparent structure and a neutral, on-the-ground monitor to
ensure proper competition.

RTOs and ISOs tend, then, to have three key functions. The first is
that these groups—which are typically non-profit organizations formed by
member   utilities,   independent   power   producers,   municipalities,
cooperatives, and other players in the electricity market—physically run,
operate, and help plan the transmission grid. Incumbent utilities that built
the grid maintain their ownership in the physical lines, but the RTO or ISO
handles day-to-day system operation. This offers potentially significant
benefits because RTOs inherently have a broader perspective of the grid:
Rather than focusing on a single system, the RTO—PJM, for example—

sees the grid over an 18-state region and can much better handle congestion, transmission outages, and other operational issues. Second, RTOs and ISOs create formalized markets, which facilitate power sales among parties. These markets, however, are not only for energy, and the energy markets themselves are disaggregated. RTOs typically run both day-ahead and real-time (or "spot") energy markets. They do this by feeding bids into complex software, which the RTOs then use to post price data for thousands of locations in the system at time intervals as short as five minutes. They often also have markets for generation capacity and other ancillary services, such as spinning reserves or voltage maintenance (*e.g.*, reactive power), plus other electricity-related products. Finally, RTOs and ISOs play a role in helping plan the expansion of the electricity grids within their footprint.

Control Room of the PJM RTO

Source: PJM Interconnection LLC (2019).

Initially, FERC pushed hard for RTOs, even looking to make membership in them mandatory for public utilities. Eventually, however, the Commission backed off this tack, instead requiring that public utilities *either* join a FERC-approved RTO *or* report on their progress toward joining one. Staunch political and industry resistance from utilities in the Southeast and the West defeated FERC's vision that the entire continental United States would be covered by RTOs. Now, RTOs manage about two-thirds of the electric power supply in the United States. *See Electric Power Markets: National Overview* Fed. Energy Reg. Comm'n (last updated July

20, 2021). Geographically, however, large swaths of the nation are still run by incumbent utilities, without any RTO presence.

RTOs and ISOs in the United States

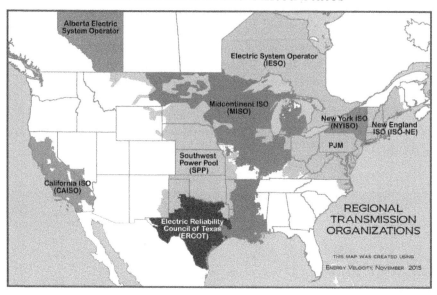

Source: Fed. Energy Reg. Comm'n.

Decisional law involving RTOs raises numerous cutting-edge issues in electricity transmission. At FERC, these tend to be sophisticated, very detailed market design and cost allocation questions. In the courts, those questions also arise, as do challenges to FERC's jurisdiction and the reasonableness of its decisionmaking in approving RTO proposals. RTOs file their tariffs and operating agreements as rate schedules at FERC, so the Commission obtains jurisdiction over their operation in part through FPA §§ 205 and 206.

The emergence of RTOs raised several important legal issues. One initial question was what rights utilities that joined RTOs gave up. In a key early case, *Atlantic City Electric Co. v. FERC*, 295 F.3d 1 (D.C. Cir. 2002), the D.C. Circuit ruled that FERC cannot force utilities who join RTOs to give up their FPA § 205 or § 206 filing rights. "The courts have repeatedly held that FERC has no power to force public utilities to file particular rates unless it first finds the existing filed rates unlawful." *Id.* at 10. FERC tried to justify its requirement by asserting that Order No. 888 firmly established that RTOs must be independent. This the court found irrelevant:

> FERC cannot rely on one of its own regulations to trump the plain meaning of a statute. . . . No matter how "bedrock" the principle of ISO independence may be, Order No. 888 is merely a regulation.

It cannot be the basis for denying the petitioners their rights provided by a statute enacted by both houses of Congress and signed into law by the president.

Id. at 11.

Likewise, the *Atlantic City Electric* court rejected FERC's attempt to compel utilities to ask permission to withdraw from an RTO after they have joined one, an effort FERC had tethered to its power to approve the disposition of jurisdictional electricity facilities under FPA § 203, 16 U.S.C. § 825b. "[T]he term 'dispose' in section 203 can only reasonably be read to refer to changes or transfers in proprietary interests or something akin thereto. . . . [Moreover,] FERC's expansive reading of its section 203 jurisdiction cannot be reconciled with section 202, which has been definitively interpreted to make clear that Congress intended coordination and interconnection arrangements be left to the 'voluntary' action of the utilities." *Atlantic City Elec.*, 295 F.3d at 12.

The courts have also found that FERC's normal FPA ratemaking powers do not give it free rein to dictate how RTOs function in practice. In *NRG Power Marketing, LLC v. FERC*, 862 F.3d 108 (D.C. Cir. 2017), for instance, PJM Interconnection—the RTO that covers much of the Mid-Atlantic and other nearby areas—submitted to FERC a proposed rate filing to change the rules it uses to run its capacity market. The idea of capacity markets is to send a price signal that new generation should be built, or that underperforming generation should be retired. Previously, PJM had in place a rule that set the minimum bid generators could put into its capacity market. However, under this prior approach, PJM could exempt generators from its minimum-price rule on a generator-by-generator (*i.e.*, unit-specific) basis. PJM's new proposal, reached through a stakeholder-based compromise, sought to shift away from this generator-specific approach for granting exemptions and instead establish categorical exemptions. It also sought to change the application of its minimum price rule from one year to three years. At FERC, the Commission found PJM's proposal unjust and unreasonable. It thus said it would approve PJM's rate filing only on the condition that (1) PJM retain its generator-by-generator exemption process, in addition to the categorical exemptions, and (2) keep the minimum price rule's application at one year, rather than extending it to three years. PJM agreed to make these changes, but several generators that operate in the PJM market challenged that choice in court. On review, the D.C. Circuit found that FERC had exceeded its authority under the Federal Power Act:

> Section 205 puts FERC in a "passive and reactive role." Under Section 205, FERC reviews the proposed rate scheme filed by a utility or Regional Transmission Organization and determines whether the proposal is just and reasonable. FERC may accept or

reject the proposal. But as this Court has held, Section 205 does not authorize FERC to impose a new rate scheme of its own making without the consent of the utility or Regional Transmission Organization that made the original proposal. *See Atlantic City Electric Co. v. FERC*, 295 F.3d 1, 10 (D.C. Cir. 2002).

Although FERC may not unilaterally impose a new rate scheme under Section 205, this Court has held that FERC has some authority to propose modifications to a utility's proposal if the utility consents to the modifications. [*See City of Winnfield v. FERC*, 744 F.2d 871, 876 (D.C. Cir. 1984).] . . .

Nonetheless, there are limits on FERC's authority to propose modifications under Section 205 even when the utility consents to those modifications. In *City of Winnfield*, we indicated that FERC would violate Section 205 if "the Commission proposal accepted by the utility involved the Commission's own original notion of a new form of rate" or an "entirely new rate scheme." . . .

We [have also held] that FERC may not go "beyond approval or rejection" of a proposal to "adoption of an entirely different rate design" than the proposal. [*Western Resources, Inc. v. FERC*, 9 F.3d 1568, 1578 (D.C. Cir. 1993).] . . . FERC may not employ a rate design that follows "a completely different strategy" than, or is "methodologically distinct" from, a proposed rate. . . .

Applying that principle here, we conclude that FERC violated Section 205. . . . First, FERC's proposed modifications resulted in an "entirely different rate design" than PJM's proposal. PJM's proposal sought to change how PJM determines which generators are exempt from the Minimum Offer Price Rule's price floor. . . . But FERC's proposed modifications went in the opposite direction. . . . Second, FERC's modifications also resulted in an "entirely different rate design" than the rate design that was "previously in effect." Under PJM's prior approach, unit-specific review was the main route to an exemption. As a result, generators had to demonstrate on a case-by-case basis that their costs fell below the price floor. Because of FERC's modifications, some generators can now claim exemptions from the price floor even if they cannot demonstrate that their costs fall below the price floor. . . .

FERC says that it did not violate Section 205 because PJM consented to FERC's proposed modifications. A utility's consent is relevant when FERC proposes "minor" modifications to the utility's proposal. But when FERC proposes its "own original notion of a new form of rate," the utility's consent does not excuse a Section 205 violation.

NRG Power Marketing, 862 F.3d at 114–16. The court thus vacated FERC's orders in part and remanded to the agency.

With FERC's authority over RTOs somewhat circumscribed, many of the legal and policy questions involving these organizations shifted to how best to design their markets and how to allocate costs among members. On this latter category, a series of important cases has emerged over the last decade. These cases, depending on one's perspective, either resurrect or recast a well-worn principle of utility regulation: "cost causation."

Although it can become more complicated in application, the basic principle of cost causation is relatively straightforward. It is not a question of whether costs should be recovered, but rather, who should pay for them. The cost causation "principle requires that 'all approved rates reflect to some degree the costs actually caused by the customer who must pay them.' The cost-causation principle has its roots in monopoly rate regulation, where rates are required to 'be based on the costs of providing service . . . plus a just and fair return on equity.' In the context of monopoly regulation, this principle helps ensure that utilities 'produce revenues from each class of customers which match, as closely as practicable, the costs to serve each class or individual customer.' " *Black Oak Energy, LLC v. FERC*, 725 F.3d 230, 237 (D.C. Cir. 2013) (citations omitted).

In 2004, the D.C. Circuit, in an opinion by Chief Justice Roberts before he was elevated to the Supreme Court, explained:

> We have described [the cost causation] principle as "requir[ing] that all approved rates reflect to some degree the costs actually caused by the customer who must pay them." *KN Energy, Inc. v. FERC*, 968 F.2d 1295, 1300 (D.C. Cir. 1992). Not surprisingly, we evaluate compliance with this unremarkable principle by comparing the costs assessed against a party to the burdens imposed or benefits drawn by that party. Also not surprisingly, we have never required a ratemaking agency to allocate costs with exacting precision. It is enough, given the standard of review under the APA, that the cost allocation mechanism not be "arbitrary or capricious" in light of the burdens imposed or benefits received.

Midwest ISO Transmission Owners v. FERC, 373 F.3d 1361, 1369–70 (D.C. Cir. 2004). Based on this analysis, the court rejected a cost causation challenge to FERC's order. That order had declined to approve an RTO fee that applied to new wholesale and unbundled retail loads but not to grandfathered or bundled retail loads. The fee was for the administrative costs of MISO. "[E]ven if they are not in some sense using the ISO," then-Judge Roberts wrote, "the MISO Owners still benefit from having an ISO":

MISO is somewhat like the federal court system. It costs a considerable amount to set up and maintain a court system, and these costs—the costs of having a court system—are borne by the taxpayers, even though the vast majority of them will have no contact with that system (will not use that system) in any given year. The public nevertheless benefits from having a system for the prompt adjudication of criminal offenses and the orderly resolution of civil disputes. Litigants bear some of the costs of using this system through the payment of filing fees and court costs. They, like utilities transmitting power under the MISO open access tariff who pay according to Schedule 1, are paying for the specific benefit of using the court system. The MISO Owners' position is tantamount to saying that if they are not a litigant, they should not be made to pay for any of the costs of having a court system. Since the MISO Owners do, in fact, draw benefits from being a part of the MISO regional transmission system, FERC correctly determined that they should share the cost of having an ISO.

Id. at 1371.

Thus, cost causation is one of the many fundamental principles of traditional utility ratemaking, including attracting capital and providing reasonably stable and predictable rates to customers, as discussed in Chapter 4. That is, while cost causation is a traditional ratemaking principle, it, like other such principles, still has important applications in today's world of electricity regulation in transition.

As you will see, because they involve RTOs, the cases excerpted here arise at the intersection of generation markets, transmission planning, and traditional and modern ratemaking principles. Together, they show FERC butting up against longstanding jurisdictional and ratemaking principles as the Commission, using a New Deal-era statute, tries to reshape the industry into something more modern, nimble, and new. This is a hallmark of electricity regulation in transition, and it pervades how regulation of the transmission system is moving forward.

As you read the cases, ask yourself whether the courts apply the principle of cost causation in a consistent way. Also consider whether such traditional principles of utility regulation have a place in the modern industry, and if you think they do not, with what legal doctrines you would replace them.

ILLINOIS COMMERCE COMMISSION V. FERC (*ICC I*)
576 F.3d 470 (7th Cir. 2009)

POSNER, CIRCUIT JUDGE.

We have before us challenges to a decision by the Federal Energy Regulatory Commission concerning the reasonableness of rates for the transmission of electricity over facilities owned by utilities that belong to a Regional Transmission Organization (that is, a power pool) called PJM Interconnection. "RTOs are voluntary associations in which each of the owners of transmission lines that comprise an integrated regional grid cedes to the RTO complete operational control over its transmission lines." Richard J. Pierce, Jr., "Regional Transmission Organizations: Federal Limitations Needed for Tort Liability," 23 *Energy L.J.* 63, 64 (2002). PJM's region stretches east and south from the Chicago area, primarily to western Michigan and eastern Indiana, Ohio, Pennsylvania, New Jersey, Delaware, Maryland, the District of Columbia, and Virginia. The region is home to more than 50 million consumers of electricity. . . .

Two issues are presented. The first . . . involves the pricing of electricity transmitted from the Midwest to the East through Ohio. [The court denied challenges to FERC's ruling on this question.] . . . The second issue relates to the financing of new transmission facilities . . . that have a capacity of 500 kilovolts or more. Heretofore all new facilities in PJM's region have been financed by contributions from the region's electrical utilities calculated on the basis of the benefits that each utility receives from the facilities. This will continue to be the rule for facilities with capacities of less than 500 kV. But for the higher-voltage facilities FERC has decided that all the utilities in PJM's region should contribute pro rata; that is, their rates should be raised by a uniform amount sufficient to defray the facilities' costs.[10]

FERC's stated reasons are that some of PJM's members entered into similar pro rata sharing agreements with each other more than forty years ago and would like to follow that precedent, that figuring out who benefits from a new transmission facility and by how much is very difficult and so generates litigation, and that everyone benefits from high-capacity transmission facilities because they increase the reliability of the entire network. Despite the stakes in the dispute—the new policy might, for example, force Commonwealth Edison to contribute hundreds of millions

---

[10] ["Pro rata" transmission pricing here is a reference to what is commonly known as postage stamp pricing. "A postage stamp rate is a fixed charge per unit of energy transmitted within a particular zone, regardless of the distance that the energy travels." Such pricing has the advantage of simplicity and the appearance of equity, but it presents several risks: inaccurate incentives, "pancaking" of rates when a transaction crosses multiple systems or zones, and a disconnect between the price paid and actual costs. For a concise primer on transmission pricing—its own (complex) subfield within energy law—see Hans-Joachim Bodenhöfer & Norbert Wohlgemuth, *Power Transmission Pricing: Issues and International Experience*, 3 INT'L ENERGY SYMP. 142 (2001).—Eds.]

of dollars to an above-500 kV eastern project called "Project Mountaineer," when it would not have had to pay a dime under the benefits-based system applicable to lower-voltage transmission facilities—no data are referred to in FERC's two opinions. . . . No lawsuits are mentioned. No specifics concerning difficulties in assessing benefits are offered. No particulars are presented concerning the contribution that very high-voltage facilities are likely to make to the reliability of PJM's network. Not even the roughest estimate of likely benefits to the objecting utilities is presented. The first sentence in this paragraph is an adequate summary of the Commission's reasoning, minus recourse to metaphor, as in the Commission's repeated references to very high-voltage facilities as the "backbone" of PJM's network. The Commission's insouciance about the basis for its ruling is mirrored by its lawyers: their brief devotes only five pages to the 500 kV pricing issue.

The objections to the Commission's ruling pivot on an asymmetry between the eastern and western portions of PJM's region. In the west the electrical generating plants usually are close to the customers—Chicago for example is ringed by power plants. As a result, relatively low-voltage transmission facilities—mainly 345 kV—are preferred. In the east, where the power plants generally are farther away from the customers, 500 kV and even higher-voltage transmission facilities are preferred, because high voltage is more efficient than low for transmitting electricity over long distances. So far as appears, few if any such facilities will be built in the objectors' service areas, that is, in the Midwest, within the foreseeable future. FERC seems not to care whether any will ever be built, because the reasons it gave for approving PJM's new pricing method are independent of where the facilities are located. . . .

That leaves for consideration the benefits that the midwestern utilities might derive from the greater reliability that the larger-capacity transmission facilities might confer on the network as a whole. The reason for building such facilities is to satisfy the demand of eastern consumers for electricity, but the more transmission capacity there is, the less likely are blackouts or brownouts caused by surges of demand for electricity on hot summer days or by accidents that shut down a part of the electrical grid. Because the transmission lines in PJM's service region are interconnected, a failure in one part of the region can affect the supply of electricity in other parts of the network. So utilities and their customers in the western part of the region could benefit from higher-voltage transmission lines in the east, but nothing in FERC's opinions in this case enables even the roughest of ballpark estimates of those benefits.

At argument FERC's counsel reluctantly conceded that if Commonwealth Edison would derive only $1 million in expected benefits from Project Mountaineer, for which it is being asked to chip in (by its estimate) $480 million, the disparity between benefit and cost would be unreasonable. The concession was prudent. As FERC itself explained in *Transcontinental Gas Pipe Line Corp.*, 112 F.E.R.C. ¶ 61,170, 61,924–61,925 (2005), "a claim of generalized system benefits is not enough to justify requiring the existing shippers to subsidize the uncontested increase in electric costs caused by the Cherokee project. . . ."

FERC is not authorized to approve a pricing scheme that requires a group of utilities to pay for facilities from which its members derive no benefits, or benefits that are trivial in relation to the costs sought to be shifted to its members. " '[A]ll approved rates [must] reflect to some degree the costs actually caused by the customer who must pay them.' " *KN Energy, Inc. v. FERC*, 968 F.2d 1295, 1300 (D.C. Cir. 1992). Not surprisingly, we evaluate compliance with this unremarkable principle by comparing the costs assessed against a party to the burdens imposed or benefits drawn by that party." *Midwest ISO Transmission Owners v. FERC*, 373 F.3d 1361, 1368 (D.C. Cir. 2004). To the extent that a utility benefits from the costs of new facilities, it may be said to have "caused" a part of those costs to be incurred, as without the expectation of its contributions the facilities might not have been built, or might have been delayed. But as far as one can tell from the Commission's opinions in this case, the likely benefit to Commonwealth Edison from new 500 kV projects is zero. . . .

No doubt there will be some benefit to the midwestern utilities just because the network is a network, and there have been outages in the Midwest. But enough of a benefit to justify the costs that FERC wants shifted to those utilities? Nothing in the Commission's opinions enables an answer to that question. Although the Commission did say that a 500 kV transmission line has twice the capacity of a 345 kV line, it added that "the reliability of 500 kV and above circuits in terms of momentary and sustained interruptions is 70 percent more reliable than 138 kV circuits and 60 percent more than 230 kV circuits on a per mile basis"—but did not compare the reliability of a 500 kV line to that of a 345 kV line, even though network reliability is the benefit that the Commission thinks the midwestern utilities will obtain from new 500 kV lines in the East.

Rather desperately FERC's lawyer, and the lawyer for the eastern utilities that intervened in support of its ruling, reminded us at argument that the Commission has a great deal of experience with issues of reliability and network needs, and they asked us therefore (in effect) to take the soundness of its decision on faith. But we cannot do that because we are not authorized to uphold a regulatory decision that is not supported by substantial evidence on the record as a whole, or to supply reasons for the decision that did not occur to the regulators. The reasons that did occur to FERC are inadequate.

We do not suggest that the Commission has to calculate benefits to the last penny, or for that matter to the last million or ten million or perhaps hundred million dollars. If it cannot quantify the benefits to the midwestern utilities from new 500 kV lines in the East, even though it does so for 345 kV lines, but it has an articulable and plausible reason to believe that the benefits are at least roughly commensurate with those utilities' share of total electricity sales in PJM's region, then fine; the Commission can approve PJM's proposed pricing scheme on that basis. For that matter it can presume that new transmission lines benefit the entire network by reducing the likelihood or severity of outages. But it cannot use the presumption to avoid the duty of "comparing the costs assessed against a party to the burdens imposed or benefits drawn by that party." . . . *Midwest ISO Transmission Owners v. FERC*, 373 F.3d at 1368.

CUDAHY, CIRCUIT JUDGE, concurring in part and dissenting in part.

. . . I write separately to express my concerns over the majority's disapproval of the proposed rate design for new transmission lines operating at voltages at or in excess of 500,000 volts.

The United States is now engaged in an urgent project to upgrade its electric transmission grid, which for years has been generally regarded as inadequate, and may become more deficient with the addition of major new anticipated loads. The existing transmission system originally served vertically integrated utilities that built their own generation relatively close to their customers. The system was not designed for long-distance power transfers between different parts of the country. The inadequacy of the present network and the urgency of the need for its improvement has only been exacerbated by the additional burdens imposed by deregulation (or restructuring), which "unbundled" generation and transmission and created a need to bring power from distant generators. Additional challenges have been posed by the demand for power from renewable generation sources (such as wind farms) that are often located in places remote from centers of electric consumption.

Long-distance transmission, which inherently presents challenges to reliability, is accomplished most efficiently by the highest levels of voltage—500 kV and above. According to FERC, "500 kV and above circuits . . . [are] 70 percent more reliable than 138 kV circuits and 60 percent more than 230 kV circuits on a per mile basis." Further, because power transfer capability increases with the square of voltage, extra-high voltage transmission also facilitates enormous transfers of power: "the maximum transfer capability at 500 kV and above is approximately 6 times greater than a similar transmission line operated at 230 kV and more than twice that at 345 kV. . . ." In light of its unique contributions to reliability and transfer capability, extra-high voltage transmission is especially fitted to be financed equally by all utilities that benefit from its role as the "backbone" of the system. Pro rata rates for extra-high voltage transmission, through their simplicity of application, also provide a strong incentive to build transmission undeterred by fruitless controversy over the allocation of costs.

It is significant that FERC's conclusion that the costs of extra-high voltage transmission facilities should be shared is consistent with the proposals of fifteen of PJM's seventeen members. In the course of this proceeding, various parties proposed voltages lower than 500 kV as the threshold above which proportional cost-sharing should apply. Although PJM's members were unable to agree on a specific voltage cutoff, they were broadly in agreement that the rate structure should be designed to share the costs of facilities providing general systemic benefits. There was thus an effort by many parties to broaden the area of rate-simplification by enlarging the set of new transmission facilities to be governed by cost-sharing, not to narrow or eliminate it. I think these efforts illustrate the value of simplification and the difficulties in the design of a transmission rate structure that attempts rigidly and in all circumstances to trace benefits to specific utilities.

However theoretically attractive may be the principle of "beneficiary pays," an unbending devotion to this rule in every instance can only ignite controversy, sustain arguments and discourage construction while the nation suffers from inadequate and unreliable transmission. Unsurprisingly, it is not possible to realistically determine for each utility and with reference to each major project the likelihood that rate-simplification will reduce litigation, or to calculate the precise value of not having to cover the costs of power failures and of not paying costs associated with congestion, and all this over the next forty to fifty years. Concerns about the real value to individual utilities of the stability and efficiency provided by improvements to the backbone grid are answered by their voluntary participation in the power pool and its collaborative "RTEP" (or regional transmission expansion planning) process. Rate-making based on cost causation is assured by this process, since universal cost-sharing is recommended only when developments are found to benefit the integrated system as a whole.

Contrary to the majority's suggestion, FERC did not violate principles of "cost causation" by failing to propose a number that would represent the specific monetary benefits to each utility of a more reliable network. Cost causation requires that "approved rates reflect to some degree the costs actually caused by the customer who must pay them." *Midwest ISO Transmission Owners v. FERC*, 373 F.3d 1361, 1368 (D.C. Cir. 2004). However, until today, no court has found that cost causation requires FERC to monetize the benefits of reliability improvements in order to share the costs. Indeed, the cases the majority cites support the opposite conclusion. Most notably, in *Midwest ISO*, the panel was quite clear that utilities that draw benefits from being a part of a power pool should share the cost of having a power pool. As then-Judge Roberts explained, "upgrades designed to preserve the grid's reliability constitute system enhancements that are presumed to benefit the entire system." *Id.* at 1369. . . . Put otherwise, the burden is on ComEd to show that it would not benefit from the newly planned transmission facilities; the burden is not on FERC to estimate how much ComEd would benefit from a more reliable grid. . . .

Because the majority's decision is based on an unusually narrow conception of cost-causation, its characterizations of FERC's and the intervenor's arguments as "insouciant" and "desperate" strike me as conspicuously misplaced. FERC responded to ComEd's objections by indicating that the proposed projects would improve reliability and reduce congestion. It did not explain how PJM's members benefit from a reliable network because no court had hitherto required it to do so. Until now, it went without saying that network reliability benefits the network's members. This is not insouciance; "[e]xplanations come to an end somewhere." LUDWIG WITTGENSTEIN, PHILOSOPHICAL INVESTIGATIONS § 1 (G.E.M. Anscombe trans., 1968).

The big picture here is that FERC's proposal to spread the cost of very high voltage transmission on a uniform basis seems to me in the interest of efficient, high-capacity transfer capability and of the closely linked improvement of reliability, which affects the system generally. Deregulation created a demand for competitive sources of power, often at a distance. Because 500 kV and above lines satisfy these new systemic needs, their separate treatment for rate-making purposes is both sensible and innovative. . . . Perhaps as important in this picture is the urgency of the need to build transmission and the need for incentives to that end. Pro rata assignment of costs eliminates not only lawsuits but nitpicking controversies of every sort and delays standing in the path of action. From that point of view, I think FERC may be in a better position to implement a policy leading to prompt improvement in a deficient transmission grid than this court, focused as it is on the inevitable complaints of utilities demanding more for their money. . . .

ILLINOIS COMMERCE COMMISSION V. FERC (*ICC II*)
721 F.3d 764 (7th Cir. 2013)

POSNER, CIRCUIT JUDGE.

Control of more than half the nation's electrical grid is divided among seven Regional Transmission Organizations. . . . Two Regional Transmission Organizations are involved in this case—Midwest Independent Transmission System Operator, Inc. (MISO) and PJM Interconnection, LLC (PJM). . . . MISO operates in the midwest and in the

Great Plains states while PJM operates in the mid-Atlantic region but has midwestern enclaves in and surrounding Chicago and in southwestern Michigan.

Each RTO is responsible for planning and directing expansions and upgrades of its grid. It finances these activities by adding a fee to the price of wholesale electricity transmitted on the grid. The Federal Power Act requires that the fee be "just and reasonable," and therefore at least roughly proportionate to the anticipated benefits to a utility of being able to use the grid. *Illinois Commerce Commission v. FERC*, 576 F.3d 470, 476 (7th Cir. 2009); *Pacific Gas & Electric Co. v. FERC*, 373 F.3d 1315, 1320–21 (D.C. Cir. 2004). Thus "all approved rates [must] reflect to some degree the costs actually caused by the customer who must pay them." *KN Energy, Inc. v. FERC*, 968 F.2d 1295, 1300 (D.C. Cir. 1992). Courts "evaluate compliance [with this principle, which is called 'cost causation'] by comparing the costs assessed against a party to the burdens imposed or benefits drawn by that party." *Midwest ISO Transmission Owners v. FERC*, 373 F.3d at 1368.

MISO began operating in 2002 and soon grew to have 130 members. . . . In 2010 it sought FERC's approval to impose a tariff on its members to fund the construction of new high-voltage power lines that it calls "multi-value projects" (MVPs), beginning with 16 pilot projects. The tariff is mainly intended to finance the construction of transmission lines for electricity generated by remote wind farms. Every state in MISO's region except Kentucky (which is barely in the region . . .) encourages or even requires utilities to obtain a specified percentage of their electricity supply from renewable sources, mainly wind farms. Indiana, North Dakota, and South Dakota have aspirational goals; the rest have mandates. The details vary but most of the states expect or require utilities to obtain between 10 and 25 percent of their electricity needs from renewable sources by 2025—and by then there may be federal renewable energy requirements as well.

"The dirty secret of clean energy is that while generating it is getting easier, moving it to market is not. . . . Achieving [a 20% renewable energy quota] would require moving large amounts of power over long distances, from the windy, lightly populated plains in the middle of the country to the coasts where many people live. . . . The grid's limitations are putting a damper on such projects already." Matthew L. Wald, "Wind Energy Bumps into Power Grid's Limits," New York Times, Aug. 27, 2008, p. A1. MISO aims to overcome these limitations.

To begin with, it has identified what it believes to be the best sites in its region for wind farms that will meet the region's demand for wind power. They are the shaded ovals in Figure 2. Most are in the Great Plains, because electricity produced by wind farms there is cheaper despite the longer transmission distance; the wind flow is stronger and steadier and land is cheaper because population density is low (wind farms require significant amounts of land).

Figure 2
Wind Development Zones and MVP Projects (dashed lines are initial proposals, solid lines approved projects)

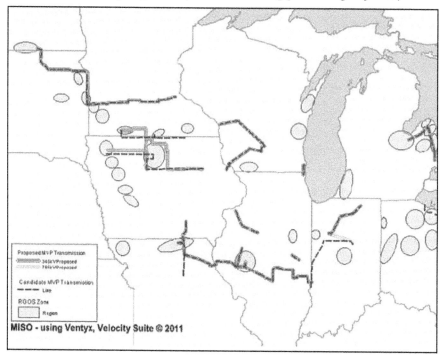

MISO - using Ventyx, Velocity Suite © 2011

MISO has estimated that the cost of the transmission lines necessary both to bring electricity to its urban centers from the Great Plains and to integrate the existing wind farms elsewhere in its region with transmission lines from the Great Plains—transmission lines that the multi-value projects will create—will be more than offset by the lower cost of electricity produced by western wind farms. The new transmission lines will also increase the reliability of the electricity supply in the MISO region and thus reduce brownouts and outages, and also increase the efficiency with which electricity is distributed throughout the region.

The cost of the multi-value projects is to be allocated among utilities drawing power from MISO's grid in proportion to each utility's share of the region's total wholesale consumption of electricity. Before 2010, MISO allocated the cost of expanding or upgrading the transmission grid to the utilities nearest a proposed transmission line, on the theory that they would benefit the most from the new line. But wind farms in the Great Plains can generate far more power than that sparsely populated region needs. So MISO decided to allocate MVP costs among all utilities drawing power from the grid according to the amount of electrical energy used, thus placing most of those costs on urban centers, where demand for energy is greatest.

FERC approved (with a few exceptions, one discussed later in this opinion) MISO's rate design and pilot projects in two orders (for simplicity well pretend they're just one), precipitating the petitions for review that we have consolidated. [We address the petitioners' challenges to FERC's ruling in turn.]

Proportionality and Procedure (best discussed together). . . . Illinois contends that the criteria for determining what projects are eligible to be treated as MVPs are too loose and as a result all MISO members will be forced to contribute to the cost of projects that benefit only a few. To qualify as an MVP a project must have an expected cost of at least $20 million, must consist of high-voltage transmission lines (at least 100kV), and must help MISO members meet state renewable energy requirements, fix reliability problems, or provide economic benefits in multiple pricing zones. None of these eligibility criteria ensures that every utility in MISO's vast region will benefit from every MVP project, let alone in exact proportion to its share of the MVP tariff. For example, Illinois power cooperatives are exempt from the state's renewable energy requirements, and so would not benefit from MVPs that help utilities meet state renewable energy requirements. But FERC expects them to benefit by virtue of the criteria for MVP projects relating to reliability and to the provision of benefits across pricing zones.

Bear in mind that every multi-value project is to be large, is to consist of high-voltage transmission . . ., and is to help utilities satisfy renewable energy requirements, improve reliability (which benefits the entire regional grid by reducing the likelihood of brownouts or outages, which could occur anywhere on it), facilitate power flow to currently underserved areas in the MISO region, or attain several of these goals at once. The 16 projects that have been authorized are just the beginning. And FERC has required MISO to provide annual updates on the status of those projects. Should the reports show that the benefits anticipated by MISO and FERC are not being realized, the Commission can modify or rescind its approval of the MVP tariff.

Illinois also complains that MISO has failed to show that the multi-value projects as a whole will confer benefits greater than their costs, and it complains too about FERC's failure to determine the costs and benefits of the projects subregion by subregion and utility by utility. But Illinois's briefs offer no estimates of costs and benefits either, whether for the MISO region as a whole or for particular subregions or particular utilities. And in complaining that MISO and the Commission failed to calculate the full financial incidence of the MVP tariff, Illinois ignores the limitations on calculability that the uncertainty of the future imposes. MISO did estimate that there would be cost savings of some $297 million to $423 million annually because western wind power is cheaper than power from existing sources, and that these savings would be "spread almost evenly across all Midwest ISO Planning Regions." It also estimated that the projected high-voltage lines would reduce losses of electricity in transmission by $68 to $104 million, and save another $217 to $271 million by reducing "reserve margin losses." That term refers to electricity generated in excess of demand and therefore (because it can't be stored) wasted. Fewer plants will have to be kept running in reserve to meet unexpected spikes in demand if by virtue of longer transmission lines electricity can be sent from elsewhere to meet those unexpected spikes. It's impossible to allocate these cost savings with any precision across MISO members.

The promotion of wind power by the MVP program deserves emphasis. Already wind power accounts for 3.5 percent of the nation's electricity, and it is expected to continue growing. . . . No one can know how fast wind power will grow. But the best guess is that it will grow fast and confer substantial benefits on the region served by MISO by replacing more expensive local wind power, and power plants that burn oil or coal, with western wind power. There is no reason to think these benefits will be denied to particular subregions of MISO. Other benefits of MVPs, such as increasing the reliability of the grid, also can't be calculated in advance, especially on a subregional basis, yet are real and will benefit utilities and consumers in all of MISO's subregions.

It's not enough for Illinois to point out that MISO's and FERC's attempt to match the costs and the benefits of the MVP program is crude; if crude is all that is possible, it will have to suffice. As we explained in [ICC I], if FERC "cannot quantify the benefits [to particular utilities or a particular utility] . . . but it has an articulable and plausible reason to believe that the benefits are at least roughly commensurate with those utilities' share of total electricity sales in [the] region, then fine. . . ." Illinois can't counter FERC without presenting evidence of imbalance of costs and benefits, which it hasn't done. . . .

Michigan . . . argues that unique features of the state's power system will cause Michigan utilities to pay a share of the MVP tariff greatly disproportionate to the benefits they will derive from the multi-value projects. A Michigan statute forbids Michigan utilities to count renewable energy generated outside the state toward satisfying the requirement in the state's "Clean, Renewable, and Efficient Energy Act" of 2008 that they obtain at least 10 percent of their electrical power needs from renewable sources by 2015. Michigan further argues that it won't benefit from any multi-value projects constructed in other states because its utilities draw very little power from the rest of the MISO grid. . . . It argues that for these reasons it should be required to contribute only to the costs of multi-value projects built in Michigan.

The second argument founders on the fact that the construction of high-voltage lines from Indiana to Michigan is one of the multi-value projects and will enable more electricity to be transmitted to Michigan at lower cost. Michigan's first argument—that its law forbids it to credit wind power from out of state against the state's required use of renewable energy by its utilities—trips over an insurmountable constitutional objection. Michigan cannot, without violating the commerce clause of Article I of the Constitution, discriminate against out-of-state renewable energy. *See Oregon Waste Systems, Inc. v. Department of Environmental Quality*, 511 U.S. 93, 100–01 (1994). . . .

Figure 3
MISO-PJM Border Region (MISO to left, PJM to right)
2004   2013

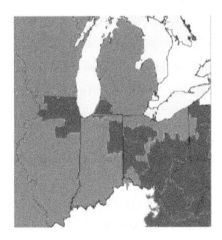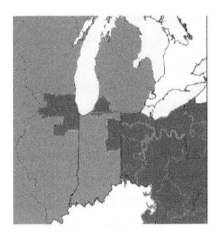

Export charges to PJM. An issue that unlike the previous ones finds MISO and FERC at loggerheads is whether the Commission is unreasonable in prohibiting MISO from adding the MVP surcharge to electricity transmitted from its grid to the grid of PJM, an adjoining Regional Transmission Organization. The Commission permits MISO to charge for transmission to other RTOs.

The prohibition arises from a concern with what in FERC-speak is called "rate pancaking" but is more transparently described as exploiting a locational monopoly by charging a toll. It is illustrated by Henrich von Kleist's classic German novella *Michael Kohlhaas*. When the book was published in 1810, what is now Germany was divided into hundreds of independent states. A road from Munich to Berlin, say, would cross many boundaries, and each state that the road entered could charge a toll as a condition for allowing entry. The toll would be limited not by the cost imposed on the state by the traveler, in wear and tear on the road or traffic congestion, but by the cost to the traveler of using a less direct alternative route. Like early nineteenth-century Germany, the American electric grid used to be divided among hundreds of independent utilities, each charging a separate toll for the right to send electricity over its portion of the grid. The multiple charges imposed on long-distance transmission discouraged such transmission. FERC promoted the creation of the Regional Transmission Organizations as a way of eliminating these locational monopolies. For it required that the RTOs embrace coherent geographic regions and that each RTO charge a single fee for use of its entire grid.

In the early 2000s Commonwealth Edison and American Electric Power had requested FERC's permission to join PJM despite being inside MISO's region (around Chicago and in southwestern Michigan, respectively). The Commission approved their requests yet was concerned that the irregular border . . . between the two regions, by creating PJM enclaves in MISO's region, violated the requirement that RTOs embrace coherent regions. The Commission was concerned for example with Michigan utilities' having to pay PJM charges on power sent from elsewhere in MISO (such as Wisconsin), because those transmissions, though beginning and ending in MISO territory, traversed a PJM enclave—the area served by Commonwealth Edison.

The Commission had another concern with the irregular border, what we'll call the "power routing" concern. Notice in the left-hand panel of Figure 3 the MISO utilities that lie (or rather lay, as of 2004) on a south to north diagonal in Kentucky and Ohio. Imagine a wholesale buyer of electricity located on the diagonal. It would be more efficient for it to draw electricity from the PJM transmission lines to its immediate west or east than from the MISO lines that snake to the northeast and thus bring electricity from a great distance. But the buyer might be deflected from the most efficient routing option because buying from PJM would cross both MISO and PJM territory and thus require paying a double toll.

So in 2003 FERC forbade export charges between MISO and PJM and ordered the two RTOs to negotiate a joint rate that would divide the costs of the cross-border transmissions between them. . . . The two RTOs negotiated a joint rate designed to share the costs of some transmission upgrades with crossborder benefits—but have not negotiated a joint rate for multi-value projects. MISO argues that the Commission should have reconsidered its 2003 prohibition of export charges to PJM and permitted such charges for multi-value projects that benefit electricity customers in PJM, in light of the changes (seen in the right-hand panel of Figure 3) in the MISO-PJM border between 2003–2004 and 2013. Those changes have straightened out the border and by doing so should have lessened the

Commission's concern that "the elongated and highly irregular seam between MISO and PJM . . . would subject a large number of transactions in the region to continued rate pancaking." . . . But with the disappearance of the MISO diagonal that we mentioned, the power-routing problem, at least, appears to have been solved, though FERC wants more data from MISO to demonstrate this. . . .

The MVPs also are not local. They will "support all uses of the system, including transmission on the system that is ultimately used to deliver to an external load," and "benefit all users of the integrated transmission system, regardless of whether the ultimate point of delivery is to an internal or external load." *Midwest Independent Transmission System Operating, Inc.*, 133 F.E.R.C. 61221, ¶ 439 (2010). . . .

MISO and PJM may eventually negotiate an allocation agreement, as they did in the pre-MVP era, but the rest of the grid is left to pay for PJM's share unless and until they do so. So far as we can tell, the Commission is being arbitrary in continuing to prohibit MISO from charging anything for exports of energy to PJM enabled by the multi-value projects while permitting it to charge for exports of energy to all the other RTOs. The Commission must determine in light of current conditions what if any limitation on export pricing to PJM by MISO is justified. This part of the Commission's decision must therefore be vacated. . . .

NOTES AND QUESTIONS

1.   In *ICC I*, the court rejected FERC's assertion that the cost of "backbone" transmission facilities should be borne by all members of the RTO. In *ICC II*, however, it affirmed FERC's spreading of the costs for multi-value projects across the RTO members, without much more evidence of exactly who benefits. Why the change? Did Judge Posner suddenly become a clean energy advocate, in favor of wind power and renewable energy? Or is the "cost causation" principle applied in the second *ICC* case different than in the first? Or does something else explain the difference? What role do FERC's underlying decisions play in the Seventh Circuit's decisions? Which case, *ICC I* or *ICC II*, do you think is more consistent with the explanation of cost causation that then-Judge Roberts gave in *Midwest ISO Transmission Owners*?

2.   In 2012, FERC issued an order basically affirming the pricing methodology struck down in *ICC I. See PJM Interconnection, L.L.C.*, 138 FERC ¶ 61,230 (2012), *order on reh'g*, 142 FERC ¶ 61,216. In 2014, in *Illinois Commerce Commission v. FERC*, 756 F.3d 556 (7th Cir. 2014) (*ICC III*), the Seventh Circuit, in a 2–1 decision authored by Judge Posner, granted the petition for review challenging FERC's decision. The *ICC III* majority took issue with the specificity of evidence FERC relied on, noting repeatedly that cost-benefit analysis was available to quantify the transmission lines' benefits.

"Much of the Commission's order on remand is devoted to handwringing over how difficult it is to estimate the benefits to PJM's western utilities of the new 500-kV lines in the east (thus reprising its original order). Yet at the same time the opinion contains detailed dollar estimates of many of the benefits—but without explaining the basis of the estimates. Studies are cited from time to time, but the evidence and analysis on which they're based are not described." *Id.* at 559. The majority also seemed convinced that even if the new high voltage transmission lines would benefit PJM as a whole, they would not advantage western PJM utilities as equally as eastern PJM utilities:

> [T]he basic fallacy of the Commission's analysis is to assume that the 500-kV lines that have been or will be built in PJM's eastern region are basically for the benefit of the entire regional grid. Not true . . . . No electric-power company would spend billions of dollars just to improve reliability in the absence of reliability violations that required fixing. There are bound to be benefits to the entire grid . . ., but they are incidental, just as repairing a major pothole in a city would incidentally benefit traffic in the city's suburbs, because some suburbanites commute to the city. So they should pay a share of the cost of repair, but a share proportionate to their use of the street with the pothole rather than proportionate to their population. The incidental-benefits tail mustn't be allowed to wag the primary-benefits dog.

Id. at 564. The court thus sent the case back to FERC. "[FERC] must try again. . . . If the Commission after careful consideration concludes that the benefits can't be quantified even roughly, it can do something [else, but it must address them somehow]. . . . If best is unattainable second best will have to do, lest this case drag on forever." *Id.* In a spirited dissent, Judge Cudahy fundamentally disagreed with the very premise of the majority's approach:

> The majority has expressed a need for more precise numbers about benefits, burdens and a variety of other aspects. Now it has enhanced that need by suggesting the use of cost-benefit analysis (a method, some think, of dressing up dubious numbers to reach more impressive solutions). I will say preliminarily that I think the majority is under the impression that somehow there is a mathematical solution to this problem, and I think that this is a complete illusion. Despite the frequency with which cost-benefit analysis is used, it does not resolve the difficulty of accurately or meaningfully measuring the costs and benefits involved with these grid strengthening projects. Cost allocation, particularly at these extraordinarily high voltages, is far from a precise science, and there are no mathematical solutions to determining benefits region by region or subregion by subregion. . . . Both parties acknowledged this much at argument. Cost allocation is a judgmental matter and should be treated as such. Cost allocation produces approximate results and requires selection of the most

appropriate methodology among many, none of which are necessarily "right."

Id. at 565 (Cudahy, J., dissenting). Who do you think is right here, the majority or dissent? What can FERC do on remand to satisfy the majority, and if you were an attorney for the agency, how would you seek to appeal-proof the agency's ruling? Is that possible?

3. In *Midwest ISO Transmission Owners*, the court compared the MISO regional transmission system to the federal court system, but in *ICC III*, the majority used the analogy of a pothole repair. Which do you think is more accurate? Does answering this question explain the difference in the cases?

4. Membership in RTOs is voluntary. Why didn't FERC make RTO membership mandatory, especially given that moving electricity over interstate areas is so critical to how our national electricity system operates? In Order No. 888, FERC made use of an OATT and the provision of open-access transmission service mandatory.

5. FERC has used incentive rates to encourage utilities to join RTOs. *See, e.g., Connecticut Dep't of Public Utility Control v. FERC*, 593 F.3d 30 (D.C. Cir. 2010); *Maine Public Utilities Comm'n v. FERC*, 454 F.3d 278 (D.C. Cir. 2006). In both of those cases, the courts upheld the incentives FERC offered utilities. How far would a financial incentive have to go to be considered arbitrary and capricious, or not supported by cost causation? Would the D.C. Circuit have a different view than the Seventh Circuit? Following President Biden's election, FERC issued a proposed rulemaking that would further enhance incentives for RTO membership. *Electric Transmission Incentives Policy Under Section 219 of the Federal Power Act*, 175 FERC ¶ 61,035 (2021).

6. FERC is not the only game in town when it comes to encouraging utilities to join RTOs. In 2021, Nevada passed legislation requiring the state to join an RTO, and Colorado adopted similar legislation mandating that all transmission utilities in the state join an organized wholesale market. Both bills set deadlines of 2030. Interest in promoting renewables was a driver of the legislation. *See* S.B. 448, 2021 Leg., 81st Sess. (Nev. 2021); S.B. 21–072, 2021 Leg., Reg. Sess. (Colo. 2021). Meanwhile, in the absence of a western RTO, the California ISO has established a real-time energy imbalance market—in which utilities in Arizona, British Columbia, Oregon, Nevada, New Mexico, Utah, and Washington participate. *See How Does the Western Energy Imbalance Market Work?*, POWER MAG (Oct. 1, 2018). Several utilities in the Southeast have also proposed forming an energy exchange market—a proposal that has sparked a fair amount of controversy to date. *See, e.g.,* Jeff St. John, *Why Utilities and Clean Energy Advocates Are Battling Over a Southeast Energy Market*, CANARY MEDIA (July 7, 2021).

7. One recurrent issue with RTOs is "market design"—that is, how to ensure that power is priced fairly considering transmission constraints across the system. One common response to this is "locational marginal pricing" or "LMP." LMP bases power prices on where the power is generated and used, so

that power which moves through more congested areas costs more. "With an LMP-based rate structure, prices are designed to reflect the least-cost of meeting an incremental megawatt-hour of demand at each location on the grid, and thus prices vary based on location and time. Each LMP consists of three components: (i) the cost of generation; (ii) the cost of congestion; and (iii) the cost of transmission losses." *Sacramento Municipal Utility District v. FERC*, 616 F.3d 520 (D.C. Cir. 2010). "Congestion costs" refer to transmission constraints. "Under the LMP system, [an ISO] takes into account the limits on available transmission capacity. . . . This results in higher energy prices at nodes that require the use of congested transmission lines and lower prices in less congested areas. . . . LMP [therefore] . . . giv[es] market participants incentives to avoid congestion-causing transactions. . . ." *Wisconsin Pub. Power, Inc. v. FERC*, 493 F.3d 239, 250–51 (D.C. Cir. 2007). "Transmission losses" refers to power that is sent to the purchasing customer but does not make it there. It is "the amount of electric energy lost when electricity flows across a transmission system. . . ." *Sithe / Independence Power Partners, L.P. v. FERC*, 285 F.3d 1, 2 (D.C. Cir. 2002). RTOs' use of locational marginal pricing has been challenged unsuccessfully in court on numerous grounds, including this methodology's justness and reasonableness and cost causation principles. *See, e.g., Sacramento Municipal Utility District v. FERC*, 616 F.3d 520 (D.C. Cir. 2010).

8.   Because RTOs operate electric generation markets, their actions deeply shape the future of the U.S. electricity system. One important example of this is a years-long dispute over the minimum offer price rule (MOPR) in PJM. Once narrowly used, that rule requires facilities bidding into the PJM capacity market to submit their bids no lower than certain pre-set prices. The idea is to avoid distorted market signals, by stopping parties from bidding lower than their actual costs. However, once states began subsidizing renewables and nuclear in order to fight climate change—especially through renewable energy credits (RECs) and zero emission credits (ZECs), addressed in more depth later in this chapter—FERC ordered PJM to apply the MOPR to all state-subsidized resources. *Calpine Corp. v. PJM Interconnection, L.L.C.*, 163 FERC ¶ 61,236 (2018), *establishing rate*, 169 FERC ¶ 61,035 (2019), *orders on reh'g*, 171 FERC ¶ 61,239, 173 FERC ¶ 61,061 (2020). This immediately spurred industrywide criticism in the renewables sector, because the MOPR prices for many of these resources would exceed the prior market clearing price, meaning they would not make money in the capacity auction. Many states within PJM also opposed the MOPR, and threatened to exit the RTO. In 2021, FERC indicated it was open to reconsidering its approach, prompting PJM to chart a new course more favorable to renewable energy interests. *See* Catherine Morehouse, *PJM Board Approves New MOPR Plan in Effort to Placate States, FERC*, UTIL. DIVE (July 9, 2021).

To better understand how RTOs influence the nation's energy future, you may want to read Shelley Welton's insightful article, *Rethinking Grid Governance for the Climate Change Era*, 109 CAL. L. REV. 209 (2021). For more on the MOPR battle, see Danny Cullenward & Shelley Welton, *The Quiet*

Undoing: How Regional Electricity Market Reforms Threaten State Clean Energy Goals, 36 YALE J. ON REG. BULL. 106 (2018); Joshua C. Macey & Robert Ward, *MOPR Madness*, 42 ENERGY L.J. 67 (2021).

9.   Notably, FERC has issued guidance indicating that it has authority to approve RTOs' market rules for carbon pricing. *See Carbon Pricing in Organized Wholesale Electricity Markets*, 175 FERC ¶ 61,036 (2021). On the worries of using markets rather than states to move to decarbonization, see Shelley Welton, *Electricity Markets and the Social Project of Decarbonization*, 118 COLUM. L. REV. 1067 (2018). What provisions of the Federal Power Act would provide FERC with authority to regulate carbon pricing in wholesale power markets? Are energy markets the right place to address GHG emissions? Is FERC the right regulator?

10.   As should be apparent by this point, the markets that RTOs operate are extraordinarily complex. In part because of this, it should also be obvious that much innovation in electricity law and policy today is occurring around, and in, RTOs, sometimes because of regulator prodding. One example of this innovation is policies that focus on the demand side of the electricity system, including by seeking to reduce electricity use rather than always relying on additional production to keep the grid in balance. One such RTO "demand response" program bubbled its way up to the Supreme Court in *FERC v. Elec. Power Supply Ass'n*, 577 U.S. 260 (2016), excerpted in Chapter 4.

As that case demonstrates, RTOs' willingness to experiment with policy innovations also can butt up against questions about who has jurisdiction to govern which parts of the grid. For more on these jurisdictional issues, see, for example, Matthew R. Christiansen & Joshua C. Macey, *Long Live the Federal Power Act's Bright Line*, 134 HARV. L. REV. 1360 (2021); Robert R. Nordhaus, *The Hazy "Bright Line": Defining Federal and State Regulation of Today's Electric Grid*, 36 ENERGY L.J. 203 (2015); Ari Peskoe, *Easing Jurisdictional Tensions by Integrating Public Policy in Wholesale Electricity Markets*, 38 ENERGY L.J. 1 (2017); and Jim Rossi, *The Brave New Path of Energy Federalism*, 95 TEX. L. REV. 399 (2016). For more on the importance of demand-side policies in energy more broadly, see Alexandra B. Klass & Elizabeth J. Wilson, *Remaking Energy: The Critical Role of Energy Consumption Data*, 104 CALIF. L. REV. 1095 (2016). And for more on RTOs' use of demand response as a grid management technique, see, for instance, Jamshid Aghaei & Mohammad-Iman Alizadeh, *Demand Response in Smart Electricity Grids Equipped with Renewable Energy Sources: A Review*, 18 RENEWABLE & SUSTAINABLE ENERGY REVS. 64 (2013); Joel B. Eisen, *Demand Response's Three Generations: Market Pathways and Challenges in the Modern Electric Grid*, 18 N.C. J. L. & TECH. 351 (2017); and the April 2010 special issue (volume 35, issue 4) of the journal, *Energy*, which devoted many of its pages to demand response programs in RTOs.

2. TRANSMISSION PLANNING: RESHAPING THE GRID

Transmission planning may not be the sexiest of topics, but it has become critical enough that virtually every major news outlet has featured a story on it in recent years. In the wake of a brutal heatwave and ensuing power outages in the Pacific Northwest in summer 2021, the *Washington Post* summarized the nation's transmission issues this way: "The American grid features stressed and often barely adequate equipment on the local level, and a region-by-region governing structure that in pursuit of market savings has become so complex that it obscures the full picture. But perhaps the central issue is chronic congestion on the transmission lines that bring power from where it's made to where it's wanted." Will Englund, *The Grid's Big Looming Problem: Getting Power to Where It's Needed*, WASH. POST (June 29, 2021); *see also* Jeff Brady, *An Aged Electric Grid Looks to a Brighter Future*, NPR (Apr. 27, 2009). Thus, Energy Secretary Jennifer Granholm has urged, "[w]e need to jam on the accelerator here. We've got to make sure the capacity is there on the grid." *Id.* Or as Bill Richardson, then-Governor of New Mexico and former Secretary of Energy, pleaded nearly two decades prior, "We are a major superpower with a third-world electrical grid. . . . Our grid is antiquated. It needs serious modernization." David Firestone & Richard Perez-Pena, *Power Failure Reveals a Creaky System, Energy Experts Believe*, N.Y. TIMES (Aug. 15, 2003).

This, then, is the triple threat of failed transmission planning in the United States: a grid that is (1) not sufficiently reliable, (2) inefficient because of transmission constraints, and (3) inadequate to integrate an increasingly renewables-based generation fleet. The solutions to these problems are not lacking because of lagging engineering. Rather, the needed answers are financial and political. For decades, transmission planning happened primarily at the state level, on a utility-by-utility basis. The inadequacy of the nation's transmission grid thus remained largely invisible, a topic relegated to industry circles, policy wonks, and energy law teachers. We discuss grid modernization in detail in Chapter 8.

By the turn of the century, the inadequacy of this piecemeal approach to transmission planning became apparent. A massive blackout across the Northeast and Canada in the summer of 2003 left "an area with an estimated 50 million people and 61,800 megawatts (MW) of electric load" without electricity for days, at a cost somewhere between $4 billion and $10 billion. U.S.-CANADA POWER SYSTEM OUTAGE TASK FORCE, FINAL REPORT ON THE IMPLEMENTATION OF THE TASK FORCE RECOMMENDATIONS 3 (2006).

Climate change has only made things worse. Winter Storm Uri, Hurricane Ida, and the western wildfires in 2021 are only the most recent of a series of climate-related impacts on the nation's electricity grid. Indeed, Hurricane Ida in August 2021 knocked out all the transmission lines leading into New Orleans, leaving more than 1 million people without electricity.

One of the more prominent disasters was the 2018 Camp Fire in California. Eventually consuming an area the size of nearly one-fifth the state of Rhode Island, the Camp Fire quickly became "the deadliest and most destructive fire in California history." It "burned a total of 153,336 acres, destroying 18,804 structures and resulting in 85 civilian fatalities and several firefighter injuries." *CAL FIRE Investigators Determine Cause of the Camp Fire*, Cal. Dep't of Forestry & Fire Protection (May 15, 2019).

The cause of this major event? It was not an earthquake or tsunami or other natural disaster. It was vegetation coming into contact with electric distribution lines owned by Pacific Gas & Electric. The result was heart-wrenching:

> In Paradise[, California, near the Sierra Nevada foothills], some residents awoke to the sound of embers raining down on their rooftops. They drove through fire and smoke too thick to see through, colliding with other cars and driving off embankments. Survivors describe the scene of horror in biblical terms. It was as if "the gates of hell had opened up." "Black and red was all you could see."

> Scott McLean arrived in Paradise around 8 a.m. as the fire was already engulfing the southern side of town. McLean is a 21-year veteran of the California Department of Forestry and Fire Protection—and Cal Fire's chief spokesperson since 2014—but he was still stunned by what he saw. "Hell," was the only word he had for it on Sunday.

> Wrecked and abandoned cars blocked the roadway, said McLean. Everywhere, there were flames, smoke, and wreckage. He thinks it was around 9 o'clock, though he can't remember for sure, that smoke filled the sky and turned the morning dark as night. As he drove around in search of safe exit routes, he came upon an elderly woman in a wheelchair alone on an empty section of road, pushing herself through the maelstrom.

> For hours, firefighters could only try to save lives. There was nothing they could do to contain the erratic, wind-whipped blaze.

Maraya Cornell, *How Catastrophic Fires Have Raged Through California*, NAT'L GEO. (Nov. 13, 2018).

So planning and maintenance of our grid matter—critically and deeply. And the nation needs new transmission lines—lots of them. What will ensure we care for the grid in a thoughtful and deliberate way? What will get these new lines built?

Two answers are the consensus: regulatory innovation and money. As Congress acknowledged shortly after the 2003 Northeast blackout: "Investment in electric transmission expansion has not kept pace with electricity demand. Moreover, transmission system reliability is suspect as demonstrated by the blackout that hit the Northeast and Midwest in August of 2003. . . . In addition, state regulatory approval delays siting of new transmission lines by many years. Even if a project is completed, there is uncertainty as to whether utilities will be able to recover all of their investment, which hinders new transmission construction." *House Report on the Energy Policy Act of 2005,* H.R. Rep. No. 109–215(I), at 171. Since 2010, the picture has improved somewhat. "[A]fter decades of decline in investment in the transmission grid, utilities and other grid operators have increased spending on grid expansion dramatically since 2010, with investor-owned utilities spending a record high $20.1 billion in investment in 2015, as compared with $10.2 billion in 2010." Alexandra B. Klass, *Transmission, Distribution, and Storage: Grid Integration, in* LEGAL PATHWAYS TO DEEP DECARBONIZATION IN THE UNITED STATES 527, 530 (Michael B. Gerrard & John C. Dernbach, eds. 2019). Still, the fundamental challenge remains. More investment is needed to relieve congestion, to allow for greater integration of growing renewable resources, and to modernize the grid.

Indeed, in many ways, the problem of grid expansion and modernization has become intractable. It derives both from a lack of investment and the thorny mess of roadblocks that fracture siting authority. One set of commentators has identified at least eleven interrelated barriers stymieing the move to a more effective transmission grid. Note how many of these are regulatory or policy-based in nature:

- Increased demand for location constrained renewable energy to power concentrated urban areas. . . .

- The "Not in My Back Yard" (NIMBY) syndrome. . . .

- Conflicts between local, statewide, and regional interests. . . .

- Inconsistent and conflicting state and local regulatory requirements. . . .

- Federal and state environmental reviews. . . .

- Federal land authorizations. . . .

- Lack of timing coordination among siting entities. . . .

- Inconsistent state policies regarding greenhouse gas emissions and renewable portfolio standards. . . .

- Short-term capacity v. long-term need. . . .

- Uncoordinated siting of transmission lines and renewable generation. . . .

- Timing of "need" determination.

JAMES A. HOLTKAMP & MARK A. DAVIDSON, TRANSMISSION SITING IN THE WESTERN UNITED STATES 7–9 (2009).

To start cutting through this regulatory red tape, Congress and regulators began implementing several policy innovations to attempt to reform how transmission planning in the United States is conducted.

NERC Regional Entities

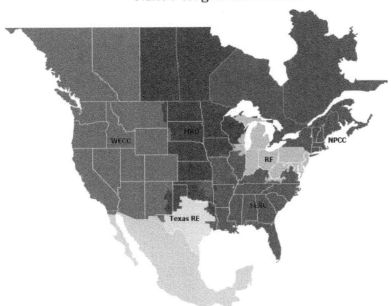

Source: North Am. Elec. Reliability Corp.

First, in direct response to the Northeast blackout of 2003, Congress in the Energy Policy Act of 2005 ordered FERC to establish an electric reliability organization (ERO) that, under FERC's purview, has oversight authority to ensure that utilities maintain their systems with adequate reliability. To no one's surprise, FERC designated the North American Electric Reliability Corporation (NERC) as the ERO. NERC divided North America into regions, establishing regional EROs, all of which are regulated according to the NERC Reliability Standards. *See* 18 C.F.R. § 40.3. These reliability standards regulate technical system reliability and engineering issues like disturbance control (to maintain the balancing of system resources and demand), return interconnection frequency (following system disturbances), and standards to avoid the loss of firm loads (following generation or transmission contingencies). NERC,

Disturbance Control Standards, Reliability Standard BAL–002–1; NERC, Contingency Reserve, Reliability Standard BAL–002–WECC–1. The reliability standards also govern the reliability of interconnections and all operating reserves to adequately balance system resources. NERC, Automatic Generation Control, Reliability Standard BAL–005–0.1b; NERC, Operating Reserves, Reliability Standard BAL–STD–002–0. To protect system safety, NERC also regulates reports of sabotage. NERC, Sabotage Reporting, Reliability Standard CIP–001–2a. NERC reliability standards "are enforceable in all interconnected jurisdictions in North America: the continental United States; the Canadian provinces of Alberta, British Columbia, Manitoba, New Brunswick, Nova Scotia, Ontario, Quebec, and Saskatchewan; and the Mexican state of Baja California Norte"—though Alaska and Hawaii are exempt. *Reliability Standards*, N. Am. Elec. Reliability Corp. (2021); *see also* ASHLEY J. LAWSON, CONG. RSCH. SERV., MAINTAINING ELECTRIC RELIABILITY WITH WIND AND SOLAR SOURCES: BACKGROUND AND ISSUES FOR CONGRESS 1 n.3 (2019).

Second, EPAct 2005 sought to give FERC more direct transmission siting authority. While FERC long has had siting authority for interstate natural gas pipelines (see Chapter 7), the idea under EPAct 2005 was different. Here FERC's siting authority would be more limited. DOE would first specify national priority areas for transmission development. Then, if states failed to approve a proposed transmission line in certain ways, or lacked the authority to do so, *see* 16 U.S.C. § 824p(1)(A), FERC could step in and site the line itself. This gave "FERC . . . 'backstop authority' for siting interstate electric transmission facilities. This limited authority is available only in areas the [DOE] identifies as a 'national interest electric transmission corridor'. . . . However, despite the promise of these provisions, similar past initiatives have failed to produce significant results." Joshua P. Fershee, *Misguided Energy: Why Recent Legislative, Regulatory, and Market Initiatives Are Insufficient to Improve the U.S. Energy Infrastructure*, 44 HARV. J. ON LEGIS. 327, 331–32 (2007); *see also* Debbie Swanstrom & Meredith M. Jolivert, *DOE Transmission Corridor Designations and FERC Backstop Siting Authority: Has the Energy Policy Act of 2005 Succeeded in Stimulating the Development of New Transmission Facilities?*, 30 ENERGY L.J. 415, 418 (2009).

Third, FERC began using different kinds of ratemaking incentives to encourage transmission construction. The basic idea here is that if a higher rate of return is allowed on new transmission lines, more lines will be built. FERC codified these incentives in its Order No. 679, Promoting Transmission Investment through Pricing Reform, Order No. 679–A, 72 Fed. Reg. 1152 (Jan. 10, 2007), FERC Stats. & Regs. ¶ 31,236 (2007) (Order No. 679–A). "In Order No. 679, FERC created eight new financial incentives intended to encourage new investment in transmission. These incentives include: (1) a return on equity ('ROE') to attract capital at the 'upper end of the zone of reasonableness;' (2) authorization to include 100 percent (rather than 50 percent) of prudently incurred construction work-in-progress in the rate base and expensing of prudently incurred 'pre-commercial costs;' (3) permission for transmission developers to base rates on hypothetical capital structures; (4) allowing accelerated depreciation for new transmission investments; (5) recovery of 100 percent of costs of abandoned transmission projects, so long as the costs were prudently incurred and the abandonment decision was not made by the developer; (6) for companies subject to retail rate moratoria, deferred cost recovery; (7) authorization to file a separate rate case for new transmission without reopening existing rates to review or litigation; and (8) a higher ROE for transmission companies participating in regional transmission organizations (RTOs) and independent system operators (ISOs)." Mary Anne Sullivan, *The Many Challenges of the "Full Portfolio" Approach: Utilities Prepare for Climate Change Regulation*, 2008 No. 3 RMMLF-INST. PAPER NO. 15.

Fourth, some states, such as Texas, created priority transmission development zones, usually for renewable resources. In Texas, these are referred to as competitive renewable energy zones, or "CREZs":

> In 2005, the Legislature enacted laws intended to encourage the development and transmission of renewable energy, such as wind energy, in Texas. . . . Among other things, this legislation required the Commission to designate "Competitive Renewable Energy Zones" (CREZs)—*i.e.*, geographic regions of Texas identified as being the best suited for cost-efficient renewable energy development such as wind farms in West Texas. The legislation also required the Commission to develop and implement a plan to build the transmission lines needed to move electricity from the CREZ locations to the state's power grid. The CREZ transmission project involves a collection of utility companies selected to build over 2,000 miles of high voltage transmission lines from West Texas to higher populated areas in the eastern portion of the state.

McMaster v. Pub. Util. Comm'n of Texas, 03–11–00571–CV, 2012 WL 3793257, n.1 (Tex. Ct. App., Aug. 31, 2012). Texas' use of CREZs generally is regarded as an "unqualified success." JULIE COHN & OLIVERA JANKOVSKA, RICE UNIVERSITY'S BAKER INST. FOR PUB. POLICY, TEXAS CREZ LINES: HOW STAKEHOLDERS SHAPE MAJOR ENERGY INFRASTRUCTURE PROJECTS 4 (Nov. 2020). "In 1999, when the legislature instituted a Renewable Portfolio Standard, the state counted 116 MW of installed wind capacity. In 2005, when the legislature authorized CREZ, the total had increased to nearly 2,000 MW. Today, Texas leads the country with 24,000 MW of installed capacity, providing upwards of 23% of the total average power generated in the state." *Id.* (For a discussion of Michigan's efforts in a similar regard, see Chapter 7.)

Finally, FERC issued a series of orders attempting to foster greater regional coordination of transmission planning. The first of these, Order No. 890, "requires public utilities to participate in open and transparent transmission-planning processes. The intent of the order was to mitigate conflict at the local and regional level by facilitating an open process and coordination." Alexandra B. Klass & Elizabeth J. Wilson, *Interstate Transmission Challenges for Renewable Energy: A Federalism Mismatch*, 65 VAND. L. REV. 1801, 1823 (2012).

Then, using Order No. 890 as its baseline, in 2011 FERC issued Order No. 1000. This regulation takes Order No. 890 to the next level, by not merely requiring utilities to engage in open planning but by compelling them to cooperate with each other in how they do so. Specifically, Order No. 1000 "establishes three requirements for transmission planning. Each public utility transmission provider must (1) participate in a regional transmission-planning process that satisfies the requirements set out in Order 890 and produce a regional transmission plan, (2) establish procedures to identify transmission needs based on public policy requirements in state or federal laws or regulations and evaluate proposed solutions to those transmission needs, and (3) coordinate with public utility transmission providers in neighboring transmission-planning regions to determine if there are more efficient or cost-effective solutions to mutual transmission needs." Klass & Wilson, *supra* at 1823–24. Rather controversially, Order 1000 also eliminates certain incumbent utilities' "right of first refusal" from federal transmission tariffs to build transmission lines within their territories; the aim is to allow market forces to spur the development of new transmission lines. Another "purpose of the order is to give more priority to lines that will serve renewable energy goals and make those lines more affordable. Significantly, in Order 1000, FERC articulated 'public policy benefits' as a new type of transmission-related benefit." *Id.* at 1824; *see also* Shelley Welton & Michael B. Gerrard, *FERC Order 1000 as a New Tool for Promoting Energy Efficiency and Demand Response*, 42 ENV'T L. REP. NEWS & ANALYSIS 11025 (2012); Steptoe & Johnson LLP, *Analysis of FERC Order No. 1000* (Aug. 3, 2011).

The following cases highlight several of the issues surrounding the transition-in-progress in U.S. transmission planning. Specifically, they outline the scope of—and limits on—FERC's authority to site and plan transmission lines—the very backbone of the nation's electricity grid—in the modern age. They show, in short, another perspective into electricity regulation in transition: a system of governance that today is clearly different from the conventional mold but also one that has not fully broken free of its old shackles.

As you read the cases, consider two questions: First, why do the cases come out differently? And second, taken together, to what degree do they limit FERC's electricity transmission siting and planning powers, how do those limits constrain the development of a more effective and efficient grid in the United States, and do you think those constraints are good or bad?

PIEDMONT ENVIRONMENTAL COUNCIL V. FERC
558 F.3d 304 (4th Cir. 2009)

MICHAEL, CIRCUIT JUDGE.

Two state utilities commissions and two community interest organizations petition for review of several rulemaking decisions made by the Federal Energy Regulatory Commission (FERC or the Commission) in connection with FERC's implementation of the new § 216 of the Federal Power Act (FPA) and the National Environmental Policy Act (NEPA). Section 216 of the FPA, which was added in 2005, gives FERC jurisdiction in certain circumstances to issue permits for the construction or modification of electric transmission facilities in areas designated as national interest corridors by the Secretary of Energy.

[W]e reverse FERC's expansive interpretation of the language in FPA § 216(b)(1)(C)(i) that grants FERC permitting jurisdiction when a state commission has "withheld approval [of a permit application] for more than 1 year." The phrase does not include, as FERC held, the denial of an application. . . .

I.

The states have traditionally assumed all jurisdiction to approve or deny permits for the siting and construction of electric transmission facilities. As a result, the nation's transmission grid is an interconnected patchwork of state-authorized facilities. In recent times increasing concerns have been expressed about the capacity and reliability of the grid. Congress has reacted to these concerns by adding a new section (§ 216) to the FPA when it passed the Energy Policy Act of 2005.

FPA § 216 authorizes the Secretary of Energy to designate areas with electric transmission constraints affecting consumers as national interest electric transmission corridors. Section 216 gives FERC the authority in national interest corridors to issue permits for the construction or modification of transmission facilities in certain instances, including the one at issue here: when a state entity with authority to approve the siting of facilities has "withheld approval for more than 1 year after the filing of an application" for a permit.

FPA § 216(c)(2) directed FERC to issue rules specifying the form of, and the information to be contained in, an application for construction or modification of electric transmission facilities in a national interest corridor. . . . In mid-December 2006 the four petitioners in this proceeding—Piedmont Environmental Council (Piedmont), the Public Service Commission of the State of New York (NYPSC), the Minnesota

Public Utilities Commission (Minnesota PUC), and CARI—filed requests for rehearing on FERC's final rule. All argued to FERC that it had erred in holding that § 216(b)(1)(C)(i)'s phrase "withheld approval [of an application] for more than 1 year" includes a denial. . . . The Commission rejected the petitioners' arguments about the meaning of § 216(b)(1)(C)(i), saying that it "continue[d] to believe that a reasonable interpretation of the language of the legislation support[ed]" its earlier conclusion. . . .

II.

. . . FERC interprets § 216(b)(1)(C)(i)'s phrase "withheld approval for more than 1 year after the filing of [a permit] application" to include a state's outright denial of an application within one year. We conclude that FERC's interpretation is contrary to the plain meaning of the statute. Simply put, the statute does not give FERC permitting authority when a state has affirmatively denied a permit application within the one-year deadline.

We begin with the word "withhold," which means "to hold back: keep from action" or "to desist or refrain from granting, giving, or allowing." WEBSTER'S THIRD NEW INT'L DICTIONARY (WEBSTER'S) 2627 (2002). We must, of course, consider the word "withheld" in the context of the statutory phrase in which it is used—"withheld approval for more than 1 year." The phrase, read as a whole, means that action has been held back continuously over a period of time (more than one year). The continuous act of withholding approval for more than a year cannot include the finite act of denying an application within the one-year deadline. The denial of an application is a final act that stops the running of time during which approval was withheld on a pending application.

To support its interpretation that withholding approval includes the denial of a permit, FERC relies on the dictionary definition of "deny" and a thesaurus entry under "refusal." Specifically, FERC quotes the following definition of "deny": "to refuse to grant: WITHHOLD." WEBSTER'S at 603 (capitalization in original). The thesaurus paragraph for "refusal" that FERC relies upon lists "deny" and "withhold" as synonyms. ROGET'S INTERNATIONAL THESAURUS, ¶ 776.4 (4th ed. 1984). The word used in the statute is "withheld," so FERC takes a backward approach to its desired result when it relies on the meaning of a word it wishes to substitute for "withheld." The word "deny" is broad enough to include "withhold" in its definition, but the word "withhold" is not broad enough to include "deny" in its definition. *Compare* WEBSTER'S at 603 (definition of deny) with WEBSTER'S at 2627 (definition of withhold). FERC therefore gets no real support from the dictionary. Moreover, just because "deny" and "withhold" are listed as synonyms does not mean that they are always interchangeable. Certainly they are not interchangeable here.

When FERC substitutes "denied" for "withheld," it ignores the context in which "withheld" is used. With FERC's word substitution the statutory phrase would read "denied approval [of an application] for more than 1 year." The substitution renders the entire phrase nonsensical because, in the context of dealing with a permit application, the final nature of "denied" conflicts with the continuing nature of "for more than 1 year." FERC would thus change the clear meaning of the provision because the denial of a permit application within one year ends the application process, and there is nothing about that terminated process that would continue for more than one year.

An examination of § 216(b)(1) as a whole, which is the broader context in which the "withheld approval for more than 1 year" phrase appears, confirms that the phrase does not encompass the denial of a permit. Section 216(b)(1) provides a carefully drawn list of five circumstances when FERC may preempt a state and issue a permit for the construction or modification of electric transmission facilities in a national interest corridor. They are when: (1) a state in which the transmission facilities are to be constructed or modified does not have the authority to approve the siting, 16 U.S.C. § 824p(1)(A)(i); (2) a state does not have the authority to consider the expected interstate benefits to be achieved by the proposed project, *id.* § 824p(1)(A)(ii); (3) a permit applicant is a transmitting utility under the FPA, but does not qualify for a permit in a particular state because it does not serve end-use customers in that state, *id.* § 824p(1)(B); (4) (the circumstance at issue here) a state commission has withheld approval for more than one year after the filing of an application or the designation of the relevant national interest corridor, whichever is later, *id.* § 824p(1)(C)(i); or (5) a state commission has conditioned its approval in such a manner that the proposed construction or modification is not economically feasible or will not significantly reduce transmission congestion in interstate commerce, *id.* § 824p(b)(1)(C)(ii).

If the circumstance of withholding permit approval is set aside, the remaining four circumstances allow FERC jurisdiction only when a state commission either is unable to act or acts inappropriately by including project-killing conditions in an approved permit. These are limited grants of jurisdiction to FERC, and they indicate that Congress meant for the "withheld [permit] approval" circumstance to be limited as well. FERC's reading of the "withheld approval" circumstance to include denial of a permit renders it completely out of proportion with the four other jurisdiction-granting circumstances in § 216(b)(1). The Commission's reading would mean that Congress has told state commissions that they will lose jurisdiction unless they approve every permit application in a national interest corridor. Under such a reading it would be futile for a state commission to deny a permit based on traditional considerations like cost and benefit, land use and environmental impacts, and health and safety. It would be futile, in other words, for a commission to do its normal work. When the five circumstances in § 216(b)(1) are considered together, they indicate that Congress intended only a measured, although important, transfer of jurisdiction to FERC. In providing for this measured transfer of jurisdiction, Congress simply makes sure that there is a utility commission available—if not a state commission, then FERC—to make a timely and straightforward decision on every permit application in a national interest corridor. . . . Indeed, if Congress had intended to take the monumental step of preempting state jurisdiction every time a state commission denies a permit in a national interest corridor, it would surely have said so directly. . . .

TRAXLER, CIRCUIT JUDGE, concurring in part and dissenting in part.

. . . In my view, the language of the statute, when considered in the context of the statute's purpose and other provisions in the statute, is susceptible to only one interpretation, the one that FERC adopted. . . .

Applying the common meaning of the word "withhold" yields a straightforward rule that a state has "withheld approval for more than 1 year" when one year after approval has been sought, the state still has not granted it, regardless of the reason. *See* FUNK & WAGNALLS STANDARD DICTIONARY 936 (1980) (defining "withhold" in part as "[t]o keep back; decline to grant"). Indeed, this is the construction that FERC adopted.

Despite the apparent clarity of the words "withhold" and "approval," Petitioners . . . argue that denying approval cannot constitute "withh[olding] approval" because a denial is a discrete event and it . . . makes no sense to speak of "denying approval for more than 1 year."

In my opinion, this argument is not sound. Under FERC's interpretation, the discrete event of denial does not constitute the withholding of approval that extends for more than one year after the application is received. The denial is merely one event that may occur during the more-than-one-year period in which approval is withheld. Under the common meaning of the words "withhold" and "approval," approval is withheld, *i.e.*, not granted, every day that no decision is issued granting approval, and it continues to be withheld on the day an application is denied (as well as every day that such a denial is not reconsidered). Thus, if a state denies an application, and then, ten months after submission of the application, reverses course and grants the application, it would certainly be the case that the state "withheld approval" for ten months before granting it. Similarly, if one year and one day after submission of an application a state has denied an application (and not reconsidered its decision), it has "withheld approval for more than 1 year." There is no other reasonable way to interpret those words.[1]

Not surprisingly, an examination of the context in which these words are used and the context of the statute as a whole confirms that Congress meant its words to be given their common meaning. First and foremost is the subsection directly following 16 U.S.C.A. § 824p(b)(1)(C)(i), which gives FERC authority when a state has granted approval but "conditioned its approval in such a manner that the proposed construction or modification will not significantly reduce transmission congestion in interstate commerce or is not economically feasible." 16 U.S.C.A. § 824p(b)(1)(C)(ii). Read together, the two subsections provide that while a state has a full year to consider and act on an application without interference from FERC, FERC nevertheless has the authority to ensure that a state does not frustrate the goal of significantly reducing transmission congestion in a national interest corridor. Petitioners, however, suggest that Congress did not intend to essentially "trump" the states' permitting decisions in order to accomplish this goal. That suggestion is completely belied, however, by Congress's undisputed willingness to do just that when a state grants a permit under conditions FERC determines to be unreasonable. The notion that Congress would have been willing to "trump" states when they thwart the goal of significantly reducing transmission congestion in a national interest corridor by granting permits subject to conditions FERC determines to be unreasonable but would not be willing to do so when states thwart the same goal by denying the permits outright makes no sense to me in light of the purpose of the legislation.

The argument that Petitioners' interpretation can be squared with § 824p(b)(1)(C)(ii) because "[w]hen a state commission grants approval with project-killing conditions, it misuses its authority, and the state licensing system has failed," but when a state simply denies an application, it "acts with transparency and engages in a legitimate use of its traditional powers," is not correct in my view. With all due respect, such a misuse of authority would occur only if a state granted its approval with conditions that it imposed for the purpose of killing the project. Section 824p(b)(1)(C)(ii) is not so narrow as to limit FERC's jurisdiction to cases in

---

[1] Petitioners contend that had Congress intended that a state could have "withheld approval for more than 1 year" in a case in which the application was denied during the one-year period, it could have conveyed that notion more clearly had it substituted "denied an application or failed to act for more than one year," for "withheld approval." Petitioners note that Congress actually employed such language in another part of the statute, see 16 U.S.C.A. § 824p(h)(6)(A) (West Supp. 2008) ("If any agency has denied a Federal authorization required for a transmission facility, or has failed to act by the deadline established . . ."). . . . Petitioners' point might have some force if the language Congress did choose were reasonably susceptible to more than one meaning, but it is not, as I have explained. Moreover, had Congress simply meant "failed to act on an application for more than 1 year," and not meant the statute to include outright denials, it could easily have used words that actually had that meaning, as it did in another part of EPAct 2005. See 16 U.S.C.A. § 824b(a)(5) (West Supp. 2008) ("If the Commission does not act within 180 days [on an application] . . .").

which such intentionally deceptive action has occurred. Rather, it clearly allows FERC to exercise jurisdiction based on simple differences of opinion between FERC and the state regarding the impact of the conditions imposed.

I recognize that several states participating in this appeal as *amici curiae* contend that FERC's interpretation would render the states' consideration of applications irrelevant. Even if the contention were true, it would not create an ambiguity in the statute, especially considering the critical national energy interests that Congress sought to protect with this legislation. FERC brings a broader national perspective to siting proposals in national interest electric transmission corridors than individual states possess, and Congress clearly intended that FERC would be authorized to act from that perspective. Nevertheless, the contention that FERC's interpretation makes the states' permitting decisions irrelevant is not correct. FERC has explained that it takes into consideration a state's decision in making its own permitting determinations. Furthermore, a state has the authority to impose on any grant of an application conditions that FERC is powerless to overturn so long as the conditions are economically feasible and would not prevent the significant reduction of transmission congestion . . . .

Although it is not determinative, it is nonetheless worth noting that FERC's construction . . . is also buttressed by the applicable legislative history. The plainest statements from the House of Representatives are from the House Committee Report on bill H.R. 1640, which . . . described the bill as allowing FERC authority "if, after one year, a state, or other approval authority is unable or refuses to site the line." H.R. Rep. No. 109–215(I), at 261 (2005). . . . Similarly, a Senate committee report summarizing a bill, S. 10 . . . described the bill as "authoriz[ing] FERC to issue siting permits if a State withholds approval inappropriately." S. Rep. No. 109–78, at 5 (2005). The use of the term "inappropriately" strongly suggests that the Committee primarily had in mind situations in which a state denied a permit that was necessary to ensure reliability of the national transmission grid, not simply situations where a state had not ruled on an application for a certain period of time. . . .

SOUTH CAROLINA PUBLIC SERVICE AUTHORITY V. FERC
762 F.3d 41 (D.C. Cir. 2014)

PER CURIAM.

This case involves challenges to the most recent reforms of electric transmission planning and cost allocation adopted by the Federal Energy Regulatory Commission pursuant to the Federal Power Act. In Order No. 1000, the Commission required each transmission owning and operating public utility to participate in regional transmission planning that satisfies specific planning principles designed to prevent undue discrimination and preference in transmission service, and that produces a regional transmission plan. The local and regional transmission planning processes must consider transmission needs that are driven by public policy requirements. Transmission providers in neighboring planning regions must collectively determine if there are more efficient or cost-effective solutions to their mutual transmission needs. The Final Rule also requires each planning process to have a method for allocating *ex ante* among beneficiaries the costs of new transmission facilities . . . and the method must satisfy six regional cost allocation principles. . . . Additionally transmission providers are required to remove from their jurisdictional tariffs and agreements any provisions that establish a federal right of first refusal to develop transmission facilities in a regional transmission plan, subject to individualized compliance review. . . .

I.

Upon enacting the FPA, Congress determined that federal regulation of interstate electric energy transmission and its sale at wholesale is "necessary in the public interest," 16 U.S.C. § 824(a), and vested the Commission with "jurisdiction over all facilities for such transmission or sale," *id.* § 824(b)(1). The States would retain authority over "any other sale of electric energy" and facilities used for "generation of electric energy," "local distribution," or "transmission of electric energy in intrastate commerce." The Commission was directed "to divide the country into regional districts for the voluntary interconnection and coordination of facilities for the generation, transmission, and sale of electric energy," and assigned the "duty" to "promote and encourage such interconnection and coordination." *Id.* § 824a(a). . . .

Congress also acted to spur investment in the electric transmission grid. Under the Electricity Modernization Act of 2005, enacted as Title XII of the Energy Policy Act of 2005, the Commission was authorized: to grant permits for construction of interstate transmission facilities in "national interest electric transmission corridors"; to subsidize the development of technology that would increase the capacity, efficiency, or reliability of transmission facilities; to provide incentive-based rates for investments in transmission infrastructure; and to require each "unregulated transmitting utility" to provide transmission services on terms and conditions "comparable to those under which [it] provides transmission services to itself and that are not unduly discriminatory or preferential." Further, the Commission . . . was to establish mandatory reliability standards for "bulk power system" operators in conjunction with the North American Electric Reliability Corporation (NERC) . . . .

In 2007, the Commission issued Order No. 890, *Preventing Undue Discrimination and Preference in Transmission Service*, 72 Fed. Reg.

12,266 (2007). Noting that the United States had "witnessed a decline in transmission investment relative to load growth," the Commission found that the resulting grid congestion "can have significant cost impacts on consumers." Concluding that transmission providers lacked incentives to plan and develop new transmission facilities in a manner consistent with the public interest, the Commission found that the "lack of coordination, openness, and transparency" in transmission planning had "result[ed] in opportunities for undue discrimination" because "participants ha[d] no means to determine whether the plan developed by the transmission provider in isolation is unduly discriminatory." To "remedy these transmission planning deficiencies" . . ., Order No. 890 required each transmission provider to establish an open, transparent, and coordinated transmission planning process that complied with nine planning principles [and to] "coordinate with customers regarding future system plans, and share necessary planning information with customers."

By late 2008, the electric industry was reporting that an estimated $298 billion of investment in new electric transmission facilities would be needed between 2010 and 2030 to maintain current levels of reliable electric service across the United States. NERC, the electric industry's self-regulator, projected that in the next decade a 9.5% to 15% increase in circuit miles of transmission would be needed to maintain reliability and to "unlock" and integrate renewable resources like wind generation that are likely to be remote from demand centers. . . .

In August 2011, the Commission issued Order No. 1000, which adopted . . . reforms [to address the problems it had identified in transmission planning and development.] . . .

II.

In adopting [Order No. 1000], the Commission relied on FPA Section 206. Petitioners contend that although "[FPA] Sections 205 and 206 empower [the Commission] to ensure that transactions involving voluntary planning arrangements are just, reasonable, and nondiscriminatory," the Commission lacks authority "to mandate transmission planning in the first instance" because the FPA "only allows [regulation of] existing voluntary commercial relationships." . . .

A.

Section 206(a) provides, in relevant part:

Whenever the Commission, after a hearing held upon its own motion or upon complaint, shall find that any rate, charge, or classification, demanded, observed, charged, or collected by any public utility for any transmission or sale subject to the jurisdiction of the Commission, or that any rule, regulation, *practice*, or contract *affecting such rate*, charge, or classification is unjust, unreasonable, unduly discriminatory or preferential, the Commission shall determine the just and reasonable rate, charge, classification, rule, regulation, practice, or contract to be thereafter observed and in force, and shall fix the same by order.

16 U.S.C. § 824e(a) (emphasis added). By its plain terms, Section 206 instructs the Commission to remedy "any ... practice" that "affect[s]" a rate for interstate electricity transmission services "demanded" or "charged" by "any public utility" if such practice "is unjust, unreasonable, unduly discriminatory or preferential." The text does not define "practice," although use of the word "any" amplifies [its] breadth . . . .

In the Final Rule, the Commission identified underlying problems with "existing transmission planning processes" and found that those processes "have a direct and discernable affect [sic] on rates," explaining that "[i]t is through the transmission planning process that ... providers determine which transmission facilities will more efficiently or cost-effectively meet the needs of the region, the development of which directly impacts the rates, terms and conditions of jurisdictional service." ... To remedy the identified systemic problems, the Commission mandated that all transmission providers not only participate in a planning process that is open and transparent as Order No. 890 requires, but also one that is regional in scope and produces a transmission plan whereby providers have the information needed to determine which projects satisfy local and regional needs more efficiently and effectively. . . .

Petitioners challenge neither the Commission's conclusion that the current transmission planning processes are "practices" under Section 206 nor its conclusion that such transmission planning practices directly affect rates. . . . Instead petitioners maintain ... that a lack of regional transmission planning was not an existing practice subject to the Commission's authority under Section 206 [because] "whether to coordinate planning is left, in the first instance, to utilities." . . .

The authority and obligation that Congress vested in the Commission to remedy certain practices is broadly stated and the only question is what limits are fairly implied. [To be sure], in *California Independent System Operator Corp. v. FERC*, 372 F.3d 395, 398 (D.C. Cir. 2004) (*CAISO*), this court held that the Commission had exceeded its authority under Section 206 by calling for the replacement of a public utility's board of directors. . . . "The word 'practices' is a word of sufficiently diverse definitions that the only realistic approach to determining Congress's 'plain meaning,' if any, is to regard the word in its context." Understood in the context of Section 206's transactional terms, the court observed, "[i]t is quite a leap" to move from the authority to regulate rates, charges, classifications and closely related matters to "an implication that by the word 'practice,' Congress empowered the Commission . . . to reform completely the governing structure of [an ISO]." . . .

[By contrast, r]eforming the practices of failing to engage in regional planning and *ex ante* cost allocation for development of new regional transmission facilities is not the kind of interpretive "leap" that concerned the court in *CAISO* but rather involves a core reason underlying Congress' instruction in Section 206. This is illustrated by the court's decision in [*Transmission Access Policy Study Group v. FERC*, 225 F.3d 667 (D.C. Cir. 2000) (*TAPS*), aff'd sub nom. *New York v. FERC*, 535 U.S. 1 (2002)]. There, the court upheld Order No. 888 mandating the unbundling of generation and transmission services and the filing of OATTs as a remedy for the refusal of transmission-owning facilities to offer transmission to emerging competitors on non-discriminatory terms. The Commission found that these facilities "c[ould] be expected to act in their own interest to maintain their monopoly" by either "denying transmission access outright" or "by providing transmission services to competitors only at comparatively unfavorable rates, terms, and conditions." Although some facilities had voluntarily opened their transmission facilities to third parties, the Commission concluded that "relying upon voluntary arrangements . . . would not remedy the fundamentally anticompetitive structure of the transmission industry." The court deferred to the Commission's reasonable interpretation that it had "authority under FPA §§ 205 and 206 to require open access as a generic remedy to prevent undue discrimination." Notably, then, in *TAPS*, the court agreed with the Commission's interpretation here that a failure to act qualifies as a "practice" under Section 206 that it must remedy [if it is unjust and unreasonable] and directly affects or is closely related to [FPA] rates.

Petitioners attempt to distinguish *TAPS* by characterizing regional transmission plans as "regional planning agreements" and "[a]greements to coordinate transmission planning" that require transmission providers to take on "binding" commercial obligations. They rely on *Otter Tail Power Co. v. United States*, 410 U.S. 366 (1973), for the proposition that Congress intended the formation of such agreements to be "voluntary" and "governed in the first instance by business judgment." This misperceives what the Commission has required . . . . In Order No. 1000, the Commission expressly "decline[d] to impose obligations to build or mandatory processes to obtain commitments to construct transmission facilities." . . . As the Commission explained on rehearing, "Order No. 1000's transmission planning reforms are concerned with process" and "are not intended to dictate substantive outcomes." . . .

[P]etitioners attempt to inject another reason the Commission lacked authority under Section 206, maintaining that the Commission's regional planning mandate "is not requiring a change to existing practices," but is instead "a directive to engage in new practices by unlawfully compelling formation of new commercial relationships," *i.e.*, "coordinated planning arrangements." . . . [T]o the extent this is not a reiteration of petitioners' *Otter Tail* argument, it is based on a false premise. Commission-mandated transmission planning is not new. The Final Rule builds on Order No. 890's requirements in light of changed circumstances and is simply the next step in a series of related reforms that began no later than Order No. 888. . . .

B.

Petitioners' principal objection, in any event, is that Section 202(a) bars the Commission from mandating transmission planning.

Section 202(a) provides, in relevant part:

> For the purpose of assuring an abundant supply of electric energy throughout the United States with the greatest possible economy and with regard to the proper utilization and conservation of natural resources, the Commission is empowered and directed to divide the country into regional districts for the *voluntary interconnection and coordination of facilities for the generation, transmission, and sale of electric energy.* . . . It shall be the duty of the Commission to promote and encourage such interconnection and coordination within each such district and between such districts.

16 U.S.C. § 824a(a) (emphasis added). The Commission concluded Section 202(a) posed no bar to adoption of the challenged transmission planning reforms because "coordination" refers to the coordinated operation of existing transmission facilities, not to the planning of future facilities. The Commission explained that the coordinated operation contemplated by Section 202(a), as a practical matter, "can occur only after the facilities are interconnected." By contrast, "[t]he planning of new transmission facilities occurs before they can be interconnected" . . . .

In petitioners' view, the meaning of "coordination" is "selfevident" and confirms that Section 202(a) precludes the Commission from requiring planning arrangements. Petitioners contend that "coordination" plainly encompasses transmission planning because "the coordination of transmission facilities is exactly what is done in transmission planning." The statutory text, however, does not unambiguously establish the meaning of "coordination" that petitioners advance. As the Supreme Court has observed, "context matters," and " '[a] word is known by the company it keeps'—a rule that 'is often wisely applied where a word is capable of many meanings in order to avoid the giving of unintended breadth to the Acts of Congress.' " The "coordination" addressed in Section 202(a) is textually limited to coordination for purposes of generation, transmission and sale, all activities that require operating facilities. Section 202(a) is silent regarding the Commission's authority with respect to pre-operational planning designed as a remedy to practices affecting rates that are unjust, unreasonable, or unduly discriminatory or preferential; that authority is addressed in Section 206. Petitioners' suggestion that "[r]eading 'coordination' to exclude coordinated transmission planning undermines the [FPA]'s purpose to preserve the voluntary nature of [commercial] relationships" misperceives the nature of the Final Rule, which, as discussed, addresses process. . . .

C.

Petitioners contend that even if Section 206 does not bar the Commission from mandating regional transmission planning, FPA Section 201(a) does. Section 201(a) [provides that FERC's authority to regulate electricity transmission in interstate commerce] "extend[s] only to those matters which are not subject to regulation by the States." . . .

Petitioners' contention that the challenged orders intrude on the States' traditional role in regulating siting and construction requires little discussion. Even assuming *arguendo* that siting and construction are matters "subject to regulation by the States" within the meaning of Section 201(a), petitioners' contention simply cannot be squared with the language of the orders, which expressly and repeatedly disclaim authority over those matters. The orders neither require facility construction nor allow a party to build without securing necessary state approvals.

Petitioners' argument that the orders interfere with state regulation of planning, however, poses a closer question. Petitioners correctly contend that [Order No. 1000] further regulate[s] the transmission planning process. And, petitioners maintain, because state regulators were already substantially involved in regulating that process, the orders encroach on their authority in violation of Section 201(a) . . . . But while petitioners' argument is not without force, relevant precedent suggests that Section 201(a) does not stand in the way of [this] planning mandate.

In *New York v. FERC*, the . . . Court's substantial discussion of Section 201 yields several insights into the provision's meaning that are helpful in resolving petitioners' argument.

First, the Commission possesses greater authority over electricity transmission than it does over sales. Even though Section 201(b) does "limit FERC's sale jurisdiction to that at wholesale," there is no textual warrant for the suggestion that the Commission lacks jurisdiction over retail transmission. That is, the FPA preserves for the States relatively more sales authority than transmission authority.

Second, Section 201(a)'s reference to a sphere of state authority is "a mere policy declaration" that should not be read in derogation of other specific provisions granting the Commission authority, including Section 201(b)'s grant of authority over "transmission of electric energy in interstate commerce." As long as the Commission's activity falls within one of these specific jurisdictional grants, the "prefatory language of section 201(a)" does "not undermine FERC's jurisdiction." . . .

Taken together, these points support the Commission's assertion of authority over transmission planning matters . . . . First, because the planning mandate relates wholly to electricity transmission, as opposed to electricity sales, it involves a subject matter over which the Commission has relatively broader authority. Second, because the orders' planning mandate is directed at ensuring the proper functioning of the interconnected grid spanning state lines, the mandate fits comfortably within Section 201(b)'s grant of jurisdiction . . . . Given that fit, *New York v. FERC* teaches that there is no reason to think that the "prefatory" statement of federalism "policy" in Section 201(a) poses an obstacle to the Commission's assertion of authority. . . .

NOTES AND QUESTIONS

1. Many commentators have criticized the Fourth Circuit's decision in *Piedmont Environmental Council* as unduly limiting FERC's ability to strengthen the grid and promote renewable energy. From a legal perspective, do you agree? That is, did the majority properly construe § 216, or did the dissent have the better argument? How about from a policy perspective? What *should* the scope of FERC's siting authority be, and why?

2. The Fourth Circuit's decision in *Piedmont* has received significant attention (and criticism) over its construction of the scope of FERC's transmission siting authority under EPAct 2005. However, another case, decided shortly after *Piedmont*, also imposed important limits on this so-called "backstop" siting authority. In *California Wilderness Coalition v. U.S. Department of Energy*, 631 F.3d 1072 (9th Cir. 2011), the Ninth Circuit addressed challenges to the Department of Energy's (DOE) designation of an area as a "national interest electric transmission corridor" (a "National Corridor," "NIET Corridor," or "NIETC"). Under EPAct 2005, FERC's backstop siting authority—circumscribed, such as it is, post-*Piedmont*—applies only in such corridors. EPAct 2005 requires DOE to conduct a transmission congestion study every three years and, based on that study, it can designate a NIETC. But EPAct 2005 also mandates that the DOE "consult" with states when it designates an NIETC. The parties in *California Wilderness Coalition* asserted that DOE had failed to satisfy this mandate, while DOE claimed that its notice-and-comment process, plus its inclusion of state representatives in a technical conference and its "reaching out" to states via the National Association of Regulatory Utility Commissioners (NARUC), were enough to fulfill its statutory obligation. The court, in a 2–1 decision that, like *Piedmont* and *South Carolina Public Service Authority*, turned heavily on statutory interpretation, disagreed: "No draft was circulated to the States, no committee was created that included representatives from the States, and the affected States were not

given access to the supporting data. Thus, DOE's efforts here fall far short of [the statute's] requirement for consultation." *Id.* at 1088. Notably, DOE has not attempted to designate any new NIETCs since the *California Wilderness Coalition* case was decided, even though transmission congestion costs, though varying widely, can be quite extensive. *See* U.S. DEP'T OF ENERGY, NATIONAL ELECTRIC TRANSMISSION CONGESTION STUDY (2015); U.S. DEP'T OF ENERGY, NATIONAL ELECTRIC TRANSMISSION CONGESTION STUDY (2020). Why might DOE have refrained from acting?

3. How do you square *Piedmont* and *South Carolina Public Service Authority*? On the one hand, *Piedmont* severely limits a specific and concrete power that Congress gave FERC, effectively creating a situation where it remains difficult to site transmission lines in the United States. On the other hand, *South Carolina Public Service Authority* recognizes rather sweeping authority for FERC, based on a statutory provision that is nearly a century old, effectively allowing the agency to reform markets and the overall shape of the grid in a way that the 1935 Congress never could have foreseen. What is this dichotomy about? States' rights? Simply the statutory language at play? An incoherent federal policy on governance of the electric grid? Something else? All of the above?

4. As the world transitions to a clean energy economy, and as congressional gridlock increasingly restrains the making of new national policies of many types, the question of what powers environmental and energy agencies can exercise under longstanding statutory provisions is a critical one. For a particularly illuminating look at this subject, see Jody Freeman & David B. Spence, *Old Statutes, New Problems*, 163 U. PA. L. REV. 1 (2014). On a corollary and related question, see, for instance, Joel B. Eisen, *FERC's Expansive Authority to Transform the Electric Grid*, 49 U.C. DAVIS L. REV. 1783 (2016); and Matthew T. Wansley, *Regulation of Emerging Risks*, 69 VAND. L. REV. 401 (2014).

5. As you might imagine, Order 1000 has furnished a hotbed of litigation. One key issue is a question that the *South Carolina Public Service Authority* court passed on as unripe: whether FERC acted lawfully in Order 1000 by requiring that utilities remove rights of first refusal from their federal tariffs and agreements? Utilities saw these rights as critical—and valuable—because they gave incumbent utilities "a first crack at constructing an electricity transmission project—that is, having the opportunity to build it without having to face competition from other firms that might also like to build it." *MISO Transmission Owners v. FERC*, 819 F.3d 329, 329 (7th Cir. 2016). As it turned out, the courts could not dodge this question for long.

In *Oklahoma Gas & Elec. Co. v. FERC*, 827 F.3d 75 (D.C. Cir. 2016), the court confronted the argument that the *Mobile-Sierra* doctrine (discussed at length in Chapter 4) foreclosed FERC's ability to eviscerate federal rights of first refusal. The court had little difficulty finding that claim unpersuasive: "Just as unfair dealing, fraud, or duress will remove a provision from the ambit of *Mobile-Sierra*, so also will terms arrived at by horizontal competitors with a common interest to exclude any future competition." *Id.* at 80; *see also MISO Transmission Owners*, 819 F.3d at 333 (rejecting challenges to MISO's removal of first refusal rights post-Order 1000, in part because "when the local firm has a right of first refusal an outsider will have little incentive to explore the need for a new transmission facility"). Although FERC eliminated federal rights of first refusal in Order 1000, it did not prohibit states from enacting or enforcing rights of first refusal enshrined in state law. *See MISO Transmission Owners*, 819 F.3d at 336. After the enactment of Order 1000, several states enacted such laws, which were then challenged on dormant Commerce Clause grounds. So far, these challenges have been rejected. *See, e.g., LSP Transmission Holdings, LLC v. Sieben*, 954 F.3d 1018 (8th Cir. 2020); *see also* Alexandra B. Klass & Jim Rossi, *Revitalizing Dormant Commerce Clause Review for Interstate Coordination*, 100 MINN. L. REV. 129, 191–95 (2015); *cf.* Melissa Powers, *Anticompetitive Transmission Development and the Risks for Decarbonization*, 49 ENV'T L. 885 (2019).

Subsequently, in *Emera Maine v. FERC*, 854 F.3d 662 (D.C. Cir. 2017), the D.C. Circuit again turned down the invitation to upend Order 1000 based on *Mobile-Sierra*. The court wrote:

> The Transmission Owners . . . point to a statement from the Supreme Court's decision in *Morgan Stanley Capital Group Inc. v. Public Utility District No. 1*, 554 U.S. 527 (2008) [that] "under the *Mobile-Sierra* presumption, setting aside a contract rate requires a finding of 'unequivocal public necessity' or 'extraordinary circumstances.'"
> . . . We reject the invitation to don blinders and read this sentence as establishing an exclusive list of phrases FERC must incant to rebut the *Mobile-Sierra* presumption. Reading just two paragraphs down in the same opinion reveals the Court's conclusion that "the FPA intended to reserve the Commission's contract-abrogation power for those extraordinary circumstances where the public will be severely harmed." In other words, severe harm to the public constitutes extraordinary circumstances. Where FERC has made a finding of such harm, it has made the requisite finding of extraordinary circumstances. FERC made such a finding here . . . .

Id. at 671. Nor was the court persuaded by resurrected claims that Order 1000 violates the FPA's division of sovereign power between the states and the national government—this time in the frame that FERC's use of RTOs for regional planning under the rule creates jurisdictional problems. "Order No. 1000," the court explained, "established a regional planning process that is agnostic as to the provenance of the transmission needs, whether resulting from population growth or federal public policy or state public policy. . . . The division of roles between ISO-NE and the states poses no jurisdictional problem for FERC. . . . ISO-NE considers transmission needs that arise from a variety of sources, one of which is the public policy requirements chosen by federal and state officials." *Id.* at 674. Thus, "[r]equiring that ISO-NE, rather than the states, evaluate transmission needs and potential solutions is a reasonable implementation of Order No. 1000's regional planning process." *Id.*

6.   There has been much talk that FERC may revisit Order No. 1000, though that has yet to occur. "Everyone seems to agree that Order 1000 is not working as intended," Neil Chatterjee said during his time as Chair of FERC. Former Commissioner Cheryl LaFleur concurred. Order No. 1000, she said, has been "a mixed success, with less change-making than we hoped for." This is in part because "the overwhelming majority of transmission development is not subject to competitive processes, which necessarily limits the savings to customers." Herman K. Trabish, *With New Transmission Urgently Needed, FERC Chair Hints at a New Order 1000 Proceeding*, UTIL. DIVE (May 31, 2019).

As Order No. 1000 has limped along, other studies have shown how to increase investment in transmission, improve the competitiveness of the process, and open up the grid to renewables. *See, e.g.*, Patrick R. Brown & Audun Botterud, *The Value of Inter-Regional Coordination and Transmission in Decarbonizing the US Electricity System*, 5 JOULE 115 (2021); ROB GRAMLICH & JAY CASPARY, PLANNING FOR THE FUTURE: FERC'S OPPORTUNITY TO SPUR MORE COST-EFFECTIVE TRANSMISSION INFRASTRUCTURE (Jan. 2021); JOHANNES P. PFEIFENBERGER ET AL., THE BRATTLE GROUP, COST SAVINGS OFFERED BY COMPETITION IN ELECTRIC TRANSMISSION: EXPERIENCE TO DATE AND THE POTENTIAL FOR ADDITIONAL CUSTOMER VALUE (Apr. 2019).

7.   Another transmission development tool that EPAct 2005 gave the federal government is Section 1222 of that law. *See* 42 U.S.C. § 16421. This provision authorizes DOE to promote transmission development by designing, developing, operating, owning, or participating with other entities in those activities for two types of projects: (1) upgrades to existing transmission facilities owned by the Southwestern Power Administration or the Western Area Power Administration and (2) new electric power transmission facilities located in a state where either of those entities operate.

In 2016, DOE exercised its Section 1222 power for the first time, announcing that it would participate in the development of the Plains & Eastern Clean Line Project, proposed to run through Arkansas, Oklahoma, and Tennessee. The project was designed to bring approximately 4,000 MW of wind energy from the Oklahoma Panhandle to the Southeast via a 700-mile, high-voltage direct current (HVDC) line. *See* Alexandra B. Klass & Jim Rossi, *Reconstituting the Federalism Battle in Energy Transportation*, 41 HARV. ENV'T L. REV. 423 (2017). Subsequently, however, DOE pulled out of the project during the Trump administration. Work on Clean Line continues, though the Oklahoma portion was sold off to NextEra Energy and other Clean Line projects have been embroiled in litigation. *See Grain Belt Express Clean Line, LLC v. Pub. Serv. Comm'n*, 555 S.W.3d 469, 471 (Mo. 2018); *Missouri Landowners Alliance v. Pub. Serv. Comm'n*, 593 S.W.3d 632 (Mo. Ct. App. 2019). These projects are also discussed in Chapter 7.

For a deeper look into extant legal authority that DOE and other agencies could use to reshape the nation's grid—even in the face of *Piedmont*—see AVI ZEVIN ET AL., BUILDING A NEW GRID WITHOUT NEW LEGISLATION: A PATH TO REVITALIZING FEDERAL TRANSMISSION AUTHORITIES (Dec. 2020). For an examination of the benefits that might inure from more HVDC projects like clean line, see AARON BLOOM ET AL., NAT'L RENEWABLE ENERGY LAB., THE VALUE OF INCREASED HVDC CAPACITY BETWEEN EASTERN AND WESTERN U.S. GRIDS: THE INTERCONNECTIONS SEAM STUDY (Oct. 2020).

8.   Energy has become so en vogue of late that many popular books and documentary films address in depth important topics, including transmission. *See, e.g.,* GRETCHEN BAKKE, THE GRID: THE FRAYING WIRES BETWEEN AMERICANS AND OUR ENERGY FUTURE (2017); RUSSELL GOLD, SUPERPOWER: ONE MAN'S QUEST TO TRANSFORM AMERICAN ENERGY (2019); *Rebuilding Paradise* (2020).

D. ELECTRICITY SUPPLY IN TRANSITION: RENEWABLE ENERGY, POLICY INNOVATION, AND FEDERALISM

Renewables could change everything. That, at least, long has been the hope of many environmentalists and others who very much would like to transform the way we produce electricity in the United States. Cleaner energy; a more reliable, distributed grid; more energy independence; more democracy, individual involvement, and choice over energy production and consumption—these all have been offered as the promises of renewable energy. "In th[is] continuity lies the key to our survival: working with, not trying to smother and replace, the life force that has brought us to this place," wrote Amory Lovins in 1977. "Sunlight leaves an earth unravished, husbanded, renewed. It leaves people unmutated, convivial, even illuminated. Above all, it respects the limits that are always with us on a little planet: the delicate fragility of life, the imperfection of human societies, and the frailty of the human design." AMORY B. LOVINS, SOFT ENERGY PATHS: TOWARD A DURABLE PEACE 218 (1977). This, say many, is what renewable energy offers—a different kind of energy future than the one we now live in.

Renewables, of course, like all energy resources, come with tradeoffs. Renewables are cleaner, less carbon-intensive, and more plentiful in the long run than their fossil fuel counterparts. However, as Chapters 2 and 3 detail, renewables also have limitations. They long were, and in some matchups still remain, more expensive than other generation alternatives, particularly natural gas in its current renaissance. They are more intermittent because the sun does not always shine and the wind does not always blow. As a result, many renewables are not easily dispatchable, and thus cannot be used as so-called "baseload" generation that runs all the time. Though grid operators have become more sophisticated in blending dispatch of renewable sources, solar and wind still often require other generation to back them up, such as gas-fired plants operating as "spinning reserves." Some argue that this need demonstrates renewables' shaky economics—the fact that arguably duplicative generation is required when they are used to meet demand. Utility-scale renewables generally also require massive amounts of new transmission investment, and they can be quite land intensive. *See generally* Uma Outka, *The Energy-Land Use Nexus*, 27 J. LAND USE & ENV'T L. 245 (2012). All these costs, others note, are particularly problematic because they will ultimately be covered by ratepayers, and those who can least afford them risk feeling the price pinch the sharpest. Finally, renewables remain an ill fit in the nation's federalist system of energy governance, so far at least, in part because where they are located (*e.g.*, the sunny Southwest, the windy Midwest) does not necessarily coincide with where energy is needed (*e.g.*, large cities). The benefits of renewables, that is, do not neatly follow state lines.

It is the first and last of these attributes—price and federalism—that have stymied a fuller U.S. transition to renewable energy the longest. That said, how renewables are treated in domestic energy law and policy is very much in transition, as with much of the rest of the field. In the last twenty years, this transition has quickly picked up momentum. The borders of federalism are changing with it.

Today, renewable energy law in the United States is dominated by three primary devices, but it is the third that is fastest growing and arguably the most important. First, there is PURPA; second, tax incentives and other subsidies such as government loan guarantees, though perhaps most notable among these is the federal production tax credit (PTC); and third, renewable portfolio standards (RPSs), which in recent years have begun to evolve into clean energy standards (CESs) more focused on climate change. *See generally* Lincoln L. Davies, *U.S. Renewable Energy Policy in Context*, 15 ENV'T L. & POL'Y 33 (2015).

Energy subsidies, including those for renewables, are addressed in Chapter 2. This section thus overviews PURPA and then focuses on RPSs and CESs. (We will also explore CESs and other legal and policy devices seeking to move the nation toward a carbon-neutral future in Chapter 11.)

Why the United States utilizes RPSs and CESs rather than feed-in tariffs (FITs)—which are popular in Europe and many other nations—to promote renewables and a transition to a clean energy economy is in part an outcome of the nation's federalist energy system and in part a product of history. The history starts with PURPA.

1. PURPA

PURPA is the grandmother of renewable energy law in the United States. PURPA's entrance onto the stage in 1978 both legitimized renewables as an alternative to "traditional" fossil and nuclear fuels and directly encouraged their use. PURPA, as noted previously, establishes a three-pronged approach to promoting renewables. First, PURPA says that incumbent utilities must purchase the electricity produced by cogeneration and certain renewable energy facilities—what PURPA calls "qualifying facilities." Second, PURPA mandates that those power purchases occur at incentivized rates—what it terms "avoided cost rates." Third, the statute exempts facilities selling power pursuant to PURPA from traditional utility regulation and compels incumbent utilities to sell power to them. Despite these changes, PURPA maintains energy law's status quo of federalism: While PURPA charges FERC with enforcing the statute, it preserves states' ability to determine at what level the statute's "avoided cost rates" are set. The D.C. Circuit aptly summarized the statutory regime:

> Congress enacted Section 210 of PURPA, 16 U.S.C. § 824a–3, to encourage the development of cogeneration and small power production facilities. *FERC v. Mississippi*, 456 U.S. 742, 750 (1982); *Conn. Valley Elec. Co. v. FERC*, 208 F.3d 1037, 1039 (D.C. Cir. 2000). A "cogeneration facility" produces both electric energy and either steam or some other form of usable energy, 16 U.S.C. § 796(18)(A); a "small power production facility" produces no more than 80 megawatts of electricity using only biomass, waste, renewable resources, or geothermal resources as the primary energy source, *id.* § 796(17)(A).

> To counter traditional electric utilities' reluctance to deal with these nontraditional facilities, the PURPA charges the Commission with implementing mandatory purchase and sell obligations, requiring electric utilities to purchase electric power from, and sell power to, qualifying cogeneration and small power production facilities (collectively, "qualifying facilities" or "QFs"). *See id.* § 824a–3(a)(1)–(2).[1] A qualifying small power production facility must "meet[ ] such requirements (including requirements respecting fuel use, fuel efficiency, and reliability) as the Commission may, by rule, prescribe." 16 U.S.C. § 796(17)(C). . . .

> Hewing to the PURPA's mandate, the Commission enacted regulations requiring a utility to purchase "any energy and capacity which is made available from a [QF]," 18 C.F.R. § 292.303(a), and to sell "any energy and capacity requested by the [QF]," *id.* § 292.303(b). While the utility must sell electricity to a QF at regulated tariff rates, the utility must buy electricity from the QF at a rate equal to the utility's full "avoided cost." 18 C.F.R. § 292.304(b)(2). The utility's avoided cost (also called the "incremental cost of alternative electric energy") is "the cost to the electric utility of the electric energy which, but for the purchase from such [QF], such utility would generate or purchase from another source." 16 U.S.C. § 824a–3(d); *see* 18 C.F.R. § 292.101(b)(6); *Am. Paper Inst., Inc. v. Am. Elec. Power Serv.*

---

[1] Congress also sought to relieve some of the regulatory burdens that discouraged development of such facilities by exempting QFs from certain state and federal laws.

Corp., 461 U.S. 402, 405–06 (1983). As a practical matter, "the rate that a QF can require a utility to pay [i.e. the avoided-cost rate] is almost always higher than the regulated tariff rate at which the QF can purchase from the utility electricity for its internal operating needs."

Southern California Edison Co. v. FERC, 443 F.3d 94, 95–97 (D.C. Cir. 2006).

It might fairly be said that the problem with PURPA is that it simultaneously did not do enough and also did too much. It got stuck in the middle.

For proponents of renewables, PURPA turned out to be less efficacious than they might have hoped, in part because it broke down only some of the barriers renewables face. It required purchases of power, but it did not prioritize those purchases above all others. It mandated an incentive price, but that price was based on other resources, not the actual cost of getting renewable facilities online. It did not compel access to the grid, and the "avoided cost" rate it offered was tremendously uncertain because it was subject to rate proceedings on a state-by-state basis. Certainty, research has shown again and again, is the lynchpin to renewable energy policy success. PURPA lacked it on multiple fronts.

For opponents of renewables, or those with vested interests in the status quo, PURPA also went too far. It put utilities in the awkward position of being compelled by federal law to buy more expensive power than they otherwise would, but then having to account to their state regulators for how they were keeping costs down. Utilities also were critical of the statute for incentivizing wastefulness. They charged that some companies built generators solely to obtain QF status and make a higher profit, not to actually increase efficiency in the system—what came to be known as "PURPA machines":

> [B]y the mid-1980s, limited incentives for QFs in PURPA had created two types of inefficiencies. First, it was difficult for any entity but an industrial generator . . . or a very small generator . . . to meet PURPA's strict size, engineering, fuel use, and ownership criteria for QFs. Some industrial suppliers continued to ensure a beneficial regulatory structure by building inefficient generators known as "PURPA machines"—power-plants which supply only enough thermal energy to ensure minimum qualification under PURPA's rules. PURPA QFs, in many instances, imposed unnecessary costs on consumers because entities had structured their projects to maintain exemptions from regulation and, in some instances, sought inefficient steam hosts to maintain QF status.

Jim Rossi, *Redeeming Judicial Review: The Hard Look Doctrine and Federal Regulatory Efforts to Restructure the Electric Utility Industry*, 1994 WIS. L. REV. 763, 782.

Caught between two hard places, Congress finally tilted the PURPA field back in favor of incumbent utilities. The Energy Policy Act of 2005 included a provision that did not quite repeal PURPA but, instead, said that in areas with effective wholesale competition, FERC could rule that PURPA's mandatory purchase requirement no longer applies to facilities over 20 MW. Since then, FERC has granted a number of these requests. As a result, PURPA effectively applies in its full scope only in limited parts of the country today. *See* Michael D. Hornstein & J.S. Gebhart Stoermer, *The Energy Policy Act of 2005: PURPA Reform, the Amendments and Their Implications*, 27 ENERGY L.J. 25, 32 (2006). Nonetheless, in those areas—and even for smaller facilities in RTOs—PURPA has continued to play an important role in promoting new renewable energy facilities.

Testament of PURPA's ongoing importance is FERC's Order No. 872. Adopted in the summer of 2020, Order No. 872 demarked the first true overhaul of FERC's PURPA regulations since the agency enacted its original implementing rules in 1980. Order No. 872 sought to modernize PURPA's implementation in an electricity landscape that had shifted substantially since 1978—a new world that had seen the rise of natural gas generation, rapid market declines in coal use, and plummeting prices for renewables, especially solar and wind. In chief, Order No. 872 effected five key changes to FERC's rules:

- *Costing flexibility*. Order No. 872 allows states to determine QFs' "avoided cost" based on several possible, non-fixed bases: price forecasts, competitive solicitation processes, and fuel hub prices. This may include locational marginal pricing or energy imbalance market prices. The Order's costing flexibility provisions apply to the energy component of the rates QFs receive, not the capacity component. The latter must remain fixed in nature.

- *Size presumptions*. EPAct 2005 allowed FERC to potentially exempt utilities from PURPA's must-purchase obligation in competitive markets. FERC initially implemented this provision by creating a rebuttable presumption that QFs larger than 20 MW are competitive in ERCOT, CAISO, ISO-NE, MISO, NYISO, and SPP, and likewise that QFs smaller than 20 MW lack nondiscriminatory access to the market. Order No. 872 lowers these thresholds from 20 MW to 5 MW.

- *One-mile rule*. FERC's old rules required affiliates sourced from the same fuel type to count as a single QF if they were within one mile of each other and, in the aggregate, comprised less than 80 MW in capacity. Utilities complained that QFs gamed this rule by breaking up a single project and moving parts just outside one mile in distance. Order No. 872 creates a rebuttable presumption that same-fuel-sourced projects more than a mile but less than ten miles apart are not located on the same site. Parties can rebut this presumption through a QF certification challenge. The Order treats projects more than 10 miles apart as separate.

- *Triggering a purchase obligation.* FERC's old rules were silent on when utilities became obligated to purchase a QF's power. Order No. 872 gives states flexibility to determine this timing. The Order specifies criteria that states may use.

- *QF certification challenges.* The old PURPA rules also did not create an easy path for utilities to challenge the certification of a project as a QF. Instead, utilities had to file a petition for a declaratory order from FERC, including tendering a $30,000-plus filing fee. Order No. 872 establishes procedures for challenging QF certifications.

See Qualifying Facility Rates and Requirements Implementation Issues Under the Public Utility Regulatory Policies Act of 1978, Order No. 872, 172 FERC ¶ 61,041, *order on reh'g*, 173 FERC ¶ 61,158 (2020).

As might be expected, multiple interests reacted differently to FERC's promulgation of Order No. 872. FERC Chair Neil Chatterjee called the rule necessary because "most" renewable projects today are developed "outside of PURPA." That, he said, "is total proof that renewables can compete in our markets." By contrast, FERC Commissioner Richard Glick, who dissented from the Order, complained that Order No. 872 "gut[s] the heart of PURPA" because the new rules "discourages QFs," when PURPA's core purpose is to encourage their development.

The utility industry was more pleased. Edison Electric Institute President Tom Kuhn, in a joint statement with the American Public Power Association and the National Rural Electric Cooperative Association, said: "For years, electricity customers have been paying billions of dollars in excess energy costs as a result of PURPA . . . . FERC [now] has helped to ensure that renewable energy can continue to grow without forcing electricity customers to pay a premium to the developers that learned how to game the system." Jeremy Dillon, *FERC Overhauls Carter-era Law Promoting Renewable Power*, GREENWIRE (July 16, 2020); Catherine Morehouse, *FERC Finalizes PURPA Overhaul in Move Glick Says "Discourages" Small Solar Development*, UTIL. DIVE (July 17, 2020) (quoting Glick and Kuhn); Catherine Morehouse, *Groups Challenge FERC's PURPA Rule, Accuse Commission of "Actively Discouraging" Small Power Facilities*, UTIL. DIVE (Aug. 24, 2020) (quoting Chatterjee).

The next chapter for PURPA unquestionably will be tied to the fate of Order No. 872. Renewable interests, unsurprisingly, were not pleased with the rule. As this book goes to print, an appeal challenging Order No. 872 brought by members of the renewable energy industry remains pending in the Ninth Circuit.

NOTES AND QUESTIONS

1.   Why do you think PURPA is so unpopular among utilities? Does it relate back to the same market power questions that gave rise to utility regulation in the first place? If so, why has utility regulation not quelled ill will toward the statute?

2.   Despite EPAct 2005's effective partial repeal of PURPA, the law has continued to play a heavy role in much of the country, particularly outside RTOs. In fact, even inside RTOs, PURPA heavily influenced renewables development post-EPAct 2005, in part because many solar installations did not approach anywhere near the 20 MW ceiling of FERC's original rebuttable presumption. As one 2016 report noted, "To date, [PURPA] has driven the largest number of non-RPS utility PV projects in the U.S." Colin Smith, *What Drives Utility Solar Growth in a Post-ITC-Extension World?*, GREENTECH MEDIA (Mar. 24, 2016). Perhaps somewhat surprisingly, then, cumulative installed capacity from PURPA-eligible QFs has only grown, not decreased, since 2005. *See North Carolina Has More PURPA-Qualifying Solar Facilities Than Any Other State*, U.S. ENERGY INFO. ADMIN. (Aug. 23, 2016); *see also* Robert Mudge et al., *New Technologies and Old Issues Under PURPA*, NORTON, ROSE, FULBRIGHT (Feb. 20, 2018) ("Virtually all net growth in QF generating capacity over the last 10 years has come from renewables . . . . Net growth in QF generating capacity over the last five years has come principally from solar. Renewable QFs have comprised about 16% of total wind and solar development over that time. . . . For example, new QFs constitute 18% of the total current capacity in North Carolina, 26% in Utah, and 24% in Montana.").

3.   Notably, PURPA interacts directly with states' RPSs, which we address in depth in the next section. Courts have sanctioned this interplay. Specifically, an RPS can serve as the benchmark for how "avoided costs" under PURPA are set. If a QF is needed to meet the state's RPS, the costs avoided must be of other eligible renewable resources—not any kind of available generation, such as natural gas. As Judge Algenon Marbley wrote for the Ninth Circuit, PURPA "require[s] an examination of the costs that a utility is *actually avoiding*. This comports with PURPA's goal to put QFs on an equal footing with other energy providers. Where a utility uses energy from a QF to meet the utility's RPS obligation, the relevant comparable energy sources are other renewable energy providers, not all energy sources that the utility might technically be capable of buying energy from." *Californians for Renewable Energy v. Cal. Pub. Utils.*

Comm'n, 922 F.3d 929, 937 (9th Cir. 2019) (emphasis in original); *see also Cal. Pub. Util. Comm'n*, 133 FERC ¶ 61,059 (2010).

FERC has also held that while state-set PURPA avoided cost rates "may not include a 'bonus' or 'adder' above the calculated full avoided cost of the purchasing utility, to provide additional compensation for, for example, environmental externalities above avoided costs," states are free to "separately provide additional compensation for environmental externalities, outside the confines of, and, in addition to the PURPA avoided cost rate, through the creation of renewable energy credits (RECs)." *Cal. Pub. Util. Comm'n*, 134 FERC ¶ 61,044 at P 31 (2011). FERC further explained that such compensation can include revenue from renewable energy credits (RECs) earned in connection with state RPSs. Can you think of a reasoned rationale for this distinction? Or is it simply the byproduct of how Congress wrote PURPA?

4. Another pro-renewables policy that interacts with PURPA is the feed-in tariff (FIT or FiT). Popular abroad—and particularly popularized by Germany's and Spain's use of the device—at least five jurisdictions in the United States—California, Indiana, New York, Washington, and Vermont—have adopted some version of these laws as well.

FITs are straightforward. They require utilities to purchase the output of eligible generators at an incentive price for a fixed period of time, with an obligation to connect the new competitor to the grid. Sound familiar? It should. Feed-in tariffs are built directly on PURPA's original architecture—with the additions of mandatory interconnection, more certainty around price, and a price structure tethered to the actual cost of renewables rather than all avoided costs.

State FITs' interaction with PURPA is largely on federalism grounds. The Ninth Circuit, for instance, found California's FIT preempted by PURPA for capping the amount of power that utilities were required to buy under the FIT. PURPA, the court said, requires purchase of the facility's produced energy—not a portion of it. *See Winding Creek Solar LLC v. Peterman*, 932 F.3d 861 (9th Cir. 2019).

Several articles are helpful if you would like to learn more about FITs: SCOTT HEMPLING ET AL., NAT'L RENEWABLE ENERGY LAB., RENEWABLE ENERGY PRICES IN STATE-LEVEL FEED-IN TARIFFS: FEDERAL LAW CONSTRAINTS AND POSSIBLE SOLUTIONS (2010); Lincoln L. Davies & Kirsten Allen, *Feed-in Tariffs in Turmoil*, 116 W. VA. L. REV. 937 (2014); John Dernbach, *Legal Pathways to Deep Decarbonization: Lessons from California and Germany*, 82 BROOK. L. REV. 825 (2017); Felix Mormann, *Enhancing the Investor Appeal of Renewable Energy*, 42 ENV'T L. 681, 694 (2012).

5. Though Order No. 872 substantially changed the ground rules for QFs, other questions about PURPA implementation remain. These are wide-ranging and important, and often influenced by state-to-state differences in applying PURPA. One, for instance, is whether states can limit PURPA's

application to facilities only that produce firm, as opposed to intermittent, power. *See Exelon Wind 1, L.L.C. v. Nelson*, 766 F.3d 380 (5th Cir. 2014). Another is whether transmission constraints can be used as a reason to limit how much of a QF's power an incumbent utility must purchase. *See, e.g., Portland Gen. Elec. Co. v. FERC*, 854 F.3d 692 (D.C. Cir. 2017). Others include curtailment of QFs and contract lengths for QF purchases. *See, e.g., In re Investigation to Review Avoided Costs That Serve as Prices for Standard-Offer Program in 2020*, 254 A.3d 178 (Vt. 2021); *Vote Solar v. Montana Dep't of Pub. Serv. Reg.*, 473 P.3d 963 (Mont. 2020); *MTSUN, LLC v. Montana Dep't of Pub. Serv. Reg.*, 472 P.3d 1154 (Mont. 2020); *Swecker v. Midland Power Co-op.*, 807 F.3d 883 (8th Cir. 2015); Robert Walton, *Idaho Regulators Reduce PURPA Contracts from 20 to 2 Years*, UTIL. DIVE (Aug. 15, 2015).

6.   One recent PURPA implementation issue that FERC resolved is whether the gross or net capacity counts in determining whether a generator counts as a QF. This issue is particularly important for solar installations, which increasingly are built with storage capacity as well. In September 2020, FERC upended four decades of precedent, ruling that the gross installed capacity was what mattered. *Broadview Solar, LLC*, 172 FERC ¶ 61,194 (2020). Less than half a year later, it reversed itself again, setting aside the September 2020 order. What matters, the Commission said, is how much electricity a facility can "send to" the grid. *Broadview Solar, LLC*, 174 FERC ¶ 61,199 (2021). What approach makes the most sense?

7.   If you are interested in differences in state implementation of PURPA, the PURPA Tracker, published by the National Regulatory Research Institute, is a helpful resource.

8.   For a short history of PURPA, see Richard D. Cudahy, *PURPA: The Intersection of Competition and Regulatory Policy*, 16 ENERGY L.J. 419 (1995). For a more in-depth look, see RICHARD F. HIRSH, POWER LOSS: THE ORIGINS OF DEREGULATION AND RESTRUCTURING IN THE AMERICAN ELECTRIC UTILITY SYSTEM (2002).

2. RENEWABLE AND CLEAN ENERGY STANDARDS

While the debate over PURPA's application was ongoing, and states considered their own restructuring legislation (discussed above), a number of states began to include statutory mandates that utilities sell a certain percentage of their energy from renewables. Instigated at the outset by the wind industry, these laws—which first came to be known as renewable portfolio standards, or RPSs, and have since begun to evolve into clean energy standards, or CESs—quickly caught on.

Indeed, it is fair to say that RPSs helped start a process that has now reshaped the U.S. energy policy landscape. In the mid-1990s, only one or two states had an RPS (Iowa and Minnesota). By 2000, a dozen states had followed suit. By 2021, 35 states plus the District of Columbia had RPSs or

CESs—while another eight had enacted non-mandatory goals of either the RPS or CES flavor.

Renewable and Clean Energy Standards and Goals (2020)

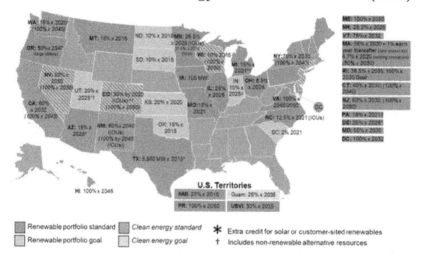

Source: Database of State Incentives for Renewables & Efficiency (DSIRE) (Sept. 2020).

This is a remarkable change for a country that still has no national renewable energy goal and barely two decades ago essentially had an absence of any state goals. Indeed, the rise of the RPS is "especially intriguing" specifically because of their pervasiveness: "so many states— both 'red' and 'blue'—have adopted some form of a mandate." Joshua P. Fershee, *When Prayer Trumps Politics: The Politics and Demographics of Renewable Portfolio Standards*, 35 WM. & MARY ENV'T L. & POL'Y REV. 53, 61 (2010); *see also* Lincoln L. Davies, *State Renewable Portfolio Standards: Is There a "Race" and Is It "To the Top"?*, 3 SAN DIEGO J. CLIMATE & ENERGY L. 3 (2011–12).

The traditional RPS features four primary components. *First*, they include a target specifying what level of renewables the state would like to reach. These targets vary widely. Some states, like Maryland and Hawaii, have set targets as high as 50% and 100%, respectively. Other states are less ambitious, like Michigan's 15% target or Ohio's 8.5% aim. *Second*, the RPS specifies how quickly the state should reach its target. These compliance dates range from 2015 to as far out as 2050. For a while, many states were adopting targets of 20% by the year 2020. The newer trend is to adopt a much higher goal by 2040, 2045, or 2050, though some states' laws have effectively lapsed, with their target dates now in the past. *Third*, these laws define what counts toward the targets. Initially, and increasingly over time, this varied. Virtually every state counted those resources that might immediately come to mind: wind, solar, and biomass. How states defined biomass, however, differed—and there were wide variations in the treatment of geothermal, ocean energy, and hydropower. *Finally*, RPSs establish compliance structures. This typically includes a jurisdictional statement regarding to whom the statute applies (just IOUs or also municipal utilities and rural electric co-ops?); a determination of how compliance will be assessed (in energy consumed—kWhs—or capacity installed—MWs—or a combination of both?); whether penalties will be assessed for failure to comply; and whether companies must report compliance, make plans for obtaining eligible energy, or both.

Of late, RPSs have begun to evolve into something else entirely. Over the last several years, numerous state legislatures have begun to adopt more aggressive laws that seek not only to promote renewables but also— and more broadly—to fight climate change. As Professor Klass has noted, in 2019 alone, "state legislatures in Maine, Nevada, New Mexico, New York, and Washington joined California and Hawaii in adopting aggressive clean energy laws to phase out the use of fossil fuels to generate electricity by 2050." Alexandra B. Klass, *Eminent Domain Law as Climate Policy*, 2020 WIS. L. REV. 49, 53 (2020). These new laws, often denominated as clean energy standards, or CESs, differ from RPSs in several respects. "First, RPSs . . . apply only in the electricity sector while many of the new clean energy policies apply to all segments of the economy that produce carbon emissions such as buildings and transportation. . . . Second, by focusing on energy that is 'carbon free' or 'zero-emission' rather than 'renewable,' the new clean energy laws allow a larger number of technologies to be used, including nuclear energy and CCS technologies, thus making it more feasible to set a 100% mandate. . . . [Third, t]hese new laws stress the urgency of addressing climate change. . . . Thus, like RPSs, the laws are future looking—designed to create a vision for a new, carbon-free energy landscape to prevent or mitigate the harms associated with climate change." *Id.*; *see also State Renewable Portfolio Standards and Goals*, Nat'l Conf. of State Legislatures (Aug 13, 2021) (detailing laws in all 50 states, with a focus on statutory amendments since 2018); Sara Kline, *Oregon Governor Signs Ambitious Clean Energy Bill*, KATU.COM (July 27, 2021) (describing Oregon's 100% clean energy law); Jeffrey Tomich, *Landmark Ill. Climate Bill Passes in Boon for Nuclear, Renewables*, ENERGYWIRE (Sept. 14, 2021) (discussing Illinois' adoption of a 100% clean energy law).

Though CESs lack a universal definition, their comparative technological neutrality bears emphasis. CESs' inclusion of non-renewable resources does not just demark a definitional shift. It also reflects an aspirational one. By counting "a broad range of zero- and low-emitting technologies as compliance options," CESs allow for higher percentage targets than RPSs typically afford. KATHRYNE CLEARY ET AL., CLEAN ENERGY STANDARDS, RESOURCES FOR THE FUTURE (Jan. 2019). Further, counting greater resources should make the laws more cost-effective. In this way, because they more accurately reflect the cost of GHG emissions reductions—rather than renewables subsidization—CESs inch closer to carbon pricing than RPSs ever did.

One common bond between RPSs and CESs is their implementing mechanism. Both laws tend to utilize renewable energy credits or certificates, sometimes referred to as RECs. These credits typically represent 1 MWh of electricity generated. Thus, in many statutes, a utility can comply with the state's law in one of three ways: build renewable or clean energy installations that generate electricity, buy eligible electricity from someone else, or acquire a credit or certificate.

The REC idea is straightforward. It is similar to how other market mechanisms work in environmental law (e.g., the SO$_x$ trading program under the Clean Air Act). RECs seek to make compliance with RPSs and CESs as low cost as possible by allowing energy producers to leverage comparative cost advantages.

Consider this simplified example: Assume that two utilities, Utility A and Utility B, both need to install 1,000 MW of wind capacity to comply with their state's CES. Assume further that Utility A is in a more densely developed area of the state and Utility B is in a less densely developed area. Thus, land prices are more expensive for Utility A, and installing wind in its service territory is $50/MWh, whereas Utility B can install wind at $35/MWh. The economically rational result is for Utility B to install all 2,000 MW of wind, use 1,000 MW for itself, and sell off the RECs for the other 1,000 MW to Utility A. In this situation, the total cost of the CES is $70,000 ($35 × 2,000). That is much cheaper than if each utility built its own wind farm. In that case, the cost of the CES would be $85,000: ($35 × 1,000) + ($50 × 1,000). So, RECs can make clean energy and renewable portfolio standards more economically efficient. *See generally* Matthew McDonnell et al., *The Potential and Power of Renewable Energy Credits to Enhance Air Quality and Economic Development in Arizona*, 43 ARIZ. ST. L.J. 809 (2011).

Given the multiple contours along which RPSs and CESs can be constructed, it does not take much imagination to envision the myriad ways these laws might manifest. In fact, there is striking diversity among both RPSs and CESs. In part, this reflects the nature by which the laws have been adopted—at the state level. Depending on one's perspective, this is either the benefit or the bane of energy federalism in the United States: a thousand flowers blooming or too many drummers marching to their own beats. *Compare, e.g.*, Lincoln L. Davies, *Power Forward: The Argument for a National RPS*, 42 CONN. L. REV. 1339 (2010) *with* David B. Spence, *The Political Barriers to a National RPS*, 42 CONN. L. REV. 1451 (2010). The remarkable diversity of these laws also owes to the sheer number of policy design choices legislators have to make when writing these laws—by one count, at least twenty choices for each statute. *See* Lincoln L. Davies, *Evaluating RPS Policy Design: Metrics, Gaps, Best Practices, and Paths to Innovation*, 4 KLRI J. L. & LEGIS. 3 (2014).

The possible intricacy of these statutory regimes belies the simplicity of their ideas—that all energy providers in the jurisdiction will supply a certain percentage of their electricity using renewables or low-GHG-emitting energy sources. While an RPS or a CES could very easily be a one-page statute, they very rarely are. To get a sense of how they are written, compare the following two statutes—Kansas' relatively early RPS and Virginia's more recently amended statute, which in many ways blurs the line between an RPS and a CES. We will return to the subject of CESs and their role in moving the energy system toward carbon neutrality in Chapter 11.

KANSAS RENEWABLE ENERGY STANDARDS ACT
(Subsequently Amended)

Kansas Stat. Ann. § 1258.   Same; renewable energy portfolio standards; rules and regulations

(a) The commission shall establish by rules and regulations a portfolio requirement for all affected utilities to generate or purchase electricity generated from renewable energy resources or purchase renewable energy credits. . . . Renewable energy credits may only be used to meet a portion of portfolio requirements for the years 2011, 2016 and 2020, unless otherwise allowed by the commission. Such portfolio requirement shall provide net renewable generation capacity that shall constitute the following portion of each affected utility's peak demand:

(1) Not less than 10% of the affected utility's peak demand for calendar years 2011 through 2015, based on the average demand of the prior three years of each year's requirement;

(2) not less than 15% of the affected utility's peak demand for calendar years 2016 through 2019, based on the average demand of the prior three years of each year's requirements; and

(3) not less than 20% of the affected utility's peak demand for each calendar year beginning in 2020, based on the average demand of the prior three years of each year's requirement.

(b) The portfolio requirements described in subsection (a) shall apply to all power sold to Kansas retail consumers whether such power is self-generated or purchased from another source in or outside of the state. The capacity of all net metering systems interconnected with the affected utilities under the net metering and easy connection act in K.S.A. 66–1263 *et seq.*, and amendments thereto, shall count toward compliance.

(c) Each megawatt of eligible capacity in Kansas installed after January 1, 2000, shall count as 1.10 megawatts for purposes of compliance. . . .

Kansas Stat. Ann. § 66–1257.   Same; definitions

As used in the renewable energy standards act:

(a) "Affected utility" means any electric public utility, as defined in K.S.A. 66–101a, and amendments thereto, but does not include any portion of any municipally owned or operated electric utility. . . .

(d) "Peak demand" means the demand imposed by the affected utility's retail load in the state. . . .

(f) "Renewable energy resources" means net renewable generation capacity from:

> (1) Wind;
>
> (2) solar thermal sources;
>
> (3) photovoltaic cells and panels;
>
> (4) dedicated crops grown for energy production;
>
> (5) cellulosic agricultural residues;
>
> (6) plant residues;
>
> (7) methane from landfills or from wastewater treatment;
>
> (8) clean and untreated wood products such as pallets;
>
> (9)
>
> > (A) existing hydropower;
> >
> > (B) new hydropower;

(10) fuel cells using hydrogen produced by one of the above-named renewable energy resources;

(11) energy storage that is connected to any renewable generation by means of energy storage equipment including, but not limited to, batteries, fly wheels, compressed air storage and pumped hydro; and

(12) other sources of energy, not including nuclear power, that become available after the effective date of this section, and that are certified as renewable by rules and regulations established by the commission pursuant to K.S.A. 66–1262, and amendments thereto.

Kansas Stat. Ann. § 66–1259. Same; renewable energy resource requirements; recovery of costs by affected utilities

The commission shall allow affected utilities to recover reasonable costs incurred to meet the new renewable energy resource requirements required in the renewable energy standards act.

Kansas Stat. Ann. § 66–1260. Same; renewable energy resource investment by affected utilities; calculation by commission; submission of information; rules and regulations; annual report

(a)

(1) For each affected utility, the commission shall determine whether investment in renewable energy resources required to meet the renewable portfolio requirement . . . causes the affected utility's total revenue requirement to increase one percent or greater.

(2) The commission shall annually determine the annual statewide retail rate impact resulting from affected utilities meeting the renewable portfolio requirement.

(b) Submission of information pertaining to an affected utility's portfolio requirement shall be determined by rules and regulations promulgated by the commission or by order of the commission.

(c) Beginning in 2013, on or before March 1 of each year, the commission shall submit a report of the annual statewide retail rate impact for the previous year to the governor, the senate committee on utilities and the house committee on energy and utilities.

VIRGINIA CLEAN ECONOMY ACT[11]

Virginia Code Ann. § 56–576. Definitions

. . . "Low-income utility customer" means any person or household whose income is no more than 80 percent of the median income of the locality in which the customer resides. The median income of the locality is determined by the U.S. Department of Housing and Urban Development. . . .

"Renewable energy" means energy derived from sunlight, wind, falling water, biomass, sustainable or otherwise, (the definitions of which shall be liberally construed), energy from waste, landfill gas, municipal solid waste, wave motion, tides, and geothermal power, and does not include energy derived from coal, oil, natural gas, or nuclear power. "Renewable energy" also includes the proportion of the thermal or electric energy from a facility that results from the co-firing of biomass. "Renewable energy" does not include waste heat from fossil-fired facilities or electricity generated from pumped storage but includes run-of-river generation from a combined pumped-storage and run-of-river facility. . . .

---

[11] Note that the Virginia statute refers to Phase I and Phase II utilities, which are defined by Virginia's utility regulations. "In practice, those terms exclusively apply to Virginia's two largest electric utilities, Dominion Energy Virginia (Phase II) and Appalachian Power Company (Phase I)." Benjamin Apple et al., *Virginia Clean Economy Act Requires Extensive New Clean Energy Measures*, JD SUPRA (May 7, 2020).

Virginia Code Ann. § 56–585.5. Generation of electricity from renewable and zero carbon sources

A. As used in this section:

. . .

"Falling water" means hydroelectric resources, including run-of-river generation from a combined pumped-storage and run-of-river facility. "Falling water" does not include electricity generated from pumped-storage facilities.

"Low-income qualifying projects" means a project that provides a minimum of 50 percent of the respective electric output to low-income utility customers as that term is defined in § 56–576. . . .

"Total electric energy" means total electric energy sold to retail customers in the Commonwealth service territory of a Phase I or Phase II Utility . . . by the incumbent electric utility or other retail supplier of electric energy in the previous calendar year, excluding an amount equivalent to the annual percentages of the electric energy that was supplied to such customer from nuclear generating plants located within the Commonwealth in the previous calendar year, provided such nuclear units were operating by July 1, 2020, or from any zero-carbon electric generating facilities not otherwise RPS eligible sources and placed into service in the Commonwealth after July 1, 2030.

"Zero-carbon electricity" means electricity generated by any generating unit that does not emit carbon dioxide as a by-product of combusting fuel to generate electricity.

B.1. By December 31, 2024, except for any coal-fired electric generating units (i) jointly owned with a cooperative utility or (ii) owned and operated by a Phase II Utility located in the coalfield region of the Commonwealth that co-fires with biomass, any Phase I and Phase II Utility shall retire all generating units principally fueled by oil with a rated capacity in excess of 500 megawatts and all coal-fired electric generating units operating in the Commonwealth.

2. By December 31, 2028, each Phase I and II Utility shall retire all biomass-fired electric generating units that do not co-fire with coal.

3. By December 31, 2045, each Phase I and II Utility shall retire all other electric generating units located in the Commonwealth that emit carbon as a by-product of combusting fuel to generate electricity.

4. A Phase I or Phase II Utility may petition the Commission for relief from the requirements of this subsection on the basis that the requirement would threaten the reliability or security of electric service to customers. The Commission shall consider in-state and regional transmission entity

resources and shall evaluate the reliability of each proposed retirement on a case-by-case basis in ruling upon any such petition.

C.   Each Phase I and Phase II Utility shall participate in a renewable energy portfolio standard program (RPS Program) that establishes annual goals for the sale of renewable energy to all retail customers in the utility's service territory, other than accelerated renewable energy buyers pursuant to subsection G, regardless of whether such customers purchase electric supply service from the utility or from suppliers other than the utility. To comply with the RPS Program, each Phase I and Phase II Utility shall procure and retire Renewable Energy Certificates (RECs) originating from renewable energy standard eligible sources (RPS eligible sources). For purposes of complying with the RPS Program from 2021 to 2024, a Phase I and Phase II Utility may use RECs from any renewable energy facility, as defined in § 56–576, provided that such facilities are located in the Commonwealth or are physically located within the PJM Interconnection, LLC (PJM) region. However, at no time during this period or thereafter may any Phase I or Phase II Utility use RECs from (i) renewable thermal energy, (ii) renewable thermal energy equivalent, (iii) biomass-fired facilities that are outside the Commonwealth, or (iv) biomass-fired facilities operating in the Commonwealth as of January 1, 2020, that supply 10 percent or more of their annual net electrical generation to the electric grid or more than 15 percent of their annual total useful energy to any entity other than the manufacturing facility to which the generating source is interconnected. From compliance year 2025 and all years after, each Phase I and Phase II Utility may only use RECs from RPS eligible sources for compliance with the RPS Program.

In order to qualify as RPS eligible sources, such sources must be (a) electric-generating resources that generate electric energy derived from solar or wind located in the Commonwealth or off the Commonwealth's Atlantic shoreline or in federal waters and interconnected directly into the Commonwealth or physically located within the PJM region; (b) falling water resources located in the Commonwealth or physically located within the PJM region that were in operation as of January 1, 2020, that are owned by a Phase I or Phase II Utility or for which a Phase I or Phase II Utility has entered into a contract prior to January 1, 2020, to purchase the energy, capacity, and renewable attributes of such falling water resources; (c) non-utility-owned resources from falling water that (1) are less than 65 megawatts, (2) began commercial operation after December 31, 1979, or (3) added incremental generation representing greater than 50 percent of the original nameplate capacity after December 31, 1979, provided that such resources are located in the Commonwealth or are physically located within the PJM region; (d) waste-to-energy or landfill gas-fired generating resources located in the Commonwealth and in operation as of January 1, 2020, provided that such resources do not use waste heat from fossil fuel combustion or forest or woody biomass as fuel; or (e) biomass-fired facilities in operation in the Commonwealth and in operation as of January 1, 2020, that supply no more than 10 percent of their annual net electrical generation to the electric grid or no more than 15 percent of their annual total useful energy to any entity other than the manufacturing facility to which the generating source is interconnected. Regardless of any future maintenance, expansion, or refurbishment activities, the total amount of RECs that may be sold by any RPS eligible source using biomass in any year shall be no more than the number of megawatt hours of electricity produced by that facility in 2019; however, in no year may any RPS eligible source using biomass sell RECs in excess of the actual megawatt-hours of electricity generated by such facility that year. In order to comply with the RPS Program, each Phase I and Phase II Utility may use and retire the environmental attributes associated with any existing owned or contracted solar, wind, or falling water electric generating resources in operation, or proposed for operation, in the Commonwealth or physically located within the PJM region, with such resource qualifying as a Commonwealth-located resource for purposes of this subsection, as of January 1, 2020, provided such renewable attributes are verified as RECs consistent with the PJM-EIS Generation Attribute Tracking System.

The RPS Program requirements shall be a percentage of the total electric energy sold in the previous calendar year and shall be implemented in accordance with the following schedule:[12]

Year	Phase I	Phase II
2021	6%	14%
2022	7%	17%
2023	8%	20%
2024	10%	23%
2025	14%	26%
2026	17%	29%
2027	20%	32%
2028	24%	35%
2029	27%	32%
2030	30%	41%
2031	33%	45%
2032	36%	49%
2033	39%	52%
2034	42%	55%
2035	45%	59%
2036	53%	63%
2037	53%	67%

---

[12] [The formatting and a few words in this table have been modified for ease of display; no substance was changed.—Eds.]

Year	Phase I	Phase II
2038	57%	71%
2039	61%	75%
2040	65%	79%
2041	68%	83%
2042	71%	87%
2043	74%	91%
2044	77%	95%
2045	80%	100% (2045
2046	84%	and thereafter)
2047	88%	
2048	92%	
2049	96%	
2050	100% (2050 and thereafter)	

A Phase II Utility shall meet one percent of the RPS Program requirements in any given compliance year with solar, wind, or anaerobic digestion resources of one megawatt or less located in the Commonwealth, with not more than 3,000 kilowatts at any single location or at contiguous locations owned by the same entity or affiliated entities and, to the extent that low-income qualifying projects are available, then no less than 25 percent of such one percent shall be composed of low-income qualifying projects.

Beginning with the 2025 compliance year and thereafter, at least 75 percent of all RECs used by a Phase II Utility in a compliance period shall come from RPS eligible resources located in the Commonwealth.

Any Phase I or Phase II Utility may apply renewable energy sales achieved or RECs acquired in excess of the sales requirement for that RPS Program to the sales requirements for RPS Program requirements in the year in which it was generated and the five calendar years after the renewable energy was generated or the RECs were created. To the extent that a Phase I or Phase II Utility procures RECs for RPS Program compliance from resources the utility does not own, the utility shall be entitled to recover the costs of such certificates at its election pursuant to § 56–249.6 or subdivision A 5 d of § 56–585.1.

D. Each Phase I or Phase II Utility shall petition the Commission for necessary approvals to procure zero-carbon electricity generating capacity as set forth in this subsection and energy storage resources as set forth in subsection E. To the extent that a Phase I or Phase II Utility constructs or acquires new zero-carbon generating facilities or energy storage resources, the utility shall petition the Commission for the recovery of the costs of such facilities, at the utility's election, either through its rates for generation and distribution services or through a rate adjustment clause pursuant to subdivision A 6 of § 56–585.1. All costs not sought for recovery through a rate adjustment clause pursuant to subdivision A 6 of § 56–585.1 associated with generating facilities provided by sunlight or onshore or offshore wind are also eligible to be applied by the utility as a customer credit reinvestment offset as provided in subdivision A 8 of § 56–585.1. Costs associated with the purchase of energy, capacity, or environmental attributes from facilities owned by the persons other than the utility required by this subsection shall be recovered by the utility either through its rates for generation and distribution services or pursuant to § 56–249.6.

1.   Each Phase I Utility shall petition the Commission for necessary approvals to construct, acquire, or enter into agreements to purchase the energy, capacity, and environmental attributes of 600 megawatts of generating capacity using energy derived from sunlight or onshore wind. [The statute contains subprovisions specifying a 2023, 2027, and 2030 schedule to achieve this goal.]

2.   By December 31, 2035, each Phase II Utility shall petition the Commission for necessary approvals to (i) construct, acquire, or enter into agreements to purchase the energy, capacity, and environmental attributes of 16,100 megawatts of generating capacity located in the Commonwealth using energy derived from sunlight or onshore wind, which shall include 1,100 megawatts of solar generation of a nameplate capacity not to exceed three megawatts per individual project and 35 percent of such generating capacity procured shall be from the purchase of energy, capacity, and environmental attributes from solar facilities owned by persons other than a utility, including utility affiliates and deregulated affiliates and (ii) pursuant to § 56–585.1:11, construct or purchase one or more offshore wind generation facilities located off the Commonwealth's Atlantic shoreline or in federal waters and interconnected directly into the Commonwealth with an aggregate capacity of up to 5,200 megawatts. At least 200 megawatts of the 16,100 megawatts shall be placed on previously developed project sites. [The statute contains subprovisions specifying a 2024, 2027, and 2030 schedule to achieve this goal.]

3.   Nothing in this section shall prohibit a utility from petitioning the Commission to construct or acquire zero-carbon electricity or from entering into contracts to procure the energy, capacity, and environmental attributes of zero-carbon electricity generating resources in excess of the requirements in subsection B. The Commission shall determine whether to approve such petitions on a stand-alone basis pursuant to §§ 56–580 and 56–585.1, provided that the Commission's review shall also consider whether the proposed generating capacity (i) is necessary to meet the utility's native load, (ii) is likely to lower customer fuel costs, (iii) will provide economic development opportunities in the Commonwealth, and (iv) serves a need that cannot be more affordably met with demand-side or energy storage resources.

Each Phase I and Phase II Utility shall, at least once every year, conduct a request for proposals for new solar and wind resources. Such requests shall quantify and describe the utility's need for energy, capacity, or renewable energy certificates. The requests for proposals shall be publicly announced and made available for public review on the utility's website at least 45 days prior to the closing of such request for proposals. The requests for proposals shall provide, at a minimum, the following information: (a) the size, type, and timing of resources for which the utility anticipates contracting; (b) any minimum thresholds that must be met by respondents; (c) major assumptions to be used by the utility in the bid evaluation process, including environmental emission standards; (d) detailed instructions for preparing bids so that bids can be evaluated on a consistent basis; (e) the preferred general location of additional capacity; and (f) specific information concerning the factors involved in determining the price and non-price criteria used for selecting winning bids. A utility may evaluate responses to requests for proposals based on any criteria that it deems reasonable but shall at a minimum consider the following in its selection process: (1) the status of a particular project's development; (2) the age of existing generation facilities; (3) the demonstrated financial viability of a project and the developer; (4) a developer's prior experience in the field; (5) the location and effect on the transmission grid of a generation facility; (6) benefits to the Commonwealth that are associated with particular projects, including regional economic development and the use of goods and services from Virginia businesses; and (7) the environmental impacts of particular resources, including impacts on air quality within the Commonwealth and the carbon intensity of the utility's generation portfolio.

4.   In connection with the requirements of this subsection, each Phase I and Phase II Utility shall, commencing in 2020 and concluding in 2035, submit annually a plan and petition for approval for the development of new solar and onshore wind generation capacity. Such plan shall reflect, in the aggregate and over its duration, the requirements of subsection D concerning the allocation percentages for construction or purchase of such capacity. Such petition shall contain any request for approval to construct such facilities pursuant to subsection D of § 56–580 and a request for approval or update of a rate adjustment clause pursuant to subdivision A 6 of § 56–585.1 to recover the costs of such facilities. Such plan shall also include the utility's plan to meet the energy storage project targets of subsection E, including the goal of installing at least 10 percent of such energy storage projects behind the meter. In determining whether to approve the utility's plan and any associated petition requests, the Commission shall determine whether they are reasonable and prudent and shall give due consideration to (i) the RPS and carbon dioxide reduction requirements in this section, (ii) the promotion of new renewable generation and energy storage resources within the Commonwealth, and

associated economic development, and (iii) fuel savings projected to be achieved by the plan. . . .

5.   If, in any year, a Phase I or Phase II Utility is unable to meet the compliance obligation of the RPS Program requirements or if the cost of RECs necessary to comply with RPS Program requirements exceeds $45 per megawatt hour, such supplier shall be obligated to make a deficiency payment equal to $45 for each megawatt-hour shortfall for the year of noncompliance, except that the deficiency payment for any shortfall in procuring RECs for solar, wind, or anaerobic digesters located in the Commonwealth shall be $75 per megawatts hour for resources one megawatt and lower. The amount of any deficiency payment shall increase by one percent annually after 2021. A Phase I or Phase II Utility shall be entitled to recover the costs of such payments as a cost of compliance with the requirements of this subsection pursuant to subdivision A 5 d of § 56–585.1. All proceeds from the deficiency payments shall be deposited into an interest-bearing account administered by the Department of Mines, Minerals and Energy. In administering this account, the Department of Mines, Minerals and Energy shall manage the account as follows: (i) 50 percent of total revenue shall be directed to job training programs in historically economically disadvantaged communities; (ii) 16 percent of total revenue shall be directed to energy efficiency measures for public facilities; (iii) 30 percent of total revenue shall be directed to renewable energy programs located in historically economically disadvantaged communities; and (iv) four percent of total revenue shall be directed to administrative costs.

For any project constructed pursuant to this subsection or subsection E, a utility shall, subject to a competitive procurement process, procure equipment from a Virginia-based or United States-based manufacturer using materials or product components made in Virginia or the United States, if reasonably available and competitively priced.

E.   To enhance reliability and performance of the utility's generation and distribution system, each Phase I and Phase II Utility shall petition the Commission for necessary approvals to construct or acquire new, utility-owned energy storage resources.

[The statute specifies a schedule for this construction: 400 MW of storage for Phase I utilities and 2,700 MW of storage for Phase II utilities, both by 2035. The law further mandates that no "energy storage project shall exceed 500 megawatts in size, except that a Phase II Utility may procure a single energy storage project up to 800 megawatts," and that the utilities will use a competitive procurement process to obtain the storage. Finally, the statute mandates that after July 1, 2020, "at least 35 percent of the energy storage facilities placed into service shall" be purchased from or owned by a party other than the utility.—Eds.]

I. Nothing in this section shall apply to any entity organized under Chapter 9.1 (§ 56–231.15 et seq.). [*i.e.*, rural electric cooperatives.—Eds.]

NOTES AND QUESTIONS

1. In 2015, the Kansas legislature amended its RPS to make it voluntary rather than mandatory. This was perhaps an odd move given that, according to some sources, Kansas had already exceeded its 2020 goal of 20% renewables in 2014. The move, however, was representative of a larger effort by the corporate-backed American Legislative Exchange Council (ALEC) and some utility interests, which have sought to roll back RPSs across the nation. These efforts have met with mixed success but have prevailed so far in at least Montana, Ohio, and West Virginia. *See* John Light, *Score One for ALEC: West Virginia Is First State to Repeal a Renewable Energy Standard*, GRIST (Feb. 5, 2015). For a summary of recent changes to RPSs, including the adoption of CESs, see Laura Shields, *State Renewable Portfolio Standards and Goals*, NAT'L CONF. OF STATE LEGIS. (Apr. 7, 2021). For a particularly insightful look into the politics behind RPSs and CESs, see LEAH CARDAMORE STOKES, SHORT CIRCUITING POLICY: INTEREST GROUPS AND THE BATTLE OVER CLEAN ENERGY AND CLIMATE POLICY IN THE AMERICAN STATES (2020).

2. At least three problems vex RPSs. First, for an RPS to be effective, it cannot stand alone. Other policy support is needed for renewables, including policies that encourage development of electric transmission lines to move renewable power to load centers. This is, in part, what has pushed some states to move to CESs rather than RPSs; non-renewable, low-emission resources like nuclear already exist, do not require new transmission, but are essential to combat climate change. Likewise, RPSs are not policy islands. They interact with other laws; for instance, financial incentives, such as the PTC have been critical, on top of an RPS mandate, to promote renewables development. This too has been a factor pushing states toward CESs—a hope for greater efficiency because "other policies (carbon tax, cap-and-trade) can interact with existing taxes on labor and capital and raise the policy's cost, while a CES has no such interactions." CLEARY ET AL., *supra*.

Second, the possible complexity of RPS design provides many ways in which loopholes, exceptions, and escape hatches can be built into these laws. This creates the risk that an RPS in actuality will not be nearly as aggressive as it might appear on its face. These loopholes can substantially dilute the strength of an RPS from its nominal percentage target. Indeed, studies have shown that taking RPS policy design into account matters significantly when assessing how well the RPS works. *See, e.g.*, Sanya Carley et al., *Empirical Evaluation of the Stringency and Design of Renewable Portfolio Standards*, 3 NATURE ENERGY 754 (2018); Miriam Fischlein & Timothy M. Smith, *Revisiting Renewable Portfolio Standard Effectiveness: Policy Design and Outcome Specification Matter*, 46 POL'Y SCI. 277 (2013). Kansas' statute provides a number of examples of how these loopholes can creep into an RPS. How many can you identify? (Hint: There are at least three.)[13] Perhaps more critical, why do you think legislators would include such loopholes in their laws? (Hint: What effect might greater reliance on renewables have on electricity prices?) Do you see any similar loopholes in Virginia's law? (Hint: Look again.) Do you think Virginia's loopholes are bigger or smaller than those in Kansas'?

A third problem RPSs face is federalism. Because some states have RPSs and others do not, lawmakers legitimately worry that a neighboring state's lack of an RPS (or use of a less aggressive RPS) will negatively impact the performance of their own statute. Giving the benefit of the doubt to state legislators, this concern might be labeled one of policy "leakage": States with non-RPS neighbors might worry that no (or less than desired) new renewables will be built in their state because existing facilities next door will simply sell their power to the RPS state. Viewed more skeptically, this concern might be framed in terms of the state trying to ensure it captures the local economic benefits it believes its RPS can deliver—a common refrain uttered by lawmakers when passing RPSs. These kinds of concerns are not far-fetched. As but one example, Rocky Mountain Power, which serves much of Utah (a state with an RPS full of enough loopholes that some call it an RPG), has built substantial wind installations in Wyoming (a state without an RPS) because the wind resources there are stronger. Take a careful look at Virginia's law. Do you see any legislative fingerprints of concern for economic gain anywhere in the statute?

3.   To combat this leakage risk, many RPSs include incentives (or sometimes requirements) to build renewables in the state. Did you see such provisions in the Kansas or Virginia statutes? Which statute is more aggressive in this way? And, importantly, do you think such provisions are a good or a bad thing? On one hand, shouldn't a state be able to capture the economic benefits of its law? On the other, isn't forcing compliance by using in-state resources only likely to drive up electricity prices farther than if cheaper, out-of-state energy could be used, thus harming local ratepayers?

Congress could fix this problem: It could adopt a national RPS or CES that applies to every state, or it could authorize states to discriminate against others to ensure their laws' effectiveness, insulating them from dormant Commerce Clause challenges. To date, however, this has not happened. Though literally dozens of national RPSs have been proposed in Congress, and both Republicans and Democrats have introduced federal CES legislation, none has passed into law. As it stands, then, two of the nation's primary tools for promoting renewables and fighting climate change remain frozen in a kind of federalism paralysis. States—not the federal government—have been the

---

[13] Section 1257(a) says that the statute does not apply to municipal utilities, automatically exempting a segment of the Kansas electricity market from the RPS. Also, what is Section 1260's objective? What happens if the RPS causes retail electricity prices to go up five percent—or more? Will the statute's requirements be waived? A number of states' RPSs say so. Likewise, note § 1257(f)(12), which allows the state commission to qualify additional technologies as renewable. Kansas' law forecloses nuclear as a possibility, but what impact does that have on climate change? Interestingly, other states count generation like advanced coal as renewable. These are only a few ways RPSs can quickly become diluted.

leaders, but federal law—not state—dictates the limits of how effective these laws might be.

4.   Juxtapose the Kansas and Virginia statutes. Notice the difference in the laws—not only in their content but also in their length, structure, complexity, and depth. Is there a reason why the Virginia statute is so much more intricate, or do you think that is simply the result of legislative style or drafting preference? Does it have anything to do with the manifold objectives the Virginia statute appears to embrace, particularly in comparison to the Kansas law's more singular focus on renewables? If you had to list the core objectives of the Virginia law, what would you say they are?

5.   On the question of federalism, do you see potential dormant Commerce Clause violations in either the Kansas or the Virginia statute—or in them both? What arguments can be made that either of the statutes is unconstitutional on these grounds? What arguments are there in response?

6.   Earlier, we suggested that the Virginia statute blurs the line between an RPS and a CES. Do you agree? Or do you think it is firmly one or the other? Did you notice how it treats nuclear energy—and how does that influence your answer?

Early lawsuits involving RPSs focused on ownership of RECs, including whether PURPA controlled this question. In *American Ref-Fuel Co.*, 105 FERC ¶ 61,004 (2003), for instance, FERC ruled that RECs "exist outside the confines of PURPA," and thus, PURPA "does not address the ownership of RECs." These disputes arose, in part, because power purchase agreements pre-dated RPSs so did not address REC ownership. Resolving these disputes, courts overwhelmingly decided that agreements which did not account for RECs effectively bestowed REC ownership on the utility purchasing the electricity from the renewable energy producer. *See, e.g., City of New Martinsville v. Pub. Serv. Comm'n of W. Virginia*, 729 S.E.2d 188 (W. Va. 2012); *ARIPPA v. Pennsylvania Pub. Util. Comm'n*, 966 A.2d 1204 (Pa. Cmwlth. 2009); *Minnesota Methane, LLC v. Dep't of Pub. Util. Control*, 931 A.2d 177 (Conn. 2007); *In re Ownership of Renewable Energy Certificates*, 913 A.2d 825 (N.J. App. Div. 2007); *Wheelabrator Lisbon Inc. v. Connecticut Dep't of Pub. Util. Control*, 526 F. Supp. 2d 295 (D. Conn. 2006), *aff'd*, 531 F.3d 183 (2d Cir. 2008).

Subsequently, a second generation of suits involving RPSs and other state efforts to fight climate change began. Those cases have centered on federalism challenges under both the Supremacy Clause and the dormant Commerce Clause.

The following cases provide examples of these suits. Both cases were decided soon after the U.S. Supreme Court rendered its decision in *Hughes v. Talen Energy Marketing, LLC*, 578 U.S. 150 (2016). There, the Court grappled with a Maryland program designed to encourage more natural gas-fired generation in the state. Maryland sought to promote this construction by requiring load-serving utilities to enter into a 20-year contract-for-differences for the capacity of a new facility. If the PJM capacity market price fell below this contractual price, the utilities had to pay the difference to the generator. But if the PJM market price exceeded the contract price, the generator had to pay the utilities the difference.

This the Court found unconstitutional. FERC regulates capacity prices, having determined that the price set by the PJM capacity market is the just and reasonable rate under the Federal Power Act. Thus, Maryland's law was preempted: "Maryland—through the contract for differences—requires CPV [the new facility that won the Maryland contract] to participate in the PJM capacity auction but guarantees CPV a rate distinct from the clearing price for its interstate sales of capacity to PJM. By adjusting an interstate wholesale rate, Maryland's program invades FERC's regulatory turf." *Id.* at 1297.

The *Hughes* Court recognized that states retain authority despite the FPA to "encourage construction of new in-state generation." But that reserved power could not save Maryland's program. "States, of course, may regulate within the domain Congress assigned to them even when their laws incidentally affect areas within FERC's domain. But States may not seek to achieve ends, however legitimate, through regulatory means that intrude on FERC's authority over interstate wholesale rates." *Id.* at 1298.

Nonetheless, the Court expressly acknowledged clear "limit[s]" on its holding in *Hughes*:

> We . . . need not and do not address the permissibility of various other measures States might employ to encourage development of new or clean generation, including tax incentives, land grants, direct subsidies, construction of state-owned generation facilities, or re-regulation of the energy sector. Nothing in this opinion should be read to foreclose Maryland and other States from encouraging production of new or clean generation through measures "untethered to a generator's wholesale market participation." So long as a State does not condition payment of funds on capacity clearing the auction, the State's program would not suffer from the fatal defect that renders Maryland's program unacceptable.

Id. at 1299.

As you will see, *Hughes* figures prominently in the two cases below. The first features a challenge to Connecticut's RPS, and the second is a more recent decision addressing a new state policy development that borrows heavily from the ideas of RECs—zero emissions credits, or ZECs, afforded by New York to support its nuclear power industry. As you read the cases, keep in mind the question whether RECs and ZECs are different and, if so, in what legally relevant ways.

ALLCO FINANCE LTD. V. KLEE
861 F.3d 82 (2d Cir. 2017)

CALABRESI, CIRCUIT JUDGE.

I.   BACKGROUND

The Federal Power Act (FPA) gives the Federal Energy Regulatory Commission (FERC) exclusive authority to regulate the sale of electric energy at wholesale in interstate commerce. *See* 16 U.S.C. § 824(b)(1); *Hughes v. Talen Energy Mktg., LLC*, 136 S. Ct. 1288, 1292 (2016). . . . Although the FPA "places beyond FERC's power, leaving to the States alone, the regulation of 'any other sale'—*i.e.*, any retail sale—of electricity," states may not regulate interstate wholesale sales of electricity unless Congress creates an exception to the FPA.

The Public Utility Regulatory Policies Act (PURPA) contains such an exception, permitting states to foster electric generation by certain power production facilities (qualifying facilities or QFs) that have no more than 80 megawatts of capacity and use renewable generation technology. A state may regulate wholesale sales of electricity made by QFs by requiring utilities to purchase power from QFs at the utilities' "avoided costs," which are the costs that the utility would have otherwise incurred in procuring the same quantity of electricity from another source. . . .

Three general categories of actors in the interstate electricity market are relevant to this opinion: generators, load serving entities (LSEs), and transmitters. Generators include power plants and other sources of electricity production. LSEs, otherwise known as utilities, sell electricity at retail to end users. Transmitters transmit the electricity from generators to the LSEs. . . .

Given the changes to the energy market that came with deregulation . . . in Connecticut and other states that have deregulated their energy markets, interstate wholesale transactions typically occur through two FERC-regulated mechanisms. The first mechanism is bilateral contracting, whereby LSEs agree to purchase a certain amount of electricity from generators at a particular rate over a specified period of time. After the parties have agreed to contract terms, FERC may review the rate to ensure it is "just and reasonable." . . . Second, RTOs and ISOs administer a number of competitive wholesale auctions. FERC extensively regulates the structure and rules of such auctions . . . .

In 2013, the Connecticut Department of Energy and Environmental Protection (DEEP) . . . issued a memorandum setting forth the state's first "Comprehensive Energy Strategy" . . . . The 2013 CES articulates a commitment (a) to promoting "diversification" of Connecticut's energy generation sources in order to mitigate "price and reliability risks," and (b) to increasing renewable energy generation in the state and in adjacent states . . . .

The Connecticut legislature enacted a statute that authorized the DEEP Commissioner, "in accordance with the policy goals outlined in the [2013 CES]," (a) to solicit proposals for renewable energy, (b) to select winners of the solicitation, and (c) to "direct [Connecticut's utilities] to enter into" bilateral contracts, called "power purchase agreements," with the chosen winners "for energy, capacity and environmental attributes, or any combination thereof, for periods of not more than twenty years." Any [such] contracts . . . also required the approval of the Connecticut Public Utilities Regulatory Authority (PURA) . . . .

In July 2013, the DEEP Commissioner solicited proposals . . . . Allco, an owner, operator, and developer of various solar projects throughout the country, submitted proposals for five solar projects, each of which had less than of 80 megawatts of capacity, and therefore were QFs under PURPA. The DEEP Commissioner did not select Allco's projects. Instead, it chose two others[, a 250 MW wind farm (not a QF) in Maine and] a QF solar project located in Connecticut . . . . The DEEP Commissioner then "directed" the Connecticut utilities to execute power purchase agreements with the generators that had been selected[, and PURA approved them]. Disappointed by its failure to receive a contract . . ., Allco sued . . . .

Allco [also] claims that a separate Connecticut program, the Renewable Portfolio Standard (RPS), Conn. Gen. Stat. § 16–245a(b), violates the dormant Commerce Clause. . . .

Connecticut's RPS program defines two types of RECs that count towards the [RPS] requirement placed on Connecticut utilities[, each of which] must be issued and tracked by the New England Power Pool Generation Information System (NEPOOL-GIS) . . . .

The first type is a REC that is generated by a renewable energy source located within the jurisdiction of ISO-NE (*i.e.*, Connecticut, Massachusetts, Vermont, New Hampshire, Rhode Island, and most of Maine). The second type is a REC that is issued by NEPOOL-GIS for energy that may be imported into the ISO-NE grid from generators in adjacent control areas[, including] ISO-New York, the Northern Maine Independent System Administrator, Inc., and Quebec and New Brunswick in Canada. Although Connecticut utilities are free to purchase RECs that do not meet these requirements . . ., such RECs will not count towards their requirements under the RPS. . . .

II. DISCUSSION

B. Preemption Claim

First, Allco alleges that the 2015 RFP allows the DEEP Commissioner to "compel" and "force" utilities to enter into contracts with specified generators at specified rates, [which it says Connecticut cannot do because that is the exclusive province of FERC under the FPA]. . . .

Plaintiff fails to provide factual allegations sufficient to support its contention . . . . Specifically, although the authorizing statutes of the 2015 RFP permit the DEEP Commissioner to "direct" Connecticut utilities to "enter into" contracts with winning bidders, the materials referenced in Allco's Complaints undermine Allco's contention that such a "direction" amounts to "compulsion." For instance, Connecticut's . . . 2015 RFP . . . provide[s] (a) that "[t]his RFP process, including any selection of preferred projects, does not obligate any [utility] to accept any bid," and (b) that the winning bidders "will enter into separate contracts with one or more [utilities] at the discretion of the [utilities]." This language makes clear, contrary to Allco's contention, that it is possible for a winning bidder to fail to reach an agreement with the utilities, or for an agreement to be terminated if a party is unable or unwilling to fulfill its terms—as apparently happened with [the Maine project]. . . .

Allco argues, however, that Connecticut's RFP process is "economically identical," to a Maryland regulatory scheme which the Supreme Court recently determined was preempted by the FPA in *Hughes*. We are not convinced . . . .

There are, we believe, important and telling distinctions between the Maryland program and Connecticut's RFPs. While Maryland sought essentially to override the terms set by the FERC-approved PJM auction, and required transfer of ownership through the FERC-approved auction, Connecticut's program does not condition capacity transfers on any such auction. Connecticut, instead, transfers ownership of electricity from one party to another by contract, independent of the auction. Moreover, the contracts at issue in the case before us are the kind of traditional bilateral contracts between utilities and generators that are subject to FERC review for justness and reasonableness . . . . They are, in other words, precisely what the *Hughes* court placed outside its limited holding. . . .

[Finally,] Allco . . . claims that the 2015 RFP exceeds the bounds of PURPA insofar as it charges fees not contemplated by PURPA, excludes bids from Allco's QFs with less than 20 megawatts of capacity, and directs utilities to enter into contracts with non-QF generators. We find, however, that the 2015 RFP process . . . is, without more, a permissible exercise of the power that the FPA grants to Connecticut to regulate its LSEs. That is, we hold that it is permitted, apart from [PURPA].

"[T]he regulation of utilities is one of the most important of the functions traditionally associated with the police power of the States." *Ark. Elec. Co-op. Corp. v. Ark. Pub. Serv. Comm'n*, 461 U.S. 375, 377 (1983). Accordingly, we believe that it is settled law that specifying the sizes and types of generators that may bid into the 2015 RFP, as well as the charging of fees to bidders, without more, lies well within the scope of Connecticut's power to regulate its utilities.

Allco, though, asserts that the contracts that will arise from the 2015 RFP will increase the supply of electricity available to Connecticut utilities, that this will place downward pressure on the "avoided cost" that Allco's QFs will be able to receive under Section 210 of PURPA, and that this pressure will have an effect on wholesale prices, thereby infringing upon FERC's regulatory authority. This incidental effect on wholesale prices does not, however, amount to a regulation of the interstate wholesale electricity market that infringes on FERC's jurisdiction. *See Hughes*, 136 S. Ct. at 1298; *cf.* [*FERC v. Elec. Power Supply Ass'n*, 136 S. Ct. 760, 776 (2016) (*EPSA*)] ("When FERC . . . takes virtually any action respecting wholesale transactions—it has some effect, in either the short or the long term, on retail rates. That is of no legal consequence."). . . .

C.   Dormant Commerce Clause Claim

[Under the dormant Commerce Clause, laws that intend to, or do, discriminate against interstate commerce are virtually *per se* invalid. By contrast, nondiscriminatory state laws that nonetheless adversely affect interstate commerce incidentally are invalid only if their burden on interstate commerce clearly exceeds their local benefits. *Pike v. Bruce Church, Inc.*, 397 U.S. 137, 142 (1970).]

Allco argues that the RPS program discriminates against Allco's Georgia facility . . . . We [disagree and find Connecticut's RPS to pass the *Pike* balancing test].

"Conceptually, of course, any notion of discrimination assumes a comparison of substantially similar entities." *Gen. Motors Corp. v. Tracy*, 519 U.S. 278, 298–99 (1997). Thus, "when the allegedly competing entities provide different products . . . there is a threshold question whether the companies are indeed similarly situated for constitutional purposes. This is so for the simple reason that the difference in products may mean that the different entities serve different markets" . . . .

In *Tracy*, the Supreme Court considered whether two allegedly similar products were, nonetheless, substantially different for the purposes of the dormant Commerce Clause because they served two different markets. These were: (1) natural gas that was sold primarily to small residential customers and was "bundled with . . . services and protections" to ensure reliability and stable rates, and (2) "unbundled" natural gas that was purchased by large, bulk buyers like General Motors, who typically did not need the same protections.

Ohio imposed a sales tax on in-state sales of goods, including natural gas, and a parallel use tax on goods purchased out-of-state for use in Ohio. Ohio, however, exempted from the sales tax state-regulated natural gas utilities, which had traditionally served the market of Ohio customers who, being in a sense "captive," had to purchase bundled natural gas, and could do so only from the state-regulated utilities. As the natural gas market evolved, however, it became possible for Ohio consumers to buy "unbundled" natural gas from independent—often interstate—marketers. General Motors—and other customers—began to purchase its gas in this way from independent non-state-regulated marketers. It was therefore charged the general use tax. . . . [Despite this, the Court found no] dormant Commerce Clause violation, in part due to the lack of competition in the in-state captive market, and in part due to] States' power to regulate and protect [natural gas supplies for their citizens]. . . .

This action [raises similar issues]. . . . Accordingly, we first ask whether the allegedly competing entities—Allco's Georgia generator, on the one hand, and generators located in ISO-NE and adjacent control areas, on the other—provide different products, *i.e.*, different RECs. We find that they do. "RECs are inventions of state property law," *Wheelabrator Lisbon, Inc. v. Conn. Dep't of Pub. Util. Control*, 531 F.3d 183, 186 (2d Cir. 2008) (per curiam), and Connecticut has invented a class of RECs that differs from Allco's Georgia facility's RECs. The two products can, therefore, be treated as different, even though they—like the unbundled and bundled gas products in *Tracy*—also have some underlying similarities.

Second, we ask whether there is a market that only one of the two entities serves, and in which competition would not be increased if the differential treatment of the two entities were removed. We answer this question in the affirmative as well.

Connecticut consumers' need for a more diversified and renewable energy supply, accessible to them directly through their regional grid or indirectly through adjacent control areas, would not be served by RECs produced by Allco's facility in Georgia—which is unable to transmit its electricity into ISO-NE. Further, this market's "characteristics"—most importantly, the boundaries of the electrical grid to which Connecticut has direct or indirect access—"appear to be independent of any effect attributable to the State's" RPS program. In other words, the RPS program's definition of qualifying RECs appears to be a response to, rather than a cause of, the fact that Connecticut has direct access only to electricity on the ISO-NE grid . . . . This suggests that competition would not be served by treating the different types of REC producers similarly.

Third, we ask whether there is also a separate market in which these two types of producers compete, and in which competition potentially would be served if Connecticut were prohibited from treating them disparately. The answer is yes. Defendants admit that there is a national market for RECs that does not distinguish between RECs on the basis of their geographic origin. In this market, "the respective sellers ... apparently do compete and may compete further." *Tracy*, 519 U.S. at 303. Eliminating Connecticut's RPS program's differential treatment "might well intensify competition ... for customers in this [national] market." This, of course, cuts in favor of treating the products as alike.

Following the Court's analysis in *Tracy*, we resolve this dilemma by asking whether the opportunity for increased competition between REC producers in the national market necessitates treating REC-producers in Georgia and New England alike for dormant Commerce Clause purposes, or whether the needs of Connecticut's local energy market permits treating the two types of REC producers differently. . . . As in *Tracy*, we find that "[a]lthough there is no *a priori* answer, a number of reasons support a decision to give greater weight" to the market for RECs that are produced by generators able to connect to Connecticut's grid . . . .

Just as the *Tracy* Court recognized the importance of Ohio's interest in protecting the captive natural gas market from the effects of competition in order to promote public health and safety, so must we here recognize the importance of Connecticut's interest in protecting the market for RECs produced within the ISO-NE or in adjacent areas. Connecticut's RPS program serves its legitimate interest in promoting increased production of renewable power generation in the region, thereby protecting its citizens' health, safety, and reliable [electricity].

These means and ends are well within the scope of what Congress and FERC have traditionally allowed the States to do in the realm of energy regulation. . . . Significantly, we note that Connecticut's RPS program makes geographic distinctions between RECs only insofar as it piggybacks on top of geographic lines drawn by ISO-NE and the NEPOOL-GIS, both of which are supervised by FERC—not the state of Connecticut. . . . In other words, it is FERC itself that has instituted a sort of regionalization of the national electricity market. And neither FERC nor Congress has given any indication that this structure is unduly harmful to interstate commerce. Congress and FERC are better-situated than the courts to supervise and to determine the economic wisdom and the health and safety effects of these geographic boundaries that Connecticut has incorporated into its RPS program. It is they that, in this setting, are best suited to decide which products ought to be treated similarly, and which should not. . . .

COALITION FOR COMPETITIVE ELECTRICITY V. ZIBELMAN

906 F.3d 41 (2d Cir. 2018)

JACOBS, CIRCUIT JUDGE.

[T]he New York Public Service Commission (PSC) adopted the Zero Emissions Credit (ZEC) program as part of a larger energy reform plan to reduce greenhouse-gas emissions by 40 percent by 2030. The program subsidizes qualifying nuclear power plants by creating "ZECs": state-created and state-issued credits certifying the zero-emission attributes of electricity produced by a participating nuclear plant. The PSC has determined that three nuclear power plants (FitzPatrick, Ginna, and Nine Mile Point) qualify for the ZEC program; other facilities, including facilities located outside New York, may be selected in the future. [Plaintiffs challenge this regime as unconstitutional.]

[I]

FERC has determined that just and reasonable rates for wholesale electricity should be set by competitive auctions. The New York Independent System Operator (NYISO) manages two types of wholesale auctions under FERC-approved rules and procedures: energy and capacity. In energy auctions, generators bid the lowest price they will accept to sell a given quantity of electrical output; in capacity auctions, generators bid (and NYISO purchases) options to call upon the generator to produce a specified quantity of electricity in the future. Both types of auction employ "stacking" of bids from lowest to highest price until demand is satisfied. The price of the highest-stacked bid sets the "market clearing price." Any generator that bids at or below the market clearing price "clears" the auction and receives the market clearing price, regardless of the price the generator actually bid. "A high clearing price in the capacity auction encourages new generators to enter the market, increasing supply and thereby lowering the clearing price .... [A] low clearing price discourages new entry and encourages retirement of existing high-cost generators."

Nuclear generators bid into the NYISO auctions as price-takers: since, unlike other types of electricity generation, they are unable to vary their output depending on price, they sell their entire output at the market clearing price, even if the price is below the cost of production.

In August 2016, the PSC issued the Clean Energy Standard (CES) Order as an overall scheme to reduce greenhouse-gas emissions by 40 percent by 2030. The CES Order created two programs that bear upon this appeal: Renewable Energy Credits (RECs) and ZECs. . . .

The REC program awards to generators one REC for each megawatt-hour (MWh) of energy that is produced from renewable sources like wind and solar. The New York State Energy Research and Development Authority (NYSERDA) purchases RECs from generators, thereby providing them a subsidy. In turn, NYSERDA sells the RECs to local utilities that sell energy to consumers at retail. The CES Order requires the utilities either to purchase RECs in an amount based on the percentage of the total load served by that utility or to make an alternative compliance payment. The utilities may (and no doubt do) pass on the cost of RECs to consumers.

The ZEC program aims to prevent nuclear generators that do not emit carbon dioxide from retiring until renewable sources of energy can pick up the slack. A ZEC is a subsidy: a "credit for the zero-emissions attributes of one megawatt-hour of electricity production by" a participating nuclear power plant. The PSC selects plants for the ZEC program based on five criteria: (1) "verifiable historic contribution . . . to the clean energy resource mix . . . in New York"; (2) the degree to which projected wholesale revenues are insufficient to prevent retirement; (3) costs and benefits of ZECs relative to clean-energy alternatives; (4) impacts on ratepayers; and (5) the public interest. . . .

The ZEC price is based on the so-called "social cost of carbon": a federal inter-agency task force's estimate of the damage from carbon emissions, which the PSC uses to measure the hypothetical environmental damage from nuclear plants' retirement. The PSC then subtracts the portion of that cost already captured through New York's participation in the Regional Greenhouse Gas Initiative (RGGI), and multiplies the result by the tons of carbon avoided per MWh of zero-emission energy. The ZEC price generated for the program's first two years is $17.48. Accordingly, "each qualifying nuclear generator will get an additional $17.48 for each MWh of electricity it generates (subject to a possible cap), in addition to the price the facility receives for the sale of the electricity and capacity in the [NYISO] market."

Beginning in 2019, the PSC intends to calculate a new ZEC price every two years. The price may be reduced based on two considerations. First, if the New York energy market experiences "additional renewable energy penetration," the price will fall, reflecting the reduced value of nuclear plants if renewable energy generation gains steam. Second, the ZEC price may be adjusted downward based on forecast wholesale prices . . . equal to the sum of forecast NYISO "Zone A" (i.e., Western New York) energy and capacity prices during the period. The reference price forecast is not paid to the ZEC plants, but rather sets a benchmark for reducing the ZEC price: if the reference price forecast exceeds $39/MWh (a historical approximation of Zone A energy and capacity prices), the two-year ZEC price is reduced by the difference.

As in the REC program, the NYSERDA purchases ZECs from the selected plants, and local utilities are required to purchase ZECs from NYSERDA in proportion to its share of total state electric load. Alternatively, the utilities may purchase both ZECs and energy directly from the generators. The utilities may then pass along these costs to consumers. . . .

[II]

The FPA divides responsibility for regulating energy between the states and the federal government. FERC has exclusive power to regulate "the sale of electric energy at wholesale in interstate commerce." . . . While FERC's authority extends to "rules or practices affecting wholesale rates," this affecting jurisdiction is limited to "rules or practices that *directly* affect the [wholesale] rate" so that FERC's jurisdiction does not "assum[e] near-infinite breadth." *FERC v. Elec. Power Supply Ass'n*, 136 S. Ct. 760 (2016).

[Likewise], "the law places beyond FERC's power, and leaves to the States alone, the regulation of 'any other sale'—most notably, any retail sale—of electricity." *Id.* The states are thus authorized to regulate energy production, and facilities used for the generation of electric energy.

When "coordinate state and federal efforts exist within a complementary administrative framework, and in the pursuit of common purposes, the case for federal pre-emption becomes a less persuasive one." . . . In this Circuit, there is a "strong presumption against finding that the [State's] powers" are preempted by the FPA, *Niagara Mohawk Power Corp. v. Hudson River-Black River Regulating Dist.*, 673 F.3d 84, 94 (2d Cir. 2012), legislation that was "drawn with meticulous regard for the continued exercise of state power," *Rochester Gas & Elec. Corp. v. PSC of N.Y.*, 754 F.2d 99, 104 (2d Cir. 1985). That presumption may be overcome only if displacing state authority was Congress' "clear and manifest purpose." *Wyeth v. Levine*, 555 U.S. 555 (2009). . . .

Plaintiffs argue that the ZEC program is indistinguishable from the Maryland program preempted in *Hughes*. The program is said to be "expressly tethered to wholesale prices resulting from the NYISO auctions" because (1) "the state requires [utilities] to make up the difference between the state's rate and the FERC-approved market rates"; (2) "the subsidy varies inversely with FERC-approved auction rates"; and (3) "the subsidy is 'received' by the favored producers 'in connection with' the sale of electricity on wholesale markets." Plaintiffs mischaracterize *Hughes* and the ZEC program.

The Maryland contract-for-differences program insulated generators from fluctuations in wholesale prices by guaranteeing that they would receive "the difference between . . . the clearing price" and the state-determined "price guaranteed in the contract for differences." New York's scheme avoids (or skirts) the *Hughes* prohibition. Until 2019, the ZEC price cannot vary from the social cost of carbon, as determined by a federal interagency workgroup. After 2019, the ZEC price is fixed for two-year periods, and does not fluctuate during those periods to match the wholesale clearing price. Because the fixed ZEC price is capped based on an independent variable (the social cost of carbon), generators are exposed to market risk in the event that energy prices fall. Moreover, the price may be fixed below the social cost of carbon, but only on the basis of *forecast* wholesale prices—forecasts based on futures prices that FERC does not regulate, *Hunter v. FERC*, 711 F.3d 155, 157 (D.C. Cir. 2013)—and there is no true-up to reconcile forecasts with actual rates. The ZEC price also adjusts based on the amount of renewable energy generation in New York. Accordingly, there is no support for Plaintiffs' contention that the "subsidy varies in almost exactly the same manner" as in *Hughes*.

Plaintiffs argue that *Hughes* preempts state programs if they are tethered to "FERC-regulated wholesale electricity prices." But the tether in *Hughes* is tied to "wholesale market *participation*," not prices; the Maryland program was unlawful because it conditioned payment on auction sales.

As the district court held, *Rochester Gas* forecloses Plaintiffs' price-tethering theory. It was argued in that case that the FPA preempted the PSC's policy of calculating intrastate retail rates by making a "reasonable estimate" of wholesale sales revenues. We held that tying retail prices (which are under state jurisdiction) to estimates of wholesale revenues (which are under FERC's) is permissible because there is "a distinction between" a state impermissibly "regulating [wholesale] sales" and a state "reflecting the profits from a reasonable estimate of those sales" when acting within its jurisdiction.

Plaintiffs attempt to distinguish *Rochester Gas* on two grounds. First, they argue that *Rochester Gas* addresses only retail rate-making, whereas the ZEC program addresses wholesale rate-making. But that argument mischaracterizes the ZEC program, which avoids setting wholesale prices and instead regulates the environmental attributes of energy generation and in the process considers forecasts of wholesale pricing.

Second, Plaintiffs distinguish *Rochester Gas* on the ground that the ZEC program has a direct impact on the generators' "position toward" the wholesale markets. But the same was true in *Rochester Gas*: the PSC policy allowed generators to keep operating, regardless of wholesale revenue, because recovery of costs was guaranteed through retail rates. What mattered in *Rochester Gas* was whether the retail rate adjustment, which factored in expected wholesale revenues, intruded on FERC's jurisdictional turf by compelling wholesale market participation. The analogous question here would be whether ZECs compel generators to make wholesale sales. [T]hey do not. . . . As the district court concluded, a generator's decision to sell power into the wholesale markets is a business decision that does not give rise to preemption concerns.

Citing *Allco*, Plaintiffs argue that the absence of a statutory compulsion for generators to sell into the wholesale market does not save a state program . . . . Plaintiffs contend that *Allco* supports their argument because the Court emphasized that the contracts were subject to FERC evaluation as just and reasonable, whereas the ZEC transactions are not. However, the evident reason that the contracts were subject to FERC review is that they were contracts for wholesale electricity sales, over which FERC has jurisdiction. Here, the only transactions New York compels are ZEC sales, and ZECs are sold separately from wholesale sales. Because there is no wholesale sale when ZECs change hands, FERC lacks jurisdiction to decide whether the ZEC transactions are just and reasonable. *Allco* is therefore inapposite.

Plaintiffs concede that the ZEC program "does not expressly mandate that the plants receiving ZEC subsidies bid into the NYISO auctions"; rather, they argue that the "practical effect" of the ZEC program is to regulate wholesale prices. Plaintiffs rely on *Northern Natural Gas Co. v. State Corporation Commission of Kansas*, 372 U.S. 84 (1963), in which a Kansas law requiring an interstate pipeline to purchase gas ratably from producers was preempted by the Natural Gas Act (NGA). The state rule did not expressly regulate wholesale prices, but the Court reasoned that "our inquiry is not at an end because the orders do not deal in terms with prices or volumes of purchases . . . . The federal regulatory scheme leaves no room either for direct state regulation of the prices of interstate wholesales of natural gas, or for state regulations which would indirectly achieve the same result."

However, *Northern Natural Gas* held that the Kansas law was preempted because it was "unmistakably and unambiguously directed at purchasers [i.e., interstate pipelines] who take gas in Kansas for resale after transportation in interstate commerce." The Court emphasized that "our cases have consistently recognized a significant distinction," with "constitutional consequences, between conservation measures aimed directly at interstate purchasers and wholesales for resale, and those aimed at producers and production."

This distinction between regulating purchasers and producers yielded the opposite result in *Northwest Central Pipeline Corp. v. State Corp. Commission of Kansas*, 489 U.S. 493 (1989). Kansas hit on another way to encourage interstate pipelines to purchase additional Kansas-Hugoton gas, but did so by regulating the producers: unless they produced their allowable quantity of gas within a certain timeframe, they would lose the right to produce it later—and of course the pipelines could not purchase gas unless it was produced. . . . FERC's brief to the Court argued that while Kansas "intended to influence" the pipeline's purchasing decisions, the state did "no more than fix[ ] limits on when producers may produce their gas" and therefore stayed within its jurisdiction, [particularly as] FERC regulation . . . does not "protect [pipelines] from the effect of state regulations that form the environment in which [they] conduct[ ] business within the state."

The Supreme Court agreed: it would be "strange indeed" to hold that Congress intended to allow the states to regulate production, but only if doing so did not affect interstate rates. In *Northern Natural Gas*, Kansas "crossed the dividing line ... by imposing purchasing requirements on interstate pipelines," but in *Northwest Central*, the state achieved the same end result by "regulat[ing] production," a matter "firmly on the States' side of that dividing line." . . .

New York has kept the line in sight, and gone as near as can be without crossing it. ZECs are created when electricity is produced in a statutorily defined manner, regardless of whether or how the electricity is ultimately sold. They are defined as "the zero-emissions attributes of one megawatt-hour of electricity *production* by an eligible Zero Carbon Electric Generating Facility." Accordingly, *Northwest Central* defeats Plaintiffs' argument premised on practical effect: even though the ZEC program exerts downward pressure on wholesale electricity rates, that incidental effect is insufficient to state a claim for field preemption under the FPA.

FERC has confirmed that REC programs fall within the jurisdiction of the states, which is telling because RECs and ZECs share many similar characteristics[:] "RECs are state-created and state-issued instruments certifying that electric energy was generated pursuant to certain requirements." *WSPP, Inc.*, 139 FERC ¶ 61,061 at P 22 (2012). When RECs are unbundled, the payment is "not a charge in connection with a wholesale sale," does not "affect wholesale electricity rates," and therefore "falls outside FERC jurisdiction." *Id.* at P 24.

As the district court observed: "Like a REC, a ZEC is a certification of an energy *attribute* that is separate from a wholesale charge or rate . . . . Like a REC, the purchase or sale of a ZEC is independent of the purchase or sale of wholesale energy. Like a REC, payment for a ZEC is not conditioned on the generator's participation in the wholesale auction; rather, RECs and ZECs are given in exchange for the renewable energy or zero-emissions *production* of energy by generators." . . .

[III]

A state law may be conflict preempted if it "stands as an obstacle to the accomplishment and execution of the full purposes and objectives of Congress," or "interferes with the method by which the federal statute was designed to reach this goal." Given the FPA's dual regulatory scheme, "conflict-pre-emption analysis must be applied sensitively in this area . . . ." So long as a state is "regulat[ing] production or other subjects of state jurisdiction, and the means chosen [are] at least plausibly . . . related to matters of legitimate state concern," there is no conflict preemption "unless clear damage to federal goals would result."

The FPA seeks to ensure, through FERC, that rates for wholesale sales remain just and reasonable, while simultaneously preserving state authority to regulate generation facilities and retail sales. As explained above, the ZEC program regulates production: its stated aspiration is to "preserve existing zero-emissions nuclear generation resources as a bridge to the clean energy future," and to "prevent backsliding" that otherwise "likely could not be avoided." Accordingly, ZEC program is not conflict preempted unless Plaintiffs can show that it would cause clear damage to federal goals.

Plaintiffs describe "the very goal of FERC's wholesale market design" as "competition from more efficient generators." ZECs, Plaintiffs argue, "enable[ ] the unprofitable plants to keep dumping substantial amounts of electricity in the FERC markets for over a decade, even though the FERC-approved price signals should cause the plants to retire," [and] "distort price signals to all other wholesale generators . . . ."

However, FERC itself has sanctioned state programs that increase capacity or affect wholesale market prices, so long as the states regulate matters within their jurisdiction. Thus, states may "grant loans, subsidies or tax credits to particular facilities on environmental or policy grounds," *Cal. PUC*, 133 FERC ¶ 61,059 (2010), including when that makes clean generation "more competitive in a cost comparison with fossil-fueled generation" or "allow[s] states to affect" the price, *S. Cal. Edison Co.*, 71 FERC ¶ 61,269, 62,080 (1995). States may "require retirement of existing generators" or construction of "environmentally friendly units, or . . . take any other action in their role as regulators of generation," even though it may "affect[ ] the market clearing price." *Conn. Dep't of Pub. Util. Control v. FERC*, 569 F.3d 477, 481 (D.C. Cir. 2009). . . .

Faced with [*Allco*'s holding that "plac[ing] downward pressure on" wholesale prices is permissible], Plaintiffs concede New York's authority to enact "measures that may have an indirect effect on . . . price signals," but insist that "New York cannot directly distort the price signals that the auctions send by setting a higher, state-approved rate for wholesale electricity sales." To the extent the ZEC program distorts an efficient wholesale market, it does so by increasing revenues for qualifying nuclear plants, which in turn increases the supply of electricity, which in turn lowers auction clearing prices. But that is (at best) an incidental effect resulting from New York's regulation of producers. . . . ZECs do not guarantee a certain wholesale price that displaces the NYISO auction price.

FERC uses auctions to set wholesale prices and to promote efficiency with the background assumption that the FPA establishes a dual regulatory system between the states and federal government and that the states engage in public policies that affect the wholesale markets.

Accordingly, the ZEC program does not cause clear damage to federal goals, and Plaintiffs have failed to state a plausible claim for conflict preemption.

NOTES AND QUESTIONS

1.   Both *Allco* and *Coalition for Competitive Electricity* involve federalism challenges to state laws. We address the doctrines of preemption and the dormant Commerce Clause in greater length in Chapters 4 and 10. There is a reason we have put so much emphasis on these doctrines. They are incredibly important in energy law (and common in energy litigation), because they are the key legal tools that delineate the contours of energy federalism.

2.   While *Allco* finds Connecticut's RPS unproblematic from a dormant Commerce Clause perspective, other courts have not been so sanguine. Recall that Judge Posner's *ICC II* decision states in dicta that any RPS (there, Michigan's) which favors in-state generation over out-of-state generation would be constitutionally invalid under the dormant Commerce Clause. What is the difference between an RPS that clearly promotes in-state generation and one like Connecticut's that promotes in-region generation? Do you find convincing Judge Calabresi's conclusion that the market that matters for the dormant Commerce Clause analysis is the local one, because Connecticut RECs are a creature of state law? Or does that reasoning prove too much, because RECs are always a function of state law, meaning that discrimination based on them must always be constitutional? What if, rather than drawing a line around ISO-NE, Connecticut had done so around its own state? Wouldn't that be unconstitutional, if not for discriminating in effect, for doing so facially?

3.   Several suits have challenged the constitutionality of RPSs, but most have been resolved out of court. Notably, RPSs differ widely in how they seek to geographically ensure their regimes' effectiveness, so it is difficult to generalize on the dormant Commerce Clause question from one state RPS to the next. In addition to *Allco*, the other key case to date is *Energy and Environment Legal Institute v. Epel*, 793 F.3d 1169, 1174 (10th Cir. 2015) (*EELI*), written by then-Judge Gorsuch and discussed in Chapter 4. *EELI* is somewhat unique among dormant Commerce Clause cases, because the party challenging Colorado's RPS focused solely on its "extraterritorial" reach. The Tenth Circuit had little trouble dismissing this argument: "EELI's . . . position would also risk serious problems of overinclusion. After all, if any state regulation that 'control[s] . . . conduct' out of state is *per se* unconstitutional, wouldn't we have to strike down state health and safety regulations that require out-of-state manufacturers to alter their designs or labels? Certainly EELI offers no limiting principle that might prevent that possibility . . . ." *Id.* at 1175. For more on the federalism questions arising around RPSs, see, e.g., Alexandra B. Klass & Jim Rossi, *Revitalizing Dormant Commerce Clause Review for Interstate Coordination*, 130 MINN. L. REV. 129 (2015); Felix Mormann, *Constitutional Challenges and Regulatory Opportunities for State Climate Policy Innovation*, 41 HARV. ENV'T L. REV. 189 (2017); Felix Mormann, *Market Segmentation vs. Subsidization:*

Clean Energy Credits and the Commerce Clause's Economic Wisdom, 93 WASH. L. REV. 1853 (2018). For a broader look at the question of the role of different government levels promoting clean energy, see Felix Mormann, *Clean Energy Federalism*, 67 FLA. L. REV. 1621 (2015).

4.   As *Allco* did, *Coalition for Competitive Electricity* involved a dormant Commerce Clause challenge to New York's ZEC regime. The Second Circuit declined to address the claim, finding that plaintiffs lacked standing to bring it. However, another ZEC case, in which Illinois' nuclear subsidization program was challenged, did entertain a dormant Commerce Clause argument—and rejected it. In *Electric Power Supply Ass'n v. Star*, 904 F.3d 518 (7th Cir. 2018), plaintiffs asserted that Illinois' ZEC scheme unconstitutionally favored in-state nuclear generators. The court demurred: "Plaintiffs observe that the credits are bound to help some Illinois firms and contend that this condemns them. But this amounts to saying that the powers reserved to the states by § 824(b)(1) are denied to the states by the Constitution, because state regulatory authority is limited to the state's territory. On this view, whenever Illinois, or any other state, takes some step that will increase or reduce the state's aggregate generation capacity, or affect the price of energy, then the state policy is invalid. That can't be right; it would be the end of federalism. The Commerce Clause does not 'cut the States off from legislating on all subjects relating to the health, life, and safety of their citizens, [just because] the legislation might indirectly affect the commerce of the country.'" *Id.* at 524–25.

5.   ZECs and RECs function in basically the same way from an economic perspective but have slightly different legal functions. Both offer certain generators—renewables facilities for RECs and nuclear facilities for ZECs—additional compensation based on their environmental attributes. This means that these generators gain an advantage in the marketplace they otherwise would not have had. RECs, however, serve an additional function. They are the currency used in most states to determine compliance with RPSs. ZECs, by contrast, do not have this separate legal function, but rather, represent a different way that some states have sought to promote nuclear power. Do you think this difference should matter for purposes of preemption and dormant Commerce Clause challenges? Why?

6.   To reach its holding, *Allco* relied in part on a market analysis of RECs. This is important—and apropos. Geographically, RECs tend to be traded in three separate markets: state-specific markets, regional markets, and, to a much lesser degree, a national market. In terms of the product market, RECs also tend to trade in two separate markets: a "compliance" market for utilities required to satisfy RPSs, and a "voluntary" market for those interested in promoting renewable energy development (or their own environmental image) by purchasing RECs. REC prices also vary widely geographically, with NEPOOL Class I RECs costing roughly $40/MWh in 2020, PJM Tier I REC prices hitting $10/MWh in 2020, but solar RECs climbing as high as $200–450/MWh in Massachusetts and New Jersey. JENNY HEETER ET AL., NAT'L RENEWABLE ENERGY LAB., MARKET BRIEF: STATUS OF THE VOLUNTARY

RENEWABLE ENERGY CERTIFICATE MARKET (2011 DATA), at 19–20 (2012); GALEN BARBOSE, LAWRENCE BERKELEY NAT'L LAB., U.S. RENEWABLES PORTFOLIO STANDARDS 2021 STATUS UPDATE: EARLY RELEASE (Feb. 2021). For more on REC markets, see Lisa Koperski, *Why the Renewable Energy Credit Market Needs Standardization*, 13 WASH. J.L. TECH. & ARTS 69 (2017); David Schraub, *Renewing Electricity Competition*, 42 FLA. ST. U. L. REV. 937 (2015).

7.   The adoption of pro-nuclear legislation such as Illinois' and New York's ZEC schemes did not happen without controversy. Another state that sought to prop up the nuclear industry—Ohio—has seen only turmoil in the wake of its law's passage. That bill, H.B. 6, effected several changes in the state. *First*, it allocated nearly $1 billion in subsidies to be paid out to nuclear generators, as well as $20 million annually for utility-scale solar projects; *second*, it reduced Ohio's RPS to 8.5%; *third*, it eliminated the RPS altogether after 2026; and *fourth*, it allowed several utilities in the state to recover the net costs of coal plants in Ohio and Indiana through 2030. *See* Ohio H.B. 6, 133rd Gen. Assemb. (2019). Grabbing even more headlines, the federal government criminally charged five men, including Ohio House Speaker Larry Householder, in a bribery case in connection with H.B. 6's passage. The charges allege that the utility that would see the most financial benefit from the law, FirstEnergy, gave $60 million to a nonprofit, which in turn used the funds to benefit lawmakers, to secure passage of the law. *Federal Grand Jury Indicts Ohio House Speaker Enterprise in Federal Public Corruption Racketeering Conspiracy Involving $60 Million*, U.S. Dep't of Justice (July 30, 2020). The U.S. Attorney for the Southern District of Ohio called the case the largest bribery and money-laundering scheme in state history: "These allegations were bribery pure and simple." Notably, in 2020, ComEd in Illinois also agreed to pay $200 million to resolve a federal probe concerning its lobbying practices there. Tony Arnold & Dave McKinney, *ComEd Charged With Bribery For Steering Jobs, Other Benefits For Speaker Michael Madigan. Speaker Denies The Feds' Claims*, WBEZ CHICAGO (July 17, 2020); Brendan O'Brien & Timothy Gardner, *Ohio House Speaker, 4 Others Charged in $60 Million Nuclear Bailout Bribery Case*, REUTERS (July 22, 2020) (quoting David DeVillers).

8.   The saga of how states treat nuclear power is far from over. In addition to Illinois and New York, New Jersey adopted a ZEC program in 2018. Connecticut also enacted pro-nuclear legislation, and Wisconsin repealed its preexisting moratorium on constructing new nuclear facilities. Meanwhile, in March 2021, Ohio reversed course, repealing its nuclear subsidy and modifying how nuclear facilities can collect their fees, leading FirstEnergy to say the company would refund $26 million to customers. Jeremy Pelzer, *Gov. DeWine Signs Repeal of Nuclear Bailout, Other Parts of Scandal-Tainted House Bill 6*, CLEVELAND.COM (Mar. 31, 2021). In all these ways, the future of nuclear power in the United States is very much tied to both state policy efforts to save existing nuclear plants and how the nation decides to grapple with climate change—a theme to which we will return in more depth in Chapters 10 and 11.

9.   Not long ago, the thought of the United States' electricity grid becoming highly penetrated with clean energy—at levels 80 percent or higher—typically

would have been dismissed as a fanciful dream. Now, with CESs in play, the idea is gaining traction. We explore this idea more in Chapter 11. For an argument in favor of a national CES, see MIKE O'BOYLE ET AL., ENERGY INNOVATION, A NATIONAL CLEAN ELECTRICITY STANDARD TO BENEFIT ALL AMERICANS (Apr. 2021).

_____

PRACTICE PROBLEM

Mississippi recently elected a new governor, Oprah Winfrey, who ran on a platform of bringing more jobs to the state. Governor Winfrey is interested in promoting job growth in Mississippi through every avenue possible, including energy development. To this end, she has asked the state legislature to adopt either a renewable portfolio standard or a clean energy standard that will "make our electricity cleaner and boost our economy by bringing more manufacturing jobs to our cities and more employment for the installation of renewable energy installations across the state."

You are legislative counsel to Brett Favre, one of the most popular state legislators in Mississippi, who has plans to introduce an RPS or a CES in support of his good friend and party-mate, Governor Winfrey. How would you draft that law? Would you choose to draft an RPS or a CES and why?

In drafting, be sure to address the key questions of RPS/CES design, including the percentage target, the time for compliance, whether there should be interim compliance targets and dates, which energy resources should "count," whether certain resources should receive extra credit toward compliance, and a compliance and reporting regime to ensure the law achieves its objectives. To advance Governor Winfrey's job growth goals, does the law need to include any geographic limits and, if so, how might you navigate the dormant Commerce Clause?

Other interests will certainly lobby hard for their own vision of the Mississippi energy future. What type of law would environmental groups prefer, and how might that differ from the version Senator Favre might introduce? What type of law do you think incumbent utilities in the state might lobby for, or what specific provisions will they want to ensure are included in the law? Likewise, what will the renewable energy industry push for, such as trade groups for wind, solar, and biomass energy? How about groups such as the American Legislative Exchange Council (ALEC)? And, perhaps most importantly, what will be the view advanced by electricity customers in the state, particularly if there is a formalized ratepayer advocate there?

If you need examples of RPSs in other states, see http://www.dsireusa.org/. On RPS design questions, see Sanya Carley et al., _Empirical Evaluation of the Stringency and Design of Renewable Portfolio Standards_, 3 NATURE ENERGY 754 (2018) and Lincoln L. Davies, _Evaluating RPS Policy Design: Metrics, Gaps, Best Practices, and Paths to Innovation_, 4 KLRI J. L. & LEGIS. 3 (2014). In designing the law, how much do you think it matters what resources

Mississippi has within its boundaries? The National Renewable Energy Laboratory has created estimates of many different renewable energy resources across states. *See* NREL, RENEWABLE ELECTRICITY FUTURES STUDY: EXECUTIVE SUMMARY 10 (2012). How much does it matter whether neighboring states have RPSs or CESs?

In considering potential approaches, you will want to look at Mississippi's current electricity mix, available on the EIA website, http://www.eia.gov/state/ analysis.cfm?sid=MS. You will also want to look at Mississippi's average electricity prices, especially compared to the rest of the country. For one data source on state electricity prices, see http://www.eia.gov/electricity/monthly/ epm_table_grapher.cfm?t=epmt_5_6_a.

CHAPTER 6

VEHICLE TRANSPORTATION
AND ENERGY USE

∎ ∎ ∎

A. OVERVIEW

Rapid and cheap transportation is one of the drivers of 21st century society. Modern transportation networks link billions of people, trillions of dollars in goods and services, and drive modern economies and communities. In this chapter we focus primarily on the energy use and policies associated with road transportation. We first explore: (1) the growth of the highway system and the policies that have supported it; and (2) sprawl and the environmental, economic, and social harms that flow from sprawl, including environmental justice concerns. We then move to oil consumption in transportation and the technology-forcing policies that have been implemented to limit the environmental harms associated with vehicle emissions through regulatory requirements on fuels and vehicles. Next, we explore the issue of alternative fuels, focusing on: (1) biofuels, including federal policies to promote the production and use of biofuels in vehicles, and the environmental and economic issues associated with its use; and (2) the more recent push worldwide to transition to electric vehicles (EVs) to address the growth of GHG emissions from the transportation sector. The electrification of vehicles and other technologies that may completely transform how we use energy in the transportation sector are also covered in Chapter 11.

Energy use and the associated air emissions in the transportation sector are driven by the number of vehicles, how much fuel they use and how cleanly they burn it, the energy efficiency and carbon intensity of the fuel used, and vehicle miles traveled. Worldwide, the transportation sector accounts for 29% of global energy consumption and is considered one of the most difficult sectors to decarbonize. Petroleum—which supplied 92% of all transport-related energy in 2018—dominates, with natural gas (4%), biofuels (3%), and electricity (1%) supplying the remainder. *See* INT'L ENERGY AGENCY, WORLD ENERGY BALANCES (2020).

Transport energy demand is projected to grow rapidly; how energy is used for transport varies significantly across and within countries. The United States and Canada consume an average of 2.3 metric tons of oil per person each year while less developed countries in Africa use less than 0.1

metric tons of oil per person each year. North America and the Middle East use more gasoline than OECD-Europe, China, and Latin America, which utilize a greater proportion of diesel fuel. WORLD ENERGY COUNCIL, GLOBAL TRANSPORT SCENARIOS 2050 (2011).

In the United States, transportation accounts for 26% of total energy use and 66% of petroleum use, with 90% of transportation energy provided by petroleum. *Energy Use for Transportation*, U.S. Energy Info. Admin. (last updated May 17, 2021). Cars and light trucks used 57% of transportation related energy in 2018, with 253 million cars and light trucks registered in 2019 and 3.4 million cars and 10.7 million light trucks sold in 2020. These numbers highlight the importance of light duty cars and trucks and their disproportionate impact in the transportation sector. By contrast, the non-highway sectors use much less energy: air—8.7%; water—4.1%; pipelines—4.1%; and all rail just 2.2%. All sources included, the U.S. transportation sector consumes a whopping 18.2% of the world's total oil production of 88 million barrels per day. STACY C. DAVIS & ROBERT G. BOUNDY, TRANSPORTATION ENERGY DATA BOOK (39th ed., Feb. 2021).

Energy use in the transportation sector is driven by economic growth, urbanization, and demographics. When the COVID-19 pandemic spread across the world, road transportation dropped 50–75% in regions with lockdowns as people were forced to stay home, with global road transport down an estimated 50% in March 2020 compared to March 2019. However, transportation energy use has increased almost 2% per year since 2000 and a rebound is expected. While shipping energy use has gotten more efficient, consumer preference for larger and heavier vehicles means that many of the fuel efficiency gains are being undermined, as SUVs now comprise 40% of the global personal vehicle market, with a 50% share in North America and Australia. Moreover, with more than half of the global population now living in cities, increased urbanization and the emergence of megacities are shaping future transportation energy trends. *See* INT'L ENERGY AGENCY, GLOBAL ENERGY REVIEW 2020 (2020).

Transportation energy use is also driven by people's behavior as they seek access to destinations and move and transport commercial goods around the world. Some technological changes, like online shopping in the United States, have massively increased the delivery of goods to U.S. households and businesses but have not led to any corresponding decreases in the miles traveled by U.S. drivers. During the pandemic, 2020 online sales increased over 32% from the year before and Q1 2021 sales were up 39% from the previous year as people were forced to stay home and shops were closed. *See Coronavirus Adds $105 Billion to US ecommerce in 2020*, DIGITAL COMMERCE 360 (June 16, 2021). This highlights both the difficulty in predicting transport changes and the "additive" nature of technological and system changes. Additionally, the energy savings from policies promoting more efficient vehicles may be partially offset by the "rebound effect," with people driving more as they spend less on fuel. *See* Kenneth A. Small & Kurt Van Dender, *Fuel Efficiency and Motor Vehicle Travel: The Declining Rebound Effect*, 28 ENERGY J. 25 (2007); Karen Turner, *"Rebound" Effects from Increased Energy Efficiency: A Time to Pause and Reflect*, 34 THE ENERGY J. (In'tl Ass'n for Energy Econ. 2013).

Policies supporting public mass transportation like intercity trains, light rail, buses, or new models of car sharing could all reduce demand for individual vehicles and the associated traffic congestion, pollution, and energy use. How widespread these policies and transportation planning approaches become depends on a host of factors and is likely to vary significantly by city, region, and country.

In addition to moving people, the transport sector moves energy resources (discussed in Chapter 7) and other goods, generally referred to as "freight." Transport of freight around the world is the lifeblood of the global economy. In the United States alone, freight networks are complex and extensive, consisting of:

- a national truck network, made up of 209,000 miles of highways, including the 47,000-mile Interstate Highway System, constituting about two-fifths of U.S. freight;

- railroads that carry freight on 140,000 miles of track, constituting about one-quarter of U.S. freight;

- barge and ship lines using 12,000 miles of shallow-draft inland waterways and about 3,500 inland and coastal port terminal facilities, making up 6% of domestic tonnage but nearly 20% of import and export tonnage; and

- air carriers offering cargo service to more than 5,000 public use airports, including more than 100 airports that handle all-cargo aircraft, making up 30% of the nation's exports.

CONG. RSCH. SERV., FEDERAL FREIGHT POLICY: IN BRIEF (Feb. 26, 2020).

NOTES AND QUESTIONS

1.   The transport sector causes many environmental and social externalities, including air pollution, noise pollution, upstream and downstream pollution from vehicle manufacturing and disposal, climate change, accidents, and infrastructure costs. Internal combustion engines burn fossil fuels and their incomplete combustion emits volatile organic compounds, nitrogen oxides, carbon monoxide, and particulate matter. Hydrocarbons from unburned fuel react with nitrogen oxides in the atmosphere and create both tropospheric

ozone and particulate matter, both harmful to human health.[1] Controlling emissions from the hundreds of millions of vehicles on the roadways presents a logistical challenge which links global vehicle manufacturing, national policies, and local air pollution.

2.   In the United States, emissions from motor vehicles have been controlled since the late 1960s. However, public health analyses suggest the health effects of particulate matter may be more serious than scientists previously realized. *See* Ki-Hyun Kim et al., *A Review on the Human Health Impact of Airborne Particulate Matter,* 74 ENV'T INT'l 136 (2015). Specifically, even very low concentrations of particulate matter have been found to be associated with increased hospitalizations due to lung and respiratory symptoms, compromised cardiac function, student absences from school, and increased mortality. *See also* AM. LUNG ASS'N, STATE OF THE AIR 2021 (2021) (reporting on areas of the United States where citizens are at highest risk of adverse health impacts from air pollution and discussing role of transportation-related emissions in contributing to those risks); Hiroko Tabuch & Nadja Popovich, *People of Color Breathe More Hazardous Air. The Sources are Everywhere*, N.Y. TIMES (Apr. 28, 2021) (focusing on disparate impacts of particulate pollution on communities of color).

3.   The transportation sector is also an important source of GHG emissions. Globally, 21% of worldwide CO_2 emissions come from the transportation sector and these are projected to increase 0.6% per year until 2050, depending on the degree of government intervention and advances in low carbon fuel systems. Passenger vehicles account for most global transportation emissions (45.1%), followed by freight (29.4%), aviation (11.6%), international shipping (10.6%), and rail and pipelines (3.2%). *See* Hannah Ritchie, *Cars, Planes, Trains: Where Do CO_2 Emissions From Transport Come From?*, OUR WORLD IN DATA (Oct. 6, 2020). Most of the global growth in transportation sector emissions is projected to take place in developing countries, where economic growth is spurring rapid increases in auto ownership, but resources to control and enforce air pollution regulations are often lacking. *See Outlook for Future Emissions*, U.S. Energy Info. Admin. (last updated Feb. 16, 2021). Worldwide, and in some U.S. states (most notably, California and New York), there is significant interest and investment in converting large percentages of passenger cars, buses, and other forms of transport to EVs to address this problem, as described later in this chapter and in Chapter 11. In 2019, transportation sector emissions constituted 29% of total U.S. GHG emissions, as compared to 25% from the electricity sector, 23% from the industrial sector, 13% from the commercial and residential sector, and 10% from the agricultural sector. *See Sources of Greenhouse Emissions*, U.S. EPA; Vicki Arroyo & Annie Bennett, *Transportation in a Changing Climate*, TR NEWS MAG. (Sept./Oct. 2020).

---

[1]   Tropospheric ozone occurs close to the ground where it acts as a pollutant with serious health consequences. The troposphere is the first atmospheric layer, extending 10–20 kilometers from earth. This is distinct from stratospheric ozone, and the "ozone hole" which occurs 20–30 kilometers above the earth.

4.   Many different policy tools are used to control pollution and incentivize change within the transportation sector, including fuel taxes, subsidies to support or promote particular technologies, command and control policies to increase vehicle efficiency or reduce polluting emissions, information policies to educate consumers and, more recently, carbon pricing. Countries also invest in research and development for transportation and invest in infrastructure and technologies to reduce energy consumption and pollution. While subsidies and information campaigns can enjoy political support, taxes and carbon policies remain politically difficult throughout the world. As you study this chapter, consider these questions: Which types of policies may be most effective in reducing vehicle emissions most rapidly? Most equitably? Most effectively without impacting economic growth? Which may be politically feasible?

5.   Although not the primary focus of this chapter, which concentrates on vehicle transportation on roads, it is important to recognize that each year 1,478 airlines fly over 33,000 planes to 3,780 airports, travelling millions of miles and burning 2.3 billion barrels of jet fuel. A ton of aviation fuel burned produces roughly 3.15 tons of CO_2, and the industry was responsible for emitting roughly 915 million tons of CO_2 in 2019. Overall, air travel uses about 11% of global transportation energy and produces 12% of transportation sector CO_2 emissions and 2% of global emissions. As the industry is growing rapidly, the aviation industry's share of transportation sector energy use and carbon emissions is projected to double by 2050. In 2019, the air industry transported 61 million tons of freight and 4.5 billion passengers. *See Facts & Figures*, Air Transport Action Group (Sept. 2020). For a discussion of GHG emissions and air travel, see JEFF OVERTON, ENV'T & ENERGY STUDY INST., FACT SHEET: THE GROWTH IN GREENHOUSE GAS EMISSIONS FROM COMMERCIAL AVIATION (Oct. 17, 2019); Hiroko Tabuchi, *"Worse Than Anyone Expected": Air Travel Emissions Vastly Outplace Predictions*, N.Y. TIMES (Sept. 19, 2019) (reporting on research from the International Council on Clean Transportation).

To reduce emissions from air travel, the industry is focusing on using more efficient planes and introducing sustainable aviation fuels (SAF). Such alternative fuels must be "demonstrably less carbon intensive" than fossil fuels and satisfy sustainability criteria. Although SAFs currently account for less than 1% of jet fuel use, this percentage is increasing. In 2021, the Biden administration, working with the national airline trade association, set a goal of reducing GHG emissions from the aviation industry by 20% by 2030, and committed to jump start the production of billions of gallons of SAFs. *See* FACT SHEET: BIDEN ADMINISTRATION ADVANCES THE FUTURE OF SUSTAINABLE FUELS IN AMERICAN AVIATION, THE WHITE HOUSE (Sept. 9, 2021). With 25% of industry revenue spent on fuel in 2019 (more than $188 billion), the economic impetus to use less fuel is strong. And even though energy use per passenger mile has decreased in the aviation sector, the number of passengers has grown steadily and thus the total amount of fuel used continues to increase. *See* AIR TRANSPORT ACTION GROUP, AVIATION BENEFITS BEYOND BORDERS (Sept. 2020).

Airplanes can become more fuel-efficient by improving the plane (e.g., reducing weight, improving engine efficiency, reducing aerodynamic drag);

improving in-flight operations (e.g., more efficient routes and better air traffic management); and improving on the ground operations (e.g., single engine taxiing, airplane tugs, auxiliary power sources at the gate). In 2021, the EPA finalized the first GHG emission standard covering the aviation industry under the Clean Air Act. The rule was immediately challenged by numerous states on grounds that it was not sufficiently stringent to protect public health. *See* XINYI SOLA ZHENG & DAN RUTHERFORD, INT'L COUNCIL ON CLEAN TRANSPORTATION REDUCING AIRCRAFT CO_2 EMISSIONS: THE ROLE OF U.S. FEDERAL, STATE, AND LOCAL POLICIES (Feb. 2021).

B. TRANSPORTATION INFRASTRUCTURE: HIGHWAYS, SPRAWL, ENVIRONMENTAL JUSTICE, AND DECARBONIZATION

The heart of the U.S. transportation system is made of roads, highways, and the vehicles that we drive to transport people and goods. This section describes (1) the creation of the U.S. highway system, its current funding structure, limitations of that funding structure, the urban sprawl arising from highways, and efforts to promote alternative modes of transportation; and (2) the environmental justice concerns from concentrating transportation infrastructure in low-income and minority neighborhoods.

1. THE FEDERAL HIGHWAY SYSTEM, GAS TAXES, MASS TRANSPORTATION AND NEW URBANISM

Officially known as the Dwight D. Eisenhower National System of Interstate and Defense Highways and commonly referred to as "the Interstate," the U.S. highway system spans 46,867 miles and is often cited as the textbook example of cooperative federalism. The original federal investment in highways began with $75 million over five years in 1916 with the passage of the Federal Aid Road Act, providing matching funds to the states for highway construction and leaving planning and road investment decisions to the states. The Federal Highway Act of 1921 provided $75 million per year and, for the first time, began to coordinate development of an interstate highway system. Many plans for interstate highway systems interconnecting major U.S. cities emerged, and the military and tactical importance of an interstate system was widely recognized. The 1956 passage of the Federal-Aid Highway Act (Public Law 84–672) authorized $25 billion for the construction of 41,000 miles of highway over a 10-year period. The project eventually cost over four times as much and took 35 years. *See* ROBERT J. DILGER, CONG. RSCH. SERV., FEDERALISM ISSUES IN SURFACE TRANSPORTATION POLICY: PAST AND PRESENT 6–10 (July 27, 2012). The following excerpt describes the laws governing the federal highway system, its funding, and limitations of the current funding structure.

FEDERAL-AID HIGHWAY PROGRAM (FAHP): IN BRIEF

Cong. Rsch. Serv. (Mar. 1, 2021)

The federal government has provided some form of highway funding to the states for more than 100 years. The major characteristics of the federal highway program have been constant since the early 1920s. First, most funds are apportioned to the states by formula and implementation is left primarily to state departments of transportation (state DOTs). Second, the states are required to provide matching funds. Until the 1950s, each federal dollar had to be matched by an identical amount of state and local money. The federal share is now 80% for non-Interstate System road projects and 90% for Interstate System projects. Third, generally, federal money can be spent only on designated federal-aid highways, which make up roughly a quarter of U.S. public roads.

The Federal-Aid Highway Program (FAHP) is an umbrella term for the separate highway programs administered by the Federal Highway Administration (FHWA). These programs are almost entirely focused on highway construction, and generally do not support operations (such as state DOT salaries or fuel costs) or routine maintenance (such as mowing roadway fringes or filling potholes). Each state is required to have a State Transportation Improvement Plan, which sets priorities for the state's use of FAHP funds. State DOTs largely determine which projects are funded, let the contracts, and oversee project development and construction. More recently, metropolitan planning organizations (MPOs) have played a growing role in project decisionmaking in urban areas, but federal project funding continues to flow through state DOTs.

The 2015 surface transportation reauthorization act, the Fixing America's Surface Transportation Act (FAST Act; P.L. 114–94), authorized funding for FY2016–FY2020. A one-year FAST Act extension, through September 30, 2021, was enacted as part of the Continuing Appropriations Act, 2021, and other Extensions Act (P.L. 116–159). Under the FAST Act as extended, about 92.5% of FAHP funding is distributed through five core programs. All five are formula programs, meaning that each state's annual share is divided up into the programs based on mathematical calculations set out in the law. The remaining programs, generally referred to as discretionary programs, are administered more directly by FHWA, but the funding distribution of some of these programs is formulaic as well. The FAHP does not provide money in advance. Rather, a state receives bills from private contractors for work completed and pays those bills according to its own procedures. The state submits vouchers for reimbursement to FHWA. FHWA certifies the claims for payment and notifies the Department of the Treasury, which disburses money electronically to the state's bank, often on the same day the state submits the voucher.

The FAHP, unlike most other federal programs, has not historically relied on appropriated budget authority. Instead, FHWA exercises contract authority over monies in the Highway Trust Fund (HTF) and may obligate (promise to pay) funds for projects funded with contract authority prior to an appropriation. Once funds have been obligated, the federal government has a legal commitment to provide the funds. This approach shelters highway construction projects from annual decisions about appropriations.

The Highway Trust Fund is financed from a number of sources, including taxes on fuels, heavy truck tires, truck and trailer sales, and a weight-based heavy-vehicle use tax. Approximately 85%–90% of trust fund revenue comes from excise taxes on motor fuels, 18.3 cents per gallon on gasoline and 24.3 cents per gallon on diesel. The HTF consists of two separate accounts—highway and mass transit. The highway account receives an allocation equivalent to 15.44 cents of the gasoline tax and the mass transit account receives the revenue generated by 2.86 cents of the tax. Because the fuel taxes are set in terms of cents per gallon rather than as a percentage of the sale price, their revenues do not increase with inflation. The fuel tax rates were last raised in 1993. . . .

Sluggish growth in vehicle travel and improved vehicle efficiency have depressed the growth of fuel consumption and therefore the growth of fuel tax revenue. Since FY2008, the revenues flowing into the highway account of the HTF have been insufficient to fund the expenditures authorized under the Federal-Aid Highway Program. Congress has resolved this discrepancy by transferring money from the general fund to the HTF. The COVID-19 pandemic has also had an impact on road travel. FHWA's December 2020 *Traffic Volume Trends* found that the 12-month cumulative travel for 2020 had changed −13.2%. This has led to a dip in revenues flowing to the HTF in FY2020 and FY2021.

A gap between dedicated HTF revenues and outlays is expected to persist after the FAST Act, as extended, expires at the end of FY2021 based on current tax rates and levels of spending adjusted for inflation. The Congressional Budget Office (CBO) projects that beginning in summer FY2022, revenues credited to the highway and transit accounts of the HTF will be insufficient to meet the fund's obligations, and that HTF receipts will fall $69.8 billion short of the amount needed to fund surface transportation programs as presently configured from FY2022 through FY2026. Congress will face the need to approve some combination of new taxes, an increase in existing fuel taxes, continued expenditures from the general fund, increased federally supported debt financing, or reductions in the scope of the federal surface transportation program if the FAST Act is replaced or again extended beyond late FY2022. . . .

NOTES AND QUESTIONS

1.   Which approaches are preferable to maintain the highway system while also encouraging sustainable driving practices? A 2021 Congressional Research Service report summarized a range of federal policy proposals, which include raising the federal fuel tax, imposing a vehicle-miles traveled (VMT) fee, taxing EVs, greater use of tolls for highway funding, and increased privatization of highway infrastructure. *See* CONG. RSCH. SERV., REAUTHORIZING HIGHWAY AND TRANSIT FUNDING PROGRAMS (Mar. 1, 2021). What are the benefits and drawbacks of these various approaches?

2.   States have begun experimenting with highway funding and incentive policies connected to the rise of EVs. California launched a series of pilot programs in 2021 to assess how mileage-based fees, rather than the traditional gas tax, might be implemented. At the federal level, President Biden's push for the electrification of the transportation sector has sparked renewed interest in a similar "by-the-mile" federal tax. With more EVs on the road, this alternative tax scheme would ensure all vehicles contribute funding for the federal highway infrastructure. *See* Emily C. Dooley, *California Tests Mileage Fee Plan as Answer to Dwindling Gas Tax*, BLOOMBERG NEWS (Dec. 3, 2020); Keith Laing, *By-the-Mile Tax on Driving Gains Steam as Way to Fund U.S. Roads*, BLOOMBERG NEWS (Mar. 12, 2021).

3.   Some experts argue that "congestion pricing" may be the best way to both fund the highway system and deal with urban sprawl, traffic, and other land use and environmental challenges associated with the nation's highways. Congestion pricing, or value pricing, shifts discretionary rush hour highway travel to mass transportation or to off-peak periods by charging a premium for particular routes or times. Congestion pricing includes express toll lanes or high occupancy toll lanes, variable tolls on entire roadways, or tolls on otherwise toll-free roads during rush hour, and variable or fixed charges to drive within or into a congested area in a city. *See What is Congestion Pricing?*, Fed. Hwy. Admin.

While cities such as New York, Minneapolis, and San Diego have implemented express lanes, bridges, or other roads with variable tolls based on time of day, congestion pricing in general has not been used widely in the United States. This may be set to change for at least one U.S. city. After being stalled by the Trump administration, in 2021, New York City obtained approval from the U.S. Department of Transportation to proceed with an environmental assessment of a congestion pricing program to mitigate traffic in Manhattan. Both San Francisco and Los Angeles are considering similar programs. *See* Tanya Snyder et al., *Driving Downtown? Get Ready to Pay Extra*, POLITICO (Mar. 21, 2021); David Shepardson, *U.S. to Speed Environmental Review of New York City Congestion Pricing Plan*, REUTERS (Mar. 30, 2021). *But see* Winnie Hu & Dana Rubinstein, *As Cuomo Exits, Will Congestion Pricing Still Come to New York City?*, N.Y. TIMES (Aug. 16, 2021). By contrast, congestion pricing is much more common in Europe in cities such as London and Stockholm. Why might there be opposition to more widespread congestion pricing in cities in the United States as opposed to in Europe or Asia? Are there equity considerations which should also be addressed?

4.   As early as the 1970s, Congress recognized that federal policies created significant incentives to build highways through parks and other government-owned land as there were few residents to object and land prices were cheap. In response, Congress enacted new statutory provisions to address this problem, namely § 4(f) of the Department of Transportation Act of 1966, as amended, and § 138 of the Federal-Aid Highway Act of 1968. These laws prohibit the Secretary of Transportation from authorizing federal funds to be used for the construction of highways through public parks if there is a "feasible and prudent" alternative route. Even when there is no feasible and prudent alternative route, the Secretary can only approve funding for the route if there has been "all possible planning to minimize harm" to the park. In the landmark case of *Citizens to Preserve Overton Park v. Volpe*, 401 U.S. 402 (1971), the Supreme Court held in 1971 that this statutory language limited the Secretary's discretion to approve highway projects, and allowed for judicial review under the Administrative Procedure Act. According to the Court, "the very existence of the statutes indicates that protection of parkland was to be given paramount importance. The few green havens that are public parks were not to be lost unless there were truly unusual factors present in a particular case or the cost or community disruption resulting from alternative routes reached extraordinary magnitudes." *Id.* at 412–13.

Despite the statute, however, many parks and entire neighborhoods were destroyed during the heyday of highway construction in the 1960s and 1970s. This resulted in community dislocation and increased air pollution, particularly in low-income and minority communities that did not have the resources to challenge highway projects. Highway planners often targeted these neighborhoods for "urban renewal" purposes and because the costs of acquiring land through voluntary agreements or eminent domain were less expensive than for more affluent neighborhoods. *See, e.g.*, Linda Poon, *Mapping the Effects of the Great 1960s "Freeway Revolts,"* BLOOMBERG CITYLAB (July 23, 2019); Joseph Stromberg, *Highways Gutted American Cities. So Why Did They Build Them?*, VOX (May 11, 2016); Deborah N. Archer, *"White Men's Roads Through Black Men's Homes": Advancing Racial Equity Through Highway Reconstruction*, 73 VAND. L. REV. 1259 (2020). What approaches can be used today to address the continuing adverse impacts of highway construction from decades ago? *See, e.g.*, Nadja Popovich et al., *Can Removing Highways Fix America's Cities?*, N.Y. TIMES (May 27, 2021) (interactive visuals).

Beyond planning and funding highways, broader factors influence transportation choices and options both in the United States and around the world. International variations in land use and population density shape urban forms as well as transportation choices and energy use.

Denser settlement patterns in European and Asian cities differ markedly from many sprawling U.S. cities. For instance, the Paris metropolitan area has 10,000 people/sq. mile (though the central city is much denser), London has 16,500 people/sq. mile, the Tokyo metro area has 12,300 people/sq. mile, and Mumbai has 57,000 people/sq. mile. By contrast, the Chicago metropolitan area has 3,300 people/sq. mile and Atlanta only 1,900 people/sq. mile. *See* DEMOGRAPHIA, DEMOGRAPHIA WORLD URBAN AREAS (17th ed. May 2021). Denser urban land use conserves productive farmland and supports mass transportation networks, making subways, light rail, and extensive bus networks more practical and affordable, while more dispersed settlement patterns favor individual vehicles. For example, U.S. pre-World War II cities are characterized by denser neighborhoods with sidewalks, which were often linked by trolley networks.

With the rise of the personal automobile and government subsidies for highways, many cities removed trolley tracks and expanded roadways to accommodate cars and parking lots. The urban sprawl that followed has locked in North American transportation patterns, consumed valuable farmland, and made North Americans particularly dependent on automobiles and oil. This type of land use also makes extensive mass transit systems in metropolitan regions logistically impractical and costly. Research suggests the costs of sprawl extend beyond energy use and affect Americans' health. A walkable neighborhood, where people can access work, shops, schools, and services has been found to correlate with lower body weights, with men weighing on average ten pounds less and women five pounds less. *See* Ken R. Smith et al., *Walkability and Body Mass Index Density, Design, and New Diversity Measures*, 35 AM. J. OF PREVENTATIVE MED. 237 (2008).

Another study explored the connection between neighborhood walkability and COVID-19 infection rates, finding more walkable neighborhoods were associated with fewer COVID-19 cases. This is hypothesized to be a result of the limited geographical mobility required when stores and other necessities are located nearby. Shigehiro Oishi, Youngjae Cha & Ulrich Shcimmack, *The Social Ecology of Covid-19 Cases and Deaths in New York City: The Role of Walkability, Wealth, and Race*, SOCIAL PSYCH. AND PERSONALITY SCI. (2021).

After significant depopulation from the 1950s to the 1970s, many urban areas in the U.S. began to re-think growth and efforts to revitalize urban communities remained widespread. New urban development is also bucking the trends of urban sprawl and embracing mixed land use and compact communities. These "smart growth" communities aim to create walkable neighborhoods with a wide range of housing options; community services like schools; and transportation choices supporting walking, biking, and mass transportation in addition to personal vehicles. Some smart growth cities are also investing in bike paths and mass transit systems. Creating more dense and diverse communities often means changing existing land use and zoning statutes. The American Planning Association has been active in creating model legislation for cities.

For example, urban planning in Paris and Barcelona has focused on restricting vehicle use and promoting walking and bicycling. Paris has banned cars along the River Seine and prohibited certain high-emissions vehicles from entering the city. Barcelona has implemented pedestrian "superblocks" that transform existing roads into vehicle-free locations. *See, e.g.*, Linda Poon et al., *Cities are Our Best Hope for Surviving Climate Change*, BLOOMBERG GREEN (Apr. 20, 2021) (interactive article showing changing streetscapes without cars in multiple cities). *See also* Somini Sengupta & Nadja Popovich, *Cities Worldwide are Reimagining Their Relationship with Cars*, N.Y. TIMES (Nov. 14, 2019); Somini Sengupta, *Trams, Cable Cars, Electric Ferries: How Cities are Rethinking Transit*, N.Y. TIMES (Oct. 3, 2021).

Within cities, rapid mass transit moves billions of people each day. Subways, light-rail systems, and bus rapid transit—where frequent buses travel on dedicated roads—allow for efficient transportation across congested urban areas. Mass transit is funded by a combination of local, state, and federal funds and both urban density and ridership shape system economics. In general, federal funding for public transportation comes through the Department of Transportation's Federal Transit Administration (FTA), with funding most recently authorized through the FAST Act. *See* CONG. RSCH. SERV., FEDERAL PUBLIC TRANSPORTATION PROGRAM: IN BRIEF (Apr. 30, 2021).

While buses are relatively inexpensive, securing the necessary infrastructure investments for developing higher cost light-rail or subway systems has proven challenging. Most medium U.S. cities have bus systems, with some of the largest metro areas supporting subway systems and/or light rail initiatives. Only seven U.S. metro areas had over 10 percent of their population commute by public transport in 2019. The top four metropolitan areas for commuters using public transport were New York City, where over 31% of all commuters take public transit to work, followed by San Francisco-Oakland-Freemont (19%), Boston-Cambridge-Newton (13.4%), and Washington D.C. (13%). *See* MICHAEL BURROWS, CHARLYNN BURD & BRIAN MCKENZIE, U.S. CENSUS BUREAU, COMMUTING BY PUBLIC TRANSPORTATION IN THE UNITED STATES: 2019 (Apr. 2021).

High-speed rail is fast, safe, energy efficient, and growing rapidly—except in the United States. Intercity rail used to be an important mode of travel in the United States but, apart from the Northeast, most American cites do not have access to rapid intercity rail. This stands in marked contrast with the rest of the industrialized world. Most other industrialized countries invest heavily in intercity rail. High-speed rail systems in

Europe, Japan, and China connect all major metropolitan areas, regularly running at speeds of 124–220 miles/hour. Investment in rail infrastructure and new technological advances like applying superconductivity to rail could reduce rail travel times by half and cut CO_2 emissions by two-thirds. New technologies are also making intercity rail faster and more efficient. In 2019, China had over 15,000 miles of high-speed rail with another 8,600 miles planned by 2025. With trains running over 200 miles/hour (300 km/hour), the network has cut travel times considerably—travel times between Shanghai and Beijing (763 miles) dropped from 18 hours in 1999 to 10 hours in 2010 to 4 hours 18 minutes in 2019. *See* MARTHA LAWRENCE, RICHARD BULLOCK & ZIMING LIU, WORLD BANK, CHINA'S HIGH-SPEED RAIL DEVELOPMENT (2019).

In the United States, the Acela Express runs from Washington D.C. to Boston with stops at other cities in between. Unlike other countries with dedicated high-speed rails, the Acela shares its track with both low speed passenger service and cargo service, and its speed averages only 78 miles/hour, though it can reach maximum speeds of 150 miles/hour. Initial funding and development for high-speed rail, which would link Anaheim and San Francisco, is underway, though the system is not projected to be fully developed until 2030. While the Midwest and Florida also developed high-speed rail plans, no projects are slated for construction as of 2021. The Texas Central Railway attempted to revive a failed attempt to build a high-speed train between Dallas and Houston and received approval from the Federal Railroad Administration. Construction could occur as early as 2021, but the project must still be approved by the Surface Transportation Board and is facing legal challenges by Texas counties. *See, e.g.,* Juan Pablo Garnham, *High-speed Train Between Dallas and Houston Gets Federal Approval*, THE TEXAS TRIBUNE (Sep. 21, 2020); Linda Chiem, *Counties, Residents Sue to Block Dallas-Houston Bullet Train*, LAW 360 (Apr. 14, 2021). For more information on the project, see http://www.texascentral.com/project/.

NOTES AND QUESTIONS

1.   City bike share programs are becoming very popular in many metropolitan areas around the world. With more than 71 participating countries and a fleet of around 20 million bikes, they are providing new non-automotive opportunities for urban travel. Shared e-scooters are another popular transportation mode, with over 150,000 scooters located in 177 U.S. and European cities. *See* JAN-PHILIPP HASENBERG & TOBIAS SCHÖNBERG, MOBILIZING MICROMOBILITY: HOW CITIES AND PROVIDERS CAN BUILD A SUCCESSFUL MODEL (Nov. 2020). In these programs, thousands of bikes and scooters are stationed across the city and people either buy a subscription for use of the vehicles or rent one on a daily or hourly basis. These programs

encourage residents and visitors to ride bikes or scooters, but they also can create tensions with auto drivers and pedestrians. *See* Daniel Libit, *Why Everyone Hates Bicyclists and Why They Hate Everyone Back*, CHICAGO BUS. (Nov. 11, 2013). While programs like these are changing the number of people who can use non-motorized transportation, they are also requiring new infrastructure development. How should these new interests be balanced with existing use of roads and sidewalks? What are the externalities from the different modes of travel? Who should pay for this and how?

2. Choices by U.S. cities about urban form and roadway patterns made early in the automobile era in the first half of the 20th century have had long-term implications for their residents' access to open space. For example, the sons of Frederick Law Olmsted, the designer of New York's Central Park, proposed a development model for Los Angeles in the 1930s that included much more green space accessed by 214 miles of interconnecting parkways. *See* Olmsted Brothers & Bartholomew and Associates, *Parks, Playgrounds and Beaches for the Los Angeles Region* 1 (1930), *reprinted in* GREG HISE & WILLIAM DEVERELL, EDEN BY DESIGN (2000). Imagine how different Los Angeles might be today if city officials followed that approach.

3. As noted above, in contrast to most of the United States, intercity rail is the transport mode of choice in most European countries as well as in Japan and China. What historical, physical, legal, and regulatory factors do you think make rail development in the United States so difficult?

4. While people in urban areas often benefit from high-speed intercity rail, passing trains do make noise and affect residents in the areas they travel. What are some of the considerations when balancing the interests of rural populations and urban residents? How do notions of individual rights and general societal welfare play out in such conflicts? What types of mechanisms are available to compensate affected communities for losses?

2. ENVIRONMENTAL JUSTICE CONCERNS

Environmental Justice (EJ) is an effort to ensure that all people, regardless of race, color, national origin, income, or other group classifications are protected against environmental harms and have access to environmental benefits. Historically, low income and minority communities were excluded from the decision-making process about policies, actions, and developments in their communities which resulted in the citizens of these communities suffering disproportionate adverse environmental and health effects from hazardous waste facilities, other industrial facilities, and highways built through their neighborhoods.

President Clinton first introduced EJ as a federal requirement in 1994, with Executive Order 12898 entitled "Federal Actions to Address Environmental Justice in Minority and Low-Income Populations." This executive order requires federal agencies to act to eliminate inequities in infrastructure planning, operation, and development. President Clinton directed EPA to implement the executive order. EPA defines EJ as "the fair treatment and meaningful involvement of all people regardless of race, color, national origin, or income with respect to the development, implementation, and enforcement of environmental laws, regulations, and policies." According to EPA, "fair treatment" requires that "no group of people should bear a disproportionate share of the negative environmental consequences resulting from industrial, governmental and commercial operations or policies." EPA states that "meaningful involvement" means that:

- People have an opportunity to participate in decisions about activities that may affect their environment and/or health;

- The public's contribution can influence the regulatory agency's decision;

- Community concerns will be considered in the decision-making process; and

- Decision makers seek out and facilitate the involvement of those potentially affected.

See Environmental Justice, U.S. EPA.

As noted earlier in this chapter, vehicle emissions in concentrated areas can result in significant adverse health impacts, and those adverse impacts fall most heavily on low income and minority neighborhoods in urban areas that are often close to highways and industry. One of the reasons that such neighborhoods are near high concentrations of auto emissions is because city planners often found it much easier to locate urban highways through poor and minority areas—property values are lower, in many cases due to historic redlining policies; communities may not be as well organized or well-financed; and residents have less access to political power and legal resources to oppose such projects. *See, e.g.*, Daniel Aaronson, *The Effects of the 1930s HOLC "Redlining" Maps*, Fed. Reserve Bank of Chicago (revised Aug. 2020). The longstanding destructive impacts of such projects are well documented and have resulted in calls to tear down existing highways through minority neighborhoods and halt construction of pending ones. *See, e.g.*, E.A. Crunden, *Highway Foes See Ally in Buttigieg*, GREENWIRE (Apr. 7, 2021); Ian Duncan, *A Woman Called for a Highway's Removal in a Black Neighborhood. The White House Singled It Out in Its Infrastructure Plan*, WASH. POST (Apr. 1, 2021); Hiroko Tabuchi & Nadja Popovich, *People of Color Breathe More Hazardous Air. The Sources are Everywhere*, N.Y. TIMES (Apr. 28, 2021). The following case, in the context of a light rail project, rather than a highway, illustrates the efforts of such neighborhoods to participate in the planning process and oppose city and regional actions that may not fully take their interests into account in transportation planning.

SAINT PAUL BRANCH OF N.A.A.C.P. v. U.S. D.O.T.

764 F. Supp. 2d 1092 (D. Minn. 2011)

DONOVAN W. FRANK, DISTRICT JUDGE.

Plaintiffs The Saint Paul Branch of the National Association for the Advancement of Colored People (the "NAACP"), Community Stabilization Project, Aurora/Saint Anthony Neighborhood Development Corporation, Shear Pleasure, Inc., Metro Bar & Grill, Inc. d/b/a Arnellia's, Carolyn Brown, Deborah Montgomery, Michael Wright, Leetta Douglas, and Gloria Presley Massey (together, "Plaintiffs") bring this action against United States Department of Transportation (US DOT), Federal Transit Administration (FTA) (together, Federal Defendants), and the Metropolitan Council (collectively, "Defendants" or "Agencies").

Plaintiffs claim that Defendants violated the National Environmental Policy Act, 42 U.S.C. § 4331 *et seq.* (NEPA), and the Administrative Procedure Act, 5 U.S.C. § 701 *et seq.* (APA), by preparing a deficient Final Environmental Impact Statement (FEIS) for the Central Corridor Light Rail Transit project (CCLRT Project or Project). Plaintiffs seek an injunction ordering Defendants to prepare an adequate environmental impact statement (EIS) and to enjoin further construction of the CCLRT Project until Defendants have complied with their NEPA obligations. Plaintiffs, Federal Defendants and the Metropolitan Council each move separately for summary judgment. For the reasons set forth below, the Court grants in part and denies in part the pending motions.

BACKGROUND

The Central Corridor refers to the area that links the central business districts of downtown Minneapolis and St. Paul, Minnesota. The Central Corridor is one of the region's most ethnically, racially, and culturally diverse areas. The Central Corridor is also experiencing rapid growth in population, housing, and employment. The Central Corridor "has a high percentage of minorities, households without automobiles, people with low incomes, and households below poverty level." Thus, a substantial percentage of the population of the Central Corridor relies on transit to get to work, healthcare facilities, schools, shopping destinations, and for recreation. Further, the Central Corridor is experiencing transportation problems due to growth and development, such as increased traffic congestion, bus ridership, and travel times. In addition, there is a decreased availability of affordable parking and a limited ability to expand existing roadways. For over 20 years, the Central Corridor has been identified as an area where mobility and capacity should be improved.

The portion of the Central Corridor that Plaintiffs describe as their community is referred to in the environmental documents as the Midway East segment. Midway East comprises the area in St. Paul along

University Avenue between Rice Street and Snelling Avenue. Midway East comprises much of what was, at one time, the Rondo neighborhood and presently contains some of the highest concentrations of minority and low-income populations in the metro area.[3]

This case involves alleged inadequacies in the planning of the proposed CCLRT Project. The Project involves approximately 11 miles of light rail line, 9.7 miles of which will run between downtown Minneapolis and downtown St. Paul. The Project will connect five major activity centers in the Twin Cities, including downtown Minneapolis, the University of Minnesota, the Midway area, the State Capitol complex, and downtown St. Paul. Approximately 1.2 miles of the line will use the existing Hiawatha LRT alignment in downtown Minneapolis and will connect with five existing stations. The CCLRT line will be built primarily along University and Washington Avenues and will include 18 new stations. In the Midway East area, the project calls for seven new stations along University Avenue in St. Paul, located at Rice Street, Western Avenue, Dale Street, Victoria Street, Lexington Parkway, Hamline Avenue, and Snelling Avenue.

The purpose of the CCLRT Project is "to meet the future transit needs of the Central Corridor LRT study and the Twin Cities metropolitan region and to support the economic development goals for the Central Corridor LRT study area. The introduction of "fixed-guideway transit to the Central Corridor" was proposed as a "cost-effective measure aimed at improving mobility by offering an alternative to auto travel for commuting and discretionary trips." . . .

Ultimately, after conducting the NEPA analysis, the Agencies concluded that the CCLRT would provide, among other things, increased transit access to employment and activity centers, significant travel time savings, and the creation of jobs through new development along the LRT route. In addition, the Agencies concluded that "substantial benefits that will accrue to the minority, low-income, and transit dependent populations more than offset nearly all of the potential adverse impacts of the Project." Moreover, the Agencies concluded that the [Alternatives Analysis and Draft Environmental Impact Statement] AA/DEIS, SDEIS, and FEIS all indicated "that there are no disproportionately 'high and adverse' effects on minority and/or low-income populations." Instead, the Agencies noted that the "potential adverse effects are not predominantly borne by a minority or low-income populations [sic]," but rather that "the potential

---

[3] The Rondo neighborhood historically was an African-American community located in St. Paul. Plaintiffs point out, and Defendants do not contest, that the Rondo area was devastated when it was divided to build Interstate Highway 94 (I-94) between Minneapolis and St. Paul. In particular, Rondo Avenue, which served as a major artery through the neighborhood, was torn up to make way for I-94. The Rondo community relocated to University Avenue along a portion of the Central Corridor.

adverse effects are shared by all populations along the proposed route, including non-minority and non-low-income populations." . . .

In their Complaint, Plaintiffs allege a single count under NEPA. Plaintiffs assert that they are entitled to summary judgment because: (1) the FEIS fails to adequately analyze the cumulative impact of displacement/gentrification caused by the CCLRT, construction of the I-94, and urban renewal policies of the 1970s; (2) the FEIS fails to adequately analyze and consider mitigation of the business interruption caused by the construction of the CCLRT; (3) the FEIS does not adequately analyze or consider mitigating the displacement of Central Corridor residents and businesses; and (4) the FEIS lacks the requisite scope because it does not analyze the entire CCLRT Project. Because of these alleged deficiencies, Plaintiffs seek an order vacating the ROD, directing the Agencies to prepare an adequate EIS, and enjoining further construction on the CCLRT until the Agencies have complied with their NEPA obligations. . . .

III. Plaintiffs' NEPA Claims

A. Cumulative Impacts of Prior Projects

Plaintiffs allege that the FEIS fails to adequately identify or consider the cumulative impacts of the construction of I-94 and the current CCLRT Project on Plaintiffs' community. Plaintiffs' community includes the African-American community of the Central Corridor as well as St. Paul's Rondo community. Plaintiffs assert that they asked the Metropolitan Council to consider prior government actions that have impacted the neighborhood, but that the FEIS did not consider the issue of the past dislocation of the Central Corridor African-American community. In particular, Plaintiffs assert that the construction of I-94 brought direct physical displacement to the Rondo neighborhood and that the CCLRT now brings indirect displacement.

As explained above, the cumulative impacts analysis must be sufficiently detailed to be "useful to the decisionmaker in deciding whether, or how, to alter the program to lessen cumulative impacts and must rely on some quantified or detailed information." . . .

Defendants assert that the FEIS, in large part, addressed the effects of the I-94 construction on the Rondo community when it considered the existing conditions. Plaintiffs contend that this analysis arbitrarily limited the required cumulative impacts analysis. . . .

Here, the administrative record demonstrates that Defendants were well aware of the negative consequences that the construction of I-94 had on the Rondo neighborhood. Indeed, the record reflects that Defendants understood that the Rondo neighborhood was devastated after being "cut in half" by the construction of I-94. In particular, the AA/DEIS noted:

Better transit would play a pivotal role in acknowledging the character and aspirations of places in the Study Area and in the region as a whole. The Central Corridor has local neighborhoods that collectively form the heart of the Twin Cities Metropolitan Area. This distinction is expressed, for example, in the annual Rondo Days festival. The Rondo area, one of the city's most diverse communities, was virtually destroyed when it was cut in half in the 1960s to build I-94 between Minneapolis and St. Paul.

In addition, the FEIS stated:

Concerns regarding community cohesion are brought into sharper relief by a sensitive understanding of the history of what was known as the Rondo neighborhood and which encompassed the environmental justice community between Lexington Parkway and Rice Street. The Rondo community, a historically African-American community, was devastated with the construction of Interstate Highway 94 in St. Paul during the 1960s.

The FEIS further indicated that "[t]he stakeholders that are engaged in the planning for the Central Corridor LRT remain committed to ensuring such disproportionate impacts are not borne again by this community." Further, in the Dale Station Area report for the CCLRT, the history of the area is set forth, noting that the Summit-University area was home to the Rondo neighborhood, the heart of St. Paul's African-American community prior to construction of I-94, and that many former residents still live in the Summit-University area.

The record also reflects that Defendants were aware of the public's concern regarding disproportionate negative impacts to the Rondo neighborhood. For example, in the chapter addressing Public and Agency Coordination and Comments, the FEIS discussed the nature of comments received regarding Neighborhood Impacts at the AA/DEIS stage of review:

The majority of comments received on the AA/DEIS concerning neighborhood impacts discussed the need to maintain community cohesion and character of the local neighborhoods, potential for land use changes and redevelopment within the corridor, and comments on livable communities. . . .

Community cohesion concerns were widely expressed by many community members, particularly in relation to the Rondo neighborhood in St. Paul. The current alignment runs through the Rondo neighborhood, the heart of St. Paul's African-American community that was devastated by the construction of I-94 in the 1960s. Community members from around the metropolitan area were concerned about maintaining the remaining neighborhood fabric and community cohesion.

Aware of the concerns regarding the Rondo neighborhood, the FEIS examined the economic and social impacts that the CCLRT Project would have under existing conditions. This examination considered the past activities in the Rondo neighborhood. For example, in its discussion of indirect and cumulative impacts of the CCLRT Project, the FEIS evaluated the effects of the CCLRT Project on the quality and cohesion and community services of the twelve neighborhoods adjacent to the proposed light rail line, including the Midway East neighborhood. The record reveals that neighborhoods in and around Midway East were examined, such as Thomas-Dale, Summit-University, and Hamline-Midway. Features and characteristics of Midway East are referenced repeatedly in the FEIS. With respect to Midway East, the FEIS noted that the CCLRT "is not expected to have long-term adverse impact [sic] on neighborhood cohesion or identity," that the "LRT should act as a catalyst for greater pedestrian activity," that "the project will reconstruct the street and sidewalks and provide a unified, clean landscape," and that the "stations are expected to become additional foci of activity and neighborhood assets." The FEIS also considered, at the neighborhood level, issues of income and poverty, housing and employment, racial and ethnic diversity, landmarks and community facilities, schools, places of worship, and public and subsidized housing. . . .

In addition, the FEIS acknowledged that the LRT alignment in the middle of University Avenue raised concerns about "connectivity between neighborhoods north and south of the tracks." In response, the FEIS explained that "no visual barrier, however, will be placed across University Avenue" and that "most currently legal pedestrian crossings will be maintained, and in many cases, will be enhanced." The FEIS also explained that:

> The Central Corridor LRT is not intended to act as a barrier to any community, but rather to enhance the access to both the adjacent communities and the metropolitan region. Physical infrastructure enhancements that will occur as a result of the project will allow for safer street crossings and improved circulation in the adjacent neighborhoods.

Chapter 3 of the FEIS discussed related social conditions in the corridor and potential effects of the LRT. Specifically, this chapter addressed potential impacts on socioeconomics, neighborhoods, community service and cohesion, cultural resources, and environmental justice. . . .

In its discussion of potential environmental justice issues, the FEIS examined both long-term implications for environmental justice communities and short-term construction impacts. The FEIS compared the effects of each alternative to protected population on air quality, noise, vibration, parking, traffic accessibility, community cohesion, acquisitions and displacements, and placement of system components. . . .

The FEIS goes on to discuss a number of accommodations added to the project to enhance community cohesion in direct response to community concerns. These accommodations include the addition of "non-signalized pedestrian crossings" to "ensure that pedestrians will be able to cross University Avenue at virtually every legal crossing that currently exists," the reconstruction of sidewalks along University Avenue, and the addition of associated streetscape elements. Additional adjustments were made to the CCLRT Project to account for potential adverse impacts to Plaintiffs' community. For example, the FEIS noted the inclusion of noise and vibration minimization, noted proportionately less loss of parking in environmental justice areas, and rejected the option of widening an intersection to avoid the demolition of existing minority businesses.

Based on its careful review of the record, the Court concludes that the FEIS complies with NEPA's requirements with respect to its cumulative impact analysis. The record demonstrates that Defendants took a "hard look" at the cumulative impacts of the proposed action and did not act arbitrarily or capriciously in its consideration of the cumulative impacts of past activities in the Rondo neighborhood. The administrative record demonstrates that the Agencies acknowledged and were cognizant of the fact that the Rondo neighborhood had been negatively impacted and nearly destroyed by the construction of I-94. The administrative record also demonstrates that the Agencies considered the comments and concerns directed at any such cumulative impacts, and considered issues of community cohesion and connectivity as they relate to the Rondo area. Finally, the Agencies considered the potential adverse impacts of the CCLRT project on the Rondo neighborhood and concluded that despite these potential impacts, the CCLRT will provide substantial benefits to the environmental justice community. NEPA ensures that agencies do not act on incomplete information, prohibits uninformed, not unwise, agency action. Here, the Court concludes that the Agencies were fully informed concerning the cumulative impacts of the CCLRT project and that the Agencies' analysis of cumulative impacts complies with NEPA.

In so holding, the Court reminds the Agencies of their commitment to "working toward resolution of community concerns that don't rise to the level of state or federal standards of adverse impacts." While the Court concludes that the Agencies have not violated NEPA in their environmental analysis of cumulative impacts, this does not diminish the valid concerns of those in the affected neighborhoods, and in particular the Rondo neighborhood that was devastated by the construction of I-94, regarding the future of their communities. The Court hopes and expects that the Agencies will continue to honor their commitment to resolving community concerns going forward, despite their technical compliance with NEPA.

[The court proceeded to find that the FEIS was deficient in its consideration of lost business revenue as an adverse impact of the construction of the CCLRT and ordered the defendants to supplement their analysis of that issue, but did not enjoin the CCLRT project.—Eds.]

CONCLUSION

The Court has concluded that the FEIS was deficient in its consideration of lost business revenue as an adverse impact of the construction of the CCLRT. The Court has also concluded that the FEIS is not deficient in its analysis of cumulative impacts of prior projects or the potential displacement of existing businesses and residents due to the gentrification of the area. Despite the latter rulings, the Court recognizes the validity and magnitude of Plaintiffs' concerns with respect to the impact that the CCLRT Project could have on the previously disrupted Rondo community and the potential impact that gentrification could have on low-income and minority populations. While the Court has concluded that the Defendants complied with the procedural requirements of NEPA, the Court expects that Defendants will continue to work with Plaintiffs to address Plaintiffs' concerns. Indeed, Defendants specifically represented that they are committed to resolving community concerns that do not rise to the level of a NEPA violation. If the relevant groups—including the Metropolitan Council, the City of St. Paul, and Ramsey County—fulfill their commitments to mitigate the displacement of the impacted communities due to gentrification of the area and to minimize impacts to the Rondo community, they will revisit these issues with Plaintiffs and resolve them in the best interest of all concerned.

The Court is hopeful that with further discussions and negotiations between the parties, along with the implementation of the mitigation measures discussed in the record, Plaintiffs' racially, ethnically, and culturally diverse community will avoid disproportionate impacts from— and will experience the anticipated benefits of—the CCLRT Project. The communities within the Central Corridor deserve no less.

———

NOTES AND QUESTIONS

1.   Light rail construction can block roads, eliminate parking, and make access to businesses difficult during construction. Additionally, after development, areas around light rail stations often become attractive for higher priced real estate development, potentially displacing existing community members. How do the impacts on a neighborhood differ as between building a highway, such as the I-94 construction in the 1960s described in the

St. Paul Branch of the N.A.A.C.P. case, and constructing a light rail project, which can disrupt local businesses, lead to gentrification, and negatively affect minority neighborhoods? For a detailed discussion of the planning and construction of the CCLRT project in the Twin Cities as well as some of the economic development impacts since completion, see Erick Trickey, *The Train That Brought the Twin Cities Back Together*, POLITICO MAGAZINE (Mar. 16, 2017). For a discussion of the history and destruction of the Rondo neighborhood mentioned in the case, see Tom Weber, *Rondo Days Festival Celebrates 34 Year This Weekend*, MPR NEWS (July 12, 2017).

2.   Low income and predominantly minority communities are often affected by the lack of access to transportation for jobs. In many urban areas, public transportation is slow and traveling from where poor residents live to higher paying jobs can involve multiple transfers and hours of travel time. This lack of access affects both earning potential and economic mobility. What are some strategies to provide access to employment and overcome the effects of geography on earnings and social mobility? *See* David Leonhardt, *In Climbing Income Ladder, Location Matters*, N.Y. TIMES (July 22, 2013).

3.   Lack of transportation from low-income and minority communities to public amenities such as beaches, parks, and recreation is another example of the connection between transportation policy and environmental justice. Robert García and Erica Flores Baltodano describe the ways in which discriminatory laws paired with transportation decisions have limited minority access to those resources. They explain, for example, that:

> In the 1980s, disproportionately white affluent communities persuaded the Southern California Rapid Transit District (RTD) to end direct bus service between South Central Los Angeles and the beachfront communities to its west. According to the sworn deposition testimony of a former Metropolitan Transportation Authority (MTA) official, bus service was changed at the request of Manhattan Beach residents so inner-city residents could not travel directly to the beach there without transferring. This not only increased the amount of time it took to reach the beach, it effectively deterred people of color from going to the beach at all because of the amount of time and hassle it took to get there. RTD also granted the request of residents of the Palos Verdes Peninsula cities that buses from the inner city not climb the Palos Verdes hill.

Robert García & Erica Flores Baltodano, *Free the Beach! Public Access, Equal Justice, and the California Coast*, 2 STAN. J. CIV. RTS. & CIV. LIBERTIES 143, 165–66 (2005). For a detailed discussion of how transportation planning and urban infrastructure in general have been used to exclude low income and minority citizens, see Sarah Schindler, *Architectural Exclusion: Discrimination and Segregation Through Physical Design of the Built Environment*, 124 YALE L.J. 1934 (2015).

C. OIL CONSUMPTION AND TECHNOLOGY-FORCING REGULATION

Roughly 14 million new cars and light trucks were sold in the United States in 2020. The average age of the U.S. car fleet is 11.9 years. On a worldwide basis, in 2018, the global registered automobile fleet was estimated at roughly 1 billion cars, with nearly 12% of all vehicles located in the United States (837 vehicles per 1000 people). This was down from 1960 when 65% of the 120 million registered cars were in the United States. Japan (61 million, 591 per 1000 people), Germany (45 million, 589 per 1000 people), Russia (41 million, 373 per 1000 people), and France (32 million, 569 per 1000 people) are other countries with large auto fleets. In these countries, average annual vehicle growth rates from 1990 to 2018 ranged from a slight decrease (−0.6% in the United States) to rapidly growing (4% in Brazil). Worldwide, the fastest growing fleets are found in China, which increased its vehicle population from 1980 to 2018 from 351,000 cars to over 194 million, making the average annual growth an astounding 18% per year between 1990 and 2018, with 173 vehicles per 1000 people. Other countries with the fastest average annual vehicle fleet growth rates are also located in Asia: Indonesia (16.5 million vehicles in 2018, 10% growth), South Korea (18.7 million vehicles, 8% growth), India (31.9 million vehicles, 10% growth), and Malaysia (13.8 million vehicles, 7.5% growth). Rapid growth in Asia is driving global demand for vehicles and oil. DAVIS & BOUNDY, *supra*; *Motorization Rate in Selected Countries as of 2018*, STATISTA (2021).

The U.S. fleet is also made up of over 14 million medium- and heavy-duty trucks which are the backbone of the U.S. transportation sector and U.S. economy. Long travel distances in the United States mean that trucks are a crucial component of transportation logistics systems. They use 23.7% of all transportation energy, 46 billion gallons of fuel, and over 6 quads of energy, with almost 90% coming from diesel fuel. Trucks are also cleaner than they were a decade ago. Low-sulfur diesel fuel requirements and advances in diesel engine technology mean that trucks today emit 90% less particulate matter and nitrogen oxides than a truck built a decade ago. *See Testimony of Derek J. Leathers before the U.S. House of Representatives Panel on 21st Century Freight Transportation* (Apr. 24, 2013); DAVIS & BOUNDY, *supra*.

The energy use and air emissions associated with the transport sector are a function of vehicle miles traveled, the number of vehicles, the fuel efficiency of vehicles, and the fuels used in vehicles. The first section discusses regulation of the fuel efficiency of vehicles while the next section discusses regulation of the fuels themselves.

1. VEHICLE FUEL EFFICIENCY
AND CAFE STANDARDS

Increasing individual vehicle fuel efficiency depends upon technological advances to make cars and trucks more efficient coupled with policies to support implementation of these changes in markets. The U.S. EIA projects a 54% increase in passenger car fuel efficiency by 2050, with light trucks achieving a 55% increase. *See* U.S. ENERGY INFO. ADMIN., ANNUAL ENERGY OUTLOOK 2021 10 (2021). Vehicle efficiency improvements vary by vehicle type. For instance, gasoline direct injection and supercharging engines to reduce their size improve fuel and combustion efficiency in internal combustion engines. DAVIS & BOUNDY, *supra*, at 4–20. For EVs, reduced battery density can increase battery pack size, allowing vehicles to drive further after charging. *See* JOHN W. BRENNAN & TIMOTHY E. BARDER, BATTERY ELECTRIC VEHICLES VS. INTERNAL COMBUSTION ENGINE VEHICLES 21 (2016). Some advances, such as reducing tire rolling resistance, improving vehicle aerodynamics to reduce drag, making cars from stronger and lighter advanced composite materials, and improving vehicle lighting and air conditioning systems, can help increase fuel efficiency for all vehicles. WORLD ENERGY COUNCIL, *supra*, at 26.

In the United States, the EPA regulates auto emissions and fuel content under the Clean Air Act while the National Highway Traffic Safety Administration (NHTSA) within the U.S. Department of Transportation regulates vehicle fuel efficiency under a separate statute. Section 202(a) of the Clean Air Act requires EPA to enact regulations setting emissions standards applicable to the emissions of air pollutants from classes of new motor vehicles that in EPA's judgment cause or contribute to air pollution that may reasonably be anticipated to endanger public health or welfare (the provision at issue in *Massachusetts v. EPA*, discussed in Chapter 1). EPA has enacted different standards for different classes of vehicles, including passenger vehicles, light duty trucks, heavy duty vehicles, and motorcycles. *See* 40 C.F.R. part 86.

Under Section 209 of the Clean Air Act, Congress has preempted (i.e., prohibited) states from setting motor vehicle emission standards that are more stringent than those set by the federal government. There is a special exception, however, for California, which is allowed to petition EPA for a preemption waiver to adopt its own, stricter standards. Once a waiver is granted, California can apply its standard to all vehicles sold in California and other states can choose to adopt the California standards. Thus, there is always the potential for two sets of vehicle emissions standards nationwide—the federal standard and the California standard. California was granted this special preemption waiver based on its history of regulating auto emissions (which predates federal regulation) and its unique problems with auto pollution, particularly in the Los Angeles area.

As a result of federal regulation as well as improved technology, pollution from cars has decreased significantly in the last 30 years, even though vehicle miles traveled have increased significantly.

In addition to EPA regulations on auto emissions under the Clean Air Act, NHTSA regulates fleet-wide automobile fuel efficiency standards by setting Corporate Average Fuel Economy (CAFE) standards. Congress established the CAFE standards in 1975 as part of the Energy Policy and Conservation Act (EPCA) in response to the 1973–74 oil crisis. The goal of the CAFE standards was to double new car fuel economy from 13.6 miles per gallon (mpg) in 1974 to 27.5 mpg by model year (MY) 1985. From 1985 until the Obama administration produced joint fuel economy and tailpipe emissions standards in 2010, discussed later in this section, the standards remained almost unchanged through 2011. *See, e.g., Light Duty Vehicles: Fuel Economy (1978–2011)*, DIESELNET; *Light Duty Vehicles: GHG Emissions and Fuel Economy*, DIESEL NET. Also, until 2011, most trucks were exempt from the CAFE standards.

The CAFE regulations require each car manufacturer to meet the standard for the sales-weighted fuel economy for the entire fleet of vehicles sold in the United States for each model year. EPA provides fuel economy data to the DOE to publish the annual Fuel Economy Guide, to NHTSA to administer the CAFE program, and to the IRS to collect Gas Guzzler taxes. EPA obtains test data from vehicle testing done at the EPA's National Vehicle and Fuel Emissions Laboratory in Ann Arbor, Michigan and by vehicle manufacturers who submit their test data to EPA. *See Fuel Economy*, U.S. EPA.

Manufacturers pay a civil penalty if their fleet of cars fails to achieve the required CAFE standard. The penalty charged is $5.50 per each tenth of a mpg under the target value multiplied by the total volume of vehicles manufactured for a given model year sold in the United States. As of 2017, manufacturers paid more than $890 million in civil penalties. *See* NHTSA, Civil Penalties, 92 Fed. Reg. 32,140 (July 12, 2017). Notably, Asian and U.S. manufacturers have never paid a civil penalty while European manufacturers have regularly paid civil penalties from less than $1 million to more than $27 million annually. *See Light Duty Vehicles: Fuel Economy (1978–2011), supra. See also CAFE Overview: Frequently Asked Questions,* NHTSA.

In 2016, the Obama administration proposed increasing the CAFE noncompliance penalties significantly—from $5.50 per tenth of a mpg to $14.00—to comply with a 2015 law that required federal agencies to increase civil penalties to account for inflation, but ultimately delayed implementation of the increase until MY 2019. When the Trump administration took office, NHTSA first attempted to delay implementation further and then to statutorily rescind the increase entirely. Both efforts were challenged in court and vacated by the U.S. Court of Appeals for the Second Circuit. The Trump administration then proposed delaying implementation of the enhanced penalties until MY 2022. *See* NHTSA, Civil Penalties, Interim Final Rule; Request for Comment; Response to Petition for Rulemaking, 86 Fed. Reg. 3016 (Jan. 14, 2021). That proposed delay was also subject to legal challenge while the Biden administration considered whether to reconsider the Trump-era rule and apply the enhanced penalties retroactively to MY 2019. *See, e.g.,* NHTSA, Supplemental Notice of Proposed Rulemaking, 86 Fed. Reg. 46811 (Aug. 20, 2021); *Tesla Urges Court to Reinstate Higher Emissions Penalties Against Automakers*, REUTERS (Mar. 28, 2021); Arianna Skibell, *Biden Admin Weighs Penalty Increase for Car Companies*, GREENWIRE (Aug. 18, 2021).

The following case explains in more detail the history of CAFE standards and EPCA's requirements.

CENTER FOR BIOLOGICAL DIVERSITY V. NATIONAL HIGHWAY TRAFFIC SAFETY ADMIN.

538 F.3d 1172 (9th Cir. 2008)

BETTY B. FLETCHER, CIRCUIT JUDGE.

Eleven states, the District of Columbia, the City of New York, and four public interest organizations petition for review of a rule issued by the National Highway Traffic Safety Administration (NHTSA) entitled "Average Fuel Economy Standards for Light Trucks, Model Years 2008–2011,".... Pursuant to the Energy Policy and Conservation Act of 1975 (EPCA), 49 U.S.C. §§ 32901–32919 (2007), the Final Rule sets corporate average fuel economy (CAFE) standards for light trucks, defined by NHTSA to include many Sport Utility Vehicles (SUVs), minivans, and pickup trucks, for Model Years (MYs) 2008–2011. For MYs 2008–2010, the Final Rule sets new CAFE standards using its traditional method, fleet-wide average (Unreformed CAFE). For MY 2011 and beyond, the Final Rule creates a new CAFE structure that sets varying fuel economy targets depending on vehicle size and requires manufacturers to meet different fuel economy levels depending on their vehicle fleet mix (Reformed CAFE).

Petitioners challenge the Final Rule under the EPCA and the National Environmental Policy Act of 1969 (NEPA), 42 U.S.C. §§ 4321–4347 (2007). First, they argue that the Final Rule is arbitrary, capricious, and contrary to the EPCA because (a) the agency's cost-benefit analysis does not set the CAFE standard at the "maximum feasible" level and fails to give due consideration to the need of the nation to conserve energy; (b) its calculation of the costs and benefits of alternative fuel economy standards assigns zero value to the benefit of carbon dioxide (CO_2) emissions reduction; . . .

I.   FACTUAL AND PROCEDURAL BACKGROUND

A.   CAFE Regulation Under the Energy Policy and Conservation Act

In the aftermath of the energy crisis created by the 1973 Mideast oil embargo, Congress enacted the Energy Policy and Conservation Act of 1975, Pub. L. No. 94–163, 89 Stat. 871, 901–16. Congress observed that "[t]he fundamental reality is that this nation has entered a new era in which energy resources previously abundant, will remain in short supply, retarding our economic growth and necessitating an alteration in our life's habits and expectations." *Id.* at 1763. The goals of the EPCA are to "decrease dependence on foreign imports, enhance national security, achieve the efficient utilization of scarce resources, and guarantee the availability of domestic energy supplies at prices consumers can afford." S. Rep. No. 94–516 (1975). These goals are more pressing today than they were thirty years ago: since 1975, American consumption of oil has risen from 16.3 million barrels per day to over 20 million barrels per day, and the percentage of U.S. oil that is imported has risen from 35.8 to 56 percent.

In furtherance of the goal of energy conservation, Title V of the EPCA establishes automobile fuel economy standards. An "average fuel economy standard" (often referred to as a CAFE standard) is "a performance standard specifying a minimum level of average fuel economy applicable to a manufacturer in a model year." 49 U.S.C. § 32901(a)(6) (2007). Only "automobiles" are subject to fuel economy regulation, and passenger automobiles must meet a statutory standard of 27.5 mpg, 49 U.S.C. § 32902(b), whereas non-passenger automobiles must meet standards set by the Secretary of Transportation, *id.* § 32902(a). Congress directs the Secretary to set fuel economy standards at "the maximum feasible average fuel economy level that the Secretary decides the manufacturers can achieve in that model year." *Id.* § 32902(a). Under this subsection, the Secretary is authorized to "prescribe separate standards for different classes of automobiles." *Id.* Congress also provides that "[w]hen deciding maximum feasible average fuel economy under this section, the Secretary of Transportation shall consider technological feasibility, economic practicability, the effect of other motor vehicle standards of the Government on fuel economy, and the need of the United States to conserve energy." *Id.* § 32902(f). . . .

The CAFE standards NHTSA sets for non-passenger automobiles or "light trucks," as referred to by the agency in its regulations, are lower than the standards for passenger automobiles. A "passenger automobile" is defined as:

> an automobile that the Secretary decides by regulation is manufactured primarily for transporting not more than 10

individuals, but does not include an automobile capable of off-highway operation that the Secretary decides by regulation—

> (A) has a significant feature (except 4-wheel drive) designed for off-highway operation; and

> (B) is a 4-wheel drive automobile or is rated at more than 6,000 pounds gross vehicle weight.

49 U.S.C. § 32901(a)(16).

The Final Rule sets CAFE standards for "light trucks," defined by NHTSA to include many SUVs, vans, and pickup trucks, for MYs 2008–2011. *See* 71 Fed. Reg. at 17,568; 49 C.F.R. § 533.5(a), (g), (h). A "light truck" is:

> an automobile other than a passenger automobile which is either designed for off-highway operation, as described in paragraph (b) of this section, or designed to perform at least one of the following functions: (1) Transport more than 10 persons; (2) Provide temporary living quarters; (3) Transport property on an open bed; (4) Provide greater cargo-carrying than passenger-carrying volume; or (5) Permit expanded use of the automobile for cargo-carrying purposes or other non-passenger-carrying purposes through [removable or foldable, stowable seats to create a flat floor].

For MYs 1996 to 2004, Congress froze the light truck CAFE standard at 20.7 mpg. After the legislative restrictions were lifted, NHTSA set new light truck CAFE standards in April 2003: 21.0 mpg for MY 2005, 21.6 mpg for MY 2006, and 22.2 mpg for MY 2007.

In response to a request from Congress, the National Academy of Sciences (NAS) published in 2002 a report entitled "Effectiveness and Impact of Corporate Average Fuel Economy (CAFE) Standards." The NAS committee made several findings and recommendations. It found that from 1970 to 1982, CAFE standards helped contribute to a 50 percent increase in fuel economy for new light trucks. In the subsequent decades, however, light trucks became more popular since domestic manufacturers faced less competition in the light truck category and could generate greater profits. The "less stringent CAFE standards for trucks . . . provide[d] incentives for manufacturers to invest in minivans and SUVs and to promote them to consumers in place of large cars and station wagons." When the CAFE regulations were originally promulgated in the 1970s, "light truck sales accounted for about 20 percent of the new vehicle market," but now they account for about half. This shift has had a "pronounced" effect on overall fuel economy. As the market share of light trucks has increased, the overall average fuel economy of the new light duty vehicle fleet (light trucks and passenger automobiles) has declined "from a peak of 25.9 MPG in 1987 to

24.0 MPG in 2000." Vehicle miles traveled (VMT) by light trucks has also been growing more rapidly than passenger automobile travel.

The NAS committee found that the CAFE program has increased fuel economy, but that certain aspects of the program "have not functioned as intended," including "[t]he distinction between a car for personal use and a truck for work use/cargo transport," which "has been stretched well beyond the original purpose." The committee also found that technologies exist to "significantly reduce fuel consumption," for cars and light trucks and that raising CAFE standards would reduce fuel consumption. Significantly, the committee found that of the many reasons for improving fuel economy, "[t]he most important ... is concern about the accumulation in the atmosphere of so-called greenhouse gases, principally carbon dioxide. Continued increases in carbon dioxide emissions are likely to further global warming." In addition, the committee found "externalities of about $0.30/gal of gasoline associated with the combined impacts of fuel consumption on greenhouse gas emissions and on world oil market conditions" that "are not necessarily taken into account when consumers purchase new vehicles.". . . .

III. DISCUSSION

A. Energy Policy and Conservation Act Issues

1. NHTSA's use of marginal cost-benefit analysis to determine "maximum feasible average fuel economy level"

With respect to non-passenger automobiles (i.e., light trucks), the fuel economy standard "shall be the maximum feasible average fuel economy level that the Secretary decides the manufacturers can achieve in that model year." "Maximum feasible" is not defined in the EPCA. However, the EPCA provides that "[w]hen deciding maximum feasible average fuel economy under this section, the Secretary of Transportation shall consider technological feasibility, economic practicability, the effect of other motor vehicle standards of the Government on fuel economy, and the need of the United States to conserve energy." *Id.* § 32902(f).

Petitioners argue that the meaning of "maximum feasible" is plain, and that NHTSA's decision to maximize economic benefits is contrary to the plain language of the EPCA because "feasible" means "capable of being done," not economically optimal. But even if "feasible" means "capable of being done," technological feasibility, economic practicability, the effect of other motor vehicle standards, and the need of the nation to conserve energy must be considered in determining the "maximum feasible" standard. . . .

The EPCA clearly requires the agency to consider these four factors, but it gives NHTSA discretion to decide how to balance the statutory factors—as long as NHTSA's balancing does not undermine the fundamental purpose of the EPCA: energy conservation. . . .

To be clear, we reject only Petitioners' contention that EPCA prohibits NHTSA's use of marginal cost-benefit analysis to set CAFE standards. Whatever method it uses, NHTSA cannot set fuel economy standards that are contrary to Congress's purpose in enacting the EPCA—energy conservation. We must still review whether NHTSA's balancing of the statutory factors is arbitrary and capricious. Additionally, the persuasiveness of the analysis in *Public Citizen [v. NHTSA*, 848 F.2d 256 (D.C. Cir. 1988)] and *Center for Auto Safety [v. NHTSA*, 793 F.2d 1322 (D.C. Cir. 1986)] is limited by the fact that they were decided two decades ago, when scientific knowledge of climate change and its causes were not as advanced as they are today. The need of the nation to conserve energy is even more pressing today than it was at the time of EPCA's enactment. *See, e.g.*, NRDC Cmt. at 4, 11 ("When fuel economy legislation was first enacted, America consumed 16.3 million barrels of oil per day and 35.8 percent of U.S. oil came from imports. In the nearly 30 years since then, oil consumption has risen to over 20 million barrels per day and 56 percent of U.S. oil is imported. If fuel economy standards are not strengthened, these trends are only expected to get worse, with transportation oil use driving 80 percent of U.S. oil demand growth through 2025 and imports rising to 68 percent of U.S. oil demand. The light duty vehicle fleet currently consumes 8.3 million barrels per day, and in the absence of stronger standards, that is projected to grow to 12.45 million barrels by 2025). What was a reasonable balancing of competing statutory priorities twenty years ago may not be a reasonable balancing of those priorities today.

2. Failure to monetize benefits of greenhouse gas emissions reduction

Even if NHTSA may use a cost-benefit analysis to determine the "maximum feasible" fuel economy standard, it cannot put a thumb on the scale by undervaluing the benefits and overvaluing the costs of more stringent standards. NHTSA fails to include in its analysis the benefit of carbon emissions reduction in either quantitative or qualitative form. It did, however, include an analysis of the employment and sales impacts of more stringent standards on manufacturers. . . .

NHTSA's reasoning is arbitrary and capricious for several reasons. First, while the record shows that there is a range of values, the value of carbon emissions reduction is certainly not zero. . . .

Second, NHTSA gave no reasons why it believed the range of values presented to it was "extremely wide"; in fact, several commenters and the NAS committee recommended the same value: $50 per ton carbon. . . .

Third, NHTSA's reasoning is arbitrary and capricious because it has monetized other uncertain benefits, such as the reduction of criteria pollutants, crash, noise, and congestion costs, and "the value of increased energy security.". . . .

Fourth, NHTSA's conclusion that commenters did not "reliably demonstrate" that monetizing the value of carbon reduction would have affected the stringency of the CAFE standard "'runs counter to the evidence'" before it. *NRDC v. U.S. Forest Serv.*, 421 F.3d 797, 806 (9th Cir. 2005) (citation omitted) . . . .

Finally, there is no merit to NHTSA's unfounded assertion that if it had accounted for the benefit of carbon emissions reduction, it would have had to account for the adverse safety effects of downweighting, and the two would have balanced out, resulting in no change to the final CAFE standards. . . .

Thus, NHTSA's decision not to monetize the benefit of carbon emissions reduction was arbitrary and capricious, and we remand to NHTSA for it to include a monetized value for this benefit in its analysis of the proper CAFE standards. . . .

6. Changing the definition of passenger and non-passenger automobiles in order to close the SUV loophole

Petitioners challenge NHTSA's decision not to reform the SUV loophole. They argue that this decision is arbitrary and capricious because it runs counter to the evidence showing that the majority of SUVs, minivans, and pickup trucks function solely or primarily as passenger vehicles, and because NHTSA has not provided a reasoned explanation for why the transition to Reformed CAFE could not be accomplished at the same time as a revision in the definitions.

The EPCA defines "passenger automobile" as "an automobile that the Secretary decides by regulation is manufactured primarily for transporting not more than 10 individuals," excluding "an automobile capable of off-highway operation that the Secretary decides . . . has a significant feature except 4-wheel drive designed for off-highway operation" and is 4-wheel drive or more than 6,000 lbs. GVWR. 49 U.S.C. § 32901(a)(16). "Non-passenger automobiles" are thus defined by exclusion. NHTSA defines an automobile other than a passenger automobile as a "light truck," a term not used in the statute. 49 C.F.R. § 523.5 (2007). Under 49 U.S.C. § 32901(a)(16), the Secretary has discretion to decide what constitutes a "passenger automobile" within the confines of the listed criteria.

NHTSA initially sought input on ways to revise the regulatory distinction because the passenger automobile/light truck distinction had become obsolete: "The application of the regulation to the current vehicle fleet (designed with the regulatory distinctions in mind) less clearly differentiates between passenger cars and light trucks than it did in the

1970s." 68 Fed. Reg. at 74,927 (ANPRM). However, in the [Notice of Proposed Rulemaking], NHTSA decided not to:

> chang[e] those classification regulations at this time in part because [NHTSA] believe[s] an orderly transition to Reformed CAFE could not be accomplished if [NHTSA] simultaneously change[s] which vehicles are included in the light truck program and because, as applied in MY 2011, Reformed CAFE is likely to reduce the incentive to produce vehicles classified as light trucks instead of as passenger cars.

70 Fed. Reg. at 51,422. Ultimately, NHTSA did not change the light truck definition other than by expanding the flat floor provision to include vehicles with folding seats, if the vehicles have at least three rows of designated seating. See 49 C.F.R. § 523.5(a)(5); 71 Fed. Reg. at 17,650–52.

We conclude that NHTSA's decision not to otherwise revise the passenger automobile/light truck definitions is arbitrary and capricious. First, NHTSA has not provided a reasoned explanation of why an orderly transition to Reformed CAFE could not be accomplished at the same time that the passenger automobile/light truck definitions are revised.

Second, NHTSA asserts that it reasonably decided to look to the purpose for which a vehicle is manufactured instead of consumers' use of a vehicle because it is a more objective way of differentiating between passenger and non-passenger automobiles. But this overlooks the fact that many light trucks today *are* manufactured primarily for transporting passengers, as NHTSA itself has acknowledged: "Many vehicles produced today, while smaller than many other passenger cars, qualify as light trucks because they have been *designed* so that their seats can be easily removed and their cargo carrying capacity significantly enhanced." 68 Fed. Reg. at 74,927 (emphasis added); . . .

One of the changes the NAS committee recommended to alleviate this problem was to "tighten" the definition of a light truck, a step the EPA has already taken for emissions standards purposes. *Id.* We agree with Petitioners that NHTSA's decision not to do the same was arbitrary and capricious, especially in light of EPCA's overarching goal of energy conservation. Thus, we remand to NHTSA to revise its regulatory definitions of passenger automobile and light truck or provide a valid reason for not doing so.

As noted earlier, after many years of little movement in the CAFE standards, significant change began in the late 2000s. First, in 2007, Congress enacted the Energy Independence and Security Act (EISA), which required NHTSA to increase combined passenger car and light truck fuel economy standards to at least 35 miles per gallon (mpg) by 2020, up from roughly 26.6 mpg for 2007. Along with requiring the higher passenger vehicle standards, EISA directed the U.S. Department of Transportation to study improvements in heavy-duty vehicles and, if feasible, issue standards for those vehicles. Also, that same year, the Supreme Court decided *Massachusetts v. EPA* (discussed in Chapter 1) and held that EPA has the authority to regulate vehicle GHG emissions under the Clean Air Act.

Adding to the activity at this time, recall that the State of California has special Congressional authorization under the Clean Air Act to set its own vehicle emission standards if it receives a preemption waiver from EPA. In 2004, the California Air Resources Board (CARB) enacted the first GHG limits on auto emissions and sought a preemption waiver from EPA. Auto manufacturers and others challenged the CARB rules on grounds that the rules were in effect fuel economy standards, that EPCA preempts states from setting fuel economy standards and delegates that authority exclusively to NHSTA, and that unlike the Clean Air Act, there is no preemption exemption for California under EPCA. Two separate courts held that EPCA did not preempt the CARB emission standards, and that such standards would be valid if the EPA granted a preemption waiver under the Clean Air Act. *See Central Valley Chrysler-Jeep, Inc. v. Goldstene,* 529 F. Supp. 2d 1151 (E.D. Cal. 2007); *Green Mountain Chrysler Plymouth Dodge Jeep v. Crombie,* 508 F. Supp. 2d 295 (D. Vt. 2007). But in 2008, the Bush administration denied California's preemption waiver request, making it the first time EPA had denied such a request from California. *See* 73 Fed. Reg. 12,156 (2008). In its denial, EPA acknowledged that climate change would have substantial effects on California but found that those effects were not sufficiently different from conditions in the nation as a whole to justify separate standards. At that time, thirteen states and the District of Columbia had adopted the California standards and other states had indicated that they would do the same.

California challenged the waiver denial in federal court but soon after, EPA, now under the Obama administration, agreed to reconsider the denial, and then granted the waiver in June 2009. Also in 2009, the Obama administration began to take its own actions regarding federal vehicle efficiency standards. In April 2010, it brokered an agreement between the auto manufacturers, California, federal agencies, and other interested parties which resulted in EPA and NHTSA promulgating a joint rulemaking to establish the first national GHG emission standards for new passenger cars, light-duty trucks, and medium-duty passenger vehicles. It also established new CAFE standards for vehicle model years 2012–2016. The rule required these vehicles to meet an estimated combined average emissions level of 250 grams of CO_2 per mile in model year 2016, equivalent to 35.5 mpg if the automotive industry were to meet this CO_2 level exclusively through fuel economy improvements. The result of this rule was that vehicles were required to meet the CAFE standards Congress mandated in EISA four years early. These new standards brought the federal standards in line with the California standards and resulted in significantly increased fuel economy and GHG emission reductions on a faster timetable. In 2011, EPA and NHTSA also issued GHG emission and fuel efficiency standards for medium- and heavy-duty engines and vehicles for model years 2014–2018. *See Regulations for Greenhouse Gas Emissions from Commercial Trucks and Buses*, U.S. EPA.

Then, in 2012, the parties reached agreement on another joint EPA and NHTSA rule for even more stringent standards for vehicle model years 2017–2025. The final standards were projected to result in an average industry fleet-wide level of 163 grams/mile of CO_2 in model year 2025, which is equivalent to 54.5 mpg if achieved exclusively through fuel economy improvements. For more information on the joint rulemaking as well as the proposed fuel savings and CO_2 emissions reductions associated with the rules, see *Regulations for Greenhouse Gas Emissions from Passenger Cars and Trucks,* U.S. EPA; BRENT D. YACOBUCCI, CONG. RSCH. SERV., AUTOMOBILE AND TRUCK FUEL ECONOMY (CAFE) AND GREENHOUSE GAS STANDARDS (Sept. 11, 2012).

The new standards showed results quickly. A 2013 EPA report showed that model year 2012 vehicles achieved an all-time high fuel economy of 23.6 miles per gallon (mpg), representing a 1.2 mpg increase over the previous year and making it the second largest annual increase in the last 30 years. Moreover, most automakers met the 2016 vehicle standards or significantly improved their performance. *See, e.g.,* JACK GILLIS ET AL., CONSUMER FEDERATION OF AMERICA, AUTOMAKERS ARE ON THE ROAD TO MEETING FUEL EFFICIENCY STANDARDS (Apr. 25, 2016); Camille von Kaenel, *American Cars on Track to Double Fuel Efficiency*, SCI. AM. (Apr. 26, 2016).

After the Trump administration took office, it repealed the Obama-era CAFE and vehicle emission standards and revoked California's preemption waiver for its Low Emission Vehicle (LEV) standards (which had been harmonized with the federal standards during the Obama administration) and its Zero Emission Vehicle (ZEV) program (which several other states had adopted and is discussed below in Section D). It replaced the Obama-era rules with new standards that reduced requirements for manufacturers to improve their fleetwide fuel economy standards from 5% per year through 2025 to only 1.4% per year through 2026. Those rules were immediately challenged in court. Around the same time, in 2019, California and several of the world's largest automakers entered into a voluntary agreement to improve fleetwide average fuel economy standards by 3.7% per year through 2026. *See, e.g.,* CONG. RSCH. SERV., VEHICLE FUEL ECONOMY AND GREENHOUSE GAS STANDARDS (Mar. 22, 2021); CONG. RSCH. SERV., VEHICLE FUEL ECONOMY AND GREENHOUSE GAS STANDARDS:

FREQUENTLY ASKED QUESTIONS (updated June 1, 2021); Brad Plumer & Nadja Popovich, *How U.S. Fuel Economy Standards Compare with the Rest of the World*, N.Y. TIMES (Apr. 3, 2018) (interactive graphs); 2020 EPA AUTOMOTIVE TRENDS REPORT (Jan. 2021).

As this book went to print, the Biden administration had proposed to reinstate the California preemption waiver and enact revised rules for yearly increases in fleetwide fuel economy and GHG emissions reductions that would reinstate, and in later years exceed, the standards from the Obama era. *See, e.g.,* NHTSA, Proposed Rule, Corporate Average Fuel Economy Standards for Model Years 2024–2026 Passenger Cars and Light Trucks, 86 Fed. Reg. 49602 (Sept. 3, 2021) (proposing to increase fuel efficiency 8% annually for MYs 2024–2026 and increase estimated fleetwide average by 12 mpg for MY 2026, relative to model year 2021); U.S. EPA, Proposed Rule, Revised 2023 and Later Model Year Light-Duty Vehicle Greenhouse Gas Emissions Standards, 86 Fed. Reg. 43726 (Aug. 10, 2021); U.S. EPA, California State Motor Vehicle Pollution Control Standards; Advanced Clean Car Program; Reconsideration of a Previous Withdrawal of a Waiver of Preemption; Opportunity for Public Hearing and Public Comment, 86 Fed. Reg. 22421 (Apr. 28, 2021); U.S. EPA, REVISED 2023 AND LATER MODEL YEAR LIGHT-DUTY VEHICLE GREENHOUSE GAS EMISSIONS STANDARDS: REGULATORY UPDATE (Aug. 2021); *Regulations for Greenhouse Gas Emissions from Passenger Cars and Trucks*, U.S. EPA.

The following chart shows the development of GHG emission standards for vehicles during the Obama era, along with the rise in CAFE standards over time.

MY2016–MY2025 Combined Passenger Car and Light Truck GHG and CAFE Standards

	2016	2017	2018	2019	2020	2021	2022	2023	2024	2025
GHG Standard (grams/mile)	250	243	232	222	213	199	190	180	171	163
GHG- Equivalent Fuel Economy (miles per gallon equivalent)	35.5	36.6	38.3	40.0	41.7	44.7	46.8	49.4	52.0	54.5
Fuel Economy (CAFE) Standard (miles per gallon)	34.1	35.4	36.5	37.7	38.9	41.0	43.0b	45.1	47.4	49.7

Source: U.S. Env't Prot. Agency and Nat'l Highway Traffic Safety Admin.

NOTES AND QUESTIONS

1.   CAFE mpg numbers and the "window sticker" mpg number you see on cars are often different because they are derived from different tests. When CAFE was first put in place, the two numbers were identical. But the laboratory tests used to compute CAFE standards do not consider the impact of high and low temperatures, use of air conditioning, and other real-world factors, which caused EPA to "downrate" the window sticker numbers first in 1985 and again in 2008. Thus, the 34.1 mpg target for 2016 was actually equal to 26 mpg on a window sticker. *See* Edmunds Car Reviews and Prices, FAQ: New Corporate Average Fuel Economy Standards (Sept. 9, 2013).

2.   Recall that the main point of contention in the *Center for Biological Diversity* case excerpted above was NHTSA's refusal to monetize the benefit of carbon emission reductions in its rulemaking setting vehicle emission standards. In 2010, a federal interagency working group was tasked with establishing values for the "social cost of carbon" (SCC) to estimate the climate benefits of federal agency rulemakings. As discussed in the *Zero Zone* case in Chapter 1, the SCC is an estimate of the economic damages associated with a small increase in CO_2 emissions, generally one metric ton, in a given year. The SCC dollar figure represents the benefit of CO_2 reduction or the value of damages avoided for reducing emissions. EPA and NHTSA used the SCC in setting the Obama-era fuel economy standards and it was used in numerous other rulemakings between 2010 and 2016, including rules governing industrial equipment efficiency, lighting standards, and air quality. *See* EPA FACT SHEET, THE SOCIAL COST OF CARBON (Dec. 2016). In 2017, the Trump administration directed federal agencies not to use SCC values in agency rulemakings and, ultimately, adjusted the SCC downward significantly (from approximately $51 per ton to $1 per ton) as part of its repeal of the Clean Power Plan. For more on the SCC and an explanation of how the two Presidential administrations determined the two different sets of SCC values, see VALUING CLIMATE DAMAGES: UPDATING ESTIMATION OF THE SOCIAL COST OF CARBON (The Nat'l Academies Press 2017); Annalee Armstrong, *Trump Administration Drops Social Cost of Carbon from $51 to $1*, S&P GLOBAL MARKET INTELLIGENCE (Oct. 23, 2017); U.S. EPA, Repeal of Carbon Pollution Emission Guidelines for Existing Stationary Sources: Electric Utility Generating Units, 82 Fed. Reg. 48035 (Oct. 16, 2017).

Nevertheless, during the Trump administration, states, including Colorado and Minnesota, continued to use the Obama administration SCC numbers (or something close to those numbers) in utility resource planning processes and other regulatory determinations. *See, e.g.*, Gavin Bade, *Minnesota Regulators Finalize Carbon Cost Rules for Utility Procurements*, UTIL. DIVE (Jan. 5, 2018); Herman K. Trabish, *Carbon Calculus: More States are Adding Carbon Costs to Utility Planning Guidelines*, UTIL. DIVE (Aug. 31, 2017). Not surprisingly, the Biden administration declared in 2021 that it would reinstate an interim SCC in federal rulemaking similar to that used by the Obama administration and determine a final number and discount rate by

2022. *See* Maxine Joselow, *Lawsuit Foreshadows Feud Over Biden's Social Cost of Carbon*, CLIMATEWIRE (Apr. 5, 2021).

3.   The United States, China, the EU, and Japan all use different approaches to measure and improve vehicle fuel economy. The U.S. CAFE standards, which focus on fleet averages, are discussed above. Many other countries, however, base allowable emissions on vehicle size rather than fleet averages. The EU, Japan, and China all set emission standards based on different vehicle weight classes and vehicles must comply with the emissions limits within its weight class. In South Korea, targets are based upon engine sizes. While Japan uses its own testing procedures, the EU and China use the New European Driving Cycle, and Korea uses the standards adopted by CAFE. Projected EU and Japanese standards for new passenger vehicles in 2030 are 81 and 71 miles per gallon, respectively, much higher than the U.S. target in 2026. Shruti Vaidyanathan, *Fuel Economy Rollback Sets the U.S. Further Behind the Leaders*, AM. COUNCIL FOR AN ENERGY-EFFICIENT ECON. (May 8, 2020). The figure below compares fuel efficiency standards in the United States, Europe, Japan, and several other countries. As you review the figure, what are the benefits and drawbacks of the United States having lower average fuel economy standards than other developed nations?

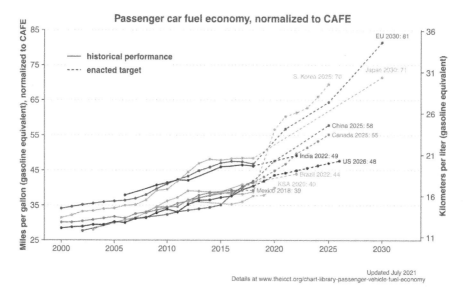

Source: The Int'l Council on Clean Transp. (last updated July 2021). For a discussion of different car testing standards, see https://theicct.org/chart-library-passenger-vehicle-fuel-economy.

4.   While the federal CAFE and GHG standards mean that today's U.S. vehicles are at near record low CO_2 emissions levels (356g/mi for 2019), fleetwide market shifts have offset these benefits. This is because passenger sedans and station wagons made up just 33% of U.S. car sales in 2019 (down from 80% market share in 1975), while SUVs, minivans, and pickup trucks were over 50% of U.S. vehicles sold that year. This trend towards bigger, more

powerful, and heavier vehicles decreases fuel savings. What should or could policy makers or regulators do to address this? *See* U.S. EPA, THE 2020 EPA AUTOMOTIVE TRENDS REPORT: GREENHOUSE GAS EMISSIONS, FUEL ECONOMY, AND TECHNOLOGY SINCE 1975, EXECUTIVE SUMMARY (Jan. 2021).

5.   The EPA's 2021 automotive trends report cited in the prior note explains that the EPA's GHG program for automobiles is an "averaging, banking, and trading (ABT) program." *Id.* at. ES-9. This means the program allows auto manufacturers to average their fleet-wide emissions, bank emissions reductions from early actions to be used later as credits towards compliance, and trade banked emissions credits with other manufacturers. For example, if a manufacturer's fleet average was lower than the standards, the difference between their fleet average and the standards would result in credits which could be banked (or traded). Compliance in future years could use banked credits or credits traded and bought from other manufacturers. According to the EPA, "[t]his provides manufacturers flexibility in meeting the standards while accounting for vehicle design cycles, introduction rates of new technologies and emission improvements, and evolving consumer preferences." *Id.* In 2019, only Tesla, Honda, and Subaru achieved compliance with the GHG standards by reducing emissions from their vehicle fleets. All other manufacturers relied on banked credits or traded (purchased) credits for compliance. *Id.* at ES-10–11. What are the benefits and drawbacks of different compliance strategies? How might such programs encourage early action or technological improvements in the industry? Given the political cycle shifts, what potential do you see for gaming the compliance system? How could you create a robust program to ensure overall emissions reductions?

6.   In 2015, researchers uncovered a "defeat device" which overrode emissions controls in the Volkswagen (VW) and Audi "clean" diesel cars. The device worked to limit emissions during EPA's dynamometer tests and meet compliance standards. However, in standard driving mode (which provides more power) the engine control system overrode the NO_x sensor and breached emissions standards. This widespread cheating resulted in a $14.7 billion settlement with EPA and the state of California. Car owners could sell their cars back to VW for between $12,500 and $44,000; if an owner decided to keep their car, they received between $5,100 and $10,000 for diminished value. Bosch, which developed the engine control system software, also settled for $327 million. *See* Clifford Atiyeh, *Everything You Need to Know about the VW Diesel-Emissions Scandal,* CAR AND DRIVER (May 11, 2017). As part of the settlement, VW is also spending $2 billion on building electric vehicle charging infrastructure through its *Electrify America* subsidiary. *See, e.g., Volkswagen Clean Air Act Civil Settlement,* U.S. EPA; Fred Lambert, *VW to Build a "Nationwide 150 kW+ Fast Charging Network" for Electric Vehicles as Part of Dieselgate Settlement,* ELECTREK (April 14, 2017).

2. REGULATION OF FUEL ADDITIVES

The CAFE standards and EPA regulation of GHG emissions from automobiles described above are examples of technology-forcing regulations imposed on vehicles to reduce fuel use and emissions. Congress and EPA have also imposed requirements on the fuels themselves to achieve similar goals. Some additives, like lead to prevent engine "knocking" or its replacement, methyl tertiary-butyl ether (MTBE), an oxygenate which boosted octane levels, were required for performance or by statute and then later removed when found to be harmful to human health and the environment.

For instance, in the 1990 Clean Air Act Amendments, Congress established the reformulated gasoline (RFG) program in certain areas, generally larger cities with high ozone levels, to reduce auto emissions of ozone forming compounds and toxic pollutants by increasing the oxygen content of gasoline. Congress required that RFG be at least two percent oxygen by weight, not more than one percent benzene by volume, and contain no heavy metals. At the time, the primary oxygenates added to RFG to make it at least two percent oxygen by weight were ethanol and MTBE. In the Energy Policy Act of 2005, Congress removed the oxygenate requirement for RFG and at the same time instituted a renewable fuel standard (discussed in detail in later in this chapter) allowing ethanol to replace MTBE as the dominant oxygenate in U.S. gasoline. For more information on the history of lead in gasoline, see F.G. Hank Hilton & Arik Levinson, *Factoring the Environmental Kuznets Curve: Evidence From Automotive Lead Emissions*, 35 J. ENV'T ECON. & MGMT. 126 (1998). For information on MTBE, see Pamela M. Franklin et al., *Clearing the Air: Using Scientific Information to Regulate Reformulated Fuels*, 34 ENV'T SCI. & TECH. 3857 (2000). *See also MTBE in Fuels*, U.S. EPA; *Reformulated Gasoline*, U.S. EPA.

The following case discusses the EPA's role in regulating lead in gasoline and the public health and environmental impacts of that action. As you read the case, consider the EPA's statutory mandate, the use of scientific evidence, and the court's role in setting and applying the burden of proof.

ETHYL CORP. V. ENVIRONMENTAL PROTECTION AGENCY
541 F.2d 1 (D.C. Cir. 1976)

J. SKELLY WRIGHT, CIRCUIT JUDGE.

Man's ability to alter his environment has developed far more rapidly than his ability to foresee with certainty the effects of his alterations. It is only recently that we have begun to appreciate the danger posed by unregulated modification of the world around us, and have created watchdog agencies whose task it is to warn us, and protect us, when technological "advances" present dangers unappreciated or unrevealed by their supporters. Such agencies, unequipped with crystal balls and unable to read the future, are nonetheless charged with evaluating the effects of unprecedented environmental modifications, often made on a massive scale. Necessarily, they must deal with predictions and uncertainty, with developing evidence, with conflicting evidence, and, sometimes, with little or no evidence at all. Today we address the scope of the power delegated one such watchdog, the Environmental Protection Agency (EPA). We must determine the certainty required by the Clean Air Act before EPA may act to protect the health of our populace from the lead particulate emissions of automobiles.

Section 211(c)(1)(A) of the Clean Air Act authorizes the Administrator of EPA to regulate gasoline additives whose emission products "will endanger the public health or welfare * * *." 42 U.S.C. s 1857f–6c(c)(1)(A). Acting pursuant to that power, the Administrator, after notice and comment, determined that the automotive emissions caused by leaded gasoline present "a significant risk of harm" to the public health. Accordingly, he promulgated regulations that reduce, in step-wise fashion, the lead content of leaded gasoline. We must decide whether the Administrator properly interpreted the meaning of Section 211(c)(1)(A) and the scope of his power thereunder, and, if so, whether the evidence adduced at the rule-making proceeding supports his final determination. Finding in favor of the Administrator on both grounds, and on all other grounds raised by petitioners, we affirm his determination.

I. THE FACTS, THE STATUTE, THE PROCEEDINGS, AND THE REGULATIONS

Hard on the introduction of the first gasoline-powered automobiles came the discovery that lead "antiknock" compounds, when added to gasoline, dramatically increase the fuel's octane rating. Increased octane allows for higher compression engines, which operate with greater efficiency. Since 1923 antiknocks have been regularly added to gasoline, and a large industry has developed to supply those compounds. Today, approximately 90% of motor gasoline manufactured in the United States contains lead additives, even though most 1975 and 1976 model automobiles are equipped with catalytic converters, which require lead-free gasoline. From the beginning, however, scientists have questioned whether the addition of lead to gasoline, and its consequent diffusion into the atmosphere from the automobile emission, poses a danger to the public health. As use of automobiles, and emission of lead particulates, has accelerated in the last quarter century, this concern has mounted. The reasons for concern are obvious (and essentially undisputed by petitioners): (1) lead in high concentrations in the body is toxic; (2) lead can be absorbed into the body from the ambient air; and (3) lead particulate emissions from gasoline engines account for approximately 90 percent of the lead in our air. Despite these apparent reasons for concern, hard proof of any danger caused by lead automotive emissions has been hard to come by. Part of the reason for this lies in the multiple sources of human exposure to lead. . . .

Human body lead comes from three major sources. In most people, the largest source is the diet. EPA estimates daily dietary lead intake for adults to average 200–300 µg per day, with a range of 100–500 µg a day. Absorption of dietary lead into the bloodstream is estimated at about 10 percent, although in children absorption may be as high as 50 percent. . . .

A second major source of the body's lead burden, at least among urban children, is regarded as controllable, although effective control may be both difficult and expensive to achieve. Ingestion of lead paint by children with pica (the abnormal ingestion of non-food substances, a relatively common trait in pre-school children, particular ages 1–3) is generally regarded as "the principal environmental source in cases of severe acute lead poisoning in young children.". . . .

The last remaining major source of lead exposure for humans is the ambient air. This source is easily the most controllable, since approximately 90 percent of lead in the air comes from automobile emissions, and can be simply eliminated by removing lead from gasoline. . . . Once the lead is in the body, however, its source becomes irrelevant; all lead in the bloodstream, from whatever source, is essentially fungible. Thus so long as there are multiple sources of lead exposure it is virtually impossible to isolate one source and determine its particular effect on the body. The effect of any one source is meaningful only in cumulative terms.

The multiple sources of human exposure to lead explain in part why it has been difficult to pinpoint automobile lead emissions as a danger to public health. Obviously, any danger is caused only by the additive effect of lead emissions on the other, largely uncontrollable, sources of lead. For years the lead antiknock industry has refused to accept the developing evidence that lead emissions contribute significantly to the total human lead body burden. In the Clean Air Act Amendments of 1970, however, Congress finally set up a legal mechanism by which that evidence could be weighed in a more objective tribunal. It gave the newly-created EPA authority to control or prohibit the sale or manufacture of any fuel additive whose emission products "will endanger the public health or welfare * * *." It is beyond question that the fuel additive Congress had in mind was lead.

Given this mandate, EPA published on January 31, 1971 advance notice of proposed rule-making. The Administrator announced he was considering possible controls on lead additives in gasolines, both because of their possible danger to health and because of their incompatibility with the newly-developed catalytic converter emission control system. Proposed regulations were issued a year later, February 23, 1972, supported by a document Health Hazards of Lead prepared by the EPA scientific staff . . . .

Under the final regulations, lead in all gasoline would be reduced over a five-year period to an average of 0.5 grams per gallon.

Petitioners, various manufacturers of lead additives and refiners of gasoline, appealed the promulgation of low-lead regulations to this court under Section 307 of the Clean Air Act, 42 U.S.C. s 1857h–5. . . .

Their primary claims . . . are that the Administrator misinterpreted the statutory standard of "will endanger" and that his application of that standard is without support in the evidence and arbitrary and capricious.

II. THE STATUTORY REQUIREMENTS

Under Section 211(c)(1)(A) the Administrator may, on the basis of all the information available to him, promulgate regulations that

> control or prohibit the manufacture, introduction into commerce, offering for sale, or sale of any fuel or fuel additive for use in a motor vehicle or motor vehicle engine (A) if any emission products of such fuel or fuel additive will endanger the public health or welfare * * *.

42 U.S.C. s 1857f–6c(c)(1)(A). The Administrator cannot act under Section 211(c)(1)(A), however, until after "consideration of all relevant medical and scientific evidence available to him, including consideration of other technologically or economically feasible means of achieving emission standards under (Section 202)." Section 211(c)(2)(A), 42 U.S.C. s 1857f–6c(c)(2)(A). Section 202 of the Act, 42 U.S.C. s 1857f–1, allows the Administrator to set standards for emission of pollutants from automobiles (as opposed to standards for the composition of the gasoline that produces the emissions), and is thus the preferred although not the mandatory alternative under the statutory scheme, presumably because it minimizes Agency interference with manufacturer prerogatives.

The Administrator is also required, before prohibiting a fuel or fuel additive under Section 211(c)(1)(A), to find, and publish the finding, that in his judgment any fuel or fuel additive likely to replace the prohibited one will not "endanger the public health or welfare to the same or greater degree * * *." Section 211(c)(2)(C), 42 U.S.C. s 1857f–6c(c)(2)(C). It is significant that this is the only conclusion the Administrator is expressly required to "find" before regulating a fuel or fuel additive for health reasons.

A. The Threshold Determination

In making his threshold determination that lead particulate emissions from motor vehicles "will endanger the public health or welfare," the Administrator provided his interpretation of the statutory language by couching his conclusion in these words: such emissions "present a significant risk of harm to the health of urban populations, particularly to the health of city children." By way of further interpretation, he added that it was his view that the statutory language * * * does not require a determination that automobile emissions alone create the endangerment on which controls may be based. Rather, the Administrator believes that in providing this authority, the Congress was aware that the public's exposure to harmful substances results from a number of sources which may have varying degrees of susceptibility to control.

Id. It is petitioners' first claim of error that the Administrator has erroneously interpreted Section 211(c)(1)(A) by not sufficiently appreciating the rigor demanded by Congress in establishing the "will endanger" standard. Therefore, petitioners argue, the Administrator's action is "short of statutory right," in violation of Section 10(e)(2)(C) of the Administrative Procedure Act (APA), 5 U.S.C. s 706(2)(C) (1970).

Petitioners argue that the "will endanger" standard requires a high quantum of factual proof, proof of actual harm rather than of a "significant risk of harm." . . . . It is our view that the Administrator's interpretation of the standard is the correct one.

. . . . Simply as a matter of plain meaning, we have difficulty crediting petitioners' reading of the "will endanger" standard. The meaning of "endanger" is not disputed. Case law and dictionary definition agree that endanger means something less than actual harm. When one is endangered, harm is threatened; no actual injury need ever occur. . . . A statute allowing for regulation in the face of danger is, necessarily, a precautionary statute. Regulatory action may be taken before the threatened harm occurs; indeed, the very existence of such precautionary legislation would seem to demand that regulatory action precede, and, optimally, prevent, the perceived threat. As should be apparent, the "will endanger" language of Section 211(c)(1)(A) makes it such a precautionary statute.

The Administrator read it as such, interpreting "will endanger" to mean "presents a significant risk of harm." We agree with the Administrator's interpretation. This conclusion is reached not only by reference to the plain meaning of the statute, but by juxtaposition of Section 211(c)(1)(A) with other sections of the Clean Air Act and by analysis of pertinent precedent. . . .

. . . . Petitioners argue that Section 211 requires the Administrator to make a "threshold factual determination" that automobile emissions "will endanger" the public health, and dispute EPA's claim that the Administrator may make "an essentially legislative policy judgment, rather than a factual determination, concerning the relative risks of underprotection as compared to overprotection." We must reject petitioners' argument, since the power to assess risks, without relying solely on facts, flows inexorably from the nature of the "will [en]danger" standard. We have already found that Section 211 allows the Administrator to regulate fuel content when he finds that emissions cause a significant risk of harm to the public health. Yet, how can the Administrator determine that a risk is a significant risk if he cannot assess risks? And how can he assess risks if he cannot make policy judgments? Surely reliance on "facts" as contemplated by petitioners will provide little guidance. However, sole reliance on facts was not demanded by Congress. . . .

Questions involving the environment are particularly prone to uncertainty. Technological man has altered his world in ways never before experienced or anticipated. The health effects of such alterations are often unknown, sometimes unknowable. While a concerned Congress has passed legislation providing for protection of the public health against gross environmental modifications, the regulators entrusted with the enforcement of such laws have not thereby been endowed with a prescience that removes all doubt from their decisionmaking. Rather, speculation, conflicts in evidence, and theoretical extrapolation typify their every action. How else can they act, given a mandate to protect the public health but only a slight or nonexistent data base upon which to draw? Never before have massive quantities of asbestiform tailings been spewed into the water we drink. Never before have our industrial workers been occupationally exposed to vinyl chloride or to asbestos dust. Never before has the food we eat been permeated with DDT or the pesticides aldrin and dieldrin. And never before have hundreds of thousands of tons of lead emissions been disgorged annually into the air we breathe. Sometimes, of course, relatively certain proof of danger or harm from such modifications can be readily found. But, more commonly, "reasonable medical concerns" and theory long precede certainty. Yet the statutes and common-sense demand regulatory action to prevent harm, even if the regulator is less than certain that harm is otherwise inevitable.

Undoubtedly, certainty is the scientific ideal to the extent that even science can be certain of its truth. But certainty in the complexities of environmental medicine may be achievable only after the fact, when scientists have the opportunity for leisurely and isolated scrutiny of an entire mechanism. Awaiting certainty will often allow for only reactive, not preventive, regulation. Petitioners suggest that anything less than certainty, that any speculation, is irresponsible. But when statutes seek to avoid environmental catastrophe, can preventive, albeit uncertain, decisions legitimately be so labeled?

The problems faced by EPA in deciding whether lead automotive emissions pose a threat to the public health highlight the limitations of awaiting certainty. First, lead concentrations are, even to date, essentially low-level, so that the feared adverse effects would not materialize until after a lifetime of exposure. Contrary to petitioners' suggestion, however, we have not yet suffered a lifetime of exposure to lead emissions. At best, emissions at present levels have been with us for no more than 15–20 years. Second, lead exposure from the ambient air is pervasive, so that valid control groups cannot be found against which the effects of lead on our population can be measured. Third, the sources of human exposure to lead are multiple, so that it is difficult to isolate the effect of automobile emissions. Lastly, significant exposure to lead is toxic, so that considerations of decency and morality limit the flexibility of experiments on humans that would otherwise accelerate lead exposure from years to months, and measure those results . . . .

While we must consider petitioners' arguments carefully, the necessary existence of limitations and inconsistencies in the data remind us to observe carefully our limited appellate function. It does not matter whether or not we agree with the Administrator's determination. Nor does it matter whether the evidence might support a conclusion contrary to that reached by the Administrator. All that is of concern to us is that there be a rational basis in the evidence for the conclusion reached. We cannot say there is not. The bulk of the evidence cited supports the Administrator. The Administrator treated all the evidence in a consistent and rational manner. This treatment disposed of most of the studies relied upon by petitioners, leaving the plain conclusion that lead emissions form a significant part of the human body burden. Particularly in light of the precautionary nature of the "will endanger" standard, we cannot find the Administrator's conclusion to be arbitrary or capricious. Accordingly, we must uphold his determination. . . .

C. Summary of the Evidence

From a vast mass of evidence the Administrator has concluded that the emission products of lead additives will endanger the public health. He has handled an extraordinarily complicated problem with great care and candor. The evidence did not necessarily always point in one direction and frequently, until EPA authorized research, there was no evidence at all. . . . From the totality of the evidence the Administrator concluded that regulation under Section 211(c)(1)(A) was warranted.

In tracking his path through the evidence we, in our appellate role, have also considered separately each study and the objections petitioners make thereto. In no case have we found the Administrator's use of the evidence to be arbitrary or capricious. Having rejected the individual objections, we also reject the overall claim of error. . . . Accordingly, we affirm his determination that lead emissions "present a significant risk of harm to the health of urban populations, particularly to the health of city children."

NOTES AND QUESTIONS

1.   Deciding to remove lead from gasoline in 1973, the issue in the *Ethyl Corp.* case, was a decision made at the end of a long political and scientific process focused on crafting health-based regulation. Key government actors providing the scientific basis and funding for the regulation were the National Institutes of Health, Centers for Disease Control (CDC), and EPA. While in hindsight, the decision is touted as one of the major environmental health successes of the 20th century, it almost did not happen but for the efforts of scientists and government officials. Over 200,000 tons of lead were emitted each year in the early 1970s and collectively the oil and lead industries had blocked efforts to regulate lead for over five decades. Industry misinformation campaigns casting doubt on scientific findings and health impacts of lead were widespread. Because the industry was the primary supporter of scientific research studying the health impacts of lead, it also shaped what was studied and ensured that industry-favorable communication dominated the public discourse. The creation of EPA, National Institutes of Environmental and Health Sciences, and expanding the mission of the CDC in the early 1970s, coupled with enabling legislation like the Clean Air Act, served to provide scientific infrastructure and a regulatory rationale to re-address these important issues.

The lead standard has been a success, with the CDC estimating that average blood lead levels in adults and children dropped over 80% between the late 1970s and the late 1990s due to the EPA's phase out of lead in gasoline. *See Blood Lead Levels Keep Dropping; New Guidelines Recommended for Those Most Vulnerable*, CDC NEWSROOM (Feb. 1997). How did the interplay between authorizing legislation and governmental scientific expertise in health and environmental impacts lead to the development of these standards? What lessons exist for other energy, health, and environmental problems? *See* Kenneth Bridbord & David Hanson, *A Personal Perspective on the Initial Federal Health-Based Regulation to Remove Lead from Gasoline*, 117 ENV'T HEALTH PERSPECTIVES 1195 (Aug. 2009). Despite the success associated with removing lead from gasoline, millions of U.S. children remain at risk for lead impairment due to exposure to lead-based paint or lead paint dust in older housing stock, in addition to exposures from lead leached from improperly maintained water pipes. *See, e.g., National Biomonitoring Program: Lead*, CDC (last updated July 12, 2013); *A Community Voice v. EPA*, 997 F.3d 983 (9th Cir. 2021) (holding EPA acted arbitrarily and capriciously in failing to sufficiently protect children from harm associated with lead based paint and lead based dust under Toxic Substances Control Act and Residential Lead-Based Paint Hazard Reduction Act); Agya K. Aning, *For the Second Time in Four Years, the Ninth Circuit Has Ordered the EPA to Set New Lead Paint and Dust Standards*, INSIDE CLIMATE NEWS (May 25, 2021) (discussing Ninth Circuit case and providing graph showing changes in lead levels in children since 1980). Why might it be more difficult for regulators to address lead exposure from these sources, as opposed to lead exposure from auto emissions?

2.   The removal of lead from gasoline did not end debates over the benefits and harms of various fuel additives. As noted in the introduction to this section,

MTBE was commonly used as an oxygenate in gasoline, until it was replaced by ethanol. Unfortunately, its use resulted in widespread water contamination when it leaked from storage tanks. *See, e.g.,* Thomas O. McGarity, *MTBE: A Precautionary Tale,* 29 HARV. ENV'T L. REV. 281, 286 (2004) (citing a 1999 EPA report indicating that "between 5 and 10% of community drinking water supplies in high MTBE-use areas contained detectable amounts of MTBE"). California, New York, and other states responded by banning the use of MTBE. States, local governments, and water suppliers ultimately sued gasoline manufacturers to recover damages arising from water pollution under various common law and statutory theories, including nuisance, negligence, civil conspiracy, and strict liability. These cases were consolidated in the U.S. District Court for the Southern District of New York for resolution of common liability issues. Although many of the gasoline manufacturers settled the claims against them, others continued to defend the suits. In 2013, a jury found ExxonMobil liable to the state of New Hampshire for $236 million in water supply damages, a verdict that was upheld on appeal. David Brooks, *N.H. To Get $235 Million-plus To Fight Gasoline Additive MTBE, Other Pollutants,* CONCORD MONITOR (May 7, 2016). For a discussion of some of the legal issues and claims in the consolidated cases, see *In re Methyl Tertiary Butyl Ether (MTBE) Products Liability Litigation,* 379 F. Supp. 2d 348 (S.D.N.Y. 2005).

D. ALTERNATIVE FUELS: ETHANOL AND ELECTRICITY

Two substitutes for using gasoline to power the transportation sector are alternative liquid fuels and electricity. As you read the materials in this section, consider the interest groups that benefit (and do not benefit) from each of these technologies, the role of federal and state policymakers in promoting them, and the environmental externalities (positive and negative) associated with their implementation.

1. ETHANOL AND THE RENEWABLE FUEL STANDARD

Two prevailing technologies for alternative liquid fuels include the transformation of coal into a liquid and the use of biofuels. "Feedstocks for biofuels include a variety of materials, such as corn, grain, grasses, forest residue, crop residue, waste biomass (including yard wastes, municipal solid waste, and construction and demolition debris), willow, soy, sugarcane, soybean oil, vegetable oil, and recycled grease." James W. Van Nostrand & Anne Marie Hirschberger, *Biofuels* in MICHAEL B. GERRARD, THE LAW OF CLEAN ENERGY 445, 446 (2011).

The United States has promoted and supported biofuels for nearly four decades. President Bush, in his 2007 State of the Union message, proposed that biofuels should replace 20% of U.S. gasoline consumption by 2017. Generous federal tax incentives, known as the Volumetric Ethanol Excise Tax Credit (VEETC), expired in 2012, but along with other subsidies, resulted in over $7 billion in tax credits to the ethanol industry in 2011 alone. *See* Randy Schnepf & Brent D. Yacobucci, Cong. Rsch. Serv., Renewable Fuel Standard (RFS): Overview and Issues (2013); Molly F. Sherlock & Jeffrey M. Stupak, Cong. Rsch. Serv., Energy Tax Incentives: Measuring Value Across Different Types of Energy Resources (2015). Additionally, the Department of Agriculture has enacted rules to help finance conversion of biomass to energy and to do so at a commercial scale. Today, every gallon of gasoline used in automobiles in the United States contains approximately 10% ethanol. For a summary of U.S. biofuels policies and implementation, see Jay Kesan et al., *An Empirical Study of the Impact of Renewable Fuel Standards (RFS) on the Production of Fuel Ethanol in the U.S.*, 2017 Utah L. Rev. 159 (2017). In addition to converting corn and other starches to ethanol, other technologies exist for creating liquid fuels, including biodiesel fuel derived from yeast, algae, and bacteria.

Government support for biofuels has the direct consequence of subsidizing corn production. Quite simply, farmers have found it more lucrative to sell corn to the biofuels market because of government financial support than to change their crop production or devote all their corn to either feedstuffs or to be sold on the retail market. One result of moving corn into the biofuels market rather than into the retail food market has been to raise the price of corn worldwide and to contribute to food shortages. Another consequence of shifting corn from food production to biofuel production is increased GHG emissions caused by the erosion of topsoil and the loss of carbon sinks when land is cleared to produce biofuels. For a discussion of the adverse environmental impacts associated with corn ethanol and the ways that Congress and EPA can address this issue through increased mandates for cellulosic ethanol and advanced biofuels, see Melissa Powers, *King Corn: Will the Renewable Fuel Standard Eventually End Corn Ethanol's Reign?*, 11 Vt. J. Env't L. 667, 669–70, 683–88 (2010).

In this section, we concentrate specifically on the federal Renewable Fuel Standard (RFS), which Congress enacted in 2005 and amended in 2007. The RFS mandates that oil producers blend a specified number of gallons of renewable fuels with gasoline and diesel fuel each year to facilitate its use as transportation energy. The RFS, like virtually all the energy policies we discuss in this book, has its proponents and opponents. These include (1) oil producers who must comply with the blending mandate; (2) auto companies and other engine manufacturers concerned about how ethanol will impact certain engines; (3) the food industry, which now faces increased competition for the nation's corn supply from the fuel industry, resulting in higher corn prices and food prices; (4) environmental groups that may support the development of advanced biofuels and cellulosic ethanol but oppose additional support for corn ethanol; (5)

ethanol producers; and (6) farmers and politicians from corn producing states. For a discussion of the actors involved in the RFS program and their interests, see Timothy A. Slating & Jay P. Kesan, *The Renewable Fuel Standard 3.0?: Moving Forward with the Federal Biofuel Mandate*, 20 N.Y.U. ENV'T L.J. 374 (2014). As you read the remainder of this section, consider the incentives of each of these groups, the arguments they make for and against the RFS, and the impacts of the RFS on energy and environmental protection goals.

KELSI BRACMORT, THE RENEWABLE FUEL STANDARD (RFS): AN OVERVIEW

Cong. Rsch. Serv. (Jan. 24, 2018)

The Statute

The RFS was established by the Energy Policy Act of 2005 and expanded in 2007 by the Energy Independence and Security Act (EISA). The RFS mandate requires that transportation fuel sold or introduced into commerce in the United States contain an increasing volume of a predetermined suite of renewable fuels. The statute required 4.0 billion gallons of renewable fuel in 2006, ascending to 36.0 billion gallons required in 2022, with EPA determining the volume amounts after 2022 in future rulemakings. The statute centers on four renewable fuel categories—conventional biofuel, advanced biofuel, cellulosic biofuel, and biomass-based diesel—each with its own target volume.

The total renewable fuel requirement for the RFS is met with the combination of fuels from two renewable fuel categories: conventional biofuel and advanced biofuel. Further, the requirement for advanced biofuel, in general, can be met with the combination of three types of advanced biofuel: cellulosic biofuel, biomass-based diesel, and other advanced biofuels. To date, the total annual volumes required have been met mostly with conventional biofuel (e.g., cornstarch ethanol). Beginning in 2015, the mandate caps the conventional biofuel volume amounts while increasing the requirement of advanced biofuels. For instance, the statutory RFS total advanced biofuel requirement increases over time from less than 7% of the RFS in 2010 to 58% of the RFS in 2022.

A key part of the statutory definition of each fuel category is whether the fuel achieves certain greenhouse gas (GHG) reductions relative to gasoline and diesel fuel. Each fuel is assigned a lifecycle GHG emission threshold (in proportion to baseline lifecycle GHG emissions for gasoline and diesel). For example, a fuel must achieve at least a 50% GHG reduction to be considered an *advanced biofuel*, at least a 60% reduction to be considered a *cellulosic biofuel*, and at least a 50% reduction to be considered *biomass-based diesel*. Similarly, biofuel from new facilities—those built after enactment of the 2007 law—must achieve at least a 20% GHG reduction to qualify as a conventional renewable fuel.

Statutory Compliance

The EPA regulates compliance with the RFS using a tradable credit system. Obligated parties submit credits—called renewable identification numbers (RINs)—to EPA that equal the number of gallons in their annual obligation. This annual obligation, referred to as the renewable volume obligation (RVO), is the obligated party's total gasoline and diesel sales multiplied by the annual renewable fuel percentage standards announced by EPA. RINs are valid for use in the year they are generated and the following year. Obligated parties may carry a deficit from one year to the next but, in the year following the deficit, the obligated party must meet compliance for that year's renewable fuel volume requirement and purchase or generate enough credits to satisfy the deficit from the previous year. RINs may be used by the party that generates them or they may be traded with other parties. The EPA Moderated Transaction System (EMTS) is used to register RIN transactions.

Different biofuels are not treated equally within the RFS, meaning that some biofuels can be used to meet the annual standard for multiple RFS categories. The categories are nested within each other, such that some fuels qualify for multiple categories (e.g., cellulosic ethanol), while others (mainly cornstarch ethanol) may only be used to meet the overall RFS but not the advanced category or its nested subcategories. For example, a gallon of cellulosic biofuel may be used to meet the cellulosic biofuel mandate, the advanced biofuel mandate, and the total renewable fuel, possibly making it a more highly valued fuel. . . .

RFS Implementation Issues

Implementation of the RFS has been complex, and compliance with some of its parts has been challenging, according to some stakeholders. This section briefly explains some of the general issues and challenges with implementing the RFS.

Administering Agency

EPA administers the RFS. This includes evaluating renewable fuel pathways eligible for the RFS. In addition, EPA is required to evaluate the ability of the biofuel industry to produce enough fuel to meet the annual volume standard, release an annual volume standard based on its research findings, and ensure that annual compliance by obligated parties is met. All of the above must be completed annually, taking into consideration comments from other government agencies, the public, and court decisions. These responsibilities could be viewed as a significant addition to EPA's regulatory workload, and have required EPA to develop new capabilities to carry them out.

For several years following the 2010 issuance of the amended RFS final rule, EPA had difficulty projecting certain volume requirements (e.g., cellulosic biofuels). One of the concerns some have raised is the accuracy of EPA's projections. Based on these projections, EPA has used its waiver authority to set annual volume requirements for cellulosic, total, advanced biofuel, and total renewable fuel different from what was stated in the statute. Legal challenges have been brought against the EPA regarding some of these annual fuel volume projections. . . .

Cellulosic Biofuel Production

By statute, cellulosic biofuel is targeted to comprise some 44% of the total renewable fuel mandate in 2022. However, the annual cellulosic biofuel production volume established by Congress is not being met. Actual cellulosic biofuel production volumes (e.g., cellulosic ethanol) are below the expectations from when the law was passed. . . . This shortfall is due to several factors, including lack of private investment, technology setbacks, and uneven support from the federal government. These factors, coupled with the fact that annual volumes in the statute were established when market conditions for raising investment capital for new biofuel technologies were more favorable, may indicate unrealistic targets for some advanced biofuels for the near future. These production limitations have raised questions about whether the statutory cellulosic biofuel volumes are attainable.

Blend Wall

The "blend wall"—the upper limit to the total amount of ethanol that can be blended into U.S. gasoline and still maintain automobile performance and comply with the Clean Air Act—has been viewed by many to be in direct conflict with the biofuel volumes mandated in the RFS. Thus far, the largest volume being met under the RFS is for the non-advanced (conventional) biofuel segment of the mandate, and this has been met mainly with cornstarch ethanol blended into gasoline. Due to a variety of factors, ethanol content in gasoline is generally limited to 10% (E10). With a relatively fixed supply of gasoline, the amount of ethanol that can be supplied this way is also limited. If the ethanol content of gasoline for the majority of vehicles remains at 10%, and given current fuel consumption rates, the conventional biofuels portion of the RFS abuts the line of just slightly requiring more ethanol than can technically be blended into gasoline. . . .

Some recent developments could alleviate blend wall concerns in the near term. One option suggested by some could be to blend higher levels of ethanol into conventional gasoline. In 2010 EPA granted a Clean Air Act waiver that allows gasoline to contain up to 15% ethanol for use in model year 2001 and newer light-duty motor vehicles. However, infrastructure and automobile warranty concerns have precluded widespread offering and purchase of E15, gasoline blended with 10.5% to 15% ethanol. Widespread use of E15 could potentially postpone hitting the blend wall for a few years.

Another option to address the blend wall would be an aggressive push for the use of ethanol in flexible-fuel vehicles capable of using E85, a gasoline-ethanol blend containing 51% to 83% ethanol. There are infrastructure concerns with the use of E85. For example, the number of E85 fueling stations is limited. To help address these infrastructure issues, the U.S. Department of Agriculture (USDA) announced $100 million in matching grants in 2015 under its Biofuel Infrastructure Partnership. The grants may be used for blender pumps, dedicated E15 or E85 pumps, and new storage tanks and related equipment associated with new facilities or additional capacity. . . .

Congressional Issues

The RFS was established at a time when Congress foresaw the need to diversify the country's energy portfolio, strengthen the economy of rural communities by encouraging certain agricultural commodities that contribute to biofuel production, bolster U.S. standing in an emerging segment of the energy technology market, and protect the environment, among other objectives. The RFS was expanded more than 10 years ago. There are indications of which components of the RFS have progressed steadily toward meeting congressional intentions and which components have not.

The RFS is a policy with an ambitious agenda. Policy questions surrounding future consideration of the RFS might include

- What should be the purposes of the RFS?

- Is the RFS properly designed to achieve those purposes?

- What happens when, and if, the RFS achieves its purposes?

At the outset, some would argue that the first question may seem straightforward; the RFS exists to introduce more biofuels into the transportation fuel market to achieve a number of transportation fuel supply and environmental objectives. However, it could be argued that the RFS exists to find another market for biomass feedstocks, or to promote the economy of rural America (e.g., the construction of biofuel facilities that create jobs). Moreover, to the extent the RFS was designed to reduce U.S. dependence on foreign oil, and to the extent that hydraulic fracturing and the growth of unconventional oil and gas production have contributed to achieving that objective, is the RFS still needed for energy security purposes? Likewise, the environmental impact of the RFS could be challenged, as the advanced biofuel component of the RFS—set to yield greater greenhouse gas emission reduction benefits—has missed the statutory targets by a large margin.

In examining whether the RFS is well designed to realize its purposes, some have inquired about the challenges in achieving the ambitious RFS targets, given concern about the slow development of some advanced biofuels. Additionally, past delays in announcing final annual standards by EPA have led to significant uncertainty for biofuel producers, feedstock growers, and refiners. Whether the RFS should be eliminated, amended to address the current challenges in the program, or maintained in its current form is an ongoing question for Congress. A related question is whether the current provisions for EPA to waive various portions of the RFS mandates, as the agency did for 2017, and to "reset" the RFS are sufficient to address the current supply challenges, or whether the use of these waivers runs counter to the goals of the program.

The third question relates to interest by some members of Congress in the elimination of the conventional biofuel (e.g., cornstarch ethanol) portion of the mandate. If a segment of the biofuels industry has consistently reached the annual mandate set by Congress, is the mandate still necessary? . . .

NOTES AND QUESTIONS

1.   The Bracmort excerpt raises three policy questions at the end of the excerpt. How would you answer them?

2.   The Bracmort excerpt describes how EISA requires EPA to conduct a "life cycle analysis" of the GHG emissions associated with the use of various types of biofuels. This requirement was added to account for the fact that even though biofuels may have reduced GHG emissions as compared to gasoline during the engine combustion stage, there are additional GHG emissions associated with the land use changes needed to grow more corn; the corn production process; the conversion of corn to ethanol, which requires the generation of electricity; and the transportation of ethanol to blending facilities. Some studies show that once these life cycle GHG emissions are considered, the GHG emissions of certain types of biofuels exceed that of gasoline. For a discussion of these studies, see, e.g., Alexandra B. Klass & Andrew Heiring, *Life Cycle Emissions and Transportation Energy*, 82 BROOKLYN L. REV. 485 (2017); Jason Hill et al., *Climate Consequences of Low-Carbon Fuels: The United States Renewable Fuel Standard*, 97 ENERGY POL'Y 351 (2016); Jay P. Kesan et al., *An Empirical Study of the Impact of the Renewable Fuel Standard (RFS) on the Production of Fuel Ethanol in the U.S.*, *supra*. However, scientific research continues regarding refining the metrics used to evaluate the impacts of different types of biofuels as well as reducing the GHG emissions and other environmental impacts associated with their use in the transportation sector. *See, e.g.*, Poritosh Roy & Aminesh Duta, *Chapter 19—Life Cycle Assessment (LCA) of Bioethanol Produced From Different Food Crops: Economic and Environmental Impacts, in* BIOETHANOL PRODUCTION

FROM FOOD CROPS: SUSTAINABLE SOURCES, INTERVENTIONS, AND CHALLENGES 385 (2019).

3.   The Bracmort excerpt discusses the "RIN" (renewable identification number) that accompanies each gallon of renewable fuel produced or imported into the United States. EPA tracks each regulated party's RINs, and if a regulated party fails to obtain an adequate number of RINs, it is subject to a penalty. Once renewable fuel is blended with gasoline, the RIN separates from the renewable fuel, and the party that blended the fuel can sell it on the market, allowing other regulated parties to acquire RINs to meet their blending requirements. In this way, the RIN market is similar to the Renewable Energy Credit (REC) market that provides a means for electricity providers to meet state renewable portfolio standards (RPSs), as discussed in Chapter 5.

The RIN market was subject to significant press and government scrutiny in 2013, when RIN prices surged to 20 times their normal price as big banks and other Wall Street financial institutions stockpiled millions of credits just as refiners were looking to buy more to meet federal requirements, causing a rise in gasoline prices and costing refiners hundreds of millions of dollars. The credits, which cost 7 cents each in January 2013, cost $1.43 in July and, by September, cost 60 cents each. *See, e.g.,* Gretchen Morgenson & Robert Gebeloff, *Wall St. Exploits Ethanol Credits, and Prices Spike*, N.Y. TIMES (Sept. 14, 2013). RIN prices spiked again during the COVID-19 pandemic in 2020 and 2021. According to the U.S. Energy Information Administration, RIN prices have typically risen in two situations: "when the cost of a biofuel was higher than the petroleum fuel it was blended into or when RFS targets increased more than market-driven biofuel consumption." During the pandemic, RIN prices rose significantly because of the first scenario—as transportation demand fell, so did the price of oil, causing declines in the price of gasoline and diesel fuel, which encouraged increased blending of ethanol and biomass-based diesel fuel. *See Ethanol and Biomass-Based Diesel RIN Prices Approaching All Time Highs*, U.S. ENERGY INFO. ADMIN. (Feb. 24, 2021).

4.   The RFS is not the only law that requires a life-cycle analysis to be used in the transportation fuel sector. The State of California, as part of its landmark Global Warming Solutions Act, also known as AB 32, enacted its own law to encourage the development of renewable fuels. This law, the Low Carbon Fuel Standard (LCFS), was intended to place a greater emphasis than the RFS on limiting the GHG emissions associated with the fuels used in the transportation sector in California. Beginning in 2011, the LCFS established a declining annual cap on the average carbon intensity (CI) of California's transportation fuel market. The goal of the LCFS is to spur the development and production of low carbon fuels, reducing overall emissions from transportation. To comply with the LCFS a fuel blender must keep the average CI of its total volume of fuel below the annual limit or purchase credits from other regulated parties who have generated excess credits by exceeding the standard's requirements, thus creating a market for fuel standard credits.

In administering the LCFS, the California Air Resources Board (CARB) calculates the life cycle emissions for all transportation fuels using the Argonne National Laboratory's Greenhouse Gases, Regulated Emissions and Energy use (GREET) life-cycle model tailored to California specifications. This model estimates and sums GHG emissions, regardless of source, over the full fuel lifecycle, including all inputs and processes associated with the production of fuel and its feedstock, fuel transport, distribution, use in California vehicles, and the emissions impacts of any co-products generated in the process. Such lifecycle emissions accounting is deemed to be appropriate for regulating emissions from transportation fuels because vehicle tailpipe emissions are not a reliable proxy for fuel emissions—tailpipe emissions represent approximately 80% of total emissions for gasoline vehicles and 0% of total emissions for EVs. For more information on the California LCFS, including amendments in 2018 strengthening the carbon-intensity benchmarks through 2030, see *Low Carbon Fuel Standard*, Cal. Air Res. Bd.; *LCFS Basics*, Cal. Air Res. Bd. (Sept. 2020) (slide deck); Cassandra B. Drotman & Raymond H. Huff, *An Overview and Next Steps for California's Low Carbon Fuel Standard*, A&WMA's 113TH ANNUAL CONFERENCE & EXHIBITION (June 29–July 2, 2020).

Midwestern ethanol producers and other fuel manufacturers challenged the LCFS in federal court on various grounds. In particular, the Midwestern ethanol producers alleged that the LCFS violated the dormant Commerce Clause because it set a higher CI for many types of ethanol produced in the Midwest. The reason for the higher CI values was because midwestern ethanol was more often produced using coal-fired electricity than ethanol in California, was transported longer distances to reach California, and resulted in land use changes that increased GHG emissions which, together, resulted in higher GHG emissions over the lifecycle of the fuel as compared with ethanol produced in California. After years of litigation, the dormant Commerce Clause claims were resolved in favor of California, as the U.S. Court of Appeals for the Ninth Circuit upheld the law in a series of decisions, finding that the law did not regulate extraterritorially and did not discriminate against interstate commerce. *See Rocky Mountain Farmers Union v. Corey*, 730 F.3d 1070 (9th Cir. 2013); *Rocky Mountain Farmers Union v. Corey*, 913 F.3d 940 (9th Cir. 2019). The Ninth Circuit also dismissed an industry challenge to a similar law enacted in Oregon. *See Am. Fuel & Petrochemical Mfrs. v. O'Keefe*, 903 F.3d 903 (9th Cir. 2018).

Should states be able to set their own standards for transportation fuels even if they impact regional and national markets for such fuels? What are the benefits? The costs? Recent data indicates that the LCFS has resulted in significant reductions in transportation related GHG emissions in California and has spurred development of a variety of renewable fuel industries throughout the United States, including the development of renewable natural gas from agricultural operations in the Midwest. *See, e.g.*, Samir Huseynov, *Does California's Low Carbon Fuel Standards Reduce Carbon Dioxide Emissions?*, 14 PLOS ONE (Sept. 2018) (finding "robust evidence" of a 10% reduction in California's transportation sector CO_2 emissions as a result of the law and that improved air quality due to the law "may have benefited California in the magnitude of hundreds of millions of dollars" as a result of increased work productivity); Daniel Sperling & Colin W. Murphy, *How (Almost) Everyone Came to Love Low Carbon Fuels in California*, FORBES (Oct. 17, 2018); Frank Jossi, *California Clean Fuel Standard Sparks Renewable Gas Boom in Midwest*, MIDWEST ENERGY NEWS (May 13, 2021). For more on the dormant Commerce Clause, lifecycle emissions, and transportation-related energy, see Alexandra B. Klass & Elizabeth Henley, *Energy Policy, Extraterritoriality, and the Commerce Clause*, 5 SAN DIEGO J. OF CLIMATE & ENERGY L. 127 (2014); Alexandra B. Klass & Andrew Heiring, *Life Cycle Emissions and Transportation Energy*, 82 BROOKLYN L. REV. 485 (2017) (discussing LCFS case). *See also* Chapter 4 (discussing dormant Commerce Clause challenges to state laws in the electricity context).

Currently, the maximum percentage of ethanol allowed in gasoline suitable for all types of engines is 10%. As noted in the Bracmort report, in 2010, EPA attempted to address "blend wall" concerns in part by granting a partial waiver of the 10% ethanol limit to allow the sale of E15 for use in model year 2001 and newer light-duty motor vehicles. The report also noted that implementation of the waiver has been difficult because of warranty concerns with regard to older engines and opposition to its use among other industry sectors, as described in the notes below. Thus, in 2015, EPA took a different tack and used a different waiver provision in the RFS to reduce the overall gallons of biofuels required to be blended with gasoline based on "inadequate domestic supply." 42 U.S.C. § 7545(*o*)(7)(A). The ethanol industry and others challenged the waiver, resulting in the decision excerpted below.

AMERICANS FOR CLEAN ENERGY, ET AL. V. EPA
864 F.3d 691 (D.C. Cir. 2017)

KAVANAUGH, CIRCUIT JUDGE.

The Clean Air Act's Renewable Fuel Program requires an increasing amount of renewable fuel to be introduced into the Nation's transportation fuel supply each year. *See* 42 U.S.C. § 7545(*o*). By mandating the replacement—at least to a certain degree—of fossil fuel with renewable fuel, Congress intended the Renewable Fuel Program to move the United States toward greater energy independence and to reduce greenhouse gas emissions.

EPA is the federal agency primarily responsible for implementing the Renewable Fuel Program's requirements. Congress has directed EPA to annually publish renewable fuel requirements that apply to certain participants in the transportation fuel market. In 2015, EPA promulgated a Final Rule setting several renewable fuel requirements for the years 2014 through 2017. In this set of consolidated petitions, various organizations, companies, and interest groups challenge that EPA Final Rule on a number of grounds. Some argue that EPA set the renewable fuel requirements too high. Others argue that EPA set the renewable fuel requirements too low.

We reject all of those challenges, except for one: We agree with Americans for Clean Energy and its aligned petitioners (collectively referred to as "Americans for Clean Energy") that EPA erred in how it interpreted the "inadequate domestic supply" waiver provision. We hold that the "inadequate domestic supply" provision authorizes EPA to consider *supply-side* factors affecting the volume of renewable fuel that is available to *refiners, blenders, and importers* to meet the statutory volume requirements. It does not allow EPA to consider the volume of renewable fuel that is available to ultimate *consumers* or the *demand-side* constraints that affect the consumption of renewable fuel by consumers. . . .

[In the Final Rule] EPA noted that the Renewable Fuel Program's requirements were "readily achieved" in the few years after Congress created the program in 2005 and amended it in 2007. That was due in large part to the fact that the industry had the capacity to produce—and the market had the capacity to consume—increasing quantities of ethanol. But by 2014, ready compliance with the statutory volume requirements was no longer possible. That is because the industry hit the "E10 blendwall": an "infrastructure and market-related constraint on ethanol demand" that "arises because most U.S. vehicle engines were not designed to handle gasoline consisting of more than 10 percent ethanol." *Monroe Energy*, [*LLC v. EPA*, 750 F.3d 909, 913–14 (D.C. Cir. 2014)]. Put differently, a few years into the amended Renewable Fuel Program, the supply of ethanol was much greater than the demand in the market. . . .

In enacting the Renewable Fuel Program, Congress chose not to place any compliance burdens on the fueling stations or consumers of transportation fuel. Instead, the statute allows EPA to designate three categories of upstream market participants—"refineries," "blenders," and "importers"—as "obligated parties" responsible for ensuring that the renewable fuel volume requirements are met. 42 U.S.C. § 7545(*o*)(3)(B)(ii)(I). To date, EPA has applied the renewable fuel obligations only to refiners and importers of fuel—not to blenders. *See* 40 C.F.R. § 80.1406(a)(1). By requiring upstream market participants such as refiners and importers to introduce increasing volumes of renewable fuel into the transportation fuel supply, Congress intended the Renewable Fuel Program to be a "market forcing policy" that would create "'demand pressure' to increase consumption" of renewable fuel. Final Rule, 80 Fed. Reg. at 77,423; *Monroe Energy*, [750 F.3d at 917] (quoting Regulation of Fuels and Fuel Additives: 2013 Renewable Fuel Standards, 78 Fed. Reg. 49,794, 49,821 (Aug. 15, 2013)). . . .

Although the Renewable Fuel Program statute establishes the annual volume requirements for the different categories of renewable fuel, Congress also granted EPA "waiver" power to reduce the statutory volume requirements in certain circumstances. Here, we consider the statute's "inadequate domestic supply" waiver provision. That provision is located within a section establishing EPA's general waiver authority. The provision gives EPA discretion to "waive" the statutory requirements applicable to obligated parties "in whole or in part" by "reducing the national quantity of renewable fuel required under paragraph (2) . . . based on a determination by the Administrator, after public notice and opportunity for comment, *that there is an inadequate domestic supply.*" 42 U.S.C. § 7545(*o*)(7)(A) (emphasis added).

Before the 2015 Final Rule, EPA had never relied upon the "inadequate domestic supply" waiver provision to reduce a statutory volume requirement. *See* Final Rule, 80 Fed. Reg. at 77,435. In the 2015 Final Rule, EPA relied on that provision to reduce the total renewable fuel volume requirements for the years 2014, 2015, and 2016. In so doing, EPA issued its first-ever interpretation of the term "inadequate domestic supply" for the purposes of establishing a renewable fuel volume requirement.

EPA began by noting its view that the statutory phrase "inadequate domestic supply" is ambiguous. That is so, according to EPA, because the text "does not specify" what "product" or "person" the "general term 'supply' refers to." Having concluded that the phrase "inadequate domestic supply" is ambiguous, EPA stated that it had interpretive authority to adopt a reading of the waiver provision that would best align with "the overall policy goals" of the Renewable Fuel Program. That "best" reading has two important elements that we consider here.

First, EPA concluded that the best reading of the "inadequate domestic supply" provision is that it refers to the supply of renewable fuel available to *consumers* for use in their vehicles—not to the supply of renewable fuel available to *refiners, blenders, and importers* for use in meeting the statutory volume requirements. Under that interpretation, EPA considered all factors that would affect the amount of renewable fuel available for sale to consumers including, among other things, the capacity and incentives of transportation fuel distributors and retail gas stations to distribute and sell blended transportation fuel.

Second, EPA concluded that the "inadequate domestic supply" waiver provision grants it authority not only to consider supply-side constraints affecting the availability of renewable fuel—such as renewable fuel production or import capacity—but also to consider *demand-side* factors affecting consumers' desire or ability to consume renewable fuels. *Id.* at 77,435–36. Those demand-side factors included, among other things, the "existence of and expansion of" vehicles and engines "capable of using" renewable fuel; the number of "retail outlets that offer renewable fuels blends"; "the attractiveness" of renewable fuel blends "to consumers"; and the "marketing effectiveness" of those promoting renewable fuel products.

An example helps crystallize the effects of EPA's interpretation. Suppose four things for a given year: (i) the statutory volume requirement is 10 million gallons; (ii) a supply of 10 million gallons of renewable fuel is available for use by refiners, blenders, and importers to meet the statutory volume requirement; (iii) due to distribution constraints, fuel retailers can make nine million gallons of renewable fuel available to consumers; and (iv) consumers can use—and therefore demand—eight million gallons of renewable fuel. Under EPA's interpretation of the "inadequate domestic supply" provision, EPA would be authorized: (i) to reduce the statutory volume requirement by one million gallons based on the distribution constraints that limit the amount of fuel offered by fuel retailers to consumers and (ii) to further reduce the volume requirement by an additional one million gallons to reflect consumer *demand* for renewable fuel. Those reductions could be made, according to EPA, notwithstanding the fact that the renewable fuel *supply* of 10 million gallons would be adequate to allow refiners, blenders, and importers to introduce enough renewable fuel into the Nation's fuel supply to meet the statutory volume requirement.

Americans for Clean Energy argues that EPA's interpretation of the phrase "inadequate domestic supply" is inconsistent with the text, structure, and purpose of the Renewable Fuel Program. According to Americans for Clean Energy, the scope of EPA's "inadequate domestic supply" waiver authority is clear: It authorizes EPA to consider *supply-side* factors affecting the volume of renewable fuel that is available to *refiners, blenders, and importers* to meet the statutory volume requirements. It does not, according to Americans for Clean Energy, allow EPA to consider factors, such as distribution capacity, affecting the supply of renewable fuel available to ultimate *consumers* for use in their vehicles. Nor does it allow EPA to consider *demand-side* constraints on the consumption of renewable fuel when determining the available renewable fuel supply.

We agree with Americans for Clean Energy that EPA's interpretation of the "inadequate domestic supply" waiver provision is inconsistent with the statute. *See Chevron U.S.A., Inc. v. Natural Resources Defense Council, Inc.*, 467 U.S. 837, 843 & n.9 (1984). . . .

The "inadequate domestic supply" provision authorizes EPA to "reduc[e] the national quantity of *renewable fuel* required" by the statute "based on a determination by" EPA "that there is an inadequate domestic supply." 42 U.S.C. § 7545(*o*)(7)(A) (emphasis added). Reading the "inadequate domestic supply" provision together with the section it modifies, the only reasonable interpretation is that the "product" at issue is the only product referenced in the provision: "renewable fuel."

Nor is the "inadequate domestic supply" waiver provision ambiguous with respect to the "person" at issue. Recall that the statute allows EPA to apply the annual renewable fuel obligations to three kinds of entities—refiners, blenders, and importers. *See id.* § 7545(*o*)(3)(B)(ii)(I). As discussed, EPA has chosen to obligate only refiners and importers. . . . Thus, it is the *refiners, blenders, and importers*—not consumers—who must "use" the statutorily required volumes of renewable fuel by incorporating that fuel into the Nation's supply of transportation fuel. It follows that it is the *refiners, blenders, and importers*—not consumers—who must have access to an adequate "supply" of renewable fuel in order to meet the Renewable Fuel Program's statutory volume requirements. When the supply of renewable fuel is "inadequate" to allow refiners, blenders, and importers to introduce enough renewable fuel to meet the statutory volume requirements, the "inadequate domestic supply" waiver provision allows EPA to reduce those requirements to reflect that fact. That reduction, in turn, benefits obligated parties—not consumers. . . .

The problems with EPA's interpretation do not end there. In the Final Rule, EPA concluded that the "inadequate domestic supply" waiver provision gives it authority not only to evaluate those factors affecting the *supply* of renewable fuel—such as feedstock availability, renewable fuel production capacity, and renewable fuel import capacity—but also to consider factors affecting the *demand* for renewable fuel—such as pricing of renewable fuel, prevalence of vehicle engines that can use renewable fuel, and marketing efforts of those promoting renewable fuel products. That interpretation, which in effect amends "inadequate domestic *supply*" to read "inadequate domestic *supply and demand*," also exceeds EPA's statutory authority. . . .

Importantly, whether a thing is "available" to someone has nothing to do with whether he or she decides to use it. (The fact that a person is on a diet does not mean that there is an inadequate supply of food in the refrigerator.) So too here: Whether there is an adequate amount of renewable fuel available to allow refiners, blenders, and importers to meet the statutory volume requirements has little to do with how much renewable fuel that refiners, blenders, and importers—much less consumers at the pump—ultimately decide to use.

EPA counters that, as a practical matter, it is unrealistic to delink "supply" and "demand." EPA argues that the "supply" of a product is a function of the "demand" for that product, and that it may therefore consider demand-side factors when deriving the available supply of renewable fuel. EPA's argument falls apart in view of the operation and structure of this statute's renewable fuel requirements.

The central problem with EPA's "supply equals demand" argument (in addition to the text of the statute, of course) is that it runs contrary to how the Renewable Fuel Program is supposed to work. By setting annual renewable fuel volume requirements that increase progressively each year, Congress adopted a "market forcing policy" intended to "overcome constraints in the market" by creating "demand pressure to increase consumption" of renewable fuels. Final Rule, 80 Fed. Reg. at 77,423; *Monroe Energy*, 750 F.3d at 917 (internal quotation marks omitted). . . . In other words, the Renewable Fuel Program's increasing requirements are designed to force the market to create ways to produce and use greater and greater volumes of renewable fuel each year. EPA's interpretation of the "inadequate domestic supply" provision flouts that statutory design: Instead of the statute's volume requirements forcing demand up, the lack of demand allows EPA to bring the volume requirements down. . . .

. . . EPA contends that its interpretation better aligns with the "overall policy goals" of the Renewable Fuel Program. Final Rule, 80 Fed. Reg. at 77,436. EPA argues that reading "inadequate domestic supply" to refer only to the available supply of biofuel—without consideration of whether that fuel can be consumed—could "impose large compliance costs on obligated parties with no corresponding increase in the use of renewable fuels, contrary to the purposes of the Act." According to EPA, its interpretation of "inadequate domestic supply" is therefore necessary to avoid causing harmful effects in the renewable fuel market such as "a significant increase in renewable fuel and RIN prices," "RIN deficits," or "non-compliance" by obligated parties. Final Rule, 80 Fed. Reg. at 77,453.

To the extent that application of the statutory volume requirements may lead to negative economic effects, we note that such effects could be addressed through other provisions of the statute. In particular, Congress authorized EPA to reduce the statutory renewable fuel volume requirements upon a determination that implementation of those requirements "would severely harm the economy or environment of a State, a region, or the United States." 42 U.S.C. § 7545(o)(7)(A)(i). EPA has not explained why Congress would have established the severe-harm waiver standard "only to allow waiver under the inadequate-supply" provision based on "lesser degrees" of economic harm. . . .

Taking a step back, moreover, we reject EPA's purposive argument on its own terms. That is because EPA's proposed interpretation of the "inadequate domestic supply" waiver provision—in which the demand for renewable fuel largely dictates the volume requirements—turns the Renewable Fuel Program's "market forcing" provisions on their head. Final Rule, 80 Fed. Reg. at 77,423. To be sure, EPA and obligated parties have raised serious concerns that the Renewable Fuel Program is not actually functioning as intended and that, as a result, the statute's requirements will only become more and more impractical to meet. But the fact that EPA thinks a statute would work better if tweaked does not give EPA the right to amend the statute. *Cf. Utility Air Regulatory Group v. EPA*, 134 S. Ct. 2427, 2445 (2014) ("An agency has no power to 'tailor' legislation to bureaucratic policy goals by rewriting unambiguous statutory terms. Agencies exercise discretion only in the interstices created by statutory silence or ambiguity; they must always give effect to the unambiguously expressed intent of Congress.") (internal quotation marks omitted). . . .

NOTES AND QUESTIONS

1.   The RFS requires the amount of ethanol to increase each year regardless of whether the amount of gasoline and other transportation fuels used each year also increases. Why might Congress have set up the program in this way? If the amount of gasoline used each year in the United States decreases, rather than increases, what strategies should refiners and renewable fuels producers use to meet the mandate? What strategies should they use to obtain relief from the mandate? For charts showing the statutory requirements for various types of biofuels as set forth in EISA, as well as EPA's adjustments to those amounts in various rulemakings, see *Overview for Renewable Fuel Standard*, U.S. EPA.

2.   In an earlier lawsuit, trade associations representing engine manufacturers, the food industry, and the petroleum industry challenged EPA's decision to approve the use of E15 for use in model year 2001 and newer vehicle engines. In a 2012 decision, the U.S. Court of Appeals for the D.C. Circuit dismissed the lawsuit on grounds that none of the parties had standing. The court found that allegations by engine product manufacturers that they might be subject to lawsuits by vehicle owners for damage to their engines after improperly using E15 in older engines was too hypothetical to support standing. Likewise, petroleum refiners and importers could not assert a sufficient injury for the labeling, distribution, and other costs associated with offering E15 because they could seek relief from EPA and Congress to avoid those burdens or find new markets for the additional ethanol. Food manufacturers and grocers, who claimed they would suffer higher prices due to additional corn being routed to fuel markets rather than food markets, met a similar fate. *See Grocery Manufacturers Association v. EPA*, 693 F.3d 169 (D.C. Cir. 2012). In the aftermath of this decision, what actions can the engine products manufacturers take to address the concerns they see with E15? How about the petroleum group plaintiffs? In 2019, the EPA enacted a rule authorizing the year-round use of E15. *See* Marc Heller, *EPA to Allow Year-Round E15 Sales*, GREENWIRE (May 31, 2021). In 2021, the D.C. Circuit vacated the rule as contrary to the plain language of the RFS. *Am. Fuel & Petrochem. Mf'rs v. EPA*, 3 F.4th 373 (D.C. Cir. 2021).

3.   Although EPA was not successful in justifying its use of the "inadequate domestic supply" waiver provision of the RFS to reduce the overall amount of required biofuels, the D.C. Circuit rejected several other challenges to the

EPA's 2015 rule in parts of the *Americans for Clean Energy* decision not included in the above excerpt. Of particular note, the court found that EPA had adequately justified the level of cellulosic ethanol suppliers were required to blend into gasoline for the relevant years covered by the Final Rule.

2.   ELECTRIC VEHICLES

As concerns grow over the rise of GHG emissions from the transportation sector, policymakers, the auto industry, and many others have focused on EVs, which are more efficient than internal combustion engines, converting about 77% of electricity used into drive train power, compared to 12–30% of energy in the fuel used for driving a conventional vehicle. *See All Electric Vehicles*, U.S. Dep't of Energy. By powering the world's vehicles with electricity, decarbonized electric grids can help reduce GHGs and local air emissions from the transportation sector. The combination of more efficient vehicles, EVs, and a cleaner grid could dramatically reduce carbon emissions from the transportation sector almost everywhere in the nation. Data from 2019 shows that the nationwide mpg-equivalent for an EV in 2019 was 93 mpg, and that in regions of the country with "cleaner" grids, that number was as high as 255 mpg. *See, e.g.*, David Ferris, *Study Shows Where EVs Do and Do—And Don't—Slash CO2*, ENERGYWIRE (June 14, 2021).

Globally, EV sales are rising, with 2.1 million vehicles sold worldwide in 2019, up 6% from 2018. In 2019, EV sales topped 1 million cars in China, 560,000 in the EU, and 326,000 in the United States. In some countries the share of EVs is very high. For example, in Norway, EVs made up 56% of all new car sales in 2019. Other countries with a high percentage of EV sales that year were Iceland (23%) and the Netherlands (15%), as compared to only 2% of total 2019 auto sales in the United States. *See* INT'L ENERGY AGENCY, GLOBAL EV OUTLOOK 2020 (June 2020). In 2021, President Biden issued an Executive Order setting a target to make 50% of all new vehicles sold in the United States zero-emission by 2030—consisting of EV, plug-in hybrid, or fuel cell vehicles. *See* FACT SHEET: PRESIDENT BIDEN ANNOUNCES STEPS TO DRIVE AMERICAN LEADERSHIP FORWARD ON CLEAN CARS AND TRUCKS, THE WHITE HOUSE (Aug. 5, 2021). New York and California have gone even further by enacting laws designed to eliminate sales of gasoline-powered cars and light trucks by 2035. The following excerpts discuss the growth in EV adoption and related policy developments at the state and federal levels.

BILL CANIS ET AL., VEHICLE ELECTRIFICATION: FEDERAL AND STATE ISSUES AFFECTING DEPLOYMENT
Cong. Rsch. Serv. (June 3, 2019)

Motor vehicle electrification has emerged in the past decade as a potentially viable alternative to internal combustion engines. Although only a small proportion of the current motor vehicle fleet is electrified, interest in passenger vehicle electrification has accelerated in several major industrial countries, including the United States, parts of Europe, and China. Despite advances in technology, electric vehicles (EVs) continue to be significantly more expensive than similarly sized vehicles with internal combustion engines. For this reason, governments in many countries have adopted policies to promote development and sales of electric vehicles. This report discusses federal and state government policies in the United States to support electrification of light vehicles and transit buses, as well as proposals to reduce or eliminate such support.

More than 92 million light vehicles—passenger cars, pickup trucks, and SUVs—were sold worldwide in 2018. The three largest markets were China (27 million vehicles sold), Europe (20 million), and the United States (17 million). Most of these vehicles are powered by internal combustion engines.

The global market for electrified vehicles is small but growing: In 2018, more than 2 million plug-in hybrid and battery electric vehicles were sold worldwide, a 64% increase over 2017. These account for about 2% of all passenger vehicle sales, both worldwide and in the United States. Demand for electric vehicles is expected to continue to grow, as some countries have called for a complete shift away from sales of new fossil-fuel vehicles by 2030.

The market for urban transit buses is smaller than the passenger car and SUV markets, but electric vehicles make up a larger part of its footprint. China leads in this category, with 106,000 electric buses put in service in 2017, bringing its total electric bus fleet to 384,000. It has been forecast to remain the largest electric bus market going forward. In the European Union (EU) and the United States, the pace of electrification is slower: More than 200 electric buses were sold in the EU in 2017, bringing the total in service to 1,700; in the United States, approximately 100 electric buses were sold, bringing the total to 300.

Two basic types of electric vehicles are now in use:

- Hybrid electric vehicles (HEVs) have both internal combustion engines and electric motors that store energy in batteries. They do not plug into external sources of electricity, but use regenerative braking and the internal combustion engine to recharge.

- Plug-in electric vehicles, of which there are two types: plug-in hybrid electric vehicles (PHEVs) use an electric motor and an internal combustion engine for power, and they use electricity from an external source to recharge the batteries. Battery electric vehicles (BEVs) use only batteries to power the motor and use electricity from an external source for recharging. In this report, electric vehicles refer to these two types of plug-in vehicles, unless otherwise noted.

Electrification of vehicles has been limited by three factors: (1) the high cost of producing the lithium-ion batteries (currently the preferred battery chemistry) that propel them; (2) their limited range; and (3) vehicle charging time and location. Not all motorists have easy access to charging stations at home or at work, and it can take several hours to fully charge the battery that powers the vehicle, depending on the type of charger used.

In 2018, more than 361,000 plug-in electric passenger vehicles (including PHEVs and BEVs) were sold in the United States, as well as more than 341,000 hybrid electric vehicles. This was the first year in which total sales of plug-in vehicles exceeded sales of hybrids. Nearly all automakers offer electric vehicles for sale: 42 different models were sold in 2018, with Tesla and Toyota recording the largest number of vehicle sales. Sales of plug-in hybrid and battery electric vehicles in 2018 rose by over 80% from the previous year, bringing the total sales of plug-in vehicles since 2010 to just over 1 million. The plug-in hybrid and battery electric share of the U.S. light vehicle market in 2018 was 2.1%. . . .

Two types of tax incentives have been used to promote electric vehicles: consumer incentives for the purchase of plug-in electric vehicles and individual and business incentives to install electric- vehicle charging stations to expand the charging network.

The credit for plug-in electric vehicles (Internal Revenue Code [IRC] § 30D) is the primary federal tax incentive for electric vehicles. The credit ranges from $2,500 to $7,500 per vehicle, depending on the vehicle's battery capacity. The tax credit is not a function of the vehicle's price. Therefore, the subsidy amount is larger (as a percentage of a vehicle's price) for less-expensive vehicles. Generally, taxpayers claim tax credits for vehicle purchases. If the purchaser or lessee is a tax-exempt organization, the seller of the vehicle may be able to claim the credit.

The plug-in electric vehicle credit begins phasing out after a vehicle manufacturer has sold 200,000 qualifying vehicles for use in the United States. General Motors (GM) and Tesla have reached the 200,000-vehicle limit . . .

Since 1956, federal surface transportation programs have been funded largely by taxes on motor fuels that flow into the highway account of the Highway Trust Fund (HTF). A steady increase in the revenues flowing into the HTF due to increased motor vehicle use and occasional increases in fuel tax rates accommodated growth in surface transportation spending over several decades. In 2001, though, trust fund revenues stopped growing faster than spending. In 2008, Congress began providing Treasury general fund transfers to keep the highway account solvent.

Electric vehicles do not burn motor fuels, and hence users do not pay motor fuels taxes. Several states have imposed some form of tax or fee on electric vehicles that is dedicated to transportation, such that EV drivers also contribute to paying for highway infrastructure. . . .

Imposing a fee on electric vehicles or other alternative vehicles would increase their cost of ownership, although as a share of the vehicle's total cost, the amount would likely be small. Exempting electric vehicles from taxes or fees imposed on other types of vehicles is one option for encouraging the purchase of electric vehicles. . . .

The DOE Clean Cities program supports local actions to reduce petroleum use in transportation. The program funds transportation projects nationwide through a competitive application process, and leverages these funds with additional public- and private-sector matching funds and in-kind contributions. . . .

Purchases of electric vehicles in the near future will depend to some extent on the steps state and local governments and private entities take to build a reliable network of charging stations.

Section 1413 of the Fixing America's Surface Transportation Act (FAST Act; P.L. 114–94) seeks to address that goal; it requires the Department of Transportation (DOT) to designate by 2020 national alternative fuel corridors (AFCs) to promote vehicle use of electricity, hydrogen, propane, and natural gas. The Federal Highway Administration (FHWA) has been working with other federal, state, and local officials and industry groups to plan AFC designations on interstate corridors FHWA has assigned designations to highways as either "corridor ready"—they have enough fueling stations to serve a corridor—or "corridor pending," where alternative fueling is insufficient. In the case of electric vehicles, a corridor-ready designation would apply if there were EV charging stations at 50-mile intervals, with a goal of establishing Level 3 DC Fast Charge infrastructure.

Under this program, FHWA has developed standardized AFC signage and other forms of public education, and encouraged regional cooperation in planning new fueling networks. FHWA has undertaken three rounds of AFC nominations, the latest announced in April 2019. FHWA has identified building out alternative corridors on the most traveled Interstates, such as I-95 and I-80, as priorities for third-round funding. An additional goal is to secure nominations for areas targeted for EV investments by Electrify America in its Zero Emission Vehicle (ZEV) investment plan. . . .

Until recently, the operation of battery electric buses in U.S. cities was seen as a long-term prospect because of their relatively high cost, range limits, and recharging infrastructure needs. But with technological improvements, public transportation agencies have begun to show interest in electric buses to replace vehicles powered by diesel and other fossil fuels. This interest is especially strong in metropolitan areas with air quality problems. The Federal Transit Administration (FTA) provides substantial support to transit agencies to purchase buses. Federal funds can be spent on most types of bus technology; the choice of technology is up to the transit agency concerned.

Transit buses typically operate over short distances with fixed routes and frequent stops. In 1996, 95% of the buses in service were powered by diesel fuel. More recently, transit agencies have integrated buses fueled by compressed natural gas (CNG), liquefied natural gas (LNG), and biodiesel into their fleets. Since the end of the last recession, the share of lower-emission hybrid buses—including diesel buses with electric motors—has also increased, rising from just under 5% of buses in use in 2009 to nearly 15% in 2016. Diesel-electric buses are powered by both an electric motor and a smaller-than-normal internal combustion engine; regenerative braking systems store energy from use of the bus's mechanical systems, giving the bus greater range. The purchase price of hybrids is less expensive than a fully electric bus, and hybrids reduce emissions compared to conventional diesel buses.

There were 300 battery electric buses in operation domestically at the end of 2017, less than 0.5% of the 65,000 buses in public transit agencies' fleets. However, the two biggest transit bus systems in the United States, Los Angeles Metro and New York City Transit, have announced plans to move to zero-emission bus fleets, most likely using battery electric buses, by 2030 and 2040, respectively.

Electric buses are typically expensive to purchase, costing as much as $300,000 more than conventional diesel buses, and require additional investment to build recharging infrastructure. On the other hand, electric buses are quieter than internal combustion engine vehicles, may have lower operating costs due to the absence of engines and transmissions requiring maintenance, and have low or zero direct emissions. The range an electric bus can travel on one charge has in the past been a limiting factor, but newer models can travel more than 200 miles, still short of the 600-mile or more range that conventional and other alternative fuel buses can travel. A study by Carnegie Mellon University found that when social costs, such as the health effects of diesel emissions, are taken into account, battery electric buses have lower total annualized costs than conventional diesel buses over the typical 12-year life cycle of a transit bus.

Electric buses are generally eligible for FTA funding under several programs, including the Bus and Bus Facilities Program. One discretionary component of the FTA bus program is the Low or No Emission Vehicle (Low-No) program, which provides funding to state and local authorities for the purchase or lease of zero-emission and low-emission transit buses as well as acquisition, construction, and leasing of required supporting facilities. Electric buses are purchased through the Low-No bus program; mandatory spending of $55 million per year through FY2020 was authorized in the FAST Act. An additional $29.5 million was appropriated for FY2018.

School buses generally have diesel engines, and they are primarily funded locally. FTA does not fund school buses, but the Environmental Protection Agency (EPA) administers the School Bus Rebate Program, which assists school districts in reducing diesel emissions. In 2017, nearly $9 million was provided to replace diesel buses with diesel-electric hybrids. . . .

In 2016, Volkswagen Group reached a number of legal settlements concerning violations of the Clean Air Act. As part of its settlement terms, Volkswagen pledged to invest $2 billion over a 10-year period in zero-emissions vehicle infrastructure and education in select U.S. cities through its Electrify America initiative. Of that amount, $800 million is to be spent in California. As an additional condition, Volkswagen was also required to fund a $2.7 billion national Environmental Mitigation Trust, funds from which are available to states and other beneficiaries for mitigating the negative impacts of the excess diesel emissions that were released by Volkswagen's noncompliant vehicles. States could choose to spend some of this special funding on bus electrification, including school buses.

Incentives vary widely from state to state. The National Conference of State Legislatures tracks vehicle and charger incentives on a state-by-state basis. Forty-five states and the District of Columbia currently offer incentives for certain hybrid or electric vehicles, or both. Those incentives include

- permitting solo drivers of electric and hybrid vehicles to use high-occupancy (carpool) lanes,

- income tax credits and rebates for the purchase of an electric vehicle,

- reduced registration fees,

- parking fee exemptions,

- excise tax and emission test waivers, and

- income tax credits for installation of a home or business charger.

These incentives have been found to vary in their effectiveness. Several analyses have shown that tax incentives for electric vehicles and infrastructure are the "dominant factors in driving PEV adoption." Rebates—which happen at the point of sale or within a short time after a vehicle purchase—have been identified as the most effective incentive because their value is clear to buyers at the time of a vehicle transaction.

The California Air Resources Board (CARB) adopted low-emission vehicle regulations in 1990, requiring automakers to sell light vehicles in that state that meet progressively cleaner emissions standards. As part of these emission regulations, CARB also established the Zero-Emission Vehicle (ZEV) program, which requires automakers to offer for sale the lowest-emission vehicles available, with a focus on battery electric, plug-in hybrid electric, and hydrogen fuel cell vehicles. The number of ZEVs each automaker is required to sell is based upon its total light-vehicle sales in California. CARB has set ZEV sales percentages through a vehicle credit system, increasing annually to 2025. Nine other states [as of 2019] have adopted the California ZEV regulations. The states affected by the regulations represent over one-third of all U.S. new light vehicle sales.

IN RE PROPOSED RULES OF THE MINNESOTA POLLUTION CONTROL AGENCY ADOPTING VEHICLE GREENHOUSE GAS EMISSION STANDARDS (CLEAN CARS MINNESOTA), MINNESOTA RULES CHAPTER 7023

Office of Administrative Hearings (OAH 71–9003–36416),
Report of the Administrative Law Judge (May 7, 2021)

As explained below, the Minnesota Pollution Control Agency (Agency or MPCA) proposes to amend its administrative rules to adopt vehicle greenhouse gas (GHG) emission standards. This rule is known as the Clean Cars Minnesota Rule. . . .

The MPCA established it has the statutory authority to adopt the proposed rules, it complied with all procedural requirements of law and rule, and that the proposed rules are needed and reasonable. Therefore, the Administrative Law Judge **APPROVES** the proposed rules and recommends they be adopted. . . .

The MPCA seeks to amend its rules governing GHG and other air pollution emissions from passenger cars, light-duty trucks, and medium-duty vehicles. Specifically, the MPCA proposes to adopt California's Low Emission Vehicle (LEV) and Zero Emission Vehicle (ZEV) standards, and to create an initial credit bank for crediting manufacturers.

Low-emission vehicles are conventional internal combustion engine (ICE) passenger cars, light-duty trucks, sports utility vehicles (SUVs) and medium-duty vehicles. Zero-emission vehicles are vehicles powered by electricity and have no tailpipe emissions.

The federal Clean Air Act (CAA) prohibits any state from adopting new motor vehicle emission standards that differ from those established under the CAA. However, the CAA permits the Environmental Protection Agency

(EPA) to waive the express preemption of state regulations for the State of California, under section 209(b), and section 177 permits other states to adopt regulations that are identical to those promulgated by California.

California developed both the LEV and ZEV standards under its section 209 authority to create two key mechanisms for reducing emissions from vehicles: first, reducing emissions from ICE passenger cars, light-duty trucks, and medium-duty vehicles; and second, increasing the proportion of ZEVs that produce no emissions from the tailpipe. . . .

At the time that this proceeding was filed, California's LEV standard governed in 14 states and the District of Columbia, and the ZEV standard applied in 12 states. During the pendency of this matter, the State of Virginia also adopted the LEV and ZEV standards. States that have adopted these standards are referred to as "Section 177 states."

Both the LEV standard and the federal standard are tailpipe emissions standards for GHGs and other air pollutants. A tailpipe emissions standard requires vehicles to emit less than a maximum amount of a given pollutant per mile and is usually written as grams per mile. California certifies vehicles as meeting the LEV standards while the federal government certifies vehicles to meet the federal standards. . . .

The transportation sector is now the largest emitter of GHGs in Minnesota, accounting for a quarter of overall GHG emissions in the state. In 2019, the Minnesota Department of Transportation (MnDOT), in collaboration with the MPCA and other state agencies, conducted public meetings and engaged in research to determine ways that Minnesota can reduce GHG emissions from transportation. MnDOT published a study, "Pathways to Decarbonizing Transportation in Minnesota," (Pathways Report) finding that action is needed across many areas of transportation, such as reducing emissions from gasoline and diesel vehicles, transitioning to electricity and biofuels as vehicle energy sources, and reducing vehicle miles traveled. The Pathways Report recommended adopting the LEV and ZEV standards.

According to the MPCA, it is imperative that Minnesota target emission reductions in the transportation sector to reduce the state's overall emissions. The MPCA anticipates the proposed rule will be an incremental, but integral, step needed for Minnesota to achieve its GHG emission reduction goals and to address Minnesota's contribution to climate change. The MPCA asserts that by targeting GHG emissions and increasing the adoption of EVs, the Clean Cars Minnesota Rule will reduce air pollution, protect public health, and advance environmental justice. . . .

The proposed rule will require automobile manufacturers to deliver for sale in Minnesota only passenger cars, light-duty trucks, medium-duty vehicles, and medium- duty passenger vehicles that are certified by California as meeting the LEV standard. Manufacturers must meet average emission requirements for the entire fleet of vehicles they deliver for sale in Minnesota, and there are separate fleet-wide emission standards for each of the different categories of vehicles.

The ZEV standard requires a certain percentage of the passenger cars and light-duty trucks that each automobile manufacturer delivers for sale in Minnesota annually to be vehicles with zero tailpipe emissions, including BEVs, PHEVs, and hydrogen-fueled vehicles.

Adoption of the ZEV standard is intended to reduce emissions by encouraging consumers to purchase EVs rather than higher-emitting vehicles. The proposed rule would increase the percentage of EVs delivered for sale in Minnesota, improving options for Minnesotans who want to purchase an EV, and for Minnesotans who might consider purchasing an EV if more were available. The proposed rule does not require any Minnesotan to purchase an EV or prohibit the sale of ICE vehicles in Minnesota.

The ZEV standard relies on a credit system under which different vehicles are accorded varying numbers of credits. For instance, long-range BEVs receive the most credits (up to 4 per vehicle) while PHEVs with short electric ranges receive the fewest. Regular (non-plug-in) hybrids and highly efficient ICE vehicles do not receive any ZEV credits.

Manufacturers are given ZEV credit percentage quotas, and the quotas increase every year until MY 2025, after which the quota remains constant. To comply with the ZEV standard, the MPCA estimates that EVs would need to make up approximately 6.2–7.4 percent of manufacturers' light-duty vehicle sales in Minnesota during the 10-year time frame spanning MY 2025 to 2034.

The LEV standard allows manufacturers to demonstrate compliance across California and all Section 177 states combined. The proposed rule would adopt a different crediting approach for ZEVs, requiring that all credits to meet the requirement must be generated by vehicles delivered for sale in Minnesota. . . .

The MPCA has conducted an analysis of the costs and benefits of this proposed rule. Overall, the MPCA has found a net benefit results from adopting both the LEV and the ZEV standards. . . .

The MPCA states that automobile dealers may incur potential costs related to marketing efforts to encourage EV purchasing. Though training of sales and service staff at dealerships is an ongoing process with any new model year introduction, the MPCA concedes that dealers will be required to offer training reflecting different product characteristics and service needs, and will need to increase understanding among their staff about EVs, charging, and how best to communicate EV-specific information to car buyers. However, the MPCA assumes any costs borne by dealers for marketing and training will be passed along to new vehicle purchasers. . . .

The MPCA notes that some dealers expressed concerns about potential lost sales resulting from the LEV standard. An LEV-certified vehicle, on average, will likely have a higher purchase price than an otherwise comparable federally certified vehicle compliant with the final SAFE rule. These dealers have expressed concerns that the potential upfront cost increases could cause diminished sales from Minnesota dealers to people living in surrounding states or that increased upfront costs would cause Minnesotans to purchase fewer new vehicles. . . .

The MPCA assumes that all costs to vehicle manufacturers and dealers attributable to the proposed rule will be passed on to consumers. It notes, however, that consumers are also the group that will accrue the benefits associated with operating LEV- certified vehicles and EVs.

The MPCA analyzed the costs and benefits of adopting the LEV and ZEV standards for the first 10 model years of implementation. The MPCA found that EVs are generally less expensive to own and operate over the life of the vehicle, due in large part to fuel and maintenance savings. EVs have higher up-front purchase costs than comparable ICE vehicles. The MPCA notes studies suggesting that BEVs will obtain cost parity with ICE vehicles, but that PHEVs are likely to continue to have an up-front pricing premium. The MPCA estimates that the average savings over the life of an EV relative to an ICE vehicle will be $11,000 or $12,400, depending on the discount rate applied. The MPCA's estimates factor in lower costs for charging vehicles and reduced maintenance costs, and an anticipated reduction in up-front costs through 2020–2030.

The MPCA acknowledges that by MY 2025, the average up-front purchase price of a new LEV-certified vehicle may be $900 to $1,200 more than a SAFE-certified vehicle subject to the current federal standard, depending on the vehicle size and type. The MPCA has estimated that an average new LEV-certified vehicle in Minnesota will be approximately $1,139, more than a new SAFE-certified vehicle, because more light-duty trucks are sold in Minnesota than passenger cars. The MPCA estimates that the increased purchase cost of LEV-certified vehicles may be mostly or entirely offset by fuel savings over the life of the vehicles. For MY 2025, the MPCA estimates an average Minnesotan who purchases a new LEV-certified vehicle will realize a reduction of $200 annually in fuel costs as compared to a SAFE-certified vehicle, resulting in estimated savings of over $1,700 over the life of the vehicle.

Depending on the choice of discount rate, the MPCA estimates that the proposed rule would result in between $23 million average annual net consumer costs to $48 million of average net consumer savings per model year over vehicles' lifetimes by model year 2034. The MPCA also estimates that over the first 10 model years of implementation, consumers would accrue between a total cost of $236 million over vehicles' lifetimes to a total benefit of $476 million. . . .

Mechanics and others who work on vehicles may experience impacts. EVs tend to require less maintenance, which may reduce demand for services from mechanics and negatively affect that industry. Mechanics may also need to obtain training and appropriate tools to be able to work on EVs, which may be a cost to that industry. However, the MPCA points out that the transition to EVs is occurring even without this proposed rule. Therefore, any economic loss or costs associated with this change for related businesses will not arise solely from adoption of the proposed rule. Moreover, with respect to mechanics, even with the ZEV standard in place, millions of ICE vehicles will remain on the road, and will need repairs and servicing, for many years to come. . . .

Electric utilities may see increased demand for electricity, which could increase their revenues. The MPCA estimates total additional revenue resulting from increased electricity consumption for the utility sector to be about $152 million over the first 10 years of the ZEV standard. At the same time, the petroleum industry may see reduced revenue from a reduction in per-vehicle demand for gasoline and diesel, as the proposed rule may lead to reduced gasoline consumption. The MPCA estimates a total reduction in gasoline consumption in Minnesota from the proposed rule will be about 700 million gallons over the first 10 years of implementation. The reduced gasoline sales may result in about a $2.1 billion reduction in revenue for the petroleum industry. The biofuels industry may experience a reduction in per-vehicle demand for liquid fuels into which biofuels such as ethanol and biodiesel are blended. This rulemaking does not regulate biofuels or limit the state's ability to take action to grow demand for biofuels. . . .

The MPCA estimates the proposed rule will result in total emissions benefit of 8.4 million tons of GHGs reduced over the first 10 model years of implementation of the proposed rule, measured in carbon dioxide equivalents (CO_2e). This includes both the tailpipe emissions from vehicles and the upstream emissions from the power sector and extracting, processing, and transporting fuel (called well-to-wheel emissions). As older ICE vehicles are replaced by lower-emitting LEV vehicles, each year's emissions benefit is greater than the previous year. The MPCA's analysis estimates that by 2034, annual well-to-wheel emissions benefits would amount to a reduction of 1.4 million tons of GHGs.

The MPCA also analyzed the expected health benefits resulting from the reduced tailpipe and upstream emissions of non-GHG pollutants. The majority of these health benefits will occur in Minnesota and virtually all of them will occur within the continental U.S. The MPCA estimates that over the first 10 years of implementation of these standards, these emissions reductions could prevent between 18–65 premature deaths from the respiratory and cardiovascular health impacts of air pollution. Additionally, numerous less severe health outcomes caused by air pollution, including emergency room visits, hospital admissions, non-fatal heart attacks, acute bronchitis, respiratory symptoms, asthma exacerbation, and work-loss days, could also be avoided as a result of these standards. The economic value of all these avoided health impacts is estimated to be between $200 million and $600 million. . . .

In addition, MPCA and MDH's recent Life and Breath Report found that air pollution contributes to the deaths of between 2,000 and 4,000 Minnesotans annually, as well as approximately 500 hospital stays and 800 emergency room visits. Transportation is the largest emitter of air pollutants that contribute to these negative health outcomes. The MPCA contends that not adopting the LEV and ZEV standards will result in business- as-usual for air pollution emissions from transportation and avoid potential public health benefits from reduced pollution exposures.

In summary, the MPCA contends that not adopting the proposed rule and allowing the weakened federal emissions standards to govern Minnesota will result in backsliding on important environmental protections and gains. . . .

Presidential Executive Order 12898, issued by President Bill Clinton in 1994, directs each federal agency to make "achieving environmental justice part of its mission by identifying and addressing disproportionately high and adverse human health or environmental effects of its programs, policies, and activities on minority and low- income populations." This order builds on the Civil Rights Act of 1964, which prohibits discrimination on the basis of race, color, and national origin; all entities that receive federal funding are required to comply with the Civil Rights Act. The MPCA is a recipient of federal funds, and so has adopted a policy for environmental justice, which states:

> The Minnesota Pollution Control Agency will, within its authority, strive for the fair treatment and meaningful involvement of all people regardless of race, color, national origin, or income with respect to the development, implementation, and enforcement of environmental laws, regulations, and policies.

The MPCA states that in Minnesota, Black, Indigenous, and People of Color (BIPOC) as well as lower-income individuals are exposed to higher levels of air pollution as a result of an ongoing history of structural racism and inequitable policies. The MPCA notes that policies such as racial covenants, red lining, and the destruction of Black communities to build Interstates 94 and 35, as well as zoning and permitting decisions that concentrate pollution sources in communities of color and under-resourced communities continue to harm these communities.

The MPCA asserts that these inequities are particularly evident in the distribution of exposure to air pollution from vehicles that have had lasting negative health effects on communities of color. The MPCA states that in this rulemaking it is dedicated to implementing a framework to advance environmental justice and ensure equitable benefits of pollution controls and reductions in Minnesota.

In developing the proposed rule, the MPCA states it sought meaningful involvement of communities of color and other under-resourced communities. The MPCA reached out to its Environmental Justice Advocacy Group, which is a 16-member advisory group representing various community groups, non-profit organizations, and environmental organizations. The MPCA shared information on the rulemaking, answered questions, took input, and asked the group to share information with their communities about commenting and public meetings on the rulemaking. The MPCA also briefed local tribal representatives at the quarterly Minnesota Tribal Environmental Council meeting about the proposed rule and sought input from them.

The Administrative Law Judge concludes that the MPCA has complied with its environmental justice policy and federal law requiring such an analysis. . . .

Many commenters expressed support for adoption of the proposed rule. Among the supporters of the rule were numerous Minnesotans who wish to buy EVs and who would like to see more EV models made available for sale in Minnesota.

Environmental advocacy organizations strongly support adoption of the rule. Conservation Minnesota, a statewide conservation organization, contends that Minnesotans are already seeing the impacts of climate change here and that, without the rule, Minnesotans will not have access to cleaner cars in the marketplace. . . .

Religious and spiritual faith organizations, members of such communities, and their leaders, expressed support for the rule stemming from their religious beliefs or moral convictions regarding environmental stewardship.

A number of businesses offered support for the rule. Ceres BICEP (Business for Innovative Climate and Energy Policy) Network (Ceres BICEP) is a coalition of 70 major employers and manufacturers across the United States, many of which have operations in Minnesota. Its members include McDonald's Corporation, the Kellogg Company and General Mills, Inc., Starbucks, Aveda, Owens Corning, and REI, among others. Ceres BICEP supports adoption of the proposed rule on behalf of its members, noting that corporate vehicle fleets are a major component of its members' emission reduction efforts and represent a significant operating cost. Ceres BICEP asserts that its members recognize that climate change represents a substantial business risk, and that deployment of LEVs and ZEVs is an important means to mitigate climate impact and reduce business costs. . . .

Numerous Minnesota governmental commenters expressed support for the rule. Several Minnesota cities submitted comments supporting the rule because adoption will assist them in meeting municipal climate goals. For example, the City of Minneapolis notes that state law prohibits municipalities from adopting more stringent standards than those adopted by the state, therefore, state support for local governments seeking to reduce GHG's is necessary for municipalities to meet their goals. . . .

Organizations representing the trucking industry and other industries, and agricultural interest groups of farmers and livestock producers, are concerned that regulations regarding emissions standards will increase transportation costs for their businesses. In particular, some of these commenters expressed concern that the rule will be expanded to include diesel-fueled vehicles in the future; they maintain that such regulations will increase costs and put them at a competitive disadvantage in the marketplace if they are forced to buy electric vehicles. . . .

Numerous commenters contended that the MPCA has not adequately considered the life-cycle emissions of EVs, including emissions generated during production, associated with charging, and connected with battery production and end-of- life disposal of EVs and their batteries. These commenters contend that factoring in these additional emissions inputs, particularly those associated with energy production for charging, means that EVs are not actually zero emission vehicles. Commenters contend that the MPCA has overstated GHG and other emissions reductions, and by so much, that the rule is not needed and reasonable. Other commenters contend that the MPCA has not adequately considered the impacts of mining lithium for use in EV batteries.

The MPCA did not address emissions generated during the manufacturing or disposal process for EVs in this rule because the rule proposes to regulate tailpipe emissions. The MPCA asserts that it did consider the upstream emissions generated by charging and found that the proposed rule would result in substantial benefits, even factoring in the emissions relating to energy generation. . . .

Automobile manufacturers, which are the only entities directly regulated by the rule, objected to adoption of the proposed rule. Auto Innovators represents automakers that produce and sell approximately 99 percent of the light-duty cars and trucks sold in Minnesota. It states that its members are committed to the goal of net zero carbon transportation, and ZEVs and EVs are critical to meeting this goal. Auto Innovators states that automobile manufacturers have made, or have committed to making, investments of more than $250 billion in ZEVs though 2023 alone, and that the auto industry is accelerating its path to electrification with aggressive goals. . . .

Despite this commitment to the electrification of transportation, Auto Innovators opposes adoption of the proposed rule. Auto Innovators disputes that the ZEV portion of the rule will spur increased EV adoption, noting that EVs have not gained market share in a number of Section 177 states. . . .

Manufacturers Tesla and Rivian are not represented by Auto Innovators and these companies support the rule. Tesla states that adoption of a ZEV standard will result in more ZEVs on Minnesota roads and reduced tailpipe emissions, and it notes that EV adoption is viewed as one reason for optimism in the effort to reduce global GHG emissions. Rivian is an independent manufacturer of "Electric Adventure Vehicles," and it intends to begin delivery of all-electric trucks, SUVS, and last-mile delivery vans during the summer of 2021. Rivian supports adoption of the rule, noting in its rebuttal comments that "[t]he entire point of regulation is to influence behavior and outcomes. If all agencies were to only implement regulations that supported 'business as usual' behavior, agencies could not affect positive outcomes via regulation in a meaningful manner."

Automobile dealers are not directly regulated by the rule, but numerous commenters expressed concerns about the impact of the rule on dealers. In particular, [Minnesota Association of Auto Dealers] MADA opposes the rule. MADA is a trade association representing 348 franchised new car dealers, which make up 98 percent of the market in Minnesota. . . .

MADA maintains that dealers will be harmed by the proposed rule. According to MADA, dealers will be required to make substantial financial investments to sell EVs, but the EV market in Minnesota is not strong enough to allow dealers to sell the number of EVs manufacturers will be required to deliver for sale here. . . .

It should be noted that opposition among automobile dealers was not universal. . . .

The MPCA responds to the concerns of dealers by noting that consumer demand for EVs in Minnesota exists, as detailed by the many commenters who wish to purchase EVs in Minnesota, but were unable to do so, and many of whom ultimately bought from dealers in other states. The MPCA notes that dealer education plays a role in EV demand, referencing commenters who indicated that they sought EVs at Minnesota dealerships, but found that dealer employees did not know about EVs and were not motivated to sell them. . . .

Some commenters believe that the proposed rule is inconsistent with Minnesota's commitment to biofuels. The Minnesota Bio-Fuels Association contends that the MPCA did not adequately consider biofuels under both the LEV and ZEV standards as a means to address GHGs. The Minnesota Soybean Growers Association expressed its belief that the proposed rule "sets Minnesota on a path where electric cars are considered the only answer to GHG reduction goals." The Minnesota Corn Growers Association supports enactment of supportive policies and programs to promote biofuels, noting that homegrown biofuels can reduce carbon emissions, and that increasing the amount of ethanol in gasoline from 10 to 15 percent could decrease carbon emissions annually by 332,000 tons. . . .

The MPCA responds that increasing the use of biofuels remains an important component of the state's response to climate change, and that the 2019 Pathways Report cited biofuels as one of the methods Minnesota could use to reduce GHG's from transportation. . . .

Many commenters expressed concerns about the up-front cost of EVs compared to ICE vehicles and increased costs for LEV-certified vehicles. . . .

The MPCA acknowledges that LEV-certified vehicles may have a higher up- front purchase price than non-LEV vehicles because manufacturers may incur costs and pass on to consumers. The MPCA asserts, however, that the reduced cost to purchase fuel, along with other reduced costs, will make the total cost of ownership of LEV-certified vehicles less than comparable non-LEV vehicles. The MPCA also contends that there are clear consumer cost savings under the ZEV rule because the costs of fueling and maintenance are greatly reduced, but it also offers the reminder that no one will be required to purchase a ZEV vehicle. . . .

[The Administrative Law Judge proceeded to approve all parts of the proposed Minnesota Clean Cars Rule, which Minnesota ultimately adopted without further amendment in July 2021.—Eds.]

NOTES AND QUESTIONS

1.   Which of the arguments against adoption of the Minnesota Clean Cars Rule did you find most persuasive? Least persuasive? In another part of the opinion not included in the above excerpt, the ALJ addressed arguments made by twenty-six Minnesota Senators and other opponents that the MPCA did not have authority under state law to adopt the rule, and that approving the rule would "rob" the legislature of authority to enact public policy legislation. The ALJ rejected that argument, finding that state law directing the MPCA to "adopt standards of air quality, including maximum allowable standards of emission of air contaminants from motor vehicles" granted the MPCA the requisite authority to adopt the rule. Do you agree? Did the Minnesota legislature intend the MPCA to make regulatory decisions regarding burdens placed on auto manufacturers that have wide ranging implications for

consumers, auto dealers, the biofuels industry, and other sectors of the economy? Or should these important policy decisions be left to the legislature? Is there anything in federal law that cabins the MPCA's authority regarding the rule?

2.   The Congressional Research Service report excerpted above discusses cities' adoption of electric city buses and school buses as part of their efforts to electrify transportation in their jurisdictions. Are there particular benefits associated with electric buses that set them apart from electric passenger vehicles? Are there particular drawbacks as well? If so, how might those be overcome? The report also discusses a variety of policy options states have adopted to spur EV adoption. Which ones do you find most effective and appropriate? Least effective and appropriate?

3.   What aspects of the Congressional Research Service report and the Minnesota ALJ decision focus on environmental justice and equity concerns? Are there particular aspects of transportation electrification in general that address these concerns?

4.   As noted in the introduction to this section, different parts of the country rely on coal and other fossil fuel resources to different degrees when generating electricity which, in turn, impacts the CO_2 reduction benefits (or lack thereof) of driving an EV that gets its power from the local electric grid. *See* Ferris, *supra*. How should EPA and NHTSA take these regional differences into account, if at all, in allowing auto manufacturers to rely heavily on EVs to meet CAFE and GHG emission standards? How should those agencies coordinate, if at all, with state and federal agencies that oversee the electric grid and electric grid resources as covered in Chapters 4 and 5?

5.   As discussed in more detail in Chapter 11, to support a widescale transition to EVs, the federal government, states, electric utilities, and a wide range of private sector actors must build out a network of EV charging stations on interstate highways as well as in workplaces, shopping centers, and single-family and multi-family residential properties. For background information on different types of EVs, EV chargers, and policies supporting EVs, see CONG. RSCH. SERV., ELECTRIC VEHICLES: A PRIMER ON TECHNOLOGY AND SELECTED POLICY ISSUES (Feb. 14, 2020). For more information on the Biden administration's plan to use interstate highways as part of an initiative to build a network of 500,000 EV charging stations, see FED. HWY. ADMIN., U.S. DEP'T OF TRANSP., FEDERAL FUNDING IS AVAILABLE FOR ELECTRIC VEHICLE CHARGING INFRASTRUCTURE ON THE NATIONAL HIGHWAY SYSTEM (Apr. 22, 2021).

6.   Transitioning to EVs requires much more than just vehicles. For an analysis of the role of civic and private actors, state legislatures, and public utility commissions in supporting electric utility investments in EV charging, see MICHAEL HAGERTY ET AL., BRATTLE GROUP, GETTING TO 20 MILLION EVS BY 2030: OPPORTUNITIES FOR THE ELECTRIC INDUSTRY IN PREPARING FOR AN EV FUTURE (June 2020); Alexandra B. Klass, *Public Utilities and Transportation Electrification*, 104 IOWA L. REV. 545 (2019). What are the benefits and

drawbacks of electric utility investment in EV charging infrastructure? What types of charging infrastructure are best funded or built by the federal government? By the states? By cities? By the private sector?

PRACTICE PROBLEM

The Biden administration has embraced EVs and has enlisted the U.S. Department of Energy and U.S. Department of Transportation to help plan, fund, and facilitate the transition to electrified transportation. In a Fact Sheet released in 2021, the White House set out the following priorities and initiatives as a "set of initial steps on the path the President's goal of a national network of 500,000 chargers to support convenient and affordable travel by drivers of zero emission vehicles across the whole country."

Supporting a Nationwide Charging Network

- Today, the Department of Transportation announced the 5th round of "Alternative Fuel Corridors" designations. This program, created by the FAST Act in 2015, recognizes highway segments that have infrastructure plans to allow travel on alternative fuels, including electricity. The first four rounds of designations included portions of 119 Interstates and 100 US highways and state roads. Round 5 includes nominations from 25 states for 51 interstates and 50 US highways and state roads.

- The cumulative designations (Rounds 1–5) for all fuel types (electric, hydrogen, propane, natural gas) include 134 Interstates and 125 US highways/State roads, covering almost 166,000 miles of the [National Highway System] NHS in 49 States plus DC. Of that total, the FHWA has designated EV corridors on approximately 59,000 miles of the NHS in 48 States plus DC. South Dakota and Mississippi are the only two states without an EV corridor designation.

- The DOT also issued a new report [cited in Note 5 above] clarifying how its programs can be used for EV charging infrastructure. Many existing programs have this as an eligible use and this guidance can expand how many funded entities take advantage of that. This could increase the use for EV charging infrastructure of $41.9 billion in federal grant funding in 15 specific programs.

Technology and Business Model Innovation

- The Department of Energy announced new research funding opportunities on three EV charging related topics:
  - $10 million to research, develop, and demonstrate innovative technologies and designs to significantly reduce the cost of electric vehicle supply equipment for DC Fast

Charging that will be needed in large number to support high volumes of EVs.

○ $20 million to accelerate the adoption of commercially available plug-in electric vehicles (PEVs) and supporting infrastructure through community-based public-private partnerships that demonstrate PEV technologies (for cars, buses, school buses, trucks) and infrastructure in various innovative applications and share resulting data, lessons learned and best practices with a broader audience. Projects that demonstrate the ability to accelerate clean energy jobs or provide new electric transportation solutions to under-served communities are of interest.

○ $4 million to encourage strong partnerships and new programs to increase workplace charging regionally or nationally which will help increase the feasibility of PEV ownership for consumers in underserved communities (e.g., demographics that currently have minimal access to home charging).

• DOE and the Electric Power Research Institute (EPRI) also announced a national EV charging technical blueprint including fast charging and grid interaction. This blueprint will assess needs in terms of connectivity, communication, protocols from utility down to vehicle, to support electrification of the full vehicle fleet. . . .

Progress on Federal Leadership

• The Council on Environmental Quality and the General Services Administration are announcing early progress in response to the Executive Order directing the federal government to transition to a zero-emission vehicle (ZEV) fleet. Since inauguration day, the administration has acquired more ZEVs than in the whole previous fiscal year. Additionally, we are on track to triple the number of total ZEVs added to the fleet this year compared to last. Installing EV charging infrastructure at federal facilities is a key component of the transition to a zero-emission fleet.

FACT SHEET: BIDEN ADMINISTRATION ADVANCES ELECTRIC VEHICLE CHARGING INFRASTRUCTURE, THE WHITE HOUSE (Apr. 22, 2021).

In light of these White House priorities, consider the following questions:

1. Is the White House focusing its efforts on the right places if its goal is to electrify transportation on a nationwide basis as quickly as possible? What other policy initiatives might it pursue? What might it be able to accomplish with additional Congressional policymaking? What would those laws look like? Are there any federal laws or policies you studied in this chapter that might serve as models?

2.   What are the environmental justice implications associated with transportation electrification in terms of land use? In terms of air quality? In terms of access to more costly EVs or EV charging infrastructure? How might states and the federal government attempt to avoid adverse impacts on environmental justice communities? *See, e.g.*, PETER HUETHER, AM. FOR AN ENERGY EFFICIENT ECONOMY (ACEEE), SITING ELECTRIC VEHICLE SUPPLY EQUIPMENT (EVSE) WITH EQUITY IN MIND (Apr. 2021).

3.   How should the federal government engage, if at all, with the electric utility industry in promoting transportation electrification? As discussed earlier in this Section, it has been primarily state legislatures and state utility commissions that have authorized, encouraged, or required electric utilities to build EV charging infrastructure, depending on the state.

4.   How should the federal government engage, if at all, with consumers to encourage EV adoption? With the auto industry? What are the policy options, funding tools, or other actions it can take?

CHAPTER 7

ENERGY INFRASTRUCTURE AND THE TRANSPORTATION OF ENERGY

■ ■ ■

A. OVERVIEW

Moving energy resources is a global endeavor. It involves many forms of transportation, including ships, pipelines, and trains—and is one of the key areas addressed by modern energy regulation. The infrastructure used to transport energy is the crucial link between energy sources and users. If energy is the lifeblood of modern society, energy infrastructure is the massive, massively complex, and far-flung vascular system used to deliver it.

Energy infrastructure has a long history. The first recorded use of natural gas transportation was by bamboo pipe in China in 2500 BC, and records from the Han Dynasty (206 BC–20 AD) suggest that Beijing was lit by natural gas transported through bamboo pipe sealed with wax. Coal and the railroads have a newer but intertwined history that emerged during the industrial revolution. Their relationship is not only physical but legal. The Interstate Commerce Act, adopted in 1887 and expanded by the Hepburn Act of 1906, regulated railways and became the model for many modern foundational energy laws, including the Federal Power Act and the Natural Gas Act.

Today, the interlinked global, national, regional, and local systems used to deliver energy are more complex and diverse than ever. An estimated 2.6 million miles of pipeline moves petroleum and natural gas products throughout the United States, creating a vital cornerstone of the energy transportation system. Oil also moves by ship across the world's oceans. In the first decade of the 21st century alone, tankers moved more than 46 trillion barrels of oil around the globe. Modern railways are used to transport both oil and coal. Over 70% of coal is moved by rail, with much of it traveling over 1,000 miles from the point of extraction to its destination by trains that can weigh over 18,000 tons. The U.S. electricity transmission system consists of roughly 700,000 circuit miles of wires, with another 6.3 million miles of distribution lines and over 180 million power poles.

In short, today, the way energy comes to our homes, schools, businesses, churches, mosques, temples, and synagogues is not so much from Point A to Point B, but rather, through a vast, intricate, interwoven, and interconnected system of systems. This far-ranging energy infrastructure is the architecture on which modern society rests.

Maintaining this infrastructure is not cheap. A recent study projects that by 2030, the United States and Canada will need an additional 28,900 to 61,900 miles of natural gas pipelines at a cost of $5 billion to $7.5 billion per year. The electricity system also is in desperate need of upgrade and expansion. In addition to the millions of miles of electric transmission lines, the U.S. electricity infrastructure consists of nearly 23,000 electric generators at over 10,000 utility-scale power plants (a utility-scale plant has a production capacity of 1 MW or more). In 2021, the American Society of Civil Engineers gave the United States' energy infrastructure a grade of a "C-". For the nation's electricity system alone, a staggering $637 billion needs to be invested from 2020 to 2029, with only $440 billion funded so far—leaving a gap of nearly $200 billion. AMERICAN SOCIETY OF CIVIL ENGINEERS, INFRASTRUCTURE REPORT CARD (2021). Even small tweaks and additions to our energy infrastructure are enormously expensive. Constructing one mile of natural gas pipeline may range from a cost of $3–13 million, high voltage transmission lines nearly $2–3 million, and one mile of new distribution line costs almost $1 million—with costs continuing to increase over time.[1]

New infrastructure, both to replace aging facilities and to accommodate new and changing demand, is a constant need in every energy sector in the United States. Of course, our energy transportation systems do not just continue to grow. The overall network shape is also shifting. Energy infrastructure may not always dominate media headlines, but it forms the core of what many energy lawyers spend their days—and careers—worrying about. Debates over whether and where to build liquefied natural gas facilities, local fights across the country over proposed electricity transmission rights-of-way, and the lightning rods that proposals such as the Keystone XL and Dakota Access oil pipelines have become are only a few examples of the pervasive disputes that our energy transport systems raise. Each demonstrates how vital and varied modern energy infrastructure is.

To be sure, the legal and policy issues that energy infrastructure and transportation present are wide-ranging. Energy transportation forges unique geopolitical alliances and dependencies. Transport of oil from the Middle East to OECD countries, as well as natural gas from Russia to

---

[1] New electric transmission line costs vary widely depending on technology. A 2014 report estimated costs of $960,000/mile for a 230 kV single circuit line, for instance, but $2.2 million/mile for a 345 kV double circuit and $3 million/mile for 500 kV double circuit lines. DC lines are less expensive: $1.5 million/mile for 500 kV HVDC bi-pole, and $1.6 million/mile for 600 kV HVDC bi-pole. BLACK & VEATCH, CAPITAL COSTS FOR TRANSMISSION AND SUBSTATIONS 2–3 (Feb. 2014). Natural gas pipeline costs also vary by diameter and geography. *See* Underground Construction, *2012 Pipeline Construction Report* (Jan. 2012); Andrew Bradford, *Gas Pipeline Costs Run Higher*, BTU ANALYTICS (Sept. 7, 2018).

Europe (and now to China), shape patterns of global trade, investment, military engagement, and policy. The movement of energy also highlights the capital-intensive nature of the energy system, the massive sunk costs, slow infrastructure turnover, and the long lifetimes of energy systems. Together, these factors contribute to a strong path dependency and highlight challenges in system transformation and change. Moreover, as the knotty question of "who decides?" repeatedly rears its head in energy transportation, the tension between states—which largely regulate energy production—and the need for regional and national coordination and cooperation in moving energy adds a geographic and political complexity that makes system evolution especially challenging.

As diverse as the types of energy infrastructure are, so too are the laws that regulate them. Nevertheless, several key themes emerge in the regulation of energy infrastructure.

First, energy infrastructure often presents the problem of "bottleneck" industries. A bottleneck occurs when a monopolistic sector of an industry exists between two competitive sectors of that industry. *See* John T. Soma et al., *The Essential Facilities Doctrine in the Deregulated Telecommunications Industry*, 13 BERKELEY TECH. L.J. 565, 595 n.235 (1998). In oil, for instance, there are a plethora of producers and millions of people want to buy refined oil in the form of gasoline. But moving the oil from the fields where it is extracted to the refineries where it is processed often takes place through pipelines, and only a limited number of companies own those facilities. Thus, because infrastructure like pipelines is so expensive to build, questions inevitably arise about who can own and use these systems, at what cost, and under what terms. A persistent risk exists that, because it cannot be easily or cheaply replicated, owners of energy infrastructure will increase transportation prices, gouge consumers, and make off with excess profits. The law in this area, then, tries to eliminate these risks. We survey them here through a discussion of the role of railways in shipping coal, followed by a case study of the regulation and, later, deregulation, of natural gas markets. Similar issues arise in the context electricity transmission, which is addressed at length in Chapters 4 and 5.

Second, the problems of siting and rights-of-way are common in energy infrastructure. Although integral to modern economies, U.S. energy transport systems tend not to be nationally planned. Rather, they typically are constructed by utilities and other private companies, and therefore must work their way through a patchwork of local, state, and national siting regimes. In this chapter, we examine some of the issues raised by energy infrastructure siting through the examples of natural gas pipelines and electric transmission lines.

Finally, energy infrastructure also raises issues of safety regulation, which might reasonably be viewed as one of the recurring questions of energy system externalities. We briefly address energy transport safety through the example of oil tankers and the Oil Pollution Act of 1990.

B. ENERGY TRANSPORT BOTTLENECKS

Bottlenecks occur in almost every type of energy transport system. The reasons are multiple. The high cost of energy infrastructure means that only so much can and should be built. The companies that build the pipes, wires, and rails used to move energy must constantly seek to balance having enough capacity to meet demand with the risk of overbuilding. Geography plays a part, as the places rich in energy resources do not necessarily align with where energy is needed. Appalachia and the Powder River Basin in Wyoming are home to wealthy deposits of coal, but that coal must be shipped elsewhere to produce electricity or run industry. Alaska, Texas, and North Dakota all have enormous oil and gas deposits, but people across the nation—and the globe—desire those products. The Southwest is sunny, the Midwest windy, and the electricity that can be produced from those renewable energy sources is needed in cities from coast to coast. Thus, inevitably, moving energy from one place to another involves system constraints. Law and public policy help manage—and sometimes can exacerbate—those limits.

Because there are bottlenecks in almost every kind of energy transportation system, common legal and policy issues emerge across resources. Many of these relate to the idea of natural monopolies, the exclusion of competitors, and discrimination among customer classes. As you read this section, you will see parallels with some of the coverage of electricity in Chapters 4 and 5. At the same time, while common issues arise in the context of transportation bottlenecks across energy resources, the laws used to address them often vary by energy type. This is important—and it shapes future system development in unexpected ways. Covering each of those areas of law in depth is a worthwhile pursuit, but it is one best suited for a treatise.

Instead, here, we seek to introduce you to some of the common issues with bottlenecks and some of the legal and policy tools used to address them. While the evolution of these tools over time has differed from resource to resource, one common trend is the move away from more top-down governmental regulation and toward market-based rules. You may have noticed this trend in our coverage of electricity transmission, particularly the discussion of Order No. 888 and the rise of RTOs and ISOs in Chapter 5. It appears again here.

An important starting point is history. Much of modern energy regulation is built on the foundation of the Interstate Commerce Act, implemented by the Interstate Commerce Commission (ICC)—the ancestral predecessor of both FERC and the Federal Communications Commission, among other agencies. The ICC regulated the rail industry, seeking to ensure that it charged fair prices, did not engage in sweetheart deals, and provided safe and reliable service.

Railways today remain essential in the nation's energy complex. Railways both use and move energy. In terms of consumption, railways account for "9% of global motorized passenger movement and 7% of freight but only 3% of transport energy use." *Rail*, Int'l Energy Agency (June 2020). In terms of energy transport, however, modern railways are most important for coal.

Coal Shipments to the Electric Power Sector by Transit Mode (2010 to 2020)

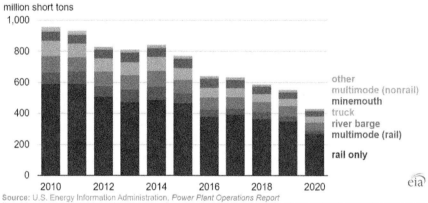

Source: U.S. Energy Information Administration, *Power Plant Operations Report*
Note: *Other* includes pipeline, other waterway, Great Lakes barge, tidewater pier, and coastal ports. Multimode rail includes some movement over railways; multimode nonrail uses multiple modes that do not include railway. Data for 2020 are preliminary.

Source: U.S. Energy Info. Admin.

Coal, rail, and electricity have a particularly special relationship. In the United States, of the 547 million short tons of coal delivered to the electricity sector in 2019, rail carried nearly 70% of the fuel. Other modes of transport paled in comparison—only 13% arrived by waterways, 11% by truck, and 7% by belts and tramways at minemouth plants. *Coal Transportation Rates in the United States Decreased for the Fifth Consecutive Year*, U.S. ENERGY INFO. ADMIN. (May 12, 2020). There is thus a direct line from the rail industry to the electricity sector; coal has been essential to the rail industry, and the rail industry has been a linchpin for electricity production.[2]

---

[2] "In 2020, coal accounted for 25% of originated tonnage for U.S. Class I railroads, far more than any other commodity, but coal tonnage in 2019 was down 46.3% from 2008's peak. Coal accounted for 14% of Class I rail revenue in 2020; only intermodal, chemicals and farm products accounted for more." *What Railroads Haul: Coal*, Ass'n of Am. Railroads (Apr. 2021). Meanwhile, even as transport costs have declined, they have been a critical component of the price of coal. "In

The history of railroad regulation also is important in the narrative arc of U.S. energy law. Rail regulation is both unique and emblematic. It is unique because it has traced its own course, different and apart from other similar fields. It is emblematic, however, because rail regulation laid much of the groundwork for legal control over other bottleneck facilities, including interstate natural gas pipelines and interstate electric transmission lines—and then, in turn, for the restructuring of these industries.

Over the course of the 20th century, the ICC's—and now the Surface Transportation Board's[3]—regulation of rail moved from a cost-of-service model to one based primarily on competition. "From its passage in 1887 until the mid-1970s, the Interstate Commerce Act provided for a strict regulatory framework to govern the federal railroad industry. This legislative approach resulted in an industry chronically plagued by capital shortfalls and service inefficiencies." Through a series of legislative reforms in the 1970s through the 1990s, however, Congress embraced "the notion that market forces would operate in the rail industry as they do in other spheres. Congress believed that free competition for rail services would ensure that consumer demand dictated the optimal rate level, while facilitating enough long-term capital investment to maintain adequate service." *MidAmerican Energy Co. v. Surface Transp. Bd.*, 169 F.3d 1099, 1105 (8th Cir. 1999); *see also* Paul Stephen Dempsey, *The Rise and Fall of the Interstate Commerce Commission: The Tortuous Path from Regulation to Deregulation of America's Infrastructure*, 95 MARQ. L. REV. 1151 (2012).

Congress' decision to deregulate the railroad industry was "largely successful." *MidAmerican*, 169 F.3d at 1106. It also levied important implications for the energy industry. Just as the Interstate Commerce Act served as the regulatory roadmap for electricity and natural gas, its demise became the blueprint for moving to competition in both industries. Riding the same de- (or, really, re-) regulatory wave that reshaped the railroad, airline, and communications industries, FERC borrowed and then imported the same idea of regulated competition into its jurisdictional sphere.

FERC started with natural gas. It then used that model to build its effort to reshape electricity. We detailed the restructuring of electricity regulation in Chapter 5. Here, we use natural gas as the core example—both to show how U.S. energy law has treated bottleneck facilities historically and as an example of how the shift toward competition has transpired over time.

2019, the average transportation cost of coal was $15.03 per ton, down from $16.07 per ton in 2018. Transportation costs accounted for about 40% of the total delivered cost of coal in 2019, down 1% compared with the previous year." *Coal Transportation Rates in the United States Decreased for the Fifth Consecutive Year, supra.*

[3]   The STB is the ICC's successor agency.

The story begins with Congress using bottlenecks in natural gas transportation to govern the natural gas production market, and it ends with FERC leveraging the same bottlenecks to open up that market to competition. Before delving into natural gas regulation, however, it is important first to understand the basics of the industry.

1. THE NATURAL GAS INDUSTRY

Natural gas has a long history in the United States—a history marked by significant changes over time. Indeed, the role of natural gas in the United States can be categorized into five key historical eras, each quite different, in natural gas use:

(1) in the early to late 1800s, as a minor, and largely opportunistic, resource for lighting, although natural gas initially lost this battle to town gas and kerosene, and then eventually to electricity;

(2) beginning in the mid-1800s and into the 1900s, as a nuisance byproduct of oil and coal extraction that producers burned off, or "flared," as waste;

(3) from the early to mid-1900s, as a growing force for home and commercial heating and appliance use, and as an industrial feedstock, made possible due largely to developments in welding and pipeline technology;

(4) beginning in the 1950s, as the centerpiece of a tumultuous regulatory story (detailed below), and then, in the 1970s (shortages) and 1980s (oversupply), as a unreliable and unpredictable resource; and

(5) beginning in the 1980s and extending to now, as an increasingly important fuel for electricity production, driven heavily by the rise of hydraulic fracturing and the abundance of shale gas resources.

Lincoln L. Davies & Victoria Luman, *The Role of Natural Gas in the Clean Power Plan*, 49 JOHN MARSHALL L. REV. 325, 329–51 (2016).

Natural gas often is found in the same formations as oil. When it is found with oil, it is known as "associated" natural gas. Today, deposits of non-associated natural gas are found more frequently and non-conventional gas resource production has boomed. Overall, natural gas constitutes approximately 34% of the country's energy profile and is used extensively for heating, manufacturing, and the production of electricity, as noted in Chapter 2.

Today, the natural gas industry can be broken into four component parts: producers, pipelines, local distribution companies or "LDCs" (such as your local utility), and end-users. Most natural gas exploration is performed by independent gas companies instead of major integrated producers. There are roughly two dozen "major" gas producers, such as Royal Dutch Shell and British Petroleum.

Pipelines play the key role in the onshore natural gas distribution system. There are several different types of pipelines:

- *Gathering lines* collect natural gas from source wells and move the product for storage or processing. There are nearly 250,000 miles of natural gas gathering lines in the United States, usually 2 to 8 inches in diameter.

- *Transmission pipelines* transport large volumes of dry natural gas from producing areas to local distribution companies, large industrial customers, electric power plants, and natural gas storage facilities. These transmission pipelines are much larger than gathering lines—8 to 24 inches in diameter. There are over 300,000 miles of interstate and intrastate onshore and offshore natural gas transmission pipelines.

- *Distribution pipelines* are the smaller lines that transport natural gas to homes and businesses and larger lines supplying industrial customers. There are roughly 1,500 such networks in the United States, comprising over 2.26 million miles of pipelines.

In addition, the nation boasts seven liquefied natural gas (LNG) terminals on the Atlantic Seaboard and Gulf Coast, and 162 active LNG storage sites plus more than "400 underground storage facilities, both of which can augment pipeline gas supplies during peak demand periods." MELISSA N. DIAZ, U.S. ENERGY IN THE 21ST CENTURY: A PRIMER, CONG. RSCH. SERV. (Mar. 16, 2021).

Globally, natural gas pipelines play a crucial geopolitical role. European Union dependence on Russian natural gas makes the pipelines connecting Russia and Europe vital to the region's economic and social well-being, highlighting the interdependence of energy and international relations. For example, it has been suggested that a 2013 deal securing 30 years of gas from Russia to China may help alleviate Chinese dependence on coal. *See* James Marson, *Russia and China in Major Natural Gas Supply Pact*, WALL ST. J. (Mar. 22, 2013).

U.S. Natural Gas Pipeline System

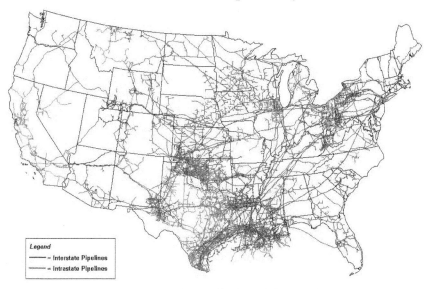

Source: Energy Information Administration, Office of Oil & Gas, Natural Gas Division, Gas Transportation Information System

Source: U.S. Energy Info. Admin.

In the United States, a vast array of over 300,000 miles of wide-diameter, high-pressure interstate and intrastate pipelines make up the "mainline" natural gas pipeline network, run by more than 250 pipeline companies. Pipeline owners historically offered two different services. They sold natural gas, thus exercising a merchant function. They also transported natural gas, thus serving a distribution function. Nearly one-sixth of natural gas transmission pipelines are located in Texas, and more than half are located in nine states: Texas, Louisiana, Kansas, Oklahoma, California, Illinois, Michigan, Mississippi, and Pennsylvania. Compressor stations every 50–100 miles along the pipe maintain pressure of the natural gas, pushing it down the pipeline. Metering stations measure the flow of natural gas as it moves through the system, which is controlled by valves throughout the pipeline. *See* FED. ENERGY REGULATORY COMM'N, ENERGY PRIMER: A HANDBOOK OF ENERGY MARKET BASICS 22 (Nov. 2015). The figure above shows intra- and interstate natural gas pipelines in the United States. About 70% of the approximately 300,000-mile transmission system are interstate lines. *See generally* U.S. DEP'T OF ENERGY, QER REPORT: ENERGY TRANSMISSION, STORAGE, AND DISTRIBUTION INFRASTRUCTURE, App. B (Apr. 2015) (Natural Gas). The laws and regulations governing the siting and approval of natural gas pipelines and liquefied natural gas (LNG) import and export facilities are discussed below in Section C.

NOTES AND QUESTIONS

1. Because natural gas production is relatively constant throughout the year but demand changes significantly with the seasons (*i.e.*, high demand in winter for heating, lower demand in summer), companies need to store the resource to accommodate the market. The prevailing method in the United States is to pump natural gas underground. These storage facilities generally come in one of three types: (1) depleted oil and gas fields; (2) aquifers; or (3) salt caverns. Depleted oil and gas fields are particularly suited for storage because they are easy to convert and tend to be close to pipeline systems. U.S. ENERGY INFO. ADMIN., UNDERGROUND NATURAL GAS STORAGE (2008); *see also* QER REPORT, *supra*, App. B.

2. In addition to pipelines, natural gas can be transported by truck and tanker as liquefied natural gas (LNG). As noted in Chapter 2, LNG is made by cooling natural gas to −260 Fahrenheit until it is in liquid form. Once LNG reaches its destination, it is reheated and returned to its gaseous state and used as traditional natural gas. LNG is especially advantageous because it makes previously unrecoverable gas economical to extract, though it is costly and energy-intensive to make. By transporting natural gas by truck, shipping companies do not have to worry about the lack of a pipeline infrastructure to get to market. For more on LNG, see Section C below.

3. Natural gas also can be transported and used as compressed natural gas (CNG). CNG is natural gas compressed to pressures above 3,100 pounds per square inch and stored in steel, aluminum, or composite tanks. It is most used to fuel vehicles. *See Transportation Natural Gas in California*, Cal. Energy Comm'n.

2. NATURAL GAS REGULATION: ENTRY, EXIT, AND THE SHIFT TO COMPETITION

Federal natural gas regulation began in earnest with the passage of the Natural Gas Act of 1938 (NGA). Prior to that time, not only was there no federal regulation, states were prohibited from regulating interstate natural gas transactions under the dormant Commerce Clause. *See Missouri v. Kansas Natural Gas Co.*, 265 U.S. 298 (1924). This prohibition strengthened the market power of the few major interstate pipeline companies operating at the time. In 1935, Congress undertook an investigation of the interstate natural gas industry. It found that natural gas pipelines were exercising monopoly-like market power in the industry's transportation sector. As a result, Congress adopted the NGA, modeled on Part II of the Federal Power Act.

Three key provisions are at the heart of the NGA. First, the NGA requires that:

> No natural-gas company or person which will be a natural-gas company upon completion of any proposed construction or

> extension shall engage in the transportation or sale of natural gas,
> subject to the jurisdiction of the Commission, or undertake the
> construction or extension of any facilities therefor, or acquire or
> operate any such facilities or extensions thereof, unless there is in
> force with respect to such natural-gas company a certificate of
> public convenience and necessity issued by the Commission
> authorizing such acts or operations.

15 U.S.C. § 717f(c)(1)(A). Sales undertaken by a gas company operating
under a certificate of public convenience and necessity are known as
jurisdictional sales, and gas so sold is "dedicated" to interstate commerce.

Second, under Section 4 of the NGA, the rates for such jurisdictional
sales must be just, reasonable, and nondiscriminatory, and under Section
5, unjust and unreasonable rates can be challenged as unlawful. 15 U.S.C.
§§ 717c, 717d. These provisions are similar to Sections 205 and 206 of the
Federal Power Act, discussed in Chapters 4 and 5.

Third, the NGA mandated that dedicated natural gas remain subject
to federal jurisdiction unless a gas company obtains federal authorization
to abandon the interstate market:

> No natural-gas company shall abandon all or any portion of its
> facilities subject to the jurisdiction of the Commission, or any
> service rendered by means of such facilities, without the
> permission and approval of the Commission first had and
> obtained, after due hearing, and a finding by the Commission that
> the available supply of natural gas is depleted to the extent that
> the continuance of service is unwarranted, or that the present or
> future public convenience or necessity permit such abandonment.

15 U.S.C. § 717f(b).

Thus, federal jurisdiction covers both entry and exit from the industry.
A natural gas company must first obtain a certificate of public convenience
and necessity to sell natural gas in interstate commerce. Then, before it
can exit the natural gas market, it must ask for permission again in the
form of a certificate of abandonment. Meanwhile, the rates it charges must
be just and reasonable.

From the NGA's passage in 1938 until the mid-1950s, natural gas
regulation was quite straightforward. The Federal Power Commission
(FPC) asserted jurisdiction over interstate pipelines but not over natural
gas producers. Thus, the FPC did not regulate producers; the prices they
charged were simply passed through to customers by pipelines, meaning
customers were not protected against excessive producer prices.

In 1947, the Supreme Court addressed the pass-through issue and
ruled that the FPC had jurisdiction over the prices that producers charged
their affiliated pipelines. *See Interstate Natural Gas Co. v. FPC*, 331 U.S.

682 (1947). Then, in 1954, the Supreme Court ruled that the FPC had jurisdiction to cover all producer prices. *See Phillips Petroleum Co. v. Wisconsin*, 347 U.S. 672 (1954).

As a consequence, the FPC had to determine whether the rate charged by each producer was "just and reasonable." This imposed a heavy burden on the agency. In response, the Commission began setting "maximum acceptable rates" for each geographic area of production. Ultimately, the Supreme Court upheld this practice, observing that the "legislative power to create price ceilings has . . . been customary from time immemorial. . . ." *Permian Basin Area Rate Cases*, 390 U.S. 747, 769–70 (1968); *see also Mobil Oil Co. v. FPC*, 417 U.S. 283 (1974).

Initially, the FPC attempted to set area rates on a cost-of-service basis, which ultimately proved infeasible due to the large number of wells and highly variable production costs. *The History of Regulation*, NATURALGAS. ORG. Then, in 1974, the agency shifted to setting national price ceilings for interstate gas sales into pipelines using a rulemaking process. *See Shell Oil Co. v. FPC*, 520 F.2d 1061 (5th Cir. 1975); *American Public Gas Ass'n v. FPC*, 567 F.2d 1016 (D.C. Cir. 1977). For an agency whose primary work was regulating energy prices, all of this ratemaking might have seemed business as usual. However, the exercise of federal jurisdiction over national rates had the effect of creating two natural gas markets: one interstate, the other intrastate.

Soon problems emerged. The federal, interstate gas market set prices based on a producer's historic average costs under traditional cost-of-service ratemaking. Meanwhile, the intrastate market took the prices that were set in world gas markets. As a result, federal market prices fell significantly below intrastate prices. Market dislocations followed. Consumers preferred lower federally set rates to the intrastate rates when they could get them. Thus, demand declined. Simultaneously, intrastate producers had an incentive to put as much of the higher priced gas on the market as they could. Likewise, interstate firms preferred to sell their gas in the intrastate market to obtain higher prices. The difficulty was that interstate producers could not take gas that was "dedicated" to interstate commerce out of the national market without a certificate of abandonment as required by the NGA. The direct consequence was a natural gas shortage: too much demand and not enough production. *See, e.g.*, PAUL W. MACAVOY, THE NATURAL GAS MARKET: SIXTY YEARS OF REGULATION AND DEREGULATION (2000); Stephen G. Breyer & Paul W. MacAvoy, *The Natural Gas Shortage and Regulation of Natural Gas Producers*, 86 HARV. L. REV. 941 (1973).

Even though the FPC was reluctant to permit widespread abandonment of service, it soon realized that a natural gas shortage was not in the national interest. The FPC then decided to liberalize its abandonment rules by first "pre-granting" abandonment of transportation services as a part of a gas company certificate of public convenience and necessity. *See FPC v. Moss*, 424 U.S. 494 (1976).

Despite the FPC's efforts, the natural gas shortage became so acute that Congress adopted the Emergency Natural Gas Act, 15 U.S.C. § 717x. This law authorized the FPC to order the transportation of large volumes of natural gas to the East Coast at prices similar to those in the intrastate/global market.

During this period, natural gas advocates also argued in favor of deregulation to alleviate the natural gas shortage. Eventually, pressure to deregulate resulted in the Natural Gas Policy Act of 1978 (NGPA), 15 U.S.C. §§ 3301 *et seq.*—the centerpiece of the five pieces of legislation that comprised President Carter's National Energy Act. *See* Pub. L. 95–91 (1977). The NGPA aimed to remedy the ill effects of price controls the FPC had been imposing on producers, unify the gas market, and stimulate production by granting the newly renamed FERC jurisdiction over both interstate and intrastate gas markets.

After the NGPA's passage, the natural gas market still did not function smoothly. Because of the natural gas shortage, pipelines and producers entered into long-term, take-or-pay contracts to ensure they would have adequate supplies to sell their customers. Under the terms of a take-or-pay contract, a pipeline was required either to take the gas or to pay for it even if the pipeline did not use it. During periods of shortage, a take-or-pay clause can be desirable, because it gives producers compensation for the scarce natural gas they are producing. In times of surplus, however, the high-cost contract gas can be burdensome because pipelines can find cheaper gas on the open market.

Given regulatory efforts to stabilize natural gas markets, a supply increase was inevitable and, indeed, the country soon experienced a natural gas bubble. As prices fell, pipelines were stuck with severe financial burdens under their take-or-pay obligations. Eventually, this built to a head. Pipelines wanted relief from their burdensome contracts. Producers wanted to capture the benefits of those contracts. And consumers across the country sought access to cheaper natural gas. The burden to restructure the natural gas market, then, rested with FERC. *See* Richard J. Pierce, Jr., *Natural Gas Regulation, Deregulation, and Contracts*, 68 VA. L. REV. 63 (1982); Richard J. Pierce, *Reconsidering the Roles of Regulation and Competition in the Natural Gas Industry*, 97 HARV. L. REV. 345 (1983).

Perhaps naturally, FERC looked to the natural gas pipelines to open the nation's natural gas markets. As noted, pipelines were the important link in the center of the natural gas market. As merchants, they could buy and sell natural gas, and as transmission providers, they could transport it for others. In other words, pipelines exercised a good degree of market power and, consequently, were the lynchpin between producers and consumers.

FERC began this market liberalization effort in 1985 by adopting Order No. 436. In that rule, FERC sought to reduce pipelines' market power by separating the merchant and transportation roles through a process known as "unbundling." Specifically, Order No. 436 created a voluntary system of "open access" pipeline transmission service. FERC offered pipelines incentives to provide transportation service on a first-come, first-served basis. The incentive was a "blanket certificate" allowing pipelines to enter into transportation arrangements with shippers without prior agency authorization. However, pipelines that chose to do this had to separate their merchant and transportation functions and could not discriminate in favor of their own merchant services. Although voluntary, all of the major pipelines eventually took part in this new scheme. This allowed their customers to save money by accessing the cheaper gas in the spot markets. It also meant, however, that pipelines' take-or-pay payments went up, because few customers wanted to pay the higher prices for that gas. The courts, in turn, largely upheld FERC's efforts. *See Associated Gas Distributors v. FERC*, 824 F.2d 981 (D.C. Cir 1987). Meanwhile, FERC began to make abandonment easier, seeking to facilitate buyers' and sellers' ability to respond to changing market conditions. *See Mobil Oil Exploration & Producing Southeast Inc. v. United Distribution Cos.*, 498 U.S. 211 (1991).

By 1989, Congress saw fit to act again. It adopted the Natural Gas Wellhead Decontrol Act (NGWDA), which completed prior efforts to deregulate wellhead prices of natural gas. Specifically, the NGWDA dictated that as of January 1, 1993, all remaining wellhead price regulations would be eliminated. This meant that the "first sales" of natural gas from the production field to pipelines, LDCs, or end users would be established without federal price regulation. The Act excluded, however, gas sales by pipelines and LDCs.

FERC finished the move toward an open natural gas market in 1992. In that year, the Commission promulgated Order No. 636, which made mandatory the unbundling of pipeline functions that Order No. 436 had voluntarily encouraged. Thus, under Order No. 636, pipelines were required to separate their transportation and marketing services. This gave "all pipeline customers ... a choice in selecting their gas sales, transportation, and storage services from any provider, in any quantity." Richard R. Bradley, *One Step in the Right Direction: An Analysis of FERC's Reporting Requirement for Status Changes for Public Utilities with Market-Based Rate Authority*, 1 ENV'T & ENERGY L. & POL'Y J. 373 (2007). It meant that pipelines would no longer engage in merchant sales, but instead would have to create arms-length affiliates to do so. Order 636 also precluded these affiliates from receiving any kind of advantage (price, volume, timing, etc.) in pipeline service over other customers. Specifically, the requirements of Order No. 636 included:

- mandatory unbundling (separation) of a pipeline's sales and transportation services;

- certification processes allowing pipelines to make unbundled sales at market-based rates;

- open access transportation service on an "equal in quality" basis regardless of seller;

- pre-granted abandonment, which authorized pipelines to abandon sales as well as engage in interruptible transportation; and

- the full recovery of "transition" costs incurred by pipelines as they complied with the order.

Eventually, in a detailed, more than 120-page-long opinion, the D.C. Circuit largely upheld Order No. 636. *See United Distribution Cos. v. FERC*, 88 F.3d 1105 (D.C. Cir. 1996). Thus, FERC's effort to restructure "the natural gas industry [by] creat[ing] a 'national gas market' with 'head-to-head, gas-on-gas competition'" marched forward. *Exxon Mobil Corp. v. FERC*, 315 F.3d 306, 307 (D.C. Cir. 2003) (citation omitted).

For a helpful summary of the history of FERC's regulation and restructuring of the natural gas industry, see JAMES H. MCGREW, FERC: FEDERAL ENERGY REGULATORY COMMISSION 55–64 (ABA Section of Environment, Energy, and Resources 2003). For more in-depth analyses, see Richard J. Pierce, Jr., *Reconstituting the Natural Gas Industry from Wellhead to Burnertip*, 9 ENERGY L.J. 1 (1988); Richard J. Pierce, Jr., *The State of the Transition to Competitive Markets in Natural Gas and Electricity*, 15 ENERGY L.J. 323 (1994).

The next case illustrates the type of questions FERC must address for pipelines and natural gas sales in the new competitive world the gas industry now inhabits. Even though FERC has facilitated a move to competition for this industry over the last decades, that does not mean it lacks a regulatory role. Instead, the type of regulation FERC engages in has changed. Rather than regulating the price of every natural gas sale, its focus is on setting rules to ensure the market properly functions—including continuing to ensure that pipelines do not exercise market power. As you read the following case, ask whether you see parallels between FERC's oversight of the natural gas sector and its regulation of electricity, as described in Chapter 5.

INTERSTATE NATURAL GAS ASS'N OF AMERICA V. FERC

617 F.3d 504 (D.C. Cir. 2010)

BROWN, CIRCUIT JUDGE.

Traditionally, an interstate natural gas pipeline "bundled" its sales and transportation services into a single package to sell to customers. In 1992, FERC, recognizing that bundling allowed pipelines to exploit their transportation monopoly to distort the sales market, issued Order No. 636, which restructured natural gas pipelines to enhance competition. Pursuant to FERC's authority under the Natural Gas Act (NGA), Order No. 636 mandated pipelines "unbundle" their sales and transportation services, effectively deregulating the sales market while preserving cost-based regulation of pipelines' transportation services. While acknowledging that Congress alone had authority to deregulate the natural gas market, FERC " 'institut[ed] light-handed regulation, relying upon market forces . . . to constrain unbundled pipeline sale for resale gas prices within the NGA's "just and reasonable" standard.' " FERC believed "open-access transportation [and] 'adequate divertible gas supplies . . . in all pipeline markets,' would ensure that the free market for gas sales would keep rates within the zone of reasonableness."

Order No. 636 also established a uniform national capacity release program to allow shippers that contracted with pipelines for rights to long-term firm transportation capacity to resell unused capacity directly to other shippers. Because FERC was concerned shippers could exercise market power over these short-term transactions, FERC capped the purchase price for capacity releases by shippers at the same cost-based maximum rates FERC set for capacity sales by pipelines.

Numerous parties from the natural gas industry filed petitions for review of Order No. 636. In *United Distribution Cos. v. FERC*, 88 F.3d 1105 (D.C. Cir. 1996) (*UDC*), we generally upheld FERC's regulatory reforms.

After studying the effects of Order No. 636 on the natural gas market, FERC discovered the cost-based price ceilings imposed on the capacity release market might be harming the very shippers they were meant to protect. During periods of peak demand, for instance, the ceilings prevented shippers willing to pay market prices for short-term capacity from purchasing unused capacity held by other shippers willing to sell it at market prices. Therefore, in 2000, FERC issued Order No. 637, which, inter alia, modified the capacity release program by eliminating, for an experimental two-year period, the price ceilings on shipper releases of long-term firm capacity into the short-term market. Nevertheless, FERC maintained the price ceilings on pipeline capacity sales.

The Interstate Natural Gas Association of America (INGAA) and other parties challenged Order No. 637 before this court in *Interstate Natural*

Gas Association of America v. FERC, 285 F.3d 18 (D.C. Cir. 2002) (*INGAA*). There, we upheld FERC's decision to lift the price ceilings on shippers . . . .

In August 2006, two shippers petitioned FERC to modify its rate cap regulations by lifting the price ceilings on shipper capacity releases. FERC responded in January 2007 by seeking comment on whether changes to the capacity release program could improve market efficiency. Later that year, FERC proposed permanently removing the price ceiling on short-term capacity release transactions of one year or less by shippers. Once again, FERC indicated it did not intend to lift the ceilings for pipelines. More than sixty entities from the natural gas industry commented on FERC's proposed rule.

In 2008, FERC issued its final rule, Promotion of a More Efficient Capacity Release Market, Order No. 712. Predictably, Order No. 712 lifted the price ceilings for short-term capacity releases by shippers but retained the ceilings for capacity sales by pipelines. INGAA and two pipelines, Spectra Energy Transmission, LLC and Spectra Energy Partners, LP, then filed the instant petitions for review.

Petitioners do not challenge FERC's decision to lift the price ceilings for shippers. Therefore, we need only address whether FERC also should have lifted the price ceilings for pipelines.

Petitioners' objections to the Orders arise from misconceptions about FERC's authority under the NGA.

First, Petitioners contend the short-term capacity market is a single market and argue that because FERC lifted the price ceilings on one category of market participants (shippers), it had to lift the ceilings for all market participants, including pipelines. Petitioners argue FERC's failure to lift the ceilings for pipeline sales has resulted in impermissible asymmetric regulation. Petitioners' argument is based on the flawed premise that FERC must regulate every category of market participant in precisely the same manner. As we discussed in *INGAA*, the NGA authorizes FERC to treat pipelines and shippers differently based on "reasonable distinctions." We "ha[ve] held that differences in rates based on relevant, significant facts which are explained are not contrary to the NGA . . . ."

Here, FERC acknowledged it was treating shippers and pipelines differently in Order No. 712, but it offered a reasonable explanation for this disparate treatment. Prior to Order No. 712, FERC already offered pipelines pricing flexibility, including negotiated and seasonal rates, and FERC thus sought to offer pricing flexibility to shippers as well. However, FERC explained it could not give identical pricing flexibility to pipelines because of concerns the pipelines could wield market power. We found this distinction between pipelines and shippers to be reasonable in *INGAA*, and we reach the same conclusion here. *See INGAA*, 285 F.3d at 35 ("[W]hereas the uncontracted capacity of a pipeline is presumptively available for the short-term market, no such presumption makes sense for the non-pipeline capacity holders: they presumably contracted for the capacity in anticipation of actually using it.").

FERC offered another important reason for treating pipelines and shippers differently. If pipelines could charge market-based rates in the short-term market, they might withhold construction of new capacity to take advantage of the opportunity to earn scarcity rents in the short-term market. Petitioners claim their construction decisions are not influenced by prices in the short-term market, but this claim relies on nothing more than assertions in an expert's affidavit. Petitioners did not adduce evidence contradicting FERC's plausible concern, informed by economic theory, that "if pipelines with market power find that maintaining scarce pipeline capacity increases their profits, then they will have much less incentive to construct long-term capacity because such capacity could result in lower profitability."

Next, Petitioners suggest FERC was obligated to remove the price ceiling for pipelines because the Commission found the short-term capacity release market was "generally competitive." If the market is truly competitive, say Petitioners, pipelines should be able to charge market-based rates. Petitioners have taken FERC's statement out of context. The key to properly interpreting FERC's finding is in the modifier "generally." Based on the evidence before it, FERC explained it could not conclude the short-term market would remain competitive if the price ceilings were removed from pipeline sales. The Commission thus found it necessary to retain the price ceilings on pipeline sales because, absent the recourse rate, pipelines might take advantage of their customers by exploiting market power. FERC reached this conclusion by analyzing data it had collected during the experimental period of Order No. 637, and more recent data that confirmed contemporary market conditions were consistent with conditions FERC had observed under Order No. 637. This data is just the sort of "real world" information we expected FERC to glean from its experiment in Order No. 637, and it provides substantial support for the Commission's policy.

Petitioners also argue Order No. 712 creates a bifurcated gas transportation market in which the capped pipeline prices will artificially inflate prices in the uncapped market for shipper-released capacity. This is a familiar argument. In *INGAA*, we noted that "distortions of [the market] seem likely in any such compromise, [which] is within the Commission's purview so long as it rests on reasonable distinctions." We again find FERC's distinction, which is "based on probable likelihood of [pipelines] wielding market power," to be reasonable. FERC acknowledged the risk of market distortion in Order No. 712 but observed it had taken steps to reduce the cost of arbitrage, thereby encouraging shippers to resell capacity to other shippers that would place a higher value on the capacity. Furthermore, by "balancing the risks of creating a somewhat bifurcated market against the possibility of the exercise of market power by the pipelines in the short-term market," FERC made a reasonable judgment to "err on the side of enhanced protection against market power." FERC's decision is consistent with the NGA's "fundamental purpose . . . to protect natural gas consumers from the monopoly power of natural gas pipelines."

FERC's decision to retain cost-based price ceilings on short-term capacity sales by pipelines is consistent with the framework set forth in *INGAA* and is supported by substantial evidence. Therefore, the petitions are

Denied.

NOTES AND QUESTIONS

1. The court in *Interstate Natural Gas Ass'n* upheld FERC's imposition of maximum prices for gas capacity sales by pipelines, even though FERC had lifted these limits for gas shippers. In part, this case thus illustrates the resilience of cost-of-service ratemaking and its persistence even in a competitive environment. What, if anything, does this tell you about how competitive the market is? If government regulation remains needed, is the market actually competitive or only somewhat so? From a pipeline's perspective, do you think the rule FERC imposed was fair? What about from the perspective of other market participants? Note that the court upheld FERC's action based in part on the administrative law idea of deference to agency expertise. Are you convinced by the reasons FERC offered for its rule?

2. Another issue that arises in the modern regulation of natural gas is what relationship pipelines can have with non-regulated players in the market. Similar to what FERC does in the electricity context, as discussed briefly in Chapter 5, pipeline operators are subject to FERC's Standards of Conduct, which limit how they can interact and share information with marketers and other parties. An illustrative case is *National Fuel Gas Supply Corp. v. FERC*, 468 F.3d 831 (D.C. Cir. 2006). There, industry interests challenged FERC's attempt to extend its Standards of Conduct from corporate affiliates that engage in marketing only to non-marketing affiliates as well. Noting that FERC had failed to marshal a factual—rather than just a theoretical—record of abuse by non-marketing affiliates, the court found the agency's decision arbitrary and capricious. The court observed, however, that FERC potentially could justify such a rule with theoretical dangers, if the Commission explained "how the potential danger of improper communications between pipelines and their non-marketing affiliates, unsupported by a record of abuse, justifies such costly prophylactic rules." *Id.* at 844. On remand, National Fuel filed a motion for clarification with FERC, but the Commission dismissed the motion because

it had adopted a new set of Standards of Conduct—Order No. 717—that, among other things, "replaced the corporate separation requirements with an employee functional approach that is based on whether an employee performs 'marketing functions.'" *National Fuel Gas Supply Corp.*, 125 FERC ¶ 61,358 (2008).

3.   FERC regulation of pipeline rates also interacts with antitrust law. In *ONEOK, Inc. v. Learjet, Inc.*, 575 U.S. 373 (2015), the Supreme Court clarified the degree to which NGA regulation preempts state antitrust law. In *ONEOK*, a group of high-volume gas purchasers brought state antitrust claims against gas pipelines for alleged manipulation of gas price indices. The pipelines sought to defend themselves by arguing that FERC price regulation foreclosed these state law claims. The Supreme Court disagreed. Finding that the scope of NGA field preemption must be determined by examining "the target at which the state law aims," the Court announced the standard for finding whether state law is preempted: "[When] a state law can be applied to [NGA] nonjurisdictional as well as jurisdictional sales," courts must "proceed cautiously, finding pre-emption only where detailed examination convinces . . . that a matter falls within the pre-empted field." *Id.* at 1599. Because, the Court said, the target of the state antitrust laws was general—any kind of violative activity, whether in the gas industry or not—as well as gas industry "practices affecting retail rates[,] which are 'firmly on the States' side of that dividing line,'" NGA preemption did not attach. *Id.* at 1600 (citation omitted). As the Court noted, the "Platonic ideal" that there is always "a clear division between areas of state and federal authority in natural-gas regulation" simply does not square with the NGA itself. *Id.* at 1601.

4.   Today's natural gas market is highly competitive and represents a tight balance between supply and demand. Thousands of natural gas producers contribute their product to daily and monthly spot markets, meaning that the gas is destined for immediate or very near-term delivery. The resource is also traded on a futures market—the New York Mercantile Exchange (NYMEX)— that requires sellers to deliver a specified amount of natural gas at a contractually-agreed-upon price on a pre-determined future date. Spot market prices reflect daily supply-and-demand balances and therefore can be highly volatile, while futures contracts seek to avoid this dilemma. Industry is the largest U.S. user of natural gas, with residential and commercial users close behind. However, because residential and commercial use is highly weather-dependent, natural gas prices vary widely over the course of a year. CHARLES AUGUSTINE ET AL., UNDERSTANDING NATURAL GAS MARKETS 1 (2006). This is particularly true in the winter when temperatures drop and heating demand increases, thus pushing up wholesale electricity prices.

5.   Over the last decade, hydraulic fracturing—a topic explored in depth in Chapter 9—has substantially changed the U.S. natural gas market, as alluded to above. Hydraulic fracturing's impact on the market has been extensive. One effect is driving prices down, with natural gas prices reaching historically low levels. A second effect is that the United States now relies more heavily on domestically produced natural gas than before—a trend that is projected to

continue, as the figure below shows. For more on the future of natural gas in the changing energy landscape, see Richard J. Pierce, Jr., *Natural Gas: A Long Road to a Promising Destination*, 32 UTAH ENV'T L. REV. 245 (2012).

U.S. Natural Gas Production and Projections 2000–2050

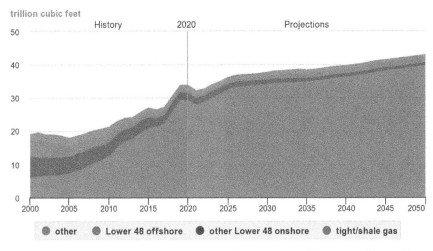

Source: U.S. Energy Information Administration, *Annual Energy Outlook 2021 Reference case*, February 2021
Note: *Other* includes Alaska and coalbed methane.

Source: U.S. Energy Info. Admin.

6. The Natural Gas Act and the Federal Power Act are companion statutes, with the former heavily modeled on the latter. Indeed, the Supreme Court has held that parallel provisions of the two laws—such as §§ 4 and 5 of the NGA and §§ 205 and 206 of the FPA—can be read together. *See, e.g., FPC v. Sierra Pacific Power Co.*, 350 U.S. 348, 353 (1956). Thus, the jurisdictional boundaries of state and federal regulation for natural gas are similar to those of the electricity world. Under the NGA, a state has regulatory authority over the direct sale of gas to consumers within its borders. *General Motors Corp. v. Tracy*, 519 U.S. 278, 290 (1997). States also have control over local distribution of natural gas, which § 1(b) of the NGA explicitly excludes from federal authority. 15 U.S.C. § 717(b). That section also reserves for states oversight of natural gas production and gathering. *See id.* § 717(c). Put another way, the NGA reserves to the states the power to regulate producers, while the federal government has control over pipeline purchasers and resellers. *See Nw. Cent. Pipeline Corp. v. State Corp. Comm'n of Kansas*, 489 U.S. 493, 507–08 (1989).

7. Given this division in federal and state authority, it should come as no surprise that federal preemption questions under the Supremacy Clause inevitably arise in the natural gas context. For example, in *Nw. Cent. Pipeline Corp. v. State Corp. Comm'n of Kansas*, 489 U.S. 493, 497 (1989), the Supreme Court addressed whether the NGA preempted a Kansas regulation "encourag[ing] timely production of gas quotas" to protect producers' correlative rights. For several reasons, the Court said no: Congress did not

intend the NGA to occupy "the entire natural-gas field to the limit of constitutional power." It was possible for federal purchasing practice and pricing regulation to coexist with state regulation of production. And Kansas' production rate regulation did not infringe on FERC's authority over abandonment because federal authority extends only to gas that "an operator . . . h[as] a right under state law to produce." *Id.* at 510, 516, 521. *But cf., e.g., N. Natural Gas Co. v. State Corp. Comm'n of Kan.*, 372 U.S. 84 (1963) (finding state regulations requiring purchasers to take gas ratably preempted by federal regulation of pipelines' cost and purchasing patterns).

C. ENERGY TRANSPORT SITING

While perhaps the most pervasive energy transportation issue is bottlenecks created by network facilities such as rail lines, pipelines, and transmission lines, another key question is how and where these facilities get built in the first place. Indeed, many energy transport bottlenecks exist in the United States because of the failure to make sufficient investments in additional facilities—or the difficulty in siting them. Historically, this has been true across industries, so many of the legal and policy issues and tools in energy infrastructure focus on siting. Siting, in short, is one of the biggest energy transport questions of our day. Energy transport siting presents several issues, but the two most important may be siting requirements and eminent domain authority.

Siting begins with governmental signoff for the construction of energy transport systems—the substance and procedure of siting. What requirements must a company that wants to build facilities satisfy, and who will enforce those requirements—local entities, state governments, or federal regulators?

Another set of issues relates to eminent domain authority, or condemnation, to obtain the property rights to build the facility if the landowner refuses to enter into a voluntary easement agreement. This implicates the Fifth Amendment of the U.S. Constitution, and similar provisions in state constitutions, which provide that private property shall only be taken for "public use" and that "just compensation" must be paid. Under what circumstances, on what grounds, using what procedures, and for what price may the governmental power of condemnation be used to erect or extend energy transportation systems? Who may exercise this power—governments alone or private companies as well? Likewise, there is the question of energy transport facilities' purpose. Are these facilities by definition public, or can they be used solely for private purposes? If the latter, should the private status of facilities impact their legal treatment? Some modern policies single out specific types of transport facilities. Should, for instance, electric transmission lines used to support renewable energy receive more favorable treatment than those used to transport electricity from fossil-fired plants?

By and large, state and local governments have exercised the bulk of authority over the siting of interstate and intrastate energy infrastructure. Federal jurisdiction has made some inroads to this traditional allocation of authority, most notably in the context of interstate natural gas pipelines. But those inroads have been far more limited when it comes to oil pipelines and electric transmission lines—even when such projects cross several states—as the electricity transmission "backstop" siting authority given to FERC in the Energy Policy Act of 2005 demonstrates (*see* Chapter 5). Here, we address the regulatory regimes governing the siting (*i.e.*, approval) of natural gas pipelines, oil pipelines, and electric transmission lines, as well as the use of eminent domain to build these projects. For each type of energy infrastructure project, pay particular attention to the ways that FERC, state agencies, courts, landowners, and other interested parties use available legal tools to promote or impede the project in question. Throughout this section, also consider the benefits and drawbacks of a regulatory regime with enhanced federal authority versus enhanced state and local authority over energy infrastructure siting and why.

1. NATURAL GAS PIPELINES AND FACILITIES

In Section B above, we saw that after many years of struggling to regulate the natural gas industry, Congress and FERC eventually moved the industry toward competition, allowing markets to supplant (and alter) FERC regulation. Despite this trend, FERC regulation remains strong when it comes to the review and approval for new or modified natural gas transport infrastructure—the interstate natural gas pipelines, compressor facilities, and import and export terminals necessary to move natural gas from where it is produced to processing facilities and markets.

Unlike interstate oil pipelines, which remain subject to virtually exclusive state siting and eminent domain authority, Congress granted FERC's predecessor (the Federal Power Commission) plenary authority over the siting and approval of interstate natural gas pipelines in the Natural Gas Act of 1938. Under Section 7 of that Act, a company must obtain a "certificate of public convenience and necessity" from FERC to build or operate either a natural gas pipeline or related facilities, like compressor stations. FERC may grant such a certificate upon request after a notice and a hearing, upon determining that the company is able and willing to comply with the federal regulations governing pipelines and that the pipeline "is or will be required by the present or future public convenience and necessity." 15 U.S.C. §§ 717f(c)–717f(e); CONG. RSCH. SERV., INTERSTATE NATURAL GAS PIPELINE SITING: FERC POLICY AND ISSUES FOR CONGRESS (May 27, 2021). Several years later, in 1947, Congress expanded federal authority by granting federally approved natural gas pipelines eminent domain authority for the pipeline's designated route if the company is unable to obtain voluntary easements from affected landowners. *See* 15 U.S.C. § 717(h).

The history of the federalization of natural gas pipeline infrastructure is notable. In the 1930s, technology had sufficiently developed to transport natural gas from extraction sites to cities hundreds of miles away. This allowed cities throughout the country to abandon their use of "manufactured gas"—which could be generated locally from coal, wood, or other combustible raw materials—in favor of natural gas—which had a much higher BTU value and emitted significantly less air pollution. Cities across the country converted their industrial operations and residential and commercial heating systems to natural gas, but they needed to import that gas from Oklahoma and Texas, which had become the new centers of U.S. natural gas development. States along the desired paths to those cities began to block pipelines as not in their own states' interests. This, in turn, created gas shortages in northeastern cities. One winter, thousands of workers were laid off from northeastern factories because of insufficient natural gas to run the plants. Those business interests complained to Congress, which responded by creating federal siting and, later, eminent domain authority so that individual state or local interests could no longer block national needs for gas resources. *See, e.g.,* Alexandra B. Klass & Danielle Meinhardt, *Transporting Oil and Gas: U.S. Infrastructure Challenges,* 100 IOWA L. REV. 947, 994–99 (2015).

As the cases below illustrate, although this regulatory regime creates a form of "one stop shopping" for pipeline operators in need of siting certificates and eminent domain authority, FERC proceedings over whether and where to build natural gas facilities can be extremely contentious. They involve a complex assessment of market factors and environmental impacts, in an effort to balance the interests of existing and potential gas customers, landowners, and communities that will be impacted, against local costs and national needs. Further, even though FERC's authority to grant certificates of public convenience and necessity is plenary, Congress reserved some discrete authority for the states through other federal laws, which can create challenges for pipeline operators.

MINISINK RESIDENTS FOR ENVIRONMENTAL PRESERVATION & SAFETY V. FERC
762 F.3d 97 (D.C. Cir. 2014)

WILKINS, CIRCUIT JUDGE.

Given the choice, almost no one would want natural gas infrastructure built on their block. "Build it elsewhere," most would say. The sentiment is understandable. But given our nation's increasing demand for natural gas (and other alternative energy sources), it is an inescapable fact that such facilities must be built somewhere. Decades ago, Congress decided to vest the Federal Energy Regulatory Commission with responsibility for overseeing the construction and expansion of interstate natural gas facilities. And in carrying out that charge, sometimes the Commission is faced with tough judgment calls as to where those facilities can and should be sited. These petitions present one such example.

In July 2012, the Commission approved a proposal for the construction of a natural gas compressor station in the Town of Minisink, New York. Many local residents, hoping to thwart that result, banded together to fight the compressor station's development. They formed a group called "Minisink Residents for Environmental Preservation and Safety" (MREPS) and mounted a vigorous, but ultimately unsuccessful, campaign opposing the project. Undeterred, MREPS and several of its individual members now petition [this court]. Though we respect the concerns they raise, we conclude that, as a legal matter, the Commission's decisions were both reasonable and reasonably explained. Consequently, we deny the petitions for review. . . .

Congress enacted the Natural Gas Act, ch. 556, 52 Stat. 821 (1938) (codified as amended at 15 U.S.C. §§ 717–717z), with the principal aim of "encourag[ing] the orderly development of plentiful supplies of . . . natural gas at reasonable prices," *NAACP v. Fed. Power Comm'n*, 425 U.S. 662, 669–70 (1976), and "protect[ing] consumers against exploitation at the hands of natural gas companies," *Fed. Power Comm'n v. Hope Natural Gas Co.*, 320 U.S. 591, 610 (1944). Along with those main objectives, there are also several " 'subsidiary purposes' " behind the NGA's passage, "includ[ing] 'conservation, environmental, and antitrust' issues." *Pub. Utils. Comm'n of Cal. v. FERC*, 900 F.2d 269, 281 (D.C. Cir. 1990) . . .

Under Section 7(c) of the Act, before an applicant can construct or extend an interstate facility for the transportation of natural gas, it must obtain a "certificate of public convenience and necessity" from the Commission. 15 U.S.C. § 717f(c)(1)(A); *Dominion Transmission, Inc. v. Summers*, 723 F.3d 238, 240 (D.C. Cir. 2013). The statute provides that a certificate "shall be issued to any qualified applicant" upon a finding that "the applicant is able and willing properly to do the acts and to perform the service proposed . . . and that the proposed service" and "construction . . . is or will be required by the present or future public convenience and necessity." 15 U.S.C. § 717f(e). FERC may, in issuing such a certificate, attach "such reasonable terms and conditions as the public convenience and necessity may require." *Id.*

The Commission has issued a policy statement outlining the criteria it considers in reviewing such certificate applications. *Certification of New Interstate Natural Gas Pipeline Facilities*, 88 FERC ¶ 61,227 (Sept. 15, 1999), *clarified*, 90 FERC ¶ 61,128 (Feb. 9, 2000), *further clarified*, 92

FERC ¶ 61,094 (July 28, 2000) (*Certificate Policy Statement*). The Commission will first confirm "whether the project can proceed without subsidies from the[ ] existing [pipeline's] customers." Then, it will "balanc[e] the public benefits against the adverse effects of the project." FERC will approve a project only "where the public benefits of the project outweigh the project's adverse impacts." . . .[1]

For years, Millennium Pipeline Company (Millennium) has owned and operated a natural gas pipeline system extending across much of New York's southern border. In July 2011, seeking to expand its service capacity, Millennium applied to the Commission for a certificate of public convenience and necessity that would allow for the construction and operation of a natural gas compressor station along its existing pipeline. The proposed site for the project was located in the Town of Minisink, New York.

As explained in its application to FERC, the aim of Millennium's project was twofold. First, the new station would allow Millennium to increase natural gas deliveries to its eastern interconnection by about 225,000 additional dekatherms per day. Second, the compressor would enable bi-directional gas flow on an existing segment of Millennium's pipeline. The project's footprint, as proposed by Millennium, would consist of: (a) two 6,130-horsepower natural gas-fired compressor units, to be housed in a newly built structure; (b) an additional 1,090 feet of pipe connecting the compressor station to the existing pipeline; (c) and several ancillary facilities, including a new mainline valve, an access driveway, a station control/auxiliary building, intake and exhaust silencers, and a filter-separator with a liquids tank. The compressor station was to be sited on a small part of a much larger, 73.4-acre parcel—a parcel acquired and owned by Millennium. We refer to Millennium's proposal as the "Minisink Project."

Consistent with agency regulations, notice of the proposed Minisink Project was published in the Federal Register. Around the same time, the Commission issued a "Notice of Intent to Prepare an Environmental Assessment," which was sent to a range of interested stakeholders . . . . In the months following, Millennium sponsored a community meeting at the Minisink Town Hall so that those interested could learn more about the proposal and voice their views. FERC also hosted its own meeting in Minisink concerning the proposal. As might be expected, the Minisink

---

[1] The "public benefits" the Commission examines "could include, among other things, meeting unserved demand, eliminating bottlenecks, access to new supplies, lower costs to consumers, providing new interconnects that improve the interstate grid, providing competitive alternatives, increasing electric reliability, or advancing clean air objectives." *Certificate Policy Statement*, 90 FERC ¶ 61,128, at 61,396. On the other side of the scale, the potential "adverse effects" the Commission will consider are "the effects on existing customers of the applicant, the interests of existing pipelines and their captive customers, and the interests of landowners and the surrounding community, including environmental impacts." *Id.*

Project sparked its fair share of local interest; during the review process, the Commission received hundreds of verbal and written comments.

Most significantly for our purposes, several residents urged Millennium and the Commission to pursue a nearby alternative site for the compressor station—what came to be known as the "Wagoner Alternative." Under the Wagoner Alternative, Millennium would construct a smaller, 5,100-horsepower compressor station directly adjacent to its existing Wagoner Meter Station, a site located along the pipeline about seven miles northwest of Minisink. This alternative, its proponents insisted, was far better suited for the project, in large part because it was less residentially dense than the site proposed in Minisink. But it came with a catch: Its implementation would require the replacement of a 7-mile segment of pipe along the pipeline—a segment the parties call the "Neversink Segment" due to its crossing of the Neversink River; according to Millennium, no such upgrade would be required by the Minisink Project. . . .

FERC released its Environmental Assessment (EA) for the Minisink Project several months later. Along with its detailed evaluation of the project's likely environmental impacts—on water resources, vegetation and wildlife, air quality and noise, and more—the EA also analyzed several alternatives to Millennium's proposal, including an in-depth comparison between the Minisink Project and the Wagoner Alternative. . . . Overall, the EA concluded that, so long as Millennium implemented certain mitigation measures, the Minisink Project was expected to have no significant environmental impact.

After receiving and reviewing a slew of comments concerning the EA, FERC ruled on Millennium's application in July 2012. By a 3–2 majority, the Commission voted to issue a certificate of public convenience and necessity to Millennium, allowing the Minisink Project to move forward. . . .

The Commission began its analysis by applying the criteria set forth in its Certificate Policy Statement, first finding the threshold factor satisfied—that the project would not require any subsidization from Millennium's existing customers. From there, the Commission weighed the project's benefits (increased capacity to customers in the high-demand northeast market, among others) against what FERC viewed as its "minimal adverse effect[s]," both market- and environmentally focused. In the end, the Commission concluded that "the public convenience and necessity require[d] approval of Millennium's proposal," subject to certain environmental conditions. . . .

In urging us to upend FERC's approval of the Minisink Project, Petitioners mount several lines of attack. Chief among them is their argument that the Commission failed to afford due consideration to the Wagoner Alternative, which Petitioners insist was undeniably superior to the Minisink Project—in their eyes, "economically, environmentally, and operationally" superior. Specifically, Petitioners claim that this alleged failure both violated the Commission's obligations under Section 7 of the NGA, and represented a misapplication of the Commission's own Certificate Policy Statement. We disagree. . . .

For one, FERC's *Certificate Order* unmistakably outlines the Commission's exploration of the Wagoner Alternative as an alternate possibility for Millennium's compressor station. . . . In keeping with the recommendations set out in the EA, however, the Commission concluded that the more significant environmental impacts associated with the Wagoner Alternative—mostly due to improvement of the Neversink Segment—rendered that option less preferable than the proposed Minisink Project. . . .

In arguing to the contrary, Petitioners marshal only one meaningful theory in their favor. They claim that the Commission's analysis was flawed because Millennium either planned or needed to upgrade the Neversink Segment all along. In other words, according to Petitioners, even if Millennium moved forward with the Minisink Project (and not the Wagoner Alternative), it still had plans to replace the Neversink Segment in the very near future. So the Commission's decision to account for the environmental impacts of a Neversink upgrade only in connection with the Wagoner Alternative and not the Minisink Project, Petitioners tell us, was unreasonable and misguided. . . . We reject their premise. . . .

In making this argument, Petitioners lean heavily on our decision in *City of Pittsburgh v. Federal Power Commission*, 237 F.2d 741 (D.C. Cir. 1956). But that decision cannot bear the weight Petitioners wish. In *City of Pittsburgh*, we reviewed the issuance of a certificate of public convenience and necessity allowing a natural gas supplier to abandon service on one pipeline and to transfer that load to another pipeline operating below capacity. In the course of contesting the Commission's order, a group of petitioners argued that the abandonment would result in rate increases associated with future expansions—increases that could be avoided, those petitioners said, if the supplier maintained service on the pipeline it sought to abandon. After review, this Court set aside the order, largely based on the Commission's failure to consider the effects of abandonment on the pipeline's future expansion. . . . Seizing on that holding, Petitioners insist it applies equally to the facts of their case because FERC glossed over and ignored the possibility of a future Neversink Segment replacement. For at least two reasons we can see, however, *City of Pittsburgh* finds no application here.

First, in *City of Pittsburgh,* it was clear and unmistakable that the pipeline intended to expand service in the future. . . . Here, on the other hand, the Commission examined the record . . . and found no concrete indication that Millennium intended, then or in the future, to upgrade the Neversink Segment. So the evidence of "future expansion" is a far cry from what we were presented with in *City of Pittsburgh*. Second, and perhaps more fundamentally, the shortcoming we took issue with in *City of Pittsburgh* was the Commission's refusal to examine the effects of future expansion *altogether*; the hearing examiner would not permit any questioning or inquiry into the supplier's plans for expansion, nor would the examiner consider several company memoranda that supposedly revealed such plans. Here, in stark contrast, FERC unquestionably did consider Petitioners' theory that Millennium planned (or needed) to upgrade the Neversink Segment. It just disagreed with their position that the prospect of such a step was sufficiently certain to require its environmental effects be taken into account in connection with the Minisink Project. . . .

Given the foregoing, we have no basis to second-guess the Commission's determination that Millennium had no firm plans to upgrade the Neversink Segment in the wake of the Minisink Project. Petitioners also press this argument with a slightly different gloss, however. They argue that even if Millennium was not *planning* to replace the Neversink Segment, circumstances would soon *require* such a step nonetheless. Absent such an upgrade, Petitioners assert, a "bottleneck" caused by the smaller-diameter pipe on the Neversink Segment would preclude Millennium's pipeline from safely handling the volume, pressure, and speed that would be generated by the Minisink Project. . . . We remain unmoved. The Commission considered this argument, too, and based on its assessment of the evidence, it again disagreed with Petitioners on the facts. FERC found no evidence that the Minisink Project would necessitate, as a structural or safety matter, an upgrade of the Neversink Segment. . . .

ENVIRONMENTAL DEFENSE FUND V. FERC
2 F.4th 953 (D.C. Cir. 2021)

EDWARDS, SENIOR CIRCUIT JUDGE.

. . . The issue in this case arose in 2016, when [Spire STL Pipeline LLC] announced its intent to build a pipeline in the St. Louis metropolitan area. In August of that year, Spire STL held an "open season" during which it invited natural gas "shippers" to enter into preconstruction contracts, also known as "precedent agreements," for the natural gas the pipeline would transport. But no shippers committed to the project during the open season. Instead, after the open season finished without any takers, Spire STL privately entered into a precedent agreement with one of its affiliates, Laclede Gas Company—now known as . . . Spire Missouri Inc.—for just 87.5 percent of the pipeline's projected capacity.

[T]he Federal Energy Regulatory Commission issued a certificate of public convenience and necessity under section 7(c) of the Natural Gas Act, 15 U.S.C. § 717f(c)(1)(A), to Intervenor-Respondent Spire STL Pipeline LLC to construct a new natural gas pipeline in the St. Louis area. The Commission may issue such a Certificate only if it finds that construction of the new pipeline "is or will be required by the present or future public convenience and necessity." *Id.* § 717f(e). . . .

Petitioner Environmental Defense Fund (EDF), along with several other parties, challenged Spire STL's Certificate application. EDF contended, *inter alia*, that the precedent agreement between Spire STL and Spire Missouri should have only limited probative value in FERC's assessment of Spire STL's application because the two companies were corporate affiliates.

I. BACKGROUND

The Natural Gas Act provides the Commission with authority "to regulate the transportation and sale of natural gas in interstate commerce." *City of Oberlin v. FERC*, 937 F.3d 599, 602 (D.C. Cir. 2019). To safeguard the public, "Section 7 of the Act requires an entity seeking to construct or extend an interstate pipeline for the transportation of natural gas to obtain [a Certificate] from the Commission." The Commission may issue Certificates only if, among other things, it finds that the proposed construction or extension "is or will be required by the present or future public convenience and necessity; otherwise such application shall be denied." 15 U.S.C. § 717f(e). In deciding whether to issue Certificates under this standard, the Commission must "evaluate *all* factors bearing on the public interest." *Atl. Refin. Co. v. Pub. Serv. Comm'n of N.Y.*, 360 U.S. 378, 391 (1959) (emphasis added). And there is good reason for the thoroughness and caution mandated by this approach: A Certificate-holder may exercise eminent domain against any holdouts in acquiring property rights necessary to complete the pipeline. 15 U.S.C. § 717f(h). . . .

[FERC's] "Certificate Policy Statement," *Certification of New Interstate Natural Gas Pipeline Facilities*, 88 FERC ¶ 61,227 (Sept. 15, 1999), *clarified*, 90 FERC ¶ 61,128 (Feb. 9, 2000), *further clarified*, 92 FERC ¶ 61,094 (July 28, 2000), . . . set[s] forth the "analytical steps" that guide its dispositions of Certificate applications. The first question the Commission considers is "whether the project can proceed without subsidies from [the applicant's] existing customers." "To ensure that a project will not be subsidized by existing customers, the applicant must show that there is market need for the project." *Myersville Citizens for a Rural Cmty., Inc. v. FERC*, 783 F.3d 1301, 1309 (D.C. Cir. 2015).

If there is market need, the Commission then determines whether there are likely to be adverse impacts on "existing customers of the pipeline proposing the project, existing pipelines in the market and their captive customers, or landowners and communities affected by the route of the new pipeline." If adverse impacts on these stakeholders will result, "the Commission balances the adverse effects with the public benefits of the project, as measured by an 'economic test.'" "Adverse effects may include increased rates for preexisting customers, degradation in service, unfair competition, or negative impact on the environment or landowners' property." Public benefits generally include "meeting unserved demand, eliminating bottlenecks, access to new supplies, lower costs to consumers, providing new interconnects that improve the interstate grid, providing competitive alternatives, increasing electric reliability, or advancing clean air objectives." . . .

The Certificate Policy Statement also specifically addresses the significance of precedent agreements in demonstrating need:

> Although the Commission traditionally has required an applicant to present [preconstruction] contracts to demonstrate need, that policy . . . no longer reflects the reality of the natural gas industry's structure, nor does it appear to minimize the adverse impacts on any of the relevant interests. Therefore, although contracts or precedent agreements always will be important evidence of demand for a project, *the Commission will no longer require an applicant to present contracts for any specific percentage of the new capacity*. Of course, if an applicant has entered into contracts or precedent agreements for the capacity, . . . they would constitute significant evidence of demand for the project.
>
> *Eliminating a specific contract requirement reduces the significance of whether the contracts are with affiliated or unaffiliated shippers*, which was the subject of a number of comments. . . .

[Certificate Policy Statement] at 61,748–49 (emphases added).

For the last two decades, natural gas consumption in the St. Louis area has been roughly flat. And when the Commission issued the Certificate Order in this case, all parties agreed that future demand projections were not expected to increase.

As of 2016, five natural gas pipelines served the St. Louis region. At that time, a majority of Spire Missouri's natural gas supply was provided via pipelines owned and operated by Enable Mississippi River Transmission, LLC. It is undisputed that, prior to Spire STL's application in this case, Spire Missouri had declined to subscribe to proposals for new natural gas pipelines in the region, stating that the proposed new pipelines did not make operational and economic sense for its customers.

In 2016, Spire STL announced its intent to construct a new natural gas pipeline to serve homes and businesses in the St. Louis area. Following an amendment to its Certificate application, the final length of the proposed pipeline was approximately 65 miles. The initial estimated cost of the project was approximately $220 million, with a proposed overall rate of return of 10.5 percent—a return on equity of 14 percent and a cost of debt of seven percent.

Between August 1, 2016 and August 19, 2016, Spire STL held an "open season," during which it sought to enter into precedent agreements with natural gas shippers. . . . Spire STL indicated that other shippers expressed interest, but it did not enter precedent agreements with any of them.

[In its Certificate application, Spire STL's] stated purpose of the pipeline was to "enhance reliability and supply security; reduce reliance upon older natural gas pipelines; reduce reliance upon mature natural gas basins . . . and eliminate reliance on propane peak-shaving infrastructure." In particular, the new pipeline would provide gas from newly accessed sources in the Rocky Mountains and Appalachian Basin; avoid transecting the New Madrid Seismic Zone, unlike other pipelines in the area; and reduce use of propane for "peaking" during periods of high demand, which purportedly has negative environmental, operational, and cost-related impacts.

Spire STL made it clear that its new pipeline "was not [being] developed to serve new demand." It further stated that "conjecture" as to whether Spire Missouri might "reduce its contract entitlements on other pipelines" as a result of contracting for capacity on the proposed pipeline "would be inappropriate." . . . Spire Missouri acknowledged that it used propane peaking on only three days between 2013 and 2018—a consecutive three-day period in January 2014.

II. ANALYSIS

Under established law, precedent agreements are "always . . . important evidence of demand for a project." *Minisink [Residents for Env't Preserv. and Safety v. FERC*, 762 F.3d 97, 11, n.10 (D.C. Cir. 2014)]. And, in some cases, such agreements may demonstrate both market need and benefits that outweigh adverse effects of a new pipeline. But there is a difference between saying that precedent agreements are always *important* versus saying that they are always *sufficient* to show that construction of a proposed new pipeline "is or will be required by the present or future public convenience and necessity." 15 U.S.C. § 717f(e).

According to the Commission's Certificate Policy Statement, "the evidence necessary to establish the need for [a] project will usually include a market study. . . . Vague assertions of public benefits will not be sufficient." In addition, the Certificate Policy Statement indicates that pipelines built for reasons other than demand growth might require greater showings of need and public benefits. . . .

In this case, the Commission was presented with strong arguments as to why the precedent agreement between Spire STL and Spire Missouri was insufficiently probative of market need and benefits of the proposed pipeline. Indeed, those arguments drew on the Commission's own Certificate Policy Statement for support. But rather than engaging with these arguments, the Commission seemed to count the single precedent agreement between corporate affiliates as conclusive proof of need. Nothing in the Certificate Policy Statement endorses this approach.

Furthermore, we can find no judicial authority endorsing a Commission Certificate in a situation in which the proposed pipeline was not meant to serve any new load demand, there was no Commission finding that a new pipeline would reduce costs, the application was supported by only a single precedent agreement, and the one shipper who was party to the precedent agreement was a corporate affiliate of the applicant who was proposing to build the new pipeline. This is hardly surprising because evidence of "market need" is too easy to manipulate when there is a corporate affiliation between the proponent of a new pipeline and a single shipper who have entered into a precedent agreement.

Moreover, in this case the Commission failed to adequately balance public benefits and adverse impacts. This is a serious problem in a case in which there is no new load demand and only one affiliated shipper. In the Certificate Order, the Commission's balancing of costs and benefits consisted largely of its *ipse dixit* "that the benefits that the [proposed pipeline] will provide to the market, including enhanced access to diverse supply sources and the fostering of competitive alternatives, outweigh the potential adverse effects on existing shippers, other pipelines and their captive customers, and landowners or surrounding communities." The Commission pointed to no concrete evidence to support these assertions.

In the Rehearing Order, the Commission made a superficial effort to remedy the obvious deficits of the Certificate Order by noting that Spire Missouri had articulated several public benefits for the proposed pipeline. However, the Commission never addressed the claims raised by EDF and others challenging whether these purported benefits were likely to occur. Instead of evaluating the legitimate claims that had been raised, the Commission simply stated that it had "no reason to second guess the business decision of" Spire Missouri as reflected in the precedent agreement. Under the circumstances presented in this case—with flat demand as conceded by all parties, no Commission finding that a new pipeline would reduce costs, and a single precedent agreement between affiliates—we agree with EDF that the Commission's approach did not reflect reasoned and principled decisionmaking.

The Commission and the Spire Intervenor-Respondents advance several arguments in response, but none carry the day. First, they rely on isolated statements this court has made while reviewing previous Commission grants of Certificates. In *Minisink*, we echoed the Certificate Policy Statement in explaining that precedent "agreements 'always will be important evidence of demand for a project.' " Similarly, in *Myersville*, we noted that the petitioners had " 'identif[ied] nothing in the policy statement or in any precedent construing it to suggest that it requires, rather than permits, the Commission to assess a project's benefits by looking beyond the market need reflected by the applicant's existing contracts with shippers.' " In *City of Oberlin*, we upheld the Commission's decision to treat both affiliated and unaffiliated precedent agreements as evidence of market need . . . . According to the Commission and the Spire Intervenor-Respondents, these cases stand for two broad propositions: (1) that the Commission generally need not look behind precedent agreements in determining whether there is market demand; and (2) that affiliated precedent agreements should almost always be treated the same as unaffiliated precedent agreements. We disagree . . . .

In both *Minisink* and *Myersville*, the precedent agreements at issue were not alleged to be between affiliated entities. Thus, those cases presented significantly different facts than the instant Certificate application. . . .

In *City of Oberlin*, the pipeline applicant had entered into four precedent agreements with affiliate shippers but had entered eight precedent agreements in total. The facts of that case are therefore easily distinguishable, and the evidence of market demand was much stronger than in the instant case, where there is but a single precedent agreement and it is with an affiliated shipper. It is true that *City of Oberlin* says that FERC can put precedent agreements with affiliates on the same footing as non-affiliate precedent agreements . . ., but only so long as FERC finds "no evidence of self-dealing" or affiliate abuse and the pipeline operator "bears the risk for any unsubscribed capacity." . . .

Here, by contrast, EDF and others have identified plausible evidence of self-dealing. This evidence includes that the proposed pipeline is not being built to serve increasing load demand and that there is no indication the new pipeline will lead to cost savings. FERC's failure to engage with this evidence did not satisfy the requirements of reasoned decisionmaking. Indeed, as noted above, FERC's ostrich-like approach flies in the face of the guidelines set forth in the Certificate Policy Statement. The challenges raised by EDF and others were more than enough to require the Commission to "look behind" the precedent agreement in determining whether there was market need. If it was not necessary for the Commission to do so under these circumstances, it is hard to imagine a set of facts for which it would ever be required. Because the Commission declined to engage with EDF's arguments and the underlying evidence regarding self-dealing, its decisionmaking was arbitrary and capricious. . . .

NOTES AND QUESTIONS

1.   Both *Minisink Residents* and *Environmental Defense Fund* illustrate how a single federal agency—FERC—is the decisionmaker for interstate natural gas pipelines. This creates a much more streamlined process for applicants than exists for interstate oil pipelines or interstate electric transmission lines (both discussed below), where the applicant must seek approval from multiple states applying multiple legal standards. It also means that the courts reviewing FERC decisions, generally the D.C. Circuit Court of Appeals, are further removed from the controversy than state courts subject to local politics. Nevertheless, FERC pipeline decisions have become much more controversial in recent years, as opposition to all types of fossil fuel infrastructure has grown. This has resulted in continued protests at FERC headquarters and disruptions of FERC proceedings, as well as repeated calls by environmental groups and EPA (at least during the Obama and Biden administrations) for FERC to require applicants to assess the upstream and downstream climate impacts of natural gas infrastructure projects. *See, e.g.*, Alexandra B. Klass & Jim Rossi, *Reconstituting the Federalism Battle in Energy Transportation*, 41 HARV. ENV'T L. REV. 423, 435, 458, 462 (2017); Arianna Skibell, *"Seismic Shift" at FERC Could Kill Natural Gas Pipelines*, ENERGYWIRE (Apr. 13, 2021). What benefits does a federal approval process for natural gas transport infrastructure provide? What costs?

Indeed, the question of downstream GHG impacts from energy infrastructure, including natural gas pipelines, has become an increasingly important issue in recent years. In 2017, for instance, the D.C. Circuit ruled that FERC was required to examine these effects in approving the Southeast Market Pipelines Project, which includes the controversial Sabal Trail Pipeline through Alabama, Georgia, and Florida. The court explained:

> It's not just the journey, though, it's also the destination. All the natural gas that will travel through these pipelines will be going somewhere: specifically, to power plants in Florida, some of which already exist, others of which are in the planning stages. Those power plants will burn the gas, generating both electricity and carbon dioxide. And once in the atmosphere, that carbon dioxide will add to the greenhouse effect, which the EIS describes as "the primary contributing factor in global climate change. The next question before us is whether, and to what extent, the EIS for this pipeline project needed to discuss these "downstream" effects of the pipelines and their cargo. We conclude that at a minimum, FERC should have estimated the amount of power-plant carbon emissions that the pipelines will make possible.

An agency conducting a NEPA review must consider not only the direct effects, but also the indirect environmental effects, of the project under consideration. . . . Effects are reasonably foreseeable if they are "sufficiently likely to occur that a person of ordinary prudence would take [them] into account in reaching a decision." *EarthReports, Inc. v. FERC*, 828 F.3d 949, 955 (D.C. Cir. 2016) (citation omitted).

[By contrast, some of our prior cases held that FERC need not look at such effects.] A question presented to us in all of these cases was whether FERC, in licensing physical upgrades for an LNG terminal, needed to evaluate the climate-change effects of exporting natural gas. Relying on [*Dep't of Transp. v. Public Citizen*, 541 U.S. 752 (2004)], we answered no in each case. FERC had no legal authority to consider the environmental effects of those exports, and thus no NEPA obligation stemming from those effects. . . .

Here, FERC is not so limited. Congress broadly instructed the agency to consider "the public convenience and necessity" when evaluating applications to construct and operate interstate pipelines. See 15 U.S.C. § 717f(e). . . . Because FERC could deny a pipeline certificate on the ground that the pipeline would be too harmful to the environment, the agency is a "legally relevant cause" of the direct and indirect environmental effects of pipelines it approves. *Public Citizen* thus did not excuse FERC from considering these indirect effects.

Sierra Club v. FERC, 867 F.3d 1357, 1371–73 (D.C. Cir. 2017). For more on the question of whether FERC must analyze upstream and downstream effects in connection with pipeline approvals, see James W. Coleman, *Beyond the Pipeline Wars: Reforming Environmental Assessment of Energy Transport Infrastructure*, 2018 UTAH L. REV. 119 (2018); Michael Burger & Jessica Wentz, *Downstream and Upstream Greenhouse Gas Emission: The Proper Scope of NEPA Review*, 41 HARV. ENV'T L. REV. 109 (2017). For more on this question broadly under NEPA, see Jamison E. Colburn, *A Climate-Constrained NEPA*, 2017 U. ILL. L. REV. 1091 (2017). Even within FERC itself, the extent to which the Commission should consider these effects remains hotly contested as of 2021. *See, e.g.*, Catherine Morehouse, *Rare FERC Move Sparks Heated Debate over Commission's Role Assessing Pipeline Climate Impacts*, UTIL. DIVE (May 21, 2021); *Birckhead v. FERC*, 925 F.3d 510 (D.C. Cir. 2019) (rejecting opponents' petition for review despite "misgivings" over FERC's "less-than-dogged efforts" to obtain relevant information on downstream GHG emissions). Notably, in 2021, the D.C. Circuit held that FERC violated both the Natural Gas Act and NEPA by failing to adequately evaluate the GHG and environmental justice impacts of three LNG terminals and associated natural gas pipelines in Texas before it authorized the projects. *See Vecinos para el Bienstar de la Commundad Costera v. FERC*, 6 F.4th 1321 (D.C. Cir. 2021).

2.   The D.C. Circuit makes short work of FERC's defense to the petitioners' objections in *Environmental Defense Fund*. From an administrative law perspective, this approach fits with what might be expected from an arbitrary and capricious analysis. FERC didn't address core arguments, which is a fundamental requirement for agency decisionmaking. But what does *Environmental Defense Fund* teach about the policy enshrined in the Natural Gas Act? On one hand, as petitioners urged, why should FERC allow affiliates to profit from a pipeline that might not be needed? On the other, as many, including Spire STL, might assert, why should FERC meddle in a business choice rather than letting the market dictate whether the project is successful?

3.   Courts repeatedly have held that "all roads lead to FERC" when it comes to natural gas pipeline siting, because the Natural Gas Act of 1938 grants FERC "exclusive jurisdiction" over interstate transportation of natural gas. *Millennium Pipeline Co., L.L.C. v. Seggos*, 860 F.3d 696 (D.C. Cir. 2017). Nonetheless, FERC's authority regularly intersects with other laws. For instance, FERC prepares environmental assessments under NEPA when authorizing natural gas pipeline construction.

Two other key legal intersections are the Clean Water Act and the Coastal Zone Management Act. Both of those statutes allow state environmental protection standards to be incorporated into the federal natural gas siting procedures as "federal standards." As a result, natural gas facility operators must obtain approvals or waivers from state agencies before the FERC certificate becomes valid. For decades, states have used this leverage, particularly Section 401 of the Clean Water Act, to place additional restrictions on federal hydropower facilities. But as fossil fuel infrastructure projects become more controversial, states have used their authority aggressively to slow down or stop such projects. Two important recent examples are the now-abandoned Constitution Pipeline and the Millennium Pipeline.

The Constitution Pipeline had been proposed to transport natural gas from the Marcellus Shale area of Pennsylvania to New York. Following federal approval in 2014, the project received particular scrutiny because the gas it sought to move was produced using hydraulic fracturing. On Earth Day 2016, the New York Department of Environmental Conservation denied Clean Water Act certification for the pipeline, resulting in significant litigation. *See Constitution Pipeline Co. v. N.Y. State Dep't of Env't Conservation*, 868 F.3d 87 (2d Cir. 2017). Eventually, in 2020, Williams, the project's owner, announced it would no longer pursue construction, stating that its profitability had become "diminished in such a way that further development is no longer supported." Scott Blanchard, *Constitution Pipeline Project Ends as Builder Cites "Diminished" Return on Investment*, NPR (Feb. 25, 2020).

The Millennium Pipeline's Eastern System Upgrade faced a different fate. Following a partial win in the D.C. Circuit, *supra*, the pipeline received authorization from FERC to proceed. *See In re Millennium Pipeline Co.*, 160 FERC ¶ 61,065 (Sept. 15, 2017). The issue before the D.C. Circuit was whether the State of New York had taken too long to issue or deny a § 401 permit under the Clean Water Act. The court ruled that a state may not take more than one year to decide, but that assertions that a state has waived its right to act must be brought in the first instance to FERC. Before FERC, the agency found that New York in fact had taken too long to act, and thus, waived its right to block the project. The Second Circuit upheld FERC's decision, and construction commenced. *N.Y. State Dep't of Env't Conserv. v. FERC*, 884 F.3d 450 (2d Cir. 2018); *see also N.Y. State Dep't of Env't Conserv. v. FERC*, 991 F.3d 449 (2d Cir. 2021) (holding New York waived its right to deny Clean Water Act certification for the Northern Access Pipeline proposed to run 99 miles from Pennsylvania to Western New York and that the state's agreement with the pipeline company to re-start the clock while the state considered additional information from the company did not extend the one-year statutory deadline).

4.   Notably, the Supreme Court has not budged on the notion that FERC is the exclusive forum for natural gas pipeline siting—even in the face of claims of state sovereignty. In *PennEast Pipeline Co. LLC v. New Jersey*, 141 S. Ct. 2244 (2021), a 5–4 Court affirmed FERC's authority to permit pipelines to use NGA eminent domain authority to seize state-owned lands for private development. In doing so, the Court rejected New Jersey's assertion that the Eleventh Amendment acted as a bar to this power. Soon after the pipeline's victory, however, PennEast canceled the project, citing state environmental permitting difficulties. *See* Niina H. Farah & Carlos Anchondo, *What the PennEast Cancellation Signals for FERC, Pipelines*, ENERGYWIRE (Sept. 28, 2021).

5.   In EPAct 2005, Congress created an expedited federal judicial review process to address state actions such as those at issue in both the Constitution and Millennium Pipeline controversies. In doing so, it was responding to Congressional testimony that natural gas pipeline projects were subject to "a series of sequential administrative and State and Federal court appeals that [could] kill a project with a death by a thousand cuts just in terms of the time frames associated with going through all those appeal processes." *Islander East Pipeline Co. v. Conn. Dep't of Env't Prot.*, 482 F.3d 79, 85 (2d Cir. 2006). Given this legislative aim and exclusive FERC jurisdiction, how were objectors able to draw the approval process out for so long?

6.   In June 2020, concerned about delays in siting approvals for natural gas pipelines, the EPA amended its § 401 Clean Water Act regulations, seeking to tighten approval timelines and limiting the scope of what might trigger the need for a § 401 permit. *Clean Water Act Section 401 Certification Rule*, 85 Fed. Reg. 42,210 (July 13, 2020). Barely a year later, following President Biden's election, the agency promptly announced that it intended to revisit the 2020 amendments. *Notice of Intention to Reconsider and Revise the Clean Water Act Section 401 Certification Rule*, 86 Fed. Reg. 29,541 (June 2, 2021). In 2021, FERC issued its own rule setting a one-year deadline for state water quality certification, specifically for proposed natural gas and LNG projects. *See* FERC, 86 Fed. Reg. 16298 (Mar. 29, 2021). How much flexibility should states be given regarding the timing of weighing in on natural gas infrastructure

projects? What are the benefits and drawbacks of increased certainty surrounding these deadlines?

7.   Another issue that has arisen in FERC's certification of pipelines is the degree to which they will be used for export. Under NGA § 3, export facilities do not have eminent domain authority, while interstate pipelines do under § 7. In *NEXUS Gas Transmission, LLC*, 160 FERC ¶ 61,022 (2017), *reh'g*, 164 FERC ¶ 61,054 (2018), FERC allowed a 250-mile-long pipeline in Ohio and Michigan to proceed on the basis of precedent agreements, some of which would export gas to Canada. The D.C. Circuit then required FERC to better explain why this was acceptable. *City of Oberlin v. FERC*, 937 F.3d 599 (D.C. Cir. 2019). On remand, The Commission provided additional reasons but stuck to its original conclusion. *NEXUS Gas Transmission, LLC*, 172 FERC ¶ 61,199 (2020), *reh'g denied*, 174 FERC ¶ 62,068 (2021). For details on the intersection of U.S. policy and exported energy, see Alexandra B. Klass & Shantal Pai, *The Law of Energy Exports*, 109 CALIF. L. REV. 733 (2021).

8.   Federal authority over natural gas infrastructure also extends to LNG import and export terminals. Such terminals are needed to import and export LNG to other nations. Prior to 2005, there was some dispute over whether federal law or state law (or both) governed the siting and approval of LNG facilities. In the early 2000s, California attempted to assert siting authority and block a proposed LNG import terminal. In response, Congress clarified federal siting authority for LNG terminals in EPAct 2005. The idea was that this would allow the nation to quickly build numerous import terminals, as many experts had expressed concerns that the United States would soon be facing natural gas shortages. Under Section 3(e) of EPAct 2005, FERC has "exclusive authority to approve or deny an application for the siting, construction, expansion, or operation of an LNG terminal." 15 U.S.C. § 717b(e). Of course, only two years later, the U.S. shale gas boom began and concerns about natural gas shortages disappeared. As a result, the LNG provisions of EPAct 2005 have been used most recently to evaluate and approve LNG *export* terminals. *See Alexandra* B. Klass, *Future-Proofing Energy Transport Law*, 94 WASH. U. L. REV. 827 (2017); Alan Kovski, *Liquified Natural Gas Export Plans Face Years of Oversupply*, BNA DAILY ENV'T REP. (July 18, 2017).

A key LNG export facility that has come under fire over the last decade is the proposed Jordan Cove LNG facility in Oregon. The facility came under attack because it facilitates fossil fuel use, because it would be the only facility on the nation's West Coast, and because indigenous interests in Oregon expressed strenuous opposition. For a time, it looked like the terminal might come to fruition. Two setbacks, however, likely have killed the project. First, FERC declined to override Oregon's disapproval of a Clean Water Act § 401 certification for the pipeline that would feed the terminal. *Pacific Connector Gas Pipeline, LP*, 174 FERC ¶ 61,057 (2021). Second, the National Oceanic and Atmospheric Administration sustained Oregon's objection to the project under the Coastal Zone Management Act.

9.   Environmental justice concerns also came heavily into play in a judicial defeat for the now-canceled $7.5 billion Atlantic Coast Pipeline project, spearheaded by Dominion Energy. Relying on state law, the Fourth Circuit found insufficient a Virginia air pollution control board's approval of air permits for a pipeline compressor station because it failed to adequately consider the likely impacts of the compressor station on the predominantly Black, rural, and low-income community where it would be built. "The Board rejected the idea of disproportionate impact on the basis that air quality standards were met. But environmental justice is not merely a box to be checked, and the Board's failure to consider the disproportionate impact on those closest to the Compressor Station resulted in a flawed analysis." *Friends of Buckingham v. State Air Pollution Control Bd.*, 947 F.3d 68, 92 (4th Cir. 2020); *see also Vecinos para el Bienstar de la Commundad Costera, supra* (criticizing FERC's evaluation of impacts of proposed LNG terminal and associated pipeline project on nearby environmental justice communities).

10. Beyond questions about the technology's environmental impacts, the two dominant narratives about hydraulic fracturing revolve, first, around its impact on fuel supplies and domestic energy security and, second, around its secondary transformation of the electricity generation sector. But has hydraulic fracturing meaningfully influenced natural gas infrastructure in the United States? What conclusion do you draw from the data below?

U.S. Natural Gas Transmission Pipeline Mileage Additions

(Miles)

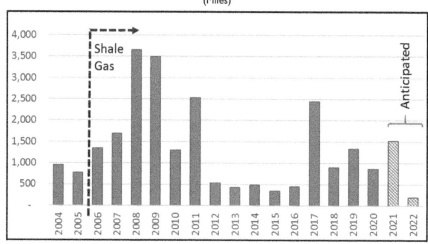

Source: Cong. Rsch. Serv.

Review Time for FERC Certificate, Pipelines over 20 Miles Long

Months After Filing

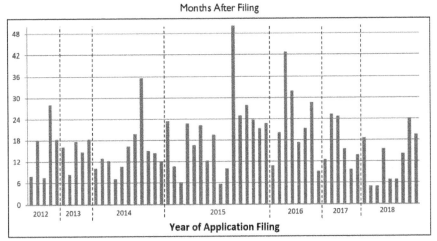

Year of Application Filing

Source: Cong. Rsch. Serv.

11. As noted earlier, opposition to all types of fossil fuel infrastructure is growing nationwide. This includes opposition to natural gas pipelines and LNG facilities in addition to coal plants and oil pipelines. In many cases, the opposition comes from new coalitions of property rights advocates who oppose the use of eminent domain for such projects and environmental groups focused on the projects' local and global environmental and climate impacts. From an environmental perspective, should all fossil fuel infrastructure projects be treated alike? What if the natural gas pipeline or LNG terminal at issue is being built to facilitate the replacement of coal-fired power with natural gas-fired power? Or to serve a power plant that is needed to backup renewable electricity generation? How should local environmental impacts be balanced against global climate impacts?

2. OIL PIPELINES

Pipelines are often the most economical way to transport large volumes of produced crude oil, with shipping from Houston to New York Harbor costing an estimated $5 per barrel, compared to $10 or $15 per barrel for rail. In more recent years, rail has garnered an increasing share of U.S. oil transport, as explained later in this chapter, but pipelines still dominate the transportation of oil and refined petroleum products. Internationally, pipelines often serve as important geopolitical links, with billions of barrels of oil transported from remote fields to refineries and international markets.

The first U.S. oil pipeline—9 miles long and made of wood—was built in Pennsylvania in 1865 to transport oil from the production fields to the rail yard. Prior to this, oil had been transported in converted whiskey barrels by horses, driven by teamsters. The following excerpt traces the fascinating early history of oil pipelines in the United States:

> . . . The first reliable petroleum supply was developed in the "Oil Region" of northwestern Pennsylvania, beginning with Drake's well at Titusville in 1859. . . . The major markets for petroleum products were located in urban areas in the United States and Europe, whereas drilling and production of the raw material occurred in relatively remote areas of Pennsylvania. Thus, transportation was a key factor in turning petroleum into a valuable commodity.
>
> The closest railroad to the 1859 Titusville oil strike was 25 miles away, accessible by wagon trail in good weather conditions. Wagon and horse teams—their drivers referred to as "teamsters"—offered oil transport at $2.50 to $4.00 per barrel and could average five to six barrels per trip between well and railroad. Prior to 1862, 6,000 teams were employed in the Oil Region, hauling oil from dispersed wellheads to rail depots in Corry, Union City, and Garland, Pennsylvania. Teams labored seven days a week, with trains of wagons sometimes extending a mile or more from rail stations. Available roads were poor: huge mud holes formed in wet weather, and leaky oil barrels led to mud and oil slurries forming on the roads. Hairless horses were a common sight, as were dead horses that had been overworked or abandoned along with broken wagons in deep mud holes. Heavy horse and oil losses were associated with this shipping method. Teamsters demanded and received high prices until water, rail, and pipeline options began to challenge teamster dominance in oil transport.
>
> By 1850, more than 80 city water systems and 50 gas distribution systems had shown that liquids and gas could be transported via pipeline. Petroleum pipelines developed as a complementary technology alongside railroads, but eventually became a transport method that would challenge railroad dominance in long-distance oil shipping. The first pipelines in the Oil Region were local "gathering lines" that collected oil and transported it across short distances. Gathering lines were initially proposed in Pennsylvania in 1860 and 1861 but teamster saboteurs, lack of capital due to the Civil War, and a state legislature unwilling to grant pipeline charters in the face of angry teamster constituents thwarted development. Yet just a few months after it denied an 1861 pipeline proposal, oil producers and railroads convinced the Pennsylvania legislature to change course and grant the Oil Creek Transportation Company the first pipeline charter. When the company failed to act immediately on its new authorization,

small, unincorporated pipelines attempted to fill the gap but largely failed due to mechanical problems and sabotage. An oil buyer built the first successful pipeline in the Oil Creek area in 1865, completed it despite teamster attacks on the line, and found the 32,000-foot line could transport about 80 barrels of oil in an hour. The pipeline and its builder had been the object of derision, but when the line proved reliable and profitable other pipelines soon appeared. By 1867 it cost 50 cents to ship a barrel of oil via pipeline, down from the $1.50 teamsters charged in 1864. Pipeline companies maintained rates just low enough to drive teamsters out of business. Pipelines also started offering storage, which allowed producers to manipulate prices by withholding oil from the market.

Pipeline companies and oil producers twice attempted and failed to get a "free pipe bill" passed in Pennsylvania to grant pipelines the eminent domain power that the railroads enjoyed. The railroads successfully blocked such efforts until a railroad price-setting scheme was revealed, angering the public and shifting opinion in favor of pipelines. When a bill was passed in Pennsylvania in 1872, the influential vice president of the Pennsylvania Railroad was successful in limiting pipeline eminent domain to eight counties in the Oil Region, excluding Allegheny County (where Pittsburgh refineries were located), and mandating that no pipeline could be constructed within five miles of the state line for the purpose of exporting oil out of state. Railroads defeated pipeline efforts to establish statewide eminent domain in Pennsylvania until 1883. A few years prior, in 1872, the Ohio Legislature passed a law granting the power of eminent domain to all pipelines acting as common carriers, and New York passed a similar law in 1878. Despite limited use of eminent domain, total pipeline mileage in the Oil Region (including gathering lines) reached 2,000 miles in 1872 and 4,000 miles in 1874. . . .

Alexandra B. Klass & Danielle Meinhardt, *Transporting Oil and Gas: U.S. Infrastructure Challenges*, 100 IOWA L. REV. 947, 954–57 (2015).

By the 1920s, the United States had over 115,000 miles of oil pipelines. During the early days of World War II, German U-boats in the Gulf of Mexico and along the Eastern Seaboard sank 48 oil tankers. As a result, building more land-based pipelines to transport oil from the Gulf Coast to the East became a national strategic priority. As the United States shifted to being a net oil importer in the 1950s and 1960s, the country further expanded its pipeline infrastructure to move oil and refined products from the Gulf Coast to the Midwest and West. Today, the U.S. pipeline system transports over 16 billion barrels of crude oil and refined petroleum products each year via nearly 220,000 miles of pipelines: over 80,000 miles of crude oil pipelines, more than 70,000 miles of natural gas liquids pipeline, and over 62,000 miles of petroleum product pipelines. Indeed, "across the U.S., natural gas is transported almost entirely by pipeline, and over 90% of crude oil and refined petroleum products are transported by pipeline at some point." E. Allison & B. Mandler, *Transportation of Oil, Gas, and Refined Products, in* PETROLEUM AND THE ENVIRONMENT (2018); *see also Where are Liquid Pipelines Located?,* Pipeline 101.

U.S. Oil Refineries and Pipelines

Source: Petroleum Geographics Corporation 2012

Source: Ass'n of Oil Pipe Lines.

Federal regulation of oil pipelines began with the Hepburn Act of 1906, which classified interstate oil pipelines as "common carriers." This made oil pipelines subject to the provisions of the Interstate Commerce Act of 1887, thus requiring pipelines to grant access to all interested and qualified shippers on a reasonable percentage of use basis. *See U.S. v. Ohio Oil Company,* 234 U.S. 548, 559 (1914) (upholding constitutionality of the Hepburn Act as applied to existing interstate oil pipelines).

In the early years, the Interstate Commerce Commission regulated interstate oil pipelines. However, in 1977, Congress transferred that authority to FERC. Today, FERC's responsibility over oil pipelines centers on rates. FERC does not regulate market entry or exit, including construction, expansion, or abandonment of oil pipelines, but rather requires pipeline operators to file tariffs containing the rates, charges, and rules for transporting oil. FERC's mandate under the Interstate Commerce Act requires "just and reasonable rates" for pipeline shipments, taking into account cost-based rates, non-cost factors, and risks associated with the regulated enterprise. *See* Interstate Commerce Act § 1(5); *Farmers Union Central Exch., Inc. v. FERC*, 734 F.2d 1486 (D.C. Cir. 1984). FERC's current regulations under the Interstate Commerce Act and the Energy Policy Act of 2005 provide for four different types of pipeline rates: (1) cost-of-service rates; (2) market-based rates; (3) settlement rates; and (4) annual index rates. For more detail on how these rates are calculated, see Elisabeth R. Myers, *Ten Years On, Oil Pipeline Deregulation Leads to Excesses—Gas, Electric Next?*, 27 NAT. GAS & ELECTRICITY 9 (Aug. 2010). Although FERC regulates roughly 200 oil pipelines, this effort comprises a small part of the agency's overall workload. In fiscal year 2012, oil pipeline regulation accounted for only 2.5% of FERC's budget. *See* Christopher J. Barr, *Unfinished Business: FERC's Evolving Standard for Capacity Rights on Oil Pipelines*, 32 ENERGY L.J. 563, 565 & n.7 (2011).

Significantly, unlike natural gas pipelines, neither FERC nor any other federal agency regulates the siting of interstate oil pipelines. Instead, pipelines must seek approval to site and build interstate and intrastate oil pipelines under state law:

> Pipelines face numerous difficulties in developing new infrastructure that are not within the FERC's regulatory purview. Like all energy projects, oil pipelines face land use restrictions and local governments increasingly at odds with new pipeline construction.
>
> *Eminent domain*. Unlike gas pipelines, oil pipelines lack the federal eminent domain authority and federal preemptive rights that accompany the FERC natural gas certificate process—eminent domain, for example, is subject to a patchwork quilt of differing state laws. Some states grant eminent domain authority to all pipelines, some to pipelines that are public utilities, some only to crude pipelines, and some provide no eminent domain authority at all. . . .
>
> *State utility commission regulation of intrastate transportation*. To the extent that oil pipelines transport petroleum in intrastate commerce, state commissions may regulate their rates and services and may indeed go further than the FERC's reach to regulate changes to facilities, leases, and changes in ownership.
>
> These and similar environmental and permitting issues loom large but are outside FERC's jurisdiction.

Christopher J. Barr, *Growing Pains: FERC's Responses to Challenges to the Development of Oil Pipeline Infrastructure*, 28 ENERGY L.J. 43, 49–51 (2007).

The lack of federal jurisdiction over oil pipeline siting means that for interstate pipelines, the pipeline must obtain approval from multiple states. Also, unlike the framework for interstate natural gas pipelines, no federal eminent domain authority is available to obtain land where an oil pipeline cannot secure voluntary agreements with all landowners in the pipeline's path. Thus, pipelines must rely on state law. In most states, a pipeline is entitled to exercise eminent domain authority so long as it is a "common carrier," meaning that the pipeline is open to any oil company willing to pay published rates. Often, oil pipelines also must receive state siting approval before they can be built, although the specifics of these requirements vary from state to state. *See* Klass & Meinhardt, *supra.*

The Keystone XL pipeline provides perhaps the highest profile recent example of a pipeline siting dispute. Because it was planned to cross the international border between the United States and Canada at Montana before traveling south to Texas, that pipeline required U.S. State Department approval in addition to approval from all the states in its path. It also provoked a stark, often bipolar debate, with those on one side urging the pipeline's necessity and economic benefits and those on the other claiming that stopping the pipeline was necessary both to limit climate change and as a symbolic turning point in efforts to reduce GHGs. The pipeline was designed to transport tar sands oil, the extraction of which can be more carbon-intensive than conventional crude oil extraction. *Compare, e.g.*, Lee Terry, *Keystone XL: The Pipeline to Energy Security*, 46 CREIGHTON L. REV. 61 (2012) *with* Allison Kilkenny, *Hundreds of Actions Are Planned to Protest Keystone XL*, THE NATION (Feb. 3, 2014). Indeed, the Keystone XL project was so controversial that it spurred legislation directly targeting it, such as Nebraska's Major Oil Pipeline Act and subsequent amendments, which instituted the first statewide review and permitting requirements for oil pipelines in the state. *See Thompson v. Heinman*, 857 N.W.2d 731 (Neb. 2015). Upon taking office in 2017, the Trump administration reversed the Obama administration's decision to deny State Department approval for the border crossing, and Nebraska had approved the pipeline, but with a different route, which required additional state and federal regulatory review. However, during the Trump administration, litigation over the environmental impacts of the pipeline continued in the courts, postponing its construction until, in 2021, President Biden revoked the border crossing permit leading to the pipeline's cancellation later that year—13 years after it was first proposed *See* John Greenberg, *Keystone XL Pipeline: Unbuilt, Opposed by Biden, Mired in Lawsuits*, POLITIFACT (Jan. 15, 2021).

But Keystone XL is not the only oil pipeline that created national controversy in the 2010s. The Dakota Access pipeline, designed to transport shale oil from North Dakota to refineries in other states, resulted in protracted protests and litigation by indigenous peoples and environmental groups. This resulted in the Obama administration denying a critical water-crossing permit for the pipeline at the eleventh hour in

2016, followed soon after by a reversal of that decision by the Trump administration in early 2017. Subsequently, the federal court vacated the project's federal easement and remanded the proceeding to the Army Corps of Engineers, but denied a proposed injunction to halt the pipeline's operations while the Corps completed required environmental review under NEPA. *Standing Rock Sioux Tribe v. U.S. Army Corps of Engineers*, 985 F.3d 1032 (D.C. Cir. 2021). As the U.S. District Court for the District of D.C. noted, "Just like the Dakota Access Pipeline, which meanders over hill and dale before carrying its crude oil underneath Lake Oahe—a large reservoir on the Missouri River between North and South Dakota—the current litigation [over the project] has wound its way through myriad twists and turns." *Standing Rock Sioux Tribe v. U.S. Army Corps of Engineers*, 2021 WL 2036662 (D.D.C., May 21, 2021).

Tribal interests, meanwhile, have been both adamant and steadfast in their opposition: "[C]onstruction and operation of the pipeline . . . threatens the Tribe's environmental and economic well-being, and would damage and destroy sites of great historic, religious, and cultural significance to the Tribe." Madison Park, *5 Things to Know About the Dakota Access Pipeline*, CNN (Aug. 31, 2016). They also—so far—have been unsuccessful. Despite all this litigation, impact on the pipeline's function has been minimal. Oil started flowing on June 1, 2017. The U.S. District Court for the District of Columbia summed it up well:

> [F]or all of the headlines and controversy that this litigation has spawned, its tangible consequences for the pipeline itself have been few. Even though this Court vacated the easement for DAPL to cross beneath Lake Oahe, and even though the D.C. Circuit affirmed such vacatur, the pipeline has maintained operations as if none of these developments had occurred. Those seeking an explanation for the persistence of this surprising state of affairs over the past ten-odd months need look no further than the Defendant in this case: the Corps.

> [A]cross two presidential administrations, the Corps has conspicuously declined to adopt a conclusive position regarding the pipeline's continued operation . . . . On the one hand, the agency has refrained from exercising its enforcement powers to halt Dakota Access's use of the pipeline, notwithstanding its status as an unlawful encroachment. At the same time, however, neither has the Corps affirmatively authorized the pipeline's occupation of the area underneath Lake Oahe . . . . Its chosen course has instead been—and continues to be—one of inaction. . . . Whatever the reason, the practical consequences of the Corps' stasis on this question of heightened political controversy are manifest: the continued flow of oil through a pipeline that lacks the necessary federal authorization to cross a key waterway of

agricultural, industrial, and religious importance to several Indian Tribes.

Those Tribes thus find themselves forced to return to this Court to seek what they have so far been unable to obtain from the Government: an order halting pipeline operations until the Corps completes its new EIS. . . .

The Court acknowledges the Tribes' plight, as well as their understandable frustration with a political process in which they all too often seem to come up just short. If they are to win their desired relief, however, it must come from that process, as judges may travel only as far as the law takes them and no further. Here, the law is clear, and it instructs that the Court deny Plaintiffs' request for an injunction.

Id.

While disputes over pipeline siting typically are neither as heated nor as high-profile as those surrounding Keystone XL or Dakota Access, they are not uncommon. The following case offers insight into both the "public convenience and necessity" findings pipelines typically need to show to be permitted (and to exercise eminent domain), and the disputes that can occur over whether eminent domain is appropriate, particularly following the Supreme Court's controversial *Kelo v. City of New London* decision in 2005, discussed below. As you read the case, consider the relative importance of whether the pipeline is considered a common carrier. The case is one piece of the multidimensional litigation over the Dakota Access pipeline.

PUNTENNEY V. IOWA UTILITIES BOARD

928 N.W.2d 829 (Iowa 2019)

MANSFIELD, JUSTICE.

The Bakken Oil Field has made North Dakota the second leading oil-producing state in our country. Almost all of America's oil-refining capacity, however, is located elsewhere in the nation. For this reason, an underground crude oil pipeline was proposed that would run from western North Dakota across South Dakota and Iowa to an oil transportation hub in southern Illinois. Following a lengthy administrative proceeding, the Iowa Utilities Board (IUB) approved the construction of this pipeline in Iowa and approved the use of eminent domain where necessary to condemn easements along the pipeline route.

Several landowners and an environmental organization sought judicial review [on statutory and constitutional grounds]. . . .

[W]e conclude that the IUB's weighing of benefits and costs supports its determination that the pipeline serves the public convenience and necessity. We also conclude that the pipeline is both a company "under the jurisdiction of the [IUB]" and a "common carrier," and therefore is not barred by Iowa Code sections 6A.21 and 6A.22 from utilizing eminent domain. In addition, we conclude that the use of eminent domain for a traditional public use such as an oil pipeline does not violate the Iowa Constitution or the United States Constitution simply because the pipeline passes through the state without taking on or letting off oil. . . .

V. Public Convenience and Necessity.

Section 479B.9gives the IUB authority to issue a permit for a pipeline that "will promote the public convenience and necessity." Iowa Code § 479B.9. Chapter 479B begins,

> It is the purpose of the general assembly in enacting this law to grant the utilities board the authority to implement certain controls over hazardous liquid pipelines to protect landowners and tenants from environmental or economic damages which may result from the construction, operation, or maintenance of a hazardous liquid pipeline or underground storage facility within the state, to approve the location and route of hazardous liquid pipelines, and to grant rights of eminent domain where necessary.

Id. § 479B.1.

Regarding the meaning of "public convenience and necessity," our court has held,

> The words are not synonymous, and effect must be given both. The word "convenience" is much broader and more inclusive than the word "necessity." Most things that are necessities are also conveniences, but not all conveniences are necessities. . . . The word "necessity" has been used in a variety of statutes . . . . It has been generally held to mean something more nearly akin to convenience than the definition found in standard dictionaries would indicate. So it is said the word will be construed to mean not absolute, but reasonable, necessity.

Thomson v. Iowa State Commerce Comm'n, 15 N.W.2d 603, 606 (Iowa 1944). In its order, the IUB looked to *Thomson* for guidance as well as an Illinois case construing the same phrase, which held,

> The word connotes different degrees of necessity. It sometimes means indispensable; at others, needful, requisite, or conducive. It is relative rather than absolute. No definition can be given that would fit all statutes. The meaning must be ascertained by reference to the context, and to the objects and purposes of the statute in which it is found.

The IUB also relied on our decision in *S.E. Iowa Cooperative Electric Association v. Iowa Utilities Board*, which approved the IUB's use of a balancing test in a related context and its determination that "the substantial benefits [of the project] outweighed the costs." 633 N.W.2d 814, 821 (Iowa 2001).

In our view, the IUB's balancing approach to public convenience and necessity should be upheld because it is not "irrational, illogical, or wholly unjustifiable." Iowa Code § 17A.19(10)(*l*). The approach is consistent with our prior caselaw and is supported by legal authority elsewhere. *See FPC v. Transcon. Gas Pipe Line Corp.*, 365 U.S. 1, 23 (1961).

Puntenney, Johnson, and the Sierra Club challenge the IUB's determination of public convenience and necessity on several grounds. First, they urge that the pipeline does not serve the public because shippers wanted it. But shippers wanted it as a way of reducing transportation costs. Given that petroleum products are commodities sold in a competitive market, lower costs for crude oil transportation tend to keep prices of crude oil derivatives lower than they otherwise would be.

Iowa is a heavy user of petroleum products. Iowa consumes the equivalent of 85.2 million barrels of oil per year but produces no oil itself. Iowa is fifth in the country in per capita energy use. Iowa ranks eighth in the country in per capita gasoline consumption. Iowa's percentage of gross domestic product from manufacturing ranks near the top in this country, and Iowa ranks sixth highest nationally in energy consumption per capita in its industrial sector. The record indicates that the Dakota Access pipeline will lead to "longer-term, reduced prices on refined products and goods and service dependent on crude oil and refined products." We agree with the IUB that these are public benefits, even though the pipeline also provides benefits to the shippers of crude oil. *See S.E. Iowa Coop. Elec.*, 633 N.W.2d at 820 (stating that "cost savings are a legitimate consideration").[2]

Next, Puntenney, Johnson, and the Sierra Club contend that drilling in the Bakken Oil Field has declined, demonstrating a reduced need for pipeline transportation. But according to the evidence before the IUB, actual crude oil production from the Bakken Oil Field has only declined about 10%, from approximately 1.2 million barrels per day to approximately 1.1 million barrels per day. At the time of the hearing, the demand for the pipeline was still there. As the IUB pointed out, shippers had executed long-term "take or pay" contracts, committing to pay for pipeline use whether they shipped oil or not.

---

[2]   The Sierra Club makes a forceful environmental argument against the Dakota Access pipeline. But this environmental argument *against* the pipeline to a degree bolsters the economic argument *for* the pipeline. That is, the Sierra Club criticizes the pipeline for making it "easier" to bring Bakken Oil Field oil to the market. Another way of saying "easier" is "cheaper" or "more economical."

Additionally, Puntenney, Johnson, and the Sierra Club maintain that rail transportation is safer than the pipeline transportation that would replace it. Various data were presented to the IUB on this issue. However, the IUB found, and the data support, that on a volume-distance basis (i.e., per barrel-mile), pipeline transportation of oil is safer than rail transportation of oil.

Lastly, Puntenney, Johnson, and the Sierra Club challenge the IUB's reliance on secondary economic benefits resulting from the construction and operation of the pipeline in Iowa. For example, the IUB observed that the pipeline would result in at least 3100 construction jobs in Iowa, at least twelve long-term jobs for Iowans, and more than $27 million annually in property tax revenue. As the Puntenney petitioners point out, Dakota Access, the IUB, and the district court cited no authority that these types of benefits can be taken into account in making a public-convenience-and-necessity determination. Yet the Puntenney petitioners cited no authority that these benefits *cannot* be considered. *See Pliura Intervenors v. Ill. Commerce Comm'n*, 942 N.E.2d 576, 585 (Ill. Ct. App. 2010) (considering, among other things, "increased revenues for local economies" resulting from a pipeline extension); *Accokeek, Mattawoman, Piscataway Creeks Cmtys. Council, Inc. v. Md. Pub. Serv. Comm'n*, 133 A.3d 1228, 1240 (Md. Ct. App. 2016) (treating "monetary benefits from construction employment and longer-term tax payments" as benefits relevant to the public-convenience-and-necessity determination). We are not persuaded that the IUB acted improperly in factoring these benefits into the public-convenience-and-necessity determination. . . .

VI. Statutory Limits on the Exercise of Eminent Domain.

The Lamb petitioners argue that Dakota Access's exercise of eminent domain over farmland would violate Iowa Code sections 6A.21 and 6A.22. Section 6A.21(1)(c) limits the authority to condemn agricultural lands by defining "public use," "public purpose," or "public improvement" in a way that requires landowner consent. Hence, section 6A.21(1)(c) reads, " '*Public use*' or '*public purpose*' or '*public improvement*' does not include the authority to condemn agricultural land for private development purposes unless the owner of the agricultural land consents to the condemnation.".

But section 6A.21 also carves out exceptions. One of them is that "[t]his limitation also does not apply to utilities, persons, companies, or corporations under the jurisdiction of the Iowa utilities board." *Id.*

The Lamb petitioners argue vigorously that Dakota Access is not a "utility." That, however, is not the full wording of the exception. We agree with the IUB and the district court that Dakota Access is a "compan[y] . . . under the jurisdiction of the [IUB]," via the permit process laid out in chapter 479B. Therefore, landowner consent is not required by section 6A.21 prior to condemnation.

The Lamb petitioners urge us to apply the canon of *ejusdem generis* to section 6A.21(2). Hence, they ask us to interpret "persons, companies, or corporations" as related to the immediately preceding word, "utilities." Their argument is difficult to follow. If the Lamb petitioners are saying that the phrase "persons, companies, or corporations" refers to *kinds* of utilities, then the word "utilities" would be sufficient by itself and the remaining language would become unnecessary. That would contravene an established principle of statutory construction. *See id.* § 4.4(2) (setting forth the presumption that "[t]he entire statute is intended to be effective"). On the other hand, if the Lamb petitioners are saying that the phrase "persons, companies, or corporations" refers to entities *other than* utilities that are nonetheless under the jurisdiction of the IUB, then Dakota Access seemingly falls in that category.

The IUB also advances an alternative ground for rejecting the Lamb petitioners' argument. It notes that section 6A.22(2) authorizes "[t]he acquisition of any interest in property necessary to the function of . . . a common carrier." In the IUB's view, Dakota Access qualifies as a common carrier.

There is no dispute that most of the pipeline capacity has been contracted to shippers in advance; however, 10% is required to be made available for walk-up business. That is all the Federal Energy Regulatory Commission requires of a common carrier. The IUB maintains it is enough here.

Based on the record before us, and our own common-carrier precedents, we agree with the IUB. It would be unrealistic to require a $4 billion pipeline to depend entirely on walk-up business, just as it would be unrealistic to require an airline to refuse all advance bookings for a flight. The key is whether spot shippers have access, and the federal agency with expertise in the matter has concluded that 10% is sufficient. We have said that "a common carrier need not serve all the public all the time." *Wright v. Midwest Old Settlers & Threshers Ass'n*, 556 N.W.2d 808, 810 (Iowa 1996) (per curiam). A common carrier may combine "other vocations" and still be considered a common carrier. *Id.* at 811. . . .

VII. Constitutional Authority for the Exercise of Eminent Domain.

This brings us to the most significant issue in the case, whether the use of eminent domain for the Dakota Access pipeline as authorized by Iowa Code section 479B.16 violates article I, section 18 of the Iowa Constitution or the Fifth and Fourteenth Amendments to the United States Constitution.

Section 479B.16 addresses the use of eminent domain for pipelines. It provides in part,

> A pipeline company granted a pipeline permit shall be vested with the right of eminent domain, to the extent necessary and as prescribed and approved by the board, not exceeding seventy-five feet in width for right-of-way and not exceeding one acre in any one location in addition to right-of-way for the location of pumps, pressure apparatus, or other stations or equipment necessary to the proper operation of its pipeline.

Article I, section 18, the takings clause in the Iowa Constitution, states in part,

> Private property shall not be taken for public use without just compensation first being made, or secured to be made to the owner thereof, as soon as the damages shall be assessed by a jury, who shall not take into consideration any advantages that may result to said owner on account of the improvement for which it is taken.

Iowa Const. art. I, § 18. The Fifth Amendment to the United States Constitution similarly provides that "private property [shall not] be taken for public use, without just compensation." U.S. Const. amend. V.

We have said that we consider federal cases interpreting the Federal Takings Clause "persuasive in our interpretation of the state provision," but "not binding."

The Lamb petitioners deny that the Dakota Access pipeline furthers a constitutionally valid public use. They contend that the indirect economic benefits of an infrastructure project, such as jobs created or tax revenues generated, cannot be considered in determining public use. They also contend that an oil pipeline that crosses Iowa but does not pick up or drop off oil within the state does not constitute a public use. We will address these arguments in order.

We begin by considering the United States Supreme Court's interpretation of the Fifth Amendment in *Kelo v. City of New London*, 545 U.S. 469 (2005). . . . There, an economic development plan was intended to remedy decades of economic decline that led to the City of New London being designated a "distressed municipality." A majority of the Court found that the City of New London could compel private homeowners to turn over their homes to a private developer because the city's plan served a "public purpose." The Court noted, "For more than a century, our public use jurisprudence has wisely eschewed rigid formulas and intrusive scrutiny in favor of affording legislatures broad latitude in determining what public needs justify the use of the takings power." *Id.* at 483.

Justice O'Connor filed a dissenting opinion in which Chief Justice Rehnquist and Justices Scalia and Thomas joined. She characterized the majority as holding "that the sovereign may take private property currently put to ordinary private use, and give it over for new, ordinary private use, so long as the new use is predicted to generate some secondary benefit for the public—such as increased tax revenue, more jobs, maybe even esthetic pleasure." *Id.* at 501. . . .

Although she did not agree that economic development alone could justify a taking, Justice O'Connor did acknowledge there were three categories of legitimate public use:

> . . . First, the sovereign may transfer private property to public ownership—such as for a road, a hospital, or a military base. Second, the sovereign may transfer private property to private parties, often common carriers, who make the property available for the public's use—such as with a railroad, a public utility, or a stadium. But "public ownership" and "use-by-the-public" are sometimes too constricting and impractical ways to define the scope of the Public Use Clause. Thus we have allowed that, in certain circumstances and to meet certain exigencies, takings that serve a public purpose also satisfy the Constitution even if the property is destined for subsequent private use.

Id. at 497–498.

The *Kelo* decision has proved controversial, not least because the development that justified the taking of Ms. Kelo's home never occurred. *See* Alberto B. Lopez, Kelo-*Style Failings*, 72 Ohio St. L.J. 777, 779–80 (2011). Several state supreme courts have held that public use must mean something more than indirect economic benefits.

Thus, in *Southwestern Illinois*, the Illinois Supreme Court held that a regional development authority could not exercise eminent domain to take a recycling facility's property and convey it to a private racetrack for a parking lot. *Sw. Ill. Dev. Auth. v. Nat'l City Env't, L.L.C.*, 768 N.E.2d 1, 4, 11 (Ill. 2002). The court concluded the purported benefit of positive economic growth in the region was not enough to satisfy public use as required under the Illinois Constitution. The court also found shorter lines to enter parking lots and the fact that pedestrians might be able to cross from parking areas to event areas in a safer manner unpersuasive as sufficient factors to satisfy the public-use requirement.

In *Southwestern Illinois*, the racetrack estimated the condemned land, which was to be used for open-field parking, would lead to an increase of $13 to $14 million in revenue per year. The Illinois court recognized that such profit could trickle down and bring revenue increases to the region. Yet it reasoned, "[R]evenue expansion alone does not justify an improper and unacceptable expansion of the eminent domain power of the government." [Courts in Michigan, Ohio, and Oklahoma have reached similar conclusions.]

Like our colleagues in Illinois, Michigan, Ohio, and Oklahoma, we find that Justice O'Connor's dissent provides a more sound interpretation of the public-use requirement. If economic development alone were a valid public use, then instead of building a pipeline, Dakota Access could constitutionally condemn Iowa farmland to build a palatial mansion, which could be defended as a valid public use so long as 3100 workers were needed to build it, it employed twelve servants, and it accounted for $27 million in property taxes.[4]

Having said that, this case is not that one. Instead, this case falls into the second category of traditionally valid public uses cited by Justice O'Connor: a common carrier akin to a railroad or a public utility. This kind of taking has long been recognized in Iowa as a valid public use, even when the operator is a private entity and the primary benefit is a reduction in operational costs. [*See Stewart v. Bd. of Supervisors*, 30 Iowa 9, 19–21 (1870); *S.E. Iowa Coop. Elec. Ass'n*, 633 N.W.2d at 820.]

In sum, because we do not follow the *Kelo* majority under the Iowa Constitution, we find that trickle-down benefits of economic development are not enough to constitute a public use. To the extent that Dakota Access is relying on the alleged economic development benefits of building and operating the pipeline, we are unmoved. But here there is more. While the pipeline is undeniably intended to return profits to its owners, the record indicates that it also provides public benefits in the form of cheaper and safer transportation of oil, which in a competitive marketplace results in lower prices for petroleum products. As already discussed, the pipeline is a common carrier with the potential to benefit all consumers of petroleum products, including three million Iowans.

The Lamb petitioners assert that even these benefits are not enough, because no Iowa business or consumer will actually use the pipeline to deliver or receive crude oil. This approach is too formalistic. Iowa has some of the most advanced and productive farming in the world. But our economy, including our agricultural economy, depends on other states to produce crude oil and refine that crude oil into petroleum products. If our consideration of public use were limited as the Lamb petitioners propose, it would be very difficult ever to build a pipeline across Iowa carrying any product that isn't produced in Iowa. Yet Iowa is crisscrossed with pipelines.

In *Enbridge Energy (Illinois), L.L.C. v. Kuerth*, the Illinois Appellate Court took a more nuanced view, which we find persuasive. There the court rejected an appeal by certain landowners and upheld a grant of eminent

---

4   In fairness to the *Kelo* majority, they did not say that any economic development benefit would meet the public-use test. If the economic benefits of merely building a project qualified as a public use, then the legislature could empower A to take B's house just because A planned to erect something new on the lot. Even the *Kelo* majority did not go that far. . . . But as Justice O'Connor noted in dissent, it is problematic to have a fact-based public-use test that allows economic development benefits to suffice in some cases, depending on whether the economic development benefit derives from "a multipart, integrated plan rather than . . . an isolated property transfer."

domain authority for an oil pipeline project. The court reasoned, "The fundamental flaw of landowners' argument is that they focus entirely upon who *uses* the pipeline rather than who *benefits* from it." . . . 99 N.E.3d [210, 218 (Ill. App. Ct. 2018)].

This reasoning applies here. The record indicates that the Dakota Access pipeline will lead to "longer-term, reduced prices on refined products and goods and service dependent on crude oil and refined products." [*See also Sunoco Pipeline L.P. v. Teter*, 63 N.E.3d 160, 171–72 (Ohio Ct. App. 2016).]

Accordingly, we hold that there was no violation of article I, section 18 of the Iowa Constitution [and] no Fifth Amendment violation. We recognize that a serious and warranted concern about climate change underlies some of the opposition to the Dakota Access pipeline. Maybe, as a matter of policy, a broad-based carbon tax that forced all players in the marketplace to bear the true cost of their carbon emissions should be imposed. The revenues from this broad-based tax could be used to offset other taxes. But policy making is not our function . . . .

NOTES AND QUESTIONS

1.   *Puntenney* raises several questions about the role of eminent domain in energy infrastructure. As noted above, most states allow private companies to exercise eminent domain to build oil pipelines and other energy-related infrastructure. Is that in the public interest? Should a for-profit pipeline be considered a "public use" allowing for the exercise of eminent domain?

2.   States vary significantly in their approach to siting and eminent domain for oil pipelines. Some states, like Texas, do not require state approval of oil pipelines but merely require the applicant to be, for instance, a common carrier. Other states, like Illinois, require a certificate of need or a certificate of public convenience and necessity, which is issued only after a full analysis of economic need and environmental impacts. Most states classify oil pipelines as a "public use" by statute, authorizing the pipeline company to exercise eminent domain authority. In some states, a certificate or other approval is required prior to exercising eminent domain, while in other states a certificate or approval is required prior to actual construction of the pipeline but not necessarily prior to initiating eminent domain proceedings. *See* Klass & Meinhardt, *supra* (providing a 50-state survey). Why might states vary so significantly in their approach to siting and eminent domain for oil pipelines? Which approach best facilitates oil transportation infrastructure? Which provides more protection for landowners and private property rights? Would a federal approach, like that used for interstate natural gas pipelines, be better? Why or why not? For an argument that pipeline siting laws inadequately assess risk, see Sara Gosman, *Planning for Failure: Pipelines, Risk, and the Energy Revolution*, 81 OHIO ST. L.J. 349 (2020).

3.   One of the longest fought battles over energy infrastructure siting took place in the 1970s and involved the Trans-Alaska Pipeline. In 1968, the Atlantic Richfield Company (ARCO) discovered large reserves of crude oil near Prudhoe Bay, Alaska. Prudhoe Bay is on Alaska's Northern Slope. To develop this oil reserve, ARCO needed to build a pipeline to carry the crude nearly 800 miles to Valdez, where it could be shipped to market by tanker. ARCO joined with several other oil companies to form the Trans-Alaska Pipeline System (TAPS), which would oversee the pipeline construction. The pipeline route would cross 641 miles of federally owned land, meaning that TAPS had to seek rights-of-way from the Bureau of Land Management to proceed. In 1969, TAPS submitted applications for those rights-of-way. Several conservation groups challenged the petitions, citing NEPA violations and violations of the right-of-way width restrictions in the Mineral Leasing Act of 1920. The plaintiffs obtained a preliminary injunction, but Interior Secretary Morton ultimately granted the pipeline applications. The D.C. District Court affirmed the Secretary's decision, but in 1973, the D.C. Circuit disagreed, finding the Secretary was bound by the Mineral Leasing Act's width restrictions. *Wilderness Society v. Morton*, 479 F.2d 842, 893 (D.C. Cir. 1973). The very next year, however, Congress passed Trans-Alaska Pipeline Authorization Act, which gave TAPS (now Alyeska) the needed rights-of-way to build the pipeline. *Trans-Alaska Pipeline History*, Am. Oil & Gas Hist. Soc'y. Construction began in 1974 and was completed in 1977 at a cost of nearly $8 billion. The dispute over the TAPS pipeline provides a case study in the controversy that can erupt around the siting of energy transportation facilities.

4.   The Keystone XL and Dakota Access controversies have drawn national attention to the role that energy transport infrastructure plays in facilitating the increased production and use of fossil fuels. But such protests and litigation have not been limited to those two pipelines. In recent years, landowners, property rights advocates, and environmental groups have joined forces to oppose oil pipelines around the country.

In 2016, for instance, local opposition to Kinder Morgan's proposed $1 billion, 360-mile, Palmetto Pipeline from South Carolina to Florida along the Georgia coast caused legislators in South Carolina and Georgia to enact moratoria on the use of eminent domain for private oil pipelines—resulting in the company abandoning the project. The moratorium in Georgia expired one year later, in 2017, but legislation enacted that year required, for the first time, oil pipeline projects to obtain a permit from the Georgia Environmental Protection Division as well as a certificate of public necessity from the Georgia Department of Transportation if eminent domain will be used. It appears that these requirements have had a significant impact on projects in the state, with Georgia's oldest and most well-known pipeline, Colonial, killing several projects due to "mounting costs and . . . opposition," Tamar Hallerman, *Land Fights, Public Opposition Left Georgia Reliant on One Pipeline*, ATLANTA J.-CONST. (May 28, 2021), and others asserting that the law has made Georgia "extremely vulnerable to supply interruptions from weather and human interference." GEORGIA ENV'T FINANCE AUTH., 2019 GEORGIA ENERGY REPORT

(Dec. 2019). The South Carolina moratorium was in place until 2020, and bills have been introduced in the state's legislature to extend the moratorium into 2022. *See* Mary Landers, *Georgia Lawmakers Pass Compromise Pipeline Bill*, SAVANNAH MORNING NEWS (Mar. 31, 2017); Gillian Neimark, *In Georgia and South Carolina, "The Game Has Changed" on Oil Pipelines*, SOUTHEAST ENERGY NEWS (Mar. 14, 2017).

Another set of controversies has revolved around two different pipelines owned and operated by the Canadian company Enbridge. These lines—Line 3 and Line 5—move crude oil from Canada into the United States. Line 5 runs through the Straits of Mackinac, which connect Lake Michigan and Lake Huron, between Michigan's Lower Peninsula and Upper Peninsula. Enbridge has promised to shore up the aging pipeline, which transports more than 500,000 barrels per day, but Michigan Governor Gretchen Whitmer ordered the company to shut down the pipeline by May 2021. As this book goes to print, the parties are in mediation. Even more controversial is Line 3—"an integrity and maintenance driven project that would involve the construction of 330 miles of new 36-inch diameter pipeline to replace 282 miles of the existing 34-inch Line 3 pipeline" from the Minnesota-North Dakota border to Enbridge's terminal near Duluth. The project is particularly controversial because it would move crude oil from tar sands in Canada, and because nearby tribal interests oppose it. As one court has described:

> In order to build, Enbridge must establish the need for replacement Line 3. That question of necessity divides state agencies—and many Minnesotans. The legislature tasked the Minnesota Public Utilities Commission to decide—after consideration of attendant environmental risks—that central question of need . . . .
>
> After considering the potential environmental impacts of replacement Line 3, the commission concluded that it was necessary. It did so leaning heavily on the comparative risks of continuing to operate existing Line 3. The commission issued the required certificate of need, and selected a route as well. . . .
>
> These decisions were not made in a vacuum. Rather, they followed vigorous public debate. In addition to everyday Minnesotans—some in favor and some opposed to replacement Line 3—the commission heard from interested groups including multiple Indian tribes with interests impacted by existing Line 3 or that would be impacted by the replacement pipeline; environmental organizations opposed to replacing the pipeline; trade organizations that hoped to use the pipeline and unions that hope to build it; and the department of commerce, which asserted a lack of need for the replacement pipeline. . . .
>
> [W]hile reasonable minds may differ on the central question of need for replacement Line 3, substantial evidence supports the commission's decision to issue a certificate of need. . . .

In re Enbridge Energy, L.P., 964 N.W.2d 173 (Minn, Ct. App., June 14, 2021). Continuing litigation over Line 3 is certain. As this book went to print, litigation was ongoing but the pipeline was scheduled to begin operating in October 2021.

5.   In addition to shining a light on the role of energy infrastructure in facilitating fossil fuel use, several pipeline controversies in recent years have underscored the environmental justice impacts these projects can have on people of color and those of lower income. This has been particularly true for the Dakota Access project. For a deep dive on Dakota Access, including the environmental racism concerns it raises, see KATHERINE WILTENBURG TODRYS, BLACK SNAKE: STANDING ROCK, THE DAKOTA ACCESS PIPELINE, AND ENVIRONMENTAL JUSTICE (2021). In contrast to the apparent outcome for Dakota Access, a pipeline project in Memphis was canceled in 2021 in the face of concerns about disproportionate impacts on people of color. Mike Soraghan, *Memphis Pipeline Canceled After Environmental Justice Feud*, ENERGYWIRE (July 6, 2021). For more details on the Trump administration approvals for the Keystone XL and Dakota Access pipelines in the face of significant public resistance, see Robinson Meyer, *Donald Trump and the Order of the Pipelines*, THE ATLANTIC (Jan. 25, 2017); Darran Simon & Eliott C. McLaughlin, *Keystone and Dakota Access Pipelines: How Did We Get Here?*, CNN (Jan. 25, 2017).

6.   Oil and natural gas are not the only energy resources transported by pipeline. Carbon dioxide is too. As noted in Chapter 2, oil is often extracted using "tertiary recovery" or enhanced oil recovery (EOR) techniques, where supercritical CO_2 is injected into oil wells to boost production. EOR is becoming increasingly profitable, and pipelines to transport CO_2 have expanded rapidly to serve well operators, who rely on them to transport CO_2 to extraction sites. There are currently nearly 4,500 miles of dedicated CO_2 pipelines and 6,000 wells using CO_2 EOR.

7. CO_2 pipelines also come into play in another way that demonstrates the interconnectedness of all our energy systems. It has been suggested that electric utilities use carbon capture and storage (CCS), discussed in Chapter 2, as a climate change mitigation tool. If that transpires, an even more extensive CO_2 pipeline network than already exists would be required. Indeed, the current CO_2 pipeline mileage would have to dramatically increase to accommodate a fully functioning CCS network. *See* PAUL PARFOMAK & PETER FOLGER, CONG. RSCH. SERV., PIPELINES FOR CARBON DIOXIDE (CO_2) CONTROL: NETWORK NEEDS AND COST (2008); Jennifer Skougard Horne, *Getting from Here to There: Devising an Optimal Regulatory Model for CO_2 Transport in A New Carbon Capture and Sequestration Industry*, 30 J. LAND RES. & ENV'T L. 357, 360 (2010). While CO_2 pipelines must meet federal safety standards and are regulated by the U.S. Department of Transportation, CO_2 pipeline siting and rates currently are not regulated by the federal government, as siting authority rests with the states. Do you think that siting authority should stay with the states or be transferred to the federal government? Why? Or is there another approach? CCS and its connection to EOR are discussed in more detail in Chapter 11.

PRACTICE PROBLEM

You are a new lawyer developing a specialty in energy law in the state of Oklahoma. Unlike many other states, Oklahoma does not have a process (like the one described in the *Puntenney* case) where a state agency reviews the economics and environmental impacts of the oil pipeline and issues a certificate or permit. This is true even though many major pipelines run through Oklahoma. You have been following the controversies surrounding the Keystone XL, Dakota Access, and Palmetto pipelines and are also aware that Nebraska and Georgia created new, statewide siting processes for major pipelines because of these controversies. You are going to a picnic at the end of the week that will likely have a mix of academics, lawyers, industry representatives, and environmental advocates present. You know that they will want to talk about the Keystone XL pipeline as well the potential for new, major pipelines in the same vicinity because of the massive increase in U.S. and Canadian oil from tar sands development and hydraulic fracturing. In your short tenure as a lawyer, you have learned that you are often called upon at cocktail parties to provide expertise on current energy law issues.

In preparation for those conversations, you want to be ready to explain the key legal and policy issues associated with the benefits and drawbacks of these pipelines, the law that applies to the siting and eminent domain surrounding their construction in Oklahoma and the rest of the region, the role of the U.S. State Department, the role of the states, the benefits and drawbacks of facilitating the import of Canadian tar sands oil to the United States, and alternative methods of transporting oil resources such as rail. You found two reports on the topic—PAUL F. PARFOMAK, CONG. RSCH. SERV., KEYSTONE XL PIPELINE: THE END OF THE ROAD? (Jan. 22, 2021) and MELISSA DENCHAK, NRDC, WHAT IS THE KEYSTONE XL PIPELINE? (June 20, 2021)—and you know there are lots of other articles and reports on the internet.

What do you plan to say on the issues above associated with recent pipeline projects? What other issues are important to a fuller understanding of the role of pipelines and their regulation in U.S. energy policy? If Oklahoma were to adopt a statewide oil pipeline siting process, should it follow Nebraska or Georgia's lead or choose another state's model?

3. ELECTRICITY TRANSMISSION

As with the natural gas, coal, and oil industries, transportation infrastructure is the spine of the nation's electricity system. In fact, large, high-voltage electric transmission lines are often referred to as just that—"backbone" facilities. They are vital to system operation and stability, and they are the core architecture around which the nation's modern electricity system is built: the capability to move power from big central power stations to distant load centers—the cities where we live.

Regulation of electricity transmission as such is covered in depth in Chapters 4 and 5. There, we address questions of transmission ratemaking, including cost allocation and incentive rates; FERC's shift to open-access, common-carrier-like transmission regulation; the emergence of ISOs and RTOs; and the changing face of electricity federalism, including limited transmission siting authority by DOE and FERC.

Here we focus on electric transmission lines as another illustration of the difficult issues surrounding energy transport siting. Transmission lines are a good example of these issues. Even a casual perusal of major newspapers reveals the pervasiveness of disputes over energy transport facility siting, often involving electric transmission lines.

One common dilemma is the NIMBY, or "not in my backyard," phenomenon. While transmission facilities benefit everyone and often are needed to keep the system running smoothly, no one wants to have a line sited near their home, parks, or schools. But if no one wants a new line near them, either it is not built and the system becomes inefficient—under-invested in and under-reliable—or those with the least amount of political clout bear the brunt of such facilities—often racial minorities and those of lower income.

Another common issue is the purpose of transmission facility use, including the actors authorized to construct them. Historically, vertically integrated utilities built transmission lines for their own use, or to buttress interconnected systems. Today, with the onset of competition and the segmentation of the industry, transmission no longer serves only this typical purpose. Many new lines are being built specifically to access renewable energy facilities or other generation owned by new competitors. And an emerging trend is the construction of transmission by non-utility, independent "merchant" transmission companies who are in the game not to serve a dedicated service area, but rather, to compete for economic profits.

We use two cases to highlight these issues and the challenges of cost allocation. The first addresses more traditional siting questions involving transmission lines. It shows how different courts address questions of eminent domain authority, specifically for a transmission line that will benefit a region rather than primarily in-state interests. The second highlights the emerging challenges associated with integrating renewable energy sources such as wind and solar farms into the existing grid, including the need for new transmission lines and capacity. Some states have adopted policies specifically to promote these types of lines, while other localities have resisted them. The map below, created by the National Renewable Energy Laboratory, illustrates how the nation could build out a network of multi-state, high-voltage direct current (HVDC) transmission lines to transport large quantities of wind and solar energy within and between the country's three interconnections, taking advantage of regional renewable energy resources as well shifting electricity demand over multiple time zones. Multiple, recent reports have similarly focused on the need for such transmission lines to meet state and federal decarbonization goals and the feasibility of building them. *See, e.g.,* MICHAEL GOGGIN ET AL., TRANSMISSION PROJECTS READY TO GO: PLUGGING INTO AMERICA'S UNTAPPED RENEWABLE RESOURCES (Apr. 2021); Patrick Brown & Audun Botterud, *The Value of Inter-Regional Coordination and Transmission in Decarbonizing the US Electricity System*, 5 JOULE 115 (Jan. 2021); U.S. ENERGY INFO. ADMIN., ASSESSING HVDC TRANSMISSION FOR IMPACTS OF NON-DISPATCHABLE GENERATION 7 & A-9 (June 2018).

"Macrogrid" Design "D3"

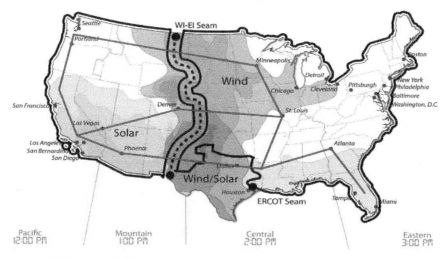

Source: Nat'l Renewable Energy Lab.

Building lines like these, however, poses multiple regulatory and political challenges. As you read the following cases and notes, consider why long-distance electric transmission lines can be so controversial. Is it because they are so visible, or is it something else? What type of policy would you prefer for the jurisdiction where you live—one that promotes construction of transmission lines or one that restricts it? What effect do those policies have on electricity service? Should it matter whether the lines will be owned by public utilities or merchant companies, whether they are for in-state or interstate use, or what type of generation they are connecting to the grid?

SQUARE BUTTE ELEC. CO-OP. V. HILKEN

244 N.W.2d 519 (N.D. 1976)

ERICKSTAD, CHIEF JUSTICE.

This is an appeal from a judgment entered in Burleigh County District Court on September 18, 1975, which denied to Square Butte Electric Cooperative the power of eminent domain for failure to establish a public use. . . .

Square Butte was incorporated in North Dakota on May 24, 1972, to generate and transmit electric power to rural electric cooperatives. It was capitalized at $1,000 through issuance of 100 shares at $10 per share. Square Butte employs only one person, its general manager Lyle Lund, who has been employed by Minnkota Power Cooperative for nearly 25 years.

Minnkota is a wholesale distributor of electricity organized in Minnesota with its principal place of business being Grand Forks, North Dakota. There are 12 Class A members of Minnkota who own and govern the distributor. Those 12 include four rural electric cooperatives in eastern North Dakota and eight rural electric cooperatives in northwestern Minnesota. . . . There are 58,000 billed customers on Minnkota's lines with the number evenly divided between North Dakota and Minnesota. . . .

In the early 1970's, according to witnesses called on behalf of Square Butte, the combination of increasing projected load growths on the Minnkota system and the curtailment of traditional Rural Electrification Administration loans led Minnkota to seek alternate sources of financing for new generating plants. An investor-owned utility serving part of northern Minnesota, including Duluth, was also looking for additional sources of power. Minnesota Power and Light [MP], through negotiations with Minnkota, ultimately agreed to guarantee bonds and securities for construction of generation and transmission facilities in exchange for delivery of electrical power to its system. . . .

For those reasons, Square Butte was incorporated with control resting in the 12 rural electric cooperatives who are Class A members of Minnkota. It subsequently entered into a power sales and interconnection agreement with MP.

The Square Butte project includes a 400 megawatt lignite [coal] fired generating plant (Center #2) near Center, North Dakota, and a direct current (DC) transmission line from the plant to Duluth, Minnesota. Center #2 will be adjacent to the Milton R. Young plant (Center #1) and will require an additional 30 employees. The DC line will cross 225.8 miles of North Dakota, including 155.1 miles of nonirrigated cropland, 63.1 miles of pasture, 2.1 miles of woodland, and 5.5 miles of wetland. Square Butte is apparently seeking easements that are 120 feet wide.

Because the line is DC, Square Butte must install a converter at Center #2 and MP must build another converter at Duluth. It is only before the power is converted from AC to DC at Center and after it is converted from DC to AC at Duluth that the power is usable by existing consumers. The system does not include any other converters and, because of the expense, none are presently planned.

Both Minnkota and MP are members of the Mid-Continent Area Power Pool (MAPP) which requires its members to maintain a 15% Reserve capacity related to annual system demand. Square Butte is not a member of MAPP. . . .

The defendants herein are landowners in Burleigh County, across whose property Square Butte seeks easements for its DC power line and structures. . . .

I.

The power of eminent domain inheres in the sovereignty of the state and is not dependent on any specific grant. It is not, however, an unfettered power. Section 14 of the North Dakota Constitution provides in pertinent part that "Private property shall not be taken or damaged for public use without just compensation having been first made to, or paid into court for the owner." . . .

By Section 32–15–02, N.D.C.C., and subject to the provisions of the chapter,

"* * * the right of eminent domain may be exercised in behalf of the following public uses:

"* * *10. Oil, gas, and coal pipelines and works and plants for supplying or conducting gas, oil, coal, heat, refrigeration, or power for the use of any county, city, or village, or the inhabitants thereof, together with lands, buildings, and all other improvements in or upon which to erect, install, place, maintain, use, or operate pumps, stations, tanks, and other machinery or apparatus, and buildings, works, and plants for the purpose of generating, refining, regulating, compressing, transmitting, or distributing the same, or necessary for the proper development and control of such gas, oil, coal, heat, refrigeration, or power, either at the time of the taking of said property or for the future proper development and control thereof . . ."

II.

As to the requisites of a public use, we find a decision of the Montana Supreme Court generally descriptive:

At the outset, we recognize that there are two conflicting lines of authority in other jurisdictions concerning the requisites of a "public use" within the meaning of eminent domain proceedings. One view, the limited or narrow view, requires in general the actual use or right to use the proposed system by the public as a whole. The other view, called the broad view, essentially requires only a use conferring a "public advantage" or a "public benefit." Montana, as with many western states, has adhered to the broad view since 1895, presumably to promote general economic development. . . .

Montana Power Company v. Bokma, 457 P.2d 769, 772–773 (Mont. 1969).

The court noted that Montana Power "is a public utility and as such has dedicated its property to the public use under regulations imposed by the Montana Public Service Commission." It sustained use of the eminent domain power for an intrastate 115 KV line designed to furnish electricity to a crude oil pumping station, but the court noted that "service from that line is available to other customers should such service be required." . . .

[In] *Adams v. Greenwich Water Co.*, 83 A.2d 177 (Conn. 1951), . . . [r]esponding to the contention that since the chartered defendant proposed to construct a reservoir greater in capacity than necessary to supply its Connecticut customers, then the reservoir was "for the exclusive benefit of nonresidents," the Connecticut Supreme Court conceded "that no state is permitted to exercise or authorize the exercise of the power of eminent domain except for a public use within its own borders." But the court concluded, "If the taking is for a public use which will provide a substantial and direct benefit to the people of the state which authorizes it, it is a proper exercise of the power of eminent domain even though it also benefits the residents of another state."

In *Gralapp v. Mississippi Power Company*, 194 So.2d 527 (Ala. 1967), . . . [r]esponding to the argument that since Mississippi Power was not subject to the control of the Alabama Public Service Commission and since Alabama Power held only a contractual right to receive power transmitted over the proposed line, the public in Alabama had no legal right to benefits from the line, the Alabama court held that as the evidence in the case established that electricity would flow in both directions along the proposed line there was sufficient benefit to the public in Alabama. . . .

In *Clark* the Florida court determined that the pleadings were insufficient to allege a public use and declared:

> * * *the sovereign's power of eminent domain, whether exercised by it or delegated to another, is limited to the sphere of its control and within the jurisdiction of the sovereign. A state's power exists only within its territorial limits for the use and benefit of the people within the state. Thus, property within one state cannot be condemned for the sole purpose of serving a public use in another state. Conjecture might be made that electrical current generated

in Georgia will flow into Florida for the benefit of Florida citizens and vice versa; however, the pleading before us indicates that a one way transmission line is contemplated from which the citizens of Florida will not derive one iota of benefit.

Clark v. Gulf Power Company, supra, 198 So.2d at 371.

From these cases, it appears that the following elements must be present for a public use to exist in the state where the property sought to be condemned lies. First, the public must have either a right to benefit guaranteed by regulatory control through a public service commission (*Bokma*) or an actual benefit (*Gralapp*). Second, although other states may also be benefited, the public in the state which authorizes the taking must derive a substantial and direct benefit [that is] . . . something greater than an indirect advantage. . . . Third, the public benefit, while not confined exclusively to the state authorizing the use of the power . . . is nonetheless inextricably attached to the territorial limits of the state because the state's sovereignty is also so constrained. . . .

To dispose of this case, we must determine whether the benefits alleged by Square Butte provide, either singly or in unison, a substantial and direct benefit to North Dakota.

III.

Reserve and Emergency Power Supplies

Square Butte alleges first that its project will increase reserve and emergency power supplies available within North Dakota. The Mid-Continent Area Power Pool requires each of its participants to hold fifteen percent of its total generating capacity in reserve to meet emergency and shortterm requirements. Since MP and Minnkota are both members of MAPP, the project will increase the reserve supply available to MAPP participants.

The trial court found "(t)hat any association of Square Butte with power pools and energy backups in not direct enough to support requirement of public use." Reserve supplies of electricity through power pooling are designed to increase the reliability of power systems and to decrease capital expenditures since each company need not install a reserve capacity equal to the size of its largest generating unit.

The Square Butte project adds 60 megawatts of reserve and emergency power supply to what would otherwise be available to the North Dakota members of MAPP. This is a significant factor relating to the adequacy and reliability of the power pool reserve. There may be, additionally, certain economic benefits to North Dakotans from Center #2 as a backup source of power. . . .

Stabilizing Effect of DC Line on Supply System

Square Butte does contend that the DC line will increase the reliability of the electrical supply system in North Dakota by reducing the frequency of phenomena known as "low frequency oscillations." Whether or not low frequency oscillation will occur depends on the combination of the amount of generation in the area, the amount of transmission and the strength of that transmission. . . .

MP's manager of system planning testified that 68 low frequency undamped oscillations were recorded in North Dakota during 1972. He indicated that seven of those resulted in system collapses: "The transmission system in North Dakota breaking up, the units tripping off the line, circuit breakers opening, et cetera." . . .

Testimony at the trial included an averment that with the stabilizing effect of the DC line on the AC system the entire generating complex in the Bismarck area will be able to operate at a higher output level than currently exists. During his deposition, Professor Krueger indicated additional generation on the AC system "with a stabilizing DC line . . . would not contribute to instability of the system, but without the line it would."

MP chose the DC line after its studies indicated that various 345 KV AC transmission schemes totaling more than 950 miles of line would not be "adequate to support the (generating) unit in North Dakota and deliver its output to the MP service area. . . ."

None of the trial court's findings of fact concern the effect of the DC line on low frequency oscillations. In his memorandum opinion, the trial judge observed, "There has been testimony regarding the stabilization of the AC lines within the State of North Dakota which this Court finds is not persuasive enough to supply public use for condemnation purposes."

. . . [W]e may not set aside findings of fact in civil actions unless such findings are clearly erroneous. . . . In light of the fact that the testimony asserting that the DC line will stabilize the existing AC generating and transmission systems in North Dakota was not disputed, it is possible that the trial court determined that the stabilizing effect is a benefit, but that such an influence is by itself insufficient to justify exercising the power of eminent domain. In any case we conclude that the trial court was clearly erroneous in not giving some effect to this influence. We think that the stabilizing influence is a factor that must be considered with other factors to determine whether there is a direct and substantial benefit to North Dakota. . . .

Because of the cumulative effect of the increase in reserve and emergency supplies, of the stabilizing effect of the DC line on the existing AC system, of the existence of [an option in the contract for Minnkota to receive power from Square Butte in specified, increasing percentage amounts after 1985], of the lower cost of that power, and of certain incidental benefits, we disagree with the trial court's conclusion that Square Butte has failed to establish a public use. None of these features alone would suffice, but the sum of the benefits does meet the requirement that North Dakota receive a substantial benefit.

Therefore, we reverse the judgment of the district court that dismissed Square Butte's complaint, reinstate the cause of action, and remand for assessment of damages. . . .

SAND and VOGEL, JUSTICES (dissenting).

. . . It is abundantly clear that the authority granted to exercise the power of eminent domain is limited by the Constitution to the taking of property for public use. The reference to public use in §§ 14 and 134 of the North Dakota Constitution obviously, and out of necessity, must refer to public use to the inhabitants of the State of North Dakota, otherwise this provision would be invalid. . . .

In the *Gralapp* case, . . . the Alabama court observed that the evidence established that the electricity would flow in both directions along the lines sought to be constructed. It then said, "We cannot agree there would be no benefits to the public in Alabama from the construction and use of this power line."

It must be observed that there is, however, a major distinction between the *Gralapp* case and the case under consideration. In the case under consideration, the transmission line is DC and will not be converted to AC until it reaches Duluth, Minnesota. Its use, if any, in North Dakota would be incidental rather than direct. The line could not be usefully "tapped" in North Dakota. We have here the reverse of the *Gralapp* case in this instance with the direct or primary benefit to Minnesota residents and indirect benefits, if any, to North Dakota residents. . . . [W]e have a DC line which would be of no avail until the direct current had been changed to AC, which does not take place in North Dakota but takes place at Duluth, Minnesota, from where the energy would be filtered back westward. . . .

The majority opinion puts the North Dakota consumer in the position of going to Midcontinent Area Power Pool (MAPP), of which Minnkota and MP are members, with hat in hand and asking, "Please, may we have some of our energy." This is the picture after North Dakota coal has been converted into electric energy, in North Dakota, and then transmitted directly to Duluth, Minnesota, by a direct current line. If the transmission lines were AC, the objection would not be as great because the line could be "tapped" and transformers could be installed and energy could be used in North Dakota, but as it is now no energy can be available to North Dakota until it has been converted to AC at Duluth and then only as it is filtered back into transmission systems in Minnesota, which may or may not bring the energy back to North Dakota. The majority opinion permits pirating North Dakota resources and land primarily for the benefit of persons other than the inhabitants of the State of North Dakota. . . .

Square Butte was designedly created as a North Dakota corporation for the purpose of building an electrical energy, DC, transmission line from Center, North Dakota, to Duluth, Minnesota. Square Butte would not control the electrical energy which is transmitted over the DC line, particularly after it reaches Duluth, Minnesota, its point of destination, where it will be converted into AC.

We thus have a situation where the condemnor is in no position to assure that the electrical transmission line will have a public use or benefit for or to the North Dakota inhabitants. The benefit, if any, that will result to any North Dakota inhabitants would come from the electrical energy which may filter back into the North Dakota network in the eastern part of the State. The benefits so obtained would be incidental, rather than direct. . . .

We would affirm the judgment of the trial court.

VOGEL, JUSTICE (dissenting [in which JUSTICE SAND joins]).

I fully agree with the dissent of Justice Sand, and add a few remarks of my own.

The benefits to North Dakota claimed in the majority opinion [rely on] . . . "incidental benefits" such as assumed lower costs in the distant future due to cheaper construction at present-day costs, and emergency backup potential.

The "incidental benefits" can be dismissed as irrelevant. . . . The "incidental benefits" are equally applicable to all plant and transmission line construction anywhere, since all lines are interconnected with others, so the construction of any line anywhere adds backup potential to all lines to which it is interconnected. Such potential, standing alone, is no reason for allowing the use of eminent domain. If the mere addition of generating capacity anywhere were enough to justify the use of eminent domain, judicial review would be meaningless. . . .

If corporate powers of eminent domain extend to this case, as the majority says they do, I find it difficult to conceive of a situation to which they would not extend. . . .

IN RE APPLICATION OF INTERNATIONAL TRANSMISSION CO.

827 N.W.2d 385 (Mich. Ct. App. 2012), *rev'd in part on other grounds*, 822 N.W.2d 23 (Mich. 2013)

PER CURIAM.

In these consolidated cases, appellant Association of Businesses Advocating Tariff Equity (ABATE) and appellants Michigan Public Power Agency (MPPA) and Michigan Municipal Electric Association (MMEA) appeal the February 25, 2011, order entered by the Michigan Public Service Commission (PSC) granting appellee International Transmission Company (ITC) an expedited siting certificate for a wind energy transmission line and authorizing construction of that line on ITC's proposed route. We hold that the PSC properly issued the siting certificate. . . .

I. BACKGROUND

Before 2008, all location and construction of electric transmission lines of a certain size and length was governed by 1995 PA 30, known as the Electric Transmission Line Certification Act, MCL 460.561 *et seq.* (Act 30). In 2008, the Legislature passed 2008 PA 295, known as the Clean, Renewable, and Efficient Energy Act, MCL 460.1001 *et seq.* (Act 295). Part 4 of Act 295, titled "WIND ENERGY RESOURCE ZONES", included provisions for the creation of a wind energy resource zone board (WERZ Board) that would issue a report determining the regions in the state with the highest wind energy harvest potential. After receiving that report, the electric utilities, affiliated transmission companies, and independent transmission companies with facilities within or adjacent to the regions identified by the state would "identify existing or new transmission infrastructure necessary to deliver maximum and minimum wind energy production potential for each of those regions" and submit that information to the WERZ Board for review. On the basis of the WERZ Board's report, the PSC would then designate an area or region of the state that would likely produce the most wind energy as "the primary wind energy resource zone." Act 295(4) also allowed electric utilities, affiliated transmission companies, and independent transmission companies to apply for and obtain an "expedited siting certificate."

The WERZ Board was created on December 4, 2008. In its final report, dated October 15, 2009, the WERZ Board identified four regions in Michigan with the highest wind energy potential. Relevant to this case, Region No. 4, covering Huron, Bay, Saginaw, Sanilac, and Tuscola Counties, had a minimum wind energy generating capacity of 2,367 megawatts (MW) and a maximum of 4,236 MW. Pursuant to MCL 460.1145(6), on November 30, 2009, ITC informed the WERZ Board that

[s]ignificant backbone transmission system enhancements would be required in [Region 4] due to the fact that the capacity of the transmission facilities in this region is already lower than the Board identified minimum and maximum wind generation capacity levels. Options presented include six 230 kV [kilovolt] high-temperature circuits at an approximate cost of $560 million to support the minimum wind generation capacity level, and eight 230 kV high-temperature circuits or four 345 kV circuits to support the maximum wind generation capacity level at approximate costs of $740 million and $510 million respectively.

On January 27, 2010, pursuant to MCL 460.1147(1), the PSC formally accepted the WERZ Board's report and designated Region 4 as the primary wind energy resource zone.

II.   UNDERLYING FACTS AND PROCEEDINGS

Pursuant to MCL 460.1149(4), on February 3, 2010, ITC submitted a letter to the PSC notifying it that, within 60 days or as soon as practicable thereafter, ITC intended to seek approval from the Midwest Independent Transmission System Operator, Inc. (MISO) for a transmission line that would enable realization of the wind power in Region 4. The PSC acknowledged receiving the letter and informed ITC that the letter fulfilled the notice requirements of MCL 460.1149(4). MISO ultimately approved ITC's proposed transmission line in August 2010.

On August 30, 2010, ITC filed an application in the PSC requesting an expedited siting certificate authorizing the construction of a transmission line to enable the wind potential of Region 4 to be realized. The proposed transmission line included "a new 345 kV double circuit tower line and four new substations." . . .

The PSC determined that "ITC's proofs fulfill[ed] all of the statutory requirements" under MCL 460.1153 and concluded that the transmission line was of "appropriate capability" because it met or exceeded the maximum load, noting that the 10 percent requirement for production of electricity with renewable energy was "a floor, not a ceiling." It also concluded that the size of the proposed transmission line was reasonable "in light of the risk that underbuilding the line now could result in substantially higher costs and additional environmental impacts in the future if transmission capacity needed to be added." . . .

. . . Under Act 30, "[i]f . . . an independent transmission company plans to construct a major transmission line in this state in the 5 years after planning commences, the . . . independent transmission company shall submit a construction plan to the [PSC]." There is no dispute that the transmission line for which ITC sought approval was a major transmission line as defined in Act 30. MCL 460.565 then provides that "[a]n . . . independent transmission company shall not begin construction of a major transmission line for which a plan has been submitted under [MCL 460.564] until the [PSC] issues a certificate for that transmission line." Both of these provisions use the term "shall," making them mandatory. Thus, under Act 30, before beginning construction, ITC was required to submit an application for a certificate of public convenience and necessity.

Appellees argue that ITC was not required to submit an application under Act 30 because the siting certificate under Act 295(4) authorized construction. The parties agree that none of the provisions in Act 295(4) expressly states that construction is authorized by issuance of a siting certificate. The PSC argues that the Legislature's use of the term "siting" to describe the certificate that is granted indicates an intent to authorize construction. Specifically, "site" means "to place in or provide with a site; locate" or "to put in position for operation[.]" RANDOM HOUSE WEBSTER'S COLLEGE DICTIONARY (1997). Similarly, "construction" is defined under Act 295(4) as "any substantial action constituting placement or erection of the foundations or structures supporting a transmission line." MCL 460.1141(a). Furthermore, certificates issued under Act 30 are not "siting" certificates but certificates of public convenience and necessity for proposed major transmission lines, and under Act 295(4), a siting certificate "is conclusive and binding as to the public convenience and necessity for that transmission line. . . ." MCL 460.1153(5). Therefore, interpreting a siting certificate to be a construction certificate would explain why there are separate construction provisions in Act 30 that are not present in Act 295(4) and why each act uses a different type of certificate.

Furthermore, given that "siting" means placement and that "construction" is statutorily defined as "any substantial action constituting placement," construction could be interpreted as a subset of siting. This reading would satisfy the principle of statutory interpretation suggesting that construction and siting have different meanings. Accepting that interpretation, the application process itself is arguably "a substantial action constituting placement" and, therefore, constitutes construction. If that is true, then Act 295(4) necessarily authorizes construction because the very act of applying constitutes construction.

Finally, authorization of construction appears implicit from MCL 460.1157, which provides, "This part does not prohibit an . . . independent transmission company from constructing a transmission line without obtaining an expedited siting certificate." It would be legitimate to interpret the express statement that Act 295(4) does not prohibit construction of transmission lines without obtaining an expedited siting certificate to mean that construction is permitted with an expedited siting certificate. Under that reading, interpreting Act 295(4) not to permit construction would render MCL 460.1157 mere surplusage in violation of the rules of statutory interpretation.

Accordingly, we hold that the PSC's interpretation of Act 295(4) to mean that issuance of an expedited siting certificate authorizes construction of the transmission line was reasonable. . . .

VI. APPROPRIATE CAPABILITY

Appellants also assert that the PSC erroneously concluded that the transmission line proposed by ITC was of an "appropriate capability" as required by MCL 460.1153(3)(d), which provides, "The proposed transmission line will be of appropriate capability to enable the wind potential of the wind energy resource zone to be realized." The PSC stated:

> Region 4 wind production capability was estimated on the record at between 2,367 MW and 4,236 MW. The proposed transmission line will have a 5,000 MW capacity. The [PSC] finds that the proposed transmission line will be of the appropriate capability to enable the wind potential of the wind energy resource zone to be realized. It is axiomatic that a planned transmission line should not be built to a size that may become overloaded. Further, building to a minimum load is wasteful and results in duplicative efforts (and costs) due to piecemeal construction. . . .

We conclude that the PSC's interpretation is consistent with the language of MCL 460.1153(3)(d). Contrary to appellants' positions, the PSC did not equate "appropriate capability" with maximum. Indeed, because ITC's proposed transmission line has a 5,000 MW capacity, it exceeds the maximum estimate. The PSC also explained that preventing duplicative efforts and costs from piecemeal construction and not building to a size that could become overloaded were considerations for determining what capability was appropriate.

ABATE argues that the PSC erred by declining to determine that appropriate capability means the minimum capacity, not the maximum capacity. However, . . . interpreting the "appropriate capability" to be the minimum wind potential is contrary to MCL 460.1153(3)(d), which requires the line "to enable the wind potential of the wind energy resource zone to be realized." Because the wind potential in Region 4 is a range that goes significantly higher than the minimum, a transmission line built only to handle the minimum wind potential would not enable the wind *potential* to be realized, only some wind *capability*. Notably, the minimum and maximum numbers were simply estimates. Thus, there is at least some possibility that *more* power could be generated. Therefore, the PSC's decision to require the capacity to be greater than the estimated maximum makes sense. . . .

NOTES AND QUESTIONS

1. As noted in the beginning of this section, transmission lines historically were built almost exclusively by public utilities, with some percentage built by public power providers and electric cooperatives. In more recent years, however, independent and merchant transmission companies have entered the transmission market, particularly to connect new sources of wind and solar energy to load centers. Private merchant companies, unlike regulated public utilities, generate revenues exclusively from contracts they sign with electric generators to transmit electricity over their lines. They do not produce or sell electricity; rather, the electricity they transmit will later be sold to utilities and other retail providers. Thus, such merchant companies do not pass on the costs of their lines to ratepayers. By contrast, independent transmission companies in some states may obtain status as a "transmission-only" utility, are regulated in many ways like a traditional public utility, and may recover costs from ratepayers. Should a merchant transmission company be able to exercise eminent domain for transmission lines just like a public utility? What about an independent transmission company? Should it matter if the service they are providing is simply for profit? For a discussion of the laws in all fifty states on this issue, see Alexandra B. Klass, *Takings and Transmission*, 91 N.C. L. REV. 1079 (2013).

2. In the *Square Butte Electric Co-op* case, the North Dakota Supreme Court held that a DC line that would not immediately provide power to North Dakota customers was still a public use for eminent domain purposes because it provided regional reliability benefits. Do you agree? Is a state court the best institution to consider such questions? Today, the Square Butte line is one of only a few HVDC lines that exist in the United States. Grid experts have conducted extensive analyses of how building more long-distance HVDC lines will be necessary to integrate the large-scale wind and solar energy into the grid that will be required to meet renewable energy and decarbonization mandates and goals. HVDC lines are more effective in transporting electric energy long distances than AC lines, making them ideal for shipping utility-scale wind and solar energy from where it can be generated to population centers that may be several states away. In a 2018 report on this issue, the U.S. Energy Information Administration highlighted the role of the Square Butte line today in transporting wind energy within the MISO RTO (which replaced "MAPP," mentioned in the case excerpt). The parent company of Minnesota Power (also discussed in the excerpt) purchased the line and related coal plant assets from Square Butte in 2009 for $71.5 million. Minnesota Power now uses the line to transport increasing amounts of wind power as it retires the coal plant in favor of the 500 MW Bison Wind Energy Center it built in North Dakota in the 2010s. *See* U.S. ENERGY INFO. AMIN., ASSESSING HVDC TRANSMISSION FOR IMPACTS OF NON-DISPATCHABLE GENERATION 7 & A-9 (June 2018).

3. The *International Transmission Co.* case raises the issue of how far into the future commissions should plan for when approving transmission lines. Clearly, it is more cost-effective in the long run to build higher capacity

transmission lines, even though they cost more up front, than to run out of capacity in ten years and build a completely new line. This is particularly important for many renewable technologies where the capacity develops over time. Should a state commission pass on the full costs of building a larger capacity line to ratepayers even though ratepayers may not use that capacity for many years? Should more of the risk fall on the transmission company? What time horizon is reasonable? Should it matter what type of generation the additional capacity will support? Why or why not?

4. The question of whether a merchant line should be able to exercise eminent domain authority arose in connection with the controversial Montana Alberta Tie Line (MATL). In October 2008, the Montana Department of Environmental Quality issued a Certificate of Compliance to MATL (which is now owned by Enbridge Energy) to build a 215-mile merchant line to transmit primarily wind energy from Great Falls, Montana to Alberta, Canada. When MATL could not obtain voluntary easements for all the land needed to build the line, it sought to exercise eminent domain authority in state court. The district court dismissed that action in 2010, holding that there was no specific grant of statutory eminent domain authority for merchant transmission companies. In 2011, the Montana legislature amended the state siting law to provide explicit eminent domain authority for all lines that obtain a certificate of compliance from the Montana Department of Environmental Quality. *See* Mont. Code Ann. § 75–20–113. Although the law was challenged on various grounds, it was ultimately upheld, and the line was completed soon after. *See MATL LLP v. Salois*, 2011 MT 126.

5. Another example of "merchant" transmission is the proposed Southern Cross Project owned by Pattern Energy, which would run approximately 400 miles of HVDC transmission lines across Louisiana and Mississippi to interconnect the ERCOT portion of the electrical grid in Texas with a portion of the Eastern Interconnection in the Southeast. The project aims to provide bi-directional power flow capability, allowing each region to either import or export power based on need or relative power price. As of 2021, the project was under development and targeted to start construction in 2022. *See Southern Cross Transmission*, Pattern Energy. An earlier set of merchant projects was proposed by Clean Line Energy Partners, including five separate long-distance HVDC lines to transport wind energy from the Midwest and Plains states to population centers to the east and west. These projects were in the permitting process for many years; received approval in many, but not all states; and were subject to litigation in others. Clean Line ultimately sold some of the projects to other developers and abandoned many of the others. For a book written about one of those lines, the Plains & Eastern Clean Line, see RUSSELL GOLD, SUPERPOWER (2020).

In 2021, the nonprofit Americans for a Clean Energy Grid published a report detailing twenty-two high-voltage DC and AC transmission projects in varying stages of development throughout the country that could begin construction in the near term if Congress, the White House, and FERC instituted new policies to support such projects. The list of projects includes the Southern Cross project and the Plains and Eastern Clean Line project discussed earlier in this note, as well as a proposed merchant HVDC underground transmission line from Iowa to Illinois that would deliver renewable energy from the MISO region to PJM. *See* MICHAEL GOGGIN ET AL., TRANSMISSION PROJECTS READY TO GO: PLUGGING INTO AMERICA'S UNTAPPED RENEWABLE RESOURCES (Apr. 2021). *See also* Mike Hughlett, *St. Louis Park Company Behind Novel $2.5B SOO Green Line Underground Power Line Project*, STAR TRIB. (Oct. 2, 2021); *SOO Green HVDC Link*, https://www.soo greenrr.com/.

6.   Michigan and Montana are not alone in using energy transport regulation to promote renewable electricity. Texas also has earned much acclaim for its renewable energy-related transmission siting laws. In 2005, the state legislature directed the Public Utility Commission of Texas to identify competitive renewable energy zones (CREZs): "areas in which renewable energy resources and suitable land areas are sufficient to develop generating capacity from renewable energy technologies." TEX. UTIL. CODE ANN. § 39.904(g)(1); *see also* WARREN LASHER, ERCOT, THE COMPETITIVE RENEWABLE ENERGY ZONES PROCESS (Aug. 11, 2014). When designating the CREZs, the PUCT considered "whether the renewable energy resources and suitable land areas [were] sufficient to develop generating capacity from renewable energy technologies; the level of financial commitments by generators; and . . . other [relevant] factors," such as the cost of new transmission and the estimated benefits of renewable energy produced in the CREZ. Kathryn B. Daniel, *Winds of Change: Competitive Renewable Energy Zones and the Emerging Regulatory Structure of Texas Wind Energy*, 42 TEX. TECH L. REV. 157, 164 (2009).

After considering recommendations from the Energy Reliability Council of Texas (ERCOT), the Texas Commission established five CREZs in 2008 in West Texas and the Panhandle and chose a transmission plan to deliver the power to demand centers throughout the state. All told, the transmission build-out cost $6.9 billion, added 3,600 miles of new 345-kV transmission lines, and now delivers nearly 18,500 megawatts of renewable energy. Lasher, *supra*; Jim Malewitz, *$7 Billion CREZ Project Nears Finish, Aiding Wind Power*, THE TEXAS TRIB. (Oct. 14, 2013); *see also* JULIE COHN & OLIVERA JANKOVSKA, TEXAS CREZ LINES, HOW STAKEHOLDERS SHAPE MAJOR ENERGY INFRASTRUCTURE PROJECTS (Nov. 2020).

7.   While Texas' build-out is perhaps the most notable example of transmission targeting renewable electricity, California, Colorado, New Mexico, and New York also have taken steps in this direction. In 2007, New Mexico passed the Renewable Energy Transmission Authority Act to "develop a renewable energy generation and export industry" and "increase in-state electric system infrastructure reliability." *HB 188: Renewable Energy Transmission Authority Act*, New Mexico Energy, Minerals, and Natural Resources Dep't. The Act created the Renewable Energy Transmission Authority Board, which has authority to exercise eminent domain power for siting transmission facilities. Pursuant to the law, the New Mexico Board has

partnered with Pattern Energy (which also owns the Southern Cross project discussed above) to build the Western Spirit transmission line. *See Western Spirit Transmission*, Pattern Energy New Mexico. Similarly, California has instituted the Renewable Energy Transmission Initiative (RETI) 2.0 to help identify transmission infrastructure needs for achieving the state's renewable energy goals. *Renewable Energy Transmission Initiative (RETI) 2.0*, Cal. Energy Comm'n.

More recently, in 2020, New York enacted the Accelerated Renewable Growth and Community Benefit Act to accelerate the permitting and construction of renewable energy generating plants over 25 MW. The law also created a "state power grid and study program" to accelerate the planning of construction of bulk and local electric transmission and distribution infrastructure. *See* Press Release, *New York State Announces Passage of Accelerated Renewable Energy Growth and Community Benefit Act as Part of 2020–2021 Enacted State Budget*, N.Y. State (Apr. 3, 2020). In 2021, Colorado enacted a new law that created "an independent Colorado electric transmission authority to establish intrastate electric transmission corridors and to operate transmission and storage facilities as needed to enable Colorado utilities to physically participate [in] regional markets." Emma Penrod, *Colorado Legislatures Direct All Transmission Utilities to Join An Organized Wholesale Market by 2030*, UTIL. DIVE (June 8, 2021). What in these laws is likely to help overcome existing barriers to new transmission lines? What barriers remain? For more on state legislatively created transmission authorities, see K. PORTER & S. FINK, NAT'L RENEWABLE ENERGY LAB., STATE TRANSMISSION INFRASTRUCTURE AUTHORITIES: THE STORY SO FAR (May 2008).

8.   Just because transmission lines benefit renewable energy development does not mean they sail to approval. Significant dispute torpedoed the 192-mile, $1.6 billion Northern Pass transmission line, which was proposed to transport nearly 1,100 MW of mostly hydroelectric power from Quebec to Massachusetts through New Hampshire. In the face of significant public opposition, the New Hampshire Site Evaluation Committee denied the facility's permit, a decision upheld unanimously by the New Hampshire Supreme Court. *Appeal of Northern Pass Transmission, LLC*, 214 A.3d 590 (N.H. 2019). Since then, developers and the state of Massachusetts pivoted to support construction of an alternative route through Maine, called the New England Clean Energy Connect, which has also been subject to sustained opposition and litigation. By contrast, in the Midwest, in 2020, another facility—the 224-mile, 500 kV Great Northern Transmission Line, which has a 250 MW capacity—began delivering hydropower from Manitoba Hydro to the utility Minnesota Power's service territory in northern Minnesota after years of planning but without litigation. *See About the Project*, Great Northern Transmission Line, Minnesota Power.

9.   In addition to state efforts, the federal government has used transmission regulation to promote renewable energy. Section 368 of the Energy Policy Act of 2005 required the Secretaries of Agriculture, Commerce, Defense, Energy, and the Interior to consult with FERC and other entities to designate

"corridors for oil, gas, and hydrogen pipelines and electricity transmission and distribution facilities on Federal land in the eleven contiguous Western States." 42 U.S.C. § 15926. Under this provision, land management agencies such as the BLM and the Forest Service can reserve land for transmission lines, pipelines, and associated energy transportation infrastructure, although the Act does not require that an agency approve any proposed project. Peter J. Schaumberg & James M. Auslander, *Power to the People: Electric Transmission Siting in the American West*, 2013 No. 5 RMMLF-INST. PAPER No. 6, 11 (Nov. 2013). *See also Energy Corridors on Federal Lands*, Office of Electricity, U.S. Dep't of Energy.

The FAST Act, discussed in the natural gas pipeline section above as well as in Chapter 6, was also designed to streamline transmission projects. *See* Andy Winkler & Sarah Kline, *10 Things You Need to Know About the FAST Act*, BIPARTISAN POLICY CENTER (Jan. 12, 2016). Moreover, since President Biden took office in 2021, the White House, DOE, and DOT have issued guidance regarding enhanced funding and use of rights of way to build transmission lines along interstate highways. *See* FACT SHEET: BIDEN ADMINISTRATION ADVANCES EXPANSION & MODERNIZATION OF THE ELECTRIC GRID, THE WHITE HOUSE (Apr. 27, 2021); *State DOTs Leveraging Alternative Uses of the Highway Right of Way Guidance*, U.S. Dep't of Transp. (Apr. 27, 2021). Based on the materials in this chapter, do you think these efforts can be successful? Why or why not? For more details on the regulatory challenges associated with building long-distance transmission lines, see James W. Coleman & Alexandra B. Klass, *Energy and Eminent Domain*, 104 MINN. L. REV. 659 (2019).

10. Although states have primary authority over the bulk of electric transmission line siting decisions, there are certain circumstances where the federal government is (or can be) the decisionmaker. First, as the previous note suggests, the federal government (often the BLM or the Forest Service) must approve any transmission lines that cross federal lands. Second, the Federal Power Act grants FERC authority to connect federal hydropower facilities with the transmission grid. Third, EPAct 2005 attempted to give FERC and DOE "backstop" siting authority to override state refusals to site transmission lines in National Interest Electric Transmission Corridors. However, as you will recall from Chapter 5, that authority has been construed by the courts to be quite narrow, rendering it a practical nullity. Fourth, in another provision of EPAct 2005—Section 1222—Congress authorized certain federal power marketing authorities, through DOE, to partner with private parties to build transmission lines in certain parts of the country if DOE determines the project will reduce transmission congestion, is needed to accommodate new capacity, and meets other requirements. DOE exercised that authority for the first time in 2016 in connection with one of the merchant transmission line projects discussed in note 5—the Plains & Eastern Clean Line project—that had obtained siting approvals from several states but was denied approval in Arkansas. Litigation over the DOE approval was underway before the Trump administration terminated the joint agreement and Clean Line sold the project

to NextEra Energy Resources. *See Plains and Eastern Clean Line*, Office of Electricity, U.S. Dep't of Energy; *Project Updates*, Clean Line Energy Partners. For details on the project, see SUPERPOWER, *supra*; Klass & Rossi, *supra*. For an in-depth discussion of siting and eminent domain authority pursuant to Sections 1221 and 1222 of EPAct 2005, see AVI ZEVIN ET AL., BUILDING A NEW GRID WITHOUT NEW LEGISLATION: A PATH TO REVITALIZING FEDERAL TRANSMISSION AUTHORITIES (Dec. 2020).

PRACTICE PROBLEM

Wind Transport, Inc. is a "merchant transmission company." Unlike a vertically integrated utility, it does not own any electric generation facilities and does not sell electricity to retail customers. Instead, it builds transmission lines and sells transmission capacity to renewable energy generators, primarily wind firms, and to the buyers of the power from these projects, primarily public utilities. One of Wind Transport's current projects is called the "Midwest Wind Express," which will deliver 3,500 MW of wind power from Kansas to Illinois, Indiana, and states farther east with strong demand for wind energy. This wind-generated electricity will be transported via an approximately 750-mile overhead, 600 kV direct current (DC) transmission line passing through several states. As explained earlier in this section, many in the industry now view DC as the most efficient and cost-effective technology to move large amounts of power over long distances, due to its lower electricity losses and smaller footprint than comparable alternating current (AC) lines. One disadvantage of a DC line, however, is that there are very few "off ramps" along the way. So, electricity may travel on the line through one or more states without providing any power to the citizens of those states.

Wind Transport must now obtain approval to site the Midwest Wind Express from each of the states through which it will pass. Assume that Missouri law grants to the state public service commission (PSC) the authority to determine whether an electric facility, including a transmission line, is "necessary or convenient" for the public service. If it makes that determination, it grants the applicant a certificate of convenience and necessity (CCN). The Missouri PSC is now holding a hearing to determine whether to grant Wind Transport a CCN to build the Midwest Wind Express. Moreover, Wind Transport may need to exercise eminent domain to build the line. Under Missouri law, a CCN will allow it to use eminent domain authority. *See* MO. STAT. ANN. §§ 393.170, 386.020(14)–(15), 523.010.

1. If you represent Wind Transport, what arguments will you make to convince the commission to issue a CCN for the line?

2. If you represent landowners who are opposed to the line, what arguments will you make in an effort to stop the line?

3. If you represent local environmental groups, what position will you take? Once you determine your position, what arguments will you make to support it?

For a discussion of some of the issues raised in this problem, see Alexandra B. Klass, *Takings and Transmission*, 91 N.C. L. REV. 1079 (2013); Klass & Rossi, *supra*; INTERCONNECTION SEAMS STUDY, *supra*; ASSESSING HVDC TRANSMISSION FOR IMPACTS OF NON-DISPATCHABLE GENERATION, *supra*; TRANSMISSION PROJECTS READY TO GO, *supra*. For a critique of certificate of convenience and necessity laws on grounds that they protect incumbent utilities over competitive merchant transmission companies, stifle competition, raise electricity costs for consumers, and obstruct clean energy projects, see Joshua C. Macey, *Zombie Energy Laws*, 73 VAND. L. REV. 1077 (2020).

D. ENERGY TRANSPORT SAFETY

A third common type of regulation of energy transportation focuses on safety. There are strong reasons for this. Throughout history, mishaps and accidents involving energy transportation have been common. These range from comparatively frequent troubles like the derailing of a rail car to more extraordinary—and far-reaching—events such as the crash of the *Exxon Valdez* oil tanker in Prince William Sound. Safety regulations apply to most parts of energy transportation systems. Perhaps most notable are the safety regulations that apply to pipelines, railroads, and certain types of shipping.

Interstate pipeline regulation in the United States takes place under the auspices of the Pipeline and Hazardous Materials Safety Administration (PHMSA), which is part of the Department of Transportation. This agency is charged with regulating nearly a half million miles of high-volume natural gas, oil, and other hazardous liquid transport pipelines. In carrying out its inspection and enforcement duties, PHMSA relies heavily on cooperation and partnerships with state pipeline safety agencies, which also oversee intrastate pipelines. Before September 11, 2001, the Department of Transportation had authority over pipeline security, but those responsibilities were subsequently transferred to the Department of Homeland Security.

PHMSA operates under a patchwork of statutes, including its two principal enabling acts: the Natural Gas Pipeline Safety Act of 1968 and the Hazardous Liquid Pipeline Act of 1979. Under these laws, government regulates the design, construction, operation, and maintenance of interstate pipeline safety. PAUL W. PARFOMAK, CONG. RSCH. SERV., DOT'S FEDERAL PIPELINE SAFETY PROGRAM: BACKGROUND AND KEY ISSUES FOR CONGRESS (May 20, 2016).

Congress updated and expanded these duties in 2011 via the Pipeline Safety Act of 2011, and again in 2016 via the Protecting our Infrastructure of Pipelines and Enhancing Safety Act of 2016 (PIPES Act). The PIPES Act seeks to improve pipeline regulation in several ways:

- Requiring PHMSA to establish safety standards for underground natural gas storage facilities;

- Authorizing emergency order authority;

- Updating regulations for certain LNG facilities;

- Increasing inspection requirements for underwater oil pipelines;

- Designating coastal, marine, and Great Lakes areas as environmentally sensitive;

- Authorizing states to participate in interstate pipeline inspections; and

- Enhancing stakeholder coordination.

For more on the likely impact of PHMSA regulations following the PIPES Act, see U.S. GOV'T ACCOUNTABILITY OFFICE, PIPELINE SAFETY: PERFORMANCE MEASURES NEEDED TO ASSESS RECENT CHANGES TO HAZARDOUS LIQUID PIPELINE SAFETY REGULATIONS (June 2021).

Pipeline safety is essential, because the United States hosts 2.6 million miles of pipelines, which in turn transport nearly two-thirds of the energy commodities consumed domestically. Overall, pipelines have proven a comparatively safe vehicle for energy transportation. Nevertheless, some incidents are inevitable. California's high-profile Aliso Canyon Underground Storage Facility leak in 2015 forced the evacuation of 2,000 homes and released 5.4 billion cubic feet of natural gas. Additional accidents this century also have raised concerns about pipeline safety. Moreover, when an incident does occur, that single pipeline event can have major environmental repercussions. See PAUL PARFOMAK, CONG. RSCH. SERV., KEEPING AMERICA'S PIPELINES SAFE AND SECURE: KEY ISSUES FOR CONGRESS 2–3 (Jan. 9, 2013).

Hazardous Liquid Pipeline Accidents
Reported by Operators

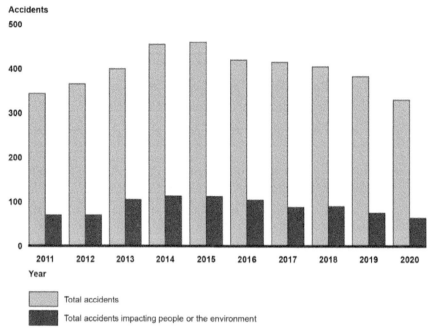

Source: U.S. GAO.

The Federal Railroad Administration (FRA), also part of the Department of Transportation, regulates railroad safety. This agency, with an inspection staff of about 400, cooperates with state safety inspectors to enforce federal law and regulations, which largely preempt state safety rules for railroads. Federal safety requirements apply to all trains operating in the United States irrespective of origin and address track safety, crossings, equipment, operating practices, and the movement of hazardous materials. PHMSA creates rules for the transportation of all hazardous materials, and the FRA enforces them as they apply to railroads. When there is a railroad incident, the National Transportation Safety Board (NTSB) investigates it. In 2014, in response to the Rail Safety Improvement Act of 2008, the FRA promulgated regulations requiring railroads to achieve specific track failure rates on their rails. *See* JOHN FRITTELLI, CONG. RSCH. SERV., U.S. RAIL TRANSPORTATION OF CRUDE OIL: BACKGROUND AND ISSUES FOR CONGRESS (2014); Fed. Railroad Admin., Track Safety Standards; Improving Rail Integrity, 79 Fed. Reg. 4234 (Jan. 24, 2014).

While railroads may be most important to energy for their transport of coal, it is the movement of oil by rail that has both increased over the last decade and drawn the most attention. There are clear reasons for the increase in rail transport of oil. Though it costs approximately $10–15 per barrel to ship oil by rail, compared to only $5 per barrel by pipeline, there have been inadequate pipeline facilities in place to move new oil resources in the United States, particularly from shale resources. Thus, the railroad industry "spent $575 billion on rail network expansion and maintenance between 1980 and 2014, and will likely continue to invest in expansion of rail facilities in light of an expected 45% overall increase in freight shipments from an estimated 19.7 billion tons in 2012 to 28.5 billion tons in 2040." Alexandra B. Klass, *Future-Proofing Energy Transport Law*, 94 WASH. U.L. REV. 827, 890 (2017). Indeed, shipments from locations where oil is hydraulically fractured, such as the Bakken Shale in Western North Dakota, rose sharply in the mid-2010s: About two-thirds of oil from the Bakken Shale traveled by rail during that time because of inadequate pipeline connections, with a full tenth of oil produced in the United States moving by rail—up from only one percent in 2009. Clifford Krauss & Jad Mouawad, *Accidents Surge as Oil Industry Takes the Train*, N.Y. TIMES (Jan. 25, 2014).

The tradeoffs for moving oil via rail or pipeline are straightforward—but intertwined. Moving oil by rail presents potentially important environmental impacts. Since 2010, the number of oil spills from rail, on a per gallon transported basis, has exceeded those from pipeline shipments in all but one year. Likewise, the amount of oil spilled, per gallon transported, from rail shipments also has exceeded the amount spilled from pipelines. JONATHAN L. RAMSEUR, CONG. RSCH. SERV., OIL SPILLS: BACKGROUND AND GOVERNANCE (Sept. 15, 2017). These impacts may become even greater if the increased use of rail continues to alter the oil transport industry. As one analysis showed, "The number of gallons spilled in the United States [in 2013] . . . far outpaced the total amount spilled by railroads from 1975 to 2012." Krauss & Mouawad, *supra*. Still, other impacts must be considered. "Pipeline supporters contend that accidents happen more frequently on railways, while rail supporters counter that when pipelines fail, they spill many more gallons of oil. According to government statistics, both claims are accurate. Data also suggests that while rail accidents cause more harm to human health and property, pipeline spills cause more harm to natural resources and ecosystems." Klass, *supra*.

The remainder of this section focuses on shipping safety, particularly with respect to oil, as the chapter's primary example of energy transport safety regulation.

Shipping plays a major role in moving energy resources. Oil tankers are designed to ship oil around the world and range in size from inland tankers carrying a few thousand tons of oil to the ultra large crude carriers (ULCCs), which can carry over 500,000 tons of oil. The global oil trade also highlights international energy security issues, with U.S. shale oil production now shifting global oil trade and increasing vulnerabilities to piracy. *See* Ajay Makan, *Oil Tanker Trade Growth Is Fastest in a Decade*, FINANCIAL TIMES (May 12, 2013).

Natural gas, in its ultra-cooled, liquefied form, known as "liquefied natural gas" or LNG, is shipped from remote locations, like fields in Qatar, Australia, Malaysia, and Indonesia, to Japan, South Korea, and Spain. Almost 47 billion cubic feet of LNG is shipped each day across the globe via an ever-growing fleet of tankers. The top global importers of LNG are Japan, China, South Korea, and India. Leading exporters include Australia, Qatar, the United States, and Russia. Indeed, the United States, with its new abundance of natural gas resources from hydraulic fracturing, has taken on a greater role in this market over the last decade: In 2016, it exported well less than 1 billion cubic feet of LNG per day; in 2020, that figure had grown to 6 billion cubic feet per day. The United States now hosts 110 LNG facilities, including seven LNG export terminals, another four that are under construction, and fourteen more that have been approved but for which construction has not commenced. FERC has approval authority over these facilities under NGA § 3, and over other, non-export facilities under NGA § 7. The export facilities—in-use, under construction, and approved—are bunched heavily along the Gulf Coast, though there are terminals also operating in Georgia and Maryland. *Global Liquefied Natural Gas Trade Was Flat in 2020 Amid Pandemic*, U.S. ENERGY INFO. ADMIN. (July 9, 2021); *North American LNG Export Terminals—Existing, Approved Not Yet Built, and Proposed*, Fed. Energy Reg. Comm'n (last updated Apr. 20, 2021).

Even coal gets in the shipping game. While most coal is used domestically and travels by truck for shorter distances or by rail for longer ones, an increasing international coal trade by ship has been growing. "Patterns of international . . . coal trade are shifting. Traditionally trade could be characterised by two geographic basins: the Pacific Basin, where Japan and Korea were the top importers; and the Atlantic Basin, where the European countries imported most of the traded coal. . . . [Still, t]he majority of seaborne thermal coal trade occurs in the Asia Pacific region, where both the largest importers and exporters are concentrated." In 2019, Indonesia led the world with 41% of exports, followed by Australia (19%), Russia (17%), South Africa (7%), Colombia (6%), and the United States (3.1%). The leading coal importer was China (21%), followed by India (17%) and Japan (13%). *Coal 2020: Report Extract—Trade*, Int'l Energy Agency.

Because oil is the largest international commodity, and roughly one-third of global maritime trade, it dominates energy transport by ship. Shipping large quantities of oil—and other energy resources—in coastal and inland waters necessarily poses risks to humans and environmental resources. Nevertheless, the more stringent safety regulations applied to shipping oil today came about only after the devastating oil spill caused by the *Exxon Valdez* tanker in Alaska in 1989. The tale of that environmental disaster has become so famous it does not require retelling in full, but a brief recounting both provides useful context and exposes some of the complexities underlying the story, which often are jettisoned in lieu of the easy version.

BRADLEY C. BOBERTZ, LEGITIMIZING POLLUTION THROUGH POLLUTION CONTROL LAWS: REFLECTIONS ON SCAPEGOATING THEORY
73 Tex. L. Rev. 711 (1995)

In March 1990, a year after the *Exxon Valdez* spilled eleven million gallons of Alaska crude into Prince William Sound, the *Frontline* television series broadcast a documentary called "Anatomy of an Oil Spill." The documentary told the following story about the immediate events leading up to the spill: At about 9:30 p.m. on March 23, 1989, the *Exxon Valdez* left port after being filled with its cargo of crude oil from the Alaska pipeline terminal and port in Valdez, Alaska. At 11:30 p.m., Captain Joseph Hazelwood radioed the Coast Guard to say that he was steering his ship outside the assigned shipping lane to avoid ice in the water. A few minutes later, Hazelwood turned over control of the tanker to Third Mate Gregory Cousins, who was licensed to operate the ship in open water, but not in Prince William Sound.

Before retiring to his quarters, Hazelwood instructed Cousins when and how to make the necessary course correction to return the ship to the proper channel. The ship made its turn at 12:03 a.m., five minutes too late. It is not clear whether Cousins waited too long to order the turn or whether the ship's helmsman (who actually operates the wheel) failed to follow the order in time. The tanker ran aground on the rocks off Bligh Reef a minute later, ripping open a large section of the hull; however, if the ship had been turned as Hazelwood had ordered, the wreck would not have occurred. At 12:26 a.m., Hazelwood radioed the Coast Guard with the news: "This is the Valdez back. We've—should be on your radar, there—we've fetched up hard aground north of Goose Island off Bligh Reef. And evidently we're leaking some oil. . . ."

The documentary rejected the conventional wisdom that blame for the spill could be pinned on one person, Hazelwood, and one corporation, Exxon. Instead, *Frontline* concluded that "the wreck and the magnitude of the damage required the bad judgment of a lot of people, in big oil and government, over a period of years." In fact, a host of institutional players shared in the blame.

First, the Coast Guard had rejected at least four critical safety measures that would have prevented the spill, including: (1) full radar coverage of Prince William Sound, (2) a system that would have provided constant updates as to tankers' positions, (3) a rule requiring trained pilots to accompany ships during their journeys through the Sound, and (4) a requirement that tankers be fitted with double hulls. The Coast Guard also routinely allowed tankers to abandon shipping lanes, exceed vessel speed limits, and violate pilotage requirements. Although much was made of the fact that the *Exxon Valdez* ran aground while being piloted by an uncertified third mate, this practice was commonplace. According to testimony at Hazelwood's criminal trial, "It was common knowledge among tanker skippers that the Coast Guard had been relaxing its pilotage regulations." Indeed, in the hours immediately preceding the spill, at least two other outbound tankers took the same detour as the *Exxon Valdez*, both piloted by officers lacking proper Coast Guard certification.

The tanker owners, for their part, had cut back on crew size and established punishing production schedules that resulted in unreasonable working hours and dangerously fatigued pilots. Union representatives claimed that "smaller crews increased the danger of accidents because of longer hours and less sleep, especially during the demanding hours when a tanker is in port being filled with or emptied of oil." The *Exxon Valdez* was designed for a crew of thirty-three, but was operating with a crew of nineteen when it ran aground.

Alyeska, the consortium of oil companies responsible for dealing with spills in the Sound, was grossly unprepared for the magnitude of the spill. The consortium had relied on a study predicting a catastrophic spill of 200,000 barrels or more only once every 241 years; a more likely spill, according to the study, would be between 1000 and 2000 barrels. Relying on this lower figure, Alyeska's contingency plan was geared for a spill 175 times smaller than that from the *Valdez*. The response was doomed from the start. According to former Alyeska President George Nelson:

> [I]f Alyeska had been out at Bligh Reef anchored to the thing— you know, ready—it wouldn't have made any difference. We didn't have—the equipment we had in our plan, as approved in the '87 plan, was to deal with a 1,000 to 2,000 barrel spill, okay? We did not have the equipment at the terminal—the plan didn't call for it, we didn't have it—to take out to deal with a 268,000 barrel spill—whatever the amount of the spill is.

Alyeska was prepared only for the small spill its models had predicted, not the massive spill that actually occurred. While Exxon took most of the blame for the botched clean-up, the company took charge only after Alyeska, hopelessly overwhelmed by the magnitude of the spill, abandoned the effort. Altogether, a complex interaction of institutional and human factors created a setting in which a major spill—at some time—was probably inevitable.

In the hours immediately following the accident, when the news of the spill first hit the media, few reporters were equipped with the essential background information that would have enabled them to understand the context of the incident. And two days later, when Exxon executive Frank Iarossi broke the story that Hazelwood had a history of alcohol problems and had alcohol on his breath after the spill, Iarossi furnished a simple, dramatic explanation that seemingly resolved the complex question of what had caused the spill. According to a reporter for the *Anchorage Times*, daily press conferences "degenerated into questions about alcohol when early on it was evident alcohol had only a small part, if any, in how the accident happened." At his criminal trial, Hazelwood was acquitted of both drunkenness and reckless operation; he was convicted only of negligently discharging oil.

Yet after the alcohol story broke, accounts of the disaster took on the guise of a morality tale involving a drunken sailor and a greedy corporation. Relying heavily on footage of the spill's victims (angry fishermen, oil-soaked birds, dead fish), television broadcasts reinforced the moralistic, innocence-despoiled-by-evil structure of the story. With few exceptions, journalists fixated on the simple and dramatic, completely disregarding (or failing to perceive) any complicating details:

> Journalists who covered the spill as a fable about a drunken sea captain and a mighty oil company that couldn't clean up after itself provided some great drama, but missed most of the story. The direct cause of the accident was a sober crew member who did not follow clear instructions, and the indirect but perhaps more important cause was a substantial deterioration of the maritime precautions administered by the Coast Guard. Since equipment and technology do[ ] not exist to contain or clean up large oil spills, the oil industry was certain to fail against public expectations no matter what its cleanup crews actually did.

Thus, an event brought about by the convergence of numerous factors was transformed into a misleading, but culturally resonant, tale of a drunken sailor and a dark-hearted company.

––––––––––

The legislative reaction to the 11 million-gallon *Exxon Valdez* spill was swift and direct. Congress passed the Oil Pollution Act of 1990, which imposed both direct and indirect safety requirements for oil tankers. The following excerpt describes how the Oil Pollution Act replaced the patchwork set of laws in place to address oil spills at the time of the *Exxon Valdez* spill.

JONATHAN L. RAMSEUR, OIL SPILLS: BACKGROUND AND GOVERNANCE

Cong. Rsch. Serv. (Sept. 15, 2017)

... With the enactment of OPA on August 18, 1990, Congress consolidated the existing federal oil spill laws under one program. The 1990 law expanded the existing liability provisions within the Clean Water Act (CWA) and created new free-standing requirements regarding oil spill prevention and response. Key OPA provisions are discussed below.

Spill Response Authority

When responding to a spill, many considered the lines of responsibility under the pre-OPA regime to be unclear, with too much reliance on spillers to perform proper cleanup. OPA strengthened and clarified the federal government's role in oil spill response and cleanup. OPA Section 4201 amended Section 311(c) of the CWA to provide the President (delegated to the U.S. Coast Guard or EPA) with authority to perform cleanup immediately using federal resources, monitor the response efforts of the spiller, or direct the spiller's cleanup activities. The revised response authorities addressed concerns "that precious time would be lost while waiting for the spiller to marshall its cleanup forces."

The federal government—specifically the On-Scene Coordinator (OSC) for spills in the Coast Guard's jurisdiction—determines the level of cleanup required. Although the federal government must consult with designated trustees of natural resources and the governor of the state affected by the spill, the decision that cleanup is completed and can be ended rests with the federal government. States may require further work, but without the support of federal funding.

National Contingency Plan

OPA expanded the role and breadth of the NCP. The 1990 law established a multi-layered planning and response system to improve preparedness and response to spills in marine environments. Among other things, the act also required the President to establish procedures and standards (as part of the NCP) for responding to worst-case oil spill scenarios.

Tank Vessel and Facility Response Plans

As a component of the enhanced NCP, OPA amended the CWA to require that U.S. tank vessels, offshore facilities, and certain onshore facilities prepare and submit oil spill response plans to the relevant federal agency. In general, vessels and facilities are prohibited from handling, storing, or transporting oil if they do not have a plan approved by (or submitted to) the appropriate agency (discussed below).

The plans should, among other things, identify how the owner or operator of a vessel or facility would respond to a worst-case scenario spill. Congress did not intend for every vessel to have onboard all the personnel and equipment needed to respond to a worst-case spill, but vessels must have a plan and procedures to call upon—typically through a contractual relationship—the necessary equipment and personnel for responding to a worst-case spill.

In 2004, Congress enacted an amendment requiring non-tank vessels (i.e., ships carrying oil for their own fuel use) over 400 gross tons to prepare and submit a vessel response plan. Congress reasoned that many non-tank vessels have as much oil onboard as small tank vessels, thus presenting a comparable risk from an oil spill. Moreover, the international standards for oil spill prevention apply to tanker and non-tanker vessels alike. Thus, the 2004 amendment brought the U.S. law more in line with international provisions.

Double-Hull Design for Vessels

The issue of double hulls received considerable debate for many years prior to OPA, and it was one of the stumbling blocks for unified oil spill legislation. Proponents maintained that double-hull construction provides extra protection if a vessel becomes damaged. However, opponents argued that a double-hulled vessel might cause stability problems if an accident occurred, thus negating the benefits. Stakeholders also highlighted the impacts that a double-hull requirement would entail for the shipping industry (e.g., cost and time of retrofitting, ship availability). The OPA requirements for double hulls reflected some of these concerns.

The act required new vessels carrying oil and operating in U.S. waters to have double hulls. However, OPA provided certain exceptions, depending on the size of the vessel (e.g., less than 5,000 gross tons) and its particular use (e.g., lightering). For older vessels, OPA established a staggered retrofitting schedule, based on vessel age and size. As of January 2010, single-hull vessels (with several exceptions, some of which expired in 2015) cannot operate in U.S. waters.

Liability Issues

OPA unified the liability provisions of existing oil spill statutes, creating a freestanding liability regime. Section 1002 states that responsible parties are liable for any discharge of oil (or threat of discharge) from a vessel or facility to navigable waters, adjoining shorelines, or the exclusive economic zone of the United States (i.e., 200 nautical miles beyond the shore).

Regarding the oil spill statutes prior to OPA, Congress recognized that "there is no comprehensive legislation in place that promptly and adequately compensates those who suffer other types of economic loss as a result of an oil pollution incident." OPA broadened the scope of damages (i.e., costs) for which an oil spiller would be liable. Under OPA, a responsible party is liable for all cleanup costs incurred, not only by a government entity, but also by a private party. In addition to cleanup costs, OPA significantly increased the range of liable damages to include the following:

- injury to natural resources,
- loss of personal property (and resultant economic losses),
- loss of subsistence use of natural resources,
- lost revenues resulting from destruction of property or natural resource injury,
- lost profits resulting from property loss or natural resource injury, and
- costs of providing extra public services during or after spill response.

OPA provided limited defenses from liability: act of God, act of war, and act or omission of certain third parties. These defenses are similar to those of the Superfund statute, established in 1980 for releases of hazardous substances (which does not include oil).

Except for certain behavior, including acts of gross negligence or willful misconduct, OPA set liability limits (or caps) for cleanup costs and other damages. OPA requires the President to issue regulations to adjust the liability limits at least every three years to take into account impacts of inflation over time. The statute directs the President to use the consumer price index (CPI) to account for these impacts. Administrations subsequent to the enactment of OPA in 1990 did not adjust the liability limits until Congress amended OPA in 2006: The Coast Guard and Maritime Transportation Act of 2006 adjusted the liability limits for vessels in statute. Subsequent limits were adjusted through agency rulemakings.

For purposes of liability limits, OPA divides potential sources of oil spills into four general categories. The liability limits differ by category, and in some cases, the scope of liability varies. The categories and their scopes of liability are:

- Tank vessels: Liability limit includes both removal costs and natural resource and economic damages. The limit is based on vessel size measured in gross tonnage.
- All other vessels: Liability limit includes both removal costs and natural resource and economic damages. The limit is based on vessel size measured in gross tonnage. The limits are lower than those for tank vessels.

- Offshore facilities (not including deepwater ports): Liability limit applies only to damages (natural resource and economic damages). Liability for removal costs is not limited.

- Onshore facilities and deepwater ports: Liability limit includes both removal costs and natural resource and economic damages.

The Oil Spill Liability Trust Fund

Prior to OPA, federal funding for oil spill response was generally considered inadequate, and damages recovery was difficult for private parties. To help address these issues, Congress supplemented OPA's expanded range of covered damages with the Oil Spill Liability Trust Fund (OSLTF).

Pursuant to Executive Order (EO) 12777, the Coast Guard created the National Pollution Funds Center (NPFC) to manage the trust fund in 1991. The fund may be used for several purposes:

- prompt payment of costs for responding to and removing oil spills;

- payment of the costs incurred by the federal and state trustees of natural resources for assessing the injuries to natural resources caused by an oil spill, and developing and implementing the plans to restore or replace the injured natural resources;

- payment of parties' claims for uncompensated removal costs, and for uncompensated damages (e.g., financial losses of fishermen, hotels, and beachfront businesses);

- payment for the net loss of government revenue, and for increased public services by a state or its political subdivisions; and

- payment of federal administrative and operational costs, including research and development, and $25 million per year for the Coast Guard's operating expenses.

Although Congress created the OSLTF in 1986, Congress did not authorize its use or provide its funding until after the Exxon Valdez incident. In 1990, OPA provided the statutory authorization necessary to put the fund in motion. Through OPA, Congress transferred balances from other federal liability funds into the OSLTF. In complementary legislation, Congress imposed a 5cent-per-barrel tax on the oil industry to support the fund. Collection of this fee ceased on December 31, 1994, due to a sunset provision in the law. However, in April 2006, the tax resumed as required by the Energy Policy Act of 2005 (P.L. 109–58). In addition, the Emergency Economic Stabilization Act of 2008 (P.L. 110–343) increased the tax rate to cents through 2016. In 2017, the rate increased to 9 cents. The tax is scheduled to terminate at the end of 2017.

Figure 6 illustrates the receipts, expenditures, and end-of-year balances for the OSLTF. At the end of FY2017, the projected balance is $5.4 billion.

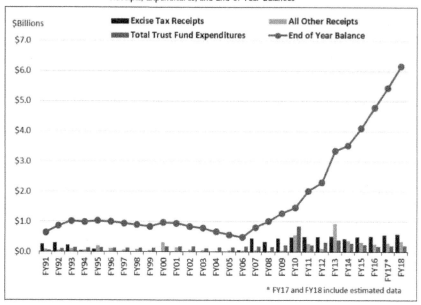

Figure 6. Oil Spill Liability Trust Fund
Receipts, Expenditures, and End-of-Year Balances

Financial Responsibility

To preserve the trust fund and ensure that responsible parties can be held accountable for oil spill cleanup and damages, OPA requires that vessels and offshore facilities maintain evidence of financial responsibility (e.g., insurance). The Coast Guard's National Pollution Funds Center (NPFC) implements the financial responsibility provisions for vessels; the Bureau of Ocean Energy Management implements this requirement for offshore facilities.

The current levels of financial responsibility are related to the current liability limits for various sources (e.g., vessels, offshore facilities) of potential oil spills. The liability limits differ by potential source. In the case of vessels, whose liability limits are a single dollar amount encompassing both removal costs and other damages, the financial responsibility levels are directly tied to the corresponding liability caps. Current law requires responsible parties for vessels to demonstrate the "maximum amount of liability to which the responsible party could be subjected under [the liability limits in OPA Section 1004; 33 U.S.C. 2704]."

Because the structure of offshore facility liability limit is different than vessels, the corresponding financial responsibility limit provisions differ. Responsible parties for offshore facilities in federal waters must demonstrate $35 million financial responsibility, unless the President determines a greater amount (not to exceed $150 million) is justified (33 U.S.C. 2716(c)). The federal regulations that are authored by this statutory provision (30 C.F.R. Part 254) base the financial responsibility amount—between $35 million and $150 million—on a facility's worst-case discharge volume (as defined in 30 C.F.R. § 253.14). For example, a facility with a worst-case discharge volume over 105,000 barrels—the highest level of worst-case discharge listed in the regulations—must maintain $150 million in financial responsibility.

Other Federal Laws

Although OPA is the primary domestic legislation for oil spills, other federal laws contain provisions that relate to oil spills. Many of these provisions were in place before OPA [and include, for example, the Clean Water Act, the Outer Continental Shelf Lands Act, the Hazardous Liquid Pipeline Act of 1979, the Ports and Waterways Safety Act of 1972, and the Port and Tanker Safety Act of 1978].

The Oil Pollution Act, like the Port and Tanker Safety Act before it, imposes direct safety requirements on the shipping of oil—namely, the law's double-hull mandate. Note, however, that the primary way the OPA deals with safety is indirectly: by creating a strict liability regime, which seeks to incentivize shippers to ensure that they operate their vessels safely. As you read the following case, which involves a straightforward application of the OPA to another kind of oil transport (by truck), consider how effective such indirect regulation of shipping safety is—and whether a different, perhaps more direct, approach might be more or less effective.

UNITED STATES V. MIZHIR

106 F. Supp. 2d 124 (D. Mass. 2000)

GORTON, DISTRICT JUDGE.

The United States brings this action for reimbursement of funds expended by the Oil Spill Liability Trust Fund for the cleanup of an oil spill allegedly caused by the defendant, George Mizhir d/b/a Mizhir Oil Co. (Mizhir). . . .

I. Background

Mizhir lives and operated an oil delivery business in Winchendon, Massachusetts. On December 20, 1994, he took his oil truck to be serviced at Bergevin's Enterprises, Inc. of Keene, New Hampshire (Bergevin's).

Bergevin's service records indicate that a mechanic inspected the truck and told Mizhir the brakes were "unsafe" and "not to drive truck."

The following day, Mizhir crashed his oil delivery truck into a house in Marlborough, New Hampshire causing a spill of 3,000 gallons of No. 2 fuel oil into the house and surrounding area. That area includes the Minnewawa Brook, which flows into the Ashuelot River. Mizhir made no attempt to remove the oil himself.

On the day after the accident, the homeowner's insurance company retained Clean Harbors Environmental Services, Inc. (Clean Harbors) to provide emergency oil removal from the house. The same day, the New Hampshire Department of Environmental Services notified the Environmental Protection Agency (EPA) of the spill. An EPA coordinator, who arrived at the scene the following day, observed oil seeping into the Minnewawa Brook. Because Mizhir made no effort to remove the oil, EPA notified the U.S. Coast Guard to secure immediate funding for the cleanup and contracted with Clean Harbors to remove the oil from the brook.

All phases of the cleanup were completed on August 4, 1995. The total cost of the cleanup was $242,587, including the EPA contract costs of $209,861 charged by Clean Harbors, $6,067 for EPA's supervisory costs, $20,759 for the cleanup of the house and interest. The homeowner's insurance company arranged for the cleanup of the house but later disclaimed liability. The government sent invoices to the defendant, but he failed to pay any portion of the cleanup costs. The government filed the instant lawsuit and thereafter the pending motion for summary judgment to be reimbursed for removal costs.

II. The Oil Pollution Act

The Oil Pollution Act provides that

> . . . each responsible party for a vessel or a facility from which oil is discharged, or which poses the substantial threat of a discharge of oil, into or upon navigable waters or adjoining shorelines . . . is liable for the removal costs . . . that result from such incident.

33 U.S.C. § 2702(a). The "responsible party" in the context of onshore facilities like a motor vehicle is defined as the person owning the facility from which oil discharged. 33 U.S.C. § 2701(32)(B). "Facility", in turn, is defined as any motor vehicle used for, inter alia, transporting oil. 33 U.S.C. § 2701(9). "Discharge" is defined as "any emission (other than natural seepage), intentional or unintentional, and includes, but is not limited to, spilling, leaking, pumping, pouring, emitting, emptying or dumping." 33 U.S.C. § 2701(7).

The OPA defines "navigable waters" as "the waters of the United States . . ." 33 U.S.C. § 2701(21). The government asserts that "waters of the United States" describes, in addition to what is obviously navigable, all waters and wetlands that are not navigable or even directly connected to navigable water. It cites two cases, *United States v. Riverside Bayview Homes, Inc.*, 474 U.S. 121, 132–39 (1985) and *Village of Oconomowoc Lake v. Dayton Hudson Corp.*, 24 F.3d 962, 964–65 (7th Cir. 1994), both of which describe the term "waters of the United States" as used in the Clean Water Act, under such broad terms. No cases address directly the term "waters of the United States" as used in the OPA, but EPA (the agency charged with enforcing the OPA) defines the term as including

> intrastate lakes, rivers, streams (including intermittent streams), mudflats, sandflats, wetlands, sloughs, prairie potholes, wet meadows, playa lakes, or natural ponds, the use, degradation or destruction of which could affect interstate or foreign commerce.

40 C.F.R. § 230.3(s)(3). Because the same language has been interpreted under the Clean Water Act and the EPA considers that term encompasses all waters, this Court concludes that "waters of the United States" as used in the OPA means all waters and wetlands, not necessarily navigable waters. In any event, Mizhir does not challenge the construction of "navigable waters".

The OPA requires the United States to remove oil spills or to oversee the removal by others. "Removal" is defined as "containment and removal of oil or a hazardous substance from water . . . or the taking of other actions as may be necessary to minimize or mitigate damage to the public health or welfare . . ." 33 U.S.C. § 2701(30). The responsible party is liable for all removal costs. 33 U.S.C. § 2702. The United States is also entitled to recover its costs in directing and monitoring all actions to remove a discharge, and interest on unpaid removal costs. 33 U.S.C. § 2705. Those removal costs may also include attorneys' fees incurred to recover the money expended by the Oil Spill Liability Fund from the responsible party.

With respect to logistics, the government usually pays expenses out of the Oil Spill Liability Trust Fund and, if the responsible party has not paid for or reimbursed the government, it may proceed against that party in a District Court "in which the discharge or injury or damages occurred or where the defendant resides . . ." 33 U.S.C. § 2717(b). Absent any defense, the OPA imposes strict liability upon the responsible party for oil removal costs. The OPA affords three defenses to such a claim, to wit: 1) an act of God, 2) an act of war or 3) an act or omission of a third party (with exceptions). 33 U.S.C. § 2703(a).

III. The Government's Motion for Summary Judgment

. . . The government asserts that this is a straightforward case in that 1) the defendant was both the operator and owner of the "facility" from which the oil was "discharged" and 2) Mizhir admittedly took no action to clean up the oil spill. Indeed Mizhir refused to accept written notification of the federal interest in the spill and did not render payment when presented with invoices for the cleanup.

Only after determining that Mizhir would undertake no cleanup action, did the EPA assume the task of oil removal. It contracted with Clean Harbors to remove all of the discharged oil and the U.S. Coast Guard, through the Oil Spill Liability fund, paid for all cleanup costs. Under the OPA, the government is entitled to reimbursement of those costs.

Mizhir asserts two defenses to the government's claim: 1) the oil discharge was the result of the act or omission of a third party and 2) the instant action was filed after the running of the applicable statute of limitations. . . .

1. *Statute of Limitations*

The OPA provides that an action for recovery of removal costs "must be commenced within 3 years after completion of the removal action." 33 U.S.C. § 2717(f)(2). The complaint in this case was filed on May 22, 1998.

Mizhir asserts that the removal action was completed on May 20, 1995, but the invoices from the cleanup clearly show that work was performed as late as August 4, 1995. Mizhir argues that 90% of the oil removal was completed before May 20 and that any action taken after that time was not part of the removal action.

By statute the government may recover all "removal costs" including 1) the cost of "containment and removal of oil or a hazardous substance from water . . . or the taking of other actions as may be necessary to minimize or mitigate damage to the public health or welfare . . ." and 2) costs of directing and monitoring all actions to remove a discharge including monitoring activities. 33 U.S.C. §§ 2701(30) and 2702.

Clean Harbors, the company retained to perform the work, conducted cleanup work on seven occasions after May 22, 1995 (three years prior to filing) and all work was completed on August 4, 1995, well within the three-year statute of limitations period. Mizhir's argument that work was complete by May 20, 1995 is groundless. Even though the date upon which removal work was completed is a question of fact, no reasonable jury could find that the government filed this action more than three years after the completion of the oil removal.

2. *Third Party at Fault*

Mizhir also claims there is a third person at fault for the accident thus exonerating him. The relevant portion of Section 2703(a) of Title 33 provides:

> A responsible party is not liable for removal costs or damages . . .
> if the responsible party establishes, by a preponderance of the

evidence, that the discharge . . . of oil and the resulting damages or removal costs were caused solely by . . .

(3) an act or omission of a third party, other than an employee or agent of the responsible party or a third party whose act or omission occurs in connection with any contractual relationship with the responsible party . . . if the responsible party establishes, by a preponderance of the evidence, that the responsible party—

(A) exercised due care with respect to the oil concerned, taking into consideration the characteristics of the oil and in light of all relevant facts and circumstances; and

(B) took precautions against foreseeable acts or omissions of any such third party and the foreseeable consequences of those acts or omissions . . .

Thus, if the oil discharge and the resulting damages were caused solely by an act or omission of a third party and the responsible party was not himself negligent, it is a complete defense to the collection of removal costs. Where the third party is an employee, agent or otherwise in a contractual relationship with the responsible party, however, that provision does not apply. Nor does that provision apply if the responsible party is himself negligent.

Mizhir contends that service of the truck brakes at Bergevin's on the day before the accident was negligent and that the failure of the brakes which caused that accident is attributable to Bergevin's and not to him.

The government response is twofold. First, the government persuasively argues that Bergevin's was an agent of Mizhir because the two were in a contractual relationship. Section 2703(a)(3) exempts from the third party defense any agent or party in a contractual relationship with the responsible party. Thus, Mizhir cannot, as a matter of law, avail himself of that defense.

The government also contends that, even if Bergevin's were found not to be an agent or otherwise in a contractual relationship with Mizhir, Section 2703 affords a third party defense only if Mizhir himself was not negligent. The service records from Bergevin's indicate that its mechanic inspected the truck and told Mizhir the brakes were "unsafe" and "not to drive truck."

Clearly, Mizhir was aware of the dangerous condition of his brakes and that it was foreseeable that they might fail. A reasonable jury could not find that Mizhir was not at least partly at fault for the accident and subsequent oil spill on December 21, 1994. For those two reasons, Mizhir cannot reasonably assert the third party defense provided by Section 2703. . . .

NOTES AND QUESTIONS

1.   While the *Exxon Valdez* spill was perhaps the most environmentally damaging in the nation's history, there have been other significant oil spills both before and after it—most notably, the 1969 Santa Barbara oil spill and the 2010 *Deepwater Horizon* spill in the Gulf of Mexico discussed in Chapter 9. Following the 1969 spill, it became clear that the "environmental disaster of unprecedented proportions . . . might have been avoided but for a failure of federal oversight." *California v. Norton*, 311 F.3d 1162, 1166 (9th Cir. 2002). As a result, the Coastal Zone Management Act and the California Coastal Act, both passed within a few years of the incident, contained provisions targeting these regulatory failures, including the waiver of safety and well construction requirements. Additionally, in the wake of the *Deepwater Horizon* spill, the Obama administration "launched the most aggressive and comprehensive reforms to offshore oil and gas regulation and oversight in U.S. history." *Regulatory Reforms*, Bureau of Ocean Energy Mgmt. These reforms ranged from well design requirements to workplace safety to corporate accountability.

2.   The fact that our legal system often waits for disasters to occur before responding has provoked criticism that U.S. environmental law is too reactionary. As one scholar put it, "disasters breed environmental law." Michael Allan Wolf, *Environmental Law Slogans for a New Millennium*, 35 U. RICH. L. REV. 91, 99 (2001). Is this the best approach to environmental protection—reacting to problems rather than trying to plan to prevent them? Many think not. One problem is that this creates "a triage approach to environmental problems"—"narrow, end-of-the-process . . . solution[s]" that do not address the root cause of environmental degradation. Amy J. Wildermuth, *The Legacy of Exxon Valdez: How Do We Stop the Crisis?*, 7 U. ST. THOMAS L.J. 130, 131, 152 (2009); *see also* David M. Driesen & Amy Sinden, *The Missing Instrument: Dirty Input Limits*, 33 HARV. ENV'T L. REV. 65 (2009). On the other hand, disasters force a reevaluation of business-as-usual and take industry to task when their "common practices" are the source of the disaster. Keith H. Hirokawa, *Disasters and Ecosystem Services Deprivation: From Cuyahoga to the Deepwater Horizon*, 74 ALB. L. REV. 543, 549 (2011).

3.   Oil spills can result in hefty economic consequences for those who cause them. As a result of the *Exxon Valdez* spill, Exxon was required to pay $900 million over ten years for restoration efforts. Sanne Knudsen, *A Precautionary Tale: Assessing Ecological Damages After the Exxon Valdez Oil Spill*, 7 U. ST. THOMAS L.J. 95, 97 (2009). The Supreme Court also upheld a punitive damages award against Exxon, although it reduced the amount from $2.5 billion to $507.5 million, which was equal to the compensatory damages Exxon had to pay. *Exxon Shipping Co. v. Baker*, 554 U.S. 471, 515 (2008).

4.   In addition to imposing civil and criminal penalties, some environmental statutes also make available liability for natural resource damages. The Oil Pollution Act is one such statute. Section 1002 of the OPA provides that those

who violate the Act are liable for "damages for injury to, destruction of, loss of, or loss of use of, natural resources, including reasonable costs of assessing the damage. . . ." 33 U.S.C. § 2702(b)(2)(A). Section 1006 then directs that these damages be calculated by adding "the cost of restoring, rehabilitating, replacing, or acquiring the equivalent of, the damaged natural resources," "the diminution in value of those natural resources pending restoration," and "the reasonable cost of assessing those damages." 33 U.S.C. § 2706(d).

PART III

ENERGY IN TRANSITION: EMERGING ISSUES

■ ■ ■

Part III is an intentional departure from traditional energy law casebooks. This part consists of case studies of the emerging energy law and policy issues that can facilitate a transition from the traditional fossil-fuel model of energy policy to a clean energy economy. While there is no shortage of challenges confronting that transition, the energy sector is developing new ideas and technologies for the future. This Part introduces you to some of the current and important topics in that transition and gives you an opportunity to explore how you would solve these cutting-edge challenges.

We start, in Chapter 8, with an examination of grid modernization. The nation's electricity grid is undergoing a major transformation. As you will learn, the traditional grid is a one-way system in which electricity is generated and ultimately sold to end-users. A modernized grid, or "smart grid," by way of contrast, will not only distribute electricity, but it will also transmit information between electricity producers and consumers. In this way, the market should function more accurately and more efficiently as we will discuss. Nevertheless, as promising as grid modernization is, barriers to its full implementation, along with concerns over privacy and cybersecurity, remain to be addressed and overcome.

In the first two decades of the 21st century, the United States, as well as other regions of the world, experienced a boom in fossil fuel discoveries both in oil and natural gas. Those resources are being recovered with new production technologies, most notably directional drilling, hydraulic fracturing, and deepwater drilling. Chapter 9 explores how these technological innovations pose new regulatory challenges and efforts made to address them. The two examples provide a particularly interesting pairing because hydraulic fracturing is governed largely at the state level, including by common law, whereas deepwater drilling has more extensive federal statutory regulation. Chapter 9 also explores developments in offshore wind energy, including the extent to which this emerging renewable energy resource in the United States can be used to overcome some of the energy transportation barriers to bringing onshore wind energy resources to coastal states.

We explore the role of nuclear power in a clean energy future in Chapter 10. Nuclear power is an important source of electricity yet remains controversial for many reasons. Issues of reactor safety continue to be a concern even though the history of nuclear power has accumulated a fairly responsible track record, with notable exceptions. The U.S. nuclear fleet of commercial reactors is aging, and new reactors have met regulatory and political barriers. Just as important, the spent fuel from the existing reactor fleet must be stored somewhere. Currently, spent fuel is stored on the reactor site. Consequently, regulators must confront the issue of relicensing reactors, expanding on-site storage, and searching for more permanent nuclear waste disposal areas. Nevertheless, carbon free nuclear power plays a key role in net-zero planning.

Finally, in Chapter 11, we turn to our energy future. We begin by describing the concept of Net Zero Energy within the context of global climate change and commitments from countries, U.S. states, and companies to manage and reduce emissions. We then examine innovation and evaluate two case studies of clean energy implementation—adoption of electric vehicles (EVs) to electrify the transportation sector and the use of carbon capture and storage (CCS) to allow the continued use of fossil fuels in the energy and industrial sectors without emitting the associated GHG emissions into the atmosphere. We end with a discussion of potential futures for the energy sector as well as concluding thoughts for this book.

CHAPTER 8

THE FUTURE OF THE ELECTRIC GRID: MODERNIZATION AND COMPLEXITY

■ ■ ■

A. OVERVIEW

As discussed in Chapters 4 and 5, the modern electric grid is a complex networked system that generates electricity and moves it in real time to millions of customers (or "load"). In the past, electric utilities, and entities like Independent System Operators (ISOs) and Regional Transmission Organizations (RTOs) ran the grid (and associated markets) with virtually no feedback from customers and limited ability to manage energy demand, except in emergency situations.

In the future, the next generation power grid will function very differently. This chapter focuses on these changes. In this chapter, we examine the needed changes in planning and policy and the resulting challenges facing grid modernization. We also explore issues like cybersecurity and consumer privacy along with new electricity system configurations presented by microgrids and community energy systems.

In doing so, we recognize that the future grid, along with the large-scale integration of distributed energy resources, requires two-way information flows between generators, markets, and consumers. This integration is facilitated by advanced power electronics, control devices, and data analytics that may simultaneously make the system more vulnerable to cyberattacks and raise privacy considerations. Increasing variable wind and solar resources on the grid also requires new system innovations in operation and planning.

In the grid of the future, system flexibility is critical. New efforts to better integrate and manage load, including buildings and EVs, can allow demand response to play an increasingly important role in grid planning and operations. At the same time, a changing climate and weather-related disruptions present new risks and require more investments to ensure reliability and resilience—addressing emergency preparedness, wildfires, cybersecurity, and more. Taken together, these drivers are shaping the future architectures of energy systems.

Modernizing the grid requires that new technologies are integrated and supported by new laws and policies. Ensuring the electric grid of the future can simultaneously remain resilient in the face of a changing climate, reduce GHGs, and support our evolving societal needs for energy is a critical goal for energy leaders, lawyers, and policymakers. A 2021 report from the National Academies of Sciences, Engineering, and Medicine on the future of the electric grid, excerpted below, identified five broad needs to consider across technologies, planning and operations, business models, and grid architectures.

THE FUTURE OF ELECTRIC POWER IN THE UNITED STATES
The Nat'l Academies of Sciences, Engineering, and Medicine (2021)

As directed by the statement of task, the committee performed an assessment and provided findings and recommendations across several topics: *technologies; planning and operations; business models; and grid architectures....* We begin by presenting the need to improve our understanding of how the system is evolving. . . .

1. **Improve our understanding of how the system is evolving.** Because of many parallel changes in technology, patterns of electricity consumption, and social expectations for electric power, it is more difficult to forecast future electricity supply, demand, and infrastructure today than it was a few decades ago. The tools for forecasting electric futures need to be capable of adaptation because the architecture of the grid will evolve in different ways in different regions and will adjust as the country reduces emissions of greenhouse gases from the overall economy through decarbonizing the electric supply and more pervasive use of electricity. As part of this effort, the nation needs to build and test new tools for simulation and experimentation to understand how the grid of the future will behave and how operators and policy makers can ensure its continued reliability.

2. **Ensure that electricity service remains clean and sustainable, and reliable and resilient.** Reducing emissions of CO_2 and other environmental impacts of electricity generation will remain a major challenge in the coming decades. While the focus of the role of electricity generation on ambient air quality may diminish as generation becomes less polluting, there is a growing focus on increasing sustainability and addressing climate change, in part through increased use of renewables. At high penetrations, this will require increasing the capacity of high-voltage, multistate transmission networks. The balance between reliability and resilience may shift over time, but

excellent overall performance will remain essential. The power system is vulnerable to a variety of natural events and accidental as well as pernicious human physical and cyberattacks that can be minimized yet not eliminated entirely. New technologies, along with continued investment in critical elements of the electric power system, such as long-distance transmission and robust distributed resources, will improve the nation's capabilities. The nation, the electric industry, and other stakeholders need to do a better job of educating and training people at all levels to design, reinforce, manage, and run a resilient and effective electric system.

3. **Improve understanding of how people use electricity and sustain the "social compact" to keep electricity affordable and equitable in the face of profound technological changes.** Already many changes in the grid reveal opportunities for new services and configurations of electric resources. Some kinds of profound changes in electric supply, such as some customers becoming less dependent on grid-delivered power, could be highly disruptive to the social compact that has been central to the electric power industry and its provision of universal service for more than a century. These changes could have large impacts on customers with low incomes. It is crucial to build tools to understand those needs along with devising regulatory responses to evolve and selectively strengthen social compacts in light of changing circumstances.

4. **Facilitate innovations in technology, policy, and business models relevant to the power system.** New technologies, such as clean generation, wide electrification, energy storage, power electronics, and systems for monitoring and control, can enable large changes in the way the power system is organized and operated. Especially large changes may occur in the distribution and retail parts of the grid where the system meets people and non-utility companies (the so-called grid edge). While supply provided by central generation and transmission and distribution wires will remain essential, technical, policy, and business-model changes could speed innovation and the introduction of new services to consumers at the grid edge. Understanding how electricity consumers behave, how devices and energy services can be aggregated for supply, and how such trends affect system loads are emerging as some of the most profound technological, regulatory, and planning challenges

and opportunities facing the future of the grid. That understanding requires situational awareness and control across potentially tens of millions of nodes and at high rates of response (milliseconds, not seconds). Such changes will require more flexible system planning and operations at both the bulk-power and local levels.

5. **Accelerate innovations in technology in the face of shifting global supply chains and the influx of disruptive technologies.** Many of the basic power system technologies were first developed in the United States. However, the supply chains and manufacturing for most critical electric power system technologies have now moved offshore. The United States has been underinvesting in the innovation needed for future electric system performance. Massive new private and public investments are needed in innovation, especially for more cutting-edge technologies on which the future grid will depend. Policies are needed to move supply chains and manufacturing for those technologies back to the United States, while recognizing that innovation and manufacturing are now global. The United States must balance competing goals—one to gain from the advantages of a global search for innovative solutions and the other to ensure U.S. control and awareness of and access to critical grid infrastructure technologies. The advantages of engagement and awareness of progress overseas will be particularly important where grids are expanding in size and function, which facilitates testing, demonstration, and deployment of new technology.

As seen in the report excerpted above, many different actors and institutions are involved in developing, financing, and building the future grid. As illustrated in this chapter, they include the Department of Energy, FERC, the National Institute of Standards and Technology (NIST), FEMA, RTOs and ISOs, state public utility commissions, public and investor-owned utilities, financial institutions, and a wide range of other public and private entities. These actors often have very different visions for the future of the grid and interact within the electric system with different constraints. For example, RTOs are charged with bulk power system planning and wholesale market operations and cover almost 70% of U.S. electricity demand. One RTO can serve a single state or stretch across many states. While all RTOs face similar technical challenges in planning and managing the transmission grid and electricity markets, there are geographic, market, and cultural variations in their orientation towards a future grid. For instance, whether RTO member states have traditionally regulated or restructured electricity markets or have adopted Renewable Portfolio Standards (RPSs) or Clean Energy Standards (CESs) can affect grid development and collective initiatives such as multi-state transmission planning.

Planning for the future electric grid must also address the resiliency and reliability of the system in the face of increasing climate and weather uncertainty. Weather related risks to the electric grid vary by location. Western states facing extreme heat, drought, or fire risk and southern states facing extreme storm and weather events need to prepare differently to ensure reliability and grid resilience. The National Oceanic and Atmospheric Administration estimates that between 2017 and 2020 there have been fifty extreme weather-related events, costing the U.S. over $237 billion. *See U.S. Billion-Dollar Weather and Climate Disasters: Overview*, NAT'L OCEANIC & ATMOSPHERIC ADMIN., https://www.ncdc.noaa.gov/billions/. It is imperative that the electric grid of the future can respond to these threats and maintain reliable service.

This is made more difficult as the future grid is being built on aging legacy infrastructure. Much of the existing electric generation, transmission, and distribution network is nearing the end of its 20–50+ year lifetime. The American Society of Civil Engineers 2020 report on the electric grid identifies a $208 billion investment gap by 2029. It concludes this investment should be targeted towards electricity generation (65%), transmission (23%), and distribution (12%) systems to support overall system reliability, noting large regional differences in spending needs. *See* AM. SOC'Y OF CIVIL ENGINEERS, FAILURE TO ACT: ELECTRIC INFRASTRUCTURE INVESTMENT GAPS IN A RAPIDLY CHANGING ENVIRONMENT (2020).

How the future grid impacts communities is also emerging as an important area of inquiry as equity and justice concerns are shaping the future energy system. The recognition that the existing energy system has unfairly impacted communities of color and the desire to ensure that future investments in the grid will help to address these inequities is an important topic. Consistent with that focus, the Biden administration created a new position of Deputy Director for Energy Justice within the Department of Energy and efforts are being made to incorporate environmental justice concerns in energy system data collection for projects like Pecan Street (mentioned below) and energy system planning and analysis. *See* Robert Walton, *Energy Equity Depends on Data, and Experts Say There Isn't Enough of It,* UTIL. DIVE (July 8, 2021); Destenie Nock & Erin Baker, *Holistic Multi-criteria Decision Analysis Evaluation of Sustainable Electric Generation Portfolios: New England Case Study,* 242 APPLIED ENERGY 655 (2019).

The frontiers of grid modernization continue to evolve. In the past it included installing smart meters, but with over 107 million smart meters installed in the United States 2020, this is no longer a driving issue. Now, flexibility has emerged as key—both on the demand side and on the supply side. On the demand side, this means integrating and coordinating energy use from buildings (including end use devices and behind the meter generation), EVs, and storage with higher levels of variable renewable resources. On the supply side, this involves continually improving the integration of variable resources into grid planning, markets, and operations. Taken together, this requires new ways of linking electricity production and energy use with management approaches and requires utilities to incorporate new planning uncertainties into their operations. It also requires the deployment of new technologies such as implementing inverter control technologies to compensate for fewer spinning reserves.

Finally, in addition to physically linking the different sectors' energy use, grid modernization also requires coordinating and managing the legal and institutional frameworks to create an integrated system. The remainder of this chapter discusses new technologies for grid modernization, the planning and policies that support the implementation of those technologies, roadblocks to implementation, cybersecurity concerns, and privacy challenges.

B. ENABLING NEW TECHNOLOGIES THROUGH NEW PLANNING AND OPERATIONS

Grid modernization efforts link electricity generation, transmission, distribution, and use in new configurations. Some technologies are used in the high-voltage transmission grid, others in the distribution network, and still others in companies or homes. Where in the system the technologies are used determines which policies and statutes apply, which incentives are effective, and what risks may arise. The following diagram shows how new grid technologies and configurations could be integrated into the electric system.

Emerging 21st-Century Electricity Two-Way Flow Supply Chain

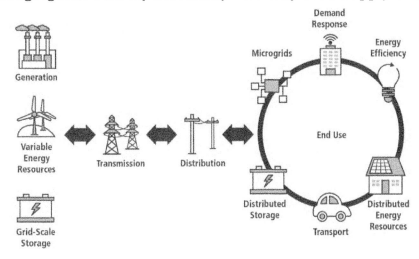

The emerging 21st-century power grid will incorporate responsive resources, storage, microgrids, and other technologies that enable increased flexibility, higher system efficiency, reduced energy consumption, and increased consumer options and value.

Source: U.S. DEP'T OF ENERGY, QUADRENNIAL ENERGY REVIEW: TRANSFORMING THE NATION'S ELECTRICITY SYSTEM (Jan. 2017).

Modernizing the electric power system is more than just new technologies arranged in different architectures. It also requires changes in how grids are planned and operated and the supporting policies, laws, and institutions. The following excerpt from the Electric Power Research Institute shows the need for additional system flexibility:

> ... Currently, most electric power systems still operate through "forecast and supply" methods that ramp up and down the controllable resources to deal with demand that is treated as variable and passively unresponsive. Integration increasingly requires a new "forecast and balance" approach through which both load and generation are forecast while supply and demand technologies are used to balance the system, often through market signals. Integrated planning for generation, transmission, and distribution systems (loosely linked until recently) can equip utilities and customers to make better use of all resources.

> Achieving this requires expanding and upgrading the electric grid. Most transmission assets were designed to move power from conventional generation (sited for access to water and fuel) to distribution systems within utility service territories. The rapid deployment of renewable energy and the closing of existing generation assets changes power flows dramatically and puts pressure on an aging transmission infrastructure. Near term, this requires inspection, assessment and monitoring, and upgrades to maintain reliability. Further, it necessitates regional

transmission expansion to connect generation from different locations. Because renewable resources (e.g., wind, solar) centered in different locations provides operational diversity, the value of transmission systems increases as they are able to link these resources with centers of load over much larger areas, while using more sophisticated, comprehensive control systems.

ELEC. POWER RSCH. INST., THE INTEGRATED ENERGY NETWORK: CONNECTING CUSTOMERS TO RELIABLE, SAFE, AFFORDABLE AND CLEANER ENERGY 16 (Feb. 2017).

One of the promises of a modern grid is that it could allow for development of microgrids through the coordinated integration of fossil sources and distributed energy resources (DER) like solar and wind. Microgrids would use control systems to link, connect, and control distributed energy technologies and energy demand in a coordinated manner. By developing new distribution network architectures and control systems, solar, wind, energy storage, and traditional natural gas or diesel generators could be linked in smaller coordinated electricity systems to ensure local electricity demand is met, while potentially increasing system reliability and resilience. While these microgrid systems could be connected and synchronous with the larger centralized power grid, or linked together in a networked fashion, they could also run independently in an "islanded" mode. In cases of extreme weather events, this could increase system reliability and resilience; in normal operating conditions it could also allow for better integration of renewables, reduce energy losses and system congestion, and improve energy efficiency and environmental outcomes. Microgrid projects have been used by military installations and are rapidly increasing worldwide, though they remain more costly than legacy grid operations. A recent NREL study reported average microgrid costs from $1.5–3 million per MW for community projects to $2.3–3.2 million per MW for utility-scale projects. *See* JULIETA GIRALDEZ ET AL., NAT'L RENEWABLE ENERGY LAB., PHASE I MICROGRID COST STUDY: DATA COLLECTION AND ANALYSIS OF MICROGRID COSTS IN THE UNITED STATES (Oct. 2018). *See also* FRANCISCO FLORES-ESPINO ET AL., NAT'L RENEWABLE ENERGY LAB., NETWORKED MICROGRID OPTIMAL DESIGN AND OPERATIONS TOOL: REGULATORY AND BUSINESS ENVIRONMENT STUDY (May 2020).

Microgrids have been supported at the state level. For instance, the New York Public Service Commission (PSC), with the support of the Governor, created an initiative called "Reforming the Energy Vision" or "REV" to "promot[e] more efficient use of energy, deeper penetration of renewable energy resources such as wind and solar, wider deployment of 'distributed' energy resources, such as microgrids, rooftop solar and other on-site power supplies, and energy storage." REV is supporting a wide variety of demonstration projects from new market platforms to electric school buses. *See About the Initiative, DPS—Reforming the Energy Vision,*

N.Y. Dept. of Pub. Serv. One of the biggest challenges in developing community level microgrids is changing the institutions. Legacy energy providers, state and federal policy makers, funders, technology providers, and the community itself all need to engage in the planning, design, construction, and operation of microgrids. While many projects are initiated for reliability and resilience reasons, some utilities do not welcome microgrids in their service territories and lenders may be reluctant to finance more costly projects. Additionally, the lack of strong state regulatory frameworks supporting microgrids or microgrid networks also hinders development. *See* FLORES-ESPINO ET AL., *supra*; Martin Warneryd et al., *Unpacking the Complexity of Community Microgrids: A Review of Institutions' Roles for Development of Microgrids,* 121 RENEWABLE AND SUSTAINABLE ENERGY REVIEWS (Apr. 2020).

Future energy system flexibility can also be supported by improved demand response, namely by better managing building energy use. As mentioned in Chapter 2, buildings use 40% of U.S. energy and 75% of electricity. FERC's Order 2222, discussed in Chapter 4, supports integrating aggregated distributed energy resources into the grid and establishes the importance of demand management approaches. If building load is viewed as a grid resource, pushes for more efficient technologies like solid state lighting, variable speed motors, and connected "smart" appliances (with controls to actively manage electric use), can provide important system attributes to both reduce energy use through efficiency and shift energy demand through demand management. Using the best available building technologies can provide enormous energy and cost savings and add system flexibility. A study by researchers at the Lawrence Berkeley National Laboratory found that nationwide deployment of efficiency and demand flexibility programs for buildings can avoid about 25% of annual electricity use (742 TWh reduction in building energy from an estimated 2030 system of 2870 TWh), reduce summer peak demand by 37% (181 GW reduced from a total of 485 GW), and reduce winter peak demand by 27% (119 GW reduction from 431 GW winter peaking demand). This study assumed high deployment levels of both energy efficiency and flexibility measures. (Note: the U.S. grid was roughly 1,100 GW in 2020, with retail sales at 3,665 billion kWh.) *See* JARED LANGEVIN ET AL., LAWRENCE BERKELEY. NAT'L LAB., U.S. BUILDING ENERGY EFFICIENCY AND FLEXIBILITY AS AN ELECTRIC GRID RESOURCE (Jan. 2021); *Electricity Explained: Electricity Generation, Capacity, and Sales in the United States,* U.S. Energy Info. Admin. (Mar. 18, 2021).

NOTES AND QUESTIONS

1. "Community energy" is another approach states and local governments are using to promote distributed energy resources, but utilities have not always been enthusiastic supporters. What sort of policies should be developed for community energy production? What types of rights *and* responsibilities should community members have? *See, e.g.*, Emma F. Merchant, *So, What Exactly Is Community Solar?*, GTM (Apr. 30, 2020).

One of the criticisms of community energy and of microgrids is that only wealthy communities and citizens can benefit from these programs. Wealthy communities and individuals may own their own homes, have enough capital to invest in rooftop solar or high enough credit scores to enroll in community solar gardens, and have the resources to plan and invest in these systems. How can low-income communities and people that rent their homes also benefit from local energy initiatives? What types of policies and incentives could help? *See* Gregory Barger, *Three Ways to Bring Solar Power to the People Who Need it Most*, WIRED MAGAZINE (Oct. 22, 2016); Kari Lydersen, *Chicago's South Side Sees First Free Solar Installations Under State Equity Program*, MIDWEST ENERGY NEWS (June 29, 2020) (discussing "Illinois Solar for All" program created under the state's 2017 Future Energy Jobs Act).

2. The February 2021 winter storm blackouts in Texas and surrounding states, where almost five million people lost power, raised questions as to whether microgrids could have helped system reliability. *See, e.g.*, Michael D. Mehta, *Texas Electricity Grid Failure Shows How Microgrids Offer Hope For A Better Future*, THE CONVERSATION (Feb. 23, 2021); Robert Hebner, *What the Texas-Freeze Fiasco Tells Us About The Future of the Grid*, IEEE SPECTRUM (Feb. 23, 2021). Microgrids can improve system reliability in the event of extreme weather, but there is a risk that they could exacerbate inequalities in electricity service between communities and undermine goals of universal access. How can this be managed? What types of coordination or incentives can help developers and regulators plan and approve projects? How should legislatures, regulators, utilities, and other stakeholders prioritize microgrid development and funding as opposed to building out a "macrogrid" connecting utility-scale renewable energy resources to remote load centers through long distance transmission lines, as discussed in Chapters 5 and 7?

3. The U.S. military uses an estimated 1% of all electric energy in the United States, has about one-third of the United States' microgrid installations, and leads in development efforts. The military spends over $11.9 billion dollars on energy, with about 30% of it on the 300,000 buildings it manages. While military investments in energy efficiency are estimated to save $1 billion a year, development of new microgrids could also help. The military uses stockpiled fuel and stand-alone diesel generators as critical backup, but additional developments and investments in microgrids could change this. *See* HEATHER L. GREENLEY, CONG. RSCH. SERV., DEPARTMENT OF DEFENSE ENERGY MANAGEMENT: BACKGROUND AND ISSUES FOR CONGRESS (JULY 25, 2019);

JEFFREY MARQUSEE ET AL., NOBLIS, POWER BEGINS AT HOME: ASSURED ENERGY FOR MILITARY BASES (Jan. 2017).

4.   Microgrids are useful in remote environments like islands and on tribal lands, where providing both heat and power are challenging. Communities in Alaska, the Canadian Arctic, Greenland, and the Russian Arctic have all experimented with different types of system configurations. *See* Lucia Mortensen et al., *How Three Key Factors are Driving and Challenging Implementation of Renewable Energy Systems in Remote Arctic Communities*, 40 POLAR GEO. 163 (May 2017). Investments in tribal microgrids could allow remote communities access to more reliable energy. *See* Andrew Burger, *$39 Million of Microgrid Funding for Tribal Lands*, MICROGRID KNOWLEDGE (Aug. 1, 2019).

5.   Early integrated infrastructure demonstration projects linking electricity, water, and gas use with solar homes and EV owners—like Pecan Street in Austin, Texas—continue to provide important research and operational insights into consumer energy use, the impact of EVs, and the integration of renewable energy into distribution grids. Launched in 2009, this ongoing project at the Robert Mueller mixed-use development (a redevelopment at the old ATX airport) in Austin, Texas was one of the first of its kind to link over 1000 home and business smart meters, in-home energy displays, and smart thermostats with 250 solar PV homes and 65 EV owners. The gas, electricity, and water use data from the project have provided detailed energy consumption and production information over time and space. This information has spurred many different research projects and publications, and has helped in the planning, development, and management of community energy systems. Efforts to ensure energy data in diverse communities is represented has led the Pecan Street project to partner with the Urban Justice Energy Lab at the University of Michigan to gather energy use data in Detroit. *See Academic Research Papers Using Pecan Street Data*, Pecan Street, https://www.pecanstreet.org/work/papers/; Robert Walton, *Energy Equity Depends on Data, and Experts Say There Isn't Enough of It,* UTIL. DIVE (July 8, 2021).

For example, poor installation of solar panels was found to decrease winter solar power production from one residence by 29%, as a small amount of shading could take out an entire solar string. There are solutions to this problem. Although more expensive, better solar installation could lead to less shading, while advanced micro-inverters (which convert the DC power produced by solar PV systems to the AC power used by the grid) could help alleviate the problem of series string design. Most of the solar PV systems at the Pecan Street Project are south or west facing. Even though west facing systems produce slightly less electricity (5% less in 2011), it was worth more to the energy system, and would have earned about 12% more money if real time prices were used, as it is better matched to actual electric loads in the Texas grid region. This makes it more valuable for utilities that are paying wholesale electric prices, but less valuable for homeowners who benefit from Austin's Value of Solar Rate, which pays $0.128 per kWh generated, regardless of the time of day. Additionally, increases in local grid variability and stability have been found on the system, and managing PV integration on the distribution network is an ongoing challenge. This "learning by doing" makes the Pecan Street Project's energy data and technical system information extremely valuable for technical and policy communities. What should be the role of the federal, state, or local governments in supporting projects like this and in making energy data available for analysis? How can such demonstration projects be used to inform policymaking? How can equity concerns be addressed in tandem with energy research? Energy innovation policy and financing are discussed in Chapter 9.

6.   As discussed, demand response can shift energy consumption and "flatten load curves" by shifting energy use to different times of the day and making the system more flexible. In some electricity markets, third party demand response aggregators have become active market participants, and demand response has become a valuable grid resource that bids into capacity and day-ahead electricity markets. Advances in smart metering allow more industrial, commercial, and residential customers to directly participate in electricity markets, potentially allowing for more efficient integration of variable resources like PV and better system energy usage. Utilities generally like demand response, as it allows them to avoid high-cost generation and postpone construction of new infrastructure. Unlike energy efficiency programs, which directly undercut utility revenues and may require special programs like demand decoupling to encourage compliance, demand response is often viewed as a utility win-win. *See* Raka Jovanovic et al., *A Multiobjective Analysis of the Potential of Scheduling Electrical Vehicle Charging for Flattening the Duck Curve,* 48 J. OF COMP. SCI. (2021).

Some of the potential benefits and challenges of demand response are illustrated by the summer heat waves in California. OhmConnect runs a "virtual power plant" connecting residential customer loads throughout California. By offering smart thermostats to shift air conditioning loads or smart plugs which can turn appliances off remotely, OhmConnect pays its customers to reduce their energy use. Currently controlling 100 MW of load reduction capacity, OhmConnect works with customers not involved in other demand response programs in the Southern California Edison, Pacific Gas and Electric, and San Diego Gas and Electric service territories. In return for controlling customers' power, OhmConnect gets paid by utilities and then pays its members for their participation in the energy market. A recent $100 million investment by Sidewalk Infrastructure Partners is aimed at allowing the company to grow rapidly and control 550 MW of load reduction over the next three years. Such third-party demand response aggregators now play a critical role in electricity system management. For example, the PJM Interconnection has over 8,900 MW of demand response available to help manage peak load and emergency situations. While these "negawatts" are critical in emergency situations, some critics question how much commercial and industrial customers will be willing to curtail electricity use as demand response becomes more routine. And as the back-up power sources are mostly diesel generation sets, the environmental impacts of demand response must be carefully weighed. *See* JAMES MCANANY, PJM, 2021 DEMAND RESPONSE OPERATIONS MARKETS ACTIVITY REPORT (June 2021). Jeff St. John, *Energy Hedging: A New Way to Make Demand Response Pay in California?* GTM (Mar. 3, 2021).

Additionally, incentives for cheating on the demand response baseline are real and several companies have been found guilty of gaming the use of demand response. A paper mill in Maine was fined $13 million for manipulating a demand response program in ISO-New England and stealing from ratepayers. In another case, citizens noticed that the lights at the Baltimore Orioles' stadium were on, even when there was no game. Investigations by FERC revealed that a Pennsylvania based demand response company, Enerwise Global Technologies Inc., was altering power use to inflate profits. They were fined $780,000 by FERC. *See* Hannah Northey, *Heat Waves Provide Critical Test for Demand Response*, GREENWIRE (July 25, 2013); José Vuelvas et al., *Limiting Gaming Opportunities on Incentive-Based Demand Response Programs*, 225 APPLIED ENERGY 668 (2018).

7.   The example above discussed buildings as a flexibility resource in energy system operations. This is especially important in places like California where rapid deployment of behind the meter solar PV, fueled by generous net metering subsidies, means that grid operations need to evolve rapidly. California had an estimated 9.4 GW of behind the meter generation in 2020 and expects up to 21 GW by 2030. Consequently, when the sun sets in California and PV stops producing electricity, the need to manage the system to rapidly meet demand is critical. This can be done by "ramping up" generators to replace the electricity from PV (which only works when there is sun) and by changing energy demand. *See* CALIFORNIA ENERGY COMMISSION, TRACKING PROGRESS, RENEWABLE ENERGY 5 (Dec. 2017). In 2013 the California Independent System Operator (CAISO) published the now iconic Duck Diagram, shown below, which highlights how behind the meter solar power can shift load times and lead to overgeneration. When the sun sets and these PV systems are no longer producing, rapid system ramping and increased flexibility may be required to compensate for increased demand. This has led to subsequent policies promoting storage, demand management, renewables integration, and other options for integrating variable resources.

CAISO Duck Diagram

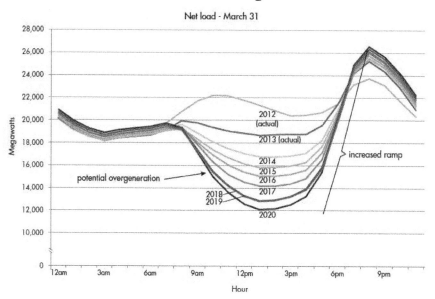

Source: California Independent System Operator (CAISO) (Licensed with permission from the California ISO. Any statements, conclusions, summaries or other commentaries expressed herein do not reflect the opinions or endorsement of the California ISO.).

While some see this as a failing of policies to promote solar energy, others see it as an opportunity to adapt our energy systems to better integrate flexible resources into the electric power grid. By making the system more flexible, larger amounts of renewable energy can be better integrated into the grid. For example, the Regulatory Assistance Project has developed a host of strategies to "teach the duck to fly," including: targeting energy efficiency to the hours when load ramps up sharply; deploying peak-oriented renewable resources; managing water and wastewater pumping loads; controlling electric water heaters to reduce peak demand and increase load at strategic hours; converting commercial air conditioning to ice storage or chilled-water storage; new rate design, which focuses utility prices on the "ramping hours" to enable price-induced changes in load; deploying electrical energy storage in targeted locations; implementing aggressive demand response programs; using inter-regional power exchanges to take advantage of diversity in loads and resources; and retiring inflexible generating plants with high off-peak, must-run requirements. *See* Jim Lazar, *Teaching the Duck to Fly* (Regulatory Assistance Project 2016); NAT'L RENEWABLE ENERGY LAB., OVERGENERATION FROM SOLAR ENERGY IN CALIFORNIA: A FIELD GUIDE TO THE DUCK CHART (Nov. 2015).

How should state and local authorities think about variable renewable resource integration? How should costs for additional efforts to integrate renewable energy into the grid be allocated? How should grid operators address the challenges associated with increasing wildfires in California in terms of smoke that decreases the ability of solar panels to generate electricity during times when it is most needed? *See Smoke from California Wildfires Decreases Solar Generation in CAISO*, ENERGY INFO. ADMIN. (Sept. 30, 2020); Mike H. Bergin et al., *Large Reductions in Solar Energy Production Due to Dust and Particulate Air Pollution*, 4 ENV'T SCI. & TECH. LETT. 339 (2017) (noting that air pollution and dust reduce PV efficiencies by 17–25%).

C. POLICIES TO PROMOTE GRID MODERNIZATION

While the technologies to create a more modern grid exist, they are not very useful unless they are used. Policy makers know that large-scale deployment depends on policies supporting and incentivizing these substantial financial investments. The following section provides a brief history and overview of the policy context for this transition.

In the United States, federal and state-level regulatory initiatives and financial investments for grid modernization have been substantial. Despite these efforts, the remaining needs are vast. The Energy Policy Act of 2005 (EPAct 2005) and the Energy Independence and Security Act of 2007 (EISA) both highlighted the need to modernize U.S. transmission and distribution grids.

EPAct 2005 was the first Congressional directive on demand response programs, which enable utility customers to contribute to energy load reduction during times of peak demand in exchange for financial incentives by shifting that load to times when electricity resources are more available and therefore cheaper. *See, e.g.,* PJM, *Demand Response*. In Section 1252 of EPAct 2005, Congress stated that pursuing demand response was in the policy interests of the United States and required the Department of Energy and FERC to conduct assessments of demand response potential and submit reports to Congress with their findings, including the need for smart meters and other technologies to enable demand response programs. Section 1252 also created new provisions under PURPA requiring state PUCs and other regulatory bodies to determine whether utilities and other electricity providers in their jurisdictions should be required to offer customers time-based rates and requiring utilities to provide suitable meters to any customer requesting such rates. Section 103 of EPAct 2005 required, to the extent possible, that advanced meters be used in all federal buildings to increase energy efficiency and reduce electricity costs and that daily and hourly data from such meters be incorporated into federal energy tracking systems and be made available to federal facility managers. *See* NAT'L COUNCIL ON ELECTRICITY POLICY, DEMAND RESPONSE AND SMART METERING ACTIONS SINCE THE ENERGY POLICY ACT OF 2005: ELECTRIC TRANSMISSION SERIES FOR STATE OFFICIALS 3–4 (Fall 2008).

EISA was signed into law in December 2007 and included an entire Title devoted to smart grid issues. EISA Section 1301's "Statement of Policy on Modernization of the Electricity Grid" declares: "It is the policy of the United States to support the modernization of the Nation's electricity transmission and distribution system to maintain a reliable and secure electricity infrastructure than can meet future demand growth. . . ." EISA Section 1301 sets forth the following goals, "which together characterize a Smart Grid":

1. Increased use of digital information and controls technology to improve reliability, security, and efficiency of the electric grid.

2. Dynamic optimization of grid operations and resources, with full cybersecurity.

3. Deployment and integration of distributed resources and generation, including renewable resources.

4. Development and incorporation of demand response, demand-side resources, and energy efficiency resources.

5. Deployment of "smart" technologies (real-time, automated, interactive technologies that optimize the physical operation of appliances and consumer devices) for metering, communications concerning grid operations and status, and distribution automation.

6. Integration of "smart" appliances and consumer devices.

7. Deployment and integration of advanced electricity storage and peak-shaving technologies, including plug-in electric and hybrid electric vehicles, and thermal-storage air conditioning.

8. Provision to consumers of timely information and control options.

9. Development of standards for communication and interoperability of appliances and equipment connected to the electric grid, including the infrastructure serving the grid.

10. Identification and lowering of unreasonable or unnecessary barriers to adoption of smart grid technologies, practices, and services.

EISA, Title XIII, Section 1301.

In addition to Section 1301 above, key provisions of EISA Title XIII also include:

*   Section 1303 establishing at DOE the Smart Grid Advisory Committee and Federal Smart Grid Task Force.

- Section 1304 authorizing DOE to develop a "Smart Grid Regional Demonstration Initiative" and allocates $100 million for this purpose for each of fiscal years 2008 through 2012.

- Section 1305 directing the National Institute of Standards and Technology (NIST), with DOE and others, including FERC and NERC, to develop a Smart Grid Interoperability Framework.

- Section 1306 authorizing DOE to develop a "Federal Matching Fund for Smart Grid Investment Costs."

EISA helped to bring needed structure to U.S. grid modernization debates. In particular, the Section 1305 interoperability standards are needed across the grid. For example, standards are necessary so that smart appliances and smart meters can tell consumers in real time how much power they are using and at what cost. Other standards will also encourage the development of infrastructure to integrate EVs into the grid and help utilities manage demand response and distributed generation resources. They will also help utilities address cybersecurity considerations. Since EISA's directive, NIST has convened numerous task forces; released reports establishing frameworks and standards for companies producing smart grid devices and software; and promoted coordination on smart grid efforts by utilities, states, regulators, and others in conjunction with the public-private Smart Grid Interoperability Panel. *See, e.g.,* NIST, NIST FRAMEWORK AND ROADMAP FOR SMART GRID INTEROPERABILITY STANDARDS, RELEASE 4.0 (July 24, 2020); NIST, GUIDELINES FOR SMART GRID CYBERSECURITY (Sept. 2014).

With the American Recovery and Reinvestment Act of 2009 (ARRA) came $4.5 billion in funding for the smart grid. While much of this money went to installing smart meters, several funded projects integrated different technologies into a larger system. These federal investments also leveraged private funds, with the $620 million in federal ARRA funds for smart grid demonstration projects matched by $1 billion from private industry. *See generally Secretary Chu Announces $620 Million for Smart Grid Demonstration and Energy Storage Projects,* U.S. Dep't of Energy (Nov. 24, 2009). For additional discussion of proposed and enacted legislation relating to the smart grid, see CONG. RSCH. SERV., THE SMART GRID: STATUS AND OUTLOOK (Apr. 10, 2018).

While utilities and private entities build the grid, FERC and state PUCs also play crucial roles in electric grid development. The 2009 FERC smart grid policy, 128 FERC ¶ 61,060 (July 16, 2009), 74 Fed. Reg. 37,098 (July 27, 2009), focused on providing guidance for developing interoperability standards and grid functionality, addressing issues like cybersecurity (discussed more below), integrating variable renewable resources, and addressing the challenges of developing electric vehicle fleets. It also adopted an interim rate policy to spur investment in smart grid technologies. While FERC's Order 1000 addresses issues of cost allocation, state PUCs must approve smart grid-related projects within their jurisdictions. *See also Cyber and Grid Security*, Fed. Energy Reg. Comm'n (last updated Dec. 17, 2020).

Moreover, FERC has been active in encouraging demand response in electricity markets. In 2011, FERC issued Order 745, which set forth requirements for compensation for demand response participants in RTO and ISO wholesale energy markets. *See* FERC Order 745, 134 FERC ¶ 61,187 (Mar. 15, 2011), 18 C.F.R. Part 35. FERC has continued to issue yearly reports assessing the role of demand response in RTO and ISO markets. *See Reports on Demand Response and Advanced Metering*, Fed. Energy Reg. Comm'n (last updated Dec. 22, 2020). As detailed in Chapter 4, in 2016, the U.S. Supreme Court upheld Order 745 in the face of legal challenges arguing that the rule went too far by "encroaching" on the states' exclusive jurisdiction to regulate the retail electricity market. *See FERC v. Elec. Power Supply Ass'n*, 577 U.S. 260 (2016).

At the state level, smart grid activities are substantial in some jurisdictions, and less prominent in others. Highly publicized problems in PG&E territory in California are contrasted with relatively smooth roll outs in the Sacramento Municipal Utility District in California and in other states like Pennsylvania. A report in 2018 from the GridWise Alliance ranked states' grid modernization policies, grid operations, and customer engagement levels. The report found California and Illinois were the top-ranked states, although they arrived there by different means. *See* GRIDWISE ALLIANCE, GRID MODERNIZATION INDEX 2018 (2018). For a more detailed discussion of how "engaged" utility customers have transformed the electric grid and grid services, see Kenneth W. Costello, *The Challenges of New Electricity Customer Engagement for Utilities and State Regulators*, 38 ENERGY L.J. 49 (2017).

D. CHALLENGES FACING GRID MODERNIZATION

Regardless of whether there is a supportive policy environment, modernizing the electric system faces numerous regulatory and economic barriers. In this section, we discuss cost and risk allocation—*i.e.*, how the significant costs and risks of smart grid investments would be shared across the wholesale power system and retail consumers. Value of solar tariffs and solar gardens serve as examples of these challenges in practice. As a more modern grid links customers, markets, utilities, regulators, grid operators, generators, and information and communication technology (ICT) companies in new configurations, the relative power balance shifts between incumbents and newcomers. This poses financial risks to incumbent utilities and their investors as it can impact industry revenues and investor returns. It also will require shifts in the regulatory regime that has governed U.S. utilities since the early 1900s, as discussed in the ratemaking section of Chapter 4. *See* PETER KIND, DISRUPTIVE CHALLENGES: FINANCIAL AND STRATEGIC RESPONSES TO A CHANGING RETAIL ELECTRIC BUSINESS (Edison Electric Institute, Jan. 2013).

As noted in earlier sections of this chapter, grid modernization allows distributed energy resources and demand technologies to be integrated into the grid, which in turn creates new market opportunities for managing and supplying electricity. In Minnesota, the legislature enacted two statutes in 2013 to spur the development of distributed and "community" solar in the state and to create a more rigorous process for determining how to value solar on the grid than exists with "net metering" (discussed in Chapters 2 and 4). One statute directed the Minnesota Public Utilities Commission (PUC) to develop and adopt a "value of solar tariff" to compensate customers for solar energy sold back to the grid in a way that evaluates and values the grid- and energy-related benefits and costs associated with solar energy. In a 2014 decision, the Minnesota PUC established the value of solar tariff but, consistent with the statute, held that power providers could either continue to compensate customers for solar using net metering, or use the new value of solar rate. *See* Minn. Pub. Utilities Comm'n, *Order Approving Distributed Solar Value Methodology*, Docket No. E–999/M–14–65 (Apr. 1, 2014). To date, utilities in Minnesota have continued to use net metering, reimbursing customers for solar they produce at the retail rate.

The other statute required the state's largest utility, Xcel Energy, to offer customers the opportunities to subscribe to "community solar gardens." Solar gardens are targeted to individuals or businesses who want to use solar power but do not want to install panels on their roof or are otherwise unable to adopt the technology themselves. Instead, such customers can pay for a subscription to a solar garden built by an independent solar energy company that builds an array (often in agricultural or exurban areas) and sells the power to Xcel for use on its distribution grid. In turn, the customer receives a credit on their electric bill for the electricity that their PV produced.

The excerpt that follows involves the question of whether Xcel Energy is required to use the value of solar rate the PUC set in its 2014 Order for solar gardens, even though Xcel has the option to stick with the retail rate (i.e., traditional net metering) for other types of distributed solar. As you read the excerpt, pay particular attention to the various positions taken by Xcel, solar developers, environmental groups, and others. Also take note of how the various parties and the PUC focus on the grid-related costs and benefits associated with solar energy and how developing sophistication regarding the grid and energy data is relevant to the decision.

IN THE MATTER OF THE PETITION OF NORTHERN STATES POWER COMPANY, DBA XCEL ENERGY, FOR APPROVAL OF ITS PROPOSED COMMUNITY SOLAR GARDEN PROGRAM

Docket No. E-002/M-13-867, 2016 WL 4701453 (Minn. P.U.C., Sept. 6, 2016)

Beverly Jones Heydinger, Chair, Nancy Lange, Dan Lipschultz, Matthew Schuerger, and John A. Tuma, Commissioners.

The community-solar-garden statute, Minn. Stat. § 216B.1641, requires Xcel to file a plan to operate a community-solar-garden program, under which its customers may subscribe to solar generating facilities (known as "community solar gardens," or simply "solar gardens") and receive bill credits for a portion of the energy generated.

Solar gardens are limited to a maximum capacity of 1 MW each. They may be owned by Xcel or by a third-party operator who contracts to sell the output to the utility.

Subscribers—customers of Xcel who live in the county where a garden is located or in an adjacent county—receive bill credits for the energy generated by the garden in proportion to the size of their subscription. Each subscription must be sized to supply no more than 120 percent of the subscriber's average annual consumption of electricity, and no subscriber may own a greater-than-40-percent share in single garden.

The statute authorizes the Commission to approve, disapprove, or modify Xcel's community-solar-garden program. Any program approved by the Commission must, among other requirements, reasonably allow for the creation, financing, and accessibility of community solar gardens and be consistent with the public interest.

Xcel opened its program to developers in December 2014. By mid-January 2015, the Company had received applications to construct solar gardens with an aggregate capacity of 431 MW. By late June that number had grown to nearly 1,000 MW. . . .

Interconnection challenges and disputes over co-location and other program rules have delayed Xcel's processing of solar-garden applications; despite the high initial volume of applications, by July 2016 only three solar gardens, representing 370 kW of capacity, were in service. But Xcel stated that it anticipated having 200 MW of solar-garden capacity online by the end of 2016, and another 200–250 MW completed by the end of 2017.

The solar-garden statute requires Xcel to purchase all energy generated by a garden at the value-of-solar rate or, until that rate has been approved by the Commission, at the applicable retail rate.

The Commission has not yet approved the value-of-solar rate for use in Xcel's solar-garden program, and the Company therefore offers solar-garden subscribers the applicable retail rate. The issue before the

Commission is whether the time has come to transition Xcel's program to the value-of-solar rate.

The value-of-solar rate is designed to reflect the value of distributed solar photovoltaic resources to a utility, its customers, and society. It is calculated according to a methodology developed by the Department [of Commerce] and approved by the Commission that accounts for avoided fuel costs, avoided operations-and-maintenance costs, avoided generation-capacity costs, avoided transmission and distribution costs, avoided environmental costs, and other benefits of distributed solar generation.[16]

The value-of-solar rate is updated annually based on changes in the input data used in the approved value-of-solar methodology. Xcel calculated the following value-of-solar rate in 2016, expressed in dollars per kilowatt hour (kWh): $0.09950

This rate represents the compensation a subscriber would receive for energy produced during a garden's first year of operation. In each succeeding year, the rate would be adjusted for inflation using the latest Consumer Price Index (CPI) data.

Xcel currently offers subscribers the applicable retail rate. For Xcel's solar-garden program, the applicable retail rate is a subscriber's full retail rate, including the energy charge, demand charge, customer charge, and applicable riders. Because retail rates are tied to customer class, Xcel offers three rates depending on which class a subscriber belongs to:

2016 APPLICABLE RETAIL RATES ($/KWH)

Residential Service: 0.12596

Small General Service: 0.12229

General Service: 0.09740

In addition, under the applicable retail rate, Xcel must offer to purchase the renewable energy credits (RECs) associated with garden energy at a rate of $0.02/kWh for large gardens and $0.03/kWh for small gardens. While these payments do not reflect a market rate for RECs, the Commission determined early in the development of Xcel's program that they were needed to reasonably allow for the creation and financing of solar gardens. . . .

In past orders, the Commission has recognized the importance of eventually transitioning to the value-of-solar rate, as contemplated by the solar-garden statute. At the same time, however, the Commission expressed doubt as to whether the value-of-solar rate would provide

---

[16] See *In the Matter of Establishing a Distributed Solar Value Methodology Under Minn. Stat. § 216B.164, Subd. 10(e) and (f)*, Docket No. E–999/M–14–65, Order Approving Distributed Solar Value Methodology, at 7–8 (April 1, 2014).

sufficient compensation to reasonably allow for the creation and financing of solar gardens, as required by the same statute.

In its April 2014 order rejecting Xcel's initial program proposal, the Commission directed the Company to file a value-of-solar tariff for solar gardens or, alternatively, to file a calculation of the value-of-solar rate for solar gardens and show cause why the rate should not be implemented for solar gardens.

In response, Xcel provided a calculation of the value-of-solar rate but argued that the rate might over incentivize solar-garden subscriptions and impose excessive costs on nonparticipating customers. It also argued that using the applicable retail rate would give the Commission greater flexibility to adjust the REC value based on market response to the program.

Other stakeholders split roughly evenly between those who supported using the value-of-solar rate and those who supported using the applicable retail rate. Those favoring the value-of-solar rate generally did so because they found it to be more transparent and predictable, while those favoring the applicable retail rate did so because, combined with the REC value, it resulted in larger payments for garden energy, at least initially.

In its September 2014 order, the Commission concluded that it was not in the public interest to approve a value-of-solar rate for solar gardens at that time and directed Xcel to continue using the applicable retail rate with an optional REC payment. The Commission also directed the parties to engage in further discussions and to file comments on potential "adders" to apply to a value-of-solar rate to ensure that the total effective rate would reasonably allow for the creation, financing, and accessibility of community solar gardens.

In its August 2015 order, the Commission concluded that changes to the bill-credit rate should wait until stakeholders had gained more experience with the program. And in its November 2015 order, the Commission directed stakeholders to file comments by April 1, 2016, addressing whether and how the Commission should modify the bill-credit rate, including switching to the value-of-solar rate.

Commenters had wide-ranging views on whether and how to transition to a value-of-solar rate. Those who supported maintaining the applicable retail rate generally did so out of a belief that there was not enough data to support any particular compensation rate, or because they believed that the applicable retail rate afforded the Commission more flexibility to adjust the rate to minimize ratepayer impact.

Commenters who supported a transition to the value-of-solar rate maintained that it would improve the financeability and accessibility of gardens by providing a transparent schedule of yearly rate increases. They also argued that adopting the value-of-solar rate would be consistent with the statute's requirement that Xcel purchase solar-garden energy at that rate.

And those commenters who supported reducing the applicable retail rate argued that it was out of line with community-solar rates in other states and threatened to cause a significant bill impact for nonparticipating ratepayers. . . .

Xcel recommended that the Commission reduce the applicable retail rate by three or four cents per kWh and replace the two-to-three-cent REC payments with competitive market rates, which Xcel suggested would be between \$0.0003 and \$0.00035 per kWh. Xcel suggested that the Commission could achieve the desired reduction in the applicable retail rate by removing the demand-charge, customer-charge, and/or rider components.

Xcel argued that a reduction was needed to bring its solar-garden rates in line with community-solar programs in other states and limit the rate impact of the program. The Company estimated that for each 100 MW of community solar gardens that comes online at current rates, ratepayers will bear an incremental fuel-cost increase of \$17 million annually. Xcel stated that as many as 400 MW of solar gardens could be built in the next year, leading to a customer bill impact of approximately 1.8 percent for nonparticipating ratepayers.

Xcel did not support transitioning to the value-of-solar rate without adjustments to the value-of-solar methodology. The Company argued that adjustments were necessary to, among other things, (1) reflect that most solar gardens are being developed in rural areas, reducing their avoided-transmission-cost benefit, (2) correct for volatility in demand-growth forecasts, and (3) allow for an "off ramp" to a lower rate if the methodology results in an unreasonably high rate. . . .

Energy CENTS Coalition, the Legal Services Advocacy Project, and Dayton's Bluff Neighborhood Housing Services were concerned about potential bill effects on low-income customers. They recommended that the Commission initiate an investigation into the scale and location of solar-garden projects, the level of costs associated with the program, and alternative solar-garden models, among other topics. And they argued that the Commission should address these issues before allowing the program to expand further. . . .

Community Power and its co-commenters recommended making no changes to the bill-credit rate at this time, arguing that it is accomplishing the goal of making solar gardens financeable and that changing it when only a handful of gardens have achieved commercial operation would create market uncertainty. In the long term, Community Power would support a value-of-solar rate but would want to see changes to the methodology to better account for the location-specific benefits of distributed solar, the economic multiplier benefits, and environmental benefits. . . .

[Other commenters] supported an immediate transition to the value-of-solar rate as calculated under the approved methodology. . . .

Fresh Energy and ELPC argued that adopting the value-of-solar rate would be consistent with the solar-garden statute's requirement that a utility purchase garden energy at the value-of-solar rate and that using that rate would satisfy the other statutory criteria for the program. Specifically, they asserted that a value-of-solar rate would be in the public interest because it is designed to compensate solar generation at a rate that matches its value, minimizing concerns about unfair impacts to nonparticipants. And they argued that the stability and predictability of the value-of-solar rate would help promote the financing and accessibility of solar gardens. . . .

Geronimo [Energy] supported the Department and Fresh Energy's recommendation to adopt the value-of-solar rate with a fixed inflation escalator for 25 years. It argued that adopting the value-of-solar rate with a consistent escalator would make bill credits more transparent. And it maintained that transparent bill credits would in turn inform customer demand, help developers determine the market for community solar, and provide a more stable platform for financing solar gardens, resulting in lower development and construction costs. . . .

Several commenters recommended using adders to create incentives for developers to construct solar gardens in economically efficient locations or in other locations that would advance program goals. Ten K Solar encouraged the Commission to adopt a multi-tiered rate structure to encourage the siting of solar gardens in locations such as brownfields, landfills, public facilities, and large commercial rooftops.

Sundial Solar argued that the Commission should incentivize true community solar, which it defined as solar generation sited within the community it serves, through an adder designed to offset the cost of siting generation in areas with higher population density. And in a similar vein, Sundial encouraged the Commission to also adopt an adder for rooftop solar gardens, which it asserted cannot compete in pricing with very large ground-mounted arrays located outside the Twin Cities urban core.

Finally, several parties also supported using an adder to make solar gardens more accessible to low-income customers.

The Commission concurs with those parties who have advocated adopting the value-of-solar rate that doing so is consistent with the intent of the solar-garden statute. Accordingly, the Commission will approve the value-of-solar rate for use as the solar-garden bill-credit rate under the conditions discussed below.

Critical to the Commission's decision is the fact that the solar-garden statute requires Xcel to purchase garden energy at the value-of-solar rate. Although the statute allows for the applicable retail rate to be used on an interim basis until the Commission has approved the value-of-solar rate for a utility, the clear intent is that a solar-garden program will eventually transition to the value-of-solar rate.

Early in the development of Xcel's program, the Commission refrained from adopting the value-of-solar rate, lacking at that time any actual experience with solar gardens, and with developers arguing that a rate lower than the applicable retail rate would not allow for financing of gardens. Now, however, it is clear that solar gardens are financeable under the applicable retail rate, and several developers have argued that the value-of-solar rate, by providing predictable yearly rate increases to adjust for inflation, will actually improve the financeability of gardens.

Because the value-of-solar rate compensates subscribers for the value—and only the value—that their generation brings to Xcel's system, it will address concerns that nonparticipating ratepayers are subsidizing the program. . . .

The Commission will also require Xcel, beginning with the 2018 value-of-solar rate, to use location-specific avoided costs in calculating avoided distribution capacity. Part of the benefit of distributed generation derives from its location on the grid; by being located near load, it reduces local peak demand and defers the need for distribution-system upgrades. . . .

Finally, several commenters recommended that the Commission adopt bill-credit adders to encourage developers to pursue residential and low-income subscribers or to construct gardens in beneficial locations. Although the record is not sufficiently developed at this time to determine the amount of any adders, the Commission agrees that these adders warrant further exploration.

The Commission will therefore request that the Department consider whether the solar-garden bill-credit rate should be adjusted with a positive or negative adder, for any of the following:

- Brownfield sites or landfills
- Public facilities
- Commercial or industrial rooftops
- Prime agricultural land
- Directly in the communities the solar gardens serve
- Residential subscribers
- Low-income residential subscribers

- Others the Department identifies as warranting modification or an adder

The Commission will request that the Department report back to the Commission on its findings by March 1, 2017. . . .

NOTES AND QUESTIONS

1.   Note that Xcel Energy was arguing for continuing to pay solar garden subscribers at the retail rate, even though that rate was higher than the value of solar rate. Why might that be? Consider what changes, if any, Xcel was arguing should be made to the retail rate as applied to solar garden payments.

2.   Think about the different positions of the parties and intervenors. Which arguments did you find most convincing and why? Did the Commission reach the "right" result? Does it depend in part on the purpose of the solar garden program and the reasons for establishing a value of solar tariff in the first place?

3.   A major controversy involving the Minnesota solar garden program was the question of "co-location" of gardens. Recall from the excerpt above that there is a statutory 1 MW limit on the size of solar gardens. In portions of the order not included in the excerpt above, the PUC explained that Xcel opened its solar program to developers in December 2014 and by June 2015 it had received nearly 1,000 MW worth of applications to construct solar gardens— far more than contemplated by the program. Many of the proposed solar gardens were clustered in a few sites in the Twin Cities metropolitan area and were "co-located"—including a group of 50 1-MW gardens by a single developer, more akin to a utility-scale facility subject to competitive bidding. Xcel then proposed to the PUC that it set a 1 MW limit on the total capacity of each co-located project. In an August 2015 order, the Commission adopted this cap with an effective date of September 25, 2015, much to the chagrin of solar developers and some large commercial and industrial electric customers. In 2016, the Minnesota Court of Appeals upheld the PUC's order setting the co-location cap. Following the PUC's establishment of the co-location cap, the rate of new applications for solar gardens dropped significantly and resulted in some applications being withdrawn. For news coverage of the dispute, see David Shaffer, *Minnesota Utility Regulators Put Limits on Solar Gardens*, STAR TRIB. (June 25, 2015); Mike Hughlett, *Size Limit Upheld for Xcel Community Solar Gardens*, STAR TRIB. (June 2, 2016). For more details on the solar garden legislation and subsequent PUC decisions, see Bob Eleff, Information Brief, Research Department, Minnesota House of Representatives, *Xcel Energy's Community Solar Garden Program* (Updated Oct. 2017). *See also* Xcel Energy, News Release, *Solar Gardens Growing in Minnesota* (Feb. 21, 2017).

4.   Is the "value of solar" the best way to move beyond the net metering controversies taking place throughout most of the rest of the United States, as illustrated by the *Westar Energy* solar case in Chapter 1? Or does establishing

a "value of solar" have similar problems? Different but equally challenging problems? Scholars like Shalanda Baker argue that the focus of the "value of solar" framing is too narrow and does not adequately encompass all the benefits of solar PV to consumers and its role in creating a more equitable energy system. *See* Shalanda H. Baker, *The Energy Justice Stakes Embedded in the Net Energy Metering Policy Debates, in* BEYOND ZERO-SUM ENVIRONMENTALISM (Sarah Krakoff et al., eds. 2019).

As noted in the Minnesota PUC solar gardens order excerpted above, different stakeholders have very different positions when it comes to system changes. Likewise, and as discussed in Chapter 4, utilities may be cautious regarding grid tariff changes, as much of their behavior boils down to their business model and their ability to secure rate recovery for investments. Some PUCs and courts have often resisted approving utility costs associated with new grid projects, creating uncertainty and making investment in major smart grid projects difficult in some cases. The following case illustrates the issues that arise in this context.

IN RE CONSUMERS ENERGY CO.

2012 WL 6766741 (Mich. Ct. App., Nov. 20, 2012)

PER CURIAM.

In these consolidated appeals, the Attorney General and the Association of Businesses Advocating Tariff Equity (ABATE)[1] appeal as of right from a November 4, 2010, order of the Public Service Commission (PSC) authorizing ... Consumer [Energy's] advanced metering infrastructure program. We affirm in part, reverse in part, and remand for further proceedings. . . .

The advanced metering infrastructure (AMI) program has been described as

> an information-gathering technology that allows [the utility] to collect real-time energy consumption data from its customers. . . . [T]he so-called "smart meters" allow the utility to remotely monitor and shut-off [sic] electricity to customers that have these meters installed. . . . The intention appears to be to allow customers to access real time energy consumption data and make alterations in their energy consumption patterns in order to reduce their own costs and to reduce the demands placed upon the

---

[1] [According to its website, "The Association of Businesses Advocating Tariff Equity (ABATE) is an organization that has been protecting the interests of industrial customers in energy and related matters since 1981. ABATE is active in a variety of forums, including the Michigan Public Service Commission, the Michigan Legislature, Michigan courts, the Federal Energy Regulatory Commission, and the U.S. Congress, when necessary." *See* http://abate-energy. org.—Eds.]

system at times of system peak. [In re Applications of Detroit Edison Co., 296 Mich. App. 101, 114, 817 N.W.2d 630 (2012) (internal quotation marks and citations omitted).]

ABATE argues that there was insufficient evidence of the program's costs and benefits, or that the new technology is necessary for the continued provision of electricity to Consumers's customers, to justify the great expense to ratepayers involved.

Instructive for present purposes is this Court's decision in *In re Applications of Detroit Edison Co.*, in which this Court reviewed an AMI program under the substantial evidence test, and concluded that the funding of the program by ratepayers was not justified by the evidence in the record. This Court noted that the program was expensive and commercially untested, exposing ratepayers to significant economic risk, while the evidence to justify the expense consisted mostly of mere "aspirational testimony" concerning expectations for the project. This Court further opined, "[w]hile we appreciate that a cost-benefit analysis for a pilot program may be more difficult to establish with record evidence, this inherent difficulty does not permit the PSC to authorize millions of dollars in rate increases without an informed assessment supported by competent, material and substantial evidence." This Court remanded *In re Applications of Detroit Edison Co.*, to the PSC for a full hearing on the AMI program, during which it shall consider, among other relevant matters, evidence related to the benefits, usefulness, and potential burdens of the AMI, specific information gleaned from pilot phases of the program regarding costs, operations, and customer response and impact, an assessment of similar programs initiated here or in other states, risks associated with AMI, and projected effects on rates.

This Court further took judicial notice that "on January 12, 2012, the PSC issued an order opening a docket to investigate the use of smart meters by electric utilities in Michigan". . . .

The question in this case, then, is whether the evidence of record better justifies the AMI funding involved than was the case in *In re Application of Detroit Edison*. We conclude that it does. Consumers Energy's Manager of Smart Grid Demand Response Programs testified to how similar programs have worked elsewhere, and opined that "[s]mart meters and a fully enabled smart grid are going to be required for the consumers of Michigan to realize the full potential of coming changes in the electric markets." Consumers' Business Technology Solutions Director of Portfolio Integration Planning and Services testified in turn that the new technology would be required to keep up with anticipated rising demands for electricity. The director of Consumers' smart-grid program also testified extensively about Consumers' collaboration with other entities to develop "interoperability" and security standards, about its monitoring of similar programs in place elsewhere, and about the anticipated timing of the eventual implementation of the new technology. Additionally, the director testified extensively on the anticipated benefits to its customers. These benefits included: more accurate meter reading, reduction of losses resulting from theft, and the opportunity to aid in energy conservation through a pricing incentive.

In its opinion and order, the PSC relied extensively on the testimony of its own expert, and summarized his testimony as follows:

> [The PSC's staff witness] testified that in general, the Commission supports utility investment in Smart Grid and AMI because these technologies have the potential to increase the reliability, security, and efficiency of Michigan's electric distribution system while allowing customers to reduce consumption. [The witness] noted, however, that Consumers' initial request included a significant level of expenditures related to full deployment of AMI/Smart Grid, rather than the pilot, and the Commission has not yet approved full deployment of these systems.

> [The witness] testified that in [an earlier case], the Commission approved $68 million in capital expenditures for Smart Grid and AMI pilots but that case did not include a lifecycle benefit cost analysis of Consumers' AMI/Smart Grid proposal. According to [the witness], the Staff reviewed Consumers' preliminary lifecycle analysis presented in this case and found that the viability of full deployment of AMI is not unequivocally demonstrated at this time. Nevertheless, [the witness] opines that continuation of the pilot is reasonable, provided that the costs of the pilot are controlled.

> [The PSC's staff witness] testified that on the basis of its review of the specific expenditures requested by Consumers, the Staff concludes that it is prudent for additional cost cutting measures to be implemented by Consumers to reduce the overall cost of the project.... [A]reas of particular concern are: 1) the level of expenditures for intangible information technology (IT) labor and expenses; 2) the level of expenditures related to architecture, assessment, and testing of metering/communication infrastructure being vetted by Consumers; and 3) the prudence of doubling the company's air conditioning load-control pilot using non-Smart Grid technology. [The witness] recommended a 20% downward adjustment to intangible IT expenditures and an adjustment to the load control pilot. [The witness] testified that the Staff is not recommending cost adjustment to the metering/communication testing category at this time, but is recommending that the Commission explore utility and vendor

practices via the Commission's Smart Grid Collaborative, or an alternative forum, with a report to be filed with the Commission.

[The staff witness] contended that in evaluating cost recovery of this Smart Grid project, the Commission should consider that the magnitude of the project on a life-cycle basis is substantial, estimated by Consumers at $2.57 billion in nominal dollars, or $0.960 billion present dollars. In addition, although Consumers estimates that the overall project will achieve a benefit cost ratio greater than one over 25 years, the costs are heavily weighted toward the beginning of the project while the benefits are not expected to accrue until the later years. In addition, over half of the expected benefits derive from difficult-to-measure demand response programs offered to customers. [The witness] further noted that Consumers did not receive a federal grant for Smart Grid/AMI like other utilities that are currently deploying these systems, and the current economic situation in the state makes investment in Smart Grid/AMI difficult for customers. [The witness] opined that these considerations increase the importance of keeping program costs low.

[The staff witness] testified that Consumers plans to spend almost $200 million on its Smart Grid/AMI pilot, or almost 20% of the cost of full deployment. [The witness] noted that the cost of the meters is only about 1% of the total cost of the pilot and that the bulk of the expenditures are for Metering, Communications, and Testing ($65 million thru 2011) and Intangible Software, Computers, and related Software ($117 million thru 2011). [The witness] calculated that Consumers proposes to spend 80% of the total IT costs in the pilot phase. [The witness] testified that front-loading so many full deployment costs onto the pilot puts ratepayers at great financial risk if the results of the pilot demonstrate that Consumers should not go forward with full deployment.

The PSC, citing its staff witness's testimony, concluded that "while it is reasonable for Consumers to continue Smart Grid and AMI pilot activities, at this time, the Commission cannot approve full deployment of the technology." The PSC further noted that "the benefit and cost information necessary for evaluating the reasonableness and prudence of full AMI and Smart Grid deployment is not yet available from the company's pilot." The PSC called for Consumers Energy to prepare and submit a report "detailing the milestones that were achieved and not achieved, decisions regarding functionality, and any other relevant information or decisions made through the piloting process," which would "facilitate the Commission's decision-making process with respect to the appropriateness of requiring customers to bear the costs of moving out of the piloting phase into full deployment." The PSC further expressed concerns and advised caution:

> Consumers should not consider the Commission's generally favorable view of AMI and Smart Grid as a blank check that will allow the company to incur staggering costs that will ultimately be borne by ratepayers. As the Staff points out, Consumers has forgone opportunities for collaboration with other utilities in customizing AMI software; collaborations that could have resulted in significantly reduced IT costs. The Commission is also concerned that Consumers' ratepayers may ultimately be paying for costs that primarily benefit vendors. . . . [T]he use of utility testing and assessment as a vehicle for vendors to develop their products is not a problem that is unique to Consumers; nevertheless, Consumers appears to have been much more accommodating to vendors than many other utilities.

The PSC credited its staff's recommendation of "a downward adjustment of $40,807,466 for AMI and Smart Grid," noting that the greater part of that related to Consumers' decision to delay deployment of the new technology. The PSC authorized an operations and maintenance expense of $3,297,000 for the continuation of the AMI program, while noting that the capital costs related to the program were included in the rate base as Construction Work in Progress, with an offset for Allowance for Funds Used during Construction, and so were not included in the rates approved in the order. The PSC further directed Consumers to "reevaluate its plan to move to full AMI deployment in mid-2012."

We conclude that the PSC's continuation of funding for the AMI program has a sufficient evidentiary basis. Consumers' witnesses covered many particulars concerning benefits and timing, and what the PSC relied on from its own staff witness was decidedly guarded. Perhaps most significantly, we note that the amount of AMI funding that the PSC approved was decidedly conservative—far below the amount requested. This case is distinguishable from *In re Applications of Detroit Edison Co.*, in that the evidence underlying the PSC's funding decision in this case went well beyond the merely "aspirational testimony," and the amount of approved funding far below, what was of concern in that case. Accordingly, our conclusion that no remand is required in this case comports with the dictates of *In re Applications of Detroit Edison Co.* . . .

NOTES AND QUESTIONS

1.   The Michigan case above illustrates the controversial nature of the costs associated with improvements to the grid, including debates over whether and how those costs should be passed on to consumers. It also illustrates the role

of state PUCs in determining whether such costs are consistent with state law and cost-effective. As you can see from the positions of the various parties involved in the proceedings, there are many interest groups that oppose new grid projects because of their impact on electricity rates for industrial, commercial, and residential sector customers. Should utilities be able to pass along the full cost of smart grid investments to their customers? Where should the risks of unnecessary costs fall when there is so much uncertainty regarding which grid technology investments will add value, which ones will fail, and which ones will become obsolete as technology advances? How does this relate to current rate-making practices?

2.   Many states have enacted statutes to guide PUC determination on how to promote new grid technologies. For instance, California SB 17, enacted in 2009, established "a state policy to modernize the state's electrical transmission and distribution system to maintain safe, reliable, efficient and secure electrical service." It was followed by SB 1222 in 2016, which consolidated reporting responsibilities and required the PUC to produce an annual report to the legislature and Governor setting forth the PUC's actions implementing the law. The report for 2020 discusses, among other issues: (1) distributed energy resource plans focusing on better grid integration and streamlining interconnection processes; (2) microgrids focusing on resiliency; (3) increased use of smart inverters to allow utilities to better understand grid operations and distributed energy resources to respond to dynamic grid needs; (4) energy storage, including procurement and integration into integrated resource planning processes, as required by other state laws; (5) transportation electrification, including installing 37,800 new charging stations, adopting new time of use rates for EV charging, and developing future plans for EV integration into the grid as specified by statute; (6) demand response covering auctions for demand response resources, analyses of how demand response resources performed in the 2020 summer heat waves, and new strategies for creating better performing demand response; and (7) reliability reporting of grid outages. The scope of the report highlights the complexities involved in changing the power system as well as the intricate legal and policy work needed to support the modernization of a state's electric infrastructure. *See* CAL. PUB. UTIL. COMM'N, CALIFORNIA'S GRID MODERNIZATION REPORT 2020 (Feb. 2021). How can these standards guide PUC decision-making when considering specific utility smart grid projects?

3.   How should state PUCs ensure that utilities implement new grid technologies that result in efficiencies that reduce the overall need for electricity? Several policy experiments to promote "decoupling" electricity industry profits from the quantity of electrons sold have been tried. For more information, see the Regulatory Assistance Project's website, http://www. raponline.org.

E. CYBERSECURITY

Critical societal infrastructure has always been a target for people or forces wishing to disrupt society. Whether it was poison in the water supplies of Kirrha to weaken the city's defenders during the First Sacred War (Greece 595–585 B.C.E.), or Allied Forces targeting Nazi Germany energy infrastructure, destroying or disrupting infrastructure is a long used military tactic. While the United States' relatively isolated location in North America has saved it from many direct physical attacks, cybersecurity is changing the scope, scale, and nature of these vulnerabilities. In this section we examine the cybersecurity of the grid and outline the challenges to effectively addressing the issue.

Cybersecurity of the electric grid is an increasingly pressing and high-profile issue. Recent cyber-attacks like the ransomware attack by hackers in May 2021 on Colonial Pipeline and constant cyber probes from China, Russia, North Korea, and Iran underscore the importance of more actively addressing security in the context of the grid and other critical infrastructure systems. While some attacks focus on obtaining confidential information and trade secrets, more recent attacks attempted to hack elections, destroy data, control machinery, and control or disable energy networks.

The May 2021 ransomware attack by DarkSide on Colonial Pipeline created a level of societal disruption which reportedly surprised even the hackers themselves. When hackers entered the Colonial Pipeline system and demanded a $5 million ransom, Colonial, a private pipeline company, shut down operations. On a normal day, the firm delivers gasoline, diesel fuel, and jet fuel from the Gulf Coast up to New York through 5,500 miles of pipeline, providing 45% of east coast fuel supply. When the pipeline shut down, panic buying of gasoline ensued and within days many gas stations ran out of fuel. While experts had warned of such vulnerabilities for years, the regular cybersecurity breaches in 2021 made the issue politically salient. *See* Clifford Krauss, *How the Colonial Pipeline Became a Vital Artery for Fuel*, N.Y. TIMES (May 12, 2021); David E. Sanger et al., *Cyberattack Forces a Shutdown of a Top U.S. Pipeline*, N.Y. TIMES (May 13, 2021). Addressing cybersecurity is made more complicated by the changing electric power grid, as this excerpt from the National Commission on Grid Resilience shows.

GRID RESILIENCE: PRIORITIES
FOR THE NEXT ADMINISTRATION
National Commission on Grid Resilience (2020)

The available "surface" of the U.S. grid that is susceptible to [cyber threat] attacks is continually expanding. In recent decades, our power grid has evolved from a centralized one-way delivery system to a bidirectional cyber-physical system that is highly complex and increasingly distributed. Several decades ago, a typical utility might have managed a few hundred assets via its manual or semi-automated supervisory control and data acquisition (SCADA) systems.

However, in recent years, significant changes have occurred at both the bulk power system and distribution utility levels. An examination of any grid operator's generator interconnection queue will reveal that instead of a handful of large assets generally well in excess of 100 megawatts (MWs), there are now hundreds of smaller assets.

In addition, much of the grid has migrated from the vertically integrated utility approach of the past to a more complex relationship between generators, transmission owners, distribution utilities and retail providers, overseen by regional grid operators. Physical failures now also have the potential to create dispatch and market-related consequences that would not have existed in the old utility environment, and create the potential for additional problems across broader regions.

At the distribution utility level, the deployment scale of devices is even more profound, as distributed and "smart devices," ranging from advanced automation, local solar arrays with smart inverters to batteries, programmable electric vehicle chargers, air conditioners, and water heaters proliferate across the system. In 2020 alone, it is estimated that up to 50,000 new residential battery systems will be installed in California, a state that already has over 1 million rooftop solar installations. Likewise, 53 utilities nationwide had control of nearly 600 MW of hot water heater capacity for demand response in 2018: operated in the aggregate, small variations in the load profiles of these consumer-side devices added up to the equivalent of a substantial power plant. In the future, it is anticipated that utilities or associated vendors could be controlling millions of smart devices, with little ability to control the access conditions of the devices themselves or enforce uniform cybersecurity standards.

In all of these cases, the implications for security are profound. Every new connected device represents a new potential attack surface for cyber assailants. At the bulk power level, that implies more opportunities for hackers to bridge across the IT environment into the critical OT environment controlling the critical assets and their operation. As these assets rapidly proliferate at the distribution utility level, at some future point it may not even be necessary to "attack the fortress" of protected centralized grid assets at all. Instead, the ability to hack into vendor systems controlling various distributed devices may be sufficient to destabilize and even take down parts of the power grid. Recent attention has been paid to the rapidly growing electric vehicle charging infrastructure, for example, where hackers could theoretically hack into charger networks, and manipulate them to cause grid instability and potential blackouts. The fastest chargers in the U.S. now deliver up to 350 kW of instantaneous demand, equivalent to that required by a large grocery store. . . .

———————

In addition to the changing technological landscape, addressing cybersecurity issues is also politically and institutionally complex, as President Biden's Executive Order on Cybersecurity excerpted below shows. President Biden issued the executive order soon after the Colonial Pipeline ransomware attack and at a time when electric utilities reported that they were under constant, daily, or frequent cyber-attacks, ranging from phishing and unfriendly probes to malware. The order highlights the critical challenges and complicated nature of dealing with cybersecurity concerns across public and private sectors and outlines some preventative measures. The excerpt below presents the summarized Fact Sheet which concisely highlights all of the issues within the Executive Order.

FACT SHEET: PRESIDENT SIGNS EXECUTIVE ORDER CHARTING NEW COURSE TO IMPROVE THE NATION'S CYBERSECURITY AND PROTECT FEDERAL GOVERNMENT NETWORKS
The White House (May 12, 2021)

Today, President Biden signed an Executive Order to improve the nation's cybersecurity and protect federal government networks. Recent cybersecurity incidents such as SolarWinds, Microsoft Exchange, and the Colonial Pipeline incident are a sobering reminder that U.S. public and private sector entities increasingly face sophisticated malicious cyber activity from both nation-state actors and cyber criminals. These incidents share commonalities, including insufficient cybersecurity defenses that leave public and private sector entities more vulnerable to incidents.

This Executive Order makes a significant contribution toward modernizing cybersecurity defenses by protecting federal networks, improving information-sharing between the U.S. government and the private sector on cyber issues, and strengthening the United States' ability to respond to incidents when they occur. It is the first of many ambitious steps the Administration is taking to modernize national cyber defenses. However, the Colonial Pipeline incident is a reminder that federal action alone is not enough. Much of our domestic critical infrastructure is owned and operated by the private sector, and those private sector companies make their own determination regarding cybersecurity investments. We encourage private sector companies to follow the Federal government's lead and take ambitious measures to augment and align cybersecurity investments with the goal of minimizing future incidents.

Specifically, the Executive Order the President is signing today will:

Remove Barriers to Threat Information Sharing Between Government and the Private Sector. The Executive Order ensures that IT Service Providers are able to share information with the government and requires them to share certain breach information. IT providers are often hesitant or unable to voluntarily share information about a compromise. Sometimes this can be due to contractual obligations; in other cases, providers simply may be hesitant to share information about their own security breaches. Removing any contractual barriers and requiring providers to share breach information that could impact Government networks is necessary to enable more effective defenses of Federal departments, and to improve the Nation's cybersecurity as a whole.

Modernize and Implement Stronger Cybersecurity Standards in the Federal Government. The Executive Order helps move the Federal government to secure cloud services and a zero-trust architecture, and mandates deployment of multifactor authentication and encryption with a specific time period. Outdated security models and unencrypted data have led to compromises of systems in the public and private sectors. . . .

Improve Software Supply Chain Security. The Executive Order will improve the security of software by establishing baseline security standards for development of software sold to the government, including requiring developers to maintain greater visibility into their software and making security data publicly available. It stands up a concurrent public-private process to develop new and innovative approaches to secure software development and uses the power of Federal procurement to incentivize the market. Finally, it creates a pilot program to create an "energy star" type of label so the government—and the public at large—can quickly determine whether software was developed securely. Too much of our software, including critical software, is shipped with significant vulnerabilities that our adversaries exploit. This is a long-standing, well-known problem, but for too long we have kicked the can down the road. We need to use the purchasing power of the Federal Government to drive the market to build security into all software from the ground up.

Establish a Cybersecurity Safety Review Board. The Executive Order establishes a Cybersecurity Safety Review Board, co-chaired by government and private sector leads, that may convene following a significant cyber incident to analyze what happened and make concrete recommendations for improving cybersecurity. Too often organizations repeat the mistakes of the past and do not learn lessons from significant cyber incidents. When something goes wrong, the Administration and private sector need to ask the hard questions and make the necessary improvements. This board is modeled after the National Transportation Safety Board, which is used after airplane crashes and other incidents.

Create a Standard Playbook for Responding to Cyber Incidents. The Executive Order creates a standardized playbook and set of definitions for cyber incident response by federal departments and agencies. Organizations cannot wait until they are compromised to figure out how to respond to an attack. Recent incidents have shown that within the government the maturity level of response plans vary widely. The playbook will ensure all Federal agencies meet a certain threshold and are prepared to take uniform steps to identify and mitigate a threat. The playbook will also provide the private sector with a template for its response efforts.

Improve Detection of Cybersecurity Incidents on Federal Government Networks. The Executive Order improves the ability to detect malicious cyber activity on federal networks by enabling a government-wide endpoint detection and response system and improved information sharing within the Federal government. Slow and inconsistent deployment of foundational cybersecurity tools and practices leaves an organization exposed to adversaries. The Federal government should lead in cybersecurity, and strong, Government-wide Endpoint Detection and Response (EDR) deployment coupled with robust intra-governmental information sharing are essential.

Improve Investigative and Remediation Capabilities. The Executive Order creates cybersecurity event log requirements for federal departments and agencies. Poor logging hampers an organization's ability to detect intrusions, mitigate those in progress, and determine the extent of an incident after the fact. Robust and consistent logging practices will solve much of this problem.

As described in Chapter 5, following the 2003 Northeast blackout, Congress enacted the Energy Policy Act of 2005 (EPAct 2005), which amended the Federal Power Act to provide for mandatory and enforceable electric reliability standards for the bulk power system. EPAct 2005 also directed FERC to create an electric reliability organization (ERO). FERC delegated the day-to-day enforcement of reliability standards to the non-profit North American Reliability Corporation (NERC). NERC reliability standards, which went into effect in 2007, apply to users, owners, and operators of the bulk power system. *See* 18 C.F.R. pt. 40. As detailed below, NERC and its reliability standards play a central role in today's efforts to address electric grid cybersecurity concerns.

NERC delegates its authority to its regional electric reliability organizations—"Regional Entities" or "Regional EROs"—to monitor and enforce compliance (shown in the map in Chapter 5). These Regional Entities oversee virtually all the electricity supplied in the United States, Canada, and the northern portion of Baja California, Mexico. Regional Entities oversee compliance for over 1,400 Registered Entities, which are the users, owners, and operators of the bulk power system. As part of its enforcement authority, NERC's Regional Entities conduct compliance audits and encourage entities to self-report issues of noncompliance. Most noncompliance issues are self-reported by Registered Entities. The Regional Entity will determine if a violation occurred and whether any mitigation measures are required.

FERC rarely directs NERC to develop a specific Reliability Standard. Rather, NERC's operating, planning, and critical infrastructure protection technical committees propose and develop Reliability Standards which FERC then approves through its rulemaking process. NERC's committees, subcommittees, task forces, working groups, and standards drafting teams are comprised of the Regional Entities' members, which include investor-owned utilities, federal power agencies, rural electric cooperatives, municipal utilities, independent power producers, power marketers, and end-use customers, along with other industry experts. The NERC Reliability Standard development process highlights the benefits of a public-private hybrid entity that can draw on the strengths of both private and government sectors. NERC and its stakeholders periodically revise Reliability Standards to ensure they align with current technology and practices on specific issues critical to promote and maintain a highly reliable and secure bulk power system.

Most notably, in addition to NERC's Operational and Planning standards, Critical Infrastructure Protection (CIP) standards have received significant attention due to recent physical and cyber-attacks to the grid, such as the ones in the Ukraine in December 2015 that caused widespread blackouts in that country. *See* Krysti Shallenberger, *Cyberattacks Raise Risks of Access to US Power System, Symantec Says*, UTIL. DIVE (Sept. 6, 2017). More recently, about 25% of U.S. electric utilities were exposed in the SolarWinds hack where a routine software update contained a malicious piece of code which wormed its way into the Orion operating system and, if installed and connected to the internet, gave system access to a third party. The hack was presumably carried out by hackers directed by the SVR, the Russian intelligence service. But despite these risks, the utility industry is not necessarily in favor of some of the federal standards requiring changes in equipment and supply chains because they have the potential to drive up costs. These tensions between business interests, compliance with CIP standards, and cyber risk are political as well as technical. *See* Blake Sobczak, *Grid Regulator Issues "Massive" Penalty Over Data Exposure*, ENERGYWIRE (Mar. 5, 2018) (discussing $2.7 million settlement between NERC and an unnamed utility); Robert Walton, *Utilities to DOE: More Information, Not New Regulations, Needed to Secure the Grid*, UTIL. DIVE (June 14, 2021); Dina Temple-Raston, *"Worst Nightmare" Cyberattack: The Untold Story Of The SolarWinds Hack*, NPR (April 16, 2021).

NOTES AND QUESTIONS

1.   According to a 2017 report by the National Academies of Sciences, Engineering, and Medicine, "[t]he electricity system, and associated supporting infrastructure, is susceptible to widespread uncontrolled cascading failure, based on the interconnected and interdependent nature of the networks," and "[a]t present, planning for all types of hazards to public infrastructure is a disorganized and decentralized activity, . . ." More problematic, "[n]o single entity is responsible for, or has the authority to implement a comprehensive approach to assure the resilience of the nation's electricity system, . . ." The report calls on regulators and industry to start "imagining the unimaginable" and plan for potentially catastrophic events. NAT'L ACADEMIES OF SCIENCES, ENG'G, AND MED., ENHANCING THE RESILIENCE OF THE NATION'S ELECTRICITY SYSTEM (2017). *See also* Peter Behr, *Grid Threats Require "Imagining the Unimaginable"—Report*, ENERGYWIRE (July 21, 2017) (quoting from and discussing the report). Who should be responsible for electric system cybersecurity across different system levels? What roles should the federal government play? What roles and responsibilities should utilities, equipment vendors, software developers, and consumers adopt? Who should pay to manage the extra costs due to cybersecurity risks? The 2017 National Academies report cited above calls on the Department of Energy to play a greater role in organizing grid operators to enhance the resiliency of the grid in the face of man-made attacks and natural disasters. Is the Department of Energy in the best position to serve in that capacity?

2.   The Presidential Executive Order on cybersecurity described in the Fact Sheet excerpted above suggests new approaches to provide better protections for cybersecurity, including grid security. But in the past few years, the prevalence of cyber and ransomware attacks has affected many different sectors. For the energy sector and beyond, what are the tradeoffs of cybersecurity protocols becoming mandatory? What are the different actor positions on voluntary versus mandatory standards for cybersecurity in the energy sector? *See* Christian Vasquez et al., *Cybersecurity: 3 Takeaways From the Colonial Pipeline Hack*, ENERGYWIRE (May 17, 2021).

F. PRIVACY

While the issues of cybersecurity illustrate the many system vulnerabilities of the modern electric grid, new technologies also collect more data, creating privacy concerns for consumers. In this section, we explore some of these issues in more detail. Smart meters or advanced meter infrastructure (AMI) record and transmit energy use data much more frequently than traditional analog meters. Some consumers worry that their data could be illegally intercepted or used by unauthorized parties to gain insights into their energy use. Industrial customers may fear that disclosing their energy use information will benefit their competitors. Residential customers may believe that home energy use data provides an unwanted window into their lives. The two major concerns are that smart meter data would reveal in-home behavior and that cybersecurity measures may be inadequate to protect and store data from misuse.

In addition to smart meters being more easily hacked and the increased cybersecurity risks mentioned above, smart meters can be used to provide almost real time data on energy use, with measurements at the sub-hourly or, with newer meters, minute level. Some worry that smart meter data could potentially show residents' personal schedules, if homes are equipped with alarm systems, electronic equipment, or even if there is medical equipment present. Such data can also highlight appliance cycles and identify when they are being used through the recorded electric load. By matching appliance load signatures to electricity use, a more detailed picture of occupant activities can be created. This can raise significant privacy concerns. Techniques like adding some "noise" to the data are being explored to preserve data privacy while still ensuring data are useful for future system operations. *See, e.g.,* Tekla S. Perry, *What Does Your Smart Meter Know About You?*, IEEE SPECTRUM (June 23, 2017).

In the past, monthly metered data was often used by law enforcement to identify suspected indoor marijuana growing operations. *See* Armand La Barge, *Indoor Marijuana Grow Operations,* 72 POLICE CHIEF MAG. (March 2005). Higher interval data could provide law enforcement with significantly more information on occupant behaviors. This tension between law enforcement and privacy concerns links to the Fourth Amendment to the U.S. Constitution, resulting in a growing number of U.S. Supreme Court decisions, several of which are discussed in the case excerpt below. Moreover, third party use of data by criminals, insurance companies, or marketers could all target consumers based on energy use patterns. *See, e.g.,* Matthew B. Kugler & Meredith Hurley, *Protecting Energy Privacy Across the Public/Private Divide,* 72 FLA. L. REV. 451 (2020).

These Fourth Amendment and privacy concerns have prompted some utility customers to resist the installation of smart meters. The following case explores this issue in more detail.

NAPERVILLE SMART METER AWARENESS V. CITY OF NAPERVILLE
900 F.3d 521 (7th Cir. 2018)

KANNE, CIRCUIT JUDGE.

The City of Naperville owns and operates a public utility that provides electricity to the city's residents. The utility collects residents' energy-consumption data at fifteen-minute intervals. It then stores the data for up to three years. This case presents the question whether Naperville's collection of this data is reasonable under the Fourth Amendment of the U.S. Constitution and Article I, § 6 of the Illinois Constitution.

The American Recovery and Reinvestment Act of 2009 set aside funds to modernize the Nation's electrical grid. The Act tasked the Department of Energy with distributing these funds under the Smart Grid Investment Grant program. Through this program, the City of Naperville was selected to receive $11 million to update its own grid. As part of these upgrades, Naperville began replacing its residential, analog energy meters with digital "smart meters."

Using traditional energy meters, utilities typically collect monthly energy consumption in a single lump figure once per month. By contrast, smart meters record consumption much more frequently, often collecting thousands of readings every month. Due to this frequency, smart meters show both the amount of electricity being used inside a home and when that energy is used.

This data reveals information about the happenings inside a home. That is because individual appliances have distinct energy-consumption patterns or "load signatures." Ramyar Rashed Mohassel et al., *A Survey on Advanced Metering Infrastructure*, 63 INT'L J. ELEC. POWER & ENERGY SYS. 473, 478 (2014). A refrigerator, for instance, draws power differently than a television, respirator, or indoor grow light. By comparing longitudinal energy-consumption data against a growing library of appliance load signatures, researchers can predict the appliances that are present in a home and when those appliances are used. *See id.*; A. Prudenzi, *A Neuron Nets Based Procedure for Identifying Domestic Appliances Pattern-of-Use from Energy Recordings at Meter Panel*, 2 IEEE POWER ENGINEERING SOC'Y WINTER MEETING 941 (2002). The accuracy of these predictions depends, of course, on the frequency at which the data is collected and the sophistication of the tools used to analyze that data.

While some cities have allowed residents to decide whether to adopt smart meters, Naperville's residents have little choice. If they want electricity in their homes, they must buy it from the city's public utility. And they cannot opt out of the smart-meter program.[1] The meters the city installed collect residents' energy-usage data at fifteen-minute intervals. Naperville then stores the data for up to three years.

Naperville Smart Meter Awareness (Smart Meter Awareness), a group of concerned citizens, sued Naperville over the smart-meter program. It alleges that Naperville's smart meters reveal "intimate personal details of

---

[1]   Residents may request that Naperville replace their analog meters with "non-wireless" smart meters. But these alternatives are smart meters with wireless transmission disabled. They collect equally rich data. The difference is that the data must be manually retrieved.

the City's electric customers such as when people are home and when the home is vacant, sleeping routines, eating routines, specific appliance types in the home and when used, and charging data for plug-in vehicles that can be used to identify travel routines and history." The organization further alleges that collection of this data constitutes an unreasonable search under the Fourth Amendment of the U.S. Constitution . . . .

The district court dismissed two of Smart Meter Awareness's complaints without prejudice. Smart Meter Awareness requested leave to file a third, but the district court denied that request. It reasoned that amending the complaint would be futile because even the proposed third amended complaint had not plausibly alleged a Fourth Amendment violation or a violation of the Illinois Constitution. . . .

The Fourth Amendment of the U.S. Constitution protects "[t]he right of the people to be secure in their persons, houses, papers, and effects, against unreasonable searches and seizures." Similarly, Article I, § 6 of the Illinois Constitution affords people "the right to be secure in their persons, houses, papers and other possessions against unreasonable searches, seizures, invasions of privacy or interceptions of communications by eavesdropping devices or other means."

We can resolve both the state and federal constitutional claims by answering the following two questions. First, has the organization plausibly alleged that the data collection is a search? Second, is the search unreasonable? For the reasons that follow, we find that the data collection constitutes a search under both the Fourth Amendment and the Illinois Constitution. This search, however, is reasonable.

"At the [Fourth Amendment's] very core stands the right of a man to retreat into his own home and there be free from unreasonable government intrusion." *Silverman v. United States*, 365 U.S. 505, 511 (1961). This protection, though previously tied to common-law trespass, now encompasses searches of the home made possible by ever-more sophisticated technology. *Kyllo v. United States*, 533 U.S. 27, 31–32 (2001). Any other rule would "erode the privacy guaranteed by the Fourth Amendment." *Id.* at 34.

"Where . . . the Government uses a device that is not in general public use, to explore details of the home that would previously have been unknowable without physical intrusion, the surveillance is a 'search.' " *Id.* at 40. This protection remains in force even when the enhancements do not allow the government to literally peer into the home. In *Kyllo*, for instance, the intrusion by way of thermal imaging was relatively crude—it showed that "the roof over the garage and a side wall of [a] home were relatively hot compared to the rest of the home and substantially warmer than neighboring homes in the triplex." *Id.* at 30. The device "did not show any people or activity within the walls of the structure" nor could it "penetrate walls or windows to reveal conversations or human activities." *Id.* Nevertheless, the Supreme Court held that law enforcement had searched the home when they collected thermal images. *Id.* at 40.

The technology-assisted data collection that Smart Meter Awareness alleges here is at least as rich as that found to be a search in *Kyllo.* Indeed, the group alleges that energy-consumption data collected at fifteen-minute intervals reveals when people are home, when people are away, when people sleep and eat, what types of appliances are in the home, and when those appliances are used. By contrast, *Kyllo* merely revealed that something in the home was emitting a large amount of energy (in the form of heat).

It's true that observers of smart-meter data must make some inferences to conclude, for instance, that an occupant is showering, or eating, or sleeping. But *Kyllo* rejected the "extraordinary assertion that anything learned through 'an inference' cannot be a search." What's more, the data collected by Naperville can be used to draw the exact inference that troubled the Court in *Kyllo.* There, law enforcement "concluded that [a home's occupant] was using halide lights to grow marijuana in his house" based on an excessive amount of energy coming from the home. Here too, law enforcement could conclude that an occupant was using grow lights from incredibly high meter readings, particularly if the power was drawn at odd hours. In fact, the data collected by Naperville could prove even more intrusive. By analyzing the energy consumption of a home over time in concert with appliance load profiles for grow lights, Naperville law enforcement could "conclude" that a resident was using the lights with more confidence than those using thermal imaging could ever hope for. With little effort, they could conduct this analysis for many homes over many years.

Under *Kyllo,* however, even an extremely invasive technology can evade the warrant requirement if it is "in general public use." While more and more energy providers are encouraging (or in this case forcing) their customers to permit the installation of smart meters, the meters are not yet so pervasive that they fall into this class. To be sure, the exact contours of this qualifier are unclear—since *Kyllo,* the Supreme Court has offered little guidance. But *Kyllo* itself suggests that the use of technology is not a search when the technology is both widely available and routinely used by the general public. *See id.* at 39 n.6 (quoting *California v. Ciraolo,* 476 U.S. 207, 215 (1986) ("In an age where private and commercial flight in the public airways is routine, it is unreasonable for respondent to expect that his marijuana plants were constitutionally protected from being observed with the naked eye from an altitude of 1,000 feet.")). Smart meters, by contrast, have been adopted only by a portion of a highly specialized industry.

The ever-accelerating pace of technological development carries serious privacy implications. Smart meters are no exception. Their data, even when collected at fifteen-minute intervals, reveals details about the home that would be otherwise unavailable to government officials with a physical search. Naperville therefore "searches" its residents' homes when it collects this data.

Before continuing, we address one wrinkle to the search analysis. Naperville argues that the third-party doctrine renders the Fourth Amendment's protections irrelevant here. Under that doctrine, a person surrenders her expectation of privacy in information by voluntarily sharing it with a third party. *See Carpenter v. United States*, 138 S. Ct. 2206, 2216 (2018) (citing *Smith v. Maryland*, 442 U.S. 735, 743–744 (1979) and *United States v. Miller*, 425 U.S. 435, 443 (1976)). Thus, when a government authority gathers the information from the third party, it does not run afoul of the Fourth Amendment. *Id.* Referencing this doctrine, Naperville argues that its citizens sacrifice their expectation of privacy in smart-meter data by entering into a "voluntary relationship" to purchase electricity from the city.

This argument is unpersuasive. As a threshold matter, Smart Meter Awareness challenges the collection of the data by Naperville's public utility. There is no third party involved in the exchange. Moreover, were we to assume that Naperville's public utility was a third party, the doctrine would still provide Naperville no refuge. The third-party doctrine rests on "the notion that an individual has a reduced expectation of privacy in information knowingly shared with another." *Carpenter*, 138 S. Ct. at 2219. But in this context, a choice to share data imposed by fiat is no choice at all. If a person does not—in any meaningful sense—"voluntarily 'assume the risk' of turning over a comprehensive dossier of physical movements" by choosing to use a cell phone, *Carpenter*, 138 S. Ct. at 2220 (quoting *Smith*, 442 U.S. at 745), it also goes that a home occupant does not assume the risk of near constant monitoring by choosing to have electricity in her home. We therefore doubt that *Smith* and *Miller* extend this far.

That the data collection constitutes a search does not end our inquiry. Indeed, "[t]he touchstone of the Fourth Amendment is reasonableness." *Florida v. Jimeno*, 500 U.S. 248, 250 (1991). Thus, if Naperville's search is reasonable, it may collect the data without a warrant. Since these searches are not performed as part of a criminal investigation, *see Riley v. California*, 134 S. Ct. 2473, 2482 (2014), we can turn immediately to an assessment of whether they are reasonable, "by balancing its intrusion on the individual's Fourth Amendment interests against its promotion of legitimate government interests." *Hiibel v. Sixth Judicial Dist. Court*, 542 U.S. 177, 187–88 (2004) (quoting *Delaware v. Prouse*, 440 U.S. 648, 654 (1979)). Although in this case, our balancing begins with the presumption that this warrantless search is unreasonable, *see Kyllo*, 533 U.S. at 40, Naperville's smart-meter ordinance overcomes this presumption.

Residents certainly have a privacy interest in their energy-consumption data. But its collection—even if routine and frequent—is far less invasive than the prototypical Fourth Amendment search of a home. Critically, Naperville conducts the search with no prosecutorial intent. Employees of the city's public utility—not law enforcement—collect and review the data.

In *Camara v. Municipal Court*, the Supreme Court noted that this consideration lessens an individual's privacy interest. 387 U.S. 523, 530 (1967). And though the Court held that a warrantless, administrative, home inspection violated the Fourth Amendment in that case, it did so based on concerns largely absent from this one. *Id.* at 530–31. Indeed, unlike the search in *Camara*, Naperville's data collection reveals details about the home without physical entry. *See id.* at 531 (highlighting the "serious threat to personal and family security" posed by physical entry). Moreover, the risk of corollary prosecution that troubled the court in *Camara* is minimal here. *See id.* (noting that "most regulatory laws, fire, health, and housing codes are enforced by criminal process."). To this court's knowledge, using too much electricity is not yet a crime in Naperville. And Naperville's amended "Smart Grid Customer Bill of Rights" clarifies that the city's public utility will not provide customer data to third parties, including law enforcement, without a warrant or court order. Thus, the privacy interest at stake here is yet more limited than that at issue in *Camara*.

Of course, even a lessened privacy interest must be weighed against the government's interest in the data collection. That interest is substantial in this case. Indeed, the modernization of the electrical grid is a priority for both Naperville, (R. 120–1, Smart Meter Agreement between Naperville and the Department of Energy), and the Federal Government, *see Smart Grid*, Federal Energy Regulatory Commission (Apr. 21, 2016).

Smart meters play a crucial role in this transition. *See id.* For instance, they allow utilities to restore service more quickly when power goes out precisely because they provide energy-consumption data at regular intervals. *See, e.g.,* Noelia Uribe-Pérez et al., *State of the Art and Trends Review of* Smart Metering *in Electricity Grids*, 6 APPLIED SCI. 68, 82 (2016). The meters also permit utilities to offer time-based pricing, an innovation which reduces strain on the grid by encouraging consumers to shift usage away from peak demand periods. *Id.* In addition, smart meters reduce utilities' labor costs because home visits are needed less frequently. *Id.*

With these benefits stacked together, the government's interest in smart meters is significant. Smart meters allow utilities to reduce costs, provide cheaper power to consumers, encourage energy efficiency, and increase grid stability. We hold that these interests render the city's search reasonable, where the search is unrelated to law enforcement, is minimally invasive, and presents little risk of corollary criminal consequences.

We caution, however, that our holding depends on the particular circumstances of this case. Were a city to collect the data at shorter intervals, our conclusion could change. Likewise, our conclusion might change if the data was more easily accessible to law enforcement or other city officials outside the utility.

Naperville could have avoided this controversy—and may still avoid future uncertainty—by giving its residents a genuine opportunity to consent to the installation of smart meters, as many other utilities have. Nonetheless, Naperville's warrantless collection of its residents' energy-consumption data survives our review in this case.

Even when set to collect readings at fifteen-minute intervals, smart meters provide Naperville rich data. Accepting Smart Meter Awareness's well-pled allegations as true, this collection constitutes a search. But because of the significant government interests in the program, and the diminished privacy interests at stake, the search is reasonable. We therefore AFFIRM the district court's denial of leave to amend.

Although concerns continue to exist around smart meters and privacy, crucial points are often absent in discussions of these issues. For example, smart meter data are different—real-time second-to-second data with homes metered at the plug-load-level is very different from hourly data that is stripped, aggregated, noise added, and used for distribution network analysis. Both the interval and the granularity of data collection and the time of release affect the contours of individual privacy but are rarely mentioned. Additionally, energy use data are vital to evaluate the effectiveness of energy efficiency programs, to target new initiatives, to scale investments in energy efficiency, and to estimate the value of demand response programs. Moreover, energy use data could provide opportunities for new products and markets. For instance, hourly energy use data for a city could allow first order estimates of solar PV sizing and generation potential. Such information is crucial for the development of microgrids and community energy systems as well as targeting new energy efficiency investments.

Finally, energy consumption data is necessary to scale energy efficiency, develop distributed generation, and create a more responsive and efficient electricity distribution network. Despite over thirty years of local, state, and federal programs offering energy efficiency incentives and educating residential, commercial, and industrial customers about cost-effective energy saving opportunities, the impacts of these programs consistently fall short and future potential is untapped.

Part of the problem is the lack of publicly available data on energy consumption. While emissions and electricity *generation* data are available at the boiler or plant level on an hourly basis through the EIA, EPA, and FERC, energy consumption data is available only as estimates through quadrennial surveys.

This lack of energy consumption data can create information asymmetries and hinder market energy transparency and investment into energy efficiency. These market failures can cause several problems:

1. *Evaluating existing programs.* Lack of energy consumption data makes it difficult to evaluate and compare current efforts. Assessing and evaluating which programs are most effective is often stymied by lack of energy use data. Post-occupancy green building performance could also be measured with energy consumption data.

2. *Targeting future energy management opportunities.* Lack of energy consumption data makes energy management program design, planning, implementation, and evaluation much more difficult. Federal, state, and local governments encourage energy efficiency through tax incentives, building standards, and appliance efficiency standards, spending vast sums of public money in the process. However, evaluating and comparing the efficiency and effectiveness of these programs often relies on modeled data, making evaluation of smaller efforts or comparing programs difficult.

3. *Scaling energy management.* Lack of energy consumption data makes targeting new opportunities and scaling up finance for energy efficient projects challenging and unable to benefit from large-scale investment.

High system penetration of energy efficiency and distributed energy resources will require additional information on energy consumption across a networked distribution grid. Unlike large wind or PV systems with a single interconnection point, targeted energy efficiency and distributed generation will enter the distribution grid at multiple points. How energy efficiency, demand management, and distributed generation are networked across time and space will be crucial for system performance and integration of variable energy resources.

While energy consumption data privacy concerns have been raised by some, it is important to distinguish between privacy and anonymity. As a society we have required data reporting transparency in very sensitive areas like health care, education, and financial markets. In each of these areas, efforts have been made to ensure individual privacy while allowing for programmatic analysis and evaluation. To do this, we have set up standardized data reporting schemes—like the U.S. Department of Energy's Green Button program which many utilities around the country have adopted—and allowed different levels of access, from highly aggregated data which is publicly available to more granular data for detailed analysis, evaluation, and planning. U.S. Census data, Surface Transportation Board data, medical data, and more all allow different levels of access for different user classes. *See* Alexandra B. Klass & Elizabeth J. Wilson, *Remaking Energy: The Critical Role of Energy Consumption Data*, 104 CALIF. L. REV. 1095 (2016); Kugler & Hurley, *supra*.

Finally, it should be noted that arguably more sensitive and also very similar data is already available. For example, public information on housing stock, value, tax rates, or street views is accessible for all of North America. Water consumption data is publicly available, and the municipal utilities that make water, natural gas, and electricity data available to the public have not met with concerns about privacy. Rather, customers ask for more data. *See, e.g.,* Gainesville Green, http://gainesville-green.com/, which lists all residences in the city of Gainesville, Florida and charts monthly gas, electric, and water use. Also, many corporations routinely disclose energy consumption data as part of voluntary carbon reporting programs and protocols, for example the Carbon Disclosure Project, Climate Registry, and others. Together, this signals that there is potentially less sensitivity around energy consumption disclosure than some parties report.

NOTES AND QUESTIONS

1.   Many other sensitive data—school and child educational performance, health care outcomes, financial data, etc.—are managed and evaluated through a host of different privacy protocols. What sort of protocols should be developed for energy consumption data analysis? What types of protections are appropriate?

2.   How should electricity use data be used to promote other social policies and evaluate investments and ensure investments are equitably made?

3.   There is no standard format or best practice for who has access to customer data and the responsibilities and protections of customer data. Rather, as the *Naperville Smart Meter Awareness* case illustrates, individual state PUCs and legislatures address privacy and third-party access issues through rulemakings, legislation, and on a case-by-case basis. The variety of approaches is also illustrated in U.S. ENERGY INFO. ADMIN., SMART GRID LEGISLATIVE AND REGULATORY POLICIES AND CASE STUDIES (Dec. 2011). *See*

also Modernizing the Electric Grid: State Role and Policy Options, Nat'l Conf. of State Legislatures (last updated Apr. 5, 2021). A U.S. Department of Energy Privacy Report outlines several consensus points for protecting smart grid data. First, customers should be able to decide if and which third parties can access their data. Second, utilities wishing to share energy data with third parties should obtain opt-in consent and record which data is to be released and the purpose of the release. Third, all third parties should ensure that the data are protected, secure, remain private, and are used only for authorized purposes. Fourth, states should enact rules governing third party access. U.S. DEP'T OF ENERGY, DATA ACCESS AND PRIVACY ISSUES RELATED TO SMART GRID TECHNOLOGIES (Oct. 5, 2010). *See also* U.S. DEP'T OF ENERGY, DATA PRIVACY AND THE SMART GRID: A VOLUNTARY CODE OF CONDUCT (VCC) (Jan. 8, 2015); Klass & Wilson, *supra*; ABRAMS ENVIRONMENTAL LAW CLINIC, UNIVERSITY OF CHICAGO LAW SCHOOL, FREEING ENERGY DATA (June 2016). How might different approaches to managing privacy affect the collection of information critical for evaluating program benefits and developing new initiatives to save energy?

4.   Over the last decade, smart meters have become widespread. Over 75% of U.S. electricity consumers now have smart meters. But for most customers, the smart meter has not allowed them to actively manage their electricity use. While this varies by jurisdiction, most areas of the country do not have retail choice. Additionally, being exposed to energy markets can pose risks to customers, as the high-profile case of the Texas 2021 winter storms illustrates. During the storm, as natural gas resources plummeted and energy markets set prices skyrocketing, electricity customers who had variable rate plans tied to wholesale market prices received bills of over $5,000. *See* Rebecca Hersher, *After Days of Mass Outages, Some Texas Residents Now Face Huge Electricity Bills*, NPR (Feb. 21, 2021). To what extent should regulators limit the ability of retail energy companies to offer rate plans like these?

* * *

PRACTICE PROBLEM

You are an energy planner for the City of Denver, Colorado and have seen your electricity demand grow 1.5% per year, with over 4% of new demand coming from hundreds of indoor commercial marijuana growing operations opened in Denver since the state of Colorado legalized recreational marijuana use in 2012. Your city has adopted aggressive greenhouse gas emissions goals—aiming to reduce CO_2 emissions to below 1990 levels—as well as goals to hold energy usage below 2012 levels while simultaneously cutting fossil fuel use by 50%. Herein lies the problem. While 36 states have some form of legal cannabis growing, the post-prohibition environment is uneven, and marijuana remains illegal at the federal level as a Schedule I drug under the Controlled Substances Act of 1970 (despite recent efforts to change this). Efforts to manage the energy and environmental impacts of the industry are patchy. As a result, cannabis grow operations cannot qualify for many federal programs or tax rebates for installing more efficient equipment or renewable power and, in some cases, utilities have been reluctant to develop industry targeted programs. As marijuana cultivation was illegal for decades, energy management was not a top priority for black market growers. Additionally, with legalization, state and local ordinances have forced marijuana cultivation indoors for security reasons.

When it is produced in large indoor industrial facilities, marijuana is an extremely energy intensive crop. It is estimated that by flower weight, it uses 500 times the energy as aluminum production, emitting an estimated 2283 to 5184 kg CO_2-equivalent per kg of dried flower and using 10–50 times the energy use per square foot of a house or office building. Energy use comes from heating, cooling, ventilation, air filtration (to prevent odors from escaping the facility) and dehumidification as well as from lighting with bright high-pressure sodium lamps. LED lighting can cut energy and heating costs substantially and locating operations in a greenhouse or outdoors can reduce emissions 25% or more. But even beyond these potential improvements, the lack of data, standards, and programs to manage the energy and environmental impacts of this once illicit sector are glaring. Rooftop solar on these facilities currently produces only roughly 10% of their electricity demand. *See* Evan Mills, *Comment on "Cannabis and the Environment: What Science Tells Us and What We Still Need to Know*, 8 ENV'T SCI. TECH. LETT. 98 (2021); Hailey M. Summers et al, *The Greenhouse Gas Emissions of Indoor Cannabis Production in the United States*, NATURE SUSTAINABILITY (Mar. 2021); Gina S. Warren, *Regulating Pot to Save the Polar Bear: Energy and Climate Impacts of the Marijuana Industry*, 40 COLUMBIA J. ENV'T L. 385 (2015). Programs in Washington and Oregon have targeted energy management in growing operations focusing on new LED lighting solutions and better HVAC controls, but they need to carefully document that power or resources from the federally funded Bonneville Power Administration is not involved or used.

1. Should your office establish cannabis customer data collection and energy analysis for city facilities? If yes, what should the process be? If no, should operations be required to report as to current practices and explain how these are reasonable and sufficient at this time?

2. How should your office address potential energy, waste, and water use concerns that the marijuana industry may raise? What are the state and federal issues to be balanced in dealing with this class of customer?

3. How should revenue be generated to support new energy efficiency or renewable energy programs in the sector?

4. Should there be a process to evaluate and manage grow operations? How should your office and the utility address additional costs associated with investments?

5. What are the opportunities for federal or state energy efficiency grants or rebates?

CHAPTER 9

ADDRESSING THE BENEFITS AND RISKS OF NEW ENERGY SOURCES AND TECHNOLOGIES: HYDRAULIC FRACTURING AND OFFSHORE ENERGY DEVELOPMENT

■ ■ ■

A. OVERVIEW

New extraction techniques have transformed the U.S. energy industry. The rapid expansion of our ability to obtain natural gas and oil from shale and from deep underwater has increased current and potential fossil fuel supplies. At the same time, industrial-scale offshore wind energy holds the potential to dramatically expand the nation's renewable energy resources. These developments have and will continue to profoundly influence energy markets. Indeed, the global energy map is being transformed as the resurgence of oil and natural gas boost domestic production in the United States and abundant offshore wind offers the prospect of carbon-free energy tantalizingly close to the country's largest population centers.

These new and developing technologies in both onshore and offshore energy resource extraction are an important part of why natural gas has become less expensive, why the United States has become less dependent on foreign oil, and why several states have recently adopted laws mandating that the state's electricity must all come from carbon free resources by dates ranging from 2030 to 2050. From the perspective of providing cheap, domestic energy, these technologies are an important, positive development. For instance, the ability to extract large reserves of onshore and offshore natural gas has played a major role in the shift away from coal in electricity production. These same extraction technologies also raise environmental and health risks that need to be managed. Lawsuits abound over water pollution from unconventional oil and gas, with dramatic depictions of flaming water and other harms in films like *Promised Land*, *Gasland*, and *Gasland 2*. Likewise, the BP *Deepwater Horizon* oil spill in 2010 (and the major motion picture with the same name) provided the public with a stark reminder of the risks posed by drilling a mile or more below the water's surface. And there remain many unanswered questions about how quickly the United States can develop offshore wind resources and the impact of that development on fisheries, endangered species, and the sea floor. How can regulation help manage these risks while encouraging innovation and economic development?

This chapter addresses these questions through a detailed examination of efforts to regulate onshore oil and gas extraction using hydraulic fracturing techniques and offshore fossil fuel and wind energy development. The chapter examines how fast-moving technology, the fragmentation of regulatory authority, and resulting federalism disputes, along with the political prominence of these developments, make these areas difficult to regulate effectively.

As you engage with the chapter's materials, consider how your perspective on our national energy policy might vary based upon your understanding of these new extraction techniques. Also consider how your views on energy regulation might be shaped based upon your position in the energy market. If you were a company that has invested significantly in a deepwater or shale gas site or an offshore wind project, what type of a regulatory approach would you prefer? If you live in a community impacted by these techniques but do not directly experience their benefits, how might your preferred approach differ? How might your opinion on these issues change if you were a local, state, or federal regulator? What is the range of views that environmental nonprofit organizations have expressed on these issues?

B. THE GROWTH OF SHALE OIL AND GAS DEVELOPMENT AND ASSOCIATED REGULATORY CHALLENGES

This section explores issues of technological change and risk, fragmentation and federalism, and regulatory reform in the context of hydraulic fracturing paired with horizontal drilling for onshore oil and gas development. Notably, the law relevant to hydraulic fracturing—like onshore oil and gas development more generally—is primarily state-based—a mix of common law property and statutory environmental and energy law—which creates problems of piecemeal regulation. As discussed in detail later in this section, the Obama administration promulgated substantial new federal regulations governing hydraulic fracturing on both public and private lands, the Trump administration made it a priority to dismantle these regulations, and the Biden administration plans to revive them.

The section begins by describing the technological developments that have allowed for a rapid expansion of onshore shale oil and gas development, as well as the risks that accompany this expansion. It then introduces the many types of applicable laws and regulations, and the difficult federalism and governance questions that emerge from both fragmentation and a rapidly evolving technological and regulatory environment.

1. THE EVOLUTION AND EXPANSION OF SHALE OIL AND GAS EXTRACTION

The United States has a massive amount of oil and natural gas trapped in shale formations. The difficulty is that this oil and gas can only be accessed through a combination of hydraulic fracturing and horizontal drilling, in which holes are made parallel to the earth's surface after vertical drilling has penetrated the surface. The impact of hydraulic fracturing and horizontal drilling on U.S. energy supplies cannot be overstated, as detailed in this 2021 Congressional Research Service report:

> Approximately 12.2 million bpd of crude oil was produced in the United States during 2019, the highest annual level in the history of the sector. . . . Oil production in the United States had been in general decline for nearly 40 years (1970–2008). However, this downward trend reversed, primarily through the application of horizontal drilling and hydraulic fracturing technology to access tight oil. . . . Between 2008 and 2019, annual production of U.S. tight oil increased by more than 7 million bpd. Tight oil represented the largest portion of domestic production volume in 2019." . . .
>
> The United States became a net exporter of natural gas in 2017, the first time since 1957. . . . The United States is the world's largest producer of natural gas. Since 2005, U.S. natural gas production rose every year until 2016, even as prices declined. Production resumed growing in 2017 and 2018, and reached a new high in 2019 of 33,657 billion cubic feet (BCF). The increase in natural gas production between 2005 and 2019 is mostly attributed to the development of shale gas resources, specifically in the Marcellus and Utica formations in the northeastern United States. Overall, shale gas production accounted for 75% of total U.S. natural gas production in 2019; the Marcellus and Utica formations accounted for 43% of the U.S. shale gas production.

MELISSA N. DIAZ, CONG. RSCH. SERV., U.S. ENERGY IN THE 21ST CENTURY: A PRIMER 6, 9–10 (Mar. 16, 2021).

The following excerpt describes the technology of hydraulic fracturing paired with horizontal drilling in the context of oil production but applies equally to natural gas production.

OIL AND PETROLEUM PRODUCTS EXPLAINED

U.S. Energy Info. Admin. (last updated Mar. 10, 2021)

Geologists often use seismic surveys on land and in the ocean to find the right places to drill wells. Seismic surveys on land use echoes from a vibration source at the surface of the earth, usually a vibrating pad under a special type of truck. Geologists can also use small amounts of explosives as a vibration source. Seismic surveys conducted in the ocean rely on blasts of sound that create sonic waves to explore the geology beneath the ocean floor.

If a site seems promising, an exploratory well is drilled and tested. If enough oil [or natural gas] is found to make it financially worthwhile to pursue, development wells are drilled. The type of well that is drilled depends on the location, geology, and oil resource.

In the past, a drilling rig drilled a single vertical well. Now, many directional or horizontal wells can be drilled from one location, or *well pad*, to access greater areas of oil- and natural gas-bearing rock.

Oil [or natural gas] may flow to the earth's surface from natural pressure in the rock formation, or it may have to be forced out of the ground and up through a well. The type of geologic formation where the oil is located determines the technologies used to start the flow of oil and natural gas from the reservoir or resource-bearing rock into the wells.

Hydraulic fracturing is used to access the oil and natural gas contained in tiny pores of rock formations composed of shale, sandstone, and carbonate (limestone). Hydraulic fracturing breaks up the rock in the formations and creates pathways that allow oil and natural gas to escape from the rock layers. Hydraulic fracturing involves forcing water, chemicals, and sand or other proppants (materials used to keep the pathways open) under high pressure into the wells. Steam, water, or carbon dioxide (CO_2) can also be injected into a rock layer to help oil flow more easily into production wells.

After the oil has been collected from wells in a production field, pipelines, barges, trains, or trucks transport the oil to refineries or to ports for shipment on oil tankers to other countries.

Production of crude oil and natural gas is sometimes called *conventional* production or *unconventional* production. Conventional production generally means that crude oil and natural gas flow to and up a well under the natural pressure of the earth. Unconventional production requires techniques and technologies to increase or enable oil and natural gas production beyond what might occur using conventional production techniques. In the United States, most of the new oil and natural gas production activities on land use unconventional production technologies.

The U.S. oil and natural gas industry uses the term *tight oil* to mean the different geologic formations producing oil at a specific well. Tight oil is produced from low-permeability sandstones, carbonates (for example, limestone), and shale formations. The U.S. Energy Information Administration (EIA) uses the term tight oil to refer to all resources, reserves, and production associated with low-permeability formations that produce oil, including shale formations.

Notable tight oil formations include

- Bakken and Three Forks formations in the Williston Basin [primarily in North Dakota]

- Eagle Ford, Austin Chalk, Buda, and Woodbine formations along the Gulf Coast [in Texas and neighboring states]

- Spraberry, Wolfcamp, Bone Spring, Delaware, Glorieta, and Yeso formations in the Permian Basin [in west Texas and eastern New Mexico]

- Niobrara formation in the Denver-Julesburg Basin [in Colorado and neighboring states]

———————

While the excerpt above focuses on the primary tight oil formations, where oil and natural gas are found together, Pennsylvania and neighboring states are home to the Marcellus Shale formation, which is now one of the nation's top producing areas for natural gas due to hydraulic fracturing technologies, but which does not contain oil. The diagram, maps, and graphs below depict the hydraulic fracturing and directional drilling process, illustrate the growth of U.S. oil and gas production since approximately 2007, and highlight the states in which that growth has occurred. According to a 2021 DOE report, fractured gas accounted for 75% of U.S. natural gas production in 2019, up from 38% in 2005, while oil production from fractured wells constituted 63% of total U.S. crude oil production, up from only 8% in 2005. *See* U.S. DEP'T OF ENERGY, ECONOMIC AND NATIONAL SECURITY IMPACTS UNDER A HYDRAULIC FRACTURING BAN 7 (Jan. 2021).

The Hydraulic Fracturing Process

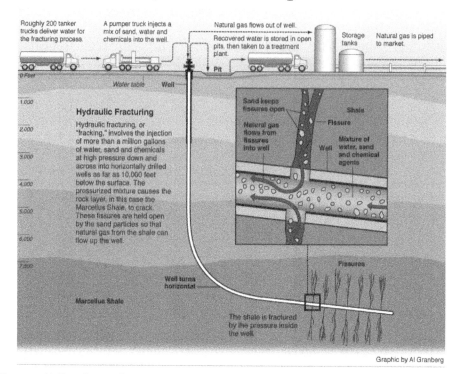

Source: Al Granberg, Illustration of Hydraulic Fracturing *in* Krista Kjellman Schmidt, *What is Hydraulic Fracturing?*, PROPUBLICA (Nov. 13, 2008).

U.S. Production of Crude Oil and Natural Gas

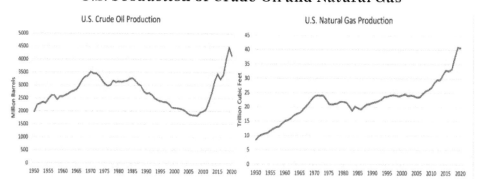

Source: U.S. Energy Info. Admin. (data files).

Top Ten U.S. Crude Oil Producing States, 2020

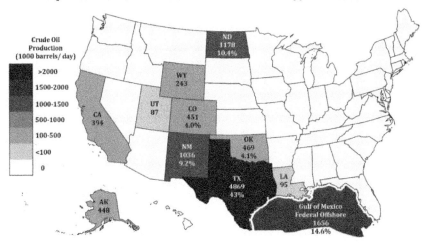

Top Ten U.S. Natural Gas Producing States, 2019

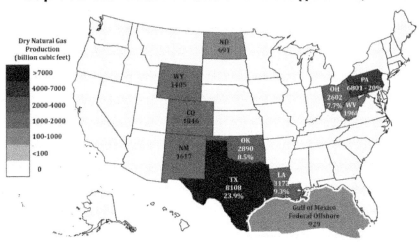

Source: U.S. Energy Info. Admin. (data files).

NOTES AND QUESTIONS

1.   A major concern associated with the use of hydraulic fracturing and directional drilling to produce oil and natural gas is water pollution. In 2016, the U.S. EPA released a study that found that the use of water withdrawal to create hydraulic fracturing fluids, the injection of those fluids into production wells, and the collection and disposal of produced water can adversely impact local and regional drinking water supplies. U.S. ENV'T PROT. AGENCY, HYDRAULIC FRACTURING FOR OIL AND GAS: IMPACTS FROM THE HYDRAULIC

FRACTURING WATER CYCLE ON DRINKING WATER RESOURCES IN THE UNITED STATES (Dec. 2020). Should these impacts be regulated at the local, state, or federal level?

2.   Although the federal government has not issued regulations regarding earthquake hazards from unconventional oil and gas, it has conducted extensive studies of this issue. The following excerpt describes the U.S. Geological Survey's 2017 findings:

> The U.S. Geological Survey (USGS) has produced a one-year 2017 seismic hazard forecast for the central and eastern United States from induced and natural earthquakes that updates the 2016 one-year forecast; this map is intended to provide information to the public and to facilitate the development of induced seismicity forecasting models, methods, and data. The 2017 hazard model applies the same methodology and input logic tree as the 2016 forecast, but with an updated earthquake catalog.
>
> The 2016 forecast indicated high seismic hazard (greater than 1% probability of potentially damaging ground shaking in one-year) in five focus areas: Oklahoma-Kansas, the Raton Basin (Colorado/New Mexico border), north Texas, north Arkansas, and the New Madrid seismic zone. During 2016, several damaging induced earthquakes occurred in Oklahoma within the highest hazard region of the 2016 forecast; all of the 21 magnitude (M) ≥ 4 and three M ≥ 5 earthquakes occurred within the highest hazard area in the 2016 forecast. Outside the Oklahoma-Kansas focus area, two earthquakes with M ≥ 4 occurred near Trinidad, Colorado (in the Raton Basin focus area), but no earthquakes with M ≥ 2.7 were observed in the north Texas or north Arkansas focus areas. Several observations of damaging ground shaking levels were also recorded in the highest hazard region of Oklahoma. The 2017 forecasted seismic rates are lower in regions of induced activity due to lower rates of earthquakes in 2016 compared to 2015, which may be related to decreased wastewater injection, caused by regulatory actions or by a decrease in unconventional oil and gas production. Nevertheless, the 2017 forecasted hazard is still significantly elevated in Oklahoma compared to the hazard calculated from seismicity before 2009.

U.S. GEOLOGICAL SURVEY, SHORT-TERM INDUCED SEISMICITY MODELS: 2017 ONE-YEAR MODEL (Mar. 2017). *See also* Ryan Schultz et al., *Hydraulic Fracturing Induced Seismicity*, 58 REVIEW OF GEOPHYSICS 1–43 (June 2020) (discussing documented cases of induced seismicity associated with hydraulic fracturing activities around the world; summarizing commonalities; and identifying issues for further research, regulation, mitigation, and documentation).

3.   Many of the technologies developed for hydraulic fracturing can also be used for enhanced geothermal technologies, discussed in Chapter 2, to develop geothermal energy in areas where it was not possible before. The advantage of

this technology is that it would allow this carbon-free baseload power to complement variable renewable resources like wind and solar. What important environmental concerns identified with fossil fracking might also be an issue for enhanced geothermal? Which would be less of an issue? Might some technological choices like closed loop or open loop systems be better at reducing environmental impacts? *See* Alice Carfrae, *Geothermal Energy: Our Oldest and Most Reliable Resource*, BBC (May 19, 2021).

2. THE ROLE OF PROPERTY LAW IN HYDRAULIC FRACTURING

For hydraulic fracturing, like onshore oil and gas development more generally, the regulatory regime is largely controlled at the state and local level. Each state approaches drilling and water regulation differently through a mix of common law, statutes, and agency regulation. Moreover, unlike deepwater drilling, which takes place on federally owned submerged lands, a significant portion of shale oil and gas exploration and drilling occurs on private property. This shale oil and gas development takes place pursuant to leases with private landowners rather than with the federal government. In response, state and local governments, nonprofit organizations, and educational institutions have been publishing guides and handbooks for landowners to assist them in making decisions on whether to sign a lease and how to negotiate appropriate lease terms and other conditions. *See, e.g.*, EMMETT ENVIRONMENTAL LAW & POLICY CLINIC, HARVARD LAW SCHOOL, A LANDOWNER'S GUIDE TO HYDRAULIC FRACTURING (2014).

A number of state and local governments, especially in areas with major shale oil and gas resources, have promulgated regulations relevant to these unconventional extraction techniques, which are explored later in this chapter. However, even with these regulations, property law remains an important way that states govern oil and gas extraction generally and hydraulic fracturing in particular.

Many of you have previously encountered the case *Pierson v. Post*, 3 Cai. R. 175, 2 Am. Dec. 264 (N.Y. 1805), in property law. In that case, the court had to decide who owned a fox that one person had chased but another person had killed. This dispute over a fox is relevant to hydraulic fracturing because, as noted in Chapters 2 and 3, it established the rule of capture, a dominant rule in oil and gas extraction. This rule allows landowners to extract as much as possible from their wells even if they end up taking oil and gas from under someone else's land due to the shared nature of the reservoir. The following case excerpt addresses the rule of capture and its application in the context of hydraulic fracturing.

COASTAL OIL & GAS CORP. V. GARZA ENERGY TRUST

268 S.W.3d 1 (Tex. 2008)

JUSTICE HECHT delivered the opinion of the Court, in which JUSTICE BRISTER, JUSTICE GREEN, JUDGE CHRISTOPHER, and JUSTICE PEMBERTON joined, and in all but Part II-B of which JUSTICE JEFFERSON, JUSTICE MEDINA, JUSTICE JOHNSON, and JUSTICE WILLETT joined.

The primary issue in this appeal is whether subsurface hydraulic fracturing of a natural gas well that extends into another's property is a trespass for which the value of gas drained as a result may be recovered as damages. We hold that the rule of capture bars recovery of such damages. . . .

We reverse the judgment of the court of appeals and remand the case to the trial court for further proceedings.

Respondents, to whom we shall refer collectively as Salinas, own the minerals in a 748-acre tract of land in Hidalgo County called Share 13, which they and their ancestors have occupied for over a century. At all times material to this case, petitioner Coastal Oil & Gas Corp. has been the lessee of the minerals in Share 13 and an adjacent tract, Share 15. Coastal was also the lessee of the minerals in Share 12 until it acquired the mineral estate in that 163-acre tract in 1995. A natural gas reservoir, the Vicksburg T formation, lies between 11,688 and 12,610 feet below these tracts. . . .

From 1978 to 1983, Coastal drilled three wells on Share 13, two of which were productive, . . . though the other . . . was not. In 1994, Coastal drilled the M. Salinas No. 3, and it was an exceptional producer. The No. 3 well was about 1,700 feet from Share 12. The closest well on Share 12 was the Pennzoil Fee No. 1 . . . but Coastal wanted one closer, so in 1996, Coastal drilled the Coastal Fee No. 1 in the northeast corner of Share 12, as close to Share 13 (and the M. Salinas No. 3) as Texas Railroad Commission's statewide spacing Rule 37 permitted—467 feet from the boundaries to the north and east. . . . In February 1997, Coastal drilled the Coastal Fee No. 2, also near Share 13.

In March, Salinas sued Coastal for breach of its implied covenants to develop Share 13 and prevent drainage. Salinas was concerned that Coastal was allowing Share 13 gas, on which Coastal owed Salinas a royalty, to drain to Share 12, where Coastal, as both owner and operator, was entitled to the gas unburdened by a royalty obligation. Salinas's suit prompted a flurry of drilling by Coastal on Share 13—eight wells in fourteen months. Not until late 1999 did Coastal drill again on Share 12.

The Vicksburg T is a "tight" sandstone formation, relatively imporous and impermeable, from which natural gas cannot be commercially produced without hydraulic fracturing stimulation, or "fracing", as the process is known in the industry. . . .

Regarding drainage, Salinas's expert, Economides, testified that because of the fracing operation on the Coastal No. 1 well, 25–35% of the gas it produced drained from Share 13. . . .

II

We begin with Salinas's contention that the incursion of hydraulic fracturing fluid and proppants into another's land two miles below the surface constitutes a trespass for which the minerals owner can recover damages equal to the value of the royalty on the gas thereby drained from the land. Coastal argues that . . . hydraulic fracturing is not an actionable trespass. . . .

Had Coastal caused something like proppants to be deposited on the surface of Share 13, it would be liable for trespass, and from the ancient common law maxim that land ownership extends to the sky above and the earth's center below, one might extrapolate that the same rule should apply two miles below the surface. But that maxim—*cujus est solum ejus est usque ad coelum et ad inferos*—"has no place in the modern world." Wheeling an airplane across the surface of one's property without permission is a trespass; flying the plane through the airspace two miles above the property is not. Lord Coke, who pronounced the maxim, did not consider the possibility of airplanes. But neither did he imagine oil wells. The law of trespass need no more be the same two miles below the surface than two miles above.

We have not previously decided whether subsurface fracing can give rise to an action for trespass. That issue, we held in *Gregg v. Delhi-Taylor Oil Corp.*, [344 S.W.2d 411 (Tex. 1961)], is one for the courts to decide, not the Railroad Commission. In 1961, when we decided *Gregg*, the Commission had never addressed the subject, and we specifically indicated no view on whether Commission rules could authorize secondary recovery operations that crossed property lines. The next Term, in *Railroad Commission of Texas v. Manziel*, [361 S.W.2d 560 (Tex. 1962)] we held that a salt water injection secondary recovery operation did not cause a trespass when the water migrated across property lines, but we relied heavily on the fact that the Commission had approved the operation. Thirty years later, in *Geo Viking, Inc. v. Tex-Lee Operating Company*, [839 S.W.2d 797 (Tex. 1992)] we issued a per curiam opinion holding that fracing beneath another's land was a trespass, but on rehearing we withdrew the opinion and expressly did not decide the issue.

We conclude that if, in the valid exercise of its authority to prevent waste, protect correlative rights, or in the exercise of other powers within its jurisdiction, the Commission authorizes secondary recovery projects, a trespass does not occur when the injected, secondary recovery forces move across lease lines, and the operations are not subject to an injunction on that basis. The technical rules of trespass have no place in the consideration of the validity of the orders of the Commission.

We acknowledge that our opinions in *Gregg* and *Manziel* are in some tension and did not perfectly delineate the Commission's authority to regulate secondary recovery operations. . . .

We need not decide the broader issue here. In this case, actionable trespass requires injury, and Salinas's only claim of injury—that Coastal's fracing operation made it possible for gas to flow from beneath Share 13 to the Share 12 wells—is precluded by the rule of capture. That rule gives a mineral rights owner title to the oil and gas produced from a lawful well bottomed on the property, even if the oil and gas flowed to the well from beneath another owner's tract. The rule of capture is a cornerstone of the oil and gas industry and is fundamental both to property rights and to state regulation. Salinas does not claim that the Coastal Fee No. 1 violates any statute or regulation. Thus, the gas he claims to have lost simply does not belong to him. He does not claim that the hydraulic fracturing operation damaged his wells or the Vicksburg T formation beneath his property. In sum, Salinas does not claim damages that are recoverable.

Salinas argues that the rule of capture does not apply because hydraulic fracturing is unnatural. The point of this argument is not clear. If by "unnatural" Salinas means due to human intervention, the simple answer is that such activity is the very basis for the rule, not a reason to suspend its application. Nothing is more unnatural in that sense than the drilling of wells, without which there would be no need for the rule at all. If by "unnatural" Salinas means unusual, the facts are that hydraulic fracturing has long been commonplace throughout the industry and is necessary for commercial production in the Vicksburg T and many other formations. And if by "unnatural" Salinas means unfair, the law affords him ample relief. He may use hydraulic fracturing to stimulate production from his own wells and drain the gas to his own property—which his operator, Coastal, has successfully done already—and he may sue Coastal for not doing so sooner—which he has also done, in this case, though unsuccessfully, as it now turns out.

Salinas argues that stimulating production through hydraulic fracturing that extends beyond one's property is no different from drilling a deviated or slant well—a well that departs from the vertical significantly—bottomed on another's property, which is unlawful. Both produce oil and gas situated beneath another's property. But the rule of capture determines title to gas that drains from property owned by one person onto property owned by another. It says nothing about the ownership of gas that has remained in place. The gas produced through a deviated well does not migrate to the wellbore from another's property; it is already on another's property. The rule of capture is justified because a landowner can protect himself from drainage by drilling his own well, thereby avoiding the uncertainties of determining how gas is migrating through a reservoir. It is a rule of expedience. One cannot protect against drainage from a deviated well by drilling his own well; the deviated well will continue to produce his gas. Nor is there any uncertainty that a deviated well is producing another owner's gas. The justifications for the rule of capture do not support applying the rule to a deviated well.

We are not persuaded by Salinas's arguments. Rather, we find four reasons not to change the rule of capture to allow one property owner to sue another for oil and gas drained by hydraulic fracturing that extends beyond lease lines.

First, the law already affords the owner who claims drainage full recourse. This is the justification for the rule of capture, and it applies regardless of whether the drainage is due to fracing. . . .

Second, allowing recovery for the value of gas drained by hydraulic fracturing usurps to courts and juries the lawful and preferable authority of the Railroad Commission to regulate oil and gas production. Such recovery assumes that the gas belongs to the owner of the minerals in the drained property, contrary to the rule of capture. While a mineral rights owner has a real interest in oil and gas in place, "this right does not extend to *specific* oil and gas beneath the property". . . . [The owner is entitled to] "a fair chance to recover the oil and gas in or under his land, *or* their equivalents in kind." The rule of capture makes it possible for the Commission, through rules governing the spacing, density, and allowables of wells, to protect correlative rights of owners with interests in the same mineral deposits while securing "the state's goals of preventing waste and conserving natural resources". . . . The Commission's role should not be supplanted by the law of trespass.

Third, determining the value of oil and gas drained by hydraulic fracturing is the kind of issue the litigation process is least equipped to handle. One difficulty is that the material facts are hidden below miles of rock, making it difficult to ascertain what might have happened. . . . But there is an even greater difficulty with litigating recovery for drainage resulting from fracing, and it is that trial judges and juries cannot take into account social policies, industry operations, and the greater good which are all tremendously important in deciding whether fracing should or should not be against the law. . . .

Fourth, the law of capture should not be changed to apply differently to hydraulic fracturing because no one in the industry appears to want or need the change. . . . [B]riefs from every corner of the industry—regulators, landowners, royalty owners, operators, and hydraulic fracturing service providers—all oppose liability for hydraulic fracturing, almost always warning of adverse consequences in the direst language. Though hydraulic fracturing has been commonplace in the oil and gas industry for over sixty years, neither the Legislature nor the Commission has ever seen fit to regulate it, though every other aspect of production has been thoroughly regulated. Into so settled a regime the common law need not thrust itself.

Accordingly, we hold that damages for drainage by hydraulic fracturing are precluded by the rule of capture. It should go without saying that the rule of capture cannot be used to shield misconduct that is illegal, malicious, reckless, or intended to harm another without commercial justification, should such a case ever arise. But that certainly did not occur in this case, and no instance of it has been cited to us. . . .

JUSTICE WILLETT, concurring.

James Michener may well be right: "Water, not oil, is the lifeblood of Texas. . . ." But together, oil and gas are its muscle, which today fends off atrophy.

At a time of insatiable appetite for energy and harder-to-reach deposits—iron truths that contribute to $145 a barrel crude and $4 a gallon gasoline—Texas common law should not give traction to an action rooted in abstraction. Our fast-growing State confronts fast-growing energy needs, and Texas can ill afford its finite resources, or its law, to remain stuck in the ground. The Court today averts an improvident decision that, in terms of its real-world impact, would have been a legal dry hole, juris-imprudence that turned booms into busts and torrents into trickles. Scarcity exists, but *above*-ground supply obstacles also exist, and this Court shouldn't be one of them.

Efficient energy production is profoundly important to Texas and to the nation. . . .

On both the supply and demand side, we inhabit an energy world transformed, and the data are growing increasingly sober. . . .

The world will doubtless diversify its energy profile in coming decades to reduce reliance on carbon-emitting fuel sources, but even assuming major advances in both efficiency and alternative sources, fossil fuels will still meet as much as 80% of global energy demand through 2030.

Bottom line: We are more and more over a barrel as "our reserves of fossil fuels are becoming harder and more expensive to find." Given this supply-side slide, maximizing recovery via fracing is essential; enshrining trespass liability for fracing (a "tres-frac" claim) is not. I join today's no-liability result and suggest another reason for barring tres-frac suits: Open-ended liability threatens to inflict grave and unmitigable harm, ensuring that much of our State's undeveloped energy supplies would stay that way—undeveloped. Texas oil and gas law favors drilling wells, not drilling consumers. Amid soaring demand and sagging supply, Texas common law must accommodate cutting-edge technologies able to extract untold reserves from unconventional fields. . . .

———————

NOTES AND QUESTIONS

1. Do you agree with the court in *Coastal Oil v. Garza* that there should be no judicial relief for the value of gas drained by hydraulic fracturing operations on neighboring property? What are the advantages and disadvantages of the court's approach?

2. *Coastal Oil v. Garza*, though only applicable directly to Texas, has had an important influence on common law claims regarding hydraulic fracturing in other states. In 2020, the Pennsylvania Supreme Court, citing the analysis in *Coastal Oil*, rejected a trespass claim under similar facts. *See Briggs v. Southwestern Energy Prod. Co.*, 224 A.3d 334 (Pa. 2020). However, not all courts have agreed with the Texas Supreme Court's rejection of trespass claims for hydraulic fracturing's ability to drain neighboring wells. For instance, in *Kerr McGee Corp. v. ANR Production Co*, 893 P.2d 698 (Wyo. 1995), the Wyoming Supreme Court found that drainage constituted a trespass. But the case hinged on the fact that the well being drained was unitized, making the circumstances sufficiently different that a direct comparison to the *Coastal Oil* case may not be helpful. For a discussion of these cases and the various types of nuisance and trespass claims associated with hydraulic fracturing, see Hannah J. Wiseman, *Beyond* Coastal Oil v. Garza: *Nuisance and Trespass in Hydraulic Fracturing Litigation*, 57 THE ADVOC. (Texas) 8 (2011); ALEXANDRA B. KLASS & HANNAH J. WISEMAN, ENERGY LAW 78–79 (2d ed. 2020) (discussing nuisance and trespass claims associated with hydraulic fracturing harms).

3. As discussed in more detail in Chapter 3, many lands used for oil and gas production are in "split estate" with one party owning the surface lands and another owning the subsurface mineral rights. When land is in split estate, state "surface accommodation" laws govern the extent to which mineral owners can make use of the surface lands to access mineral resources. If a mineral owner can make use of the overlying surface lands to access mineral rights below it, should it also be able to use those same surface lands to access adjacent mineral rights? In *EQT Prod. Co. v. Crowder*, 828 S.E.2d 800 (W. Va. 2019), the West Virginia Supreme Court held as a matter of first impression that even though a mineral owner has "an implied right to use the surface of a tract in any way reasonable and necessary to the development of minerals underlying the tract" it cannot use the surface to access mining or drilling on other lands without an express agreement with the surface owner. Is this the right result? What are the implications of this limitation on surface access? Do you see why this issue would arise more frequently as hydraulic fracturing and directional drilling become the dominant means of extracting onshore oil and gas resources?

3. THE ROLE OF FEDERAL REGULATION IN HYDRAULIC FRACTURING

While the common law of property plays an important role in unconventional oil and gas regulation, the federal government and many states have adopted regulations to deal with hydraulic fracturing directly. This section focuses on the rapidly evolving federal regulation of the industry.

Prior to the Obama administration, federal regulation of unconventional oil and gas was extremely limited. One major constraint on federal regulation, which still exists, is an exemption enacted under the Energy Policy Act of 2005, referred to by many environmental groups as the "Halliburton Loophole." This exemption provides that the requirements of the Safe Drinking Water Act governing underground injection of wastewater do not apply to hydraulic fracturing operations, except when diesel fuels are used.

The Obama administration significantly expanded federal regulation of onshore oil and gas development on both private and public lands. With respect to water pollution, the EPA promulgated Clean Water Act regulations in June 2016 that prohibited oil and gas companies from sending the wastewater produced in their shale oil and gas operations to wastewater treatment plants. *See* U.S. EPA, Effluent Limitations Guidelines and Standards for the Oil and Gas Extraction Point Source Category, 81 Fed. Reg. 41,845 (June 28, 2016). It also issued permitting guidance for underground injection involving diesel fuel. U.S. EPA, Revised Guidance: Permitting Guidance for Oil and Gas Hydraulic Fracturing Activities Using Diesel Fuels: Underground Injection Control Program Guidance #84 (Feb. 2014).

Another major focus of federal regulation has been air emissions—particularly methane emissions—resulting from the rapid rise in domestic oil production made possible by hydraulic fracturing and directional drilling technologies. Every shale oil well also produces what is known as "associated" or "casinghead" gas consisting primarily of methane. Although this natural gas is valuable in its own right, oil producers often will flare (burn off) or otherwise dispose of the gas into the atmosphere if allowed by federal and state laws, unless an adequate network of gas capture pipelines is available for them to collect, transport, and sell the gas at a profit. *See, e.g.,* Gunnar W. Schade, *The Problem with Natural Gas Flaring,* TEXAS, A&M TODAY (Aug. 3, 2020); *Natural Gas Flaring and Venting in North Dakota and Texas Increased in 2019,* U.S. ENERGY INFO. ADMIN. (Dec. 8, 2020) (U.S. flared gas reached an all-time high in 2019, with Texas and North Dakota accounting for 85% of the total). This increase in gas flaring, coupled with inadvertent leaks and other releases from oil and gas infrastructure, has become a major contributor to climate change and localized air pollution. *See, e.g.*, Robert W. Howarth, *Ideas and Perspectives: Is Shale Gas a Major Driver of Recent Increase in Global Atmospheric Methane?*, 16 BIOGEOSCIENCES 3033 (2019); Hiroko Tabuchi, *Halting the Vast Release of Methane is Critical for the Climate*, N.Y. TIMES (Apr. 25, 2021); *Emissions Return to Pre-Pandemic Levels in Nation's Largest Oilfield*, ENV'T DEF. FUND (Mar. 24, 2021).

Even beyond flaring, NASA satellites, drones, and other aircraft are now documenting formerly undetected, significant methane leaks from oil and gas production sites, tanks, pipelines, and processing plants. These methane leaks have not previously been included in the lifecycle GHG emissions associated with natural gas production. *See, e.g.*, Eric Roston, *Permian Study Finds Overproduction Leading to More Methane Leaks*, BLOOMBERG LAW (June 2, 2021); *Permian Methane Analysis Project*, Env't Def. Fund (website); Z.R. Barkley et al., *Analysis of Oil and Gas Ethane and Methane Emissions in the Southcentral and Eastern United States Using Four Seasons of Continuous Aircraft Ethane Measurements*, 126 JGR ATMOSPHERES (May 27, 2021) (finding that regulators are underestimating methane emissions from the U.S. oil and gas sector by 48%–76%). Moreover, data reported to EPA shows that methane emissions associated with oil and gas production vary widely across producers and geographic areas. *See Benchmarking Methane and Other GHG Emissions of Oil & Natural Gas Production in the United States*, M.J. BRADLEY & ASSOC. (June 2021); Hiroko Tabuchi, *Here are America's Top Methane Emitters. Some Will Surprise You*, N.Y. TIMES (June 2, 2021); Carlos Anchondo, *10 Companies Emit 36% of Oil and Gas Methane—Report*, ENERGYWIRE (June 3, 2021).

In 2016, the EPA published a final rule on methane emissions from new, reconstructed, and modified sources that required oil and gas companies to install technology to detect and fix methane leaks from wells, pipelines, and storage sites. *See* U.S. EPA, Oil and Natural Gas Sector: Emission Standards for New, Reconstructed, and Modified Sources, 81 Fed. Reg. 35,824 (June 3, 2016). This was in addition to regulatory action by the Bureau of Land Management (BLM) within the U.S. Department of Interior, which had published two rules that applied to oil and gas wells on federal public lands. *See* U.S. Dep't of Interior, Bureau of Land Management, Oil and Gas; Hydraulic Fracturing on Federal and Indian Lands, 80 Fed. Reg. 16,128 (Mar. 26, 2015); U.S. Dep't of Interior, Bureau of Land Management, Waste Prevention, Production Subject to Royalties, and Resource Conservation, 81 Fed. Reg. 83008 (Nov. 18, 2016). The excerpt below discusses the extensive litigation over the second of these BLM rules, often referred to as the "Waste Prevention Rule" or the "BLM Methane Rule."

WYOMING V. U.S. DEP'T OF INTERIOR
493 F. Supp. 3d 1046 (D. Wyo. 2020)

SCOTT W. SKAVDAHL, UNITED STATES DISTRICT JUDGE.

On November 18, 2016, the Department of the Interior (DOI), Bureau of Land Management (BLM) issued its final rule "promulgating new regulations to reduce waste of natural gas from venting, flaring, and leaks during oil and natural gas production activities on onshore Federal and Indian (other than Osage Tribe) leases" and "clarify[ing] when produced gas lost through venting, flaring, or leaks is subject to royalties, and when oil and gas production may be used royalty-free on-site." *Waste Prevention, Production Subject to Royalties, and Resource Conservation*, 81 Fed. Reg. 83,008 (Nov. 18, 2016) (the Waste Prevention Rule or Final Rule or Rule). Petitioners [Wyoming and other oil and gas producing states] contemporaneously initiated this litigation, contending the Rule represents unlawful agency action because it exceeds BLM's statutory authority and is otherwise arbitrary and capricious. . . .

During oil production, operators frequently dispose of the associated gas by venting or flaring, if the gas cannot be easily captured for sale or used on-site. Associated gas is the natural gas produced from an oil well during normal production operations that is either sold, re-injected, used for production purposes, vented (rarely) or flared, depending on whether the well is connected to a gathering line or other method of capture. In addition, emergency flaring or venting may be necessary for safety reasons. Venting is the release of gases into the atmosphere, such as opening a valve on a tank to relieve tank pressure. Flaring is the controlled burning of emission streams through devices called flares or combustors, releasing the byproducts of that combustion into the atmosphere. While venting or flaring is sometimes unavoidable, it is also sometimes done in the absence of infrastructure to transport the gas to market.

The DOI has regulated venting and flaring to prevent the waste of Federal and Indian natural gas since 1979 when it issued Notice to Lessees and Operators of Onshore Federal and Indian Oil and Gas Leases, which the Waste Prevention Rule purports to replace. NTL-4A prohibits venting and flaring of gas produced by oil wells, except when the gas is "unavoidably lost" as defined in NTL-4A and when the operator has sought and received BLM's approval to vent or flare. While unavoidably lost gas and gas vented or flared with BLM approval are exempted from royalty obligation, gas that is "avoidably lost"—that is, gas lost due to an operator's negligence or failure to comply with the law—is subject to royalties. NTL-4A also requires operators to measure and report each month the volume of gas sold, avoidably or unavoidably lost, vented or flared, or used for beneficial purposes.

In the decade prior to issuance of the Rule, oil and natural gas production in the United States, and on BLM-administered leases, increased dramatically. Domestic production from over 96,000 Federal oil and gas wells now accounts for 11 percent of the Nation's natural gas supply and 5 percent of its oil supply. In FY 2015, Federal and Indian leases produced oil and gas valued at $20.9 billion, which generated over $2.3 billion in royalties. BLM represents that this increase in oil production has been accompanied by "significant and growing quantities of wasted natural gas." . . . For purposes of the Rule, BLM considered data provided by the DOI's Office of Natural Resources Revenue (ONRR), evidencing that over a 7-year period (from 2009 through 2015), operators reported venting or flaring about 2.7 percent of the natural gas produced from both oil and gas wells on BLM-administered leases—purportedly enough natural gas to supply over 6.2 million households for one year, assuming all of that gas was "avoidably lost" and the existence of infrastructure to transport the gas to market. According to the BLM, the growing problem of natural gas lost on BLM-administered leases is also evidenced by a 318 percent increase in reported volumes of flared oil-well gas and an increased number of operator applications to vent or flare royalty-free (between 2005, 2011, and 2014, the number of applications per year went from 50, to 622, to 1,248).

While acknowledging that flaring is sometimes unavoidable, the BLM determined the majority of flaring on its leases results from the rate of new well construction outpacing the existing infrastructure capacity. The other situation resulting in substantial flaring of associated gas on BLM-administered leases is when capture and processing infrastructure has not yet been built out. Flaring in these circumstances may be due to insufficient information about how much gas will be produced or to an operator's decision to focus on near-term oil production rather than investing in the gas capture and transmission infrastructure necessary to realize a profit from the associated gas.

. . . In 2010, the DOI's Office of Inspector General and the U.S. Government Accountability Office (GAO) recommended BLM's regulations regarding the royalty-free use of gas be updated to take advantage of new capture technologies. The GAO estimated that the economically recoverable volume of natural gas being wasted through venting and flaring at oil and gas production sites on Federal and Indian lands represents about $23 million in lost royalties. The GAO determined that around 40 percent of the natural gas vented and flared on onshore Federal leases could be economically captured using currently available technologies. In 2016, the GAO issued another report finding that BLM's regulations failed to provide operators clear guidance on accounting for and reporting lost gas.

Concluding there is a "compelling need to update [NTL-4A's] requirements to make them clearer, more effective, and reflective of modern technologies and practices," BLM [issued the Final Rule] with an effective date of January 17, 2017.

The Final Rule prohibits venting, except in certain limited situations such as emergencies or when flaring the gas is technically infeasible. . . . [T]he Final Rule adopts a [ ] flexible capture-percentage approach, modeled on North Dakota's regulations, that requires operators to capture a certain percentage of the gas they produce each month, excluding specified volumes of allowable flared gas. Both the capture percentage and the flaring allowance were designed to phase in over a ten-year period. The Final Rule allows operators to choose whether to comply with the capture targets on a lease-by-lease, county-wide, or state-wide basis.

The Final Rule retains NTL-4A's distinction between avoidably and unavoidably lost gas—with royalties owed on the former but not the latter—but eliminates BLM's discretion to make unavoidable loss determinations on a case-by-case basis and instead lists twelve categories in which a loss is always considered unavoidable. Any gas flared in excess of the capture requirements is deemed an avoidable loss. The Rule also requires operators to measure and report the amount of gas vented or flared above 50 million cubic feet per day. For leaks, the Rule requires that all operators inspect equipment twice a year and timely repair any leaks found. It also requires that operators update old and inefficient equipment that contributes to waste and minimize gas lost from storage vessels and during well maintenance, drilling, and completion.

The BLM identified the costs of the Rule to "include engineering compliance costs and the social cost of minor additions of carbon dioxide to the atmosphere, resulting from the on-site or downstream use of gas that is newly captured." BLM measured the Rule's benefits as "the cost savings that the industry would receive from the recovery and sale of natural gas and the environmental benefits of reducing the amount of methane (a potent GHG [greenhouse gas]) and other air pollutants released into the atmosphere." BLM also identified "numerous ancillary benefits"— including improved quality of life for nearby residents "who note that flares are noisy and unsightly at night," reduced release of hazardous air pollutants, and reduced production of nitrogen oxides and particulate matter which can cause respiratory and heart problems—and estimated the Rule would produce additional royalties of $3–$14 million per year (depending on the discount percentage used). Overall, "the BLM estimates that the benefits of this rule outweigh its costs by a significant margin."

Petitioners contend the Rule is an attempt by BLM, under the pretense of regulating mineral waste, to regulate air pollution associated with oil and gas production, a problem squarely within the EPA's scope of authority and expertise. Congress expressly delegated authority to the States and the EPA to "protect and enhance the quality of the Nation's air resources so as to promote the public health and welfare and productive capacity of its population." 42 U.S.C. § 7401(b)(1). The Clean Air Act (CAA) provides that "[e]ach State shall have the primary responsibility for assuring air quality within the entire geographic area comprising such State[.]" *Id.* § 7407(a). . . .

The Mineral Leasing Act of 1920 (MLA) creates a program for leasing mineral deposits on Federal lands. Congress authorized the Secretary "to prescribe necessary and proper rules and regulations and to do any and all things necessary to carry out and accomplish *the purposes of [the MLA]*." 30 U.S.C. § 189 (emphasis added). "The purpose of the Act is to promote the orderly development of oil and gas deposits in publicly owned lands of the United States through private enterprise," *Geosearch, Inc. v. Andrus*, 508 F. Supp. 839, 842 (D. Wyo. 1981) (citing *Harvey v. Udall*, 384 F.2d 883 (10th Cir. 1967)), and "to obtain for the public reasonable financial returns on assets belonging to the public," *Mountain States Legal Found. v. Andrus*, 499 F. Supp. 383, 392 (D. Wyo. 1980). . . .

The Federal Oil and Gas Royalty Management Act of 1982 (FOGRMA), 30 U.S.C. § 1751, creates a thorough system for collecting and accounting for Federal mineral royalties. FOGRMA reiterates Congress' concern about wasted oil and gas: "Any lessee is liable for royalty payments on oil or gas lost or wasted from a lease site when such loss or waste is due to negligence on the part of the operator of the lease, or due to the failure to comply with any rule or regulation, order or citation issued under this chapter or any mineral leasing law." 30 U.S.C. § 1756. Like the MLA, FOGRMA contains a broad grant of rulemaking authority to achieve its objectives. 30 U.S.C. § 1751 ("The Secretary shall prescribe such rules and regulations as he deems *reasonably necessary to carry out this chapter*.") (emphasis added).

The terms of the MLA and FOGRMA make clear that Congress intended the Secretary, through the BLM, to exercise rulemaking authority to prevent the waste of Federal and Indian mineral resources and to ensure the proper payment of royalties to Federal, State, and Tribal governments. . . . The question here, then, is not whether the MLA and FOGRMA specifically grant BLM the authority to regulate venting, flaring, and equipment leaks, but rather whether these statutes unambiguously grant BLM authority to regulate oil and gas production activities *for the prevention of waste*. The answer to that question, largely undisputed by Petitioners, is "yes." "The [MLA] was intended to promote wise development of these natural resources and to obtain for the public a reasonable financial return on assets that 'belong' to the public." *California Co. v. Udall*, 296 F.2d 384, 388 (D.C. Cir. 1961).

The rub here, however, is whether the Rule, or at least certain provisions of the Rule, was promulgated *for the prevention of waste* or instead for the *protection of air quality*, which is expressly within the "substantive field" of the EPA and States pursuant to the Clean Air Act. The Intervenor-Respondents argue the Rule's ancillary benefits to air quality do not undermine its waste prevention purpose—to be sure, a regulation that prevents wasteful losses of natural gas from venting and flaring necessarily reduces emissions of that gas. The Court further agrees that the BLM is entitled to at least some level of deference in determining how best to minimize losses of gas due to venting, flaring, and leaks, and to incentivize the capture and use of produced gas. In doing so, the Federal Land Policy and Management Act (FLPMA) directs BLM to consider any impact to "the quality of . . . air and atmospheric . . . values." 43 U.S.C. § 1701(1)(8). While the statutory obligations of two separate agencies may overlap, the two agencies must administer their obligations to avoid inconsistencies or conflict. *See Massachusetts v. E.P.A.*, 549 U.S. 497, 532 (2007). . . .

Although the Rule's overlapping regulations themselves appear consistent with EPA regulations, the Rule has potential conflict and inconsistency with the implementation and enforcement provisions of the CAA. The Rule upends the CAA's cooperative federalism framework and usurps the authority to regulate air emissions Congress expressly delegated to the EPA and States. *See* 42 U.S.C. § 7401(a)(3) ("air pollution prevention . . . and air pollution control at its source is the *primary responsibility of States and local governments*") (emphasis added); 42 U.S.C. § 7407(a) ("Each *State shall have the primary responsibility* for assuring air quality within the entire geographic area comprising such State . . . .") (emphasis added). For example, the Rule recognizes compliance with the EPA's oil and gas production facility performance standards as compliance with the Rule; but no similar automatic compliance recognition exists for State, local, or tribal standards approved by the EPA. Instead, the Rule requires States and Tribes to request a variance from a particular BLM regulation, placing the burden on the States and Tribes to prove its already EPA-approved rules "would perform at least as well as the BLM provision to which the variance would apply, in terms of reducing waste of oil and gas, reducing environmental impacts from venting and/or flaring of gas, and ensuring the safe and responsible production of oil and gas." In doing so, the BLM disregards the States' "wide discretion in formulating [their] [implementation] plan[s]" under the CAA. *Union Elec. Co. v. EPA*, 427 U.S. 246, 250 (1976). . . .

Furthermore, although the stated purpose of the Rule is waste prevention, significant aspects of the Rule evidence its primary purpose being driven by an effort to regulate air emissions, particularly greenhouse gases. First is the Rule's apparent preference for flaring over venting. For waste minimization and resource conservation purposes, no difference exists between eliminating excess methane by venting it or flaring it—the same amount is wasted in either event. There is, however, a difference for air quality purposes. Emissions that occur through leaking and venting are transformed into different emissions when flared. For air quality agencies, the choice between venting or flaring is an opportunity to choose between different general sets of pollutants, based on comparative local and regional air quality concerns. Flaring methane changes it from a potent greenhouse gas with global impacts into nitrogen oxides, which can trigger localized air pollution concerns. Thus, the Rule's venting prohibition prioritizes global climate change over regional ozone control, without changing the amount of natural gas that is wasted. Regulation of "a broad array of air pollutants without inadvertently causing additional air quality concerns" is not a matter within the BLM's substantive field of expertise. . . .

Finally, the BLM's cost-benefit analysis is, perhaps, the most telling in revealing that the Rule is not independently justified as waste prevention measures pursuant to BLM's statutory authority. The BLM acknowledged the Rule "will require operators to incur costs to reduce flaring, replace outdated equipment, implement or contract for leak detection and repair programs, install measurement equipment, and administer these programs." BLM estimates the Rule would impose costs of about \$114–279 million per year or \$110–275 million per year, depending on the discount rate. It then considered the monetized benefits of the Rule, determining the "cost savings" to industry would be \$20–157 million per year. But BLM valued the environmental benefits from reduced methane emissions to be \$189–247 million per year. The BLM arrived at this value using estimates for the "social cost of methane" on a global scale. Thus, the Rule only results in a net benefit if the ancillary benefits to global climate change are factored in—without these "indirect" benefits, the costs of the Rule likely more than double the benefits every year. . . .

While the BLM can consider environmental impacts to the public lands when it chooses to regulate, there is nothing in any of the statutes empowering the agency to consider or work to address *global* climate change in the process. Absent the ancillary benefits monetized by the BLM, the Waste Prevention Rule is arbitrary and capricious, as it will cost likely more than double what it saves annually. . . .

NOTES AND QUESTIONS

1.   In *Wyoming v. U.S. Dep't of Interior*, Judge Skavdahl focuses heavily on BLM's alleged motives in enacting the Waste Prevention Rule separate and apart from the purpose stated in the rule itself. Do you find that focus

appropriate? If there are multiple motives behind a rule, should a court consider all of them in determining whether the rule is arbitrary and capricious?

2. The Waste Prevention Rule has had a long and tortured history. After the election of Donald Trump in 2016, Congress attempted to use the Congressional Review Act to legislatively repeal it, but it failed by three votes in the Senate. Soon after, the BLM under President Trump first postponed and then suspended the rule, but a federal district court in California found those actions arbitrary and capricious. That decision revived litigation pending in the Wyoming federal court that had been stayed while the Trump administration attempted to roll back the rule administratively, ultimately resulting in the decision excerpted above. For additional details, see *BLM Methane Waste Prevention Rule*, Regulatory Rollback, Harvard Law School Env't & Energy L. Program. As of 2021, the Biden administration was expected to enact a new rule to address venting and flaring on federal public lands. What advice would you give it on how to proceed?

3. Can you articulate precisely what Judge Skavdahl found wanting in the BLM's cost-benefit analysis for the rule? Is the judge's analysis of the social cost of methane consistent with regulatory or judicial assessments you've seen in earlier chapters of the book regarding the social cost of carbon? Should it be?

4. What should be the role of the federal government in regulating unconventional oil and gas? What can be most effectively regulated at that scale, and what should be addressed at state and local levels? In 2021, Congress used the Congressional Review Act to vacate the Trump administration's repeal of the Obama-era EPA's methane reduction rule discussed in both the text prior to Judge Skavdahl's opinion and the opinion itself. *See* Mike Lee & Carlos Anchondo, *Obama-Era Methane Rules Return. Are Lawsuits Next?*, ENERGYWIRE (July 1, 2021). If the EPA's 2016 methane reduction rules are reinstated, is there any reason for the BLM to impose its own rules to regulate the same emissions? For details on the Biden administration EPA's proposed methane reduction rules as of 2021, see Jean Chemnick, *Methane Rule to Eclipse Past Regulation, Including Obama's*, CLIMATEWIRE (Sept. 8, 2021).

5. As discussed in the text prior to the case excerpt, new satellite and other technologies now allow researchers to document significant methane leaks from the oil and gas production and transportation process that were previously invisible. As a result of this data, along with different modeling approaches, some scientists have concluded that EPA has underestimated methane releases from U.S. oil and natural gas production by 90% and 50%, respectively. *See* Joannes D. Maasakkers et al., *2010–2015 North American Methane Emissions, Sectoral Contributions, and Trends: A High-Resolution Inversion of GOSAT Observations of Atmospheric Methane*, 21 ATMOSPHERIC CHEMISTRY & PHYSICS 4339 (Mar. 2021); Carlos Anchondo, *Study: EPA Far Underestimates Methane Emissions*, ENERGYWIRE (Mar. 30, 2021). Should this cause policymakers at the federal and state levels to reconsider the role of

natural gas in the nation's energy mix? What should be the response of the oil and gas industry to these studies?

6.   The federal government is not alone in attempting to regulate methane releases from the oil and gas industry. As discussed in the Practice Problem at the end of this chapter, Colorado and New Mexico are two oil and gas producing states that have enacted stricter regulations governing flaring and other methane releases in recent years. *See, e.g.*, Mike Lee, *N.M. Finalizes Landmark Oil Methane Rules*, ENERGYWIRE (Mar. 26, 2021) (discussing rules in New Mexico and Colorado governing venting and flaring from oil wells in the state).

4.   THE ROLE OF STATE AND LOCAL REGULATION IN HYDRAULIC FRACTURING

Especially with federal regulations in flux, state regulation of a variety of aspects of unconventional oil and gas plays a crucial role in shaping how hydraulic fracturing paired with horizontal drilling will move forward. These laws focus on numerous aspects of operations and production, including both water pollution and methane emissions.

State approaches vary widely, and depending on their formulation, these laws face criticism at times from environmental groups, industry, and even government. Some states have even banned hydraulic fracturing paired with horizontal drilling entirely. For example, New York decided in 2014, after completing an extensive study, that it would no longer allow high volume hydraulic fracturing. In addition, complex federalism dynamics occur between state and local governments. States vary in how they resolve these conflicts. Compare, for example, the following Pennsylvania and Colorado Supreme Court cases in which local governments challenged state approaches to unconventional oil and gas development.

ROBINSON TOWNSHIP V. COMMONWEALTH OF PENNSYLVANIA
83 A.3d 901 (Pa. 2013)

CHIEF JUSTICE CASTILLE.

In this matter, multiple issues of constitutional import arise in cross-appeals taken from the decision of the Commonwealth Court ruling upon expedited challenges to Act 13 of 2012, a statute amending the Pennsylvania Oil and Gas Act (Act 13). Act 13 comprises sweeping legislation affecting Pennsylvania's environment and, in particular, the exploitation and recovery of natural gas in a geological formation known as the Marcellus Shale. The litigation proceeded below in an accelerated fashion, in part because the legislation itself was designed to take effect quickly and imposed obligations which required the challengers to formulate their legal positions swiftly; and in part in recognition of the obvious economic importance of the legislation to the Commonwealth and its citizens.

The litigation implicates, among many other sources of law, a provision of this Commonwealth's organic charter, specifically Section 27 of the Declaration of Rights in the Pennsylvania Constitution, which states:

> The people have a right to clean air, pure water, and to the preservation of the natural, scenic, historic and esthetic values of the environment. Pennsylvania's public natural resources are the common property of all the people, including generations yet to come. As trustee of these resources, the Commonwealth shall conserve and maintain them for the benefit of all the people.

PA. CONST. art. I, § 27 (the "Environmental Rights Amendment"). Following careful deliberation, this Court holds that several challenged provisions of Act 13 are unconstitutional, albeit the Court majority affirming the finding of unconstitutionality is not of one mind concerning the ground for decision. This Opinion, representing the views of this author, Madame Justice Todd, and Mr. Justice McCaffery, finds that several core provisions of Act 13 violate the Commonwealth's duties as trustee of Pennsylvania's public natural resources under the Environmental Rights Amendment; other challenges lack merit; and still further issues require additional examination in the Commonwealth Court. Mr. Justice Baer, in concurrence, concurs in the mandate, and joins the Majority Opinion in all parts except Parts III and VI(C); briefly stated, rather than grounding merits affirmance in the Environmental Rights Amendment, Justice Baer would find that the core constitutional infirmity sounds in substantive due process. Accordingly, we affirm in part and reverse in part the Commonwealth Court's decision, and remand for further proceedings consistent with specific directives later set forth in this Opinion.

I.   Background

The Marcellus Shale Formation has been a known natural gas reservoir (containing primarily methane) for more than 75 years. Particularly in northeastern Pennsylvania, the shale rock is organic-rich and thick. Early drilling efforts revealed that the gas occurred in "pockets" within the rock formations, and that the flow of natural gas from wells was not continuous. Nonetheless, geological surveys in the 1970s showed that the Marcellus Shale Formation had "excellent potential to fill the needs of users" if expected technological development continued and natural gas prices increased. Those developments materialized and they permitted shale drilling in the Marcellus Formation to start in 2003; production began in 2005.

In shale formations, organic matter in the soil generates gas molecules that absorb onto the matrix of the rock. Over time, tectonic and hydraulic stresses fracture the rock and natural gas (*e.g.*, methane) migrates to fill the fractures or pockets. In the Marcellus Shale Formation, fractures in the rock and naturally-occurring gas pockets are insufficient in size and number to sustain consistent industrial production of natural gas. The industry uses two techniques that enhance recovery of natural gas from these "unconventional" gas wells: hydraulic fracturing or "fracking" (usually slick-water fracking) and horizontal drilling. Both techniques inevitably do violence to the landscape. Slick-water fracking involves pumping at high pressure into the rock formation a mixture of sand and freshwater treated with a gel friction reducer, until the rock cracks, resulting in greater gas mobility. Horizontal drilling requires the drilling of a vertical hole to 5,500 to 6,500 feet—several hundred feet above the target natural gas pocket or reservoir—and then directing the drill bit through an arc until the drilling proceeds sideways or horizontally. One unconventional gas well in the Marcellus Shale uses several million gallons of water. The development of the natural gas industry in the Marcellus Shale Formation prompted enactment of Act 13.

In February 2012, the Governor of Pennsylvania, Thomas W. Corbett, signed Act 13 into law. Act 13 repealed parts of the existing Pennsylvania Oil and Gas Act and added provisions re-codified into six new chapters in Title 58 of the Pennsylvania Consolidated Statutes. The new chapters of the Oil and Gas Act are:

— Chapter 23, which establishes a fee schedule for the unconventional gas well industry, and provides for the collection and distribution of these fees;

— Chapter 25, which provides for appropriation and allocation of funds from the Oil and Gas Lease Fund;

— Chapter 27, which creates a natural gas energy development program to fund public or private projects for converting vehicles to utilize natural gas fuel;

— Chapter 32, which describes the well permitting process and defines statewide limitations on oil and gas development;

— Chapter 33, which prohibits any local regulation of oil and gas operations, including via environmental legislation, and requires statewide uniformity among local zoning ordinances with respect to the development of oil and gas resources;

— Chapter 35, which provides that producers, rather than landowners, are responsible for payment of the unconventional gas well fees authorized under Chapter 23.

See 58 Pa. C.S. §§ 2301–3504. Chapter 23's fee schedule became effective immediately upon Act 13 being signed into law, on February 14, 2012, while the remaining chapters were to take effect sixty days later, on April 16, 2012.

In March 2012, the citizens promptly filed a fourteen-count petition for review in the original jurisdiction of the Commonwealth Court, broadly requesting a declaration that Act 13 is unconstitutional, a permanent injunction prohibiting application of Act 13, and legal fees and costs of litigation. The citizens claimed that Act 13 violated the Pennsylvania Constitution, specifically, Article I, Section 1 (relating to inherent rights of mankind); Article 1, Section 10 (relating in relevant part to eminent domain); Article I, Section 27 (relating to natural resources and the public estate); Article III, Section 3 (relating to single subject bills); and Article III, Section 32 (relating in relevant part to special laws). . . .

II. Justiciability: Standing, Ripeness, Political Question

[The Court finds the claims justiciable.]

III. The Constitutionality of Act 13

. . . To describe this case simply as a zoning or agency discretion matter would not capture the essence of the parties' fundamental dispute regarding Act 13. Rather, at its core, this dispute centers upon an asserted vindication of citizens' rights to quality of life on their properties and in their hometowns, insofar as Act 13 threatens degradation of air and water, and of natural, scenic, and esthetic values of the environment, with attendant effects on health, safety, and the owners' continued enjoyment of their private property. The citizens' interests, as a result, implicate primarily rights and obligations under the Environmental Rights Amendment—Article 1, Section 27. We will address this basic issue, which we deem dispositive, first. . . .

Initially, we note that the Environmental Rights Amendment accomplishes two primary goals, via prohibitory and non-prohibitory clauses: (1) the provision identifies protected rights, to prevent the state from acting in certain ways, and (2) the provision establishes a nascent framework for the Commonwealth to participate affirmatively in the development and enforcement of these rights. Section 27 is structured into three mandatory clauses that define rights and obligations to accomplish these twin purposes; and each clause mentions "the people." . . .

Act 13 is not generalized environmental legislation, but is instead a statute that regulates a single, important industry—oil and gas extraction and development. Oil and gas resources are both privately owned and partly public, *i.e.*, insofar as they are on public lands. Act 13 does not remotely purport to regulate simply those oil and gas resources that are part of the public trust corpus, but rather, it addresses the exploitation of all oil and gas resources throughout Pennsylvania. Act 13's primary stated purpose is not to effectuate the constitutional obligation to protect and preserve Pennsylvania's natural environment. Rather, the purpose of the statute is to provide a maximally favorable environment for industry operators to exploit Pennsylvania's oil and natural gas resources, including those in the Marcellus Shale Formation. The authority to regulate the oil and gas industry in this context derives, therefore, from the General Assembly's plenary power to enact laws for the purposes of promoting the general welfare, including public convenience and general prosperity, rather than from its corresponding duties as trustee of Pennsylvania's public natural resources. The public natural resources implicated by the "optimal" accommodation of industry here are resources essential to life, health, and liberty: surface and ground water, ambient air, and aspects of the natural environment in which the public has an interest. As the citizens illustrate, development of the natural gas industry in the Commonwealth unquestionably has and will have a lasting, and undeniably detrimental, impact on the quality of these core aspects of Pennsylvania's environment, which are part of the public trust.

. . . Pennsylvania has a notable history of what appears retrospectively to have been a shortsighted exploitation of its bounteous environment, affecting its minerals, its water, its air, its flora and fauna, and its people. The lessons learned from that history led directly to the Environmental Rights Amendment, a measure which received overwhelming support from legislators and the voters alike. . . .

The type of constitutional challenge presented today is as unprecedented in Pennsylvania as is the legislation that engendered it. But, the challenge is in response to history seeming to repeat itself: an industry, offering the very real prospect of jobs and other important economic benefits, seeks to exploit a Pennsylvania resource, to supply an energy source much in demand. The political branches have responded with a comprehensive scheme that accommodates the recovery of the resource. By any responsible account, the exploitation of the Marcellus Shale Formation will produce a detrimental effect on the environment, on the people, their children, and future generations, and potentially on the public purse, perhaps rivaling the environmental effects of coal extraction. The litigation response was not available in the nineteenth century, since there was no Environmental Rights Amendment. The response is available now.

The challenge here is premised upon that part of our organic charter that now explicitly guarantees the people's right to an environment of quality and the concomitant expressed reservation of a right to benefit from the Commonwealth's duty of management of our public natural resources. The challengers here are citizens—just like the citizenry that reserved the right in our charter. They are residents or members of local legislative and executive bodies, and several localities directly affected by natural gas development and extraction in the Marcellus Shale Formation. Contrary to the Commonwealth's characterization of the dispute, the citizens seek not to expand the authority of local government but to vindicate fundamental constitutional rights that, they say, have been compromised by a legislative determination that violates a public trust. The Commonwealth's efforts to minimize the import of this litigation by suggesting it is simply a dispute over public policy voiced by a disappointed minority requires a blindness to the reality here and to Pennsylvania history, including Pennsylvania constitutional history; and, the position ignores the reality that Act 13 has the potential to affect the reserved rights of every citizen of this Commonwealth now, and in the future. We will proceed now to the merits.

1.   Section 3303

We begin by addressing the citizens' claims regarding the constitutionality of Section 3303 of Act 13 [prohibiting local regulation of oil and gas operations]. We recognize that, as the Commonwealth states, political subdivisions are "creations of the state with no powers of their own." *Fross v. County of Allegheny*, 610 Pa. 421, 20 A.3d 1193, 1202 (2011). Municipalities have only those powers "expressly granted to them by the Constitution of the Commonwealth or by the General Assembly, and other authority implicitly necessary to carry into effect those express powers." *Id.* Within this construct, the General Assembly has the authority to alter or remove any powers granted and obligations imposed by statute upon municipalities. By comparison, however, constitutional commands regarding municipalities' obligations and duties to their citizens cannot be abrogated by statute. Moreover, the General Assembly has no authority to remove a political subdivision's implicitly necessary authority to carry into effect its constitutional duties.

With respect to the public trust, Article I, Section 27 of the Pennsylvania Constitution names not the General Assembly but "the Commonwealth" as trustee. We have explained that, as a result, all existing branches and levels of government derive constitutional duties and obligations with respect to the people. The municipalities affected by Act 13 all existed before that Act was adopted; and most if not all had land use measures in place. Those ordinances necessarily addressed the environment, and created reasonable expectations in the resident citizenry. To put it succinctly, our citizens buying homes and raising families in areas zoned residential had a reasonable expectation concerning the environment in which they were living, often for years or even decades. Act 13 fundamentally disrupted those expectations, and ordered local government to take measures to effect the new uses, irrespective of local concerns. The constitutional command respecting the environment necessarily restrains legislative power with respect to political subdivisions that have acted upon their Article I, Section 27 responsibilities: the

General Assembly can neither offer political subdivisions purported relief from obligations under the Environmental Rights Amendment, nor can it remove necessary and reasonable authority from local governments to carry out these constitutional duties. Indeed, if the General Assembly had subsumed local government entirely by Act 13—it did not, instead it required local government essentially to be complicit in accommodating a new environmental regime irrespective of the character of the locale—the General Assembly could not eliminate the commands of Article I, Section 27. Rather, the General Assembly would simply have shifted the constitutional obligations onto itself. And those obligations include the duty to "conserve and maintain" the public natural resources, including clean air and pure water, "for the benefit of all the people." The Commonwealth, by the General Assembly, declares in Section 3303 that environmental obligations related to the oil and gas industries are of statewide concern and, on that basis, the Commonwealth purports to preempt the regulatory field to the exclusion of all local environmental legislation that might be perceived as affecting oil and gas operations. Act 13 thus commands municipalities to ignore their obligations under Article I, Section 27 and further directs municipalities to take affirmative actions to undo existing protections of the environment in their localities. The police power, broad as it may be, does not encompass such authority to so fundamentally disrupt these expectations respecting the environment. Accordingly, we are constrained to hold that, in enacting this provision of Act 13, the General Assembly transgressed its delegated police powers which, while broad and flexible, are nevertheless limited by constitutional commands, including the Environmental Rights Amendment.

2. Section 3304

Next, we address the Commonwealth's claims regarding the constitutionality of Section 3304, a provision that elaborates upon local regulation of oil and gas development in Pennsylvania. In regulating the oil and gas industry, the General Assembly exercises its constitutional police powers (to promote general welfare, convenience, and prosperity) but it must also exercise its discretion as trustee of the public natural resources (to "conserve and maintain" public natural resources for the benefit of the people), permitting changes to the corpus of the trust to encourage sustainable development where appropriate. . . .

We have explained that, among other fiduciary duties under Article I, Section 27, the General Assembly has the obligation to prevent degradation, diminution, and depletion of our public natural resources, which it may satisfy by enacting legislation that adequately restrains actions of private parties likely to cause harm to protected aspects of our environment. We are constrained to hold that Section 3304 falls considerably short of meeting this obligation for two reasons.

First, a new regulatory regime permitting industrial uses as a matter of right in every type of pre-existing zoning district is incapable of conserving or maintaining the constitutionally-protected aspects of the public environment and of a certain quality of life. . . . Protection of environmental values, in this respect, is a quintessential local issue that must be tailored to local conditions. . . . Oil and gas operations do not function autonomously of their immediate surroundings. Act 13 emerged upon this complex background of settled habitability and ownership interests and expectations.

Despite this variety in the existing environmental and legislative landscape, Act 13 simply displaces development guidelines, guidelines which offer strict limitations on industrial uses in sensitive zoning districts; instead, Act 13 permits industrial oil and gas operations as a use "of right" in **every zoning district throughout the Commonwealth,** including in residential, commercial, and agricultural districts. *See* 58 PA. C.S. § 3304(a), (b)(1), (5)–(9). Insofar as Section 3304 permits the fracking operations and exploitation of the Marcellus Shale at issue here, the provision compels exposure of otherwise protected areas to environmental and habitability costs associated with this particular industrial use: air, water, and soil pollution; persistent noise, lighting, and heavy vehicle traffic; and the building of facilities incongruous with the surrounding landscape. The entirely new legal regimen alters existing expectations of communities and property owners and substantially diminishes natural and esthetic values of the local environment, which contribute significantly to a quality of environmental life in Pennsylvania. Again, protected by their organic charter, these communities and property owners could reasonably rely upon the zoning schemes that municipalities designed at the General Assembly's prompt, schemes in which participation was mandatory and which imposed costs (for example, land use restrictions) upon participants, in addition to benefits. The costs, under the local schemes, presumably were rationally related to the scheme's benefits. For communities and property owners affected by Act 13, however, the General Assembly has effectively disposed of the regulatory structures upon which citizens and communities made significant financial and quality of life decisions, and has sanctioned a direct and harmful degradation of the environmental quality of life in these communities and zoning districts. In constitutional terms, the Act degrades the corpus of the trust. . . .

A second difficulty arising from Section 3304's requirement that local government permit industrial uses in all zoning districts is that some properties and communities will carry much heavier environmental and habitability burdens than others. . . . This disparate effect is irreconcilable with the express command that the trustee will manage the corpus of the trust for the benefit of "all the people." PA. CONST. art. I, § 27. A trustee must treat all beneficiaries equitably in light of the purposes of the trust.

Again, we do not quarrel with the fact that competing constitutional commands may exist, that sustainable development may require some degradation of the corpus of the trust, and that the distribution of valuable resources may mean that reasonable distinctions are appropriate. But, Act 13's blunt approach fails to account for this constitutional command at all and, indeed, exacerbates the problem by offering minimal statewide protections while disabling local government from mitigating the impact of oil and gas development at a local level. *See* 58 PA. C.S. § 3304(b)(2)–(4), (10)–(11). Section 3304 requires either that no "conditions, requirements or limitations" be imposed on certain aspects of oil and gas location or operations or that such conditions, requirements, or limitations be no "more stringent" than those imposed on other industrial uses in the municipality (relating to construction activities) or other land development in the zoning district (relating to heights of structures, screening and fencing, lighting or noise). Remarkably, Section 3304 then goes even further, as it prohibits local government from tailoring protections for water and air quality (*e.g.*, through increased setbacks) and for the natural, scenic, and esthetic characteristics of the environment (*e.g.*, through increased setbacks, screening, fencing, reduced hours of operation requirements) in the affected areas within a municipality. *Id.* Imposing statewide environmental and habitability standards appropriate for the heaviest of industrial areas in sensitive zoning districts lowers environmental and habitability protections for affected residents and property owners below the existing threshold and permits significant degradation of public natural resources. The outright ban on local regulation of oil and gas operations (such as ordinances seeking to conform development to local conditions) that would mitigate the effect, meanwhile, propagates serious detrimental and disparate effects on the corpus of the trust. . . .

For these reasons, we are constrained to hold that the degradation of the corpus of the trust and the disparate impact on some citizens sanctioned by Section 3304 of Act 13 are incompatible with the express command of the Environmental Rights Amendment. . . .

CITY OF LONGMONT V. COLO. OIL AND GAS ASS'N
369 P.3d 573 (Colo. 2016)

JUSTICE GABRIEL delivered the Opinion of the Court.

Hydraulic fracturing, commonly known as fracking, is a process used to stimulate oil and gas production from an existing well. *See* Patrick H. Martin & Bruce M. Kramer, *The Law of Oil and Gas* 14–15 (9th ed. 2011). Viscous fluid containing a proppant such as sand is injected into the well at high pressure, causing fractures that emanate from the well bore. The pressure is then released, allowing the fluid to return to the well. *Id.* The proppant, however, remains in the fractures, preventing them from closing. When the fluid is drained, the cracks allow oil and gas to flow to the wellbore. *Coastal Oil & Gas Corp. v. Garza Energy Tr.*, 268 S.W.3d 1, 7 (Tex. 2008). First used commercially in 1949, the process is now common worldwide.

As the briefing in this case shows, the virtues and vices of fracking are hotly contested. Proponents tout the economic advantages of extracting previously inaccessible oil, gas, and other hydrocarbons, while opponents warn of health risks and damage to the environment. We fully respect these competing views and do not question the sincerity and good faith beliefs of any of the parties now before us. This case, however, does not require us to weigh in on these differences of opinion, much less to try to resolve them. Rather, we must confront a far narrower, albeit no less significant, legal question, namely, whether the City of Longmont's bans on fracking and the storage and disposal of fracking waste within its city limits are preempted by state law.

Applying well-established preemption principles, we conclude that an operational conflict exists between Longmont's fracking bans and applicable state law. Accordingly, we hold that Article XVI [of Logmount's Home Rule Charter] is preempted by state law and, therefore, is invalid and unenforceable. We thus affirm the district court's order enjoining Longmont from enforcing Article XVI and remand this case for further proceedings consistent with this opinion.

In the fall of 2012, the residents of Longmont, a home-rule municipality, voted to add Article XVI to Longmont's home-rule charter. Article XVI provides:

> It shall hereby be the policy of the City of Longmont that it is prohibited to use hydraulic fracturing to extract oil, gas, or other hydrocarbons within the City of Longmont. In addition, within the City of Longmont, it is prohibited to store in open pits or dispose of solid or liquid wastes created in connection with the hydraulic fracturing process, including but not limited to flowback or produced wastewater and brine.

Later that year, the Colorado Oil and Gas Association . . ., an industry organization, sued Longmont, seeking a declaratory judgment invalidating, and a permanent injunction enjoining Longmont from enforcing, Article XVI. . . .

[The court proceeded to hold that "home rule" cities like Longmont may enact local regulations that supersede conflicting state laws in matters of local concerns but not in matters of statewide concern or in matters of mixed state and local concern. The court then held that regulations governing hydraulic fracturing were a matter of statewide concern.—Eds.]

The state's interest in oil and gas development is expressed in the Oil and Gas Conservation Act and the regulations promulgated thereunder by the Commission. The Act declares:

> It is the intent and purpose of this article to permit each oil and gas pool in Colorado to produce up to its maximum efficient rate of production, subject to the prevention of waste, consistent with the protection of public health, safety, and welfare, including protection of the environment and wildlife resources, and subject further to the enforcement and protection of the coequal and correlative rights of the owners and producers of a common source of oil and gas, so that each common owner and producer may obtain a just and equitable share of production therefrom.

§ 34–60–102(1)(b), C.R.S. (2015).

Pursuant to the Act, the Commission is empowered to make and enforce rules, regulations, and orders, § 34–60–105(1), C.R.S. (2015), and to regulate, among other things, the "drilling, producing, and plugging of wells and all other operations for the production of oil or gas," the "shooting and chemical treatment of wells," and the spacing of wells, § 34–60–106(2)(a)–(c), C.R.S. (2015).

The Commission, in turn, has promulgated an exhaustive set of rules and regulations "to prevent waste and to conserve oil and gas in the State of Colorado while protecting public health, safety, and welfare." Dep't of Nat. Res. Reg. 201, 2 Colo. Code Regs. 404–1 (2015). The rules and regulations define terms related to fracking, including "base fluid," "hydraulic fracturing additive," "hydraulic fracturing fluid," "hydraulic fracturing treatment," and "proppant," among others. Dep't of Nat. Res. Reg. 100 Series, 2 Colo. Code Regs. 404–1 (2015). They also regulate the fracking process. For example, Rule 205a of the Department of Natural Resources' Regulations, 2 Colo. Code Regs. 404–1 (2015), which is titled, "Hydraulic Fracturing Chemical Disclosure," requires operators to disclose substantial information about wells that they have fracked, including the chemicals used. *See also* Dep't of Nat. Res. Regs. 305.c(1)(C)(iii), 308B, 316C.a, 2 Colo. Code Regs. 404–1 (2015) (providing for additional reporting and notice of an intent to conduct fracking activities). Other rules and regulations govern the disposal of "exploration and production waste," including waste associated with the fracking process. *See, e.g.*, Dep't of Nat. Res. Reg. 603.h(2)(D), 2 Colo. Code Regs. 404–1 (2015) (prohibiting certain production, special purpose, and flowback pits containing exploration and production waste within defined floodplains).

The Oil and Gas Conservation Act and the Commission's pervasive rules and regulations, which evince state control over numerous aspects of fracking, from the chemicals used to the location of waste pits, convince us that the state's interest in the efficient and responsible development of oil and gas resources includes a strong interest in the uniform regulation of fracking. Article XVI, however, prevents operators [in Longmont] from using the fracking process even if they abide by the Commission's rules and regulations, rendering those rules and regulations superfluous. Thus, by prohibiting fracking and the storage and disposal of fracking waste, Article XVI materially impedes the effectuation of the state's interest.

Accordingly, we conclude that in its operational effect, Article XVI, which bans both fracking and the storage and disposal of fracking waste within Longmont, materially impedes the application of state law, namely, the Oil and Gas Conservation Act and the regulations promulgated thereunder. We therefore hold that state law preempts Article XVI. . . .

The citizen intervenors assert that the inalienable rights granted to citizens by article II, section 3 of the Colorado Constitution "reign supreme over any state statute." Accordingly, they contend that because Article XVI's fracking ban protects citizens' inalienable rights, no state statute may preempt it. We are not persuaded.

Article II, section 3 of the Colorado Constitution provides, "All persons have certain natural, essential and inalienable rights, among which may be reckoned the right of enjoying and defending their lives and liberties; of acquiring, possessing and protecting property; and of seeking and obtaining their safety and happiness." This provision protects fundamental rights from abridgment by the state absent a compelling government interest. *See People in the Interest of J.M.*, 768 P.2d 219, 221 (Colo. 1989) (noting that "as to adults, the rights of freedom of movement and to use the public streets and facilities in a manner that does not interfere with the liberty of others are basic values inherent in a free society," and describing these interests as "fundamental"). As the citizen intervenors concede, however, no authority supports application of that provision to the preemption analysis in this case.

Moreover, under the citizen intervenors' interpretation of the inalienable rights provision, no local regulation alleged to concern life, liberty, property, safety, or happiness could *ever* be preempted, and thus, such local regulations would *always* supersede state law. Such a result would arguably render the home-rule provision of our constitution, art. XX, § 6, unnecessary, and we cannot countenance such a result. *See Colo. Educ. Ass'n v. Rutt*, 184 P.3d 65, 80 (Colo. 2008) (noting that courts must avoid any construction that would render a constitutional provision either superfluous or a nullity).

The decision of the Pennsylvania Supreme Court in *Robinson Township v. Commonwealth*, 83 A.3d 901 (Pa. 2013), on which the citizen intervenors rely, is inapposite. In *Robinson Township*, 83 A.3d at 985, the Pennsylvania court struck down a state law prohibiting local regulation of oil and gas operations. In doing so, the court relied on a "relatively rare" provision in the Pennsylvania Constitution, the Environmental Rights Amendment, which, in part, established the public trust doctrine. *Id.* at 955–56, 962 (plurality opinion); . . . .

The Colorado Constitution does not include a similar provision, and the citizen intervenors have not cited, nor have we seen, any applicable Colorado case law adopting the public trust doctrine in this state. We therefore conclude that the inalienable rights provision of the Colorado Constitution does not save Article XVI.

NOTES AND QUESTIONS

1.   Why do the Pennsylvania and Colorado courts reach different results? What rights and interests do the courts balance? Does one approach seem more appropriate than the other, or do they simply reflect differences in state law? The courts of Pennsylvania and Colorado are not the only ones to address whether local regulation of hydraulic fracturing operations conflict with state law. Courts in Ohio, Louisiana, and New Mexico have issued decisions upholding state laws that preempt local regulation, while the New York Court of Appeals ruled against preemption of local law. *See, e.g., Energy Mgmt. Corp. v. City of Shreveport*, 467 F.3d 471, 475 (5th Cir. 2006) (applying Louisiana law); *State ex rel. Morrison v. Beck Energy Corp.*, 37 N.E.3d 128 (Ohio 2015); *SWEPI v. Mora Cty.*, 81 F. Supp. 3d 1075 (D.N.M. 2015); *Wallach v. Town of Dryden*, 16 N.E.3d 1188 (N.Y. 2014). Should the power to make such decisions be vested at the state level exclusively? Or also at the local level, even putting aside differences in state constitutions? What legal challenges might oil and gas operators bring to challenge New York's ban on hydraulic fracturing?

2.   In 2019, the Colorado legislature granted local governments the right to enact regulations that are "more protective or stricter than state requirements"; to regulate "the surface impacts of oil and gas operation in a reasonable manner"; and to regulate the siting of oil and gas facilities as well as water quality, vibrations, noise, traffic, and other impacts associated with oil and gas development within their jurisdictions. *See* Colorado SB 19–181; *Colorado's Sweeping Oil and Gas Law: One Year Later*, GIBSON DUNN (Apr. 30, 2020). Does this law change the outcome of the *Longmont* case? Why or why not?

3.   For more on the *Robinson Township* case, the Pennsylvania Environmental Rights Amendment, and subsequent cases involving the application of the Pennsylvania Constitution to hydraulic fracturing practices, see *Pennsylvania Env't Defense Found. v. Commonwealth*, 161 A.3d 911, 916–19 (Pa. 2017); John Dernbach et al., Robinson Township v. Commonwealth of Pennsylvania: *Examination and Implications*, 67 RUTGERS U. L. REV. 1169 (2015); John Dernbach, *The Potential Meanings of a Constitutional Public Trust*, 45 ENV'T L. 463 (2015). For further discussion of the integration of public trust principles into state constitutions and state statutes in the 1970s, see

Alexandra B. Klass, *Fracking and the Public Trust Doctrine: A Response to Spence*, 93 TEXAS L. REV. *SEE ALSO* 47 (2015); Alexandra B. Klass, *Modern Public Trust Principles: Recognizing Rights and Integrating Standards*, 82 NOTRE DAME L. REV. 699 (2006).

4.   Federal, state, and local are not the only relevant levels of government. Concerns about the limited federal regulation and adequacy of state regulation of hydraulic fracturing have at times led other stakeholders to take action. One example of such regulatory innovation is a 2010 decision by the Delaware River Basin Commission, a regional entity with a focus on regional water resources in New Jersey, Delaware, New York, and Pennsylvania, to promulgate regulations on hydraulic fracturing under its authority. This move was very controversial and led to challenges that were dismissed on jurisdictional grounds. *New York v. U.S. Army Corps of Engineers*, 896 F. Supp. 2d 180 (E.D.N.Y. 2012); *Senator Gene Yaw, et al. v. The Delaware River Basin Comm'n*, 2021 WL 2400765 (E.D. Pa., June 11, 2021). After ten years of additional analysis and study, the Commission (made up of the Governors of each of the basin states) voted to permanently ban fracking in the basin. *See New DRBC Regulation Prohibits High Volume Hydraulic Fracturing in the Delaware River Basin*, Delaware River Basin Comm'n (Feb. 25, 2021).

5.   Even when states or local governments enact new regulations to mitigate the environmental externalities associated with hydraulic fracturing, states have struggled with adequate enforcement. For instance, in a 2012 article, Professor Hannah Wiseman documented how oil and gas commissions in numerous states have struggled to maintain sufficient enforcement staff and resources to inspect the quickly growing number of new oil and gas wells and to take meaningful enforcement action in the case of environmental, health, and safety violations. *See* Hannah Wiseman, *Fracturing Regulation Applied*, 22 DUKE ENV'T L. & POL'Y F. 361 (2012). *See also* NATHALIE EDDY, EARTHWORKS, NEW MEXICO'S MOVING AHEAD: RESTORING THE OIL CONSERVATION DIVISION'S STRENGTH AND AUTHORITY (Jan. 2019) (report documenting how limited personnel, resources, funding, and regulatory authority have made it difficult for the state's oil and gas agency to address operator violations in the face of the rapid growth of oil and gas activity in New Mexico due to hydraulic fracturing); *N.M. Amends Rule to Prohibit Oil and Gas Spills*, ENERGYWIRE (June 14, 2021) (reporting on revised New Mexico rule prohibiting liquid waste spills from oil and gas operations, replacing rule that previously had only required reporting of spills, after data showing roughly 12,000 spills and releases between 2010 and 2020).

PRACTICE PROBLEM

You are advising the Governor of New Mexico regarding where she should focus her priorities in terms of regulation and economic development associated with oil and gas production in the state. In 2021, New Mexico became the second-largest oil-producing state and eighth-largest natural gas-producing state due to widespread use of hydraulic fracturing in the Permian Basin, which is located primarily in western Texas and eastern New Mexico. *See New Mexico Profile Analysis*, ENERGY INFO. ADMIN. (last updated Mar. 18, 2021); Heather Richards, *Biden Paused Leasing. Oil Boomed Anyway*, ENERGYWIRE (Jul. 13, 2021).

However, unlike Texas, the bulk of the increased production in New Mexico has taken place on federal public lands, rather than on private lands. You have seen an analysis showing that oil and natural gas production on federal lands in New Mexico brought in $1.5 billion in revenue and accounted for 18% of total state spending in fiscal year 2020. *See New Analysis: Oil and Gas on Federal Lands Provided $1.5 Billion to New Mexico Budget*, N.M. OIL & GAS ASS'N (Feb. 2, 2021). Much of this revenue is a result of royalties paid by oil and gas operators to the federal government, of which 50% goes to the states in which production is located under federal law. In the wake of President Biden's "pause" on new oil and gas wells on federal lands (discussed in Chapter 3), there is concern that development in the basin will shift more heavily to Texas, where shale oil resources are located on private lands, rather than public lands. Kevin Robinson-Avila, *NM Oil and Gas Industry Wary of Regulatory Future*, ALBUQUERQUE J. (Mar. 22, 2021). At the same time, one of the stated reasons for the pause was to evaluate whether to raise federal royalty rates.

While New Mexico has welcomed the additional revenues from increased oil and gas production, it is also concerned about the rapid increase in natural gas flaring from oil wells. Data shows that methane releases from the Permian Basin are three times the national average and 15 times larger than methane reduction targets set by industry. *See New Data: Permian Oil & Gas Producers Releasing Methane at Three Times National Rate*, ENV'T DEF. FUND (Apr. 7, 2020). In 2019, the New Mexico legislature enacted a law granting the state Oil Conservation Division of the Energy, Minerals, and Natural Resources Department enhanced authority to issue civil penalties against producers for violating provisions of the state oil and gas law. In 2021, the Oil Conservation Commission adopted new rules requiring the reduction of 98% of vented and flared natural gas from production wells and equipment, creating some of the strictest standards in the nation. *See* Oil Conserv. Div., N.M. Energy, Minerals & Nat. Res. Dept., http://www.emnrd.state.nm.us/OCD/rules.html (providing links to department rules and commission order explaining rules); Trent Jacobs, *New Mexico Regulators Move to End Flaring and Venting*, J. OF PETROLEUM TECH. (Mar. 29, 2021) (discussing new rules and comparing them to rules in other states). Likewise, New Mexico has also enacted an ambitious clean energy standard, illustrating its commitment to a transition away from fossil fuels, at least in the electricity sector.

The Governor has asked you for advice regarding priorities associated with future state regulation and investment relating to the oil and gas industry. However, she has also asked you to keep in mind the important role of the federal government in the oil and gas industry in the state, as well as the state's commitment to a clean energy transition. Based on the information contained in this Practice Problem, as well as the remainder of this chapter, please consider the following questions in connection with advising the Governor.

1.   To what extent does current state and local regulation of hydraulic fracturing seem adequate to address the oil and gas industry? What are the benefits and limitations of an approach to regulation in which state and local governments play the most significant role? Are there economic or environmental benefits for New Mexico associated with the federal government's enhanced role in the state's mineral production due to the large percentage of production on federal lands in the state? What are some of the drawbacks?

2.   What are the benefits and drawbacks of the Biden administration's pause on federal oil and gas leases in terms of production, royalty rates, and environmental externalities? One of the stated reasons for the pause in federal leasing was to allow the administration to consider "whether to adjust royalties associated with coal, oil, and gas resources extracted from public lands and offshore waters, or take other appropriate action, to account for corresponding climate costs." *See* EXECUTIVE ORDER ON TACKLING THE CLIMATE CRISIS AT HOME AND ABROAD, THE WHITE HOUSE (Jan. 27, 2021). What position should New Mexico take regarding these federal actions?

3.   In what areas of hydraulic fracturing regulation is a federal role most appropriate? To what extent should states cover these areas if the federal government is not inclined to regulate or is not allowed to regulate because of statutory restrictions or court intervention? How should federal regulation deal with state and local authority over land use planning?

4.   When should laws provide very specific standards and when is it appropriate for companies to be given more flexibility? What role does monitoring and enforcement capacity play in the answer to this question? What are the potential economic benefits and costs of New Mexico having some of the strictest venting and flaring laws in the nation?

C. OFFSHORE ENERGY DEVELOPMENT

Unlike hydraulic fracturing, which is governed primarily by state law, offshore energy development—both oil and gas exploration and offshore wind energy development—takes place primarily on the Outer Continental Shelf (OCS), which is subject to exclusive federal regulation with important input from affected coastal states. The materials that follow explain the federal regulatory regime that governs the OCS in the context of both offshore oil and gas development and offshore wind energy.

Congress set the boundaries between state and federal jurisdiction over submerged lands in coastal waters in 1953, in the Submerged Lands Act (SLA), 43 U.S.C. §§ 1301, *et seq.* The SLA established state jurisdiction over submerged lands within 3 nautical miles (3.45 miles or 5.6 kilometers) of the coastline except for Texas and the west coast of Florida, where the

SLA extends the states' Gulf of Mexico jurisdiction to 9 nautical miles (10.35 miles or 16.7 kilometers). Also in 1953, in the Outer Continental Shelf Lands Act (OCSLA), Congress defined the OCS as submerged waters beyond state jurisdiction and confirmed federal jurisdiction and control over the OCS. 43 U.S.C. §§ 1331, *et seq.* The OCSLA also sets forth the process for leasing and developing oil and gas resources in the OCS. The Bureau of Ocean Energy Management (BOEM) within the U.S. Department of Interior oversees leasing and other activities within the OCS. Despite the primacy of federal authority over the OCS, after the devastating Santa Barbara Oil Spill in 1969 (discussed in Chapter 3), Congress enacted the Coastal Zone Management Act (CZMA) in 1972 to provide states with additional oversight authority for offshore oil and gas drilling in the OCS. *See* 16 U.S.C. §§ 1451, *et seq.* Finally, in the Energy Policy Act of 2005 (EPAct 2005), Congress granted authority to BOEM to administer offshore wind leases in the OCS, thus placing a single federal agency in charge of leasing and administering both fossil fuel and renewable energy resource development in the OCS.

As you read the materials that follow, consider the three themes of energy law introduced in Chapter 1. Regarding regulation of markets, you will see that a complex array of statutes and regulations govern virtually every aspect of the production of offshore energy resources, creating both limits and opportunities with regard to demand, supply, and energy markets. As for federalism, when it comes to the OCS, federal law dominates through application of the OCSLA and EPAct 2005, but there remains a significant role for state regulation through the CZMA. Regarding a clean energy transition, political debates and litigation over the use of the OCS for energy development often center on the environmental externalities associated with continued offshore oil and gas drilling, as well as how to harness offshore wind resources to accomplish a clean energy transition. Across these themes, environmental justice issues also arise, most notably because the externalities of offshore oil and gas development, including major oil spills, have unequal impacts.

1. OFFSHORE OIL AND GAS LEASING AND PRODUCTION

In recent years, as hydraulic fracturing technologies have opened up vast resources of lower-cost onshore oil and gas development on both federal and nonfederal lands, the percentage of domestic oil and natural gas produced from the OCS has declined. In 2019, offshore oil and natural gas production constituted 15.6% and 2.6% respectively of total domestic oil and gas production, as compared to 2005, when production of oil and natural gas from the OCS constituted over 30% and 25% respectively of total production. *Compare* MELISSA N. DIAZ, CONG. RSCH. SERV., U.S. ENERGY IN THE 21ST CENTURY: A PRIMER 39 (Mar. 16, 2021) *with* THE

WHITE HOUSE NAT'L ECON. COUNCIL, ADVANCED ENERGY INITIATIVE 15 (Feb. 2006). *See also* LAURA E. COMAY ET AL., CONG. RSCH. SERV., FIVE-YEAR PROGRAM FOR OFFSHORE OIL AND GAS LEASING: HISTORY AND PROGRAM FOR 2017–2022 13–14 (Aug. 23, 2019).

Nevertheless, offshore oil and gas development remains a significant source of federal revenue, as well as an economic driver in many coastal states such as Louisiana and Mississippi. In FY 2019, offshore oil and gas leases constituted $5.57 billion in federal revenues, made up of monies collected from royalties, bonus bids, rents, and other sources. *See* DIAZ, *supra* at 39–41.

As discussed above, the OCSLA, enacted in 1953, sets out the process for the federal government to plan for and issue leases for offshore oil and gas drilling in the OCS. In 1982, Congress passed the Federal Oil and Gas Royalty Management Act, 30 U.S.C. §§ 1701, *et seq.* to ensure that offshore federal lands have proper accounting and enforcement mechanisms. Today, offshore energy development is managed by BOEM (described above); the Bureau of Safety and Environmental Enforcement (BSEE); and the Office of Natural Resources Revenue (ONRR), which manages the royalties and other revenues associated with offshore leasing. *See Nat. Res. Revenue Data*, U.S. Dep't of Interior. These agencies and the federal laws that govern them are explored in the excerpts below.

CENTER FOR BIOLOGICAL DIVERSITY
v. U.S. DEP'T OF INTERIOR
563 F.3d 466 (D.C. Cir. 2009)

SENTELLE, CHIEF JUDGE:

In August 2005, the United States Department of Interior (Interior) began the formal administrative process to expand leasing areas within the Outer Continental Shelf (OCS) for offshore oil and gas development between 2007 and 2012. This new five-year Leasing Program included an expansion of previous lease offerings in the Beaufort, Bering, and Chukchi Seas off the coast of Alaska. Petitioners filed independent petitions for review challenging the approval by the Secretary of the Interior (Secretary) of this Leasing Program on various grounds. . . .

The Outer Continental Shelf is an area of submerged lands, subsoil, and seabed that lies between the outer seaward reaches of a state's jurisdiction and that of the United States. 43 U.S.C. § 1331(a). The OCS generally extends from 3 miles to 200 miles off the United States coast. This action concerns a Leasing Program approved by Interior that includes a potential expansion of previous lease offerings in the Beaufort, Bering, and Chukchi Seas off the coast of Alaska. Each of these seas is home to a number of species of wildlife. For instance, the Beaufort and Chukchi Seas are home to two polar bear populations. The North Pacific right whale, an endangered marine mammal, is known to inhabit the Bering Sea. Bowhead whales are also known to feed and migrate through each of these seas. In addition, a number of other species of whale, seals, the Pacific walrus, and various seabirds are indigenous to these seas.

OCSLA establishes a procedural framework under which Interior may lease areas of the OCS for purposes of exploring and developing the oil and gas deposits of the OCS's submerged lands. *See* 43 U.S.C. §§ 1334, 1337; *see also California v. Watt (Watt I)*, 668 F.2d 1290, 1295–1300 (D.C. Cir. 1981). In order to ensure "the expeditious but orderly development of OCS resources," *Watt I*, 668 F.2d at 1297, OCSLA provides that Interior undertake a four-stage process in order to develop an offshore oil well. *See Sec'y of the Interior v. California*, 464 U.S. 312, 337 (1984). As we noted in *Watt I*, the leasing program's four-stage process is "pyramidic in structure, proceeding from broad-based planning to an increasingly narrower focus as actual development grows more imminent." *Watt I*, 668 F.2d at 1297. This multi-tiered approach was designed "to forestall premature litigation regarding adverse environmental effects that ... will flow, if at all, only from the latter stages of OCS exploration and production." *Sec'y of Interior*, 464 U.S. at 341.

First, during the preparation stage, Interior creates a leasing program by preparing a five-year schedule of proposed lease sales. 43 U.S.C. § 1344. At this stage, "prospective lease purchasers acquire no rights to explore, produce, or develop" any of the areas listed in the leasing program. *Sec'y of Interior*, 464 U.S. at 338. Second, during the lease-sale stage, Interior solicits bids and issues leases for particular offshore leasing areas. 43 U.S.C. § 1337(a). Third, during the exploration stage, Interior reviews and determines whether to approve the lessees' more extensive exploration plans. 43 U.S.C. § 1340. Interior allows this exploration stage to proceed only if it finds that the lessees' exploration plan "will not be unduly harmful to aquatic life in the area, result in pollution, create hazardous or unsafe conditions, unreasonably interfere with other uses of the area, or disturb any site, structure, or object of historical or archeological significance." 43 U.S.C. § 1340(g)(3). Fourth and final is the development and production stage. During this stage, Interior and those affected state and local governments review an additional and more detailed plan from the lessee. 43 U.S.C. § 1351. If Interior finds that the plan would "probably cause serious harm or damage ... to the marine, coastal or human environments," then the plan, and consequently the leasing program, may be terminated. 43 U.S.C. § 1351(h)(1)(D)(i).

The Leasing Program at issue has only completed its first stage—preparation of the five-year program under Section 18 of OCSLA, 43 U.S.C. § 1344. Under Section 18, the Secretary is required to prepare, periodically revise, and maintain "an oil and gas leasing program" that consists of "a schedule of proposed lease sales indicating, as precisely as possible, the size, timing, and location of leasing activity which he determines will best meet national energy needs for the five-year period following its approval or reapproval." 43 U.S.C. § 1344(a). The Secretary must prepare and maintain a leasing program consistent with several principles. First, the Secretary must ensure that a leasing program is "conducted in a manner which considers economic, social, and environmental values of the renewable and nonrenewable resources contained in the [OCS], and the potential impact of oil and gas exploration on other resource values of the [OCS] and the marine, coastal, and human environments." 43 U.S.C. § 1344(a)(1). Second, the Secretary must consider additional factors with respect to the timing and location of exploration, development, and production of oil and gas in particular OCS areas. These factors include, *inter alia:* a region's "existing information concerning the geographical, geological, and ecological characteristics"; "an equitable sharing of developmental benefits and environmental risks among the various regions"; "the interest of potential oil and gas producers in the development of oil and gas resources"; "the relative environmental sensitivity and marine productivity of different areas of the [OCS]"; and "relevant environmental and predictive information for different areas of the [OCS]." 43 U.S.C. §§ 1344(a)(2)(A), (B), (E), (G), (H). Next, Interior must ensure, "to the maximum extent practicable," that the timing and location of leasing occurs so as to "obtain a proper balance between the potential for environmental damage, the potential for the discovery of oil and gas, and the potential for adverse impact on the coastal zone." 43 U.S.C. § 1344(a)(3). Finally Interior's leasing activities must ensure that winning lessees receive "fair market value for the lands leased and the rights conveyed by the Federal Government." 43 U.S.C. § 1344(a)(4).

The Five-Year Leasing Program in this case was first developed on August 24, 2005. After developing and publishing a draft proposed plan, and reviewing commentary to that draft plan, Interior published a "Proposed Plan" and an accompanying draft EIS. Finally, Interior published its "Proposed Final Plan" in April 2007 along with its Final EIS for the approval stage of the Leasing Program. This was submitted to Congress and the President, and was later approved by the Secretary of Interior. In total, the Leasing Program has scheduled 21 potential lease-sales between July 1, 2007 and June 30, 2012 in eight areas of the OCS. Four of those potential leasing areas are in the Beaufort, Bering, and Chukchi Seas off the Alaska coast. At the time the petitions challenging the approval of the Leasing Program were brought before this court, Interior had not yet conducted any lease-sales in these regions. Since that time, however, Interior has approved one lease-sale in the disputed Alaskan sea areas, Chukchi Sea Lease-Sale 193, which occurred on February 6, 2008. Petitioner[s] challenged this lease-sale in the federal district court for the District of Alaska. . . .

Petitioners claim that Interior violated both OCSLA and NEPA because Interior failed to consider both the economic and environmental costs of the greenhouse gas emissions associated with the Program and the effects of climate change on OCS areas. . . .

[The court evaluated the NEPA climate change and baseline data claims and the ESA claims and found they were not ripe because of the multiple stage nature of the leasing program.—Eds.]

Petitioners raise two distinct but related OCSLA-based climate change claims. First, Petitioners argue that the Secretary violated sections 18(a)(1) and (a)(3) of OCSLA by failing to account for the environmental costs resulting from consumption of the fossil fuels extracted from the OCS. Second, Petitioners contend that Interior violated section 18(a)(2) of OCSLA because Interior failed to adequately consider climate change caused by consumption of these fossil fuels and the present and future impact of climate change on OCS areas as section 18(a)(2)(H) requires. To the extent these claims concern Interior's alleged failure to consider the effects brought about by *consumption* of oil and gas extracted under the Program, we hold that OCSLA does not require Interior to consider the global environmental impact of oil and gas consumption before approving a Leasing Program. Therefore, OCSLA does not require Interior to consider the further derivative environmental impact that oil and gas consumption has on OCS areas. Accordingly, Petitioners' OCSLA climate change claims fail.

Contrary to Petitioners' claims, the text of OCSLA does not require Interior to consider the impact of *consuming* oil and gas extracted under an offshore Leasing Program. Under Section 18(a) of OCSLA, Interior must prepare Leasing Programs so that "the size, timing, and location of leasing activity . . . will best meet national energy needs." 43 U.S.C. § 1344(a). Section 18(a)(1) states further that Interior must consider the values of resources "contained in the outer Continental Shelf," as well as "the potential impact of oil and gas *exploration* on other resource values of the [OCS] and the marine, coastal and human environments." 43 U.S.C. § 1344(a)(1) (emphasis added). Similarly, section 18(a)(3) states that "[t]he Secretary shall select the timing and location of leasing . . . so as to obtain a proper balance between the potential for environmental damage, the potential for the discovery of oil and gas, and the potential for adverse impact on the coastal zone." 43 U.S.C. § 1344(a)(3). We noted in *Watt I* that such a cost-benefit analysis of oil and gas extraction under section 18(a)(3) is satisfactory when an individual area's potential benefits are weighed against its potential costs. *See Watt I*, 668 F.2d at 1318. The Secretary therefore need only consider the "potential for environmental damage" on a localized area basis. And, under section 18(a)(2), Interior is required to determine the impacts of "exploration, development, and production" of oil and gas. As the statutory language and our precedent show, Interior's obligations under OCSLA extend to assessing the relative impacts of production and extraction of oil and gas on the localized areas in and around where the drilling and extraction occurred. Interior need not consider the impacts of the *consumption* of oil and gas after it has been extracted from the OCS. OCSLA therefore concerns the local environmental impact of leasing activities in the OCS and does not authorize—much less require—Interior to consider the environmental impact of post-exploration activities such as consuming fossil fuels on either the world at large, or the derivative impact of global fossil fuel consumption on OCS areas. . . .

Petitioners' consumption-related claims appear to stem from the flawed premise that, before Interior approves an offshore oil and gas Leasing Program, it must first consider whether it should extract oil and gas from the OCS at all. But Congress has already decided that the OCS should be used to meet the nation's need for energy. Indeed, OCSLA instructs Interior to ensure that oil and gas are extracted *from the OCS* in an expeditious manner that minimizes the *local* environmental damage to the OCS. *See* 43 U.S.C. § 1344. Interior simply lacks the discretion to consider any global effects that oil and gas consumption may bring about. Interior was therefore correct to point out in its EIS that the more expansive effect of oil and gas consumption is a matter for the Congress to consider "when decisions are made regarding the role of oil and gas generally, including domestic production and imports, in the Nation's overall energy policy." Consequently, it was unnecessary for Interior to consider the climate change effects brought about by the consumption of oil and gas—either as oil and gas consumption affects the global environment generally or the OCS areas specifically.

Interior's decision to limit its inquiry to the effect of the Program's *production* activities on climate change is consistent with its obligations under OCSLA, and was not error. Here, there is no doubt that Interior considered the effects of the Program's production activities on climate change generally, and the present and future impact of climate change on the local OCS areas. In the EIS, which Interior incorporated by reference in its Program approval, Interior estimated the total amount of greenhouse gas emissions that would result from leasing, exploration, and development in the OCS, and examined the cumulative impact of these emissions on the global environment. Interior also noted that potential impacts are "most pronounced in [the] Arctic Subregion," and could affect the areas of Alaska in which Petitioners assert an interest. Accordingly, Petitioners' OCSLA-based climate change claims fail. . .

Section 18(a)(2)(G) of OCSLA requires agencies to consider "the relative environmental sensitivity of . . . different areas of the outer Continental Shelf." 43 U.S.C. § 1344(a)(2)(G). In its efforts to comply with this requirement, Interior ranked the environmental sensitivity of various program areas in terms of only one factor: the "physical characteristics" of the shoreline of those areas. This ranking was based on Interior's use of the Environmental Sensitivity Index, developed by NOAA, which considered the sensitivity of different shoreline areas to oil spills, and ranked them on that basis. The study ranked each area on a scale of 1 to 10 (with 10 being a rating for an area most likely to be damaged long-term by oil spills). Petitioners contend that Interior's sole reliance on this study to measure the environmental sensitivity of the potential OCS leasing areas in the Leasing Program renders the Program improper. Interior counters that this court has stated that Section 18(a)(2)(G) "provides no method by which environmental sensitivity . . . [is] to be measured." *Watt I*, 668 F.2d at 1311. Accordingly, Interior argues that its adoption of the NOAA shoreline study to determine environmental sensitivity of OCS areas is a policy judgment that is entitled to substantial deference. . . .

Interior's interpretation of Section 18(a)(2)(G) is irrational. It was not based on a consideration of the relevant factors set forth therein. Section 18(a)(2)(G) states clearly that an agency must assess the environmental sensitivity of "different areas *of the outer Continental Shelf*" in order to make its determination of when and where to explore and develop additional areas for oil. 43 U.S.C. § 1344(a)(2)(G) (emphasis added). Based on this language alone, Interior's use of the NOAA study runs afoul of this provision because it assesses only the effects of oil spills on shorelines. Interior provides no explanation for how the environmental sensitivity of coastal shoreline areas can serve as a substitute for the environmental sensitivity of OCS areas, when the coastline and proposed leasing areas are so distant from each other. This interpretation runs directly counter to the statutory language. . . .

Our conclusion that Interior failed to properly conduct an environmental sensitivity analysis under Section 18(a)(2)(G) does not end our inquiry. We have consistently linked the adequacy of Interior's analysis under Section 18(a)(2) with its analysis under Section 18(a)(3). *See Watt II*, 712 F.2d at 599 & n. 75; *Watt I*, 668 F.2d at 1318. Section 18(a)(3) requires that, when preparing a leasing program, Interior select, "to the maximum extent practicable," the "timing and location of leasing . . . so as to obtain a proper balance between the potential for environmental damage, potential for the discovery of oil and gas, and the potential for adverse impact on the coastal zone." 43 U.S.C. § 1344(a)(3). . . . Though Section 18(a)(3) does not define specifically how Interior shall balance these three elements, *Watt I*, 668 F.2d at 1315, it stands to reason that a flawed consideration of Section 18(a)(2) factors hinders Interior's ability to obtain a proper balance of the factors under Section 18(a)(3). Interior's failure to properly consider the environmental sensitivity of different areas of the OCS—areas *beyond* the Alaskan coastline—has therefore also hindered Interior's ability to comply with Section 18(a)(3)'s balancing requirement.

Consequently, on remand, the Secretary must first conduct a more complete comparative analysis of the environmental sensitivity of different areas *"of the outer Continental Shelf,"* 43 U.S.C. § 1344(a)(2)(G) (emphasis added), and "must at least attempt to identify those areas whose environment and marine productivity are most and least sensitive to OCS activity." *Watt I,* 668 F.2d at 1313. Though Interior may ultimately conclude as a result of this additional analysis that the shorelines of the Beaufort, Bering, and Chukchi Seas are the areas that are most sensitive to OCS development, such a conclusion cannot be reached without considering the effects of development on areas of the OCS in addition to the shoreline. Once Interior has conducted its Section 18(a)(2)(G) analysis, Interior must then determine whether its reconsideration of the environmental sensitivity analysis warrants the exclusion of any proposed area in the Leasing Program. *See Watt I,* 668 F.2d at 1314. Finally, having reconsidered its Section 18(a)(2) analysis, Interior must reassess the timing and location of the Leasing Program "so as to obtain a proper balance between the potential for environmental damage, the potential for the discovery of oil and gas, and the potential for adverse impact on the coastal zone," as required by Section 18(a)(3). 43 U.S.C. § 1344(a)(3).

... In light of Interior's failure to properly consider the relative environmental sensitivity and marine productivity of different areas of the OCS under Section 18(a)(2)(G), and its derivative failure to strike a proper balance incorporating environmental and coastal zone factors under Section 18(a)(3), ... we vacate the Leasing Program and remand the Program to the Secretary for reconsideration in accordance with this opinion.

CALIFORNIA V. NORTON
311 F.3d 1163 (9th Cir. 2002)

D.W. NELSON, SENIOR CIRCUIT JUDGE.

Appellants (United States) granted "suspensions" of thirty-six oil leases offshore of central California pursuant to 43 U.S.C. § 1334(a)(1). The purpose of the lease suspensions was to extend the lives of the leases and to allow the lessees to "facilitate proper development of the lease[s]." 43 U.S.C. § 1334(a)(1). Without the suspensions, the leases would have expired and the lessees would have lost all production rights because the lessees had not begun production in paying quantities and the term of the leases had elapsed. *Id.*

Appellee (California) asserted authority to review the lease suspensions for consistency with California's Coastal Management Program pursuant to the Coastal Zone Management Act, 16 U.S.C. §§ 1451–1465. ... The United States refused to submit the lease suspensions to California for review, claiming that lease suspensions are not subject to review by California under the terms of the Coastal Zone Management Act. . . .

California filed suit in federal district court seeking to enjoin the lease suspensions until it was afforded the opportunity to review them. . . .

This case implicates California's ability to review and influence decisions of the federal government regarding oil drilling in federal waters off of California's coast. Our decision today necessarily involves a rather long and complex textual journey through an interwoven scheme of federal and State statutes and regulations. Before we embark, we briefly recollect the failures that these environmental protections are designed to prevent by providing for substantial State involvement in federal decisions concerning offshore oil drilling.

Five miles off the shore of the small beach town of Summerland, California, at 10:45 a.m. on Tuesday, January 28, 1969, crews on Union Oil Company offshore Platform Alpha were pulling the drilling tube out of well A-21 in order to assess their progress. Mud began to ooze up from the depths through the well shaft, signaling that something had gone wrong below. Within minutes, tons of mud spewed out of the top of the well propelled by a blast of natural gas. . . . The unlined walls of the well shaft gave way and oil poured into the surrounding geological formation under the sea floor. . . . The flow continued at thousands of gallons per hour for more than a week, spreading a tar-black patch seaward over eight hundred square miles of ocean. . . .

Then on the evening of Tuesday, February 4, the wind shifted and blew hard onshore, driving the oil into Santa Barbara harbor and fouling thirty miles of beaches up and down the coast. For weeks on end "[a] dense acrid stench clung to the shoreline as a force of 1000 men—many of them prisoners—pitchforked tons of straw onto the stained sand and murky tide to soak up the mess." *Great Oil Slick Cleanup—The 'Impossible' Task*, S.F. Chron., Feb. 10, 1969 at 2. The cleanup efforts proved largely ineffective against the mass of oil, and thousands of sea birds were killed along with seals and other marine mammals. *See Oil Slick Killing Off Wild Life*, S.F. Chron., Feb. 2, 1969 at 1; *Oil Thickens on Beach—'Months of Work Ahead'*, S.F. Chron., Feb. 6, 1969 at 1. By February 24, another well on Platform Alpha had blown out, and the oil-gushing fractures had spread over acres of ocean floor.

The nation was confronted with an environmental disaster of unprecedented proportions that might have been avoided but for a failure of federal oversight. A federal regulator had approved Union Oil's request to waive safety requirements that called for well shafts to be lined with hardened casing to prevent just the type of accident that occurred. . . .

In the aftermath of the spill, California Congressman John V. Tunney took to the well of the House to declare that "ill-planned offshore oil drilling" was a manifestation of "centuries of careless neglect of the environment [that] have brought mankind to a final crossroads," and that "the quality of our lives is eroded and our very existence threatened by our abuse of the natural world." 116 Cong. Rec. 498 (1970). President Richard Nixon personally viewed the damage and agreed that the Santa Barbara spill "frankly touched the conscience of the American people." *The Santa Barbara Oil Spill: A Retrospective* at 3.

As President Nixon aptly observed, the Santa Barbara spill changed the nation's attitudes towards the environment. Some would trace the current framework of environmental protections in substantial measure directly to the Santa Barbara spill. *See, e.g.,* Miles Corwin, *The Oil Spill Heard 'Round The Country',* L.A. Times, Jan. 28, 1989. Of particular relevance here, the federal Coastal Zone Management Act and California's Coastal Act followed in the wake of the spill and both provided California substantial oversight authority for offshore oil drilling in federally controlled areas. . . .

If a State determines that a proposed federal activity is not consistent with that State's Coastal Management Program and the United States disagrees, the State may seek mediation of the dispute, 15 C.F.R. § 930.44 (1999), or may seek relief in federal court, *see, e.g., Akiak Native Comty. v. United States Postal Serv.,* 213 F.3d 1140 (9th Cir. 2000). Alternatively, coastal States have the right to review any "Federal license or permit" required for activities that affect the coastal zone. 16 U.S.C. § 1456(c)(3)(A). . . .

In 1972 the voters of California approved the California Coastal Zone Conservation Act by popular initiative. Subsequently, the California legislature codified the protections of the initiative in the California Coastal Act of 1976. The California Legislature declared that the California Coastal Act was "to provide maximum state involvement in federal activities allowable under federal law." Cal. Pub. Res. Code § 30004.

Acting under its authority pursuant to the California Coastal Act, the California Coastal Commission developed California's Coastal Management Program, as contemplated in the federal Coastal Zone Management Act. The federal government approved California's Coastal Management Program. *Am. Petroleum Inst. v. Knecht,* 456 F. Supp. 889, 893–94 (C.D. Cal. 1978).

Thus, California is authorized by federal law to review specified federal activities for consistency with its Coastal Management Program. . . .

The term for off shore leases is set by statute at five to ten years. 43 U.S.C. § 1337(b)(2)(A) & (B). After the initial term of the lease elapses, the lease continues in effect so long as oil and gas are being produced in paying quantities or drilling operations are underway. *Id.* If production or approved drilling are not underway at the end of the term, the lease expires and the leaseholder loses rights to exploit resources in the lease area.

If the lessee is not able to begin production within the term of the lease, a procedure exists to avoid expiration of the lease and extend the lease term. These extensions are referred to as "suspensions." 43 U.S.C. § 1334(a)(1). The effect of a lease suspension is to extend the life of the lease and to allow the lessee to "facilitate proper development of a lease." *Id.* . . .

The thirty-six leases that are the subject of this litigation were issued between 1968 and 1984. They have not yet begun producing paying quantities of oil or gas and would have expired but for previous suspensions. The latest round of suspensions, which are challenged in this lawsuit, were issued to prevent the leases from expiring in 1999. . . . The oil companies paid the United States approximately $1.25 billion for the leases. The leaseholds are located between the Channel Islands National Marine Sanctuary and the Monterey Bay National Marine Sanctuary, which contain many species that are particularly sensitive to the impacts of spilled oil. . . .

In May of 1999, the lessees submitted requests for suspensions of all thirty-six leases. Shortly thereafter, California informed the United States that it had determined to assert its authority under the Coastal Zone Management Act to review the lease suspensions for consistency with California's Coastal Management Plan. The United States responded that California had no authority to review the lease suspensions because the lease suspensions in and of themselves did not have the potential to affect the land or water use or natural resources of California's coastal zone. Despite California's objections, the United States granted the suspension requests for the thirty-six leases without providing California an opportunity for consistency review. . . .

Section (c)(1) [of the CZMA] provides for consistency review for federal agency activities. Section (c)(3) provides for consistency review for federal licenses or permits. Sections (c)(1) and (c)(3) are mutually exclusive because section 1456(c)(1)(A) provides that an "activity shall be subject to this paragraph unless it is subject to paragraph (2) or (3)."

Under (c)(1) review, the federal agency makes a "consistency determination" and submits it to the State. Under (c)(3) review, the applicant for the license or permit prepares a "consistency certification," which is submitted to the State. . . .

The United States does not dispute that activities that will ultimately take place under the extended leases will affect the natural resources of the coastal zone. The United States also does not dispute that approval of lease suspensions is a federal agency activity within the meaning of the statute. However, the United States argues that reviewing the lease suspensions for consistency would be duplicative, because any activities that take place under the extended terms of the leases will themselves be reviewed for consistency when exploration plans or development and production plans are approved. The United States points out that any exploration activities must be preceded by submission of an exploration plan. 43 U.S.C. § 1340(e)(2). These plans are formal documents that must be submitted to California for consistency review. 16 U.S.C. § 1456(c)(3)(B); 43 U.S.C. § 1340(c)(2). Once oil or gas is discovered, a development and production plan must also be submitted before production commences and the development and production plan must also be submitted to California for consistency review. 16 U.S.C. § 1456(c)(3)(B); 43 U.S.C. § 1351(d). . . .

Congress did mandate that once an exploration plan or development and production plan is submitted to California and found to be consistent with California's Coastal Management Plan, the subsidiary licenses and permits needed to carry out the activities specifically described in the plan are not themselves subject to another round of consistency review. 16 U.S.C. § 1456(c)(3)(B). From this, the United States goes on to extrapolate that federal agency activities antecedent and prerequisite to exploration and development and production plans (i.e., the lease suspensions) could not logically be subject to consistency review because consistency review occurs once, and once only—at the exploration and development and production plan stage.

However, it does not follow that lease suspensions, which are not subsidiary to exploration and development and production plans, are not subject to consistency review. In fact, the same extrapolation used here by the United States—that because activities following exploration and development and production plans are not subject to consistency review, those activities preceding the plans aren't either—has been specifically rejected by Congress.

In 1984, the Supreme Court held that a lease sale (the original sale of the lease as opposed to the lease extensions at issue here) was not subject to consistency review by California. *Sec'y of the Interior v. California,* 464 U.S. 312, 343 (1984). In reaching this decision, the Supreme Court held that specific activities affecting the coastal zone would be reviewed at the exploration plan or development and production plan stage and that Congress intended to limit State consistency review to these later two phases of offshore oil and gas development. In 1990, Congress amended the statute specifically "to overturn the decision of the Supreme Court in *Secretary of the Interior v. California,* 464 U.S. 312 (1984), and to make clear that Outer Continental Shelf oil and gas lease sales are subject to the requirements of section 307(c)(1) [16 U.S.C. § 1456(c)(1)]." H.R. Conf. Rep. No. 01–508 at 970 (1990). In subjecting lease sales to consistency review, Congress has made it clear that the statute does not prohibit consistency review of federal agency activities that are not subsidiary to exploration and development and production plans. . . .

In determining that these lease suspensions are subject to review, we note that the leases at issue have *never* been reviewed by California. Because these leases were issued prior to 1990, when Congress amended the statute to make clear that lease sales are subject to consistency review, California was not afforded an opportunity to review the leases. These lease suspensions represent a significant decision to extend the life of oil exploration and production off of California's coast, with all of the far reaching effects and perils that go along with offshore oil production. As the Counties point out, all but one of the lease sales for these leaseholds predate the approval of California's Coastal Management Plan. One of the lease dates back all the way to 1968. Subsequent to the sale of the leases, the Counties have enacted policies regarding oil transportation that have in turn been certified by the California Coastal Commission. The leases have never been reviewed for consistency with these policies. The Environmental Groups point out that numerous other factors have changed since the leases were sold, including the expansion in the range of the threatened sea otter toward the lease area and the creation of the Monterey Bay Marine Sanctuary.

Based on the foregoing, we affirm the district court's decision that the suspensions of these thirty-six leases are subject to consistency review pursuant to 16 U.S.C. § 1456(c)(1)(A). . . .

We note that Congress specifically subjected lease sales to section (c)(1). Although a lease suspension is not identical to a lease sale, the very broad and long term effects of these suspensions more closely resemble the effects of a sale than they do the highly specific activities reviewed under section (c)(3). We also note that for some of the leases being extended new exploration plans will be issued and these plans will be subject to section (c)(3) review. For other leases, existing exploration plans will be revised, which may also trigger section (c)(3) review. Thus, section (c)(3) review will be available to California at the appropriate time for specific individual new and revised plans as they arise, and section (c)(1) review is available now for the broader effects implicated in suspending the leases. . . .

LAURA B. COMAY ET AL., FIVE-YEAR PROGRAM FOR OFFSHORE OIL AND GAS LEASING: HISTORY AND PROGRAM FOR 2017–2022
Cong. Research Serv. (Aug. 23, 2019)

Under the Outer Continental Shelf Lands Act (OCSLA), as amended, the Department of the Interior (DOI) must prepare and maintain forward-looking five-year plans—referred to by DOI as *five-year programs*—that indicate proposed public oil and gas lease sales in U.S. waters over a five-year period. In preparing each program, DOI must balance national interests in energy supply and environmental protection. The lead agency within DOI responsible for the program is the Bureau of Ocean Energy Management (BOEM). . . .

On November 18, 2016, then-Secretary of the Interior Sally Jewell submitted to Congress the third and final version of BOEM's oil and gas leasing program for 2017–2022. . . . The final program scheduled 11 lease sales on the OCS: 10 in the Gulf of Mexico region, 1 in the Alaska region, and none in the Atlantic or Pacific regions. . . . On January 4, 2018, the Trump Administration released a [draft proposed program] DPP for a five-year program for 2019–2024, which would replace the final years of the Obama Administration program. This DPP proposes a total of 47 lease sales during the five-year period, covering all four OCS regions. . . .

During development of the 2017–2022 program, U.S. offshore crude oil production was declining in absolute terms and as a percentage of total U.S. production. Offshore production volumes declined by about 12% between 2010 and 2015, whereas U.S. total crude oil production increased by about 73% over 2010 levels. Offshore natural gas production also fell—by nearly 50%—between 2010 and 2015, while during the same period, U.S. total annual natural gas production rose by more than 30%. The surge in total U.S. crude oil and natural gas production was the result of increased production of shale gas and shale oil in several unconventional onshore formations throughout the United States (e.g., Marcellus, Bakken, Permian Basin, and Eagle Ford). The onshore shale oil plays have lower production costs than the deepwater plays being explored and developed offshore. A low oil and natural gas price environment during the period of the program's development also contributed to softer demand for the acquisition of new offshore leases. Numbers of active and producing offshore leases declined between 2010 and 2015, and the Energy Information Administration (EIA) anticipated lower domestic investment in oil and gas projects over the 2015–2020 period. . . .

The Gulf of Mexico is the most mature BOEM region, with "the most abundant proven and estimated oil and gas resources, broad industry interest, and well-developed infrastructure." The region accounts for about 97% of all U.S. offshore and gas production. Also, the Central and Western Gulf states (Louisiana, Texas, Mississippi, and Alabama) are supportive of offshore oil and gas activities. For all these reasons, the majority of the lease sales in the 2017–2022 program, as in previous programs, were scheduled in the Gulf region (10 of 11 proposed sales). . . .

Interest in exploring for offshore oil and gas in the Alaska region of the U.S. OCS has grown as the region sees decreases in the areal extent of summer polar ice, allowing for a longer drilling season. Recent estimates of substantial undiscovered oil and gas resources in Arctic waters have also contributed to the increased interest. However, the region's severe weather and perennial sea ice, and its lack of infrastructure to extract and transport offshore oil and gas, continue to pose challenges to new exploration. Among 15 BOEM planning areas in the region, the Beaufort and Chukchi Seas are the only two areas with existing federal leases, and only the Beaufort Sea has any producing wells in federal waters (from a joint federal-state unit). Stakeholders including the state of Alaska, as well as some Members of Congress, seek to expand offshore oil and gas activities in the region. Other Members of Congress as well as some environmental groups oppose offshore oil and gas drilling in the Arctic, due to concerns about potential oil spills and about the possible contributions of these activities to climate change. . . .

The final program for 2017–2022 excluded a lease sale in the Atlantic region that had been proposed in the DPP version of the program. If conducted, it would have been the first offshore oil and gas lease sale in the Atlantic since 1983. The lack of oil and gas activity in the Atlantic region in the past 30 years was due in part to congressional bans on Atlantic leasing imposed in annual Interior appropriations acts from FY1983 to FY2008, along with presidential moratoria on offshore leasing in the region during those years. Starting with FY2009, Congress no longer included an Atlantic leasing moratorium in annual appropriations acts. In 2008, President George W. Bush also removed the long-standing administrative withdrawal for the region. These changes meant that lease sales could now potentially be conducted for the Atlantic. However, no Atlantic lease sale has taken place in the intervening years. . . .

For both the DPP and [proposed program] PP versions of the 2017–2022 program, BOEM analyzed of a variety of factors for the Atlantic region under Section 18 of the OCSLA. These factors included the region's resource potential and infrastructure needs, ecological and safety concerns, competing uses of the areas—especially by the Department of Defense and the National Aeronautics and Space Administration (NASA)—and state and local attitudes toward drilling, among others. . . .

BOEM further cited the broader U.S. energy situation as a factor in its decision not to hold an Atlantic lease sale in the 2017–2022 period. The agency observed that the increases over the past decade in onshore oil and gas production have made national energy needs less pressing. BOEM stated that "domestic oil and gas production will remain strong without the additional production from a potential lease sale in the Atlantic." . . .

Like other recent five-year programs, the 2017–2022 program scheduled no lease sales for the Pacific region. No federal oil and gas lease sales have been held for the region since 1984, although some active leases with production remain in the Southern California planning area. Like the Atlantic region, the Pacific region was subject to congressional and presidential leasing moratoria for most of the past 30 years. Although these restrictions were lifted in FY2009, the governors of California, Oregon, and

Washington continue to oppose offshore oil and gas leasing in the region. . . .

NOTES AND QUESTIONS

1.   As described in the Comay excerpt, what aspects of the Obama administration's approach to leasing did the Trump administration attempt to change? What were the potential economic and environmental implications of that policy shift?

2.   As referenced in the Comay excerpt, in early 2018, U.S. Secretary of the Interior Ryan Zinke announced a new five-year leasing plan that significantly changed how much of the Outer Continental Shelf would be available for oil and gas leasing—from 94% off limits to 90% available. After Florida objected to the proposed plan and was granted an exemption, other states asked to be exempt as well. The Trump administration ultimately did not follow through on its expanded leasing program and the Biden administration does not plan to pursue it. Why might the Trump administration have backed away after publicly announcing its plan to open all Atlantic and Pacific waters to offshore oil and gas development? Should states be able to obtain blanket exemptions from oil and gas development off their shores? What are the arguments in favor? Against? Do you feel the same way about states or local governments that may want to ban or severely limit onshore wind or solar farms? Why or why not?

3.   In *Center for Biological Diversity v. U.S. Dep't of Interior*, Judge Sentelle declares that the Interior Department does not have the discretion to consider the impacts of oil and gas consumption in making leasing decisions, and thus need not evaluate that information as part of the NEPA process. On what grounds does he reach that conclusion? In light of that analysis, can a President issue an executive order imposing a moratorium on oil and gas leasing in the OCS? If so, on what grounds? If not, why not? *See* EXECUTIVE ORDER ON TACKLING THE CLIMATE CRISIS AT HOME AND ABROAD § 208 (Jan. 27, 2021) ("To the extent consistent with applicable law, the Secretary of the Interior shall pause new oil and natural gas leases on public lands or in offshore waters pending completion of a comprehensive review and reconsideration of Federal oil and gas permitting and leasing practices in light of the Secretary of the Interior's broad stewardship responsibilities over the public lands and in offshore waters, including potential climate and other impacts associated with oil and gas activities on public lands or in offshore waters.").

4.   The *California v. Norton* excerpt illustrates how Congress created a role for states to provide input into federal oil and gas leasing and permitting in the OCS through the enactment of the CZMA. Why might Congress have provided states with the ability to review and object to resource development that the federal government has already determined is in the national interest?

Note that under the CZMA, states do not have true "veto" power over federal actions and approvals in the OCS. Even if a state finds a federal action is not consistent with its approved coastal management plan, the Secretary of Commerce can override a state's objection if it finds that the project is in fact consistent with the coastal management plan or finds that the proposed action is necessary for national security. For more information on the CZMA, see EVA LIPIEC, CONG. RSCH. SERV., COASTAL ZONE MANAGEMENT ACT (CZMA): OVERVIEW AND ISSUES FOR CONGRESS (Jan. 15, 2019).

2. THE PROMISE AND PERILS OF DEEPWATER DRILLING

Offshore drilling has evolved over the past two decades. Ultra-deepwater drilling—at depths of over 1,500 meters—barely existed prior to the early 2000s, because the technological challenges were simply too daunting. Now, companies are increasingly accessing the large quantities of oil located in ultra-deep locations, where drilling often takes place a mile below the surface. *See, e.g., Global Deepwater Production Hits 10 Million BOE/D*, J. OF PETROLEUM TECH. (Dec. 29, 2019) (figure showing increasing depths of deepwater drilling over time); *Offshore Oil Production in Deepwater and Ultra-Deepwater is Increasing*, ENERGY INFO. ADMIN. (Oct. 28, 2016) (graphs showing growth in deepwater and ultra-deepwater drilling in Brazil, United States, Norway and rest of the world between 2005 and 2015).

The following excerpt, prepared by Curry Hagerty and Jonathan Ramseur for Congress in the aftermath of the BP *Deepwater Horizon* oil spill, describes the expansion of deepwater and ultra-deepwater drilling, the technologies that make it possible, and the regulations that attempt to minimize its risks.

CURRY L. HAGERTY & JONATHAN L. RAMSEUR, DEEPWATER HORIZON OIL SPILL: SELECTED ISSUES FOR CONGRESS
Cong. Rsch. Serv. (July 30, 2010)

On April 20, 2010, the Deepwater Horizon oil drilling rig—under contract to BP, the leaseholder of the tract approximately 50 miles offshore of Louisiana—was nearing completion of a deepwater oil well when an explosion occurred. An apparent equipment failure, perhaps of the blowout protector, at the wellhead released oil and natural gas; explosions and fire on the oil rig killed 11 of the crew, and the rig sank within days. In the aftermath, the oil spill became the largest in U.S. waters. . . .

Setting: Oil and Gas Recovery in the Gulf of Mexico

Sediments buried deep below the seafloor in the Gulf of Mexico host large quantities of oil and gas that have been the target of exploration activities for decades. Most of the undiscovered oil and gas on the U.S. outer continental shelf (OCS) is thought to occur in the Gulf, particularly in the central and western regions. The central and western Gulf account for about 48% of the undiscovered technically recoverable resource (UTRR) for oil and about 50% of the UTRR for natural gas in the entire U.S. OCS, according to the Department of the Interior. (In comparison, Alaska accounts for about 31% of the UTRR for oil and gas in the OCS.)

Recent attention has focused on oil and gas resources underlying deep water in the Gulf (i.e., deeper than 1,000 feet), because that is where the largest resource potential exists and where the majority of OCS leases are held. Since 2006, there has been a 44% increase in proven deepwater discoveries in the Gulf, even though most of the deepwater leases are as yet undrilled. (For example, 272 of nearly 1,900 ultra-deepwater leases— those at a water depth greater than 5,000 feet—were drilled between 1996 and 2007.) Deepwater and ultra-deepwater exploration and development have been the focus of OCS oil and gas development in recent years, and the potential for new and large discoveries in that part of the Gulf has been viewed as key to slowing or stopping the decline in OCS oil and gas reserves. . . .

Offshore Oil and Gas Drilling Technology

In comparison with nearshore oil and gas activities, deepwater and ultra-deepwater exploration and production require technologies that can withstand high pressures and low temperatures at the seafloor, and require the operator to control the process remotely from a surface vessel thousands of feet above the actual well. Seawater temperatures are lower in these waters (for example, at 5,000 feet deep in the Gulf, the seafloor water temperature is about 40°F, or 4.4°C); and pressures are greater (at 5,000 feet deep the seafloor pressure is about 2,500 psi). Consequently, equipment and operations at the seafloor are accessible only by remotely operated vehicles (ROVs). Drilling technologies built to withstand the harsher conditions in deep water and ultradeep water are complicated, difficult to repair, and expensive. In addition, long lengths of pipe, or marine "riser," extending from the seafloor to the drill rig, are needed, requiring a large and complex surface platform to conduct operations through the longer pipe. One of the most common types of drilling platforms for deep water and ultra-deep water is a semisubmersible rig, which has an upper and lower hull. During the drilling operation, the lower hull is filled with water, partially submerging the rig but leaving the upper hull floating above the drill site. Transocean's Deepwater Horizon rig was a semisubmersible platform, kept in place above the drill site by a dynamic positioning system (i.e., not permanently anchored to the seafloor) and connected to the well by the marine riser.

During drilling operations, the drill bit and drill pipe (or drill string) extend through the riser from the drill platform and through a subsea drilling template—essentially a large metal box embedded in the seafloor—into the marine sediments and rocks down to the hydrocarbon-bearing zone. A special fluid called drilling mud (a mixture of water, clay, barite, and other materials) is circulated down to the drill bit and back up to the drilling platform. The drilling mud, which has higher viscosity and density than water, serves several purposes: it lubricates the drill bit, helps convey rock cuttings from the drill bit back to the surface, and exerts a column of weight down the hole to control pressure against a possible blowout. A blowout can occur if the subterranean pressure encountered down the hole exceeds the pressure exerted by the weight of the drill assembly and drilling mud. The Deepwater Horizon rig experienced a blowout on April 20, 2010, and the role of the drilling fluid is under investigation.

Drilling a deepwater or ultra-deepwater well is a multi-step process. At different stages the drill string is removed and steel casing is inserted into the wellbore, telescoping down from the largest-diameter casing at the top of the well to the smallest diameter at the bottom. Casing serves, among other things, to stabilize the wellbore, prevent the formation from caving in, maintain control of fluid pressure, and prevent crossflow of fluids from one part of the formation to another. The bottommost interval of casing, usually called the production casing, is inserted through the interval in the formation containing hydrocarbons that the operator wishes to produce. The casing is cemented in place over various intervals; cement is injected between the well casing and the surrounding rock. In addition, cement may be injected into intervals of the casing itself when the well is to be temporarily or permanently plugged. At the Deepwater Horizon well, Halliburton (as a contractor for BP) had finished cementing the final production casing string about 20 hours before the blowout on April 20, according to congressional testimony.

As a last line of defense against a blowout, a blowout preventer (BOP) is installed at the seafloor and connected to the marine riser. The BOP is essentially a system of valves designed to be closed in the event of anomalous wellbore pressure (such pressure is sometimes referred to as a "kick"). At the depth and pressures encountered by the Deepwater Horizon well, BOEMRE/MMS regulations require at least four such valves, or rams, which must be remote-controlled and hydraulically operated during offshore operations. During the Deepwater Horizon blowout, all of the rams on the BOP failed to close properly.

BOPs can have backup systems that would attempt to engage the rams in case of loss of direct communication to the drilling vessel at the surface. One type of backup system, referred to as a "deadman switch," is intended to operate automatically if communication to the surface is disrupted. A second type of backup system, referred to as an "autoshear," would automatically activate one of the rams if the lower marine riser pipe disconnected. Another form of backup system includes the use of remotely operated vehicles (ROVs), controlled from the surface, which can operate control panels on the BOP itself at the seafloor. In the Deepwater Horizon incident, the BOP was reportedly equipped with a deadman switch and an autoshear device, and ROVs were used to attempt to activate the BOP after the blowout occurred. These systems appear to have failed to fully engage the BOP.

NOTES AND QUESTIONS

1.   A 2015 Congressional Research Service report by Jonathan Ramseur summarizes the BP *Deepwater Horizon* initial spill response:

> In the wake of the explosion of the Deepwater Horizon offshore drilling rig in the Gulf of Mexico on April 20, 2010, federal agencies, state and local government agencies, and responsible parties faced an unprecedented challenge. An oil discharge continued for 87 days, resulting in the largest ever oil spill in U.S. waters.
>
> Led by the U.S. Coast Guard, response activities were extensive for several years but have diminished substantially:
>
> - At the height of operations (summer of 2010), response personnel numbered over 47,000.
>
> - As of April 2015, 30 response personnel, including federal officials and civilians, are working on activities related to the Deepwater Horizon incident.
>
> - In February 2015, a Coast Guard memorandum announced that in March 2015, the Gulf Coast Incident Management Team (GCIMT) would "transition from Phase III (Operations) . . . and reconstitute as a Phase IV Documentation Team." As part of that transition, Coast Guard field unit commanders would respond to reports of oil spills in their respective areas of responsibility.
>
> As one of the responsible parties, BP has spent over $14 billion in cleanup operations. In addition, BP has paid over $15 billion to the federal government, state and local governments, and private parties for economic claims and other expenses, including reimbursements for response costs related to the oil spill. BP and other responsible parties have agreed to civil and/or criminal settlements with the Department of Justice (DOJ). Settlements from various parties, to date, total almost $6 billion. BP's potential civil penalties under the Clean Water Act (CWA), which could be considerable, are not yet determined.

JONATHAN L. RAMSEUR, CONG. RSCH. SERV., DEEPWATER HORIZON OIL SPILL: RECENT ACTIVITIES AND ONGOING DEVELOPMENTS (Apr. 17, 2015). In 2016, BP entered into a settlement agreement with the federal government, five Gulf states, and affected local governments for $20.8 billion—the largest environmental damages settlement in U.S. history. The settlement includes amounts for civil penalties, natural resources damages, and economic damages.

2.   Under the Oil Pollution Act, several federal agencies, states, and tribes were designated trustees to both evaluate spill impacts and develop and implement a restoration plan. *See Trustees*, Gulf Spill Restoration. The trustees produced a comprehensive assessment of affected natural resources and developed a programmatic restoration plan, which was funded by up to $8.8 billion from the settlement with BP. *See* DEEPWATER HORIZON OIL SPILL: FINAL PROGRAMMATIC DAMAGE ASSESSMENT AND RESTORATION PLAN AND FINAL PROGRAMMATIC ENVIRONMENTAL IMPACT STATEMENT (Feb. 2016). For an evaluation of post-spill response actions and reforms ten years after the disaster, see Lisa Friedman, *Ten Years After Deepwater Horizon, U.S. Is Still Vulnerable to Catastrophic Spills*, N.Y. TIMES (Apr. 19, 2020); Eric L. Pulster et al., *A First Comprehensive Baseline of Hydrocarbon Pollution in Gulf of Mexico Fishes*, 10 SCI. REPORTS 1 (2020).

3.   The impacts of the BP *Deepwater Horizon* oil spill, like those of other major oil spills, were not equally distributed. For an analysis of the environmental justice concerns, including with respect to the spill response, compensation, and workers, see Hari M. Osofsky et al., *Environmental Justice and the BP Deepwater Horizon Oil Spill*, 20 N.Y.U. ENV'T L.J. 99 (2012).

4.   As climate change make the Arctic more accessible for deepwater drilling, major questions arise about how to drill safely in that environment, especially in the aftermath of the BP *Deepwater Horizon* oil spill. A 2014 report by the Brookings Energy Security Initiative describes these issues:

> First, climate change is opening new regions of the Arctic for commercial development. Second, not only is there a strong prospect for extensive oil and gas discoveries, but there is also growing commercial interest and activity in the region's hydrocarbon resources, with all the littoral states having enacted policies to enable their development. Third, the Arctic environment poses unique challenges to offshore oil and gas development. Fourth, and perhaps most importantly, despite some recent positive policy developments, there is near unanimous consensus that the U.S. government is not sufficiently prepared to address these changing dynamics.

> . . . [T]he Deepwater Horizon oil spill in April 2010, along with the setbacks experienced by Shell in the Chukchi Sea in 2012, have had major impact on this evolving policy environment, specifically on drilling in fragile frontier areas. Opponents of developing offshore Arctic hydrocarbons are skeptical that the risks associated with oil and gas development in the Arctic can be reduced to an acceptable

level. They stress that the existing governance regime in the Arctic is inadequate; the very limited resources available to respond to a loss of well control combined with pristine and highly diverse ecosystems would make a Deepwater Horizon-type incident have far more dire consequences in the Arctic than it did in the Gulf of Mexico. Furthermore, critics argue that existing standards are not Arctic-tested for operations in ice-covered waters, and that there is no equipment and infrastructure in the region to respond to an oil spill. In contrast, supporters of Arctic drilling favor appropriately regulated access to resources to support economic development, generate revenues for local and national governments, and create jobs.

CHARLES K. EBINGER ET AL., OFFSHORE OIL AND GAS GOVERNANCE IN THE ARCTIC: A LEADERSHIP ROLE FOR THE U.S. 1–2 (Brookings Energy Security Initiative, Mar. 2014). For more details and a case study on the physical and financial hazards associated with deepwater drilling in the Arctic, see McKenzie Funk, *The Wreck of the Kulluk*, N.Y. TIMES MAG. (Dec. 30, 2014).

3.   OFFSHORE WIND ENERGY

For years, the federal government, coastal states, and the renewable energy industry have promoted offshore wind energy as a potential breakthrough technology to integrate large quantities of renewable energy into the U.S. electric grid. With high-quality sustained winds, proximity to major populations centers on U.S. coasts, and sophisticated and well-funded companies with deep experience financing and building projects in European waters, one might wonder why development has so far been limited to two, small projects off the coasts of Rhode Island and Virginia. *See, e.g.*, Ivan Penn, *Offshore Wind Farms Show What Biden's Climate Plan Is Up Against*, N.Y. TIMES (June 7, 2021) (discussing promise and challenges of offshore wind development in the United States and noting that Europe has 5,400 offshore turbines providing renewable energy while the United State has only seven). In 2021, President Biden announced a target of employing tens of thousands of workers to deploy 30 GW of offshore wind energy by 2030, expedited permitting for key offshore wind projects, enhanced support for research and development, and new priority offshore areas for development. *See* FACT SHEET: BIDEN ADMINISTRATION JUMPSTARTS OFFSHORE WIND ENERGY PROJECTS TO CREATE JOBS, THE WHITE HOUSE (Mar. 29, 2021). As you read the materials that follow, consider what barriers stand in the way of widescale deployment of offshore wind energy in the United States and potential strategies to overcome them.

ADAM VANN, WIND ENERGY: OFFSHORE PERMITTING
Cong. Rsch. Serv. (Mar. 8, 2021)

. . . The production of energy on federal and federally controlled lands, including the [Outer Continental Shelf] OCS, requires some form of permission, such as a right-of-way, easement, or license. For *onshore* wind projects on federal public lands, the Department of the Interior (DOI), through the Bureau of Land Management, has created a regulatory program under the Federal Land Policy and Management Act, but a federal statute expressly governing *offshore* wind energy development was not enacted until August 2005 as part of the Energy Policy Act of 2005 (EPAct). Before enactment of EPAct, some permitting in support of offshore wind energy development had taken place, but the use of the laws existing at that time proved controversial and was challenged in court. . . .

Section 388 of EPAct sought to address some of the uncertainty related to federal jurisdiction over offshore wind energy development by amending OCSLA to establish legal authority for federal review and approval of various offshore energy-related projects. Section 388 authorized the Secretary of the Interior, in consultation with other federal agencies, to grant leases, easements, or rights-of-way on the OCS for certain activities—wind energy development among them—not authorized by other relevant statutes. A memorandum of understanding between the Department of the Interior and the Federal Energy Regulatory Commission (FERC) signed in April of 2009 confirmed the exclusive jurisdiction of the Secretary of the Interior, exercised through what was then the Bureau of Ocean Energy Management, Regulation, and Enforcement, over "the production, transportation, or transmission of energy from non- hydrokinetic renewable energy projects on the OCS."

EPAct also made clear that federal agencies with permitting authority under other federal laws retain their jurisdiction. Thus, offshore development continues to require a Corps permit pursuant to the RHA. Federal agencies that take actions with respect to energy development must also, for example, comply with environmental review requirements and species protection laws. . . .

The law directs the Secretary of the Interior to consult with other agencies as a part of its leasing, easement, and right-of-way granting process. DOI is also responsible for ensuring that activities carried out pursuant to its new authority provide for "coordination with relevant federal agencies." The law also directs the Secretary to establish a system of "royalties, fees, rentals, bonuses, or other payments" that will ensure a fair return to the United States for any property interest granted under this provision.

While Section 388 of EPAct provided DOI with significant flexibility in crafting a regulatory regime for offshore wind energy development, the act specifically addressed certain aspects of the process related to the grant of property interests. First, the act directed that leases, easements, and rights-of-way are to be issued on a competitive basis, subject to limited exceptions. The Secretary is further authorized to provide for the duration of any property interest granted under this subsection and to provide for suspension and cancellation of any lease, easement, or right-of- way.

In general, an offshore wind energy developer that is granted a lease, easement or right-of-way is responsible for royalties or other payments. Section 388 of EPAct also established the method for allocating those payments among states. . . .

In addition, EPAct authorized considerable regulation of impacts associated with offshore development. It required the Secretary to ensure that "any activity under this subsection" be carried out in a manner that adequately addresses specified issues, including environmental protection, safety, protection of U.S. national security, and protection of the rights of others to use the OCS and its resources. It also established specific financial security requirements for projects. The law requires the holder of a Section 388 property interest to "provide for the restoration of the lease, easement, or right-of-way" and to furnish a surety bond or other form of security, leaving the amount and the exact purposes to which any forfeited sums will be applied to the Secretary's discretion. Further, in conjunction with the authority to require some form of financial assurance, the Secretary is empowered to impose "such other requirements as the Secretary considers necessary to protect the interests of the public and the United States." Thus the Secretary, depending on how these authorities are exercised, may potentially regulate many aspects of any industry that is permitted to operate on the OCS under this subsection of the OCSLA.

EPAct also contained a provision expressly providing for a state consultative role in the permitting process. Section 388 requires the Secretary of the Interior to provide for coordination and consultation with a state's governor or the executive of any local government that may be affected by a lease, easement, or right-of-way granted under this new authority. In addition, the law makes clear that it does not affect any state's claim to "jurisdiction over, or any right, title, or interest in, any submerged lands."

In 2009, DOI issued a final rule establishing the permitting process and setting forth a royalty collection and allocation structure for OCS energy projects, as directed by EPAct. The rulemaking authorized BOEM to issue two types of OCS leases. Limited leases grant access and operational rights to the lessee for activities related to the production of energy, including assessment and testing activities, but do not authorize production of energy products for sale or distribution. Such leases generally support exploration and allow the lessee to develop a fuller proposal for energy production, potentially leading to the potential sale of a commercial lease. Commercial leases would give the lessee full rights to receive authorizations necessary to assess, test, and produce renewable energy on a commercial scale over the long term (approximately 30 years).

The rulemaking sets forth a formula for determining payment amounts, including lease payments and royalties, owed by parties participating in OCS renewable energy projects. The rulemaking also establishes how federal revenues from lessees will be allocated. As mandated by EPAct, BOEM shares 27% of revenues for any project "located wholly or partially within the area extending three nautical miles seaward of State submerged lands" with any "eligible state," which is defined as a "coastal State having a coastline (measured from the nearest point) no more than 15 miles from the geographic center of a qualified project area." To determine each eligible state's share of those revenues, the agency uses an "inverse distance formula, which apportions shares according to the relative proximity of the nearest point on the coastline of each eligible State to the geographic center of the qualified project area." . . .

Potential environmental impacts of offshore wind energy projects include, but are not limited to, impacts on existing resources of alternative sites in terms of physical oceanography and geology; impacts on wildlife, avian, shellfish, finfish and benthic habitat; impacts on aesthetics, cultural resources, socioeconomic conditions; and impacts on and air and water quality. Human uses such as boating and fishing may also be affected, and must be considered in a NEPA analysis. . . .

In addition to the role interested parties and cooperating agencies may play under NEPA, certain federal agencies have independent sources of jurisdiction over specific ocean resources. Some of the most relevant authorities are the Endangered Species Act (ESA), the Marine Mammal Protection Act (MMPA), and the Migratory Bird Treaty Act (MBTA). The agencies that administer those statutes do not have final authority over leasing decisions, but are likely to be involved in the environmental review process leading to a final DOI decision.

Briefly, each of these laws sets parameters for federal activities that potentially harm designated species of plants and animals. Offshore wind energy projects may impact marine species due to their obstructive, noise, or water quality impacts, and they may impact avian species primarily as a navigational hazard (i.e., birds striking wind turbine blades in motion). . . .

PUBLIC EMPLOYEES FOR ENV'T
RESPONSIBILITY V. HOPPER
827 F.3d 1077 (D.C. Cir. 2016)

The Cape Wind Energy Project is a proposal to generate electricity from windmills off the coast of Massachusetts. It calls for the "construction, operation and maintenance . . . of 130 wind turbine generators" in the Horseshoe Shoal region of Nantucket Sound. The turbines have an estimated life-span of twenty years, and during that time they are expected to generate up to three-quarters of the electricity needs for Cape Cod and the surrounding islands. The project's "underlying purpose" is to help the region achieve Massachusetts's renewable energy requirements, which "mandate that a certain amount of electricity come from renewable energy sources, such as wind." *See* Mass. Gen. Laws ch. 25A, § 11F.

Offshore energy providers like Cape Wind must comply with a slew of federal statutes designed to protect the environment, promote public safety, and preserve historic and archeological resources on the outer continental shelf. They must also go through "several regulatory and administrative procedures" to satisfy regulations promulgated under these statutes.

Cape Wind first sought government approval for its project in 2001 when it filed a permit application with the United States Army Corps of Engineers, the federal agency then regulating outer continental shelf wind energy projects. Four years later, the Energy Policy Act of 2005, Pub. L. No. 109–58, § 388(a), 119 Stat. 594, 744, amended the Outer Continental Shelf Lands Act, *see* 43 U.S.C. § 1337(p), and transferred primary regulatory authority over offshore renewable energy projects to the Bureau of Ocean Energy Management, an agency within the Department of the Interior.... Since then, this Bureau has promulgated regulations governing the development of "renewable" energy production on the outer continental shelf. *See* 30 C.F.R. § 585.100 *et seq.* ("Renewable Energy and Alternate Uses of Existing Facilities on the Outer Continental Shelf"). The regulations require the Bureau both to collect information about projects and to "consult with relevant [f]ederal agencies," including *inter alia* the United States Coast Guard and the Fish and Wildlife Service. Although Cape Wind submitted its application before the regulations issued, the Bureau decided that the regulations would nonetheless "be applicable as the Cape Wind Energy Project moves forward through the construction, operation, and decommissioning phases." ...

Plaintiffs challenge the Bureau's decision to issue the lease for Cape Wind's project without first obtaining "sufficient site-specific data on seafloor and subsurface hazards" in Nantucket Sound. They argue that the Bureau violated the National Environmental Policy Act, 42 U.S.C. § 4332, by relying on inadequate "geophysical and geotechnical" surveys.... We agree.

Under NEPA, an agency must "consider every significant aspect of the environmental impact of a proposed action." *Balt. Gas & Elec. Co. v. NRDC*, 462 U.S. 87, 97 (1983); *see* 42 U.S.C. § 4332(2). The agency must then "inform the public that it has indeed considered environmental concerns in its decisionmaking process." 462 U.S. at 97. In other words, agencies must "take a 'hard look' at [the] environmental consequences" of their actions, and "provide for broad dissemination of relevant environmental information." *Robertson v. Methow Valley Citizens Council*, 490 U.S. 332, 350 (1989) (quoting *Kleppe v. Sierra Club*, 427 U.S. 390, 410 n.21 (1976)). This "hard look" requirement applies to the "authorization or permitting of private actions" like the Cape Wind Project. *Sierra Club v. U.S. Army Corps of Engineers*, 803 F.3d 31, 36–37 (D.C. Cir. 2015).

The principal way the government informs the public of its decisionmaking process is by publishing environmental impact statements. *See* 42 U.S.C. § 4332(2)(C). Agencies must "prepare and make publicly available" these statements for all "major [f]ederal actions significantly affecting the quality of the human environment. . . ." *Sierra Club*, 803 F.3d at 37. Among other things, impact statements must describe a proposed "action's anticipated direct and indirect environmental effects." 803 F.3d at 37.

In 2004, the Army Corps of Engineers issued a draft impact statement for the Cape Wind project. After the Bureau assumed authority, it reviewed the Corps's draft statement, "identified information requirements and/or issue areas that [were] incomplete," and announced that it would issue its own impact statement. The Bureau published draft and final impact statements in 2008 and 2009, respectively.

Plaintiffs argue that the Bureau's 2009 impact statement is arbitrary and capricious because it does not adequately assess the seafloor and subsurface hazards of the Sound. They claim that the statement relies on inadequate geological surveys, which according to the Bureau's internal guidance, help determine whether "the seafloor [is] able to support large structures," and whether "important archaeological and prehistoric features [can] be protected." In support, plaintiffs refer to a series of internal Bureau emails describing "the dearth of geophysical data over the entire area" of the proposed wind farm. . . .

We do not think the Bureau has "fulfilled its duty to take a 'hard look' at the geological and geophysical environment" in Nantucket Sound. NEPA requires federal agencies to prepare impact statements for all "major [f]ederal actions significantly affecting the quality of the human environment." *Sierra Club*, 803 F.3d at 37. The Bureau does not contest that issuing a renewable energy lease constitutes a major federal action. Therefore, the question is whether the Bureau "consider[ed] every significant aspect of the environmental impact" of the project, including the subsurface environment. *Balt. Gas*, 462 U.S. at 97. The Bureau distinguishes between the *"initial* decision" to issue a lease and the consequences of that decision. Cape Wind also points out that the impact statement required "additional geophysical . . . surveys" once the project was authorized, and claims these surveys were completed in 2012. But there is no evidence the Bureau relied on any additional surveys in its impact statement, and NEPA does not allow agencies to slice and dice proposals in this way. Agencies must take a "hard look" at the environmental effects of a major federal action "*and consequences* of that action." *Robertson*, 490 U.S. at 352 (italics added). The impact statement must therefore look beyond the decision to offer a lease and consider the predictable consequences of that decision. By relying solely on data so roundly criticized by its "own experts," the Bureau failed to fulfill this duty. . . . Of course, an agency need not be clairvoyant. In some cases it may be appropriate for an impact statement to provide for ongoing monitoring in order to gather more data. . . . But that does not excuse the Bureau from its NEPA obligation to gather data about the seafloor. Without adequate geological surveys, the Bureau cannot "ensure that the seafloor [will be] able to support" wind turbines.

The Bureau therefore violated NEPA, but that does not necessarily mean that the project must be halted or that Cape Wind must redo the regulatory approval process. . . . To decide whether "the project should be halted pending completion of an [impact statement]," we must perform a "particularized analysis of the violations that have occurred," "the possibilities for relief," and "any countervailing considerations of public interest," including "the social and economic costs of delay. . . ." *NRDC v. U.S. Nuclear Regulatory Comm'n*, 606 F.2d 1261, 1272 (D.C. Cir. 1979) (internal quotation marks omitted); . . . Delaying construction or requiring Cape Wind to redo the regulatory approval process could be quite costly. The project has slogged through state and federal courts and agencies for more than a decade. *See, e.g., All. to Protect Nantucket Sound, Inc. v. U.S. Dep't of Army*, 288 F. Supp. 2d 64 (D. Mass. 2003), *aff'd*, 398 F.3d 105 (1st Cir. 2005); *All. to Protect Nantucket Sound, Inc. v. Energy Facilities Siting Bd.*, 858 N.E.2d 294 (Mass. 2006). Meanwhile, Massachusetts's renewable energy requirements continue to increase. *See* Mass. Gen. Laws ch. 25A, § 11F. Allowing the project to move forward could help meet these requirements. On the other hand, it would be imprudent to allow Cape Wind to begin construction before it can "ensure that the seafloor [is] able to support" its facilities. Cape Wind has "no prior experience developing/operating offshore wind farms," and the construction site "lie[s] in the frontier areas of the [outer continental shelf,] where *detailed* geological, geophysical, and geotechnical data and information is generally lacking." Therefore, we will vacate the impact statement and require the Bureau to supplement it with adequate geological surveys before Cape Wind may begin construction. We will not, however, vacate Cape Wind's lease or other regulatory approvals based on this NEPA violation. . . .

[The court also found that U.S. Fish & Wildlife Service violated the Endangered Species Act by insufficiently analyzing the risk of bird collisions during periods of poor visibility.—Eds.]

NOTES AND QUESTIONS

1.   After 16 years of permitting efforts and litigation, the Cape Wind project surrendered its federal lease at the end of 2017, bringing an end to the first major effort to site a large-scale wind farm in the Atlantic OCS. Permitting delays, litigation like the case excerpted above, and contract uncertainty for power sales ultimately led to the project's demise. *See* Michelle Froese, *Lessons Learned from Cape Wind*, WINDPOWER ENG'G & DEV. (July 30, 2019). Should traditional environmental laws like NEPA and the Endangered Species Act apply to renewable energy projects in the same way as for fossil fuel and other industrial-scale projects? Or should Congress or state legislatures create exemptions for certain clean energy projects? *See, e.g.*, J.B. Ruhl, *What Happens When the Green New Deal Meets the Old Green Laws?*, 44 VT. L. REV. 693 (2020).

2.   As of December 2020, BOEM managed 16 active offshore wind leases, none of which had yet begun producing electricity. DIAZ, *supra* at 41. In FY 2019, offshore wind leases on the OCS brought in $411 million in federal revenue consisting of bonuses, rents, royalties, and other fees. *See id.* The offshore wind project furthest along as of 2021 was Vineyard Wind, a 800 MW project 15 miles off the coast of Massachusetts south of Martha's Vineyard. The project was expected to consist of more than sixty 13 MW turbines spaced approximately one nautical mile apart. After considerable delay during the Trump administration, BOEM approved the Record of Decision under NEPA for the project in 2021, paving the way for the required federal permits. *See Overview, Vineyard Wind 1*, Vineyard Wind. The project required over 25 state and federal permits, with the first applications made in 2017. *Id.* For information on offshore wind leases, see BOEM, OCS RENEWABLE ENERGY LEASES, MAP BOOK (Mar. 2021). *See also* WALTER MUSIAL ET AL., U.S. DEP'T OF ENERGY, OFFSHORE WIND MARKET REPORT: 2021 EDITION ix (Aug. 2021) (map showing other offshore wind projects in the permitting process).

3.   Part of the reason for the focus on projects off the coast of Massachusetts, is that the state was one of the first to create policies supporting the procurement of wind energy to meet the state's renewable energy mandates. In 2016, the state enacted the "Act to Promote Energy Diversity," which allowed for the procurement of up to 1,600 MW of offshore wind energy by 2027 through an RFP process. Vineyard Wind was selected to provide 800 MW through that project, and the state enacted additional legislation in 2019 to procure an additional 1,600 MW of offshore wind energy. As you might imagine, offshore wind energy is far more expensive to build than onshore wind energy in the United States, at least for now. Why might a state like Massachusetts focus on offshore wind energy to meet its renewable energy mandates despite the cost? Are there other renewable or carbon-free resources it should rely on instead? Consider the information you have learned in other chapters about the availability of renewable energy resources in various parts of the United States and challenges associated with permitting and constructing interstate electric transmission lines, as well as adaptations required to integrate those resources into the electric grid.

4.   Until recently, there has been far less focus on offshore wind energy in the OCS in the Pacific, due to the greater water depths in that region as well as the potential interference with military operations. However, in 2021, the Departments of Interior, Energy, and Defense announced an agreement with the State of California to develop areas on the Pacific OCS to build up to 4.6 GW of floating offshore wind, with a lease sale auction targeted for 2022. *See* Iulia Gheorghiu, *Biden Administration Opens Up 4.6 GW of Offshore Wind Development*, UTIL. DIVE (May 26, 2021) (discussing federal funding, expected price per MW, and technical aspects of offshore floating wind turbines); Coral Davenport, *Biden Opens California's Coast to Wind Farms*, N.Y. TIMES (May 25, 2021). What barriers to development might you anticipate will arise as these projects move forward? What might developers and regulators learn from the Cape Wind saga? How much emphasis should states or the federal government place on offshore wind as part of their clean energy transition policies?

5.   In 2021, The Biden administration announced it would also focus offshore wind development in the Gulf of Mexico OCS as part of its goal to deploy 30 GW of offshore wind by 3030. *See Press Release, Interior Department to Explore Offshore Wind Development in the Gulf of Mexico*, U.S. Dep't of Interior (June 8, 2021). What are the benefits and drawbacks of focusing development efforts on the Gulf of Mexico?

6.   In addition to the OCS, developers have focused on the Great Lakes as a potential site for offshore wind energy development. What benefits and barriers might be associated with Great Lakes wind development, as compared with development in the Atlantic and Pacific OCS? *See, e.g.*, NICHOLAS WALLACE, STANFORD SCHOOL OF EARTH, ENERGY, & ENV'T SCIENCES, OFFSHORE WIND IN THE GREAT LAKES: FOSTERING DEVELOPMENT THROUGH STATE POLICY (Apr. 2021); John Funk, *Nation's First Freshwater Windfarm All But Approved as Ohio Siting Board Removes "Poison Pill,"* UTIL. DIVE (Sept. 18, 2020).

7.   Financing offshore wind projects is big business in the United States and globally. Vineyard Wind I is being built by Copenhagen Infrastructure Partners (CIP) in Denmark and Avangrid Renewables, which is part of Iberdrola, a global company headquartered in Spain with renewables projects all over the world. *See Vineyard Wind 1 Offshore Wind Farm*, Iberdrola. Avangrid is also involved in the proposed Kitty Hawk 2,550 MW project off the coast of North Carolina and the Park City 804 MW project off the coast of Connecticut. *See Flagship Projects*, Iberdrola. Equinor, a Norwegian company, is also a global renewable energy finance leader developing major projects off the coast of New York and elsewhere. *See Offshore Wind, United States*, Equinor. Given the development trajectory of offshore wind, why might European finance be playing such an important role in U.S. projects?

CHAPTER 10

NUCLEAR ENERGY

■ ■ ■

A. OVERVIEW

Nothing in energy law evokes emotions like nuclear power. This energy source seemed destined to do so from the beginning. Transferred as a technology from the most devastating military weapon ever created to a peaceful, civilian purpose—a transformation the Supreme Court would later dub the "turning of swords into plowshares," *Pacific Gas & Elec. Co. v. State Energy Resources Conservation & Dev. Comm'n*, 461 U.S. 190, 193–94 (1983)[1]—nuclear energy continues to elicit strong, often diametrically opposed views.

Take a single example. In the aftermath of the 2011 tsunami-induced meltdown at the Fukushima Daiichi plant in Japan, a tragedy that, according to the World Nuclear Association, indirectly resulted in 2,313 deaths[2] and displaced over 160,000 from their homes—including more than 40,000 who have still not been able to return—demands for abandoning atomic energy inevitably arose. Germany heeded this call, boldly announcing it would shutter its seventeen nuclear plants making up roughly one quarter of its electricity production. It began just that process, closing half of its facilities, with the other half slated to cease operation by 2022. The United States, by contrast, repeatedly asserted its devotion to nuclear power, with President Barack Obama declaring: "[I]n light of what's happened in Japan, I've requested a comprehensive safety review by the Nuclear Regulatory Commission to make sure that all of our existing nuclear energy facilities are safe. And we're going [to] incorporate those conclusions and lessons from Japan in design and the building of the next generation of plants. But we can't simply take it off the table." *Remarks by*

---

[1] The original phrase is biblical. *See Isaiah* 2:4. Early nuclear research in the United States focused mostly on weapon creation for World War II, under the code name the *Manhattan Project*. U.S. DEPARTMENT OF ENERGY, THE HISTORY OF NUCLEAR ENERGY 7–8. A later government program, led by the Atomic Energy Commission, carried out nuclear explosions in an attempt to find additional civil applications for atomic energy. They called their effort the "Plowshare Program." *See* SCOTT KAUFMAN, PROJECT PLOWSHARE: THE PEACEFUL USE OF NUCLEAR EXPLOSIVES IN COLD WAR AMERICA (2012).

[2] These deaths are considered "disaster related," caused by the forced evacuation and psychological impacts, not by radiation exposure. "It has been established that there has been a dramatic increase in depression, PTSD, substance abuse, and suicides, driven partially by the evacuations, partially by stigmatisation, and partially by an amplified perception of radiation risks which goes far beyond the scientific evidence." *Fukushima Daiichi Accident FAQ*, World Nuclear Org. (last updated 2020).

the President on America's Energy Security, The White House (Mar. 30, 2011). Meanwhile, energy-isolated Japan insisted that atomic energy would remain part of its generation portfolio even as most of its plants went into shutdown. In the meltdown's immediate aftermath, citizens and grid operators showed an immense capacity for conserving power while resurgent environmentalists protested in the streets. So far, however, the likely continued future use of nuclear power in Japan remains.[3] Nonetheless, no matter the circumstance—disaster or everyday electricity production—the issues that nuclear energy raises are always diverse, important, and thorny.

1. THE NUCLEAR INDUSTRY

The complexity of the policy issues that nuclear energy introduces stands in stark contrast to the conceptual simplicity of the technology. Nuclear energy is, at bottom, one more way to boil water to turn an electric turbine. As Amory Lovins so colorfully put it, nuclear electricity is in some ways the equivalent of "cutting butter with a chainsaw." Amory B. Lovins, *Energy Strategy: The Road Not Taken?*, 55 FOREIGN AFF. 65, 79 (1976). Of course, the details of nuclear power technology are much more complicated, and demand precision engineering and careful plant operation by true experts in the field.

Boiling Water Reactor

Source: U.S. Energy Info. Admin.

As Chapter 2 introduced, there are two basic types of nuclear reactors: (1) boiling water reactors and (2) pressurized water reactors. The primary difference between these technologies is that the former actually boils

---

[3] Japan restarted two reactors in 2015, with seven more joining that tally since; another sixteen operable reactors are currently in the process of seeking restart approval. World Nuclear Ass'n, *Nuclear Power in Japan* (June 2021).

water to create steam, while "pressurized" systems circulate supercritical water in a continuous piped loop. In both cases, however, the reactor's primary function is the same. It is to turn turbines to generate electricity.

Pressurized Water Reactor

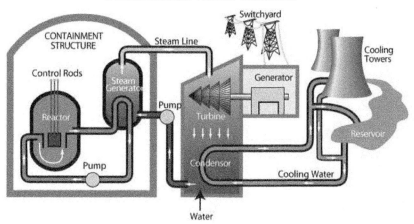

Source: U.S. Energy Info. Admin.

A typical nuclear power station consists of four main parts. First, the *reactor core* is where the nuclear fuel rods, which contain fingertip-sized pellets of enriched uranium (the "nuclear fuel"), are lowered into heavy water. This begins the fission reaction—the splitting of atoms—that produces heat to run the turbine. This reaction is moderated by the shape of the fuel rod array and the "control rods," which are most commonly made of hafnium, silver, indium, cadmium, and boron. The control rods, which can also be lowered in and out of the core, moderate the reaction by absorbing neutrons. The reactor core is encased by thick walls of steel and concrete. It is located within a larger containment building.

Second, the *generation turbine* is connected to the reactor by piping that conveys the steam to make the turbine turn. Cooled water also circulates to the core to keep its temperature down, that is, to stop it from overheating. Have you ever seen white "smoke" rising out of a nuclear power plant's cooling towers? It is not smoke at all but merely water vapor from the cooling tower evaporating into the air.

Third, the *control room* is the nuclear power station's nerve center. It consists of computers and other instruments that the plant operators use to monitor and operate the plant. If you have ever watched the television program, *The Simpsons*, you may have a basic, if extremely oversimplified, notion of what a nuclear power station's control room looks like. The photo below shows an actual control room, at the Davis-Bess Nuclear Power Station in Oak Harbor, Ohio.

Nuclear Reactor Control Room

Source: Nuclear Regulatory Comm'n.

Fourth, nuclear power plant sites include two different kinds of *storage facilities*. The first is "cooling ponds"—large, indoor structures that hold fuel rods after they are removed from the reactor. Cooling ponds are necessary because fuel rods are both literally (thermally) and figuratively (radioactively) "hot" following use. Circulating water in the pond reduces their temperature and acts as a shield against radiation. Originally, cooling ponds were designed as short-term storage facilities. However, in the absence of a national nuclear waste repository, cooling ponds have become the de facto long-term storage area for nuclear power plants in the United States. Today, the cooling ponds at many reactors are larger, and have remained open longer, than originally planned. Reliance on these ponds is one point of criticism of the nation's nuclear policy, although some argue that onsite storage is positive because it makes the spent nuclear fuel more available for reuse as technology improves. *See* Denise Renee Foster, *Utilities: De Facto Repositories for High-Level Radioactive Waste?*, 5 DICK. J. ENV'T L. & POL'Y 375, 392 (1996); *Arizona Pub. Serv. Co. v. United States*, 93 Fed. Cl. 384, 385 (Fed. Cl. 2010); *Yankee Atomic Elec. Co. v. United States*, 73 Fed. Cl. 249, 253 (Fed. Cl. 2006), *aff'd in part, rev'd in part and remanded*, 536 F.3d 1268 (Fed. Cir. 2008).

Cooling Pond

Source: Sellafield Ltd./Nuclear Decommissioning Auth.

The other kind of storage facility at nuclear power sites is "dry cask" storage. Dry casks are giant steel-and-cement tubes that hold fuel rods which have sufficiently reduced their temperature after time in a cooling pond. Welded shut, the cement-and-steel casks block radiation, while a passive ventilation system uses air circulation to further cool the rods. Later in this chapter, we will visit in more depth why nuclear power stations have dry cask storage. The short answer is that Nuclear Regulatory Commission (NRC) rules limit how much on-site cooling pond storage power plants can have, *see* 10 C.F.R. § 50, and the nation has been unable to forge a permanent storage solution for the high-level nuclear waste that atomic power plants produce.

Dry Cask Storage

Source: Am. Nuclear Soc'y.

Regulation of nuclear energy in the United States has a long history—beginning, effectively, with the introduction of the technology itself. Nuclear technology for civilian use began shortly after World War II. Following the first demonstration of an atomic reaction at the University of Chicago on December 2, 1942—underneath the football field—the first atomic reactor was built at the Idaho National Laboratory in southeastern Idaho. On December 20, 1951, that facility produced enough electricity to power four light bulbs. Less than two years later, on December 8, 1953, President Dwight D. Eisenhower gave his famous "Atoms for Peace" speech to the United Nations, in which he declared:

> Against the dark background of the atomic bomb, the United States does not wish merely to present strength, but also the desire and the hope for peace. The coming months will be fraught with fateful decisions. In this Assembly; in the capitals and military headquarters of the world; in the hearts of men everywhere, be they governed or governors, may they be the decisions which will lead this world out of fear and into peace. To the making of these fateful decisions, the United States pledges before you—and therefore before the world—its determination to help solve the fearful atomic dilemma—to devote its entire heart and mind to find the way by which the miraculous inventiveness

of man shall not be dedicated to his death, but consecrated to his life.

Dwight D. Eisenhower, *Atoms for Peace*, Dec. 8, 1953.

From there, nuclear energy consumption would only grow. By 1957, the first commercial-scale nuclear reactor was operational: the Shippingport Atomic Power Station in Pennsylvania. That plant had a production capacity of 60 MW, or about a third of a single modern combined cycle natural gas generator. Shippingport was also the first nuclear power plant to be decommissioned, in the late 1980s. Today, the cost and time for decommissioning plants in the United States varies but may run over $500 to nearly $900 million per reactor—and take several years to over a decade to complete. *Decommissioning Nuclear Facilities*, World Nuclear Ass'n (updated May 2021). NRC regulations govern decommissioning. *See* 10 C.F.R. §§ 20.1401 *et seq.*

Shippingport Reactor Being Lowered Into Place

Source: Library of Congress.

Decommissioning is not just a domestic issue. Germany began the process of decommissioning its entire nuclear fleet following the 2011 Fukushima Daiichi disaster. Though the cost of shuttering its 23 nuclear units has ballooned from nearly $60 billion to a new estimate of $130 billion, Germany has remained steadfast to its promise of replacing its full nuclear production with other energy sources by 2023. As it does so, the government must also cope both with finding new production and the chance that energy companies could fold before the work is complete, leaving the public responsible for the expensive decommissioning process. *See, e.g., Germany's Atomic Phaseout: How to Dismantle a Nuclear Power Plant*, DEUTSCHE WELLE (Mar. 11, 2019).

Operating U.S. Commercial Nuclear Reactors (2020)

License Renewals Granted for Operating Nuclear
Power Reactors

Licensed to Operate (94)

⚓ Original License (8) ⚓ License Renewal Granted (82) ⚓ Subsequent License Renewal Granted (4)

Note: The NRC has issued a total of 96 license renewals; 8 of these units have permanently shut down. Data are as of August 2020. For the most recent information, go to the Dataset Index Web page at https://www.nrc.gov/reading-rm/doc-collections/datasets/.

Source: Nuclear Reg. Comm'n.

As the above figure shows, as of 2020, the United States had 94 nuclear reactors licensed to operate across the country, primarily in the Midwest and East. These facilities account for roughly a fifth of the nation's electricity production—a figure that has remained remarkably stable even as the nuclear industry and the U.S. electricity sector have undergone significant transformation over the years. By comparison, France, the country with the second most installed nuclear capacity in the world, has 58 nuclear reactors capable of generating 61 GW, comprising 72% of its electricity production.

2. NUCLEAR REGULATION

The United States' remarkable growth in atomic energy was made possible—and largely encouraged—by the regulatory structure Congress put in place. After World War II, in the Atomic Energy Act of 1946, Congress declared that the regulation and control of nuclear power technology the military had developed would move into the civilian realm. Diane Carter Maleson, *The Historical Roots of the Legal System's Response to Nuclear Power*, 55 S. CAL. L. REV. 597, 598 (1982). Eight years later, the Atomic Energy Act of 1954, 42 U.S.C. §§ 2011 *et seq.*, created the NRC's predecessor, the Atomic Energy Commission (AEC), and directed it to institute a licensing scheme to allow private companies to build and operate nuclear power plants.

Under the Atomic Energy Act, the NRC has exclusive regulatory authority over nuclear power plants and atomic materials, which it exercises through licenses for the possession, transfer, and use of nuclear materials. Thus, the NRC licenses both nuclear power plants and the spent fuel they produce. "While the AEA does not specifically refer to the storage or disposal of spent nuclear fuel, it has long been recognized that the AEA confers on the NRC authority to license and regulate the storage and disposal of such fuel." *Bullcreek v. NRC*, 359 F.3d 536, 539 (D.C. Cir. 2004).

In short, the core of NRC proceedings is licensing. One way to think of the NRC's licensing activity is to break it down into five categories following the nuclear energy lifecycle: laws and regulations governing (1) uranium mining, processing, and handling; (2) nuclear power plant licensing; (3) atomic incident liability regimes, namely, the Price-Anderson Act; (4) low-level nuclear waste disposal; and (5) high-level nuclear waste disposal.

The NRC carries out its licensing activities in the first instance through its Atomic Safety and Licensing Board (ASLB). The ASLB panel "conducts all licensing and other hearings as directed by the Commission, primarily through individual Atomic Safety and Licensing Boards or single presiding officers appointed by either the Commission or the Chief Administrative Judge. The Panel . . . is composed of administrative judges (full-time and part-time) who are lawyers, engineers, and scientists. Administrative judges serve as single presiding officers or on three-member boards, which generally are chaired by a lawyer, for a broad range of proceedings." *Atomic Safety and Licensing Board Panel*, U.S. Nuclear Reg. Comm'n. Decisions by the ASLB are then subject to review by the Commission.

Although the details of how the AEC, and now the NRC, have implemented this licensing scheme have evolved over time, the bedrock principle is that Congress defers to the agency's technical expertise to ensure that nuclear plants run safely and reliably. Thus, while legislative policy choices and administrative procedure permeate the nuclear regulatory field, even a brief perusal of NRC regulations reveals that the agency's rules are as much about applied science and engineering as they are about energy law as such. This is the charge the Atomic Energy Act gives the NRC—to license nuclear activities to ensure they operate safely and to keep atomic materials secure. "All nuclear power plant applications must undergo a safety review, an environmental review and antitrust review by the NRC." *Backgrounder on Nuclear Power Plant Licensing Process*, U.S. Nuclear Reg. Comm'n (last updated Aug. 2020).

For nuclear reactors, there are effectively two types of licenses available. Under the NRC's old system, nuclear plants went through a two-step licensing process. The first step was receiving a construction permit, and the second was obtaining an operating license. In this process, the NRC would include safety, economic, emergency, and environmental factors, focusing on "characteristics of the site, including surrounding population, seismology, meteorology, geology and hydrology; design of the nuclear plant; anticipated response of the plant to hypothetical accidents; plant operations including the applicant's technical qualifications to operate the plant; discharges from the plant into the environment (i.e., radiological effluents); and emergency plans." *Id.* The Supreme Court thus summarized this two-step licensing process:

> Under the Atomic Energy Act of 1954 . . ., a utility seeking to construct and operate a nuclear power plant must obtain a separate permit or license at both the construction and the operation stage of the project. In order to obtain the construction permit, the utility must file a preliminary safety analysis report, an environmental report, and certain information regarding the antitrust implications of the proposed project. This application then undergoes exhaustive review by the Commission's staff and by the Advisory Committee on Reactor Safeguards (ACRS), a group of distinguished experts in the field of atomic energy. Both groups submit to the Commission their own evaluations, which then become part of the record of the utility's application. The Commission staff also undertakes the review required by the National Environmental Policy Act. . . . Thereupon a three-member Atomic Safety and Licensing Board conducts a public adjudicatory hearing, and reaches a decision which can be appealed to the Atomic Safety and Licensing Appeal Board, and currently, in the Commission's discretion, to the Commission itself.

Vermont Yankee Nuclear Power Corp. v. Natural Resources Defense Council, 435 U.S. 519, 525–26 (1978).

This two-step licensing process was often criticized as slow and cumbersome. To respond to these concerns, the NRC adopted three significant regulatory innovations aimed at streamlining the licensing process and encouraging nuclear plant construction. First, proposed nuclear facilities can now obtain a single "combined" construction and operation license (COL), rather than going through the old, two-step process. Second, parties can obtain from the agency an early site permit (ESP) that "resolves site safety, environmental protection, and emergency preparedness issues independent of a specific nuclear plant design." *Backgrounder on Nuclear Licensing Process, supra.* "The early site permit also allows for a limited work authorization to perform non-safety site preparation activities, subject to redress, in advance of issuance of a combined license. . . . [It] is initially valid for no less than 10 and no more than 20 years and can be renewed for 10 to 20 years." *Id.* Third, the NRC will now approve standard nuclear plant designs—independent of any specific facility site—using a rulemaking process. This "design certification" process seeks to further reduce licensing costs and time, because "[a]n application for a combined license . . . can incorporate by reference a design certification and/or an early site permit. The advantage of this approach is that the issues resolved during the design certification rulemaking and the early site permit hearing processes are precluded from reconsideration later at the combined license stage." *Id.*

Nuclear Reactor Licensing by the NRC

Source: Nuclear Regulatory Comm'n.

The NRC conducts its combined license review pursuant to Part 52 of its regulations. *See* 10 C.F.R. pt. 52. The agency has summarized this process as follows:

> By issuing a combined license (COL), the U.S. Nuclear Regulatory Commission (NRC) authorizes the licensee to construct and (with specified conditions) operate a nuclear power plant at a specific site, in accordance with established laws and regulations. A COL is valid for 40 years from the date of the Commission finding . . .

that the acceptance criteria in the combined license are met. A COL can be renewed for an additional 20 years. . . .

In a COL application, the NRC staff reviews the applicant's qualifications, design safety, environmental impacts, operational programs, site safety, and verification of construction with ITAAC [Inspections, Tests, Analyses, and Acceptance Criteria]. The staff conducts its review in accordance with the Atomic Energy Act, NRC regulations, and the National Environmental Policy Act. All stakeholders (including the public) are given notice as to how and when they may participate in the regulatory process, which may include participating in public meetings and opportunities to request a hearing on the issuance of a COL.

Combined License Applications for New Reactors, U.S. Nuclear Reg. Comm'n; *see also Inspections, Tests, Analyses, and Acceptance Criteria (ITAAC)*, U.S. Nuclear Reg. Comm'n.

The NRC's COL innovation has met mixed success. As of August 2020, the agency had received COL applications for reactors at nineteen different sites. Of these, two of the applications were suspended, one was under review, eight were withdrawn, and eight had been issued. *Combined License Applications for New Reactors, supra.* However, as described below, many of the facilities that have received COL approval will not be completed, and broader changes in the industry have called into question whether any further full-scale reactors will be built in the United States. Indeed, of the eight projects for which the NRC has issued COL licenses, as of 2021, three of the operators had affirmatively terminated their licenses. The Tennessee Valley Authority, for instance, withdrew its applications, citing lower than expected load growth and the efficacy of its non-nuclear energy efficiency measures. *Id.*; Wayne Barber, *TVA Considers Sale of Bellefonte Nuclear Plant Site*, POWER ENGINEERING (Feb. 17, 2016).

While the broad concept of how the NRC regulates is easily grasped, the technical detail involved in the process is far more complicated. By necessity, courts often defer heavily to the NRC, in part because its licensing process must rely so extensively on engineering and technical analyses. The paradox is how the field provokes such an impassioned discourse despite the regulation's extremely technical nature. Indeed, it is perhaps in part because the scientific and technical details involved in nuclear licensing are so complex that decisions to license or relicense nuclear power plants can be so controversial in the public realm.

The following case provides an example of the application of NRC's licensing regulations. In addition to exposing you to the reactor design certification, ESP, and COL processes, the case is notable because it involves the only commercial-scale reactors currently being constructed in the United States, the Southern Company's Vogtle Units 3 and 4. As you read the case, consider what you think about the amount and quality of public participation in the underlying NRC proceeding—whether it is not enough, too much, or just right. The parties' arguments in the case were based, in part, on the implications of the disaster at the Fukushima Daiichi facility in Japan, a subject that is addressed at length later in this chapter through the lenses of technology risk and NEPA.

BLUE RIDGE ENVIRONMENTAL DEFENSE LEAGUE V. NRC
716 F.3d 183 (D.C. Cir. 2013)

EDWARDS, SENIOR CIRCUIT JUDGE.

This case arises from actions taken by the Nuclear Regulatory Commission (NRC or Commission) approving (1) an application by Southern Nuclear Operating Company (Southern) for combined licenses to construct and operate new Units 3 and 4 of the Vogtle Nuclear Power Plant and (2) an application by Westinghouse Electric Company (Westinghouse) for an amendment to its already-approved AP 1000 reactor design on which the Vogtle application relied. . . .

I. REGULATORY BACKGROUND

A. Reactor Design Certification

Under 10 C.F.R. Part 52, Subpart B, a party may request a "standard design certification" for the approval of a nuclear power plant design. *See* 10 C.F.R. § 52.41. Once a design is certified through this generic process, a future applicant may rely on the already-approved design. Design certification by NRC requires notice-and-comment rulemaking and culminates in publication in the Federal Register as a "design certification rule." *See id.* § 52.54.

When a proposed design certification rule is published, NRC's associated [Environmental Assessment (EA) under the National Environmental Policy Act (NEPA)] is published for comment at the same time. Because a reactor design is certified without reference to any specific plans for its construction, NRC has determined by rule that every proposed design certification or amendment requires only an EA, not a more comprehensive Environmental Impact Statement (EIS).

The EA for a design certification addresses only one topic: the costs and benefits of any Severe Accident Mitigation Design Alternatives that were considered and not incorporated into the final design. When a proposal is made to modify an approved design certification rule . . ., modifications to the original EA are necessary only if the proposed design change amendment alters the cost-benefit calculus concerning any Severe Accident Mitigation Design Alternatives.

B. Combined Operating Licenses

The Atomic Energy Act authorizes NRC to issue a combined operating license for both the construction and operation of new reactors after a public hearing. *See* 42 U.S.C. § 2235(b). Any such license must be accompanied by a full EIS, 10 C.F.R. §§ 51.75, 51.92(b), (d), (e), and may rely on and incorporate by reference an approved standard design certification, *id.* § 51.75(c)(2).

NRC must afford interested parties an opportunity to participate in a contested hearing subject to additional procedural requirements. *See* 42 U.S.C. § 2239(a). However, in order to initiate such a contested hearing, NRC regulations require that interested parties submit contentions that are supported by "sufficient information to show that a genuine dispute exists with the applicant/licensee on a material issue of law or fact." 10 C.F.R. § 2.309(f)(1)(vi). In addition, interested parties "must set forth with particularity the contentions sought to be raised" and [meet other specificity and procedural requirements]. *Id.* § 2.309(f)(1)(ii), (v), (vii). When interested parties are allowed to intervene, "[t]he scope of the Intervenors' participation in adjudications is limited to their admitted contentions, *i.e.*, they are barred from participating in the uncontested portion of the hearing." *Exelon Generation Co., LLC*, 62 N.R.C. 5, 49 (2005).

NRC also holds a separate "mandatory" hearing before issuing a combined license. *See* 42 U.S.C. §§ 2235(b), 2239(a). The mandatory hearing does not address contentions raised by the parties, and participation is limited to the applicant and NRC staff. The mandatory NRC hearing determines the adequacy of the NRC . . . review of the application. . . .

C. Environmental Requirements

NEPA mandates that a federal agency take a "hard look" at any major undertaking by assembling an EIS. . . . The EIS must address all reasonably foreseeable environmental impacts, including reactor accidents, even if the probability of such an occurrence is low.

As a major federal action, NRC's issuance of a combined operating license requires an EIS. NRC regulations require preparation of an EIS both at the early site permit stage and at the combined operating license stage.

Once NRC has prepared an EIS, it must continue to evaluate the environmental consequences of the project and supplement the EIS, as necessary, even after initial approval. This ongoing duty is mitigated, however, by a "rule of reason," which excuses the agency from supplementing an environmental report based only on "remote and highly speculative consequences." *Deukmejian v. NRC*, 751 F.2d 1287, 1300 (D.C. Cir. 1984).

The EIS must be submitted for public comment. [W]e have held that "the agency has significant discretion in determining when public comment is required with respect to EAs."

D. Fukushima Accident and NRC Fukushima Task Force

On March [11], 2011, a catastrophic accident occurred at the Fukushima Dai-ichi Nuclear Power Station in Honshu, Japan. NRC appointed a Task Force to study the regulatory implications of the accident for the United States. . . .

NRC's Fukushima Task Force issued its report in July 2011, concluding that NRC's "current regulatory approach, and more importantly, the resultant plant capabilities" demonstrate "that a sequence of events like the Fukushima accident is unlikely to occur in the United States and some appropriate mitigation measures have been implemented, reducing the likelihood of core damage and radiological releases." The Task Force supported completing work on the then-pending AP1000 design certification rulemaking "without delay" and noted that "all of the current early site permits [e.g., Vogtle Units 3 and 4] already meet the requirements" of the Task Force Report recommendation governing seismic and flooding analysis. . . .

The Task Force offered twelve recommendations[, which the] Task Force grouped . . . into five categories: "Clarifying the Regulatory Framework," "Ensuring Protection," "Enhancing Mitigation," "Strengthening Emergency Preparedness, and "Improving the Efficiency of NRC Programs." . . .

II. FACTUAL BACKGROUND

A. AP1000 Design Certification

NRC first issued a design certification rule approving Westinghouse's AP1000 design in 2006. Along with this design certification rule, NRC prepared an EA that analyzed sixteen Severe Accident Mitigation Design Alternatives and rejected all sixteen on cost-benefit grounds.

Westinghouse subsequently applied for an amendment to the approved AP1000 reactor design. NRC received and considered over 200 public comments, most of which urged delaying resolution of the AP1000 design amendment proceeding until the lessons learned from the Fukushima accident were applied to NRC regulations.

On December 30, 2011, after considering these comments, NRC declined to suspend or delay the design certification rulemaking proceeding, emphasizing that the AP1000 design was already compliant with many of the Task Force recommendations. NRC concluded that no Severe Accident Mitigation Design Alternatives were cost-beneficial and that no supplemental EA was necessary.

NRC certified the AP1000 design and stressed the ongoing nature of Commission review of designs . . . .

B. Vogtle Combined Operating Licenses

On August 15, 2006, Southern applied for an early site permit for Vogtle Units 3 and 4. A coalition of community action organizations, including several Petitioners in this case, sought a hearing on the application and intervened on three admitted contentions related to NRC's draft EIS for the site. NRC assigned the conduct of the licensure proceeding to a three-member Atomic Safety and Licensing Board (Board), which considered Petitioners' contentions in a series of on-the-record hearings. The Board ruled against Petitioners on all three contentions, and NRC denied review, ending the contested portion of the hearing. The Board issued its final initial decision in August 2009, after holding its mandatory sufficiency review and questioning Southern and NRC staff, and approved the Vogtle early site application.

Southern subsequently applied for combined operating licenses for Vogtle Units 3 and 4. As with the early site permit proceeding, NRC prepared an EIS for this licensing action, which included consideration of the potential for severe accidents and their consequences.

In response, Petitioners brought three contentions to the Board, which denied two and admitted the third, a safety-related contention. After consideration of the contention, the Board granted summary disposition against the intervenors, finding that the contention failed to present a material factual dispute. The Board declined to admit an additional environmental contention and concluded the contested portion of the proceeding. A second licensing Board was established to consider another contention in April 2010; it denied the request, and NRC affirmed.

In April 2011, shortly after the Task Force was appointed, Petitioners and other organizations submitted an Emergency Petition, asking NRC to suspend all pending licensing decisions, including the decision whether to issue a combined license for Vogtle 3 and 4, while it investigated the implications of the Fukushima accident. The Commission denied these requests for a suspension.

At the same time, Petitioners submitted a petition requesting that NRC immediately suspend the rulemaking for the amendment of the AP1000 design certification pending evaluation of the implications of the Fukushima accident. . . . The Commission denied the request for immediate postponement as premature, but directed NRC staff to consider the submissions as comments to the AP1000 rulemaking. . . .

Petitioners [then filed several additional comments and motions over the next months, requesting the NRC to reopen proceedings and modify its actions, including EISs, based on concerns it believed were raised by the Fukushima disaster. The Commission declined these invitations.]

On February 9, 2012, the Commission handed down its opinion resulting from its September 27 and 28, 2011, mandatory hearing on the Vogtle licensing application. . . . At the hearing, NRC technical staff confirmed that the AP1000 design certification and the Vogtle licenses met current safety and environmental standards. . . . The Commission considered the likelihood and consequences of potential severe accidents similar to the Fukushima accident and found that the risks to the AP1000 reactor design at the Vogtle site were "lower than those for current generation plants."

NRC approved the combined license applications for the Vogtle 3 and 4 reactors at the conclusion of the mandatory hearing. The Commission found that the staff's review adequately supported the requisite safety and environmental findings under 10 C.F.R. §§ 52.97, 51.107(a) & (d), and 50.10, that all NEPA requirements had been met, and that the staff had followed an appropriate process for assessing "new and significant" information. In addition, the Commission restated that no plant, including Vogtle, would be exempt from Task Force recommendations enacted in the future . . . .

IV. ANALYSIS

A. NRC's Refusal to Admit Petitioners' Contentions

NRC regulations dictate the criteria that a party's contention must meet in order to initiate a contested hearing. Because we have held that NRC's "procedural rules [under 10 C.F.R. § 2.309(f)] do not facially violate the Atomic Energy Act or the APA [and] they are also consistent with NEPA," and because we find that NRC reasonably applied these rules in evaluating Petitioners' contentions, we defer to NRC's rejection of Petitioners' contentions. . . .

1. The Task Force Report Alone Was Not a "New and Significant" Circumstance Requiring a Supplemental EIS

. . . Under NEPA, NRC is obligated to undertake a supplemental EIS only when presented with "substantial changes in the proposed action that are relevant to environmental concerns" or "new and significant circumstances or information relevant to environmental concerns and bearing on the proposed action or its impacts" after the EIS is assembled. 10 C.F.R. § 51.92(a)(1)–(2) . "New and significant" information presents "a seriously different picture of the environmental impact of the proposed project from what was previously envisioned." The determination as to whether information is either new or significant "requires a high level of technical expertise"; thus, we "defer to the informed discretion of the [Commission]."

Petitioners contend that the Task Force recommendations give rise to an obligation to supplement the Vogtle EIS because the recommendations may alter NRC regulations in the years ahead. Thus, in Petitioners' view, the Vogtle licenses necessarily must be delayed until the recommendations are finalized. We [disagree] . . . .

In this case, NRC's original EIS for Vogtle considered precisely the types of harm that occurred as a result of the Fukushima accident. The EIS considered consequences and mitigation of severe accidents involving reactor core damage and the release of fission products. In addition, the EIS for the Vogtle early site permit evaluated the human health impacts, economic costs, and land contamination risks, concluding that the environmental risks associated with severe accidents from an AP1000 reactor at the Vogtle site "would be small compared to risks associated with operation of the current-generation reactors at [Vogtle]" and were "well below NRC safety goals."

Petitioners' contentions provide no explanation as to how the Task Force Report recommendations raise previously unaddressed issues. The Commission reasonably concluded that, for their contentions to be admitted for consideration, Petitioners were required to cite particular information that was missing from the Vogtle EIS based on particular recommendations from the Task Force. Petitioners failed to do this.

Petitioners argue that, once NRC described the Fukushima accident as "significant," the agency was obligated to generate new environmental reports for all implicated pending sites and reactor designs. This argument is clearly unavailing, as it relies on Petitioners' elision of "safety significance" with "environmental significance." In the case on which Petitioners chiefly rely, *San Luis Obispo Mothers for Peace v. NRC*, 449 F.3d 1016 (9th Cir. 2006), NRC had categorically declined to consider any environmental consequences resulting from terrorism-related threats. . . . The situation here is quite different. In this case, NRC thoroughly analyzed the environmental consequences of severe accidents for Vogtle. Chairman Jaczko, the lone dissenter from the issuance of the Vogtle licenses, objected because he sought greater assurances that the Vogtle reactors would remain in compliance with future safety regulations. The Chairman did not contend that his concerns about safety standards created present environmental concerns; and he did not claim that there were any present shortcomings at the Vogtle site or any need for additional NEPA review. . . .

2. Petitioners' Contentions Lacked Specific Links Between the Fukushima Accident and the Vogtle Site

[Petitioners' arguments also fail because they did not show a specific nexus between the risks present in the Fukushima disaster and the Vogtle site.] The First Circuit, addressing an appeal from NRC's denial of other post-Fukushima objections to plant licensing actions, held that a petitioner's "mere pointing to a piece of information and speculating that the results of the [environmental risk analysis] may be different was not sufficient to meet" the Commission's stringent standards for reopening a closed proceeding. *Massachusetts v. NRC*, 708 F.3d 63, 76–77 (1st Cir. 2013). We agree. . . .

In light of the Commission's decision [that if "new and significant information comes to light that requires consideration as part of the ongoing preparation of application-specific NEPA documents, [we] will assess the significance of that information, as appropriate,"], Petitioners were obligated to present a contention sufficiently detailed and specifically related to the challenged reactor location to demonstrate how the contention differed from the "premature" generic request that the Commission denied . . . . Absent any evidence—or even allegation—linking the conditions at the Vogtle site itself to the Task Force recommendations, NRC appropriately applied the applicable contention-specificity regulations in declining to admit Petitioners' contentions. . . .

C. Approval of AP1000 Reactor Design Certification

Finally, we hold that NRC properly declined to supplement its existing EA for the AP1000 design certification amendment before adopting the final rule. The EA for a design certification amendment considers only whether the design change that is the subject of the proposed amendment renders a previously rejected Severe Accident Mitigation Design Alternative cost beneficial or identifies a new alternative necessitating its own cost-benefit analysis. *See* 10 C.F.R. § 51.30(d). The Commission reasonably found that the existing AP1000 EA adequately considered Severe Accident Mitigation Design Alternatives.

In considering the AP1000 design certification amendment, NRC reexamined the probability that a severe accident might occur and concluded that potential design changes did not affect its original evaluations. NRC erred "on the side of high consequences" and concluded that the AP1000 EA "make[s] a convincing case that no identified [Severe Accident Mitigation Design Alternative] is worth the expense." Petitioners do not challenge this analysis, nor do they connect any of the Task Force recommendations to any alternative that NRC failed to consider. Without an explicit challenge, NRC appropriately relied on its 2011 EA in approving the final AP1000 rule amendment. Indeed, the Task Force Report "supports completing [the AP1000] design certification rulemaking activities without delay."

Petitioners have failed to demonstrate that NRC acted less than reasonably in declining to order a supplemental EA for the AP1000 design certification amendment. We therefore defer to the Commission's conclusion that such a supplement was unnecessary.

NOTES AND QUESTIONS

1.   *Blue Ridge Environmental Defense League* puts front and center the question of public participation in NRC licensing proceedings. Do you think the public interest groups in that case were able to adequately participate? Do you think they felt their input received sufficient weight? The NRC says that it "considers public involvement in . . . our activities to be a cornerstone of strong, fair regulation of the nuclear industry." U.S. Nuclear Reg. Comm'n, *Public Participation* (updated Aug. 15, 2017). Was that objective fulfilled in *Blue Ridge Environmental Defense League?*

2.   The issue of public participation before the NRC has a long and somewhat tortured history. "It is an article of faith—albeit a false one—among many nuclear power proponents that public participation in the original adjudicatory licensing process created under the Atomic Energy Act was the primary cause of the industry's travails during the implosion of the first nuclear build-out." Christopher E. Paine, *The Nuclear Fuel Cycle, Global Security, and Climate Change: Weighing the Costs and Benefits of Nuclear Power Expansion*, 44 U. RICH. L. REV. 1047, 1060 (2010). Thus, while some pro-nuclear interests have criticized public participation in NRC licensing as crippling, others have suggested that the NRC unduly limits the scope and nature of public involvement.

One hurdle is that the NRC requires a party to show that it has standing to intervene in a licensing proceeding, meaning that not just any member of the public can participate. *See* David A. Repka & Tyson R. Smith, *Proximity, Presumptions, and Public Participation: Reforming Standing at the Nuclear Regulatory Commission*, 62 ADMIN. L. REV. 583 (2010). Another is that NRC procedures are quite unique among agencies, even though they were overhauled in 2004 to increase efficiency and efficacy. As one set of commentators has suggested, "Even if a member of the public overcomes all the hurdles and actually manages to meet the requirements for a hearing, the path to full and fair exploration of the few issues that survived the procedural gauntlet is littered with potholes and roadside bombs designed to further impede a full exploration of the issues pressed by a public participant." Anthony Z. Roisman et al., *Regulating Nuclear Power in the New Millennium (The Role of the Public)*, 26 PACE ENV'T L. REV. 317, 344 (2009). Others have urged that public participation at the NRC, when it does occur, is not meaningful because the agency has been "captured" by the nuclear industry. *See, e.g.*, UNION OF CONCERNED SCIENTISTS, NUCLEAR POWER AND GLOBAL WARMING 6 (2007); Tom Zeller Jr., *Nuclear Agency Is Criticized as Too Close to Its Industry*, N.Y. TIMES (May 7, 2011). *But see* Hope M. Babcock, *A Risky Business: Generation of Nuclear Power and Deepwater Drilling for Offshore Oil and Gas*, 37 COLUM. J. ENV'T L. 63, 133–34 (2012) (documenting steps the NRC has taken to avoid regulatory capture).

What level of public involvement in NRC proceedings do you think is appropriate? Is public participation critical, both to have an agency watchdog and to ensure that safety is adequately monitored? Or is the very idea of public participation in nuclear proceedings a myth because the average citizen cannot meaningfully comment on such highly technical matters? *Cf.* Harold P. Green, *Public Participation in Nuclear Power Plant Licensing: The Great Delusion*, 15 WM. & MARY L. REV. 503, 516 (1974). One view is that these questions are irrelevant, because public participation is necessary as a practical matter. *See* Richard Goldsmith, *Regulatory Reform and the Revival of Nuclear Power*, 20 HOFSTRA L. REV. 159, 209–10 (1991) ("The need for meaningful public participation in nuclear regulation is a political reality even if it is entirely 'delusional,' as one of its most thoughtful critics has charged.").

3.   The type of reactor discussed in *Blue Ridge Environmental Defense League*—the Westinghouse AP1000—is part of a newer category of technology typically referred to as Generation III or III+ reactors. In this nomenclature, Generation I reactors were those built in the 1950s and 1960s, with the last of its generation having been shut down in the United Kingdom in 2015. Generation II reactors "are typified by the present US and French fleets and most in operation elsewhere." *Advanced Nuclear Power Reactors*, World Nuclear Ass'n (last updated Apr. 2021). Generation III and III+ reactors are those now being built or recently put into operation, though some suggest that their "distinction from Generation II is arbitrary." *Id.* Generation IV reactor designs are in research and development. A U.S.-led international task force of thirteen countries is working on seven design concepts, some of which are fast reactors (and thus more efficient at uranium use), "with a view to commercial deployment by 2030." *Id.*

Several features set apart Generation III reactors from their predecessors. First, they tend to use more passive safety features, such as stored water and control rods that can be released via gravity in case of emergency, rather than "active" safety features that require electricity to operate, such as heat pumps or forced air ventilation. The intent is to reduce the risk of Fukushima-style meltdowns and explosions in the case of an earthquake or other event. Second, these reactors are built through modular construction. That is, different components are prefabricated and assembled on site, rather than the entire facility being built step-by-step on site. The aim is twofold: to reduce overall construction time because different components can be manufactured simultaneously rather than sequentially, and to allow for standardization of facilities. Third, Generation III reactors are designed to be load-following. That is, they can ramp up and down in terms of production as demand for electricity fluctuates. In addition, Generation III units tend to have a larger installed capacity—the measure of how much electricity they can produce—while taking up less space than their predecessors. *See id.*

The AP1000 bears each of these features. It includes nine separate passive safety systems that seek to ensure the plant will "achieve and maintain safe shutdown condition without operator action, and without the need for ac power or pumps," for at least 72 hours. *AP1000 Nuclear Power Plant—Passive Safety*

Systems, Westinghouse Elec. Co. LLC. It is composed of 149 structural and 198 mechanical modules that all can be manufactured off-site. It is designed to operate as a load-following unit as needed when it is running between 25 and 100 percent of capacity. And it is much more compact than prior units. When compared to similar power units built in the 1970s and 1980s, for instance, the AP1000 requires only about one-quarter the footprint and one-fifth the concrete and steel for construction.

4.   The AP1000 was announced to much acclaim. Westinghouse boasted that the design meant that "[t]he future of nuclear energy is here" because the AP1000 offers the "most advanced safety systems," is "[q]uicker to construct," requires "[l]ess maintenance," and is "ideal for new baseload generation." *AP1000 Nuclear Power Plant Design*, Westinghouse Elec. Co. LLC.

Indeed, as mentioned in *Blue Ridge Environmental Defense League*, the NRC gave this reactor final design certification in December 2005, the first Generation III+ reactor to receive such approval. That certification was "the culmination of a 1300 man-year and $440 million design and testing program." World Nuclear Ass'n, *Advanced Nuclear Power Reactors* (Aug. 2017). In an effort to offer a globally standardized design, Westinghouse then applied for pre-licensing design approval in the United Kingdom in 2007. That application garnered support from European utilities and "was granted in 2017." *Id.*

While other advanced designs have been deployed across the globe, the Westinghouse design quickly became the most dominant advanced reactor option globally. The four most prominent facilities to undergo construction in the United States—Southern Company's Vogtle Units 3 and 4 in Georgia, and SCANA's and Santee Cooper's now-abandoned Summer Units 2 and 3 in South Carolina—were slated to use the AP1000. Westinghouse also built four AP1000 units in China—Haiyang Units 1 and 2, completed in 2020, and Sanmen Units 1 and 2, completed in 2018—and has many more slated for completion there. *Advanced Nuclear Power Reactors, supra.*

Overall, since 2011, 58 nuclear reactors have begun operation globally, with the most—34—starting operation in China, followed by Russia (10) and then South Korea (5). *World Nuclear Power Plants in Operation*, Nuclear Energy Inst. (Mar. 2020). As of May 2021, another roughly 50 power reactors were under construction in 16 countries, with China again leading the way. *Plans for New Reactors Worldwide*, World Nuclear Ass'n (May 2021).

5.   Despite the auspiciousness with which the AP1000 was announced, the design has run into significant setbacks. While the control room for Haiyang Unit 1 in China was declared operational in May 2015, cost overruns and construction delays at all four U.S. units started having large, negative ripple effects.

In early 2008, Westinghouse submitted to the NRC an amended plan to alter the AP1000 design, specifically, to address concerns whether the reactor containment would be able to withstand impact from an aircraft. Although the NRC granted this revised design certification in December 2011, the change increased capital costs. In turn, other construction cost overruns and delays began to mount.

In March 2017, Westinghouse filed for Chapter 11 bankruptcy and was subsequently acquired by Brookfield, an asset management company, for about $4.6 billion. Westinghouse's financial demise was a direct result of the escalating construction costs at the Vogtle and Summer plants, which also left its parent company, Toshiba, in near financial ruin. *How Two Cutting Edge U.S. Nuclear Projects Bankrupted Westinghouse*, REUTERS (May 1, 2017); *Westinghouse Purchase Pulls It Out of Bankruptcy*, POWER TECH. (Aug. 3, 2018).

In July 2017, Santee Cooper announced that it would abandon the Summer project in South Carolina due to cost overruns, with SCANA then declaring that the project would be canceled altogether. Although Toshiba had offered the companies $2.2 billion toward construction costs, Santee Cooper's analysis showed that the facility would be completed four years later than even its latest, quite-delayed estimate and cost the company $11.4 billion for its 45% share in the facility—more than double the original budget of $5.1 billion. Predictably, litigation began almost immediately over the stranded costs from the plant, and in July 2020, Santee Cooper agreed to provide $520 million in refunds to its 1.7 million customers as a settlement of a class action against the utility. *See* Peter Maloney, *SCE&G, Santee Cooper Face More Litigation over Summer Nuclear Project Abandonment*, UTIL. DIVE (Aug. 31, 2017); *$520 Million Settlement Approved in Santee Cooper Lawsuit*, U.S. NEWS & WORLD REPORT (July 21, 2020). In 2021, former SCANA CEO Kevin B. Marsh was sentenced to two years in federal prison for counts of conspiracy to commit mail and wire fraud after he asserted that the Summer project was on track when in fact it was not. Acting U.S. Attorney M. Rhett DeHart declared, "Due to this fraud, an $11 billion nuclear ghost town, paid for by SCANA investors and customers, now sits vacant in Jenkinsville, S.C." *Former SCANA CEO Sentenced to Two Years for Defrauding Ratepayers in Connection with Failed Nuclear Construction Project*, U.S. ATTORNEY'S OFFICE FOR THE DIST. OF S.C. (Oct. 7, 2021).

Meanwhile, Southern Company has proceeded with construction at Vogtle in Georgia, even though that project has run more and more behind schedule and is expected to cost more than $27 billion, "nearly twice the original amount budgeted." *Georgia PSC Supports Continuing Plant Vogtle Project*, ATLANTA BUS. CHRON. (Aug. 15, 2017); *see also* Jeff Amy, *Georgia Nuclear Plant Costs Top $27 Billion As More Delays Unveiled*, AP (July 29, 2021). Toshiba agreed to pay $3.7 billion to the Vogtle project to complete construction, which Georgia regulators indicated was necessary for the project to continue. As of July 2021, Georgia Power expected that the first reactor would begin operation in the second quarter of 2022 and the second reactor in early 2023—six years behind schedule. *See* Matt Kemper, *Georgia Power Discloses More Vogtle Nuclear Delays, Big Extra Costs*, ATLANTA J.-CONST. (July 29, 2021).

6.   The continuing retirement of reactors from the U.S. nuclear fleet, due to plant aging as well as cost competitiveness difficulties, has created significant concern among those worried about climate change. Between 2012 and 2021, there have already been eleven nuclear plant shutdowns in the United States. In 2021, Illinois passed a bill providing substantial climate-based subsidies to its nuclear power plants after Exelon threatened to shutter the facilities. *See* Dan Petrella, *Gov. J.B. Pritzker Says He'll Sign Sweeping Energy Proposal That Bails Out Nuclear Plants, Sets Ambitious Clean-energy Targets, Following Senate Approval*, CHI. TRIB. (Sept. 13, 2021). One estimate shows that if no further investments are made to extend the operating life of the existing nuclear fleet, nuclear power production capacity will decline by two-thirds by 2040—causing a rise of 4 billion tons of CO_2 emissions. INT'L ENERGY AGENCY, NUCLEAR POWER IN A CLEAN ENERGY SYSTEM (May 2019).

To address these concerns, some U.S. states—Connecticut, Illinois, New Jersey, New York, and Ohio (though Ohio later reversed course)—have begun offering compensation to nuclear reactors for producing zero-GHG-emission electricity. The compensation comes in the form of zero emission credits (ZECs) and other subsidies, as discussed in Chapter 5. *Five States Have Implemented Programs to Assist Nuclear Power Plants*, U.S. Energy Info. Admin. (Oct. 7, 2019). Do you think lawmakers should take action to help keep nuclear reactors running? Why or why not? Does it change your mind to know that renewables such as wind and solar long have enjoyed significant federal tax credits and other financial subsidies? Does it color your thinking at all to know that in July 2020, federal prosecutors arrested the Speaker of the Ohio House of Representatives, Larry Householder, for allegedly accepting approximately $61 million in exchange for his assurance that the state's nuclear subsidization legislation would be passed?

7.   Given the ongoing difficulty in constructing new, large reactors like Vogtle and Summer, perhaps the most intriguing nuclear technology under development is the small modular reactor (SMR). SMRs have several potential advantages over their extant counterparts. The fact that they are small means they can use entirely passive technology for cooling, reducing their cost and creating a larger safety margin. Their size also means that they can match existing load growth, rather than depressing market prices by creating a glut of supply as soon as they come online. Further, their modularity means that they can be combined into a bundle if more generation capacity is needed—particularly helpful since units can be prefabricated and mass-produced. And, because they are smaller, SMRs can be used as load-following generation, which is what is most needed in the market as penetration of renewables continues to increase. *See generally* Robert Fares, *3 Ways Small Modular Reactors Overcome Existing Barriers to Nuclear*, SCI. AM. (May 19, 2016).

Two entities in the United States have expressed clear interest in developing SMRs. In 2016, the Tennessee Valley Authority (TVA) applied for an early site permit at Clinch River to potentially develop two or more SMRs (up to 800 MW). TVA received its early site permit in late 2019 and is working with the University of Tennessee to evaluate feasibility. In addition, the Utah

Associated Municipal Power Systems (UAMPS)—a political subdivision of the State of Utah that serves municipal and other public power systems in Utah, Arizona, California, Idaho, Nevada, New Mexico, Oregon, and Wyoming— plans to build several SMRs at the Idaho National Laboratory site in southeastern Idaho. UAMPS intends to use technology developed by NuScale, which received the first NRC approval of an SMR design in August 2020. Each NuScale module is 15 feet in diameter and 76 feet tall. James Conca, *NuScale's Small Modular Nuclear Reactor Keeps Moving Forward*, FORBES (Mar. 16, 2017). In January 2021, UAMPS and NuScale announced that they expect to place the first order for modules in 2022, with plans to submit a Combined License Application in 2023 and begin construction in 2025 or 2026. *NuScale and UAMPS Agreements Progress Plans for SMR Plant*, WORLD NUCLEAR NEWS (Jan. 12, 2021).

8.   One challenge for new reactor technologies is that many of them will demand a more highly enriched form of uranium than traditional reactors use. Some projections suggest a twenty-fold increase in demand for this fuel to meet climate goals—with not nearly enough production facilities in the pipeline and a construction schedule that often takes seven years to complete a facility. *See* Matthew Bandyk, *Nuclear Reactors of the Future Have a Fuel Problem*, UTIL. DIVE (Aug. 30, 2021).

9.   Students with additional interest in nuclear regulation as a standalone subject will do well to consult sources such as JAY M. GUTIERREZ & ALEX S. POLONSKY, FUNDAMENTALS OF NUCLEAR REGULATION IN THE UNITED STATES (2007), which provides an excellent introduction to understanding NRC regulation. For a more international perspective, see HELEN COOK, THE LAW OF NUCLEAR ENERGY (2d ed. 2017); ABDULLAH AL FARUQUE, NUCLEAR ENERGY REGULATION, RISK AND THE ENVIRONMENT (2019); CARLTON STOIBER ET AL., HANDBOOK ON NUCLEAR LAW (2003); and STEPHEN TROMANS, NUCLEAR LAW: THE LAW APPLYING TO NUCLEAR INSTALLATIONS AND RADIOACTIVE SUBSTANCES IN ITS HISTORIC CONTEXT (2d ed. 2010).

3.   NUCLEAR POWER AND ENERGY LAW

Controversy surrounding the use of nuclear energy is not unique. As illustrated throughout this book, virtually every issue in energy law and policy presents difficult, sometimes irresolvable, questions and conflicts. That is part of what makes energy law so fascinating. It touches every part of our lives.

What makes nuclear energy special, then, is the passion that parties tend to bring to the debate. Perhaps the nuclear discussion is so fervent, in part, because atomic energy also epitomizes the broad themes that run through U.S. energy law. This chapter thus uses atomic energy as a case study to highlight, and re-weave, the three core themes that dominate energy law. It is our hope that by drawing out these themes in the nuclear context, you may be able to see them more clearly—and apply them to— other substantive areas of energy law.

The three broad themes of energy law form the remainder of this chapter, which is organized around two case studies designed to bring out all three of the themes. Those themes are:

1. *Markets or planning?* The choice between "technology-forcing regulation" and "letting markets decide" is starkly apparent in nuclear energy. Should Congress encourage nuclear power because it is a relatively "clean" energy with next to no greenhouse gas or other air pollution emissions? Or is nuclear power really a "dirty," risky technology that should be used only if plants can compete against other sources on their own merit, without help from the law? From the outset, government has levied a heavy hand in nuclear power utilization. Proponents and opponents of the technology have good arguments that government intervention in this part of the energy market has both advanced and limited nuclear energy use.

2. *Who decides?* Although traditional "vertical" federalism questions long have arisen—and continue to arise—in the nuclear context, with states pitted against the federal government, the question of who decides in atomic energy is bound only to become even more complicated over time. Who should decide whether a nuclear power plant can be built in a local community, and on what basis? Should the local community's interest matter most, or something else—the regional need for more electricity, expert regulators' view of the facility's environmental safety, or national citizen preferences for low-emission electricity? In many states, local authorities have begun to flex more muscle over whether nuclear plants should operate there. Often, multiple state entities also play important roles in nuclear power, creating "horizontal" federalism questions, such as the debate over the state water board's approval of water rights for a proposed generator in southern Utah. *See HEAL Utah v. Kane Cnty. Water Conservancy Dist.*, 378 P.3d 1246 (Utah Ct. App. 2016). These efforts inevitably intersect with, and butt up against, governance roles that have been statutorily allocated to federal and state governments. And this is just one type of knotty governance question that nuclear power raises.

3. *Toward clean energy?* Perhaps more than any other resource, nuclear power highlights the difficulty in transitioning to a clean energy economy, precisely because nuclear is seen both as "clean" and "dirty" by different camps. For decades, nuclear energy was the filthiest of words in many environmental circles, but the imminence of climate change

forced many to reconsider. Then disaster struck at Fukushima Daiichi, and the "nuclear renaissance" many industry hawks long had called for fell immediately into doubt. Today, nuclear energy rests in as precarious a place as ever. Is the reliable, essentially emissions-free electricity that nuclear produces worth it, or are the risks too high? Is it really "cheap" electricity, or is the price of nuclear low only because the government subsidizes it? How do we balance the environmental demands of our energy use against our ever-growing thirst for more power? Nuclear power brings the fact that every energy source presents environmental and other tradeoffs into sharp contrast.

B. ATOMIC POWER AND THE ENERGY-ENVIRONMENT NEXUS

Today, the energy-environment debate around nuclear power focuses primarily on climate change. The tradeoffs are clear. Those concerned about continued utilization of nuclear facilities worry both about the risks of an atomic catastrophe and about the apparently unsolvable problem of disposing of nuclear waste. Those more in favor of the technology point to its key role in mitigating climate change, as roughly half of the United States' carbon-free emissions in electricity production come from this generation source.

The starkness of these environmental tradeoffs complicates the debate around nuclear power—and drives home how difficult energy law and policy choices are. As one astute observer has noted, "If you approach nuclear power as a policy question, on the merits, you will find that, like most things, it's complicated; there are multiple, overlapping issues involved, and the answers cannot be captured in a single binary." David Roberts, *A Beginner's Guide to the Debate over Nuclear Power and Climate Change*, VOX (Dec. 19, 2019). This is why it's true "that 'pro-nuclear' and 'anti-nuclear' are not considered policy positions. They are identities, ways of signaling membership in a tribe. You sign up for one team and then scold the other team on social media (you will have lots of company)." *Id.* To parse the question meaningfully requires delving more deeply into the tradeoffs that nuclear power poses—especially those at the intersection of energy and environment.

From a climate perspective, nuclear energy offers tangible benefits. "Nuclear power is a large-scale, concentrated energy source that provides round-the-clock electricity. Yet it is flexible enough to contribute effectively to low carbon energy systems with large shares of variable renewable sources like wind and solar. Its GHG emissions per kilowatt-hour are 40 times less than those of an efficient gas-fired power plant." *Climate Change and Nuclear Power 2020*, Int'l Atomic Energy Ass'n. Thus, as the world contemplates the possibilities of electricity consumption growing anywhere between 20% to 330% by 2050, the need for low-carbon electricity production sources will only heighten. *See id.* at 2. Whether nuclear should be at the center of that solution certainly can be contested. Whether, however, it should play a role in the mix of sources that helps address climate change is not a question that can be avoided.

Recognizing the complexity of that question, one useful lens for considering nuclear energy's role in mitigating climate change is to parse the technology by the different ways it is—or could be—deployed. In this connection, there are three separate issues that must be considered around nuclear power use and climate change:

- *Existing facilities*: What, if anything, should be done to help nuclear power plants that are operating today keep running in coming years? And how might the risks of pushing older plants beyond their original sunset dates be managed?

- *Modern construction*: Taking their climate change benefits into account, what path should be pursued in building new nuclear facilities, particularly as this solution to reducing greenhouse gas emissions tends to be quite expensive while renewables continue to beat the most optimistic cost forecasts?

- *New technologies*: How should traditional nuclear technology, even if more "advanced," be promoted or encouraged, particularly as compared to other new competing technologies, such as small modular nuclear reactors?

See Roberts, *supra.*

On this final point, a key challenge that nuclear power has faced over time is how to manage risk around its technologies. Originally, the Atomic Energy Commission relied on a "defense in depth" approach that sought to identify specific risks and then engineer multiple layers of protection and safeguards to prevent that risk. Over time, the AEC, and then its successor, the Nuclear Regulatory Commission, shifted to a different strategy: "probabilistic risk assessment." Under this approach, rather than defining specific threats, the agency would ask "more broadly what emergencies were most likely based on reactors' operating data in order to draw up defenses." In this way, probabilistic risk assessment "gave the NRC and reactor builders a cost-effective way to prioritize safety measures to avoid piling 'one safety system on the back of another.'" Peter Behr, *NRC Historian Details 'Safe Enough' Reactor Debate*, ENERGYWIRE (June 21, 2021). The idea, in short, is that no energy technology is risk-free. So, the question around nuclear power cannot be how to make the technology perfectly safe; it is how to make nuclear "safe enough." *See generally*

THOMAS R. WELLOCK, SAFE ENOUGH? A HISTORY OF NUCLEAR POWER AND ACCIDENT RISK (2021).

Although today nuclear energy's environmental tradeoffs are often seen through a climate change lens, historically that was not the case. The question of safety long predominated the nuclear power discourse. That perspective, of course, continues to matter deeply. The risk of environmental disaster from nuclear power is never far from the center of the discourse.

Indeed, disasters have heavily shaped the nuclear industry's fate. Three are most crucial. In 1979, the Three Mile Island facility in Dauphin County, Pennsylvania partially melted down, causing fear and panic in the United States. Although the accident was contained and no one was killed, the incident catalyzed and helped solidify an anti-nuclear sentiment among some in the public. *See Backgrounder on the Three Mile Island Accident*, U.S. Nuclear Reg. Comm'n (last updated June 2018). This might have been in part because the film *The China Syndrome* was released on March 16, 1979—only twelve days before the Three Mile Island accident. The film featured a storyline involving cover-ups of safety breaches and fabricated safety records at a nuclear facility near Los Angeles. Although the film was fictitious, it successfully stoked the fears of industry cover-ups in U.S. nuclear plants. In fact, nuclear opposition was growing in the United States before Three Mile Island, and it only increased after. In 1975, fifty different bills were introduced in twenty-four state legislatures prohibiting or restricting the use and development of commercial nuclear power plants. Arthur W. Murphy & D. Bruce La Pierre, *Nuclear "Moratorium" Legislation in the States and the Supremacy Clause: A Case of Express Preemption*, 76 COLUM. L. REV. 392 (1976). As of 2017, fourteen states had restrictions on the construction of new nuclear plants, but only one state, Minnesota, placed an outright ban on new nuclear power plants. The limits states have put on the construction of new nuclear plants include state legislature approval, voter approval, and findings of economic feasibility for ratepayers. *State Restrictions on New Nuclear Power Facility Construction*, Nat'l Conf. of State Legis. (updated May 2017). Notably, a few states, like Kentucky and Wisconsin, have repealed longstanding bans on new nuclear plants in recent years or are reconsidering existing bans. *Id.*

The 1986 Chernobyl disaster in what is now the Ukraine (formerly the U.S.S.R.) was far worse. The meltdown of that facility resulted in the immediate death of two workers, and the subsequent deaths of twenty-eight people within a few weeks of the accident. The event forced the immediate evacuation of approximately 115,000 people. Eventually, resettlements out of the most contaminated zones totaled over 500,000. ADRIANA PETRYNA, LIFE EXPOSED: BIOLOGICAL CITIZENS AFTER CHERNOBYL 82 (2002). The blast deposited large amounts of radioactive debris nearby and, more ominously, formed a radioactive cloud that traveled over Russia, Belarus, Ukraine, and much of Europe. A walk through a hospital ward serving infants of those who were working or evacuated from the areas closest to Chernobyl and received high doses of radiation revealed children with missing lungs, extra fingers, and "guts" outside the body. *Id.* The impact was far-reaching enough that it affected the safe use of sheep in the United Kingdom; today, Germans still are urged not to consume wild boars, which remain radioactive, or the mushrooms they eat. By 2000, about 4,000 children exposed to radiation from Chernobyl were diagnosed with thyroid cancer. Although the reactor used at Chernobyl was different in kind from those in the United States, the tragedy captivated the public's imagination and further cemented the link between nuclear power and the risk of disaster. *See Backgrounder on Chernobyl Nuclear Power Plant Accident*, U.S. Nuclear Reg. Comm'n (last updated Aug. 2018). The Chernobyl disaster was so defining for the nuclear industry that in 2019—more than thirty years after the meltdown—HBO premiered an award-winning miniseries dramatizing the 1986 crisis.

Yet for twenty-five years after Chernobyl, the nuclear industry operated largely without incident. Then, in 2011, just as it looked like nuclear energy might make a resurgence as a climate change mitigation tool, disaster struck at the Fukushima Daiichi plant on Japan's eastern coast.

1.   THE DISASTER AT FUKUSHIMA DAIICHI

Fukushima started with an earthquake, but the shockwaves it sent through the nuclear industry were just as far-reaching. Across the globe, governments responded to the disaster in myriad ways, including a rather cautious but business-as-usual course in the United States and the resurrection of a flat ban—and a process for closing all the country's nuclear power plants—in Germany.

The unfolding of the Fukushima disaster is itself a fascinating tale, one full of mistakes, miscommunication, heroism, human folly, engineering hubris, and, as some would observe, the inevitability that no technology is accident-proof.

EVAN OSNOS, THE FALLOUT: LETTER FROM FUKUSHIMA
New Yorker (Oct. 17, 2011)

On the afternoon of March 11th—a Friday—the Fukushima Daiichi Nuclear Power Station, on Japan's Pacific coast, had more than six thousand workers inside. The plant, about a hundred and fifty miles north of Tokyo, is painted white and pale blue and is a labyrinth of boxy buildings and piping on a campus larger than the Pentagon's. It has six reactors. Yusuke Tataki was in the concrete building that contains Reactor No. 4.

He is a tobi worker—a scaffolder—and, at thirty-three, is small and nimble. Like many of the plant's employees, he grew up nearby. He often skipped classes to surf, and after high school he worked, unhappily, on an assembly line welding circuit boards, until he got into scaffolding, which has kept him employed, on and off, at nuclear plants ever since. "Even when there's no work elsewhere, there is work at the plants," he told me recently.

At 2:46 P.M. on March 11th, an earthquake began to rattle the building, more violent than any Tataki could remember. It knocked him to the ground, and the lights failed. In darkness, he heard steel crashing against steel and men shouting. The building groaned. Heavy objects fell around him from heights of three or four stories. When the shaking stopped and emergency lights came on, the air was thick with a chalky haze of dust and concrete. Tataki knew that the only way out of the building was through an air lock—a set of parallel doors designed to prevent contamination—but the quake had jammed it shut. The workers around him were disciplined but anxious, and they banged on the door for help. "We all knew that during a quake everything in there could become contaminated with radiation," he told me.

The quake had erupted beneath the ocean floor two hundred and thirty miles northeast of Tokyo, at a magnitude of 9.0—the strongest ever recorded in Japan. On that day, three of the Fukushima plant reactors were down for routine maintenance; the other three shut down automatically, as intended.

After a few minutes, a guard managed to open the jammed door, and Tataki hurried toward the parking lot. He has a wife and two children, and wanted to check on them and on his house. About seven hundred employees remained. "We had trained for this," Keiichi Kakuta, a forty-two-year-old father of two, who worked in the public-affairs department, told me. "Of course, the mood was tense, but after someone said the reactors had shut down I saw the plant chief calmly instructing people what to do." . . .

In the imagination, tsunamis are a single towering wave, but often they arrive in a crescendo, which is a cruel fact. After the first wave, survivors in Japan ventured down to the water's edge to survey who could be saved, only to be swept away by the second. In all, twenty thousand people died or disappeared along a stretch of the Japanese coast greater than the distance from New York to Providence.

At the plant, the first wave arrived at 3:27 P.M., but it did not overtop a thirty-three-foot concrete seawall. Eight minutes later, the second wave appeared: a churning white mass of water, four stories tall, that leaped over sixty thousand concrete blocks and barriers—designed to defend against typhoons, not tsunamis—and advanced toward the reactors. First, the water approached the turbine buildings, which had been built with large shutters facing the sea. It burst through the closed shutters and swamped the buildings. Inside, the plant's emergency diesel generators, each the size of an eighteen-wheeler, were stored on the ground floor and in the basements. They were destroyed, and two workers who had been sent underground to check for leaks were killed. The water hurled pickup trucks pinwheeling end over end into delicate pipes and equipment, and it swamped the campus in roiling brown pools, fifteen feet deep, leaving the nuclear reactors protruding like boulders in a river. And then it recoiled into the sea.

Two minutes after the water arrived, the plant's main control rooms began to lose electrical power. Hundreds of gauges and instruments went dark or froze. A worker who was keeping a log of the deteriorating situation scribbled something unprecedented in a Japanese nuclear plant: "SBO"—station blackout. Kakuta said to himself, "What happens now?" Without a constant source of coolant, the nuclear fuel rods in the heart of the three active reactors would eventually boil away the water that prevents them from melting down. The log entry was grim: "Water levels unknown." Workers desperate for electricity had to improvise: they fanned out into the parking lot to scavenge car batteries from any vehicles that had survived the wave.

When the earthquake struck, the top ranks of Japan's government were already in one place: at a meeting in a wood-paneled chamber of the national legislature, in Tokyo, discussing whether the Prime Minister, Naoto Kan, had taken illegal campaign donations. . . . At 7:03 P.M., Kan declared a nuclear emergency, and shortly afterward he ordered people within three kilometres of the plant to evacuate; the number of nuclear refugees eventually expanded to eighty thousand. But that evening Kan's spokesman, Yukio Edano, projected calm: "Let me repeat that there is no radiation leak, nor will there be a leak."

Gregory Jaczko, the chairman of the United States Nuclear Regulatory Commission, learned of the tsunami before dawn, in Washington, D.C., from his clock radio. The quake had struck overnight, D.C. time, and his first concern was about any tsunami effects on the West Coast of the United States. Once it was clear that there were none, he turned to Fukushima, but his staff was having a difficult time determining the details of what was happening. Over the phone, Japanese counterparts were vague or inconsistent, leaving exasperated American officials at the N.R.C.'s headquarters, in Rockville, Maryland, to watch the unfolding drama helplessly. "We were getting a lot of our information from the same source that everybody else was: open source, CNN, Japanese television," Patricia Milligan, a senior N.R.C. emergency-preparedness specialist, recalled. Initially, Jaczko was not surprised; the tsunami had created an epic humanitarian crisis. He figured Japanese authorities were too busy to keep him updated. But gradually he reached a more disturbing conclusion. "It wasn't a question of them not providing the information to us," he told me. "The information just didn't exist." . . .

As night fell on March 11th, it became clear that the Fukushima Daiichi plant's operator, the Tokyo Electric Power Company, which produces a third of the country's electricity, had been unprepared for such a disaster. After the lights went out in the plant, engineers had to borrow flashlights from nearby homes in order to creep through dark, waterlogged passageways to study the gauges.

There was no mystery about what they were facing: the core of each operating reactor held at least twenty-five thousand twelve-foot fuel rods— slender metal tubes filled with pellets of enriched uranium. When things were working normally, the nuclear reaction in the core produced enormous amounts of heat, used to boil water for steam. . . . The reaction also produced radioactive isotopes, which are safely contained within a series of steel-and-concrete defenses arranged like nesting dolls. But, with the power out, and emergency systems down, there was no way to cool the hot fuel; it was rapidly boiling away the water around it—creating huge pressure in the reactor—and eventually it would begin to melt, eating through the shells encasing it.

In a log later filed with the International Atomic Energy Agency, workers recorded frantic efforts to get water on the fuel. They tried to use a fire truck, but waves had thrown a storage tank across the road, making it impassable. To restore electricity, they called for emergency power vehicles, but those were stymied by traffic on damaged roads. . . .

Of the six reactors, No. 1 needed the most urgent help: the uranium was melting through the fuel rods, and when the damaged rods mixed with steam they gave off hydrogen, which is highly combustible. In order to prevent an explosion, the steam had to be released through a vent, and that meant piping radiation straight into the air. But the alternative was worse: wait too long, and an explosion would release a far larger burst of radiation. By 3 A.M., the government and Tokyo Electric knew that the vent had to be opened, but four hours later it was still closed. Later, the company said that it was waiting to make sure that all nearby residents had evacuated. Government officials have alleged that the company didn't want to release radiation, because it would have immediately invited comparisons to the Chernobyl disaster, in the U.S.S.R., in 1986.

Finally, Prime Minister Kan flew by helicopter to the plant and demanded that Tokyo Electric open the vent. According to *Yomiuri Shimbun*, the chief of the plant replied, "We'll form a suicide squad to do it."

Opening the vent was such an unusual prospect that workers needed the blueprints to figure out how to do it, but the prints were in a building whose ceiling had collapsed. Only after they were retrieved did workers learn how the vent could be opened manually.

Six workers divided into three teams of two. Going in alone would be impossible, because the men would be operating in darkness, amid aftershocks, without radio contact with headquarters. According to the log, the teams would work in a relay, so that no one would be exposed to too much radiation.

The six workers assembled in the main control room. They had swallowed tablets that flooded their thyroid glands with iodine and hindered their bodies from absorbing radioactive iodine from the air; they wore dosimeters—portable radiation detectors that would warn them when they were nearing the legal limits of exposure. They were outfitted in heavy firefighting suits with oxygen tanks, gear that would shield them from inhaling and absorbing through their skin tiny particles that emit alpha and beta radiation, which can linger in the body for years, causing organ damage. The equipment, however, would provide little protection against gamma rays, so their only true defense would be to get out of danger as fast as possible.

At 9:04 A.M., the first two workers, carrying flashlights, set off into the darkness of Reactor Building No. 1. They found the manual gate valve, which can be opened by laboriously cranking a metal handle through hundreds of revolutions, like a man pumping an old-fashioned handcar down a railroad track. They cranked it open a quarter of the way and retreated. They had been inside for eleven minutes. The second team went in, but, with the vent partly ajar, the radiation level was climbing fast, and the men were driven back before they could even reach their target. They had been inside for no more than six minutes, but one of them received a radiation dose greater than the legal limits allowed for five years of work in the plant. It was deemed too risky to try again, and the third team was disbanded.

Despite those efforts, that afternoon, at 3:36 P.M., Reactor Building No. 1 exploded, hurling chunks of concrete that injured five workers and destroyed cables that had been laid in the hope of restoring electricity. With that explosion, the crisis passed an invisible line, as each problem triggered another. High radiation levels hampered workers trying to vent Reactor No. 3, and on the third day after the tsunami it, too, exploded. The following day, another blast occurred, this time at No. 4. On television screens throughout the world, three exposed steel carcasses were seen smoldering. An American aircraft carrier and its fleet left waters downwind of the plant after seventeen helicopter crew members returned from missions with traces of radiation.

By Tuesday, March 15th, conditions at the plant were becoming untenable. Radiation in part of the plant had climbed to four hundred millisieverts per hour; after less than thirty minutes of exposure at that level, the risk of cancer increases measurably. "It was the worst day of my life," the Prime Minister's nuclear adviser, Goshi Hosono, recalled. . . . Japanese leaders, who had been working without sleep for days, were beginning to buckle under the demands. One suspected that he was having a stroke. Prime Minister Kan's thoughts veered toward the apocalyptic. He imagined "deserted scenes of Tokyo without a single man," he later told a Japanese reporter. . . .

After Chernobyl, many countries suspended plans to expand nuclear power, but Japan did not. Within two years, it had begun construction on five more plants. Although public opinion soured, the industry responded with a major investment in the visitors' centers attached to its plants, adding swimming pools, golf courses, tennis courts, gardens, and IMAX theatres. . . . Where the centers once targeted men interested in science, they now focused on attracting women and children, according to Noriya Sumihara, a cultural anthropologist at Tenri University. . . . "The companies believed that mothers were key decision-makers in the family," he said. "If women felt the plants were relatively safe, then men would, too."

Not far from Tokyo, the Tokaimura nuclear power plant maintains a complex called Atom World, which has two floors of games and interactive exhibits. When I visited recently, kids were being greeted by a young woman in a red apron printed with the image of a smiling uranium atom. . . . Exhibits were narrated by cartoon characters, such as Uranium Boy and Little Pluto Boy, short for plutonium, who dispensed advice. "No need to worry too much!" he said on a poster about food with legal traces of radiation. When Japan was debating the use of a plutonium-fuelled reactor, in 1993, visitor centers added a video of Little Pluto Boy helping a child drink liquid plutonium, assuring him, "It's unthinkable that I could cause any effects on the human body!" The video is no longer used. (It's still available on YouTube.)[4]

The visitors' center at Tokaimura showed a short film that described uranium as "a gift from God" and "the fire of hope in the twenty-first century." . . .

The myth of total safety went beyond public relations and degraded the industry's technical competence. According to Taro Kono, a legislator in the Liberal Democratic Party, emergency drills in the plants were scheduled to fit within an eight-hour workday, rather than simulating realistic conditions. A 2002 report by Tokyo Electric and five other companies declared, "There is no need to take a hydrogen explosion into consideration," the *Yomiuri Shimbun* reported. (After the third hydrogen explosion at Fukushima, a company official conceded . . . that "we were

---

4   [*See* http://www.youtube.com/watch?v=Q_6yomWh05o.—Eds.]

overly confident.") Government regulators adopted a similar posture. A 1990 set of Nuclear Safety Commission guidelines announced, "We do not need to take into account the danger of a long-term power severance." Even basic precautions were declared obsolete: Japan once developed a set of radiation-resistant robots to use in the event of a nuclear accident; in 2006, all but two of them were donated to a university and a museum. After the Fukushima meltdowns, Japan had to depend on devices from iRobot, an American manufacturer best known for producing the Roomba vacuum cleaner. . . .

By March 15th, . . . [i]t was clear that in the process of bringing the plant under control some people would receive doses previously considered illegal. Normally, Japanese workers were barred from receiving more than a hundred millisieverts over five years; now the Health Ministry officially raised that limit to two hundred and fifty millisieverts—five times the maximum exposure permitted for American workers. . . .

Japan's defense forces arrived the next day. The results were not reassuring. Chinook helicopters scooped up buckets of seawater from the Pacific and nosed in toward Reactor No. 3, but they were forced back by high radiation. Lead plates were bolted to the bellies of the choppers for a second attempt, the next morning, but most of the water scattered in the wind. . . .

A more decisive maneuver had been gathering strength, with far less attention, for several days. Even as buildings exploded, some of the workers had hooked up a train of fire trucks capable of generating enough pressure to inject water directly into the fuel cores. (As with the helicopters, they drew water from the ocean—a desperate measure, because a multibillion-dollar reactor that has been bathed in saltwater can never be used again.) The drenching continued around the clock, and it went on for months—an approach known as "feed and bleed." Casto, of the N.R.C., said, "No one ever envisioned steam-cooling reactors for long periods of time. In reactor world, this is all new." The process was ungainly, and it produced millions of gallons of radioactive water that is dangerous to store, but it probably did more than any other measure to avert a far worse disaster. . . .

The effects of the Fukushima disaster were severe. Fukushima's meltdown impacted not just the workers from Tokyo Electric Power but also the surrounding community, region, and environment:

> The release of radiation forced the evacuation of approximately 86,000 people from around the facility. The Japanese government established a six-mile evacuation perimeter, a perimeter it later doubled . . . .

The failure to contain Fukushima resulted in substantial environmental contamination. The scope of immediate fallout was so vast it included an area as large as Chicago. . . . Six months after the meltdowns, local fishermen and cattle farmers were still banned from selling their yields. . . .

A half-year after the explosions at the reactors, work remained ongoing to strip local land of contaminated soil . . . . One government estimate suggested that nearly 2500 square kilometers of contaminated soil would need to be cleared—an area bigger than Tokyo itself. Consequently, the region . . . became home to scores of "nuclear gypsies" who traveled from across the country to work on the cleanup. As one report put it, "anyone who isn't [in Fukushima] on business simply isn't there." . . .

Although the International Atomic Energy Agency confirmed that the site had become "essentially stable" six months after the tragedy began, doubts about the area's future remain. . . . Trying to quell fears that cleanup efforts were ineffective at decontaminating water at the site, a government official in November took the dare of a journalist, went on television, and drank half a glass of water collected from the reactor buildings. The Japanese government also . . . acknowledged that . . . much of the area will remain evacuated indefinitely—for decades at least. "We cannot deny a possibility that some of the residents may not be able to return to their homes for a long time," acknowledged Chief Cabinet Secretary Yukio Edano in an August news conference. "We are very sorry."

Lincoln L. Davies, *Beyond Fukushima: Disasters, Nuclear Energy, and Energy Law*, 2011 B.Y.U. L. REV. 1937.

A decade hence, the impacts of this disaster continue to linger—in Fukushima prefecture and beyond. The Japanese government has spent ¥32 trillion ($295 billion) on recovery efforts for the region, including constructing a controversial gray concrete seawall, as high as 50 feet in some places, to try to quell future tsunamis. Fukushima Daiichi's operator, Tokyo Electric Power Company, has estimated it will pay ¥21.5 trillion to decommission the site, compensate evacuees, and decontaminate materials outside the plant's boundary. Worse, the triple earthquake-tsunami-nuclear disaster displaced almost 500,000 people; nearly 43,000, including over 35,000 from Fukushima, still have not been able to return home. "No-go zones remain in nine Fukushima municipalities surrounding the wrecked nuclear plant," accounting for 2.4% of prefectural land. *Fukushima Anniversary: Loss of Life Is Still 'Unbearable,'* DEUTSCHE WELLE (Mar. 11, 2021). Radioactive materials remain far from the Daiichi site. Enough radioactive soil, trees, and other waste to fill 11 baseball stadiums has been collected and remains in "waste bags piled at temporary storage sites." *Id.* "Greenpeace has been taking thousands of radiation readings for years in the towns around the Fukushima nuclear plant. It says radiation levels in parts in Namie[, a town just north of the Daiichi facilities and] where evacuation orders have been lifted[,] will remain well above international maximum safety recommendations for many decades, raising the risks of leukemia and other cancers to 'unjustifiable levels,' especially for children. In the rural areas around the town, radiation levels are much higher and could remain unsafe for people beyond the end of this century . . . . When it rains, the radioactive cesium in the mountains flows into rivers and underground water sources close to the town." Simon Denyer, *Near Site of Fukushima Nuclear Disaster, a Shattered Town and Scattered Lives*, WASH. POST (Feb. 3, 2019).

NOTES AND QUESTIONS

1.   How much should risk play a role in deciding what our energy system looks like? Disasters such as Fukushima are obviously serious, but they are also comparatively rare. One observer noted that the 9.0-magnitude earthquake which gave rise to the Fukushima Daiichi disaster was "one of the most powerful and destructive displays of nature in recorded human history. . ., [t]he earth convuls[ing] for a full six minutes," so strong that it "shoved Japan's main island several feet to the east." Chico Harlan, *The Fukushima Tsunami 10 Years Later: A Correspondent Recounts the Day That Changed Japan*, WASH. POST (Mar. 10, 2021). Does all the good created by the carbon-free electricity from nuclear power plants make up for the small chance that catastrophic events like Fukushima will occasionally happen? Or does the long-lasting nature of any realized risk from a nuclear disaster outweigh the technology's benefits?

2.   Does the risk of nuclear energy look more reasonable in the face of natural risks that humans face? Note that more people died from the tsunami that caused the meltdowns in Japan than from all three of the nuclear disasters at Three Mile Island, Chernobyl, and Fukushima.

3.   How should the cost of the risk of events like Fukushima be accounted for in nuclear electricity prices? One of the core arguments that proponents of renewable energy make is that "conventional" (fossil fuel and nuclear) resources impose negative externalities that are not fully captured in the price of electricity. Is the mere *risk* of a Fukushima-like disaster an externality, or must the disaster be realized first? For more on risk and nuclear power, see, for instance, Emily Hammond, *Nuclear Power, Risk, and Retroactivity*, 48 VAND. J. TRANSNAT'L L. 1059 (2015); Anni Huhtala, *Quantifying the Social Costs of Nuclear Energy: Perceived Risk of Accident at Nuclear Power Plants*, 105 ENERGY POL'Y 320 (2017); Amanda Leiter, *The Perils of a Half-Built*

Bridge: Risk Perception, Shifting Majorities, and the Nuclear Power Debate, 35 ECOLOGY L.Q. 31 (2008).

4.   While nuclear disasters often capture popular headlines, historically one of nuclear power's biggest risks is its cost, a fact made clear by the above notes and questions that follow the *Blue Ridge Environmental Defense League* case. Initially, many companies believed that nuclear technology would provide cheap power. Quickly, however, cost overruns plagued nuclear construction— especially as federal regulation became more stringent in response to environmental and safety concerns after events like Three Mile Island. Thus, until recently, no new nuclear construction had occurred in the United States for decades, with plants instead expanding their output through increased performance and uprating. These cost overruns also led to extensive legal proceedings, in which utilities sought to recover "stranded costs" for planned or partially constructed facilities they abandoned because of cost overruns, a topic discussed in Chapter 4. *See also, e.g., CenterPoint Energy, Inc. v. Pub. Util. Comm'n of Texas*, 143 S.W.3d 81 (Tex. 2004); *Indianapolis Power & Light Co. v. Pennsylvania Pub. Util. Comm'n*, 711 A.2d 1071 (Pa. Commw. Ct. 1998). New stranded cost battles emerged immediately in the wake of the Summer project's cancellation in South Carolina, eventually resulting in a 2020 settlement in which Santee Cooper agreed to pay more than $500 million in customer refunds. *$520 Million Settlement Approved in Santee Cooper Lawsuit*, U.S. NEWS & WORLD REP. (July 21, 2020).

5.   In February 2013, The World Health Organization completed a comprehensive assessment of the health risks associated with the Fukushima disaster. The assessment concluded that for the general population outside the areas exposed to the highest amount of radiation, the predicted health risks are low, with no expected increases in baseline cancer rates. By contrast, for people in the most contaminated locations, the estimated increases are:

- all solid cancers—around 4% in females exposed as infants;

- breast cancer—around 6% in females exposed as infants;

- leukemia—around 7% in males exposed as infants;

- thyroid cancer—up to 70% in females exposed as infants.

WORLD HEALTH ORGANIZATION, HEALTH RISK ASSESSMENT FROM THE NUCLEAR ACCIDENT AFTER THE 2011 GREAT EAST JAPAN EARTHQUAKE AND TSUNAMI BASED ON PRELIMINARY DOSE ESTIMATION (2013).

6.   After Fukushima, many asserted that part of the cause of the disaster was regulatory and government acquiescence to the nuclear industry. As Evan Osnos recounted:

> Over the years, nuclear regulators became so submissive to the industry that critics named the alliance Japan's "nuclear village." To some extent, Taro Kono blamed the fact that the agency charged with policing power plants—the Nuclear and Industrial Safety Agency— was part of the very ministry in charge of promoting them. "There's

no reason for you to regulate something, because when you go back to the ministry everyone's going to be mad at you," he said.... Japanese nuclear regulators, like their American counterparts, have frequently been criticized for following a revolving door into lucrative jobs in the industries they police, and vice versa....

Nuclear-safety scandals began to emerge. In June, 2002, Tokyo Electric was forced to reveal that for two decades it had faked hundreds of repair records, at the Fukushima Daiichi plant and at several other reactors. Five years later, it conceded that it had lied in its previous acknowledgment of lying and owned up to six more emergencies at Fukushima Daiichi that had been concealed....

Of all the warnings that were ignored, the most significant was from the past. On June 24, 2009, two senior Japanese seismologists appeared before a government-led safety panel to warn that the Fukushima Daiichi plant was acutely vulnerable to tsunamis. They pointed to the words of ancient historians who described a wave in the year 869 so large that it left "no time to get into boats or climb the mountains"; it devastated a castle and left "everything utterly destroyed." According to a transcript of the hearing, a Tokyo Electric official responded that "future research should evaluate" the claim, because it appeared that "there isn't much evidence of damage." The plant was designed to absorb swells of up to about nineteen feet in height; the tsunami that arrived in March was more than twice that tall.

Osnos, *supra*. Is this kind of regulatory failure unique to Japan, or to the nuclear industry? Certainly, we do not promote atomic power as blatantly in the United States as Mr. Osnos describes here, but there is a long history of encouraging energy use domestically. After all, one of the early selling points of nuclear power, even if it was offered somewhat symbolically, was that it eventually would be "too cheap to meter." *Abundant Power from Atom Seen*, N.Y. TIMES (Sept. 17, 1954), at 5 (quoting Lewis L. Strauss, Chairman, Atomic Energy Comm'n, Address at the Twentieth Anniversary of the National Association of Science Writers (Sept. 16, 1954)); *see also* Sheldon L. Trubatch, *How, Why and When the U.S. Supreme Court Supports Nuclear Power*, 3 ARIZ. J. ENV'T L. POL'Y 1 (2012). Is it even possible to avoid industry-government cooperation when a field as technically complex as nuclear energy is involved?

7.   Fukushima's effects were also felt in the United States. A proposal to build a nuclear plant in Texas was canceled due, at least partially, to the shadow Fukushima cast on the technology's future. Further, as described in *Blue Ridge Environmental Defense League* case, thirteen existing U.S. reactors use designs like those at Fukushima Daiichi, so the NRC established a special Task Force to assess the disaster and propose next steps. The Task Force made twelve specific recommendations, though it concluded that "continued operation and continued licensing activities do not impose an imminent risk to the public health and safety and are not inimical to the common defense and

security." CHARLES MILLER ET AL., RECOMMENDATIONS FOR ENHANCING REACTOR SAFETY IN THE 21ST CENTURY: THE NEAR-TERM TASK FORCE REVIEW OF INSIGHTS FROM THE FUKUSHIMA DAI-ICHI ACCIDENT (July 12, 2011). Following on those recommendations, the NRC itself then implemented several measures to prevent a Fukushima-like accident at home. For more on the NRC's response to Fukushima, see, *Japan Lessons Learned*, U.S. Nuclear Reg. Comm'n.

8.   What happens if there is a nuclear accident in the United States? The Price-Anderson Nuclear Industries Indemnity Act (typically referred to as the "Price-Anderson Act" or just "Price-Anderson"), 42 U.S.C. §§ 2210 *et seq.*, governs liability from such "nuclear incidents." *See id.* § 2014(q). Adopted in 1957 to promote deployment of civilian reactors (by allaying concerns that liability could bankrupt nuclear energy operators), the Act requires reactor owners to obtain $450 million in private insurance to cover offsite liability. This is referred to as the "first tier" of coverage under Price-Anderson and applies to each reactor site, not each reactor. The "second tier" of coverage under the Act is a pool of liability among all reactors. "In the event a nuclear accident causes damages in excess of $450 million, each licensee would be assessed a prorated share of the excess, up to $131.056 million per reactor. With 98 reactors currently in the insurance pool, this secondary tier of funds contains about $12.9 billion." *Backgrounder on Nuclear Insurance and Disaster Relief*, Nuclear Reg. Comm'n (May 2019) (noting that NRC regulations do not distinguish between operating and closed reactors).

Reactor owners pay about $1 million annually in insurance premiums. That payment is for the first reactor on a site. American Nuclear Insurers, the only pool that writes nuclear insurance in the United States, typically offers a discount for additional reactors on the same site. In addition to the private insurance reactor owners must obtain under Price-Anderson, "NRC regulations require licensees to maintain a minimum of $1.06 billion in onsite property insurance at each reactor site." *Id.*

The Energy Policy Act of 2005 extended Price-Anderson to reactors constructed through 2025. Statutory coverage includes disease, bodily injury, death, property damage, and living expenses for anyone evacuated because of a nuclear incident. If 15 percent of the second-tier funds are expended, a federal district court determines priority for payout of remaining funds. Price-Anderson caps liability to owners at the level of statutory coverage, and if an incident causes damage in excess of that coverage, the NRC "may request additional funds from Congress. Alternatively, if the courts determine, based on a damage assessment conducted by the NRC, that public liability exceeds the funds available in the pool, the President of the United States can make a recommendation to Congress on additional sources of funding." Kevin T. Colby et al., *International Nuclear Liability: From the Perspective of the U.S. Engineering and Construction Industry*, 4 J. AM. C. CONSTRUCTION LAW. 37 (2010).

How much do you think a single nuclear incident would cost in terms of potential liability? Is the coverage that Price-Anderson provides likely to be sufficient? Even more to the point, does it matter? Why or why not? By point of reference, the Three Mile Island disaster in 1979, which was determined to result in at most de minimis releases of radiation into the environment, accumulated payouts of $71 million in claims and litigation costs. The total estimated cost for the Fukushima Daiichi disaster, including decommissioning the plant, compensating those affected, and completing decontamination in surrounding areas, has only escalated with time, and most recently was put at ¥22 trillion, or roughly $200 billion. *See* Mari Yamaguchi, *Japan Revises Fukushima Cleanup Plan, Delays Key Steps*, AP NEWS (Dec. 27, 2019).

9.   In addition to the critically important legal, economic, and policy questions that the risk of nuclear disasters raises, the lessons that these events teach about the limits of technology—and the limits of humankind's ability to contain technological side-effects—are fascinating. For more on the history of key nuclear power disasters, see, for example, SVETLANA ALEXIEVICH, VOICES FROM CHERNOBYL: THE ORAL HISTORY OF A NUCLEAR DISASTER (2005); KATE BROWN, PLUTOPIA: NUCLEAR FAMILIES, ATOMIC CITIES, AND THE GREAT SOVIET AND AMERICAN PLUTONIUM DISASTERS (2013); DAVID LOCHBAUM ET AL., FUKUSHIMA: THE STORY OF A NUCLEAR DISASTER (2014); JAMES MAHAFFEY, ATOMIC ACCIDENTS: A HISTORY OF NUCLEAR MELTDOWNS AND DISASTERS FROM THE OZARK MOUNTAINS TO FUKUSHIMA (2014).

PRACTICE PROBLEM

Only one nuclear power plant remains operating in California—the Diablo Canyon facility near San Luis Obispo, operated by Pacific Gas & Electric. Diablo Canyon's NRC licenses are set to expire in 2024 and 2025 (each of the two reactors has a different license), and PG&E has decided not to seek renewal.

PG&E's decision has potentially momentous consequences for California. With an operating capacity of 2,100 MW, the Diablo Canyon facility provides electricity to about 3 million Californians. It does so quite cleanly. Estimates show that if the facility closes, natural gas power plants are likely to fill the gap, resulting in 15.5 million metric tons of new GHG emissions by 2030—in short, the same impact as 306,000 gasoline-powered automobiles.

Different groups want different outcomes. Many Californians, wary of nuclear power and the state's seismic profile, point out that an earthquake fault has been identified near Diablo Canyon. Looking to the Fukushima Daiichi disaster, they think PG&E has it right. Diablo Canyon should close, and California should remain nuclear-free in perpetuity.

Others think that nuclear power might have a role in California's future. They worry about climate change and recognize the state's goal of a carbon-free electricity system by 2050 is a tall order. Other pathways might be possible to achieve that goal, but they wonder if nuclear might be a necessary part of the mix—if not by building new plants at least by keeping Diablo Canyon open.

Some Californians—including many pragmatic and more modern environmentalists—are much more pro-nuclear. They assert that Diablo Canyon is essential to addressing climate change, and that it thus would be a grave mistake not to renew the facilities' licenses. They note nuclear energy's strong safety record—suggesting that it is the safest electricity generation technology per megawatt-hour in the world—and that renewables need backup power. This is generally true but especially so given climate change, which is shifting weather patterns and increasing wildfire risks: Solar power production plummeted during the most recent California wildfires.

California's Governor faces political pressure from every side. Pro-business interests urge more energy development, but also worry about increasing energy costs. Environmentalists seem fractured; they want action on climate change, but some only want renewables while others are more broadminded about solutions. Criticism has come frequently and regularly for the handling of wildfires that have marred the state; rolling brown- and black-outs were deeply unpopular, and some blame climate change for the growing phenomenon while others point the finger at the Governor's office.

The Governor is weighing whether to pressure PG&E to renew the Diablo Canyon licenses—or to ask another utility to take on the facilities and keep running them.

You are her energy advisor. What counsel would you give? Why?

If you'd like to read more about Diablo Canyon, or ongoing changes in California, as you prepare your advice, several resources may be helpful: Kavya Balaraman, *California's Last Nuclear Plant Is Poised to Shut Down. What Happens Next?*, UTIL. DIVE (Mar. 23, 2021); Rebecca Tuhus-Dubrow, *The Activists Who Embrace Nuclear Power*, NEW YORKER (Feb. 19, 2021); ENERGY FUTURES INITIATIVE, OPTIONALITY, FLEXIBILITY & INNOVATION—PATHWAYS FOR DEEP DECARBONIZATION: SUMMARY FOR POLICYMAKERS (Apr. 2019); Sammy Roth, *California's Next Climate Challenge: Replacing Its Last Nuclear Plant*, L.A. TIMES (May 18, 2021).

2. ADDRESSING NUCLEAR POWER'S ENVIRONMENTAL RISKS

Citizens opposed to atomic energy often invoke environmental concerns as a reason not to license, or relicense, nuclear power plants. This is yet one more way that the intrinsic connection between energy and environmental questions arises. How should society balance the environmental benefits of atomic energy, including its low carbon footprint, against its environmental risks, such as events like Fukushima?

There are effectively five ways that groups opposed to a nuclear power plant might use environmental concerns as a lever to limit, or prevent, the facility's operation.

First, as shown in the *Blue Ridge Environmental Defense League* case excerpted above, a group can participate in the NRC licensing or relicensing proceeding. Groups often do this, but many also claim that the NRC's decisionmaking process is slanted heavily in favor of promoting atomic energy. They note that the agency assumes that compliance with NRC regulations and rules adequately mitigates environmental risks.

Second, as also seen in *Blue Ridge Environmental Defense League*, groups use the environmental review process under the National Environmental Policy Act (NEPA), 42 U.S.C. § 4321 *et seq.*, to argue that the NRC must review certain environmental questions related to the facility.

Third, groups may participate in the facility's approval through the Emergency Planning and Community Right to Know Act of 1986 (EPCRA), 42 U.S.C.A. § 11001 *et seq.* The EPCRA has two main purposes: It seeks to compile accurate information on the presence of toxic chemicals and to make that information available on a local level. And it seeks to facilitate the use of reported information to create local emergency response plans in order to limit damage in the event of an accident. Thus, if an owner or operator of a nuclear facility fails to report the use of toxic chemicals, EPCRA offers a cause of action for private individuals to bring a civil suit.

Fourth, groups may use various state laws, such as public service commission prudency reviews or environmental licensing statutes, to try to stop nuclear plants.

Fifth, groups may resort to the political process. Indeed, in the wake of the Supreme Court's decision in *Pacific Gas & Electric Co. v. State Energy Resources Conservation & Development Comm'n*, 461 U.S. 190 (1983), discussed in the next section of this chapter, it became clear that states may ban nuclear power for economic, but not safety, reasons. *See also Entergy Nuclear Vermont Yankee, LLC v. Shumlin*, 733 F.3d 393 (2d Cir. 2013). Currently, fourteen states have placed restrictions on the construction of new nuclear power facilities. *State Restrictions on New Nuclear Power Facility Construction*, Nat'l Conf. of State Legis. (last updated May 2017).

The leading Supreme Court case involving the second avenue for opposing a nuclear power plant—NEPA—is *Metropolitan Edison Co. v. People Against Nuclear Energy*, 460 U.S. 766 (1983). *Metropolitan Edison* involved a challenge to the reopening of the Three Mile Island nuclear power plant after the March 1979 accident at that facility. A public interest group comprised of residents from the Harrisburg, Pennsylvania area asserted that the environmental impact statement the NRC prepared in connection with its decision allowing the facility to reopen was deficient because it "failed to consider whether the risk of an accident at TMI-1 might cause harm to the psychological health and community well-being of residents of the surrounding area." *Id.* at 768.

The D.C. Circuit agreed. It reasoned that NEPA requires agencies to assess environmental impacts; the environment includes humans; and reopening Three Mile Island would impact humans' psychological health. This, however, the Supreme Court said, went too far. Analogizing to the distinction between "but for" and "proximate" causation in tort law, the Court explained:

> If we were to seize the word "environmental" out of its context and give it the broadest possible definition, the words "adverse environmental effects" might embrace virtually any consequence of a governmental action that some one thought "adverse." But we think the context of the statute shows that Congress was talking about the physical environment—the world around us, so to speak. NEPA was designed to promote human welfare by alerting governmental actors to the effect of their proposed actions on the physical environment. . . .

> To determine whether § 102 requires consideration of a particular effect, we must look at the relationship between that effect and the change in the physical environment caused by the major federal action at issue. . . . Some effects that are "caused by" a change in the physical environment in the sense of "but for" causation, will nonetheless not fall within § 102 because the causal chain is too attenuated. . . . For example, residents of the Harrisburg area have relatives in other parts of the country. Renewed operation of TMI-1 may well cause psychological health problems for these people. . . . However, this harm is simply too remote from the physical environment to justify requiring the NRC to evaluate the psychological health damage to these people that may be caused by renewed operation of TMI-1.

> Our understanding of the congressional concerns that led to the enactment of NEPA suggests that the terms "environmental effect" and "environmental impact" in § 102 be read to include a requirement of a reasonably close causal relationship between a change in the physical environment and the effect at issue. This requirement is like the familiar doctrine of proximate cause from tort law. . . .

> PANE argues that the psychological health damage it alleges "will flow directly from the risk of [a nuclear] accident." But a risk of an accident is not an effect on the physical environment. A risk is, by definition, unrealized in the physical world. In a causal

chain from renewed operation of TMI-1 to psychological health damage, the element of risk and its perception by PANE's members are necessary middle links. We believe that the element of risk lengthens the causal chain beyond the reach of NEPA.

Id. at 775.

The next two cases involve more recent nuclear facility disputes where the parties invoked *Metropolitan Edison*. The Practice Problem that follows asks you to apply the case law.

SAN LUIS OBISPO MOTHERS FOR PEACE V. NRC
449 F.3d 1016 (9th Cir. 2006)

THOMAS, CIRCUIT JUDGE.

This case presents the question as to whether the likely environmental consequences of a potential terrorist attack on a nuclear facility must be considered in an environmental review required under the National Environmental Policy Act. The United States Nuclear Regulatory Commission (NRC) contends that the possibility of a terrorist attack on a nuclear facility is so remote and speculative that the potential consequences of such an attack need not be considered at all in such a review. [Petitioners] disagree . . . .

While NEPA requires the NRC to consider environmental effects of its decisions, the AEA is primarily concerned with setting minimum safety standards for the licensing and operation of nuclear facilities. The NRC does not contest that the two statutes impose independent obligations, so that compliance with the AEA does not excuse the agency from its NEPA obligations. The AEA lays out the process for consideration of the public health and safety aspects of nuclear power plant licensing, and requires the NRC to determine whether the licensing and operation of a proposed facility is "in accord with the common defense and security and will provide adequate protection to the health and safety of the public." 42 U.S.C. § 2232(a).

On December 21, 2001, PG&E applied to the NRC pursuant to 10 C.F.R. Part 72 for a license to construct and operate a Storage Installation at Diablo Canyon. The Storage Installation would permit the necessary and on-site storage of spent fuel, the byproduct of the two nuclear reactors at that site. PG&E expects to fill its existing spent fuel storage capacity at Diablo Canyon sometime this year. Therefore, unless additional spent fuel storage capacity is created, the Diablo Canyon reactors cannot continue to function beyond 2006.

PG&E proposes to build a dry cask storage facility. The basic unit of the storage system is the Multi-Purpose Canister (Canister), a stainless steel cylinder that is filled with radioactive waste materials and welded shut. The Canisters are loaded into concrete storage overpacks that are designed to permit passive cooling via the circulation of air. The storage casks, or the filled Canisters loaded into overpacks, are then placed on one of seven concrete pads. The Storage Installation would house a total of 140 storage casks, 2 more than the 138 projected to be required for storage of spent fuel generated at Diablo Canyon through 2025. . . .

[T]he NRC decided categorically that NEPA does not require consideration of the environmental effects of potential terrorist attacks. . . . We review each of [the agency's proffered] grounds for reasonableness, and conclude that these grounds, either individually or collectively, do not support the NRC's categorical refusal to consider the environmental effects of a terrorist attack.

A

The Commission relied first on finding that the possibility of a terrorist attack is too far removed from the natural or expected consequences of agency action. . . .

The Commission claims that its conclusion that the environmental impacts of a possible terrorist attack on an NRC-licensed facility is beyond a "reasonably close causal relationship" was a reasonable application of this "proximate cause" analogy [from *Metropolitan Edison*].

The problem with the agency's argument, however, is that *Metropolitan Edison* and its proximate cause analogy are inapplicable here. . . .

The appropriate analysis is instead that developed by this court in *No GWEN Alliance v. Aldridge*, 855 F.2d 1380 (9th Cir. 1988). In *No GWEN*, the plaintiffs argued that NEPA required the Air Force to consider the threat of nuclear war in the implementation of the Ground Wave Emergency Network (GWEN). We held "that the nexus between construction of GWEN and nuclear war is too attenuated to require discussion of the environmental impacts of nuclear war in an [EA] or [EIS]."

The events at issue here, as well as in *Metropolitan Edison* and *No GWEN*, form a chain of three events: (1) a major federal action; (2) a change in the physical environment; and (3) an effect. *Metropolitan Edison* was concerned with the relationship between events 2 and 3 (the change in the physical environment, or increased risk of accident resulting from the renewed operation of a nuclear reactor, and the effect, or the decline in the psychological health of the human population). The Court in *Metropolitan Edison* explicitly distinguished the case where the disputed relationship is between events 1 and 2: "we emphasize that in this case we are considering effects caused by the risk of accident. The situation where an agency is asked to consider effects that will occur if a risk is realized, for example, if an accident occurs . . . is an entirely different case." In *No GWEN*, we followed the Court's admonition and, in addressing the relationship between events 1 and 2, we held that the *Metropolitan Edison* analysis did not apply "because it discusse[d] a different type of causation than that at issue in this case . . . [which] require[d] us to examine the relationship between the agency action and a potential impact on the environment." *No GWEN* [thus held that NEPA did not require consideration of] the plaintiffs' claims that the military GWEN system's installation would "increase the probability of nuclear war," [because those] propositions [were] "remote and highly speculative" . . . .

In the present case, as in *No GWEN*, the disputed relationship is between events 1 and 2 (the federal act, or the licensing of the Storage Installation, and the change in the physical environment, or the terrorist attack). The appropriate inquiry is therefore whether such attacks are so "remote and highly speculative" that NEPA's mandate does not include consideration of their potential environmental effects.

The NRC responds by simply declaring without support that, as a matter of law, "the possibility of a terrorist attack . . . is speculative and simply too far removed from the natural or expected consequences of agency action to require a study under NEPA." In doing so, the NRC failed to address Petitioners' factual contentions that licensing the Storage Installation would lead to or increase the risk of a terrorist attack because (1) the presence of the Storage Installation would increase the probability of a terrorist attack on the Diablo Canyon nuclear facility, and (2) the Storage Installation itself would be a primary target for a terrorist attack. We conclude that it was unreasonable for the NRC to categorically dismiss the possibility of terrorist attack on the Storage Installation and on the entire Diablo Canyon facility as too "remote and highly speculative" to warrant consideration under NEPA.

In so concluding, we also recognize that the NRC's position that terrorist attacks are "remote and highly speculative," as a matter of law, is inconsistent with the government's efforts and expenditures to combat this type of terrorist attack against nuclear facilities. In [a prior case], the NRC emphasized the agency's own post-September 11th efforts against the threat of terrorism:

> At the outset, however, we stress our determination, in the wake of the horrific September 11th terrorist attacks, to strengthen security at facilities we regulate. We currently are engaged in a comprehensive review of our security regulations and programs, acting under our AEA-rooted duty to protect "public health and safety" and the "common defense and security." We are reexamining, and in many cases have already improved, security and safeguards matters such as guard force size, physical security

exercises, clearance requirements and background investigations for key employees, and fitness-for-duty requirements. . . .

We find it difficult to reconcile the Commission's conclusion that, as a matter of law, the possibility of a terrorist attack on a nuclear facility is "remote and speculative," with its stated efforts to undertake a "top to bottom" security review against this same threat. Under the NRC's own formulation of the rule of reasonableness, it is required to make determinations that are consistent with its policy statements and procedures. Here, it appears as though the NRC is attempting, as a matter of policy, to insist on its preparedness and the seriousness with which it is responding to the post-September 11th terrorist threat, while concluding, as a matter of law, that all terrorist threats are "remote and highly speculative" for NEPA purposes. . . .

B

[Relying on precedent, the NRC also sought to justify its decision here by suggesting that the risk of terrorist attacks cannot be adequately determined. This rationale also is] not reasonable. First, the NRC's dismissal of the risk of terrorist attacks as "unquantifiable" misses the point. The numeric probability of a specific attack is not required in order to assess likely modes of attack, weapons, and vulnerabilities of a facility, and the possible impact of each of these on the physical environment, including the assessment of various release scenarios. Indeed, this is precisely what the NRC already analyzes in different contexts. It is therefore possible to conduct a low probability-high consequence analysis without quantifying the precise probability of risk. The NRC itself has recognized that consideration of uncertain risks may take a form other than quantitative "probabilistic" assessment:

> In addressing potential accident initiators (including earthquakes, sabotage, and multiple human errors) where empirical data are limited and residual uncertainty is large, the use of conceptual modeling and scenario assumptions in Safety Analysis Reports will be helpful. They should be based on the best qualified judgments of experts, either in the form of subjective numerical probability estimates or qualitative assessments of initiating events and casual [sic] linkages in accident sequences.

48 Fed. Reg. at 16,020.

No provision of NEPA, or any other authority cited by the Commission, allows the NRC to eliminate a possible environmental consequence from analysis by labeling the risk as "unquantifiable." If the risk of a terrorist attack is not insignificant, then NEPA obligates the NRC to take a "hard look" at the environmental consequences of that risk. . . .

NEW JERSEY DEPARTMENT OF
ENVIRONMENTAL PROTECTION V. NRC

561 F.3d 132 (3d Cir. 2009)

ROTH, CIRCUIT JUDGE.

The issue presented by this appeal is whether the Nuclear Regulatory Commission (NRC), when it is reviewing an application to relicense a nuclear power facility, must examine the environmental impact of a hypothetical terrorist attack on that nuclear power facility. The New Jersey Department of Environmental Protection (NJDEP) contends that the National Environmental Policy Act of 1969 (NEPA), requires the analysis. NJDEP has petitioned for review of an NRC decision denying its request to intervene in relicensing proceedings for the Oyster Creek Nuclear Generating Station (Oyster Creek). . . .

NJDEP's petition suffers from two insurmountable flaws, each of which independently supports our denial [of its petition]. First, NJDEP has not shown that there is a "reasonably close causal relationship" between the Oyster Creek relicensing proceeding and the environmental effects of a hypothetical aircraft attack. Accordingly, such an attack does not warrant NEPA evaluation. *See DOT v. Pub. Citizen*, 541 U.S. 752, 767 (2004); *Metro. Edison Co. v. People Against Nuclear Energy*, 460 U.S. 766, 774 (1983). Second, the NRC has already considered the environmental effects of a hypothetical terrorist attack on a nuclear plant and found that these effects would be no worse than those caused by a severe accident. NJDEP has not provided any evidence to challenge this conclusion and has not demonstrated that the NRC could undertake a more meaningful analysis of the specific risks associated with an aircraft attack on Oyster Creek.

A. Causation

In rejecting NJDEP's contention, the NRC held that "there simply is no proximate cause link between an NRC licensing action, such as [in this case] renewing an operating license, and any altered risk of terrorist attack. Instead, the level of risk depends upon political, social, and economic factors external to the NRC licensing process." NJDEP, on the other hand, asserts that the government has a duty to protect against foreseeable danger, even if that danger comes from intentional criminal conduct, and that here the risk of environmental harm caused by terrorists is foreseeable given the September 11, 2001, attacks on the World Trade Center and Oyster Creek's proximity to important urban centers. NJDEP also finds significant the NRC's efforts to improve security at nuclear facilities, asserting that these efforts demonstrate the NRC's recognition that a terrorist attack is foreseeable.

The Supreme Court has spoken on two occasions regarding the circumstances in which NEPA requires an agency to prepare an EIS. [The court discussed the Supreme Court's decision in *Metropolitan Edison*.] The Supreme Court again discussed NEPA's causation requirement in *Department of Transportation v. Public Citizen*, 541 U.S. 752 (2004). *Public Citizen* concerned the operation of Mexican tractor-trailer trucks in the United States. [In 1982], Congress suspended [the] certification [of Mexican trucks] in light of concerns about Mexico's discriminatory treatment of American trucks operating in Mexico. . . . [Following adoption of the North American Free Trade Agreement], the Federal Motor Carrier Safety Administration (FMCSA) published proposed safety regulations and procedures for the certification of Mexican trucks. The FMCSA also prepared an environmental assessment (EA) focusing on the effects of its proposed regulations. The EA did not consider the environmental impact of increased Mexican truck traffic because the FMCSA attributed this increase not to the regulations but to NAFTA and the President's decision to lift the moratorium.

The Supreme Court upheld the FMCSA's decision. The Court noted that an EIS is required only for " 'major Federal actions,' " defined to include " 'actions with effects that may be major and which are potentially subject to Federal control and responsibility.' " The Court then noted that "effects" were limited by regulation to (1) "[d]irect effects, which are caused by the action and occur at the same time and place," and (2) "indirect effects, which are caused by the action and are later in time or farther removed in distance, but are still reasonably foreseeable." . . .

NJDEP argues that neither *Metropolitan Edison* nor *Public Citizen* is apposite, asserting that those decisions involved cause and effect relationships that are far more attenuated than the one presented here. We disagree. The Supreme Court has directed that we "draw a manageable line between those causal changes that may make an actor responsible for an effect and those that do not." In the cases, this line appears to approximate the limits of an agency's area of control. For example, in *Metropolitan Edison*, the NRC could control the nuclear facility and its operation but not how individuals perceived the risks of renewed operation and the possibility of another accident; therefore, these risks were too remote to require a NEPA analysis. Likewise, in *Public Citizen*, the FMCSA controlled the certification process, but it could not control the admission or volume of Mexican trucks; the FMCSA's role was limited to certification.

In the instant case, the NRC controls whether equipment within a facility is suitable for continued operation or could withstand an accident, but it has no authority over the airspace above its facilities, which is largely controlled by Congress and the Federal Aviation Administration (FAA). The NRC has explicitly noted its limited ability to address airborne threats, articulating its consistent view that "security from terrorist attacks on nuclear facilities [i]s best approached by enhancing aviation security, including intelligence gathering and security at airports and on airplanes." *Riverkeeper, Inc. v. Collins,* 359 F.3d 156, 161 (2d Cir. 2004). . . .

NRC's lack of control over airspace supports our holding that a terrorist aircraft attack lengthens the causal chain beyond the "reasonably close causal relationship" required by those cases. Indeed, an aircraft attack on Oyster Creek requires at least two intervening events: (1) the act of a third-party criminal and (2) the failure of all government agencies specifically charged with preventing terrorist attacks. . . .

B.   The NRC'S Prior Analysis of the Terrorism Threat

Even if NEPA required an assessment of the environmental effects of a hypothetical terrorist attack on a nuclear facility, the NRC has already made this assessment. As described above, the GEIS addresses the risks associated with a terrorist attack, stating that "estimates of risk from sabotage" are impossible to quantify but nonetheless characterizing the risks as "small." The GEIS goes on to say that, should the unlikely event occur, the effects would be "no worse than those expected from internally initiated events." The NRC rules codify these generic findings, and by regulation, license renewal applicants are excused from discussing generic issues in their environmental reports.

Generic analysis "is clearly an appropriate method of conducting the hard look required by NEPA." *Baltimore Gas & Elec. Co. v. NRDC,* 462 U.S. 87, 101 (1983). Indeed, it is "hornbook administrative law that an agency need not—indeed should not—entertain a challenge to a regulation" in an individual adjudication. NJDEP's contention challenges the NRC's generic findings, essentially arguing that certain characteristics of Oyster Creek make the risk of a terrorist attack more than "small" and the environmental effects of a terrorist attack somehow different from "those expected from internally initiated events." These arguments thus amount to collateral attacks on the licensing renewal regulations, and the proper way to raise them would have been in a petition for rulemaking or a petition for a waiver based on "special circumstances." . . .

NOTES AND QUESTIONS

1.   Did either *San Luis Obispo Mothers for Peace* or *New Jersey Department of Environmental Protection* correctly apply the Supreme Court's decision in *Metropolitan Edison*? Why or why not?

2.   Why did the NRC insist on not considering the effects raised by the public interest groups and state government in the above cases? Given that NEPA does not require agencies to mitigate environmental impacts they consider, wouldn't it have been easier for the NRC simply to evaluate these risks as part

of its NEPA process rather than fighting the principle—all the way to the Supreme Court and before multiple circuits?

3.   If you were representing a group opposed to a nuclear power plant, what is the strongest argument you could make that possible terrorist attacks should be considered in the NEPA process? What is the strongest contrary argument you could make if you were representing the NRC or the facility owner and wanted to exclude terrorism risks from the NEPA analysis?

4.   Just as it does in the reactor licensing and relicensing context, NEPA plays a crucial role in the NRC's consideration of environmental concerns when it approves nuclear waste storage facilities. In *Baltimore Gas & Electric Co. v. NRDC*, 462 U.S. 87 (1983), the Supreme Court addressed a challenge to the NRC's generic rulemaking determination that "licensing boards should assume, for purposes of NEPA, that the permanent storage of certain nuclear wastes would have no significant environmental impact and thus should not affect the decision whether to license a particular nuclear power plant." *Id*. at 89. In a unanimous decision authored by Justice O'Connor, the Court held that the NRC's decision complied with NEPA: "[W]e think that the zero-release assumption—a policy judgment concerning one line in a conservative Table designed for the limited purpose of individual licensing decisions—is within the bounds of reasoned decisionmaking. It is not our task to determine what decision we, as Commissioners, would have reached. Our only task is to determine whether the Commission has considered the relevant factors and articulated a rational connection between the facts found and the choice made. Under this standard, we think the Commission's zero-release assumption, within the context of Table S-3 as a whole, was not arbitrary and capricious." *Id*. at 105–06. Does this decision affect how you view the difference between the Ninth Circuit's ruling in *San Luis Obispo Mothers for Peace* and the Third Circuit's decision in *New Jersey Department of Environmental Protection*? Why?

5.   Would the NEPA analysis in *New Jersey Department of Environmental Protection* change if terrorists had recently posted a video to the internet stating that they will "imminently propagate attacks on American nuclear power facilities"? For a discussion on NEPA, terrorism risks, and nuclear power, see Sheldon L. Trubatch, *Nuclear Terrorism Under NEPA: A Meta-Legal Analysis of the Split Between the Third and Ninth Circuits*, 36 COLUM. J. ENV'T L. & POL'Y 1 (2011).

6.   Are there differences, relevant to NEPA, between a terrorist attack and hurricanes? Between terrorist attacks and tsunamis? *See Blue Ridge Environmental Defense League*, excerpted above, as well as *Massachusetts v. NRC*, 708 F.3d 63 (1st Cir. 2013) (rejecting Massachusetts' challenge to the adequacy of the NRC's EIS based on the events at Fukushima).

PRACTICE PROBLEM

Coastal Carolina Electric & Gas (CCEG) is the largest electricity provider in the fifty-first state in the Union, East Carolina. CCEG has a large generation portfolio, consisting of three coal-fired power plants, several natural gas combined cycle units, several hundred megawatts of installed wind and solar capacity, and two nuclear power facilities, Blue Devil 1 and Tar Heel 2.

Blue Devil 1 is the older of these two units. It was built forty years ago and thus is in the process of being relicensed by the NRC. Tar Heel 2 was built ten years after Blue Devil 1 and thus has several years left on its operating license.

Both Blue Devil 1 and Tar Heel 2 have excellent operating records. Neither facility has ever been cited by the NRC for improper maintenance or operation, nor has either plant ever had a single incident of malfunction or radiation release. In fact, last year, the Atomic Power Producers Alliance (APPA), the umbrella industry organization for utilities that run nuclear power plants in the United States, awarded CCEG its prize for "Best Nuclear Operator of the Decade." The prize was based on CCEG's exemplary record of performance at Blue Devil 1 and Tar Heel 2.

Notwithstanding CCEG's track record, two citizen groups have formed in opposition to the relicensing application CCEG recently filed with the NRC for Blue Devil 1. The groups are Fathers Against Nuclear Generation (FANG) and Carolinians Lobbying Against Waste (CLAW).

Both groups are seeking to intervene in the NRC relicensing proceeding, with the objective of stopping Blue Devil 1 from further operation. They insist that if the NRC fully accounts for the environmental impacts of the plant, including the risk of radioactive exposure from a meltdown, it will be clear that Blue Devil 1 should not be relicensed. The groups make their arguments on four bases:

1. The fact that Blue Devil 1 was originally planned only to run for forty years and the groups' assertion that "once a facility is past its originally scheduled operating life, its ability to withstand severe weather is severely reduced";

2. Historical evidence showing that hurricanes regularly strike East Carolina, almost on an annual basis and sometimes more often, and a statement in the most recent Intergovernmental Panel on Climate Change (IPCC) assessment that East Carolina is "significantly likely to begin suffering more frequent, and much stronger, hurricanes than in the past";

3. New evidence from seismologists at East Carolina State University showing that a "major" earthquake, which "may well cause tsunamis to strike the East Coast, especially the Carolinas," is "likely" to occur within the next fifteen years and "almost certain" to occur within the next fifty years; and

4. The groups' assertion that "the tragedy at Fukushima Daiichi shows the horrendous environmental impacts that can occur when a nuclear power plant is allowed to run past its planned useful life."

Blue Devil 1 sits one-quarter of a mile from East Carolina's Atlantic shoreline, well within the projected flooding zone shown by the East Carolina University seismologists' models for a tsunami's potential path. Blue Devil 1 also uses the same reactor design as the facility at Fukushima Daiichi.

If the NRC refuses to consider the hurricane and tsunami evidence offered by FANG and CLAW as part of its NEPA analysis, how should a court rule?

C. HIGH-LEVEL NUCLEAR WASTE—ENERGY FEDERALISM AND "SUPER WICKED PROBLEMS"

Another aspect of nuclear power that spotlights the technology's environmental tradeoffs is the intractable problem of high-level nuclear waste. Unquestionably, this is nuclear energy's Achilles' heel. Although Finland is set to open a long-term waste repository in 2023, no other nation has been able to solve the dilemma of what to do with nuclear fuel rods once they are "spent," or become "waste."

Disposal of nuclear waste thus might be accurately characterized as what some commentators have termed a "super wicked problem." *See, e.g.,* Richard J. Lazarus, *Super Wicked Problems and Climate Change: Restraining the Present to Liberate the Future,* 94 CORNELL L. REV. 1153 (2009). A key problem with nuclear waste is how long-lasting and highly radioactive it is. As a result, no one wants the waste, almost no one is willing to take it, and finding a solution to deal with it has proven elusive. The D.C. Circuit summarized the problem:

> After four to six years of use in a reactor, nuclear fuel rods can no longer efficiently produce energy and are considered "spent nuclear fuel" (SNF). Fuel rods are thermally hot when removed from reactors and emit great amounts of radiation—enough to be fatal in minutes to someone in the immediate vicinity. Therefore, the rods are transferred to racks within deep, water-filled pools for cooling and to protect workers from radiation. After the fuel has cooled, it may be transferred to dry storage, which consists of large concrete and steel "casks." Most SNF, however, will remain in spent-fuel pools until a permanent disposal solution is available.

> Even though it is no longer useful for nuclear power, SNF poses a dangerous, long-term health and environmental risk. It will remain dangerous "for time spans seemingly beyond human comprehension." Determining how to dispose of the growing volume of SNF, which may reach 150,000 metric tons by the year 2050, is a serious problem. Yet despite years of "blue ribbon"

commissions, congressional hearings, agency reports, and site investigations, the United States has not yet developed a permanent solution. That failure, declared the most recent "blue ribbon" panel, is the "central flaw of the U.S. nuclear waste management program to date." Experts agree that the ultimate solution will be a "geologic repository," in which SNF is stored deep within the earth, protected by a combination of natural and engineered barriers. Twenty years of work on establishing such a repository at Yucca Mountain was recently abandoned when the Department of Energy decided to withdraw its license application for the facility. At this time, there is not even a prospective site for a repository, let alone progress toward the actual construction of one.

New York v. NRC, 681 F.3d 471, 474 (D.C. Cir. 2012).

In the United States, federal policy favoring atomic energy has contributed to the waste dilemma. Effectively, the United States adopted a policy in favor of deploying a large nuclear fleet without first coming up with a plan to handle the fleet's eventual byproduct.

Three statutes encouraged construction of large nuclear plants in the United States. The Atomic Energy Act of 1954 first facilitated nuclear adoption by offering the technology to the private sector and instituting a licensing regime that allowed use of the technology for civilian purposes. *See* 42 U.S.C. § 2011 *et seq.*

Next, the Price-Anderson Act of 1957 erected what is for all intents and purposes a governmental insurance program for nuclear power. *See* 42 U.S.C. § 2210 *et seq.* Large utilities insisted they could not afford to install nuclear plants given the potentially enormous liability in the case of a nuclear catastrophe. Price-Anderson was the government's response:

> Congress [adopted] the Price-Anderson Act for the purpose of "protect[ing] the public and . . . encourag[ing] the development of the atomic energy industry. The Price-Anderson Act had three main features: 1) It "established a limit on the aggregate liability of those who wished to undertake activities involving the handing or use of radioactive materials"; 2) It channeled public liability resulting from nuclear incidents to the federal government; and 3) It established that all public liability claims above the amount of required private insurance "protection would be indemnified by the Federal Government, up to the aggregate limit on liability."

O'Conner v. Commonwealth Edison Co., 13 F.3d 1090, 1095 (7th Cir. 1994). Since adopting the Price-Anderson Act, Congress has amended it three times. In 1966, Congress amended the Act to address concerns that its statute of limitations was too short because radiation effects can manifest years after exposure. In 1975, the Act was amended to increase the insurance ceiling of each individual company to $140 million. Amendments in 1988 increased the amount of insurance for each generator to $200 million and created federal jurisdiction for public liability actions arising from nuclear incidents. In the Energy Policy Act of 2005, Price-Anderson was extended to 2025. The Supreme Court rejected due process and equal protection challenges to the Act in *Duke Power Co. v. Carolina Environmental Study Group*, 438 U.S. 59 (1978).

Finally, the government assured the nuclear industry that it would resolve the problem of what to do with nuclear waste once enough waste was produced. Although the first nuclear generator in the United States began operating in 1957, Congress gave no official answer on how it would handle the waste until the early 1980s. Then, in the Nuclear Waste Policy Act of 1982 (1982 NWPA), the government took action. The Act instituted a special fee on nuclear generation to promote a program for government-owned and -operated geologic nuclear waste "repositories." Under the Act, nuclear-owning utilities were required to enter into a disposal contract with the Department of Energy, creating an obligation on the part of the federal government to begin disposing of the utilities' nuclear waste no later than January 31, 1998. The 1982 NWPA also called for a study of suitable repository sites. The Secretary of Energy was required to determine and nominate five sites suitable for the first repository site and, no later than January 1, 1985, to recommend to the President three of those sites as candidate sites. Meanwhile, the Act also mandated the Department of Energy to conduct "a detailed study" of the need and feasibility for "one or more" monitored retrievable storage (MRS) facilities where high-level nuclear waste could be continuously observed and, if necessary, withdrawn. This study had to be completed by June 1, 1985. The Act specified that the government would take title to and assume responsibility for managing the waste when it was received at either an MRS or a permanent geologic storage site.

The solution brokered by the 1982 NWPA, however, would not last. Only five years later, Congress overhauled its prior plan and instituted a new one. The Nuclear Waste Policy Act of 1987 (1987 NWPA) called for the phaseout of all candidate sites other than Yucca Mountain, Nevada, and required the Secretary to receive specific authorization from Congress to conduct site-specific activities in connection with a second repository. The 1987 NWPA also authorized the Secretary to site an MRS, and established the Nuclear Waste Negotiator, appointed by the President, to facilitate the MRS. The Nuclear Waste Negotiator had the responsibility to work with states and Indian tribes to find a repository or MRS site, and then to negotiate with any state or tribe that expressed interest. The position, though created in 1987, went unfilled until 1990. In 1991, the Nuclear Waste Negotiator invited states, localities, and tribes to apply for $100,000 grants to study the possibility of siting an MRS in their area. Four counties and sixteen tribes applied. *See* DOUG EASTERLING & HOWARD KUNREUTHER, THE DILEMMA OF SITING A HIGH LEVEL NUCLEAR WASTE REPOSITORY 72 (1995); Jon D. Erickson et al., *Monitored Retrievable Storage of Spent Nuclear Fuel in Indian Country: Liability, Sovereignty, and Socioeconomics*, 19 AM. INDIAN L. REV. 73, 79–81 (1994).

Thus began a long—and still ongoing—saga of how and where to dispose of spent nuclear fuel in the United States. Depending on how one measures it, the U.S. policy has failed to find an answer to the nuclear waste dilemma at least four times. First, the Department of Energy's plan to put an MRS site in Oak Ridge, Tennessee failed in 1986, when statewide opposition, including a legal challenge by the state and vetoes by the governor and state legislature, put a stop to the plan. Second, following the 1987 NWPA, the Mescalero Band of Apache Indians expressed interest in taking the waste on a temporary basis, but then broke off negotiations in April 1996. *See* Noah Sachs, *The Mescalero Apache Indians and Monitored Retrievable Storage of Spent Nuclear Fuel: A Study in Environmental Ethics*, 36 NAT. RES. J. 641 (1996). Third, following the Mescalero Apaches' withdrawal, a small tribe of roughly 130 people—the Skull Valley Band of Goshute Indians—proposed to store up to 40,000 metric tons of the waste for up to forty years on a 100-acre cement pad in their tiny reservation in the northwest Utah desert. The NRC was in the process of licensing the site and had finished one of the last hurdles for the project, preparing an environmental impact statement. But political pressure and congressional maneuvering prevented the Goshutes from receiving the waste. *See* Lincoln L. Davies, *Skull Valley Crossroads: Reconciling Native Sovereignty and the Federal Trust*, 68 MD. L. REV. 290, 292 (2009). Finally, a longstanding battle to permanently store the waste underground in Yucca Mountain, Nevada continues.

The Yucca Mountain fight has a life all its own. The 1987 NWPA designated Yucca Mountain as the permanent repository of U.S. nuclear waste, and since that time, the Department of Energy has spent more than $15 billion studying, preparing, and constructing the repository. The arguments for Yucca center around a variety of benefits that many contend the site possesses: a stable environment; natural rock that creates barriers to the movement of radionuclides; and a mountain location allowing construction hundreds of meters below the surface but still hundreds of meters above the water table. Despite this, doubts about the site's long-term stability repeatedly have been raised, with some questioning how well the natural barriers will contain waste after the man-made barrier systems have failed. *See generally* ALLISON M. MACFARLANE & RODNEY C. EWING, UNCERTAINTY UNDERGROUND: YUCCA MOUNTAIN AND THE NATION'S HIGH-LEVEL NUCLEAR WASTE (2006).

Yucca Mountain

Source: U.S. Dep't of Energy.

Not a single cask of waste has yet made its way to Yucca Mountain. The NWPA promised that Yucca would open in 1998. In 2006, DOE asserted that waste could be received in Yucca Mountain by 2017. And so on. Nevada has long opposed locating the waste there, and litigation over the site has been extensive. *See, e.g., In re Aiken County,* 645 F.3d 428 (D.C. Cir. 2011); *Nevada v. DOE,* 457 F.3d 78 (D.C. Cir. 2006); *Nevada v. DOE,* 400 F.3d 9 (D.C. Cir. 2005); *Nuclear Energy Inst., Inc. v. EPA,* 373 F.3d 1251 (D.C. Cir. 2004); *Northern States Power Co. v. DOE,* 128 F.3d 754 (D.C. Cir. 1997).

As a result of the delays in opening a long-term repository, nearly 100 cases have resulted in settlements or payouts from the DOE for breaching the standard contract it signed with utilities, in which it promised to begin accepting waste in 1998. As of 2020, another 16 cases remained pending. U.S. DEP'T OF ENERGY, AGENCY FINANCIAL REPORT: FISCAL YEAR 2020 (2020); *see also Indiana Michigan Power Co. v. U.S. Dep't of Energy,* 88 F.3d 1272 (D.C. Cir. 1996); *Northern States Power Co., v. U.S. Dep't of Energy,* 128 F.3d 754 (D.C. Cir. 1997); *S. California Edison Co. v. United States,* 655 F.3d 1319 (Fed. Cir. 2011); *Carolina Power & Light Co. v. United States,* 573 F.3d 1271, 1273 (Fed. Cir. 2009); Richard B. Stewart & Jane B. Stewart, *Solving the Spent Nuclear Fuel Impasse,* 21 N.Y.U. ENV'T L.J. 1, 82–85, 102–11 (2014). The federal government's tab for unaccepted waste has thus grown to $8.6 billion, with the Department of Energy estimating that it may be liable for another $30.6 billion. AGENCY FINANCIAL REPORT: FISCAL YEAR 2020, *supra*.

Meanwhile, following his election, President Obama announced that Yucca Mountain was not the right solution. The DOE thus withdrew its licensing application for Yucca from the NRC, and a legal battle erupted. *See In re Aiken County*, 645 F.3d 428, 430 (D.C. Cir. 2011). A Blue Ribbon Commission convened by President Obama found that the "approach laid out under the 1987 Amendments to the Nuclear Waste Policy Act (NWPA)—which tied the entire U.S. high-level waste management program to the fate of the Yucca Mountain site—has not worked to produce a timely solution for dealing with the nation's most hazardous radioactive materials. . . . The United States has traveled nearly 25 years down the current path only to come to a point where continuing to rely on the same approach seems destined to bring further controversy, litigation, and protracted delay." BLUE RIBBON COMMISSION ON AMERICA'S NUCLEAR FUTURE, DRAFT REPORT TO THE SECRETARY OF ENERGY, DEPARTMENT OF ENERGY iii (July 2011). The Blue Ribbon Commission thus suggested a different "consent-based approach" with a "new organization dedicated solely to implementing the waste management program" to create "one or more geologic disposal facilities" and "one or more consolidated interim storage facilities." *Id.* at iv.

Today, the resolution of how to handle spent nuclear fuel in the United States is as uncertain as ever. Five years into the Obama administration, the D.C. Circuit ruled that the federal government could no longer collect a storage fee from nuclear power generators because it had withdrawn support for Yucca Mountain while offering no other viable alternatives for long term waste storage. *See Nat'l Ass'n of Regulatory Util. Comm'rs v. U.S. Dep't of Energy*, 736 F.3d 517 (D.C. Cir. 2013). The court flatly rejected the Department of Energy's suggested range of costs it was relying upon to keep collecting the fee: "According to the Secretary, the final balance of the fund to be used to pay the costs of disposal could be somewhere between a $2 trillion deficit and a $4.9 trillion surplus. This range is so large as to be absolutely useless. . . . (This presentation reminds us of the lawyer's song in the musical, 'Chicago,'—'Give them the old razzle dazzle.')" *Id.* at 519. The court also referred to the Department's 2011 report, "Strategy for the Management and Disposal of Used Nuclear Fuel and High-Level Radioactive Waste," as a "so-called strategy." *Id.* And it found unconvincing the government's position that "completion of a permanent depository (located somewhere) not until 2048" could be reconciled with the NWPA, which, it noted, mandated completion by 1998. "That is truly 'pie in the sky.' " *Id.* Thus, given the NWPA's command that the government build Yucca Mountain, it took the court barely three pages to reject the Department of Energy's decision to abandon the site:

> The government claims it is . . . in a catch-22 position . . ., [b]ut the government's problem is of its own making. It certainly could have used Yucca Mountain's costs if it were still pursuing that site, but it cannot have it both ways. It cannot renounce Yucca Mountain and then reasonably use its costs as a proxy. The government was hoist on its own petard.

Id. at 520. "The NRC resumed work on its technical and environmental reviews of the Yucca Mountain application using available funds in response to" the D.C. Circuit's ruling, with NRC staff completing the "final volumes of the safety evaluation report in January 2015. The staff completed and issued an Environmental Impact Statement supplement in May 2016. The adjudicatory hearing, which must be completed before a licensing decision can be made, remains suspended." Nuclear Regulatory Comm'n, *High-Level Waste Disposal: NRC's Yucca Mountain Licensing Activities.*

The D.C. Circuit's decision notwithstanding, the future of Yucca Mountain remains very much in limbo. While the Trump Administration's first three proposed budgets included requests of roughly $120 million to restart licensing of the facility, President Trump subsequently reversed course. In February 2020, he tweeted that he would respect the opinion of Nevadans and pursue innovative options for nuclear waste storage. President Biden, for his part, has said that there will not be disposal of nuclear waste in Nevada.

The United States, of course, is not alone in this nuclear waste stalemate. Germany continues to search for a solution despite its ongoing efforts to shutter all its nuclear power plants by 2022. The 2009 documentary film, *Into Eternity*, chronicled Finland's process of constructing a nuclear waste disposal site comparable to Yucca Mountain. Among the dilemmas faced in that project: What signage to use to mark the site, given that the waste will remain highly radioactive for 250,000 years? Because it is unknowable what language will be spoken so far into the future, one suggestion was simply to post permanent placards with copies of Edvard Munch's famous painting, *The Scream*, around the site. As one group of experts wrote in 2003, "[D]isposal of high-level radioactive spent fuel . . . is one of the most intractable problems facing the nuclear power industry throughout the world. No country has yet successfully implemented a system for disposing of this waste." MASSACHUSETTS INSTITUTE OF TECHNOLOGY, THE FUTURE OF NUCLEAR POWER 10 (2003).

The Nuclear Energy Institute estimates that reactors in the United States have already produced over 78,000 tons of high-level waste, with another 2,000–2,300 tons being produced annually. It remains scattered across the country at 75 operating and shuttered nuclear plant sites. Nuclear Energy Inst., *Used Fuel Storage and Nuclear Waste Fund*

Payments by State (updated Feb. 2017); *Funding Increased for Yucca Mountain Review*, WORLD NUCLEAR NEWS (June 8, 2012). Eventually, some worry, this will become the de facto "policy" for storing nuclear waste—on-site, even though those facilities were never designed for that purpose.

For more on the Yucca Mountain saga, see WILLIAM M. ALLEY & ROSEMARIE ALLEY, TOO HOT TO TOUCH: THE PROBLEM OF HIGH-LEVEL NUCLEAR WASTE (2013); JOHN D'AGATA, ABOUT A MOUNTAIN (2010); MACFARLANE & EWING, *supra*; J. SAMUEL WALKER, THE ROAD TO YUCCA MOUNTAIN: THE DEVELOPMENT OF RADIOACTIVE WASTE POLICY IN THE UNITED STATES (2009); Bruce R. Huber, *Checks, Balances, and Nuclear Waste*, 48 ARIZ. ST. L.J. 1169 (2016).

NOTES AND QUESTIONS

1.   Why doesn't the United States "reprocess" spent nuclear fuel, which can reduce the amount of (though not completely eliminate) the waste? France, which, as noted earlier, relies heavily on nuclear power for its electricity supply, long has reprocessed its fuel. Used nuclear fuel can be processed to extract fissile materials for recycling and to reduce the volume of high-level wastes by recovering a significant amount of plutonium and small amounts of uranium. *Processing of Used Nuclear Fuel*, World Nuclear Ass'n. Indeed, as noted above, one of the reasons some advocates of onsite nuclear storage back that idea is to limit the movement of spent nuclear fuel, and thus, they argue, the risk of these materials falling into the wrong hands. In the United States, the commercial reprocessing of plutonium was indefinitely suspended by President Gerald Ford due to concerns of nuclear weapons proliferation. But if France can reprocess without proliferating nuclear weapons, couldn't the United States as well?

2.   Nonproliferation concerns are not the only reason the United States does not reprocess spent nuclear fuel. Economic and environmental factors also play a part. It is much cheaper to mine uranium than to reprocess spent nuclear fuel. *See* Heba Hashem, *Recycling Spent Nuclear Fuel*, NUCLEAR ENERGY INSIDER (Nov. 21, 2012). Thus, unless uranium prices dramatically increase or reprocessing costs become more competitive, reprocessing will continue to face an uphill battle in the United States. *See* U.S. NUCLEAR REG. COMM'N, BACKGROUND, STATUS, AND ISSUES RELATED TO THE REGULATION OF ADVANCED SPENT NUCLEAR FUEL RECYCLE FACILITIES (2008). Ecological risks posed by reprocessing, including the chance of leaks and the need for long-term storage, also present obstacles to domestic reprocessing. *See* R. STEPHEN BERRY ET AL., NUCLEAR FUEL REPROCESSING: FUTURE PROSPECTS AND VIABILITY 14–16 (2010). For more on the question of reprocessing in the United States, see Paige Lambermont, *Why Won't the U.S. Reprocess Spent Nuclear Fuel?*, INST. FOR ENERGY RSCH. (June 2021).

3.   Fuel for nuclear power plants can also be derived from military warheads. In 1993, the United States and Russia struck a deal in which Russia agreed to sell the United States the uranium from Russia's surplus of nuclear weapons, and the United States would then sell the uranium to privately owned nuclear power plants—a program called "Megatons to Megawatts." Ultimately, this agreement resulted in the disarmament of approximately 500 tons of weapons-grade uranium into nuclear fuel and provided 10% of all electricity in the United States. On December 11, 2013, the program concluded, when the last shipment of uranium arrived in the United States.

4.   Is geologic storage really the best option for disposing nuclear waste? Or does putting it underground—where it later could be more difficult to access in the case of, for instance, an earthquake—only result in exacerbated risk? Might it be better to leave the waste above ground, where it can be more easily monitored? How about other options, like launching it into space? That actually has been considered. *See Pacific Gas & Electric Co. v. State Energy Resources Conservation & Development Comm'n*, 461 U.S. 190, 196 (1983) ("A number of long-term nuclear waste management strategies have been extensively examined. These range from sinking the wastes in stable deep seabeds, to placing the wastes beneath ice sheets in Greenland and Antarctica, to ejecting the wastes into space by rocket."). For more on what appears to be, for now, the *de facto* solution to storing nuclear waste in the United States, see Steven D. Melzer, *Nuclear Stalemate: Indefinite Above-Ground Storage Is A Temporary, Albeit Safe Band-Aid for A Serious Wound*, 91 NOTRE DAME L. REV. 847 (2015).

5.   Would above-ground storage at or near operating nuclear power plants also be more equitable than a centralized repository like Yucca Mountain? Note that the vast majority of nuclear facilities are east of the Mississippi River, while three of the four locations that have been seriously considered for storing the waste have been in the Intermountain West, which has only eight nuclear power plants. Shouldn't the people who benefit from the consumption of nuclear electricity also be the ones who bear the burden of its waste? To date, concerns over groundwater contamination and terrorist threats have been stumbling blocks toward above-ground storage options.

1. WHO DECIDES?: JURISDICTION IN ENERGY GOVERNANCE

The federal government's encouragement of nuclear energy, first by allowing licensing without any waste solution in place and then by assuring utilities it would solve the predicament, might well be considered an adverse consequence of government pushing a certain technology. Indeed, a common criticism in U.S. energy policy is that government should not "pick winners and losers." Gary E. Marchant, *Sustainable Energy Technologies: Ten Lessons from the History of Technology Regulation*, 18 WIDENER L.J. 831 (2009). At the same time, the U.S. nuclear energy industry has produced an enormous amount of electricity, with effectively no critical air pollution emissions and a remarkably safe record of operation. Nuclear power thus tees up perfectly the debate of what role government should play in influencing energy outcomes. What matters more—atomic energy's abundant electricity or the long-term risk of exposure to radioactivity from a Fukushima-like event or leaking high-level nuclear waste?

Another question is, "Who decides which is more important?" Nuclear energy puts this on stark display as well. Here, there are two key legal doctrines that appear again and again in energy law, not just in the nuclear context but throughout the field. Both are constitutional.

The first is the concept of federal "preemption" of state law pursuant to the Supremacy Clause of the U.S. Constitution. Under Supreme Court precedent, federal law may preempt state law in one of three ways. First, federal law may *expressly* preempt state law by saying that it does so. Second, federal law may *impliedly* preempt state law when that law creates so significant an obstacle to carrying out federal law that it "conflicts with," "frustrates," or "stands as an obstacle" to the accomplishment of" the national regime—a category often referred to as "conflict preemption." Finally, federal law may *impliedly* preempt state law when the national regime is so pervasive that it effectively occupies the field of regulation, leaving no room for states to legislate. This last type of preemption is often called "field preemption." *See, e.g., City of Morgan City v. South Louisiana Elec. Co-op. Ass'n*, 31 F.3d 319, 321–22 (5th Cir. 1994).

The second important, recurring constitutional concept in energy law is the "dormant" or "negative" Commerce Clause, which was discussed earlier in Chapters 4 and 5. This doctrine is called "dormant" or "negative" because it does not appear on the face of the Constitution. Instead, courts have found that the Commerce Clause's affirmative grant of power to Congress to regulate interstate commerce also forecloses states from using law to "Balkanize"—fractionalize or segment—the national economic market. States may not prefer their citizens to those of other states in an effort to give their own citizens an economic advantage. The idea, in short, is free trade among states.

Courts also use a multi-part test to decide whether a state law violates the dormant Commerce Clause. First, a state law becomes subject to "strict scrutiny"—and thus is "virtually *per se*" invalid—if it discriminates against interstate commerce. Discrimination can arise in three circumstances: where state law (1) intends to discriminate against out-of-state commerce; (2) discriminates against out-of-state commerce on the statute's face; or (3) discriminates against out-of-state commerce in its application or practical effect. *C & A Carbone, Inc. v. Town of Clarkstown*, 511 U.S. 383, 386 (1994). Alternatively, a state law that is neutral in its application but imposes a burden on interstate commerce may still be found unconstitutional if it fails the so-called *Pike* balancing test. That test states: "Where the statute regulates even-handedly to effectuate a legitimate local public interest, and its effects on interstate commerce are only incidental, it will be upheld unless the burden imposed on such commerce is clearly excessive in relation to the putative local benefits." *Pike v. Bruce Church, Inc.*, 397 U.S. 137, 142 (1970).

As is true throughout the field of energy law, understanding these constitutional principles is essential to attorneys practicing in the area. They delineate the contours of where states and the federal government can regulate, and they regularly form the substance of litigation among parties in the energy industry. These doctrines, in short, provide the primary legal substance used to answer one of the key questions in all of energy law: Who decides?

2. THE FAILED SKULL VALLEY PLAN

To explore in greater depth these challenging constitutional concepts, a more detailed case study of the dispute over siting a nuclear waste storage facility in Skull Valley, Utah is useful. We first present a narrative account of the dispute, followed by case extracts and a Practice Problem for a more in-depth discussion of the application of the Supremacy and dormant Commerce Clauses in the nuclear energy context.

DAVID RICH LEWIS, SKULL VALLEY GOSHUTES AND THE POLITICS OF NUCLEAR WASTE: ENVIRONMENT, IDENTITY, AND SOVEREIGNTY

Native Americans and the Environment: Perspectives on the Ecological
Indian (Michael E. Harkin & David Rich Lewis eds., 2007)

"Over my dead body!" thundered Utah governor Michael Leavitt. Normally, every committed environmentalist in Utah and the Intermountain West would have lined up to accommodate the Republican governor's challenge. But this time, there was a resounding silence, even an endorsement of the governor's stand. At issue was an agreement between the Skull Valley Band of Goshute Indians and Private Fuel Storage LLC to store forty thousand metric tons of high-level radioactive waste for up to forty years on a concrete pad forty-five miles southwest of Salt Lake City. The eighteen-thousand-acre Skull Valley Goshute Reservation is already surrounded by military bombing ranges, federal nerve agent storage facilities, and private hazardous waste sites, and it affords the approximately 124 band members few if any options for economic development. The agreement would bring the Goshutes jobs and millions of dollars annually. For Skull Valley tribal chairman Leon Bear, the issue is about cultural survival and tribal sovereignty, the paternalism of the state, and the environmental racism of Goshute critics. For Governor Leavitt, the state legislature, and environmental opponents, it is about the lack of state control or fiscal benefit, the fear of having two million residents live downwind from a nuclear repository, the environmental racism of the nuclear industry, and the conflicting images of ecological Indians versus Indians as modern human beings. . . .

But first, the question: Who in their right mind would store highly radioactive nuclear waste in their own backyard, and why? . . .

[Like many tribes, the Skull Valley Goshutes faced immense cultural and environmental pressure from non-native "settlers." For the Skull Valley Goshutes, this was the Mormon pioneers that came to northern Utah, though the tribe continued to cling to its ancestral land even after the Mormons arrived.] Every few years after 1863—even as they ignored Goshutes in general—federal officials proposed relocating Goshutes to the Fort Hall Shoshone or Uintah-Ouray Ute reservation, but each time their proposals met stiff resistance by Goshutes deeply attached to their homeland. In 1871 Skull Valley Goshutes voiced their concerns through William Lee, longtime Grantsville resident who was helping them operate a small farm. "They have a decided objection to go to Uintah or any other place," wrote Lee. "They are willing to do anything on their own land, the land of their fathers which their Great Father at Washington may wish them to do, but they are not willing to go to the land of the strangers. The land of their fathers is sacred to them. On it they wish to live. And in it they wish their bodies laid when dead." . . .

Over time, Goshutes began to divide between those living and attempting to farm under the limited supervision of federal agents and Mormon missionary settlers in the Deep Creek Valley, and a much smaller group in Skull Valley who did some farming and wage work but refused to relocate. Populations dwindled to fewer than two hundred Goshutes, and according to one ethnographer, "The old men weep at the doom of extinction which they believe plainly to see ahead of their people." After years of neglect, the federal government codified those two Goshute communities, establishing the 34,000-acre Deep Creek Reservation by executive order in 1914 and the 18,000-acre Skull Valley Reservation in 1917 and 1918. No one paid much attention to the Skull Valley Goshutes after that. By 1921 the BIA had closed its school and withdrawn its farm agent . . . .

That few lived in Skull Valley was, in part, a result of World War II, when the very isolation and barrenness of Utah's west desert made it perfect for the military. Air crews training at Wendover and Hill Air Force bases bombed the Utah Test and Training Range. The army opened Dugway Proving Grounds and Tooele Army Depot to develop and store weapons. During the ensuing cold war, Dugway, Tooele, and the Deseret Chemical depots evolved to develop, test, and store the nation's chemical and biological weapons. Dugway, surrounding Skull Valley on the west and south, was the worst and most secretive. Between 1951 and 1969 there were 1,635 open-air tests involving more than fifty-five thousand chemical rockets, artillery shells, bombs, and land mines, as well as low- and high-altitude aerial spraying tests in all sorts of weather conditions. Cameras rolled to record the deadly effects on animals caged in the test range. Weapons released a half million pounds of nerve agent, equivalent to 3.5 trillion lethal doses. Spent and unexploded army ordinance was scattered over fourteen hundred square miles of public land in Utah, not all of it within the recognized test ranges. Accidents were common. Nerve agents released at altitude dispersed widely, and 10 to 30 percent target hits were not unusual. In 1962, only 4 percent of a test drop of twenty-eight hundred pounds of VX nerve agent reached the target grid. In 1968 a Phantom jet leaked twenty pounds of VX that drifted thirty miles into Skull Valley, sickening ranchers and killing wildlife and sixty-four hundred grazing sheep. The government denied responsibility but took the sheep for testing and then buried them back on the reservation, without tribal knowledge. . . .

The Skull Valley Indian Reservation is surrounded by these live-fire zones and toxic sites. "And I think the federal government snuck one in on us also because surrounding our reservation we have all those things," observed Skull Valley band chairman Leon Bear. "And we were never consulted on those issues whether we liked it or not. They didn't tell us that these things were dangerous. They didn't come out and tell the Goshute band or the Council, 'How would you guys like to have a hazardous and toxic waste dump by you? Or how would you like to have a low level radioactive dump by you? Or how would you like to have the biological labs by you? Or the storage of nerve agents by you?'" But in 1997 the tables were about to turn.

"When I saw the proposal and it was going out to the Indian community," recalled Danny Quintana, former attorney for the Skull Valley Goshute, "I suggested . . . that we get the proposal because my intent was to gather the data and put together a report and kill the proposal. Because I had thought initially what was occurring was the Department of Energy and the utility companies were in a conspiracy to dump high level nuclear waste on reservations." Longtime band chairman Richard Bear (Leon's father) agreed. But after using $300,000 in federal study grants to investigate temporary waste storage and thinking seriously about the long-term health of their territory and their people, Quintana said, "it became crystal clear [to the council] that this could be done safely."

Even though Congress canceled the National Waste Negotiator's budget for 1994, Richard Bear and the Skull Valley Goshutes continued educating band members about dry-cask storage by touring national and international nuclear facilities. "We also went to . . . Governor Leavitt, and we had told him that this was our plan," says Leon Bear . . . .

On May 20, 1997, Chairman Leon Bear and the Skull Valley Band of Goshutes signed a lease with PFS to accept up to forty thousand metric tons of high-level radioactive waste and to store that waste above ground in an independent spent fuel storage installation for twenty years, renewable to forty years. Ten million spent nuclear fuel rods—3.5- to 4.5-meter-long zirconium alloy tubes packed with thousands of pencil-eraser-size uranium pellets and bundled into groups of two hundred—will be removed from their water-cooling tanks and dry packed into four-inch-thick steel casks, encased in two feet of concrete. Packaged casks from the PFS member utilities will be shipped via rail to the 820-acre Skull Valley [Independent Spent Fuel Storage Installation (ISFSI)] and placed inside stainless steel containers capable of holding ten metric tons of waste. Some four thousand containers, each eighteen feet tall, will sit spaced out for cooling on a one-hundred-acre pad of reinforced concrete, three feet thick, surrounded by a low wall. Surrounding the perimeter of the ISFSI will be two eight-foot-high chain-link fences. Construction costs are estimated at $500 million, creating four hundred temporary and forty to sixty permanent jobs. Contract payments to the Skull Valley band [would have been for approximately $40 million]. PFS project manager Scott Northand estimated total operation costs at $3.1 billion over the forty-year life of the project.

So, back to the fundamental question: Who in their right mind would support storing highly radioactive waste in their own backyard, and why? Obviously, Leon Bear and the Skull Valley Band of Goshutes. They studied the issue intensively and voted two to one to support the project as a means of revitalizing the band, politically and socially. In the 1960s the band had only fifteen adult members. "People just gave up," recalled Bear. "They just got up and left. June grass moved in, houses fell apart. Skull Valley pretty much died off at that point." Bear said a few older people like his mother tried to maintain seasonal subsistence traditions of gathering pine nuts and chokecherries, while his father served as tribal chairman and worked at Deseret Chemical Depot. "So we did most of our gathering at Safeway," he joked.

Today between 25 and 30 of 124 band members live on the reservation. Only four are fluent Goshute speakers. The rest live nearby in Grantsville, Stockton, and Tooele or in cities along Utah's Wasatch Front. Unemployment and poverty are three times the national average. . . .

Opportunities for economic development have always been limited given Skull Valley's isolated location surrounded by toxic neighbors. Ninety percent of band income came from their Tekoi Rocket Test Facility . . ., but that has ended. The band operated a convenience store ironically named the Pony Express Station, and they lease some land to local ranchers. In the last decade they were majority owners of Earth Environmental Services, selling dumpsters to government agencies and private industry, and they tried a landfill recycling company that failed. PepsiCo and a local water company both approached them about setting up bottling plants until they heard about Dugway. Other corporations have approached them about storing municipal wastes and mining by-products or operating hazardous waste incinerators. . . .

With no other economic options, with hopelessness, alcoholism, migration, and language loss threatening their political and cultural existence, Skull Valley leaders view the ISFSI as a bottom-line tool for cultural survival. The project will create jobs, bringing people back to the reservation. It will help build houses, roads, utilities, businesses, a school, and a health clinic to keep them there. It will support education scholarships and health insurance and put money in people's pockets. "That's why they put me in office," says Chairman Bear, "so that we can make money and so that we can prosper and build infrastructure on our reservation. That's the whole purpose of this whole thing. And also, to keep our traditions and our cultural resources intact at the same time." Ultimately, he says, "it's up to the people themselves to determine how much culture or traditions they want to maintain." Bear recognizes the potential dangers of an ISFSI but stresses the industry's safety record, the assurances of science and scientists, federal over-sight and liability responsibility, and his personal commitment that this is a temporary storage facility, not a permanent waste dump. "[We] would never compromise . . . to harm any of our children, the tribe, the land or the territory around it." "We'll always be part of this land," says Bear. "We're not going anywhere. We're survivors." . . .

Just off the reservation, Tooele County officials welcomed the facility, acknowledging that site construction and operation would generate jobs for their non-Indian citizens who are already surrounded by and working at such hazardous facilities. In May 2000 county commissioners signed an agreement with PFS that will net the county between $90 and $250 million over the forty-year life of the project. "Our interest was to make sure again that if something was going to happen that we had no control over, we protected our citizens to the best of our ability," said former county commissioner Gary Griffith. And in the realm of what had been located in his county, Griffith found the proposed ISFSI innocuous: "I would submit to you that it probably would be the safest, cleanest business that we could bring into this county." . . .

But fear and opposition to the project is strong across the state, in Tooele County, and within the small Skull Valley band itself. "This project is a no-brainer for a politician," said attorney Danny Quintana. "It involves high level radioactive waste. It involves a Native American community and it involves an opportunity to appear green even if they're not. So for a politician to oppose this is a slam dunk." Until he resigned in 2003 to head the Environmental Protection Agency in the George W. Bush administration, Governor Leavitt led the opposition, making it acceptable for Utah Republicans—particularly Utah's ultraconservative "Cowboy Caucus"—to embrace environmentalism and partner with environmental organizations as distasteful as Greenpeace, the Sierra Club, the Southern Utah Wilderness Alliance, and the Green Party. Long-term opponent of environmentalists, Utah representative James Hansen (Republican) and his First District successor Rob Bishop (Republican) even appropriated the rhetoric of wilderness advocates in a disingenuous plan to create the Cedar Mountain Wilderness area, adjacent to Utah's Test and Training Range, thereby preventing road or rail construction in order to derail the Goshute project. Likewise, Utah environmentalists, religious leaders, and citizen groups such as HEAL Utah, Utah Down-winders, and Citizens Against Nuclear Waste in Utah have swallowed their pride to partner with their environmental opponents against this Native American minority . . . .

Together, opponents of the Skull Valley ISFSI argue that the environmental impact assessments are flawed and the science is wrong; that transporting nuclear waste through the state is dangerous; that this will become a permanent nuclear waste dump by default; that accidents are inevitable; that in the event of an accident or abandonment, financial liability is not clear; and that the region is seismically unstable. After the events of September 11, 2001, they argue, the facility will be an easy target for similar terrorist attacks, or military jets from Hill Air Force Base might crash into the facility on their way to bomb the Utah Test and Training Range. All of these are legitimate concerns, especially in a state that remembers how the federal government used it as a cold war guinea pig for fallout from the Nevada Nuclear Test site.

But as the argument extends, elements of financial self-interest emerge. Leavitt has made it clear, "We don't produce it. We don't benefit from it, and we don't want to store it for those who do. . . . [H]aving lethally hot nuclear waste 40 miles from where I sit now and within a very close range of the major population center of this state is inconsistent with our vision of what we want this state to be." Yet radioactive waste is a national phenomenon, from locally generated low-level medical and industrial waste to the national power grid . . . .

The arguments also reveal the troubling paternalism and underlying thread of racism that permeates the history of Mormon-Indian relations in Utah. Opponents of the Skull Valley ISFSI claim that PFS enticed the Goshutes with money and misinformation. Representative James Hansen voiced this brand of paternalism: "I guess our concerns is, and I don't mean to be unkind to anybody but it [PFS] put an awful lot of money on some of our Indian friends out there . . . the financial reward was maybe overwhelming to some folks who probably haven't seen much money in their lifetime, and we didn't think that was a proper thing to do." . . .

In April 1997 Governor Leavitt went on the offensive, forming an Office of High Level Waste Storage Opposition within the state's Department of Environmental Quality to mobilize opposition to the Skull Valley ISFSI proposal. That summer he met with Leon Bear and asked him to "step away" from the project or face active opposition. Bear refused, later suggesting to journalist Kevin Fedarko that "the governor's request might have carried a bit more weight if the people of Utah hadn't spent the better part of the past 170 years treating the Goshutes like pariahs." . . .

In 2001, following NRC approval of the draft environmental impact statement, the gloves came off as the Utah Legislature passed three measures: the first levied steep taxes and security bonds on PFS to drive it away; the second authorized $1.1 million for a dream team of lawyers to tie PFS in legal knots; and the third offered the Skull Valley band $2 million for economic development if they would step away from their agreement with PFS. All three bills passed, but only the Goshute economic development bill carried no appropriation, no action. [Meanwhile, by 2005, the state had spent roughly $5 million] trying to defeat the project . . . .

In 1997, Margene Bullcreek organized Ohngo Gaudadeh Devia . . ., a grass-roots coalition of fifteen to twenty tribal members along with environmental supporters. As part of its "try-everything" strategy, the state has covered more than $500,000 in legal bills for OGD to challenge the BIA lease approval and to file an environmental justice contention with the NRC against PFS, all without success. Undeterred, Bullcreek and [Sammy] Blackbear[, another Skull Valley Goshute opposed to the nuclear storage proposal,] have waged a very public and acrimonious debate in the press and courts . . . .

Bullcreek and Blackbear frame their most potent arguments in cultural terms, as "traditionalists," where "seventh generation" decision making and environmental standards define Indian identity. "The land is not ours," says Sammy Blackbear. "We're caretakers of the land . . . for the next generation and I don't see us doing that putting a nuclear facility there." Bullcreek calls the facility "an insult to American Indians and all people who believe in their ways and that the Earth is sacred" and blames the young people of the tribe who are turning their backs on "tradition." "The real issue is not the money," says Bullcreek. "The real issue is who we are as Native Americans and what we believe in. If we accept these wastes, we're going to lose our tradition." Bullcreek and Blackbear fear that the ISFSI will drive them away from the valley . . . and toward an urban melting pot that obliterates Indianness. . . .

Bear bristles at suggestions that he is not acting like a traditional Indian, and he points out what Goshute traditions are—survival as mobile and adaptive desert dwellers in a harsh environment. "Look, I'm not here to lay down and die like the buffalo. . . . This is a survival issue for us. But in order to bring my people back to the reservation, we're going to have to provide them with a livelihood. That means real jobs, real houses. As far as being traditional and protecting Mother Earth, I don't understand how we can do that. . . . There's no way we can go back to living off the land. Not with what they've done to it." . . .

NOTES AND QUESTIONS

1.   Given both the Skull Valley Goshutes' and Mescalero Apaches' interest in interim storage, and Congress' specific inclusion of tribes in the statute as eligible to take the waste, do the charges of environmental racism in this context have some ring of truth? Or are those claims too complicated by the tribes' desire to site the facility on their land? In other words, did Congress' inclusion of tribes in the statute buoy tribes' interests in case they wanted to be included in a process that offered access to federal funds, or did it merely reify longstanding structural racism?

2.   Tribes' status as sovereign entities in the United States' tripartite (federal-state-tribal) system of government complicated the already complex decisionmaking process for siting a spent nuclear fuel storage facility. For instance, under existing statutory law, the Skull Valley Goshutes could not just decide to take the waste but first had to obtain approval from the Department of the Interior to be able to lease the land to PFS. Nevertheless, the Goshutes' decision to put the waste on their land is emblematic of the many jurisdictional conflicts in energy law. Who should make the tough calls on energy policy: states, the federal government, or some other governmental entity? Why didn't Congress just assign the NRC the task of finding a depository and then let that agency work it out?

3.   The Goshutes continued to push for the ability to take the PFS waste after the State of Utah passed its legislative package trying to thwart that effort, and even after Congress created a wilderness area around the tribe's reservation, effectively derailing their arrangement with PFS. In fact, in 2010, the federal District Court in Utah ruled that the Bureau of Land Management acted unlawfully when it denied the request for a right-of-way across federal land to the Goshute reservation, remanding the application back to the Department of the Interior for reconsideration. *Skull Valley Band of Goshute Indians v. Davis*, 728 F. Supp. 2d 1287 (D. Utah 2010). Despite this ruling, the Goshute's proposal has stalled, seemingly permanently.

4.   For an example of a controversy surrounding the storage of spent nuclear fuel and the opposition by cities, municipalities, and other groups, see *New York v. Nuclear Regulatory Comm'n*, 681 F.3d 471 (D.C. Cir. 2012) (remanding an NRC rulemaking for failing to adequately evaluate environmental risks in assessing a temporary storage facility's ability to safely house spent fuel in on-site storage pools for sixty years post plant licensure). For an example of local opposition over the relicensing of a nuclear reactor, see *Entergy Nuclear*

Vermont Yankee, LLC v. Shumlin, 733 F.3d 393 (2d Cir. 2013) (holding that states cannot effectively foreclose nuclear power by adopting safety statutes that make facility operation impossible).

5.   The question of federal preemption also arises in the context of the Price-Anderson Act, which, as discussed earlier, governs liability from nuclear incidents. For instance, in *Cook v. Rockwell Int'l Corp.*, 790 F.3d 1088 (10th Cir. 2015), a divided Tenth Circuit panel ruled that Price-Anderson did not preempt property owners' state law nuisance claims against a nuclear weapons manufacturing plant, where the property owners had not proven that a Price-Anderson "nuclear incident" had occurred. While the Act defines "nuclear incident" broadly—it includes "any occurrence" that causes "bodily injury, sickness, disease, or death, or loss of or damage to property, or loss of use of property, arising out of or resulting from the radioactive, toxic, explosive, or other hazardous properties" of nuclear materials, 42 U.S.C. § 2014(q)—the court held that because plaintiffs had abandoned their effort to prove that a "nuclear incident" had occurred, Price-Anderson was not triggered. Wrote then-Judge Gorsuch: "Not only can federal claims for larger nuclear incidents subject to the Act's limitations and benefits coexist with state law claims for lesser nuclear occurrences, they can do so quite sensibly. Larger occurrences that qualify as nuclear incidents can threaten to bankrupt nuclear power providers and leave victims un-(or under-) compensated. In these cases, it's understandable why Congress might intercede to provide liability caps and indemnification. Meanwhile, smaller occurrences are less likely to raise the same concerns, so it's equally understandable why Congress might not prevent state law from running its course with respect to them. Our case illustrates the point. At trial, Dow and Rockwell's liability for compensatory damages totaled roughly $177 million. The Act, meanwhile, currently caps federal contractors' liability for nuclear incidents at approximately $12.7 *billion*." *Id.* at 1096 (emphasis in original). For two contrasting examples, where courts found state claims preempted by Price-Anderson, see *McMunn v. Babcock & Wilcox Power Generation Grp., Inc.*, 869 F.3d 246 (3d Cir. 2017); *Steward v. Honeywell Int'l, Inc.*, 469 F. Supp. 3d 872 (S.D. Ill. 2020).

What Utah legislators wanted to do about the Skull Valley Band of Goshutes' plan did not necessarily coincide with the authority they could constitutionally exercise, either under the Supremacy Clause or the dormant Commerce Clause. The following cases provide some examples of the application of these doctrines in energy law, including in the Skull Valley dispute. The Practice Problem that follows then asks you to apply the doctrines to a hypothetical contest involving nuclear waste.

VIRGINIA URANIUM V. WARREN
139 S. Ct. 1894 (2019)

JUSTICE GORSUCH announced the judgment of the Court and delivered an opinion, in which JUSTICE THOMAS and JUSTICE KAVANAUGH join.

Virginia Uranium insists that the federal Atomic Energy Act preempts a state law banning uranium mining, but we do not see it. True, the AEA gives the Nuclear Regulatory Commission significant authority over the milling, transfer, use, and disposal of uranium, as well as the construction and operation of nuclear power plants. But Congress conspicuously chose to leave untouched the States' historic authority over the regulation of mining activities on private lands . . . .

Virginia Uranium thought its plan was pretty straightforward. First, the company wanted to use conventional mining techniques to extract raw uranium ore from a site near Coles Hill, Virginia. Next, it intended to mill that ore into a usable form. Typically performed at the mine site, milling involves grinding the ore into sand-sized grains and then exposing it to a chemical solution that leaches out pure uranium. Once dried, the resulting mixture forms a solid "yellowcake," which the company planned to sell to enrichment facilities that produce fuel for nuclear reactors. Finally, because the leaching process does not remove all of the uranium from the ore, the company expected to store the leftover "tailings" near the mine to reduce the chances of contaminating the air or water.

But putting the plan into action didn't prove so simple. Pursuant to the AEA, the NRC regulates milling and tailing storage activities nationwide, and it has issued an array of rules on these subjects. None of those, though, proved the real problem for Virginia Uranium. The company hit a roadblock even before it could get to the point where the NRC's rules kick in: State law flatly prohibits uranium mining in Virginia. *See* Va. Code Ann. §§ 45.1–161.292:30, 45.1–283 (2013). . . .

We begin with the company's claim that the text and structure of the AEA reserve the regulation of uranium mining for the purpose of addressing nuclear safety concerns to the NRC alone—and almost immediately problems emerge. Unlike many federal statutes, the AEA contains no provision preempting state law in so many words. Even more pointedly, the statute grants the NRC extensive and sometimes exclusive authority to regulate nearly every aspect of the nuclear fuel life cycle except mining. Companies like Virginia Uranium must abide the NRC's rules and regulations if they wish to handle enriched uranium, to mill uranium ore or store tailings, or to build or run a nuclear power plant. *See* 42 U.S.C. §§ 2111(a), 2113(a), 2073. But when it comes to mining, the statute speaks very differently, expressly stating that the NRC's regulatory powers arise only "*after* [uranium's] removal from its place of deposit in nature." § 2092 (emphasis added). . . .

What the text states, context confirms. After announcing a general rule that mining regulation lies outside the NRC's jurisdiction, the AEA carves out a notably narrow exception. On federal lands, the statute says, the NRC may regulate uranium mining. § 2097. And if the federal government wants to control mining of uranium on private land, the AEA tells the NRC exactly what to do: It may purchase or seize the land by eminent domain and make it federal land. § 2096. Congress thus has spoken directly to the question of uranium mining on private land, and every bit of what it's said indicates that state authority remains untouched.

Later amendments to the AEA point to the same conclusion. Some years after the statute's passage, Congress added a provision, currently codified in § 2021, allowing the NRC to devolve certain of its regulatory powers to the States. Unsurprisingly, Congress indicated that the NRC must maintain regulatory control over especially sensitive activities like the construction of nuclear power plants. § 2021(c). But under § 2021(b) the NRC may now, by agreement, pass to the States some of its preexisting authorities to regulate various nuclear materials "for the protection of the public health and safety from radiation hazards." Out of apparent concern that courts might (mis)read these new provisions as prohibiting States from regulating any activity even tangentially related to nuclear power without first reaching an agreement with the NRC, Congress added subsection (k):

> "Nothing in this section [that is, § 2021] shall be construed to affect the authority of any State or local agency to regulate activities for purposes other than protection against radiation hazards."

Section 2021, thus, did nothing to extend the NRC's power to activities, like mining, historically beyond its reach. Instead, it served only to allow the NRC to share with the States some of the powers previously reserved to the federal government. Even then, the statute explained in subsection (k) that States remain free to regulate the activities discussed in § 2021 for purposes other than nuclear safety without the NRC's consent. Indeed, if anything, subsection (k) might be described as a non-preemption clause.

Virginia Uranium's case hinges on a very different construction of subsection (k). The company suggests that, properly read, the provision greatly expands the preemptive effect of the AEA and demands the displacement of any state law (touching on mining or any other subject) if that law was enacted for the purpose of protecting the public against "radiation hazards." And, the company adds, Virginia's law bears just such an impermissible purpose.

In our view, this reading nearly turns the provision on its head. Subsection (k) does not displace traditional state regulation over mining or otherwise extend the NRC's grasp to matters previously beyond its control.

It does not expose every state law on every subject to a searching judicial inquiry into its latent purposes. Instead and much more modestly, it clarifies that "nothing in this [new] section [2021]"—a section allowing for the devolution-by-agreement of federal regulatory authority—should be construed to curtail the States' ability to regulate the activities discussed in that same section for purposes other than protecting against radiation hazards. So only state laws that seek to regulate the activities discussed in § 2021 without an NRC agreement—activities like the construction of nuclear power plants—may be scrutinized to ensure their purposes aim at something other than regulating nuclear safety. . . .

If the best reading of the AEA doesn't require us to hold the state law before us preempted, Virginia Uranium takes another swing in the same direction. . . . [It] points to this Court's decision in *Pacific Gas & Elec. Co. v. State Energy Resources Conservation and Development Comm'n*, 461 U.S. 190 (1983).

But here, too, problems quickly appear. *Pacific Gas* rejected a preemption challenge to a state law prohibiting the construction of new nuclear power plants. Along the way, the Court expressly dismissed the notion that § 2021 establishes the federal government as "the sole regulator of all matters nuclear." The Court observed that subsection (k) addresses itself only to "the preemptive effect of 'this section,' that is [§ 2021]." And the Court acknowledged that subsection (k) does not "cut back on pre-existing state authority outside the NRC's jurisdiction," a field that surely includes uranium mining. . . .

Still, Virginia Uranium seeks to make the best of a bad situation. The company points out that *Pacific Gas* upheld the state law at issue there only after observing that it was enacted out of concern with economic development, not for the purpose of addressing radiation safety hazards. From this, the company reasons, we should infer that any state law enacted with the purpose of addressing nuclear hazards must fall . . . .

But even that much does not follow. Since the passage of the AEA, the NRC has always played a significant role in regulating the construction of nuclear power plants. Indeed, under § 2021(c) this remains one area where the NRC generally cannot devolve its responsibilities to the States. And because § 2021 classifies the construction of nuclear power plants as one of the core remaining areas of special federal concern, any state law regulating that activity risks being subjected to an inquiry into its purposes under subsection (k). But the activity Virginia's law regulates—mining on private land—isn't one the AEA has ever addressed, and it isn't one § 2021 discusses, so subsection (k) does not authorize any judicial inquiry into state legislative purpose in this case.

Admittedly, there is a wrinkle here. *Pacific Gas* seemed to accept California's argument that its law addressed whether new power plants may be built, while the NRC's regulatory power under § 2021(c) extends only to the question how such plants are constructed and operated. And accepting (without granting) these premises, it would appear that California's law did not implicate an activity addressed by § 2021, so an inquiry into state legislative purpose under subsection (k) was not statutorily authorized. Yet *Pacific Gas* inquired anyway, perhaps on the unstated belief that the state law just came "too close" to a core power § 2021(c) reserves to the federal government. . . .

[But j]ust because *Pacific Gas* may have made more of state legislative purposes than the terms of the AEA allow does not mean we must make more of them yet. It is one thing to do as *Pacific Gas* did and inquire exactingly into state legislative purposes when state law prohibits a regulated activity like the construction of a nuclear plant, and thus comes close to trenching on core federal powers reserved to the federal government by the AEA. It is another thing to do as Virginia Uranium wishes and impose the same exacting scrutiny on state laws prohibiting an activity like mining far removed from the NRC's historic powers. . . . Being in for a dime doesn't mean we have to be in for a dollar.

This Court's later cases confirm the propriety of restraint in this area. In a decision issued just a year after *Pacific Gas* (and by the same author), this Court considered whether the AEA preempted state tort remedies for radiation injuries after a nuclear plant accident. *Silkwood v. Kerr-McGee Corp.*, 464 U.S. 238 (1984). In doing so, the Court did not inquire into state legislative purposes, apparently because it thought state tort law (unlike a law prohibiting the construction of a nuclear power plant) fell beyond any fair understanding of the NRC's reach under the AEA. . . . Some years later, this Court in *English v. General Elec. Co.*, 496 U.S. 72 (1990), went further still, casting doubt on whether an inquiry into state legislative purposes had been either necessary or appropriate in *Pacific Gas* itself. 496 U.S. at 84–85, n.7 ("Whether the *suggestion* of the majority in *Pacific Gas* that legislative purpose is relevant to the definition of the pre-empted field is part of the *holding* of that case is not an issue before us today" (emphasis added)). . . .

If the AEA doesn't occupy the field of radiation safety in uranium mining, Virginia Uranium suggests the statute still displaces state law through what's sometimes called conflict preemption. In particular, the company suggests, Virginia's mining law stands as an impermissible "obstacle to the accomplishment and execution of the full purposes and objectives of Congress" [because, it says,] Virginia's moratorium disrupts the delicate "balance" Congress sought to achieve [in the AEA between promoting nuclear power while limiting environmental harms]. Maybe the text of the AEA doesn't touch on mining in so many words, but its authority to regulate later stages of the nuclear fuel life cycle would be effectively undermined if mining laws like Virginia's were allowed.

A sound preemption analysis cannot be as simplistic as that. No more than in field preemption can the Supremacy Clause be deployed here to elevate abstract and unenacted legislative desires above state law; only federal laws "made in pursuance of" the Constitution, through its prescribed processes of bicameralism and presentment, are entitled to preemptive effect. . . .

As an alternative to proceeding down the purposes-and-objectives branch of conflict preemption, Virginia Uranium might have pursued another. Our cases have held that we can sometimes infer a congressional intent to displace a state law that makes compliance with a federal statute impossible. But Virginia Uranium hasn't pursued an argument along any of these lines, and understandably so. Not only can Virginia Uranium comply with both state and federal laws; it is also unclear whether laws like Virginia's might have a meaningful impact on the development of nuclear power in this country. Some estimate that the United States currently imports over 90 percent of the uranium used in this country. Domestic uranium mines currently exist on federal lands as well and are thus beyond the reach of state authorities. And if the federal government concludes that development of the Coles Hill deposit or any other like it is crucial, it may always purchase the site (or seize it through eminent domain) under the powers Congress has supplied. All this may be done without even amending the AEA, itself another course which Congress is always free to pursue—but which this Court should never be tempted into pursuing on its own.

NEW ENGLAND POWER CO. V. NEW HAMPSHIRE
455 U.S. 331 (1982)

CHIEF JUSTICE BURGER delivered the opinion of the Court.

These three consolidated appeals present the question whether a state can constitutionally prohibit the exportation of hydroelectric energy produced within its borders by a federally licensed facility, or otherwise reserve for its own citizens the "economic benefit" of such hydroelectric power.

I

Appellant New England Power Co. is a public utility which generates and transmits electricity at wholesale. It sells 75% of its power in Massachusetts and much of the remainder in Rhode Island; less than 6% of New Hampshire's population is serviced by New England Power's wholesale customers. New England Power owns and operates six hydroelectric generating stations on the Connecticut River, consisting of 27 generating units. Twenty-one of these units—with a capacity of 419.8 megawatts, or about 10% of New England Power's total generating capacity—are located within the State of New Hampshire. The units are licensed by the Federal Energy Regulatory Commission pursuant to Part I of the Federal Power Act. . . . Since hydroelectric facilities operate without significant fuel consumption, these units can produce electricity at substantially lower cost than most other generating sources. . . .

A New Hampshire statute, enacted in 1913, provides:

"No corporation engaged in the generation of electrical energy by water power shall engage in the business of transmitting or conveying the same beyond the confines of the state, unless it shall first file notice of its intention so to do with the public utilities commission and obtain an order of said commission permitting it to engage in such business." N.H. Rev. Stat. Ann. § 374:35 (1966).

The statute empowers the New Hampshire Commission to prohibit the exportation of such electrical energy when it determines that the energy "is reasonably required for use within this state and that the public good requires that it be delivered for such use."

Since 1926, New England Power or a predecessor company periodically applied for and obtained approval from the New Hampshire Commission to transmit electricity produced at the Connecticut River plants to points outside New Hampshire. However, on September 19, 1980, after an investigation and hearings, the Commission withdrew the authority formerly granted New England Power to export its hydroelectric energy, and ordered the company to "make arrangements to sell the previously exported hydroelectric energy to persons, utilities and municipalities within the State of New Hampshire. . . ." In its report accompanying the order, the Commission found that New Hampshire's population and energy needs were increasing rapidly; that, primarily because of its low "generating mix" of hydroelectric energy, the Public Service Company of New Hampshire, the State's largest electric utility, had generating costs about 25% higher than those of New England Power; and that if New England Power's hydroelectric energy were sold exclusively in New Hampshire, New Hampshire customers could save approximately $25 million a year. The Commission therefore concluded that New England Power's hydroelectric energy was "required for use within the State" of New Hampshire, and that discontinuation of its exportation would serve the "public good."

II

The Supreme Court of New Hampshire recognized that, absent authorizing federal legislation, it would be "questionable" whether a state could constitutionally restrict interstate trade in hydroelectric power. Our cases consistently have held that the Commerce Clause of the Constitution, Art. I, § 8, cl. 3, precludes a state from mandating that its residents be given a preferred right of access, over out-of-state consumers, to natural resources located within its borders or to the products derived therefrom. . . .

The order of the New Hampshire Commission, prohibiting New England Power from selling its hydroelectric energy outside the State of New Hampshire, is precisely the sort of protectionist regulation that the Commerce Clause declares off-limits to the states. The Commission has made clear that its order is designed to gain an economic advantage for New Hampshire citizens at the expense of New England Power's customers in neighboring states. Moreover, it cannot be disputed that the Commission's "exportation ban" places direct and substantial burdens on transactions in interstate commerce. Such state-imposed burdens cannot be squared with the Commerce Clause when they serve only to advance "simple economic protectionism."

The Supreme Court of New Hampshire nevertheless upheld the order of the New Hampshire Commission on the ground that § 201(b) of the Federal Power Act expressly permits the State to prohibit the exportation of hydroelectric power produced within its borders. It is indeed well settled that Congress may use its powers under the Commerce Clause to "[confer] upon the States an ability to restrict the flow of interstate commerce that they would not otherwise enjoy." *Lewis v. BT Investment Managers, Inc.*, 447 U.S. 27, 44 (1980). The dispositive question, however, is whether Congress in fact has authorized the states to impose restrictions of the sort at issue here.

III

. . . In 1935, Congress enacted Part II of the Federal Power Act, which delegated to the Federal Power Commission, now the Federal Energy Regulatory Commission, exclusive authority to regulate the transmission and sale at wholesale of electric energy in interstate commerce, without regard to the source of production. The 1935 enactment was a "direct result" of this Court's holding in *Public Utilities Comm'n v. Attleboro Steam & Electric Co.* that the states lacked power to regulate the rates governing interstate sales of electricity for resale. Part II of the Act was intended to "fill the gap" created by *Attleboro* by establishing exclusive federal jurisdiction over such sales.

Section 201(b) of the Act provides, *inter alia*, that the provisions of Part II "shall not . . . deprive a State or State commission of its lawful authority now exercised over the exportation of hydroelectric energy which is transmitted across a State line." However, this provision is in no sense an affirmative grant of power to the states to burden interstate commerce "in a manner which would otherwise not be permissible." In § 201(b), Congress did no more than leave standing whatever valid state laws then existed relating to the exportation of hydroelectric energy; by its plain terms, § 201(b) simply saves from pre-emption under Part II of the Federal Power

Act such state authority as was otherwise "lawful." The legislative history of the Act likewise indicates that Congress intended only that its legislation "tak[e] no authority from State commissions." Nothing in the legislative history or language of the statute evinces a congressional intent "to alter the limits of state power otherwise imposed by the Commerce Clause," or to modify the earlier holdings of this Court concerning the limits of state authority to restrain interstate trade. Rather, Congress' concern was simply "to define the extent of the federal legislation's pre-emptive effect on state law."

To support its argument to the contrary, New Hampshire relies on a single statement made on the floor of the House of Representatives during the debates preceding enactment of Part II. Congressman Rogers of New Hampshire stated:

> "[T]he Senate bill as originally drawn would deprive certain States, I think five in all, of certain rights which they have over the exportation of hydroelectric energy which is transmitted across the State line. This situation has been taken care of by the House committee, and I hope when you come to it, section 201 of part II, that you will grant us the privilege to continue, as we have been for 22 years, to exercise our State right over the exportation of hydroelectric energy transmitted across State lines but produced up there in the granite hills of old New Hampshire."

From this expression of "hope," New Hampshire concludes that Congress specifically intended to preserve the very statute at issue here.

Reliance on such isolated fragments of legislative history in divining the intent of Congress is an exercise fraught with hazards, and "a step to be taken cautiously." However, even were we to accord significant weight to Congressman Rogers' statement, it would not support New Hampshire's contention that § 201(b) was intended to permit states to regulate free from Commerce Clause restraint. Congressman Rogers simply urged his colleagues not to "deprive" the State of New Hampshire of "rights" it already possessed—*i.e.*, to ensure that the Act itself would not be read as pre-empting otherwise valid state legislation.

To be sure, some Members of Congress may have thought that no further protection of state authority was needed. Indeed, given that the Commerce Clause—independently of the Federal Power Act—restricts the ability of the states to regulate matters affecting interstate trade in hydroelectric energy, § 201(b) may in fact save little in the way of "lawful" state authority. But when Congress has not "expressly stated its intent and policy" to sustain state legislation from attack under the Commerce Clause, we have no authority to rewrite its legislation based on mere speculation as to what Congress "probably had in mind." We must construe § 201(b) as it is written, and as its legislative history indicates it was intended—as a standard "non pre-emption" clause. . . .

We conclude, therefore, that New Hampshire has sought to restrict the flow of privately owned and produced electricity in interstate commerce, in a manner inconsistent with the Commerce Clause. . . .

SKULL VALLEY BAND OF GOSHUTE INDIANS V. NIELSON
376 F.3d 1223 (10th Cir. 2004)

HENRY, CIRCUIT JUDGE.

I. Background

This case is one of many arising out the vexing problem of transporting and storing the spent nuclear fuel (SNF) that is generated by nuclear power plants. Because SNF remains radioactive for thousands of years, long-term storage strategies are essential. However, the search for the safest solution has been long and difficult. . . .

PFS is a consortium of utility companies, which formed in order to seek temporary storage options for the SNF storage problem. In May 1997, PFS entered into a lease of Skull Valley Band tribal land located fifty miles from Salt Lake City. PFS sought to build an SNF storage facility there. The Bureau of Indian Affairs of the United States Department of Interior has conditionally approved the lease, and PFS has submitted an application for licensure of the facility with the NRC, which remains pending. Under the federal regulations, the proposed facility is characterized as an "independent spent fuel storage installation," and must satisfy detailed requirements before it may be constructed. *See* 10 C.F.R. § 72.1. . . .

[T]he state of Utah passed a series of statutes between 1998 and 2001 that regulate the storage and transportation of SNF. As the district court explained, the statutes are comprised of four general categories: (1) amendments to Utah's Radiation Control Act, which establish state licensing requirements for the storage of SNF, and which revoke statutory and common law grants of limited liability to stockholders in companies engaged in storing SNF; (2) "the County Planning Provisions," which require county governments to impose regulations and restrictions on SNF storage; (3) "the Road Provisions," which vest the Governor and the state legislature with authority to regulate road construction surrounding the proposed SNF storage site on the Skull Valley reservation; and (4) "the Miscellaneous Provisions," which require drug and alcohol testing of employees of companies engaged in SNF storage and which authorize litigation to determine water rights in areas under consideration for SNF storage. [O]nly the first three categories are at issue here. . . .

III. Supremacy Clause Claim

. . . Three Supreme Court decisions have addressed the preemptive effect of this extensive federal [nuclear] regulatory scheme in considerable detail: *Pacific Gas* [& *Elec. Co. v. State Energy Res. Conserv. & Dev. Comm'n*, 461 U.S. 190 (1938)]; *Silkwood* [*v. Kerr-McGee Corp.*, 464 U.S. 238, 248–57 (1984)]; and *English* [*v. Gen. Elec. Co.*, 496 U.S. 72, 80–90 (1990)]. Interestingly, in all three cases, the Court concluded that the state laws at issue were not preempted. . . .

In *Pacific Gas*, . . . the Court identified "a field in which the federal interest is . . . dominant"—"the radiological safety aspects involved in the construction and operation of a nuclear plant." Accordingly state laws within "the entire field of nuclear safety concerns" are preempted, even if they do not directly conflict with federal law. Thus, "[a] state moratorium grounded in safety concerns falls squarely within the prohibited field". . . . However, if state regulation is grounded in "a non-safety rationale," it may fall outside the preempted field. . . . The Court concluded that a non-safety rationale supported California's moratorium: the economic costs of allowing construction of additional nuclear power plants before adequate SNF storage facilities could be developed. . . . The Court also concluded that the moratorium did not conflict with the objectives of federal law. Although the primary purpose of the Atomic Energy Act is the promotion of nuclear power, that power is not to be developed "at all costs." Congress had left to the states to determine whether, as a matter of economics, a nuclear power plant should be constructed.

In *Silkwood*, the Court applied these preemption principles to a state law punitive damages award arising out of exposure to radioactive materials at a nuclear power plant. . . . The Court acknowledged a tension between the federal government's exclusive power to regulate "the radiological safety aspects involved in the construction and operation of a nuclear plant," and "the conclusion that a state may nevertheless award damages based upon its own law of liability." [Nonetheless, f]ocusing on the legislative history of the Price-Anderson Act . . ., the Court held that the punitive damages award was not preempted and found "ample evidence" that Congress did not intend to bar such a remedy . . .:

> insofar as damages for radiation injuries are concerned, preemption should not be judged on the basis that the federal government has so completely occupied the field of safety that state remedies are foreclosed but on whether there is an irreconcilable conflict between the federal and state standards or whether the imposition of a state standard in a damages action would frustrate the objectives of the federal law.

In *English*, the Supreme Court considered another state law cause of action, concluding that, like the state law in *Silkwood*, it too was not preempted. An employee of nuclear fuel production facility had filed a claim for intentional infliction of emotional distress arising out of her employer's allegedly retaliating against her for having reported suspected violations of nuclear safety violations to the NRC. The Court held that the state law claim "d[id] not fall within the pre-empted field of nuclear safety," and did not conflict with a provision of the 1978 amendments to the Atomic Energy Act that encourages employees to report safety violations and establishes a procedure to protect them from any resulting retaliation. . . . Under the preemption inquiry established by *Pacific Gas*, the Court reasoned, "part of the pre-empted field is defined by reference to the purpose of the state law in question," and "another part of the field is defined by the state law's actual effect on nuclear safety." . . . The Court then noted that the state tort law at issue was not motivated by safety concerns. Thus, the preemption inquiry should focus upon the effect of the state law, asking whether the law had "some direct and substantial effect on the decisions made by those who build or operate nuclear facilities concerning radiological safety levels." Because such a direct and substantial effect was lacking, the Court concluded that the state law claim did not fall within the preempted field of nuclear safety. . . .

[Here], the Utah officials . . . contend [1] that PFS and the Skull Valley Band have failed to offer sufficient evidence that the statutes have "some direct and substantial effect" on decisions made by those who would operate the SNF storage facility . . . [and 2] that the challenged statutes are analogous to the state laws upheld in *Silkwood* and *English*. . . .

1. *The County Planning Provisions*

The . . . County Planning Provisions . . . allow a county to either (a) adopt an ordinance barring the transportation and storage of SNF, or (b) allow such transportation and storage, but only if the county adopts a comprehensive land use plan containing detailed information regarding the effects of any proposed SNF site upon the health and general welfare of citizens of the State. Counties are indemnified if they choose the former option. The County Planning Provisions also prohibit counties from providing "municipal-type services," including fire protection, garbage disposal, water, electricity, and law enforcement, to SNF transportation and storage facilities within the county. . . .

We agree with the district court that the County Planning Provisions are preempted. In requiring county land use plans to "address the effects of the proposed [SNF storage] site upon the health and general welfare of the citizens of the state," including "specific measures to mitigate the effects of high-level nuclear waste . . . [to] guarantee the health and safety of citizens of the state," these provisions address matters of radiological safety that are addressed by federal law and that are the exclusive province of the federal government.

Although the provision requiring a county to address radiological safety issues in its land use plan may not apply if a county adopts an ordinance banning the storage of high level nuclear waste within its borders, that alternative provision is itself grounded in safety concerns. That conclusion follows from the text of the County Planning Provisions, which refers to the effects of nuclear waste on the health and welfare of Utah citizens. Moreover, unlike the state officials in *Pacific Gas*, the Utah officials here have failed to offer evidence that the provision allowing a county to ban SNF transportation and storage is supported by a non-safety rationale. . . .

Silkwood and *English* do not save the County Planning Provisions. In holding in *Silkwood* that a $10 million award of punitive damages on a state law claim was not preempted, the Court relied upon "ample evidence that Congress had no intention of forbidding the states from providing" "state-law remedies [to] those suffering injuries from radiation in a nuclear plant." *English* relies on the same evidence. The Utah officials identify no analogous evidence that Congress intended to allow detailed regulation of nuclear facilities by county governments, and we have found none.

Moreover, *Silkwood* and *English* both involve generally applicable state tort law that existed before Congress began to regulate nuclear power. Neither case concerns state laws that target the nuclear industry, as the Utah provisions do here. . . .

2. *The Unfunded Potential Liability Provisions*

. . . At issue here are the sections of the Utah licensing scheme that require the operator of a SNF storage facility to pay to the state of Utah an amount equal to at least 75% of the "unfunded potential liability" of the project. That amount is determined by the Department of Environmental Quality, based upon "the health and economic costs expected to result from a reasonably foreseeable accidental release [of SNF]."

According to the Utah officials, these unfunded liability provisions are designed to "fill in the gaps" in the liability coverage established by the Price-Anderson Act. . . .

[The court discussed the parties' dispute over whether "conflict" or "field" preemption analysis applied.] In the absence of controlling Supreme Court precedent, we will afford the Utah officials the benefit of the doubt, assuming without deciding, that Utah's unfunded liability provisions concern "damages for radiation injuries," in that they seek to ensure that there are adequate resources to allow injured parties to recover for those injuries. Nevertheless, even under the more limited preemption inquiry set forth in *Silkwood*, we conclude that the unfunded liability provisions are preempted. In our view, the fact that there may be gaps in the Price-Anderson Act's indemnification and insurance scheme does not establish that states are free to fill those gaps, as Utah has done here.

That conclusion follows from the response of the NRC's Atomic Safety and Licensing Board to the potential gaps in the Price-Anderson scheme. In reviewing PFS's license application, the Licensing Board has recognized that the Price-Anderson Act may not apply to certain aspects of the proposed storage facility. Nevertheless, the Licensing Board proceeded to determine whether PFS had obtained liability insurance "sufficient to cover cost recovery for any foreseeable accident at the PFS facility." As to offsite liability, the Board found sufficient PFS's $200 million nuclear energy liability policy, the largest one currently available. . . .

Thus, in requiring PFS to demonstrate the sufficiency of its insurance coverage regarding operations not necessarily covered by the Price-Anderson Act, the Licensing Board has itself filled some of the gaps in that regulatory scheme. Those gap-filling measures are authorized by the Atomic Energy Act and accompanying regulations.

In light of the "gap-filling" undertaken by the NRC and its Licensing Board, Utah's unfunded liability provisions conflict with the objectives of federal law. Those statutes allow the state of Utah to make an independent determination of "the dollar amount of the health and economic costs expected to result from a reasonably foreseeable accidental release of waste involving a transfer or storage facility, or during transportation of waste, within the exterior boundaries of the state" and subject the operator of an SNF storage facility to the loss of its license unless it pays 75% of that amount to the DEQ. Under the federal licensing scheme however, it is not the states but rather the NRC that is vested with the authority to decide under what conditions to license an SNF storage facility. . . .

3. *Abolition of Limited Liability*

. . . Because Utah's abolition of limited liability "frustrate[s] the objectives of federal law," we agree with the district court that the challenged statute is preempted. Under Utah law, stockholders are generally not personally liable for the debts of a corporation. . . . Section 19–3–316 removes this well-established protection, and does so for reasons that the Utah officials concede are related to radiological safety concerns. *See* Aplts' Br. at 96 (stating that "[t]he Legislature was aware that a PFS-type enterprise would create risks of an almost unfathomable magnitude and that the scope of the [Price-Anderson Act] relative to a PFS-type facility was uncertain" and therefore abolished limited liability).

In contrast, in enacting the Atomic Energy Act and subsequent amendments, "Congress' purpose was to remove the economic impediments in order to stimulate the private development of electric energy by nuclear power while simultaneously providing the public compensation in the event of a catastrophic nuclear incident." *Duke Power Co. v. Carolina Env't Study Group, Inc.,* 438 U.S. 59, 83 (1978). By upending a fundamental principle of corporate law as applied to SNF storage facilities, § 19–3–316 disrupts the balance that Congress sought to achieve. . . .

Moreover, we again reject the Utah officials' contention that the state laws that survived preemption in *Silkwood* and *English* are analogous to the Utah statute. Here, the abolition of limited liability attempts a sea change in the law of corporations and is targeted at the nuclear industry only. The statutes do not involve a state tort remedy that existed prior to the enactment of federal legislation regarding nuclear power and that Congress intended to preserve.

4. *The Road Provisions*

[T]hese provisions amend the Utah statutes by (1) requiring the concurrence of the governor and the legislature to resolve disputes arising out of the request to construct a railroad crossing made by an entity engaged in SNF storage and transportation; (2) designating certain county roads and trails near the Skull Valley Reservation as "statewide public safety interest highways," and providing that the state Department of Transportation has jurisdiction and control over them; (3) removing control of the only road permitting access to the Skull Valley Reservation and PFS's proposed facility from the county by designating it as a state highway; and (4) requiring the consent of the governor and the state legislature before the Department of Transportation may grant a right of way to a company engaged in the transportation or storage of SNF.

. . . [T]he evidence cited by the district court indicates that the Road Provisions were enacted in order to prevent the transportation and storage of SNF in Utah. The state legislator who sponsored the Road Provisions explained that they established a "moat" around the proposed SNF site, and the Governor added that the Road Provisions "will add substantially to our ability as a state to protect the health and safety of our citizens against the storage of high-level nuclear waste." In the 1999 State of the State address, the Governor announced that he would deny permission for the rail crossings needed to provide access to the proposed SNF facility.

The Utah officials do not attempt to contest any of this evidence; nor is it likely that they could. The record thus establishes that the Road Provisions were enacted for reasons of radiological safety and are therefore preempted. Moreover, as the district court concluded, by jeopardizing access to the proposed SNF storage facility, the Road Provisions directly and substantially affect decisions regarding radiological safety levels by those operating nuclear facilities. . . .

NOTES AND QUESTIONS

1.   The Court's decision in *Virginia Uranium* presents as plurality-like, but actually there were six votes in favor of the outcome; Justice Ginsburg, joined by Justices Kagan and Sotomayor, wrote a concurring opinion. Notably, the reasoning of her opinion tracked the logic of Justice Gorsuch's almost step-for-step. The key difference? She disagreed with portions of his opinion, largely excluded from the excerpt above, suggesting multifarious "perils of inquiring into legislative motive," which she thought "sweep[ed] well beyond the confines of this case, and therefore seems to me inappropriate in an opinion speaking for the Court, rather than for individual members of the Court." *Virginia Uranium*, 139 S. Ct. at 1909.

2.   *Virginia Uranium* created unusual alignments among the justices. Chief Justice Roberts, joined by Justices Alito and Breyer, dissented. He took issue with the Court's decision to devote "its analysis to whether the field of uranium mining safety is preempted" by the AEA. That, he said, was not in dispute. "Rather, the question we agreed to address is whether a State can purport to regulate a field that is not preempted (uranium mining safety) as an indirect means of regulating other fields that are preempted (safety concerns about uranium milling and tailings)." On this question, Chief Justice Roberts explained, "[O]ur precedent is clear." *Pacific Gas* controls. "Like California's ban in that case, Virginia's ban on its face regulates a non-preempted field—uranium mining safety. Like the plaintiffs challenging the California ban, the mining company argues that the statute's purpose is really to regulate a preempted field—safety concerns about uranium milling and tailings. But unlike California in *Pacific Gas*, Virginia in this case has not put forward a 'nonsafety rationale.' That should have been the end of the story." *Id.* at 1916, 1918.

3.   All three opinions in *Virginia Uranium* relied heavily on the Court's prior decision in *Pacific Gas*. That case, as both *Virginia Uranium* and *Skull Valley Band of Goshute Indians* explained, established an intent-based standard for determining whether the AEA preempts a state law: "A state moratorium on nuclear construction grounded in safety concerns falls squarely within the prohibited field. [Likewise, a] state prohibition on nuclear construction for safety reasons would also be in the teeth of the Atomic Energy Act's objective to insure that nuclear technology be safe enough for widespread development and use—and would be preempted for that reason. That being the case, it is necessary to determine whether there is a non-safety rationale for [California's law]." What do you make of this standard? What areas of regulation does it leave to the states, and what does it preserve exclusively for the NRC?

4.   Is the *Pacific Gas* standard too easy to manipulate—for instance, if a state legislature is actually motivated by nuclear safety concerns but wants to pretend it is not? Might the intent-based pliability of the *Pacific Gas* standard be why the six justices who found no preemption in *Virginia Uranium* came out the way they did, rather than siding with Chief Justice Roberts? Is that

the real difference between the Justice Gorsuch/Ginsburg opinions and Chief Justice Roberts'—whether *Pacific Gas* remains binding precedent?

5.   If it is true that the *Pacific Gas* standard is too easily manipulable, why didn't the Utah legislature simply invoke non-safety rationales to justify its legislation—and avoid the preemption problem—in *Skull Valley Band of Goshute Indians*? Are there portions of that legislation that could have been justified using non-safety rationales, thus rendering them constitutional, as opposed to other portions of the laws that could not feasibly escape *Pacific Gas*'s reach?

PRACTICE PROBLEM

The Commonwealth of New Oaxaca is the fifty-first state in the United States. Located in the desert Southwest, New Oaxaca is rich in many natural resources, including uranium. For several decades now, five different commercial uranium extractors, millers, and processors have run operations in New Oaxaca, near the Azul River.

Although the uranium companies operating in New Oaxaca try to fully comply with applicable regulations, accidents still happen. In the process of mining, they have created large piles of uranium tailings, many of which are within 100 yards of the Azul River. Moreover, in the wake of the disaster at Fukushima Daiichi, three of the five uranium mining operations have gone out of business.

When heavy rains fall near the uranium tailings piles, radioactive water often washes into the Azul River. This is of obvious concern. The Azul River is home to an endangered species of fish, the Green-Eyed Rock Minnow. The river's water also is used for agricultural production in New Oaxaca (mostly watermelons and different varieties of lettuce), and the tributary ultimately runs into the Colorado River, on which the entire region heavily relies. Accordingly, the United States Congress recently adopted a joint resolution declaring the sites where the tailing piles are located—dubbed "Montezuma Alley" by locals—a "national radiological disaster area."

In response to this congressional pronouncement, the United States Department of Energy (DOE) has instigated an "emergency" cleanup process for the area. However, because not all the companies that caused the contamination still exist, and because DOE's own funding is limited, the cleanup is proceeding much more slowly than local residents would prefer.

Spurred on by its citizenry's dissatisfaction, the New Oaxaca legislature recently adopted a statute aimed at "facilitating the cleanup of the radiological waste in this Commonwealth and protecting the economic well-being of all New Oaxacans." This so-called Montezuma Alley Disaster Cleanup Facilitation Act includes two key provisions:

First, the law specifies that:

No new nuclear power plants shall be built or operate in this Commonwealth, and the New Oaxaca Department of Economic and Environmental Regulation shall not issue any required land use or other permits for such facilities, until the United States Department of Energy declares that the Montezuma Alley Radiological Disaster Area has been fully and completely decontaminated and remediated. The Legislature hereby finds that, until such time, the addition of any nuclear material to New Oaxaca is not appropriate because the presence of radiological contamination in the state serves as an economic deterrent to new industry and corporations locating their facilities in our Commonwealth.

New Oaxaca currently has one operating nuclear power plant within its borders, the Alto Azul Nuclear Power Station in the northern part of the state.

Second, the law establishes certain tax measures for uranium consumed and mined in the state:

Because cleanup of the Montezuma Alley Radiological Disaster Area is critical to promoting the economic well-being of New Oaxaca, the Legislature hereby establishes a fund to be used in the cleanup and remediation of the Area. Beginning on August 1 of this year, all uranium consumed in the Commonwealth shall be subject to a $12,500 per pound tax (hereinafter, the "New Oaxaca Uranium Tax"), with such poundage measured prior to use. For uranium contained in nuclear fuel rods, the entire weight of the rod shall be counted for purposes of calculating the tax. Provided further, however, that any nuclear plant operating in the state that utilizes in its nuclear power production facilities uranium originating from New Oaxaca shall receive a deduction from its annual state corporate taxes equivalent to one-half the amount of the New Oaxaca Uranium Tax it owes for the year.

Pasadena Power & Gas (Pasadena), a large California utility that also owns extensive uranium mining holdings nearby, recently purchased a large amount of land and millions of dollars in water rights to construct a new nuclear power station in New Oaxaca.

Pasadena has filed suit challenging the constitutionality of the Montezuma Alley Disaster Cleanup Facilitation Act. Pasadena argues that the law: (1) violates the Supremacy Clause by "regulating in the area of nuclear materials, which is the sole province of the United States Nuclear Regulatory Commission"; (2) violates the Supremacy Clause by "imposing an unnecessary and unwanted tax on uranium consumption, which in turn threatens to render the use of nuclear energy uneconomic, frustrating the Atomic Energy Act's goal of promoting nuclear power use"; and (3) "violates the Commerce Clause of the United States Constitution by erecting a protectionist and nefarious regime that favors in-state economic resources over out-of-state players."

How should the court rule?

CHAPTER 11

ENERGY FUTURES: NET-ZERO ENERGY AND DISRUPTIVE INNOVATION

■ ■ ■

A. OVERVIEW

Throughout this book, we contrast traditional U.S. energy policy based on fossil fuel combustion with the policies needed to support an energy transition. Envisioning such an energy transition is no small task. Ensuring that the nation's energy system is up to the challenges of reducing greenhouse gas (GHG) emissions, of adapting critical infrastructure to new weather and climate regimes, and of responding to emerging cybersecurity risks requires rethinking traditional energy sector roles. Responding to climate change is energy policy. How future lawyers will work to create an energy system that remains resilient and reliable in the face of these system risks is the subject of this chapter.

Here, we focus on GHG reductions, highlighting both the scale of needed reductions and accompanying policy goals affecting the energy sector. We discuss the reductions needed to stabilize atmospheric GHG levels and limit climate warming. We examine the goals of the Paris Climate Accords and developing policies in the United States, the European Union (EU), and China, as well as in individual U.S. states. In general, these policies aim to reach "Net Zero Energy" and stabilize atmospheric GHG concentrations.

From these high-level aspirations, we focus on details necessary to make it happen. While there is a growing consensus that an energy transition from fossil fuels to cleaner energy is inevitable and economically and environmentally desirable, this opinion is not universally shared. Given the long-lived nature of energy infrastructure and the networked nature of the system, large-scale transitions to a Net Zero Energy world will take time. However, the pace of change is neither gradual nor regular, and things currently impossible can rapidly become possible.

This chapter explores this challenge in three parts. First, we describe the concept of Net Zero Energy within the context of global climate change and commitments from countries, states, and companies to manage and reduce emissions. Second, we examine innovation and evaluate two case studies of clean energy implementation—electric vehicle (EV) adoption and the use of carbon capture and storage (CCS). Last, we close with a discussion of potential futures for the energy sector, as well as concluding thoughts for this book.

B. CLIMATE TARGETS AND NET ZERO ENERGY

A core challenge of moving to Net Zero Energy is the long-lived nature of GHGs. Stabilizing GHGs is different than controlling conventional air pollutants. Criteria pollutants like SO_x or NO_x have atmospheric lifetimes of a few hours, so reducing emissions from tailpipes or smokestacks will reduce atmospheric emissions in just a few hours to days. This is not true for GHGs, which have long atmospheric residence times—tens to hundreds to thousands of years. CO_2 emitted from generating electricity or burning fossil fuels in our cars persists in the atmosphere for roughly a hundred years.

The United Nations Intergovernmental Panel on Climate Change's (IPCC) periodic reports are developed by the world's leading experts on climate change and draw from extensive studies to present consensus views of the scientific community. In 2021, the IPCC published Assessment Report 6, which states:

> The scale of recent changes across the climate system as a whole and the present state of many aspects of the climate system are unprecedented over many centuries to many thousands of years. In 2019, atmospheric CO_2 concentrations were higher than at any time in at least 2 million years (high confidence), and concentrations of CH_4 and N_2O were higher than at any time in at least 800,000 years (very high confidence). Since 1750, increases in CO_2 (47%) and CH_4 (156%) concentrations far exceed, and increases in N_2O (23%) are similar to, the natural multi-millennial changes between glacial and interglacial periods over at least the past 800,000 years. . . . Human-induced climate change is already affecting many weather and climate extremes in every region across the globe. Evidence of observed changes in extremes such as heatwaves, heavy precipitation, droughts, and tropical cyclones, and, in particular, their attribution to human influence, has strengthened since [Assessment Report 5].

WORKING GROUP I CONTRIBUTION TO THE SIXTH ASSESSMENT REPORT OF THE INTERGOVERNMENTAL PANEL ON CLIMATE CHANGE, CLIMATE CHANGE 2021: THE PHYSICAL SCIENCE BASIS, SUMMARY FOR POLICYMAKERS 9–10 (Aug. 7, 2021).

If the goal is to limit damage from climate change, Net Zero Energy strategies are critical. Energy policy *is* climate policy.

1. DEFINITIONS AND INTERNATIONAL GOALS

The idea of Net Zero Energy is simple. For every ton of carbon dioxide emitted into the atmosphere, a ton must be removed—keeping atmospheric carbon in balance. That is, atmospheric carbon no longer increases: the emissions reach net zero.

Though simple in concept, the implementation of Net Zero Energy is tricky. It demands global action but political and economic power rests with individual countries and their subnational governments, companies, and projects. Its scope is also immense. Net Zero Energy requires leaving at least an estimated 60% of natural gas and oil and 90% of coal reserves in the ground. *See* Jonathan Foley, *The World Needs Better Climate Pledges,* GLOBALECOGUY.ORG (June 16, 2021); Dan Welsby et al., *Unextractable Fossil Fuels in a 1.5°C World,* 597 NATURE 230 (2021). Carbon emissions are not just persistent; they are extensive, typically being measured by the ton. (To give you an idea of what a ton is, an average car weighs about 1.5 tons, and a standard pickup truck is approximately 3 tons.) In 2019, the world emitted over 59 billion metric tons of CO_2 equivalent GHGs (GtCO$_2$e), with emissions on track to warm global temperatures by over 3.2°C before the end of the century.

The push towards Net Zero Energy is an outgrowth of international climate agreements dating back to the Rio Declaration in 1992 and including the Paris Climate Agreement, which was signed in 2015 and entered into force in 2016. The Paris Climate Agreement was signed by 195 nations, including the United States, and targets reducing GHG emissions to limit global temperature increases by the end of the century to 2° Celsius (3.6°F) above preindustrial levels—while pledging to limit the increase to 1.5°C (2.7°F). Note that since the mid-1900s, a 1°C (2°F) temperature increase has been documented. To achieve these reductions, the signatories submitted their Nationally Determined Contributions (NDCs) outlining how they would reduce their emissions. As all countries are on different trajectories, the targets and timelines vary. Under the Obama administration, the United States agreed to reduce emissions 26–28% below 2005 levels by 2025, with plans to cut emissions through the Clean Power Plan, vehicle efficiency standards, and other initiatives. The Trump administration withdrew from the Paris Agreement and worked to roll back emission reduction policies. In 2021, the Biden administration rejoined the Paris Agreement and committed to reduce emissions more aggressively. The Paris Agreement provides an accounting framework for measuring reductions. It also seeks to support developing countries in both mitigation and adaptation. *See* Melissa Denchak, *The Paris Climate Agreement: Everything You Need to Know,* NRDC (Feb. 19, 2021).

The Paris Agreement's effort to limit global temperature increases to 1.5°C relies on climate research from the IPCC. To date, measured increases in global temperatures chart a warming planet, with shifting precipitation patterns, droughts and fires, flooding, and increased cyclones. *See Climate Change Indicators: U.S. and Global Temperature,* U.S. EPA (Apr. 2021).

The goal of 1.5°C is also the focus of Net Zero Energy policies. To meet the 1.5°C target, the world would need to reach Net Zero Energy by 2040–2055 and adopt negative emission technologies that actively remove GHGs from the atmosphere. As of 2021, over 31 countries had made Net Zero Energy pledges in law or policy, with over 100 countries considering such pledges. *See Net Zero Targets: Which Countries Have Them and How They Stack Up,* WORLD RES. INST. (June 2, 2021); INTERGOVERNMENTAL PANEL ON CLIMATE CHANGE, SPECIAL REPORT: GLOBAL WARMING OF 1.5°C (2018); *Evaluation Methodology for National Net Zero Targets,* Climate Action Tracker (June 23, 2021).

The world is not on target to meet the Paris Agreement goals. Indeed, "[t]he levels of ambition in the Paris Agreement must be roughly tripled for the 2°C pathway and increased at least fivefold for the 1.5°C pathway." *See* UN ENV'T PROGRAMME, EMISSIONS GAP REPORT 2020: KEY MESSAGES (2020). The more aggressive (and safer) 1.5°C target means decreasing global emissions by an additional 29–32 $GtCO_2e$ in 2030 from the current NDC commitments in the Paris Agreement. *See id.; Climate Action Tracker,* https://climateactiontracker.org/. Understanding the scope of what will be required to meet Net Zero Energy can be seen through the lens of the three largest global emitters: the United States, the EU, and China.

In 2019, the United States emitted 6.5 $GtCO_2e$—or 11% of all emissions—making it the second largest global emitter. To meet the United States' original NDC goals under the Paris Agreement, U.S. economy-wide emissions need to decrease 26–28% from the 2005 baseline by 2025. Between 2005 and 2019, U.S. GHG emissions decreased 12%. Meeting the original Paris Agreement NDC means reducing emissions to 4.7–4.9 $GtCO_2e$ in 2025—or 1–1.2 $GtCO_2e$ less than current levels. When the Biden administration rejoined the Paris Agreement in 2021, the United States submitted a more aggressive NDC, targeting reductions of 50–52% below the 2005 baseline by 2030. The new goal is thus 3.2–3.3 $GtCO_2e$ by 2030, a reduction of 2.4 $GtCO_2e$. *See Inventory of U.S. Greenhouse Gas Emissions and Sinks,* U.S. EPA; *Greenhouse Gas Inventory Data Explorer,* U.S. EPA.

Even with the new, more aggressive NDC, the United States is not on track for Net Zero Energy, which is a 5–10% larger goal. For the Biden administration to meet Net Zero Energy goals by 2050, total GHG emissions (minus any sequestration) need to be reduced to zero. To be on track for Net Zero Energy, proponents argue that 2030 emissions levels need to decrease by 50%, or 57–63% from the U.S. 2005 baseline year levels

(2.5–2.9 GtCO₂e). *See* 1.5°C-CONSISTENT BENCHMARKS FOR THE US 2030 CLIMATE TARGET, CLIMATE ACTION TRACKER (Mar. 2021). This will require a vastly different energy landscape—massive investments in wind and solar power, a rebuilt electric grid, and millions of EVs, just to start. The figure below shows the old and new targets and Net Zero Energy goals.

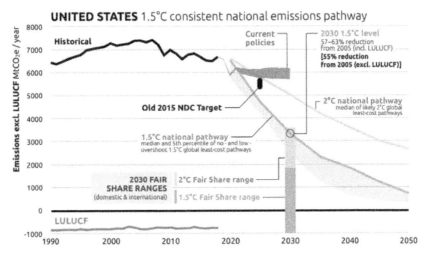

Source: *Country Summary*, Climate Action Tracker.

There are many proposed policies to help the United States achieve Net Zero Energy, including a goal for a carbon-free power sector by 2035 and a decarbonized economy by 2050. This would include updating building codes and increasing building electrification and energy efficiency with technologies like heat pumps and induction stoves. In the transportation sector, the goal is to make vehicles more efficient; to support charging infrastructure for EVs; to develop renewable fuels for aviation; and to support infrastructure investments for rail, transit, and biking. *See* FACT SHEET: PRESIDENT BIDEN SETS 2030 GREENHOUSE GAS POLLUTION REDUCTION TARGET AIMED AT CREATING GOOD-PAYING UNION JOBS AND SECURING U.S. LEADERSHIP ON CLEAN ENERGY TECHNOLOGIES, THE WHITE HOUSE (Apr. 22, 2021). President Biden has also set ambitious goals for a decarbonized electricity system by 2035, significant offshore wind development, and a massive investment in solar energy. *See, e.g.,* Ivan Penn, *From 4% to 45%: Energy Department Lays Out Ambitious Blueprint for Solar Power*, N.Y. TIMES (Sept. 8, 2021) (reporting on President Biden's climate and energy targets); U.S. DEP'T OF ENERGY, SOLAR FUTURES STUDY (Sept. 2021).

Turning to the EU, in 2019 it was the third largest global contributor, emitting 4.2 GtCO₂e, or roughly 8% of global emissions. The EU also has Net Zero Energy goals. The original EU NDC target was for economy-wide GHG emissions to reach 40% below 1990 levels by 2030. The long-term goal is 91–94% below 1990 levels. In 2021, the EU announced its "Fit for 55" proposal, targeting GHG emissions reductions of 55% below 1990 levels by 2030.

The proposed initiative is far-reaching. It will expand the EU's Emission Trading Scheme (ETS), which targets energy and carbon-intensive industries by lowering the emissions cap and increasing the rate of reduction. It proposes including aviation and shipping within the EU ETS and setting up a parallel ETS for fuel distribution for road transport and buildings. There are proposed efficiency targets, including a target of 3% reduction in public building energy use, and a pledge to plant 3 million trees for carbon storage by 2030. In the transportation sector, there is a proposed 55% decrease in emissions from new cars by 2030, and a 100% decrease by 2035—essentially forbidding sales of new internal combustion cars beyond that date. The proposals support developing charging infrastructure for EVs, with chargers required every 60 km (37 miles) on major highways. Greening aviation fuels and setting limits on ship emissions at EU ports are also included.

The EU also proposed revising the Energy Taxation Directive between EU member states and proposed a Carbon Border Tax Adjustment to help ensure that EU and non-EU trade does not lead to "carbon-leakage." A proposal for a Social Climate Fund, financed by ETS revenue, would provide an estimated €72.2 billion ($85 billion) from 2025–2032 to help EU citizens pay for cleaner cars, energy efficiency, and heating and cooling systems. *See* EU Press Release, *European Green Deal: Commission Proposes Transformation of EU Economy and Society to Meet Climate Ambitions*, EUROPEAN COMM'N (July 14, 2021); *Climate Action Tracker*, *supra*.

As for China, in 2019 it was the world's largest emitter at 13.5 $GtCO_2e$, or 22% of global emissions. China is a rapidly industrializing country with strong economic growth and an expanding energy system. In 2005, China's emissions were just 7.9 Gt CO_2e, or 70% less than current levels. China's NDC calls for peaking economy-wide carbon emissions around 2030, with 20% of energy coming from non-fossil sources. The plan also has carbon intensity targets (reducing emissions per unit of GDP) of 60–65% below 2005 levels for 2030. (The Chinese NDC only covers carbon, not all GHGs, and its position on land sequestration of carbon is not clear.) In 2020, Chinese President Xi Jinping announced that the country would scale up its NDC commitment: Not only would China's emissions peak *before* 2030, but for the first time, China stated its intention to reach carbon neutrality by 2060.

As of 2021, specific policies and goals were under development and no formal revised NDC had been submitted. It is important to note that China remains very dependent on coal. China accounted for over half of the world's electricity generated from coal in 2021, and it has another 250 GW of coal plants in the development queue. Additionally, Chinese investment in energy resources—both coal and renewables—is driving energy installations around the world. Over 25%, or 102 GW, of global coal projects in development are linked to Chinese finance companies. *See* Ranping Song, *4 Questions About China's New Climate Commitments*, WORLD RES. INST. (Sept. 30, 2020); John Kemp, *China's Five-Year Plan Focuses on Energy Security* REUTERS (Mar. 19, 2021); *Climate Action Tracker, supra.*

A final, important idea to keep in mind about such a broadscale move to address climate change: Net Zero Energy strategies also have distributional justice challenges. Historically large emitters like the United States and the EU not only contribute more heavily to climate change, but also have used and continue to use more energy per person. Moreover, developing country major emitters, like China, have grown in their per capita emissions. In this sense, a ton of carbon is not just a ton of carbon, as making such a reduction may be more difficult or problematic for one nation compared to another. An understanding of carbon emitted per capita and historical differences in emissions patterns are thus needed to explore distributional justice issues. In 2019, the rate of per capita emissions (emissions divided by population) in the United States was 19.8 tons CO_2e/capita; in the EU, 9.4 tons CO_2e/capita; and in China, 9.6 tons CO_2e/capita. However, in other developing countries like Ethiopia, the rate was only 1.2 tons CO_2e/capita. The energy (and carbon equity) questions drive the conversation in critically important directions. Countries have a right to ensure energy is available for their development and for their citizens, including for climate adaptation. Energy justice must be global and must also address the fact that nearly a billion people have no access to electricity—and that there are billions more who lack access to reliable and affordable energy. *See* Raphael J. Heffron & Daren McCauley, *The Concept of Energy Justice Across the Disciplines*, 105 ENERGY POL'Y. 658 (June 2017); Rose Mutiso, *The Energy Africa Needs to Develop and Fight Climate Change,* TED Talk (Oct. 2020).

2. IMPLEMENTING NET ZERO ENERGY

As should be plain, creating policies and programs to support a global goal of Net Zero Energy demands both incredible ambition and careful attention to detail in the implementation. But while the goal is global, implementing policies to support Net Zero Energy transitions will happen in many different jurisdictions and spaces, from nations to U.S. states to private sector companies. In this section, we first examine some of the studies adapting the concept and mapping out Net Zero Energy. We then discuss U.S. state government policies, private sector actions, and the role of financial institutions.

a. Studies on Implementing Net Zero Energy

A 2021 Lawrence Berkeley National Laboratory report for the Department of Energy (DOE) detailed the progress that the United States has made toward a carbon-free electric power sector. CO_2 emissions in 2020 were more than 50% lower than 2005 levels. Both wind and solar outperformed expectations; renewable energy contributions were nearly 90% higher than projected. Utilities also switched to natural gas, and energy demand declined both in the Great Recession of 2008 and the COVID-19 pandemic of 2020. Further, there was little change in the cost of electricity to consumers, but major reductions in climate damage and related health costs. Climate damage from power sector carbon emissions dropped 50%. Healthcare costs were 90% lower than 2005 estimates. And there was a more than 90% reduction in premature deaths from power sector air pollution. Additionally, nearly 1 million renewable energy jobs were created. RYAN WISER, LAWRENCE BERKELEY NAT'L LAB., HALFWAY TO ZERO: PROGRESS TOWARD A CARBON-FREE POWER SECTOR (Apr. 2021).

Princeton University's 2020 Net Zero Energy study maps several possible pathways to a net-zero economy for the United States, from a high electrification scenario to a 100% renewable energy scenario. The study asserts that each pathway will result in a net increase of energy sector employment, with significant reductions in air pollution leading to public health benefits. Further, the estimated annual spending on energy for each pathway is comparable or lower as a percentage of GDP than what is currently being spent on energy. To achieve a net-zero economy, the report focuses on six pathways: (1) increasing energy efficiency and electrification; (2) clean electricity based on wind and solar generation, transmission, and a reliance on firm power; (3) increasing use of bioenergy and other zero carbon fuels; (4) carbon capture, storage, and utilization; (5) reducing emissions from non-carbon gases; and (6) enhancing carbon sinks. The report thus lists the following 2030 priorities:

- Adding 50 million electric cars on the road and installing at least 3 million public charging stations.

- Quadrupling wind and solar electricity generation.

- Doubling high voltage transmission capacity for renewable electricity.

- Increasing the uptake of carbon stored in forests and in agricultural soils.

- Improving permitting and siting of electric transmission for renewable resources.

- Investing in key technologies to make them cheaper, scalable, and ready for widespread adoption.

ERIC LARSON ET AL., PRINCETON UNIVERSITY, NET-ZERO AMERICA:
POTENTIAL PATHWAYS, INFRASTRUCTURE, AND IMPACTS (2020).

In 2021, the National Academies of Sciences, Engineering and
Medicine (NAS) issued a study detailing a proposed system-wide
decarbonization plan for the United States. The NAS study recommended
a $40/ton carbon price, which would then increase at 5% per year, and the
creation of additional government agencies to support the energy
transition. The report also recommended a "green bank," capitalized
initially at $30 billion, and tripling DOE's clean energy research funding
over the next decade. The report acknowledged that approximately $2
trillion in capital investments would be needed over the next decade with
$350 billion in federal spending. *See* NAT'L ACADEMIES OF SCIENCES, ENG'G,
AND MED., ACCELERATING DECARBONIZATION OF THE U.S. ENERGY SYSTEM
(2021). The report also laid out specific goals for different energy
technologies, many of which we have discussed in detail in earlier chapters
of this book. These include investing in energy efficiency and productivity;
electrifying energy services in transportation, buildings, and industry;
producing carbon-free electricity; planning, permitting, and building
critical infrastructure like electric transmission lines; and expanding
innovation. On the last point, the report proposed "a tripling of federal
investment in clean energy [research, development, and demonstration
(RD&D)] to provide new technological options, to reduce costs of existing
options, and to better understand how to manage a socially just energy
transition." *Id.* at 7.

In addition to government laboratories and universities, the
International Energy Agency's (IEA) 2021 Net Zero Energy study presents
a global goal of limiting global temperature increases to 1.5°C by 2050.
INT'L ENERGY AGENCY, NET ZERO BY 2050: A ROADMAP FOR THE GLOBAL
ENERGY SECTOR (May 2021). The IEA is an independent organization with
representatives from approximately 120 countries. The IEA's energy sector
focus is on over 400 milestones for all sectors and technologies for the
energy transformation, with no offsets and with low reliance on negative
emissions technologies like CCS to remove carbon from the atmosphere.
When the IEA's Net Zero Energy report was published, countries emitting
70% of global CO_2 had made Net Zero Energy commitments. The report
urged further extending these commitments and setting a target for a 40%
larger global economy in 2030 using 7% less total energy. The IEA study
assumed all technologies were available, but it also recognized that
advanced batteries, green hydrogen, and direct air capture and storage
were at either the demonstration or prototype phases and would require
additional investments to bring them to scale. Government R&D would be
used to leverage private funds, a key tactic to meet the study's goals.

The IEA study also acknowledged the need for consumer participation
as consumers purchase vehicles, household goods, and install efficient

technologies. It projected that by 2050, nearly 90% of electricity generation would come from renewable resources, with the remaining 10% from nuclear power. This rapid transition away from fossil fuels would require that there be no new oil and gas fields approved for development and no new coal mines or extensions after 2021. The IEA found that the transition would have economic benefits, including new jobs in the renewable energy, infrastructure development, manufacturing, and construction sectors. The IEA also estimated that there would be 2 million fewer premature deaths globally from air pollution in 2030 than there are today.

<hr />

NOTES AND QUESTIONS

1.   Do research organizations and universities have the same or different constituencies and audiences as international and governmental bodies? What role does each play relative to regulators and politicians?

2.   Climate change is a global problem, but action is often national, and deployment is state and local. How do studies taking a global perspective differ from national ones? The NAS study recommendations are targeted and specific. Do you think they are politically feasible? Why or why not? Where are compromises made and what are some of the implicit and underlying assumptions?

3.   The ambition of Net Zero Energy is breathtaking. Do you think achieving these goals is realistic? Feasible? What are the tradeoffs if countries don't try? Or if they try but fail?

b.   Government Net-Zero Policies

Studies by government labs, universities, and think tanks can help to inform and evaluate different policy pathways, but, for the most part, the organizations writing these reports have no authority to create or implement programs. Earlier in this chapter, we introduced the 2015 Paris Agreement and national NDCs, which provide a broad framework to examine Net Zero Energy goals. The materials below examine how U.S. states are working to reduce GHG emissions and transform the energy systems in their jurisdictions.

As discussed in Chapter 5, many U.S. states began enacting Renewable Portfolio Standards (RPSs) in the 1990s, requiring utilities to procure or produce a minimum percentage of electricity from renewable resources. In the late 2010s, several states went further and enacted 100% clean energy standards (CESs), requiring utilities to completely decarbonize their electricity sources. Chapter 5 explored the design of many of these statutes. This section focuses on the state decarbonization commitments and implementation measures, using CES laws in California and Virginia as examples.

CALIFORNIA 100 PERCENT CLEAN
ENERGY ACT OF 2018 (SB 100)

2021 SB 100 Joint Agency Report: Achieving 100 Percent Clean Electricity in
California: An Initial Assessment Executive Summary (Mar. 15, 2021)

The 100 Percent Clean Energy Act of 2018 (Senate Bill 100, De León, Chapter 312, Statutes of 2018) is a landmark policy that establishes a target for renewable and zero-carbon resources to supply 100 percent of retail sales and electricity procured to serve all state agencies by 2045. The bill also increases the state's Renewables Portfolio Standard (RPS) to 60 percent of retail sales by December 31, 2030 and requires all state agencies to incorporate these targets into their relevant planning. . . .

California has long led the nation and the world in setting ambitious renewable energy and climate policies, working toward a clean economy that is healthier and more just. The state now aims to achieve carbon neutrality by 2045 and net negative emissions thereafter.

Decarbonizing the electric grid is imperative to achieve economywide carbon neutrality. The Renewables Portfolio Standard (RPS) has been a primary driver for increasing clean electricity generation, requiring the state's electric utilities to make renewable energy sources like solar and wind an ever-greater percentage of their power base. Although California is ahead of schedule in meeting its 33 percent renewable energy target by 2020 and on track to achieve 60 percent renewable energy by 2030, deep decarbonization of the electricity sector to meet climate change objectives will require continued transformational change in the state's electric system.

As California enters a new climate reality and moves toward a majority renewable grid, the state's planning processes likewise need to evolve to meet the needs of all Californians who depend on safe, affordable, and reliable electricity every day. Effectively integrating 100 percent renewable and zero-carbon electricity and achieving carbon neutrality in the state by 2045 will require rigorous analysis of implementation considerations, as well as coordinated planning across state agencies. While there remains work to do, achieving 100 clean electricity is a core pillar in the transition to a clean energy economy enjoyed by all Californians.

In addition to serving as a central policy in the state's efforts to address climate change, successful implementation of SB 100 can benefit residents across the state . . .

Implementing SB 100 is expected to reduce criteria air pollution emissions as renewable and zero-carbon resources replace fossil fuel in generating electricity. Today, more than 28 million Californians live in areas that exceed the federal health-based standards for ozone and fine particulate matter (PM2.5). Disadvantaged communities . . . will reap the highest health benefits from the phaseout of fossil fuels in generating electricity; half of the state's natural gas power plants are in communities that rank among the 25 percent most disadvantaged.

The public health benefits are expected to grow substantially throughout the state as the transition from fossil fuels to clean electricity accelerates in transportation and buildings. Increased conversion of cars, trucks, and buses, as well as home appliances to electric technologies can improve health and reduce mortalities associated with air pollution across the state.

The joint agencies are committed to ensuring the benefits of cleaner, more efficient energy are enjoyed by all Californians, including those in low-income and disadvantaged communities, as well as tribal and rural communities. To ensure equitable outcomes, SB 100 will need to be implemented in ways that help these communities overcome barriers to clean energy, including:

- Keeping electricity affordable, with an emphasis on vulnerable populations and households that pay a disproportionately high share of their household income on energy.

- Reducing air pollution from local power plants, particularly in communities that experience a disproportionate amount of air pollution.

- Strengthening communities' ability to function during power outages and enjoy reliable energy in a changing climate.

- Funding of training for high-quality jobs and careers in the growing clean energy industry . . . .

Successful implementation of SB 100 alone will not achieve statewide carbon neutrality, but it is pivotal to the success of California's climate-fighting efforts that collectively can reach the target. A clean electricity grid can serve as a backbone to support the decarbonization of transportation, buildings, and some industries. Together, with the electricity sector, these sectors account for 92 percent of the state's GHG emissions.

Figure 2: California GHG Emissions by Sector

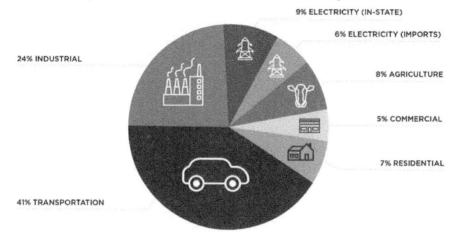

Source: CARB Emissions Inventory.

SB 100 sits within a portfolio of related key clean energy efforts to reduce climate and air pollution emissions while maintaining a reliable and affordable electric grid. These efforts include:

- **Transportation Electrification**—While the transportation sector remains among the state's biggest decarbonization challenges, California has already positioned itself as a leader in clean transportation with more than 566,000 zero-emission vehicles (ZEVs) on the road and nearly half of the total U.S. ZEV sales. Building on this success, Governor Gavin Newsom issued an executive order in September 2020 requiring all new passenger car and truck sales to be zero-emission by 2035. This transformation will require close coordination and planning across the electric and transportation sectors.

- **Building Decarbonization**—The construction of and conversion to zero-emission buildings has rapidly emerged as a key decarbonization strategy in recent years. State agencies are assessing pathways to reduce emissions from this important sector and considering implications of migrating more building energy uses, such as space and water heating, to the electric grid.

- **Energy Efficiency**—Prioritizing cost-effective energy efficiency measures remains critical as the state moves toward 100 percent clean electricity. Taking steps to reduce energy demand can offset the need for additional generation capacity, saving customers money while reducing land-use and other environmental impacts associated with the construction of new generation facilities.

- **Load Flexibility**—Load flexibility—the ability to shift electricity consumption to other parts of the day—is critical to supporting grid reliability, especially in a high-renewables future, and reducing the total cost of the electric system. The state has efforts underway to research and implement a variety of load flexibility applications.

- **Research and Innovation**—Given the urgency of achieving an electricity system powered by renewable and carbon-free electricity, continued prioritization of research and development of new and more cost-effective solutions is imperative. State agencies are also working to ensure these investments benefit all Californians. . . .

VIRGINIA CLEAN ECONOMY ACT (2020)

Press Release: "Governor Northam Signs Clean Energy Legislation"
Office of the Governor, Commonwealth of Virginia (Apr. 12, 2020)

RICHMOND—Governor Ralph Northam is accelerating Virginia's transition to clean energy by signing the Virginia Clean Economy Act and by amending the Clean Energy and Community Flood Preparedness Act that requires Virginia to join the Regional Greenhouse Gas Initiative.

"These new clean energy laws propel Virginia to leadership among the states in fighting climate change," said Governor Northam. "They advance environmental justice and help create clean energy jobs. In Virginia, we are proving that a clean environment and a strong economy go hand-in-hand."

The Virginia Clean Economy Act was passed as House Bill 1526 and Senate Bill 851, which were sponsored by Delegate Richard C. "Rip" Sullivan, Jr. and Senator Jennifer McClellan, respectively. The Act incorporates clean energy directions that the Governor issued in Executive Order Forty-Three in September 2019. It results from extensive stakeholder input and incorporates environmental justice concepts related to the Green New Deal.

The law requires new measures to promote energy efficiency, sets a schedule for closing old fossil fuel power plants, and requires electricity to come from 100 percent renewable sources such as solar or wind. Energy companies must pay penalties for not meeting their targets, and part of that revenue would fund job training and renewable energy programs in historically disadvantaged communities. The Act accomplishes the following broad goals:

- **Establishes renewable portfolio standards**. The Act requires Dominion Energy Virginia to be 100 percent carbon-free by 2045 and Appalachian Power to be 100 percent carbon-free by 2050. It requires nearly all coal-fired plants to close by the end of 2024.

- **Establishes energy efficiency standards**. The Act declares energy efficiency pilot programs to be "in the public interest." It creates a new program to reduce the energy burden for low-income customers, and it requires the Department of Social Services and the Department of Housing and Community Development to convene stakeholders to develop recommendations to implement this program. The Act sets an energy efficiency resource standard, requiring third party review of whether energy companies meet savings goals.

- **Advances offshore wind**. The Act provides that 5,200 megawatts of offshore wind generation is "in the public interest." It requires Dominion Energy Virginia to prioritize Commonwealth to advance apprenticeship and job training, and to include an environmental and fisheries mitigation plan.

- **Advances solar and distributed generation**. The Act establishes that 16,100 megawatts of solar and onshore wind is "in the public interest." The law expands "net metering," making it easier for rooftop solar to advance across Virginia. The new law requires Virginia's largest energy companies to construct or acquire more than 3,100 megawatts of energy storage capacity.

NOTES AND QUESTIONS

1.   What differences do you see between the California and the Virginia 100% clean energy laws described above? What decarbonization efforts do they emphasize? How do they differ from the national policies in terms of definition, mechanisms, and scope?

2.   California has placed a significant focus on EVs in its decarbonization efforts. Why might that state prioritize transportation electrification more than other states at this juncture? Are there any equity considerations that it should focus on in its EV policies?

3.   Virginia's law emphasizes offshore wind energy. Think about the benefits of offshore wind for an Atlantic coastal state like Virginia as compared to California or midwestern states. Why might it be more difficult for Virginia to procure other forms of lower-cost, large-scale renewable energy?

4.   Both states make energy efficiency a highlight of their implementation plans. States have decades of experience with energy efficiency programs, but

with varying results. In some states, utilities run the programs; in others, non-profits do. Serving low-income customers or renters is often a challenge. *See Customer Energy Efficiency Programs*, Am. Council for an Energy-Efficient Econ.; RACHEL CLUETT ET AL., AM. COUNCIL FOR AN ENERGY-EFFICIENT ECON., BUILDING BETTER ENERGY EFFICIENCY PROGRAMS FOR LOW-INCOME HOUSEHOLDS (Mar. 2016). How can states work to ensure energy efficiency programs contribute to climate goals and address equity considerations?

c. Corporate Commitments and Initiatives

Over 200 major corporations—such as Amazon, Verizon, IBM, and Microsoft—have signed a climate pledge to reach net zero carbon emissions across their businesses by 2040. The pledge commits these corporations to regular reporting, carbon elimination, and the use of credible offsets. *See The Climate Pledge*, https://www.theclimatepledge.com/us/en/the-pledge. IKEA and Microsoft have net zero goals that include their supply chains. Microsoft also announced intentions to neutralize all the CO_2 emitted since its 1975 founding.

In 2017, over a thousand businesses, including some of the major corporations listed above, as well as state and local governments and faith and cultural institutions, formed the group "America is All In." The group is focused on "pushing and partnering with the federal government to develop an ambitious, all-in national climate strategy that meets the urgency of the climate crisis; scaling climate action around the country to accelerate the transition to a 100 percent clean energy economy; and promoting the leadership of non-federal actors on the world stage." *See* Press Release, *American Is All In Unveils Clear and Actionable Blueprint to Cut U.S. Emissions in Half by 2030*, AMERICA IS ALL IN (Sept. 20, 2021). In 2021, the group released its "Blueprint 2030: An All-In Climate Strategy for Faster, More Durable Emissions Reductions," with specific proposals to reduce U.S. emissions by at least 50% by 2030 and to create a decarbonized economy before the middle of this century. Across the Atlantic, ACI Europe, representing over 500 European airports, has a net zero target for 2050 that covers its buildings and operations on land but not emissions from airplanes. Joeri Rogelj et al., *Three Ways to Improve Net-Zero Emissions Targets*, 591 NATURE 365 (2021).

As companies continue to develop their carbon reduction pledges and proposals, accountability and transparency are critical. The non-profit Carbon Disclosure Project (CDP) has been helping corporations, states, regions, and cities track GHG emissions from their facilities and across their supply chains for over two decades. This information allows investors and business managers to track and manage environmental impacts. Over 9,600 companies disclosed GHG emissions through the CDP in 2020, representing over 50% of global market capitalization. The CDP collects data in line with the recommendations of the Task Force on Climate-related Financial Disclosure (TCFD), a group established in 2015 by G20 finance ministers and central bankers. The CDP cites tangible business benefits from disclosing emissions, and from uncovering risks and opportunities in tracking climate and environmental progress. CPD publishes a full environmental and GHG reporting dataset for companies and investors. *See* CDP, https://www.cdp.net/en.

Accountability and transparency are particularly important for energy companies and electric utilities. Analyst Richard Heede's work with the Carbon Accountability Institute has shown that just 90 fossil fuel and cement companies were responsible for over two-thirds of global carbon emissions between 1965 and 2018. *See* Richard Heede, *Carbon Majors 2018 Data Set Released December 2020: Update of Top Twenty Companies 1965– 2018*, Climate Accountability Inst. (Dec. 2020). These companies include Saudi Aramco, Gazprom, Chevron, ExxonMobil, BP, and Royal Dutch Shell, to name a few. *Cf.* Dario Kenner & Richard Heede, *White Knights, or Horsemen of the Apocalypse? Prospects for Big Oil to Align Emissions With a 1.5°C Pathway*, ENERGY RES. & SOCIAL SCI. (Apr. 15, 2021).

While the biggest oil companies in the United States have been unwilling to make their own Net Zero Energy targets, oil companies in the EU exist in a different political environment and have adopted a different strategy. Both BP and Shell Oil have pledged to become "integrated energy companies" and have adopted Net Zero Energy goals to transform their operations to emit zero net emissions by 2050. BP aims to do this by investing in renewables, bioenergy, hydrogen, and CCS in addition to more efficient upstream operations. Shell seeks to reduce the carbon intensity of the products it sells (6–8% reduction from a 2016 baseline). Shell also announced that its oil production had peaked, and that future production would decrease 1–2% per year until 2030. The company plans to invest $2– 3 billion per year in its "Renewables and Energy Solutions" group, focusing on electricity, renewables, and hydrogen, as well as energy access. It plans to use CCS for another 25 million tons of CO_2.

Like oil companies, some electric utilities have adopted Net Zero Energy goals. Unlike international oil companies, however, electric companies are governed largely by the countries and states in which they operate. The electric industry is responsible for about one-third of GHG emissions in the United States, and so achieving Net Zero Energy depends on a decarbonized electricity industry, especially as pushes to electrify everything increase. Yet, creating a carbon-free utility also requires major operational changes.

For example, in 2019 and 2020, Northern States Power Co., an electric utility subsidiary of Xcel Energy, which operates in multiple states, submitted an Integrated Resource Plan (IRP) for 2020–2034 to the Minnesota PUC. *See* XCEL ENERGY, UPPER MIDWEST INTEGRATED

RESOURCE PLAN 2020–2034, REPLY COMMENTS, Docket No. E002/RTP–19–368 (June 25, 2021). That plan encountered several challenges, including demands by stakeholders for alternatives to building new natural gas generation; more aggressive retirements of coal plants; and increased use of renewable resources, including local generation. A major point of contention was Xcel's plan to convert a coal-fired plant (Sherco) to a combined-cycle natural gas plant. Xcel responded to stakeholder feedback by creating an Alternate Plan that eliminated plans for the Sherco plant and included development of solar at the Sherco site. By 2030, the company now aims to eliminate coal-fired power plants from its system while acquiring more utility-scale solar and wind generation. It also seeks to extend operation of its nuclear plants and increase investments in energy efficiency. This Alternate Plan offers other benefits too, including creating a 2030 generation portfolio that will be 54% renewables and 81% carbon-free—reducing the utility's 2030 carbon emissions by 86% from 2005 levels. *See id.*; Scott Voorhis, *Xcel Plans to Roll out 10,000 MW of Renewable Energy in Minnesota, Colorado by 2030*, UTIL. DIVE (July 30, 2021).

But the plan also presents some risks. Xcel found that if it did not build a combined cycle gas plant at Sherco, it would be required to operate and plan its system differently to account for the lack of central station power. The utility also noted that property taxes for the host city would be lower, and some job losses could be expected, though the company committed to ensuring all current employees remain employed. Those risks aside, the new plan would free up electric transmission capacity for additional renewable energy. Xcel found that "[o]n balance . . . we believe the Alternate Plan . . . represents the best path forward for our customers, stakeholders, and the states we serve. It is projected to reduce customer costs over the planning period, achieve substantially greater carbon reduction, and allow us to move faster in pursuing a more renewable and carbon-free generation system, all while preserving reliability." UPPER MIDWEST INTEGRATED RESOURCE PLAN REPLY COMMENTS, *supra*, at 3.

For Duke Energy in the Carolinas, the transition to a Net Zero Energy system looks very different. Duke submitted a 2020 IRP to North Carolina and South Carolina regulators covering a 15-year planning horizon. *See* DUKE ENERGY CAROLINAS INTEGRATED RESOURCE PLAN 2020 (corrected Nov. 6. 2020). The utility proposed to expand its system to serve 560,000 new customers and add 1.6 GW of winter peak demand. While the utility planned to expand energy efficiency and demand response programs, new capacity was needed as it retired older resources, including plans to retire all coal by 2030. Duke Energy committed to reducing 2030 CO_2 emissions by 50% from 2005 levels to meet a 2050 net-zero goal. In North and South Carolina, the utility operates six nuclear power plants (11 GW), for which it sought to renew 11 nuclear unit licenses; in 2018, these plants provided half of customers' electricity. The utility also operates 26 hydro plants (3.4

GW) and owns or buys 4 GW of solar. Duke Energy's 2020 IRP developed six different scenarios for an array of generation portfolios. According to the company, "[t]hese portfolios explore the most economic and earliest practicable paths for coal retirement; acceleration of renewable technologies including solar, onshore and offshore wind; greater integration of battery and pumped-hydro energy storage; expanded energy efficiency and demand response and deployment of new zero-emitting load following resources (ZELFRs) such as small modular reactors (SMRs)." *Id.* at 11. Notably, Duke later revised its IRP after South Carolina state regulators rejected its 2020 filing on grounds that the company did not sufficiently address how it would address customers' energy needs through increased solar power and for failing to choose a single "preferred" alternative among the proposed planning scenarios. *See* DUKE ENERGY CAROLINAS INTEGRATED RESOURCE PLAN: 2020 MODIFIED (filed Aug. 27, 2021); Scott Van Voorhis, *Duke Explores Shutting Coal-Fired Plants by 2030 in South Carolina Plans*, UTIL. DIVE (Sept. 1, 2021).

NOTES AND QUESTIONS

1. What responsibility do major emitters have to reduce emissions? While we currently hold countries responsible for tracking emissions, how does work like the CDP and the Carbon Accountability Institute change the way companies are or could be held responsible for their emissions?

2. How are the operating environments of oil companies like BP and Shell different from U.S. firms or other big oil companies? What role will fossil fuel production play in their futures, and how will those futures be shaped? Do their status as legacy energy companies add or subtract from their societal legitimacy to operate in a carbon-managed world? How might European oil companies position themselves differently than U.S.-based companies to shareholders? To policymakers and regulators? Employees? Customers? Management? The general public? In response to a lawsuit brought by environmental groups, a Dutch court held in 2021 that Shell needed to reduce its emissions more rapidly to reach a 45% reduction by 2030 from 2019 levels. How might such lawsuits spur a firm's action? Or not? *See* Jeff Brady, *In A Landmark Case, A Dutch Court Orders Shell To Cut Its Carbon Emissions Faster,* NPR (May 26, 2021).

3. In the late 2010s, states and local governments across the country began to file lawsuits against the fossil fuel industry to recover for harm associated with climate change, raising a variety of state law tort and consumer protection claims. Some of these claims were based on allegations that the industry had not been honest about its knowledge of and contributions to climate change. *See State Suits Against Oil Companies*, State Energy and Env't Impact Center, NYU Law (providing descriptions of cases and links to court filing and orders); *Local Suits Against Oil Companies*, State Energy and Env't Impact Center,

NYU Law (same); *see also* LEAH CARDAMORE STOKES, SHORT CIRCUITING POLICY: INTEREST GROUPS AND THE BATTLE OVER CLEAN ENERGY AND CLIMATE POLICY IN THE AMERICAN STATES (2020). How does this affect how the public and regulators should view the industry's Net Zero Energy claims? How should different oil companies be treated in this regard?

4. Compare the Duke Energy and Xcel IRP goals and plans. Where are they similar and where do they differ? Are there other issues that should be included? Both utilities state that they utilized broad stakeholder engagement, but that not all issues were resolved. Are the companies' responses to stakeholders adequate? What role do the utilities think natural gas should play in a transition to a clean energy economy?

5. Regardless of positive steps towards a clean energy future, a 2020 study showed that levels of carbon abatement by utilities fell short of their potential. DELOITTE INSIGHTS, UTILITY DECARBONIZATION STRATEGIES: RENEW, RESHAPE, AND REFUEL TO ZERO (2020).

d. Financial Institutions

The success of all Net Zero Energy plans depends upon securing the financing and funds to build new carbon-free energy systems. As noted, the NAS study estimates the need for $2 trillion in capital project investments over the next decade for the United States to reach Net Zero Energy. While some of this money would be from federal investment, the bulk would come from the private sector. Globally, financing the transition is even more costly, with one study estimating that Net Zero Energy finance will be in the range of $1–5 trillion per year globally, for a thirty-year total of $100–150 trillion. BOSTON CONSULTING GROUP & GLOBAL FINANCIAL MARKETS ASS'N, CLIMATE FINANCE MARKETS AND THE REAL ECONOMY: SIZING THE GLOBAL NEED AND DEFINING THE MARKET STRUCTURE TO MOBILIZE CAPITAL 9 (Dec. 2020).

On the private side, large-scale financing is available from commercial banks. For more experimental or higher risk projects, venture capitalists (VC) or private equity funds (PE) can be used. Commercial banks are more risk adverse than VC/PE firms, and they expect a lower rate of return on their investments. Consequently, commercial banks are more likely to loan to established borrowers than to new ventures. While both VC and PE expect high rates of return—often more than 10 times the value of their capital investment—they differ from each other in certain respects. PE firms generally invest in companies that are not publicly listed or traded. VC firms also invest in such companies; however, they tend to focus on startups. Both PE and VC firms take equity positions in their borrowers with the intent of ultimately exiting those investments by equity financing through initial public offerings.

Financial institutions are also making Net Zero Energy pledges, as well as evaluating the GHG liabilities of their investments (see CDP information above). These firms are committing to aligning their lending practices with their Net Zero Energy pledges. First, lending institutions screen their investments and evaluate their own portfolios to evaluate GHG emissions and investments in zero-emission technologies and projects. Many firms already use some sort of ESG (Environment, Social, Governance) screen for their investments. Financial institutions also assess future investments' climate and environmental risks. A lender is more likely to invest where technological and regulatory requirements are clear and markets are stable.

Similarly, financial firms can choose to loan money to borrowers who can demonstrate that their climate pledges (and climate risks) are backed with rigorous reporting and analysis. Ensuring the borrower's climate goals are transparent and evaluated with sound and standardized methodologies using high-quality data makes the borrower more attractive (assuming the project is worthy of investment). Thus, tools like the CDP become an invaluable resource to evaluate investments.

This need for rigorous and transparent evaluation drives the recommendation for establishing uniform disclosure requirements and reporting. Chaired by Michael Bloomberg, a task force of global representatives of financial institutions including large banks, insurance companies, pension funds, and asset managers, together with consumers, developed a list of recommendations to make climate risk disclosures transparent and uniform. Uniform disclosures center around four themes: institutional governance, investment strategy, risk management, and having specific metrics and targets.

Notice that the first theme of these recommendations is governance. The organization must be committed to its Net Zero Energy goals from the boardroom through leadership, management, and operations. Additionally, financial planning and disclosing climate-related risks to an organization's businesses must be part of regular reporting. Further, the climate disclosures must demonstrate how the organization identifies and manages risks through specified metrics and targets. *See* WHITNEY MANN ET AL., RMI, ZEROING IN: THE US FINANCIAL SECTOR PERSPECTIVE ON NET-ZERO LENDING AND INVESTING (2021); GROUP OF THIRTY, MAINSTREAMING THE TRANSITION TO A NET-ZERO ECONOMY (Oct. 2020).

Because of their riskiness, new technologies may not have access to commercial capital and, depending upon the magnitude of the perceived risk, may have limited access to PE and VC capital. Consequently, there is a role for public funding to support innovative clean energy technologies and demonstration projects. There is also a role for "green banks." There are roughly 60 green banks worldwide and 20 in the United States. Green banks are nonprofits generally established through state legislation that use public capital to promote clean energy projects and serve other objectives, like serving low-income communities. These are mission-driven institutions that can help fund Net Zero Energy goals and clean energy projects. They look for scalable projects that are past the R&D stage. In calendar year 2020, green banks made a total investment of $442 million, which leveraged over a billion dollars of private capital for a total investment of $1.9 billion. To date, cumulative green bank investments are $7 billion.

Some green bank projects include creating community solar pilot projects designed to assist low-income households; developing a farm waste-to-energy project; and funding clean energy projects by local entrepreneurs. *See, e.g.*, AMERICAN GREEN BANK CONSORTIUM & COALITION FOR GREEN CAPITAL, GREEN BANKS IN THE UNITED STATES: 2021 U.S. GREEN BANK ANNUAL INDUSTRY REPORT (May 2021); ADRIANA BECERRA CID ET AL., STATE OF GREEN BANKS 2020 (Rocky Mtn. Inst. 2020); *Green Banks*, State, Local, and Tribal Governments, Nat'l Renewable Energy Lab; STEPHANY GRIFFITH-JONES & KELLY SIMS GALLAGHER, POLICY BRIEF: HOW A U.S. GREEN BANK COULD MAKE THE ECONOMY GREENER AND FAIRER (Sept. 2021).

A second form of public financing to complement green banks is an accelerator bank. Accelerator banks would finance larger scale projects than green banks, have research capabilities to assess capital needs, make investments based on a project's significant public benefits (such as emissions reductions) without being constrained by earning a return, and have some administrative capacity to help manage risks. FRANK GRAVES ET AL., CLEAN ENERGY AND SUSTAINABILITY ACCELERATOR (Jan. 14, 2021). Like the green bank, the accelerator bank would have a clean energy focus and be publicly funded. The key difference is the accelerator bank does not necessarily anticipate a return on its investments. Also, the accelerator would be federally financed. *See* H.R. 806—Clean Energy and Sustainability Accelerator Act, 117th Cong., 1st Sess. (Feb. 4, 2021); SUSAN F. TIERNEY & PAUL J. HIBBARD, ACCELERATING JOB GROWTH AND AN EQUITABLE LOW-CARBON ENERGY TRANSITION: THE ROLE OF THE CLEAN ENERGY ACCELERATOR (Jan. 14, 2021). Examples of accelerator funding include financing the electrification of municipal bus fleets, retrofitting and modernizing homes in communities of low- and moderate-income households, investing in community solar, and reducing urban heat islands. *Id.* at 3–4.

***

NOTES AND QUESTIONS

1.   While the availability of money to transform the energy system is critical, renewable energy projects are very sensitive to interest rates and the cost of capital. Unlike natural gas or coal plants, they do not have high O&M costs,

making upfront financing particularly important. What types of fiscal policies could help prevent the slowing down of renewable deployment if interest rates rise? *See* Florian Egli et al., *Cost of Capital for Renewable Energy: The Role of Industry Experience and Future Potentials, in* GREEN BANKING 335 (2020); Bjarne Steffen et al., *The Role of Public Banks in Catalyzing Private Renewable Energy Finance, in* RENEWABLE ENERGY FINANCE: FUNDING THE FUTURE OF ENERGY (2020).

2.   Energy projects in developing countries often have difficulty accessing capital. While the UN's Sustainable Development Goal 7 (SDG 7) focuses on Energy for All, 600 million people in Sub-Saharan Africa still lack access to electricity. Multilateral development banks have financed most energy infrastructure, and their engagement with renewable energy has been growing. How can this be supported? What lessons and risks from experience may be applicable? *See Executive Summary: Scaling-up Energy Investments in Africa for Inclusive and Sustainable Growth*, SEI PLATFORM (2020); Bjarne Steffen & Tobias Schmidt, *A Quantitative Analysis of 10 Multilateral Development Banks' Investment in Conventional and Renewable Power-Generation Technologies From 2006 to 2015*, 4 NATURE ENERGY 75 (Jan. 2019).

PRACTICE PROBLEM

You have been tasked with evaluating the GHG liabilities for your investment firm's $2 billion investment portfolio to align your firm's investments with its new Net Zero Energy policy. After considering all the materials above: (1) What corporate initiatives would you undertake to address Net Zero Energy? (2) What relationships do you build and cultivate? (3) Whom do you consult? (4) What are the components of your investment firm's Net Zero Energy plan? One of the companies your firm invests in is Duke Energy Carolinas, mentioned above. How would you evaluate its GHG liabilities as it develops its next operational plan?

C. THE INNOVATION PROCESS

In the United States, we like to trumpet our spirit of innovation and entrepreneurship. Innovators such as Edison, Westinghouse, and others created the electric industry and built a national infrastructure that fueled a robust economy. While those innovators worked in the private sector, the role of delivering reliable and affordable electricity throughout the United States depended on a public-private partnership—and was supported by over a century's worth of government legislation, regulation, policy, research, and investment. Today, while the energy industry is larger and more complex than ever, and technological innovation is global, deploying new technologies remains local. The private sector plays an important role in developing and implementing the new energy technologies to achieve Net Zero Energy. But government is also critical, particularly in the early stages of innovation, as described below. *See, e.g.*, LAURA DIAZ ANDON ET AL., TRANSFORMING U.S. ENERGY INNOVATION (Nov. 2011).

The DOE plays a major role in energy innovation in the United States. Part of its role is conducting most of the nation's basic scientific research in energy, through 17 national laboratories, each of which is engaged in a wide variety of activities—from fusion to bioenergy, and from nanomaterials to solar projects. The national laboratories began with defense-related research but have since expanded to energy and environmental matters across the board. The primary research division within the DOE is known as the Advanced Research Projects Agency-Energy or ARPA-E, which is an outgrowth of the Defense Advanced Research Projects Agency (DARPA), operated by the Department of Defense. DARPA is best known for the development of ARPANET—the foundation for the Internet. DOE operates a variety of energy projects, including Energy Innovation Hubs and Energy Frontier Research Centers. These hubs and centers constitute a new configuration for technological innovation. They bring together public and private sectors, including universities and industries, to explore a full panoply of energy technologies, including advanced nuclear reactors, energy storage, superconductors, biofuels, and the like.

In the energy sector, most actors prefer (or claim to prefer) that the government not "pick winners." Instead, they say, public energy innovation funding should be targeted to stimulate a wide variety of technologies and let the private sector manage deployment. A primary reason for governments around the world to invest in energy innovation, particularly basic science, is because these activities are underfunded by the private sector. Moreover, even if new energy technologies are viable, the private sector will continue to underinvest until commercialization and marketability can be clearly seen on the horizon. Thus, energy innovation is a joint public/private affair, as the following excerpt describes.

JOSEPH P. TOMAIN, CLEAN POWER POLITICS: THE DEMOCRATIZATION OF ENERGY
Cambridge Univ. Press pp. 109–27 (2017)

The fundamental idea [behind the energy innovation system] is to create an environment where inventions can occur and then move those inventions into the commercial marketplace. . . . [E]nergy innovation . . . generate[s] a wide range of low- or no-carbon technologies. Also, along the innovation continuum, different public and private actors have distinct roles to play and the dynamic interaction between government and private firms is . . . central to the full development of useful energy technologies. [There are four stages of the innovation process: basic research, valleys of death, private finance, and assessment. The relationship between government and private investments in energy innovation changes along a funding continuum.]

At the beginning of the innovation cycle, it may be necessary for government to invest in fundamental science and technological research . . . because the private sector is reluctant to invest. In the initial stages of the innovation system, government bears more risk than private actors and reaps little to no reward for those risks. At the other extreme, after the system has run its course, as specific technologies reach market, private actors control the commercialization of the new technologies. In short, "[a]s an innovation approaches deployment and investment prospects begin to rise, it is typical for private sector involvement to increase and public sector involvement to decrease." . . .

The first stage addresses *basic research*. Initial research involves scientific investigation as well as the initial application of a scientific discovery through the development of a new technology. The second stage addresses two *valleys of death* that must be traversed as a new technology moves from idea to market—the technological valley of death (i.e. moving from idea to demonstration) and the commercial valley of death (i.e. moving from demonstration commercialization.) Both valleys involve financial risks that many entrepreneurs are unwilling to bear. The third stage in the process is referred to as either *deployment* or full commercialization at which time government involvement recedes and private involvement expands. At this point, *private finance* replaces government funding. . . .

Government investment in demonstration projects is made for the same reason that private actors do not commit capital in the early stages of innovation. Currently, demonstration projects are underway on a variety of activities including, the smart grid and offshore wind power, and to some extent to carbon capture and sequestration and advanced nuclear power, both of which have proven to be expensive and a long way from marketability given their high costs and canceled or inactive projects. . . .

[Another] financial challenge is known as the commercialization valley of death. Even though the idea in the lab may have proven itself in government-sponsored demonstration projects, it remains to be seen whether a particular innovation is marketable and, therefore, profitable. It is at this stage in the innovation cycle that begins to attract more substantial private funding because of its profit potential. At this stage in the process, [venture capital] VC and [private equity] PE are seen as the vehicles to bridge projects to bring them to the point of commercial investment. . . . Commercialization efforts for energy technologies are costly easily running to hundreds of millions of dollars. Too often, these financial requirements are perceived as too risky for most VC/PE firms. Consequently, to increase the chance of commercialization it is often necessary for government regulations to establish incentives to make commercialization more likely. Government incentives, such as subsidies and tax breaks, that reduce the cost of doing business can push technologies into the market.

Innovation policy can also stimulate market activity through standard-setting or technology requirements, which have the effect of pulling those technologies into the market. In the clean energy sector, innovation policy employs both devices. R&D funding, for example, can help push new technologies such as smart meters into the market while pollution control requirements will have the effect of pulling technologies into the market. . . .

We have moved along the innovation continuum from idea to proof of concept, to development and demonstration, and we are now poised for marketability and commercialization. This last stage, sometimes referred to as diffusion or deployment, can only successfully occur with large-scale private sector involvement. . . . The goal of energy innovation is commercialization, and commercialization means private sector involvement and ownership even though government involvement occurs from R&D through demonstrations and deployment right through to commercialization.

NOTES AND QUESTIONS

1.   Sketch out the innovation continuum: can you identify which actors are involved and the roles they play at different stages? What roles should universities, private industry, non-governmental organizations, foundations, or government play in developing energy technologies? Which actor(s) should be responsible for bringing a particular technology to market? Consider the funding and financial support across the technology's development lifecycle. Should the support be in the form of direct investments? Loans? Legal standards? Taxes? For a discussion of recent public-private partnerships in clean energy innovation, see David Iaconangelo, *Landmark DOE, Bill Gates Partnership Targets "Valley of Death,"* ENERGYWIRE (Aug. 13, 2021) (reporting on Bill Gates' pledge of $1.5 billion to DOE for demonstration of new technologies, including "renewable hydrogen, direct air capture, long-duration energy storage, and low-carbon aviation fuel.").

2.   The World Economic Forum estimates that in 2019, total global clean energy investments reached $282.2 billion. *This is How Much Was Invested in Clean Energy in 2019*, World Economic Forum (June 2020). Bloomberg New Energy Finance, however, reports that total global investments reached $501.3 billion in 2020, up from $458.6 billion in 2019. *Energy Transition Investment Trends: Tackling Global Investment in the Low-Carbon Energy Transition*, Bloomberg NEF (2021); *see also* REN21, RENEWABLES 2021: GLOBAL STATUS REPORT Ch. 5 (2021). Domestically, one estimate showed that in 2020, U.S.

investments in clean energy were $55 billion. *Investment in US Clean Energy to Total $55 Billion in 2020*, S&P GLOBAL (Nov. 23, 2020).

3.   Innovation in the energy sector is crucial to a Net Zero Energy transition. When the 2016 Paris Climate Agreement was signed, a group of over 20 billionaires announced the formation of Breakthrough Energy Coalition to support a new, clean energy mix for the future, with a 2050 Net Zero Energy target. *See* Breakthrough Energy, https://www.breakthroughenergy.org/.

4.   Mission Innovation (MI) was also an outcome of the Paris Agreement. MI is a global initiative of 22 countries and the European Commission (on behalf of the EU) focused on meeting Paris Agreement goals by generating investment in research, development, and demonstration to make clean energy affordable and accessible. *See* Mission Innovation, http://mission-innovation.net/.

5.   Government and private financial support for energy system innovation can take many forms. Some sources covered here and in prior chapters include taxes and credits, loans, subsidies, mandates such as RPSs and CESs, vehicle emission and fuel economy standards, government funding, and utility regulation. At this point in your studies, which mix of financial support, incentives, and regulation do you think is optimal? How dependent is it on the particular market in question?

D.   DECARBONIZING TECHNOLOGIES: TWO CASE STUDIES

The innovation policy principles discussed above illuminate the ways that new technologies can help meet Net Zero Energy goals. Here, we explore two potentially transformational technology shifts in detail: (1) electrifying the transportation sector through EVs and (2) removing carbon from the atmosphere with CCS. We chose these two examples because both technologies require fundamental shifts of larger embedded technological systems. This means changes not just in technologies like vehicles or coal plants, but also in the laws, policies, finances, and operations that govern these technologies. Moreover, both transportation electrification and CCS have received significant federal and state financial subsidies and are part of global shifts in energy systems. In the United States, their deployment is either well underway (EVs) or at the early commercialization stage (CCS). Both technologies have strong supporters and detractors. Other Net Zero Energy technologies under development include direct air capture; green hydrogen; zero-carbon cement, steel, and aviation fuels; nuclear fission and small modular nuclear reactors; and solar engineering. *See, e.g.*, BILL GATES, HOW TO AVOID A CLIMATE CATASTROPHE (2021).

1.   ELECTRIC VEHICLES

The phrase "electrifying transportation" links two primary energy sources and sectors in new ways—oil and electricity. Technologically, it includes EVs, EV charging infrastructure, batteries, and changes in consumer buying and behavior. On the policy side, it includes subsidies, taxes, standards, ratemaking, innovation policy, and other legislative and regulatory actions. EV deployment also requires public and private financial investments. We saw in Chapters 4 and 5 how the electricity sector is already far down the path to reduce fossil fuel use. EVs could do the same for the transportation sector. While many political, technological, and economic barriers remain, significant progress has occurred since the early 2000s. This section provides an overview of EVs today and discusses several of the important remaining issues: batteries, grid integration, and charging infrastructure.

Writing this section of the book is challenging for at least two reasons. First, domestic and international policies, along with the technologies these policies aim to support, are developing rapidly. Second, COVID-19 created data anomalies in 2020 and vehicle supply issues in 2021. This latter problem is larger than EVs, but it does make trend predictions tricky.

To meet Net Zero Energy goals, a Bloomberg New Energy Finance report estimates the following actions are needed:

- EVs need to represent almost 60% of global new passenger vehicle sales by 2030 and 95% of medium- and heavy-duty truck sales by 2040.

- Early adoption is important for building infrastructure and broader consumer interest.

- Government policies should include tighter fuel economy or CO_2 standards for trucks; mandates for the electrification of government fleets; tighter regulations for vehicles entering urban areas; and accelerated development of charging infrastructure.

- Sales of gasoline-powered vehicles must be phased out by or shortly after 2035.

- Electric batteries need to be lighter and cheaper, and new fuels such as hydrogen cells need to be incorporated in ZEVs.

The report also stresses that EVs represent a $7 trillion market opportunity between 2021 and 2030, and $46 trillion between 2021 and 2050. *See* Colin McKerracher et al., *Electric Vehicle Outlook 2021*, Bloomberg NEF (2021).

The U.S. transportation sector consumes over 13 million barrels of oil per day (mbd) (of 19 mbd total oil used) and emits about one-third of U.S. GHG emissions, or 4% of global emissions. The average U.S. vehicle is driven 13,500 miles per year, with over 3 trillion miles driven annually. There are many ways to reduce GHG from the transportation sector, as discussed in Chapter 6: more efficient vehicles, cleaner transportation fuels, more use of public transportation, and better urban land planning—such as expanding bike paths and vehicle sharing. Decarbonizing the U.S. transportation sector also requires new fuel. Here, we focus on EVs.

Battery Electric Vehicles (BEV) are built with rechargeable batteries and use 100% electricity to power their driving. Their driving ranges are increasing rapidly. In 2020, BEVs had ranges from 110 to 380 miles per charge. BEVs are Zero Emission Vehicles, as they do not emit pollutants from their tailpipes. In 2021, there were 26 BEV models for sale in the United States, with at least 39 more planned over the next four to five years. *See EV (BEV and PHEV) Models Currently Available in the U.S.,* EVAdoption (Apr. 4, 2021); *Future EVs,* EVAdoption (2021).

Plug-in Electric Vehicles (PHEV) are hybrid cars, which use both a rechargeable battery and a smaller internal combustion (IC) engine. They can drive using gasoline or can be plugged in to recharge the battery. While they may only have a 25–50-mile range per electric charge, this covers a large percent of average trips. They also use hybrid technologies like regenerative braking when driving in hybrid mode, so engine efficiencies are relatively high. As of 2021, there were 30 PHEV vehicles for sale in the United States, with plans for 16 more over the next four to five years.

The EV market share in the United States was 2% of all light-duty vehicles sold in 2018 (328,000 vehicles) and slightly less in 2019 and 2020 (320,000 and 295,000 vehicles sold, respectively) as federal tax credits were phased out. There are substantial regional differences. For instance, in 2020, over 8% of the new cars sold in California were EVs, and those sales were concentrated in metro areas like San Jose, San Francisco, and Los Angeles. In other states and outside the 50 largest U.S. metro areas, there were relatively few EVs sold. *See* ANH BUI ET AL., THE INT'L COUNCIL ON CLEAN TRANSP., UPDATE ON ELECTRIC VEHICLE ADOPTION ACROSS U.S. CITIES (Aug. 2020). So, like many clean energy technologies discussed in this book, EV deployment is patchy and dependent on many factors, with urban areas leading the way for EV sales and associated charging infrastructure. Nevertheless, the overall projections for EV growth remain strong. EV industry groups estimate that 500,000 EVs will be sold in the United States in 2021 (3.4% of all sales), with a projected 30% (4.7 million cars) by 2030. *See id.;* EV *Sales Forecasts,* EVAdoption (2021).

Given the new EV models coming online in the next four to five years and increasing consumer comfort with the technology, the potential for EVs to become a dominant technology within the next decade seems much more likely than it did even four years ago. To keep things in perspective, in 2021 there were nearly 290 million vehicles on American roads, and roughly 1.8 million were EVs. The average lifetime of a car is 200,000 miles or 12.5

years. The EV industry projects 25 million EVs on the road in 2030, slightly under 10% of the total fleet. *See EV Sales Forecasts,* EVAdoption (2021).

With over 2.2 million cars sold around the world in 2019, the global EV market is concentrated in Europe and China. In Europe, EVs have a 10% market share, with the same country by country market variation seen in U.S. states. In Norway, nearly three quarters of the cars sold are EVs due to generous financial incentives. Other northern European countries like Sweden, the Netherlands, Finland, and Denmark also have EV sales above 15%. Over 5% of new cars sold in China are EVs, and the country has an EV growth rate of 36%, compared to 17% for the United States. Market expansion is driven partly by different jurisdictions' incentives and rebates. *See* Drew Silver, *Today's Electric Vehicle Market: Slow Growth in U.S., Faster in China, Europe,* PEW RESEARCH CENTER (June 7, 2021). The EU's decision to phase out all internal combustion engine sales by 2035 should create a strong growth trend for EV adoption.

Batteries are one of the main cost components of an EV. EV batteries have increased in performance and decreased in price. As car batteries must be cheaper, lighter, and capable of storing enough electricity to increase EV driving ranges, technological advances are impressive. In 2011, the Nissan Leaf had a 73-mile driving range on a single charge; in 2019, the same vehicle had a 226-mile range. With a driving range of 250 miles per charge, it is estimated that with "average driving" of 15,000 miles per year, EV owners will be able to charge at home 92% of the time and require only 6 stops at fast charging stations each year (compared to 40 gas station stops for internal combustion engine vehicles). Chris Harto, *Electric Vehicle Ownership Costs,* CONSUMER REPORTS (Oct. 2020). Notably, "[m]oving from 250 to 300 miles of range per charge adds 20 percent to the cost, weight, and volume of batteries but reduces the percentage of total annual miles that require public charging by only 2 percent." *Id.* at 15.

Innovations in battery technologies and EV efficiency are supported by investments in energy storage and are happening around the world. The EU is investing heavily in battery technologies and manufacturing. U.S. national laboratories like the National Renewable Energy Laboratory (NREL) are engaged in improving storage, materials, and grid integration, as well as renewable energy resources. *See* Brad Plumer, *Energy Department Targets Vastly Cheaper Batteries to Clean Up the Grid,* N.Y. TIMES (July 14, 2021); *Transportation and Mobility Research,* Nat'l Renewable Energy Lab.

Battery charging times are also decreasing. Level 1 charging involves a standard 120-volt outlet like the ones found in your home. At this level, it takes about 24 hours to recharge an EV to 80%. Level 2 charging at a minimum of 240 volts can take up to 8 hours for a full charge. The fastest charging available is the DC fast charger, which can recharge up to 80% in twenty minutes. For most drivers, charging at home at night will be a workable solution for the majority of driving. K.C. Colwell, *How Long Does It Take to Charge an Electric Vehicle?*, CAR AND DRIVER (May 22, 2020).

As EVs become more widespread, they will require more energy from the electric grid. Chapter 8 discussed grid modernization and how EVs may shape the future grid. To recap, EVs use electricity to recharge their batteries. When EVs are not in use (note that the average car is parked over 95% of the time), it is possible that they could serve as batteries for the grid and help manage demand peaks and ramping. This type of integration could increase system reliability. *See Electric Vehicle Grid Integration*, Nat'l Renewable Energy Lab. Developing smart charging, wireless charging, and estimating EV and grid impacts are all fruitful areas of research and development. However, grid integration cannot happen without government regulation and new standards.

Clean and low-carbon electricity are also critical for EVs, as a carbon-intensive and polluting grid could have negative impacts. If tens of millions EVs are charged by the grid, understanding how the increased load impacts grid operations is critical. Innovative charging strategies and developing charge management protocols are needed to ensure EVs do not increase GHG emissions due to higher electricity demands. Maintaining grid reliability and managing cybersecurity concerns associated with EVs is also key.

Even though this section is about EVs, remember that fossil fuels provided about 90% of U.S. transportation energy in 2020—and the nation and the world have spent over a century constructing a massive network of fueling stations to support the delivery and use of fossil fuels. The Volkswagen (VW) emission cheating scandal discussed in Chapter 6 resulted in a multi-billion settlement with the U.S. EPA and the State of California that included VW paying $2.9 billion into a fund called the Environmental Mitigation Trust, which has been distributed to states over time to help fund emissions reductions products, including EV charging investments. In addition, the settlement required VW to create an entirely new company, called Electrify America, to invest $2 billion in EV charging infrastructure nationwide over a period of 10 years. *See, e.g., Our Investment Plan*, Electrify America; *Volkswagen Settlement FAQs*, Minn. Pollution Control Agency; Conner Smith, *Nearly 80 Percent of VW Funds Remain Two Years After First Awards*, EV HUB (July 10, 2020).

The DOE's Alternative Fuels Data Center tracks EV charging infrastructure. In July 2021, there were 43,492 stations offering 106,338 charging outlets. Of these, 5,250 stations offered fast DC charging (with 18,800 outlets), and almost 40,000 stations offered Level 2 charging (86,113 outlets). Chargepoint is by far the largest EV charging network open to the public, with over 24,000 stations offering 45,000 outlets. Other companies like Electrify America, Greenpoint, and Tesla also offer charging. *See Alternative Fuels Data Center,* U.S. Dep't of Energy.

***

NOTES AND QUESTIONS

1.   At first glance, it may appear that plugging EVs into the grid is not much different than plugging a toaster into a wall. However, millions of EVs connecting to the grid shifts energy demand and requires charge management. New vehicle grid integration and smart charging are fruitful areas of future research, standards development, and regulation. There is also a new language of EV charging and vehicle specifications. For a useful reference, see Chris Nelder, *Electric Vehicle Charging for Dummies*, ROCKY MTN. INST. (June 10, 2019).

2.   Another benefit of EVs is that they can connect to the electric grid and serve as a grid resource. The concept is known as vehicle-to-grid, or V2G. By connecting to the grid using a smart charging protocol, an owner's EV can potentially help balance electric load, integrate renewables, and support system reliability. One estimate shows that by 2050, up to 45% of households will provide V2G services, thus contributing to a Net Zero Energy economy. NATIONALGRID ESO, FUTURE ENERGY SCENARIOS (July 2020).

3.   In 2021, the EU announced a decision to phase out all internal combustion engine car sales by 2035 and committed to install EV chargers every 60 kilometers on major highways. *European Green Deal: Commission Proposes Transformation of EU Economy and Society to Meet Climate Ambitions,* EUROPEAN COMM'N (July 14, 2021). What other actions beyond installing EV chargers must the EU take to meet its goal of eliminating internal combustion engine car sales by 2035? In the United States, President Biden issued a 2021 Executive Order setting a national goal that EVs make up 50% of new car sales by 2030. *See* FACT SHEET: PRESIDENT BIDEN ANNOUNCES STEPS TO DRIVE AMERICAN LEADERSHIP FORWARD ON CLEAN CARS AND TRUCKS, THE WHITE HOUSE (Aug. 5, 2021). New York and California have adopted laws designed to eliminate sales of gasoline-powered cars and light trucks by 2035. How do you think these actions might affect the trajectory for EV deployment domestically?

***

A shift to EVs requires a massive infrastructure investment in EV charging. As a result, many states that have enacted 100% clean energy standards like those discussed above also have adopted incentives for electric utilities to build that charging infrastructure. Even in states without specific legislation, many electric utilities see EV adoption as an important business opportunity and have sought permission from state PUCs to invest in EV charging infrastructure and recover those costs from ratepayers. The following excerpts provide examples of state utility commission reviews of these efforts. Note that, as covered in Chapter 4,

PUCs are obligated to set rates that are just, reasonable, and nondiscriminatory. So, while public funding of clean innovation may be desirable, regulators are watchful of impacts on ratepayers.

IN THE MATTER OF A COMMISSION INQUIRY INTO ELECTRIC VEHICLE CHARGING AND INFRASTRUCTURE

Docket No. E–999/CI–17–879, 2019 WL 446228 (Minn. P.U.C., Feb. 1, 2019)

BEFORE: Dan Lipschultz, Matthew Schuerger, Katie J. Sieben and John A. Tuma Commissioners.

EVs have the potential to benefit Minnesota in numerous ways, but could also adversely impact the electric system if their integration is not planned. In order to facilitate EV integration in a manner consistent with the interests of the public and of ratepayers, the Commission initiated this investigation into EV charging and infrastructure. . . .

EVs have the potential to deliver a variety of benefits to Minnesota, especially environmental and public health benefits. Replacing fossil fuel powered vehicles with EVs can reduce greenhouse gas and other harmful emissions, especially as the rise of EVs coincides with the rise of renewable energy and the decline in coal-fired electric generation.

Reducing greenhouse gas emissions is key to stopping climate change, and Minnesota has accordingly established greenhouse gas emissions reduction goals. But according to [the Minnesota Pollution Control Agency] MPCA, the transportation sector is a leading source of greenhouse gas emissions in Minnesota and has not significantly reduced emissions levels. Increasing the adoption of EVs in Minnesota can help the state meet its emissions reduction goals and fight climate change.

Fossil-fuel powered vehicles also emit harmful pollutants that can cause adverse public health effects. These harmful pollutants tend to disparately impact minority and low-income areas where emissions are higher. Switching to EVs can help reduce emissions of these harmful pollutants and improve health outcomes in these vulnerable communities.

By using more electricity, EVs can benefit all ratepayers. An increase in electricity sales can drive down rates for all ratepayers "by spreading the utilities' fixed costs over a greater amount of kilowatt-hour sales," especially if EV charging occurs during times of low demand when not as much electricity is consumed by customers. It is estimated that an EV driver uses 4,000–5,000 kilowatt hours annually, but the Department concluded that significant growth in EVs is necessary before it would noticeably impact electric consumption.

Utilities can play a role in advancing these wide-ranging potential benefits by helping facilitate the growth of EVs through education of the public and development of EV charging infrastructure.

Widespread EV adoption is not a given due to conditions that can hamper the growth of EVs. The two main barriers to EVs that have been identified in this docket are insufficient charging infrastructure and lack of consumer awareness of EVs and their benefits.

These barriers are intertwined, because a great way to remind consumers about EVs and show that EVs are a viable and convenient option is for consumers to encounter charging infrastructure as they go about their day. Potential EV owners have reported concerns about being able to complete their driving trips on a single charge, a phenomenon that has been labeled "range anxiety." Installing plenty of chargers that potential EV owners encounter regularly can help counteract range anxiety and encourage EV adoption. Developing charging infrastructure is therefore a potential prerequisite to significant growth in EVs. However, third-party charging providers can face difficulties in developing charging infrastructure without robust EV ownership to support it. Utilities can play a role in facilitating and developing charging infrastructure in order to help bridge this gap.

The electric system is designed to provide safe and reliable service at all times, including times of peak demand, which is the time of day when electricity use by the public is at its highest. In Minnesota, peak demand generally occurs during the evening hours when most people have returned from work, with the lowest demand occurring overnight. The growth of EVs has the potential to significantly impact the electric grid, because scores of EVs charging during times of peak demand could necessitate large investments in generation and distribution infrastructure to handle this new load. Fortunately, rate design can be an efficient and effective tool for avoiding these costly investments.

Time-of-use rates adjust the price of electricity based on the time that it is consumed, with low prices during low-demand periods and high prices during peak demand. A time-of-use rate could therefore encourage charging during times of low demand and impose higher rates for usage when demand is high to reflect the additional costs this usage imposes on the system. Using rate design to encourage charging during times of low demand can help the electric grid absorb and accommodate the new load created by EVs without the need for new generation or distribution infrastructure, thereby enhancing the efficient use of existing infrastructure and potentially driving down electricity rates.

Rate design mechanisms intended to encourage off-peak charging through lower rates at those times can be particularly effective for persuading public and private fleet managers to switch to EVs. Fleet managers "tend to be very sensitive to operations and maintenance costs, and so are more accustomed to thinking in terms of total cost of ownership" and therefore more likely to consider fuel cost savings in choices about vehicle types.

Another benefit of encouraging charging during times of low demand is that overnight electricity consumption also tends to correlate with high generation of Minnesota's most abundant renewable resource: wind power. Matching EV charging with wind generation could allow utilities to make better use of the wind resource and potentially support increased wind generation, which can help Minnesota meet its greenhouse gas and harmful emission reduction goals.

Smart or managed charging takes rate design a step further by enabling the utility to actively manage the charging load. Chargers can be equipped with two-way communication capabilities between the utility and the EV, which allows the utility to remotely control the rate of EV charging in order to meet a local or regional system need. For example, the utility could ramp up EV charging during times of high wind generation, and the utility could curtail charging during peak demand in areas with high EV penetration to defer the need for distribution infrastructure upgrades.

The EV tariff statute allows utilities to recover costs incurred "to inform and educate customers about the financial, energy conservation, and environmental benefits of electric vehicles and to publicly advertise and promote participation in the customer-optional tariff." A plain reading of this provision authorizes cost recovery for education efforts by a utility that go beyond simply encouraging customers to enroll in the utility's EV tariff. The statute contemplates that utilities could disseminate information to customers about the overall benefits of EVs, such as the financial benefits to the individual customer in the form of lower fuel costs and broader environmental benefits of widespread EV adoption.

Utilities are uniquely situated to educate the public about the benefits of EVs because of their existing relationships and frequent contact with their customers. Education efforts could even target public and private fleet managers to encourage the transition of vehicle fleets to EVs—a high-impact opportunity for boosting EV adoption. Since lack of awareness about the benefits of EVs is a major barrier to EV adoption, utility efforts to educate ratepayers about benefits of EVs can be an efficient and effective way to encourage EV growth.

Because EV charging infrastructure must connect to the electric grid, utilities inevitably play a role in the development of that infrastructure. At a minimum, the utility will treat a customer hosting charging infrastructure like any new customer by providing a service connection to the customer, including any necessary distribution upgrades, up to and including the meter. The costs of the service connection are then allocated to the customer hosting the charging infrastructure in the same manner as any new customer.

Utilities can take on a larger role in developing EV charging infrastructure by assuming more of the costs and spreading them across all ratepayers. Under the "make-ready" approach, the utility could cover the cost of connecting the charging infrastructure up to the point where the charger connects to the grid. This approach could reduce the cost of building charging infrastructure, which could increase the economic viability of that infrastructure.

Utilities could build and own EV chargers, which would ensure development of charging infrastructure and strongly support the growth of EVs. A less direct approach could involve the utility offering financial incentives to third-party charging providers to build charging infrastructure.

Another factor to consider regarding EV charging infrastructure is the type of infrastructure that will be installed. For example, direct current fast charging (DCFC) infrastructure allows users to recharge in 10–30 minutes, drastically reducing charging time compared with traditional EV chargers and enhancing the potential for combined charging and parking services. . . .

Any discussion of utility investments raises the issue of how the utility will recover the cost of those investments from ratepayers. Utilities recover costs from ratepayers through a variety of mechanisms, depending on the type of cost being recovered. Different types of cost recovery can incentivize certain investments and behaviors of the utility.

In the course of this investigation, stakeholders suggested a variety of approaches to cost recovery for EV-related costs. A utility's capital investments in EV infrastructure could be added to rate base through a rate case and earn a rate of return on the investment. The Commission has also authorized cost recovery outside of a rate case through riders. Utilities could be allowed to earn a higher rate of return on EV-related investments as an incentive. Attaching performance metrics to EV-related costs could tie cost recovery to the utility's achievement of certain goals, such as customer participation or satisfaction. Allowing the utility to recover EV-related costs as operating expenses would distribute cost recovery across all ratepayers but without the utility earning a rate of return on those costs. To be clear, the Commission generally decides recovery of a utility's cost of service on a case-by-case basis considering factors such as the purpose, nature, magnitude, and potential benefits of the costs incurred.

For investments serving only one customer, such as home charging equipment, it may be appropriate to recover the cost from that customer. These costs could be recovered over time using on-bill financing, which would recover a portion of the cost through the customer's electric bill each month, thereby easing the burden of the cost to that customer. . . .

Utilities occasionally propose pilot programs, which are temporary programs that allow the utility to test new technology or policies on a smaller scale. Pilot programs can be useful in the EV context because they allow utilities to experiment with different approaches to rate design, emerging technologies, infrastructure build-out, and other EV issues.

The purpose of a pilot is to determine whether a proposal is beneficial enough to warrant expansion to a full-scale program. A pilot proposal should articulate clear goals for the pilot and detail the evaluation metrics that will be used to measure and assess whether those goals have been met. Once the pilot has been adequately evaluated, the Commission can turn to the question of whether the approaches that were tested in the pilot should be expanded. . . .

. . . The Commission affirms that EVs hold the potential for significant benefits to all Minnesota ratepayers, and that utilities will play a role in educating ratepayers about the benefits of EVs and helping integrate EVs into the electric system.

The Commission will require Minnesota's three investor-owned utilities—Minnesota Power, Otter Tail Power, and Xcel Energy—to submit . . . filings . . . . [The Commission then directed the state's three investor-owned utilities to file reports identifying transportation electrification plans with next steps over two years for facilitating customer awareness of public and residential charging infrastructure, the benefits of EVs, plans for truck and bus fleet electrification, low-income and equitable access to EV charging, and other issues.—Eds.]

IN THE MATTER OF THE PETITION OF THE ELECTRIC VEHICLE WORK GROUP FOR IMPLEMENTATION OF A STATEWIDE ELECTRIC VEHICLE PORTFOLIO, MARYLAND PUBLIC SERVICE COMMISSION

Order No. 88997, Case No. 9478, 2019 WL 249400 (Md. P.S.C., Jan. 14, 2019)

[This PSC proceeding involved a petition for a Statewide Electric Vehicle Portfolio. Local utilities, environmental groups, community groups, and think tanks participated in the case. Ultimately, many were signatories to a request to the PSC to approve the overall portfolio. The general portfolio was also broken into sub-portfolios for residential, non-residential, public, innovation, and technology service. The utilities offered different programs for each of the sub-portfolios, and intervenors responded to the utilities' plans. A key contested aspect of the proposals was cost recovery. In part, many of the costs would be recovered in electric consumer rates. Additionally, utilities offered rebates to customers that installed charging capacity. Portions of the Commission's decision addressing the residential sub-portfolio follow.—Eds.]

Maryland has adopted several policies related to the advancement of electric vehicles and electric vehicle service equipment (EVSE) in the State. In 2015, Governor Larry Hogan signed into law an extension of the Maryland Electric Vehicle Infrastructure Council (EVIC). EVIC is tasked with evaluating incentives for EV and EVSE adoption, developing recommendations for a statewide EV infrastructure plan, and proposing policies to promote successful EV integration in Maryland. . . .

In 2016, Governor Hogan signed into law the reauthorization of Maryland's Greenhouse Gas Emissions Reduction Act, which targets a 40 percent reduction in statewide greenhouse gas (GHG) emissions from 2006 levels by 2030. The legislation tasked the Maryland Department of the Environment (MDE) with developing and implementing a GGRA Plan to mitigate carbon emissions while considering, among other things, the impact on electricity costs to Maryland customers. MDE has since identified the electrification of Maryland's transportation sector as a key GHG mitigation strategy for meeting the State's reduction targets. In recognition of the fact that the transportation sector currently accounts for approximately one-third of Maryland's GHG emissions, the State has adopted a goal of having 300,000 zero-emission electric vehicles (ZEVs) on Maryland roadways by 2025. Further, the Maryland Commission on Climate Change has requested that EVIC "assess policies that employ Maryland's public utilities to aid in efforts to rapidly and equitably expand EV infrastructure in Maryland, with specific targets in rural areas; and policies that make it easier to install EV charging infrastructure at multi-family housing locations with attention to high density, urban populations."

Additionally, State programs and initiatives through the Maryland Energy Administration (MEA), MDE and other agencies offer funding to deploy EV charging in Maryland. Recently, MDE, in conjunction with MEA and the Maryland Department of Transportation (MDOT), announced a draft spending plan to invest approximately $11.3 million from Maryland's portion of the Volkswagen settlement toward the deployment of EV charging infrastructure, among other strategies to help improve air quality. MEA "runs multiple grant, rebate, and funding programs in order to accelerate the adoption of [plug-in electric vehicles] throughout the State."

The proposed EV Portfolio and its various Utility program offerings are designed to incentivize the deployment of charging infrastructure in furtherance of state policy goals and commitments for the electrification of Maryland's transportation sector. Specifically, the Signatory Parties maintain that development of a robust charging network is necessary to help Maryland achieve the adoption of 300,000 ZEVs by 2025 and a 40 percent reduction in GHG emissions, from 2006 levels, by 2030. To that end, the Petition aims to (1) alleviate EV range anxiety, (2) help customers understand and manage their charging load, (3) increase interest and investment in smart charging, as well as encourage workplace and fleet charging, (4) provide information regarding EV charging behavior to facilitate future TOU rates, managed charging, and other EV programs, and (5) evaluate grid impacts to determine opportunities for integrating additional technology as well as maximize economic and technical benefits of an EV charging infrastructure.

The Commission supports many aspects of the Petition and applauds the Work Group for its development, but the Commission must balance these goals against other considerations, such as coordination with the full suite of State programs and initiatives, the appropriate size of an EV charging program, the level of utility involvement, the ratepayer impacts, the cost-effectiveness of the program, the overall benefits to all Maryland ratepayers, and the potential impediments to competition by market participants.... [T]he Commission finds that the Petition's pilots, as proposed, are overly broad and costly to ratepayers in the service territories .... However, as modified, components of the Petition can inform the Commission and the public of potential impacts and implications for the electric distribution grid, including reliability, load management, improved system efficiency, and whether a wider expansion of a ratepayer funded EV charging network would be appropriate in the future....

The Utilities' Residential sub-portfolios are comprised of three types of offerings: rebate incentives for chargers, time variant rates, and FleetCarma [a specific type of charger offered by the utilities]. In sum, the Residential sub-portfolios have a combined cost of approximately $17.8 million across all four Utilities. As proposed, only Delmarva and Pepco expressly offer the Discounted L2 smart charger rebate program, which couples the rebate incentive with an EV-only residential time-of-use tariff.... Next, all of the Utilities offer a residential smart charger rebate-only program, designed to incent customers to install smart L2 chargers at their residence and enable them to participate in future programs from the Utilities....

The EV Portfolio proposes to advance Maryland's goal of increasing EV adoption and usage by offering, among other things, customer rebates toward the purchase and installation of smart L2 chargers. These residential rebates are designed to offset the higher costs associated with purchasing a smart charger, up to 50 percent of the costs to purchase and install the charger, net of other available rebates and discounts, with some variation among the programs. Further, the residential rebates are generally capped at a maximum of $500 per rebate. The combined total costs for the Utilities' smart charger rebate-only programs are estimated at approximately $13.5 million.... Additionally, as a condition of receiving the rebate, PE would require its customers to also agree to share their charging data with the company; the other Utilities include no such requirement in their rebate-only Residential offerings.

Several participants . . . object to the use of ratepayer funds to finance rebates for residential chargers because it leads to customer cross-subsidization. . . . [T]he goal of the residential rebates is to provide enough incentive for a residential customer to choose an advanced L2 charger over a cheaper alternative that lacks the "smart"[1] functionality.

The Commission finds there is value in collecting usage data and determining how load management profiles can be shaped by using smart chargers. It also stands to reason that an increase in EV usage would also increase a Utility's distribution revenues, which could lower electric distribution rates for all ratepayers. Indeed, Staff points out that the increase in load from EVs could pay back the costs of the rebates in short time. Thus, in view of maximizing smart charger functionality to assess potential grid impacts and mitigation strategies, the Commission finds that it is in the public interest to approve the Petition's rebate incentive program, with modification, as discussed below.

The State agencies raise concerns regarding the size and cost of the BGE and PE rebate-only programs. MEA [Maryland Energy Administration] believes that "ratepayers should not solely bear the burden of one-third of the State's infrastructure gap, as determined by the NREL gap analysis." Staff argues that the proposed $500 rebate caps are too high and unsubstantiated. And OPC [Office of People's Counsel] states that the residential rebates should be based on "a percentage of the difference in cost between a standard L2 charger and a smart L2 charger."

For pilot study purposes, the Commission finds it appropriate to reduce the size of the proposed rebate-only programs to a smaller number of rebates, which would lower the overall cost to ratepayers and could mitigate cross-subsidization between EV owners and non-EV owners. Scaling down the rebate measures would also provide time and opportunity over the course of the pilot to assess the effectiveness of these programs to incent EV adoption while limiting risk to ratepayers in paying for these programs.

To further allay cost and cross-subsidization concerns, Staff and OPC recommend that the Commission reduce the rebate amount. According to Staff, the Utilities' selection of $500 as the maximum rebate amount was not based on any study or analysis that demonstrates this amount is optimal. Rather, the Utilities explain that $500 reflects the difference in price between a smart charger and a non-smart charger. However, according to an analysis by BGE, the average difference in price between a smart and non-smart charger is $371.70. Staff explains that the Utilities

---

[1] ["Smart chargers" are automated through microprocessors and use multiple steps in order to maintain a full charge.—Eds.]

rounded this number to $500 "to cover the costs of the more expensive residential chargers and associated infrastructure." The Commission agrees that reducing the rebate amount will further lower ratepayer impact, ratepayer risk, and customer cross-subsidization. The Commission therefore adopts Staff's recommendation to limit the maximum rebate amount for smart L2 chargers to $300 for residential customers.

Lastly, as an alternative to the residential rebates, Staff suggests that creative rate design can further reduce or remove the residential rebate program altogether. Staff contends that offering a reduced distribution rate for overnight hours to encourage off-peak EV charging, or a reduced rate to encourage charging during times when renewable energy penetration is highest, can lower the costs of the residential programs, reduce cross-subsidization, and produce environmental benefits. Staff also notes that the Utilities can offer distribution bill credits for off-peak use equal to a rebate. Under this approach, the EV customer would receive a rate credit for a certain amount energy for EV charging during off-peak periods. While Staff's alternative proposals could, in theory, serve the same purpose as the proposed residential rebate programs, Staff has not shown that either approach will incentivize customers to purchase a smart charger in the same manner as receiving a rebate in hand. For this reason, the Commission declines to eliminate the rebate incentive entirely. However . . . the Commission finds that lower distribution rates for off-peak charging yields additional benefits that warrant development and evaluation.

NOTES AND QUESTIONS

1. After the Minnesota commission decision requiring the state's investor-owned utilities to file reports with EV charging proposals, Xcel Energy, the state's largest utility, submitted a proposal for several residential and commercial EV pilot programs, along with a public charging program. The Minnesota commission approved the program, and it was upheld on appeal after a challenge by a group of Xcel's large industrial customers. *See Matter of Xcel Energy's Petition for Approval of Electric Vehicle Pilot Programs*, Case Nos. A19–1785, A20–0116, 2020 WL 5626040 (Minn. Ct. App., Sept. 21, 2020). Why might the utility's large industrial customers oppose these programs?

2. Maryland wanted to develop its EV program and offered rebates, as described in the order. Why would utilities offer rebates, and how would that system work? As customers who install EV chargers receive a reduced electricity bill, the rebates will come from all the utility's ratepayers. This is a type of cross-subsidization that the PSC addresses. Is such a cross-subsidization appropriate?

3.   Although not in your excerpt, one of the participants that opposed the rebate program in Maryland was the American Petroleum Institute. What stake would it have in the proceedings, and why might it oppose the EV program? To what extent should state utility commissions take the views of the oil industry into account?

4.   How important is it for states to enact legislation directing state utility commission action on proposals for EV charging infrastructure? Might commissions be more hesitant to approve large investments, paid by ratepayers, without such legislation? What authority can commissions rely on in the absence of EV-related legislation? For a discussion, see Alexandra B. Klass, *Public Utilities and Transportation Electrification*, 104 IOWA L. REV. 545 (2019); Alexandra B. Klass, *Regulating the Energy "Free Riders,"* 100 B.U. L. REV. 581, 621–641 (2020).

5.   Both the Minnesota and Maryland commission decisions were relatively early on in each state's process of evaluating EV infrastructure proposals. However, as of 2021, utility commissions from 21 states and the District of Columbia had approved such utility investments totaling almost $2.4 billion in EV charging infrastructure. These investments support almost 200,000 charging stations, with billions of dollars of additional funding under consideration. *See* PETER HEUTHER, AM. COUNCIL FOR AN ENERGY-EFFICIENT ECON., SITING ELECTRIC VEHICLE SUPPLY EQUIPMENT (EVSE) WITH EQUITY IN MIND 12–15 (Apr. 2021). *See also* MICHAEL HAGERTY ET AL., THE BRATTLE GROUP, GETTING TO 20 MILLION EVS BY 2030: OPPORTUNITIES FOR THE ELECTRIC INDUSTRY IN PREPARING FOR AN EV FUTURE (June 2020); Scott Voorhis, *Southern California Edison Plans for 38,000 Charging Stations, In Largest IOU Effort of Its Kind*, UTIL. DIVE (July 13, 2021).

6.   There has also been a growing emphasis on equity considerations in evaluating utility proposals, with state legislatures and commissions requiring utilities to ensure that investments are made in low-income and minority communities. HUETHER, *supra. See also* Robert Walton, *Colorado Approves Xcel's $100M Transportation Electrification Plan, with Strong Equity Emphasis*, UTIL. DIVE (Jan. 14, 2021). Why should legislatures, regulators, and utilities focus so heavily on EV charging investments in low-income and minority communities? Is there the potential for a market failure in the absence of regulation? What concerns are associated with cross-subsidies by utility ratepayers? How should policymakers consider the fact that low-income and minority communities are the most impacted by vehicle tailpipe emissions because of decades of building highways through those communities, as discussed in Chapter 6?

7.   The Biden administration has expressed support for EV charging infrastructure, proposing a $15 billion federal investment to build 500,000 charging stations on U.S. highways and roads. The investment would utilize grants and incentive programs with assistance from the U.S. Department of Transportation and the DOE. *See* FACT SHEET: BIDEN ADMINISTRATION ADVANCES ELECTRIC VEHICLE CHARGING INFRASTRUCTURE, THE WHITE HOUSE

(Apr. 22, 2021). How much of this investment in EV charging infrastructure should be paid for by EV users? By federal taxpayers? By utility ratepayers? What justifications exist for anyone other than current EV owners to pay for the infrastructure that today supports only a small percentage of vehicles on the road? For a discussion of the critical need for EV charging infrastructure to support EV adoption, see Niraj Chokshi et al., *Biden's Electric Car Plans Hinge on Having Enough Chargers*, N.Y. TIMES (Sept. 7, 2021).

PRACTICE PROBLEM

You are a California lawyer and housing and energy advocate working to ensure that all Californians have access to clean and affordable transportation. You know that the poorest Californians are exposed to the worst air quality, and that climate change is making this worse.

California, with its aggressive climate goals, is a leader in EV sales and associated infrastructure. It has several programs to help low-income citizens buy EVs. These include CleanCars4All, a program paying $9,500 to scrap older polluting cars and offering a free EV charger; a $7,000 rebate to purchase or lease an EV; and a program offering $5,000 in down payment assistance to help low-income citizens with an EV purchase or charger installation. Yet, ensuring the programs serve all Californians, including low-income residents, remains a challenge. This is especially true for EV charging.

EVs with a range of 250 miles or greater per charge can charge at home roughly 92% of the time, but over 40% of Americans do not live-in single-family homes. How can your organization ensure that charging infrastructure is accessible for people living in multi-unit dwellings (MUDs) like condos, apartments, or denser urban areas? Installing chargers in MUDs is also difficult. While changes in the building code can help to ensure new buildings have access to charging, estimates from California suggest that this would impact no more than 10% of buildings by 2030—and its impact on lower income communities would not be sufficient to ensure access, as many of the MUD residents are renters, lower-income, and people of color. Many of these areas also have higher-than-average pollution levels, so there are important equity and justice considerations embedded in the transition to EVs.

In 2021, there were 73,000 EV chargers installed in California (with 6,000 fast DC chargers). There are an additional 123,000 chargers planned (including 3,600 fast chargers), but the state estimates that it needs 1–1.2 million chargers by 2030 to support the projected 7.5 million new EVs on the road. This massive investment, as you just read, will involve utilities and ratepayers. The California Energy Commission issued a report estimating that MUDs will need 265,000 to 395,000 Level 1 and 2 chargers. As at-home charging uses cheaper residential electricity rates, it can be much less expensive than public charging stations. *See* CAL. ENERGY COMM'N, ASSEMBLY

BILL 2127 ELECTRIC VEHICLE CHARGING INFRASTRUCTURE ASSESSMENT (July 2021).

Your organization is partnering with Southern California Edison to address energy justice issues. Southern California Edison's territory is diverse. Over 50% of the customers live in MUDs, and approximately 45% of the residential households are in low-income communities, with many ratepayers qualifying for subsidized electric rates. These areas also have some of the worst air quality in the nation. Southern California Edison has established a Charge-Ready program to promote EV charging infrastructure in multi-family housing, with availability for disadvantaged communities. The utility also just announced plans to install 38,000 new charging stations. This $436 million program will be financed by ratepayers and is the largest of its kind, according to the utility. The utility plans to install 18,000 of the new stations at MUDs, with 2,500 targeted to disadvantaged neighborhoods. *See* Scott Voorhis, *Southern California Edison Plans for 38,000 EV Charging Stations,* UTIL. DIVE (July 13, 2021); *Clean Energy Access Working* Group, Southern California Edison (June 24, 2019); *Charge Ready Opportunities for Multi-Family Property Owners and Operators,* Southern California Edison. How will you help Southern California Edison ensure that low-income residents can benefit from EVs and the pollution reductions they provide?

2.   CARBON CAPTURE AND STORAGE (CCS)

We must remove CO_2 from the economy and the atmosphere to achieve Net Zero Energy. While electrifying the transportation sector using cleaner fuels can help prevent GHG emissions, there are some industrial activities that cannot be easily decarbonized. Making cement, steel, or other energy-intensive industrial processes are examples.

As introduced in Chapter 2, carbon capture and storage (CCS) is a system that (1) captures carbon at its source, such as from coal- or gas-fired power plants, ethanol plants, and cement kilns and (2) transports that CO_2 through a pipeline network to be (3) injected deep into suitable geologic formations where it will remain. It is sometimes referred to as carbon capture, utilization, and storage (CCUS)—to account for the possibility of utilizing the captured CO_2 instead of, or in addition to, storing it in the subsurface.

Although it has been around for decades, CCS uptake has been slow, with about 20 projects around the world in 2020. Projects have received minimal private sector financial support as compared to energy efficiency or clean energy technologies. Moreover, over 80% of proposed U.S. CCS projects have not been built. *See* Ahmed Abdulla et al., *Explaining Successful and Failed Investments in U.S. Carbon Capture and Storage Using Empirical and Expert Assessments,* 16 ENV'T RES. LETTERS 014036 (2020); *A New Era for CCUS,* Int'l Energy Agency; George Peridas & Briana Mordick Schmidt, *The Role of Carbon Capture and Storage in the*

Race to Carbon Neutrality, 34 ELEC. J. 106996 (2021); Chris Grieg & Sam Uden, *The Value of CCUS in Transitions to Net-Zero Emissions*, 34 ELEC. J. 107004 (2021).

Most of today's CCS projects use captured CO_2 for enhanced oil recovery (EOR), where it is injected into the subsurface to help recover more oil. Subsurface storage space is plentiful, with enough estimated space to store 2,000–22,000 billion tons of CO_2. Advocates for CCS often focus on the possibility of beneficial carbon reuse, sometimes referred to as carbontech, where captured CO_2 is repurposed into useful products. However, CCS experts opine that EOR is projected to continue to be more attractive than other uses. *See* NAT'L ENERGY TECH. LAB., OFFICE OF FOSSIL ENERGY, U.S. DEP'T OF ENERGY, CARBON STORAGE ATLAS (5th ed. 2015); David Roberts, *Could Squeezing More Oil Out of the Ground Help Fight Climate Change?*, VOX (Dec. 6, 2019).

Advocates say that CCS projects can reduce carbon emissions from power plants by as much as 90%, provide state and local tax revenues, and create new jobs while preserving old ones. Challenges include cost, both of carbon capture itself (in dollars and energy penalties) and of suitable and safe long-term sequestration. *See* Lincoln L. Davies et al., *Understanding Barriers to Commercial-Scale Carbon Capture and Sequestration in the United States: An Empirical Assessment*, 59 ENERGY POL'Y 745 (2013). From a GHG perspective, CCS is an end-of-pipe carbon disposal technology. Individual CCS projects could avoid millions to tens of millions of tons of CO_2 from being emitted into the atmosphere. But at scale, CCS would be injecting billions of tons of CO_2 into the subsurface annually to be sequestered for hundreds to thousands of years.

CCS projects associated with oil and gas development—like those using captured CO_2 for enhanced oil recovery (EOR)—could continue to be permitted by state oil and gas agencies. There is little regulatory experience for large-scale dedicated CCS injection sites. EPA permitting could be critical to CCS success, as the agency oversees injections into deep saline geologic formations through its Underground Injection Control (UIC) program under the Safe Drinking Water Act. To date, only two geologic saline permits have been issued. *See, e.g.*, John Larson et al., *The Economic Benefits of Carbon Capture: Investment and Employment Opportunities for the Contiguous United States*, RHODIUM GROUP (Apr. 20, 2021); Elizabeth Anderson & Jennifer Christensen, *Game-Changing SCALE Act Could Enable Carbon Capture Infrastructure Needed for Net-Zero Goals*, GREAT PLAINS INST. (Apr. 14, 2021).

Ahmed Abdulla et al.'s analysis, cited above, evaluating of all U.S. CCS projects (existing and failed) suggests that a successful CCS project depends on several factors. First, lower capital costs are better, as "engineering megaprojects" are complex and can run into delays and cost overruns. Second, technological readiness matters, and projects using proven technologies have higher success rates. Third, credible revenue sources are important; linking CCS to EOR projects with "bilateral offtake agreements" aid success. Fourth, and perhaps counterintuitively, the successful CCS projects rely *less* on government incentives than the failed projects. The authors state that "[p]rojects with high price tags have generally received government incentives; they are flagship, high-profile, sometimes high-risk, demonstration projects. It is precisely these types of projects that often fail, often because they are vulnerable to 'vetoes' if policy makers waver in their support, especially given their potentially long lead times." Abdulla et al., *supra*, at 6. Taken together, this research can inform future projects, policies, CCS deployments, and your work on the Practice Problem below. For an interactive map showing the location of U.S. CCS projects, as well as details on those projects, see *U.S. Carbon Capture Activity and Project Map*, Clean Air Task Force, https://www.catf.us/ ccsmapus/.

To date, government agencies have taken mixed approaches to CCS projects, as illustrated in the excerpts below.

COUNCIL ON ENVIRONMENTAL QUALITY REPORT TO CONGRESS ON CARBON CAPTURE, UTILIZATION, AND SEQUESTRATION
Executive Office of the President (June 2021)

To reach the President's ambitious domestic climate goal of net-zero emissions economy-wide by 2050, the United States will likely have to capture, transport, and permanently sequester significant quantities of carbon dioxide (CO_2). In addition, there is growing scientific consensus that carbon capture, utilization, and sequestration (CCUS) and carbon dioxide removal (CDR) will likely play an important role in decarbonization efforts globally; action in the United States can drive down technology costs, accelerating CCUS deployment around the world.

For CCUS to be widely used, CCUS technologies must advance in the context of a strong regulatory regime informed by science and experience. Responsible CCUS projects should include meaningful public engagement and help address cumulative pollution for overburdened communities. CCUS can reduce the costs of meeting climate goals, and maintain and create well-paying union jobs nationwide and globally.

To broadly scale CCUS in an manner that is efficient, orderly, and responsible, the President has committed to increasing support for CCUS research, development, demonstration, and deployment (RDD&D), enhancing the Section 45Q tax incentive for CCUS, advancing a technology-inclusive Energy Efficiency and Clean Electricity Standard, ensuring a robust and effective regulatory regime, and supporting efforts to ensure that CCUS technologies are informed by community perspectives and deliver desired climate, public health, and economic goals, as outlined in this report.

CCUS is likely to be especially important for decarbonizing the industrial sector. While the first priority for addressing climate change must be to reduce emissions rapidly, CDR technologies, such as direct air capture (DAC) and permanent sequestration, are likely needed to deliver on the Paris Agreement. Some CDR approaches, including DAC and bioenergy carbon capture and sequestration (BECCS), may incorporate geologic sequestration. CCUS is therefore an emission reduction strategy where it is applied to new and existing sources of emissions, and an enabler of CDR from the atmosphere.

In the United States, there are 5,200 miles of dedicated CO_2 pipelines, and 52 million tons of CO_2 were supplied to EOR for injection underground in 2019. And there are approximately 45 CCUS facilities in operation or in development in the United States today. The costs of carbon capture have decreased by 35% between a first-of-a-kind power plant with carbon capture and the second facility using the same technology. But if the United States is to achieve its climate goals, research suggests that CCUS deployment should increase tenfold over the next decade. Deploying CCUS at a larger scale will require robust governance to ensure these systems are delivering desired societal outcomes and have broad and deep public support. Successful widespread deployment of responsible CCUS will therefore require strong and effective permitting and regulatory regimes and meaningful public engagement early in the technological deployment process.

As this report reveals, CCUS is progressing in the United States in part because such a framework is taking shape. The Environmental Protection Agency (EPA) has a regulatory framework that was finalized in 2010 under the authorities of the Safe Drinking Water Act and the Clean Air Act that ensures the long-term, safe and secure geologic sequestration of CO_2. The Utilizing Significant Emissions with Innovative Technologies (USE IT) Act made CCUS infrastructure eligible for the permitting review process created under Fixing America's Surface Transportation Act (FAST-41). And the President's American Jobs Plan seeks to build on this momentum, all while reducing pollution for overburdened communities and maintaining and growing well-paying union jobs. . . .

Earlier in this chapter, we highlighted several states that have enacted 100% clean energy standards. For many of those states, the focus is on replacing coal- and gas-fired power plants with renewable energy and battery storage. In addition, these standards generally allow for the continued expansion of nuclear energy, hydropower, and CCS. In other states, particularly those with historic fossil fuel economies, there has been a greater emphasis on CCS development as a bridge to allow continued fossil fuel electricity generation. The following materials focus on these states. The first case, from Wyoming, involves the state utility commission's review of a utility's integrated resource plan (IRP). Recall from Chapter 4 that many traditionally regulated states, inside and outside of RTOs, use an IRP process to determine utility investments over a 10–15-year period. The second case, from New Mexico, illustrates challenges with CCS deployment, including financing the technology.

IN THE MATTER OF THE COMMISSION'S INVESTIGATION PURSUANT TO WYO. STAT. § 37–2–117 OF THE INTEGRATED RESOURCE PLAN FILED BY ROCKY MOUNTAIN POWER ON OCTOBER 18, 2019

Docket No. 90000–147–XI–19 (Record No. 15389),
2021 WL 365177 (Wyo. P.S.C., Jan. 15, 2021)

RMP is a division of PacifiCorp, an Oregon corporation, engaged in the business of supplying electric utility service to customers throughout its six-state service territory, including Wyoming. RMP is a public utility, as defined in Wyo. Stat. § 37–1–101(a)(vi)(C), subject to the Commission's jurisdiction pursuant to Wyo. Stat. § 37–2–112. Commission Rule Chapter 3, Section 33 requires RMP to file an IRP with the Commission.

RMP engages in an ongoing process of developing and updating its IRP, a 20-year plan intended to identify the least-cost, least-risk portfolio of generation and transmission resources needed to meet the Company's obligation to serve. RMP produces and files an IRP every two years, and generally produces and files an update between IRPs. Each IRP includes an "Action Plan" that identifies specific resource additions and retirements for the initial 5 years of the entire 20-year planning period contemplated.

On April 27, 2018, the Oregon Public Utility Commission (Oregon PUC) ordered PacifiCorp to perform "system optimizer runs for each coal unit." The Company completed the study in December 2018, yielding results favoring the closure of 16 coal-fired units. After running stacked analyses, the Company concluded "Results from the coal studies informed the portfolio-development phase of the 2019 IRP by driving coal retirement assumptions in the initial portfolio development step of the portfolio-development process."

RMP filed its IRP on October 18, 2019. Over the 20-year planning horizon, the Preferred Portfolio calls for the replacement of 4,500 MW of coal-fired generation with: 6,300 MW of solar resources; 4,600 MW of new wind resources; more than 2,800 MW of battery storage; front office transactions; and increases in energy efficiency. The Action Plan also includes the construction of Energy Gateway South and other transmission upgrades, resulting in an investment of more than $17 billion, with approximately $14.5 billion for generation and storage resources and $2.5 billion for transmission.

The Commission initiated its investigation of the Coal Study by Order dated June 20, 2019. The Order states "[g]iven the potential influence of the Coal Study's results on the development of RMP's preferred generation portfolio, expected to be included with the Company's 2019 IRP filing, it is necessary and desirable that a public process be commenced to provide a mechanism for the Commission and other interested parties to explore all aspects of the Coal Study, including but not limited to, its origins, methodology and results."

The Commission initiated its investigation of the IRP by Order dated November 13, 2019. . . . In addition to the Parties, Commission Staff conducted a thorough analysis of the IRP and publicly issued its recommendations prior to the hearing. . . .

Commission Staff noted the IRP did not consider local/state economic impacts, supply chain emissions or siting costs. Specifically, the Company did not calculate whether the devastating economic impacts to communities and the State of Wyoming caused by early retirement of a coal unit were larger than the [Present Value Revenue Requirement] PVRR benefits of the Preferred Portfolio. In addition, the Company's analysis related to emission reductions only focused on generation and did not include emission implications of the fabrication, transportation, and construction of new resources. The selection of the Preferred Portfolio did not include consideration of potential impact of specific siting, decommissioning or land/water usage on resource cost and performance which Commission Staff views as material.

All these concerns taken together resulted in Commission Staff concluding that it is unclear whether RMP would have chosen the Preferred Portfolio if the IRP incorporated a broader analysis of uncertainties and risks into the evaluation process. . .

We first briefly address the novelty of this investigation and the criticism directed toward the Commission for initiating and conducting this investigation. There have been claims in some Parties' pleadings, public comments, and media reports that this action is unprecedented and unusual. To a certain extent, these claims are accurate, while the criticism is misplaced. In light of the drastic transformation of the Company's generation resources proposed in the 2019 IRP compared to the 2017 IRP, our obligation to safeguard the public interest compelled us to open an investigation and conduct a thorough review of the IRP process, the resulting 2019 IRP, and the associated Action Plan.

The generation "transformation" that RMP witness Mr. Link testified to during the hearing is not gradual in nature and the accelerated change in generation resources between 2017 and 2019 came with little notice. This Preferred Portfolio results in investments that nearly double RMP's existing net plant investment so it is incumbent on the Commission to thoroughly understand such a transformative investment no matter the resource mix proposed. To not do so would be a dereliction of our duties to ratepayers. Given that this 20-year plan has the highest price tag in the history of the Company, a thorough and impartial review was necessary and warranted. . . .

Much of the discussion in pre-filed testimony and during the hearing focused on the significant negative socioeconomic impacts that would result from the Company's proposal to prematurely retire coal-fired generation units in Wyoming. We are especially grateful to the Wyoming Coalition of Local Governments for participating as an intervenor in this investigation and providing extensive information regarding these impacts through its two witnesses, Lincoln County Commission Chairman Kent Connolly and Sweetwater County Commissioner Wally Johnson. The information and testimony provided was heart wrenching and could only have come directly from a source intimately familiar with the role RMP's generation facilities play in their communities and the potential impact of new transmission and generation facilities included in the Action Plan.

The question for the Commission, however, is whether and how to consider these socioeconomic impacts both in the 2019 IRP and in future IRPs. This Commission's customary role is principally that of a traditional economic regulator. As personally moved as each member of the Commission was by the evidence showing the devastating economic and social impacts of early coal facility closings, we have concluded that socioeconomic impacts are not properly considered in an IRP. However, this type of analysis, while not appropriate for the IRP, is critically important. All PacifiCorp and RMP states, along with the Company, must quantify and understand these impacts in order to make fully informed decisions about how to proceed. The Company should want to know the implications of its decisions to the communities and employees who have dedicated more than forty years to the success of the utility. If the economics of early retirement are a close call, as we believe they are and discuss further below, the economic devastation caused by early retirements should weigh heavily in final decisions on the fate of RMP's facilities. It is incumbent on the utility to prepare an Employee Transition Plan and a Community Action Plan to mitigate these impacts. While some have expressed their view that such plans would mitigate the impact of the proposed early closures, we agree with Commissioner Johnson that there is no adequate mitigation for the economic loss facing several Wyoming communities. Additionally, while a Transition Plan may be able to assist some employees in a new trade, there will be a segment of employees that will simply be left without their livelihood. As critical as these plans are, the Commission is suited for a relatively limited role in their preparation. While we certainly want to be aware and informed, we have insufficient subject matter expertise to play a leading role in developing these plans. Instead, PacifiCorp should leverage the expertise of other state agencies such as Workforce Services, the Community Colleges, the Business Council and others to develop these plans. . . .

We find the Coal Study is fundamentally flawed given the limited scope prescribed by the Oregon Public Utilities Commission, RMP's manual inputs, the inconsistent analysis between phases, and the sole reliance on the medium gas and medium carbon dioxide assumption.

Once the results of the Coal Study were incorporated into the IRP, the resource portfolios without early coal unit retirements were not fully analyzed or considered for comparison purposes as potential candidates for the Preferred Portfolio.

One of our principal interests in this investigation was to determine whether the Preferred Portfolio is economically sound. In the most basic analysis, for the Preferred Portfolio to be consistent with the best interest of ratepayers, operational costs of existing coal-fired generation facilities units would have to be greater than stranded investment resulting from early closure plus the cost of replacement generation and associated required transmission investment. While we understand and appreciate that the calculation is in fact much more complex, after considering the entire record, including the filed testimony and exhibits, the evidence and comments provided during the hearing, and the post hearing briefs, we are not convinced that this basic premise has been satisfied.

We were reminded by [Office of Consumer Advocate] OCA that RMP has long been a low-cost provider of electric service in Wyoming and that the drastic changes in generation profile proposed by RMP must be scrutinized with that fact in mind.

OCA posed an interesting question given its conclusion that there is a relatively small difference in PVRR between several scenarios: "Do we really want to upend the economics and reliability of a system that has been developed over many decades on the promise of speculative and nearly imperceptible savings?"

The most speculative assumption in the 2019 IRP is the cost of carbon since currently there is no national carbon price or tax imposed on RMP. Yet, on page 612 of Volume II of the IRP, the Company acknowledges that "CO_2 emission cost savings account for 77% of the overall benefit associated with early retirement." The modeling added a carbon price beginning in 2025, instead of 2030, without justification other than "stakeholder input." In the absence of a specific regulation or carbon tax, accelerating the imposition of the pricing further inflated operating costs of Wyoming coal units. That significant reduction to the already minimal projected ratepayer savings render the Preferred Portfolio unjustifiable from an economic perspective.

The speculative nature of the economic assumptions in the Preferred Portfolio makes it an insufficient basis for early retirement of coal plants, especially considering the devastating economic impacts to Wyoming communities and the State's economy. . . .

RMP failed to adequately analyze carbon capture technologies in the 2019 IRP. Glenrock and Commission Staff provided information in the record about the IRP's early exclusion of carbon capture technologies from any meaningful consideration. This was disappointing, given the numerous informal efforts the State of Wyoming has made to encourage the Company to actively engage in a carbon capture project in Wyoming.

There are significant potential benefits to the Company and ratepayers from a successful carbon capture project: [i] reliable and dispatchable electricity; [ii] reduced emissions; [iii] preservation of jobs; [iv] potential creation of new jobs; [v] reduction or elimination of the risk of stranded assets; and [vi] potential revenue to the Company and savings to ratepayers from CO_2 sale revenues. To allow these potential benefits to be ignored without thorough examination is contrary to our duty to regulate RMP consistent with the public interest and to ensure safe, adequate, and reliable service at just and reasonable rates.

Because of PacifiCorp's investment in its coal fleet, the Company has the opportunity to be the first utility in the country to provide low carbon electricity from a coal plant, which would assist other states in its service territory in meeting their carbon reduction targets.

Wyoming has now codified its policy, consistent with its informal efforts to encourage carbon capture, in HB200. The newly enacted law, effective July 1, 2020, among other things, requires "each public utility to demonstrate in each integrated resource plan submitted to the commission the steps the public utility is taking to achieve the electricity standard established" by the Commission.

While the standard will not be set prior to filing of its next IRP, PacifiCorp's 2021 IRP should identify and quantitatively demonstrate the coal units that have the most potential for retro-fit and consider the numerous options for financing these projects. There was some confusion during the hearing as to the provisions of HB200 so it is fitting to provide a brief summary of the relevant portions here. The statute expands the Commission's innovative ratemaking authority and includes both ratepayer and utility protections. Specifically for ratepayers, the rate recovery mechanism that would collect a surcharge from customers shall not exceed 2% of each customer's total bill. Importantly, the concept in the statute of a carbon capture facility "integral or adjacent to" creates a wide range of financing possibilities to include a scenario where no ratepayer funds are involved, but instead customers would benefit from revenues of CO_2 sales, which would decrease rates. To incentivize the utility, the statute allows the Commission to authorize a higher rate of return on any utility investment in carbon capture, imposition of a sharing band between shareholders and customers for revenues from the sale of capture CO_2, and recovery of prudently incurred incremental costs if the previously collected rates are insufficient.

The type of analysis contained in the recent report issued by the Department of Energy titled "Wyoming Carbon Capture, Utilization and Storage Study" provides RMP with a starting point for providing technical and economic information regarding carbon capture in its 2021 IRP. The Commission appreciates the comments we received from the Company and the University of Wyoming Enhanced Oil Recovery Institute. The comments paint a stark contrast of views of the study results and prospects for a carbon capture project in Wyoming. We will not recite an exhaustive list of disagreements between these two entities. There are many. Suffice it to say that RMP's dismissal of the study in its comments will not serve as an adequate response to the study's conclusions in the 2021 IRP, particularly its conclusion that "The weight the Commission gives to the Study should, therefore, be zero". (RMP Comments on Late Filed Exhibits, p.19). RMP commented that it "maintains an interest" but yet it was eager to point out the challenges facing CCUS. Given the potential benefits of CCUS previously mentioned, we believe the Company has a responsibility to the communities and employees who have supported it for decades to make its best efforts to pursue these options. The Company shall make a more thorough and meaningful effort to evaluate carbon capture options on its Wyoming coal fleet. . . .

IN THE MATTER OF THE PUBLIC SERVICE COMPANY OF NEW MEXICO'S ABANDONMENT OF SAN JUAN GENERATING STATION UNITS 1 AND 4

Case No. 19–00018–UT, 2020 WL 1667396 (N.M. Pub. Reg. Comm'n, Feb. 21, 2020)

[In 2019, New Mexico passed Senate Bill 489 which included, as two of its components, the Energy Transition Act and an amendment to the state's Renewable Energy Act. As described in the excerpt, the goal of the Energy Transition Act was to facilitate the closure of the two-remaining coal-fired units of the San Juan Generating Station owned by the Public Service Company of New Mexico (PNM). The plant originally consisted of four coal-fired units totaling 1,684 MW, but PNM had closed two of them in 2007 pursuant to a settlement with U.S. EPA, leaving the plant with two remaining units totaling 847 MW. In the proceeding below, the New Mexico commission considered PMN's application to abandon the remaining two units; replace it with a mix of alternative energy resources, including renewable energy; and for approval for financing the plant abandonment with $361 million of transition bonds paid for through customer charges. Additionally, PNM sought approval for new generating sources to make up for 497 MW of retired capacity. The new sources included power purchase agreements (PPA) and storage agreements for solar power; utility-owned energy storage systems; and a utility-owned natural gas-fired unit. As part of the proceeding the commission discussed the potential to convert the two remaining coal units to CCUS.—Eds.]

The four coal-fired generating units of the San Juan Generating Station came on line in 1976 through 1982. The Station has been operated by PNM on behalf of the Station's nine owners pursuant to the San Juan Project Participation Agreement (Participation Agreement). The Participation Agreement is set to expire on July 1, 2022.

Four of the owners negotiated the exit of their participation in 2015 rather than be responsible for their shares of the costs required to install pollution control technology required by the U.S. Environmental Protection Agency and the New Mexico Environment Department to comply with the Regional Haze requirements of the federal Clean Air Act.

To minimize the costs of complying with the EPA requirements, PNM and the remaining owners negotiated their ability to install a pollution control technology . . . based upon the owners' willingness to close Units 2 and 3. . . .

With the upcoming expiration of the ownership and coal supply agreements on July 1, 2022, four of the five owners . . . announced their intentions . . . not to continue their participation past July 1, 2022. The City of Farmington, however, which owns a 5.076% interest in the plant, notified the exiting owners on June 14, 2018 of its interest in continuing the plant's operation.

The City has subsequently indicated its intention to exercise its right under the Participation Agreement to acquire the exiting owners' interests in an effort to continue the plant's operation. The City has entered into a series of preliminary agreements with an investment group and developer, Enchant Energy Corporation and Enchant Energy LLC (collectively "Enchant Energy"), and several equipment manufacturers and construction companies to investigate and pursue the potential retrofit of the plant with Carbon Capture and Utilization Storage (CCUS) technology. The CCUS technology could potentially enable the plant's continued operation with CO_2 emissions that satisfy the 1,100 pounds CO[2]/MWh emissions limits specified in the ETA to become effective in 2023. The Sargent and Lundy engineering firm has conducted a pre-feasibility study that suggests that the CCUS retrofit could be feasible and the U.S. Department of Energy recently awarded $ 2.7 million in funding for a

Front-End Engineering Design Study (FEED Study) to further investigate the project's feasibility and provide the support for the further development of the project. Farmington states that the study will be completed by the first quarter of 2021.

Preliminary negotiations have begun with PNM and the other exiting owners for the transfer of their ownership interests to the City, but it is too early to know whether the City's efforts will be successful. Nevertheless, the City's efforts draw into question whether the plant will, in fact, close on July 1, 2022 . . . and the extent to which certain of the funds sought in PNM's securitization request (i.e., for decommissioning, reclamation, severance and job training for plant and mine workers, and funding for state Indian Affairs, economic development and displaced worker programs) will need to be expended.

Senate Bill 489 (2019 N.M. Laws, ch. 65) and the Energy Transition Act are often considered one and the same legislation. But the ETA is only one part of Senate Bill 489.

Senate Bill 489 includes 82 pages of double-spaced provisions. It contains primarily a new 49-page chapter of the Public Utility Act entitled Energy Transition Act (ETA), major revisions to the Renewable Energy Act (REA), an amendment to the Air Quality Control Act, and several other related amendments to the Public Utility Act.

The ETA establishes mechanisms to facilitate the abandonment of PNM's interests in two coal-fired generating plants—the remaining Units 1 and 4 of the San Juan Generating Station in 2022 and PNM's interests in the Four Corners Generating Station in 2031. The ETA provides for the use of bonds, i.e., securitization, to recover for PNM the undepreciated costs of its interests in the two plants; the estimated costs of decommissioning and reclamation; the estimated costs of severance and job training for affected employees at the plants and mines; financing costs associated with the securitization; and payments required to the state-administered funds for Indian affairs, energy transition economic development, and the assistance of displaced workers. The bonds would be issued by a wholly-owned subsidiary of PNM newly created as a special purpose entity (SPE).

The ETA then provides for the establishment of non-bypassable charges, i.e., Energy Transition Charges (ETCs), to be paid by PNM customers to cover the bonds' debt service costs over the estimated 25-year life of the bonds. The ETA also provides for ratemaking mechanisms designed (1) to eliminate the costs of the abandoned facilities at the time the ETC rates are first collected (upon the abandonment of the units), (2) to recover for PNM, separately from the ETCs, the difference between the estimated costs recovered through the bonds and PNM's future actual costs, and (3) to adjust the ETCs throughout the life of the bonds to ensure the full and timely payment of the bonds' debt service payments.

The amendment to the Air Quality Control Act is intended to facilitate the potential closure of the two generating stations. It requires the state Environmental Improvement Board to establish standards of performance for coal-fired electric generating facilities with an original installed capacity exceeding 300 MW to limit carbon dioxide emissions to no more than 1,100 pounds per MWh on and after January 1, 2023—level that is not attainable with the pollution controls used by most coal-fired generating plants.

The amendments to the Renewable Energy Act are intended more generally to increase the use of renewable energy by the state's electric public utilities. Senate Bill 489's amendments to the Renewable Energy Act require that renewable energy comprise the following minimum percentages of each public utility's total retail sales to New Mexico customers:

(1)   20% by January 1, 2020;

(2)   40% by January 1, 2025;

(3)   50% by January 1, 2030; and

(4)   80% by January 1, 2040.

Ultimately, the REA amendments require, by January 1, 2045, that zero carbon resources supply 100% of all retail sales of electricity in New Mexico. . . .

PNM asks the Commission to approve the abandonment of PNM's interests in the operation of the San Juan coal plant effective on or around July 1, 2022, to authorize PNM to take steps to abandon the coal plant, and to thereafter expend funds for the purposes of plant decommissioning and mine reclamation.

PNM cites four reasons for its decision to abandon its remaining interest in Units 1 and 4 of the San Juan plant. PNM witness, Nicholas Phillips, stated that the analysis performed to support PNM's Application shows that, by abandoning its share of the San Juan coal plant and supplanting this capacity with PNM's recommended replacement portfolio . . ., PNM's customers can expect economic and environmental benefits over the next 20 years. He said PNM's analysis is consistent with PNM's recommendation in its 2017 IRP to pursue retirement of the remainder of PNM's interest in Units 1 and 4 at the San Juan coal plant. . . .

Second, Phillips stated that retiring the San Juan coal plant will provide the opportunity for PNM to replace the plant with resources that better match varying loads and are better suited to accommodate the anticipated deployment of more renewable energy in New Mexico and the regional market.

Third, Phillips said the recent enactment of the ETA adopts an energy policy favoring the closure of coal generation facilities and the development of more renewable and carbon-free energy. The ETA imposes new and costly emissions limitations in 2023 which will render the San Juan coal plant even less economic to operate.

Fourth, the decision by the other remaining plant owners, except the City of Farmington, not to continue operations after the San Juan coal agreement and ownership agreements expire in 2022 is also a driver for a plant closure in 2022. PNM witness Thomas Fallgren said any continued operation would have to be under a very different ownership structure than currently exists. He said there is no economic or practical way for the plant to continue to serve PNM customers past 2022. . . .

Finally, [PNM witness Mark Fenton] maintained the retirement will further the public interest and the public policy under the ETA. He said the ETA makes clear that there will be public benefits arising from abandonment of coal-fired generation using securitization and establishes new emissions and renewable energy standards that make abandonment of the San Juan coal plant consistent with the state's newly adopted energy policy. Fenton concluded that the ETA focuses the Commission's attention on the economic impacts of the closure of the San Juan coal plant on the Four Corners region by expressing a preference for replacement resources located in the region, as well as creating an economic development assistance fund for the affected region. . . .

Only [the Utility Division] Staff [of the Commission] recommends that PNM's request be denied, but they recommend that it only be denied at this time. Staff believes that PNM should further evaluate the economics of continuing the plant's operation with carbon capture technology. Staff recommends that PNM re-file an abandonment application if PNM's further analysis continues to show that abandonment is less costly than continued operations with carbon capture technology. . . .

. . . PNM contends there was no valid reason for PNM to have modeled a carbon capture retrofit in its original filing. PNM states it was well aware of the excessive costs and risks presented by a carbon capture retrofit of the San Juan coal plant based on a 2010 study of carbon capture retrofit on the four units at the San Juan coal plant. PNM also maintains that it is common knowledge in the utility industry that carbon capture technology is still in the development stage in terms of retrofitting large coal plants such as the San Juan plant and is not considered an established, commercialized technology for large coal plants. . . .

The Hearing Examiners find that PNM's request to abandon San Juan Units 1 and 4 should be approved. The statutory standard for abandonment of a facility is whether the present and future public convenience and necessity requires the continued use of the facility. The "public convenience and necessity" standard has been interpreted as requiring the showing of a "net benefit to the public." . . .

The evidence indicates that the abandonment of PNM's interest in San Juan Units 1 and 4 satisfies both the net public benefit and [other applicable] standards. The modeling presented at the hearing shows that the abandonment will cost ratepayers less over the next 20 years than PNM's continued operation of the plant. The modeling conducted by PNM also shows that the abandonment will cost substantially less than PNM's continued operation of the plant retrofitted with carbon capture technology, and no party has presented contrary evidence. Furthermore, PNM and other parties have presented modeling that shows that a variety of generating resources can be acquired to replace the San Juan capacity by the date of the proposed abandonment and that the costs to do so will be less than PNM's continued operation of the plant.

The evidence also shows that, for additional reasons, it would not be in the public interest for the Commission to require PNM to install CCUS technology to continue operation of the plant. The Commission would have to require PNM to acquire the interests of the other San Juan owners, likely including their liabilities for the decommissioning and reclamation. It would also require PNM to spend at least $1.3 billion to install the CCUS technology.

What's more, the potential for the project's success is far from clear. And the federal tax credits on which its potential success depends are set to expire in 12 years, after which time even the promoters of the project anticipate its potential closure. Given that the Commission will have ordered PNM to acquire the plant and make the capital expenditures, it is likely that PNM's ratepayers would be held responsible for the undepreciated costs of the investment at that time. Those undepreciated costs would be significantly greater than the undepreciated costs PNM ratepayers are being held responsible for with the abandonment of San Juan Units 1 and 4.

Moreover, the abandonment of PNM's interest in San Juan Units 1 and 4 will not, in itself, necessitate the plant's closure. The City of Farmington and Enchant will still be able to negotiate the plant's acquisition from PNM and the current owners, and they will be able to seek private financing to install the carbon capture technology and operate the plant. They may also be able to prepare a PPA proposal for PNM in the future if the plant's retrofitted operation is successful. The risk of proceeding on this latter path, however, will be on Enchant and its investors and not on PNM's ratepayers. . . .

NOTES AND QUESTIONS

1.   How did each of the state commissions describe the benefits and drawbacks of CCS? What about the benefits and drawbacks associated with plant closure? How did legislation in each state influence the commission's decision?

2.   After the Wyoming commission's decision, PacifiCorp issued a Request for Expressions of Interest (REOI) to "identify and engage with interested parties to explore the feasibility and design of a carbon capture, utilization and sequestration (CCUS) facility or facilities to remove carbon dioxide (CO_2) from exhaust gases for PacifiCorp Wyoming operating coal-fueled generation facilities and subsequently utilize and/or sequester all removed CO_2." *See* PACIFICORP, 2021 WYOMING CARBON CAPTURE, UTILIZATION AND SEQUESTRATION (CCUS) REQUEST FOR EXPRESSIONS OF INTEREST (REOI) (June 29, 2021).

3.   As of this book's publication, the owner of San Juan Generating Station, Enchant Energy, planned to invest in CCS to continue operating the plant, citing both the cutting-edge technology that would be developed as well as the retention of jobs, taxes, and other economic benefits in the region associated with the plant. *See The Story of the San Juan Generating Station*, Enchant Energy. However, Enchant was having difficulty obtaining financing for the estimated $1.4 billion CCS project. *See* David Schlissel, *Investors Hesitate to Fund San Juan Generating Station CCS Retrofit*, INST. FOR ENERGY ECON. & FIN. ANALYSIS (May 27, 2021); Kevin Robinson-Avila, *Setbacks to San Juan Coal Plant Retrofit Plans Raise Feasibility Questions*, ALBUQUERQUE J. (June 14, 2021). In the meantime, the New Mexico commission approved a 100% renewable energy replacement plan for the plant proposed by the Santa Fe, N.M.-based Coalition for Clean Affordable Energy. *See* Darrell Proctor, *DOE Supports CCUS Retrofit for San Juan Coal Plant*, POWER MAG. (Oct. 6, 2020).

How should states, the federal government, and the private sector take economic hardship and energy poverty concerns into account when engaging in energy transition? *See, e.g.*, N.M. INDIAN AFFAIRS DEP'T, THE PROJECTED IMPACT OF THE ENERGY TRANSITION ACT ON NATIVE AMERICAN COMMUNITIES IN NEW MEXICO (June 2019) (discussing provisions of the Energy Transition Act that include $40 million for affected communities and displaced workers from the San Juan Generating Station plant closure; $30 million for cleanup and remediation of the plant, job training, replacement power; and funds for community engagement). Is there also a role for CCS in addressing these concerns? Under what circumstances?

4.   Wyoming is not the only state that has enacted legislation to support CCS use for continued fossil fuel reliance. North Dakota enacted significant financial incentives for developing and implementing CCS generally within the state, as well as specifically for "Project Tundra"—a proposal to implement CCS at a major coal-fired power plant. *See Project Tundra*, https://www.projecttundrand.com/; Press Release, *Burgum Signs Bill Incentivizing Use of Carbon Capture for Enhanced Oil Recovery*, Office of the Governor (Apr. 24,

2019); Adam Willis, *Carbon Capture Loans Could Leave North Dakota Taxpayers on the Hook for $250M*, GRAND FORKS HERALD (June 21, 2021).

5.   The above materials raise issues about how to finance CCS and whether electric utility ratepayers, taxpayers, or both, should pay those costs. As a matter of financial incentives, the DOE has $8.5 billion available in its Advanced Fossil Fuel Energy Project solicitation program that can be used for CCS project development. Section 45Q of the Internal Revenue Code provides tax incentives for CCS and other advanced coal projects. *See* CONG. RSCH. SERV., THE TAX CREDIT FOR CARBON SEQUESTRATION (SECTION 45Q) (June 8, 2021); Marc Jaruzel, *Carbon Capture in the U.S. Is Growing Like Never Before, But Further Policy Support Is Crucial*, CLEAN AIR TASK FORCE (July 28, 2021); Emeka Richard Ochu & S. Julio Friedmann, *CCUS in a Net-Zero U.S. Power Sector: Policy Design, Rates, and Project Finance,* 34 ELEC. J. 107000 (2021). Between 2016 and 2021, DOE gave out more than $500 million in grant money to CCS-related projects. See Leslie Kaufman, *To Test Carbon-Capture Tech, Firms Visit this Wyoming Facility*, BLOOMBERG LAW (July 26, 2021). President Biden's American Jobs Plan also supports CCS through financial incentives for CCS-related transportation projects, clean technologies, and storage projects.

At the state level, tax-related incentives include tax credits, exemptions from or reductions of property taxes, severance taxes, gross receipt taxes, and sales tax. Non-tax incentives include low carbon fuel standards, declaring CO_2 storage to be in the public interest, clarifying CO_2 ownership laws, and transferring long-term liability to the state. CCS is also incentivized through agreements that provide guaranteed buyers for the electricity or output from CCS projects, and by including CCS as an eligible resource in state clean energy standards. *See, e.g.,* Tripp Baltz, *States Spur Carbon Capture with Tax Breaks, Regulatory Support*, BLOOMBERG LAW (Mar. 4, 2021); Sasha Mackler et al., *A Policy Agenda for Gigaton-Scale Carbon Management,* 34 ELEC. J. 1016999 (2021).

6.   The Massachusetts Institute of Technology has engaged in a wide variety of collaborative endeavors to address decarbonization, with CCS comprising a significant part of those efforts. *See Carbon Capture, Utilization, and Storage Center*, MIT Energy Initiative. Through its CCUS Center, MIT works on new technologies to capture and store carbon, reduce carbon emissions, and develop safe geologic storage. Moreover, the Gulf Coast Carbon Center at the Texas Bureau of Economic Geology has been a long-standing leader in studying deep subsurface sequestration of CO_2.

PRACTICE PROBLEM

You manage the investments for an eccentric multi-billionaire, Dr. X. She wants to ensure that her future investments are contributing to her portfolio's Net Zero Energy goals. She recently heard about the sale of Great River Energy's Coal Creek Station in North Dakota to Rainbow Energy Marketing and the plans to make it a CCS project. She asks for your advice and analysis on investing in this project. Dr. X grew up in North Dakota and is aware that both the Biden administration and the state of North Dakota support CCS technology and that there may be tax subsidies available for projects. She has also expressed concern that there be a "just transition" for fossil fuel communities, like those in North Dakota and other states with economies based on extractive industries. *See, e.g.,* Ann M. Eisenberg, *Just Transitions*, 92 S. CAL. L. REV. 271 (2019).

The facts: Coal Creek Station is a two-unit lignite-fired (1.2 GW) coal plant in McClean County, North Dakota adjacent to the Falkirk mine, which supplies lignite coal energy to power the plant. Great River Energy, a Minnesota-based rural electric cooperative, owns the plant and uses it to provide power to its customers in Minnesota. The plant has been producing electricity since 1981 and is connected by a 473-mile-long, high-voltage direct current (HVDC) transmission line to Buffalo, Minnesota in Great River Energy's service territory. In 2019, the plant emitted 9.5 million tons of CO_2 and suffered losses of $170 million. *Annual Emission Comparison*, U.S. EPA. In 2020, Great River Energy announced that it would try to sell the plant and, if no buyer emerged, close the plant in 2022 while spending $1.5 billion to develop new wind resources in the area, to be serviced by the existing transmission line. But that plan was scuttled when McClean County placed a moratorium on new feeder lines for wind farms, which would have connected them to the HVDC line, and a neighboring county enacted a moratorium on new wind farms. Both actions were taken in an effort to save the plant. The plant employs 240 people, the mine 450; coal mining and power plant jobs are important in the rural county, which sees itself as "coal country."

The sale of the plant to Rainbow Energy (reported to be $225 million for the transmission line and $1 for the power plant) came as a surprise to many and was a cause for celebration for North Dakota lawmakers and local officials. Rainbow says that it plans to develop a CCS project at Coal Creek Station, disposing of the captured CO_2 into a saline aquifer below the site. Given federal and state support for developing the technology and keeping the plant operating, there could be some investment opportunities. Dr. X is excited about CCS and wants to invest.

However, there are reasons to be skeptical. First, Coal Creek Station was "subeconomic" before the sale, and CCS technologies will make it more expensive, not less. Second, Rainbow is an energy trading company with no experience developing or operating power plants or CCS facilities. Third, except for the short-lived Petra Nova plant in Texas, no commercial-scale U.S. CCS projects have involved retrofitting coal plants. Fourth, the captured CO_2 would be injected on-site into a saline reservoir, as there is no nearby EOR project. While North Dakota does produce over a million barrels of oil per day from the Williston Basin, there are no EOR projects in the Bakken formation, as it is a "stacked field," making it uncertain how or if EOR will work in that geology. The University of North Dakota is investigating the use of CCS for

EOR projects in a similar stacked oil field pursuant to a $3.2 million grant from the DOE. *See* Jan Orvik, *Bakken Game Changer?*, UND TODAY (Feb. 19, 2019).

Rainbow contacted Dr. X through a third party to see if she was interested in investing in the Coal Creek Station CCS project. Given the Abdulla et al. research on successful and failed CCS projects in the United States cited earlier in this chapter, please structure an analysis for her, addressing these questions: What would make the project a go? What should she seriously consider? What might be a potential counterproposal from Dr. X? Are there any public-private partnerships that would be fruitful? For more information, see Dan Gearino, *A Lifeline for a Coal Plant Gives Hope to a North Dakota Town. Others See It as a Boondoggle,* INSIDE CLIMATE NEWS (July 17, 2021); Dan Gearino, *Plan to Save North Dakota Coal Plant Faces Intense Backlash from Minnesotans Who Would Help Pay for It*, INSIDE CLIMATE NEWS (July 23, 2021).

E. YOUR ROLE IN THE ENERGY FUTURE

Congratulations! You have arrived at the last section of a very intensive dive into energy law and policy. We hope that you have gained new insights and perspectives into how the energy system came to be and how it works today. We also hope that you have some thoughts on where it needs to go next. Whether or not you choose to work in energy law and policy, it supports your life every time you turn on a light, cook food, or stream *The Mandalorian*. It also shapes how our communities work, live, and breathe—and our planet's future.

The future of energy law and policy is changing and evolving every day. As part of the next generation of energy lawyers and policymakers, you can shape this future. We wrote this casebook to provide you with a solid foundation from which to understand the history of the sector and to create the next energy systems. We tried to provide information and tools to help you understand and analyze the challenges facing the energy system. The field of energy law and policy is rich and dynamic, both in the United States and globally.

We recognize that, globally, our energy futures will take many different paths. We also appreciate that we are tied together on one planet and dependent on each other for the functioning of our societies and economies. We recognize that accurately predicting technological and societal change, especially around energy, is impossible. "[M]ore than 100 years of long-term forecasts of energy affairs . . . have, save for a few proverbial exceptions confirming the rule, a manifest record of failure." VACLAV SMIL, ENERGY AT THE CROSSROADS: GLOBAL PERSPECTIVES AND UNCERTAINTIES 121 (2003).

What we do know is that energy lawyers and policy makers will be in the middle of it all. They will be directly involved in negotiating new energy and climate treaties; writing national, state, and local energy legislation; drafting and promulgating new regulations and market rules; and carrying out the transactions, investments, and deals which will create that energy future.

The major changes in technology, markets, and institutions explored throughout this book happen globally and locally. If society chooses, we can create opportunities for cleaner energy futures and economies that support jobs and justice. The good news is that, as you have seen, energy systems around the world are changing rapidly. That too is the challenge.

We trust that your study of energy law and policy has given you a new perspective on the world in which we all live. The best energy lawyers and policymakers leverage the existing regulatory and policy foundation to build the energy system needed for the future. We hope that this book helps you to develop a vision for what the energy system can become, and advocate for and help realize the transition you believe is right.

INDEX

References are to Pages